Ethical Issues

Ethical Issues

Perspectives for Canadians

edited by Eldon Soifer

Second Edition

broadview press

Cataloguing in Publication Data

Soifer, Eldon, 1960–
    Ethical issues

ISBN 1-55111-109-8

1. Social Ethics. 2. Ethics. 3. Social problems. I. Title.

BJ1012.S6   1996   170   C92-093422-6

broadview press   OR   **broadview press**
P.O. Box 1243   3576 California Road
Peterborough, Ontario   Orchard Park, NY
K9J 7H5   Canada   14127   USA

printed in Canada

DEDICATION

I dedicate this book to Lynn Loutzenhiser, whose encouragement, help, and belief in me have made this project, as so much else in my life, both easier and more enjoyable.

CONTENTS

Introduction

This book contains discussions of a number of moral issues which are currently being debated in a variety of places: in government and other policy-making bodies, in the courts, in the press, within professional organizations, and in ordinary everyday conversations. What makes them "issues" is that reasonable people disagree about how to act in regard to these subjects, yet agree that it is important to decide how to act. (There would be little point to discussing whether torturing innocent people is wrong, or whether one should tie one's left shoe before one's right.) No doubt most readers have already discussed many of these issues with friends, family, and others. The purpose of this book is to provide thought-provoking ideas and systematic presentations of various positions which will help readers to try to sort out their own views on these issues. There are likely to be new aspects one has never thought of before, and even points one *has* considered may be put in ways which make them seem much more difficult to ignore or re-

ject. Ultimately, however, each individual must decide his or her own views on these matters. It is no part of the purpose of this book to try to sway people to any particular stance. Rather, the purpose is to provide readings which will entertain the reader, promote further discussion of the issues, and stimulate thought.

There are many different ways of thinking about these issues. This book is first and foremost "philosophical" in its orientation. I do not mean this word in the off-hand sense it often has in everyday speech of being resigned, as in "she took her friend's anger philosophically," but it has proven notoriously difficult to provide an exact account of what *is* meant by this term. The word derives from ancient Greek, meaning "love of wisdom," and originally applied to virtually every area of human search for knowledge (hence today's "Doctor of Philosophy" degree in every subject from English literature to atomic physics). The readings in this book are "philosophical" in the sense that they attempt to proceed (in connection with their respective issues) by a certain sort of method involving reasoning, argument, criticism and insight. The fact that the authors included here take a calm, reasoned approach to their subjects should not be taken to mean that they do not feel passionately about the issues they discuss. It is possible to have strong opinions, and yet be able to discuss them (and the reasons for holding them) in a cool and rational manner. It is assumed here that there is a sort of communal interest in discussing these issues and progressing in some way toward truth, or consensus, or at least an appreciation of the basis of disagreement.

This book is also Canadian in its orientation. The issues it deals with apply to people everywhere, and most of the points raised here could be applied very broadly, but there are places where specific aspects of the issues may be viewed from a distinctly Canadian perspective. This book tries to reflect that perspective by including references to Canadian law and policy, and by including many selections written by Canadians.

The book contains readings which are organized into nine categories, dealing with nine different issues. Needless to say, these are not the only moral issues of interest to people today. The issues here have been chosen largely because they seem to be of particular interest to a large number of people, and because they provide an indication of the broad range of concerns being discussed in the philosophical community today. It is important to note, however, that there is something a bit artificial about dividing contemporary moral concerns into distinct areas. People who discuss one issue usually find they need to say something about some other matter as well. To give just one example of such an interlocking chain, one issue which arises in connection with free expression involves speech which is thought to be damaging to members of traditionally oppressed groups. This can lead to questions about how we are to separate and identify groups, which in turn can lead to discussions about multiculturalism and group rights. One way in which different groups are often identified is in terms of different understandings of the world. For instance, it has been claimed that European cultures have imposed their views of such things as a justice system and the relationship of humans to the environment on others. This in turn raises questions about what different views are available on, say, the environment. In discussing that, one might wonder how to decide what sorts of entities have moral status. That issue has implications not only for environmental ethics, but also for our treatment of non-human animals, abortion, assisted reproduction, and euthanasia. And so it goes. This spilling over of one issue into another is characteristic of philosophy. It is nevertheless useful to consider different aspects of these questions separately (one has to start somewhere!), and thus the division into different issues helps make the debates manageable. It should also be noted that it is not necessary to read the sections of this book in order—each of the "issues" can be considered on its own, at least up to a point.

There is another way in which the different issues are linked as well. This is that they are all *moral* issues. (Note: many people distinguish between "moral" and "ethical," and the distinction is drawn in a variety of different ways. For the purposes of this book, however, I see no need to draw such a distinction, and so these words will be used interchangeably.) "Moral" is another word notoriously difficult to define. I will take it that calling an issue a "moral" issue implies that it has something to do with how people *should* act; with what is right or wrong, or what states of affairs are good or bad. In this broad sense, it seems everyone has *some* moral beliefs—people who say they "don't believe in morality" usually mean that they do not accept the particular moral "rules" dominant in their societies at the time, not that they have no beliefs whatsoever about what sorts of things people should or should not do.

It is not necessary, of course, for individuals to have a fully worked out moral system, or a firmly established set of moral rules. People can function perfectly well with only a vague set of moral beliefs or intuitions. Nevertheless, philosophers have often tried to provide some sort of systematic account of morality. There is considerable debate within philosophy about whether it is even possible to develop such a "moral theory," and I do not want to pre-judge that issue here. Nevertheless, I believe it to be useful for any reader interested in these issues to have some sort of background understanding of how the issues might be described in terms of various moral theories. (For one thing, writers on these issues often refer to these theories, assuming a background knowledge. For example, writers on scarcity of medical resources often refer to a "utilitarian" method of deciding who should get scarce medical resources, without explaining the moral theory this word describes.) Accordingly, this book begins with an introduction to some of the most influential strands of moral theory. I leave it to the reader to decide how these might apply to the issues at hand.

Utilitarianism

Perhaps the single most influential moral theory over the past couple of centuries has been one called "utilitarianism." One of its best known advocates, John Stuart Mill, described utilitarians in the 1860s as people who believe that "actions are right in proportion as they tend to promote happiness; wrong as they tend to produce the reverse of happiness."[1] The basic intuition here seems to be that, if anything matters, happiness does, and it makes sense to try to get as much as possible of what matters. There are other theories that tell us to aim at the maximum possible amount of some other thing held to have value, such as beauty, knowledge, etc. Any such theories are commonly called "consequentialist," because they claim that the rightness of an act depends on its having the right sort of *consequences*. Utilitarianism, then, is a particular form of consequentialist theory, which states that the value to be maximized is happiness (or "utility"). Utilitarianism adds to this an emphasis on equality —the belief that each entity capable of happiness is entitled to having that happiness counted equally with all others. Of course one might not get what one wants, if more people want something else, or indeed if only a few people want something else, but they want it very much. Still, nobody's well-being is simply to be ignored. Therefore, according to utilitarianism, the way to decide which action to pursue is to add up the increase in happiness for each individual affected by the action (subtracting all unhappiness, if there is any) for each possible action, and do whichever action will produce the most happiness.

Before getting into more detail about utilitarianism, it is worth mentioning another theory which is also concerned with bringing about happiness and which is commonly called "ethical egoism." According to this view, the right thing for individuals to do is to aim at their own happiness, whether or not that coincides with the happiness of others. This view should be separated from a view known as "psychological egoism," which holds that, as a matter of fact, human beings always do try to act in their own interests. Psychological egoism makes an empirical claim about human nature and how people *do* act (although it is sometimes hard to see what evidence could possibly be taken to disprove the claim, which casts doubt on its credentials as an empirical claim at all.) Ethical egoism, on the other hand, makes a claim about how people *should* act, and indeed it might seem ethical egoism depends on the falsity of psychological egoism, since it makes little sense to say one *should* act in a particular way if it is in fact impossible to act in any other way.

Some people would deny that ethical egoism is a "moral" theory at all, maintaining that morality requires people to be self-sacrificing, at least sometimes. (Egoism does recommend that people sacrifice their current interests for their long-term interests, e.g. by forcing oneself to study for an exam so as to further one's career, even when one is more inclined to watch a movie on TV. But that might not be considered self-sacrificing.) In any case, insofar as egoism tries to provide a guide for how people should live, it deserves some mention when discussing morality.

One argument often put forward for ethical egoism is that, if people pursue their own interests, everyone will be better off. This could be because each person knows his or her own interests best, and so will be in the best position to achieve them, or because such an approach would avoid the ill effects of people's "butting in" and generally interfering with others' business. It has also been suggested along these lines that charity is always demeaning to the recipient, and that only ethical egoism can avoid some such element of charity.

Of course, all of these are empirical claims, which might turn out to be false. For example, there could be cases where people are *not* the best judges of what is

in their best interests, or it may be that such an egoist approach might turn out to be in the interests of some at the expense of others, rather than being better for everyone. But the main thing to note here is that these arguments are not really arguments for egoism at all, so much as arguments for a particular view of utilitarianism. The expressed goal here is "everyone's happiness," or "maximum happiness," not just one's own good. It is simply that having each pursue his or her own good is held to be the best means for bringing about the utilitarian goal. There may be other arguments which really are for ethical egoism directly, but for now I will return to utilitarianism.

There is an obvious appeal to a theory that tells us to aim at maximum happiness, but there are problems as well. This is not the place to recite all of the arguments for and against this theory, but I will touch on some of the most important aspects of the ongoing debate.

The first point to be noted is that, in order to use this theory, we have to have a pretty good idea of what sorts of things contribute to a person's happiness. Although everyone has at least some rough idea about this, there are certainly cases where people might disagree; for instance, about whether a particular action has made a given individual "better off" or not. Utilitarians generally try to explain what is meant by "happiness" either in terms of some pleasant mental state, or in terms of having one's desires satisfied. (Note that there may be cases in which these accounts have to separate, such as times when satisfaction of one's desires does not produce the mental state one expected.) Some people, however, might claim that people can be better off in one conditions than another, whether they realize it or not. For example, someone might think a person is better off doing something active with one's leisure time, rather than sitting around watching television. Calling this sort of being better off a state of "happiness" might involve stretching the term a bit, but nevertheless there have been "utilitarians" who have claimed that happiness along these lines is what is to be maximized.

Another problem utilitarianism faces is in deciding how to compare one person's happiness with another's. To take a simple case: if two children each want the last candy, how can one decide which one to give it to? Utilitarianism seems to say we should give it to the one who will enjoy it more, but it may be very hard to tell which one that is. When it comes to making decisions for large numbers of people, the problem is even greater. If a town has to decide whether to build a theatre or a gymnasium, each of which would be used by different people, how can we compare the amounts of happiness involved in either decision? These problems are compounded by the fact that we cannot foresee *all* the consequences of our actions, and so can't even tell exactly how many people will be affected in the long run.

These are certainly problems utilitarians should consider, but they may not be strong enough to destroy the theory. Perhaps utilitarians can claim that all we need for guiding our decisions are rough estimates. After all, nobody claims that human beings will always succeed in doing the right moral thing all the time. Perhaps *trying* to bring about the most happiness is all we can demand. And it seems clear that people often do use such considerations in trying to make decisions. For example, if several people want to go out to dinner together and are trying to decide where to go, it seems likely they will use elements of utilitarian reasoning. If some people like Chinese food and others prefer Italian, for example, often the decision will be made by some sort

of estimate of which choice will maximize the overall happiness.

Even if utilitarianism is able to deal with these problems, however, it is still not off the hook. One of the most persistent criticisms of utilitarianism has been that it fails to give the required prominence to considerations of justice. Utilitarianism says that utility is to be maximized overall, but what if the way to achieve that is to sacrifice some individual (or group of individuals) so that others may enjoy greater benefits? Is it all right to do so, or do the individuals involved have rights that they not be treated in certain ways?

A classic example of the sort of question at issue here goes as follows: suppose you are a law officer, and you are holding a person in custody. There is a mob outside threatening to riot unless you turn this person over to them, in which case the person will be abused and ultimately killed. You know that this person has done no wrong, and the mob would therefore be killing an innocent person. On the other hand, you know that if you do not turn the person over, there will be no way to prevent the mob from rioting (assume it is too late for any rational persuasion). If they do riot, there is a very good chance not only of a great deal of damage to property in the neighbourhood, but also that more innocent people (say, local residents) will be killed in the chaos. Assuming that each person's life would contain equal happiness, it seems that the way to maximize utility would be by turning over this individual, thereby stopping the riot and saving the lives of some innocent residents. Yet many people believe that the person in custody has a right not to be treated in this way, and that one is not allowed to sacrifice this one person for the overall good. What should one do in such a case?

Cases such as the one involving the innocent person in custody are often used as criticisms of utilitarianism. The claim is that the only way to maximize happiness overall is by doing something which we are not morally allowed to do. Since utilitarianism tells us to maximize happiness overall, it tells us to do something we are not morally allowed to do. No theory which sometimes tells us to do what is wrong can be the ultimate test of what is right.

Utilitarians can respond to such a challenge in several ways. One way is to accept that the theory would tell us to perform actions which would be commonly considered wrong, but claim that they in fact are not wrong in the rare circumstances in which the theory says to do them. Indeed, it might be asked how we can know with certainty that certain actions (such as sacrificing an innocent person) are always wrong. How reliable are our intuitions? A second sort of response a utilitarian might offer is to deny that the proposed "wrong" action really would have the best consequences. It might be claimed, for example, that the situation as described fails to take into account long-term consequences, such as loss of trust in the law, or the guilt members of the angry mob would feel when the truth came out at a later time. Perhaps killing the innocent person appears to maximize happiness only when one fails to look at the big picture. One final sort of response utilitarians might use would be to argue that there are adequate resources within the theory to prohibit it from requiring any grossly wrong actions.

One version of utilitarianism which has been claimed to have such resources is sometimes known as "indirect utilitarianism," the best-known version of which is called "rule utilitarianism."[2] (The account of utilitarianism discussed above might then be called "direct" or "act" utilitarianism, for contrast.) The rule utilitarian believes that

one should figure out which rules, if generally followed, would bring about the most happiness. When faced with a particular decision, this view then states that one should simply follow the rule which applies to the situation in which one finds oneself. For instance, it seems likely that a rule saying "do not kill," if followed, would have good consequences overall, and thus it is one it seems a rule utilitarian would be likely to endorse. In the sort of "innocent person" case above, then, the rule utilitarian might simply note that that rule applies, and accordingly decide not to kill the innocent person, without needing to calculate the consequences in this particular case. This might be thought particularly valuable because people are not likely to be able to evaluate consequences accurately in the heat of the moment when action is called for.

Act utilitarians have two main reasons for resisting rule utilitarianism. The first is that one may be virtually certain that following the generally good rule would *not* have the best consequences in some situations in which one finds oneself. Should one stick to the rule anyway in such a situation? What would be the justification for doing so? Since the purpose of the rule was to bring about the best consequences, it might seem odd to follow it even in cases in which it is not likely to fulfill its purpose. Indeed, philosopher J. J. C. Smart has claimed that adhering to rules in such situations amounts to "rule-worship," and should be dismissed as irrational.[3] Thus the act utilitarian claims that rules may be useful as general guidelines, but following a rule can never be an adequate substitute for calculating consequences.

The second, related, objection act utilitarians raise against rule utilitarianism has to do with the specificity of the rules the rule utilitarian advocates. The rule "do not kill" does seem, at first glance, likely to maximize happiness overall, but careful thought reveals a number of possible exceptions. Perhaps the rule should be "do not kill, except in self-defense," or "except when killing an enemy soldier while fighting a just war," and so on. If there are too many exceptions, the rule might prove unmanageable for everyday use, and yet there might seem to be compelling reasons to allow such exceptions. Ultimately, the act utilitarian might claim that the rule would have to become something like "do not kill, except when utility would be maximized by doing so," but that is not really anything different from what an act utilitarian would say. In other words, it could be claimed that rule utilitarianism "collapses" back into act utilitarianism.

Both act and rule utilitarians believe that the ultimate moral standard lies in good consequences, specifically maximizing happiness. Theories which maintain that there are some moral considerations which do not depend on the consequences of our actions are sometimes called "deontological" theories.

Deontological Theories

Deontological theories do not have say consequences are *always* unimportant, but they do have to say that the rightness of an action at least sometimes depends on qualities of the action itself, rather than its consequences. A deontologist might claim, for example, that it is always wrong to tell a lie, even if that lie will not harm anyone. Deontological theories often begin with either rights or duties. In recent political debate, it has become popular to try to draw support for one's cause by describing it in terms of rights. Thus, people make claims ranging from "a right to treatment as an equal" and a "right to life," through "animal rights" and "rights to national self-

determination," to "rights to a university education" and "rights to holidays with pay." Often, people on each side of an issue claim rights which seem to conflict with those claimed by the other side.

In philosophy, some care must be taken in introducing a rights claim. It may be that some moral claims cannot properly be put in terms of rights. What sorts of entities can have rights? Must right-holders be individuals, or can there be collective rights? What is the relationship between interests and rights? Must rights be the sort of things one can choose whether or not to exercise, such as the right to free expression? Can there be "special" rights which belong to some people and not others (for example, rights police officers must have, but others should not)? And what happens when rights claims conflict?

It has been suggested that rights claims should be understood in terms of several elements. One way to do this is in terms of a formula such as the following: "X has a right to Y against Z in virtue of V." In these terms, if people make rights claims, it is permissible to press them to explain exactly what is to be substituted for each of the letters in the formula. Who has the right (X)? How did they qualify for it (V)? What is it a right to (Y)? And what does its existence imply by way of duties for others (Z)? With regard to the last of these questions, it is also possible to ask whether others have a "positive" duty to provide something for the right-holder (e.g., health care), or merely a "negative" duty not to interfere (e.g., with one's right to express oneself). Raising these questions will often make rights claims less obvious than they may have seemed at first.

The other common forms of deontological theories take "duties" as the central notion of morality. Certainly much of our common moral discourse can be described in terms of duties. For example, one might assert we have a duty to refrain from murdering, or a duty not to make promises we do not intend to keep. It is possible, though, that some aspects of morality are more difficult to describe in this way. For example, if we see someone trapped in a burning building, do we have a duty to try to rescue him or her, even at the risk of our own lives, or is that something which it would be nice to do, but which is "beyond the call of duty"?

Even if there is a way to describe all of our moral beliefs in terms of duties, however, there is still a problem. How do we come to know which duties we have? Where do they come from? This problem becomes more acute when we discover that different duties conflict with each other, and that people (both in different cultures and within a single one) disagree about which duties they have. For example, if I have promised to keep a secret, but it turns out someone I care about will be harmed if I do, I may be unsure about what to do. It may seem that in these sorts of cases I have two conflicting duties, and I need some way of knowing which one should give way. Similarly, at the inter-personal level, people might disagree about whether there is a duty to abstain from pre-marital sex, for example. How are we to decide which is right in such cases?

A) Intuitionism

Some deontological theorists have claimed that we have a faculty called "intuition" which informs us about our duties. This faculty is often seen as being similar to our senses. Just as sight can perceive colour and hearing can perceive sound, so intuition might be said to perceive moral facts.

One problem many people have with this view is that there may not be any moral "facts" out there waiting to be perceived. The most common objection, however, is that talk of this faculty does not really explain how different people can have such different moral beliefs, nor indeed how it can come to be that whole cultures can agree within themselves, but disagree with other cultures.

The intuitionist can reply that some people are simply better than others at using this faculty, just as some people may have better vision or hearing than others. Perhaps also the faculty needs to be "trained" by proper upbringing. Such a reply raises questions, however, about how we can tell which people are using the faculty "correctly" and which are not. Furthermore, a person who is uncertain how to act is not given much useful guidance if told simply to follow his or her intuition. For these sorts of reasons, many people do not find this intuitionist approach satisfactory.

B) Kantian Ethics

How else might we learn which duties we have? Perhaps the most influential deontological theorist of all has been eighteenth-century philosopher Immanuel Kant, who believed that we could discover our moral duties through the use of reason alone. He suggested that any time we are contemplating an action we should apply a rational test to it, and if it fails the test, it is an action we are not allowed to perform. This test, known as the "categorical imperative," has a few different formulations. The best known of these are, first, that we should act as if the principle we were acting on were to become a universal law,[4] and, second, that we must "treat humanity...always at the same time as an end and never simply as a means."[5] There has been a great deal of debate about how these principles are to be interpreted. One way to understand the first one might be by considering the question often raised when someone does a thing of which we do not approve, which is "What if everyone did that?" (or, perhaps, "How would you like it if people did that to you?"). The second one might be understood as a requirement that we treat people with respect and concern for their integrity as people.

Few would deny that these are good general guidelines for action, but many would question whether they give a full account of morality, or whether they are indeed given by reason alone. For example, one might ask what it means to treat a person as an end and not simply as a means. Does that mean we should consider each person's well-being before we act? But that is exactly what a utilitarian would say, and Kant's deontological approach was supposed to solve some of the problems utilitarianism runs into. And as for the "universalizing" version of the test, does it matter how we describe the circumstances? If we describe a given action as an act of lying, then it would seem we could not want that universalized. But if we describe it as an act of lying to a would-be murderer so as to save the life of a friend, we might come to a very different conclusion.

It is not clear whether a rational test such as the categorical imperative can provide us with all the moral guidance we might want. Kant's principles have unquestionably inspired many moral philosophers, but there is still no consensus as to how successfully he addressed the pressing ethical questions. It is also not clear whether there is another way to discover which duties apply, such as through a faculty of intuition. These deontological approaches raise some promising ideas, but cannot be said to have provided unquestionable solutions to the problems of moral philosophy.

Virtue Ethics

As we have seen, utilitarianism and deontology each has its appeal, but each has problems as well. Many philosophers continue to believe that one of these approaches is the best one to take, and the debate rages on. Others, however, have decided that some alternative must be found.

One such alternative which has been around for centuries but which has become increasingly popular in recent years is what is often known as "virtue ethics." This approach focuses on the state of character of a morally good person, rather than on a state of affairs (as utilitarianism seems to do) or on particular actions (as deontology seems to do). According to this view, the primary usage of moral terminology should be to evaluate individuals' characters as "good" or "bad," where a "good" person is one who chooses actions because they are of the right moral kind. Such a person acts out of a disposition to do what is morally right, rather than by weighing the alternatives of what one could do and applying a general principle to decide between them.

One way of conceptualizing the difference between virtue ethics and the other types of ethical views discussed here is in terms of the central questions asked. Whereas the other views seem to focus on the question of what one should do, virtue ethics focuses on the question of what sort of person one should be. This might be thought to have the advantage of putting moral actions within the context of entire lives, rather than seeing ethical life as a series of unconnected actions. This in turn might make sense of a number of types of moral judgements we actually make.

Clearly, we often do make judgements about people's ethical character (e.g., "she's dishonest," or "he's weak-willed"). What's more, these judgements can be made even if there are some actions by the person which do not fit with the characterization. For example, a generous person may sometimes act selfishly, and still be considered a generous person. We might say the selfish action is "out of character" for that person.

Another element of our moral judgements which relates to character is the element of integrity. People differ from each other in terms of their individual projects and commitments and their personal relationships. The sorts of ethical views discussed above seemed to require the same action from *anyone* placed in the same circumstances. Perhaps morality should not be seen as "agent-neutral" in this sense, however. Perhaps one's obligations depend upon facts about who one is, as an individual. It might make a difference, for example, whether one is the parent of one of the people affected by an action, or whether one is a committed pacifist, or whether one has devoted hours to studying a particular type of architecture. To demand that everyone be required to act the same way in order to be moral might be to require people to act in ways which conflict with their deeply held convictions. Such a demand might be seen, however, to conflict with the integrity of the individual, and thus to miss a major aspect of our moral experience.

One specific ethical outlook which might be considered a kind of virtue ethics is the "Ethic of Care" approach, which deserves special mention. This approach is often associated with feminism, and suggested differences between women and men (either biologically based or as a result of socialization). In particular, it has been claimed that women tend to think about moral situations largely in terms of caring responses to individuals involved, whereas men are more likely to try to apply general abstract principles. It has been further stated that traditional consequentialist and deontological theories have not sufficiently appreciated the value of emotional caring responses (thereby excluding women's experience from discussion of morality). It has also been suggested that responding sympathetically to the needs and desires of others might lead to a less confrontational approach to ethics, and a greater possibility of finding mutually acceptable solutions to moral problems. This approach may also be thought to have the advantage, common to virtue ethics approaches, of allowing the flexibility needed to deal with the fact that no two situations are alike.

The most common objection to virtue ethics is that it is too vague to be of much use in moral decision-making. For one thing, there is a problem of knowing which character traits should be seen as "virtues," especially in view of differences between cultures in terms of which character traits have been considered virtuous. Both utilitarians and deontologists would claim that we can decide which character traits to encourage as "virtues" only because we already know what sorts of actions we believe to be right, and then can decide which personal characteristics are most likely to lead one to perform the right actions. Even if we knew which traits were virtues, however, it might be difficult to use this information to help decide how to act in the face of moral dilemmas. If honesty and avoiding harm to others are both virtues, for example, how is one to decide whether to tell the truth when one knows doing so will cause harm? The ethical issues discussed in this book give rise to a large number of cases in which there appears to be a conflict between virtues.

Deontologists and consequentialists could agree that we do evaluate people in terms of having or not having various good characteristics, but insist that we do so only because those people generally do the right sort of actions, or bring about the right sort of consequences. The fact that we do make evaluations of these various types does not by itself establish anything about which of them is most fundamental.

Ethical Relativism

When faced with the various difficulties which confront the leading moral theories, some philosophers have suggested that there are no universal moral truths at all—that what is "right" in a given society is whatever people in that society *believe* is right. This view is often called "relativism," or, to distinguish it from other theories which sometimes go by this name, it could be called "cultural ethical relativism."

In order to assess this relativist claim, it may be useful to distinguish several different issues. First of all, it should be noted that relativists say more than that there are different beliefs in different cultures. They also make the claim that what each of these cultures believes to be right *is* right. One could believe the first without believing the second, however—one might think that one culture has it right while another has it wrong. It may be very difficult to *prove* that one is right and the other wrong, but that does not necessarily mean that it is not true to say it. For example, people might have different theories about why the dinosaurs died out, only one of which could be true, even if it were never possible to prove which one is correct.

On the other hand, even if one is convinced that a particular culture has a mistaken moral belief, that does not automatically tell us anything about what we are allowed to do to try to change the situation. Certainly much harm has been done over the years by people who felt certain

about their own moral beliefs and tried to impose these beliefs on others. Mistakes of that sort have no doubt helped convince many people that a relativist approach is the only one we can adopt, practically speaking. However, one might think that tolerance of others' difference is a very important moral value all by itself, and therefore one might disapprove of such impositions of moral belief, even while believing that one particular set of beliefs is morally best in some objective sense. Indeed, many people's common-sense moral beliefs seem to reflect such a value, but also place a limitation upon it. If, for example, the dominant view in another culture is that women should not be treated as equals, or that slavery or torture is acceptable, many people might think we have an obligation to try to convince that culture of the error of its ways. We may or may not be entitled to use force to bring about the change, but many would say we should do more than simply say "Well, that's their business" and stay out of the picture.

Indeed, if relativism is correct, it becomes hard to see how people can engage in ethical debate even within a single culture. One might wonder how we are to determine what a culture believes (Does everyone within the culture have to believe it? Nearly everyone? Just over half the people?). Once one has settled that, however, it seems one needs merely to take a vote in order to discover whether something is morally acceptable. Consider as an example the issue of capital punishment. If most people think capital punishment is acceptable, and I do not think so, it seems there is nothing I could say to convince them. The simple fact that they *think* it is uacceptable would be enough to settle the issue, if the test of moral rightness is what people believe to be right.

It should also be noted that the same sort of reasoning which supports cultural ethical relativism might be taken to support what me might call "individual ethical relativism," the claim that what each individual thinks is right is right for that individual. Note, however, that accepting this would make it virtually impossible to justify any sort of moral criticism of others (and might also make it difficult to explain what it is one does if one changes one's mind about an ethical matter).

One other problem which cultural ethical relativists must face is in explaining how to identify a culture. Many countries (including Canada) are made up of several different cultural groups. Whether one refers to them as "cultures" or "sub-cultures" or by some other name, the problem remains that it is difficult to make any strong claims about what the present culture of Canada believes. (Note: some issues relating to this observation are among those discussed in the chapter on "Multiculturalism, Nationalism, and Aboriginal Rights"). Nevertheless, presumably issues such as those raised in this book must be approached from within some sort of cultural framework, and some of the questions (such as what laws, if any, there should be governing such things as abortion, treatment of the environment, and distribution of pornography) seem to require answers which can be applied to all Canadians.

I have suggested that cultural ethical relativism has problems, but it is still possible that these problems could be overcome, and convincing reasons put forward for accepting cultural ethical relativism. To that extent, relativism is still a live issue. Perhaps it is best to approach the ethical issues discussed in this book with the aim of discovering answers which apply here and now, and postpone the question of whether these answers can be universally applicable. Clearly relativism does raise interesting questions about the very nature of moral reasoning,

but one should not conclude from the fact that people disagree about an issue that there is no possibility of establishing that one view about it is better than others.

Application

As we have seen, there is a great deal of question about which moral theory is the best, or even about whether we should aim for moral theories at all. Much interesting work is being done in this area, and it is well worth investigating further, but this is not the place to do so. Instead, I will now turn to the question of how moral theories might apply to specific moral issues.

The classic view has been that one should work out the best moral theory, and then apply it to specific issues (hence the common term "applied ethics" for discussion of such contemporary moral issues). According to this view, one might decide, for example, that utilitarianism is the best view available, and then simply resolve the issues by trying to determine which action or policy would maximize happiness. Alternatively, one might test various policies to see if they conform to the categorical imperative, and so on.

Not everyone would accept this approach, however. Some argue that we can be much more certain of our beliefs about these concrete cases than we can about rather abstract moral theories. Others point out that in the heat of the moment, we often do not have time to calculate what our chosen moral theory dictates, and so must simply apply, as well as we can, general common-sense rules which we have adopted earlier.

I do not propose to settle these issues here. One could write a whole book on whether moral issues are best dealt with by applying moral theories—but that would be a different book. The information in this introduction is meant to familiarize the reader with some of the terms which may be referred to in the pieces which follow, and to provide some introductory background information about the nature of moral philosophy. What you make of that information, and of the arguments and ideas which follow, is up to you.

Notes

1 J. S. Mill, *Utilitarianism*, originally published 1861, Hackett edition (Indianapolis: Hackett, 1979), p. 7.

2 Another version of indirect utilitarianism, which might be called "disposition utilitarianism," might tell a person to foster whichever dispositions are most likely to maximize happiness overall, and then simply act in accordance with one's dispositions in various situations.

3 J. J. C. Smart, "Extreme and Restricted Utilitarianism," as printed in P. Foot (ed.), *Theories of Ethics* (Oxford: Oxford University Press, 1967), pp. 176–177.

4 I. Kant, *Grounding for the Metaphysics of Morals*, (J. W. Ellington, trans.), (Indianapolis: Hackett, 1981), p. 30, or p. 421 in the standard pagination.

5 *Ibid.*, p. 36, or p. 429 in the standard pagination.

CHAPTER 1

The Moral Status of Non-Human Animals

Ordinarily, our moral beliefs are geared toward other human beings. However, we share this universe with many other sorts of beings: rocks, pinball machines, computers, fetuses, biospheres, non-human animals, and works of art, for example. Some of these may lack the characteristics which "normal" adult human beings have. Can moral statements be extended so as to apply to some or all of these other beings?

One way this question is often approached is by asking what sorts of beings "matter" (or "count") morally. It is common to assert that normal adult human beings matter morally, but that rocks (for example) do not. A person who hits a rock has probably not done anything wrong, but a person who hits another adult human being probably has. What makes the difference here? Is there some relevant characteristic which the human has, but the rock does not?

Several possible criteria have been suggested for the moral status of a being. If it is true that all normal adult human beings count, then the criterion will have to be something which is common to all such beings. Suggestions for what this characteristic might be have included the capacity to feel pain, the capacity to use language or to think abstractly or rationally, the sense of oneself as continuing through time, or the property of having a soul.

Of course there is also disagreement about which particular beings *have* these characteristics. Is there such a thing as a soul at all, and if so, do non-human animals have them? (From now on, for convenience, I will use the word "animals" to refer to non-human animals.) Can fish feel pain? Can insects, or plants? Are non-human primates capable of abstract thought? Do whales use language? The questions are endless.

One way of describing this line of questioning is in terms of an attempt to discover which beings should be considered "persons." One might claim that "persons" count morally, and then leave open the question of which beings might qualify as persons. Of course, in ordinary usage "person" is virtually synonymous with "human being," and indeed many people might claim that human beings count morally, and other beings do not. It is fair to ask, however, what is so special about human beings.

Clearly we are predisposed to favour members of our own group over "outsiders," and it is much easier to identify with other human beings than with rocks or biospheres or even other animals. However, much of what is commonly considered political progress over the past century or two can be usefully understood in terms of an expansion of the circle of beings people have been willing to consider members of their own group. For example, favouring people whose skin colour is the same as one's own has been commonly denounced as "racism," denial of rights to people on the basis of gender has been commonly denounced as "sexism," and so on. Some people would claim that this broadening process should continue, and that failure to include animals in one's own group should be denounced as "speciesism."

It should be noted that saying that certain beings count morally does not necessarily imply that they have to be counted as equals. One might think that the suffering of dogs counts for something, and should be avoided if possible, but that if one has to choose between allowing a dog to suffer and allowing a human being to suffer, one should not be indifferent about the choices. But what if the choice was between one human being and a hundred dogs? Is there any amount of dog suffering which can outweigh the suffering of a human being? If so, how much? If not, why not?

This question of how to compare human well-being with animal well-being is important for the broader issue of how we should treat animals. What if many people enjoy eating meat, but could survive on a strictly vegetarian diet? Is it morally acceptable to sacrifice an animal's life in order to provide the increased pleasure of a tasty meal? How about for a bit of leather, or fur, or ivory?

Many people believe that it is acceptable to use animals for human purposes if the purpose is important enough, but not for "trivial" things such as improved cosmetics. Explaining how this distinction between important and unimportant purposes works may be a difficult task, especially since human beings obviously get different amounts of pleasure from different things. Is eating meat somehow more important than wearing fur, for example? But even in cases where the goal is clearly important, such as medical experimentation which could potentially save many lives, it is not clear what principle is at stake here. Again, the question is how we compare human well-being with that of animals.

Some people, at the extreme "animal rights" end of the scale, argue that it is never permissible to use animals in a way it would not be permissible to use human beings. They point out that many human beings do not have all the capacities of "normal" adult humans. Human infants and severely mentally handicapped people, not to mention people in comas and perhaps fetuses, seem incapable of abstract thought, use of language, etc. Indeed, some animals may seem more advanced in these regards than the human beings in question. Yet most people would claim that it would be wrong to use infants or severely mentally handicapped people for experiments, or to kill them for food. The animal rights advocate might claim that treating animals but not these humans in these ways reveals an unreasonable double standard, and that using animals in such ways should be seen as abhorrent.

Other people might claim that causing

the death of animals is not wrong, but causing their suffering is. In this case, if, for example, it is true that the present-day meat industry causes animals to live miserable lives, then that would be a reason to stop eating meat. If, however, it were possible to kill animals humanely after comfortable lives, perhaps eating meat would not be wrong.

Another view which would provide only limited protection for animals maintains that animals do not have any standing in their own right, but that there are good reasons for people to treat them well in any case. One such reason might be that people often grow emotionally attached to animals (pets, etc.) and that hurting those animals would indirectly hurt the people who care about them, which is morally impermissible. This is analogous to an argument which might be raised for showing consideration toward works of art, which other people might appreciate. Another such indirect reason for being kind to animals might be that people should foster dispositions of kindness and consideration, for the well-being of human society, and that cruelty toward animals tends to disrupt those dispositions.

Other human-based arguments in favour of some sort of consideration for animals have to do with wastefulness and distribution of resources. It has been claimed that a great deal of plant protein is wasted in the process of nourishing an animal for consumption, so that fewer people can be fed successfully on animal meat than on the grain the animal itself is fed on. It has also been claimed that great quantities of water are similarly used inefficiently in meat production. Further concerns about the impact of the meat industry on human well-being have been raised because of practices within the meat industry which have given rise to medical conditions such as "mad cow disease." It is important to note, however, that these arguments do not depend on the animals' counting morally at all—the claim is simply that human beings will be better off if we adopt certain attitudes toward the use of animals.

The selections in this chapter consider some of the alternative views on the moral status of non-human animals, and try to provide answers to the question of how we should view our relationship to them.

Cruelty to Animals

Section 446, Canadian Criminal Code

In current Canadian law, non-human animals do not have standing in their own right, but there are limitations on the ways in which people can treat them. The following is the existing law against cruelty to animals.

★   ★   ★

CAUSING UNNECESSARY SUFFERING / Punishment / Failure to exercise reasonable care as evidence / Presence at baiting as evidence / Order of prohibition / Breach of order.

446. (1) Every one commits an offence who

(a) wilfully causes or, being the owner, wilfully permits to be caused unnecessary pain, suffering or injury to an animal or a bird;

(b) by wilful neglect causes damage or injury to animals or birds while they are being driven or conveyed;

(c) being the owner or the person having the custody or control of a domestic animal or a bird or an animal or a bird wild by nature that is in captivity, abandons it in distress or wilfully neglects or fails to provide suitable and adequate food, water, shelter and care for it;

(d) in any manner encourages, aids or assists at the fighting or baiting of animals or birds;

(e) wilfully, without reasonable excuse, administers a poisonous or an injurious drug or substance to a domestic animal or bird or an animal or a bird wild by nature that is kept in captivity or, being the owner of such an animal or a bird, wilfully permits a poisonous or an injurious drug or substance to be administered;

(f) promotes, arranges, conducts, assists in, receives money for or takes part in any meeting, competition, exhibition, pastime, practice, display or event at or in the course of which captive birds are liberated by hand, trap, contrivance or any other means for the purpose of being shot when they are liberated; or

(g) being the owner, occupier, or person in charge of any premises, permits the premises or any part thereof to be used for a purpose mentioned in paragraph (f).

(2) Every one who commits an offence under subsection (1) is guilty of an offence punishable on summary conviction.

(3) For the purposes of proceedings under paragraph (1)(a) or (b), evidence that a person failed to exercise reasonable care or supervision of an animal or a bird thereby causing it pain, suffering, damage or injury is, in the absence of any evidence to the contrary, proof that the pain, suffering, damage or injury was caused or was permitted to be caused wilfully or was caused by wilful neglect, as the case may be.

(4) For the purpose of proceedings under paragraph (1)(d), evidence that an accused was present at the fighting or baiting of animals or birds is, in the absence of any evidence to the contrary, proof that he encouraged, aided or assisted at the fighting or baiting.

(5) Where an accused is convicted of an offence under subsection (1), the court may, in addition to any other sentence that may be imposed for the offence, make an order prohibiting the accused from owning or having the custody or control of an animal or a bird during any period not exceeding two years.

(6) Every one who owns or has the custody or control of an animal or a bird while he is prohibited from doing so by reason of an order made under subsection (5) is guilty of an offence punishable on summary conviction. R.S., c.C-34, s. 402; 1974-75-76, c. 93, s. 35.

The Rights of Animals and Unborn Generations

Joel Feinberg

In this selection, Feinberg tries to determine what characteristics a being must have in order to have rights. His announced intention is to see if future generations of humans can have rights against us, but in the process of exploring that, he considers the claim of non-human animals, vegetables, whole species, dead persons, human vegetables, and fetuses. He claims that in order to have rights, a being must have interests, and tries to separate authentic uses of that description from metaphorical or mistaken uses.

★　★　★

Every philosophical paper must begin with an unproved assumption. Mine is the assumption that there will still be a world five hundred years from now, and that it will contain human beings who are very much like us. We have it within our power now, clearly, to affect the lives of these creatures for better or worse by contributing to the conservation or corruption of the environment in which they must live. I shall assume furthermore that it is psychologically possible for us to care about our remote descendants, that many of us in fact do care, and indeed that we ought to care. My main concern then will be to show that it makes sense to speak of the rights of unborn generations against us, and that given the moral judgement that we ought to conserve our environmental inheritance for them, and its grounds, we might well say that future generations *do* have rights correlative to our present duties toward them. Protecting our environment now is also a matter of elementary prudence, and insofar as we do it for the next generation already here in the persons of our children, it is a matter of love. But from the perspective of our remote descendants it is basically a matter of justice, of respect for their rights. My main concern here will be to examine the concept of a right to better understand how that can be.

The Problem

To have a right is to have a claim[1] *to* something and *against* someone, the recognition of which is called for by legal rules or, in the case of moral rights, by the principles of an enlightened conscience. In the familiar cases of rights, the claimant is a competent adult human being, and the claimee is an officeholder in an institution or else a private individual, in either case, another competent adult human being. Normal adult human beings, then, are obviously the sorts of beings of whom rights can meaningfully be predicated. Everyone would agree to that, even extreme misanthropes who deny that anyone in fact has rights. On the other hand, it is absurd to say that rocks can have rights, not because rocks are morally inferior things unworthy of rights (that statement makes no sense either), but because rocks belong to a category of entities of whom rights cannot be meaningfully predicated. That is not to say that there are no circumstances in which we ought to treat rocks carefully, but only that the rocks themselves cannot validly claim good treatment from us. In between the clear cases of rocks and normal human beings, however, is a spectrum of less obvious cases, including some bewildering borderline ones. Is it meaningful or conceptually possible to ascribe rights to our dead ancestors? to individual animals? to whole species of animals? to plants? to idiots and madmen? to fetuses? to generations yet unborn? Until we know how to settle these puzzling cases, we cannot claim fully to grasp the concept of a right, or to know the shape of its logical boundaries.

One way to approach these riddles is to turn one's attention first to the most familiar and unproblematic instances of rights, note their most salient characteristics, and then compare the borderline cases with them, measuring as closely as possible the points of similarity and difference. In the end, the way we classify the borderline cases may depend on whether we are more impressed with the similarities or the differences between them and the cases in which we have the most confidence.

It will be useful to consider the problem of individual animals first because their case is the one that has already been debated with the most thoroughness by philosophers so that the dialectic of claim and rejoinder has now unfolded to the point where disputants can get to the end game quickly and isolate the crucial point at issue. When we understand precisely what is at issue in the debate over animal rights, I think we will have the key to the solution of all the other riddles about rights.

Individual Animals

Almost all modern writers agree that we ought to be kind to animals, but that is quite another thing from holding that animals can claim kind treatment from us as their due. Statutes making cruelty to animals a crime are now very common, and these, of course, impose legal duties on people not to mistreat animals; but that still leaves open the question whether the animals, as beneficiaries of those duties, possess rights correlative to them. We may very well have duties *regarding* animals that are not at the same time duties *to* animals, just as we may have duties regarding rocks, or

buildings, or lawns, that are not duties *to* the rocks, buildings, or lawns. Some legal writers have taken the still more extreme position that animals themselves are not even the directly intended beneficiaries of statutes prohibiting cruelty to animals. During the nineteenth century, for example, it was commonly said that such statutes were designed to protect human beings by preventing the growth of cruel habits that could later threaten human beings with harm too. Prof. Louis B. Schwartz finds the rationale of the cruelty-to-animals prohibition in its protection of animal lovers from affronts to their sensibilities. "It is not the mistreated dog who is the ultimate object of concern," he writes. "Our concern is for the feelings of other human beings, a large proportion of whom, although accustomed to the slaughter of animals for food, readily identify themselves with a tortured dog or horse and respond with great sensitivity to its sufferings."[2] This seems to me to be factitious. How much more natural is it to say with John Chipman Gray that the true purpose of cruelty-to-animals statutes is "to preserve the dumb brutes from suffering."[3] The very people whose sensibilities are invoked in the alternative explanation, a group that no doubt now includes most of us, are precisely those who would insist that the protection belongs primarily to the animals themselves, not merely to their own tender feelings. Indeed, it would be difficult even to account for the existence of such feelings in the absence of a belief that the animals deserve the protection in their own right and for their own sakes.

Even if we allow, as I think we must, that animals are the intended direct beneficiaries of legislation forbidding cruelty to animals, it does not follow directly that animals have legal rights, and Gray himself, for one,[4] refused to draw this further inference. Animals cannot have rights, he thought, for the same reason they cannot have duties, namely, that they are not genuine "moral agents." Now, it is relatively easy to see why animals cannot have duties, and this matter is largely beyond controversy. Animals cannot be "reasoned with" or instructed in their responsibilities; they are inflexible and unadaptable to future contingencies; they are subject to fits of instinctive passion which they are incapable of repressing or controlling, postponing or sublimating. Hence, they cannot enter into contractual agreements, or make promises; they cannot be trusted; and they cannot (except within very narrow limits and for the purposes of conditioning) be blamed for what would be called "moral failures" in a human being. They are therefore incapable of being moral subjects, of acting rightly or wrongly in the moral sense, of having, discharging, or breeching duties and obligations.

But what is there about the intellectual incompetence of animals (which admittedly disqualifies them for duties) that makes them logically unsuitable for rights? The most common reply to this question is that animals are incapable of *claiming* rights on their own. They cannot make motion, on their own, to courts to have their claims recognized or enforced; they cannot initiate, on their own, any kind of legal proceedings; nor are they capable of even understanding when their rights are being violated, of distinguishing harm from wrongful injury, and responding with indignation and an outraged sense of justice instead of mere anger or fear.

No one can deny any of these allegations, but to the claim that they are grounds for disqualification of rights of animals, philosophers on the other side of this controversy have made convincing rejoinders. It is simply not true, says W.D. Lamont,[5] that the ability to understand what a right is and the ability to set legal machinery in motion by one's own initiative are necessary for the possession of rights. If that were the case, then neither human idiots nor wee babies would have any legal rights at all. Yet it is manifest that both of these classes of intellectual incompetents have legal rights recognized and easily enforced by the courts. Children and idiots start legal proceedings, not on their own direct initiative, but rather through the actions of proxies or attorneys who are empowered to speak in their names. If there is no conceptual absurdity in this situation, why should there be in the case where a proxy makes a claim on behalf of an animal? People commonly enough make wills leaving money to trustees for the care of animals. Is it not natural to speak of the animal's right to his inheritance in cases of this kind? If a trustee embezzles money from the animal's account,[6] and a proxy speaking in the dumb brute's behalf presses the animal's claim, can he not be described as asserting the animal's *rights*? More exactly, the animal itself claims its rights through the vicarious actions of a human proxy speaking in its name and on its behalf. There appears to be no reason why we should require the animal to understand what is going on (so the argument concludes) as a condition for regarding it as a possessor of rights.

Some writers protest at this point that the legal relation between a principal and an agent cannot hold between animals and human beings. Between humans, the relation of agency can take two very different forms, depending upon the degree of discretion granted to the agent, and there is a continuum of combinations between the extremes. On the other hand, there is the agent who is the mere "mouthpiece" of his principal. He is a "tool" in much the same sense as is a typewriter or telephone; he simply transmits the instructions of his principal. Human beings could hardly be the agents or representatives of animals in this sense, since the dumb brutes could no more use human "tools" than mechanical ones. On the other hand, an agent may be some sort of expert hired to exercise his professional judgement on behalf of, and in the name of, the principal. He may be given, within some limited area of expertise, complete independence to act as he deems best, binding his principal to all the beneficial or detrimental consequences. This is the role played by trustees, lawyers, and ghost-writers. This type of representation requires that the agent have great skill, but makes little or no demand upon the principal, who may leave everything to the judgement of his agent. Hence, there appears, at first, to be no reason why an animal cannot be a totally passive principal in this second kind of agency relationship.

There are still some important dissimilarities, however. In the typical instance of representation by an agent, even of the second, highly discretionary kind, the agent is hired by a principal who enters into an agreement or contract with him; the principal tells his agent that within certain carefully specified boundaries "You may speak for me," subject always to the principal's approval, his right to give new directions, or to cancel the whole arrangement. No dog or cat could possibly do any of those things. Moreover, if it is the assigned task of the agent to defend the principal's rights, the principal may often decide to release his claimee, or to waive his own rights, and instruct his agent accordingly. Again, no mute cow or horse can do that. But although the possibility of hiring, agreeing, contracting, approving, directing, canceling, releasing, waiving, and instructing is present in the typical (all-human) case of agency representation, there appears to be no reason of a logical or conceptual kind why that *must* be so, and indeed there are some special examples involving human principals where it is not in fact so. I have in mind legal rules, for example, that require that a defendant be represented at his trial by an attorney, and impose a state-appointed attorney upon reluctant defendants, or upon those tried *in absentia*, whether they like it or not. Moreover, small children and mentally deficient and deranged adults are commonly represented by trustees and attorneys,

even though they are incapable of granting their own consent to the representation, or of entering into contracts, of giving directions, or waiving their rights. It may be that it is unwise to permit agents to represent principals without the latters' knowledge or consent. If so, then no one should ever be permitted to speak for an animal, at least in a legally binding way. But that is quite another thing than saying that such representation is logically incoherent or conceptually incongruous—the contention that is at issue.

H. J. McCloskey,[7] I believe, accepts the argument up to this point, but he presents a new and different reason for denying that animals can have legal rights. The ability to make claims, whether directly or through a representative, he implies, is essential to the possession of rights. Animals obviously cannot press their claims on their own, and so if they have rights, these rights must be assertable by agents. Animals, however, cannot be represented, McCloskey contends, and not for any of the reasons already discussed, but rather because representation, in the requisite sense, is always of interests, and animals (he says) are incapable of having interests.

Now, there is a very important insight expressed in the requirement that a being have interests if he is to be a logically proper subject of rights. This can be appreciated if we consider just why it is that mere things cannot have rights. Consider a very precious "mere thing"—a beautiful natural wilderness, or a complex and ornamental artifact, like the Taj Mahal. Such things ought to be cared for, because they would sink into decay if neglected, depriving some human beings, or perhaps even all human beings, of something of great value. Certain persons may even have as their own special job the care and protection of these valuable objects. But we are not tempted in these cases to speak of "thing-rights" correlative to custodial duties, because, try as we might, we cannot think of mere things as possessing interests of their own. Some people may have a duty to preserve, maintain, or improve the Taj Mahal, but they can hardly have a duty to help or hurt it, benefit or aid it, succor or relieve it. Custodians may protect it for the sake of a nation's pride and art lovers' fancy; but they don't keep it in good repair for "its own sake," and for "its own true welfare," or "well-being." A mere thing, however valuable to others, has no good of its own. The explanation of that fact, I suspect, consists in the fact that mere things have no conative life: no conscious wishes, desires, and hopes; or urges and impulses; or unconscious drives, aims, and goals; or latent tendencies, direction of growth, and natural fulfillments. Interests must be compounded somehow out of conations; hence mere things have no interests. *A fortiori*, they have no interests to be protected by legal or moral rules. Without interests a creature can have no "good" of its own, the achievement of which can be its due. Mere things are not loci of value in their own right, but rather their value consists entirely in their being objects of other beings' interests.

So far McCloskey is on solid ground, but one can quarrel with his denial that any animals but humans have interests. I should think that the trustee of funds willed to a dog or cat is more than a mere custodian of the animal he protects. Rather his job is to look out for the interests of the animal and make sure no one denies it its due. The animal itself is the beneficiary of his dutiful services. Many of the higher animals at least have appetites, conative urges, and rudimentary purposes, the integrated satisfaction of which constitutes their welfare or good. We can, of course, with consistency treat animals as mere pests and deny that they have any rights; for most animals, especially those of the lower orders, we have no choice but to do so. But it seems to me, nevertheless, that in general, animals *are* among the sorts of beings of whom rights can meaningfully be predicated and denied.

Now, if a person agrees with the conclusion of the argument thus far, that animals are the sorts of beings that *can* have rights, and further, if he accepts the moral judgement that we ought to be kind to animals, only one further premise is needed to yield the conclusion that some animals do in fact have rights. We must now ask ourselves for whose sake ought we to treat (some) animals with consideration and humaneness? If we conceive our duty to be one of obedience to authority, or to one's own conscience merely, or one of consideration for tender human sensibilities only, then we might still deny that animals have rights, even though we admit that they are the kinds of beings that *can* have rights. But if we hold not only that we ought to treat animals humanely but also that we should do so for the animals' own sake, that such treatment is something we owe animals as their due, something that can be claimed for them, something the withholding of which would be an injustice and a wrong, and not merely a harm, then it follows that we do ascribe rights to animals. I suspect that the moral judgements most of us make about animals do pass these phenomenological tests, so that most of us do believe that animals have rights, but are reluctant to say so because of the conceptual confusions about the notion of a right that I have attempted to dispel above.

Now we can extract from our discussion of animal rights a crucial principle for tentative use in the resolution of the other riddles about the applicability of the concept of a right, namely, that the sorts of beings who *can* have rights are precisely those who have (or can have) interests. I have come to this tentative conclusion for two reasons: (1) because a right holder must be capable of being represented and it is impossible to represent a being that has no interests, and (2) because a right holder must be capable of being a beneficiary in his own person, and a being without interests is a being that is incapable of being harmed or benefitted, having no good or "sake" of its own. Thus, a being without interests has no "behalf" to act in, and no "sake" to act for. My strategy now will be to apply the "interest principle," as we can call it, to the other puzzles about rights, while being prepared to modify it where necessary (but as little as possible), in the hope of separating in a consistent and intuitively satisfactory fashion the beings who can have rights from those which cannot.

Vegetables

It is clear that we ought not to mistreat certain plants, and indeed there are rules and regulations imposing duties on persons not to misbehave in respect to certain members of the vegetable kingdom. It is forbidden, for example, to pick wildflowers in the mountainous tundra areas of national parks, or to endanger trees by starting fires in dry forest areas. Members of Congress introduce bills designed, as they say, to "protect" rare redwood trees from commercial pillage. Given this background, it is surprising that no one[8] speaks of plants as having rights. Plants, after all, are not "mere things"; they are vital objects with inherited biological propensities determining their natural growth. Moreover, we do say that certain conditions are "good" or "bad" for plants, thereby suggesting that plants, unlike rocks, are capable of having a "good." (This is a case, however, where "what we say" should not be taken seriously: we also say that certain kinds of paint are good or bad for the internal walls of a house, and this does not commit us to a conception of walls as being possessed of a good or welfare of their own.) Finally, we are capable of feeling a kind of affection for particular plants, though we rarely personalize them, as we do in the case of animals by giving them proper names.

Still, all are agreed that plants are not the kinds of beings that can have rights. Plants are

never plausibly understood to be the direct intended beneficiaries of rules designed to "protect" them. We wish to keep redwood groves in existence for the sake of human beings who can enjoy their serene beauty, and for the sake of generations of human beings yet unborn. Trees are not the sorts of beings who have their "own sakes," despite the fact that they have biological propensities. Having no conscious wants or goals of their own, trees cannot know satisfaction or frustration, pleasure or pain. Hence, there is no possibility of kind or cruel treatment of trees. In these morally crucial respects, trees differ from the higher species of animals.

Yet trees are not mere things like rocks. They grow and develop according to the laws of their own nature. Aristotle and Aquinas both took trees to have their own "natural ends." Why then do I deny them the status of beings with interests of their own? The reason is that an interest, however the concept is finally to be analyzed, presupposes at least rudimentary cognitive equipment. Interests are compounded out of *desires* and *aims*, both of which presuppose something like *belief*, or cognitive awareness. A desiring creature may want X because he seeks anything that is $\emptyset$, and X appears to be $\emptyset$ to him; or he may be seeking Y, and he believes, or expects, or hopes that X will be a means to Y. If he desires X in order to get Y, this implies that he believes that X will bring Y about, or at least that he has some sort of brute expectation that is a primitive correlate of belief. But what of the desire for $\emptyset$ (or for Y) itself? Perhaps a creature has such a "desire" as an ultimate set, as if he had come into existence all "wound up" to pursue $\emptyset$-ness or Y-ness, and his not to reason why. Such a propensity, I think, would not qualify as a desire. Mere brute longings unmediated by beliefs—longings for one knows not what—might perhaps be a primitive form of consciousness (I don't want to beg that question) but they are altogether different from the sort of thing we mean by "desire," especially when we speak of human beings.

If some such account as the above is correct, we can never have any grounds for attributing a desire or a want to a creature known to be incapable even of rudimentary beliefs; and if desires or wants are the materials interests are made of, mindless creatures have no interests of their own. The law, therefore, cannot have as its intention the protection of their interests, so that "protective legislation" has to be understood as legislation protecting the interests human beings may have in them.

Plant life might nevertheless be thought at first to constitute a hard case for the interest principle for two reasons. In the first place, plants no less than animals are said to have needs of their own. To be sure, we can speak even of mere things as having needs too, but such talk misleads one into thinking of the need as belonging, in the final analysis, to the "mere thing" itself. If we were so deceived we would not be thinking of the mere thing as a "mere thing" after all. We say, for example, that John Doe's walls need painting, or that Richard Roe's car needs a washing, but we direct our attitudes of sympathy or reproach (as the case may be) to John and Richard, not to their possessions. It would be otherwise, if we observed that some child is in need of a good meal. Our sympathy and concern in that case would be directed at the child himself as the true possessor of the need in question.

The needs of plants might well seem closer to the needs of animals than to the pseudo-needs of mere things. An owner may need a plant (say, for its commercial value or as a potential meal), but the plant itself, it might appear, needs nutrition or cultivation. Our confusion about this matter may stem from language. It is a commonplace that the word *need* is ambiguous. To say that A needs X may be to say either: (1) X is necessary to the achievement of A's goals, or to the perform-

ance of one of its functions, or (2) X is good for A; its lack would harm A or be injurious or detrimental to him (or it). The first sort of need-statement is value-neutral, implying no comment on the value of the goal or function in question; whereas the second kind of statement about needs commits its maker to a value judgement about what is good or bad for A in the long run, that is, about what is in A's interests. A being must have interests, therefore, to have needs in the second sense, but any kind of thing, vegetable or mineral, could have needs in the first sense. An automobile needs gas and oil to function, but it is no tragedy for it if it runs out—an empty gas tank does not hinder or retard its interests. Similarly, to say that a tree needs sunshine and water is to say that without them it cannot grow and survive; but unless the growth and survival of trees are matters of human concern, affecting human interests, practical or aesthetic, the needs of trees alone will not be the basis of any claim of what is "due" them in their own right. Plants may need things in order to discharge their functions, but their functions are assigned by human interests, not their own.

The second source of confusion derives from the fact that we commonly speak of plants as thriving and flourishing, or withering and languishing. One might be tempted to think of these states either as themselves consequences of the possession of interests so that even creatures without wants or beliefs can be said to have interests, or else as grounds independent of the possession of interests for the making of intelligible claims of rights. In either case, plants would be thought of as conceivable possessors of rights after all.

Consider what it means to speak of something as "flourishing." The verb *to flourish* apparently was applied originally and literally to plants only, and in its original sense it meant simply "to bear flowers: BLOSSOM"; but then by analogical extension of sense it came also to mean "to grow luxuriantly: increase, and enlarge," and then to "THRIVE" (generally) and finally, when extended to human beings, "to be prosperous," or to "increase in wealth, honor, comfort, happiness, or whatever is desirable."[9] Applied to human beings the term is, of course, a fixed metaphor. When a person flourishes, something happens to his interests analogous to what happens to a plant when it flowers, grows, and spreads. A person flourishes when his interests (whatever they may be) are progressing severally and collectively toward their harmonious fulfillment and spawning new interests along the way whose prospects are also good. To flourish is to glory in the advancement of one's interests, in short, to be happy.

Nothing is gained by twisting the botanical metaphor back from humans to plants. To speak of thriving human interests as if they were flowers is to speak naturally and well, and to mislead no one. But then to think of the flowers or plants as if they were interests (or the signs of interests) is to bring the metaphor back full circle for no good reason and in the teeth of our actual beliefs. Some of our talk about flourishing plants reveals quite clearly that the interests that thrive when plants flourish are human not "plant interests." For example, we sometimes make a flowering bush flourish by "frustrating" its own primary propensities. We pinch off dead flowers before seeds have formed, thus "encouraging" the plant to make new flowers in an effort to produce more seeds. It is not the plant's own natural propensity (to produce seeds) that is advanced, but rather the gardener's interest in the production of new flowers and the spectator's pleasure in aesthetic form, color, or scent. What we mean in such cases by saying that the plant flourishes is that our interest in the plant, not its own, is thriving. It is not always so clear that that is what we mean, for on other occasions there is a correspondence between our interests and the plant's natural propensities, a coinciding of what we want

from nature and nature's own "intention." But the exceptions to this correspondence provide the clue to our real sense in speaking of a plant's good or welfare.[10] And even when there exists such a correspondence, it is often because we have actually remade the plant's nature so that our own interests in it will flourish more "naturally" and effectively.

Whole Species

The topic of whole species, whether of plants or animals, can be treated in much the same way as that of individual plants. A whole collection, as such, cannot have beliefs, expectations, wants, or desires, and can flourish or languish only in the human interest related sense in which individual plants thrive and decay. Individual elephants can have interests, but the species elephant cannot. Even where individual elephants are not granted rights, human beings may have an interest—economic, scientific, or sentimental—in keeping the species from dying out, and *that* interest may be protected in various ways by law. But that is quite another matter from recognizing a right to survival belonging to the species itself. Still, the preservation of a whole species may quite properly seem to be a morally more important matter than the preservation of an individual animal. Individual animals can have rights but it is implausible to ascribe to them a right to life on the human model. Nor do we normally have duties to keep individual animals alive or even to abstain from killing them provided we do it humanely and nonwantonly in the promotion of legitimate human interests. On the other hand, we do have duties to protect threatened species, not duties to the species themselves as such, but rather duties to future human beings, duties derived from our housekeeping role as temporary inhabitants of this planet.

We commonly and very naturally speak of corporate entities, such as institutions, churches and national states having rights and duties, and an adequate analysis of the conditions for ownership of rights should account for that fact. A corporate entity, of course, is more than a mere collection of things that have some important traits in common. Unlike a biological species, an institution has a charter, or constitution, or bylaws, with rules defining offices and procedures, and it has human beings whose function it is to administer the rules and apply the procedures. When the institution has a duty to an outsider, there is always some determinant human being whose duty it is to do something for the outsider, and when the state, for example, has a right to collect taxes, there are always certain definite flesh and blood persons who have rights to demand tax money from other citizens. We have no reluctance to use the language of corporate rights and duties because we know that in the last analysis these are rights and duties of individual persons, acting in their "official capacities." And when individuals act in their official roles in accordance with valid empowering rules, their acts are imputable to the organization itself and become "acts of state." Thus, there is no need to posit any individual superperson named by the expression "the State" (or for that matter, "the company," "the club," or "the church.") Nor is there any reason to take the rights of corporate entities to be exceptions to the interest principle. The United States is not a superperson with wants and beliefs of its own, but it is a corporate entity with corporate interests that are, in turn, analyzable into the interests of its numerous flesh and blood members.

Dead Persons

So far we have refined the interest principle but we have not had occasion to modify it. Applied to dead persons, however, it will have to be stretched to near the breaking point if it is to explain how our duty to honor commitments to the dead can be thought to be linked to the rights of the dead against us. The case against ascribing rights to dead men can be made very simply: a dead man is a mere corpse, a piece of decaying organic matter. Mere inanimate things can have no interests, and what is incapable of having interests is incapable of having rights. If, nevertheless, we grant dead men rights against us, we would seem to be treating the interests they had while alive as somehow surviving their deaths. There is the sound of paradox in this way of talking, but it may be the least paradoxical way of describing our moral relations to our predecessors. And if the idea of an interest's surviving its possessor's death is a kind of fiction, it is a fiction that most living men have a real interest in preserving.

Most persons while still alive have certain desires about what is to happen to their bodies, their property, or their reputations after they are dead. For that reason, our legal system has developed procedures to enable persons while still alive to determine whether their bodies will be used for purposes of medical research or organic transplantation, and to whom their wealth (after taxes) is to be transferred. Living men also take out life insurance policies guaranteeing that the accumulated benefits be conferred upon beneficiaries of their own choice. They also make private agreements, both contractual and informal, in which they receive promises that certain things will be done after their deaths in exchange for some present service or consideration. In all these cases promises are made to living persons that their wishes will be honored after they are dead. Like all other valid promises, they impose duties on the promisor and confer correlative rights on the promisee.

How does the situation change after the promisee has died? Surely the duties of the promisor do not suddenly become null and void. If that were the case, and known to be the case, there could be no confidence in promises regarding posthumous arrangements; no one would bother with wills or life insurance policies. Indeed the duties of courts and trustees to honor testamentary directions, and the duties of life insurance companies to pay benefits to survivors, are, in a sense, only conditional duties before a man dies. They come into existence as categorical demands for immediate action only upon the promisee's death. So the view that death renders them null and void has the truth exactly upside down.

The survival of the promisor's duty after the promisee's death does not prove that the promisee retains a right even after death, for we might prefer to conclude that there is one class of cases where duties to keep promises are not logically correlated with a promisee's right, namely, cases where the promisee has died. Still, a morally sensitive promisor is likely to think of his promised performance not only as a duty (i.e., a morally required action) but also as something owed to the deceased promisee as his due. Honoring such promises is a way of keeping faith with the dead. To be sure, the promisor will not think of his duty as something to be done for the promisee's "good," since the promisee, being dead, has no "good" of his own. We can think of certain of the deceased's interests, however, (including especially those enshrined in wills and protected by contracts and promises) as surviving their owner's death, and constituting claims against us that persist beyond the life of the claimant. Such claims can be represented by proxies just like the claims of animals. This way of speaking, I believe, reflects more accurately than any other an important fact about the human condition: we have an interest while alive that other interests of ours will continue to be recognized and served after we are dead. The whole practice of honoring wills and testaments, and the like, is thus for the sake of the living, just as a particular instance of it may be thought to be for the sake of one who is dead.

Conceptual sense, then, can be made of talk about dead men's rights; but it is still a wide open moral question whether dead men in fact have rights, and if so, what those rights are. In particular, commentators have disagreed over whether a man's interest in his reputation deserves to be protected from defamation even after his death. With only a few prominent exceptions, legal systems punish a libel on a dead man "only when its publication is in truth an attack upon the interests of living persons."[11] A widow or a son may be wounded, or embarrassed, or even injured economically, by a defamatory attack on the memory of their dead husband or father. In Utah defamation of the dead is a misdemeanor, and in Sweden a cause of action in tort. The law rarely presumes, however, that a dead man himself has any interests, representable by proxy, that can be injured by defamation, apparently because of the maxim that what a dead man doesn't know can't hurt him.

This presupposes, however, that the whole point of guarding the reputations even of living men, is to protect them from hurt feelings, or to protect some other interests, for example, economic ones, that do not survive death. A moment's thought, I think, will show that our interests are more complicated than that. If someone spreads a libelous description of me, without my knowledge, among hundreds of people in a remote part of the country, so that I am, still without my knowledge, an object of general scorn and mockery in that group, I have been injured, even though I never learn what has happened. That is because I have an interest, so I believe, in having a good reputation *simpliciter*, in addition to my interest in avoiding hurt feelings, embarrassment, and economic injury. In the example, I do not know what is being said and believed about me, so my feelings are not hurt; but clearly if I did know, I would be enormously distressed. The distress would be the natural consequence of my belief that an interest other than my interest in avoiding distress had been damaged. How else can I account for the distress? If I had no interest in a good reputation as such, I would respond to news of harm to my reputation with indifference.

While it is true that a dead man cannot have his feelings hurt, it does not follow, therefore, that his claim to be thought of no worse than he deserves cannot survive his death. Almost every living person, I should think, would wish to have this interest protected after his death, at least during the lifetimes of those persons who were his contemporaries. We can hardly expect the law to protect Julius Caesar from defamation in the history books. This might hamper historical research and restrict socially valuable forms of expression. Even interests that survive their owner's death are not immortal. Anyone should be permitted to say anything he wishes about George Washington or Abraham Lincoln, although perhaps not everything is morally permissible. Everyone ought to refrain from malicious lies about Nero or King Tut, though not so much for those ancients' own sakes as for the sake of those who would now know the truth about the past. We owe it to the brothers Kennedy, however, as their due, not to tell damaging lies about them to those who were once their contemporaries. If the reader would deny that judgement, I can only urge him to ask himself whether he now wishes his own interest in reputation to be respected, along with his interest in determining the distribution of his wealth, after his death.

Human Vegetables

Mentally deficient and deranged human beings are hardly ever so handicapped intellectually that they do not compare favorably with even the highest of the lower animals, though they are commonly so incompetent that they cannot be assigned duties or be held responsible for what they do. Since animals can have rights, then, it follows that human idiots and madmen can too. It would make good sense, for example, to ascribe to them a right to be cured whenever effective therapy is available at reasonable cost, and even those incurables who have been consigned to a sanatorium for permanent "warehousing" can claim (through a proxy) their right to decent treatment.

Human beings suffering extreme cases of mental illness, however, may be so utterly disoriented or insensitive as to compare quite unfavorably with the brightest cats and dogs. Those suffering from catatonic schizophrenia may be barely distinguishable in respect to those traits presupposed by the possession of interests from the lowliest vegetables. So long as we regard these patients as potentially curable, we may think of them as human beings with interests in their own restoration and treat them as possessors of rights. We may think of the patient as a genuine human person inside the vegetable casing struggling to get out, just as in the old fairy tales a pumpkin could be thought of as a beautiful maiden under a magic spell waiting only the proper words to be restored to her true self. Perhaps it is reasonable never to lose hope that a patient can be cured, and therefore to regard him always as a person "under a spell" with a permanent interest in his own recovery that is entitled to recognition and protection.

What if, nevertheless, we think of the catatonic schizophrenic and the vegetating patient with irreversible brain damage as absolutely incurable? Can we think of them at the same time as possessed of interests and rights too, or is this combination of traits a conceptual impossibility? Shocking as it may at first seem, I am driven unavoidably to the latter view. If redwood trees and rosebushes cannot have rights, neither can incorrigible human vegetables.[12] The trustees who are designated to administer funds for the care of these unfortunates are better understood as mere custodians than as representatives of their interests since these patients no longer have interests. It does not follow that they should not be kept alive as long as possible: that is an open moral question not foreclosed by conceptual analysis. Even if we have duties to keep human vegetables alive, however, they cannot be duties *to* them. We may be obliged to keep them alive to protect the sensibilities of others, or to foster humanitarian tendencies in ourselves, but we cannot keep them alive for their own good, for they are no longer capable of having a "good" of their own. Without awareness, expectation, belief, desire, aim, and purpose, a being can have no interests; without interests, he cannot be benefited; without the capacity to be a beneficiary, he can have no rights. But there may nevertheless be a dozen other reasons to treat him as if he did.

Fetuses

If the interest principle is to permit us to ascribe rights to infants, fetuses, and generations yet unborn, it can only be on the grounds that interests can exert a claim upon us even before their possessors actually come into being, just the reverse of the situation respecting dead men whose interests are respected even after their possessors have ceased to be. Newly born infants are surely noisier than mere vegetables, but they are just barely brighter. They come into existence, as Aristotle said, with the capacity to acquire concepts and dispositions, but in the beginning we suppose that their consciousness of the world is a "blooming, buzzing confusion." They do have a capacity, no doubt from the very beginning, to feel pain, and this alone may be sufficient ground for ascribing both an interest and a right to them. Apart from that, however, during the first few hours of their lives, at least, they may well lack even the rudimentary intellectual equipment necessary to the possession of interests. Of

course, this induces no moral reservations whatever in adults. Children grow and mature almost visibly in the first few months so that those future interests that are so rapidly emerging from the unformed chaos of their earliest days seem unquestionably to be the basis of their present rights. Thus, we say of a newborn infant that he has a right now to live and grow into his adulthood, even though he lacks the conceptual equipment at this very moment to have this or any other desire. A new infant, in short, lacks the traits necessary for the possession of interests, but he has the capacity to acquire those traits, and his inherited potentialities are moving quickly toward actualization even as we watch him. Those proxies who make claims in behalf of infants, then, are more than mere custodians: they are (or can be) genuine representatives of the child's emerging interests, which may need protection even now if they are to be allowed to come into existence at all.

The same principle may be extended to "unborn persons." After all, the situation of fetuses one day before birth is not strikingly different from that a few hours after birth. The rights that our law confers on the unborn child, both proprietary and personal, are for the most part, placeholders or reservations for the rights he shall inherit when he becomes a full-fledged interested being. The law protects a potential interest in these cases before it has even grown into actuality, as a garden fence protects newly seeded flower beds long before blooming flowers have emerged from them. The unborn child's present right to property, for example, is a legal protection offered now to his future interest, contingent upon his birth, and instantly voidable if he dies before birth. As Coke put it: "The law in many cases hath consideration of him in respect of the apparent expectation of his birth";[13] but this is quite another thing than recognizing a right actually to be born. Assuming that the child will be born, the law seems to say, various interests that he will come to have after birth must be protected from damage that they can incur even before birth. Thus prenatal injuries of a negligently inflicted kind can give the newly born child a right to sue for damages which he can exercise through a proxy-attorney and in his own name any time *after* he is born.

There are numerous other places, however, where our law seems to imply an unconditional right to be born, and surprisingly no one seems ever to have found that idea conceptually absurd. One interesting example comes from an article given the following headline by the *New York Times*: "Unborn Child's Right Upheld Over Religion."[14] A hospital patient in her eighth month of pregnancy refused to take a blood transfusion even though warned by her physician that "she might die at any minute and take the life of her child as well." The ground of her refusal was that blood transfusions are repugnant to the principles of her religion (Jehovah's Witnesses). The Supreme Court of New Jersey expressed uncertainty over the constitutional question of whether a non-pregnant adult might refuse on religious grounds a blood transfusion pronounced necessary to her own survival, but the court nevertheless ordered the patient in the present case to receive the transfusion on the grounds that "the unborn child is entitled to the law's protection."

It is important to reemphasize here that the questions of whether fetuses do or ought to have rights are substantive questions of law and morals open to argument and decision. The prior question of whether fetuses are the kind of beings that can have rights, however, is a conceptual, not a moral, question, amenable only to what is called "logical analysis," and irrelevant to moral judgement. The correct answer to the conceptual question, I believe, is that unborn children are among the sorts of beings of whom possession of rights can meaningfully be predicated, even though

they are (temporarily) incapable of having interests, because their future interests can be protected now, and it does make sense to protect a potential interest even before it has grown into actuality. The interest principle, however, makes perplexing, at best, talk of a noncontingent fetal right to be born; for fetuses, lacking actual wants and beliefs, have no actual interest in being born, and it is difficult to think of any other reason for ascribing any rights to them other than on the assumption that they will in fact be born.[15]

Future Generations

We have it in our power now to make the world a much less pleasant place for our descendants than the world we inherited from our ancestors. We can continue to proliferate in ever greater numbers, using up fertile soil at an even greater rate, dumping our wastes into rivers, lakes, oceans, cutting down our forests, and polluting the atmosphere with noxious gases. All thoughtful people agree that we ought not to do these things. Most would say that we have a duty not to do these things, meaning not merely that conservation is morally required (as opposed to merely desirable) but also that it is something due our descendants, something to be done for their sakes. Surely we owe it to future generations to pass on a world that is not a used up garbage heap. Our remote descendants are not yet present to claim a livable world as their right, but there are plenty of proxies to speak now in their behalf. These spokesmen, far from being mere custodians, are genuine representatives of future interests.

Why then deny that the human beings of the future have rights which can be claimed against us now in their behalf? Some are inclined to deny them present rights out of a fear of falling into obscure metaphysics, by granting rights to remote and unidentifiable beings who are not yet even in existence. Our unborn great-great-grandchildren are in some sense "potential" persons, but they are far more remotely potential, it may seem, than fetuses. This, however, is not the real difficulty. Unborn generations are more remotely potential than fetuses in one sense, but not in another. A much greater period of time with a far greater number of causally necessary and important events must pass before their potentiality can be actualized, it is true; but our collective posterity is just as certain to come into existence "in the normal course of events" as is any given fetus now in its mother's womb. In that sense the existence of the distant human future is no more remotely potential than that of a particular child already on its way.

The real difficulty is not that we doubt whether our descendants will ever be actual, but rather that we don't know who they will be. It is not their temporal remoteness that troubles us so much as their indeterminacy—their present facelessness and namelessness. Five centuries from now men and women will be living where we live now. Any given one of them will have an interest in living space, fertile soil, fresh air, and the like, but that arbitrarily selected one has no other qualities we can presently envision very clearly. We don't even know who his parents, grandparents, or great-grandparents are, or even whether he is related to us. Still, whoever these human beings may turn out to be, and whatever they might reasonably be expected to be like, they will have interests that we can affect, for better or worse, right now. That much we can and do know about them. The identity of the owners of these interests is now necessarily obscure, but the fact of their interest-ownership is crystal clear, and that is all that is necessary to certify the coherence of present talk about their rights. We can tell, sometimes, that shadowy forms in the spatial distance belong to human beings, though we know not who or how many they are; and this imposes a duty on us not to throw bombs, for example, in their direction. In like manner, the vagueness of the human future does not weaken its claim on us in light of the nearly certain knowledge that it will, after all, be human.

Doubts about the existence of a right to be born transfer neatly to the question of a similar right to come into existence ascribed to future generations. The rights that future generations certainly have against us are contingent rights: the interests they are sure to have when they come into being (assuming of course that they will come into being) cry out for protection from invasions that can take place now. Yet there are no actual interests, presently existent, that future generations, presently nonexistent, have now. Hence, there is no actual interest that they have in simply coming into being, and I am at a loss to think of any other reason for claiming that they have a right to come into existence (though there may well be such a reason). Suppose then that all human beings at a given time voluntarily form a compact never again to produce children, thus leading within a few decades to the end of our species. This of course is a wildly improbable hypothetical example but a rather crucial one for the position I have been tentatively considering. And we can imagine, say, that the whole world is converted to a strange ascetic religion which absolutely requires sexual abstinence for everyone. Would this arrangement violate the rights of anyone? No one can complain on behalf of presently nonexistent future generations that their future interests which give them a contingent right of protection have been violated since they will never come into existence to be wronged. My inclination then is to conclude that the suicide of our species would be deplorable, lamentable, and a deeply moving tragedy, but that it would violate no one's rights. Indeed if, contrary to fact, all human beings could ever agree to such a thing, that very agreement would be a symptom of our species' biological unsuitability for survival anyway.

Conclusion

For several centuries now human beings have run roughshod over the lands of our planet, just as if the animals who do live there and the generations of humans who will live there had no claims on them whatever. Philosophers have not helped matters by arguing that animals and future generations are not the kinds of beings who can have rights now, that they don't presently qualify for membership, even "auxiliary membership," in our moral community. I have tried in this essay to dispel the conceptual confusions that make such conclusions possible. To acknowledge their rights is the very least we can do for members of endangered species (including our own). But that is something.

Appendix

The Paradoxes of Potentiality

Having conceded that rights can belong to beings in virtue of their merely potential interests, we find ourselves on a slippery slope; for it may seem at first sight that anything at all can have potential interests, or much more generally, that anything at all can be potentially almost anything else at all! Dehydrated orange powder is potentially orange juice, since if we add water to it, it will be orange juice. More remotely, however, it is also potentially lemonade, since it will become lemonade if we add a large quantity of lemon juice, sugar, and water. It is also a potentially poisonous brew (add water and arsenic), a potential orange cake (add flour, etc., and bake), a potential orange-colored building block (add cement and harden), and so on, *ad infinitum*. Similarly a two-celled embryo, too small to be seen by the unaided eye, is a potential human being; and so is an unfertilized ovum; and so is even an "uncapacitated" spermatozoan. Add the proper nutrition to an implanted embryo (under certain other necessary conditions) and

it becomes a fetus and then a child. Looked at another way, however, the implanted embryo has been combined (under the same conditions) with the nutritive elements, which themselves are converted into a growing fetus and child. Is it then just as proper to say that food is a "potential child" as that an embryo is a potential child? If so, then what isn't a "potential child?" (Organic elements in the air and soil are "potentially food," and hence potentially people!)

Clearly, some sort of line will have to be drawn between direct and proximate potentialities and indirect or remote ones; and however we draw this line, there will be borderline cases whose classification will seem uncertain or even arbitrary. Even though any X can become a Y provided only that it is combined with the necessary additional elements, a, b, c, d, and so forth, we cannot say of any given X that it is a "potential Y" unless certain further—rather strict—conditions are met. (Otherwise the concept of potentiality, being universally and promiscuously applicable, will have no utility.) A number of possible criteria of proximate potentiality suggest themselves. The first is the criterion of causal importance. Orange powder is not properly called a potential building block because of those elements needed to transform it into a building block, the cement (as opposed to any of the qualities of the orange powder) is the causally crucial one. Similarly, any pauper might (misleadingly) be called a "potential millionaire" in the sense that all that need be added to any man to transform him into a millionaire is a great amount of money. The absolutely crucial element in the change, of course, is no quality of the man himself but rather the million dollars "added" to him.

What is causally "important" depends upon our purposes and interests and is therefore to some degree a relativistic matter. If we seek a standard, in turn, of "importance," we may posit such a criterion, for example, as that of the ease or difficulty (to some persons or other) of providing those missing elements which, when combined with the thing at hand, convert it into something else. It does seem quite natural, for example, to say that the orange powder is potentially orange juice, and that is because the missing element is merely common tap water, a substance conveniently near at hand to everyone; whereas it is less plausible to characterize the powder as potential cake since a variety of further elements, and not just one, are required, and some of these are not conveniently near at hand to many. Moreover, the process of combining the missing elements into a cake is rather more complicated than mere "addition." It is less plausible still to call orange powder a potential curbstone for the same kind of reason. The criterion of ease or difficulty of the acquisition and combination of additional elements explains all these variations.

Still another criterion of proximate potentiality closely related to the others is that of degree of deviation required from "the normal course of events." Given the intentions of its producers, distributors, sellers, and consumers, dehydrated orange juice will, in the normal course of events, become orange juice. Similarly, a human embryo securely imbedded in the wall of its mother's uterus will in the normal course of events become a human child. That is to say that if no one deliberately intervenes to prevent it happening, it will, in the vast majority of cases, happen. On the other hand, an unfertilized ovum will not become an embryo unless someone intervenes deliberately to make it happen. Without such intervention in the "normal" course of events, an ovum is a mere bit of protoplasm of a very brief life expectancy. If we lived in a world in which virtually every biologically capable human female became pregnant once a year throughout her entire fertile period of life, then we would regard fertilization as something that happens to every ovum in "the natural course of events." Perhaps we would regard every unfertilized ovum, in such a world, as a potential person even possessed of rights corresponding to its future interests. It would perhaps make conceptual if not moral sense in such a world to regard deliberate nonfertilization as a kind of homicide.

It is important to notice, in summary, that words like *important, easy*, and *normal* have sense only in relation to human experiences, purposes, and techniques. As the latter change, so will our notions of what is important, difficult and usual, and so will the concept of potentiality, or our application of it. If our purposes, understanding, and techniques continue to change in indicated directions, we may even one day come to think of inanimate things as possessed of "potential interests." In any case, we can expect the concept of a right to shift its logical boundaries with changes in our practical experience.

Notes

1 I shall leave the concept of a claim unanalyzed here, but for a detailed discussion, see my "The Nature and Value of Rights," *Journal of Value Inquiry* 4 (Winter 1971): 263–277.

2 Louis B. Schwartz, "Morals, Offenses and the Model Penal Code," *Columbia Law Review* 63 (1963): 673.

3 John Chipman Gray, *The Nature and Sources of the Law*, 2d ed. (Boston: Beacon Press, 1963), p. 43.

4 And W.D. Ross for another. See *The Right and the Good* (Oxford: Clarendon Press, 1930), app. 1, pp. 48–56.

5 W.D. Lamont, *Principles of Moral Judgment* (Oxford: Clarendon Press, 1946), pp. 83–85.

6 Cf. H.J. McCloskey, "Rights," *Philosophical Quarterly* 15 (1965): 121, 124.

7 *Ibid.*

8 Outside of Samuel Butler's *Erewhon*.

9 *Webster's Third New International Dictionary*.

10 Sometimes, of course, the correspondence fails because what accords with the plant's natural propensities is not in our interests, rather than the other way round. I must concede that in cases of this kind we speak even of weeds flourishing, but I doubt that we mean to imply that a weed is a thing with a good of its own. Rather, this way of talking is a plain piece of irony, or else an animistic metaphor (thinking of the weeds in the way we think of prospering businessmen). In any case, when weeds thrive, usually no interests, human or otherwise, flourish.

11 William Salmond, *Jurisprudence*, 12th ed., ed. P.J. Fitzgerald (London: Sweet and Maxwell, 1966), p. 304.

12 Unless, of course, the person in question, before he became a "vegetable," left testamentary directions about what was to be done with his body just in case he should ever become an incurable vegetable. He may have directed either that he be preserved alive as long as possible, or else that he be destroyed, whichever he preferred. There may, of course, be sound reasons of public policy why we should not honor such directions, but if we did promise to give legal effect to such wishes, we would have an example of a man's earlier interest in what is to happen to his body surviving his very competence as a person, in quite the same manner as that in which the express interest of a man now dead may continue to exert a claim on us.

13 As quoted by Salmond, *Jurisprudence*, p. 303. Simply as a matter of policy the potentiality of some future interests may be so remote as to make them seem unworthy of present support. A testator may leave property to his unborn child, for example, but not to his unborn grandchildren. To say of the potential person presently in his mother's womb that he owns property now is to say that certain property must be held for him until he is "real" or "mature" enough to possess it. "Yet the law is careful lest property should be too long withdrawn in this way from the uses of living men in favor of generations yet to come; and various restrictive rules have been established to this end. No testator could now direct his fortune to be accumulated for a hundred years and then distributed among his descendants"—Salmond, *ibid*.

14 *New York Times*, 17 June 1966, p. 1.

15 In an essay entitled "Is There a Right to be Born?" I defend a negative answer to the question posed, but I allow that under certain very special conditions, there can be a "right *not* to be born." See *Abortion*, ed. J. Feinberg (Belmont, Calif.: Wadsworth, 1973).

Questions for Discussion

1 What is the relationship between legal rights and moral rights? Does having one qualify one for the other?

2 Is it possible to make sense of the claim that people should not be cruel to animals without attributing moral weight to the animals themselves?

3 Is Feinberg correct in saying that the kinds of appetites and purposes which animals have should count as the sort of interests needed to have rights?

4 How important is it that a right-holder be able to claim rights on its own behalf? Should we accept such a requirement, even if it means some human beings (e.g., babies and severely mentally handicapped persons) do not qualify as right-holders?

Animal Liberation[1]

Peter Singer

Peter Singer has been one of the leaders in the movement to change common attitudes toward treatment of animals for many years now. The following landmark article first appeared in 1973. Both it and Singer's later elaborations of its basic claims have been extremely influential. Singer argues that all suffering counts equally, no matter whose it is, and that non-human animals are capable of suffering.

★　★　★

I

We are familiar with Black Liberation, Gay Liberation, and a variety of other movements. With Women's Liberation some thought we had come to the end of the road. Discrimination on the basis of sex, it has been said, is the last form of discrimination that is universally accepted and practiced without pretense, even in those liberal circles which have long prided themselves on their freedom from racial discrimination. But one should always be wary of talking of "the last remaining form of discrimination." If we have learned anything from the liberation movements, we should have learned how difficult it is to be aware of the ways in which we discriminate until they are forcefully pointed out to us. A liberation movement demands an expansion of our moral horizons, so that practices that were previously regarded as natural and inevitable are now seen as intolerable.

Animals, Men and Morals is a manifesto for an Animal Liberation movement. The contributers to the book may not all see the issue this way. They are a varied group. Philosophers, ranging from professors to graduate students, make up the largest contingent. There are five of them, including the three editors, and there is also an extract from the unjustly neglected German philosopher with an English name, Leonard Nelson, who died

in 1927. There are essays by two novelist/critics, Brigid Brophy and Maureen Duffy, and another by Muriel the Lady Dowding, widow of Dowding of Battle of Britain fame and the founder of "Beauty without Cruelty," a movement that campaigns against the use of animals for furs and cosmetics. The other pieces are by a psychologist, a botanist, a sociologist, and Ruth Harrison, who is probably best described as a professional campaigner for animal welfare.

Whether or not these people, as individuals, would agree that they are launching a liberation movement for animals, the book as a whole amounts to no less. It is a demand for a complete change in our attitudes to nonhumans. It is a demand that we cease to regard the exploitation of other species as natural and inevitable, and that, instead, we see it as a continuing moral outrage. Patrick Corbett, Professor of Philosophy at Sussex University, captures the spirit of the book in his closing words:

> ...we require now to extend the great principles of liberty, equality and fraternity over the lives of animals. Let animal slavery join human slavery in the graveyard of the past.

The reader is likely to be skeptical. "Animal Liberation" sounds more like a parody of liberation movements than a serious objective. The reader may think: We support the claims of blacks and women for equality because blacks and women really are equal to whites and males—equal in intelligence and in abilities, capacity for leadership, rationality, and so on. Humans and nonhumans obviously are not equal in these respects. Since justice demands only that we treat equals equally, unequal treatment of humans and nonhumans cannot be an injustice.

This is a tempting reply, but a dangerous one. It commits the non-racist and non-sexist to a dogmatic belief that blacks and women really are just as intelligent, able, etc., as whites and males—and no more. Quite possibly this happens to be the case. Certainly attempts to prove that racial or sexual differences in these respects have a genetic origin have not been conclusive. But do we really want to stake our demand for equality on the assumption that there are no genetic differences of this kind between the different races or sexes? Surely the appropriate response to those who claim to have found evidence for such genetic differences is not to stick to the belief that there are no differences, whatever the evidence to the contrary; rather one should be clear that the claim to equality does not depend on IQ. Moral equality is distinct from factual equality. Otherwise it would be nonsense to talk of the equality of human beings, since humans, as individuals, obviously differ in intelligence and almost any ability one cares to name. If possessing greater intelligence does not entitle one human to exploit another, why should it entitle humans to exploit nonhumans?

Jeremy Bentham expressed the essential basis of equality in his famous formula: "Each to count for one and none for more than one." In other words, the interests of every being that has interests are to be taken into account and treated equally with the like interests of any other being. Other moral philosophers, before and after Bentham, have made the same point in different ways. Our

concern for others must not depend on whether they possess certain characteristics, though just what that concern involves may, of course, vary according to such characteristics.

Bentham, incidentally, was well aware that the logic of the demand for racial equality did not stop at the equality of humans. He wrote:

> The day *may* come when the rest of the animal creation may acquire those rights which never could have been withholden from them but by the hand of tyranny. The French have already discovered that the blackness of the skin is no reason why a human being should be abandoned without redress to the caprice of a tormentor. It may one day come to be recognized that the number of the legs, the villiosity of the skin, or the termination of the *os sacrum*, are reasons equally insufficient for abandoning a sensitive being to the same fate. What else is it that should trace the insuperable line? Is it the faculty of reason, or perhaps the faculty of discourse? But a full-grown horse or dog is beyond comparison a more rational, as well as a more conversable animal, than an infant of a day, or a week, or even a month old. But suppose they were otherwise, what would it avail? The question is not, Can they *reason?* nor Can they *talk?* but, Can they *suffer?*[2]

Surely Bentham was right. If a being suffers, there can be no moral justification for refusing to take that suffering into consideration, and, indeed, to count it equally with the like suffering (if rough comparisons can be made) of any other being.

So the only question is: do animals other than man suffer? Most people agree unhesitatingly that animals like cats and dogs can and do suffer, and this seems also to be assumed by those laws that prohibit wanton cruelty to such animals. Personally, I have no doubt at all about this and find it hard to take seriously the doubts that a few people apparently do have. The editors and contributors of *Animals, Men and Morals* seem to feel the same way, for although the question is raised more than once, doubts are quickly dismissed each time. Nevertheless, because this is such a fundamental point, it is worth asking what grounds we have for attributing suffering to other animals.

It is best to begin by asking what grounds any individual human has for supposing that other humans feel pain. Since pain is a state of consciousness, a "mental event," it can never be directly observed. No observations, whether behavioral signs such as writhing or screaming or physiological or neurological recordings, are observations of pain itself. Pain is something one feels, and one can only infer that others are feeling it from various external indications. The fact that only philosophers are ever skeptical about whether other humans feel pain shows that we regard such inference as justifiable in the case of humans.

Is there any reason why the same inference should be unjustifiable for other animals? Nearly all the external signs which lead us to infer pain in other humans can be seen in other species, especially "higher" animals such as mammals and birds. Behavioral signs— writhing, yelping, or other forms of calling, attempts to avoid the source of pain, and many others, are present. We know, too, that these animals are biologically similar in the relevant respects, having nervous systems like ours which can be observed to function as ours do.

So the grounds for inferring that these animals can feel pain are nearly as good as the grounds for inferring other humans do. Only nearly, for there is one behavioral sign that humans have but nonhumans, with the exception of one or two specially raised chimpanzees, do not have. This, of course, is a developed language. As the quotation from Bentham indicates, this has long been regarded as an important distinction between man and other animals. Other animals may communicate with each other, but not in the way we do. Following Chomsky, many people now

mark this distinction by saying that only humans communicate in a form that is governed by rules of syntax. (For the purposes of this argument, linguists allow those chimpanzees who have learned a syntactic sign language to rank as honorary humans.) Nevertheless, as Bentham pointed out, this distinction is not relevant to the question of how animals ought to be treated, unless it can be linked to the issue of whether animals suffer.

This link may be attempted in two ways. First, there is a hazy line of philosophical thought, stemming perhaps from some doctrines associated with Wittgenstein, which maintains that we cannot meaningfully attribute states of consciousness to beings without language. I have not seen this argument made explicit in print, though I have come across it in conversation. This position seems to me very implausible, and I doubt that it would be held at all if it were not thought to be a consequence of a broader view of the significance of language. It may be that the use of a public, rule-governed language is a precondition of conceptual thought. It may even be, although personally I doubt it, that we cannot meaningfully speak of a creature having an intention unless that creature can use a language. But states like pain, surely, are more primitive than either of these, and seem to have nothing to do with language.

Indeed, as Jane Goodall points out in her study of chimpanzees, when it comes to the expression of feelings and emotions, humans tend to fall back on nonlinguistic modes of communication which are often found among apes, such as a cheering pat on the back, an exuberant embrace, a clasp of hands, and so on.[3] Michael Peters makes a similar point in his contribution to *Animals, Men and Morals* when he notes that the basic signals we use to convey pain, fear, sexual arousal, and so on are not specific to our species. So there seems to be no reason at all to believe that a creature without language cannot suffer.

The second, and more easily appreciated way of linking language and the existence of pain is to say that the best evidence that we can have that another creature is in pain is when he tells us that he is. This is a distinct line of argument, for it is not being denied that a non-language-user conceivably could suffer, but only that we could know that he is suffering. Still, this line of argument seems to me to fail, and for reasons similar to those just given. "I am in pain" is not the best possible evidence that the speaker is in pain (he might be lying) and it is certainly not the only possible evidence. Behavioral signs and knowledge of the animals' biological similarity to ourselves together provide adequate evidence that animals do suffer. After all, we would not accept linguistic evidence if it contradicted the rest of the evidence. If a man was severely burned, and behaved as if he were in pain, writhing, groaning, being very careful not to let his burned skin touch anything, and so on, but later said he had not been in pain at all, we would be more likely to conclude that he was lying or suffering from amnesia than that he had not been in pain.

Even if there were stronger grounds for refusing to attribute pain to those who do not have a language, the consequences of this refusal might lead us to examine these grounds unusually critically. Human infants, as well as some adults, are unable to use language. Are we to deny that a year-old infant can suffer? If not, how can language be crucial? Of course, most parents can understand the responses of even very young infants better than they understand the responses of other animals, and sometimes infant responses can be understood in the light of later development.

This, however, is just a fact about the relative knowledge we have of our own species and other species, and most of this knowledge is simply derived from closer contact. Those who have studied the behavior of other animals soon learn to understand their responses at least as well as we understand those of an infant. (I am not just referring to Jane Goodall's and other well-known studies of apes. Consider, for example, the degree of understanding achieved by Tinbergen from watching herring gulls.[4]) Just as we can understand infant human behavior, so we can understand the behavior of other species in the light of our own behavior (and sometimes we can understand our own behavior better in the light of the behavior of other species).

The grounds we have for believing that other mammals and birds suffer are, then, closely analogous to the grounds we have for believing that other humans suffer. It remains to consider how far down the evolutionary scale this analogy holds. Obviously it becomes poorer when we get further away from man. To be more precise would require a detailed examination of all that we know about other forms of life. With fish, reptiles, and other vertebrates the analogy still seems strong, with molluscs like oysters it is much weaker. Insects are more difficult, and it may be that in our present state of knowledge we must be agnostic about whether they are capable of suffering.

If there is no moral justification for ignoring suffering when it occurs, and it does occur in other species, what are we to say of our attitudes toward these other species? Richard Ryder, one of the contributors to *Animals, Men and Morals*, uses the term "speciesism" to describe the belief that we are entitled to treat members of other species in a way in which it would be wrong to treat members of our own species. The term is not euphonious, but it neatly makes the analogy with racism. The non-racist would do well to bear the analogy in mind when he is inclined to defend human behavior toward nonhumans. "Shouldn't we worry about improving the lot of our own species before we concern ourselves with other species?" he may ask. If we substitute "race" for "species" we shall see that the question is better not asked. "Is a vegetarian diet nutritionally adequate?" resembles the slaveowner's claim that he and the whole economy of the South would be ruined without slave labor. There is even a parallel with skeptical doubts about whether animals suffer, for some defenders of slavery professed to doubt whether blacks really suffer in the way that whites do.

I do not want to give the impression, however, that the case for Animal Liberation is based on the analogy with racism and no more. On the contrary, *Animals, Men and Morals* describes the various ways in which humans exploit nonhumans, and several contributors consider the defenses that have been offered, including the defense of meateating mentioned in the last paragraph. Sometimes the rebuttals are scornfully dismissive, rather than carefully designed to convince the detached critic. This may be a fault, but it is a fault that is inevitable, given the kind of book this is. The issue is not one of which one can remain detached. As the editors state in their Introduction:

> Once the full force of moral assessment has been made explicit there can be no rational excuse left for killing animals, be they killed for food, science, or sheer personal indulgence. We have not assembled this book to provide the reader with yet another manual on how to make brutalities less brutal. Compromise, in the traditional sense of the term, is simple unthinking weakness when one considers the actual reasons for our crude relationships with the other animals.

The point is that on this issue there are few critics who are genuinely detached. People who eat pieces of slaughtered nonhumans every day find it hard to believe that they are doing wrong; and they also find it hard to imagine what else they could eat. So for those who do not place nonhumans beyond the pale of morality, there comes a stage when further argument seems pointless, a stage at which one can only accuse one's opponent of hypocrisy and reach for the sort of sociological account of our practices and the way we defend them that is attempted by David Wood in his contribution to this book. On the other hand, to those unconvinced by the arguments, and unable to accept that they are rationalizing their dietary preferences and their fear of being thought peculiar, such sociological explanations can only seem insultingly arrogant.

II

The logic of speciesism is most apparent in the practice of experimenting on nonhumans in order to benefit humans. This is because the issue is rarely obscured by allegations that nonhumans are so different from humans that we cannot know anything about whether they suffer. The defender of vivisection cannot use this argument because he needs to stress the similarities between man and other animals in order to justify the usefulness to the former of experiments on the latter. The researcher who makes rats choose between starvation and electric shocks to see if they develop ulcers (they do) does so because he knows that the rat has a nervous system very similar to man's, and presumably feels an electric shock in a similar way.

Richard Ryder's restrained account of experiments on animals made me angrier with my fellow men than anything else in this book. Ryder, a clinical psychologist by profession, himself experimented on animals before he came to hold the view he puts forward in his essay. Experimenting on animals is now a large industry, both academic and commercial. In 1969, more than 5 million experiments were performed in Britain, the vast majority without anesthetic (though how many of these involved pain is not known). There are no accurate US figures, since there is no federal law on the subject, and in many cases no state law either. Estimates vary from 20 million to 200 million. Ryder suggests that 80 million may be the best guess. We tend to think that this is all for vital medical research, but of course it is not. Huge numbers of animals are used in university departments from Forestry to Psychology, and even more are used for commercial purposes, to test whether cosmetics can cause skin damage, or shampoos eye damage, or to test food additives or laxatives or sleeping pills or anything else.

A standard test for foodstuffs is the "LD50." The object of this test is to find the dosage level at which 50 percent of the test animals will die. This means that nearly all of them will become very sick before finally succumbing or surviving. When the substance is a harmless one, it may be necessary to force huge doses down the animals, until in some cases sheer volume or concentration causes death.

Ryder gives a selection of experiments, taken from recent scientific journals. I will quote two, not for the sake of indulging in gory details, but in order to give an idea of what normal researchers think they may legitimately do to other species. The point is not that the individual researchers are cruel men, but that they are behaving in a way that is allowed by our speciesist attitude. As Ryder points out, even if only 1 percent of the experiments involve severe pain, that is 50,000 experiments in Britain each year, or nearly 150 every day (and about fifteen times as many in the United States, if Ryder's guess is right). Here then are two experiments:

O.S. Ray and R.J. Barrett of Pittsburgh gave electric shocks to the feet of 1,042 mice. They then caused convulsions by giving more intense shocks through cup-shaped electrodes applied to the animals' eyes or through pressure spring clips attached to their ears. Unfortunately some of the mice who "successfully completed Day One training were found sick or dead prior to testing on Day Two." [*Journal of Comparative and Physiological Psychology,* 1969, Vol. 67, pp. 110–116]

At the National Institute for Medical Research, Mill Hill, London, W. Feldberg and S.L. Sherwood injected chemicals into the brains of cats—"with a number of widely different substances, recurrent patterns of reaction were obtained. Retching, vomiting, defaecation, increased salivation and greatly accelerated respiration leading to panting were common features,"...

The injection into the brain of a large dose of Tubocuraine caused the cat to jump "from the table to the floor and then straight into its cage, where it started calling more and more noisily whilst moving about restlessly and jerkily...finally the cat fell with legs and neck flexed, jerking in rapid clonic movements, the condition being that of a major [epileptic] convulsion...within a few seconds the cat got up, ran for a few yards at high speed and fell in another fit. The whole process was repeated several times within the next ten minutes, during which the cat lost faeces and foamed at the mouth."

This animal finally died thirty-five minutes after the brain injection. [*Journal of Physiology,* 1954, Vol. 123, pp. 148–167]

There is nothing secret about these experiments. One has only to open any recent volume of a learned journal, such as the *Journal of Comparative and Physiological Psychology,* to find full descriptions of experiments of this sort, together with the results obtained—results that are frequently trivial and obvious. The experiments are often supported by public funds.

It is a significant indication of the level of acceptability of these practices that, although these experiments are taking place at this moment on university campuses throughout the country, there has, so far as I know, not been the slightest protest from the student movement. Students have been rightly concerned that their universities should not discriminate on grounds of race or sex, and that they should not serve the purposes of the military or big business. Speciesism continues undisturbed, and many students participate in it. There may be a few qualms at first, but since everyone regards it as normal, and it may even be a required part of a course, the student soon becomes hardened and, dismissing his earlier feelings as "mere sentiment," comes to regard animals as statistics rather than sentient beings with interests that warrant consideration.

Argument about vivisection has often missed the point because it has been put in absolutist terms: would the abolitionist be prepared to let thousands die if they could be saved by experimenting on a single animal? The way to reply to this purely hypothetical question is to pose another: Would the experimenter be prepared to experiment on a human orphan under six months old, if it were the only way to save many lives? (I say "orphan" to avoid the complication of parental feelings, although in doing so I am being overfair to the experimenter, since the nonhuman subjects of experiments are not orphans.) A negative answer to this question indicates that the experimenter's readiness to use nonhumans is simple discrimination, for adult apes, cats, mice, and other mammals are more conscious of what is happening to them, more self-directing, and, so far as we can tell, just as sensitive to pain as a human infant. There is no characteristic that human infants possess that higher mammals do not have to the same or a higher degree.

(It might be possible to hold that what makes it wrong to experiment on a human infant is that the infant will in time develop into more than the nonhuman, but one would then, to be consistent, have to oppose abortion, and perhaps contraception, too, for the fetus and the egg and sperm have the same potential as the infant. Moreover, one would still have no reason for experimenting on a nonhuman rather than a human with brain

damage severe enough to make it impossible for him to rise above infant level.)

The experimenter, then, shows a bias for his own species whenever he carries out an experiment on a nonhuman for a purpose that he would not think justified him in using a human being at an equal or lower level of sentience, awareness, ability to be self-directing, etc. No one familiar with the kind of results yielded by these experiments can have the slightest doubt that if this bias were eliminated the number of experiments performed would be zero or very close to it.

III

If it is vivisection that shows the logic of speciesism most clearly, it is the use of other species for food that is at the heart of our attitudes toward them. Most of *Animals, Men and Morals* is an attack on meat-eating—an attack which is based solely on concern for nonhumans, without reference to arguments derived from considerations of ecology, macrobiotics, health, or religion.

The idea that nonhumans are utilities, means to our ends, pervades our thought. Even conservationists who are concerned about the slaughter of wild fowl but not about the vastly greater slaughter of chickens for our tables are thinking in this way—they are worried about what we would lose if there were less wildlife. Stanley Godlovitch, pursuing the Marxist idea that our thinking is formed by the activities we undertake in satisfying our needs, suggests that man's first classification of his environment was into Edibles and Inedibles. Most animals came into the first category, and there they have remained.

Man may always have killed other species for food, but he has never exploited them so ruthlessly as he does today. Farming has succumbed to business methods, the objective being to get the highest possible ratio of output (meat, eggs, milk) to input (fodder, labor costs, etc.). Ruth Harrison's essay "On Factory Farming" gives an account of some aspects of modern methods, and of the unsuccessful British campaign for effective controls, a campaign which was sparked off by her *Animal Machines* (Stuart: London, 1964).

Her article is in no way a substitute for her earlier book. This is a pity since, as she says, "Farm produce is still associated with mental pictures of animals browsing in the fields...of hens having a last forage before going to roost...." Yet neither in her article nor elsewhere in *Animals, Men and Morals* is this false image replaced by a clear idea of the nature and extent of factory farming. We learn of this only indirectly, when we hear of the code of reform proposed by an advisory committee set up by the British government.

Among the proposals, which the government refused to implement on the grounds that they were too idealistic, were: *"Any animal should at least have room to turn around freely."*

Factory farm animals need liberation in the most literal sense. Veal calves are kept in stalls five feet by two feet. They are usually slaughtered when about four months old, and have been too big to turn in their stalls for at least a month. Intensive beef herds, kept in stalls only proportionately larger for much longer periods, account for a growing percentage of beef production. Sows are often similarly confined when pregnant, which, because of artificial methods of increasing fertility, can be most of the time. Animals confined in this way do not waste food by exercising, nor do they develop unpalatable muscle.

"A dry bedded area should be provided for all stock." Intensively kept animals usually have to stand and sleep on slatted floors without straw, because this makes cleaning easier.

"Palatable roughage must be readily available to all calves after one week of age." In order to produce the pale veal housewives are said to prefer, calves are fed on an all-liquid diet un-

til slaughter, even though they are long past the age at which they would normally eat grass. They develop a craving for roughage, evidenced by attempts to gnaw wood from their stalls. (For the same reason, their diet is deficient in iron.)

"Battery cages for poultry should be large enough for a bird to be able to stretch one wing at a time." Under current British practice, a cage for four or five laying hens has a floor area of twenty inches by eighteen inches, scarcely larger than a double page of the *New York Review of Books*. In this space, on a sloping wire floor (sloping so the eggs roll down, wire so the dung drops through) the birds live for a year or eighteen months while artificial lighting and temperature conditions combine with drugs in their food to squeeze the maximum number of eggs out of them. Table birds are also sometimes kept in cages. More often they are reared in sheds, no less crowded. Under these conditions all the birds' natural activities are frustrated, and they develop "vices" such as pecking each other to death. To prevent this, beaks are often cut off, and the sheds kept dark.

How many of those who support factory farming by buying its produce know anything about the way it is produced? How many have heard something about it, but are reluctant to check up for fear that it will make them uncomfortable? To nonspeciesists, the typical consumer's mixture of ignorance, reluctance to find out the truth, and vague belief that nothing really bad could be allowed seems analogous to the attitudes of "decent Germans" to the death camps.

There are, of course, some defenders of factory farming. Their arguments are considered, though again rather sketchily, by John Harris. Among the most common: "Since they have never known anything else, they don't suffer." This argument will not be put by anyone who knows anything about animal behavior, since he will know that not all behavior has to be learned. Chickens attempt to stretch wings, walk around, scratch, and even dustbathe or build a nest, even though they have never lived under conditions that allowed these activities. Calves can suffer from maternal deprivation no matter at what age they were taken from their mothers. "We need these intensive methods to provide protein for a growing population." As ecologists and famine relief organizations know, we can produce far more protein per acre if we grow the right vegetable crop, soy beans for instance, than if we use the land to grow crops to be converted into protein by animals who use nearly 90 percent of the protein themselves, even when unable to exercise.

There will be many readers of this book who will agree that factory farming involves an unjustifiable degree of exploitation of sentient creatures, and yet will want to say that there is nothing wrong with rearing animals for food, provided it is done "humanely." These people are saying, in effect, that although we should not cause animals to suffer, there is nothing wrong with killing them.

There are two possible replies to this view. One is to attempt to show that this combination of attitudes is absurd. Roslind Godlovitch takes this course in her essay, which is an examination of some common attitudes to animals. She argues that from the combination of "animal suffering is to be avoided" and "there is nothing wrong with killing animals" it follows that all animal life ought to be exterminated (since all sentient creatures will suffer to some degree at some point in their lives). Euthanasia is a contentious issue only because we place some value on living. If we did not, the least amount of suffering would justify it. Accordingly, if we deny that we have a duty to exterminate all animal life, we must concede that we are placing some value on animal life.

This argument seems to me valid, although one could still reply that the value of animal life is to be derived from the pleasures that life can have for them, so that, provided their lives have a balance of pleasure over pain, we are justified in rearing them. But this would imply that we ought to produce animals and let them live as pleasantly as possible, without suffering.

At this point, one can make the second of the two possible replies to the view that rearing and killing animals for food is all right so long as it is done humanely. This second reply is that so long as we think that a non-human may be killed simply so that a human can satisfy his taste for meat, we are still thinking of nonhumans as means rather than as ends in themselves. The factory farm is nothing more than the application of technology to this concept. Even traditional methods involve castration, the separation of mothers and their young, the breaking up of herds, branding or ear-punching, and of course transportation to the abattoirs and the final moments when the animal smells blood and senses danger. If we were to try rearing animals so that they lived and died without suffering, we should find that to do so on anything like the scale of today's meat industry would be a sheer impossibility. Meat would become the prerogative of the rich.

I have been able to discuss only some of the contributions to this book, saying nothing about, for instance, the essays on killing for furs and for sport. Nor have I considered all the detailed questions that need to be asked once we start thinking about other species in the radically different way presented by this book. What, for instance, are we to do about genuine conflicts of interests like rats biting slum children? I am not sure of the answer, but the essential point is just that we *do* see this as a conflict of interests, that we recognize that rats have interests too. Then we may begin to think about other ways of resolving the conflict—perhaps by leaving out rat baits that sterilize the rats instead of killing them.

I have not discussed such problems because they are side issues compared with the exploitation of other species for food and for experimental purposes. On these central matters, I hope that I have said enough to show that this book, despite its flaws, is a challenge to every human to recognize his attitudes to nonhumans as a form of prejudice no less objectionable than racism or sexism. It is a challenge that demands not just a change of attitudes, but a change in our way of life, for it requires us to become vegetarians.

Can a purely moral demand of this kind succeed? The odds are certainly against it. The book holds out no inducements. It does not tell us that we will become healthier, or enjoy life more, if we cease exploiting animals. Animal Liberation will require greater altruism on the part of mankind than any other liberation movement, since animals are incapable of demanding it for themselves, or of protesting against their exploitation by votes, demonstrations, or bombs. Is man capable of such genuine altruism? Who knows? If this book does have a significant effect, however, it will be a vindication of all those who have believed that man has within himself the potential for more than cruelty and selfishness.

Notes

1 This article originally appeared as a book review of *Animals, Men and Morals*, edited by Stanley and Roslind Godlovitch and John Harris.

2 *The Principles of Morals and Legislation*, Ch. XVII, Sec. 1, footnote to paragraph 4. (Italics in original.)

3 Jane van Lawick-Goodall, *In the Shadow of Man* (Houghton Mifflin, 1971), p. 225.

4 N. Tinbergen, *The Herring Gull's World* (Basic Books, 1961).

Questions for Discussion

1 Is it "speciesist" to believe that human suffering counts more than that of non-human animals? Is this term conceptually analogous to "racist" and "sexist"?

2 Is there any good reason to allow experiments on non-humans which one would not allow on, say, a human orphan under six months old?

3 If there is a part of a city in which rats are biting children, how would we go about weighing the interests of the rats against those of the children?

Utilitarianism and Vegetarianism

Roger Crisp

In this selection, Roger Crisp argues that people who believe that the pleasures and sufferings of animals count may be not only permitted but morally required to eat meat. He claims this will be true so long as the animals live pleasant lives (which is not the case in factory farms), because the meat industry may be responsible for the very existence of the animals, who are better off living and then being killed than never living at all. In the process, Crisp critiques several of the common arguments against eating meat.

★   ★   ★

The condition of non-human animals—especially those consumed as food by human beings—has been a major concern of many thinkers in the utilitarian tradition. Two main lines of thought have been taken on the ethics of eating meat. It is claimed either that utilitarianism requires Vegetarianism (V)[1], or that it does not, but permits one to eat meat.[2] In this paper, I shall develop a third line: that utilitarianism does not permit V, requiring a form of non-V. This view I shall call the Compromise Requirement view (CR). I shall claim that one is morally required both to abstain from the flesh of intensively reared animals and to eat the flesh of certain non-intensively-reared animals.

The paper will proceed primarily in a negative way, through consideration and refutation of the main utilitarian arguments for V. But a positive case for CR will emerge, particularly in the discussion of the Argument from Suffering.

Before proceeding to the first argument, it might be helpful to outline the utilitarian positions under consideration:

Vegetarianism (V): One is morally required to abstain from meat.

The Compromise Permission View (CP): One is morally required to abstain from the flesh of intensively reared animals, but permitted to eat the flesh of certain non-intensively-reared animals.

The Compromise Requirement View (CR): One is morally required both to abstain from the flesh of intensively reared animals and to eat the flesh of certain non-intensively-reared animals.

The Raymond Frey View (RF): One is morally permitted to eat all kinds of meat, but required to campaign against intensive farming, by means such as political lobbying.

The Full Meat-eating Requirement View (FR): One is morally required to eat all kinds of meat.

1 The Argument from Killing

1. The widespread practice of Meat-eating requires killing sentient beings.

2. Killing sentient beings is wrong.
3. Therefore, the widespread practice of Meat-eating is wrong.

The first premise of this argument is undeniable. Therefore, it can only be vulnerable as regards its second premise. The premise can be supported, in turn, by three subsidiary utilitarian arguments intended to demonstrate the wrongness of killing. Replies to each will show that these arguments do not apply to the case of killing animals for food, and thus that the Argument from Killing fails.

1(a) The Argument from Direct Diminution of Utility

1. Killing a sentient being for food directly reduces the amount of utility in the world by removing that being from the world.
2. Reducing the amount of utility is wrong.
3. Therefore, killing a sentient being for food is wrong.

The second premise here is correct by definition in utilitarian terms. Thus, we must focus on the first. It is not clear that this is correct.

The reason for this is that utilitarianism is committed to replaceability. The replacing of one being by another at a similar level of utility is, other things being equal, morally neutral.

It may be objected that if the utility levels of both the animal to be killed and that intended as a surrogate are above zero, then it would be better that both live. There are two replies to this. The first is that we are concerned with Meat-eating as a widespread practice. And an inherent feature of this practice is that over time some animals will be killed for food, and others will take their places. If animals were not killed, the practice could not exist. The second is that the objection is not anyway to the point. All that needs to be shown is that killing an animal need not be wrong, not that failing to increase the overall level of utility is not wrong. Replaceability makes morally neutral killing a possibility.[3]

In what does an animal's utility consist? Primarily it must be sheer pleasurable experience, and the fulfillment of desires for those experiences.[4] And the pleasures of even the more intelligent domestic animals, such as pigs, will tend to be of the 'low' variety.[5] Indeed, one would not have to be a Socrates dissatisfied to have a life preferable to that of a contented pig. Not all the desires of animals are for pleasurable experiences, however. For example, they also have desires connected with their relations with other animals. If a cow sees her calf being mistreated, she will show signs of acute distress, and perhaps attempt to protect her offspring. It would be more plausible to explain her actions by ascribing to her the desire that her offspring not suffer, than the desire that she not experience the sight of her offspring suffering. No cow is so stupid as not to realize that a more effective way of fulfilling the latter desire would be to turn tail and head for the other end of the field.

The Vegetarian may use the notion of the sophistication of animal desires in the following way. She may accept that merely replacing one pleasurable experience with another is morally neutral. But, she may continue, desires are not like this. An animal may have desires for the future. The frustration of these desires is not counter-balanced by the bringing into existence of a new animal.

The fulfillment of future-related desires, however, does not differ from mental states, as far as replaceability is concerned.[6] Utilitarian theories are neutral as to when or where utility is located. Thus, the surrogate animal will also have future-related desires, and if these desires are fulfilled, replaceability once again ensures the moral neutrality of the killing.[7]

In the context of a widespread practice of Meat-eating, of course, the surrogate animal is highly unlikely to go on living for very long. It too will be killed and eaten. It might be thought that to ensure the moral neutral-ity of the process one has only to stipulate that the *final* animal in the process will be allowed to survive. Given that the process of rearing animals for food is nowhere near its end, this is a worry that need not afflict us at present.

But this claim misses the same point as the original Vegetarian argument based on desires. Desire-fulfillment, and hence frustration, like pleasure and pain is cumulative. As the process continues, more and more future-related desires will be frustrated, and these are not counter-balanced by the fulfillment of one such set of desires at the end of the process.

To solve the problem, one has to be aware of another mistaken assumption underlying the original Vegetarian argument. This is the view that there is something special about these *particular* future-related desires. The utilitarian must accept that the value of their fulfillment can be outweighed by the value of the fulfillment of other desires (and, depending on the type of utilitarianism in question, other values, such as pleasure or aesthetic appreciation).

Thus, the frustration of the future-related desires of the animal killed is counter-balanced by: i) the utility of the life of the surrogate animal; ii) the utility of the desire-satisfaction, pleasure, or aesthetic appreciation in eating the animal; and (which surely tips the balance in favour of Meat-eating here) iii) the utility of the life of the animal killed, given that, in the context of a widespread practice of Meat-eating, it would not have existed had it not been intended for slaughter. (It is important to bear in mind that i) and iii) will not apply in the case of intensively reared animals, who live at levels of negative utility. But these animals are better off not existing, so killing them is not wrong.)

1(b) The Argument from Indirect Diminution of Utility

1. Killing a sentient being causes grief, anxiety, and thereby suffering in other sentient beings.

2. Thus, killing a sentient being indirectly reduces the amount of utility in the world.
3. Reducing the amount of utility is wrong.
4. Therefore, killing a sentient being is wrong.

Premise 3 is correct by definition, and premise 2 is true if premise 1 is true. Thus, we must attend to premise 1.

Now it cannot be denied that killing *certain* sentient beings, in particular humans and other higher primates, almost always causes grief and anxiety among other such beings. But this does not seem to be the case with domestic animals. We are not unduly perturbed at the killing of animals, especially if we do not see it happen. And those who kill them are similarly unaffected.

It may be said that animals become distressed when members of their group are killed in their presence. In the case of domestic animals, this could only occur at the slaughter-house. But there is no argument for not killing, if it is possible to alter the circumstances of the death. And surely it is possible to do this, by changing the methods of slaughtering. Animals could be killed in separate pens, for example.

Animals can also be distressed at the death of a mate. Pair-bonding, however, is not found among the animals we eat. And finally there is the problem of distress caused by the death of a parent or offspring. This again is not an argument for not killing. The problem can be dealt with *either* by slaughtering both parent and offspring at the same time *or* by slaughtering neither parent nor offspring at times when the offspring is young enough to experience distress at the loss or to cause the parent distress at the loss of the offspring.

1(c) The Argument from Autonomy

1. Killing a sentient being, other things being equal, violates its autonomy and deprives it of liberty.
2. Autonomy and liberty are productive of utility.
3. Thus, killing a sentient being reduces the amount of utility in the world.

4. Reducing the amount of utility is wrong.
5. Therefore, killing a sentient being is wrong.

Some utilitarians have appealed to respect for autonomy as a moral principle.[8] And a Vegetarian might think that an ideal utilitarian theory, which included the claim that autonomy is itself *part of utility*, would also support her case.

She will be disappointed, however. For animals do not possess autonomy.[9] They do have desires, and they do make choices. But their choices are not about how their lives should go. They are about immediate things, such as whether to walk in this or that direction, to lie in the shade or under the sun, to flee or stay. Autonomy requires at least some degree of a global conception of one's life, and this it seems clear animals do not have.[10]

Animals can, however, be free. Indeed, the basis of the ethical criticism of our treatment of animals for many people is that we deprive them of liberty. But by killing an animal we do not deprive it of liberty alone. We deprive it of everything. And, if my critique of the Argument from Direct Diminution of Utility is correct, depriving a being of everything including liberty can be justified by replaceability. Thus, even if animals possess liberty, it is not always wrong to deprive them of it.

2 The Argument from Suffering

1. The widespread practice of Meat-eating causes suffering.
2. The causing of suffering is wrong.
3. Therefore, Meat-eating is wrong.

The second premise of this argument requires attention. Utilitarians do, of course, claim that suffering is bad, and that causing suffering is *in itself* a bad thing to do. But causing suffering *can* be a good thing to do when it is not considered in itself. It may lead to better consequences occurring than if suffering had not been caused (*e.g.* the action of a dentist filling a cavity), or it may be part of a series of actions which, taken overall, are productive of utility (*e.g.* the punishing of a child). Thus, as I noted in the discussion of replaceability, doing something that causes a drop in the level of utility can be counter-balanced by doing something else that causes an increase.

In the case of rearing animals for food, it may well be that the suffering they will inevitably endure is analogous to that experienced by a child who is punished in the normal run of things.[11] Most non-intensively-reared animals lead worthwhile lives[12], and we enjoy eating them. The worthwhileness of their lives, and the pleasure we gain from eating them, justify the practice of rearing them, although it inevitably involves causing suffering. And if we were not to eat them, both of these sources of utility would disappear. Thus, there is here the beginning of a case for CR.

Intensively-reared animals, however, fall into a different category. Their lives are frustrating, painful, stunted, and devoid of anything but the slightest pleasure.[13] It would have been better for such animals if they had not been born. The only consideration counter-balancing the severe suffering endured by intensively reared animals is our pleasure in eating them. When we consider the fact that alternative meals are available, it seems patently clear that this consideration will not justify factory-farming.

Thus far, I have ruled out V as an option, and suggested that there is a requirement on us to eat non-intensively-reared meat. This gives *prima facie* support to CR, RF, and FR. I have also suggested that intensively rearing animals cannot be justified in utilitarian terms. This narrows the field to CR and RF.

RF is still in play for the reason that from the claim that the *practice* of intensively rearing animals is wrong, in that it causes more suffering than pleasure overall, one cannot conclude that an *individual* is therefore required to desist from eating the products of factory-farms. For it may be that an individual's actions will have no effect on the practice.

This problem is similar to the Problem of Collective Action in Marxism[14]: *just as* it is not in the interest of individual workers to struggle for socialism, even if they see socialism as a desirable goal, since what an ordinary individual does makes no difference to what others do, and so whether socialism comes about or not does not depend on the actions of that individual; *so* whether or not I abstain from intensively reared meat, given the vast scale of modern meat-production, will be irrelevant as to whether any good effects arise from a widespread practice of abstaining from intensively reared meat.

One response to this problem might be that it is unfair to take advantage of others. If we assume that intensive rearing will decrease in scale if a certain number of people give up eating meat reared in that way, and that no one accepts that this is a good thing, then when others are boycotting such meat, it is unfair not to join them.

This claim, however, is counter to the consequentialism at the heart of utilitarianism. If the consequences alone determine the moral standing of an act, and the only consequences relevant to this determination are benefits and harms, then to claim that an act is wrong, although it does no harm and indeed produces a benefit (the pleasure of eating meat), seems not only churlish, but also contradictory.[15]

A more promising response might be to claim that characterizing the problem in this way makes what Parfit calls the 'fifth mistake in moral mathematics.'[16] One makes this mistake if one thinks that:

If some act has effects on other people that are imperceptible, this act cannot be morally wrong *because* it has these effects. An act cannot be wrong because of its effects on other people if none of these people could ever notice any difference. Similarly, if some act would have imperceptible effects on other people, these effects cannot make this act what someone ought to do.

Developing Parfit's analysis, one might claim that in order to avoid the paradox that, if imperceptible acts are never wrong, many people who increase the suffering of a person until it is severe, each by an imperceptible amount, are doing no wrong, we should attend to the consequences of what *we together* do.

This response also fails, however, in that it still provides no reason for the *individual* to join the boycott. The group will go on doing the good whether or not any one individual partakes in the boycott.

The following response to the Problem of Collective Action is more successful. There are three possible effects of an individual boycotting intensively reared meat. It will either have no effect, being below the threshold required to make a difference; or a great effect, 'tipping the balance' over a threshold; or a small effect, if thresholds do not exist and the effect on intensive farming is direct.

If thresholds do exist, the action will have one or other of the first two effects. It might be thought that this gives the individual a reason not to join the boycott, in the same way that the fact that there is a very small probability of having an effect in a general election might be thought to supply a good reason for any one individual not to vote. This, however, is to make Parfit's third mistake, that of ignoring small chances.[17] According to utilitarianism, we should act so as to maximize *expected* utility. Thus, a small chance of bringing about a great good does give me a reason to act.

It is also possible that boycotting intensively reared meat will have an effect on intensive farming, regardless of the effects of the acts on others. In fact, it seems likely that this will sometimes be the case. Imagine that I am a Meat-eating individual, who, like most people, enjoys the taste of chicken. In a year, I

might buy, say, five chickens. Now information-transfer in a corporate market economy is not perfect. If I chose to boycott Bernard Matthews' chickens, he would not be able to find out that *I* had done so. But neither is it entirely inefficient. If I buy my chickens from the same store, and then stop buying them, the figures for chicken sales for the next year will be less by five than if I had not joined the boycott. The store may order fewer chickens over the next year, and the farmer produce fewer chickens. For farmers surely will supply fewer chickens if demand drops. If this scenario appears unlikely, however, the argument based around thresholds still suffices to solve the Collective Action Problem.

It is also the case that an individual's boycott can be a symbolic gesture, and thus have indirect effects on intensive farming through influencing others to reflect upon the reasons for the boycott and to join it.

On the basis of the discussion so far, then, CR emerges as the most plausible utilitarian view on Meat-eating.

3 The Argument from Callousness

1. The practice of rearing animals and killing them for food engenders a callous attitude in human beings towards other human beings.
2. This attitude will be expressed in callous actions towards other human beings, which cause suffering.
3. Causing suffering is wrong.
4. Therefore, the practice is wrong.

One way to criticize this old argument would be to point out that, once again, only the *bad* consequences are being taken into account. The number of people actually involved in the practice is small, relative to the number of people who benefit from it (the Meat-eaters). Thus, even if animal-farmers and employees of slaughter-houses do cause more suffering to other human beings than they might otherwise have done if employed in a different area, it is still possible that the benefits gained by those who enjoy their products will more than suffice to counter-balance that suffering.

But it seems questionable whether the first premise is anyway correct. If those involved in the practice are made aware of the justifications for it, there need be no presumption that they will become callous in their attitude towards other animals or humans. And even if not only are they not aware of the justifications, but also (as is often claimed) they must think of animals as in some sense inanimate if they are to do their job, there is no reason to think that this is the first step on a slippery slope leading to callous actions towards human beings. For this attitude to animals would be based on the notion that they are even more unlike humans than they in fact are.

The truth of the matter is that there is a place for compassion in the rearing of animals for food, and that even where callousness takes the place of compassion, there is no reason to think that this will spill over into callousness towards human beings.

4 The Argument from Paternalism

1. There is strong evidence that Meat-eating is not conducive to the health of a population.
2. It is the utilitarian duty of a government to minimize harm.
3. Therefore, Meat-eating ought to be forbidden.

The first premise is loosely worded. There is strong evidence that the eating of red meat—and fatty foods in general—in large quantities is linked with conditions such as heart-disease. But there is little, if any, evidence that eating meat, in particular white meat or fish, in moderation is harmful.

The proponent of the argument may then attempt to weaken the conclusion to the claim that eating *red* meat ought to be forbidden. But this ignores the direct and indirect harms of paternalism. Paternalism, by definition, violates a person's autonomy, and infringes upon his or her liberty. And banning red meat would also have obvious bad side-effects, simi-

lar to those which occurred during the era of Prohibition of alcohol in the United States. Indeed, it is likely that any such measure would have to be repealed. The conclusion, then, must be weakened still further. The argument can only require a government to disseminate information concerning the dangers to the individual of consuming large amounts of food with a high fat content.

5 The Argument from Starvation

1. The widespread practice of Meat-eating requires the feeding of large amounts of protein to animals.
2. This protein could be used to feed those human beings who are starving.
3. By eating meat, we are causing the deaths of these human beings.
4. Causing the death of human beings is wrong.
5. Therefore, we ought to cease to eat meat.

Utilitarians cannot accept that there is a moral distinction between acts and omissions. Thus, the obvious common-sense reply to the argument, that we are not killing those who starve to death, but merely allowing them to die, is not open to me in a dispute with a utilitarian.

Could I claim that we have property-rights over this protein, in that it is purchased on the open market from its legal owners, either at home, or in other countries, where people may or may not be starving? It is true that utilitarianism does offer a strong rationale for the institution of property.[18] But, given that goods diminish marginally in value, any utilitarian theory of property which would permit the present inequality of wealth, and hence control over resources, between northern and southern hemispheres must be entirely unconvincing.[19]

The problem with this argument is the simplistic conception of economics on which its main assumption rests. This is that the practices of Meat-eating use protein which would otherwise have been available for the starving. But famines are not usually *caused* by shortages of food, but rather more complex issues such as sudden changes in entitlement relations.[20] What those who are starving need is wealth, to buy food and long-term productive capacity, not our ceasing to eat meat. This would be likely to disturb the world grain-market to such an extent that very bad consequences could occur. For example, countries relying on grain-export would become poorer, with adverse effects on their population. And a further likely consequence would be that there would be *less* grain available to those who are starving. This was suggested by a number of economists, reacting to the statement in the nineteen-seventies by the American senator Earl Butt that each American citizen ought to eat one less hamburger a week, with a view to easing starvation in the Third World.[21] Third World grain supplies fluctuate according to surpluses in the First World. Supply in the First World in turn fluctuates according to demand. And the greater the demand, the greater the likely surplus. Thus, as it turned out, Butt should have urged Americans to eat one *more* hamburger a week!

If the proponent of the argument then claims to be aware of these problems, and to be offering a purely tactical or protreptic thesis, designed to bring about a change in people's diets, there is a requirement that V be shown to be justified on grounds *other* than those allegedly supplied by the Argument from Starvation.[22] And those grounds we have yet to find. The Argument from Starvation is valid and true if re-interpreted as a demand that an individual give money to a charity concerned with aid to the Third World. But becoming a Vegetarian will not aid those who are starving.

6 The Argument from Future Generations

1. Extra sentient beings in the world would raise the level of utility.

2. Human beings are the most efficient producers of utility.
3. Therefore, it is wrong to rear animals for food, since the protein consumed by these animals would produce more utility if used to feed extra human beings, until an optimum population is reached.

This argument relies on Total, as opposed to Average, utilitarianism.[23] According to the Total view, we are required to maximize the level of total utility over time, not, say, average utility (total utility divided by the number of beings living).

One important objection to the argument is of course that people do not believe in the Total view, including most members of most governments. Thus, even if more protein becomes available, it is unlikely to support programs of population-growth. It is not only the economics, but also the politics of this argument which are simplistic.

A more trenchant point, however, is that the Total view does not support increasing population in our world. Unless there is some disaster, it will be many millions of years before life on this planet dies out through the sun's being extinguished. Thus, our conception of 'the future' ought to be far broader than that implied by the Argument from Future Generations.

Human beings at present are heavy users of finite resources, such as fossil-fuels and metals. These resources are being used very inefficiently. Imagine future generations classified into three groups: the short-term, the medium-term, and the long-term. And consider the effects of two policies: Depletion of resources, through increasing the population; and Conservation, through maintaining present levels of population. Depletion will benefit the short-term generations, but at the expense of the medium-term. Conservation will benefit the medium-term, but at the expense of the short term. There are two relevant considerations, here. Keeping the population steady will (i) give us more time to develop substitutes for these resources, and (ii) enable us to contrive more efficient ways of using resources that remain. If we fail to develop substitutes, there could be a global disaster. Conservation gives us more time for research, and thus is less likely to result in disaster for medium- *and* long-term generations. And any amount of resources used in the medium-term will almost certainly provide more utility, because of increased efficiency.

Meanwhile, renewable resources, such as protein, should be put to their most efficient use. And the most efficient use of protein will involve feeding both human beings and domestic animals.

I conclude, then, that none of the main utilitarian arguments for V succeeds. The suffering endured by intensively reared animals rules out eating them. Thus RF, FP, and FR are incorrect. The practice of rearing animals non-intensively is productive of utility. Thus, CP is incorrect, and CR is the most plausible utilitarian view on Meat-eating.[24]

Acknowledgement

I am indebted to Raymond Frey, James Griffin, Richard Hare, Michael Lockwood, Peter Singer, and Eldon Soifer for their comments on previous drafts of this paper.

Notes

1 See *e.g.* P. Singer, *Animal Liberation,* London: Jonathan Cape, 1976; *Practical Ethics*, Cambridge: Cambridge University Press, 1979. In 'Killing animals and killing humans,' *Inquiry 22*, 1979, and 'Utilitarianism and vegetarianism,' *Philosophy and Public Affairs* 7, 1979–80, Singer's position becomes more sympathetic to what I call the Compromise Permission view (CP). Singer does, however, appear to qualify his adherence to CP: i) it may only be suited to a society of 'sophisticated philosophers'; ii) it may be the first step onto a slippery slope leading us back to Full Meat-eating in a factory-farming society. Singer's arguments will be discussed further below.

2 See *e.g.* R. Frey, *Rights, Killing, and Suffering*, Oxford: Basil Blackwell, 1983. Frey does not advocate the Full Meat-eating Permission view (FP) (according to which one can eat all kinds of meat without qualms), but is sympathetic to the motivation behind the Compromise views. One is morally permitted to eat any kind of animal flesh, but also morally required to campaign for the end of intensive farming, by means such as political lobbying. I shall call this the R. Frey view (RF).

3 This incidentally is why one should take care in interpreting Singer's claim about replaceability:

> ...that even if it is valid when the animals in question have a pleasant life, it would not justify eating the flesh of animals reared in modern 'factory farms,' where the animals are so crowded together and restricted in their movements that their lives seem to be more of a burden than a benefit to them. [*Practical Ethics*, p. 100]

4 It has been argued in Frey, *Interests and Rights*, Oxford: Clarendon Press, 1980 and elsewhere that animals cannot have desires. Common sense suggests that this is false, and is supported by *e.g.* T. Regan, *The Case for Animal Rights*, London, Routledge & Kegan Paul, chap. 2.

5 J.S. Mill, *Utilitarianism*, repr. in (ed.) M. Warnock, *Utilitarianism*, London: Fontana, 1962, chap. 2.

6 See M. Lockwood, 'Singer on killing and the preference for life,' *Inquiry* 22, 1979, p. 61.

7 Singer appears to believe that a Desire theory can supply special reasons for not killing 'self-conscious' beings (those with the desire to go on living). See *Practical Ethics*, 80f.; ch. 5; 'Killing humans and killing animals.' He says:

> The replaceability principle applies, regardless of species, to beings who have never had the capacity to desire continued life. ['Killing humans and killing animals,' 154f.]

> He also seems to believe that domestic animals lack self-consciousness, and do not therefore have the desire to go on living. The latter claim seems to me false, and I suspect that the former is either false or confused. But as the main text shows the point is not relevant here, and so does not deserve further discussion.

8 E.g., Singer, *Practical Ethics*, 83ff.; J. Glover, *Causing Death and Saving Lives*, Harmondsworth: Penguin, 1977, chap. 5; J. Griffin, *Well-Being*, Oxford: Clarendon Press, 1986, p. 67.

9 For the opposing view, see Regan, *The Case for Animal Rights*, ch. 3.

10 Again, I am concerned with *domestic* animals here. If someone were to claim that certain chimpanzees or gorillas are autonomous to some degree, I should be less inclined to dismiss her.

11 Singer sometimes seems to pass by this point. For example:

> ...the important question is not whether animal flesh *could* be produced without suffering, but whether the flesh that we are considering buying *was* produced without suffering. Unless we can be confident that it was, the principle of equal consideration of interests implies that it was wrong to sacrifice important interests of the animal to satisfy less important interests of our own; consequently we should boycott the end result of this process. [*Practical Ethics*, p. 56f.]

12 Although they do of course often experience severe suffering. See Singer, *Animal Liberation*, 152ff.

13 See Singer, *Animal Liberation*, Chap. 3; and J. Mason and Singer, *Animal Factories*, New York: Crown Publishers, 1980.

14 See M. Olson, *The Logic of Collective Action*, Cambridge, Mass.: Harvard University Press, 1965.

15 For a different view, see Griffin, 'Some problems of fairness,' *Ethics 96*, 1985.

16 D. Parfit, *Reasons and Persons*, Oxford: Clarendon Press, 1984, pp. 28–9.

17 *Reasons and Persons*, p. 27. See also Singer, 'Utilitarianism and vegetarianism,' p. 336.

18 See A. Ryan, *Property and Political Theory*, Oxford: Basil Blackwell, 1984, chap. 4.

19 See Singer, 'Famine, affluence and morality,' *Philosophy and Public Affairs* 1, 1972.

20 See A. Sen, *Poverty and Famines*, Oxford: Clarendon Press, 1981.

21 Butt's claim was brought to my attention by Lockwood.

22 I discuss another tactical argument concerning animals in 'The argument from marginal cases,' *Journal of Applied Philosophy* 2, 1985. If the utilitarian offers this as an argument for V—on the ground that we would think it wrong to eat mentally defective people—it will fail on grounds similar to those on which the Argument from Indirect Diminution of Utility (1b) failed. The side-effects in each case are markedly different.

23 See H. Sidgwick, *The Methods of Ethics*, London: Macmillan, 1907, p. 415f.

24 It should be noted that CR requires only the consumption of artificially-reared meat. Wild animals, including fish, will not be replaced, and so should not be eaten.

Questions for Discussion

1 Can the pleasures and satisfactions of one animal simply be "replaced" by those of another?

2 What is the relationship between the ethics of eating meat at the individual level, and the ethics of the institution of meat-production?

Do Animals Feel Pain?

Peter Harrison

Many of the arguments which try to establish that we have moral obligations toward non-human animals hinge on the claim that non-human animals can suffer, and that suffering is morally bad. In this selection, Peter Harrison challenges the claim that non-human animals can suffer. Harrison points out the difficulty in inferring anything about mental states from physical phenomena, and introduces evidence which casts doubt on the claim that entities with similar neurological systems must have similar mental states. He also suggests that non-human animals may have evolved so as to react to pain stimuli, without having the mental experience of pain. He claims it is the behaviour, not the mental experience, which can be seen to have evolutionary value.

★ ★ ★

In an oft-quoted passage from *The Principles of Morals and Legislation* (1789), Jeremy Bentham addresses the issue of our treatment of animals with the following words: 'the question is not, Can they *reason?* nor, can they *talk?* but, Can they *suffer?*'[1] The point is well taken, for surely if animals suffer, they are legitimate objects of our moral concern. It is curious therefore, given the current interest in the moral status of animals, that Bentham's question has been assumed to be merely rhetorical. No-one has seriously examined the claim, central to arguments for animal liberation and animal rights, that animals actually feel pain. Peter Singer's *Animal Liberation* is perhaps typical in this regard. His treatment of the issue covers a scant seven pages, after which he summarily announces that 'there are no good reasons, scientific or philosophical, for denying that animals feel pain'.[2] In this paper I shall suggest that the issue of animal pain is not so easily dispensed with, and that the evidence brought forward to demonstrate that animals feel pain is far from conclusive.

Three kinds of argument are commonly advanced to support the contention that animals feel pain. The first involves the claim that animal behaviours give us clues to alleged mental states, about what animals are feeling. Thus animals confronted with noxious stimuli which would cause human beings pain, react in similar ways. They attempt to avoid the stimulus, they show facial contortions, they may even cry out. From these 'pain behaviours' it is inferred that the animals must be experiencing pain.

A second argument asserts that by virtue of a similarity in structure and function of nervous systems it is likely that human beings and animals closely related to the human species will experience the external environment in much the same way. It is assumed, for example, that primates have visual experiences similar to our own, feel hunger and thirst as we do, and so on. Presumably when they encounter noxious stimuli, they, like us, feel pain.

A third line of argument is derived from evolutionary theory. Organic evolution implies that there is no radical discontinuity between human and other species. It is likely, on this view, that human minds evolved from animal minds, and that closely related species would experience similar mental events. The evolutionary model would also suggest that pain is an essential adaptation for organisms in that it helps them avoid those things which would reduce their chances of survival and reproduction.

Let us consider these arguments in turn.

I

The argument based on 'pain behaviours' is the most intuitive. Considered in isolation, however, it is the least compelling. Even the simplest representatives of the animal kingdom exhibit rudimentary 'pain behaviours'. Single-celled organisms, for example, will withdraw from harmful stimuli. Insects struggle feebly after they have been inadvertently crushed underfoot. Yet few would want to argue that these behaviours resulted from the experience of pain. Certainly we show little sympathy for those unfortunate ants which are innocent casualties of an afternoon stroll, or the countless billions of microorganisms destroyed by the chlorination of our water supplies. For all practical purposes we discount the possibility that such simple forms of life feel pain, despite their behaviours.

In more elevated levels of the animal kingdom there are also instances of 'pain behaviours' which undoubtedly occur in the absence of pain. Some parent birds, for instance, will feign injury to lure predators away from their young. The converse is also true. Animals might have sustained considerable tissue damage, but display none of the signs which we imagine would usually attend such trauma. This is because immobility is the best response to certain kinds of injury.[3] Pain behaviours, in any case, can be ably performed by non-living entities. If we were to construct a robot which was devoid of speech, yet was to have an active and independent existence, it would be necessary to programme it with mechanisms of self-preservation. Of the many objects it might encounter, it would need to be able to detect and respond to those likely to cause it most harm. Properly programmed, such a machine would manifest its own 'pain behaviour'. If we lit a fire under it, it would struggle to escape. If it found itself in a dangerous situation from which it could not extricate itself (say it fell into an acid bath) it would attempt to summon aid with shrill cries. If it were immobilized after a fall, it might, by facial contortions, indicate that it was damaged. But this 'pain behaviour' would convey nothing about what it was feeling, for robots, on most accounts, can feel nothing. All that could be learned from such behaviour was how well the robot had been programmed for self-preservation. *Mutatis mutandis,* the 'pain behaviours' of animals demonstrate, in the first instance, how well natural selection has fitted them for encounters with unfriendly aspects of their environment. For neither animals, nor our imaginary robot, is 'pain behaviour' primarily an expression of some internal state.

I think these examples are sufficient to show that the argument from behaviours *alone* is fairly weak. But the reason we are inclined to deny that simple animals and computers feel pain is that despite their competent performance of 'pain behaviours', their internal structure is sufficiently dissimilar to our own to warrant the conclusion that they do not have a mental life which is in any way comparable. Animals closely related to the human species, however, possess at least some of the neural hardware which in human beings is thought to be involved in the experience of pain. It might be that the behavioural argument is stronger when considered together with the second argument—that based on the affinity of nervous systems.

II

Pain is a mental state. It might be caused by, or correlated with, brain states. It might have behavioural or psychological indicators. Yet it remains intractably mental. Herein lies the stumbling block of the second argument, for the closest scrutiny of the nervous systems of human beings and animals has never progressed beyond, and arguably never will progress beyond, the description of brain states to arrive at mental states. Thus the introduction of the structure and function of nervous systems into this discussion brings with it that whole constellation of difficulties which revolve around the problem of psycho-physical reductionism. Can mental states be reduced to physical states, and is it possible to project mental states from appropriate anatomical and physiological data? To be successful, the second argument for animal pain must answer both of these questions in the affirmative.

Descartes, in his *Meditations* (1641), quite correctly pointed out that there is no necessary *logical* relation between propositions about mental states and propositions about physical states. We may doubt the existence of our bodies, but not our minds. A disembodied mind is a logical possibility. Conversely, there is no logical impropriety in imagining bodies behaving in quite complex ways, without those behaviours being necessarily accompanied by relevant mental processes. Our robot, for example, would fit the bill, and indeed for Descartes, animals too were merely automatons, albeit organic ones.

Of course from the fact that there is no *logical* connection between mental states and physical states it cannot be inferred that no *contingent* connection is possible. Descriptions of mental and physical states may be linked in a number of ways, and it is upon such linkages that the second argument for animal pain depends. The most compelling evidence of connection between the physical state of the brain and the mental life of the individual comes from instances of brain pathology or brain surgery. The fact that damage to the cerebral cortex can reduce individuals to a 'mindless' state would suggest that observable brain states cause mind states, or at the very least are a necessary condition of mind states. More specifically, neurologists have had some success in identifying those parts of the brain which seem to be responsible for particular conscious states.

Our experience of pain, for example, seems to be mediated through a complicated physical network involving the neospinothalamic projection system (sensory aspects of pain), reticular and limbic structures (motivational aspects of pain), and the neocortex (overall control of sensory and motivational systems).[4] (It may be significant that this latter structure we share only with the primates. An argument could be made on this basis alone that the experience which we designate 'pain' is peculiar to us and a few primate species.) But despite such well-established connections between observable brain structures and more elusive mental states, it would be rash to attempt to predict the mental states of individuals on the basis of the presence or absence of certain structures, or even on the basis of the physiological status of those structures.[5] The well-known literature on the psychology of pain illustrates that the same stimulus may prove intensely painful to one individual, and

be of little concern to another. The use of placebos to control pain, the influence of hypnosis or suggestion to influence pain perception, national differences in pain thresholds, all such aspects of the psychology of pain illustrate that the presence of certain brain structures and requisite sensory inputs are not sufficient conditions for the prediction of mental states.

Not only does the psychology of pain afford instances in which the same neural hardware might give rise to a variety of different conscious states, but the human brain itself exhibits an amazing ability to generate certain mental states in the absence of the relevant physical structures. Phantom pain is perhaps the most obvious example. Amputees frequently report awareness of a limb which has been recently amputated. In a minority of cases a phantom limb may become an ongoing source of severe pain. Often the pain is located in a quite specific part of the missing appendage.

An even more compelling illustration of the generation of certain mental states in the absence of appropriate structures comes from John Lorber's engaging paper 'Is Your Brain Really Necessary?'[6] Paediatric neurologist Lorber reports on a number of individuals with hydrocephalus—a condition which resulted in their having virtually no cerebral cortex. The most intriguing case cited by Lorber is that of a mathematician with IQ of 126. A brain scan revealed that this young man had, in Lorber's words, 'virtually no brain'. The supratentorial part of the intracranial cavity contained only a thin layer of brain tissue, between one and two millimetres thick, attached to the skull wall. No 'visual cortex' was evident, yet the individual, who by all accounts should have been blind, had above average visual perception. It is likely that the functions which would normally have taken place in the missing cerebral cortex had been taken over by other structures. Cases such as this show that certain aspects of human consciousness have a tenacity which confounds our understanding of the link between brain structure and consciousness.

Lorber's discoveries are a striking example of the fact that an advancing neuroscience, far from establishing concrete links between brain states and mental states, is actually deepening the mystery of how the brain is causally related to human consciousness. It need hardly be said that when we cross the species boundary and attempt to make projections about animals' putative mental lives based on the structures of their nervous systems we are in murky waters indeed. Two further examples illustrate this.

The brains of birds, such as they are, do not contain a 'visual cortex'. Thus if we are to argue that similar brain structures give rise to similar experiences, then it is unlikely that the visual experiences of birds will be qualitatively similar to our own. On the other hand, the behaviour of birds would seem to indicate that they can 'see'. While we assume from the behaviour of birds that their visual experience of the world is much the same as ours, if we are committed to the view that like mental states are generated by like brain structures, we are bound to admit that this assumption is unfounded. We might of course be tempted to revert to the first argument—that behaviour, not structure, gives the correct cues to mental states. But this seems to commit us to the view that computers, flies, and amoebas have states of consciousness like our own.

Another illustration which concerns visual experiences is the much-discussed phenomenon of 'blind-sight'.[7] As we have already mentioned, the 'visual' or striate cortex is thought to be necessary for human vision. Individuals suffering from damage to the striate cortex may lose sight in part of their visual field. Larry Weisenkrantz and his colleagues have carried out a number of experiments on one such individual who claimed to be blind

in his left field of view. Simple shapes were presented to this subject in his blind field of view. Though he denied being able to see anything, the subject could, with reasonable consistency, describe the shape of the object and point to it. In each instance he insisted that his correct response was merely a guess.[8] Examples of blindsight indicate, amongst other things, that it is possible to have visual experiences of which we are unaware. The blindsight phenomenon thus opens up the possibility that there might be *non-conscious* experiences to which we can nonetheless respond with the appropriate behaviour.[9] Blindsighted individuals can learn to respond *as if* they see, even though they have no conscious awareness of seeing anything. The significance of this for a discussion of animal behaviours is that animals might respond to stimuli as if they were conscious of them, while in fact they are not. Thus birds which lack the human apparatus of conscious vision (as do blindsighted subjects) might not simply have qualitatively different visual experiences as suggested above, they might not have conscious visual experiences at all. It may be concluded that an animal's experience of stimuli which we would find painful might be qualitatively different (that is, not painful) or may even be non-conscious. Animals might react to such stimuli by exhibiting 'pain behaviour' and yet not have that mental experience which we call 'pain', or perhaps not have any conscious experience at all.[10]

So far our discussion of neural circuitry and how it relates to putative mental states has focused upon the inability of contemporary neuroscience to bridge the gap between brain and mind. There are those, of course, who have asserted that it is impossible in principle to bridge that gap. It is significant that Thomas Nagel, one of the chief spokesmen for this group, has alluded to animal consciousness to make his point.

In the seminal paper 'What is it Like to

be a Bat?',[11] Nagel leads us into the subjective world of the bat. These curious mammals, he reminds us, perceive the external world using a kind of sonar. By emitting high-pitched squeals and detecting the reflections, they are able to create an accurate enough image of their environment to enable them to ensnare small flying insects, while they themselves are air-borne. Nagel points out that we might observe and describe in detail the neurophysiology which makes all this possible, but that it is unlikely that any amount of such observation would ever give us an insight into the bat's subjective experience of the world—into what it is like to be a bat. As Nagel himself puts it:

> For if the facts of experience—facts about what it is like *for* the experiencing organism-are available only from one point of view, then it is a mystery how the true character of experience could be revealed in the physical operation of that organism.[12]

Nagel thus asserts that the construction of subjective experiences from the observation of brain states is *in principle* impossible.[13]

For our present purposes it is not necessary to enter into the argument about whether mind states are reducible to brain states. Suffice it to say that there is sufficient confusion about how brain structure and function relate to mental states to rule out any simple assertion that animal nervous systems which resemble our own will give rise to mental states like ours.

It seems then, that pain, a mental state, can be neither perceived nor inferred by directing the senses on to behaviours or on to the brain itself. But what of the third argument for animal pain—that based on evolutionary theory?

III

Evolutionary theory provides the most convincing case for animal pain. Because evolu-tion stresses continuities in the biological sphere, it breaks down the distinction between human and animal. Thus any special claims made on behalf of the human race—that they alone experience pain, for example—require justification. Before examining how, in evolutionary terms, we might justify treating *Homo sapiens* as a unique case, we ought to consider first how animal pain might conceivably fit into the evolutionary scheme of things.

Natural selection 'designs' animals to survive and reproduce. An important sort of adaptation for organisms to acquire would be the ability to avoid aspects of the environment which would reduce their chances of survival and reproduction. Pain, we might suppose, plays this adaptive rôle by compelling organisms to avoid situations in their world which might harm them. This view of the matter receives some measure of support from cases of individuals born with a congenital insensitivity to pain. Such unfortunate people frequently injure themselves quite severely in their early childhood, and must be taught how to avoid inflicting damage upon themselves. That such a condition can lead eventually to permanent disability or death would suggest that pain has considerable adaptive value for human beings at least.[14] Animals which were similarly insensitive to damaging stimuli, we might reasonably infer, would have little chance of survival. Yet there are difficulties with this interpretation.

Strictly, it is not pain (real or imputed) which is the adaptation, but the *behaviour* which is elicited when the damaging stimulus is applied. Those who are insensitive to pain are not disadvantaged by the absence of unpleasant mental states, but by a lack of those behavioural responses which in others are prompted by pain. We tend to lose sight of the primacy of behaviour because we get caught up in the connotations of 'expression'. That is to say, we consider some animal behaviours to be expressions of a particular mental state.

Even Darwin, who should have known better, was guilty of this infelicity when he spoke of the 'expression of the emotions in man and animals'. Such locutions are misleading because they suggest that certain aspects of behaviour are arbitrary outward signs which signify some conscious state. But the simplest application of the theory of natural selection would only allow that such behaviours as violent struggling, grimacing and crying out, serve some more direct purpose in enhancing an animal's chances of survival and reproduction. (Darwin admittedly stressed the communicative aspects of these signs.) To exploit another example which I have drawn upon in another context, a wildebeest which is being torn apart by dogs will die in silence, while a chimpanzee will screech out in response to some trivial hurt like a thorn puncturing its foot.[15] It seems that the chimp gives expression to its pain, whereas the wildebeest does not. Yet neither expresses its pain. Rather, each behaves in a way likely to enhance the survival of the species. The chimpanzee communicates either to warn its conspecifics, or to summon aid. The wildebeest remains silent so that others will not be lured to their deaths. It is the behaviour, rather than some hypothetical mental state, which adapts the organism.

Another linguistic usage which holds us in thrall is the language of 'detection'. We assume that 'detection' entails 'conscious awareness of'. This leads us to believe that an animal cannot respond to a stimulus unless in some sense it consciously 'knows' what it has encountered. The reason such insectivorous plants as the venus fly trap capture our imagination is that they behave as if they are aware. How, we ponder, do they 'know' that the fly is there? Again we need to remind ourselves that the simplest of organisms are able to detect and respond to stimuli, yet we are not thereby committed to the view that they have knowledge or beliefs. The same is true of more neurologically complex organisms. There is an important truth in that litany of behaviourists: animals acquire behaviours, not beliefs.

If it is granted that the behaviour rather than some postulated mental state is what adapts an organism, we are next led to inquire whether organisms might exhibit 'pain behaviours' without that attendant mental state which we call 'pain'. As we noted at the outset, many invertebrates to which we do not generally attribute feelings of pain exhibit 'pain behaviour'. In higher animals too, as we have already seen, it is possible that relevant behaviours might be performed in the absence of any conscious experience. But is it probable? Must pain be introduced to cause the behaviours, or might these be caused more directly by the stimulus, or perhaps by indifferent conscious states? We might at this point simply opt for the most parsimonious explanation. This is in fact the upshot of Lloyd Morgan's famous dictum: 'In no case may we interpret an action as the outcome of the exercise of a higher psychical faculty, if it can be interpreted as the outcome of the exercise of one which stands lower in the psychological scale.'[16] We must ask, in other words, if we can explain all animals' reactions to noxious stimuli without recourse to particular mental states. Our blindsight examples show that it is possible for organisms to respond appropriately to stimuli in the complete absence of mental states. If the general case is true, then the same might be said for the specific performance of 'pain behaviours' in the absence of pain.

The thrust of Morgan's canon can be reinforced epistemologically with the arguments of Descartes. As we know, Descartes' radical doubt led him to propose that all we can know for certain are the truths of logic and the existence of our own mental states.[17] Fortunately one of the truths of logic was the existence of a God who could guarantee, to some extent, the veracity of perceptions of the world. Yet strict application of the criterion of doubt permits us to ascribe minds to other creatures only if they demonstrate (verbally, by signs, or by rational behaviour) evidence of mental activity. From the lack of such indications from animals, Descartes concluded that we have no evidence which would enable us legitimately to infer that animals have minds.[18] Not having minds, they cannot feel pain. Descartes thus provides *epistemological* grounds for denying that animals feel pain.[19]

If we adopt the conservative stance of Morgan or Descartes, then it seems that we have no grounds, *scientific* or *philosophical*, for asserting that animals feel pain. Yet this is a much weaker claim than the positive assertion that we have good reasons for believing that animals do not feel pain, or, to put it another way, that only human beings feel pain.[20] Certainly a reasonable case could be advanced that given our admitted ignorance, we have *moral* grounds for giving animals the benefit of the doubt. We shall return to this point later. For the moment, let us consider the positive statement of the case. Do we have reasons for believing that only human beings feel pain? Or, recasting the question in evolutionary terms, why should pain have adaptive value for the human species, if it would serve no purpose in other species?

IV

Pain is a mental state, and mental states require minds. Our inquiry, then, is in part an investigation of the selective advantage conferred by the possession of a mind. A mind's reflection on its own activities, amongst other things, enables us to predict the behaviour of other human beings, and to a lesser extent, animals. By reflecting upon our reasons for behaving in certain ways, and by assuming that our fellow human beings are similarly motivated, we can make predictions about how they are likely to behave in certain situations. But more than this, by ascribing consciousness and intelligence to other organisms we

can also make predictions about how they will behave. Such ascriptions, whether they have any basis in fact or not, can thus help the human species survive. As H. S. Jennings remarked almost ninety years ago, if an amoeba 'were as large as a whale, it is quite conceivable that occasions might arise when the attribution to it of the elemental states of consciousness might save the unsophisticated human from destruction that would result from lack of such attribution.'[21] Along with human self-awareness, then, came a tendency to attribute a similar awareness to other creatures. That animals might have beliefs, mental images, intentions and pains like our own could be nothing more than a useful fiction which gives us a shorthand method of predicting their behaviour.

There is, then, some value in the belief that animals suffer pain, for it provides a reasonably reliable guide to how they will behave. But it is not an infallible guide. If, for example, we were to pit ourselves against a chess-playing computer, the best strategy to adopt would be to act as if the machine were a skilled human opponent, possessed of certain intentional states—a desire to win, particular beliefs about the rules, and so on. However, there might be occasions when it would be better to adopt another attitude towards the computer. Let us imagine that the computer was programmed to play at three levels—beginner, intermediate, and advanced. Set at the 'beginner' level, the computer might show itself to be vulnerable to a basic 'fool's mate', so that whenever this simple gambit was used, it inevitably lost. A human opponent could thus be confident of beating the computer whenever he or she wished. Now this exploitation of the computer's weakness would result from the adoption of quite a different stance. No longer would the computer be treated as if it had desires and beliefs (or more importantly as if it had the ability to acquire new beliefs), for a human opponent in the same situation would quickly learn to counter the 'fool's mate'. Instead, predictions of the computer's behaviour would be based on the way it had been designed to operate. Thus, our wildebeest, on an intentional account, should exhibit 'pain behaviour'. Only when we adopt a 'design stance' (the animal was 'designed' by natural selection to behave in ways which would enhance the survival of the species) do we get a reasonable explanation of why it dies in silence.[22] The general point is this. The ascription to animals of certain mental states usually enables us to predict their behaviour with some accuracy (such ascription increasing our own chances of survival). But there will always be instances where this intentional model will break down and explanations which refer to selective advantages will be preferred.

Another reason for attributing pain experiences only to human beings is to do with free-will and moral responsibility. While there has been some dispute about whether animals ought to be the object of our moral concern, we do not usually consider animals to be moral agents. Animals are not generally held to be morally responsible for their own acts, and notwithstanding some rather odd medieval judicial practices, animals do not stand trial for antisocial acts which they might have committed. What is absent in animals which is thought to be crucial to the committing of some wrong is the *mens rea*—the evil intent. Animals are not morally responsible for the acts they commit because while they may have behavioural dispositions, they do not have thoughts and beliefs about what is right and wrong, nor can they, whatever their behavioural disposition, form a conscious intent. Or at least, so we generally believe. Animals, in short, are not 'free agents', and this is why they are not regarded as being morally responsible. But what does the determined nature of animal behaviour have to do with pain? Simply this, that if animals' behaviours are causally

determined, it makes no sense to speak of pain as an additional causal factor.

One way of seeing the force of this is to explore some of the contexts in which we use the term 'pain'. There are many ways we have of talking about pain which exclude animals. Consider the following: (1) 'For the long-distance runner, it is a matter of mind over matter. He must break through the pain barrier'. (2) 'The hunger striker finally succumbed and died'. (3) 'Even though she knew it would mean a horrible death at the stake, she refused to recant'. (4) 'The pain became unbearable. He cried out'. If we attempt to substitute animals for the human agents in these statements, the result becomes complete nonsense. Our inability to fit animals into the logic of these expressions is not merely because animals are not (contingently) long-distance runners, or hunger strikers, or religious martyrs. The key lies in statement (4). We must ask: Do animals ever find pain unbearable?, and, What reasons could they have for bearing it?

Consider this sentence in which a suitable substitution might be made. 'The man's hand reached into the flames, and was immediately withdrawn with a cry'. We could easily substitute 'ape' for 'man' here and the statement will retain its sense. But what about this: 'The man plunged his hand into the flames again, knowing that only he could reach the valve and stem the flow of petrol which threatened to turn the sleepy village into an inferno'. Now the substitution becomes impossible, for what could conceivably cause the ape to plunge its hand back into the flames? Nothing, I suspect, for apes do not have reasons for bearing pain.

Now it may seem unsatisfactory to proceed on the basis of certain linguistic practices to make some claim about how things really are. (This, I suspect, is why Anselm's ontological argument always leaves one feeling a little uneasy.) But the exclusive nature of the grammar of pain, or more correctly of 'bearing pain', reveals the unique province of pain. Pain operates as one kind of reason which free agents are bound to take into consideration when they decide on a particular course of action. Pain can be borne if there are *reasons*. But an animal never has reasons either to bear pain, or to succumb to pain. And if pain never need be brought into the sphere of reasons—the mind—then there is no need for it, *qua* unpleasant mental event, at all. Thus, while it is undeniable that animals sense noxious stimuli and react to them, these stimuli only need be represented as unpleasant mental states if they are to become the body's reasons in the context of other reasons. Only as various degrees of unpleasantness can they be taken seriously amongst reasons, and this is only necessary in the mind of a rational agent.

Another way of thinking about this is to consider the attributes of the long-distance runner, the hunger striker, the martyr, the hero of the sleepy village. We could say that they had mental strength, great courage, or moral character. But we would never predicate these of animals. The wildebeest dies silently and does not endanger the herd. But does it die courageously? Does it bear the pain to the end? Does it have a reason for remaining silent? No, because it does not have a choice. All wildebeest behave in this fashion. And if it does not have a choice, there is no requirement for the dismemberment of its body to be represented mentally as pain.

Pain is the body's representative in the mind's decision-making process. Without pain, the mind would imperil the body (as cases of insensitivity to pain clearly show). But without the rational, decision-making mind, pain is superfluous. Animals have no rational or moral considerations which might overrule the needs of the body. It is for this reason that Descartes referred to pain, hunger and thirst as 'confused modes of *thought*', which can only be predicated of creatures which can think.[23]

V

We may now return to the original issue which prompted this examination of the reasons for ascribing pains to animals—the moral question of how we should treat animals. The arguments set out above do not constitute a conclusive disproof of animal pain. Indeed if the mind-body problem is as intractable as I have suggested, then the best we can manage is to arrive at some degree of probability. This much should be clear, however: First, there are reasons for claiming that only human beings feel pain; second, our treatment of animals cannot be based on dubious speculations about their mental lives. It follows, at the very least, that Bentham's question cannot provide a sound basis for an ethic which is to extend to animals. How then do we proceed from here?

It will seem to some that while there remains even a small possibility that animals (or certain kinds of animals) feel pain, these creatures ought to be given the benefit of the doubt. This is true to a point. Animal liberationists and animal rights activists have performed a valuable service in exposing many frivolous and mischievous practices which resulted in the unnecessary mutilation and deaths of animals. Such practices should cease, and many have. On the other hand, there are many animal experiments which improve, or might lead to the improvement of, the human lot. Even if a utilitarian equation which balances net pleasures over net pains can provide a rational basis for making moral choices in these matters (and this is doubtful), the balance should be tipped in favour of human beings, given our uncertainty about animal pain. Further, it virtually goes without saying that if it is doubtful that animals experience physical pain, even more groundless are claims that animals have other kinds of mental states—anxiety, the desire for freedom, and so on. Concerns for the psychological well-being of battery hens, veal calves, penned dolphins, and the like, would seem to be fundamentally misplaced. Our moral sensibilities have gone sadly awry when we expend effort on determining 'what animals prefer' before inquiring into whether 'preference' can be sensibly applied to animals. This is especially so when we are in little doubt as to what human beings prefer, and yet so many of them exist in conditions little different from those of battery hens.

None of this means, however, that there are no strictures on how we ought to behave towards animals. Other considerations—aesthetic, ecological, sentimental, psychological, and pedagogical—can give us a more solid foundation for an 'animal ethic'. Briefly, it would be morally wrong to attack Michelangelo's 'Pieta' with a hammer, despite the fact that this beautifully crafted piece of marble cannot feel pain. If animals are mere machines, they are, for all that, intricate and beautiful machines (most of them), which like old buildings, trees and works of art, can greatly enrich our lives. Accordingly, rational arguments can be mounted against acts which would damage or destroy them.

There is also a growing awareness in the Western world that human beings and animals form part of a global biological community. While at times this awareness expresses itself in rather silly ways, it is still true that if we carelessly alter the balance of that community by the slaughter of certain animals for pleasure or short-term economic gain, we place at risk the quality of life of ourselves and that of future generations.

At a more personal level, many people form strong emotional attachments to animals. Domestic animals traditionally have served as playmates for children and as company for the elderly. If mistreating these animals causes human beings to suffer, then such mistreatment is clearly wrong. Moreover, as the notorious Milgram experiments have shown, the belief that one is causing pain to another, even if false, can do great psychological harm.[24]

When we believe we are being cruel to animals we do ourselves damage, even though our belief might be mistaken.

Finally, there is surely some value in the observation of Thomas Aquinas that kindness to animals might help to teach kindness to human beings.[25] Considerations of these kinds, though they require further development, can provide a far more certain guide to how we should treat animals.

Notes

1 (Oxford: Clarendon Press, 1907), 310f. n. 1 (XVII, 1, iv).

2 Peter Singer, *Animal Liberation* (London: Cape, 1976), 16.

3 Thus Dennis and Melzack: 'The appropriate behavioural response to overt damage may be inactivity; pain arising from trauma should presumably promote such behaviour. However, the appropriate behavioural response to threat may be vigorous activity; pain arising from threat should therefore promote this sort of activity. Thus the overt expression of pain sensation may actually be a combination of inherently contradictory processes and behavioural tendencies.' S. Dennis and R. Melzack, 'Perspectives on Phylogenetic Evolution of Pain Expression', *Animal Pain: Perception and Alleviation,* R. L. Kitchell and H. H. Erickson (eds), (Bethesda: American Physiological Society, 1983), 155.

4 See, e.g., Ronald Melzack, *The Puzzle of Pain* (Ringwood: Penguin, 1973) 93–103, 162f.

5 Thus Theodore Barber reports of individuals chronically insensitive to pain that for most, if not all, 'no distinct localized damage exists in the central nervous system'. 'Toward a Theory of Pain', *Psychological Bulletin* 56(1959), 443. It is true that Barber cites no evidence from autopsies, and that more sophisticated scanning apparatus has been developed since this publication, but the fact that this insensitivity to pain can be reversed without surgical intervention would support Barber's observation.

6 See David Paterson's article of the same name in *World Medicine* 3 May 1980, 21–24. Also see Norton Nelkin, 'Pains and Pain Sensations', *The Journal of Philosophy* 83 (1986), 129–148.

7 On 'blindsight' see Larry Weisenkrantz, 'Varieties of Residual Experience', *Quarterly Journal of Experimental Psychology* 32 (1980), 365–386; Thomas Natsoulas, 'Conscious Perception and the Paradox of "Blindsight"', in *Aspects of Consciousness*, III, Geoffrey Underwood (ed.), (London: Academic Press, 1982), 79–109.

8 Larry Weisenkrantz, 'Trying to Bridge some Neurophysiological Gaps between Monkey and Man', *British Journal of Psychology* 68 (1977), 431–435.

9 On the possibility of 'non-conscious experience', see Peter Carruthers, 'Brute Experience', *The Journal of Philosophy* 86 (1989), 258–269.

10 This is also suggested by Carruthers, ibid., 266–269.

11 *The Philosophical Review* 83 (1974), 435–450.

12 Ibid., 442.

13 Colin McGinn has made a similar point from a different perspective. He argues that the mystery of our mental life arises out of the fact that we simply do not possess the cognitive faculties necessary to solve the mind-body problem. 'Cognitive closure' prevents our ever having access to that vital natural link which presumably exists between brain states and conscious states. See Colin McGinn, 'Can We Solve the Mind-Body Problem?', *Mind* 98 (1989), 349–366.

14 On congenital insensitivity to pain see Melzack, *The Puzzle of Pain,* 15f.

15 David McFarland, 'Pain', *The Oxford Companion to Animal Behaviour,* David McFarland (ed.), (Oxford University Press, 1981), 439.

16 Quoted in Robert Boakes, *From Darwin to Behaviourism* (Cambridge University Press, 1984), 40. This dictum is actually a version of the Aristotelian principle, 'Nature does nothing in vain', couched in evolutionary terms.

17 *Meditations* II.

18 Descartes' clearest explanation of the matter comes in a letter to the English Platonist, Henry More. See Descartes, *Philosophical Letters,* Anthony Kenny (ed.), (Oxford: Clarendon Press, 1970), 243–245.

19 It may seem that Morgan and Descartes are making the same point, but they are not. Morgan's canon was virtually a biological application of the second law of thermodynamics, asserting that a complex biological system would not evolve if a simpler one could perform the same function. Of course, in applying this canon to 'psychical' functions, Morgan seems to have committed himself to the view that more complex mental states require a more complex physical apparatus.

20 Thus Descartes admitted in his letter to More that his thesis about animals was only probable. *Philosophical Letters,* 244.

21 Quoted in Larry Weisenkrantz, 'Neurophysiology and the Nature of Consciousness', *Mindwaves,* C. Blakemore and S. Greenfield (eds), (Oxford: Blackwell, 1987), 309.

22 The terms 'intentional stance' and 'design stance' are D. C. Dennett's. See his *Brainstorms* (Hassocks: Harvester Press, 1978), 3–22.

23 *Meditation IV (HR* I, 192) my emphasis. Cf. Norton Nelkin, who states that pain is an attitude, not a sensation. 'Pains and Pain Sensations', 148.

24 See Stanley Milgram, *Obedience to Authority: An Experimental View* (London: Tavistock, 1974).

25 *Summa theologiae,* la, 2ae. 102, 6.

Questions for Discussion

1 Harrison provides a variety of reasons to think we should not draw conclusions about mental states from evidence of brain structures and activity. Does this refute the claim that non-human animals can feel pain because they have neural systems like ours? How does the answer to this question affect our ability to judge that another human being is in pain?

2 Does it matter whether non-human animals actually feel pain, if the attribution of pain to them is a reliable guide to predicting their behaviour?

3 Harrison describes how a wildebeest will die in silence, while a chimpanzee will cry out, and he claims the behaviour of each has survival value for its species. Does this indicate that neither is really expressing pain?

4 If we are uncertain as to whether non-humans can feel pain, should we treat them as if they can in any case?

The Prospects for Consensus and Convergence in the Animal Rights Debate

Gary E. Varner

Varner offers a summary of the main philosophical views about the moral status of non-human animals, and argues that these views are not as far apart as many people believe. He suggests that a more careful philosophical understanding of the views involved might ease political confrontations, and enhance genuine conversation.

★ ★ ★

Controversies over the use of nonhuman animals (henceforth animals) for science, nutrition, and recreation are often presented as clear-cut standoffs, with little or no common ground between opposing factions and, consequently, with little or no possibility for consensus formation. As a philosopher studying these controversies, my sense is that the apparent intransigence of opposing parties is more a function of political posturing than theoretical necessity, and that continuing to paint the situation as a clear-cut standoff serves the interests of neither side. A critical look at the philosophical bases of the animal rights movement reveals surprising potential for convergence (agreement at the level of policy despite disagreement at the level of moral theory) and, in some cases, consensus (agreement at both levels).[1] Recognizing this should make defenders of animal research take animal rights views more seriously and could refocus the animal rights debate in a constructive way.

In response to the growth of the animal rights movement, animal researchers have begun to distinguish between animal rights views and animal welfare views, but they have not drawn the distinction the way a philosopher would. Researchers typically stress two differences between animal welfarists and animal rightists. First, welfarists argue for reforms in research involving animals, whereas rightists argue for the total abolition of such research.

Second, welfarists work within the system, whereas rightists advocate using theft, sabotage, or even violence to achieve their ends. A more philosophical account of the animal rights/animal welfare distinction cuts the pie very differently, revealing that many researchers agree with some animal rights advocates at the level of moral theory, and that, even where they differ dramatically at the level of moral theory, there is some potential for convergence at the level of policy.

Animal Welfare: The Prospects for *Consensus*

Peter Singer's *Animal Liberation* is the acknowledged Bible of the animal rights movement. Literally millions of people have been moved to vegetarianism or animal activism as a result of reading this book. PETA (People for the Ethical Treatment of Animals) distributed the first edition of the book as a membership premium, and the number of copies in print has been cited as a measure of growth in the animal rights movement. However, Singer wrote *Animal Liberation* for popular consumption, and in it he intentionally avoided discussion of complex philosophical issues.[2] In particular, he avoided analyzing the concepts of 'rights' and 'harm,' and these concepts are critical to drawing the animal rights/animal welfare distinction in philosophical terms.

In *Animal Liberation*, Singer spoke loosely of animals having moral "rights," but all that he intended by this was that animals (at least some of them) have some basic moral standing and that there are right and wrong ways of treating them. In later, more philosophically rigorous work—summarized in his *Practical Ethics*, a second edition of which has just been issued[3]—he explicitly eschews the term *rights*—noting that, as a thoroughgoing utilitarian, he must deny not only that animals have moral rights, but also that human beings do.

When moral philosophers speak of an individual "having moral rights," they mean something much more specific than that the individual has some basic moral standing and that there are right and wrong ways of treating him or her. Although there is much controversy as to the specifics, there is general agreement on this: to attribute moral rights to an individual is to assert that the individual has some kind of special moral dignity, the cash value of which is that certain things cannot justifiably be done to him or her (or it) for the sake of benefit to others. For this reason, moral rights have been characterized as "trump cards" against utilitarian arguments. Utilitarian arguments are based on aggregate benefits and aggregate harms. Specifically, utilitarianism is the view that right actions maximize aggregate happiness. In principle, nothing is inherently or intrinsically wrong, according to a utilitarian; any action could be justified under some possible circumstances. One way of characterizing rights views in ethics, by contrast, is that there are some things which, regardless of the consequences, it is simply wrong to do to individuals, and that moral rights single out these things.

Although a technical and stipulative definition of 'rights,' this philosophical usage reflects a familiar concept. In day-to-day discussions, appeals to individuals' rights are used to assert, in effect, that there is a limit to what individuals can be forced to do, or to

the harm that may be inflicted upon them, for the benefit of others. So the philosophical usage of rights talk reflects the common-sense view that there are limits to what we can justifiably do to an individual for the benefit of society.

To defend the moral rights of animals would be to claim that certain ways of treating animals cannot be justified on utilitarian grounds. But in *Practical Ethics* Peter Singer explicitly adopts a utilitarian stance for dealing with our treatment of nonhuman animals. So the author of "the Bible of the animal rights movement" is not an animal *rights* theorist at all, and the self-proclaimed advocates of animal research are appealing to precisely the same tradition in ethics as is Singer. Both believe that it is permissible to sacrifice (even involuntarily) the life of one individual for the benefit of others, where the aggregated benefits to others clearly outweigh the costs to that individual. (At least they agree on this as far as animals are concerned. Singer is a thoroughgoing utilitarian, whereas my sense is that most animal researchers are utilitarians when it comes to animals, but rights theorists when it comes to humans.)

Many researchers also conceive of harm to animals very similarly to Singer, at least where nonmammalian animals are concerned. In *Animal Liberation*, Singer employs a strongly hedonistic conception of harm. He admits that the morality of killing is more complicated than that of inflicting pain (p. 17) and that although pain is pain wherever it occurs, this "does not imply that all lives are of equal worth" (p. 20). This should be stressed, because researchers commonly say that according to animal rights philosophies, of which Singer's is their paradigm, all animals' lives are of equal value. No fair reading of Singer's *Animal Liberation* would yield this conclusion, let alone any fair reading of *Practical Ethics,* where he devotes four chapters to the question of killing.

The morality of killing is complicated by competing conceptions of harm. In *Animal Liberation* Singer leaves the question of killing in the background and uses a strongly hedonistic conception of animal welfare. He argues that the conclusions reached in the book, including the duty to refrain from eating animals, "flow from the principle of minimizing suffering alone" (p. 21). To conceive of harm hedonistically is to say that harm consists in felt pain or lost opportunities for pleasure. For a utilitarian employing a hedonistic conception of harm, individuals are replaceable in the following sense. If an individual lives a pleasant life, dies a painless death, and is replaced by an individual leading a similarly pleasant life, there is no loss of value in the world. Agriculturalists appear to be thinking like hedonistic utilitarians when they defend humane slaughter in similar terms. Researchers employ a similarly hedonistic conception of harm when they argue that if all pain is eliminated from an experimental protocol then, ethically speaking, there is nothing left to be concerned about.

Singer conceives of harm to "lower" animals in hedonistic terms and thus agrees with these researchers and agriculturalists. He even acknowledges that the replaceability thesis could be used to defend some forms of animal agriculture, although not intensive poultry systems, where the birds hardly live happy lives or die painless deaths. However, Singer argues that it is implausible to conceive of harm in hedonistic terms when it comes to "self-conscious individuals, leading their own lives and wanting to go on living" (p. 125), and he argues that all mammals are self-conscious in this sense.

Singer equates being self-conscious with having forward-looking desires, especially the desire to go on living. He argues that such self-conscious individuals are not replaceable, because when an individual with forward-looking desires dies, those desires go unsatis-fied even if another individual is born and has similar desires satisfied. With regard to self-conscious individuals, Singer is still a utilitarian, but he is a *preference* utilitarian rather than a *hedonistic* utilitarian. Singer cites evidence to demonstrate that the great apes are self-conscious in his sense (pp. 11–16) and states, without saying what specific research leads him to this conclusion, that neither fish nor chickens are (pp. 95, 133), but that "a case can be made, though with varying degrees of confidence," that all mammals are self-conscious (p. 132).

It is easy to disagree with Singer about the range of self-consciousness, as he conceives of it, in the animal kingdom.[4] Probably most mammals have forward-looking desires, but the future to which they look is doubtless a very near one. Cats probably think about what to do in the next moment to achieve a desired result, but I doubt that they have projects (long-term, complicated desires) of the kind suggested by saying that they are "leading their own lives and wanting to go on living."

However, even if we grant Singer the claim that all mammals have projects, so long as we remain utilitarians this just means that research on mammals carries a higher burden of justification than does research on "lower" animals like reptiles or insects, a point many researchers would readily grant. A preference utilitarian is still a utilitarian, and in at least some cases, a utilitarian must agree that experimentation is justified.

In the following passage from *Practical Ethics,* Singer stresses just this point:

> In the past, argument about animal experimentation has often ... been put in absolutist terms: would the opponent of experimentation be prepared to let thousands die from a terrible disease that could be cured by experimenting on one animal? This is a purely hypothetical question, since experiments do not have such dramatic results, but as long as its hypothetical nature is clear, I think the question should be an-

swered affirmatively—in other words, if one, or even a dozen animals had to suffer experiments in order to save thousands, I would think it right and in accordance with equal consideration of interests that they should do so. This, at any rate, is the answer a utilitarian must give. (p. 67)

Singer doubts that most experiments are justified, not because he believes experimentation is wrong *simpliciter,* but because he doubts that the benefits to humans significantly outweigh the costs to the animals. In the pages preceding the passage just quoted, Singer cites examples of experiments he thinks cannot plausibly be said "to serve vital medical purposes": testing of new shampoos and food colorings, armed forces experiments on the effects of radiation on combat performance, and H. F. Harlow's maternal deprivation experiments. "In these cases, and many others like them," he says, "the benefits to humans are either nonexistent or uncertain, while the losses to members of other species are certain and real" (p. 66).

So the disagreement between Singer and the research establishment is largely empirical, about how likely various kinds of research are to lead to important human benefits. Researchers often argue that we cannot be expected to know ahead of time which lines of research will yield dramatic benefits. Critics respond that these same scientists serve on grant review boards, whose function is to permit funding agencies to make such decisions all the time. Here I want only to emphasize that this is an empirical dispute that cannot be settled *a priori* or as a matter of moral theory. One of the limitations of utilitarianism is that its application requires very detailed knowledge about the effects of various actions or policies. When it comes to utilitarian justifications for animal research, the probability—and Singer is correct that it is never a certainty—that various lines of research will save or significantly improve human lives must

be known or estimated before anything meaningful can be said. Singer is convinced that most research will not meet this burden of proof; most researchers are convinced of just the opposite.

Animal Rights: The Prospects for *Convergence*

Most animal researchers agree to a surprising extent with the Moses of the animal rights movement. Their basic ethical principles are the same (at least where nonhuman animals are concerned), and they apply to all animals the same conception of harm which Singer applies to all animals except mammals. Where they disagree with Singer is at the level of policy; they see the same ethical theory implying different things in practice. Dramatic disagreement at the level of moral theory emerges only when we turn to the views of Tom Regan, whose ethical principles and conception of harm are dramatically different from Singer's and the researchers'.

Regan's *The Case for Animal Rights*[5] is a lengthy and rigorous defense of a true animal rights position. It is impossible to do justice to the argument of a 400-page book in a few paragraphs, so here I will simply state the basic destination Regan reaches, in order to examine its implications for animal research.

For Regan, there is basically one moral right: the right not to be harmed on the grounds that doing so benefits others, and all individuals who can be harmed in the relevant way have this basic right. Regan conceives of harm as a diminution in the capacity to form and satisfy desires, and he argues that all animals who are capable of having desires have this basic moral right not to be harmed. On Regan's construal, losing an arm is more of a harm than stubbing one's toe (because it frustrates more of one's desires), but death is always the worst harm an individual can suffer because it completely destroys one's capacity to form and satisfy desires. As to which animals have desires, Regan explicitly defends only the claim that all mentally normal mammals of a year or more have desires, but he says that he does this to avoid the controversy over "line drawing," that is, saying precisely how far down the phylogenetic scale one must go to find animals that are incapable of having desires. Regan is confident that at least all mammals and birds have desires, but acknowledges that the analogical evidence for possession of desires becomes progressively weaker as we turn to herpetofauna (reptiles and amphibians), fish, and then invertebrates.[6]

Regan defends two principles to use in deciding whom to harm where it is impossible not to harm someone who has moral rights: the miniride and worse-off principles. *The worse-off principle* applies where *noncomparable* harms are involved, and it requires us to avoid harming the worse-off individual. Regan's discussion of this principle makes it clear that for him, harm is measured in absolute, rather than relative terms. If harm were measured relative to the individual's original capacity to form and satisfy desires, rather than in absolute terms, then death would be uniformly catastrophic wherever it occurs. But Regan reasons that although death is always the greatest harm which any individual can suffer (because it forecloses all of that individual's opportunities for desire formation and satisfaction), death to a normal human being is noncomparably worse than death to any nonhuman animal, because a normal human being's capacity to form and satisfy desires is so much greater. To illustrate the use of the worse-off principle, Regan imagines that five individuals, four humans, and a dog are in a lifeboat that can support only four of them. Since death to any of the human beings would be noncomparably worse than death to the dog, the worse-off principle applies, and it requires us to avoid harming the human beings, who stand to lose the most.

The *miniride principle* applies to cases where *comparable* harms are involved, and it requires us to harm the few rather than the many. Regan admits that, where it applies, this principle yields the same conclusions as the principle of utility, but he emphasizes that the reasoning is nonutilitarian. The focus, he says, is on individuals rather than the aggregate. What the miniride principle instructs us to do is minimize the overriding of individuals' rights, rather than to maximize aggregate happiness. To illustrate the miniride principle's application, Regan imagines that a runaway mine train must he sent down one of two shafts, and that fifty miners would be killed by sending it down the first shaft but only one by sending it down the second. Since the harms that the various individuals in the example would suffer are comparable (only humans are involved, and all are faced with death), the miniride principle applies, and we are obligated to send the runaway train down the second shaft.

Regan argues that the rights view (as he labels his position) calls for the total abolition of animal research. In terms of the basic contrast drawn above between rights views and utilitarianism, it is easy to see why one would think this. The fundamental tenet of rights views is opposition to utilitarian justifications for harming individuals, and as we saw above, researchers' justification for animal research is utilitarian. They argue that by causing a relatively small number of individuals to suffer and die, a relatively large number of individuals can live or have their lives significantly improved.

However, Regan's worse-off principle, coupled with his conception of harm, would seem to imply that at least *some* research is not only permissible but required, even on a true animal rights view. For as we just saw, Regan believes that death for a normal human is noncomparably worse than death for any nonhuman animal. So if we knew that by performing fatal research on a given number of nonhuman animals we could save even one human life, the worse-off principle would apply, and it would require us to perform the research. In the lifeboat case referred to above, Regan emphasizes that where the worse-off principle applies, the numbers do not matter. He says:

> Let the number of dogs be as large as one likes; suppose they number a million; and suppose the lifeboat will support only four survivors. Then the rights view still implies that, special considerations apart, the million dogs should be thrown overboard and the four humans saved. To attempt to reach a contrary judgment will inevitably involve one in aggregative [i.e., utilitarian] considerations. (p. 325)

The same reasoning, in a hypothetical case like that described by Singer (where we *know*, with absolute certainty, that one experiment will save human lives) would imply that the experiment should be performed.

One complication is that the empirical dispute over the likelihood of significant human benefits emerging from various lines of research, which makes utilitarian justifications of experimentation so complex, will reappear here. Having admitted that some research is justified, animal rights advocates would doubtless continue to disagree with researchers over which research this is. Nevertheless, the foregoing discussion illustrates how the implications of a true animal rights view can converge with those of researchers' animal welfare philosophy. Even someone who attributes moral rights in the philosophical sense to animals, and whose ethical theory thus differs dramatically from most animal researchers', could think that some medical research is justified. This warrants stressing, because researchers commonly say things like, "According to animal rightists, 'a rat is a pig is a dog is a boy,'" and, "Animal rightists want to do away with all uses of animals, including life-saving medical research." However, no fair reading of either Singer or Regan would yield the conclusion that they believe that a rat's or a pig's life is equal to a normal human's. And, consequently, it is possible for someone thinking with Singer's or Regan's principles to accept research that actually saves human lives.

It is *possible*, but Regan himself continues to oppose all animal research to benefit humans. His basis is not the worse-off principle, but that the principle applies, "special considerations apart." One of those considerations is that "risks are not morally transferrable to those who do not voluntarily choose to take them," and this, he claims, blocks application of the worse-off principle to the case of medical experimentation (p. 377). For example, subjects used to screen a new vaccine run higher risks of contracting the disease when researchers intentionally expose them to it. Humans can voluntarily accept these risks, but animals cannot. Consequently, the only kind of research on "higher" animals (roughly, vertebrates) that Regan will accept is that which tests a potential cure for a currently incurable disease on animals that have already acquired the disease of their own accord.

However, most people believe that in at least some cases, we can justifiably transfer risks without first securing the agreement of those to whom the risks are transferred. For instance, modifying price supports can redistribute the financial risks involved in farming, and changing draft board policies in time of war can redistribute the risk of being killed in defense of one's country. Yet most people believe such transfers are justifiable even if involuntary. In these cases, however, the individuals among whom risks are redistributed are all members of a *polis* through which, arguably, they give implicit consent to the policies in question. Still, in some cases there cannot plausibly be said to be even implicit consent: When we go to war, for instance, we impose dramatic risks on thousands or even millions of people who have no political influence in our country. But if the war is justified, so too, presumably, are the involuntarily imposed risks.

The Prospects for Conversation

It has not been my purpose in this paper to decide which particular forms of experimentation are morally justifiable, so I will not further pursue a response to Regan's abolitionist argument. My goal has been to refocus the animal rights debate by emphasizing its philosophical complexity. The question is far more complicated than is suggested by simplistic portrayals by many researchers and in the popular media.

According to the common stereotype, an animal rights advocate wants to eliminate all animal research and is a vegetarian who even avoids wearing leather. But the first "serious attempt ... to assess the accuracy of" this stereotype, a survey of about 600 animal activists attending the June 1990 "March for Animal Rights" in Washington, D.C., found that: nearly half of all activists believe the animal rights movement should not focus on animal research as its top priority; over a third eat red meat, poultry, or seafood; and 40 percent wear leather.[7] I have often heard agriculturalists and scientists say that it is hypocritical for an animal rights advocate to eat any kind of meat, wear leather, or use medicines that have been developed using animal models. But it would only be hypocritical if there were a single, monolithic animal rights philosophy that unambiguously ruled them all out.

In this essay, I have stressed the philosophical diversity underlying the animal rights movement. The "animal rights philosophies" of which many researchers are so contemptuous run the philosophical gamut from a utilitarianism very similar to their own to a true animal rights view that is quite different from their own. On some of these views, certain kinds of animal agriculture are permissible, but

even on a true animal rights view like Regan's, it is possible to endorse some uses of animals, including experimentation that is meaningfully tied to saving human lives.

Continuing to paint all advocates of animal rights as unreasoning, anti-science lunatics will not make that movement go away, any more than painting all scientists who use animal models as Nazis bent on torturing the innocent will make animal research go away. Animal protection movements have surfaced and then disappeared in the past, but today's animal rights movement is squarely grounded in two major traditions in moral philosophy and, amid the stable affluence of a modern, industrialized nation like the United States, cannot be expected to go away. By the same token, twentieth-century medical research has dramatically proven its capacity to save lives and to improve the quality of human life, and it cannot be expected to go away either. So the reality is going to involve some level of some uses of animals, including some kinds of medical research.

A more philosophical understanding of the animal welfare/animal rights distinction can help replace the current politics of confrontation with a genuine conversation. Researchers who understand the philosophical bases of the animal rights movement will recognize similarities with their own views and can rest assured that genuinely important research will not be opposed by most advocates of animal rights. In the last analysis, what animal rights views do is increase the burden of proof the defenders of research must meet, and this is as it should be. Too often, pain and suffering have been understood to be "necessary" whenever a desired benefit could not be achieved without them, without regard to how important the benefit in question was.[8]

When it comes to research on animals, "academic freedom" cannot mean freedom to pursue any line of research one pleases, even in the arena of medical research. In most areas of research, someone who spends her career doing trivial work wastes only the taxpayers' money. But a scientist who spends his career doing trivial experiments on animals can waste the lives of hundreds or even thousands of sentient creatures. There will be increasing public oversight of laboratory research on animals, because major traditions in Western ethical theory support at least basic moral consideration for all sentient creatures. Researchers who react by adopting a siege mentality, refusing to disclose information on research and refusing to talk to advocates of animal rights, only reinforce the impression that they have something to hide.

References

1. I owe this account of the consensus/convergence distinction to Bryan G. Norton, *Toward Unity among Environmentalists* (New York: Oxford University Press, 1991), pp. 237–43.

2. Peter Singer, *Animal Liberation,* 2nd ed. (Avon Books: 1990), pp. x–xi.

3. Peter Singer, *Practical Ethics*, 2nd ed. (New York: Cambridge University Press, 1993).

4. In any case, as Raymond Frey has pointed out, it is not clear that having forward-looking desires is a necessary condition for being self-conscious. R.G. Frey, *Rights, Killing, and Suffering: Moral Vegetarianism and Applied Ethics* (Oxford: Basil Blackwell, 1983), p. 163.

5. Tom Regan, *The Case for Animal Rights* (Berkeley and Los Angeles: University of California Press, 1983).

6. This evidence is reviewed in my *In Nature's Interests? Interests, Animal Rights, and Environmental Ethics,* in manuscript.

7. S. Pious, "An Attitude Survey of Animal Rights Activists," *Psychological Science* 2 (May 1991): 194–96.

8. Susan Finsen, "On Moderation," in *Interpretation and Explanation in the Study of Animal Behavior*, ed. Marc Bekoff and Dale Jamieson, vol. 2 (Boulder: Westview Press, 1990), pp. 394–419.

Questions for Discussion

1 Under what circumstances, if any, is it morally acceptable to conduct experiments on non-human animals?

2 Is there a difference between minimizing the overriding of individuals' rights (the "miniride" principle) and aggregating happiness? If so, which should be used for considering the interests of non-human animals?

3 To what extent should individual researchers be allowed to determine whether a research project is important enough to justify the death or injury of non-human animals?

4 Do the principles which govern research with non-human animals also apply to using them for teaching purposes? Should special provisions be made for students who object to using animals in ways required in their courses?

Trapped

J. Barber

In the following article, Barber argues that the anti-fur movement may be doing more damage than good, both to the environment and to human beings. He offers a critical examination of some of the claims of the anti-fur movement and discusses the plight of the trappers who depend on the fur trade for their livelihood.

★　★　★

As a wildlife biologist employed by the state of Louisiana, Greg Linscombe fields a lot of calls from journalists on the enormous problems facing his state's magnificent coastal marshes. At four million acres, they form one of the most productive wildlife habitats on the continent. Dozens of species of Canadian waterfowl, among innumerable other animals, depend on them for survival. And they are eroding so fast that they could soon disappear.

When reporters ask him what people can do to help save the marshes, Linscombe always repeats the same message. "If you're really concerned about the wetlands," he says, "buy a fur coat."

Linscombe explains that the marshes face a host of manmade problems. But one of the biggest threats today comes from the otherwise innocuous nutria. A kind of outsize muskrat native to South America, the nutria was accidentally let loose in the bayou country more than 50 years ago. As long as nutria pelts were in demand, trappers combined with alligators to keep them in check. Now that the price of fur of all kinds has collapsed like a penny stock, trappers don't bother much with nutria and the marsh-eating interlopers are multiplying crazily. "They're eating the marshes right down to the mud," says Linscombe.

The solution doesn't exactly jibe with the preconceptions of his callers, most of whom accept uncritically the fashionable view that fur coats are the ultimate symbol of environmental insensitivity. So, like a fourth-grade teacher, Linscombe repeats himself a lot. "Buy a nutria coat and help save the marsh. Wear it with pride."

Linscombe is a biologist, not a moralist, so he doesn't dwell on the obvious irony of the situation: the fact that certain animal lovers who are intent on destroying the fur trade—and would be delighted to claim full responsibility for the worldwide crash in fur prices—are in the process helping to destroy one of the richest wildlife habitats in North America. But it is worth noting, because the nutria explosion is just one of the unintended consequences of their campaign.

The logic and the morality are so simple: You shouldn't kill animals for the sake of luxury and vanity. The images of terrified animals struggling in steel leg-hold traps are so persuasive. The suffering seems inarguable. The targets, the furriers and their wealthy clientele, are so easy. Never mind that virtually every Native group in Canada thinks of the anti-fur campaign as nothing less than the white man's attempt at cultural genocide. Or that biologists from Siberia to the Yukon predict that its victory will result in outright environmental disaster. That the movement, in the words of Valerius Geist, a professor of environmental science at the University of Calgary, "stands ultimately for brutalized landscapes and wildlife depleted and squeezed into tiny enclaves." That view, like Linscombe's, is irritatingly complex. It has no validity amid the cozy simplicities of the anti-fur protest. Never mind that it's right.

There is no hint of the anti-fur protest at Montreal's huge and bustling Canadian International Fur Fair, not a single sidewalk placard. Inside the Place Bonaventure there are literally miles of coat racks groaning with the weight of fur. There are buyers and sellers from around the world, rural Louisianians mingling with Milanese couturiers—all the brisk chaos of a long-established, nuts-and-bolts trade fair. Even the army of models, dressed identically in their uniform of black, have an air more businesslike than glamorous as they don coat after coat for stony-faced buyers sitting behind order books and pocket calculators.

Yet there is a pervasive unease in Montreal this year. Nothing reflects that better than the variety of excuses being offered for the second straight year of rock-bottom prices. Retailers and manufacturers talk about the overall decline in the fashion industry. European over-production of ranch mink—anything but the effects of the fur protest. But those effects are undeniable: Fur coat sales have almost disappeared in many European countries, where the campaign is most active and where simply appearing on the streets in fur invites attack from paint-throwing zealots. British department stores, most famously Harrods, have abandoned the fur business altogether, while specialty furriers, who are stuck with it, learn to live with constant vandalism and death threats. In magazines and on television, the issue is presented as a "debate" that pits the hollow legal rights of furriers to engage in a distasteful business against the shocking cruelty and barbarism of the trappers. Guess which side is winning. A recent survey found that almost 80 per cent of Americans think it is wrong to kill an animal for a fur coat.

Nothing, it would seem, provokes easier outrage in 1990 than wearing fur. "They come at me with such incredible fanatical energy and such hatred on their faces, I'm afraid they're going to attack me physically," says one Toronto woman who persists in wearing a fur coat. Men leading small children shout obscenities; others stalk her along the street, sometimes for blocks at a time.

Respectable and sincere anti-fur activists understandably distance themselves from the lunatics and terrorists. Nevertheless, the movement seems infested with people who are addicted to the pleasure of moral disapproval and, as all the old orthodoxies crumble away, turn to fur for their fix. As *The Wall Street Journal* pointed out last February, "These are not your typical pet lovers. Their actions show less a love for furry rodents than a certain hatred for their own species."

At Montreal this year, the fur trade is countering with its own propaganda. Exhibitors wear buttons that say "FUR, naturally yours," part of a campaign to promote fur as a "green" product. It is questionable whether anyone will be persuaded to buy a fur coat by the fact that it is biodegradable, but not all of the fur trade's efforts are so feeble. It learned important lessons from the destruction of the seal hunt earlier this decade. One is that if it's going to survive, the fur trade needs to become as slick as its media-savvy opposition. For this year's fair they have assembled a crack team of pro-fur activists to send the message out. The keynote speaker is Pierre Berton.

Berton is impressively thunderous. A seasoned campaigner against animal rights extremism, mainly in support of scientific research, he calls the anti-fur movement "a tragedy and a scandal, and whenever I get a chance to say it I do. Nothing short of an all-out campaign will prevent these people from ruining the country." Anti-fur activists "are at best misinformed and at worst fanatics, and whether misinformed or fanatics, they are certainly dangerous." The story of what happened to the Inuit of the eastern Arctic as a result of the European ban on imports of sealskin is depressingly familiar. "Their lives have been ruined and the result has been suicide, drugs, alcohol and murder. That's what's going on in the high Arctic. The suicide rate is due entirely to the animal rights movement.

"We've got to ask ourselves when cruelty to animals stops and cruelty to humans begins."

Berton's speech is the emotional equivalent of an anti-fur film, the kind that shows foxes struggling desperately to free themselves from the steel jaws of a leg-hold trap. (Berton argues that most such films are fakes, like the notorious footage obtained by activists who paid a hunter to skin a seal pup alive; on the other hand, less passionate observers hesitate to attribute all Inuit suicides to the destruction of the seal hunt.) But the problem with more rational appeals is that they invariably run into an impassable emotional roadblock. How do you justify death?

Alcide Giroux has come up against that question many times, and has never been able to provide a soothing answer. The Ontario trapper has come to Montreal to do business and speak up for his cause and he doesn't go in for euphemisms like "harvest." He talks about killing animals, plain talk that sets him apart from the PR apparatus as clearly as his Rotarian suit, white socks and bent nose. "It's a fact of life that people who don't even know where milk comes from cannot accept that you can kill an animal," says Giroux.

He can't fight people who oppose swatting mosquitoes and eating fish. He doesn't even try to argue against animal-rights activists. What he can and does fight are the misconceptions they foster about trappers. "When people say that trapping's cruel and inhumane, they don't have a clue what trapping is and what a trapper does," says Giroux.

Giroux was one of the first trappers in Canada to urge his colleagues to get serious about animal welfare, and he takes personal pride in the wave of new humane trapping regulations quickly advancing across the country. The anti-fur campaign continues to focus dogmatically on the steel-jawed leg-hold trap, a device that can lead to a lingering and painful death. But as Giroux points out, the propaganda bears no relationship to the trap's role in the fur trade today. About three-quarters of all animals trapped in Canada every year die in quick-kill traps. And in the vast majority of cases in which the leg-hold trap is still used, it is set so the animal drowns within a few minutes. Giroux says that 98 per cent of all fur-bearers trapped in Canada die either instantly or within a few minutes of being caught. Federal officials, more cautious, would lower that figure—many trappers continue to resist the new methods. Even so, says Giroux, "It's the law of the land. We made it the law of the land and a trapper must abide by it or lose his licence."

Currently Giroux is helping government

researchers field-test a new padded trap that could eliminate the use of conventional leg-holds on wolves, coyotes, foxes, bobcats and lynx. Although it is uncommon even for standard traps to injure these animals, padded traps promise to cause no pain and minimal stress to the animals held in them, even over a period of several hours.

Such innovations are the result of campaigns initiated decades ago by old-fashioned animal-welfare groups. Modern anti-fur campaigners flatly dismiss them, saying that humane trapping is a contradiction in terms. But, as Giroux points out, trapping will continue even if wearing fur becomes a capital offence in every country on earth. Northerners will trap for food and people all over the world will trap nuisance animals like rats and moles. Dutch trappers kill 200,000 muskrats per year to prevent the country's dikes from washing away into the North Sea—and now, with knowledge gained from Canadian research, they can do it humanely. "No matter what people say, animals will still be killed," says Giroux. "So what responsibility do we have? It's to use the most humane and effective trapping programs possible." In response, anti-fur campaigners distribute pictures of wolves with stakes shoved down their throats, saying, "This is how a trapper kills an animal caught in a trap"; they capture animals out of season in illegal traps and shove cameras in their faces, filming as the animal struggles desperately to get away; they produce videos showing corrupt paparazzi at a fashion show being showered with blood. Blood is a favorite tool. Giroux recalls the disappointment of a CBC film crew that spent a week on his trap line. "They kept asking me, `Where's the blood?'" he says. He couldn't show them blood, because there wasn't any. All the animals in his traps were dead.

As well as characterizing trappers as blood-thirsty brutes, many anti-fur campaigners take it as a matter of faith that they are also wiping out whole populations of animals. Faith is necessary in this case, because no fur-bearing species in Canada is endangered or even threatened by trapping. Charles Dauphine, the biologist who advises the Canadian government on the application of the Convention on International Trade in Endangered Species, keeps a close watch on the rarest fur-bearers—especially when prices for their pelts are high—and has consistently concluded that trapping does not threaten their numbers. The only animal about which he has doubts is the prairie long-tailed weasel. "I have told this to the anti-trapping groups and they just go, 'Ho hum,'" says Dauphine. "They just want more exciting animals."

As evidence for their charge that wildlife is being wiped out indiscriminately, anti-fur campaigners say there is insufficient data to prove that it is not being wiped out. It is a conveniently endless argument. But the truly astonishing thing about fur-bearing animals in Canada is that there are so many of them, especially large predators such as wolves, bears and coyotes. Wild wolves in Europe are all but extinct; meanwhile there are as many wolves in Alcide Giroux's backyard—Ontario cottage country—as anywhere else on earth.

Gazing down from the moral high ground, anti-fur campaigners care little for the complexities of conservation policy or humane trapping. Some of them say it is wrong to kill animals, period; they would like to see an end to commercial fisheries as well as the fur trade. Others, more realistic, say merely that it is wrong to kill for frivolous reasons, adding that nothing could be more frivolous than "luxury furs." It seems like a reasonable argument, except when one considers that trappers are among the poorest-paid people in the country; to them, fur is hardly a luxury. But more important, it ignores the vital role they play in environmental protection.

For Bob Stevenson, the imposing, long-haired Métis who heads the Aboriginal Trap-

pers Federation of Canada, that role is as real as the bearclaw necklace around his neck. Stevenson has set up his fur-draped teepee right at the entrance to the Montreal show, where he functions as a kind of moral doorman and an irresistible magnet for the long-legged models killing time between shows. "The trapper is the true environmentalist," he says simply. "He will always be the first to complain about pollution or oil spills or clear-cutting. You can't take him away from the land. Once you do, these people come bulldozing in, they destroy the land and create all kinds of problems for the animals."

Trappers and hunters have a vested interest in maintaining an unspoiled environment. The wildlife they rely on cannot survive on land polluted by mine tailings or flooded by hydro megaprojects. And anyone who has paid the slightest attention to northern development in Canada, especially since the historic Berger Inquiry quashed the Mackenzie Valley pipeline, knows the vital role played by trappers and hunters who live on the land. Their role as guardians is real, not theoretical.

Canadian hunters and trappers are the exact equivalent of the Brazilian rubber-tree trappers whose heroic defence of the rain forest against slash-and-burn cattle ranchers transformed them into international heroes. The lessons of that struggle have led environmentalists to search frantically for other renewable resources that could be extracted from the rain forest without harming it, creating sustainable economic activity to forestall destructive practices like ranching and logging. In other words, making the rain forest more valuable intact than in ashes. A luxury trade, which by definition is characterized by high prices and an eager market, would be perfect. The Canadian fur trade provides the ideal model. If there was anything like it in the tropics, the future of the rain forest would not be nearly so grim.

The argument that fur is a luxury, ergo bad, has an impregnable simplicity that complicated facts can't breach. What knocks it all to hell is strictly human: the tens of thousands of Native families who rely on trapping as one of their last links with an embattled way of life. They saw what happened to the Inuit of the eastern Arctic in the wake of the European ban on sealskin—the widespread social breakdown is well documented by academics and by the federal government's Royal Commission on the seal hunt—and they know that the anti-fur campaign threatens more than their livelihood. It threatens a way of life that, despite intense persecution, has persisted for thousands of years. Stephen Kakfwi, former president of the Dene Nation, notes that the anti-fur campaign is "potentially far more dangerous than the threat to our lands posed by resource developers and far more oppressing than colonial governments." In the eyes of Bob Stevenson, its goal—perhaps unintended but no less real for that—is simply "cultural genocide." On that subject, of course, Natives are expert.

European anti-fur activists generally dismiss the Native right to continue trapping with straightforward utilitarian arguments. "If you look at the figures it turns out that one-tenth of one per cent of fur coming onto the international market comes from those northern communities," says Mark Glover of the British animal-rights group Lynx. "For me that's not a good enough reason for us to stop the campaign." The Europeans are far enough away from the 50,000 human victims of their campaign that they can afford to treat them like statistics. Many Canadians, however, confronted with real people demanding they take responsibility for their actions, respond with evasion, sanctimonious lectures and outright contempt.

The attitude was typified by an exchange that took place at a forum on the fur trade held at McGill University in 1987. Thomas Coon, a James Bay Cree and executive of the Native pro-fur lobby, Indigenous Survival International, was talking to Cynthia Drummond, coordinating director of the Canadian Society for the Prevention of Cruelty to Animals. Coon said, "Those people who killed the seal market will eventually kill the fur trade and the fur market. But the people who are truly suffering, people who are facing hardships, my people, want an answer to this question: What are the alternatives?"

Drummond refused to answer, "because our position with the SPCA is to speak about what's happening to the animals."

"What is happening to the human beings?" asked Coon. "Us, people that are suffering? What about us? Do animal rights supersede human rights? What about us? What about me? What am I going to feed my little ones with?"

There was no answer.

When there is an answer, however, it tends to be offensive. Anti-fur people often suggest that Natives who argue against them—and that includes virtually every Native in the country—are simply being "manipulated" by the fur industry. The assumption is that Natives haven't the wit to recognize their real self-interest and that if they did, they would oppose the fur trade. They are merely, in the words of Stephen Best, the Toronto-based vice-president of the International Wildlife Coalition, "a public relations tool."

Best is famous for his anti-Native arguments. He has made a close study of the poverty and desperation that exists on many Canadian reserves, and in a speech he has given more than once he describes it in astonishing detail—long lists of all the most depressing statistics. "This is what the heritage of the fur fashion industry has wrought," he declares. Past exploitation by the fur trade is something no Native denies, even though the historical fur trade allowed Natives an important measure of independence and figures strongly in much of their nostalgia for the good old days. But Best's audacious claim that all contemporary Native problems are exclusively due to the fur trade—"There does not appear to be anything else in particular that caused it," he says—is palpably absurd.

What, then, is the point of describing Native despair in such loving detail? One suspects that Best merely enjoys rubbing their noses in it. Here are his views on Native culture: "I own the Native culture. I bought it with my taxes.... There would be no Indian culture today if it wasn't for the fact that southern Canadians pay for it. Native people have got to develop a culture that is sufficiently apart from southern interests, and they have to do it on their own terms. When they do, they will be able to call all their own shots." Until then, of course, they will remain "public relations tools" mired in desperate poverty, with no ability—and presumably no right—to run their own lives.

The depressing thing about such arguments is that they are so familiar. They were invented by missionaries and educators who used them to justify their deliberate attempt to eradicate a stubbornly persistent Native culture. As Justice Berger noted in his famous report, long before anyone had heard of Stephen Best, the exact same arguments were adopted holus-bolus by the powerful industrial interests urging him to approve a pipeline down the Mackenzie Valley. The argument that Native culture is "a pathetic and diminishing remnant of what existed in the past," wrote Berger, "arises as much from our attitudes toward Native people as from any process of reasoning.... We simply do not see Native culture as defensible. Many of us do not even see it as a culture at all."

Among the nonracist arguments brought against Native people, the most serious one claims that they are no longer engaged in subsistence hunting and trapping, that using snowmobiles and accepting cash disqualifies

them from the right to trap. Such simplistic assertions ignore the reality of life in the north. For the Native people, the food value of the animals they hunt and trap far outweighs the price they receive for the pelts: The replacement value of food obtained from fur-bearing animals in the Northwest Territories alone amounts to $50 million a year. But the cash they do earn can be vital in sustaining their independence—keeping them off welfare and on the land. That is why they hold on to trapping so seriously.

Life in the high Arctic presents a classic study in the nature of true subsistence, which has little to do with the artifacts of technology. The Inuit readily adopt high technology, but they do it to improve their life: For them, satellite TV is a means to preserve and promote their language and culture, not a cheap way to get *Mork and Mindy* reruns. So it is with hunting and trapping. George Wenzel, a professor of geography at McGill University who has spent 20 years studying the Inuit of Baffin Island, points out that subsistence is a matter of cooperation, of perpetuating the system of social relations that is centred on the hunt. Those relations haven't changed with modern technology or with the cash needed to buy gas and bullets. But without the hunt, they disappear. Without the hunt, says Wenzel, Inuit lose their economic independence and the basic organizing principle of their culture. "The anti-fur movement is an ideology, just like capitalism, and it takes no account of the Native perspective at all. It's basically saying, 'We're right and you're wrong.' That's what white men have always done."

The consequences of imposing rigid definitions of subsistence on Native hunters—in effect forcing them into unworkable museum cultures—were revealed tragically in the Pribilof Islands of Alaska, where in 1983 animal-rights campaigners succeeded in halting a centuries-old seal hunt conducted by local Aleuts. The ban ostensibly permitted subsistence hunting. But John Grandy, vice-president of the Humane Society of the United States, explains that when the Aleuts tried to sell the pelts of seals killed for food, "we frankly said, 'No way, José. You can't do that. That's not what we mean by subsistence.'" The absurd result, duplicated in the Canadian arctic, is that the Aleuts are now forced to bury those pelts—a criminal waste that offends every principle of traditional culture and true subsistence.

Another result, not incidental, was that a formerly self-sufficient society was plunged into desperate poverty. Domestic violence and alcohol abuse reached crisis proportions among the 700 Aleuts of the Pribilofs, and over a single year there were four suicides, 100 documented suicide attempts and three murders. Meanwhile, US animal-rights activists stepped up their campaign, demanding an end to the "subsistence" hunt.

Clearly, the only endangered animals in the fur trade are human beings. Not just any humans, but the last of the hunter-gatherers, the stubborn survivors of the greatest epic of human evolution.

Two years after Greenpeace succeeded in destroying the seal hunt, a British representative of the group visited Greenland for the first time to see the conditions prevailing in the seal-hunting communities along the west coast. He said, "We didn't really know what it was like in a community like this.... Maybe if we had known about these things earlier, it [the anti-sealing campaign] wouldn't have happened like that." The admission gave little solace to the Inuit people, who might well have asked why Greenpeace didn't research the facts before it launched its long and vigorous campaign. But as a result, the group has dropped out of the wider anti-fur campaign. The fur trade "is just not a priority for us," says a spokesperson.

It seems incredible that so many other groups, despite clear evidence of the human suffering they threaten to cause, remain implacably determined to wipe out the entire fur trade. The reason probably lies in the philosophical gulf that separates the two sides. That gulf is so wide that the Native people have virtually become invisible to their oppressors; they are seen only as statistics, or distant criminals.

"The further you are from the wilderness," says Pierre Berton, "the more chance you have of becoming an animal rights advocate." The statement is not merely funny; it is a fact. For people raised in cities and garden-like countrysides, where nature is strictly controlled if not downright suppressed, nature becomes a marvellous park. For people who buy their meat in cellophane packages and are raised on stories in which hedgehogs wear aprons and muskrats smoke pipes, it becomes impossible not to see all wild animals as pets. Who would not protect their pet against a killer?

People who live close to nature can never afford such a cozy view. If an Inuk's dog faltered in its traces, it was cut loose and left to freeze to death on the tundra. People who live close to nature know that there is no such thing as old age in the animal world, that every wild animal meets a horrible, often violent death. They know that for man to live, he must kill. The same Mother Nature that succors and supports them is also fundamentally and utterly hostile. As the myths of every aboriginal culture prove, intimacy with nature breeds attitudes and beliefs that are so complex they are incomprehensible to civilized people. When they are trying to explain their "side" in the fur debate, Native people invariably attempt to describe their relationship with nature. It's a lost cause; they might as well lecture on Martian ballet.

The most pragmatic behave like Dave Monture, secretary-treasurer of Indigenous Survival International. Monture wears a three-piece suit, speaks in well-crafted sound bites

Ethical Issues

and is a veteran of the bureaucratic corridors in cities such as Brussels and Strasbourg. His latest campaign was to stop the European Community from moving up the deadline on its proposed ban on fur imports, currently scheduled to take effect January 1, 1995. To that end he organized a tour, wittily titled "A Few Acres of Snow," that took five key members of the European Parliament to northern Manitoba in the dead of winter. They gained a "first-time glimpse of reality," says Monture. "They saw what the price of hamburger was at the 59th parallel, and at minus-30 Centigrade they didn't notice any banana plantations."

The diplomacy, actively supported by the federal government, is having some effect. The European ban will be enforced if by 1995 there are no international standards for humane trapping. Canada recently put a proposal to that effect before the International Organization for Standardization and appears to have secured the agreement of the European Community to help in its development.

But such successes, as anti-fur activists are quick to point out, mean little. The fact is, they are winning the hearts and minds of virtually all well-intentioned people who like animals. As Stephen Best said, testifying before a parliamentary committee four years ago, "I may be completely morally bankrupt in dealing with this, and all the people I deal with and all the people who support us, who are in the millions, may all be wrong; but they exist.... It is a practical fact you have to deal with, whether it is right or wrong...."

Never mind all the tedious arguments— the fur trade is dying. Thomas Coon knows it. "We are the weak, we are the poor, we will lose," he says simply. A hard fact of life. "Taking life is definitely a cruelty," says Coon. "No matter how we die as human beings, no matter how we take life, it is cruelty. Killing a culture, killing a society and killing a way of life is definitely a cruelty. My culture will die in agony."

Questions for Discussion

1 Does the fact that a species was accidentally introduced into an environment by human beings (such as occurred with the nutria) justify more interference with the environment than would otherwise have been the case? Is there an obligation to try to "undo" what was done, and restore the environment to its condition before the accidental introduction?

2 Can concern for the interests of non-human animals ever be a sufficient reason to force humans to abandon their modes of employment (e.g., hunting and trapping)? Does it matter whether the humans involved are members of a traditionally oppressed group, carrying out their traditional practices?

CHAPTER 2

Ethics and the Environment

The twentieth century has witnessed an unprecedented increase both in the number of human beings and in our technological capability. As a result, we now create larger changes in the world around us than ever before. With this increased impact, there has been a growth in concern about those changes. What will be the long-term costs of our actions? Are we doing irreparable harm to our environment? How much change in ordinary attitudes is required to reflect this concern?

It is clear that people have often acted without knowing the full consequences of their actions, often with tragic results. For example, when the United States was conducting experiments with nuclear weapons after the Second World War, it warned visitors to cover their eyes to protect themselves from the radiation. Now we know that such "protection" was woefully inadequate and that many people were needlessly harmed. The same can be said about unseen hazards such as underground toxic wastes and asbestos fibres. Even visible pol-

lution, such as industrial smoke, was once believed to dissipate harmlessly; now it is thought to be responsible for (among other things) acid rain and the corresponding deaths of many kinds of fish and wildlife.

There are many different views about what follows from these sorts of observations. The most straightforward approach—people should take greater care to discover the consequences of their actions—agrees with the traditional view that nature is there for our use, but emphasizes that we must take care to make *good* use of it. This approach has led to the imposition of "environmental impact assessments" of many major projects. Before people do anything which might have a serious impact on the environment, they should conduct a study to determine exactly what consequences can be expected, and perhaps to investigate alternatives with their accompanying costs in both financial and environmental terms. After the assessment is completed, it is then possible to decide whether the benefits of the project are important enough to warrant the foreseen risks to the environment.

Practical objections to this approach point out that, the way the system stands, some people's environmental concerns may not be given a full hearing in environmental assessments. For example, it has been claimed that the people proposing the projects in question are likely to be fairly wealthy, organized groups, who have a vested interest in the project's success. Those who are likely to suffer the consequences, on the other hand, are often isolated individuals, in many cases already socially disadvantaged, who are less able to mount an organized opposition. Indeed, some potential victims may not even be aware of proposed changes. Furthermore, there is sometimes a question about who is allowed to have standing to make a presentation before the body conducting the assessment. Some viewpoints may be shut out of the process, simply because the process is not public enough.

Another objection to environmental impact assessments is that they tend to view things in exclusively economic terms, and systematically undervalue some societal "goods." For example, it is very difficult to place a monetary value on the benefit of a pleasing natural landscape, and so such values may fail to be taken into account when considering the "costs" of a proposed project.

Extremists opposed to environmental impact assessments as commonly practiced claim that no interference with natural environments should be tolerated. This could be maintained on the ground that we know too little about the interconnectedness of different aspects of the environment, and simply cannot estimate the full consequences of our actions.

Making a claim as strong as saying we should freeze all interference with the environment might require one to explain what counts as an "interference." Any human activity, even one as basic as breathing, has *some* impact on the environment; certainly activities such as building shelters and consuming food can have negative effects on the non-human world. Nevertheless, it is clear that some human activities have more broad-ranging and intrusive effects than others, and one could argue that no activities of the larger sort should be undertaken. Whether one believes we should put a "hold" on all projects with significant environmental ramifications will depend in part on how serious one believes the long-term harm is likely to be. Of course nobody knows for certain, but perhaps people should simply make their best estimate of what will have the best consequences, and act accordingly.

One objection to freezing our activities at the status quo is that this would be unfair to people who have not yet been able to benefit from the advantages of technology. For example, it might be claimed that the "developed" nations have benefitted from exploiting the "third world" nations, and that it is only fair now to give those nations a chance to catch up, even if this means further destruction of the environment. It may be that North Americans, for example, could live reasonably well without any further major development of the environment, but that some nations which face tremendous poverty have no choice but to exploit their resources to avoid a tremendous human cost. Furthermore, it might be argued that it is technological advance which makes it possible to keep more people alive, by making more efficient use of existing resources. If humankind suddenly stopped employing its technology, the results might be even greater infringement of the environment, or a great extension of human poverty and suffering. This then seems to become an empirical question, about whether technology tends to do more harm or good.

Many people would argue that the threats to the environment cannot be overcome without serious changes in common attitudes toward material goods. The "consumerism" of people in wealthy nations seems to be responsible for much of the rampant depletion of resources in the poverty-stricken third world. Meanwhile, the industries, transportation, and conveniences of the developed nations require increasing amounts of energy. Using traditional sources of energy such as coal, oil, and gas not only depletes the world's irreplaceable resources, but also leaves a polluting residue and generates heat which may affect the climate of the planet. What is more, it has been argued that our economic system is based on a notion of continuous exponential growth which simply cannot be maintained. To what extent must we change our assumptions, attitudes, and behaviour in order to preserve our planet?

One question this gives rise to concerns the goal of preserving the planet itself. Should we be concerned only with the long-term interests of human beings (and perhaps other sentient beings), or should we be concerned about the interests of entities such as trees, prairies, or wetlands? The dominant tradition in Canada has been for people to see themselves as somehow separate from nature, having either been given, or simply legitimately taking, dominion over it. However, it is possible to view ourselves as *part* of the environment—as one more feature which should try to fit in to the whole. One way to put this view would be to say that we should stop viewing ourselves as the only things which have value in the universe, and come to recognize the intrinsic value of such things as forests, species, and perhaps even rock forma-

tions. We might also want to assert that the whole earth (or at least everything living on it) has value, and that people should view their relationship to it as one of stewardship rather than ownership. People who advocate attributing intrinsic moral value to things independently of their impact on human lives are sometimes known as "deep ecologists."

It is very difficult to tell what properties something must have in order to have value in its own right. (For more on this issue, see the chapter on "The Moral Status of Non-Human Animals.") Can the "biosphere" as a whole have rights? Can individual plants? How about species? This issue about whether our environmental concern should be based, ultimately, on human good, or on some broader good, is one of the central issues of environmental ethics.

Some people argue that, although of course most people do feel some sorrow at the prospect of a species dying out, or of a beautiful forest that has existed for centuries being felled to make room for a shopping mall or equivalent, this feeling can be associated with the sense of loss we feel when we hear someone has destroyed a priceless painting. Perhaps our appreciation of such objects is aesthetic rather than moral, and perhaps it does not reveal a belief that the species, or tree, has any moral status in its own right, any more than works of art do. If this is the case, then it is still an open question how such value should be balanced against other values, such as the well-being of human beings.

Another objection often raised against deep ecologists has to do with the question of whether concern for non-human entities does necessarily lead (as deep ecologists commonly suggest) to non-interference on our part. If diversity of species is itself a good, should we feel an obligation to use our technology to produce new species? If forests (for example) have interests, should we go out and water them in times of drought, or trim the trees so that they can reach their full potential?

A similar objection to deep ecology grows from the claim that we should view ourselves as simply one part of nature. If that is true, it would seem that any intervention we make in the world around us could be viewed as a "natural" development. To call ourselves "stewards" with an obligation to protect the natural world (of a sort plants, habitats, and species presumably do not have) does seem to involve set-

ting ourselves apart from the rest of the world in some way.

This chapter explores some of the alternatives for how we might view the relationship between human beings and the non-human environment. Virtually everyone would agree that we must change some of our behaviours and attitudes in light of a new appreciation of the interconnectedness of things in the natural order and the long-term consequences of our activities. However, the degree of change required is still very much open to debate.

Crimes Against the Environment

Law Reform Commission of Canada

Traditionally, the legal remedy for excessive pollution has been the imposition of fines on the polluters. Some people have objected that this amounts to the same thing as establishing a licensing fee for polluting—would-be polluters can simply calculate whether it will cost them more to change their behaviour so as to avoid the fine, or pay it and continue polluting. In 1985, the Law Reform Commission of Canada published a working paper which considered the idea that damaging the environment might be considered a criminal offense. In the process, the Commission considered several aspects of environmental ethics, including the question of which rights (if any) are violated by harm to the environment, and whether the environment should be protected for its own sake, apart from any relevance it may have for human beings.

★　★　★

The present *Criminal Code* in effect prohibits offences against persons and property. It does not, in any explicit or direct manner, prohibit offences against the natural environment itself. In this Working Paper, the Commission makes and supports the proposition that the natural environment should now become an interest explicitly protectable in some cases in the *Criminal Code*. Some acts or omissions seriously harmful or endangering to the environment should, if they meet the various tests of a real crime, be characterized and prohibited

for what they really are in the first instance, crimes against the environment....

In terms of harm done, risks caused, degree of intent and values threatened, environmental pollution spans a continuum from minor to catastrophic; from what is harmless, to what is tolerable if controlled in view of various social benefits thereby achieved, to what is intolerable and deserving of social abhorrence and denunciation; from what is only accidental, careless or negligent, to what is grossly negligent, reckless or intentional....

That wide range regarding harm, values threatened and degree of intent calls for a similar range of legal controls and responses. In this Working Paper, the focus is on those pollution activities at the most serious end of the scale, those which in the view of this Commission, merit the most severe societal deterrence, repudiation and sanction available, namely, that provided by their clear and explicit prohibition in the *Criminal Code*. The problems addressed are those of: determining at what point on the pollution continuum these offences should be considered real crimes; deciding what the essential elements of environmental crimes should be; and demonstrating that their prohibition fulfils an urgent need which cannot otherwise be met.

It must be emphasized at this point that no claim will be made that the explicit prohibition by the *Criminal Code* of some pollution activity will provide in one stroke the solution to all pollution problems. In fact it is almost certain that from a practical and long-range point of view, a number of other existing and evolving legal and administrative approaches, controls and incentives, especially those focused on prevention and compliance, will do much more to limit and lessen pollution than will recourse to the *Criminal Code*. It should be acknowledged that what will count far more towards environmental protection than *any* law reform, criminal or otherwise, is an increasingly informed and environmentally sensitive public combined with an evolution in economic and political priorities.

It is the view of this Commission that a fundamental and widely shared value is indeed seriously contravened by some environmental pollution, a value which we will refer to as the *right to a safe environment*.

To some extent, this right and value appears to be new and emerging, but in part because it is an extension of existing and very traditional rights and values already protected

by criminal law, its presence and shape even now are largely discernible. Among the new strands of this fundamental value are, it may be argued, those such as *quality of life*, and *stewardship* of the natural environment. At the same time, traditional values as well have simply expanded and evolved to include the environment now as an area and interest of direct and primary concern. Among these values fundamental to the purposes and protections of criminal law are the *sanctity of life*, the *inviolability and integrity of persons*, and the *protection of human life and health*. It is increasingly understood that certain forms and degrees of environmental pollution can directly or indirectly, sooner or later, seriously harm or endanger human life and human health.

"Environmental Rights": The Options

An indisputable task in exploring and justifying our proposal to add environmental crimes to the *Criminal Code* is that of determining, with as much precision as possible, the particular value and interest legitimately within the scope of criminal law protection. There can, in other words, be a number of reasons why one might wish to make serious harm or danger to the environment a crime. But it does not follow that each reason has the same weight, or that each of the interests in mind equally merit the involvement of criminal law. The principle of restraint in the use of criminal law obliges us not to extend its already wide scope, except to include identifiable and deserving targets.

Expressed very broadly and in terms of environmental rights, there are potentially five related but different levels of "environmental rights" one might wish to enshrine in law, and corresponding activities one may wish the law to prohibit:

(1) *A right not to have one's life or health harmed or endangered as a result of environmental pollution, the health effects of which are*

known, predictable, serious, and relatively immediate.

In effect this category can be thought of as an extension and application of the more general right and interest already the primary focus of the *Criminal Code*—that of physical integrity and security.

(2) *A right to a reasonable level of environmental quality, even when a specific pollutant or pollution source cannot now be identified with certainty as the cause of specific health damage or risk, on the grounds that sooner or later serious pollution of the environment will threaten human life and health as well.*

Although the right in this case would be to environmental quality, the ultimate concern and basis, as in the first category, is human health. Unlike the first category, however, its scope would extend beyond just those instances of pollution with known, predictable and serious dangers to human life and health, to include all instances of serious environmental pollution. Proponents of this view would and do argue that, in the long run, to badly damage particular aspects of the natural environment, especially in an irreversible manner, may do serious harm to human health—if not to those now living, then to those in a future generation; in other words that, from an ecological perspective, there is no discontinuity between serious environmental harm and harm to the health of humans in general. Because of that risk, the law should directly prohibit all pollution which seriously harms or endangers environmental quality. This level and category of right does not assume or promote victimless crimes. Rather, it assumes that there will be specific and identifiable victims; it is simply that we do not yet know their identity or the particular form of their victimization.

(3) *A right to a reasonable level of environmental quality, but one which is violated by pollution instances which deprive people of the use and enjoyment of the environment, even when*

there are no health effects or dangers.

This right and category differs from the previous two in that the interest underlying the right is not the protection of human life and health, but a wide range of uses of the natural environment and natural resources which can be seriously interfered with by pollution ranging from noise to toxic contamination. These amenity considerations could range from a dirty (but not unhealthy) river, to the ability to exploit a particular natural resource for commercial purposes because of pollution damage. The fundamental question which must be faced in this regard is whether the scope of criminal law should be extended into the environmental arena to protect amenity rights alone, when there are no significant human health implications. Important rights can, of course, be infringed in both cases, and various branches of law other than criminal already are involved in protecting, for various purposes, the use and enjoyment of the environment; but the case for involving the *criminal* law would appear to be much stronger when claims to the use and enjoyment of the environment also involve direct or indirect health risks. In other words, the emission of very large quantities of highly carcinogenic or mutagenic compounds into city air would appear to constitute a much more serious and hence potentially criminal infringement of environmental rights than the emission of pollutants making a river objectionable to swim in, but not unhealthy.

(4) *A right of the environment to be protected from serious pollution for its own sake, even if pollution incidents should result in no direct or indirect risk or harm to human health or limitation upon the use and enjoyment of nature.*

The previous three categories permit the focus upon, and protection of, the environment *itself*, although ultimately for the sake of human life, human health, and the use and enjoyment of the environment by humans. However, this last right would protect the environment *for its own sake*, quite apart from health or amenity considerations. From this perspective, it is the environment which should have various rights, not people who should have environmental rights. The implications of environmental pollution for humans would be quite incidental to this right. The extension of criminal law protection to encompass the first three rights could be considered *evolutionary* (although not necessarily justifiable in each case). However, for the criminal law, or law generally for that matter, to acknowledge this fourth category and right in the strict and literal sense would be truly *revolutionary*. It would be, in effect, to assign rights to nonhuman entities, and it has always been thought that only humans can have rights. Interesting and tempting though it may be to do so, efforts to argue that case have so far not been met with anything approaching general support, whether in philosophical or legal thinking. Some very real conceptual problems stand in the way of such efforts.[1] In our view, there are more than adequate grounds for more rigorous environmental protection right now, whether or not nonhuman entities are granted legal rights at some future date.

(5) *A right to have one's private property protected from damage by pollution caused by others.*

It is doubtful in our view that this new environmental crime should include within its scope pollution which only damages or endangers the private property of others. The implications of some pollution for private property can be very serious; but when there are no serious dangers to human health or the environment itself as well, what is at issue is not environmental rights, but (private) property rights. To include property considerations as a direct and exclusive object of this new crime against the environment would be to blunt its focus and diffuse its effect. It is in part at least

to focus clearly on the environment itself as opposed to (private) property that this new environmental crime is being proposed. When only private property is harmed or endangered by pollution, the more direct and effective legal routes would seem to be the civil route for prosecutions for crimes against property....

The Public Trust Doctrine, Environmental Quality and Bills of Environmental Rights

Another strand of an environmental ethic given increased attention in our times is the notion of "public trust" applied to environmental rights and duties. That notion is contributing to an evolution in our concept of private ownership. At present, most environmental protection legislation in Canada gives governments (through their environmental agencies) only a discretionary role *vis-à-vis* protection of the environment. That is, it *may* apply and enforce the legislation, but it *need not*. There are few obligations imposed on those who administer statutes.

However, the emerging public trust notion would impose duties to manage and use resources *in trust* for the public. It is already generally accepted that *governments* have public trust duties, in that land and resources owned by the government cannot be disposed of to private interests without taking into account the broad public interest. However, many argue that this notion should be applied to business as well, and to the land resources they own. While industries and developers would continue to be allowed the reasonable use of resources they own, their ownership and use would be qualified by their "public trustee" responsibilities.[2] Involved in this notion is in effect an evolution in our concept of ownership. The right to the private ownership and use of its land and resources by an industry would not be denied, but a new dimension would be added. That new dimension would be a responsibility to use it not only for private gain but also in the light of the common good. Consideration of the common good and the public heritage dimension of privately owned land and resources would rule out, for example, disposal of one's industrial wastes in ways likely to create public harm or risk.

This general notion of a dimension of common ownership is not in reality entirely new to law. It is only being rediscovered in our times. It was already expressed in the Institutes of Justinian:

> By natural law the following things belong to all men, namely: air, running water, the sea, and for this reason the shores of the sea.[3]

The concept of public trust—of the environment as a public heritage—is one of the foundations of efforts on many fronts in recent years to establish environmental Bills of Rights....

They seek to shift at least some of the burden of proof from the plaintiff and Crown to the defendant and accused. Not only would a plaintiff, for example, not have to claim *personal* injury to have standing to bring an environmental action before a court, but if the activity complained of could be shown to endanger the environment, then the burden would shift to the alleged polluter to establish the safety of that activity.

From a "Homocentric" to an "Ecocentric" Ethic

A number of commentators have observed that the dominant environmental ethic both politically and intellectually until about the 1960s envisaged humans at the centre of the universe. Generally speaking that view made two assumptions as a result: that humans have dominion over all other forms of life and inanimate entities; and that we could and would make perpetually greater demands on the natural environment by way of production, consumption, and waste.[4] To a large extent,

that "mankind at the centre" perspective characterized as well the arguments and positions of those pushing for a safer and cleaner environment. What counted as the measure of defensible environmental policies was the value of the environment to us—the need to protect it because it is indispensable to the satisfaction of human needs and desires. That view also fueled the environmental legislation in the United States and Canada. Harm to the environment was to be avoided and controlled, implicitly because we humans would otherwise be affected in some manner; continuing and expanding resource consumption and production would be constrained, our enjoyment of nature curtailed, and our health put at risk.

However, more recently environmentalists and others have underlined what they see as some serious limitations of that homocentric or "mankind at the centre" perspective, and many promoted instead an ecocentric or "environment at the centre" stance. They claim, for instance, that the older view was wrong to assume that we could have adequate environmental protection at no cost to our appetites, desires or life-styles—that we could continue and expand production, consumption and waste and at the same time have a safe and clean environment—that nature is infinitely resilient and flexible. They now argue that there are always costs, some payable now, some later, that some resources are not renewable, and that there are thresholds and limits to what can be used and destroyed in the environment and in each ecosystem. They maintain that there is a balance, harmony and interdependence in nature to be protected and respected for its own sake.

Some environmentalists also argue that, pushed to its logical conclusion, a policy of environmental protection based only on *human* goals and rights could progressively weaken claims for the protection of endangered aspects of the environment, the pollution or destruction of which would not constitute economic or aesthetic loss, or danger to human health. Some fear that as our capacity increases to supply by artificial means those human needs and desires now supplied by the natural environment, the checklist of those forms of life and inanimate entities in nature which we deem worthy of protecting would progressively shrink.

To some extent then, these and similar views constitute a shift away from a largely homocentric ethic, one which in effect seeks the protection of the environment *for its own sake*, quite apart from its relevance to humans. There are, of course, many important and laudable insights provided by proponents of this more recent stage of environmental concerns. At the very least, they further demonstrate that the environment itself in the view of many ought to be a legally protectable interest; but, as already suggested above, there remain some serious conceptual and practical obstacles to the provision of legal protection to the natural environment *for its own sake*, apart from considerations of human benefits, wishes, uses and health risks. It would amount to granting rights to nonhuman entities. From a practical standpoint, it is inconceivable that natural resources could ever be totally insulated from economic and political considerations. Nor is it evident that we cannot provide adequate protection for the natural environment itself by continuing to permit a homocentric ethic to underlie our environmental regulations and laws, but one which now gives more scope to the *quality* of human life, and to our responsibility of *stewardship* or trusteeship over the natural environment.

Conclusions

In view of the preceding analyses about fundamental values and interests, we are now able to make the first of our conclusions. At this point, this first set of conclusions will encompass only the matter of the particular environmental values and interests to which the

Criminal Code could and should legitimately extend. The five options in this regard were described above....

1. The scope of a *Criminal Code* offence against the environment should not extend to protecting the natural environment for its own sake, apart from human values, rights and interests.

2. However, a fundamental value is seriously contravened by some instances of environmental pollution, one which can be characterized as the right to a safe environment, or the right to a reasonable level of environmental quality.

3. This value may not as yet be fully emerged or universally acknowledged, but its existence and shape are already largely discernible. In protecting it, the *Criminal Code* would be essentially reflecting public perceptions and expanding values traditionally underlined in the *Code*—the sanctity of life, the integrity of persons, and the centrality of human life and health. At the same time, the *Criminal Code* would be playing an educative and advocacy role by clearly articulating environmental concerns and dangers not always perceived as such, and by incorporating newer concerns such as quality of life and stewardship of the natural environment.

4. More specifically, the scope of a *Criminal Code* pollution offence should extend to prohibiting environmental pollution which seriously damages or endangers the *quality of the environment*, and thereby seriously harms or endangers *human life or health*.

5. The pollution activities prohibited by a *Code* offence should include not only those which are presently known to constitute immediate and certain health harms and risks, but also those *likely* to cause serious harm to human health in the foreseeable future.

6. The scope of a *Criminal Code* pollution offence should not normally extend to prohibiting pollution which deprives others of the *use and enjoyment* of a natural resource but

causes no serious present or likely harm or risks to human health. Only by express exception should an interest other than life or health fall within the scope of such an offence. Such an exception would be, for example, when a form of pollution would deprive an entire community of its livelihood.

7. Environmental pollution which destroys or damages *private property* without, as a result, causing or risking serious harm to human life or health, should not fall within the scope of a *Code* offence against the environment, but should be the object of civil remedies or prosecuted as a crime against property.

Seriously Harmful or Endangering Conduct

...One explanation of the mechanics and implications of environmental damage and destruction is that provided by the ecosystem approach. That approach is not without its limitations when pushed to extremes, and it is not our intention to promote it or to justify legal prohibitions and reforms purely on the basis of one or another environmental school of thought. Nevertheless, some findings of ecologists are not disputed, and the general lines of the approach help to underline the potential seriousness of some environmental pollution.[5]

This relatively new approach is a synthesis of the insights and skills of a number of disciplines, especially biology, chemistry, geography and climatology. Whereas those and other fields study the threads of nature, the ecosystem approach studies its "whole cloth." Its proponents insist especially upon two points. They argue first of all that it is erroneous to speak of man *and* environment, or of man as *external* to the natural environment. Rather, humans are internal to, and partners with, the rest of nature. They argue, secondly, that serious harm done to one element in an ecosystem will invariably lead to the damage or even destruction of other elements in that and other ecosystems.

What ecologists mean by an "ecosystem" is any relatively homogeneous and delineated unit of nature in which nonliving substances and living organisms interact with an exchange of materials taking place between the nonliving and living parts. The term "ecosystem" is somewhat flexible and the boundaries between them somewhat arbitrary. Those boundaries are generally based upon what is most convenient for measuring the movement of energy and chemicals into and out of the system. Typical and important interrelated and overlapping ecosystems are: units of land along with the surrounding air and water, or lakes, or river basins, or forests, or climatic zones, or the earth itself or the biosphere (the outer sphere of the earth inhabited by living organisms and including lakes, oceans, soil and living organisms, including man). Within each ecosystem there is, they maintain, a delicate balance and interdependence between all the elements. Systems can cope with and adapt to some interferences, but not others. The overall long-range effect of some intrusions is not yet known with certainty or in detail. Ecologists argue that ecosystems are now known to be subject to very definable and immutable processes, which impose corresponding ecological constraints. They stress two organizational rules, namely, the first two of the three laws of thermodynamics. The first rule (that of conservation of matter and energy) is that matter and energy cannot be destroyed, only *transformed*. The second (the law of entropy) is that all energy transformations are *degradations*, whereby energy is transformed from more organized to less organized forms. In simpler terms, they explain those rules by the following principles and examples.

The first is that *everything in the environment or individual ecosystems is related.* If one breaks a link in the food-chain, for example, or introduces a substance not biodegradable, there are consequences for the entire ecosystem. Examples of the serious and often irreversible harm are DDT and mercury. Since its massive use in the 1940s, the footsteps of DDT can be followed from wheat, to insects, to rodents, to larger animals and birds, and to man. In its wake it left whole species of animals more or less extinct or with serious reproductive problems. To illustrate the degree of interaction involved and the insignificance of time and distance, traces of DDT can now be found in the flesh of polar bears. The industrial discharge of *mercury* is another illustration. It has been followed from its discharge by pulp and paper industries into the air and water, to its transformation in the water into methyl-mercury by the water's micro-organisms, to its accumulation in the sediment of lakes or its absorption by the fish. Among its victims in the next stage, it is argued, have been the Indians of northern Ontario and Quebec, who eat the fish and are frequently afflicted with the horrors of what has come to be known as Minamata disease.

The second principle underlined by ecologists is that *unless neutralized, every contaminating substance remains harmful somewhere to something or someone* in the natural environment. Sooner or later we will pay, in some cases dearly, for discarding, for example, nonrecycled industrial toxins into rivers and dumps. Matter cannot be destroyed—only transformed. The atoms and molecules of matter are always preserved by ecosystems in some form. Moreover, if they are not or cannot be transformed, degraded, recycled or neutralized, it is an illusion to hope that that form will become a benign and harmless one.

Limitations of an Unqualified Ecosystem Approach

From the perspective of harm, however, there may be some difficulties and limitations of the ecosystem approach pushed to its extreme. It has been observed that some (by no means all)

of its proponents are unjustifiably pessimistic and too rigorous. Some imply that each now stable and healthy ecosystem has inherent worth, and must be preserved exactly as it is, that any harm or modification to it would be immoral, and that all human impacts upon, or changes to, an aspect of the environment are necessarily unnatural. However, that view has at least three limitations.

(1) Viruses and Diseases: Good or Bad?

First of all, if every ecosystem, every species, is to be preserved and protected "as is" in its natural state, if human values, human judgement and human benefit are to be considered irrelevant, we would be forced to *tolerate many threats and diseases* generally perceived to be themselves harmful if not attacked and even wiped out if possible. An unqualified ecosystem approach pushed to its logical extreme might, for example, force a conclusion that the extinction of the smallpox virus was not a good thing, or that grasshoppers, mosquitoes, noxious weeds, various pests and disease organisms should not be combatted but protected, or that the building of human settlements was wrong because some ecosystems were necessarily harmed in the process. Few if any ecologists seem actually to intend these conclusions, but they do perhaps illustrate the sort of dilemmas implicit in attempts to determine and evaluate environmental harm, and the need to qualify the "deep ecology" stance in the light of some other considerations.

(2) The Adaptive Capacity of the Environment

A second limitation of an extreme and rigorous ecosystem approach used to measure environmental harm, is that ecosystems are not only in many respects vulnerable, but also *adaptive and evolutionary.* Up to a point and in some respects, ecosystems can respond to and accommodate change. Some man-made alterations of an element of the environment can, in particular cases, trigger adaptive responses. Ecosystems are not in all respects fixed; there is a degree of rhythm and fluctuation. It becomes important in this regard to weigh impacts of polluting contaminants and activities as to whether they are degradable and noncumulative (for example, mercury, lead, PCBs), reversible or irreversible, natural yet likely to cause damage to some environments in large concentrations (for example, sulphates, chlorides). There are undoubtedly good reasons for policy makers to give more attention to the "inherent worth" view of the natural environment, but this adaptive mechanism itself of ecosystems has an inherent worth and should be added to the calculations of harm. In some cases, the conclusion will be that a substance or activity goes well beyond the adaptive capacity of an ecosystem; in other cases it may not.

(3) Tolerating Pollution for Legitimate Social Purposes: Balancing the Human Health Standard

There is yet a third and most important factor to be weighed in calculations of serious pollution harm, a factor more or less incompatible with an ecosystem approach which is strict and absolute. It is generally acknowledged in our political and economic system, and in our environmental policies and laws, that there are a number of legitimate social purposes which can justify, at least for a period of time, varying degrees of pollution, deterioration and risk—which permit downgrading the pollution harm and risk from serious and intolerable to less-than-serious and tolerable. It is not, of course, uncommon for the law to conclude that what would be reckless and unacceptable behaviour in some circumstances, can be justified if socially desirable for one reason or another. For example, a very

risky medical operation can, in some circumstances, be acceptable and even desirable if it offers the only chance to save a life.

Primary among the goals and purposes implicitly or explicitly underlying environmental policies, regulations and statutes are economic ones. An environmental agency may judge, for example, that a particular existing industry should be allowed to exceed, at least for a specified time, the statutory emission standard for a particular contaminant, because there may be good reason to believe the expense of strict compliance will bankrupt the company and cause widespread unemployment. Similarly, it may be judged that the only way to secure the establishment of a new industry in an economically depressed area and to develop and market local resources is to permit it to do some widespread ecological damage, and/or, at least for a time, exceed by a considerable margin the statutory emission standards. It would, of course, be naive and unrealistic to assume that all such judgements are equally defensible, or that the economic viability and employment arguments of industry should be accepted uncritically by agencies. However, it would be equally naive and Utopian to expect that environmental decision-making can ever be completely insulated from economic and political considerations.

It should be noted that the mere emission of a particular contaminating substance beyond the standard established in the relevant statute or regulations need not in itself always imply serious (or even minor) environmental and health harm. In the first place, the standard itself may be open to legitimate debate as to its accuracy and appropriateness. In some cases the standard may, by some criteria, be too strict, or based upon uncertain evidence. On the other hand, it may be felt by some to be not strict enough. Secondly, it is at least the intention of regulation and standard makers to build into the emission standards a certain margin of safety.

The "social utility" and other factors just indicated demonstrate that judgements before or after the event about the types and degrees of pollution which will be characterized and treated as serious and intolerable, as opposed to minor and tolerable within regulated limits, are not and cannot be strictly and exclusively "scientific" in nature. Determinations of harm and degree of harm are to a large degree value-judgements, rather than scientific calculations. More precisely, such judgements are based upon criteria which themselves imply or import value-judgements. Therefore, these judgements about the acceptability of harm and risk should not be made only by the scientist as scientist.[6]

There is, then, a major distinction to be made between pollution offences and the "paradigm" (criminal) offences of homicide, assault and theft, as regards seriousness. The latter are *always* considered seriously harmful to individuals and fundamental societal values, and therefore criminal (if the *mens rea* conditions are met), no matter what the degree of injury or loss. However, especially given the "social utility" factor, it is possible at present for pollution which by some criteria is endangering to the environment (and human health) to be characterized in the final analysis as not serious and even tolerable. To characterize the harm and danger as not serious need not, of course, mean that the conduct should be subject to no legal prohibitions and sanctions, only that the conduct in question would not fall within the scope of the *Criminal Code*.

That balancing of the environmental risks involved in permitting harmful pollution, with (for example) the economic implications of prohibiting it, is to at least some extent inescapable "before the event" in the formulation of environmental policies, standards and regulations. However, that same balancing is also legitimate "after the event," that is, in determining the seriousness of the alleged offence. At this stage, the social utility factor as a cri-

terion of gravity can be one of the considerations in the choice among various compliance mechanisms authorized by the relevant statute, and in the decision about how rigorously to enforce the statute in this case, including whether or not to prosecute.

However, weighing the social utility of an alleged incidence of pollution to determine its seriousness is also inevitable if we go the further step being proposed in this Paper and characterize some of these activities as potentially *criminal in nature*. One of the criteria of pollution as a crime would be that it must be proved to be seriously harmful. That would be determined, at least in part, by whether conduct which is harmful or endangering by some scientific criteria, may in the final analysis be less than seriously harmful and endangering, or even justifiable and tolerable, in part because it promotes valid social goals. It has been suggested to us by one of those consulted that an alternate or more specific way of highlighting the social utility factor would be to make it a defence, or simply leave it to guide prosecutorial discretion. Both approaches appear to us essentially compatible with the analysis to this point. However, we feel that the jury may have a unique and important role to play in the balancing of harm and social utility.

In any event, the life and health of others cannot be traded off for other apparent benefits, whether economic or not. We do not permit such a trade-off for other criminal offences involving serious harms or dangers to human life and bodily integrity. That being so, we may formulate the following by way of a general criterion: (1) the more certain is the evidence or likelihood of present or future harm and danger to human life and health, and the more serious the nature of that harm and danger, the less legitimate and persuasive should be other socially useful goals as justifications for the pollution or for reducing its classification from serious to minor, and the more compelling would be arguments for the criminal nature of that activity; (2) the less likely are the serious present and future human health harms and dangers, and the more likely the interests affected are exclusively those of the use and enjoyment of the environment, the more relevant and legitimate is the weighing of other societal goals by way of mitigating its classification as potentially serious harm.

Notes

1 See generally on this approach, C.D. Stone, "Should Trees Have Standing?—Toward Legal Rights for Natural Objects" (1972), 45 *Southern California Law Review* 450; L.H. Tribe, "Ways Not to Think about Plastic Trees: New Foundations for Environmental Law" (1974), 83 *Yale Law Journal* 1315; D.P. Emond, "Co-operation in Nature: A New Foundation for Environmental Law" (1984) 22 *Osgoode Hall Law Journal* 323.

2 One of the strongest and earliest proponents of the relevance of this doctrine to environmental protection was Joseph Sax. See his *Defending the Environment: A Strategy for Citizen Action* (New York: Alfred A. Knopf, 1971). See also Constance D. Hunt, "The Public Trust Doctrine in Canada," in John Swaigen, ed., *Environmental Rights in Canada* (Toronto: Butterworths, 1981), pp. 151–94. A related approach encouraged by many argues for a new substantive right to environmental quality which could be enforced by government or any member of the public against business, or by any member of the public against the government. See John Swaigen and Richard Woods, "A Substantive Right to Environmental Quality," in *Environmental Rights in Canada, supra*, pp. 195–241.

3 Institutes of Justinian, Book II, Title I, para. 1, in *The Civil Law*, a translation by S.P. Scott (Cincinatti: The Central Trust Company, 1932), vol. 2, p. 33.

4 See, for example, N. Morse and D.A. Chant, *An Environmental Ethic: Its Formulation and Implications* (Ottawa: Canadian Environmental Advisory Council, 1975); R. Cahn, *Footprints on the Planet: A Search for an Environmental Ethic* (New York: Universe Books, 1978).

5 For details on the meaning and significance of the ecosystems approach, see: E.P. Odum, *Fundamentals of Ecology*, 3rd ed. (London: Saunders, 1971); H.T. Odum, *Environment, Power and Society* (New York: Wiley, 1971); B. Commoner, *L'encerclement* (Paris: Le Seuil, 1972); P. Lebreton, *Les chemins de l'écologie* (Paris: Éditions Denoël, 1978); A. Schnaiberg, *The Environment* (Oxford: Oxford U. Press, 1980).

6 See T. Page, "A Framework for Unreasonable Risk in the Toxic Substances Control Act (TSCA)" in W. Nicholson, ed., *Management of Assessed Risk for Carcinogens* (1981), 363 *Annals of the New York Academy of Sciences,* New York.

Questions for Discussion

1 Should people who cause harm to the environment be made criminally liable for their actions? If so, should such liability ever extend to harms such as depriving people of the use and enjoyment of natural resources, or should it be limited to harm to life and health?

2 Does the claim that ecosystems have inherent value, independently of human beings, lead us to the conclusion that "the extinction of the smallpox virus was not a good thing, or that grasshoppers, mosquitoes, noxious weeds, various pests and disease organisms should not be combatted but protected"? How does the answer to this question affect our understanding of our relationship to the environment?

3 The Commission suggests that environmental agencies should sometimes judge that environmental considerations must lose out to economic ones. Under which circumstances, if any, would this be true?

Identification as a Source of Deep Ecological Attitudes

Arne Naess

Arne Naess coined the phrase "deep ecology" in a 1973 paper. This phrase is now often used to describe a number of views which hold that nature has intrinsic value, apart from its contribution to human well-being, and that major changes are required in the ways in which humans (especially in the West) think about and interact with nature. In this 1988 paper, Naess elaborates some of the ideas of "deep ecology," and describes the sort of identification with nature he believes is called for.

★   ★   ★

The Shallow and the Deep Ecological Movement

In the 1960s two convergent trends made headway: a deep ecological concern, and a concern for saving deep cultural diversity. These may be put under the general heading "deep ecology" if we view human ecology as a genuine part of general ecology. For each species of living beings there is a corresponding ecology. In what follows I adopt this terminology which I introduced in 1973 (Naess 1973).

The term *deep* is supposed to suggest explication of fundamental presuppositions of valuation as well as of facts and hypotheses. Deep ecology, therefore, transcends the limit of any particular science of today, including systems theory and scientific ecology. *Deepness of normative and descriptive premises questioned* characterizes the movement.

The difference between the shallow and deep ecological movement may perhaps be illustrated by contrasting typical slogans, here formulated very roughly:[1]

Shallow Ecology	Deep Ecology
Natural diversity is valuable as a resource for us.	Natural diversity has its own (intrinsic) value.
It is nonsense to talk about value except as value for mankind.	Equating value with value for humans reveals a racial prejudice.
Plant species should be saved because of their value as genetic reserves for human agriculture and medicine.	Plant species should be saved because of their intrinsic value.
Pollution should be decreased if it threatens economic growth.	Decrease of pollution has priority over economic growth.
Third World population growth threatens ecological equilibrium.	World population at the present level threatens ecosystems but the population and behavior of industrial states more than that of any others. Human population is today excessive.
"Resource" means resource for humans.	"Resource" means resource for living beings.
People will not tolerate a broad decrease in their standard of living.	People should not tolerate a broad decrease in the quality of life but in the standard of living in overdeveloped countries.
Nature is cruel and necessarily so.	Man is cruel but not necessarily so.

Deep ecological argumentation questions both the left-hand and the right-hand slogans. But tentative conclusions are in terms of the latter.

The shallow ecological argument carries today much heavier weight in political life than the deep. It is therefore often necessary for tactical reasons to hide our deeper attitudes and argue strictly homocentrically. This colors the indispensable publication *World Conservation Strategy.*[2]

As an academic philosopher raised within analytic traditions it has been natural for me to pose the questions: How can departments of philosophy, our establishment of professionals, be made interested in the matter? What are the philosophical problems explicitly and implicitly raised or answered in the deep ecological movement? Can they be formulated so as to be of academic interest?

My answer is that the movement is rich in philosophical implications. There has, however, been only moderately eager response in philosophical institutions.

The deep ecological movement is furthered by people and groups with much in common. Roughly speaking, what they have in common concerns ways of experiencing nature and diversity of cultures. Furthermore, many share priorities of life style, such as those of "voluntary simplicity." They wish to live "lightly" in nature. There are of course differences, but until now the conflicts of philosophically relevant opinion and of recommended politics have, to a surprisingly small degree, disturbed the growth of the movement.

In what follows I introduce some sections of a philosophy inspired by the deep ecological movement. Some people in the movement feel at home with that philosophy or at least approximately such a philosophy; others feel that they, at one or more points, clearly have different value priorities, attitudes, or opinions.

To avoid unfruitful polemics, I call my philosophy "Ecosophy T," using the character *T* just to emphasize that other people in the movement would, if motivated to formulate their world view and general value priorities, arrive at different ecosophies: Ecosophy "A," "B," ..., "T," ..., "Z."

By an "ecosophy" I here mean a philosophy inspired by the deep ecological movement. The ending *-sophy* stresses that what we modestly try to realize is wisdom rather than science or information. A philosophy, as articulated wisdom, has to be a synthesis of theory and practice. It must not shun concrete policy recommendations but has to base them on fundamental priorities of value and basic views concerning the development of our societies.[3]

Which societies? The movement started in the richest industrial societies, and the words used by its academic supporters inevitably reflect the cultural provinciality of those societies. The way I am going to say things perhaps reflects a bias in favor of analytic philosophy intimately related to social science, including academic psychology. It shows itself in my acceptance in Ecosophy T of the theory of thinking in terms of "gestalts." But this provinciality and narrowness of training does not imply criticism of contributions in terms of trends or traditions of wisdom with which I am not at home, and it does not imply an underestimation of the immense value of what artists in many countries have contributed to the movement.

Selected Ecosophical Topics

The themes of Ecosophy T which will be introduced are the following:

- The narrow self (ego) and the comprehensive Self (written with capital S)
- Self-realization as the realization of the comprehensive Self, not the cultivation of the ego

- The process of identification as the basic tool of widening the self and as a natural consequence of increased maturity
- Strong identification with the whole of nature in its diversity and interdependence of parts as a source of active participation in the deep ecological movement
- Identification as a source of belief in intrinsic values. The question of "objective" validity.[4]

Self-Realization, Yes, but Which Self?

When asked about *where* their self, their "I," or their ego is, some people place it in the neighborhood of the *larynx*. When thinking, we can sometimes perceive movement in that area. Others find it near their eyes. Many tend to feel that their ego, somehow, is inside their body, or identical with the whole of it, or with its functioning. Some call their ego spiritual, or immaterial and not within space. This has interesting consequences. A Bedouin in Yemen would not have an ego nearer the equator than a whale-hunting eskimo. "Nearer" implies space.

William James (1890: Chapter 10) offers an excellent introduction to the problems concerning the constitution and the limits of the self.

> The Empirical Self of each of us is all that he is tempted to call by the name of *me*. But it is clear that between what a man calls *me* and what he simply calls *mine* the line is difficult to draw. We feel and act about certain things that are ours very much as we feel and act about ourselves. Our fame, our children, the work of our hands, may be as dear to us as our bodies are, and arouse the same feelings and the same acts of reprisal if attacked. And our bodies, themselves, are they simply ours, or are they *us?*

> The body is the innermost part of *the material Self* in each of us; and certain parts

of the body seem more intimately ours than the rest. The clothes come next.... Next, our immediate family is a part of ourselves. Our father and mother, our wife and babes, are bone of our bone and flesh of our flesh. When they die, a part of our very selves is gone. If they do anything wrong, it is our shame. If they are insulted, our anger flashes forth as readily as if we stood in their place. Our *home* comes next. Its scenes are part of our life; its aspects awaken the tenderest feelings of affection.

One of his conclusions is of importance to the concepts of self-realization: "We see then that we are dealing with a fluctuating material. The same object being sometimes treated as a part of me, at other times as simply mine, and then again as if I had nothing to do with it all."

If the term *self-realization* is applied, it should be kept in mind that "I," "me," "ego," and "self" have shifting denotations. Nothing is evident and indisputable. Even *that* we are is debatable if we make the question dependent upon answering *what* we are.

One of the central terms in Indian philosophy is *ātman*. Until this century it was mostly translated with "spirit," but it is now generally recognized that "self" is more appropriate. It is a term with similar connotations and ambiguities as those of "self"—analyzed by William James and other Western philosophers and psychologists. Gandhi represented a *maha-ātman*, a *mahatma*, a great (and certainly very wide) self. As a term for a kind of metaphysical maximum self we find *ātman* in *The Bhagavadgita*.

Verse 29 of Chapter 6 is characteristic of the truly great *ātman*. The Sanskrit of this verse is not overwhelmingly difficult and deserves quotation ahead of translations.

sarvabhūtastham atmānam
sarvabhutāni cā'tmani
Itsate yogayuktātmā
sarvatra samadarśanah

Radhakrisnan: "He whose self is harmonized by yoga seeth the Self abiding in all beings and all beings in Self; everywhere he sees the same."

Eliot Deutsch: "He whose self is disciplined by yoga sees the Self abiding in all beings and all beings in the Self; he sees the same in all beings."

Juan Mascaró: "He sees himself in the heart of all beings and he sees all beings in his heart. This is the vision of the Yogi of harmony, a vision which is ever one."

Gandhi: "The man equipped with *yoga* looks on all with an impartial eye, seeing *Atman* in all beings and all beings in *Atman*."

Self-realization in its absolute maximum is, as I see it, the mature experience of oneness in diversity as depicted in the above verse. The minimum is the self-realization by more or less consistent egotism—by the narrowest experience of what constitutes one's self and a maximum of alienation. As empirical beings we dwell somewhere in between, but increased maturity involves increase of the wideness of the self.

The self-realization maximum should not necessarily be conceived as a mystical or meditational state. "By meditation some perceive the Self in the self by the self; others by the path of knowledge and still others by the path of works *(karma-yoga)* [*Gita:* Chapter 13, verse 24]. Gandhi was a *karma-yogi,* realizing himself through social and political action.

The terms *mystical union* and *mysticism* are avoided here for three reasons: First, strong mystical traditions stress the dissolution of individual selves into a nondiversified supreme whole. Both from cultural and ecological points of view diversity and individuality are essential. Second, there is a strong terminological trend within scientific communities to associate mysticism with vagueness and confusion.[5] Third, mystics tend to agree that mystical consciousness is rarely sustained under normal, everyday conditions. But strong, wide identification *can* color experience under such conditions.

Gandhi was only marginally concerned with "nature." In his *ashram* poisonous snakes were permitted to live inside and outside human dwellings. Anti-poison medicines were frowned upon. Gandhi insisted that trust awakens trust, and that snakes have the same right to live and blossom as the humans (Naess, 1974).

The Process of Identification

How do we develop a wider self? What kind of process makes it possible? One way of answering these questions: There is a process of ever-widening identification and ever-narrowing alienation which widens the self. The self is as comprehensive as the totality of our identifications. Or, more succinctly: Our Self is that with which we identify. The question then reads: How do we widen identifications?

Identification is a spontaneous, non-rational, but not irrational, process through which *the interest or interests of another being are reacted to as our own interest or interests.* The emotional tone of gratification or frustration is a consequence carried over from the other to oneself: joy elicits joy, sorrow sorrow. Intense identification obliterates the experience of a distinction between *ego* and *alter,* between me and the sufferer. But only momentarily or intermittently: If my fellow being tries to vomit, I do not, or at least not persistently, try to vomit. I recognize that we are different individuals.

The term *identification, in the sense used here,* is rather technical, but there are today scarcely any alternatives. "Solidarity," and a corresponding adjective in German, "solidarisch;' and the corresponding words in Scandinavian languages are very common and useful. But genuine and spontaneous solidarity with others already presupposes a process of identification. Without identification, no solidarity.

Thus, the latter term cannot quite replace the former.

The same holds true of empathy and sympathy. It is a necessary, but not sufficient condition of empathy and sympathy that one "sees" or experiences something similar or identical with oneself.[6]

A high level of identification does not eliminate conflicts of interest: Our vital interests, if we are not plants, imply killing at least some other living beings. A culture of hunters, where identification with hunted animals reaches a remarkably high level, does not prohibit killing for food. But a great variety of ceremonies and rituals have the function to express the gravity of the alienating incident and restore the identification.

Identification with individuals, species, ecosystems, and landscapes results in difficult problems of priority. What should be the relation of ecosystem ethics to other parts of general ethics?

There are no definite limits to the broadness and intensity of identification. Mammals and birds sometimes show remarkable, often rather touching, intraspecies and cross-species identification. Konrad Lorenz tells of how one of his bird friends tried to seduce him, trying to push him into its little home. This presupposes a deep identification between bird and man (but also an alarming mistake of size). In certain forms of mysticism, there is an experience of identification with every life form, using this term in a wide sense. Within the deep ecological movement, poetical and philosophical expressions of such experiences are not uncommon. In the shallow ecological movement, intense and wide identification is described and explained psychologically. In the deep movement this philosophy is at least taken seriously: reality consists of wholes which we cut down rather than of isolated items which we put together. In other words: there is not, strictly speaking, a primordial causal process of identification, but one of

largely unconscious alienation which is overcome in experiences of identity. To some "environmental" philosophers such thoughts seem to be irrational, even "rubbish."[7] This is, as far as I can judge, due to a too narrow conception of rationality.

The opposite of *identification* is *alienation,* if we use these ambiguous terms in one of their basic meanings.[8]

The alienated son does perhaps what is required of a son toward his parents, but as performance of moral duties and as a burden, not spontaneously, out of joy. If one loves and respects oneself, identification will be positive, and, in what follows, the term covers this case. Self-hatred or dislike of certain of one's traits includes hatred and dislike of the beings with which one identifies.

Identification is not limited to beings which can reciprocate: Any animal, plant, mountain, ocean may induce such processes. In poetry this is articulated most impressively, but ordinary language testifies to its power as a universal human trait.

Through identification, higher level unity is experienced: from identifying with "one's nearest," higher unities are created through circles of friends, local communities, tribes, compatriots, races, humanity, life, and, ultimately, as articulated by religious and philosophic leaders, unity with the supreme whole, the "world" in a broader and deeper sense than the usual. I prefer a terminology such that the largest units are not said to comprise life *and* "the not living." One may broaden the sense of "living" so that any natural whole, however large, is a living whole.

This way of thinking and feeling at its maximum corresponds to that of the enlightened, or yogi, who sees "the same," the *ātman,* and who is not alienated from anything.

The process of identification is sometimes expressed in terms of loss of self and gain of Self through "self-less" action. Each new sort of identification corresponds to a widening of the self, and strengthens the urge to further widening, furthering Self-seeking. This urge is in the system of Spinoza called *conatus in suo esse perseverare,* striving to persevere in oneself or one's being *(in se, in suo esse).* It is not a mere urge to survive, but to increase the level of *acting out* (ex) *one's own nature or essence,* and is not different from the urge toward higher levels of "freedom" *(libertas).* Under favorable circumstances, this involves wide identification.

In western social science, self-realization is the term most often used for the competitive development of a person's talents and the pursuit of an individual's specific interests (Maslow and others). A conflict is foreseen between giving self-realization high priority and cultivation of social bonds, friends, family, nation, nature. Such unfortunate notions have narrow concepts of self as a point of departure. They go together with the egoism-altruism distinction. Altruism is, according to this, a moral quality developed through suppression of selfishness, through sacrifice of one's "own" interests in favor of those of others. Thus, alienation is taken to be the normal State. Identification precludes sacrifice, but not devotion. The moral of self-sacrifice presupposes immaturity. Its relative importance is clear, in so far we all are more or less immature.

Wideness and Depth of Identification as a Consequence of Increased Maturity

Against the belief in fundamental ego–alter conflict, the psychology and philosophy of the (comprehensive) Self insist that the gradual maturing of a person *inevitably* widens and deepens the self through the process of identification. There is no need for altruism toward those with whom we identify. The pursuit of self-realization conceived as actualization and development of the Self takes care of what altruism is supposed to accomplish. Thus, the distinction egoism-altruism is transcended.

The notion of maturing has to do with getting out what is latent in the nature of a being. Some learning is presupposed, but thinking of present conditions of competition in industrial, economic growth societies, specialized learning may inhibit the process of maturing. A competitive cult of talents does not favor Self-realization. As a consequence of the imperfect conditions for maturing as persons, there is much pessimism or disbelief in relation to the widening of the Self, and more stress on developing altruism and moral pressure.

The conditions under which the self is widened are experienced as positive and are basically joyful. The constant exposure to life in the poorest countries through television and other media contributes to the spread of the voluntary simplicity movement (Elgin, 1981). But people laugh: What does it help the hungry that you renounce the luxuries of your own country? But identification makes the efforts of simplicity joyful and there is no feeling of moral compulsion. The widening of the self implies widening perspectives, deepening experiences, and reaching higher levels of activeness (in Spinoza's sense, not as just being busy). Joy and activeness make the appeal to Self-realization stronger than appeal to altruism. The state of alienation is not joyful, and is often connected with feelings of being threatened and narrowed. The "rights" of other living beings are felt to threaten our "own" interests.

The close connection between trends of alienation and putting duty and altruism as a highest value is exemplified in the philosophy of Kant. Acting morally, we should not abstain from maltreating animals because of their sufferings, but because of its bad effect on us. Animals were to Kant, essentially, so different from human beings, that he felt we should not have any moral obligations toward them. Their unnecessary sufferings are morally indifferent and norms of altruism do not apply in our relations to them. When we decide ethically to be kind to them, it should be because of the favorable effect of kindness on us—a strange doctrine.

Suffering is perhaps the most potent source of identification. Only special social conditions are able to make people inhibit their normal spontaneous reaction toward suffering. If we alleviate suffering because of a spontaneous urge to do so, Kant would be willing to call the act "beautiful," but not moral. And his greatest admiration was, as we all know, for stars and the moral imperative, not spontaneous goodness. The history of cruelty inflicted in the name of morals has convinced me that increase of identification might achieve what moralizing cannot: beautiful actions.

Relevance of the Above for Deep Ecology

This perhaps rather lengthy philosophical discourse serves as a preliminary for the understanding of two things: first, the powerful indignation of Rachel Carson and others who, with great courage and stubborn determination, challenged authorities in the early 1960s, and triggered the international ecological movement. Second, the radical shift (see Sahlins, 1972) toward more positive appreciation of nonindustrial cultures and minorities—also in the 1960s, and expressing itself in efforts to "save" such cultures and in a new social anthropology.

The second movement reflects identification with threatened cultures. Both reactions were made possible by doubt that the industrial societies are as uniquely progressive as they usually had been supposed to be. Former haughtiness gave way to humility or at least willingness to look for deep changes both socially and in relation to nature.

Ecological information about the intimate dependency of humanity upon decent behavior toward the natural environment offered a much needed rational and economic

justification for processes of identification which many people already had more or less completed. Their relative high degree of identification with animals, plants, landscapes, were seen to correspond to *factual relations* between themselves and nature. "Not man apart" was transformed from a romantic norm to a statement of fact. The distinction between man and environment, as applied within the shallow ecological movement, was seen to be illusory. Your Self crosses the boundaries.

When it was made known that the penguins, of the Antarctic might die out because of the effects of DDT upon the toughness of their eggs, there was a widespread, *spontaneous* reaction of indignation and sorrow. People who never see penguins, and who would never think of such animals as "useful" in any way, insisted that they had a right to live and flourish, and that it was our obligation not to interfere. But we must admit that even the mere appearance of penguins makes intense identification easy.

Thus, ecology helped many to know more *about themselves.* We are living beings. Penguins are too. We are all expressions of life. The fateful dependencies and interrelations which were brought to light, thanks to ecologists, made it easier for people to admit and even to cultivate their deep concern for nature, and to express their latent hostility toward the excesses of the economic growth societies.

Living Beings Have Intrinsic Value and a Right to Live and Flourish

How can these attitudes be talked about? What are the most helpful conceptualizations and slogans?

One important attitude might be thus expressed: "Every living being has a *right* to live." One way of answering the question is to insist upon the value in themselves, the autotelic value, of every living being. This opposes the notion that one may be justified in treating any living being as just a means to an end. It also generalizes the rightly famous dictum of Kant "never use a person solely as a means:' Identification tells me: if *I* have a right to live, *you* have the same right.

Insofar as we consider ourselves and our family and friends to have an intrinsic value, the widening identification inevitably leads to the attribution of intrinsic value to others. The metaphysical maximum will then involve the attribution of intrinsic value to all living beings. The right to live is only a different way of expressing this evaluation.

The End of the Why's

But why has *any* living being autotelic value? Faced with the ever returning question of "why?", we have to stop somewhere. Here is a place where we well might stop. We shall admit that the value in itself is something shown in intuition. We attribute intrinsic value to ourselves and our nearest, and the validity of further identification can be contested, and is contested by many. The negation may, however, also be attacked through series of "whys?" Ultimately, we are in the same human predicament of having to start somewhere, at least for the moment. We must stop somewhere and treat where we then stand as a foundation.

The use of "Every living being has a value in itself" as a fundamental norm or principle does not rule out other fundamentals. On the contrary, the normal situation will be one in which several, in part conflicting, fundamental norms are relevant. And some consequences of fundamental norms *seem* compatible, but in fact are not.

The designation "fundamental" does not need to mean more than "not based on something deeper," which in practice often is indistinguishable from "not derived logically from deeper premises." It must be considered a rare case, if somebody is able to stick to one

and only one fundamental norm. (I have made an attempt to work with a *model* with only one, Self-realization, in Ecosophy T.)

The Right to Live Is One and the Same, but Vital Interests of Our Nearest Have Priority of Defense

Under symbiotic conditions, there are rules which manifest two important factors operating when interests are conflicting: vitalness and nearness. The more vital interest has priority over the less vital. The nearer has priority over the more remote—in space, time, culture, species. Nearness derives its priority from our special responsibilities, obligations, and insights.

The terms used in these rules are of course vague and ambiguous. But even so, the rules point toward ways of thinking and acting which do not leave us quite helpless in the many inevitable conflicts of norms. The vast increase of consequences for life in general, which industrialization and the population explosion have brought about, necessitates new guidelines.

Examples: The use of threatened species for food or clothing (fur) may be more or less vital for certain poor, nonindustrial, human communities. For the less poor, such use is clearly ecologically irresponsible. Considering the fabulous possibilities open to the richest industrial societies, it is their responsibility to assist the poor communities in such a way that undue exploitation of threatened species, populations, and ecosystems is avoided.

It may be of vital interest to a family of poisonous snakes to remain in a small area where small children play, but it is also of vital interest to children and parents that there are no accidents. The priority rule of nearness makes it justifiable for the parents to remove the snakes. But the priority of vital interest of snakes is important when deciding where to establish the playgrounds.

The importance of nearness is, to a large degree, dependent upon vital interests of communities rather than individuals. The obligations within the family keep the family together; the obligations within a nation keep it from disintegration. But if the nonvital interests of a nation, or a species, conflict with the vital interests of another nation, or of other species, the rules give priority to the "alien nation" or "alien species."

How these conflicts may be straightened out is of course much too large a subject to be treated even cursorily in this connection. What is said only points toward the existence of rules of some help (for further discussion, see Naess [1979]).

Intrinsic Values

The term "objectivism" may have undesirable associations, but value pronouncements within the deep ecological movement imply what in philosophy is often termed "value objectivism" as opposed to value subjectivism, for instance, "the emotive theory of value." At the time of Nietzsche there was in Europe a profound movement toward separation of value as a genuine aspect of reality, on a par with scientific, "factual" descriptions. Value tended to be conceived as something projected by man into a completely value-neutral reality. The *Tractatus Philosophico-Logicus* of the early Wittgenstein expresses a well-known variant of this attitude. It represents a unique trend of *alienation of value* if we compare this attitude with those of cultures other than our technological-industrial society.

The professional philosophical debate on value objectivism—which in different senses, according to different versions, posits positive and negative values independent of value for human subjects—is of course very intricate. Here I shall only point out some kinds of statements within the deep ecological movement which imply value objectivism in the sense of intrinsic value:

- Animals have value in themselves, not only as resources for humans.
- Animals have a right to live even if of no use to humans.
- We have no right to destroy the natural features of this planet.
- Nature does not belong to man.
- Nature is worth defending, whatever the fate of humans.
- A wilderness area has a value independent of whether humans have access to it.

In these statements, something *A* is said to have a value independent of whether *A* has a value for something else, *B*. The value of *A* must therefore be said to have a value inherent in *A*. *A* has *intrinsic value*. This does not imply that *A has* value for *B*. Thus *A* may have, and usually does have, both intrinsic and extrinsic value.

Subjectivistic arguments tend to take for granted that a subject is somehow implied. There "must be" somebody who performs the valuation process. For this subject, something may have value.

The burden of proof lies with the subjectivists insofar as naive attitudes lack the clear-cut separation of value from reality and the conception of value as something projected by man into reality or the neutral facts by a subject.

The most promising way of defending intrinsic values today is, in my view, to take gestalt thinking seriously. "Objects" will then be defined in terms of gestalts, rather than in terms of heaps of things with external relations and dominated by forces. This undermines the subject–object dualism essential for value subjectivism.

Outlook for the Future

What is the outlook for growth of ecological, relevant identification and of policies in harmony with a high level of identification?

A major nuclear war will involve a setback of tremendous dimensions. Words need not be wasted in support of that conclusion. But continued militarization is a threat: It means further domination of technology and centralization.

Continued population growth makes benevolent policies still more difficult to pursue than they already are. Poor people in megacities do not have the opportunity to meet nature, and shortsighted policies which favor increasing the number of poor are destructive. Even a small population growth in rich nations is scarcely less destructive.

The economic policy of growth (as conceived today in the richest nations of all times) is increasingly destructive. It does not *prevent* growth of identification but makes it politically powerless. This reminds us of the possibility of significant *growth* of identification in the near future.

The increasing destruction plus increasing information about the destruction is apt to elicit strong feelings of sorrow, despair, desperate actions, and tireless efforts to save what is left. With the forecast that more than a million species will die out before the year 2000 and most cultures be done away with, identification may grow rapidly among a minority.

At the present about 10% to 15% of the populace of some European countries are in favor of strong policies in harmony with the attitudes of identification. But this percentage may increase without major changes of policies. So far as I can see, the most probable course of events is continued devastation of conditions of life on this planet, combined with a powerless upsurge of sorrow and lamentation.

What actually happens is often wildly "improbable," and perhaps the strong anthropocentric arguments and wise recommendations of *World Conservation Strategy* (1980) will, after all, have a significant effect.

Notes

1. For a survey of the main themes of the shallow and the deep movement, see Naess (1973); elaborated in Naess (1981). See also the essay of G. Sessions in Schultz (1981) and Devall (1979). Some of the 15 views as formulated and listed by Devall would perhaps more adequately be described as part of "Ecosophy D" (D for Devall!) than as parts of a common deep ecology platform.

2. Commissioned by The United Nations Environmental Programme (UNEP) which worked together with the World Wildlife Fund (WWF). Published 1980. Copies available through IUNC, 1196 Gland, Switzerland. In India: Department of Environment.

3. This aim implies a synthesis of views developed in the different branches of philosophy—ontology, epistemology, logic, methodology, theory of value, ethics, philosophy of history, and politics. As a philosopher the deep ecologist is a "generalist."

4. For comprehensive treatment of Ecosophy T, see Naess (1981, Chapter 7).

5. See Passmore (1980). For a reasonable, unemotional approach to "mysticism," see Stahl (1975).

6. For deeper study more distinctions have to be taken into account. See, for instance, Scheler (1954) and Mercer (1972).

7. See, for instance, the chapter "Removing the Rubbish" in Passmore (1980).

8. The diverse uses of the term *alienation* *(Entfremdung)* has an interesting and complicated history from the time of Rousseau. Rousseau himself offers interesting observations of how social conditions through the process of alienation make *amour de soi* change into *amour propre*. I would say: How the process of maturing is hindered and self-love hardens into egotism instead of softening and widening into Self-realization.

References

Elgin, Duane. 1981. *Voluntary Simplicity,* New York: William Morrow.

James, William. 1890. *The Principles of Psychology.* New York. Chapter 10: The Consciousness of Self.

Kohler, W. 1938. *The Place of Value in a World of Facts.* New York. On thinking in terms of gestalts.

Meeker, Joseph W. 1980. *The Comedy of Survival*. Los Angeles: Guild of Tutor's Press.

Mercer, Philip. 1972. *Sympathy and Ethics*. Oxford: The Clarendon Press. Discusses forms of identification.

Naess, A. 1973. "The Shallow and the Deep, Long Range Ecology Movement," *Inquiry* 16: 95–100.

Naess, A. 1974. *Gandhi and Group Conflict*. 1981, Oslo: Universitetsforlaget.

Naess, A. 1979. "Self-realization in Mixed Communities of Humans, Bears, Sheep and Wolves," *Inquiry*, Vol. 22, pp. 231–241.

Naess, A. 1981. *Ekologi, sämhalle och livsstil. Utkast til en ekosofi*. Stockholm: LTs förlag.

Passmore, John. 1980. *Man's Responsibility for Nature*. 2nd ed., London: Duckworth.

Rodman, John. 1980. "The Liberation of Nature," *Inquiry* 20: 83–145.

Sahlins, Marshall. 1972. *Stone Age Economics*. Chicago: Aldine.

Scheler, Max. 1954. *The Nature of Sympathy*. London: Routledge & Kegan Paul.

Schultz, Robert C. and J.D. Hughes (eds.). 1981. *Ecological Consciousness*. University Press of America.

Schumacher, E.F. 1974. *The Age of Plenty: A Christian View*. Edinburgh: Saint Andrew Press.

Sessions, George. 1981. *Ecophilosophy* (mimeo), Department of Philosophy, Sierra College, Rocklin, CA. Survey of literature expressing attitudes of deep ecology.

Stahl, Frits. 1975. *Exploring Mysticism*. Berkeley: University of California Press.

Stone, Christopher D. 1974. *Should Trees Have Standing?* Los Altos, CA: Kaufmann.

World Conservation Strategy. 1980. Prepared by the International Union for Conservation of Nature and Natural Resources (IUCN).

Questions for Discussion

1 Are there limits to the sorts of entities we can, or should, identify with? Is it *better* (or more important) to identify with some entities than with others?

2 Do human beings begin as alienated individuals who have to learn to identify with others as they mature, or do they begin as individuals who identify broadly with the world around them, and learn alienation from their social and economic environment?

3 Naess says that "self-hatred or dislike of certain of one's traits includes hatred and dislike of the beings with which one identifies." What is the relationship between individual mental health, and acceptance of deep ecology?

4 Some cultures may have a high degree of identification with non-human animals, yet still hunt and kill them. Is this consistent?

5 If all humankind were moving to a different planet, would it matter what condition we left the earth in?

Deeper than Deep Ecology:
The Eco-Feminist Connection

Ariel Kay Salleh

"Deep ecologists" such as Naess are sometimes accused of not going far enough in their analysis. For example, it is suggested that they fail to look at the links between the traditional view that humans can dominate and control nature, and the ways in which some humans can dominate and control others. In particular, it is sometimes suggested that attention to the ways in which men dominate women might cast light on our relationship to nature. In this selection, Salleh outlines some reasons for favouring such an "eco-feminist" way of critiquing modern western society.

★ ★ ★

... beyond that perception of otherness lies the perception of psyche, polity and cosmos, as metaphors of one another....

John Rodman[1]

In what sense is eco-feminism "deeper than deep ecology"? Or is this a facile and arrogant claim? To try to answer this question is to engage in a critique of a critique, for deep ecology itself is already an attempt to transcend the shortsighted instrumental pragmatism of the resource-management approach to the environmental crisis. It argues for a new metaphysics and an ethic based on the recognition of the intrinsic worth of the nonhuman world. It abandons the hardheaded scientific approach to reality in favor of a more spiritual consciousness. It asks for voluntary simplicity in living and a nonexploitive steady-state economy. The appropriateness of these attitudes as expressed in Naess' and Devall's seminal papers on the deep ecology movement is indisputable.[2] But what is the organic basis of this paradigm shift? Where are Naess and Devall "coming from," as they say? Is deep ecology a sociologically coherent position?

The first feature of the deep ecology paradigm introduced by Naess is replacement of the Man/Nature dualism with a *relational total-field image*, where man is not simply "in" his environment, but essentially "of" it. The deep ecologists do not appear to recognize the primal source of this destructive dualism, however, or the deeply ingrained motivational complexes which grow out of it.[3] Their formulation uses the generic term *Man* in a case where use of a general term is not applicable. Women's monthly fertility cycle, the tiring symbiosis of pregnancy, the wrench of childbirth and the pleasure of suckling an infant, these things already ground women's consciousness in the knowledge of being coterminous with Nature. However tacit or unconscious this identity may be for many women, bruised by derogatory patriarchal at-

titudes to motherhood, including modern male-identified feminist ones, it is nevertheless "a fact of life." The deep ecology movement, by using the generic term *Man*, simultaneously presupposes the difference between the sexes in an uncritical way, and yet overlooks the significance of this difference. It overlooks the point that if women's lived experience were recognized as meaningful and were given legitimation in our culture, it could provide an immediate "living" social basis for the alternative consciousness which the deep ecologist is trying to formulate and introduce as an abstract ethical construct. Women already, to borrow Devall's turn of phrase, "flow with the system of nature."

The second deep ecology premise, according to Naess is a move away from anthropocentrism, a move toward *biological egalitarianism* among all living species. This assumption, however, is already cancelled in part by the implicit contradiction contained in Naess' first premise. The master–slave role which marks man's relation with nature is replicated in man's relation with woman. A self-consistent biological egalitarianism cannot be arrived at unless men become open to both facets of this same urge to dominate and use. As Naess rightly, though still somewhat anthropocentrically, points out, the denial of dependence on Mother/Nature and the compensatory drive to mastery which stems from it, have only served to alienate man from his true self. Yet the means by which Naess would realize this goal of species equality is through artificial limitation of the human population. Now putting the merits of Naess' "ends" aside for the moment, as a "means" this kind of intervention in life processes is supremely rationalist and technicist, and quite at odds with the restoration of life-affirming values that is so fundamental to the ethic of deep ecology. It is also a solution that interestingly enough cuts right back into the nub of male dependence on women as mothers and creators of life—

another grab at women's special potency, inadvertent though it may be.

The third domain assumption of deep ecology is the *principle of diversity and symbiosis:* an attitude of live and let live, a beneficial mutual coexistence among living forms. For humans the principle favors cultural pluralism, an appreciation of the rich traditions emerging from Africa, China, the Australian Aboriginal way, and so on. These departures from anthropocentrism, and from ethnocentrism, are only partial, however, if the ecologist continues to ignore the cultural inventiveness of that other half of the human race, women; or if the ecologist unwittingly concurs in those practices which impede women's full participation in his own culture. The annihilation of seals and whales, the military and commercial genocide of tribal peoples, are unforgivable human acts, but the annihilation of women's identity and creativity by patriarchal culture continues as a fact of daily existence. The embrace of progressive attitudes toward nature does little in itself to change this.

Deep ecology is an *anti-class posture;* it rejects the exploitation of some by others, of nature by man, and of man by man, this being destructive to the realization of human potentials. However, sexual oppression and the social differentiation that this produces is not mentioned by Naess. Women again appear to be subsumed by the general category. Obviously the feminist ecological analysis is not "in principle" incompatible with the anti-class posture of deep ecology. Its reservation is that in bypassing the parallel between the original exploitation of nature as object-and-commodity resource and of nurturant woman as object-and-commodity resource, the ecologist's anti-class stance remains only superficially descriptive, politically and historically static. It loses its genuinely deep structural critical edge. On the question of political praxis though, there is certainly no quarrel between the two positions. Devall's advocacy of loose activist

networks, his tactics of nonviolent contestation, are cases in point.[4] Deep ecology and feminism see change as gradual and piecemeal; the violence of revolution imposed by those who claim "to know" upon those who "do not know" is an anathema to both.

The fight against *pollution and resource depletion* is, of course, a fundamental environmental concern. And it behooves the careful activist to see that measures taken to protect resources do not have hidden or long-term environmental costs which outweigh their usefulness. As Naess observes, such costs may increase class inequalities. In this context he also comments on the "after hours" environmentalist syndrome frequently exhibited by middle-class professionals. Devall, too, criticizes what he calls "the bourgeois liberal reformist elements" in the movement—Odum, Brower, and Lovins, who are the butt of this remark. A further comment that might be made in this context, however, is that women, as keepers of *oikos,* are in a good position to put a round-the-clock ecological consciousness into practice. Excluded as many still are from full participation in the social-occupational structure, they are less often compromised by the material and status rewards which may silence the activist professional. True, the forces of capitalism have targeted women at home as consumer par excellence, but this potential can just as well be turned against the systematic waste of industrialism. The historical significance of the domestic labor force in moves to recycle, boycott, and so on, has been grossly underestimated by ecologists.

At another level of analysis entirely, but again on the issue of pollution, the objectivist attitude of most ecological writing and the tacit mind-body dualism which shapes this, means that its comprehension of "pollution" is framed exclusively in external material terms. The feminist consciousness, however, is equally concerned to eradicate ideological pollution, which centuries of patriarchal conditioning have subjected us all to, women and men. Men, who may derive rather more ego gratification from the patriarchal status quo than women, are on the whole less motivated to change this system than women are. But radical women's consciousness-raising groups are continually engaging in an intensely reflexive political process; one that works on the psychological contamination produced by the culture of domination and helps women to build new and confident selves. As a foundation for social and political change, this work of women is a very thorough preparation indeed.

The sixth premise of Naess' deep ecology is the *complexity, not complication principle.* It favors the preservation of complex interrelations which exist between parts of the environment, and inevitably, it involves a systems theoretical orientation. Naess' ideal is a complex economy supported by division, but not fragmentation of labor; worker alienation to be overcome by opportunities for involvement in mental and manual, specialized and nonspecialized tasks. There are serious problems of implementation attached to this vaguely sketched scenario, but beyond this, the supporting arguments are also weak, not to say very uncritical in terms of the stated aims of the deep ecology movement. The references to "soft future research," "implementation of policies," "exponential growth of technical skill and intervention," are highly instrumental statements which collapse back into the shallow ecology paradigm and its human chauvinist ontology. What appears to be happening here is this: the masculine sense of self-worth in our culture has become so entrenched in scientistic habits of thought, that it is very hard for men to argue persuasively without recourse to terms like these for validation. Women, on the other hand, socialized as they are for a multiplicity of contingent tasks and practical labor functions in the home and out, do not experience the inhibiting constraints of status validation to the same extent. The tra-

ditional feminine role runs counter to the exploitive technical rationality which is currently the requisite masculine norm. In place of the disdain that the feminine role receives from all quarters, "the separate reality" of this role could well be taken seriously by ecologists and reexamined as a legitimate source of alternative values. As Snyder suggests, men should try out roles which are not highly valued in society; and one might add, particularly this one, for herein lies the basis of a genuinely grounded and nurturant environmentalism. As one eco-feminist has put it:

> If someone has laid the foundations of a house, it would seem sensible to build on those foundations, rather than import a prefabricated structure with no foundations to put beside it.[5]

A final assumption of deep ecology described by Naess is the importance of *local autonomy and decentralization.* He points out that the more dependent a region is on resources from outside its locality, the more vulnerable it is ecologically and socially: for self-sufficiency to work, there must be political decentralization. The drive to ever larger power blocs and hierarchical political structures is an invariant historical feature of patriarchal societies, the expression of an impulse to compete and dominate the Other. But unless men can come to grips honestly with this impulse within themselves, its dynamic will impose itself over and over again on the anatomy of revolution. Women, if left to their own devices, do not like to organize themselves in this way. Rather they choose to work in small, intimate collectivities, where the spontaneous flow of communication "structures" the situation. There are important political lessons for men to learn from observing and participating in this kind of process. And until this learning takes place, notions like autonomy and decentralization are likely to remain hollow, fetishistic concepts.

Somewhat apologetically, Naess talks about his ecological principles as "intuitive formulations" needing to be made more "precise." They are a "condensed codification" whose tenets are clearly "normative"; they are "ecophilosophical," containing not only norms but "rules," "postulates," "hypotheses," and "policy" formulations. The deep ecology paradigm takes the form of "subsets" of "derivable premises," including at their most general level "logical and mathematical deductions." In other words, Naess' overview of ecosophy is a highly academic and positivized one, dressed up in the jargon of current science-dominated standards of acceptability. Given the role of this same cultural scientism in industry and policy formulation, its agency in the very production of the eco-crisis itself, Naess' stance here is not a rationally consistent one. It is a solution trapped in the given value, the very term *policy* implies a class separation of rulers and ruled. Devall, likewise, seems to present purely linear solutions—"an objective approach," "a new psychology"; the language of cost-benefit analysis, "optimal human carrying capacity," and the language of science, "data on hunter gatherers," both creep back in. Again, birth "control programs" are recommended, "zoning," and "programming," the language of technocratic managerialism. "Principles" are introduced and the imperative *should* rides roughshod through the text. The call for a new epistemology is somehow dissociated in this writing from the old metaphysical presuppositions which prop up the argument itself.

In arguing for an eco-phenomenology, Devall certainly attempts to bypass this ideological noose—"Let us think like a mountain," he says—but again, the analysis here rests on what is called "a gestalt of person-in-nature": a conceptual effort, a grim intellectual determination "to care"; "to show reverence" for Earth's household and "to let" nature follow "its separate" evolutionary path. The residue of specular instrumentalism is overpowering;

yet the conviction remains that a radical transformation of social organization and values is imminent: a challenge to the fundamental premises of the dominant social paradigm. There is a concerted effort to rethink Western metaphysics, epistemology, and ethics here, but this "rethink" remains an idealism closed in on itself because it fails to face up to the uncomfortable psychosexual origins of our culture and its crisis. Devall points by turn to White's thesis that the environmental crisis derives from the Judeo-Christian tradition, to Weisberg's argument that capitalism is the root cause, to Mumford's case against scientism and technics. But for the eco-feminist, these apparently disparate strands are merely facets of the same motive to control which runs a continuous thread through the history of patriarchy. So, it has been left to the women of our generation to do the theoretical housework here—to lift the mat and sweep under it exposing the deeply entrenched epistemological complexes which shape not only current attitudes to the natural world, but attitudes to social and sexual relations as well.[6] The accidental convergence of feminism and ecology at this point in time is no accident.

Sadly, from the eco-feminist point of view, deep ecology is simply another self-congratulatory reformist move; the transvaluation of values it claims for itself is quite peripheral. Even the Eastern spiritual traditions, whose authority deep ecology so often has recourse to—since these dissolve the repressive hierarchy of Man/Nature/God—even these philosophies pay no attention to the inherent Man/Woman hierarchy contained within this metaphysic of the Whole. The suppression of the *feminine* is truly an all pervasive human universal. It is not just a suppression of real, live, empirical women, but equally the suppression of the feminine aspects of men's own constitution which is the issue here. Watts, Snyder, Devall, all want education for the spiritual development of "personhood." This is the self-estranged male reaching for the original androgynous natural unity within himself. The deep ecology movement is very much a spiritual search for people in a barren secular age; but how much of this quest for self-realization is driven by ego and will? If, on the one hand, the search seems to be stuck at an abstract cognitive level, on the other, it may be led full circle and sabotaged by the ancient compulsion to fabricate perfectability. Men's ungrounded restless search for the alienated Other part of themselves has led to a society where not life itself, but "change," bigger and better, whiter than white, has become the consumptive end. The dynamic to overcome this alienation takes many forms in the post-capitalist culture of narcissism—material and psychological consumption like karma-cola, clown workshops, sensitivity training, bio-energetics, gay lib, and surfside six. But the deep ecology movement will not truly happen until men are brave enough to rediscover and to love the woman inside themselves. And we women, too, have to be allowed to love what we are, if we are to make a better world.

Notes

1 John Rodman, "The Liberation of Nature?" *Inquiry* 20 (1977): 83–145; quoted by Bill Devall in "The Deep Ecology Movement," *Natural Resources Journal* 20 (1980): 317.

2 Arne Naess, "The Shallow and the Deep, Long Range Ecology Movement," *Inquiry* 16 (1973): 95–100; Bill Devall, "The Deep Ecology Movement," pp. 299–322.

3 See Ariel Kay Salleh, "Of Portnoy's Complaint and Feminist Problematics," *Australian and New Zealand Journal of Sociology* 17 (1981): 4–13; "Ecology and Ideology," *Chain Reaction* 31 (1983): 20–21; "From Feminism and Ecology," *Social Alternatives* (1984): forthcoming.

4 And on this connection, see Ariel Kay Salleh, "The Growth of Eco-feminism," *Chain Reaction* 36 (1984): 26–28; also comments in "Whither the Green Machine?" *Australian Society* 3 (1984): 15–17.

5 Ann Pettitt, "Women Only at Greenham" *Undercurrents* 57 (1982): 20–21.

6 Some of this feminist writing is discussed in Ariel Kay Salleh, "Contributions to the Critique of Political Epistemology," *Thesis Eleven* 8 (1984): 23–43.

Questions for Discussion

1 Is it true, as Salleh suggests, that women have more direct knowledge of their link with nature than men?

2 Salleh claims that the use of words such as "policy," "norm," and "hypotheses" is inherently "scientist," and reveals a narrowness of outlook which is linked to the attitudes which cause our ecological crisis. Is it possible to avoid using such words in discussion? Is it desirable? What alternatives are there?

3 Are the Judeo-Christian tradition, capitalism, and faith in science and technology all "facets of the same motive to control"?

Legal Rights for Nature

The Wrong Answer to the Right(s) Question

P.S. Elder

In the following article, Elder argues that there is no convincing reason to accept the view of the "deep ecologists" that there are subjects of moral value other than individual sentient creatures. Elder goes on to claim that the existing moral and legal systems are adequate for dealing with environmental problems.

★ ★ ★

Some years ago, Christopher Stone gave an affirmative answer to his own question, "Should Trees Have Standing?"[1] He was independently supported in this conclusion by Laurence Tribe.[2]

I reject Stone's claim that non-animal and perhaps non-living objects ought to have legal standing. The only stone which could be of moral concern and hence deserving of legal rights, is one like Christopher. This may tell today's "deep ecologist" that "anthropocentric" thinkers such as myself, are "shallow"; but epithets do not replace analysis.

In this essay, I will highlight the differences between "shallow" and "deep" ecology, and briefly criticize Stone's position. I will then claim that Stone and the deep ecologists, even if not philosophically confused, do not take us anywhere in solving environmental disputes, that conventional ethics and law do not already go.

Shallow and Deep Ecology

My disagreement with Stone reflects the current debate between the self-described deep ecologists and their shallow opponents.[3] Each term represents a constellation of views about how humans should relate to the natural order. Different camps co-exist under each banner, but shallow ecologists tend to see moral value only in individual sentient creatures, if not solely in human beings. For this reason, they have been called "anthropocentric"[4] as opposed to the "ecocentric" views of deep ecologists. Different proponents in the latter group argue that not only sentient creatures, but all living things, all species, all ecosystems, possibly all things in the entire universe have inherent value and have moral significance independent of their use by human beings, or even of human existence. They decry the "species-ism" in the claim that human beings have unique moral importance. They also reject the "sentientism" which claims that some level of consciousness or capacity for experience is a prerequisiste for moral significance. Indeed, some ecologists have adopted a mystical, ineffable vision of the unity of all:

> [It] then follows...that the distinction between 'life' and 'lifeless' is a human construct. Every atom in this body existed before organic life emerged.... Remember your own childhood as minerals, as lava, as rocks?...We are the rocks dancing. Why do we look down on them with such a condescending air?[5]

Although I have neither the space nor the background to assess the many arguments for each species of shallow or deep ecology, I note that Stone is clearly deep and that I am shallow. Also, animal rights advocates like Tom Regan,[6] whose case rests on sentientism, are shallow ecologists.

Stone's Position

In his article, Stone is "quite seriously proposing that we give legal rights to forests, oceans, rivers and other so-called 'natural objects' in the environment—indeed to the natural environment as a whole."[7] He specifically limits himself to "non-animal but natural objects."[8] This extraordinary leap is based on the following implicit argument. Our environment is seriously degraded by human action which has been based upon a serious ethical mistake. We have failed to see that natural objects, both animate and inanimate, have moral worth in themselves. Our "anthropocentric" ethics value the natural world as a resource to be manipulated at will for human benefit, without regard for the rights of non-animate things. On such a view, even conservationists make anthropocentric utilitarian arguments. Creating rights for these things and allowing the appointment of guardians to invoke these rights will enable us to improve the environmental quality. Presumably for Stone, nothing short of this new "ethical" framework will enable us to do this.

In discussing the legal implications of his thesis, Stone describes what it means to be a holder of legal rights: first, no entity has a right "unless and until *some public authoritative body* is prepared to give *some amount of review* to actions that are colorably inconsistent with that 'right'"; secondly, "the thing can institute legal actions at his *behest*"; thirdly, "the court must take *injury to it* into account" and fourthly, "relief must run to the *benefit of it.*"[9] Naturally, the inanimate object could institute proceedings only through its guardian.

Stone does admit that even if trees had rights, they could still be cut down on certain conditions. Indeed, the environment might have a different body of rights than humans.[10] He believes that an expansion of environmental impact assessment procedures would be a major step toward protecting rights of the environment.[11] Beyond procedural protection, however, Stone suggests that "some [relatively] absolute rights be defined for the environment by setting up a constitutional list of 'preferred objects.'"[12] Proposals threatening injury to them would "be reviewed with the highest level of scrutiny at all levels of government."[13] Also, Stone argues that plants can communicate their "needs,"[14] but does not explain how rocks can do so. He also believes that economic analysis can quantify loss either on a replacement cost basis or, in the case that is question-begging, on a normative basis of how much something should be valued. Payment into a trust fund for the environment would presumably follow development approval.[15]

Stone believes that this shift in conceptual framework would work into the language of judges and steer their thoughts in the right direction.[16] Perhaps, for example, the burden of proof would be interpreted "far more liberally from the point of view of the environ-ment."[17] Stone even suggests that at the legislative level the natural environment should perhaps be given some sort of proportional representation.[18]

Criticism of Stone

Unfortunately, Stone never reveals why the natural environment has a moral claim. He argues that, since we have progressed morally by extending rights to blacks, women and children, and even to some animals that can suffer, we can (and should) progress further by giving plants and inanimate objects rights.[19] But this is obviously a non sequitur: people and plants are not in the same category, which would be necessary to justify such a conclusion. Even if the grass and plants "need" water, in the sense that they will die without it, why does it follow that we have a duty to water them? Do they have any moral importance?

Stone clearly believes they do, and that is the heart of the matter. But they lack any of the relevant characteristics which make persons of moral importance—awareness, self-consciousness, the ability to formulate goals, act to attain them and to appreciate their attainment. It is, therefore, a distortion of our concepts to claim that plants or non-living natural objects can "want" to survive or remain undisturbed. There is "nobody home" who would care, or who could suffer. And if they do not care, why should we? In short, to paraphrase Gertrude Stein, "When you get there, there's no *their* there."

Deep ecologists admit that trees and canyons lack the human characteristics which we all agree make people of moral importance. They deny, however, that these are the only criteria for an object to have value in and of itself. Yet, following Kant, does not the notion of value presuppose a rational conception of self as subject rather than object? This second order self-awareness or,

[R]eflective capacity of persons...makes them the *source of value*, the objects of moral concern. The reason that persons are the source of value is that the choice of an alternative must *matter* to the chooser; the choice must make the difference, it must be valued. The idea of a choice being valued is intelligible only if the choice is consistent with a concept of one's self.[20]

Stone uses another non sequitur when he argues that, since we can give rights to fictional entities such as corporations, and can create guardians for people who cannot speak for themselves, we can do so for the environment. Maybe we can; certainly these examples have met legal and individual needs in our complex society. The question, again, is why is it morally appropriate to do so? Stone is, remarkably, silent on the matter.

If it cannot matter to canyon or trees if they are irreparably damaged, how are their guardians to know what to argue on their behalf, other than by using their own values? Even if trees "want" less smog in the air, why would they want it? One answer might be to reduce biological strain and to allow the tree to grow bigger or produce more seeds. But equally, the tree could ask that other trees competing with it be cut down for the same reason. Down with survival of the fittest (and perhaps, implicitly, with wilderness)! Civilized trees, bears or deer might reasonably ask that they, like people, be protected from the dangers of the natural environment and be fed and watered by people through the long rigorous winter (or summer in arid regions). As Sagoff comments:

> Are labour saving conveniences only good for people? Environmentalists always assume that the interests of those objects [rivers, mountains, lakes and other natural things] are *opposed to development*. How do they know this? Why wouldn't Mineral King want to host a ski resort, after doing nothing for a billion years? The sea-shore...indicates its willingness to entertain poor people...by becoming covered with great quantities of sand.[21]

At root, therefore, are the deep ecologists themselves not being "anthropocentric" in believing they know what is best for the natural environment? And, what if we disagree about what is best? In the case of an environment with rights, one can imagine government, industry and public interest groups litigating to see who will be named as guardian and thus give content to these "rights."

Suppose we agree with Stone that humans are indeed part of the biosphere and should not be seen as separate and apart. We could draw a radically different conclusion from his: people are a part of nature, and in manipulating the environment to their own ends have simply proven to be better suited for survival. Over the eons of natural processes, ninety-nine percent of species have already become extinct. Why may we now not cause other species to become extinct, by being the stronger competitor? The deep ecologists' answer, one assumes, is that we owe these species moral duties. Why? *Because we're different and the deep ecologists' case rests on this difference.* We are not simply "part of nature." We can understand morality. Indeed, it is the essence of being human which leads to respecting the rights of morally important beings.

Ordinary Ethics Gets Us There Too

The fundamental question is why moral obligations exist and toward whom. Stone is quite right to point out that we already accept obligations to other than fully aware human persons—to babies, idiots and to some extent human vegetables. Who then has rights?

This essay is meant only to show that Stone has not made his case; it is not intended to argue the case for ordinary morality. I would simply state my conclusion: first, that any self-conscious being who can have hopes and wishes about the future, weigh alternatives, freely choose among them and appreciate their attainment, is an object of moral concern. Second, a creature's capacity to feel pain (not merely show some physical reactions as plants and styrofoam cups do) clearly establishes its right not to have unnecessary suffering inflicted even if the creature is not in the first category. Third, there is no other category of morally relevant creatures or things. Thus, if whales, dolphins, apes or fruit flies can be shown to meet the first test, we cannot murder them for food or any other purpose nor can we enslave them. On the other hand, if they can feel pain, but cannot conceptualize (an impossibility to at least one serious thinker[22]) we can kill them for food and even experiment on them as long as they are not caused to suffer unduly.

These conclusions may not seem emotionally satisfying. Deep ecologists may even think such views can be held only by vandals or philistines. This is not so. They need not lead to pillage or to Coney Island. Many shallow ecologists, including myself, feel peace, delight and awe when in the wilderness. We respect life. We also feel great personal distress about the diminishing wilderness or impending extinction of beautiful animals or plants. But here are human reasons for us to let them or wilderness environments, survive—so that many people, shallow or deep, will not suffer anguish at their disappearance. Thus, rigorous environmental protection follows from shallow ecology as well as deep. Indeed, of Arne Næss's seven characteristics of deep ecology, I can support at least five.[23]

Conventional Law Can Do It

Whether or not Stone's murky intuitive claims are philosophically sound, a great deal of philosophic and legal fuss can be avoided if our present, conventional legal notions can achieve the same result. Since all of law is a human construct, it follows that we can identify any matter of concern and legislate about it, if we want to. Whether or not non-humans have rights, only humans can be actors in the legal system and it must follow that only human concerns could ever be addressed by it. If society has the will to create rights for non-humans, we can a fortiori use sovereign legislating power to protect the environment by giving new rights to people.[24] A wide range of policy and legal techniques is available within existing legal and moral paradigms. For the moment, I will ignore the real problem, lack of political will; this exists whether or not a conceptual or merely technical shift is required.

Stone's main policy thrust seems to be an extension of environmental impact assessment and procedures to ensure a heavier weighting of environmental criteria.[25] Clearly, this can be done with our existing notions. Many suggestions have been made: legislate environmental criteria which must be considered by decision-makers and allow court challenges under broader rules of standing for failure to meet minimum standards of procedure or substance in decision-making;[26] guarantee the rights to public interest groups or concerned citizens to participate in open hearings with full information and financial aid to intervenors; extend environmental impact assessment to include the social and economic environments; and mandate a more searching inquiry of broad alternatives to the proposed project. For instance, decision-makers (and thus public hearing bodies) could be required to consider evidence that insulation and other energy conservation policies would be a cheaper "source" of new energy than developing tar sands or frontier hydrocarbons and, in addition, that conservation creates more employment.[27]

Further, the ambit of impact assessment could be extended to both private and public projects, and even to those which are individually insignificant if a predicted series of them would, in the aggregate, cause a significant impact. Programs or even legislative proposals would require assessment.[28] Funds for environmental mitigation or reclamation could be established. Decision makers in all levels of government involved in this assessment could be required to use legislated criteria, which presumably Stone would favour. For example, projects having significant environmental impacts might be authorized only "if no feasible and prudent alternative exists" and "if all possible planning to minimize harm" has been done.[29]

It is widely agreed that our society has failed to protect its citizens adequately from harm caused by the production or use of many chemicals and from manufacturing processes. Technology assessment might prevent the production or use of new chemicals or processes until society is satisfied that no unreasonable long range human health problems or environmental damage will occur. Legislatively, a particular burden and standard of proof could be placed on the proponent of the technology; the weight of the burden could be statutorily defined. If scientific uncertainty and difficulty in the prediction of harm is inevitable,[30] development may have to be slowed down dramatically. Also, we must think more carefully about whether limited or pilot approvals should be considered.

In Canada, for instance, the law of standing has been a potential barrier in constitutional, public nuisance and administrative law disputes. Basically, the courts require that a person who sues must demonstrate a particular interest, usually property or person, which has been damaged or threatened, before the lawsuit can proceed. Although the rules, at least in constitutional cases, have been relaxed,[31] legislation can entirely abolish the standing problem if this is thought desirable. Also, lax pollution standards could become more restrictive. However, sophisticated judge-

ment will be necessary to decide if the criminal law model is unsatisfactory.[32] Possibly effluent fees or regional pollution treatment authorities should be considered. Legislation such as *Michigan Environmental Protection Act*[33] can create a substantive right for any citizen to sue to prevent significant environmental harm and even to challenge the adequacy of agency standards. Numerous other techniques are available to the government to shape or even require or prevent behaviour: income tax deductions or credits; compulsory standards (zero pollutant discharge, if deemed feasible); subsidies; education, training and public information programs; pilot or demonstration programs; government procurement requirements; paid advertising; price setting; and constitutional amendments.

For example, the Charter of Rights and Freedoms could be amended to provide some form of a right to a healthy, safe environment. It should be remembered that, although this reform would protect only legal persons, preventing harmful pollutants protects many other species than our own.

No doubt other more imaginative legal innovations and prescriptions for radical social transformation can and should be developed. But enough has been said to suggest that the limiting factor in environmental protection is not the paucity of available legal techniques based on anthropocentric theories of rights. I cannot think of one environmental protection reform which is beyond present institutional or legal scope. Of course, this is not to imply that there exists the will to restore the environment to pristine condition or even that it is necessary to try to do so. But the debate on this is intelligible and capable of resolution within our traditional ethics. We do, however, need rigorous public debate about the failure in many spheres of policy to apply traditional moral principles of justice (rights) and consequentialist goals, such as maximized happiness or minimized suffering. Stone, Tribe and the deep ecologists are right when they criticize society for favouring values which in the long run are wrong, both from a prudential and a moral point of view. Polluters who fail to internalize their externalities are really solving their disposal or economic problems at the expense of others—the paradigm of ignoring other people's rights. And rights, properly understood, include more than protection of property and the physical person, although again taking these seriously would go far toward solving our problems. Persons have psychological needs, but ethical policy formulation can take these into account.

Environmental and social reform require decisions in the political process, and until the necessary shifts in public attitudes or values occur, the fundamental direction of our society will continue as it is. Participatory decision-making processes may allow us to argue the case for the conserver society, social control over production, zero discharge of highly toxic chemicals, and alternative energy. But, precisely because the legal techniques await policy decisions, it seems a waste of time for either Stone or myself to discuss in detail how legal techniques could help us clean up the environment, if there were the will. There is not. However, the collective lack of will need not render reformers impotent. Careful analysis and tireless political action are both badly needed. Ultimately, decision-makers, in appropriate circumstances, must be persuaded to favour environmental over other interests. Careful ethical analysis will be needed to show the thoughtful ones why they should. Once sound theory is in place, sophisticated political action will be needed to show the others why they had better follow such a lead.

But to return to Stone. He is also right to criticize the casual treatment of the world as a resource, a factory and a dump. It is, first of all, our home and as it is effectively a closed ecological system (save for energy from the sun), decision-makers owe us all a moral duty to respect our rights to "life, liberty and the security of the person."

Our present economic and political systems have failed us. Most people sense this, even if they cannot articulate it. It is now up to political, economic and environmental thinkers to show whether capitalism, socialism or a third, environmentally based political theory can provide guidance for the future. Personally, I doubt that a shared perception of environmental problems and of general prescriptions like decentralized, small-scale institutions, appropriate technology or the conserver society can unite people of the left, right and centre for very long. Ultimately, people will still have to choose who will own or control the means of production and how distribution will occur; "economistic"[34] analysis may not be sufficient, but it is necessary. This is why environmental political parties like the Green Party[35] may be doomed, even though they add other issues like feminism and nuclear disarmament to their program.

The Canadian mixed economy has tried brilliantly to fuse capitalism and socialism. Social welfare programs and Crown enterprises have been accepted by private capital as the price for the latter to remain fundamentally in control. We can opt for this mixed capitalist economy with social mobility for the most able, but in a future without continual growth, the present pattern of distribution will come under increased pressure. In light of these life and death decisions about toxic and carcinogenic pollutants, human starvation, oppression and the threat of nuclear holocaust, deep ecology's argument supporting rights for canyons, trees and mule deer is really a trivial pursuit. It is not the direction in which environmental political philosophy should go.

Postscript

In reading the editors' preface [to *Environmental Ethics: Volume II*], I am struck by the claim that my criticism of nonanthropocentrists is itself a non sequitur because they are "indulging...in theory construction." I think this suggestion is wrong.

First, I doubt that deep ecologists are constructing an entirely new theory such that criticism from within the traditional paradigm of ethics would be irrelevant or, as the editors prefer, a non sequitur. If the deep ecologists' theory were unconnected with morality, it could never accommodate *any* let alone all of the present moral data. Indeed, "moral" would have no meaning like its present one. Nor couled they claim, as they seem to do, that any one (morally) should support their theory.

To try to persuade people that deep ecology is a morally sureior theory is to admit its dependence on conventional ethical theory. It is also to demonstrate that the choice of theory rests on rational argument and that pointing contradictions and non sequiturs is legitimate. Unless deep ecology has also jettisoned logical rules like the principle of noncontradition (in which case the theory cannot even be expressed), rational dialogue entails justification. Justification of something morally just or right is "a matter of the mutual support of many considerations, of everything fitting together in one coherent view."[36]

As I argue here and in "Is Deep Ecology the Way?"[37] deep ecology fails this test.

Notes

1 *Southern California Law Review* 45 (1972): 450. Herinafter, "Standing."

2 Tribe, "Ways Not to Think About Plastic Trees: New Foundations for Environmental Law," *Yale Law Journal* 83 (1974): 1315.

3 Næss, "The Shallow and the Deep, Long-Range Ecology Movement. A Summary," *Inquiry* 16 (1973): 95.

4 "Anthropocentrism" is a somewhat misleading term. First, all environmental ethics are anthropocentric in that, as far as we know, they can only be prescribed and consciously followed by humans. Second, few people believe that only humans are the object of any moral concern whatever. Almost everybody accords some limited moral significance to those animals who we think are capable at least of having experience of pain and pleasure.

5 Seed, "Anthropocentrism?," in Sessions and Devall (eds.), *Ecophilosophy* 5 (1983): 11-12.

6 See Regan, *The Case for Animal Rights* (Berkeley: The University of California Press, 1983).

7 "Standing," 456.

8 "Standing," 26n.

9 "Standing," 458 (emphasis in original).

10 "Standing," 458.

11 "Standing," 483–86.

12 "Standing," 486.

13 "Standing," 486.

14 "Standing," 471.

15 "Standing," 480.

16 "Standing," 488.

17 "Standing," 488.

18 "Standing," 487.

19 "Standing," 450–57.

20 Thomas L. Harper and Stanley M. Stein, "Persons as the Source of Value: An Alternative Basis for Rational Planning," a paper presented to the Association of Collegiate Schools of Planning, San Francisco (October 1983): 3.

21 Mark Sagoff, "On Preserving the Natural Environment," *Yale Law Journal* 84 (1974): 222 (words in brackets supplied).

22 Janet M. Keeping, *Pain*, unpublished Master's thesis, Department of Philosophy, University of Calgary, 1977.

23 See note 3 above. I support the following five of Næss's seven normative principles of deep ecologists (all emphasis in the original):

1. "Rejection of the Man-in-environment image in favour of the *relational, total-field image*." (p. 95.) Human[s] should not be

seen as isolated from, but intrinsic to, the environment.

2. *"Principles of diversity and symbiosis."* (p. 96.)

3. "Fight against *pollution and resource depletion."* (p. 97.)

4. *"Complexity, not complication"* (p. 97), because of the existence of unifying principles which help us to explain ecosystems.

5. *"Local autonomy and decentralization."* (p. 98.)

I disagree with:

1. *"Biosphere egalitarianism—in principle."* (p. 95.) Næss believes that the equal right to live inheres in all living creatures not just humans subject to some rights of self-defence.

2. *"Anti-class posture"* (p. 96), but only if Næss means to imply that being anti-class involves a refusal to divide living creatures into those having, and those not having, moral significance.

24 The "supremacy of Parliament" may be subject to constitutionally protected rights, but if the constitution interferes with achieving social goals such as rigorous environmental protection, legal machinery exists which can amend the constitution.

25 "Standing," 482-85.

26 See P.S. Elder, "A Survey of Developments in American Environmental Law," in *Pollution Environmental Law Reference Material* (Toronto: Department of Continuing Education, Law Society of Upper Canada, 11 and 12 May, 1972): 149–50. Stone cites one of the same cases. *Scenic Hudson Preservation Conference v. Federal Power Commission,* 354 F. 2nd 608 (1965) (sub. nom., *Consolidated Edison Co. of New York Inc. v. Scenic Hudson Preservation Conference et al.,* cert. denied, 384 US 941, 86 S.Ct. 1462 (1966)) to show this is already happening. Curiously he takes developments in the law of standing as support for his position.

27 See P.S. Elder, *Heating Up Cold Lake—Public Participation and Esso Resources' Heavy Oil Project* (Faculty of Environmental Design, The University of Calgary, Occasional Paper Series, October 1981).

28 Section 102(c) of the *US National Environmental Policy Act* of 1969 requires environmental impact statement on "proposals for legislation and other major federal actions...."

29 This was the legislation binding on the US Secretary of Transportation in *Citizens to Preserve Overton Park Inc. v. Volpe,* 401 US 402, 91 S.Ct. 814 (1971). See Elder, "A Survey of Developments in American Environmental Law," 150.

30 See Thompson, "Water Law—The Limits of the Management Concept," in *Environmental Law in the 1980s: A New Beginning Proceedings* (Calgary: Canadian Institute of Resources Law, 1982), 45; and Howard R. Eddy, "Problems in Resolving Scientific Uncertainty Through Legal Process," *ibid.,* 131.

31 John Swaigen, "Environmental Law 1975–1980," *Ottawa Law Review* 12 (1980): 459. See this useful article for a discussion of various ideas referred to herein.

32 Thompson, "Water Law."

33 See Joseph L. Sax and Joseph F. Dimento, "Environmental Citizen Suits: Three Years' Experience Under the Michigan Environmental Protection Act," *Ecology Law Quarterly* 4 (1974): 1; John Swaigen and Richard E. Woods, "A Substantive Right to Environmental Quality," in Swaigen, (ed.), *Environmental Rights in Canada* (Toronto: Butterworths, Canadian Environmental Law Research Foundation, 1981), 195. This collection is fundamental to the area being discussed herein.

34 Murray Bookchin, *Toward an Ecological Society* (Montreal: Black Rose Books, 1980).

35 The Green Party is a well known political faction in Europe, especially in France and Germany. As well as being environmentalist, its members are deeply democratic (favouring concensus over majority rule) and tend to believe more in direct action than in Parliamentary representation. As well as environmentalism, they support feminism and nuclear disarmament.

The existence of green parties (they are being organized in several provinces in Canada, including British Columbia, Alberta and Ontario) is a source of frustration to socialists who argue that they have the same program. However, "Greens" point out that many socialists support nuclear power, centralized planning and increase material production, all of which are anathema to many environmentalists.

36 John Rawls, *A Theory of Justice* (Cambridge: Harvard University Press, 1971), 23 and 579.

37 *Alternatives* 15 (April/May 1988): 70.

Questions for Discussion

1 Is Elder right to say that, in thinking they know what is in the interests of the environment, "deep ecologists" are being just as anthropocentric as "shallow ecologists"?

2 Is there more of a burden of proof on the "deep ecologists" to show that a whole new perspective is required, or on the "shallow ecologists" to show that the existing approach can handle environmental problems?

3 Elder claims that the existing legal system can provide adequate protection for the environment, but that what is required is a change in public attitudes. Can the law be used as a vehicle for changing attitudes, and if so, how?

Resources and Environmental Policy

Jan Narveson

Canadian philosopher Jan Narveson is a supporter of the libertarian view that liberty is the most important individual value, and thus that restrictions on liberty such as those imposed by taxes (e.g., for welfare or health care) should be eliminated or minimized. In this article, he combines that view with some arguments about the nature of resources and population pressures to arrive at the conclusion that there are no real global shortages calling for collective action to combat them. In short, Narveson not only disagrees with some of the other authors here about how to deal with environmental problems, he denies there are any real environmental problems which need dealing with.

★   ★   ★

Introduction

No one needs to have it proven that the big news these days is The Environment. People are persuaded that we are "endangering the planet"; walls are decorated with "I love the Earth" or "Every Day is Earth Day", and so forth. Canada has put Out a "Green Paper", detailing lots of expensive legislation allegedly designed to "protect the environment". Styrofoam cups are the object of derision (and, of course, restrictive legislation); DDT has long since been stricken from the list of available resources; a pound of PCB is worth half a million dollars of politically-engendered expenditure. And we have been told for decades that the earth is finite, that resources are limited, scarce, that there is danger of a "population explosion", about which we must "do something"; and so on.

We cannot take on all of this at once here, but I shall devote attention in this paper to one very major—indeed, in obvious ways, *the* major—assumption underlying all this, namely, the claim that natural resources are scarce, fixed, finite, limited. From this premise all sorts of interesting and important conclusions are drawn. The most important, perhaps, from the general human point of view is the inference that population "problems" threaten us, and thus that we need to restrict population growth. This translates especially, in current circumstances, into policies that could easily look, to the impartial observer, pretty racist: for the "we" who need to do the restricting, and the "populations" that allegedly need restricting turn out to be quite different in racial respects: of course it is we enlightened middle-class white folks in the rich countries who need to do something to impose restrictions on the supposedly burgeoning populations of the unenlightened brown, black, or yellow folks.

By way of counterbalance to this racist-looking tendency, there is ample room for upper-middle-class hair-shirtism as well—in the end, we are impartially hard on everybody, on balance. For it is often claimed that there is a horrendous "imbalance" between, say, the North and the South. Thus I have heard it said that Canada, the per capita most energy-use-intensive country in the world, uses something like 40 times the energy per capita that India does. Those who point this out seem to think that something important follows from this—not that the Indians could maybe use a bit more, but rather that *we* need to use quite a lot *less*. And why? Because energy is "finite", limited, and so more for us is less for them, which is thought to be *unfair*.

I shall not discuss here the subject of whether it would be unfair even if it were true,[1] since my main interest in this is to persuade you that it is not true, that people's reasons for thinking it is true rest partly on ignorance of fact, but far more on conceptual confusion, propelled by politically-engendered boondoggling.[2] Admittedly the realm of facts used to be thought to lie beyond the province of us Olympian philosophers—we were not to sully our hands with such things. While there is still *some* reason to think something of the sort, we should draw the line at levels of ignorance that leave us out of touch with reality, which is the situation today in regard to matters environmental. Besides, typically philosophers have taken this plunge. It's too late to retreat to pristine a priorism.

But the main burden of this paper, which is addressed not just to philosophers[3] but to all those who are currently involved with these issues, is the conceptual point about the nature of resources.

One cautionary note. My paper, as befits a philosopher, concerns the *global* situation, the situation for humankind at large and the whole planet on which we live. Scarcities for particular people and groups of people are, of course, a fact of life and always, indeed necessarily, will be. Part of the object here, indeed, will be to define, or rather, since it's so simple a matter to do so, to remind us of the meaning of the notion of scarcity. But today we are told on all fronts that it is indeed *the world* that faces scarcities. It is that claim that I wish to lay firmly to rest. In the senses in which these claims are put forward, they are all *false*.

This is very good news for us humans, though for some reason it seems to fall very unwelcomely on intellectuals' ears these days. That, indeed, is one of the reasons I am discussing this. The other is that it is extremely important for policy at all levels: personal, local, Provincial or State, national, and global. Wrong assumptions about this matter make a drastic difference to our lives, and on a reasonably liberal and humane normative perspective, the differences made by errors on the matter are all very much for the worse.

Natural Resource Scarcity: The Argument

In general reaction to most of the global environmentalist fearmongers, I shall propose in this essay a general theorem about resources. To explore this, let us look at what would have to be shown by the pessimists. Their standard form of argument must go something like this:

1. There are particular kinds of natural resource, X such that people *require* some amount of X in order to live [or [1a], a critically important variant, to live at such-and-such a "level"];

2. Resource X is *finite;*
3. *Therefore,* Resource X is *scarce;*
4. Therefore, "we" must *do something* before it's too *late.*

The conclusion, (4), is invariably of the form that *collective, politically imposed* control must be exercised over the relevant population [the world's, ours, or whichever is in question], and/or that population's consumption of X—and *soon,* before people start dying in droves, or their "quality of life" declines below some threshold (implicitly or explicitly defined by the theorist or researcher issuing the admonition in question).

The argument in form seems plausible, and has proven remarkably seductive. I am among those formerly seduced: in all of my own earlier work on population questions[4], abstract though it was, I assumed that *some* such argument must be sound: that there are at least some values of X, relevant to the argument, for which some such conclusion holds. But it is, as I will show, wrong. It is wrong in fact, and more importantly for high-level policy purposes, it is wrong *in principle.* Specifically, I shall argue:

1. Its opening premise, for all interesting and relevant values of X, is simply *false.*
2. The reasoning from premise (2) to premise (3) is *fallacious*: scarcity just does not follow from finitude. Even for many important specific types of what are currently considered resources, indeed, finitude is perfectly compatible with the resource being *empirically unlimited*, in relation to *any feasible* level of demand, extending indefinitely into the future.
3. It is wildly off in its third premise, that resources are (globally) scarce in any sense that would support the conclusion; it is empirically refuted at every turn of the clock, for reasons of a very general and fundamental type, of interest to social theorists.

4. The fourth claim wouldn't strictly *follow* even if the first three were true; under the circumstances, of course, it is blatantly erroneous.

Conclusion: insofar as the conclusion of this argument is thought to follow from the types of premises considered, it should be rejected. There are other and darker reasons why people would want to limit other people's family sizes, consumption of various things those people enjoy, and so on. I shall touch on these at the end, but they are not the immediate concern of this essay. Let us now proceed to detailed analysis.

On being "necessary"

The opening premise is crucial: that there are at least some resources to which the rest of the argument applies, some specific kinds of things which are essential to life, or at least to a "decent" life or a good one. And it does seem plausible at first glance. Don't we require food and water, say, and surely living space? Of course, we do. But none of these is necessary for life, or for life at any particular "level", in any sense in which it is either *inherently* or in any *relevant* sense "finite" or necessarily "scarce". Air, for instance, is actually a source of oxygen, which in a pinch can be supplied independently of "air"—witness astronauts and deep-sea divers, etc. Water we may grant (a similar manœuvre as for air can be made, but is not worth making). But of course water is, as we will see further below, not even in fantasy "scarce" on a global level. Food is, of course, necessary: however, nature does not contain any "food". All it contains are things like apples, mollusks, yaks, and a very few, very primitive (and no longer much used) varieties of certain grains. *No one* of these is "necessary for life". Indeed, if nutritional needs is what we are talking about, then probably all of them, even now, could be met by *wholly* synthetic substances, just as probably all of them now are met, for most people we know, by specific substances which never existed prior to a century ago—e.g., specific varieties of grains that never grew in the wilds but were created by geneticists and agricultural biologists.

The point here is that as regards *specific substances*—the only things that there are—no one of them and no few of them can plausibly be regarded as essential to life, either "quantitatively" or at any "quality" level you might wish to specify. Of course there are normative issues kicking around here. You can always find some enthusiast who insists that you "haven't lived" until you've tried X, where X range over Wheaties, oat bran, single-malt Scotch, and no end of other items. Need I say more?

Minima and Decency

The first premise is made to look more plausible by insisting, not on the minimum level of X needed to keep a human life going at all, but on the minimum needed for a "decent" or "acceptable" level. Of course as soon as you get into this, you are into highly debatable and subjective matters. American welfare cases have income levels that would be the envy of any but upper-class Pakistanis. Yet lower class Pakistanis *exist,* they are and have for thousands of years *lived.* Not too many theorists in the West are quite arrogant enough to say that we should go and exterminate all those below-the-minimum low-lifers, but a surprising number of them seem to think that it is nevertheless our moral duty to prevent them from coming into existence in the first place. Why?, one might ask. (We'll return to that point later.)

Meanwhile, I will shortly go farther out on my limb and propose that there is *no* minimum level high enough to make the argument go through.

Substitution

One main general point in respect to premise (1) is that for any actual specific substance you can name—call it X—we can *do without* X just fine, by utilizing something else, Y, instead. And the availability of Y depends, for all practical purposes, *entirely* on *technology* (which, of course, also requires human energy) and scarcely at all on the existence of definite quantities of particular natural substances. With the very doubtful exceptions of water, air, and space, there are no other instances in which premise (1) holds true at the global level. And in the case of water, air, and space, substitution (depending on what you count as a "substitute") is unnecessary, as will be detailed below, since they are in no relevant sense "finite" anyway.

Finitude

Plato loved mathematics, and philosophers have always been greatly impressed by mathematical notions, among them the notion of the "infinite" and hence the "finite". But when we are arguing about resources, the fact that the number of cubic meters of this or that is not *infinite,* which is as near as never mind to being a necessary truth anyway, is obviously not relevant. A *resource* is relative to a *use.* The word "resource" is incomplete: to be a resource is to be useful *for* some purpose. When it is said that "resources are finite", it is of no relevance to point out that the available quantity of a given substance that currently supplies the demand in question is measured by what mathematicians call one of the "natural" numbers. What matters is whether it is *realistically conceivable* that we might *run out* of the stuff some day. If a resource is adequate to *any realistically possible need,* then it is not *relevantly* "finite". "Finite" should, in these contexts, imply "potentially scarce", on some reasonable criterion of scarcity (as will be discussed in the next point). The claim that stuff is in the out-

and-out mathematical sense finite is of no interest for present purposes. No argument whose premise is merely that something or other is "finite" is, as it stands, capable of supporting *any* of the interesting conclusions we are looking at here.

From Finitude to Scarcity?

We drink water in at one end—but then, out it comes at the other (and through our pores and in our breath). Clean it up, and it's all ready to be used again. And again, and again. (The astronauts are merely a specially high-tech case of this.) The amount of water in the world is, of course, "finite" (though immense). But in global terms, it is in no interesting way "scarce". It can be very scarce at certain points in the Sahara if you are an ill-prepared traveller, to be sure, and the cost of supplying clean water for populations with fabulously high standards of cleanliness in such matters, such as ourselves, may sometimes go up for awhile. But globally? Forget it!

The same is true of food and air (more details below). In goes the food at one end, and out the other comes fertilizer and materials for replenishing the earth. The earth's "biomass", as the current jargon has it, does not decrease. Astronauts live in a closed-cycle environment: 100% of what they take in is converted into reusable food, water, and air. For us terrestrials, resources are, at the global level, *infinite in relation to any conceivable demand.* Finitude does not entail scarcity.

The same analysis, more surprisingly, applies to those more specific, less "essential" resources of which we are so fond, such as iron, copper, gold, oil, and you-name-it. To a considerable extent, of course, these too are reusable and recyclable. More important, as has already been noted, is that they are *indefinitely substitutable.* Who can straightfacedly claim to *know* what the houses, means of transportation, etc., etc. of typical North Americans will

be mostly made of 100 years hence? Perhaps interesting to the philosophically inclined is that, given enormous amounts of energy, we could probably literally *make* all of these substances if we really wanted to: new and far more sensible versions of alchemy have turned out to be distinctly possible, just as the production of new plants and animals by selective breeding and by genetic splicing. But for the foreseeable term, it is unnecessary, because in fact we are not anywhere near to running out of anything, even with present technologies. Nor will we be. Ever.

With regard to these other sorts of resource, there is a further basic reason why "finite" doesn't entail "scarce": it is that we learn to use these substances *more efficiently.* We get more miles per gallon, more bridge per ton of steel, and so on. If the rate at which we dig into the earth's resources declines even as we make more and more things with those resources, then of course the picture of a supply that is dwindling remorselessly already begins to lose its ominous quality. Technology, in other words, is again the essential catalyst. And technology is, of course, driven by the market. (It is also, as we will be emphasizing further below, in principle literally unlimited.) The very fact that known resources are getting harder to come by, when that is so, spurs research on how to use them better. And the research is always successful, a fact which it is a major purpose of this essay to persuade readers should be utterly unsurprising.

Scarcity

Some basic resources are not in any sense even finite, not even potentially scarce. What about the rest, though? Aren't we running low on some resources, such as oil, copper, iron? And what about food? Isn't there starvation? Isn't there reason for concern? The short answers to these questions are, again, negative. We are not "running low" on anything, and there is no reason to think that we will, either sooner *or later*. And the kind of concern we need to have about starvation has nothing to do with global scarcity—or at least not of *food*. Brains, decency, political savvy, yes—but not food or the means to produce it.

Here are a few broad empirical points regarding some major cases, to buttress the analysis.

Food

People just love to prophesy that we are running short of food, even as the surpluses mount skyward in those countries foolish enough to subsidize its production; indeed, those same countries often resort to paying their farmers *not* to grow crops on their agricultural land. (Yet the Government of Ontario is so short-sighted as to impose severe restrictions on the conversion of "prime agricultural land", which Canada with its trivial population needs like another hole in the head, to residential area, which it can really use, or commercial, manufacturing, sports, and other uses. It's *billed* as "far-sighted", of course. But as the number of acres needed to grow a given amount of food declines year after year, and the amount grown continues to mount anyway, this is an odd sort of "far-sightedness"—it consists in staring fixedly backwards on the technological front, and of course averting your gaze from the expressed interests of mere people.)

Food is, of course, locally scarce in countries foolish enough to keep food prices artificially low, and heartless enough to block entry to the mountains of provisions so readily extended by generous wealthy nations. Coercive restriction of agricultural prices, as in Nicaragua and various African countries, provides highly efficient disincentives to their farmers, and outright starvation can indeed result, especially if you then turn loose plenty of well-armed troops to drive people from their land they know how to farm to land they

don't. But that is no reflection on the capacity of either the land or the farmers in those countries to produce food. And the cure for it is by now utterly obvious: *don't do it*. Let farmers and consumers agree on their prices, i.e., let the food production and distribution system be market-driven, and those farmers will cheerfully supply the demand.

All of the actual starvation in the world, since the first half of this century, has been due to politics, and some of it to poor management and technology; *none* of it can be ascribed to globally limited resources (and almost none even to locally limited resources). And this too is unsurprising, again for essentially the same reason. Basically, as I say, the food that goes into us at one end and comes out in different forms at the other converts, by assorted familiar processes, back into food. It is an *inherently* recycled class of products. Malthus was wrong *in principle*.

Land

People talk of a finite supply of agricultural land, for instance, or of fertilizer, and the like, and infer doom from such considerations. Part of the problem with such arguments is conceptual, and we will take that up a little later. But for the moment consider that on recent estimates, enough food can be grown to supply the minimal nutritional needs of an average human on a mere *27 square meters* of earth—about the size of the average living room for a "bourgeois" homeowner. If my mathematics isn't too far off, then at this best-currently-possible output, that's enough to feed 37,000 people with the output from *one* square kilometer (or close to 100,000 per square mile). At that rate, the entire current population of the world could be fed on an area the size of, say, New Brunswick—one of Canada's smallest Provinces. If we suppose that even 1/4 of that efficiency is pretty realistically possible on good farmland, then to feed everyone in the world nowadays would require an area roughly the size of the State of Kansas. With hydroponic farming technology, now beginning to come on stream, food output per unit could beat that by a wide margin. *And there is no limit to this process.* You have to keep your head *very* firmly fixed in the technological sand to mouth Malthusian slogans about food production in the face of what we now know—not to mention what we will know in the future.

Obviously much agriculture is currently far less efficient than that. But the doomsayers need to be talking about *necessary* limits—about resources being *inherently* so limited as to pose serious obstacles to sustained development, even at (mere) current rates. It is to them that we have to point out that both their figures *and their reasoning* are wildly off base. The intrinsic capabilities of known resources even with current technologies are so far beyond requirements that talk of scarcity of resources in this connection is, to put it bluntly, in cloud-cuckooland—as the facts keep on confirming. Agricultural production keeps going up and up, at a pace in advance of population; so does industrial production of all sorts (and would far more still, of course, if the human resources siphoned off into the administration of programs designed to repress it were instead utilized for its further enhancement).

Here's a lovely example of what people who are bound and determined to find a crisis around every corner will say about this matter. Anne Ehrlich tells us that "between 1950 and 2000, acreage of land planted in grains per person worldwide will have shrunk by half. Nearly all the 2.6-fold increase in grain production since 1950 has come from increasing yields (production per acre)."[5] But supposing that she wasn't wrong about that situation (as she is), just what is supposed to be wrong with *that?* She doesn't say—despite the obvious inference from what she does say. For the population of the world has *not* increased by anything like 2.6x since 1950 (it's more like

1.4), so that in fact the amount of food available, on a *per capita* basis, has *greatly increased.* So even if her "facts" about the absolute amount of "farmland" available were correct, what her claims would imply is that the amount of farmland available is becoming increasingly *irrelevant,* that humans can take care of their needs for food admirably on a decreasing amount of land. Her facts are wildly off anyway—acreage under cultivation has *increased* steadily over the past century and is still doing so[6]—yet even if they weren't, why would it *matter,* so long as we can extract more from a given acre, and our capacity to make an acre yield more continues? There is, of course, no reason whatever why the food supply *per person* should keep expanding: individual *people* are not expanding at exponential rates—why should their food supply? (If anything, Americans and Canadians are struggling to keep their food intake *down!*) Alas, Ehrlich's report is no worse than most.

Living Space

If we think in terms of units of space on the surface of the earth, then let us concede abstractly that this is in principle "finite". But again, no conclusions follow. To begin with, consider the fact that most living space nowadays is not *on* the ground. And there is no literally necessary limit to the height to which buildings can be built, thus accommodating many more people on the same area of the earth's surface. When a one-hundred story apartment building comfortably housing 40,000 people could be built on one acre of land, the meaning of the claim that living-space is limited becomes exceedingly unclear. Recall that the term "finite" in these contexts must be interpreted in a *relevant* manner: if a resource is adequate to any realistically conceivable need, then it is not relevantly "finite".

As regards "lebensraum" for people, scarcity is *strictly* academic (in the bad sense).

Julian Simon points out that one million people were claimed to have gathered at once in Tiananmen Square in Beijing. At that density, *every last one* of the one billion Chinese could stand in an area *smaller than the city of Beijing alone*—and it occupies a minuscule percentage of the whole area of China. For that matter, the *entire population of the world* could stand in the area occupied by a town of quite modest size, such as my own modest city in Ontario, Canada (300,000 occupants at present). Of course we don't want to be standing elbow to elbow on the earth. But there is no humanly conceivable scenario in which people would multiply to that extent, making the point utterly academic.

The most densely populated country on earth is Holland. If the whole inhabitable part of the earth were populated as densely as it, there would be more than *fifty billions* of us— a figure which there are excellent and familiar reasons to think will in fact never be reached in any case (in all of the "advanced" countries, natural population change from live births is *negative* and has been for years). Yet the visitor to Holland has no impression of "overcrowding". There are open spaces, forests, meadows, lots and lots of flowers, lots of purely ornamental buildings, walks, and so on. Talk of a world population that is "burgeoning out of control", with catastrophe around the next corner or so, is simply out of line with reality. The fact, in short, is that the present population of the world could increase *tenfold* and it would still *not* be "overcrowded" in any interesting sense of the word. Since there is little reason to think that it will do anything of the sort anyway, *there is no "space issue";* it is a non-issue. The case for imposing artificial restrictions on population growth from limited *global* resources of either food or space is, in short, *nonexistent*.

Other Resources

When people think that things are scarce and must get scarcer, their argument is probably about a scarcity of something else which they suppose is essential to the production of food: not only land, which we have just discussed, but fertilizer, say, or water, or the energy necessary to desalinate or otherwise clean up the water, or something else. It is for this reason that I address the argument in terms of "all *interesting* values of X". What makes a value of X interesting for this purpose is that it is at least in principle plausible to regard it as finite in a sense sufficiently robust to get the rest of the argument off the ground. Iron, for instance, or oil, or whatever, are sometimes claimed to be in such a state of in situ supply that the world must expect serious shortages in the foreseeable future. We can then formulate my "theorem" concerning resources: namely, that in regard to all such resources, the premise of this argument concerning "scarcity" is flatly false, wildly off base. There are *no* relevant global scarcities for this purpose. Arguments based on the contrary are utterly unsound.

Energy

When any particular resource begins to run short or become more difficult to get, substitution of some other resource usually requires an input of energy, and in any case we do— thus far![7]—need energy for heat and the like. And pundits have been quite hyperactive about predicting energy scarcities looming before us, unless we adopt a more primitive lifestyle[8] quite soon. It is useful to appreciate that they are *entirely* wrong in all such predictions, and that there is from the point of view of resource availability *no* reason for concern. There's only the same old familiar reason that each of us always has to economize on our use of resources: so we can have more money to spend on something else. But it is energy supplies especially that bring up the need to be clear about what scarcity is. We turn to that first, and then present some points about energy sources and resources.

Assessing Scarcity: Two Conceptual Approaches

Scarcity is a relative notion, for one thing: a thing is scarce in relation to *need* or *interest,* to what economists call *demand.* And it is also, of course, quantitatively variable. Things aren't just "scarce" or "plentiful", but rather, they are more or less scarce. But what measures that? Here I am indebted (even more than elsewhere) to Julian Simon's revelatory discussion of these matters. Simon distinguishes two ways of "measuring" resources: the "technological", and the "economic" (UR[9], 15–41). The *technological* method consists in trying to come up with some sort of figure purporting to represent the quantity of a certain kind of stuff left in the earth as a whole, such as crude oil. The *economic* method, on the other hand, consists, much more simply, in noting price trends for the resource on the market. To do this, of course, you have to *have* a market; if "prices" are strictly artifacts of the prevailing government's ideology, then they may imply nothing at all about real supply. Luckily, many commodities are on *world* markets, so that no matter what some benighted country may do, it can't keep met prices from telling their story.)

When headline-writers, politicians, and environmentally-inclined philosophers talk of scarcity, they invariably produce forecasts of the first, or technological sort. There turn out to be excellent reasons why this procedure is certain to do nothing but obfuscate the issues. For purposes of global resource estimation— the primary purpose for which doomsday-scenario writers use them—such reports are essentially useless. Here's why.

First: no technologist, no expert, knows now or will in the foreseeable future know what is supposed to be at stake here, namely, the *absolute* amount of oil, iron, gold, and so forth left in the earth as a whole. Simon gives just one small but extremely pregnant example of the problem here: In assessing copper

resources, do we count the copper salts dissolved in the sea? (UR, 31) We can add to that from familiar cases. Is oil from shale and the Athabasca tar sands to be included in the amount of oil left? What about alcohol that can be made from grains, or gasoline from coal? Grain is an open-ended resource—we can grow an indefinitely large amount. Given what has already been said about food production, this means straight off that there is no practical upper bound to the amount of liquid fuel the world could avail itself of. Coal? That is already known by technological methods to be so plentiful that the earth's supply would last millennia even at current rates of consumption, and even without the more efficient utilization that is no doubt possible and is improving daily. And so on.

... Bear in mind ... that whatever the precise truth may turn out to be regarding anything in this area at any given time in the future, it will be to the effect that we have even more than we thought. What we know at any given time is that relative to current methods, we have such-and-such an amount. What we don't know, because we can't, is how much more there *absolutely* is. And what we have every reason to believe is that it will in general be *vastly* more than anybody thought. (For one small example: The amount of copper estimated to be retrievable by current techniques in 1970 was 179% of what it was in 1950.)

The other way of forecasting is the "economist's" way, which consists simply in noting general price trends over reasonably long terms. Prices, of course, fluctuate locally and "prices" that are wholly artificial don't count, since they reflect nothing except the political interests of those who impose them. But prices of commodities relative, say, to the typical income of a working class family do give us a useful measure. If over the long term prices in those terms are declining, then there *cannot* be real scarcity; scarcity cannot be increasing if prices are decreasing on a free market. For of course the owners of resources will hold out for the highest price they can get, and if quantities available decline relative to demand, then prices must go up. Moreover, if the prospects in the nearish future were for restricted supply, people would invest in futures for such products.

But the fact is, that they have gone *down*. *All* of them have, over the years, as Simon details.[11] Not just computers, CD players, and so on, but also coal, iron, oil, electricity—you name it, and a curve drawn over many decades shows a decline. The supply of resources available to satisfy our various desires has in fact been increasing, right along with the increase of population and the rest. It's been increasing for hundreds of years; it is still doing so; and there is every reason to argue, as Simon does, that this can continue *indefinitely*. There is *no* problem of scarce natural material resources, *no* clear-eyed view of the future showing only blackness and its attendant support for imposed restrictions.

Resources and Technology

A further and more "philosophical" reflection on the nature of resources is now in order. Let us ask: What does it mean to say that resources "exist"? Are there kinds of material entities which just simply *are,* as they stand, *resources?* It is quickly apparent on modest reflection that the answers to these questions are, even to a superficial view, almost entirely negative. A deeper look will persuade you that they are in fact *entirely* negative.

Whether something is a resource depends on two things: (1) whether there is a demand (a need, an interest, a positive valuation by someone) for what can be made out of it; and (2) whether somebody knows how to make things that people want out of that stuff. The two factors are by no means independent. We don't generally "demand" what is known to be

unattainable, and of course, as Marx and others observed, we do come to demand what newly becomes attainable despite being previously undreamed of. We develop technologies because we have a fairly good idea what people do and will want—that is, because it is supposed that the results will serve to satisfy demands. We can view technology, and therefore, of course, the people who do the thinking and research necessary to produce it, as a resource, and if we do, then of course it is by every rational measure the *primary* resource.

... The true resource, above all, is the human mind, employed in thinking up better ways to use the world around us. Without it we are nowhere. But without much in the way of gross material stuff, and plenty of ingenuity, we can do very well indeed.

Technology Unlimited

One nice thing about technology is that it is intrinsically extremely easy, in "material" terms, to transfer and replicate. Jones thinks up a good idea, writes it up, and anyone who can read will soon have that same idea, with no further effort on Jones' part plus appropriate use of what has now become a trivial amount of merely "material resources" (with e-mail technology, the quantity of energy and wear and tear on any strictly material resources required is vanishingly close to zero). It was not always so: in ancient Sumeria, inscribing rudimentary messages on clay tablet was a good day's work. And even now you will find philosophical periodicals asking their readers to buy copies of articles at 10¢/page and enormous waiting periods, when you could photocopy them immediately for 2¢/page.

Even if our engineer's or scientist's idea is not shared *very* widely, still, if they and a very few others can translate that good idea into concrete terms, multitudes of consumers can soon be benefiting from it, despite their total ignorance of the underlying technology. Others will then get into the act, finding ways to improve things still more, making the resultant products cheaper so that still more people can enjoy the benefits. *That* is economic growth, and what enables it to happen is technology, including the technology of information transfer.

Our ancestors in the stone age lived in the very same natural world that we did, and the stock of strictly material substances from which they and we draw is presumably pretty much identical with what it was then. Yet we are (comparatively) rich and they were (in the same sense) poor, indeed sub-destitute. The amount of "labor" available *per capita,* remember, was the same then as now: the day is still but 24 hours long for each of us. *100% of the difference* lies in *know-how.* It is the software of humankind that is its true capital, its true wealth.

What is important about this, in turn, is that with each new human added to the world's population, we have one more usable brain, with a concomitant capacity to add to the world's wealth. As Julian Simon points out, children, while they are children, are usually a net cost[12] (and the cost is increasing as the amount of education needed to produce useful skills increases). In primitive countries, children are very soon a net benefit; we in the "developed" world must wait a little longer. But in the normal case, that individual will, in the course of his or her life, make a positive contribution to the world's wealth—*not a negative one.* And of course some among those extra brains will make very great contributions—they will invent, say, the light bulb or the Macintosh computer, or compose Beethoven's symphonies.

That is why resources are, in the final analysis, *not finite* in any relevant senses. That is to say: a "finite" material stock, i.e., a bunch of substances that are in some way quantifiable and when so measured yield "finite" numbers in toto, suffices to enable people with their minds engaged to make themselves and (there-fore) all of us *indefinitely* better off in "material" (as well as any other) respects. What this means is that *more for us* does *not* mean *less for them*—or vice versa. So long as wealth grows by free means, that is, by a series of individually agreeable exchanges rather than by some extracting it from others by force, use of "material" resources is a *positive sum* activity. Then the producers and the users are better off, and those who do not use or produce it at that time are no worse off at that time, either; but in future, they too are better off, for they will be able to avail themselves of goods or services they could not otherwise choose.

It has been insufficiently noticed that to deny the hypothesis of non-finite resources requires a heroic assumption: viz., that we *can predict future technology* sufficiently well to know that, for certain resources, in principle nothing can ever be made that will substitute for them, or that no application of any new methods can ever hope to otherwise improve their supply. To make good on this, one would have to *know already what we do not yet know*—which of course one cannot. Or one would have to show good reason to think that mankind is running out of intellect or creativity. But that is wildly contrary to the facts, on (again) any reasonable view. Indeed, the sheer fact of population increase makes the reverse enormously likely: creative technological thought will increase rather than decrease.

Population Morals

This aspect of the argument ends here. *Every* specific argument for population restriction on the basis of scarcity depends on a premise to the effect that some particular resource is *both necessary and irremediably scarce.* All such arguments are unsound. Either the resource in question is not relevantly finite or it is not literally necessary—something else can be used for the same purpose. If we run out of iron, cars and girders will be made of plastics, which are made out of sand, which is not relevantly scarce. And so on.

A general point must be made about these matters. In all fields of production, everywhere, the familiar story is one of decreasing costs with increasing scale. A firm that produces virtually anything will find itself getting more and more efficient as time goes by, even without revolutionary improvements in its technology. This is due to what has come to be called "the learning curve": the people who do the work simply find ways to do it better, quicker, or with less effort. It is a very, very widely observed phenomenon;[13] equally important, it is a phenomenon that makes excellent sense in common-sense terms. Even academics get better at what they do over the years, despite the initial implausibility of supposing that one can find out better how to have abstract ideas. When we get to the toolroom and the assembly line, the scope for improvements in efficiency is essentially unlimited.

It is a consequence of these facts—that goods cannot be simply identified with quantities of material objects (especially not with quantities of "resources") and that technology is both potent and open-ended—that the very idea that costs of resources will increase as population increases is fundamentally wrongheaded. More people means more brains; more brains means more and better ideas; more and better ideas means more and better genuinely desired goods and services forthcoming from the *same* "finite" stock of material resources. There is every reason to expect that as population increases, so will resources of all the requisite kinds. A working doomsday scenario absolutely requires the assumption that we are stuck in the same technological rut we are in during the period over which the prophet in question gathers his data for the projected shortage. In any but the most short-term context, this procedure is utterly wrong, because the data in question are becoming obsolete with each passing day.

"The Environment"

What I have been saying is directly relevant to the general subject vaguely referred to in the currently modish term "The Environment". "Natural" resources are, of course, part of our environment. But we now need to turn to two other general issues. First, there are extensive questions these days about supposed "environmental deterioration". Those questions raise the underlying issue of just what counts as "deterioration" for something so ubiquitous and varied as the world around us. There are three sorts of answers to consider. The first concerns the potential of our environment for making our lives worse in respect of our organic welfare, e.g. by making them less healthy or shorter. But the others concern the status of environmental considerations themselves. We may divide these in turn into two. One is the matter of aesthetics: we may be interested in a more beautiful environment, independently of its conduciveness to survival and flourishing in physical respects. The other concerns the sort of thing that has been labelled "deep ecology": Is there a separate set of values to be attached to the environment *as such?* Does it, in fact, make any sense to say that *x* or *y harms* a definite entity that one could appropriately call "the environment"? I shall address these, in very general terms, in the next part of this inquiry.

Pollution

In no area are we more bedeviled with the same general type of ill-conceived reasoning, harnessed to emotions and instinctive snap judgments, as in the general area of pollution. It is too large a one to go into great detail here, but the thoughtful reader will already have begun, I daresay, to anticipate the point.

Three Concerns

Pollution concerns may be divided into three sorts, to judge from current statements:

First, and primarily, there are the pollutions that are so considered because they (at least allegedly, in any given case) negatively affect human health.

Second, there are *aesthetic* pollutants: things that are thought, by those who consider them to be pollutants, to make the world around us in some way less attractive.

Third, there are the "deep ecology" people who seem to think that animals, plants, canyons, indeed the "earth" *itself* are actually just like us, more moral agents who have rights on their own account.

Beauty

A few quick remarks on the differences among these are in order. Clearly health is a pervasive and reasonable concern of all of us, and the questions to be asked in that regard are basically about whether the measures that people propose and enact really do promote the goal they are allegedly aimed at, and promote it in a rational way. That will be the main burden of my next remarks. But beauty is another matter.

This second kind of concern raises very difficult problems of how to resolve disagreements. We all have our tastes, our special aesthetic values. Some can express these better than others, but then, why should the aesthetic views of the articulate outweigh those of the people whose aesthetic values would be steamrollered by his proposals? Those who love uninhabited wildernesses, for instance, can have them if the rest of us commit suicide—in an environmentally clean way, of course. But is this a good reason why we should do so? We must at least appreciate that as soon as aesthetic concerns are what are really being invoked, then we are into a very different ball game from claims about health and safety. Moreover, there is no escape, at the public level, from the time-honored principle of "beauty is in the eye of the beholder". We can't expect agreement

on matters of taste. Therefore, the public agenda simply can't specify what is beautiful and what isn't, or which beauties shall be respected and which not. Instead, there is a way to handle this. Each person may incorporate his own selection of beauties on his *own* property; when he deals with others, he must either convince them of the rectitude of his own tastes, or else he must negotiate with them, perhaps buying the other person's property, at a mutually agreed price, so that he can redecorate it on his own terms. The same can be true of nature. If you and I think that such-and-such a bit of nature should be "preserved", or altered, then the rule is easy: buy it, and go to it! Nobody will like this suggestion, because it is the only rational one: the only one that can work with anybody's tastes. We'd all like to dictate the public taste. But we can't, if we are serious about us all being in this together, on equal terms.

Environmental Depth

The third kind of claim has it that the environment has, so to speak, rights of its own, that "the environment" is *intrinsically* valuable. Dealing fully with this view would take a fair amount of separate discussion, for it raises fundamental issues about the very meaning of moral notions. I shall say only a little, but I will say that little. Namely, that morals are rules and principles for appraising our actions in relation to each other. Anything other than people comes into the discussion *only* under the aegis of being *somebody's* interest of some kind. Now, the view that Nature Itself is a sort of moral agent in her own right is, I am bound to say, one of the most deeply incoherent views in the whole philosophical world, not easily matched by any of the legendary metaphysicians. It is also, not coincidentally, a gold mine for "rent-seekers"—people interested in power-trips and bilking an uncomprehending and thus gullible public. Of course it also, and necessarily, shares all the problems of the second category—of which it might charitably be regarded as a species, for that matter. For as soon as it is admitted that one is *not* claiming that cutting the trees, or whatever, will actually damage some human's health or happiness, and yet it is insisted that we should desist *for the sake of the trees themselves,* one is treating trees and other nonhuman entities as though they too were moral beings, with interests, desires, values of their own, to be taken into account in their own right. It is that aspect of "deep ecology" that one has to see to be strictly incoherent. For *there is no such thing as "the interest of the environment",* taken as a moral being in itself, apart from human interests. To say any such thing is on all fours with saying that we should all accept policy X on the ground that that's what the great god Vishnu wants. Those of us who don't accept that there is any such personage will not give any weight to such a demand, and rightly so. We can and ought to do exactly the same with those who advance the interests of canyons, rocks, and forests in their own right. (In fact, it is not at all unfair to describe such views as a sort of pantheistic religion.)

Moreover, there is a single utterly fair and just way of treating them: tell them they're welcome to buy some property and build their own preferred kind of church on it, or get together with fellow believers and preserve weird endangered species, trees, whatever. No problem! But as to considering such claims for one moment as legitimate bases of *public policy,* forget it! Yet you will find much legislation nowadays devoted to protecting endangered species, swamps, you name it, quite irrespective of what such "protection" does to the poor blokes who thought they *owned* the areas in question. This is not liberal government, it is government gone berserk, government sold out to bizarre special interests.

Health and Us

That leaves health. And here too there is a definite message: namely, that the paramount need is to appreciate that health, for any remotely normal person, is *one good among others.* It is *not* a special *kind* of good that takes total priority over all others. In virtually all of the things we do, we take risks to our health and life: when we drive to the grocery store, when we eat too much dessert, and so on and so on. Those risks are, in general, *perfectly rational.* Yet obviously if risks were too great, they would reasonably change our activities. If the probability of getting run over on my way to the store were 80% instead of .00000008%, then of course I'd want to reconsider walking there. *It is, necessarily, all a matter of degree.* We are *always* weighing benefits and costs, where the "costs" are in the form of *risks* engendered by or in the course of the activities we consider engaging in.

Those who impose heavy costs on us on the ground that they are necessary in order to effect a *scarcely measurable decrease* in the likelihood that we or somebody will get cancer, or whatever else your current favorite disease is, are asking us to behave *irrationally.* And the result is that we are worse off; not better. People in Los Angeles, with all of its smog and even with its panoply of social problems, are much better off now than were the bands of natives who occupied the area five centuries earlier, despite the complete absence of smog (maybe—for we don't know how many wood fires they burned!).

Canada currently spends well over two thousand dollars per individual per year on health care. This is a level of expenditure that probably makes no sense from the point of view of most of the people who "benefit" from it. Spending a lot less on medical attention and a lot more on other things that matter a lot more to them would, in most cases, make sense. And when it would, only bad arguments about resources stand in their way, "justifying" governments in forcing those people to shift their personal resources in the medical direction rather than elsewhere. Health is no more a fixed, finite, global resource than anything else. And any policies on pollution, and on a "green" environment, based on such assumptions can only work ill—work to make us worse off on the whole.

Tiny Effects, Linearity, and Paracelsus' Principle

Many centuries ago the famous doctor Paracelsus observed, in response to a question about which things are poisons, that *everything* is, if you take enough of it in the right circumstances; and also that *nothing* is, given small enough quantities and, again, the right circumstances. He had the right answer. But almost all modern regulations depend on violating Paracelsus' dictum. All it takes for an enterprising politician to get on a bandwagon for prohibiting free market access to item X is a "finding" by "scientists" to the effect that X is poisonous, as shown by the fact that if you force-feed some poor unsuspecting rat with an incredibly large amount of the stuff, that rat will get very sick, probably with cancer. For the politician's purposes, the news that substance Y is a "known carcinogen" is great news; and to establish this, all he needs is the information that it *can* cause cancer. The next move is to trot out the latest fancy scientific measuring devices and discover that there is a bit of stuff Y in, say, the water supply, or your favorite brand of ice cream, or whatever. In no time at all, Y will be *verboten*. In Canada you can't buy saccharine over the counter, and manufacturers aren't permitted to install it in your favorite drinks. And why? Because somebody discovered that if you force-feed rats with more of the stuff than any human could conceivably consume (let alone want to), then the rat's grandchildren show a higher likelihood of getting cancer. Neat!

Two general assumptions are needed to justify this kind of regulation, and one specific one. The general ones are (1) Linearity: if X is bad for you, then *any* amount, no matter how tiny, is also bad for you; and (2) that the goal of promoting health is sufficient to justify imposing *any* amount of inconvenience, expense and for that matter danger on the public. The special assumption needed is (3) that rats are good models for people, and that it is reasonable to infer from the bad effects of huge quantities inflicted on rats that normal, voluntary exposures by humans will also result in bad effects.

The interesting thing about these assumptions is that *all* of them are *known* to be false. Linearity down to vanishing input levels is practically unknown in the biological portions of nature, which just aren't that simple, and there is ample new evidence of its falsity regarding various specific substances or processes. No rational person values his health to the absolute subordination of all else. And rats aren't good models for people; moreover, forced consumption isn't a good model of normal consumption. (Force-feeding of anything, such as water, will hasten the onset of cancer, for instance. Paracelsus strikes again!)

…Assumption No. 2 has already been discussed in a general way. But it is useful to add a further dimension to it. It turns out that what's wrong with it isn't just that we reasonably weigh health against other values without assigning it absolute priority. For it is also true that *wealth translates into health.* The wealthier are in general healthier, and this too can be quantified. We can say pretty definitely that if we reduce income, we reduce life expectancy. And so if we tax away a whole lot of money from some people in order to try to "save" the lives of others, then at some point, the transfer becomes *medically* uneconomic: the *cost in life expectancy* of the transfer *outweighs the proposed saving.* When does this happen? Precise figures would be hard to give and of course vary, but it seems to be in the range of a half to one million dollars per saved life. Programs that spend fifty million dollars to save ten lives are not just wasting a lot of money—they are also costing a net of forty *lives* lost. Even those who think that health must take priority over all else will have to be impressed by this, if (as seems very likely) the premises are right.

The Sad Tale of DDT

Back in the sixties everybody was reading Rachel Carson's *The Silent Spring,* a runaway best-seller whose message was that chemical crop treatments, with DDT at the top of the list, were doing in the birds and, at the rate we were going, their merry chatter would become a thing of the past. She seems to have found the ideal time for her message, which to this day influences all kinds of well-meaning people. One of the things it influenced such people to do in her day was to get DDT officially pronounced to be Evil (poisonous). Evidence on the subject had nothing to do with this, it seems—people who tried to detect the alleged poisons were very hard put to do so, except for one thing: its effects on mosquitoes were very poisonous indeed. So poisonous, in fact, that careful use in those areas of the world in which malaria and yellow fever were major killers all but eradicated those diseases. In Sri Lanka, for example, there had been almost 3 million cases of malaria in 1948, the year Dr. Paul Muller was given a Nobel Prize for discovering DDT. By 1963, after 15 years of spraying, there were 17 (yes, *seventeen).* But then the U.S. ceased the spraying, under the influence of the Carsonites, and within a few years the number was back up to 2.5 million. World-wide, there was real hope by 1970 of eradicating this major killer from the face of the earth. But six years after the U.S. ban was imposed, there were 800 million cases, with 8.2 million deaths per year.

Moreover, due to the timing of the halt, resistant strains of malaria developed which travellers could bring home, so that even the United States can look forward to a recrudescence of these deadly scourges,[14] though no doubt Americans can afford to substitute more expensive and less effective chemicals for the amazingly effective and inexpensive DDT, thus continuing its track-record of quasi-racism in such matters.

The story against DDT turns out to have been just about 100% fabrication, but that is not typical. What is typical is to ban things on the ground that they contain *some* traces of, say, carcinogens, by far the favorite target. Banning things with all but undetectable levels of carcinogens turns out to be one of the more irrational activities that legislators have ever turned their fertile minds to. It is now well established that virtually all carcinogenic materials are found in our daily diets—fruits, for instance, are loaded with them—so that if you wanted to eliminate all carcinogens from your diet, your only alternative would be starvation. These natural carcinogens absolutely overwhelm any residuals from plant sprays or most other sources of *synthetic* chemicals in our diets.[15] ...

Economizing

Let me conclude by emphasizing a note on which I began. Each particular person on this world operates in an environment of scarcities. There are lots of things we would like more of, but our limited budget, of time, energy, money, or of specific other resources, requires us to choose among them. Economy is optimization: trading some resources for others that we suppose have higher value for us.

But from the fact that each person rationally operates in this manner, it does not follow that there are *global* scarcities, "shortages" in *the world as a whole,* such that *collective* policies are required to deal with them, even though these policies impose *uneconomic* costs on the individuals concerned. Thus we are required to use paper cups instead of styrofoam, despite the fact that the former costs several times as much, is in every respect worse from the disposal and energy-consumption points of view, and is much less convenient—cold coffee, burned fingers, and so on. And why? Because of a highly speculative[16] *hypothesis* about the influence of styrofoam on the ozone layer and its alleged implications for our ultimate health. That the risks involved even if the hypothesis were correct would, when related to any particular individual, show the cure to be much worse than the disease does not deter environmentally rabid governments from imposing those costs on us gullible citizens. But that is the story of virtually all of the currently contemplated legislation, and its reasoning is the same. Clean air, health, etc., are held to be resources superior to others even if you or I would, given our choice over the actual values involved, prefer the others. And they are held to be intrinsic goods, *necessary,* and globally scarce.

The moral is: don't you believe it. By all means, let us have more technical investigation into pollution, water purity, and so on. But let's integrate all this important information into rational decisions, rather than having it operate as the minor premise in an argument whose major premises have to do with globally finite resources and the like. What we have today is a classic case of misuse of science by government. It has already cost us considerable, and it will continue to do so. I hope to have shown that a major part of the reasoning behind most environmental policy forays is hopelessly unsound. And the policy implications from their erroneous premises are certainly going to make life worse for you and me.

Science and Politics

It is time to summarize and provide some explanation of a continuing theme in the fore-

going. If you read the newspapers or listen to politicians, the story you will hear will be by and large diametrically opposite to the one I have been recounting above. Why should you believe me instead of them? You should, of course, delve into the responsible literature on these matters and find out for yourselves....

But I do owe you an explanation of why the news from the "pop" sources is so largely disastrous, in both senses of the term. There is an answer, and it's one that we really have to be aware of in democratic countries. The first point is an important one about human psychology: *Good News is boring.* News about disasters turns us on; "news" about one more good day on top of all the others puts us to sleep. It's not surprising, but it is something that should make us a bit wary. If what we want is disaster, then the message for reporters is clear: *exaggerate!* So is the message for politicians. If you want to get elected, find yourself a disaster which you can proclaim your readiness to Do Something About. And *every* politician wants to get elected, right?

There's another thing. When you walk into the voting booth, the apparent cost to you of voting for one candidate or one policy rather than another is essentially zero. Your protective instincts and your huge supply of human sympathy and brother love and suchlike will induce you to vote for the politicians who will proclaim that things *are* on the brink of disaster *but* you can help by voting for Me, who will fix them up! A clearheaded, rational calculation of the risks of trying to use this candidate's means for the proposed ends isn't at all likely. That takes hard work and thought—quite the reverse of what it takes to come up with a rousing cheer for the candidate who proclaims that *His* Administration will "Get the Country Back on its Feet" with a vigorous program of this or that. (In my country, Canada, "Job-Creation" was the magic slogan that swept the new leaders into power in the last election; I'm told it had something to do with Mr. Clinton's presence in the White House as well. There is, and is known to be, no rational sense to top-down "job-creation" as a supposed economic policy—but in which politician's interest is it to mention *that,* anyway? People who know things like that hate politics, and the rest wouldn't have a prayer of getting elected.) Similarly with someone who will spend a whole lot of your money Protecting you from Cancer by stamping out carcinogens in trivial quantities from harmless substances. All *you* see is the looming disaster and the magnitude of the effort. You do *not* see the paucity of underlying reasoning, the numerous large facts that render the few little ones supporting the politicians or the "environmental activists" not only ungrounded but counterproductive. You won't get elected and you won't get newspapers sold if you insist on confining yourself to the truth. It's a familiar story from centuries of human experience—but its price tag today is probably the highest it's ever been, due to the inimitable characteristics of Democracy which, as you know, is rule by the ignorant. The issues in this area are, in any case, more technical than they've ever been, making the unsuspecting layman a prime target—where typical PhD's are ignoramuses, how can we possibly imagine that ordinary people won't be?

In my old-fashioned view, though, government is justified *only* by its service to people. People are not well served by half-truths or by bad reasoning. And academics, it seems to me, should be devoting themselves to the truth as well, rather than to what will get them bigger grants from those very politicians. As between two rival scientific hypotheses, which will we opt for: the more plausible one? Or the one that will get us the bigger grant? When the grant is provided by a government agency or by a group that seeks or depends on political favor for its support, it is not an accident that the two do not coincide very well. And when the results of research are re-

ported to the public through newspapers that are much more interested in selling a titillating story than telling us what's going on in the world, then the results are hardly surprising. Which doesn't make them any more acceptable, in my or, I trust, *your* book.

Notes

1 I don't think it would be, in fact, and argue this in "Property Rights: Original Acquisition and Lockean Provisos"—currently unpublished but available from the author.

2 In the sixties and seventies, especially, other prophets were busy forecasting mass starvation, and it became popular for everyone, including philosophers, to think of the earth as a sort of "lifeboat". At the same time that all this forecasting was being publicized at a remarkable rate, the facts were busy proving them wrong, as they had been doing in the previous century or so that had elapsed since the publication of Thomas Malthus' *Essay on Population.*

3 This paper was prepared for the meetings of the Ontario Philosophical Society in Ottawa, Canada, October, 1991.

4 The main ones are: "Utilitarianism and New Generations" *Mind,* 1967 Reprinted: M. Bayles, *Ethics and Population* (Cambridge: Schenkman, 1976); "Moral Problems of Population" *The Monist,* Winter 1973; "Future People and Us", R.I. Sikora and Brian Barry, eds., *Obligations to Future Generations,* Philadelphia: Temple University Press, 1978.

5 Anne H. Erhlich, "People and Food", *Population and Environment,* vol. 12, No. 3, Spring 1991, pp. 223–224.

6 Julian Simon, *Population Matters* (New Brunswick, NJ: Transaction Press, 1990), pp. 115–117.

7 Advances in the art of house insulation, however, can reduce our requirements of energy for this purpose virtually to zero. Super-insulated houses—which are by no means uneconomic to build, costing only perhaps 20% more than conventional ones of similar size—already require *no* energy to heat beyond that supplied by the people in them, plus their usual burning of lightbulbs.

8 Most primitive people, in fact, squander energy and generate massive pollutions while they are at

it. Those following this course have to accompany their recommendations with proposals to severely reduce population on top of it, not realizing that this is due precisely to the inefficiency of the proposed alternatives.

9 "UR" = Julian Simon, *The Ultimate Resource* (Princeton, 1981). ...

11 Julian Simon, *Population Matters* (New Brunswick, NJ: Transaction Press, 1990), Ch. 2, pp. 63–158, presents a wealth of information on these matters.

12 See his *Population Matters* (Rutgers, NJ: Transaction Publishers, 1990), p. 177: "To be sure, in the short run an additional person—baby or immigrant—inevitably means a lower standard of living for everyone; every parent knows that."

13 See George Gilder, *The Spirit of Enterprise* (NY: Simon & Schuster, 1984), for many examples.

14 The story is to be found in Dixie Lee Ray's *Trashing the Planet* (Washington: Regenery, 1990), pp. 68–77.

15 Dixie Lee Ray and Lou Guzzo, *Trashing the Planet* (Regnery Gateway, 1990), pp. 76–77.

16 For the full story, see Ray & Guzzo, *op. cit.*, Ch. 6.

Questions for Discussion

1 What does it mean to say a resource is "scarce"? Is there more than one way to interpret this claim?

2 Narveson suggests that environmentalism is like a religion, which (like other religions) should not be imposed on those who do not accept it, but which people can practice freely on the land they own themselves. Is he right?

3 To what extent can a free capitalist market be expected to protect the environment?

The Sinking Ark

N. Myers

Human beings have been responsible, directly or indirectly, for the extinction of many different species of plants and animals. In the following selection, Myers discusses the relationship between consumerism and such extinctions, and argues that environmental issues must be understood within a network of interdependent global problems. In particular, the relationship between the developed nations and the developing nations must be changed if we are to put an end to the extinction of species which is spiralling out of control.

★   ★   ★

Ask a man in the street what he thinks of the problems of disappearing species, and he may well reply that it would be a pity if the tiger or the blue whale disappeared. But he may add that it would be no big deal, not as compared with crises of energy, population, food and pollution—the "real problems." In other words, he cares about disappearing species, but he cares about many other things more: he simply does not see it as a critical issue. If the tiger were to go extinct tonight, the sun would still come up tomorrow morning.

In point of fact, by tomorrow morning we shall almost certainly have one less species on Planet Earth than we had this morning. It will not be a charismatic creature like the tiger. It could well be an obscure insect in the depths of some remote rainforest. It may even be a creature that nobody has ever heard of. A unique form of life will have been driven from the face of the earth for ever.

Equally likely is that by the end of the century we shall have lost 1 million species, possibly many more. Except for the barest handful, they will have been eliminated through the hand of man.

Extinction Rates

Animal forms that have been documented and recognized as under threat of extinction now amount to over 1000. These are creatures we hear much about—the tiger and the blue whale, the giant panda and the whooping crane, the orangutan and the cheetah. Yet even though 1000 is a shockingly large number, this is only a fractionally small part of the problem. Far more important are those many species that have not even been identified by science, let alone classified as threatened. Among the plant kingdom, these could number 25,000, while among animals, notably insects, the total could run to hundreds of thousands....

...By the time human communities establish ecologically sound life-styles, the fallout of species could total several million. This would amount to a biological débâcle greater than all mass extinctions of the geological past put together.

Loss to Society

We face, then, the imminent elimination of a good share of the planetary spectrum of species that have shared the common earth-home with man for millenia, but are now to be denied living space during a phase of a mere few decades. This extinction spasm would amount to an irreversible loss of unique resources. Earth is currently afflicted with other forms of environmental degradation, but, from the standpoint of permanent despoilation of the planet, no other form is anywhere so significant as the fallout of species. When water bodies are fouled and the atmosphere is treated as a garbage can, we can always clean up the pollution. Species extinction is final. Moreover, the impoverishment of life on earth falls not only on present society, but on all generations to come.

In scores of ways, the impoverishment affects everyday living right now. All around the world, people increasingly consume food, take medicines and employ industrial materials that owe their production to genetic resources and other startpoint materials of animals and plants. These pragmatic purposes served by species are numerous and growing. Given the needs of the future, species can be reckoned among society's most valuable raw materials. To consider the consequences of devastating a single biome, the tropical moist forests: elimination of these forests, with their exceptional concentration of species, would undermine the prospects for modernized agriculture, with repercussions for the capacity of the world to feed itself. It could set back the campaign against cancer by years. Perhaps worst of all, it would eliminate one of our best bets for resolving the energy crisis: as technology develops ways to utilize the vast amount of solar energy stored in tropical-forest plants each day, these forests could generate as much energy, in the form of methanol and other fuels, as almost half the world's energy consumption from all sources in 1970. Moreover, this energy source need never run dry like an oil well, since it can replenish itself in perpetuity.

Any reduction in the diversity of resources, including the earth's spectrum of species, narrows society's scope to respond to new problems and opportunities. To the extent that we cannot be certain what needs may arise in the future, it makes sense to keep our options open (provided that a strategy of that sort does not unduly conflict with other major purposes of society). This rationale for conservation applies to the planet's stock of species more than to virtually any other category of natural resources.

The situation has been well stated by Dr. Tom Lovejoy of the World Wildlife Fund:

> If we were preparing for a new Dark Age, and could take only a limited number of books into the monasteries for the dura-

tion, we might have to determine which single branch of knowledge would have the greatest survival value for us. The outstanding candidate would be biology, including its applied form such as medicine, agriculture, forestry and fisheries. Yet we are doing just the contrary, by busily throwing out the biology books before they have been written.

Many other biologists—switched-on scientists, not "case-hardened eco-nuts"—believe that man is permanently altering the course of evolution, and altering it for the worse. The result will be a grossly impoverished version of life's diversity on earth, from which the process of evolution will be unlikely to recover for many millions of years. And it is not going too far to say that, by eliminating an appreciable portion of earth's stock of species, humanity might be destroying life that just might save its own.

Species Conservation and Economic Advancement

There is another major dimension to the problem, the relationship between conservation of species and economic advancement for human communities.

As indicated, the prime threat to the species lies with loss of habitat. Loss of habitat occurs mainly through economic exploitation of natural environments. Natural environments are exploited mainly to satisfy consumer demand for numerous products. The upshot is that species are now rarely driven extinct through the activities of a few persons with direct and deliberate intent to kill wild creatures. They are eliminated through the activities of many millions of people, who are unaware of the "spill-over" consequences of their consumerist lifestyles.

This means that species depletion can occur through a diffuse and insidious process. An American is prohibited by law from shooting a snowy egret, but, by his consumerist life-

style, he can stimulate others to drain a marsh (for croplands, highways, housing) and thereby eliminate the food supply for a whole colony of egrets. A recent advertisement by a utility corporation in the United States asserted that "Something we do today will touch your life," implying that its activities were so far-reaching that, whether the citizen was aware or not, his daily routine would be somehow affected by the corporation's multifaceted enterprise. In similar fashion, something the citizen does each day is likely to bear on the survival prospects of species. He may have no wanton or destructive intent toward wildlife. On the contrary, he may send off a regular donation to a conservation organization. But what he contributes with his right hand he may take away with his half-dozen left hands. His desire to be a consumer as well as conservationist leads him into a Jekyll-and-Hyde role. Unwitting and unmalicious as this role might be, it becomes even more significant and pervasive every day.

Equally important, the impact of a consumerist lifestyle is not confined to the home country of the fat-cat citizen. Increasingly the consequences extend to lands around the back of the earth. Rich-world communities of the temperate zones, containing one-fifth of earth's population, account for four-fifths of raw materials traded through international markets. Many of these materials derive from the tropical zone, which harbors around three-quarters of all species on earth. The extraction of these materials causes disturbance of natural environments. Thus affluent sectors of the global village are responsible—unknowingly for sure, but effectively nonetheless—for disruption of myriad species' habitats in lands far distant from their own. The connoisseur who seeks out a specialty-import store in New York or Paris or Tokyo, with a view to purchasing some much-sought-after rosewood from Brazil, may be contributing to the destruction of the last forest habitat of an Amazon monkey. Few factors of the conservation scene are likely to grow so consequential in years ahead as this one of economic-ecologic linkages among the global community.

True, citizens of tropical developing countries play their part in disruption of natural environments. It is in these countries that most of the projected expansion of human numbers will take place, 85 percent of the extra 2 billion people that are likely to be added to the present world population of 4 billion by the end of the century. Of at least as much consequence as the outburst in human numbers is the outburst in human aspirations, supported by expanding technology. It is the combination of these two factors that will precipitate a transformation of most natural environments throughout the tropics. Equally to the point, impoverished citizens of developing nations tend to have more pressing concerns than conservation of species. All too often, it is as much as they can do to stay alive themselves, let alone to keep wild creatures in being.

Plainly, there is a lot of difference between the consumerdom of the world's poor majority and of the world's rich minority. For most citizens of developing countries, there is little doubt that more food available, through cultivation of virgin territories (including forests, grasslands, wetlands, etc.), would increase their levels of nutrition, just as more industrial products available would ease their struggle for existence in many ways. It is equally likely that the same cannot be said for citizens of the advanced world: additional food or material goods do not necessarily lead to any advance in their quality of life. The demand for products of every kind on the part of the 1 billion citizens of affluent nations—the most consummate consumers the world has ever known, many making Croesus and Louis XIV look like paupers by comparison—contributes a disproportionate share to the disruption of natural environments around the earth.

For example, the depletion of tropical moist forests stems in part from market demand on the part of affluent nations for hardwoods and other specialist timbers from Southeast Asia, Amazonia and West/Central Africa. In addition, the disruptive harvesting of tropical timber is often conducted by multinational corporations that supply the capital, technology and skills without which developing countries could not exploit their forest stocks at unsustainable rates. Such is the role of Georgia Pacific and Weyerhauser from the United States, Mitsubishi and Sumitomo from Japan and Bruyzneel and Borregaard from Europe. Similarly, the forests of Central America are being felled to make way for artificial pasture-lands, in order to grow more beef. But the extra meat, instead of going into the stomachs of local citizens, makes its way to the United States, where it supplies the hamburger trade and other fast-food business. This foreign beef is cheaper than similar-grade beef from within the United States—and the American consumer, looking for a hamburger of best quality at cheapest price, is not aware of the spillover consequences of his actions. So whose hand is on the chainsaw?

A further source of destruction in tropical forests is the shifting cultivator. There are at least 140 million of these people, subsistence peasants who often have nowhere to sink a digging hoe except the virgin territories of primeval forests. Theirs is a form of agriculture that tends, by its very nature, to be inefficient: it is highly wasteful of forestlands.

It could be made intensive rather than extensive, and thus relieve the pressure on virgin forests, through the perquisites of modern agriculture, notably fertilizer to make a crop patch productive year after year. But since the OPEC price hike in 1973, the cost of petroleum-based fertilizer has been driven sky-high—and has been kept sky-high through inflated demand on the part of affluent nations (Americans and Europeans use as much fertilizer on their gardens, golf courses and cemeteries as is used by all the shifting cultivators of tropical forestlands). As long as the price of fertilizer remains beyond the reach of subsistence peasants, there is less prospect that they will change their agricultural practices. Part of the responsibility for this situation lies with the OPEC cartel, part with the excessively consumerist communities of the advanced world.

An Interdependent Global Community

Looked at this way, the problem of declining tropical forests can be seen to be intimately related to other major issues of an interdependent global community: food, population, energy, plus several other problems that confront society at large. It is difficult to make progress on all the others at the same time. This aspect of the plight of tropical forests—the inter-relatedness of problems—applies to the problem of disappearing species in general.

Similarly, the advanced-nation citizen can hardly support conservation of species while resisting better trade-and-aid relationships with developing nations. The decline of tropical forests could be slowed through a trade cartel of Tropical Timber Exporting Countries. If the countries in question could jack up the price of their hardwood exports, they could earn more foreign exchange from export of less timber. For importer countries of the developed world, the effect of this move would be a jump in the price of fine furniture, specialist panelling and other components of better housing. Would an affluent-world citizen respond with a cry of protest about inflation, or with a sigh of relief at improved prospects for tropical forests? For a Third-World citizen, it is difficult to see how a conservationist can be concerned with the International Union for Conservation of Nature and Natural Resources, without being equally concerned with the New International Economic Order.

A second example concerns paperpulp. There could soon be a shortage of paperpulp to match present shortages of fuel and food. The deficit could be made good through more intensive exploration of North American forests, or through more extensive exploitation of tropical forests—both of which alternatives might prompt outcries from environmental groups. A third alternative would be for developed-world citizens, who account for five-sixths of all paperpulp consumed world-wide, to make do with inadequate supplies, in which case the cost of newsprint would rise sharply. So perhaps a definition of a conservationist could be a person who applauds when he finds that his daily newspaper has once again gone up in price.

In accord with this view of the situation, this book emphasizes that problems of threatened species and disappearing forests can be realistically viewed only within a framework of relationships between the developed world and the developing world.

A prime conservation need everywhere, and especially in tropical regions, is for countries to set aside representative examples of their ecosystems in order to protect their stocks of species. In other words, to expand their present networks of parks, such as they are, by establishing systems of protected areas. However, many developing countries are in no position to designate large tracts of their territory as "off limits" to development. (Through their present efforts to safeguard the bulk of the earth's species, they in effect subsidize the rest of the global community.) If emergent regions of the tropics are to help protect the global heritage of species for the community at large, the community should see to it that their development prospects are not thereby penalized. In short, ways must be devised to make conservation programs economically acceptable and politically palatable for developing nations.

How Far Should We Go to Save Species?

Just as the whooping crane is not worth more than a mere fraction of the United States' GNP to save it, so the preservation of species in all parts of the planet, and especially in tropical regions, needs to be considered within a comprehensive context of human well-being. Anthropocentric as this approach may appear, it reflects the way the world works: few people would be willing to swap mankind, a single species, for fishkind with its thousands of species.

So the central issue is not "Let's save the species, come what may." Rather we should ask whose needs are served by conservation of species, and at what cost to whose opportunities for a better life in other ways. Instead of seeking to conserve species as an over-riding objective, we should do as much as we can within a framework of trying to enhance long-term human welfare in all manner of directions.

As we have seen, people already make "choices" concerning species. Regrettably they do not make deliberate choices after careful consideration of the alternatives. Rich and poor alike, they unconsciously contribute to the decline of the species, in dozens of ways each day. Not that they have malign intentions toward wild creatures. According to a 1976 Gallup Poll, most people would like to see more done to conserve wildlife and threatened species—87 percent in the United States, 89 percent in Western Europe, 85 percent in Japan, 75 percent in Africa, and 94 percent in Latin America (though only 46 percent in crowded India). Subsistence communities of the developing world have limited scope to change the choice they implicitly make through their ways of making a living. Rich-world people, by contrast, have more room to maneuver, and could switch to a stronger expression of their commitment in favor of species. Meantime, through their commitment to extreme consumerism, they in effect express the view that they can do without the orangutan and the cheetah and many other species—and their descendants, for all ages to come, can likewise do without them. In theory, they would like the orangutan and the cheetah to survive in the wild, but in practice they like many other things more. However unwittingly, that is the way they are making their choice right now.

Fortunately, affluent-world citizens will have plenty of scope to make a fresh choice. They may find it turns out to be no easy choice. If they truly wish to allow living space for millions of species that existed on the planet before man got on his hind legs, they will find that entails not only a soft-hearted feeling in support of wildlife, but a hard-nosed commitment to attempt new lifestyles. While they shed a tear over the demise of tropical moist forests with their array of species, they might go easy on the Kleenex....

How Species Arrive and Disappear

The evolutionary process that throws off new species, speciation, has been under way virtually since life first appeared. As a species encounters fresh environments, brought about by factors such as climatic change, it adapts, and so alters in different ways in different parts of its range. Eventually a new form becomes differentiated enough to rank as a new species. The parent form, if unable to fit in with changed circumstances, disappears, while the genetic material persists, diversified and enriched.

By contrast, some species are not so capable at the process of adaptation and differentiation. This applies especially to those that have become so specialized in their lifestyles that they cannot cope with transformed environments. They fade away, and their distinctive genetic material is lost forever.

Since life began about 3.5 billion years ago, vast amounts of unique genetic formulations have been eliminated. The total number of species that is believed to have existed is put at somewhere between 100 and 250 million,[1] which means that the present stock of species, estimated at 5–10 million, represents between 2 and 10 percent of all species that have ever lived on earth. It also means that extinction is not only a biological reality, but it is a frequent phenomenon under natural circumstances. Moreover, whereas the process of speciation is limited by the rate of genetic divergence, and so generally throws up a new species only over periods of thousands or millions of years, the process of extinction is not limited by any such constraint, and can occur, through man's agency, within just a year or two, even less.

How many species have existed at each stage of evolutionary history is only roughly known. The fossil record is so limited that it is a pitiful reflection of past life. But it now appears likely that, after a gas cloud solidified into the present planet approximately 6 billion years ago, earth remained lifeless for another 2.5 billion years. When life eventually appeared, it left virtually no trace of its existence for a long time, except for micro-fossils of early algae such as have been found in Swaziland. Not until about 1500 million years ago did nuclear-celled organisms appear, and not until about 700 million years ago, following an outburst of evolutionary activity during the Cambrian period, did most modern phyla become recognizable. This array of species diversified only gradually, or even remained pretty constant, for the best part of 400 million years, until it crashed spectacularly with the extinction of many marine organisms towards the end of the Permian period. Thereafter the abundance and variety of species steadily increased, until a further mass extinction during the late Cretaceous period, 70 million years ago, put an end to around one-quarter of all families, including the dinosaurs and their kin. Since that time the trend has been generally towards ever-greater diversity

of species. In short, the evolutionary record does not show a steady upward climb in earth's total of species, rather a series of step-wise increases. The current stock of species is reckoned to be 10 or even 20 times larger than the stock of species inhabiting the Paleozoic seas before the Permian crash.[2]

During the past few million years, however, extinction rates seem to have speeded up. At the time of the late Pliocene, some 5 million years ago, there may have been one-third more bird species than today.[3] During the early Pleistocene, around 3 million years ago, a bird species probably had an average life expectancy of 1.5 million years. This span progressively contracted until, by the end of the Pleistocene, it could have amounted to only 40,000 years.[4] Equally likely is that the pace of speciation has probably speeded up, and full speciation among certain classes of birds could now be far more rapid than the quarter of a million years once believed necessary. Indeed, it conceivably takes place in as little as 15,000 or even 10,000 years.

The house sparrow, introduced into North America in the 1850s, has thrown off a number of clear subspecies during the course of only 110–130 generations.[5] In certain circumstances, for instance when new variations are radiating from an unspecified ancestor, a new plant species can evolve, it is estimated, in only 50–100 generations.[6] (Experiments with fruit flies, under special laboratory conditions that serve to "force the pace," show that speciation can occur in less than a dozen generations.) Among mammals, with generally slower breeding rates than birds, the average life expectancy for a species could now be, under natural circumstances, around half a million years.

Man's Impact on Extinction Rates

More recently, extinction has stemmed increasingly from the hand of man. For much of his last 50,000 years as a hunter-gatherer, primitive man, perhaps in conjunction with climatic upheavals, proved himself capable of eliminating species through over-hunting and through habitat modification by means of fire.[7] In the main, the process was relatively rare and gradual. By around the year A.D. 1600, however, man became able, through advancing technology, to disrupt extensive environments ever more rapidly, and to employ modern weapons to over-hunt animals to extinction in just a few years. It is from this recent watershed stage that man's impact can no longer be considered on a par with "natural processes" that lead to extinction. Of course, this is not to say that natural extinction is not still taking place. The Labrador duck appears to have disappeared through no discernible fault of man, while the white-nosed saki of Brazil has been losing more of its range to other Amazon monkeys than to man.

To reduce the history of species on earth to manageable proportions, suppose the whole existence of the planet is compressed into a single year. Conditions suitable for life do not develop for certain until May, and plants and animals do not become abundant (mostly in the seas) until the end of October. In mid-December, dinosaurs and other reptiles dominate the scene. Mammals, with hairy covering and suckling their young, appear in large numbers only a little before Christmas. On New Year's Eve, at about five minutes to midnight, man emerges. Of these few moments of man's existence, recorded history represents about the time the clock takes to strike twelve. The period since A.D. 1600, when man-induced extinctions have rapidly increased, amounts to 3 seconds, and the quarter-century just begun, when the fallout of species looks likely to be far greater than all mass extinctions of the past put together, takes one-eighth of a second—a twinkling of an eye in evolutionary times.

It is sometimes suggested that, as some sort of compensation for the outburst of extinctions now under way, two evolutionary processes may gather pace, one a natural process and the other contrived by man. The argument in support of the first process is that as species disappear, niches, or "ecological living space," will open up for newly emerging species to occupy. In fact so many vacant niches could appear that they might well stimulate a spurt of speciation. Sound as this argument is in principle, it is a non-starter in practice. The present process of extinction, vastly speeded up, will not lead to anything near a similarly speeded up process of speciation. As natural environments become degraded under man's influence, there will be few areas with enough ecological diversity to encourage many new species to emerge. Furthermore, as natural environments become homogenized, there will be little geographical isolation of populations, and hence little reproductive isolation of genetic reservoirs, to enable speciation to continue as it would under less disturbed conditions.

The second argument deals with man-contrived speciation. Opportunities are now emerging to synthesize genes in the laboratory by combining segments of the master molecule of life, DNA, from different species. This opens the way to creation of forms of life distinct from any that now exist. Regrettably this argument too is not valid. Producing a new species will be costly in the extreme, far more so than conserving the gene pool of virtually any species in its natural habitats. Moreover, a synthetic species may not be adapted to conditions outside the laboratory, in which case it may either quickly be eliminated or may encounter no natural controls to restrict its increase.

Meantime, man's activities, especially his mis-use and over-use of natural environments, continue to drive species extinct at an increasing rate. From A.D. 1600 to 1900, man was certainly accounting for one species every 4 years. From the year 1900 onwards, the rate increased to an average of around one per year. These figures refer, however, almost entirely to mammals and birds; and they are limited to species which man knows have existed and which man knows have disappeared. When we consider the other 99 percent of earth's stock of species, the picture appears far different from a "mere" one species per year.

...[I]t is likely that during the last quarter of this century we shall witness an extinction spasm accounting for 1 million species. The total fallout could turn out to be lower; it could also, and more probably, turn out to be higher. Taking 1 million as a "reasonable working figure," this means an average of over 100 extinctions per day. The rate of fallout will increase as habitat disruption grows worse, i.e., toward the end of the period. Already, however, the process is well underway. In the region where rainforest destruction is most advanced, Southeast Asia, we can expect a wave of extinctions by the mid-1980s. Thus it is not unrealistic—in fact, probably optimistic—to say that we are losing one species per day right now. Within another decade, we could be losing one every hour.

Notes

1 Brodkorb, B.P., 1971, Origin and evolution of birds, *Avian Biology* 1:19–55.

2 Gould, S.J., 1975, Diversity through time, *Natural History* 84 (8):24–32: Stebbins, G.L., 1971, *Processes of Organic Evolution*, Prentice-Hall, Englewood Cliffs, New Jersey.

3 Fisher, J. and Peterson, R.J., 1964, *The World of Birds*, Macdonald Publishers, London.

4 Moreau, R.E., 1966, *The Bird Faunas of Africa and Its Islands*, Academic Press, New York.

5 Johnstone, R.F. and Selander, R.K., 1971, Evolution in the house sparrow, *Evolution* 25:1–28.

6 Huxley, A., 1974, *Plant and Planet*, Allen Lane Publisher, London.

7 Martin, P.S. and Wright, H.E. (editors), 1967, *Pleistocene Extinctions: The Search for a Cause*, Yale University Press, New Haven, Connecticut.

Questions for Discussion

1 Why should we be concerned with the loss of species, as opposed to limiting our concern to individual sentient beings? Is this a *moral* concern, or is it of some other type (e.g., aesthetic)? Does it matter that extinction is, to some extent, a "natural" phenomenon?

2 Myers claims that the possible uses of genetic materials for medicines, food, and industrial purposes make them among our most valuable resources. How should we balance such potential benefits against more certain immediate benefits of land-use, etc?

3 How much limitation on consumerism should be imposed in the name of environmental concern? If some such change is desirable, how should it be brought about?

New and Future People

What Should We Do About Future People?

Trudy Govier

It is often argued that we have an obligation to protect the environment now for the benefit of future generations. There are a number of problems which arise, however, when we try to take future people into consideration in our moral reasoning. Many of these flow from the fact that these people do not exist yet (and thus are what are sometimes called "possible people"), and sometimes our decisions will affect whether they will exist at all, and which particular people will exist, as well as what the quality of life will be for any people who exist in the future. How are the interests of future people to be weighed against those of people who already exist? In this article, Govier considers a number of problems raised by the notion of future people, and provides an account which attempts to solve some of the most complicated of these issues.

★   ★   ★

There are primarily two kinds of contexts in which the question arises as to whether and how we ought to take into account the interests of people who do not yet exist. One kind of context is that in which an action we are contemplating would significantly affect those people who do not exist at present but are likely to exist in the future. The other is that in which we are deciding whether or not to have children. I shall argue that these two kinds of contexts are importantly different in that the interests of prospective, but non-existent, people bear differently on each. The contrast which is involved here is tied to the contrast between *predicting whether someone will exist*, on the one hand, and *deciding whether to produce him,* on the other. In this paper I shall propose an account of the moral status of prospective, but nonexistent, people which is based largely on this contrast.

The account I shall propose fulfills what I think are three very desirable conditions. First, it makes intelligible the moral requirement that we pay some attention to the needs of future generations. Second, it is compatible with an asymmetrical view about reproductive morality: it is wrong to have a child who

would likely be miserable if born, but not wrong to refrain from having a child who would be happy if born. And third, though it gives prospective people *some* moral status, it does not entail that their interests should weigh equally in our moral calculations with those of already existent people.

Concerning the second two conditions mentioned, some references to philosophical literature are perhaps in order. First of all, there is the matter of asymmetry. It has been argued that while the very likely unhappiness of a prospective person is a good reason not to bring him into existence, happiness which he would be likely to experience if born does not provide good reason to produce him. This view was put forward by Jan Narveson in his book *Morality and Utility* and in several published papers.[1] Critics have questioned whether the asymmetry to which Narveson committed himself in these works can be justified. Recently he himself expressed certain misgivings about it.[2] It might well appear that if we are to consider the pain and unhappiness which a prospective person would likely experience as constituting reason *not* to produce him, then we ought also to consider whatever pleasure and happiness he would be likely to experience as reason for producing him. On this issue, I am strongly inclined to agree with the view which Narveson initially held and has repeatedly argued for in print. I think that some of the considerations brought out later in the paper can help to buttress this very plausible asymmetry.

Then there is the matter of weighing the interests of those who do not exist yet against those of people who already do exist. Philosophers have often written as though future people are just as real as present ones. They just happen to differ from present people with respect to the time at which they exist. Time, these philosophers would argue, is no more a morally significant property than hair color or number of freckles. Therefore, this view has it, the interests of future people are every bit as important as those of present people; future people should be accorded all the rights accorded to present people. L. W. Sumner once claimed that if we give a preference to presently existing people in our moral reasoning, if we weight their needs and interests more heavily than those of people who do not exist yet, we are *violating moral canons of impartiality*.[3] I think that it is a mistake to go this far in defending the interests of future generations; the account I shall put forward here provides reasons for the belief that this is a mistake.

Much of the philosophical literature to which I shall allude from time to time concerns the issue as to whether utilitarianism has as its most reasonable interpretation the *total view* or the *average view*. On the total view, utilitarianism directs us to maximize the happiness in the world and minimize the misery in the world. If people could be produced who would be *even slightly happy* and whose existence would not lessen the total happiness of existing people more than their own happiness would increase the happiness in the world, then, on the total view, such people

ought to be produced. This consequence does not hold on the average view, wherein it is permissible to produce only those new people whose happiness will result in an increase in the happiness of the whole population *on the average*. The present paper does not address itself to this issue of total versus average utilitarianism. It is intended to be relatively independent of specific moral theories and to be compatible with any moral theory which allows that the rightness or wrongness of actions *depends at least in part on their effects on people's well-being*.[4] My account shares with defenses of average utilitarianism the refusal to allow that there is any obligation to bring people into existence which arises from the likelihood that they would be happy if they existed. However, it departs from some current versions of that doctrine by taking into account the interests of prospective people in other contexts.

In some contexts where we must consider the interests of prospective people, we are making a decision which is *not* a reproductive one. We are making a decision about some non-reproductive activity—say damming a river or using an insecticide. And the problem is that pursuing the activity is likely to change *those who are likely to exist in the future*. In this kind of context, there is a high probability that there will be people to be affected by our action and this probability is *relatively independent of the performance of the action*. If, for instance, we consider damming the river above Peterborough, we ought to consider how that action would affect people who are likely to exist in Peterborough in 100 years' time. Most of those people, whoever they will be, do not exist now, but there *are* likely to be people in Peterborough in 100 years. This likelihood is relatively independent of whether we dam the river or not.

In such a context these prospective people whose interests bear on our decision are possible people, possible in an epistemic sense. By saying this, I mean that there is some likelihood that they will come to exist; that we in effect *predict* their existence with some degree of probability. It is in order to do this when the moral issue which concerns us is *not* a reproductive one. If a moral agent, *A,* is making a decision, D_1, about an action, Q_1, wherein the likelihood of the existence of prospective persons, *X* and *Y,* is relatively independent of the performance of Q_1, *X* and *Y* are *epistemically possible* for *A,* in the context of that decision.

If, however, an agent is making a moral decision which is a reproductive one, that is a context in which it is inappropriate to think of her prospective child as epistemically possible. Someone who contemplates having a child cannot properly *simply* calculate a probability of her child coming into existence for that probability depends on what she decides to do. Where *X* is the prospective child, the probability of *X*'s existence is precisely *not* independent of her action. If she decides to have a child and takes steps in that direction, then there is typically a fairly *high* probability that a child of hers will exist. And if she decides not to have one, and takes steps in that direction, there is typically a fairly *low* probability that a child of hers will exist. In this context, the prospective but non-existent child is *volitionally possible;* the agent is deciding whether to produce it, not estimating whether it will come to exist. To be more precise, if an agent, *A,* is making a decision, D_2, about an action, Q_2, wherein the likelihood of the existence of some prospective person, *X,* is highly dependent on Q_2, then *X* is volitionally possible for *A,* in the context of D_2.

For stylistic convenience, I shall speak of epistemically possible people and of volitionally possible people. But this way of speaking should not be taken to indicate some kind of ontological division among possible people. It is merely a convenience to omit a full reference to the context. However, the distinction between epistemic and volitional possibility is one which is relative to context. Persons who

might come to exist are *epistemically possible* in that there is some probability of their coming to exist and *volitionally possible* for their prospective parents, or for someone else.

Of course, the clearest and most common case in which possible persons are volitionally possible for us is when we are prospective parents. A child is volitionally possible for someone who is deciding whether to use contraceptives or whether to have an abortion. For a god creating a world, its inhabitants are volitionally possible, and if a mad scientist set out to furnish a rocket with sperm and ova which would form developing embryos, the prospective inhabitants of that world would be volitionally possible for him. The god, or scientist, would have to decide whether to produce people and how many to produce. So volitional possibility is not logically tied to prospective parenthood.

There are less fanciful cases in which people are volitionally possible for others who are not their prospective parents, but most have morally problematic aspects to them. A doctor can be in a position where he has effective control over whether his patient has offspring, and in that case her children are for him volitionally possible. A guardian might similarly control whether one of his wards had offspring. And in some circumstances a government could be in such a position that future citizens of a country would be volitionally possible for that government. But the control needed for this would be extraordinary indeed. In any normal case governments only formulate and implement policies which provide incentives or disincentives to parenthood, and they do not decide whether to bring people into existence or not. It is not my purpose in this paper to pursue the question of who should decide whether more children are born. I have a strong inclination to think that prospective parents, and particularly prospective mothers, should make this decision in almost all cases, but I shall not argue for this view here.

Most of the time when we reason about nonexistent people, these people are for us epistemically possible, not volitionally possible. Those future generations whom we believe to have rights to clean air and an aesthetically tolerable environment are epistemically possible; so too are my great-grandchildren, and those people who will grow to adulthood in the northern environment resulting from pipeline construction in the Yukon. Though none of these people exist, all are epistemically possible and there are contexts in which we feel intuitively that their interests should bear on our decisions.

I would contend that it is slightly misleading to talk about future people. Future people are those epistemically possible people the probability of whose existence is very high. We do not know that there will be future generations; we do not even know that there will be human beings alive in 2095, much less in the year 4000. When we speak of future generations, we do so in the belief that it is highly probable that there will be humans at the time in question, and on the assumption that *whether* there will be people then is very largely out of our individual control. For instance, it is highly probable that there will be people living in Peterborough, Ontario, in 2095; those possible people identified as the inhabitants of Peterborough in 2095 are *epistemically possible* for us. They likely will exist, and there is not much that we as individuals can do about this one way or the other. Given the high probability of their coming to exist, and our almost total lack of control over this, it is understandable that we should speak and think of these "future generations" of Peterborough as though they will quite certainly come along. This may explain why some philosophers maintain that "future people" differ from us only in the morally incidental respect that their birthdays just happen to be on dates later than ours and later than the present date.

However, we do not know that there will be any future people, and we cannot know that there will be any. In moral deliberations, the best we can do is to base our decisions on the very best evidence we have. With reference to "future people," this evidence can never tell us that some people *do* have birthdays later than the present date; it can only tell us that it is very likely that people will be born. For the purposes of moral reasoning, it is misleading to think that *there are future people,* who differ from us only with respect to the time at which they exist. Rather, there are people who for us are epistemically possible and whose existence is highly probable.

I shall pause here to try to defend what I am saying, as it is definitely at odds with the view other philosophers have taken. Jan Narveson says:

> Now *future persons,* as the term implies, *are simply persons* whose birth dates lie some temporal distance in the future relative to us. Apart from that, *they are real people,* actual people, flesh and blood people like ourselves. And it would be difficult to think of a more elementary requirement of morality than that the mere fact that someone's birth date is what it is cannot justify treating him in accordance with a quite different basic set of moral rules from others. Whatever we want to claim are the basic rights of persons, we will be committed to the implication that persons existing a hundred or five hundred years hence also have them.[5] (my emphasis)

The italicized statement seems rather at odds with Narveson's later claim, in the same paper, that "it is at any rate in principle (or perhaps 'ideally') always due to a decision (certainly an act) of ours that the next generation contains just the persons it does, and therefore, *partly due to our decisions that any future earthlings exist.*"[6] If future persons are as real as we are, and if we have genuine alternatives when we decide, how can it be a matter of our decision whether there are any future persons at all? There seems to be some tension in Narveson's view here. The answer to this dilemma, I think, is that it is not up to anyone *individually* whether there will be future people; nor are there future people who are as real as we are. The word "future" here can be misleading. *If* there are future people, then they are real and have all the basic human rights; but *whether* there will be any such people is not known for certain, it is merely highly probable. In another paper, Narveson repeats his statement that future persons are "just like ourselves"[7] but later seems to recognize the probabilistic element when he says "there is no difficulty identifying future generations, in the ordinary meaning of those terms; they are the collections of individuals who will be living in the future *if any do live*"[8] (my emphasis).

Like Narveson, Derek Parfit contrasts future people [with those] whose existence is "merely possible." He says:

> Suppose that we must act in one of two ways. Future people are the people who will exist whichever way we act. Possible people are the people who exist if we act in one way, but who won't exist if we act in the other way. To give the simplest case, the children we could have are possible people.[9]

Parfit goes on to compare people who are distant in time with those who are distant in space, saying that our actions can affect those who do not exist *now* just as they can affect those who do not exist *here*. But Parfit, like Narveson, gets into some trouble with this contrast, as he later argues that, due to the wide-sweeping effects of different social policies, *different specific people* will emerge depending on what action we take.[10] This would entail that there are *no specific people who will exist whichever way we act,* on Parfit's own account.

Parfit's suggestion that future people be compared with past people and with distant people is not a promising one. We can in principle know what people have existed and what people do exist far away. But we cannot know just which people will exist in the future. Indeed, we cannot know that there will be future people at all. In making this claim, I wish to assert more than a simple wholesale scepticism about all future propositions. (Though I think that such scepticism does have much to be said in its favor, I am not basing my case on this doctrine here.)

In saying that we do not know that future persons will exist, I mean to assert the following three propositions:

(1) We do not know that any conceptions which have not yet occurred will occur, be followed by healthy and completed pregnancies, and issue in infants who develop into persons.

(2) We do not know that any conceptions which have occurred will be followed by healthy and completed pregnancies, and will issue in infants who develop into persons.

(3) We do not know that any infants successfully delivered but still very young will develop into persons.

Why do we not know these things? It is not only because these propositions are about the future: special considerations apply. These should be obvious: they have to do with the chanciness of conception; the possibility of natural catastrophes, world war, or accidental nuclear explosion; side-effects from drugs, food additives, pesticides, or any number of other things; the risks of pregnancy and childbearing; and the possibilities of childhood disease. There are simply too many factors which could intervene, even in cases where we might think that conceptions, healthy pregnancies and deliveries, and normal infancies were virtual certainties. Since world-wide catastrophe as a result of nuclear or germ warfare, or accidents involving sophisticated weaponry are among these factors, and since the likelihood of these is not insignificant, it is unreasonable to claim that we know now that people not born yet will be born and will develop into persons. This is why I insist that when we speak of future persons, we can only legitimately mean those persons who in all probability will exist after us and whose existence we have no reason to regard as being dependent on our individual will.

If the preceding arguments are accepted, then we are left with the basic distinction between those prospective people who are epistemically possible for us in a context and those prospective people who are volitionally possible for us in a context. "Future people" are those epistemically possible people whose existence is highly probable and not properly regarded, in the context in question, as a matter for our decision.

Let us first consider a fairly standard sort of context where consideration of the interests of epistemically possible people is morally required. We have an insecticide, which will increase crop production and which is not known to have any harmful effects on people or animals now living. However, it is known that over a number of years, the residue from this insecticide will combine with other chemicals to produce a substance which can cause blindness in human beings. We are deciding whether to use this insecticide. It is certainly *relevant* to this decision that the insecticide is likely ultimately to produce blindness in people who probably will exist, though they do not exist now. We run the risk of seriously harming those people likely to exist if we use the insecticide. Although in certain circumstances this might not provide an absolutely *conclusive* reason not to use the substance, it always provides a good reason not to use it. The decision in question is not a decision as to whether there will be people existing at later dates; it is a decision whether to use something now which is likely to harm people who likely will exist at later dates.

In such a case I think that it is natural and correct to take account of the interests of non-existent, but possible, people. The relevant factors are the likelihood of their coming to exist, the extent and likelihood of effects of one's action upon them, and the cost to existing people of not doing the contemplated action.

What distinction we make between benefiting and harming nonexistent people should depend on the distinction we make for existing people. There is a greater importance to not harming people than there is to benefiting them. Nevertheless, I think that benefits to epistemically possible people should have some bearing on our actions. Imagine a case in which, by spending an extra half hour with my lawyer, I could ensure that my spacious lakeside property would be preserved as parkland for generations-to-come of deprived children. If this could be done, and if there is a significant probability that there will be children in future years who would greatly benefit from having such a park area, then I think that it would be proper to consider the interests of these not-yet-existent children, and that these provide *some reason* to take the trouble to make the arrangement. I shall not say that in this case I would have an obligation to spend the extra time with my lawyer; whether one wants to posit an obligation in this case will depend on one's more general view about whether we have obligations to benefit other people.

It is entirely appropriate here to treat epistemically possible people in a way strictly analogous to the way in which we treat actual people, the difference being only that we should take into account the fact that their existence is only probable. Since the probability that an epistemically possible person will exist is always less than one, the interests of epistemically possible people always count for something less than those of actual people. This is so whenever our decision is not a decision as to whether there will be people or not, and whenever the existence of the people in question is determined by factors other than the matter about which we are deliberating.

When we are the ones who are deciding whether to produce a child or not, it does not make sense to weigh the interests of that prospective child against the probability of his coming to exist. We decide whether he will exist or not. This is why it is crucial to distinguish between contexts of epistemic and volitional possibility when we are reasoning about possible people. There are cases in which people are not exactly volitionally possible for an agent, but wherein the probability of their coming to exist does depend significantly upon his decision. Where there is this interdependence, the model outlined for taking into account the interests of epistemically possible people cannot properly be applied. This is because something which will vary considerably depending upon what our decision is cannot properly be used as a basis on which that decision is made.

Suppose that someone could release a gas which would sharply diminish the safe food supply and make it impossible for human life to survive on the earth in 100 years' time. Those people who might exist in 120 years need not be considered when we assess the morality of this action, for the probability of their existing depends on whether the action is performed or not. Thus their interests cannot be balanced against the probability of their existence. This consequence might seem so implausible as to constitute an objection to the present account. Nevertheless we can arrive at the result that the gas should not be released and that the reason for this is that the gas would affect future people as well as actual people. We can reach this conclusion without including these prospective people in our calculations.

If the gas is released, then there are people alive when it is released, and their food supply will be adversely affected by it. Either they will be able to produce children or they will not. If the former, their children are epistemically possible and their interests in a safe food supply and in being able to reproduce must be taken into account. If the latter, then actual people are harmed in that they are not able to fulfill the very basic and natural desire to have children. There are enough actual and epistemically possible people whose existence is independent of the decision and who will be harmed by the prospective action that we can generate the decision that the gas should not be released. We need not appeal to the interests of those prospective people whose existence depends on the performance of the action in question.

At this point I wish to consider an important argument put forward by Derek Parfit. Parfit considers two alternative policies toward resources which he refers to as Depletion and Conservation. He maintains that there is no future person whose existence is independent of which of these policies is pursued.

> The people who will live more than a century from now would be different on the different policies. Given the effects of two such policies on the details of people's lives, different marriages would increasingly be made. More simply, even in the same marriages the children would increasingly be conceived at different times. This would be enough to make them different children.... Depletion would lower the quality of life in the further future. But the people who would then be alive would not have existed if instead, we had Conserved. So if we Deplete, *there would never be anyone who is worse off than he would have otherwise been.* Depletion would be worse for no one.[11]

Parfit is not advocating depletion of our resources. Rather, he takes this argument to be a kind of paradox; he does not propose any solution to it. The paradox is that, whereas we would find it natural to believe that future generations will be harmed by depletion, this apparently cannot be true, in that there is no particular person in the future who will be worse off under a depletion policy than under a conservation policy. Because of the variation in which specific people come to exist, it appears that *no one* is harmed by a depletion policy. And this seems paradoxical; would we not want to say that *those who will exist will fare badly if we deplete the resources* and that this, indeed, is why we should *not deplete?* I shall refer to this problem as Parfit's Paradox.

I have said that whenever an action of ours is such that the existence of prospective people is probabilistically independent of the performance of that action, the interests of such people ought to be considered. Given this independence, such prospective people are, on my account, *epistemically possible* in the context in question. Parfit seems to be arguing in effect that no prospective person is ever epistemically possible in this sense, as which specific people come to exist depends on what we decide to do. If we use the insecticide mentioned in my first example, one set of specific people will result in the world of one hundred years hence; if we do not use it, another set of specific people will result. On this account, then, there is no specific person whose existence is (or can be known to be) probabilistically independent of our decision to do anything. Parfit's argument might be seen as generating the conclusion that in effect *all* prospective people are volitionally possible in *all* contexts. But this would be a misleading interpretation: a prospective person is volitionally possible for someone who can decide whether to produce a person, and people do not decide whether to produce *specific* persons. If Beethoven's mother had considered an abortion, she would not have been deciding whether or not to produce Ludwig van Beethoven, but rather whether to carry the child in her womb to term.

Parfit's Paradox is difficult to resolve satisfactorily. My approach to it is along the following lines: people in the future are not to be regarded as volitionally possible in the context of the depletion/conservation issue. This is because in such a context *whether some people will exist in the future* does not depend on whether we deplete or conserve. It is very likely that people will be here on earth in 100 years, and the likelihood of there being some people alive on earth at that time does not depend on this particular social policy.[12] Our concern for people who are likely to exist can never be a concern for some *specific* prospective persons *as opposed to others,* for when we are making decisions which require a reference to prospective persons, we are never in a position to identify *specific* ones. (The first part of what I have said here is acknowledged by Parfit.)[13] The reason we should not deplete the resources is primarily that those who are likely to exist will be badly off if we deplete. If someone should say that "the people under depletion" owe their very existence to a depletion policy, and still live a life better than no life at all, the correct reply is "that's irrelevant." It is irrelevant because consideration of *these specific* people who would exist under depletion and will not exist under conservation is logically out of order. First, we cannot sensibly consider *specific* prospective people. Secondly, when we are deciding to conserve, there is *of course* no need to consider specific prospective people identified as "those who would exist if we deplete but would not exist if we conserve." *By definition,* the probability of their existence, given the decision to conserve, is zero. The people we ought to consider when we are deciding whether to deplete or to conserve are *those people who will likely exist at a future time.* Those people will be badly off if we deplete; therefore we ought not to deplete.

We move now to a consideration of contexts where prospective people *are* for us volitionally possible. Typically these are contexts where moral agents are deciding whether to reproduce. If a moral agent is deciding whether to reproduce, then the probability that a prospective child of hers will exist is very largely dependent on what she decides to do. It is not logically appropriate for her to consider the probability that this child will exist as a factor on which her decision is based: that probability depends on the decision. She will have to base the decision on other factors—on the interests of those already alive whose lives would be affected if the child were born. This does not take us yet to the asymmetry which Narveson has argued for. But I think that this asymmetry becomes comprehensible and justifiable if we think about reasons which this moral agent might have for changing her mind, once her decision is made.

Suppose that she has decided to have a child. She ought, then, to consider the interests of this child-that-is-to-be, for if her decision is successfully implemented, he will be an actual person. If there seems to be every chance that he will lead an acceptable happy life, no special problem arises. Since she wants to have a child and after due consideration of the difference this child's existence will make to herself and others, has decided to have one, she can go ahead and do so. The child is likely to be happy and she has judged that any harm or inconvenience to others as a result of his existence is not of over-riding importance. Things are otherwise, though, if it seems likely that the child she wants to bear would lead a miserable life if born. She will have produced a miserably unhappy person; she can anticipate that she will regret her decision, *out of regard for him,* and he could legitimately complain about his miserable fate, perhaps even to bemoan the very fact of his existence. If she implements her decision to have a child, then, if the child will be miserable, this will be the result. So if there is evidence that the prospective child would be miserable, there is reason to reverse the decision to produce him. By "miserable," in this context, I mean so badly off that his life

would be worse than no life at all. If one can predict that the child one would have would be so miserable that he would be better off not having been born at all, then there is conclusive reason not to have him. Here it is appropriate to take the interests of the child one would have *into account, since the typical and intended effect of deciding to have a child is that there will be a child to consider.*

But now let us look at the other decision. Suppose that our prospective parent has decided not to have a child. She may then reflect on this decision; can she predict that she will have cause to regret it, or that others will complain of it? She may think of happiness a child of hers could have had; should she anticipate that this can rationally be a source of guilt or sadness? She should not, for if she implements her decision not to have a child, there will be no child; there will be "lack of a happy child," not an unhappy child. And the lack of a happy child should not bring guilt or regret unless the prospective parent wants a child. If she does, she will decide to have one—so that is not the case we are considering. And if she comes to want a child in the future she can decide then to have one. Similarly, if others want her prospective child, this can have a bearing on her decision-making now or in the future. But the child itself can provide no basis for regret, no guilt, and no complaints with regard to a decision not to have it. For the decision is precisely a decision not to have the child. The fact that *if* one had a child, that child would be happy provides no reason to have a child and no reason to change one's mind if one has decided not to have a child.

In this way, I think that we can support the asymmetry for which Narveson has argued. There is reason to reverse a decision to have a child if that child would likely be miserable, and there is no comparable reason to reverse a decision to have a child if that child would be happy. Hence, asymmetry.[14]

This asymmetry is in accord with the pre-philosophical convictions of many people. People do not normally argue that others should produce children on the grounds that those children would be happy if they existed. And yet they do hold it reprehensible to knowingly bring into the world children who will be seriously deformed, in dire poverty, or desperately in need of loving care. Even people who oppose a liberal abortion policy often favor abortion in those cases where the fetus is seriously deformed or handicapped, out of consideration for that person who would exist if the fetus were not aborted.

Before leaving this matter of asymmetry, it is in order to say more about the claim that some prospective persons would be better off if "they" did not exist. For this seems a puzzling assertion. *Who* is better off when "he" does not exist? And just what is better than life: nothingness? The problem may be approached, I think, by comparing birth with death.[15] It is said sometimes that people whose circumstances are absolutely desperate would be better off dead. This is to say that no life at all would be better *for these people* than the life they are leading. And yet, with no life, there is no subject for things to be better *for*. There is no consciousness, no awareness of anything. And yet we do sometimes think that a very desperate life, in which there is no hope at all, is worse *for the person living it* than death. If a person is extremely deprived, or if he is in continual and acute pain, and if there is no hope at all for improvement, then he might very well come to believe that he would be "better off dead." This expression suggests that such a person is making a comparison between two states which he could be in: he could be alive, having these kinds of experiences, or he could be dead, having no experiences at all. And of course this way of looking at the matter is all wrong, for *he won't be* in one of the states. A judgment by someone that he would be "better off dead" should

be interpreted as a judgment that his continuance as an experiencing subject should be terminated, because the experiences he has and can expect to have, are so dreadful. People sometimes do judge that they would be better off dead, and when they do this, it is possible that they hold the belief rationally and that what they believe is true.

Let us turn from the context of death to the one which is directly relevant to reproductive morality: that in which we compare the life which we would anticipate for a volitionally possible person with no life at all, *for that person*. Since such a comparison must, of necessity, be made before the prospective person is born, we cannot consult him in the matter. And we cannot go very far in the direction of using his specific interests and ambitions as a basis for making our judgment. We must make the comparison between the kind of life we think he would have and no life at all from the viewpoint of a representative human being, attributed normal, fundamental human emotions and needs. If a prospective parent can anticipate that the child she might have will not have sufficient food, that he will be seriously deformed and in almost constant pain, or that there will be no one interested in loving and caring for him, she can anticipate that he will be miserable, as in his case, fundamental human needs will not be met.

If we say, then, that it would be better, from the point of view of a prospective child, if he did not exist, we define the viewpoint of the prospective child with reference to fundamental human needs. Once this is done, then judging that such a life is absolutely not worth having is similar in principle to comparing a particular life which some particular person is leading with death for that person. It is to say, in effect, that experiences of the type which he could expect just should not be suffered by any human being, and that if these are the only kinds of experiences he is likely to have, then it is better for there to be no subject of experience at all.

There is no insurmountable *logical* difficulty, then, in the judgment that some prospective people would be better off if "they" did not exist. But we must be very cautious in making these judgments, for actual people vary in their needs, and we do not want to underestimate the adjustments which a deformed or handicapped person can make. It is possible to see how to make logical sense of the judgment that a prospective person would be "better off" if "he" did not exist. However, we must take every precaution in particular cases to see that we do not make this judgment insensitively or prematurely.

On the basis of the account just given, I would sum up the moral status of prospective people as follows:

(1) The moral worth of an action, *A*, depends at least in part on the harm or benefit it is likely to bring to those who exist or who are likely to exist, where in the latter case the probability of their existing is largely independent of whether *A* is performed or not.
(2) We are never obliged to bring someone into existence merely because he is likely to be very happy if he exists.
(3) We are generally obliged not to bring someone into existence if he is likely to be very miserable if he exists.
(4) It is generally permissible to bring into existence people who are likely to lead happy, or moderately happy, lives.

The word "generally" is used in (3) and (4) to allow for balancing the interests of prospective people against those of already-existing people. It is arguable at least that it would be permissible to produce someone who would be unhappy if his existence would greatly alleviate the unhappiness of people already alive. And certainly the permissibility of producing people who would likely be happy is contingent upon their lives not seriously diminishing the well-being of those who were already alive at the time of their conception.

Notes

1 "Utilitarianism and New Generations," *Mind* 76 (1967), 62–72; and "Moral Problems of Population," *The Monist* 57 (1973), 62–86.

2 At a lecture given at Trent University in March 1977, Narveson said that he did not think that he could adequately defend the asymmetry; however, more recently he has put forward additional arguments in its favor, in a draft paper written in June 1977.

3 L.W. Sumner, "The Absurdity of Average Utilitarianism," paper presented at the Canadian Philosophical Association meetings in Fredericton. New Brunswick, June 1977.

4 It may also be used in some of its essentials, in conjunction with moral theories which do not share this presupposition. For instance, Nozick's theory bases morality on respecting rights to life and property. One could deny a right to life for people not yet born or conceived, and who are volitionally possible; and weigh rights of the epistemically possible as less than those of already existing people, on grounds essentially the same as those presented in this paper.

5 "Harm to the Unconceived?—A Utilitarian (In Spirit) Comment on Professor Bayles' Paper," presented at the Kalamazoo Conference on the Philosophy of Law, Spring 1976, 4.

6 *Ibid.*, 5–6.

7 "Semantics, Future Generations, and the Abortion Problem," *Social Theory and Practice* 6 (1975), 468.

8 *Ibid.*, 473.

9 "Rights, Interests, and Possible People," in Gorovitz *et al.*, eds., *Moral Problems in Medicine* (Englewood Cliffs, N.J., 1976) 369–75.

10 Parfit, draft of a paper entitled "Overpopulation."

11 "Overpopulation," 12. See also Section IX, 3:

> If we Deplete, the quality of life in the further future will be lower. But the particular people who would then be alive would not have existed if we had Conserved. So if those people's lives would still be worth living, Depletion would be better for them. Since it would also be better for existing people, it would be better for everyone who ever lives.

12 If one is convinced that the likelihood of there being any people at all depends on whether we deplete, the case then becomes analogous to that of the gas which would affect future food supply, and should be treated in the same way. See above, 140.

13 "Overpopulation," 19–20.

14 This line of reasoning is quite similar to that in "Moral Problems of Population," 96–7:

> If you bring these people into existence, then of course you must treat them in accordance with their moral status as human beings. And if you can foresee that it will not be possible to do that, or that no matter how much you or anyone tries, you won't be able to succeed in enabling them to live a worthwhile life, then that is a reason for not starting on the project in the first place.... But the solubility of such problems, the fact that one would be able to treat, and that others would be able to treat, the newcomer in a satisfactory way, does not seem of itself any reason at all for having him.

Compare also R.I. Sikora, "Utilitarianism: The Classical Principle and the Average Principle," *Canadian Journal of Philosophy,* 5 (1975), 409–17. This reasoning more easily justifies asymmetry when the distinction between epistemic and volitional possibility is kept in mind.

15 I owe a debt here to L.W. Sumner, "A Matter of Life and Death," *Nous* 10 (1976), 145–71.

Questions for Discussion

1 Govier discusses the asymmetry between the claim that "we are never obliged to bring someone into existence merely because he is likely to be very happy if he exists" and the claim that "we are generally obliged not to bring someone into existence if he is likely to be very miserable if he exists." Is this asymmetry a problem? Does Govier provide an adequate resolution of the problem?

2 "Parfit's Paradox" notes that if we follow a policy which damages the environment, there may never be anyone who is worse off than he or she would have been if we had followed a different policy. This could be true because our choice of policy might affect which particular people are born, and thus people who bear the brunt of our environmental damage would not even have existed (and thus would not have been better off) if we had not acted as we did. How big a problem is this? Does Govier offer an adequate solution for it?

3 Can we make sense of the claim that a future person's life would be so miserable that he or she would be better off not existing at all?

4 Does Govier's discussion of "volitionally possible" people involve an unstated assumption that human beings will almost always be able to reproduce when they want to? How does this aspect of the discussion connect with issues about infertility and assisted reproduction?

CHAPTER 3

Distribution of Scarce Resources

It has been suggested that there would be no need for morality at all if there were enough material goods around for all people to have whatever they wanted. Whether this is correct or not, it is certainly the case that one of the problems of today's world concerns the distribution and use of limited resources. This problem arises at several different levels. There is the global dilemma of how relatively wealthy nations should act toward poorer nations, and (what may be a different issue) how individual citizens of wealthy nations should respond to widespread poverty in many parts of the world. There is also the problem of how the goods within society should be distributed among members of that society—for example, the extent to which some sort of social welfare system is required by considerations of justice. A related question concerns decisions about which of several competing groups should receive government support.

One of the most visible areas in which the problem of distribution of scarce re-sources within a society has arisen is in relation to medical resources. Obviously health has a tremendous influence on how well people live; indeed, sometimes medical assistance is needed if people are to go on living at all. Modern medical technology has made it possible to extend the lives of a great many people. However, much of this technology is very expensive, and providing everyone with all treatments which could be expected to benefit them may not be feasible. Of course, that might be a reason to advocate a large-scale reorganization of society's priorities, a reorganization that might well have other consequences which would outweigh its benefits. In any case, in society as it stands, there is a very real question about the best way to distribute medical care.

This issue is often divided into two major sub-categories: "macro-allocation" and "micro-allocation," although in practice the distinction may not be completely clear-cut. Macro-allocation has to do with the broad questions about how nations should go about providing health care for their citizens. Should the government provide all necessary health care, or leave medical care to market forces? Assuming society takes some responsibility for medical care, what proportion of its resources should be devoted to such care? Macro-allocation is also concerned with providing rough guidelines for how allocated resources are to be divided. For example, one might ask how much should be spent on treatment of the unhealthy, how much on education and preventative measures, and how much on research to improve our ability to do each of the first two things in the future. For another example, one might wonder how much should go to treatment of life-threatening conditions (such as heart disease) and how much to conditions which are not life-threatening but seriously impair the sufferers' quality of life (such as arthritis).

Micro-allocation, on the other hand, is concerned with the specific distribution of resources at an individual level. For example, if a hospital can only afford to provide dialysis for ten patients, and there are twenty who could benefit from such treatment, how are the fortunate ten to be selected? Should they be evaluated on the basis of likely contribution to the community at large? Past contributions? Likelihood of responding well to treatment? First-come first-served? The questions multiply.

As mentioned above, the distribution of medical resources is only one question about how resources should be used within a community, albeit an important and much-discussed one. A similar quandary concerns the notion of a welfare state. To what extent do needy people have a legitimate claim against those better off within their society? How did those who control more of society's resources come to be in such a position? Are people entitled to whatever they are able to "earn" under existing systems, or should government intervene to redistribute wealth?

Finally, there are questions about how much responsibility members of societies should take for those of other societies who are less well off. It might be the case that one could always do more good by sending money for food for a starving child rather than spending it on a movie or new clothes. Are we morally required to keep giving rather than spending on ourselves so long as the recipient of the money can use it for greater benefit than we can? Or would giving to poor countries in that way be counter-productive, or foolhardy?

There are many facets to the question of how scarce resources should be distributed. The writings which follow cannot possibly cover all of them adequately, but do serve to introduce some of the important issues, and suggest ways of approaching them.

Excerpts from "Anarchy, State, and Utopia"

Robert Nozick

One issue concerning distribution of scarce resources involves the question of how people come to "own" particular resources at all. The classical view has been that natural resources are originally unowned, but people may then stake a claim to the unowned property. One of the most famous accounts of how this might take place was offered by John Locke in the seventeenth century. Locke claimed people acquire previously unowned objects by mixing their labour with them. Contemporary philosopher Robert Nozick follows in this tradition, maintaining that we can determine whether people have a just claim to their holdings simply by seeing if they have acquired them justly ("justice in acquisition," if converted directly from an unowned state, or "justice in transfer," if originally appropriated by someone else but then transferred to the current owner). In the following selection from his influential book, Nozick outlines his "entitlement theory," and offers a critical discussion of Locke's account of property acquisition, including an attempt at understanding Locke's "proviso" that others not be made worse off by one's acquisition. Nozick believes that a free market system, with a minimal social safety net, will satisfy the requirements of justice, viewed in this way.

★　　★　　★

The Entitlement Theory

The subject of justice in holdings consists of three major topics. The first is the *original acquisition of holdings,* the appropriation of unheld things. This includes the issues of how unheld things may come to be held, the process, or processes, by which unheld things may come to be held, the things that may come to be held by these processes, the extent of what comes to be held by a particular process, and so on. We shall refer to the complicated truth about this topic, which we shall not formulate here, as the principle of justice in acquisition. The second topic concerns the *transfer of holdings* from one person to another. By what processes may a person transfer holdings to another? How may a person acquire a holding from another who holds it? Under this topic come general descriptions of voluntary exchange, and gift and (on the other hand) fraud, as well as reference to particular conventional details fixed upon in a given society. The complicated truth about this subject (with placeholders for conventional details) we

shall call the principle of justice in transfer. (And we shall suppose it also includes principles governing how a person may divest himself of a holding, passing it into an unheld state.)

If the world were wholly just, the following inductive definition would exhaustively cover the subject of justice in holdings.

1. A person who acquires a holding in accordance with the principle of justice in acquisition is entitled to that holding.
2. A person who acquires a holding in accordance with the principle of justice in transfer, from someone else entitled to the holding, is entitled to the holding.
3. No one is entitled to a holding except by (repeated) applications of 1 and 2.

The complete principle of distributive justice would say simply that a distribution is just if everyone is entitled to the holdings they possess under the distribution.

A distribution is just if it arises from another just distribution by legitimate means. The legitimate means of moving from one distribution to another are specified by the principle of justice in transfer. The legitimate first "moves" are specified by the principle of justice in acquisition.* Whatever arises from a just situation by just steps is itself just. The means of change specified by the principle of justice in transfer preserve justice. As correct rules of inference are truth-preserving, and any conclusion deduced via repeated application of such rules from only true premises is itself true, so the means of transition from one situation to another specified by the principle of justice in transfer are justice-preserving, and any situation actually arising from repeated transitions in accordance with the principle from a just situation is itself just. The parallel between justice-preserving transformations and truth-preserving transformations illuminates where it fails as well as where it holds. That a conclusion could have been deduced by truth-preserving means from premises that are true suffices to show its truth. That from a just situation a situation *could* have arisen via justice-preserving means does *not* suffice to show its justice. The fact that a thief's victims voluntarily *could* have presented him with gifts does not entitle the thief to his ill-gotten gains. Justice in holdings is historical; it depends upon what actually has happened. We shall return to this point later.

Not all actual situations are generated in accordance with the two principles of justice in holdings: the principle of justice in acquisition and the principle of justice in transfer. Some people steal from others, or defraud them, or enslave them, seizing their product and preventing them from living as they choose, or forcibly exclude others from competing in exchanges. None of these are permissible modes

---

* Applications of the principle of justice in acquisition may also occur as part of the move from one distribution to another. You may find an unheld thing now and appropriate it. Acquisitions also are to be understood as included when, to simplify, I speak only of transitions by transfers.

of transition from one situation to another. And some persons acquire holdings by means not sanctioned by the principle of justice in acquisition. The existence of past injustice (previous violations of the first two principles of justice in holdings) raises the third major topic under justice in holdings: the rectification of injustice in holdings. If past injustice has shaped present holdings in various ways, some identifiable and some not, what now, if anything, ought to be done to rectify these injustices? What obligations do the performers of injustice have toward those whose position is worse than it would have been had the injustice not been done? Or, than it would have been had compensation been paid promptly? How, if at all, do things change if the beneficiaries and those made worse off are not the direct parties in the act of injustice, but, for example, their descendants? Is an injustice done to someone whose holding was itself based upon an unrectified injustice? How far back must one go in wiping clean the historical slate of injustices? What may victims of injustice permissibly do in order to rectify the injustices being done to them, including the many injustices done by persons acting through their government? I do not know of a thorough or theoretically sophisticated treatment of such issues.[1] Idealizing greatly, let us suppose theoretical investigation will produce a principle of rectification. This principle uses historical information about previous situations and injustices done in them (as defined by the first two principles of justice and rights against interference), and information about the actual course of events that flowed from these injustices, until the present, and it yields a description (or descriptions) of holdings in the society. The principle of rectification presumably will make use of its best estimate of subjunctive information about what would have occurred (or a probability distribution over what might have occurred, using the expected value) if the injustice had not taken place. If the actual description of holdings turns out not to be one of the descriptions yielded by the principle, then one of the descriptions yielded must be realized.*

The general outlines of the theory of justice in holdings are that the holdings of a person are just if he is entitled to them by the principles of justice in acquisition and transfer, or by the principle of rectification of injustice (as specified by the first two principles). If each person's holdings are just, then the total set (distribution) of holdings is just. To turn these general outlines into a specific theory we would have to specify the details of each of the three principles of justice in holdings: the principle of acquisition of holdings, the principle of transfer of holdings, and the principle of rectification of violations of the first two principles. I shall not attempt that task here. (Locke's principle of justice in acquisition is discussed below.) ...

Locke's Theory of Acquisition

Locke views property rights in an unowned object as originating through someone's mixing his labor with it. This gives rise to many questions. What are the boundaries of what labor is mixed with? If a private astronaut clears a place on Mars, has he mixed his labor with (so that he comes to own) the whole planet, the whole uninhabited universe, or just a particular plot? Which plot does an act bring under ownership? The minimal (possibly disconnected) area such that an act decreases entropy in that area, and not elsewhere? Can virgin land (for the purposes of ecological investigation by high-flying aiplane) come under ownership by a Lockean process? Building a fence around a territory presumably would make one the owner of only the fence (and the land immediately underneath it).

Why does mixing one's labor with something make one the owner of it? Perhaps because one owns one's labor, and so one comes to own a previously unowned thing that becomes permeated with what one owns. Ownership seeps over into the rest. But why isn't mixing what I own with what I don't own a way of losing what I own rather than that a way of gaining what I don't? If I own a can of tomato juice and spill it in the sea so that its molecules (made radioactive, so I can check this) mingle evenly throughout the sea, do I thereby come to own the sea, or have I foolishly dissipated my tomato juice? Perhaps the idea, instead, is that laboring on something improves it and makes it more valuable; and anyone is entitled to own a thing whose value he has created. (Reinforcing this, perhaps, is the view that laboring is unpleasant. If some people made things effortlessly, as the cartoon characters in *The Yellow Submarine* trail flowers in their wake, would they have lesser claim to their own products whose making didn't *cost* them anything?) Ignore the fact that laboring on something may make it less valuable (spraying pink enamel paint on a piece of driftwood that you have found). Why should one's entitlement extend to the whole object rather than just to the *added value* one's labor has produced? (Such reference to value might also serve to delimit the extent of ownership; for example, substitute "increases the value of" for "decreases entropy in" in the above entropy criterion.) No workable or coherent value-added property scheme has yet been devised, and any such scheme presumably would fall to objections (similar to those) that fell the theory of Henry George.

---

* If the principle of rectification of violations of the first two principles yields more than one description of holdings, then some choice must be made as to which of these is to be realized. Perhaps the sort of considerations about distributive justice and equality that I argue against play a legitimate role in *this* subsidiary choice. Similarly, there may be room for such considerations in deciding which otherwise arbitrary features a statute will embody, when such features are unavoidable because other considerations do not specify a precise line; yet a line must be drawn....

It will be implausible to view improving an object as giving full ownership to it, if the stock of unowned objects that might be improved is limited. For an object's coming under one person's ownership changes the situation of all others. Whereas previously they were at liberty (in Hohfeld's sense) to use the object, they now no longer are. This change in the situation of others (by removing their liberty to act on a previously unowned object) need not worsen their situation. If I appropriate a grain of sand from Coney Island, no one else may now do as they will with *that* grain of sand. But there are plenty of other grains left for them to do the same with. Or if not grains of sand, then other things. Alternatively, the things I do with the grains of sand I appropriate might improve the position of others, counterbalancing their loss of the liberty to use that grain. The crucial point is whether appropriation of an unowned object worsens the situation of others.

Locke's proviso that there be "enough and as good left in common for others" (sect. 27) is meant to ensure that the situation of others is not worsened. (If this proviso is met is there any motivation for his further condition of nonwaste?) It is often said that this proviso once held but now no longer does. But there appears to be an argument for the conclusion that if the proviso no longer holds, then it cannot ever have held so as to yield permanent and inheritable property rights. Consider the first person Z for whom there is not enough and as good left to appropriate. The last person Y to appropriate left Z without his previous liberty to act on an object, and so worsened Z's situation. So Y's appropriation is not allowed under Locke's proviso. Therefore the next to last person X to appropriate left Y in a worse position, for X's act ended permissible appropriation. Therefore X's appropriation wasn't permissible. But then the appropriator two from last, W, ended permissible appropriation, and so, since it worsened X's

position, W's appropriation wasn't permissible. And so on back to the first person A to appropriate a permanent property right.

This argument, however, proceeds too quickly. Someone may be made worse off by another's appropriation in two ways: first, by losing the opportunity to improve his situation by a particular appropriation or any one; and second, by no longer being able to use freely (without appropriation) what he previously could. A *stringent* requirement that another not be made worse off by an appropriation would exclude the first way if nothing else counterbalances the diminution in opportunity, as well as the second. A *weaker* requirement would exclude the second way, though not the first. With the weaker requirement, we cannot zip back so quickly from Z to A, as in the above argument; for though person Z can no longer *appropriate*, there may remain some for him to *use* as before. In this case Y's appropriation would not violate the weaker Lockean condition. (With less remaining that people are at liberty to use, users might face more inconvenience, crowding, and so on; in that way the situation of others might be worsened, unless appropriation stopped far short of such a point.) It is arguable that no one legitimately can complain if the weaker provision is satisfied. However, since this is less clear than in the case of the more stringent proviso, Locke may have intended this stringent proviso by "enough and as good" remaining, and perhaps he meant the non-waste condition to delay the end point from which the argument zips back.

Is the situation of persons who are unable to appropriate (there being no more accessible and useful unowned objects) worsened by a system allowing appropriation and permanent property? Here enter the various familiar social considerations favoring private property: it increases the social product by putting means of production in the hands of those who can use them most efficiently (profitably); experimentation is encouraged, because with separate persons controlling resources, there is no one person or small group whom someone with a new idea must convince to try it out; private property enables people to decide on the pattern and types of risks they wish to bear, leading to specialized types of risk bearing; private property protects future persons by leading some to hold back resources from current consumption for future markets; it provides alternate sources of employment for unpopular persons who don't have to convince any one person or small group to hire them, and so on. These considerations enter a Lockean theory to support the claim that appropriation of private property satisfies the intent behind the "enough and as good left over" proviso, *not* as a utilitarian justification of property. They enter to rebut the claim that because the proviso is violated no natural right to private property can arise by a Lockean process. The difficulty in working such an argument to show that the proviso is satisfied is in fixing the appropriate base line for comparison. Lockean appropriation makes people no worse off than they would be *how?*[1] This question of fixing the baseline needs more detailed investigation than we are able to give it here. It would be desirable to have an estimate of the general economic importance of original appropriation in order to see how much leeway there is for differing theories of appropriation and of the location of the baseline. Perhaps this importance can be measured by the percentage of all income that is based upon untransformed raw materials and given resources (rather than upon human actions), mainly rental income representing the unimproved value of land, and the price of raw material *in situ*, and by the percentage of current wealth which represents such income in the past.[*]

We should note that it is not only persons favoring *private* property who need a theory of how property rights legitimately originate. Those believing in collective property, for example those believing that a group of persons living in an area jointly own the territory, or its mineral resources, also must provide a theory of how such property rights arise; they must show why the persons living there have rights to determine what is done with the land and resources there that persons living elsewhere don't have (with regard to the same land and resources).

The Proviso

Whether or not Locke's particular theory of appropriation can be spelled out so as to handle various difficulties, I assume that any adequate theory of justice in acquisition will contain a proviso similar to the weaker of the ones we have attributed to Locke. A process normally giving rise to a permanent bequeathable property right in a previously unowned thing will not do so if the position of others no longer at liberty to use the thing is thereby worsened. It is important to specify *this* particular mode of worsening the situation of others, for the proviso does not encompass other modes. It does not include the worsening due to more limited opportunities to appropriate (the first way above, corresponding to the more stringent condition), and it does not include how I "worsen" a seller's position if I appropriate materials to make some of what he is selling, and then enter into competition with him. Someone whose appropriation otherwise would violate the

---

[*] I have not seen a precise estimate. David Friedman, *The Machinery of Freedom* (N.Y.: Harper & Row, 1973), pp. xiv, xv, discusses this issue and

suggests 5 percent of US national income as an upper limit for the first two factors mentioned. However he does not attempt to estimate the percentage of current wealth which is based upon such income in the past. (The vague notion of "based upon" merely indicates a topic needing investigation.)

proviso still may appropriate provided he compensates the others so that their situation is not thereby worsened; unless he does compensate these others, his appropriation will violate the proviso of the principle of justice in acquisition and will be an illegitimate one.* A theory of appropriation incorporating this Lockean proviso will handle correctly the cases (objections to the theory lacking the proviso) where someone appropriates the total supply of something necessary for life.†

---

* Fourier held that since the process of civilization had deprived the members of society of certain liberties (to gather, pasture, engage in the chase), a socially guaranteed minimum provision for persons was justified as compensation for the loss (Alexander Gray, *The Socialist Tradition* (New York: Harper & Row, 1968), p. 188). But this puts the point too strongly. This compensation would be due those persons, if any, for whom the process of civilization was a *net loss*, for whom the benefits of civilization did not counterbalance being deprived of these particular liberties.

† For example, Rashdall's case of someone who comes upon the only water in the desert several miles ahead of others who will also come to it and appropriates it all. Hastings Rashdall, "The Philosophical Theory of Property," in *Property, its Duties and Rights* (London: MacMillan, 1915). We should note Ayn Rand's theory of property rights—"Man's Rights" in *The Virtue of Selfishness* (New York: New American Library, 1964), p. 94—wherein these follow from the right to life, since people need physical things to live. But a right to life is not a right to whatever one needs to live; other people may have rights over these other things (see Chapter 3 of [Nozick's] book). At most, a right to life would be a right to have or strive for whatever one needs to live, provided that having it does not violate anyone else's rights. With regard to material things, the question is whether having it does violate any right of others. (Would appropriation of all unowned things do so? Would appropriating the water hole in Rashdall's example?) Since special considerations (such as the Lockean proviso) may enter with regard to material property, one *first* needs a theory of property rights before one can apply any supposed right to life (as amended above). Therefore

A theory which includes this proviso in its principle of justice in acquisition must also contain a more complex principle of justice in transfer. Some reflection of the proviso about appropriation constrains later actions. If my appropriating all of a certain substance violates the Lockean proviso, then so does my appropriating some and purchasing all the rest from others who obtained it without otherwise violating the Lockean proviso. If the proviso excludes someone's appropriating all the drinkable water in the world, it also excludes his purchasing it all. (More weakly, and messily, it may exclude his charging certain prices for some of his supply.) This proviso (almost?) never will come into effect; the more someone acquires of a scarce substance which others want, the higher the price of the rest will go, and the more difficult it will become for him to acquire it all. But still, we can imagine, at least, that something like this occurs: someone makes simultaneous secret bids to the separate owners of a substance, each of whom sells assuming he can easily purchase more from the other owners; or some natural catastrophe destroys all of the supply of something except that in one person's possession. The total supply could not be permissibly appropriated by one person at the beginning. His later acquisition of it all does not show that the original appropriation violated the proviso (even by a reverse argument similar to the one above that tried to zip back from *Z* to *A*). Rather, it is the combination of the original appropriation *plus* all the later transfers and actions that violates the Lockean proviso.

Each owner's title to his holding includes the historical shadow of the Lockean proviso on appropriation. This excludes his transferring it into an agglomeration that does violate the Lockean proviso and excludes his using it in a way, in coordination with others or independ-

---

the right to life cannot provide the foundation for a theory of property rights.

ently of them, so as to violate the proviso by making the situation of others worse than their baseline situation. Once it is known that someone's ownership runs afoul of the Lockean proviso, there are stringent limits on what he may do with (what it is difficult any longer unreservedly to call) "his property." Thus a person may not appropriate the only water hole in a desert and charge what he will. Nor may he charge what he will if he possesses one, and unfortunately it happens that all the water holes in the desert dry up, except for his. This unfortunate circumstance, admittedly no fault of his, brings into operation the Lockean proviso and limits his property rights.* Similarly, an owner's property right in the only island in an area does not allow him to order a castaway from a shipwreck off his island as a trespasser, for this would violate the Lockean proviso.

Notice that the theory does not say that owners do have these rights, but that the rights are overridden to avoid some catastrophe. (Overridden rights do not disappear; they leave a trace of a sort absent in the cases under discussion.)[2] There is no such external (and *ad hoc?*) overriding. Considerations internal to the theory of property itself, to its theory of acquisition and appropriation, provide the means for handling such cases. The results, however, may be coextensive with some condition about catastrophe, since the baseline for comparison is so low as compared to the productiveness of a society with private appropriation that the question of the Lockean proviso being violated arises only in the case of catastrophe (or a desert-island situation).

The fact that someone owns the total supply of something necessary for others to stay

alive does *not* entail that his (or anyone's) appropriation of anything left some people (immediately or later) in a situation worse than the baseline one. A medical researcher who synthesizes a new substance that effectively treats a certain disease and who refuses to sell except on his terms does not worsen the situation of others by depriving them of whatever he has appropriated. The others easily can possess the same materials he appropriated; the researcher's appropriation or purchase of chemicals didn't make those chemicals scarce in a way so as to violate the Lockean proviso. Nor would someone else's purchasing the total supply of the synthesized substance from the medical researcher. The fact that the medical researcher uses easily available chemicals to synthesize the drug no more violates the Lockean proviso than does the fact that the only surgeon able to perform a particular operation eats easily obtainable food in order to stay alive and to have the energy to work. This shows that the Lockean proviso is not an "end-state principle"; it focuses on a particular way that appropriative actions affect others, and not on the structure of the situation that results.[3]

Intermediate between someone who takes all of the public supply and someone who makes the total supply out of easily obtainable substances is someone who appropriates the total supply of something in a way that does not deprive the others of it. For example, someone finds a new substance in an out-of-the-way place. He discovers that it effectively treats a certain disease and appropriates the total supply. He does not worsen the situation of others; if he did not stumble upon the substance no one else would have, and the others would remain without it. However, as time passes, the likelihood increases that others would have come across the substance; upon this fact might be based a limit to his property right in the substance so that others are not below his baseline position; for example, its bequest might be limited. The theme of

---

* The situation would be different if his water hole didn't dry up, due to special precautions he took to prevent this. Compare our discussion of the case in the text with Hayek, *The Constitution of Liberty*, p. 136; and also with Ronald Hamowy, "Hayek's Concept of Freedom; A Critique," *New Individualist Review*, April 1961, pp. 28–31.

someone worsening another's situation by depriving him of something he otherwise would possess may also illuminate the example of patents. An inventor's patent does not deprive others of an object which would not exist if not for the inventor. Yet patents would have this effect on others who independently invent the object. Therefore, these independent inventors, upon whom the burden of proving independent discovery may rest, should not be excluded from utilizing their own invention as they wish (including selling it to others). Furthermore, a known inventor drastically lessens the chances of actual independent invention. For persons who know of an invention usually will not try to reinvent it, and the notion of independent discovery here would be murky at best. Yet we may assume that in the absence of the original invention, sometime later someone else would have come up with it. This suggests placing a time limit on patents, as a rough rule of thumb to approximate how long it would have taken, in the absence of knowledge of the invention, for independent discovery.

I believe that the free operation of a market system will not actually run afoul of the Lockean proviso.

Note to "The Entitlement Theory"

1 See, however, the useful book by Boris Bittker, *The Case for Black Reparations* (New York: Random House, 1973).

Notes to "Locke's Theory of Acquisition"

1 Compare this with Robert Paul Wolff's "A Refutation of Rawls' Theorem on Justice," *Journal of Philosophy*, March 31, 1966, sect. 2. Wolff's criticism does not apply to Rawls' conception under which the baseline is fixed by the difference principle.

2 I discuss overriding and its moral traces in "Moral Complications and Moral Structures," *Natural Law Forum*, 1968, pp. 1–50.

3 Does the principle of compensation (Chapter 4) introduce patterning considerations? Though it requires compensation for the disadvantages imposed by those seeking security from risks, it is not a patterned principle. For it seeks to remove only those disadvantages which prohibitions inflict on those who might present risks to others, not all disadvantages. It specifies an obligation on those who impose the prohibition, which stems from their own particular acts, to remove a particular complaint those prohibited may make against them.

Questions for Discussion

1 Should natural resources be viewed as "unowned" but there for the taking?

2 Is "mixing one's labour" with something a good enough explanation of how we can come to acquire unowned things?

3 What should the relevant comparison be for saying that a person has been made worse off by a series of acquisitions and transfers? Can this assessment be made in material terms alone? Can a resulting inequality provide a justification for requiring people to surrender some of their possessions to those worse off?

Excerpts from "Equality and Liberty"

A Defense of Radical Egalitarianism

Kai Nielsen

*In addition to his many other philosophical interests, Kai Nielsen has for many years been one of the leading Canadian advocates of adjusting society in the direction of greater equality. In the following selection from his book, **Equality and Liberty**, Nielsen defines a view he calls "radical egalitarianism," and defends it against a number of objections, including the claim that redistribution of wealth violates individuals' entitlements.*

★   ★   ★

3. Radical Egalitarian Justice: Justice as Equality

I

Put somewhat crudely and oversimply, my intention in this [paper] is to explicate and defend an egalitarian conception of justice both in production and in distribution that is even more egalitarian than John Rawls' conception of justice. I shall argue that such a conception of justice requires, if it is to be anything other than an ideal which turns no machinery, a socialist organization of society. It is clear that there are a host of very diverse objections that will immediately spring to mind. I shall try to make tolerably clear what I am claiming and why, and I shall consider and try in some degree to meet, some of the most salient of these objections.

I shall first give four formulations of such a radical egalitarian conception of justice: formulations which, if there is anything like a concept of social justice, hopefully capture something of it, though it is more likely that such a way of putting things is not very helpful and what we have here are four conceptualizations of social justice which together articulate what many on the left take social justice to be. I shall follow that with a statement of what I take to be the two most

fundamental principles of radical egalitarian justice.

Four Conceptions of Radical Egalitarian Justice

1. Justice in society as a whole ought to be understood as requiring that each person be treated with equal respect irrespective of desert and that each person be entitled to the social conditions supportive of self-respect irrespective of desert.[1]
2. Justice in society as a whole ought to be understood as requiring that each person be so treated such that we approach, as close as we can, to a condition where everyone will be equal in satisfaction and in such distress as is necessary for achieving our commonly accepted ends.[2] (We must recognize that we cannot achieve this for the severely handicapped and for people in analogous positions and we cannot do that for people with expensive tastes. The latter are not so worrisome, but even for them, in conditions of great abundance, we should work towards such a state.)
3. Justice in society as a whole ought to be understood as a complete equality of the overall level of benefits and burdens of each member of that society.[3] (This should be understood as ranging over a person's life as a whole.)
4. Justice in society as a whole ought to be understood as a structuring of the institutions of society so that each person can, to the fullest extent compatible with all other people doing likewise, satisfy her/his genuine needs.

These conceptualizations are, of course, vague and in various ways indeterminate.

What counts as "genuine needs," "fullest extent," "complete equality of overall level of benefits," "as close as we can," "equal respect" and the like? Much depends on how these notions function and in what kind of a theory they are placed. However, I will not pursue these matters in this chapter. These conceptualizations, in any case, should help us locate social justice on the conceptual and moral map.

The stress and intent of these egalitarian understandings of the concept of social justice is on equal treatment in various crucial respects of all humankind. The emphasis is on attaining, in attaining social justice, some central equality of condition for everyone. Some egalitarians stress some prized condition such as self-respect or a good life; others, more mundanely, but at least as crucially, stress an overall equal sharing of the various good things and bad things of the society. And such talk of needs postulates a common condition of life that is to be the common property of everyone.

When egalitarians speak of equality, they should be understood as asserting that everyone should be treated equally in certain respects, namely that there are certain conditions of life that should be theirs. What they should be understood as saying is that all human beings should be treated equally in respects F_1, F_2, F_3, ... F_n, where the predicate variable will range over the conditions of life which are thought to be things that it is desirable that all people have. Here equality is being treated as a goal. To say, where "X" refers to "human beings," "All X's should be treated equally in respects F_1, F_2, F_3, ... F_n." can be expressed, for those who go in for that sort of thing, in the logically equivalent form of the usual universal quantification, "For anything, if it is X, then it should have F_1, F_2, F_3, . . . F_n." This is to say that each person should have them, but this is not to say, or to give to understand, that each person, like having equal amounts of an equally divided pie, should have identical or uniform amounts of them. Talking about identical or uniform amounts has no clear sense in such matters as respect, self-respect, satisfaction of needs or attaining the best life of which a person is capable. The equality of condition to be coherently sought is that they all have F_1, F_2, F_3, ... F_n. Not that they must all have them equally, since for some F's this does not even make sense. Even in speaking of rights, as when we say that everyone has a right to respect and to an equal respect in that none can be treated as second-class people, this still does not mean, or give to understand, that in treating them with respect you treat them in an identical way. In treating with equal respect a baby, a young person, or an enfeebled old man out of his mind on his death-bed, we do not treat them equally, i.e., identically or uniformly, but with some kind of not very clearly defined proportional equality.[4] (It is difficult to say what we mean here but we know how to work with the notion.) Similarly, in treating an Andaman Islander and a Bostonian with respect, we do not treat them identically, for what counts as treating someone with respect will not always be the same.

I want now to turn to a statement and elucidation of my egalitarian principles of justice. They are principles of just distribution, and it is important to recognize at the outset that they do not follow from any of my specifications of the concept of social justice. Someone might accept one of those specifications and reject the principles, or conversely accept the principles and reject any or all of those specifications, or indeed believe that there is no coherent concept of social justice at all but only different conceptualizations of justice that different theorists with different aims propound. But there is, I believe, an elective affinity between my principles and the egalitarian understanding of what the concept involves specified above. I think that if one does take justice in this egalitarian way one will find it reasonable to accept these principles.

I state my principles in a way parallel to those of John Rawls for ease of comparison ...

Principles of Egalitarian Justice

1. Each person is to have an equal right to the most extensive total system of equal basic liberties and opportunities (including equal opportunities for meaningful work, for self-determination and political and economic participation) compatible with a similar treatment of all. (This principle gives expression to a commitment to attain and/or sustain equal moral autonomy and equal self-respect.)
2. After provisions are made for common social (community) values, for capital overhead to preserve the society's productive capacity, allowances made for differing unmanipulated needs and preferences, and due weight is given to the just entitlements of individuals, the income and wealth (the common stock of means) is to be so divided that each person will have a right to an equal share. The necessary burdens requisite to enhance human well-being are also to be equally shared, subject, of course, to limitations by differing abilities and differing situations. (Here I refer to different natural environments and the like and not to class position and the like.)

...

II

...

A central intent of my second principle of egalitarian justice is to try to reduce inequalities in primary social goods or basic goods. The intent is to reduce inequalities in goods that are the source of or ground for distinctions that will give one person power or control over another. All status distinctions should be viewed with suspicion. Everyone should be treated equally as moral persons and, in spite of what will often be rather different moral conduct, everyone should be viewed as having equal moral worth.

The second principle is meant as a tool in trying to attain a state of affairs where there are no considerable differences in life prospects between different groups of people because some have a far greater income, power, authority or privilege than others. My second principle argues for distributing the benefits and burdens so that they are, as far as is compatible with people having different abilities and needs, equally shared. It does not say that all wealth should be divided equally, like equally dividing up a pie. Part of the social product must be used for things that are public goods, e.g., hospitals, schools, roads, clean air, recreation facilities and the like. And part of it must be used to protect future generations. Another part must be used to preserve the society's productive capacity so that there will be a continuous and adequate supply of goods to be divided. However, we must beware—coming out of an economically authoritarianly controlled capitalist society geared to production for profit and capital accumulation and only secondarily to meet needs—of becoming captivated or entrapped by productivism. We need democratically controlled decisions about what is to be produced, who is to produce it and how much is to be produced. The underlying rationale must be to meet, as fully as possible, and as equally as possible, allowing for their different needs, the needs of all the people. Care must be taken, particularly in the period of transition out of a capitalist society, that the needs referred to are needs people would acknowledge when they were fully aware of the various hidden persuaders operating on them. And the satisfaction of a given person's needs must, as far as possible, be compatible with other people being able similarly so to satisfy their needs.

A similar attitude should be taken toward preferences. People at different ages, in different climates, with different needs and preferences will, in certain respects, need different treatment. They all, however, must start with a baseline in which their basic needs are met—needs that they will have in common. (Again what exactly they are and how this is to be ascertained is something which needs careful examination.)

Rawls' primary goods captures something of what they are. What more is required will be a matter of dispute and will vary culturally and historically. However, there is enough of a core here to give us a basis for consensus and, given an egalitarian understanding of the concept of social justice, there will be a tendency to expand what counts as "basic needs." Beyond that, the differing preferences and needs should, as far as possible, have equal satisfaction, though what is involved in the rider "as far as possible" is not altogether evident. But it is only fair to give them all a voice. No compossible need should be denied satisfaction where the person with the need wishes its satisfaction when he/she is well-informed and would continue to want its satisfaction were he/she rationally to deliberate. Furthermore, giving them all a voice has, as well, other worthwhile features. It is evident enough that people are different. These differences are sometimes the source of conflict. Attaching the importance to them that some people do, can, in certain circumstances, be ethnocentric and chauvinist. But it is also true that these differences are often the source of human enrichment. Both fairness and human flourishing are served by the stress on giving equal play to the satisfaction of all desires that are compossible.

So my second principle of justice is not the same as a principle which directs that a pie be equally divided, though it is like it in its underlying intent, namely that fairness starts with a presumption of equality and only modifies a strict equal division of whatever is to be divided in order to remain faithful to the underlying intent of equal treatment. For example, two sisters may not both be given skates—one is given skates, which is what she wants, and the other is given snowshoes, which is what she wants. Thus both, by being in a way treated differently, are treated with equal concern for the satisfaction of their preferences. Treating people like this catches a central part of our most elemental sense of what fair treatment comes to.

It should also be noted that my second principle says that each person, subject to the above qualifications, has a right to an equal share. That is, they will have, where sufficient abundance makes this possible, an equal right to the resources necessary to satisfy their needs in a way that is compatible with others likewise satisfying their needs. But this does not mean that all or even most people will exercise that right or that they will feel that they should do so. This is generally true of rights. I have a right to run for office and to make a submission to a federal regulatory agency concerning the running of the C.B.C. But I have yet even to dream of exercising either of those rights, though I would be very aggrieved if they were taken away; and, in not exercising them, I have done nothing untoward. People, if they are rational, will exercise their rights to shares in what Rawls calls the primary goods, since having them is necessary to achieving anything else they want, but they will not necessarily demand equal shares and they will surely be very unlikely to demand equal shares of all the goodies of the world. People's wants and needs are simply too different for that. I have, or rather should have, an equal right to have fish pudding or a share in the world's stock of jelly beans. *Ceteris paribus,* I have an equal right to as much of either as anyone else, but, not wanting or liking either, I will not demand my equal share.

When needs are at issue something even stronger should be said. If I need a blood transfusion, I have, *ceteris paribus,* a right equal to anyone else's. But I must actually need it before I have a right to an equal share or indeed to any blood plasma at all. Moreover, people who need blood have an equal right to the amount they require, compatible with others who are also in need of having the same treatment; but, before they can have blood at all, they must need it. My wanting it does not give me a right to any of the common stock, let alone an equal share. And, even for the people actually getting the blood, it is unlikely that a fair share would be an equal share. Their needs here would probably be too different.

How does justice as equality work where it is impossible to give equal shares? Consider the equal right to have a blood transfusion. Suppose in a remote community at a given time two people both need, for their survival, an immediate transfusion and it was impossible to give them both a transfusion at that time. There is no way of getting blood of the requisite type in time, and in order to live each person needs the whole supply of available plasma—thus it cannot be divided. There can, at least for people who are being even remotely reasonable, be no equal division here. Still are not some distributions just and others unjust? If there are no relevant differences between the people needing the plasma, the only just thing to do is to do something like flipping a coin. But there almost always are relevant differences and then we are in a somewhat different ball game.

It might be thought that, even more generally in such a situation, the radical egalitarian should say: "In such a situation a coin should be tossed" but suppose the two people involved were quite similar in all relevant respects except that A had been a frequent donor of blood and B had never given blood. There is certainly a temptation to bring in desert and say that A is entitled to it and B is not. A had done his fair share in a cooperative situation and B had not, so it is only fair that A gets it. (We think of justice not only as equality but also as reciprocity.) Since "ought" implies "can" and, since we cannot divide it equally, it does not violate my second principle or the conception of justice as equality to so distribute the plasma.

I would not say that to do so is unjust, but, given my reservations about giving a central place to the category of desert ... I would hesitate to say that justice requires it. But the central thing to see here is that such a distribution according to desert does not violate my second principle or run counter to justice as equality.

Suppose, to take a different example, the individuals involved were an A′ and a B′. They are alike in all relevant respects except that A′ is a young woman who, with the transfusion would soon be back in good health and who has three children, and B′ is a woman ninety years of age, severely mentally enfeebled, without dependents and who would most probably die within the year anyway. It seems to me that the right thing to do under the circumstances is to give the plasma to A′. Again it does not violate my second principle for an equal division is rationally impossible. But it is not correct to say A′ deserves it more than B′ or even, in a straightforward way, needs it more. We can, however, relevantly say, because of the children, that more needs would be satisfied if A′ gets it than B′. This is bringing in utilitarian reasoning here; but, whatever we would generally say about utilitarianism as a complete moral theory, it seems to me perfectly appropriate to use such reasoning in this context. We could also say—and notice the role universalizability and role reversal play here—that, after all, B′ had lived her life to the full, was now quite incapable of having the experiences and satisfactions that we normally can be expected to prize and indeed will soon not have any experiences at all, while A′, by contrast, has much of the fullness of her life before her. Fairness here, since we have to make such a horrible choice, would seem to require that we give the plasma to A′ or, if "fairness" is not the correct notion here, a certain conception of rightness seems to dictate that, everything considered, that is the right thing to do.

Let me briefly consider a final pair A″ and B″. Again they are alike in every respect except that A″ is the community's only doctor while B″ is an unemployable, hopeless drunk. Both are firm bachelors and they are both middle-aged. B″ is not likely to change his ways or A″ to stop supplying needed medical services to the community. Here it seems to me we again quite rightly appeal to social utility—to the overall good of the community—and give the plasma to A″. Even if, since after all he is the only doctor, A″ makes the decision himself in his favor, it is still something that can be impartially sustained. Again my second principle has not been violated since an equal division is impossible.

I think that all three of those cases—most particularly the last two with their utilitarian rationale—might be resisted because of the feeling that they, after all, violate not only my second principle, but, more generally, that they also run against the underlying rationale of justice as equality by not giving equal treatment to persons. B, B′ and B″ are simply treated as expendable in a utilitarian calculation. They are treated merely as means.

This response seems to me to be mistaken. B, B′ and B″ are no more than the As simply being ignored. If the roles were reversed and they had the features of the A they are paired with, then they should get the plasma. They are not being treated differently as *individuals*. We start from a baseline of equality. If there were none of these differences between them, if there were no other relevant differences, there would be no grounds to choose between them. We could not, from a moral point of view, simply favor A because he was A. Just as human beings, as moral persons or persons who can become capable of moral agency, we do not distinguish between them and we must treat them equally. In the limiting case, where they are only spatiotemporally distinct, this commitment to equality of treatment is seen most clearly. Morality turns into favoritism and

privilege when this commitment is broken or ignored. *Within* morality there is no bypassing it; that is fixed by the very language-game of morality (by what the concept is, if you don't like that idiom).

III

...

[A] glance at my two radical egalitarian principles should make it evident that I do not want to reduce people to a uniform sameness of condition, such that they all get the same things, do the same things, have the same interests and in general behave in the same way. That is not what my conception of equal wealth aims at or would result in. I stress the importance of recognizing differences in need and stress that they must be catered to by an equal distribution principle. This is built into the formulation of my second principle. I also stress that, where we have full abundance, need should be a criterion of distribution, though not the sole criterion. I only claim that, once allowances are made for human differences and the like, in a world of moderate scarcity, each individual should have a right to an equal share of the available resources where, of course, such sharing is possible.

What I am *most* concerned to avoid, ... is not income differentials but inequality in whole life prospects between members of different classes and strata. With such differences, there exists control, domination and privilege by one group over another. It is a control etc. that makes the lives of some groups quite arbitrarily better and more autonomous than those of other groups. Since this is so, there must be, to achieve social justice, a levelling such that a society will come into existence that has neither classes nor strata. This I call a *statusless* society. Essential for the existence of such a society—not the whole of it but something without which the rest is impossible—is an equality in political and economic power.

It is essential for equal autonomy and equal autonomy in turn provides the rational basis for equal self-respect. This in turn is necessary if there is to obtain a situation in which there is an equal respect for all human beings.

However, I also argue, ... that in a socialist reconstruction of society, where the society is one of relative abundance and tending toward classlessness, the underlying general conception should be that of everyone having a right to an equal share, where there is something like an equal need, of the available resources that can be shared.

We should start with this presumption, a presumption showing an equal concern for all human beings, and a belief—rooted in that equal concern—that there should in the normal case at least be an equality of the overall level of benefits and burdens. Departures from that initial presumption must be justified first on the basis of differing genuine needs and differing situations (where differences in rank do not count as being in a different situation) and secondly on differing preferences where the first two are satisfied or irrelevant. The case of handicapped people is an obvious case where some adjustments must be made. But plainly this is not the normal case, and a theory of social justice set for the design of a just society must first set itself out for the normal case and then add the qualifications necessary for the exceptional cases. This, as I have already shown, in a very literal sense, is not to treat everyone the same and it avoids what I believe is one of the most persistent criticisms of radical egalitarianism, namely that it advocates, or would result in, a grey, uniform world of sameness where human freedom, creativeness and diversity would be destroyed.

4. Impediments to Radical Egalitarianism

...

In asking about justice as equality, three questions readily spring to mind: (1) Why is a greater equality in the conditions of life desirable? (2) Is anything like my radical egalitarianism something that could actually be achieved or even be reasonably approximated? (3) Given the steep inequalities that actually exist, if they (or at least most of them) are eradicable, are they only so at an unacceptable cost? In short, is the cost of equality too high?

There is no complete answer to (1), (2), and (3) which is entirely independent. There is, that is to say, reason for not considering them in utter isolation. ... A short answer to (1) ... is that a greater equality is desirable because it brings with it greater moral autonomy and greater self-respect for more people. It isn't, as some conservative critics assume, so much equality *per se* which is so desirable but what it brings in the way of human flourishing, though there is in such egalitarian thinking the assumption that the most extensive equal realization of that is an end devoutly to be desired. What I argued for [elsewhere] I shall assume here, namely, that equality, if its costs are not too high, is desirable. I shall assume, that is, that (1) has a positive answer at least when it is not considered in relation to (2) and (3). But, as (3) asks, are the costs of this equality, after all, just too high? Many conservative critics claim that they are.[2] I shall, before I turn to (2), consider (3), as it is more closely linked to (1).

It is pointed out by conservative critics that we cannot in our assessments of what is just and what is unjust start from scratch. Goods to be distributed do not come down, like manna from heaven; they come with entitlements. Certain people have produced them, bought them, been given them, inherited them, found them, struggled to make them and to preserve them. To think that we can override their entitlements in setting out ideal distributive patterns is to fail to respect people. It is to be willing to run over their rights in redistributing goods—to treat some people as means only. A society in which a state or a class can take from people what is rightfully theirs cannot be a just society The ideals of equality and the ideals of justice are different ideals. Equality is a forward looking virtue concerned, some conservative theorists claim, with seeing that it is the case that people have their various and not infrequently unequal entitlements.[3] Justice will be done in a society when people have what they are entitled to. The idea isn't to establish a certain distributive pattern, but to protect people's entitlements. Because this is what justice really is, rather than anything about equality, it will sometimes be the case that an individual, a family, or even a class will quite justly achieve certain advantages on which the rest of the society can have no proper claim. Our maxim for justice should *not* be "Holdings ought to be equal unless there is a weighty moral reason they ought to be unequal," where the burden of proof is always to justify unequal treatment. Rather, our maxim should be "People are entitled to keep whatever they happen to have unless there is a weighty moral reason why they ought to give it up." The burden of proof has now shifted to the redistributivist to justify a redistribution.[4] The normal situation will be that people will be entitled to what they have properly acquired. These entitlements are rooted in the particular situations and activities of people. They cannot in the typical situation be equal. Fairness doesn't come to distributing things equally, even with allowance for differing needs, but to *not* taking from people what they are entitled to. Particular entitlements can be challenged, but if anyone with a passion for justice sets out "systematically and at a stroke to devalue the lot, in the interests of a new strictly forward-looking distribution, he is, by this move, abandoning the whole notion of justice in favour of another alternative ideal."[5]

I shall return to this objection in a moment. However, even if it is the case that some

distinction between social justice and individual justice or justice in distribution and justice in acquisition should show this criticism to be mistaken, there are still two related objections that remain in place and again have to do with the value of individual autonomy. (It is the three together which seem to me to constitute a formidable cluster of objections.) Firstly, it is claimed that if we treat social justice as equality, we will repeatedly have to use state intervention to keep the pattern of distribution at the requisite level of equality, for people in their ordinary transactions will continually upset the pattern whatever the pattern may be. But such continual intervention constitutes an intolerable interference in the lives of people. No one who cares about individual liberty and moral autonomy could support that. Secondly, in a democratic society people would not support with their votes a redistributive policy that was egalitarian, let alone the radical egalitarianism that I propose. It would have to be imposed from above by some dictatorial elite. It will not be accepted in a democratic society. Again, its costs would be too high because it could only be achieved by abandoning democracy.

I shall start with the last objection for that one seems to me the weakest. It seems to me that it is not at all a question of imposing or trying to impose egalitarianism on anyone. In the first place, it is unrealistic because it cannot be done; but, even if it could and such a procedure were not self-undermining, it still would be undesirable. Justice as equality is set out as an ideal of social justice which, radical egalitarians argue, best captures what is fundamental to the very idea of justice. The thing is, by moral argumentation in "the public sphere," to use Jurgen Habermas' conception, to convince people of it. There is no question at all of imposing it or of an "egalitarian clerisy" indoctrinating people. Whatever the morality of it, it is impractical to try in such circumstances to impose equality or such an understanding of justice. The only road here is through patient and careful social argumentation to make the case for egalitarianism.

Socialists are well aware that the consciousness industry will be turned against radical egalitarianism and that there will be a barrage of propaganda directed against it, some (depending on the audience) subtle and some unsubtle. It will not get a fair hearing, but there is nothing else to be expected from a class society in the hands of a class who must be deeply opposed to egalitarianism. But this is just a specific application of the general political problem of how social change can be achieved in an increasingly managed class society. This is one of the deep and intractable social problems of our time—one of the problems Max Horkheimer and Theodore Adorno anguished over—and, particularly for those of us in developed capitalist societies, it is a very puzzling and intractable problem indeed. But whatever we should say and do here, it will not be the case that we intelligentsia should try to impose egalitarian ideals on an unwilling working class. Until the working class—the vast majority of people—see fit to set about the construction of a genuinely egalitarian society, the role of the intellectual can, and should, be that of someone who through the employment of critical analysis and ideology critique makes attempts at consciousness raising in his society. (This is, of course, also perfectly compatible with an unflinching search for truth.)

II

I want now to consider the second objection, namely, the claim that any patterned distribution, and most particularly the patterned distributions of radical egalitarianism, would require such continuous and massive state intervention that it would undermine individual liberty and the moral autonomy essential for the good of self-respect.

This objection uncritically makes all the background assumptions of laissez-faire capitalism—a social order which has not existed for a long time and probably could not exist in our contemporary world. But a society committed to radical egalitarianism would also be a genuinely socialist society and would have very different background conditions. The objection just unrealistically assumes a genuinely free market society where people are busy, possessive individualists devoted to accumulating and bargaining and are concerned very centrally with protecting their private property. It simply assumes that human beings, independently of the particular type of socialization they have been subject to, have very little sense of or feeling for community or cooperativeness, except in the form of bargaining (again the free market being the model). But a society in which radical egalitarianism could flourish would be an advanced socialist society under conditions of considerable abundance. People would not have a market orientation. They would not be accumulators or possessive individualists, and the aim of their economic organization would not be profit maximization but the satisfaction of the human needs of everyone. The more pressing problems of scarcity would have been overcome. Everyone would have a secure life, their basic needs would be met, and their level of education, and hence their critical consciousness, would be much higher than it is now, such that, in their situation, they would not be committed to Gomper's dictum of "more." Furthermore, the society would be thoroughly democratic and this would mean industrial democracy as well as political democracy. That would mean that working people (which would include all able-bodied adults) would control—collectively control in a fair democratic manner—their own work: that is, the production relations would be in their hands as well as the governmental functions of the society, which in this changed environment would have become essentially administrative functions. In fine, the institutions of the society and the psychological motivations of people would be very different than those implicitly appealed to in the objection. Under these conditions, the state, if that is the best thing still to call it, would not be the instrument of class oppression and management that it now is. People would democratically manage their own lives and the design of their society in a genuine *gemeinschaft* so that there would no longer exist structures of class domination interfering with people's liberties. People would be their own masters with a psychology that thinks in terms of "we" and not just, and most fundamentally, in terms of "I," where the protection of my rights is the crucial thing. Moreover, now the society would be so organized that cooperation made sense and was not engaged in just to avoid the "state of nature." The society would be a secure society of relative abundance. (Communism and radical egalitarianism are unthinkable in any other situation.) It would be a society in which the needs of everyone would be met. Since the society would be geared, within the limits of reasonable growth, to maximize for everyone, and as equally as possible, the satisfaction of their needs, a roughly egalitarian pattern would be in a steady state. It would not have to be constantly tinkered with to maintain the pattern. People would not, in such a secure situation, have such a possessive hankering to acquire things or to pass them on. Such acquisitiveness would no longer be such a major feature of our psychologies. Moreover, given the productive wealth of the society, there would be no need to worry if in practice distributions sometimes swayed a little from the norm of equality. Everyone would have plenty and have security; people would not be possessive individualists bent on accumulating and obsessively concerned with mine and thine. There would, moreover, be no way for anyone to become a capitalist and

exploit others and indeed there would be precious little motivation to do so.

If, in spite of this, an elite did show signs of forming, there would be firmly in place democratic institutions sufficient to bring about the demise of such deviations from the norm. This should not be pictured as an impersonal dictatorial state interfering with people's liberties, but as the people acting collectively to protect their liberties against practices which would undermine them. Yet that things like this would actually happen— that such elitist practices would evolve—in such a situation of abundance and cooperation is rather unlikely. In such circumstances, the pattern of distribution of justice as equality would be stable and, when it did require adjustment, it would be done by a democratic government functioning to protect and further the interests of everyone. This patterning would not upset liberty and undermine moral autonomy and self-respect.

III

I will now turn to the first objection—the objection that justice is entitlement and not anything even like equality. ... It may be that justice as entitlement is that part of justice which is concerned with justice in initial acquisition and in transfer of what is initially justly acquired and is not distributive justice at all, the justice in social schemes of cooperation. It may be that these are two different species of justice that need capturing in some larger overall theory. Be that as it may, the challenge of justice as entitlement seems, at least on the surface, to be a very real one. Entitlement theorists certainly have a hold of something that is an essential part of justice.[6]

... [H]ere I believe I can ... give a practical answer which will show that such a challenge is not a threat to justice as equality. In doing this I want to show that such a conception of justice is consistent with the rights of entitlement. Recall that a radical egalitarian will also be a socialist. He will be concerned with justice in the distribution of products, but he will be centrally concerned as well with justice in production.[7] His concern with the justice to be obtained in production will come, most essentially, to a concern with transforming society from a society of private ownership and control of the means of production to one of a social ownership and control of the means of production, such that each worker—in a world of workers—will have an equal say in the disposition and rationale of work. (Control here seems to me the key notion. In such new production relations, the very idea of ownership *may* not have any unproblematic meaning.) It will, that is, be work which is democratically controlled. The aim will be to end class society and the dominance of an elite managerial stratum. Justice as equality most essentially requires a society with no bosses. The demand for equality is most fundamentally a demand to end that state of affairs and to attain a situation of equal moral autonomy and self-respect.

These considerations are directly relevant when we consider that entitlement conceptions of justice are most at home in situations where a person has mixed his labor and care with something, say built and lovingly cared for a house or built up a family farm. It would, *ceteris paribus,* be wrong, plainly unjust, to take those possessions away from that person and give them to someone else. But a radical egalitarian is not challenging entitlements of this type. Socialists do not want to take people's houses or family farms from them. In a Communist society there are consumer durables and there is individual property, e.g., people can own their own car, house, family farm, family fishing boat, and the like. The private property socialists seek to eliminate is private ownership and control of the major means of production. This is the private property that is the central source and

sustainer of class divisions, of the great power of one person over another and the great advantages of one group over another. This form of private ownership is at the root of much existing exploitation and injustice. This is most crucially true of the great industries controlling vast resources and employing wage labor. Family farms and family fishing boats, as long as they do not sprout into empires employing many wage-laborers, are not the problem.[8] The equality aimed at by radical egalitarians is that of a classless, statusless society. But in such a society the type of personal entitlements that we have been speaking of can perfectly well remain intact. And it is just such entitlements that are allowed for in the articulation of my second principle of justice. It is over entitlements of this last sort that our moral convictions remain firmest.

The entitlement theorist will surely respond by saying "If the person who builds a house or works a farm up out of a wilderness is entitled to it, why isn't a capitalist who, through his own initiative, creativeness, and dogged determination, creates an industrial empire entitled to keep his property as well?" They both are the effect of something we prize in human nature, namely, we see here human beings not merely as satisfiers of desires but as exercisers of opportunities. At least in some cases, though less and less typically now, they can be his hard-earned and creatively-struggled-for holdings.

This creates a presumption of entitlement, but only a presumption. (Alternatively, we can say it creates an entitlement but a defeasible one that can be rightly overridden.) We have, as is not the case with the house or the family farm, very good grounds indeed for overriding this presumption and requiring a redistribution. Remember the conservative principle was "People are entitled to keep whatever they happen to have, unless there is a weighty moral reason why they should relinquish it." Well, in this situation, there are weighty moral reasons, entirely absent in cases like that of the fishing boat, family farm or house. First, in our historical circumstances, such capitalist ownership and control of the means of production causes extensive misery and impoverishment that could otherwise be avoided. Secondly, it gives capitalists and a small managerial elite (who are often also capitalists themselves) control over people's lives in such a way as to lessen their effective equal citizenship and undermine their self-respect and moral autonomy. Moreover, these are not inevitabilities of human life but the special and inescapable features of a class society, where there must be a dominant capitalist class who owns and controls the means of production. But they are not inescapable features of the human condition and they have not been shown simply to be something that must come with industrial society.

Someone determined to defend laissez-faire capitalism and an entitlement theory of justice might tough it out and claim that the error in the above entitlement theorist's conduct of his case is in stating his account in such a conditional way, namely, that "People are entitled to keep whatever they happen to have, unless there is a (weighty) moral reason why they ought to relinquish it." It should instead be stated as "People are entitled to their holdings if the initial acquisition was just and any transfer from it just; the initial acquisition, in turn, was just if it accords with the Lockean proviso that it was taken from unclaimed land and if the initial appropriation left enough in kind for everyone else." This principle of justice is designed, in the way the first entitlement account was not, to normatively block any attempt by the state or any group of people to justifiably compel any transfer, under any circumstances not specified in the above formulation, of any holdings to satisfy any redistributive scheme. Any person, quite categorically, may justifiably and justly hold on to whatever he initially justly acquired, no

matter what the consequences. There is the obvious point that we do not know how to go about ascertaining whether in fact the patterns of holdings now in effect result from just acquisitions via just transfers. But this obvious point aside, such a categorical entitlement account has plain defects. To take such a right of property to be a moral absolute is unduly to narrow even a right-based moral theory. A society organized with that as its fundamental moral principle—a principle of justice which could never rightly be overridden—would lead to the degradation of large numbers of people. They would, in circumstances such as our own, have the *formal* rights to acquire property but in actuality they would have little or no property and their impoverishment and loss of autonomy and self-respect would be very great indeed. To hold on to an unqualified right to property in those circumstances would be not only arbitrary and morally one-sided, it would be morally callous as well. Moreover, it is not a commitment that clearheadedness and a devotion to rationality dictates. What such a one-valued absolutism neglects is that we are morally obliged to respond to suffering. On such an entitlement theory we would not be obliged to relieve the suffering of another even when we could do so without serious loss to ourselves. What it gains here in categoricalness, it *loses* in moral coherence. To have an understanding of the moral language-game, to have an understanding of what morality requires, we need to understand that we cannot be indifferent to the sufferings of others. Are we morally justified in holding onto even a *minuscule* bit of our property, say food which could be shared with a starving person, when sharing it could be done without any serious inconvenience to ourselves? To think that, morally speaking, our options are open in such a situation is not only to exhibit moral callousness, it is also to reveal a failure even to understand what it is to take a moral point of view. To avoid harming others and violating their rights is, of course, as this entitlement account stresses, central to morality, but morality requires—taking a moral point of view requires—that, under certain circumstances, preventing or alleviating or remedying the misery of others is also part of our duty. The recognition of such duties undermines such a categorical commitment to entitlements to private property. Sometimes we are morally compelled to redistribute. Anything else would be grossly unjust and immoral. Whether we feel compassion or not, the relief of human misery, where this is reasonably within our capacities, is something that is morally required of us. What we otherwise would be entitled to, we can hardly be entitled to when we could, by sharing it, save the life of another and (to put it concessively and minimally) not cause any great distress to ourselves. My last remark can easily be misunderstood. It is not so much demands placed on individuals within an unjust social system that are crucial but a commitment on the part of individuals to alter the social system. In a period of political stagnation, to demand of a tolerably well off suburbanite that he greatly diminish his holdings and send a not inconsiderable sum of money to the Sahel comes too close to requiring him to be a Don Quixote. What needs to be altered is the social system. To maintain that severe sacrifices are required of individuals when there is little prospect of turning the society around is to ask them to be martyrs if, by so acting, there is not a chance for significant social change. Still, morally speaking, there has to be redistribution, and where we genuinely could relieve misery to not acknowledge that such a *sharing* is required of us is to fail to grasp something very essential to morality. Failure here is as much a moral failing as an intellectual one and no amount of cleverness can get around that.

IV

I want now to turn to the second general problem about radical egalitarianism I mentioned [earlier]. Some critics of egalitarianism maintain that however abstractly desirable egalitarianism may be, it still is an impossible ideal, for it is impossible to achieve or even reasonably to approximate.[9] Such a criticism would apply doubly to my radical form of egalitarianism. We must just come to recognize, so the criticism goes, that inequality is inevitable and erect our account of justice in the light of this inevitability.

Are there any basic features or functional prerequisites of society or human nature that make inequality inevitable in all societies or at least in all industrial societies? I shall limit my answer to remarks about industrial societies and consider the claim that classes, bureaucracies (with their hierarchical social relations) and social stratification are inevitable. The inevitability of any of them would ensure that any future industrial society would also be to some degree a status society with a ranking of people, and not just a society with differentiations, according to social roles. With these inequalities in status there would be the differences in power and authority that have plagued societies in the past and continue to plague our societies.

It has been claimed that inequalities are functionally necessary to any industrial society. There will be a division of labor and a differentiation of social roles in those societies. Since certain social roles are functionally more important than others—being a doctor at the Crisis Center is functionally more important than being a ski instructor—and since suitable performance in these more important roles requires suitable training and discipline, it is necessary to induce with adequate rewards those with the appropriate talents to delay gratification and take on the required training—the long years of struggle in medical school, graduate school, or law school. This is done by assuring them that at the end of their training they will be rewarded more highly for their sacrifice in taking on that training. This requires the inequalities of differential incentives. People, the argument goes, simply will not make the sacrifice of going to medical school or going to law school unless they have very good reason to believe that they will make much more money than they would by selling cars or running a little shop. To stream people into these functionally necessary occupations, there must be differential rewards and with those rewards social stratification with its concomitant inequalities in prestige, power, and authority. Moreover, we must do this to make sure that the most talented people will continue to occupy the most functionally important positions and to work at their maximal capacity. The very good of the society requires it.

The first thing to note is that all this, even if sound, does not add up to an inevitability. Still, some might say that it is all the same a "rational inevitability," given that it is a functional prerequisite for the proper functioning of an industrial society. But is it actually a functional prerequisite? Again, like some of the previous criticisms of egalitarianism we have examined, it simply uncritically assumes something like contemporary capitalism as being the norm for how any industrial society must operate, but there is no reason why the additional training should be a form of sacrifice or even be regarded as a sacrifice. It too much takes the ideology of the present as an accurate depiction of social reality. In an egalitarian society, by contrast, everyone would be materially secure and there would be no material loss in remaining in medical school, law school, or graduate school. Once that becomes so and once the pace is slowed down, as it really could be, so that students are not rushed through at great stress and strain, it would be, for many people at least, far less of

a sacrifice to go through medical school than to be a bank-teller, rug salesman, or assembly line workman all day. For many people, perhaps for most people of normal intelligence, the work both during their school years and afterwards would be more rewarding and challenging than present-day routine jobs. There is no need to provide special incentives, given other suitable changes in society, changes which are quite feasible if we do not continue to take a capitalist organization of society as normative. It is a particular social structure with its distinctive value scheme (scheduling of values) that requires such incentives and such attitudes towards incentives—not anything in the nature of industrial society itself. (I leave aside whether we can, for a whole range of cases, and not just in some obvious cases, identify, in a non-ethnocentric manner, what the functionally important positions are. Are ministers more important than garage mechanics? Are lawyers more important than dental technicians? Are marriage counsellors more important than airline stewardesses?)

A more interesting argument for the inevitability of inequality is Ralf Dahrendorf's claim that the very concept of a society is such that, when we think of its implications, we realize that there could not—logically could not—be a society without inequalities.[10] A society by definition is a moral, as distinct from amoral, community. We might say of a way of life of a society that we deeply disapprove of that it is an immoral society. It makes sense to say (that is, it is not a deviation from a linguistic regularity to say) "Swedish sexual morality is immoral," but it makes no sense to speak of an amoral society. In that sense every society is a moral community. It will have a cluster of norms, tolerably integrated, which regulate the conduct of its members. Moreover, these norms carry one or another kind of sanction which ensure their obligatory character by providing rewards for conforming to them and penalties for deviation from them. Dahrendorf concludes from that that "the sanctioning of human behaviour in terms of social norms necessarily creates a system of inequality of rank and that social stratification is therefore an immediate result of the control of social behaviour by positive and negative sanctions."[11] But, given the very idea of what it is for a mass of people to be a society, there could not be a society without such norms; but, if there are such norms, then there must also be a schedule of inequalities.

Steven Lukes, quite succinctly, exposes the crucial mistakes in Dahrendorf's influential argument.[12] "It does not follow," Lukes argues, "from the mere existence of social norms and the fact that their enforcement discriminates against those who do not or cannot (because of their social position) conform to them that a society-wide system of inequality and 'rank order of social status' are 'bound to emerge.'"[13] From the fact that a society, actually to be a society at all, must have norms, spelling out what it is right and wrong to do, and that it must apply sanctions to assure general compliance, it does not follow that these norms are the sort of norms that would provide a social stratification with a hierarchy of power, status, and authority. An egalitarian society would have norms and the associated sanctions too, only they would be far less oppressive and pervasive. As Lukes nicely puts it, "Dahrendorf slides unaccountably from the undoubted truth that within groups norms are enforced which discriminate against certain persons and positions ... to the unsupported claim that, within a society as a whole, a system of inequality between groups and positions is inevitable."[14] Dahrendorf gives us no grounds for believing that all societies must, because they have various norms carrying sanctions, be organizations which have a system of stratification, either implicit or explicit, in which their various norms and behavior are ranked within a single system of stratification.

V

I now turn to what I, at least, take to be the most troubling arguments about the inevitability of inequality in industrial societies. They turn on the claim that the empirical evidence, when linked to reasonable theories and arguments, shows that a status society is inevitable under the conditions of modern life. There is no way of making industrial societies free of bureaucracy with the cluster of privileges and differential power and authority which go with such inegalitarian structures.

It is reasonable to argue that there are, when we look at the various modern societies (including Russia, China, Cuba, and Yugoslavia), no classless societies, or what is more relevant, and from a leftist perspective more disturbing, no societies which are clearly tending in the direction of classless societies. Given this, isn't radical egalitarianism implausible? Would it not be better, given these empirical facts, to opt for a more modest egalitarianism with principles something like Rawls'? We must not tell ourselves Marxist fairy tales!

...

First the facts. We have not had any proletarian revolutions yet, though we have had revolutions made in the name of a very small and undeveloped proletariat.[15] We have yet to have a dictatorship of the proletariat—a society controlled by the proletariat and run principally in its own interests. The state socialist societies that exist are not socialist societies that developed in the conditions that Marx said was propitious for the development of socialism but (East Germany and Czechoslovakia aside as isolated exceptions) in economically backward societies that had yet to experience a bourgeois revolution. It is also a fact that these socialist societies (if that is the right name for them) [have been] surrounded by strong capitalist societies which are, naturally enough, implacably hostile to socialism.

... If the instability of monopoly capitalism increases and if the Third World remains unpacified, conditions in the industrially developed capitalist countries may change. A militancy and a sense of class may arise and class conflict may no longer be merely a muted and disguised reality. That could lead to the first social transformation by an actual proletarian class, a class developed enough, educated enough, numerous enough, and strong enough to democratically run things in its own interests and to pave the way for a society organized in the interests of everyone, namely a classless society. I do not maintain that we have good grounds for saying that it will happen. I say only that that scenario is a coherent possibility. Minimally I do not believe that anyone has shown this to be a mere dream, a fantastic bit of utopianism. If it is also, as I believe it to be—everything considered—a desirable possibility, it is something to be struggled for with all the class conflict that that will involve.

VI

However, even if all this is so, there remains another worrying objection which tends to engender the anxiety that a statusless radically egalitarian society may still be pie in the sky by and by. Suppose we can achieve a strictly classless society, that is, a society in which there is no structural means by which a historically extendable (intra-generational) group, by means of its social role, can extract surplus value from another group because all remuneration is according to work and there is no land-rent or profits from shares and the like. However, even in such a society, as Mihailo Marković observes, ... there still could be political elites or at least bureaucratic elites.[16] These elites could come to exert considerable domination over other people and, even if there was only a bureaucratic elite and that bureaucratic elite had little political power,

something which is actually not very likely while it remained an elite, still their high status would make for considerable social inequality and would plainly be harmful to the egalitarian commitment to equal self-respect and to equal moral autonomy. Thus, even though in a strict sense classes were no more, it could be the case that a status society of rank and privilege could still exist with a rather sharp social stratification which would still contain considerable differences in whole life prospects. Differences which are clearly incompatible with a radical egalitarianism.

Marković is no doubt right in saying that it is at least "theoretically conceivable how the emergence of a hierarchy of power may be prevented."[17] Marković's prescription is like Marx's and Mao's. There is "democratic election, replaceability, and vertical rotation for all functions of social management."[18] While there will continue to be a division of labor, the persistent aim is to prevent the formation of a group of professional managers and to break down the class-impregnated and status-engendering traditional distinction between mental and manual labor. This will also cut down at least the extent of the bureaucracy. There will under such conditions be no persistent and stable group of people who alone will know how to manage the society and who can claim a kind of technical expertise in management that must simply be accepted and taken as authoritative and which will lead to a high status and, very likely, again to political power. The power of occupational roles and particularly of bureaucratic occupational roles is both understandable in an industrial society and threatening to egalitarianism and moral autonomy.

It surely is not known that status society can be overcome. It is simplistic wishful thinking to say that we know that it will be overcome. But it is also a too easy *realpolitik* to claim that we know that conditions cannot arise in which a society other than a hunting and gathering or an agricultural society could come into being and flourish which had no such elites. Whether it is probable that such a society is on the historical agenda is hard to say. Indeed it is not evident what, if anything, is on the historical agenda, but as far as I can see, it has not been shown not to be a reasonable historical possibility. Similar considerations obtain to those we noted in discussing class. The facts about the conditions under which state socialist societies emerged make the existence of status distinctions under such conditions practically speaking unavoidable. That they emerged is surely hardly surprising. It is those factors that can, when we reflect on them, make us prematurely pessimistic. But what would emerge out of a socialist revolution in an advanced industrial society, with an established bourgeois democratic tradition, is another thing again. Surely the bourgeoisie, and particularly the haute bourgeoisie who run our societies, would like us to be cultural pessimists, would like us not to believe in the possibility of "the art of the impossible." But what is reasonable to hope for, and to struggle for, should not be so culturally defined, defeating our hopes for a more human future. Given a humanistic conception of what sort of society is worth bringing into being, such a hope, given the stark alternatives, is not an unreasonable hope of human beings who are not blind to social reality.

Notes to "3. Radical Egalitarian Justice: Justice as Equality"

1 David Miller, "Democracy and Social Justice," *British Journal of Political Science* 8 (1977): 119.

2 Ted Honderich, *Three Essays on Political Violence* (Oxford: Basil Blackwell, 1976), pp. 37–44.

3 Christopher Ake, "Justice as Equality," *Philosophy and Public Affairs* 5, no. 1 (Fall 1975): 69–89.

4 Sidney Hook, *Revolution, Reform and Social Justice* (Oxford: Basil Blackwell, 1975), pp. 269–87.

Notes to "4. Impediments to Radical Egalitarianism"

...

2 Robert Nozick's *Anarchy, State, and Utopia* (New York: Basic Books, 1974) is the best known current example of such a conservative critique. But it has also been developed by Robert Nisbet in his "The Pursuit of Equality," *The Public Interest 35* (spring 1971): 103–20 and in his "The Costs of Equality" in *Small Comforts for Hard Times*, eds. Michael Mooney and Florian Stuber (New York: Columbia University Press, 1977), pp. 3–47; and Irving Kristol, "About Equality," *Commentary*, November, 1972.

3 Nozick, of course, argues this, but it has most intransigently been argued by Antony Flew in two articles: "Equality or Justice?" *Midwest Studies in Philosophy* 3 (1978): 176–94; and "A Theory of Social Justice" in *Contemporary British Philosophy*, ed. H.D. Lewis (New York: Humanities Press, 1976), pp. 69–85.

4 Flew, "Equality or Justice?" p. 183.

5 Ibid., p. 186.

6 Thomas Nagel, in his *Mortal Questions* (Cambridge, England: Cambridge University Press, 1979) and in his discussion of Nozick, indicates how entitlement conceptions and distributive conceptions may in reality mesh as complementary parts of a coherent conception of justice. See Thomas Nagel, *Mortal Questions* (Cambridge, England: Cambridge University Press, 1979), pp. 106–27; and his "Libertarianism Without Foundations," *Yale Law Journal* 85, no. 1 (November 1975): 136–49.

7 Ziyad I. Husami, "Marx on Distributive Justice," *Philosophy and Public Affairs* 8, no. 1 (Fall 1978): 27–64; Gary Young, "Justice and Capitalist Production: Marx and Bourgeois Ideology," *Canadian Journal of Philosophy* 8, no. 3 (September 1978): 421–55; Allen Buchanan, "The Marxian Critique of Justice and Rights," *Canadian Journal of Philosophy*, Supplementary Volume 7, pp. 269–306.

8 Nancy Holmstrom, "Exploitation," *Canadian Journal of Philosophy* 7, no. 2 (1977): 353–69; Allen Buchanan, "Exploitation, Alienation and Injustice," *Canadian Journal of Philosophy* 9, no. 1 (March 1979), pp. 121–39.

9 Ralf Dahrendorf, "On the Origin of Social Inequality" in *Philosophy, Politics and Society: Second Series,* eds. Peter Laslett and W.G. Runciman (Oxford: Basil Blackwell, 1962), pp. 83–109.

10 Dahrendorf, op. cit.

11 Ibid., p. 107.

12 Steven Lukes, "Socialism and Equality" in *The Socialist Idea,* eds. Leszek Kolakowski and Stuart Hampshire (London: Weidenfeld and Nicolson, 1974), pp. 74–95.

13 Ibid., p. 92.

14 Ibid., p. 93.

15 Irving Fetscher, "Karl Marx und die 'Marxistischen' Revolutionen," *Neue Züricher Zeitung,* September 30, 1977, pp. 35–36.

16 Mihailo Marković, *The Contemporary Marx* (Nottingham, England: Spokesman Books, 1974), pp. 128–39.

17 Ibid., p. 133.

18 Ibid.

Questions for Discussion

1 Is it too idealistic to suggest a society in which people aim at the satisfaction of the human needs of everyone, rather than personal accumulation of profit? To what extent are a person's goals determined by the society in which the person grows up?

2 Nielsen claims that equality is meant to promote "greater moral autonomy and greater self-respect for more people." Are these the only, or the most important, goals of society? Is equality, as Nielsen describes it, the best way of acquiring them? Should we aim to *equalize* or *maximize* autonomy and self-respect?

3 Is there a greater burden of proof on one who wants to justify unequal distributions of resources, or on one who wants to redistribute so as to promote equality?

A Definition of Health

From Preamble to the Constitution of the World Health Organization

World Health Organization

One reason often put forward for being concerned about the distribution of scarce resources is that people have a right to a fair chance at a healthy life. Whether there is such a right or not, it is clear that health is a very important moral value. However, it is not easy to define exactly what is meant by "health." The World Health Organization has offered the following broad definition.

★ ★ ★

The States Parties to this Constitution declare, in conformity with the Charter of the United Nations, that the following principles are basic to the happiness, harmonious relations and security of all peoples:

Health is a state of complete physical, mental and social well-being and not merely the absence of disease or infirmity.

The enjoyment of the highest attainable standard of health is one of the fundamental rights of every human being without distinction of race, religion, political belief, economic or social condition.

The health of all peoples is fundamental to the attainment of peace and security and is dependent upon the fullest co-operation of individuals and States.

The achievement of any State in the promotion and protection of health care is of value to all.

Unequal development in different countries in the promotion of health and control of disease, especially communicable disease, is a common danger.

Healthy development of the child is of basic importance; the ability to live harmoniously in a changing total environment is essential to such development.

The extension to all peoples of the benefits of medical, psychological and related knowledge is essential to the fullest attainment of health.

Informed opinion and active co-operation on the part of the public are of the utmost importance in the improvement of the health of the people.

Governments have a responsibility for the health of their peoples which can be ful-

filled only by the provision of adequate health and social measures.

Accepting these principles, and for the purpose of co-operation among themselves and with others to promote and protect the health of all peoples, the Contracting Parties agree to the present Constitution and hereby establish the World Health Organization as a specialized agency within the terms of Article 57 of the Charter of the United Nations.

Questions for Discussion

1 Does the WHO definition go too far in equating health with "complete physical, mental and social well-being"? If this broad definition is accepted, is it still plausible to claim that people have a "right to health care"?

2 To what extent would the full promotion of health require a restructuring of the existing economic order? Is this desirable?

Allocating Scarce Medical Resources

Case Presentation: Selection Committee for Dialysis

Ronald Munson

One of the central cases where issues arise with respect to how to distribute scarce resources is the case in which there is not enough medical care available for the number of people who need it. How is one to decide which people will receive the needed care, and which will have to do without? In the following somewhat speculative account of such a decision procedure, Ronald Munson raises some of the factors which might be considered relevant.

★   ★   ★

In 1966 Brattle, Texas, proper had a population of about ten thousand people. In Brattle County there were twenty thousand more people who lived on isolated farms deep within the pine forests, or in crossroads towns with a filling station, a feed store, one or two white, frame churches, and maybe twenty or twenty-five houses.

Brattle was the marketing town and county seat, the place all the farmers, their wives, and children went to on Saturday afternoon. It was also the medical center because it had the only hospitals in the county. One of them, Conklin Clinic, was hardly more than a group of doctors' offices. But Crane Memorial Hospital was quite a different sort of place. Occupying a relatively new three-story brick building in downtown Brattle, the hospital offered new equipment, a well-trained staff, and high quality medical care.

This was mostly due to the efforts of Dr. J.B. Crane, Jr. The hospital was dedicated to the memory of his father, a man who practiced medicine in Brattle County for almost fifty years. Before Crane became a memorial hospital, it was Crane Clinic. But J.B. Crane, Jr., after returning from the Johns Hopkins Medical School, was determined to expand the clinic and transform it into a modern hospital. The need was there, and private investors were easy to find. Only a year after his father's death, Dr. Crane was able to offer Brattle County a genuine hospital.

It was only natural that when the County Commissioner decided that Brattle County should have a dialysis machine, he would turn to Dr. Crane's hospital. The machine was bought with county funds, but Crane Memorial Hospital would operate it under a contract agreement. The hospital was guaranteed against loss by the county, but the hospital was also not permitted to make a profit on dialysis. Furthermore, although access to the machine was not restricted to county residents, residents were to be given priority.

Dr. Crane was not pleased with this stipulation. "I don't like to have medical decisions influenced by political considerations," he told the Commissioner. "If a guy comes in and needs dialysis, I don't want to tell him that he can't have it because somebody else who doesn't need it as much is on the machine and that person is a county resident."

"I don't know what to tell you," the Commissioner said. "It was county tax money that paid for the machine, and the County Council decided that the people who supplied the money ought to get top priority."

"What about the kind of case that I mentioned?" Dr. Crane asked. "What about somebody who could wait for dialysis who is a resident as opposed to somebody who needs it immediately who's not a resident?"

"We'll just leave that sort of case to your discretion," the Commissioner said. "People around here have confidence in you and your doctors. If you say they can wait, then they can wait. I know you won't let them down. Of course if somebody died while some outsider was on the machine.... Well, that would be embarrassing for all of us, I guess."

Dr. Crane was pleased to have the dialysis machine in his hospital. Not only was it the only one in Brattle County, but none of the neighboring counties had even one. Only the big hospitals in places like Dallas, Houston, and San Antonio had the machines. It put Crane Memorial up in the top rank.

Dr. Crane was totally unprepared for the problem when it came. He hadn't known there were so many people with chronic renal disease in Brattle County. But when news spread that there was a kidney machine available at Crane Memorial Hospital, twenty-three people applied for the dialysis program. Some were Dr. Crane's own patients or patients of his associates on the hospital staff. But a number of them were ones referred to the hospital by other physicians in Brattle and surrounding towns. Two of them were from neighboring Lopez County.

Working at a maximum, the machine could accommodate fourteen patients. But the staff decided that maximum operation would be likely to lead to dangerous equipment malfunctions and breakdowns. They settled on ten as the number of patients that should be admitted to the program.

Dr. Crane and his staff interviewed each of the program's applicants, reviewed their medical history, and got a thorough medical workup on each. They persuaded two of the patients to continue to commute to Houston, where they were already in dialysis. In four cases, renal disease had already progressed to the point that the staff decided that the patients could not benefit sufficiently from the program to make them good medical risks. In one other case, a patient suffering intestinal cancer and in generally poor health was rejected as a candidate. Two people were not in genuine need of dialysis but could be best treated by a program of medication.

That left fourteen candidates for the ten positions. Thirteen were from Brattle County and one from Lopez County.

"This is not a medical problem," Dr. Crane told the Commissioner. "And I'm not going to take the responsibility of deciding which people to condemn to death and which to give an extra chance at life."

"What do you want me to do?" the Commissioner asked. "I wouldn't object if you made the decision. I mean, you wouldn't have to tell everybody about it. You could just decide."

"That's something I won't do," Dr. Crane said. "All of this has to be open and above-board. It's got to be fair. If I decide, then everybody will think I am just favoring my own patients or just taking the people who can pay the most money."

"I see what you mean. If I appoint a selection committee, will you serve on it?"

"I will. So long as my vote is the same as everybody else's."

"That's what I'll do then," the Commissioner said.

The Brattle County Renal Dialysis Selection Committee was appointed and operating within the week. In addition to Dr. Crane, it was made up of three people chosen by the Commissioner. Amy Langford, a Brattle housewife in her middle fifties whose husband owned the largest automobile and truck agency in Brattle County, was one member. Reverend David Johnson was another member. He was the only black on the committee and the pastor of the largest predominantly black church in Brattle. The last member was Jacob Sims, owner of a hardware store in the nearby town of Silsbee. He was the only member of the committee not from the town of Brattle.

"Now I'm inclined to favor this fellow," said Mr. Sims at the Selection Committee's first meeting. "He's twenty-four years old, he's married and has a child two years old."

"You're talking about James Nelson?" Mrs. Langford asked. "I had some trouble with him. I've heard that he used to drink a lot before he got sick, and from the looks of his record he's had a hard time keeping a job."

"That's hard to say," said Reverend Johnson. "He works as a pulp-wood hauler, and people who do that change jobs a lot. You just have to go where the work is."

"That's right," said Mr. Sims. "One thing, though. I can't find any indication of his church membership. He says he's a Methodist, but I don't see where he's told us what his church is."

"I don't either," said Mrs. Langford. "And he's not a member of the Masons or the Lions Club or any other sort of civic group. I wouldn't say he's made much of a contribution to this community."

"That's right," said Reverend Johnson. "But let's don't forget that he's got a wife and baby depending on him. That child is going to need a father."

"I think he is a good psychological candidate," said Dr. Crane. "That is, I think if he starts the program he'll stick to it. I've talked with his wife, and I know she'll encourage him."

"We should notice that he's a high school dropout," Mrs. Langford said. "I don't think we can ever expect him to make much of a contribution to this town or to the county."

"Do you want to vote on this case?" asked Mr. Sims, the chairman of the committee.

"Let's talk about all of them, then go back and vote," Reverend Johnson suggested.

Everyone around the table nodded in agreement. The files were arranged by date of application, and Mr. Sims picked up the next one from the stack in front of him.

"Alva Algers," he said. "He's a fifty-three-year-old lawyer with three grown children. His wife is still alive, and he's still married to her. He's Secretary of the Layman's Board of the Brattle Episcopal Church, a member of the Rotary Club and the Elks. He used to be a scoutmaster."

"From the practical point of view," said Dr. Crane, "he would be a good candidate. He's intelligent and educated and understands what's involved in dialysis."

"I think he's definitely the sort of person we want to help," said Mrs. Langford. "He's the kind of a person who makes this a better town. I'm definitely in favor of him."

"I am too," said Reverend Johnson. "Even if he does go to the wrong church."

"I'm not so sure," said Mr. Sims. "I don't think fifty-three is old—I'd better not, because I'm fifty-two myself. Still, his children are grown, he's led a good life. I'm not sure I wouldn't give the edge to some younger fellow."

"How can you say that," Mrs. Langford said. "He's got a lot of good years left. He's a person of good character who might still do a lot for other people. He's not like that Nelson, who's not going to do any good for anybody except himself."

"I guess I'm not convinced that lawyers and members of the Rotary Club do a lot more good for the community than drivers of pulp-wood trucks," Mr. Sims said.

"Perhaps we ought to go on to the next candidate," Reverend Johnson said.

"We have Mrs. Holly Holton, a forty-three-year-old housewife from Mineral Springs," Mr. Sims said.

"That's in Lopez County, isn't it?" Mrs. Langford asked. "I think we can just reject her right off. She didn't pay the taxes that bought the machine, and our county doesn't have any responsibility for her."

"That's right," said Reverend Johnson. Mr. Sims agreed and Dr. Crane raised no objection.

"Now," said Mr. Sims, "here's Alton Conway. I believe he's our only black candidate."

"I know him well," said Reverend Johnson. "He owns a dry cleaning business, and people in the black community think very highly of him."

"I'm in favor of him," Mrs. Langford said. "He's a married man and seems quite settled and respectable."

"I wouldn't want us to take him just because he's black," Reverend Johnson said. "But I think he's got a lot in his favor."

"Well," said Mr. Sims, "unless Dr. Crane wants to add anything, let's go on to Nora Bainridge. She's a thirty-year-old divorced woman whose eight-year-old boy lives with his father over in Louisiana. She's a waitress at the Pep Cafe."

"She is a very vital woman," said Dr. Crane. "She's had a lot of trouble in her life, but I think she's a real fighter."

"I don't think she's much of a churchgoer," said Reverend Johnson. "At least she doesn't give us a pastor's name."

"That's right," said Mrs. Langford. "And I just wonder what kind of morals a woman like her has. I mean, being divorced and working as a waitress and all."

"I don't believe we are trying to award sainthood here," said Mr. Sims.

"But surely moral character is relevant," said Mrs. Langford.

"I don't know anything about her moral character," said Mr. Sims. "Do you?"

"I'm only guessing," said Mrs. Langford. "But I wouldn't say that a woman of her background and apparent character is somebody we ought to give top priority to."

"I don't want to be the one to cast the first stone," said Reverend Johnson. "But I wouldn't put her at the top of our list either."

"I think we had better be careful not to discriminate against people who are poor and uneducated," said Dr. Crane.

"I agree," said Mrs. Langford. "But surely we have to take account of a person's worth."

"Can you tell us how we can measure a person's worth?" asked Mr. Sims.

"I believe I can," Mrs. Langford said. "Does the person have a steady job? Is he or she somebody we would be proud to know? Is he a churchgoer? Does he or she do things for other people? We can see what kind of education the person has had, and consider whether he is somebody we would like to have around."

"I guess that's some of it all right," said Mr. Sims. "But I don't like to rely on things like education, money, and public service. A lot of people just haven't had a decent chance in this world. Maybe they were born poor or have had a lot of bad luck. I'm beginning to think that we ought to make our choices just by drawing lots."

"I can't approve of that," said Reverend Johnson. "That seems like a form of gambling to me. We ought to choose the good over the wicked, reward those who have led a virtuous life."

"I agree," Mrs. Langford said. "Choosing by drawing straws or something like that would mean we are just too cowardly to make decisions. We would be shirking our responsibility. Clearly, some people are more deserving than others, and we ought to have the courage to say so."

"All right," said Mr. Sims. "I guess we'd better get on with it then. Simon Gootz is a forty-eight-year-old baker. He's got a wife and four children. Owns his own bakery—probably all of us have been there. He's Jewish."

"I'm not sure he's the sort of person who can stick to the required diet and go through with the dialysis program," Dr. Crane said.

"I'll bet his wife and children would be a good incentive," said Mrs. Langford.

"There's not a Jewish church in town," said Reverend Johnson. "So of course we can't expect him to be a regular churchgoer."

"He's an immigrant," said Mr. Sims. "I don't believe he has any education to speak of, but he did start that bakery and build it up from nothing. I think that says a lot about his character."

"I think we can agree he's a good candidate," said Mrs. Langford.

"Let's just take one more before we break for dinner," Mr. Sims said. "Rebecca Scarborough. She's a sixty-three-year-old widow. Her children are all grown and living somewhere else."

"She's my patient," Dr. Crane said. "She's a tough and resourceful old woman. I believe she can follow orders and stand up to the rigors of the program, and her health in general is good."

Reverend Johnson said, "I just wonder if we shouldn't put a lady like her pretty far down on our list. She's lived a long life already, and she hasn't got anybody depending on her."

"I'm against that," Mrs. Langford said. "Everybody knows Mrs. Scarborough. Her family has been in this town for ages. She's one of our most substantial citizens. People would be scandalized if we didn't select her."

"Of course I'm not from Brattle," said Mr. Sims. "And maybe that's an advantage here, because I don't see that she's got much in her favor except being from an old family."

"I think that's worth something," said Mrs. Langford.

"I'm not sure if it's enough, though," said Reverend Johnson.

After dinner at the Crane Memorial Hospital cafeteria, the Selection Committee met again to discuss the seven remaining candidates. It was past ten o'clock before their final decisions were made. James Nelson, the pulp-wood truck driver, Holly Holton, the housewife from Mineral Springs, and Nora Bainridge, the waitress, were all rejected as candidates. Mrs. Scarborough was rejected also. The lawyer, Alva Algers, the dry cleaner, Alton Conway, and the baker, Simon Gootz,

were selected to participate in the dialysis program. Others selected were a retired secondary school teacher, an assembly-line worker at
the Rigid Box Company, a Brattle County
Sheriff's Department patrolman, and a twenty-
seven-year-old woman file clerk in the office
of the Texas Western Insurance Company.

Dr. Crane was glad that the choices were
made so that the program could begin operation. But he was not pleased with the selection method and resolved to talk to his own
staff and with the County Commissioner
about devising some other kind of selection
procedure.

Without giving any reasons, Mr. Sims sent
a letter to the County Commissioner resign-
ing from the Renal Dialysis Selection Committee.

Mrs. Langford and Reverend Johnson also
sent letters to the Commissioner. They
thanked him for appointing them to the
Committee and indicated their willingness to
continue to serve.

Questions for Discussion

1 Among the factors considered relevant by various
members of the committee were: number of de-
pendants, civic participation, expected future contribution to the community, conformity to
accepted moral standards, likelihood of sticking
with the treatment, and age. Are all of these factors worth taking into account? How should they
be ranked in order of importance?

2 Should the likelihood of a person's sticking to
treatment be considered, even if there is a practical tendency for it to work against already disadvantaged groups?

3 Is it true that making selections on the basis of a
random process such as drawing straws is "cowardly" and amounts to shirking the responsibility
of deciding which people are most deserving?

Four Unsolved Rationing Problems

A Challenge

Norman Daniels

*In this selection, Norman Daniels articulates four specific questions about the principles which should govern the
distribution of scarce medical resources. These are: 1) How much should we favour producing the best outcome
with our limited resources? 2) How much priority should we give to treating the sickest or most disabled patients?
3) When should we allow an aggregation of modest benefits to larger numbers of people to outweigh more significant benefits to fewer people? and 4) When must we rely on a fair democratic process as the only way to determine what constitutes a fair rationing outcome?*

★   ★   ★

Faced with limited resources, medical providers and planners often ask bio-ethicists how
to limit or ration the delivery of beneficial
services in a fair or just way. What advice
should we give them? To focus our thinking
on the problems they face, I offer a friendly
challenge to the field: solve the four rationing problems described here.

We have generally ignored these problems
because we think rationing an unusual phenomenon, associated with gas lines, butter
coupons, or organ registries. But rationing is
pervasive, not peripheral, since we simply cannot afford, for example, to educate, treat
medically, or protect legally people in all the
ways that their needs for these goods require

or that accepted distributive principles seem to demand. Whenever we design institutions that distribute these goods, and whenever we operate those institutions, we are involved in rationing.

Rationing decisions, both at the micro and macro levels, share three key features. First, the goods we often must provide—legal services, health care, educational benefits—are not sufficiently divisible (unlike money) to avoid unequal or "lumpy" distributions. Meeting the educational, health care, or legal needs of some people, for example, will mean that the requirements of others will go unsatisfied. Second, when we ration, we deny benefits to some individuals who can plausibly claim they are *owed them in principle*; losers as well as winners have plausible claims to have their needs met. Third, the general distributive principles appealed to by claimants as well as by rationers do not by themselves provide adequate reasons for choosing among claimants. They are too schematic; like my "fair equality of opportunity" account of just health care, they fail to yield specific solutions to these rationing problems. Solving these problems thus bridges the gap between principles of distributive justice and problems of institutional design.

The Fair Chances/Best Outcomes Problem

> *How much should we favor producing the best outcome with our limited resources?*

Like the other problems, the fair chances/best outcomes problem arises in both micro and macro contexts. Consider first its more familiar microrationing form: which of several equally needy individuals should get a scarce resource, such as a heart transplant? Suppose that Alice and Betty are the same age, have waited on queue the same length of time, and will each live only one week without a transplant. With the transplant, however, Alice is expected to live two years and Betty twenty.

Who should get the transplant?[1] Giving priority to producing best outcomes, as in some point systems for awarding organs, would mean that Betty gets the organ and Alice dies (assuming persistent scarcity of organs, as Dan Brock notes).[2] But Alice might complain, "Why should I give up my only chance at survival—and two years of survival is not insignificant—just because Betty has a chance to live longer?" Alice demands a lottery that gives her an equal chance with Betty.

To see the problem in its macroallocation version, suppose our health care budget allows us to introduce one of two treatments, T1 and T2, which can be given to comparable but different groups. Because T1 restores patients to a higher level of functioning than T2, it has a higher net benefit. We could produce the best outcomes by putting all our resources into T1; then patients treatable by T2 might, like Alice, complain that they are being asked to forgo any chance at a significant benefit.

The problem has no satisfactory solution at either the intuitive or theoretical level. Few would agree with Alice, for example, if she had very little chance at survival; more would agree if her outcomes were only somewhat worse than Betty's. At the level of intuitions, there is much disagreement about when and how much to favor best outcomes, though we reject the extreme positions of giving full priority to fair chances or best outcomes. Brock proposes breaking this deadlock by giving Alice and Betty chances proportional to the benefits they can get (e.g., by assigning Alice one side of a ten-sided die). Frances Kamm proposes a more complex assignment of multiplicative weights.[3] Both suggestions seem ad hoc, adding an element of precision our intuitions lack. But theoretical considerations also fall short of solving the problem. For example, we might respond to Alice that she already has lost a "natural" lottery; she might have been the one with twenty years expected survival, but it turned out to be Betty instead.

After the fact, however, Alice is unlikely to agree that there has already been a fair "natural" lottery. We might try to persuade her to decide behind a veil of ignorance, but even then there is controversy about what kinds of gambling are permissible.

The Priorities Problem

How much priority should we give to treating the sickest or most disabled patients?

Suppose Xs are much sicker or more disabled patients than Ys and suppose that we can measure the units of benefit that can be given each patient, for example, in QUALYs or some other unit. Most people believe that if a treatment can deliver equal benefit to Xs or Ys, we should give priority to helping Xs, who are worse off to start with. This intuition is ignored by some uses of cost-effectiveness or cost-benefit methodologies, which may be neutral between Xs and Ys if the benefits and costs are the same. Similarly, we may be willing to forgo some extra benefits for Ys in order to provide lesser benefits to Xs. We favor Xs in more than tiebreaking cases, though we intuitively reject giving full priority to them. How much priority we give to Xs rather than Ys may also depend on whether Xs end up much better than Ys after treatment.

As in the previous problem, we intuitively reject extreme positions but we have no satisfactory theoretical characterization of an intermediary position.

The Aggregation Problem

When should we allow an aggregation of modest benefits to larger numbers of people to outweigh more significant benefits to fewer people?

In June of 1990, the Oregon Health Services Commission released a list of treatment-condition pairs ranked by a cost-benefit calculation. Critics were quick to seize on rankings that seemed completely counterintuitive. For example, as David Hadorn noted, tooth capping was ranked higher than appendectomy.[4] The reason was simple: an appendectomy cost about $4,000, many times the cost of capping a tooth. Simply aggregating the net medical benefit of many capped teeth yielded a net benefit greater than that produced by one appendectomy.

As David Eddy pointed out, our intuitions in these cases are largely based on comparing treatment-condition pairs for their importance on a one-to-one basis.[5] One appendectomy is more important than one tooth capping because it saves a life rather than merely reducing pain and preserving dental function. Our intuitions are much less well developed when it comes to making one-to-many comparisons, though economists have used standard techniques to measure them.[6] Kamm shows that we are not straightforward aggregators of all benefits, though we do permit some forms of aggregation. Nevertheless, our moral views are both complex and difficult to explicate in terms of well-ordered principles. While we are not aggregate maximizers, as presupposed by the dominant methodologies derived from welfare economics, we do permit or require some forms of aggregation. Are there principles that govern the aggregation we accept? Failing to find justifiable principles would give us strong reason to rely instead on fair procedures.

The Democracy Problem

When must we rely on a fair democratic process as the only way to determine what constitutes a fair rationing outcome?

There is much that is appealing about relying on people's preferences and values in deciding how it is fair to ration medical services. Which preferences and values must we take at face value, however, regardless of the outcomes they imply? In Oregon, for example, people's attitudes were included in the process of ranking medical services in several ways. Adapting Kaplan's "quality of well-being" scale for use in measuring the benefit of medical treatments, Oregon surveyed residents, asking them to judge on a scale of 0 (death) to 100 (perfect health) what the impact would be of having to live the rest of one's life with some physical or mental impairment or symptom; for example, wearing eyeglasses was rated 95 out of 100, for a weighting of -0.05, which is about the same as the weight assigned to not being able to drive a car or use public transportation and to having to stay at a hospital or nursing home. Are these weightings the result of poor methodology? If they represent real attitudes, must we accept them at face value? Whose attitudes should we rely on, the public as a whole or the people who have experienced the condition in question? Those who do not have a disabling condition may suffer from cultural biases, overestimating the impact of disability. But those who have the condition may rate it as less serious because they have modified their preferences, goals, and values in order to make a "healthy adjustment" to their condition. Their overall dissatisfaction—tapped by these methodologies—may not reflect the impact that would be captured by a measure more directly attuned to the range of capabilities they retain. Insisting on the more objective measure has a high political cost and may even seem paternalistic.

The democracy problem arises at another level in procedures that purport to be directly democratic. The Oregon plan called for the OHSC to respect "community values" in its ranking of services. Because prevention and family planning services were frequently discussed in community meetings, the OHSC assigned the categories that included those services very high ranking. Consequently, in Oregon, vasectomies are ranked more important than hip replacements. Remember the priority and aggregation problems: it would

seem more important to restore mobility to someone who cannot walk than to improve the convenience of birth control through vasectomy in several people. But, assuming that the commissioners properly interpreted the wishes of Oregonians, that is not what Oregonians wanted the rankings to be. Should we treat this as error? Or must we abide by whatever the democratic process yields?

Thus far I have characterized the problem of democracy as a problem of error: a fair democratic process, or a methodology that rests in part on expressions of preferences, leads to judgments that deviate from either intuitive or theoretically bad judgments about the relative importance of certain health outcomes or services. The problem is how much weight to give the intuitive or theoretically based judgments as opposed to the expressed preferences. The point should be put in another way as well. Should we in the end think of the democratic process as a matter of pure procedural justice? If so, then we have no way to correct the judgment made through that process, for what it determines to be fair is what counts as fair. Or should we really consider the democratic process as an impure and imperfect form of procedural justice? Then it is one that can be corrected by appeal to some prior notion of what constitutes a fair outcome of rationing. I suggest that we do not yet know the answer to this question, and we will not be able to answer it until we work harder at providing a theory of rationing.

Acknowledgments

This work was generously supported by the National Endowment for the Humanities (RH 20917) and the National Library of Medicine (1R01LM05005). This paper is adapted from my "Rationing Fairly: Programmatic Considerations," *Bioethics* 7, nos. 2/3 (1993): 224–33.

References

1 Frances M. Kamm, "The Report of the U.S. Task Force on Organ Transplantation: Criticisms and Alternatives," *Mt. Sinai Journal of Medicine* (June 1989): 207–20.

2 Dan Brock, "Ethical Issues in Recipient Selection for Organ Transplantation," in *Organ Substitution Technology: Ethical, Lega, and Public Policy Issues*, ed. Deborah Mathieu (Boulder: Westview, 1988), pp. 86–99.

3 Frances M. Kamm, *Morality, Mortality*, vol. 1, *Death and Whom to Save from It* (New York: Oxford University Press, 1993); see also Kamm, "Report of the U.S. Task Force."

4 David Hadorn, "Setting Health Care Priorities in Oregon: Cost-Effectiveness Meets the Rule of Rescue," *JAMA* 265, no. 17 (1991): 2218–25.

5 David Eddy, "Oregon's Methods: Did Cost-Effectiveness Analysis Fail?" *JAMA* 266, no. 15 (1991): 2135–41.

6 Eric Nord, "The Relevance of Health State after Treatment in Priorities between Different Patients," unpublished manuscript in author's possession.

Question for Discussion

1 To what extent would a moral theory, such as utilitarianism, be useful in answering the questions Daniels raises?

Quality-Adjusted Life-Years

Ethical Implications for Physicians and Policymakers

John La Puma and Edward F. Lawlor

*One proposal which has been made for allocating scarce medical resources involves measuring "quality-adjusted life-years," or "QALYs." The idea here is that it might take several years of life with diminished health to have the same worth for an individual as a single year of complete health. Then, if we are considering which of two treatments to provide, this approach might tell us to consider the number of years of life we can expect to gain by each, but also "adjust" that result in light of the expected **quality** of those years. In the following article, La Puma and Lawlor discuss some of the ways in which QALYs might be thought helpful in attaining cost-effective systems of health care and rational approaches to rationing scarce resources. The authors also discuss some ethical problems the use of QALYs can give rise to.*

★   ★   ★

A quality-adjusted life-year (QALY) is a numerical description of the value that a medical procedure or service can provide to groups of patients with similar medical conditions. Quality-adjusted life-years attempt to combine expected survival with expected quality of life in a single metric: if an additional year of healthy life is worth a value of 1 (year), then a year of less healthy life is worth less than 1 (year).[1] Quality-adjusted life-years represent a progression in the cost-effectiveness analysis of health care, as concepts of health, quality of life, and utility are inherently amorphous and elusive. Albert Mulley, MD, calls this "the stuff of poets and philosophers," but in QALY assessment they are also the stuff of economists and psychometricians. Health economists have struggled for decades to estimate the value of life and many have been uncomfortable with life-years gained as an outcome, but have had little more to offer.[2]

Serious clinical ethical questions, however,

have been raised about QALYs.[3–9] We review herein QALY methods and historical development and attempt to identify the ethical issues they present.

QALY Methods

Calculations of QALYs are based on measurements of the value that individuals place on expected years of life. Measurements can be made in several ways: by simulating gambles about preferences for alternative states of health, by inferring willingness to pay for alternative states of health, or through "trading off" some or all likely survival time that a medical intervention might provide to gain less survival time of higher quality.

A reference gamble reveals preference by asking the respondent to choose the consequences of a hypothetical game (such as choosing balls out of an urn) with known probabilities. Willingness-to-pay estimates rely either on statements of the sacrifice an individual is willing to make to obtain alternative outcomes or on the analysis of actual observed behavior. Estimates of QALYs can also be derived by asking respondents to explicitly trade years of life for different presentations of quality of life.

In theory, these techniques could be employed to elicit QALYs for an individual patient who faces a choice between alternative therapies that yield different probabilities for pain reduction, abilities to engage in activities of daily living, and life expectancies. A patient with severe angina and triple-vessel disease will likely generate different QALYs with bypass surgery, without surgery, and with medications; a patient with severe angina and single-vessel disease would generate still different QALYs than the former patient.

How much survival time groups of patients would trade off for what degree of quality may change as more is learned about disease. New data may be folded into the analysis as they become available, e.g., cyclosporine has improved survival after organ transplantation, requiring QALY recalculations to higher, more accurate values. In effect, QALYs "discount" years of life saved by a health care intervention by how much patients' subjective well-being is diminished by discomfort or distress.

The methods used to calculate QALYs are still under development.[10] Quality-adjusted life-year assessments have been shown to vary by how health states are described, how outcomes are reported, how scales are generated, and how surveys are administered.[11] We will not belabor the technical issues involved in utility measurement[12] and quality-of-life assessment,[13] but they are controversial and variable.

Cost-Effectiveness Analysis in Health Policy

Cost-effectiveness analyses attempt to assess how efficiently interventions are being used, given how much they cost. When divided by cost, QALYs can yield a measure of cost-effectiveness[14] and help establish priorities for funding. Interventions of highest priority (yielding the most QALYs per unit of cost) would receive the most resources: the more QALYs per dollar, the more resources and the greater development of that intervention. In theory, QALYs can help provide for an efficient use of those resources that already exist and for the allocation of new resources.

Quality-adjusted life-years are also a potential result of community medical ethics: the public identification, prioritization, and implementation of an equitable, virtuous distribution of health care resources. Accurate, detailed knowledge of community preferences is essential to allocate resources fairly. At least 10 state programs in community clinical ethics now exist.[15] Oregon Health Decisions, for example, helped persuade the state legislature not to fund organ transplantation because it received a lower community priority than preventive programs.[16] Although coverage for transplantation was reinstated after a public outcry,[17] the concept of small town meetings to allocate resources has broad appeal.

QALYs as a Rationing Tool

Most QALY proponents expect QALYs to inform resource allocation decisions, especially large-scale decisions that deploy resources across disease states and population groups. In theory, a QALY analysis compares the merits of devoting resources to an intervention likely to extend the lives of a population for a specific period, but with high levels of disability and distress, with another intervention, which may not yield as many years of life saved, but generates higher levels of subjective well-being.

Cost-per-QALY analyses are motivated by scarcity: if resources were unlimited, rationing would be unnecessary. In the United Kingdom, there is explicit rationing of some health care services, requiring physicians to be both caretakers and resource agents. In the United States, rationing is accomplished through patients' differential ability to pay: 87 million uninsured people do not have equal access to health care.[18] Aaron and Schwartz[19] found that British physicians most often find medical reasons to deny a needed treatment (e.g., dialysis) to a patient. Such patients are said to be too old, too sick, or too unlikely to benefit; physicians generally do not say that the resource is relatively scarce and unavailable.

Explicit health care rationing, with selected priorities for funding, has been proposed in Oregon[20] and by scholars.[21] Oregon state officials hope to ration Medicaid services by July 1, 1990, using the "Quality of Well-Being Scale" and "Well-Years" very similar to QALYs.[22] These plans call on physicians to ration care at the bedside and could benefit from a clear explication of how QALYs have developed.

Historical Development

Technical Development

Derived from operations research in engineering and mathematics, QALYs were first introduced by decision analysts and researchers in the United States.[23,24] Weinstein and Stason[25] described QALYs as a way of elucidating the trade-offs between quality of life and additional survival, representing "the net health effectiveness of the program or practice in question."

In 1978 in Britain, Rosser and Kind[26] reported the results of psychometric testing of 70 selected patients, volunteers, physicians, and nurses. The authors devised a scale that assigned a numerical value to 29 hypothetical states of disability and distress. The resulting Rosser index has been the foundation of most British work on QALYs, pioneered by health economist Alan Williams.

Clinical Decision Making

Quantitative analytic techniques such as those of economic analysis can make the components of clinical decision making more clear; these techniques are most effective when their underlying value assumptions are made explicit. The algorithms and decision trees of health status assessment are not readily accepted as clinical tools,[27] however, as they miss the complexity and subtlety necessary for many clinical decisions. Still, Jennett and Buxton[28] have suggested that QALYs can and should be part of clinical considerations about quality of life and should be used at the bedside.

The process of clinical decision making, itself an outcome, is not taken into account by measures such as QALYs. The significance of this criticism is undervalued. Many interactions between physician and patient do not result in a tangible intervention or easily measurable data. Patients often seek physicians for attention, information, reassurance, encouragement, and permission, not just prescriptions and procedures. In QALYS, there is no attempt to integrate the therapeutic value and outcome of talking with patients[29] or their families: patient care is evidenced by the boxes checked on the office encounter sheet.

Health Policy Proposals

Calculations for numerous interventions have been reported. Weinstein and Stason[25] applied QALYS to the resources allocated to manage hypertension and proposed a threshold value of blood pressure below which it would not be cost-effective to treat patients. It costs less than £200 ($350) to gain 1 year of quality-adjusted life for general practitioners to counsel patients not to smoke, £1000 ($1500) for coronary artery bypass grafting for left main disease with mild angina, and £15,000 ($22,500) for hospital hemodialysis.[30] Policy implications of these findings are that treatments with costs-per-day QALY above £5000 ($7500) "should be taken off the ... budget completely and financed only as research and development activities."[30] More recently in America, QALYs and quality-adjusted life-months have been calculated for estrogen use in postmenopausal women,[31] neonatal intensive care,[32] dialysis,[33] coronary artery bypass grafting,[34] and prostatectomy.[35]

In 1985, Williams[36] compared the QALY costs and benefits of coronary artery bypass grafting with renal transplantation, concluding that bypass grafting for left main disease with severe or moderate angina and for triple-vessel disease should be funded before renal transplantation.

In 1986, Gudex[37,38] reported the results of the preliminary use of QALYs in the North Western Regional Health Authority in Brit-

ain, which, like other health authorities, receives monies from the National Health Service to fund its health care activities. Gudex compared the QALY efficiency of several unrelated interventions, using life-expectancy data from current literature and a revised Rosser index.[39] Surgery for a "neuromuscular" patient had the lowest cost per QALY (£194 [$291]), corrective surgery for an adolescent scoliotic patient had a higher cost per QALY (£2619 [$3929]), and chronic ambulatory peritoneal dialysis lasting 4 years had the highest cost per QALY (£13,434 [$20,151]). The North Western Regional Health Authority has not continued the studies and the Department of Health and Social Services has not made a formal statement about QALYs, although it continues to fund the work of Williams, Rosser, and Gudex.

The need for outcome management in American and British health care is increasingly newsworthy; the brief, efficient, accurate measurement of quality of life is an important part of that management. Ellwood[40] has encouraged the Health Care Financing Administration to define the quality-of-life data set, and more than 100 scales can be used to measure quality of life. Despite continuing uncertainty about how to deploy these measurements in health policy,[41,42] we can identify the ethical assumptions that underlie QALYs.

QALYs and Medical Ethics

The debate about QALYs occurs on at least four levels. First, there are methodological problems of theory, measurement, and interpretation. Second, practical questions of implementation arise, assuming the technical properties of QALY-based policy guidance are clarified and agreed on. Third, QALYs present moral and professional challenges to the fundamental values and assumed prerogatives of physicians. Fourth, QALYs hold an uneasy, conspicuous, critical place in the recent evolution of health policy, an evolution preoccupied with the agenda of cost containment.

QALYS' Ethical Assumptions

The formal use of QALYs and QALY-like scales makes six ethical assumptions. First, quality of life can be accurately measured and should have "standing" in determining resource allocation. Second, utilitarianism ("the greatest good for the greatest number") is the appropriate ethical theory for resolving resource allocation dilemmas. Third, equity and efficiency are compatible and should be balanced in QALY construction. Fourth, projections of community preferences for interventions can ethically substitute for the preferences of individual patients when allocating and rationing resources. Fifth, older and sicker patients have less "capacity to benefit" from interventions than those who are younger and healthier. Sixth, physicians will be able to differentiate between a patient's medical need and a resource's availability and between being a patient advocate and a public agent, will favor the measurable outcome of clinical decision making over its process, and will not use QALYs as clinical maxims.

Quality of Life

The President's Commission for the Study of Ethical Problems in Medicine and Biomedical and Behavioral Research noted that "quality of life [is] an ethically essential concept that focuses on the good of the individual, what kind of life is possible given the person's condition, and whether that condition will allow the individual to have *a life that he or she views as worth living* [italics added]." One prominent philosopher has recently suggested that quality-based societal limits are needed and are morally correct.[43] In a recent national survey, nearly three fourths of Americans felt that an unconscious, terminally ill patient should be removed from life-support systems because of his or quality of life and that of his or her family.[44]

Quality-adjusted life-years assume that quality of life can be measured well enough to make policy judgments about it. They also assume that at some point—the same point for all persons—life becomes so miserable that it is worse than death.[45] Incalculables such as freedom from the fear of dependency on a ventilator or the value of time spent awake, alert, and participatory are part of quality of life.

We do not say that such incalculables render impossible the useful measurement of quality of life. Some patients, though, would rather live no matter what their disability/distress score. Other patients cannot or will not decide and have no one to speak for them. The lives of these patients—the demented, the mentally ill, and the "old-old"—QALYs judge to be of inadequate worth; for these patients, quality-of-life assessments cannot be made accurately.

The Greatest Good for the Greatest Number

Consider the estimation of QALYs generated by a zidovudinelike therapy for patients infected with the human immunodeficiency virus. Whose utility assessments count? Should a representative sample of the public be interviewed? Or should potential candidates for the therapy be interviewed? Should some form of weighing be developed for respondents with knowledge of or experience with the relevant health states? How should the valuation of outcomes in the distant future be treated?[46] How should individual preferences and attitudes about risk taking be accommodated?[47] How should resources for individuals with impaired decision making be handled? How should these assessments be summed or interpreted, particularly if there are major differences in assessments among respondents?

These questions are not new or unfamiliar to health planners and analysts, but the answers may be contained within the ideology of cost containment and the moral perspective of utilitarianism. As Caplan[48] has said, "The quantification of value ... often is ideology masquerading as a moral point of view."

Equity and Efficiency

Legitimate concerns arise about how QALYs may influence the conduct and direction of health policy. Our society continues to evolve toward a utilitarian ethic, one that appreciates medicine for what it can measurably produce, rather than for humanistic care. Quality-adjusted life-years are controversial not only for what they are, but also for the new financial ethos they represent. They symbolize a movement to make health a commodity and to shift the balance of power in and philosophy of clinical practice from highly discretionary physician-patient encounters to more standardized, quantified, and regulated protocols.[49] Thus, many critics of QALYs are fundamentally concerned with the problems of integrating explicit economic guidance and formulas with clinical decision making, fearing that policymakers will conflate efficiency and equity[50] and that physicians will be forced to choose between being a patient advocate or a public agent,[51] to the disadvantaged patient's disadvantage.[14]

Whose Autonomy? Whose Justice?

Quality-adjusted life-years risk projecting community preferences over those of individual patients. The ethical principle of autonomy or self-determination, generally most important for individual patients, would be trumped by that of justice or fairness, generally most important for a community. The preferences of a selected population sample or the preferences of a representative sample of patients in hypothetical medical situations would be used as if they were individual patient preferences. For example, Williams, Rosser, and Gudex use an assessment of community values in QALY calculations. Their assessment for an individual patient would come from the preferences of the average member of the public, not the average patient and not the patient himself.

This departure from codes of medical ethics and from clinical ethics reflects underlying QALY assumptions—that the projections of healthy others can be generalized to any patient with a particular medical condition. If all members of the public were reliably asked how many years of life they would trade off for different conditions and their verified responses were analyzed, a sound public policy statement on health care resources could be made. Using such a policy to allocate resources at a high level could be tenable, but does not obviate the physician's professional responsibility to work at the bedside for a patient's medical interests. In the current era of cost containment, the physician should not be in the position of defending public policy: patient advocate or public agent should be an easy choice.

Finally, individual patient preferences cannot always be accurately assessed by others. One study has suggested that chronically ill elderly outpatients believe their quality of life is better than their physicians believe it is.[52] Another study found that quality of life is a poor predictor of individual patient preferences for intensive care.[53] Although the preferences of family members and others can be included in technology evaluation, even family preferences may not represent those of the patient. Spouses may overestimate patient preferences for many intensive therapies, including cardiopulmonary resuscitation, and physicians both underestimate and overestimate patients' preferences.[54,55] Given the variability and difficulty of assessing individual preferences[53] and the potential for misuse when grouped, implementation of QALY-like standards in clinical practice would present significant risks to patients.

What is 'Capacity to Benefit'?

Several studies of QALYs assume that patients' "capacity to benefit" from an intervention is a relevant measure of QALYs. Researchers define "capacity to benefit" as the ability of an intervention to provide more life-years of adjusted quality. This definition would likely direct care away from patients who have a poor quality of life and little or no "capacity to benefit" (e.g., terminally ill, locked-in, and comatose patients),[56,57] because their care would yield few QALYs at a relatively high cost. While the care of the terminally ill and the neurologically impaired may not be QALY efficient, it is part of the traditional role of health professionals. Attending to time-consuming patients and their families is part of this compassionate, although QALY-inefficient ethos of medicine.

Although straight counting of life-years undervalues the lives of the elderly,[3] they have less "capacity to benefit" than the young. If QALYs are calculated with patients' families in mind, reducing the disability or distress of patients with dependents will be preferable to reducing the disability or distress of patients without dependents. Patients who are more critically ill or whose quality of life is poorer would probably receive treatments *after* those who were less critically ill or whose quality of life was better.

QALYs as Clinical Maxims: The New Diagnosis Related Groups?

Much of the concern about QALY implementation appears to have less to do with their technical properties than with how they might be abused. Clinician reaction to a 1977 *Hastings Center Report* article, for example, is in-

structive.[58] A simple didactic quality-of-life equation (not a QALY) was presented; the equation was intended to aid decision making for incompetent individuals. It was misinterpreted by many as a decision-making rule—an algorithm to be interpreted strictly and applied uncritically to individual cases. Neither the author nor critics envisioned any such use for this formulation.

Diagnosis related groups were similarly conceived to provide guidance about use for relatively large numbers of cases,[59] but instead of simply guiding prospective payment they have been employed directly in clinical decision making about individual cases.[60,61] The overall effect of diagnosis related groups has been to force hospitals to economize, accepting fewer uninsured patients, reducing patients' length of stay, and increasing the acuity of illness at discharge. While there is nothing wrong with encouraging physicians to be efficient, the point is that both QALYs and diagnosis related groups try to combine efficiency with equity to yield a blunt, economically driven tool. Whether QALYs will be used as clinical maxims remains to be seen.

QALYs and Clinical Practice

Quality-adjusted life-years attempt to clarify judgments about quality of life. Clinicians make quality, cost, and survival judgments implicitly and individually, based on their experience with different patients and on the particular needs of an individual patient. These judgments are often subjective and always difficult to quantify. By identifying specific quality states, survival estimates, and societal preferences, QALYs may improve the efficiency and objectivity of medical decision making, reducing the subjectivity of judgments about quality of life.[62]

Quality-adjusted life-years are intended to be a "macro" tool. Quality-adjusted life-years use aggregate community preferences and trade-offs to determine what is best for an individual patient, regardless of whether societal preferences and an individual's preferences are the same. Using QALYs as a "micro" clinical decision-making tool has health system-wide implications that may promote decision making not by the numbers from physical examination and laboratory measurement, but by single metrics, e.g., QALYs, diagnosis related groups, and age. Such decision making impoverishes medicine as a science of numbers and robs it of the richness of clinical detail.

Quality-adjusted life-years assume that the duration and quality of an individual patient's life are not different from most other commodities that can be purchased. While utilitarianism may be an acceptable ethical theory with which to make health policy at the macro level, at present, clinical practice is not primarily conducted to benefit society as a whole, the public interest, or the common good. The physician's primary duty is to meet the patient's medical needs as they together find them, the physician with technical knowledge and expertise and the patient with his or her personal history and values. Conserving society's resources is secondary or tertiary; if such conservation is brought about by considering some patients expendable or by serving opposing masters of patient and society,[63–66] the seemingly imminent role of public agent must be acknowledged, appealed, and refuted.

Using resources in response to patient need, however, as assessed by health professionals and as differentiated from patient or physician want, and in proportion to the expected benefit, should be the objective of clinical encounters. If rational, reasonable health policies are constructed and physicians are constrained from offering expensive technologies of marginal benefit,[67] then can we keep straight the difference between what is medically needed and medically available? Civil suits, licensure actions, courts of public opinion,[68,69] ethics consultants,[70] and the

media have already appealed these constraints, but the real question is whether the physician's role must be redefined to include "negotiator" and "advocate" at the policy level. Understanding QALYs will help physicians influence policy in a way that preserves a level of choice within the reality of increasing fiscal constraints on patient care.

Conclusion

Quality-adjusted life-years are a new health measurement tool that many health care economists and decision analysts believe has promise to provide health care to those who have the greatest capacity to benefit. Despite interest in the deployment of QALYs, there are significant computational problems of utility theory, instrumentation, measurement, and interpretation and ethical dilemmas of equity, justice, autonomy, beneficence, and discrimination.

Policymakers who wish to use QALYs to allocate resources must fully identify and disclose QALYs' ethical assumptions, so that they can be debated. How to reconcile variability in individual medical values and preferences with cost-per-QALY calculations is still uncertain. What is certain is that QALY analyses have bedside implications for patients and physicians.

If physicians use community-derived QALYs to determine which of their patients will receive treatment, full disclosure to patients will not help. Medical treatments are not like other commodities that can be proffered and purchased. Patients' preferences and needs for health care may be replaced by an economic analysis that relies on selected community opinions, giving insufficient weight to the patient's preferences or the clinician's judgment. Physicians' social responsibility to use resources carefully may supplant our professional responsibility to care for our patients medically.

It is unclear whether resources available for research should be directed toward cost-effectiveness analyses such as QALYs or toward superior outcome measures. The improper or overzealous deployment of QALYs may mask a simpler and more arbitrary cost-containment agenda. Policymakers should consider quality-of-life factors in decision making, but must do so with better data and great compassion. Excluding needy patients must be an anathema to both policy-makers and physicians. The tension between selected societal and individual interests will continue and heighten; guarding against economic analyses' imposition of selected societal interests on individual patients will increasingly become the physician's duty and charge, one that physicians must seize and defend.

This work was supported in part by the American College of Physicians in Philadelphia, through an American College of Physicians A. Blaine Brower Traveling Scholarship for 1988 through 1989 (Dr. La Puma).

References

1 Williams A. The importance of quality of life in policy decisions. In: Walker SR, Rosser RM, eds. *Quality of Life: Assessment and Application*. Lancaster, England: MTP Press Ltd; 1988:279–290.

2 Avorn J. Benefit and cost analysis in geriatric care. *N Engl J Med*. 1984; 310:310–322.

3 Melzel PT. *Medical Costs, Moral Choices*. New Haven, Conn: Yale University Press; 1983:185–195.

4 Maynard A, Devlin JB. Economists v clinicians: the crucial debate. *Health Soc Service J*. July 18, 1985:7–8.

5 Jarret RJ. Economics or coronary artery bypass grafting. *Br Med J*. 1985; 291:600.

6 Smith A. Qualms about QALYs. *Lancet*, 1987; 1:1134–1136.

7 Harris J. QALYfying the value of life. *J Med Ethics*., 1987; 13:117–123.

8 *The Ian Ramsey Centre Working Party Report on Decision-Making and Quality of Life*. Oxford, England: The Ian Ramsey Centre; 1989.

9 Rawles J. Castigating QALYs. *J Med Ethics*. 1989; 15:143–147.

10 Smith GT, ed. *Measuring Health: A Practical Approach*. New York, NY: John Wiley & Sons Inc; 1988.

11 Mulley AG. Assessing patient utilities: can the ends justify the means? *Med Care*. 1989; 27(suppl): S269–S281.

12 Eisenberg JM. Clinical economics: a guide to the economic analysis of clinical practices. *JAMA*. 1989; 262:2879–2886.

13 Guyatt GH. Measuring quality of life in clinical trials. *Can Med Assoc J*. 1989; 140:1441–1448.

14 Emery DD, Schneiderman LJ. Cost-effectiveness analysis in health care. *Hastings Cent Rep*. 1989; 19(4):8–13.

15 Jennings B. A grassroots movement in bioethics. *Hastings Cent Rep*. 1988; 18(suppl to No. 3):1–16.

16 Garland MJ, Crawshaw R. Oregon's decision to curtail funding for organ transplantation. *N Engl J Med*. 1988; 319:1420.

17 Welch HG, Larson EB. Dealing with limited resources: the Oregon decision to curtail funding for organ transplantation. *N Engl J Med*. 1988; 319:171–173.

18 Todd J. It is time for universal access, not universal insurance. *N Engl J Med*. 1989; 321:46–47.

19 Aaron HJ, Schwartz WB. *The Painful Prescription: Rationing Health Care*. Washington, DC: The Brookings Institute; 1984.

20 Lund DS. Health care rationing plan OK'd in Oregon, stymied in California. *Am Med News*. July 21, 1989:1.

21 Churchill LR. *Rationing Health Care in America: Perceptions and Principles of Justice*. University of Notre Dame (Ind) Press; 1987.

22 Meyer H. Oregon Medicaid plan gets boost from health care executives' poll. *Am Med News*. March 16, 1990:2.

23 Patrick DL, Bush HW, Chen MM. Toward an operational definition of health. *J Health Soc Behav.* 1973; 14:6–23.

24 Torrance GW, Sackett DL, Thomas WH. Utility maximization model for program evaluation: a demonstration application, Health Status Indexes. In: Berg RL, ed. *Proceedings of a Conference Conducted by Health Services Research Tucson, Arizona, 1972.* Chicago, Ill: Hospital Research and Educational Trust; 1973.

25 Weinstein MC, Stason WB. Foundations of cost-effectiveness analysis for health and medical practices. *N Engl J Med.* 1977; 296:716–721.

26 Rosser R, Kind P. A scale of valuations of states of illness: is there a social consensus? *Int J Epidemiol.* 1978; 7:347–358.

27 Deyo R, Patrick DL. Barriers to the use of health status measures in clinical investigation, patient care and policy research. *Med Care.* 1989; 27(suppl):S254–S268.

28 Jennett B, Buxton M. Economics and the management of cancer: placing a value on human life. In: Stoll B, ed. *Social Impact of Cancer.* London, England: Macmillan Publishers Ltd; 1989.

29 Cassell EJ. *Talking With Patients: Clinical Technique.* Cambridge, Mass: MIT Press; 1985:2.

30 Williams A. The cost-effectiveness approach to the treatment of angina. In: Patterson DLH, ed. *The Management of Angina Pectoris.* Dobbs Ferry, NY: Castle House Publications; 1987:131–146.

31 Weinstein MC. Estrogen use in postmenopausal women. *N Engl J Med.* 1980; 303:308–316.

32 Boyle MS, Torrance GW, Sinclair JC, Horwood SP. Economic evaluation of neonatal intensive care of very-low-birth-weight infants. *N Engl J Med.* 1983; 308:1330–1337.

33 Churchill DN, Lemon BC, Torrance GW. A cost-effectiveness analysis of continuous ambulatory peritoneal dialysis and hospital hemodialysis. *Med Decis Making.* 1984; 4:489–500.

34 Weinstein MC, Stason WB. Cost-effectiveness of coronary artery bypass surgery. *Circulation.* 1982; 66(suppl III):III-56–III-66.

35 Barry MJ, Mulley AG, Fowler FJ, Wennberg JW. Watchful waiting vs immediate transurethral re-section for symptomatic prostatism. *JAMA.* 1988; 259:3010–3017.

36 Williams A. Economics of coronary artery bypass grafting. *Br Med J.* 1985; 291:326–329.

37 Gudex C. *QALYs and Their Use by the Health Service.* University of York (England) Centre for Health Economics; 1986. Discussion Paper 20.

38 Gudex C. QALYs: an explicit outcome measure for today's NHS. *Public Finance Accountancy.* November 13, 1987:13–15.

39 Kind P, Rosser R, Williams A. Valuation of quality of life: some psychometric evidence. In: Jones-Lee MW, ed. *The Value of Life and Safety.* Amsterdam, the Netherlands: Elsevier/North Holland; 1982.

40 Ellwood PM. Shattuck Lecture: outcomes management: a technology of patient experience. *N Engl J Med.* 1988; 318:1549–1556.

41 Drummond MF. Resource allocation decisions in health care: a role for quality of life assessments? *J Chronic Dis.* 1987; 40:605–616.

42 Sisk JE. Discussion: Drummond's 'Resource Allocation Decisions in Health Care: A Role for Quality of Life Assessments?' *J Chronic Dis.* 1987; 40:617–19.

43 Callahan D. *Setting Limits.* New York, NY: Simon & Schuster Inc Publishers; 1987.

44 Blendon RJ. The public's view of the future of health care. *JAMA.* 1988; 259:3587–3593.

45 McNeil BJ, Pauker SG, Sox HC, Tversky A. On the elicitation of preferences for alternative therapies. *N Engl J Med.* 1982; 306:1259–1262.

46 Lipscomb J. Time preference for health in cost-effectiveness analysis. *Med Care.* 1989; 27(suppl):S233–S248.

47 Piliskin JS, Shepard DS, Weinstein MC. Utility functions for life years and health status. *Operations Res.* 1980; 28:206–224.

48 Caplan AL. How should values count in the allocation of new technologies in health care? In: Bayer R, Caplan AL, Daniels N, eds. *In Search of Equity: Health Care Needs and the Health Care System.* New York, NY: Plenum Press; 1983:95–124.

49 Siegler M. The progression of medicine: from physician paternalism to patient autonomy to bu-

reaucratic parsimony. *Arch Intern Med.* 1985; 145:713–715.

50 Mendeloff J. Measuring elusive benefits: on the value of health. *J Health Politics Policy Law.* 1983; 8:554–580.

51 Abrans FR. Patient advocate or secret agent. *JAMA.* 1986; 256:1784–1785.

52 Pearlman RA, Uhlmann RF, Cain KC. Quality of life in chronic diseases: perceptions of elderly patients. *J Gerontol.* 1988; 43(2):M25–M30.

53 Danis M, Patrick DL, Southerland LI, Green ML. Patients' and families' preferences for medical intensive care. *JAMA,* 1988; 260:797–802.

54 Uhlmann RF, Pearlman RA, Cain KC. Physicians' and spouses' predictions of elderly patients' resuscitation preferences. *J Gerontol.* 1988; 43(5): M115–M121.

55 Zweibel NR, Cassel CK. Treatment choices at the end of life: a comparison of decisions by older patients and their physician-selected proxies. *Gerontologist.* 1989; 29:615–621.

56 La Puma J, Schiedermayer DL, Gulyas AE, Siegler M. Talking to comatose patients. *Arch Neurol.* 1988; 45:20–22.

57 Wolf SM. The persistent problem of PVS. *Hastings Cent Rep.* 1988; 18(1):26.

58 Shaw A. QL revisited. *Hastings Cent Rep.* 1988; 18(2):10–12.

59 Vladeck BC. Medicare hospital payment by diagnosis-related groups. *Ann Intern Med.* 1984; 100:576–591.

60 Hsiao WC, Dunn DL. The impact of DRG payment on New Jersey hospitals. *Inquiry.* 1987; 24:2120.

61 Greer EG, Kronenfeld JJ, Baker SL, Amidon RL. An appraisal of organizational response to fiscally constraining regulation: the case of hospitals and DRGs. *J Health Soc Behav.* 1989; 30:41–55.

62 Kruse JA, Thill-Baharozian MC, Carlson RW. Comparison of clinical assessment with APACHE II for predicting mortality risk in patients admitted to a medical intensive care unit. *JAMA.* 1988; 260:1739–1742.

63 Levinson DF. Toward full disclosure of referral restrictions and financial incentives by prepaid health plans. *N Engl J Med.* 1987; 317:1729–1731.

64 Reagan MD. Physicians as gatekeepers: a complex challenge. *N Engl J Med.* 1987; 317:1731–1734.

65 Hillman AL. Financial incentives for physicians in HMOs: is there a conflict of interest? *N Engl J Med.* 1987; 317:1743–1748.

66 La Puma J, Cassel CK, Humphrey H. Ethics, economics, and endocarditis: the physician's role in resource allocation. *Arch Intern Med.* 1988; 148:1809–1811.

67 Morreim EH. Fiscal scarcity and the inevitability of bedside budget balancing. *Arch Intern Med.* 1989; 149:1012–1015.

68 In the courts. *Hastings Cent Rep.* 1986; 16(6):32.

69 *Wickline v California,* 2nd Appellate District, Division 5, No. B010156, July 30, 1986.

70 Schiedermayer DL, La Puma J, Miles SH. Ethics consultations masking economic dilemmas in patient care. *Arch Intern Med.* 1989; 149:1303–1305.

Questions for Discussion

1 Can QALYs be measured well enough for use in decision-making?

2 Does use of QALYs accord with the principles of justice? Are there any other factors which need to be taken into consideration? Are there any better alternatives?

Living on a Lifeboat

Garrett Hardin

Looking at distribution of resources on a global scale, Hardin argues against the common view that wealthy nations have some obligation to help the starving of the world. Using the image of a lifeboat in a sea full of drowning people, Hardin argues that the eventual result of giving large amounts of humanitarian aid and loosening immigration laws would not be a raising of the disadvantaged to the level of the well-off, but rather a lowering of the wealthy to the level of the poor. This paper was first published in the mid-1970s, but remains one of the classic statements of warning against large-scale humanitarian aid.

★ ★ ★

Susanne Langer (1942) has shown that it is probably impossible to approach an unsolved problem save through the door of metaphor. Later, attempting to meet the demands of rigor, we may achieve some success in cleansing theory of metaphor, though our success is limited if we are unable to avoid using common language, which is shot through and through with fossil metaphors. (I count no less than five in the preceding two sentences.)

Since metaphorical thinking is inescapable it is pointless merely to weep about our human limitations. We must learn to live with them, to understand them, and to control them. "All of us," said George Eliot in *Middlemarch*, "get our thoughts entangled in metaphors, and act fatally on the strength of them." To avoid unconscious suicide we are well advised to pit one metaphor against another. From the interplay of competitive metaphors, thoroughly developed, we may come closer to metaphor-free solutions to our problems.

No generation has viewed the problem of the survival of the human species as seriously as we have. Inevitably, we have entered this world of concern through the door of metaphor. Environmentalists have emphasized the image of the earth as a spaceship—Spaceship Earth. Kenneth Boulding (1966) is the principal architect of this metaphor. It is time, he

says, that we replace the wasteful "cowboy economy" of the past with the frugal "spaceship economy" required for continued survival in the limited world we now see ours to be. The metaphor is notably useful in justifying pollution-control measures.

Unfortunately, the image of a spaceship is also used to promote measures that are suicidal. One of these is a generous immigration policy, which is only a particular instance of a class of policies that are in error because they lead to the tragedy of the commons (Hardin 1968). These suicidal policies are attractive because they mesh with what we unthinkingly take to be the ideals of "the best people." What is missing in the idealistic view is an insistence that rights and responsibilities must go together. The "generous" attitude of all too many people results in asserting inalienable rights while ignoring or denying matching responsibilities.

For the metaphor of a spaceship to be correct the aggregate of people on board would have to be under unitary sovereign control (Ophuls 1974). A true ship always has a captain. It is conceivable that a ship could be run by a committee. But it could not possibly survive if its course were determined by bickering tribes that claimed rights without responsibilities.

What about Spaceship Earth? It certainly has no captain, and no executive committee. The United Nations is a toothless tiger, because the signatories of its charter wanted it that way. The spaceship metaphor is used only to justify spaceship demands on common resources without acknowledging corresponding spaceship responsibilities.

An understandable fear of decisive action leads people to embrace "incrementalism"—moving toward reform by tiny stages. As we shall see, this strategy is counterproductive in the area discussed here if it means accepting rights before responsibilities. Where human survival is at stake, the acceptance of responsibilities is a precondition to the acceptance of rights, if the two cannot be introduced simultaneously.

Lifeboat Ethics

Before taking up certain substantive issues let us look at an alternative metaphor, that of a lifeboat. In developing some relevant examples the following numerical values are assumed. Approximately two-thirds of the world is desperately poor, and only one-third is comparatively rich. The people in poor countries have an average per capita GNP (Gross National Product) of about $200 per year; the rich, of about $3,000. (For the United States it is nearly $5,000 per year.) Metaphorically, each rich nation amounts to a lifeboat full of comparatively rich people. The poor of the world are in other, much more crowded lifeboats. Continuously, so to speak, the poor fall out of their lifeboats and swim for a while in the water outside, hoping to be admitted to a rich lifeboat, or in some other way to benefit from the "goodies" on board. What should the passengers on a rich lifeboat do? This is the central problem of "the ethics of a lifeboat."

First we must acknowledge that each lifeboat is effectively limited in capacity. The land of every nation has a limited carrying capac-

ity. The exact limit is a matter for argument, but the energy crunch is convincing more people every day that we have already exceeded the carrying capacity of the land. We have been living on "capital"—stored petroleum and coal—and soon we must live on income alone.

Let us look at only one lifeboat—ours. The ethical problem is the same for all, and is as follows. Here we sit, say fifty people in a lifeboat. To be generous, let us assume our boat has a capacity of ten more, making sixty. (This, however, is to violate the engineering principle of the "safety factor." A new plant disease or a bad change in the weather may decimate our population if we don't preserve some excess capacity as a safety factor.)

The fifty of us in the lifeboat see 100 others swimming in the water outside, asking for admission to the boat, or for handouts. How shall we respond to their calls? There are several possibilities.

One. We may be tempted to try to live by the Christian ideal of being "our brother's keeper," or by the Marxian ideal (Marx 1875) of "from each according to his abilities, to each according to his needs." Since the needs of all are the same, we take all the needy into our boat, making a total of 150 in a boat with a capacity of sixty. The boat is swamped, and everyone drowns. Complete justice, complete catastrophe.

Two. Since the boat has an unused excess capacity of ten, we admit just ten more to it. This has the disadvantage of getting rid of the safety factor, for which action we will sooner or later pay dearly. Moreover, *which* ten do we let in? "First come, first served?" The best ten? The neediest ten? How do we *discriminate*? And what do we say to the ninety who are excluded?

Three. Admit no more to the boat and preserve the small safety factor. Survival of the people in the lifeboat is then possible (though we shall have to be on our guard against boarding parties).

The last solution is abhorrent to many people. It is unjust, they say. Let us grant that it is.

"I feel guilty about my good luck," say some. The reply to this is simple: *Get out and yield your place to others.* Such a selfless action might satisfy the conscience of those who are addicted to guilt but it would not change the ethics of the lifeboat. The needy person to whom a guilt-addict yields his place will not himself feel guilty about his sudden good luck. (If he did he would not climb aboard.) The net result of conscience-stricken people relinquishing their unjustly held positions is the elimination of their kind of conscience from the lifeboat. The lifeboat, as it were, purifies itself of guilt. The ethics of the lifeboat persist, unchanged by such momentary aberrations.

This then is the basic metaphor within which we must work out our solutions. Let us enrich the image step by step with substantive additions from the real world.

Reproduction

The harsh characteristics of lifeboat ethics are heightened by reproduction, particularly by reproductive differences. The people inside the lifeboats of the wealthy nations are doubling in numbers every eighty-seven years; those outside are doubling every thirty-five years, on the average. And the relative difference in prosperity is becoming greater.

Let us, for a while, think primarily of the US lifeboat. As of 1973 the United States had a population of 210 million people, who were increasing by 0.8% per year, that is, doubling in number every eighty-seven years.

Although the citizens of rich nations are outnumbered two to one by the poor, let us imagine an equal number of poor people outside our lifeboat—a mere 210 million poor people reproducing at a quite different rate. If

we imagine these to be the combined populations of Colombia, Venezuela, Ecuador, Morocco, Thailand, Pakistan, and the Philippines, the average rate of increase of the people "outside" is 3.3% per year. The doubling time of this population is twenty-one years.

Suppose that all these countries, and the United States, agreed to live by the Marxian ideal, "to each according to his needs," the ideal of most Christians as well. Needs, of course, are determined by population size, which is affected by reproduction. Every nation regards its rate of reproduction as a sovereign right. If our lifeboat were big enough in the beginning it might be possible to live *for a while* by Christian-Marxian ideals. *Might.*

Initially, in the model given, the ratio of non-Americans to Americans would be one to one. But consider what the ratio would be eighty-seven years later. By this time Americans would have doubled to a population of 420 million. The other group (doubling every twenty-one years) would now have swollen to 3,540 million. Each American would have more than eight people to share with. How could the lifeboat possibly keep afloat?

All this involves extrapolation of current trends into the future, and is consequently suspect. Trends may change. Granted: but the change will not necessarily be favorable. If—as seems likely—the rate of population increases falls faster in the ethnic group presently inside the lifeboat than it does among those now outside, the future will turn out to be even worse than mathematics predicts, and sharing will be even more suicidal.

Ruin in the Commons

The fundamental error of the sharing ethics is that it leads to the tragedy of the commons. Under a system of private property the man (or group of men) who own property recognize their responsibility to care for it, for if they don't they will eventually suffer. A farmer, for instance, if he is intelligent, will allow no more cattle in a pasture than its carrying capacity justifies. If he overloads the pasture, weeds take over, erosion sets in, and the owner loses in the long run.

But if a pasture is run as a commons open to all, the right of each to use it is not matched by an operational responsibility to take care of it. It is no use asking independent herdsmen in a commons not to act responsibly, for they dare not. The considerate herdsman who refrains from overloading the commons suffers more than a selfish one who says his needs are greater. (As Leo Durocher says, "Nice guys finish last.") Christian-Marxian idealism is counterproductive. That it *sounds* nice is no excuse. With distribution systems, as with individual morality, good intentions are no substitute for good performance.

A social system is stable only if it is insensitive to errors. To the Christian-Marxian idealist a selfish person is a sort of "error." Prosperity in the system of the commons cannot survive errors. If *everyone* would only restrain himself, all would be well; but it takes *only one less than everyone* to ruin a system of voluntary restraint. In a crowded world of less than perfect human beings—and we will never know any other—mutual ruin is inevitable in the commons. This is the core of the tragedy of the commons.

One of the major tasks of education today is to create such an awareness of the dangers of the commons that people will be able to recognize its many varieties, however disguised. There is pollution of the air and water because these media are treated as commons. Further growth of population and growth in the per capita conversion of natural resources into pollutants require that the system of the commons be modified or abandoned in the disposal of "externalities."

The fish populations of the oceans are exploited as commons, and ruin lies ahead. No technological invention can prevent this fate; in fact, all improvements in the art of fishing merely hasten the day of complete ruin. Only the replacement of the system of the commons with a responsible system can save oceanic fisheries.

The management of western range lands, though nominally rational, is in fact (under the steady pressure of cattle ranchers) often merely a government-sanctioned system of the commons, drifting toward ultimate ruin for both the rangelands and the residual enterprisers.

World Food Banks

In the international arena we have recently heard a proposal to create a new commons, namely an international depository of food reserves to which nations will contribute according to their abilities, and from which nations may draw according to their needs. Nobel laureate Norman Borlaug has lent the prestige of his name to this proposal.

A world food bank appeals powerfully to our humanitarian impulses. We remember John Donne's celebrated line, "Any man's death diminishes me." But before we rush out to see for whom the bell tolls let us recognize where the greatest political push for international granaries comes from, lest we be disillusioned later. Our experience with Public Law 480 clearly reveals the answer. This was the law that moved billions of dollars worth of US grain to food-short, population-long countries during the past two decades. When P.L. 480 first came into being, a headline in the business magazine *Forbes* (Paddock and Paddock 1970) revealed the power behind it: "Feeding the World's Hungry Millions: How it will mean billions for US business."

And indeed it did. In the years 1960 to 1970 a total of $7.9 billion was spent on the "Food for Peace" program, as P.L. 480 was called. During the years 1948 to 1970 an additional $49.9 billion were extracted from

American taxpayers to pay for other economic aid programs, some of which went for food and food-producing machinery. (This figure does *not* include military aid.) That P.L. 480 was a giveaway program was concealed. Recipient countries went through the motions of paying for P.L. 480 food—with IOUs. In December 1973 the charade was brought to an end as far as India was concerned when the United States "forgave" India's $3.2 billion debt (Anonymous 1974). Public announcement of the cancellation of the debt was delayed for two months; one wonders why.

"Famine—1974!" (Paddock and Paddock 1970) is one of the few publications that points out the commercial roots of this humanitarian attempt. Though all US taxpayers lost by P.L. 480, special interest groups gained handsomely. Farmers benefited because they were not asked to contribute the grain—it was bought from them by the taxpayers. Besides the direct benefit there was the indirect effect of increasing demand and thus raising prices of farm products generally. The manufacturers of farm machinery, fertilizers, and pesticides benefited by the farmers' extra efforts to grow more food. Grain elevators profited from storing the grain for varying lengths of time. Railroads made money hauling it to port, and shipping lines by carrying it overseas. Moreover, once the machinery for P.L. 480 was established an immense bureaucracy had a vested interest in its continuance regardless of its merits.

Very little was ever heard of these selfish interests when P.L. 480 was defended in public. The emphasis was always on its humanitarian effects. The combination of multiple and relatively silent selfish interests with highly vocal humanitarian apologists constitutes a powerful lobby for extracting money from taxpayers. Foreign aid has become a habit that can apparently survive in the absence of any known justification. A news commentator in a weekly magazine (Lansner 1974), after exhaustively going over all the conventional arguments for foreign aid—self-interest, social justice, political advantage, and charity—and concluding that none of the known arguments really held water, concluded: "So the search continues for some logically compelling reasons for giving aid...." In other words, *Act now, justify later*—if ever. (Apparently a quarter of a century is too short a time to find the justification for expending several billion dollars yearly).

The search for a rational justification can be short-circuited by interjecting the word "emergency." Borlaug uses this word. We need to look sharply at it. What is an "emergency?" It is surely something like an accident, which is correctly defined as *an event that is certain to happen, though with a low frequency* (Hardin, 1972a). A well-run organization prepares for everything that is certain, including accidents and emergencies. It budgets for them. It saves for them. It expects them—and mature decision-makers do not waste time complaining about accidents when they occur.

What happens if some organizations budget for emergencies and others do not? If each organization is solely responsible for its own well-being, poorly managed ones will suffer. But they should be able to learn from experience. They have a chance to mend their ways and learn to budget for infrequent but certain emergencies. The weather, for instance, always varies and periodic crop failures are certain. A wise and competent government saves out of the production of the good years in anticipation of bad years that are sure to come. This is not a new idea. The Bible tells us that Joseph taught this policy to Pharaoh in Egypt more than 2,000 years ago. Yet it is literally true that the vast majority of the governments of the world today have no such policy. They lack either the wisdom or the competence, or both. Far more difficult than the transfer of wealth from one country to another is the transfer of wisdom between sovereign powers or between generations.

"But it isn't their fault! How can we blame the poor people who are caught in an emergency? Why must we punish them?" The concepts of blame and punishment are irrelevant. The question is, what are the operational consequences of establishing a world food bank? If it is open to every country every time a need develops, slovenly rulers will not be motivated to take Joseph's advice. Why should they? Others will bail them out whenever they are in trouble.

Some countries will make deposits in the world food bank and others will withdraw from it; there will be almost no overlap. Calling such a depository-transfer unit a "bank" is stretching the metaphor of *bank* beyond its elastic limits. The proposers, of course, never call attention to the metaphorical nature of the word they use.

The Ratchet Effect

An "international food bank" is really, then, not a true bank but a disguised one-way transfer device for moving wealth from rich countries to poor. In the absence of such a bank, in a world inhabited by individually responsible sovereign nations, the population of each nation would repeatedly go through a cycle of the sort shown in Exhibit A. P_2 is greater than P_1, either in absolute numbers or because a deterioration of the food supply has removed the safety factor and produced a dangerously low ratio of resources to population. P_2 may be said to represent a state of overpopulation, which becomes obvious upon the appearance of an "accident," e.g., a crop failure. If the "emergency" is not met by outside help, the population drops back to the "normal" level—the "carrying capacity" of the environment—or even below. In the absence of population control by a sovereign, sooner or later the population grows to P_2 again and the cycle repeats. The long-term population curve (Hardin 1966) is an irregularly fluctuating one, equilibrating more or less about the carrying capacity.

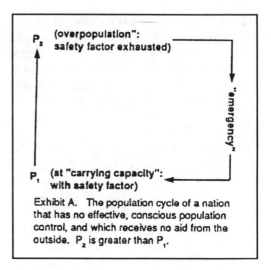

Exhibit A. The population cycle of a nation that has no effective, conscious population control, and which receives no aid from the outside. P_2 is greater than P_1.

A demographic cycle of this sort obviously involves great suffering in the restrictive phase, but such a cycle is normal to any independent country with inadequate population control. The third century theologian Tertullian (Hardin, 1969a) expressed what must have been the recognition of many wise men when he wrote: "The scourges of pestilence, famine, wars, and earthquakes have come to be regarded as a blessing to overcrowded nations, since they serve to prune away the luxuriant growth of the human race."

Only under a strong and farsighted sovereign—which theoretically could be the people themselves, democratically organized—can a population equilibrate at some set point below the carrying capacity, thus avoiding the pains normally caused by periodic and unavoidable disasters. For this happy state to be achieved it is necessary that those in power be able to contemplate with equanimity the "waste" of surplus food in times of bountiful harvests. It is essential that those in power resist the temptation to convert extra food into extra babies. On the public relations level it is necessary that the phrase "surplus food" be replaced by "safety factor."

But wise sovereigns seem not to exist in the poor world today. The most anguishing problems are created by poor countries that are governed by rulers insufficiently wise and powerful. If such countries can draw on a world food bank in times of "emergency," the population *cycle* of Exhibit A will be replaced by the population *escalator* of Exhibit B. The input of food from a food bank acts as the pawl of a ratchet, preventing the population from retracting its steps to a lower level. Reproduction pushes the population upward, inputs from the world bank prevent its moving downward. Population size escalates, as does the absolute magnitude of "accidents" and "emergencies." The process is brought to an end only by the total collapse of the whole system, producing a catastrophe of scarcely imaginable proportions.

Such are the implications of the well-meant sharing of food in a world of irresponsible reproduction.

I think we need a new word for systems like this. The adjective "melioristic" is applied to systems that produce continual improvement; the English word is derived from the Latin *meliorare*, to become or make better. Parallel with this it would be useful to bring in the word *pejoristic* (from the Latin *pejorare*, to become or to make worse). This word can be applied to those systems that by their very nature, can be relied upon to make matters worse. A world food bank coupled with sovereign state irresponsibly in reproduction is an example of a pejoristic system.

This pejoristic system creates an unacknowledged commons. People have more motivation to draw from than to add to the common store. The license to make such withdrawals diminishes whatever motivation poor countries might otherwise have to control their populations. Under the guidance of this ratchet, wealth can be steadily moved in

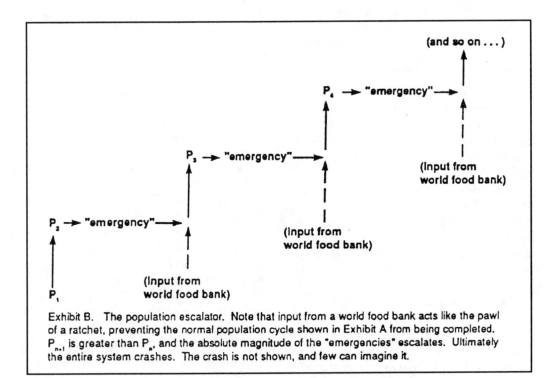

Exhibit B. The population escalator. Note that input from a world food bank acts like the pawl of a ratchet, preventing the normal population cycle shown in Exhibit A from being completed. P_{n+1} is greater than P_n, and the absolute magnitude of the "emergencies" escalates. Ultimately the entire system crashes. The crash is not shown, and few can imagine it.

one direction only, from the slowly-breeding rich to the rapidly-breeding poor, the process finally coming to a halt only when all countries are equally and miserably poor.

All this is terribly obvious once we are acutely aware of the pervasiveness and danger of the commons. But many people still lack this awareness and the euphoria of the "benign demographic transition" (Hardin 1973) interferes with the realistic appraisal of pejoristic mechanisms. As concerns public policy, the deductions drawn from the benign demographic transition are these:

> 1. If the per capita GNP rises the birth rate will fall; hence, the rate of population increase will fall, ultimately producing ZPG (Zero Population Growth).
>
> 2. The long-term trend all over the world (including the poor countries) is of a rising per capita GNP (for which no limit is seen).
>
> 3. Therefore, all political interference in population matters is unnecessary; all we need to do is foster economic "development"—*note the metaphor*—and population problems will solve themselves.

Those who believe in the benign demographic transition dismiss the pejoristic mechanism of Exhibit B in the belief that each input of food from the world outside fosters development within a poor country thus resulting in a drop in the rate of population increase. Foreign aid has proceeded on this assumption for more than two decades. Unfortunately it has produced no indubitable instance of the asserted effect. It has, however, produced a library of excuses. The air is filled with plaintive calls for more massive foreign aid appropriations so that the hypothetical melioristic process can get started.

The doctrine of demographic laissez-faire implicit in the hypothesis of the benign demographic transition is immensely attractive. Unfortunately there is more evidence against

the melioristic system than there is for it (Davis 1963). On the historical side there are many counter-examples. The rise in per capita GNP in France and Ireland during the past century has been accompanied by a rise in population growth. In the twenty-five years following the Second World War the same positive correlation was noted almost everywhere in the world. Never in world history before 1950 did the worldwide population growth reach one percent per annum. Now the average population growth is over two percent and shows no signs of slackening.

On the theoretical side, the denial of the pejoristic scheme of Exhibit B probably springs from the hidden acceptance of the "cowboy economy" that Boulding castigated. Those who recognize the limitations of a spaceship, if they are unable to achieve population control at a safe and comfortable level, accept the necessity of the corrective feedback of the population cycle shown in Exhibit A. No one who knew in his bones that he was living on a true spaceship would countenance political support of the population escalator shown in Exhibit B.

Eco-destruction via the Green Revolution

The demoralizing effect of charity on the recipient has long been known. "Give a man a fish and he will eat for a day; teach him how to fish and he will eat for the rest of his days." So runs an ancient Chinese proverb. Acting on this advice the Rockefeller and Ford Foundations have financed a multipronged program for improving agriculture in the hungry nations. The result, known as the "Green Revolution," has been quite remarkable. "Miracle wheat" and "miracle rice" are splendid technological achievements in the realm of plant genetics.

Whether or not the Green Revolution can increase food production is doubtful (Harris

1972, Paddock 1970, Wilkes 1972), but in any event not particularly important. What is missing in this great and well-meaning humanitarian effort is a firm grasp of fundamentals. Considering the importance of the Rockefeller Foundation in this effort it is ironic that the late Alan Gregg, a much-respected vice-president of the Foundation, strongly expressed his doubts of the wisdom of all attempts to increase food production some two decades ago. (This was before Borlaug's work—supported by Rockefeller—had resulted in the development of "miracle wheat.") Gregg (1955) likened the growth and spreading of humanity over the surface of the earth to the metastasis of cancer in the human body, wryly remarking that "Cancerous growths demand food; but, as far as I know, they have never been cured by getting it."

"Man does not live by bread alone"—the scriptural statement has a rich meaning even in the material realm. Every human being born constitutes a draft on all aspects of the environment—food, air, water, unspoiled scenery, occasional and optional solitude, beaches, contact with wild animals, fishing, hunting—the list is long and incompletely known. Food can, perhaps, be significantly increased, but what about clean beaches, unspoiled forests, and solitudes? If we satisfy the need for food in a growing population we necessarily decrease the supply of other goods, and thereby increase the difficulty of equitably allocating scarce goods (Hardin 1969b, 1972b).

The present population of India is 600 million, and it is increasing by fifteen million per year. The environmental load of this population is already great. The forests of India are only a small fraction of what they were three centuries ago. Soil erosion, floods, and the psychological costs of crowding are serious. Every one of the net fifteen million lives added each year stresses the Indian environment more severely. *Every life saved this year in*

a poor country diminishes the quality of life for subsequent generations.

Observant critics have shown how much harm we wealthy nations have already done to poor nations through our well-intentioned but misguided attempts to help them (Paddock and Paddock 1973). Particularly reprehensible is our failure to carry out post-audits of these attempts (Farvar and Milton 1972). Thus have we shielded our tender consciences from knowledge of the harm we have done. Must we Americans continue to fail to monitor the consequences of our external "do-gooding?" If, for instance, we thoughtlessly make it possible for the present 600 million Indians to swell to 1,200 million by the year 2001—as their present growth rate promises—will posterity in India thank *us* for facilitating an even greater destruction of *their* environment? Are good intentions ever a sufficient excuse for bad consequences?

Immigration Creates a Commons

I come now to the final example of a commons in action, one for which the public is least prepared for rational discussion. The topic is at present enveloped by a great silence that reminds me of a comment made by Sherlock Holmes in A. Conan Doyle's story, "Silver Blaze." Inspector Gregory had asked, "Is there any point to which you wish to draw my attention?" To this Holmes responded:

> "To the curious incident of the dog in the night-time."
> "The dog did nothing in the night-time," said the Inspector.
> "That was the curious incident," remarked Sherlock Holmes.

By asking himself what would repress the normal barking instinct of a watch dog Holmes realized that it must be the dog's recognition of his master as the criminal trespasser. In a similar way we should ask ourselves what repression keeps us from discussing something as important as immigration?

It cannot be that immigration is numerically of no consequence. Our government acknowledges a *net* inflow of 400,000 a year. Hard data are understandably lacking on the extent of illegal entries, but a not implausible figure is 600,000 per year. (Buchanan 1973). The natural increase of the resident population is now about 1.7 million per year. This means that the yearly gain from immigration is at least nineteen percent and may be thirty-seven percent, of the total increase. It is quite conceivable that educational campaigns like that of Zero Population Growth, Inc., coupled with adverse social and economic factors—inflation, housing shortage, depression, and loss of confidence in national leaders—may lower the fertility of American women to a point at which all of the yearly increase in population would be accounted for by immigration. Should we not at least ask if that is what we want? How curious it is that we so seldom discuss immigration these days!

Curious, but understandable—as one finds out the moment he publicly questions the wisdom of the status quo in immigration. He who does so is promptly charged with *isolationism, bigotry, prejudice, ethnocentrism, chauvinism,* and *selfishness.* These are hard accusations to bear. It is pleasanter to talk about other matters, leaving immigration policy to wallow in the crosscurrents of special interests that take no account of the good of the whole—*or of the interests of posterity.*

We Americans have a bad conscience because of things we said in the past about immigrants. Two generations ago the popular press was rife with references to *Dagos, Wops, Pollacks, Japs, Chinks,* and *Krauts*—all pejorative terms that failed to acknowledge our indebtedness to Goya, Leonardo, Copernicus, Hiroshige, Confucius, and Bach. Because the implied inferiority of foreigners was *then* the justification for keeping them out, it is *now*

thoughtlessly assumed that restrictive policies can only be based on the assumption of immigrant inferiority. *This is not so.*

Existing immigration laws exclude idiots and known criminals; future laws will almost certainly continue this policy. But should we also consider the quality of the average immigrant, as compared with the quality of the average resident? Perhaps we should, perhaps we shouldn't. (What is "quality" anyway?) But the quality issue is not our concern here.

From this point on, *it will be assumed that immigrants and native-born citizens are of exactly equal quality,* however quality may be defined. The focus is only on quantity. The conclusions reached depend on nothing else, so all charges of ethnocentrism are irrelevant.

World food banks move food to the people, thus facilitating the exhaustion of the environment of the poor. By contrast, unrestricted immigration moves people to the food, thus speeding up the destruction of the environment in rich countries. Why poor people should want to make this transfer is no mystery, but why should rich hosts encourage it? This transfer, like the reverse one, is supported by both selfish interests and humanitarian impulses.

The principal selfish interest in unimpeded immigration is easy to identify: it is the interest of the employers of cheap labor, particularly that needed for degrading jobs. We have been deceived about the forces of history by the lines of Emma Lazarus inscribed on the Statue of Liberty:

> *Give me your tired, your poor,*
> *Your huddled masses yearning to breathe free,*
> *The wretched refuse of your teeming shore,*
> *Send these, the homeless, tempest-tossed to me:*
> *I lift my lamp beside the golden door.*

The image is one of an infinitely generous earth-mother, passively opening her arms to hordes of immigrants who come here on their own initiative. Such an image may have been adequate for the early days of colonization, but by the time these lines were written (1886) the force for immigration was largely manufactured inside our own borders by factory and mine owners who sought cheap labor not to be found among laborers already here. One group of foreigners after another was thus enticed into the United States to work at wretched jobs for wretched wages.

At present, it is largely the Mexicans who are being so exploited. It is particularly to the advantage of certain employers that there be many illegal immigrants. Illegal immigrant workers dare not complain about their working conditions for fear of being repatriated. Their presence reduces the bargaining power of all Mexican-American laborers. Cesar Chavez has repeatedly pleaded with congressional committees to close the doors to more Mexicans so that those here can negotiate effectively for higher wages and decent working conditions. Chavez understands the ethics of a lifeboat.

The interests of the employers of cheap labor are well served by the silence of the intelligentsia of the country. WASPs—White Anglo-Saxon Protestants—are particularly reluctant to call for a closing of the doors to immigration for fear of being called ethnocentric bigots. It was, therefore, an occasion of pure delight for this particular WASP to be present at a meeting when the points he would like to have made were made better by a non-WASP speaking to other non-WASPs. It was in Hawaii, and most of the people in the room were second-level Hawaiian officials of Japanese ancestry. All Hawaiians are keenly aware of the limits of their environment, and the speaker had asked how it might be practically and constitutionally possible to close the doors to more immigrants to the islands. (To Hawaiians, immigrants from the other forty-nine states are as much of a threat as those from other nations. There is only so much room in the islands, and the islanders know

it. Sophistical arguments that imply otherwise do not impress them.)

Yet the Japanese-Americans of Hawaii have active ties with the land of their origin. This point was raised by a Japanese-American member of the audience who asked the Japanese-American speaker: "But how can we shut the doors now? We have many friends and relations in Japan that we'd like to bring to Hawaii some day so that they can enjoy this beautiful land."

The speaker smiled sympathetically and responded slowly, "Yes, but we have children now and someday we'll have grandchildren. We can bring more people here from Japan only by giving away some of the land that we hope to pass on to our grandchildren some day. What right do we have to do that?"

To be generous with one's own possessions is one thing; to be generous with posterity's is quite another. This, I think, is the point that must be gotten across to those who would, from a commendable love of **distributive justice**, institute a ruinous system of the commons, either in the form of a world food bank or that of unrestricted immigration. Since every speaker is a member of some ethnic group it is always possible to charge him with ethnocentrism. But even after purging an argument of ethnocentrism the rejection of the commons is still valid and necessary if we are to save at least some parts of the world from environmental ruin. Is it not desirable that at least some of the grandchildren of people now living should have a decent place in which to live?

The Asymmetry of Door-Shutting

We must now answer this telling point: "How can you justify slamming the door once you're inside? You say that immigrants should be kept out. But aren't we all immigrants, or the descendants of immigrants? Since we refuse to leave, must we not, as a matter of justice and symmetry, admit all others?"

It is literally true that we Americans of non-Indian ancestry are the descendants of thieves. Should we not, then, "give back" the land to the Indians, that is, give it to the now-living Americans of Indian ancestry? As an exercise in pure logic I see no way to reject this proposal. Yet I am unwilling to live by it, and I know no one who is. Our reluctance to embrace pure justice may spring from pure selfishness. On the other hand, it may arise from an unspoken recognition of consequences that have not yet been clearly spelled out.

Suppose, becoming intoxicated with pure justice, we "Anglos" should decide to turn our land over to the Indians. Since all our other wealth has also been derived from the land, we would have to give that to the Indians, too. Then what would we non-Indians do? Where would we go? There is no open land in the world on which men without capital can make their own living (and not much unoccupied land on which men with capital can either). Where would 209 million putatively justice-loving, non-Indian Americans go? Most of them—in the persons of their ancestors—came from Europe, but they wouldn't be welcomed back there. Anyway, Europeans have no better title to their land than we to ours. They also would have to give up their homes. (But to whom? And where would *they* go?)

Clearly, the concept of pure justice produces an **infinite regress**. The law long ago invented statutes of limitations to justify the rejection of pure justice, in the interest of preventing massive disorder. The law zealously defends property rights—but only *recent* property rights. It is as though the physical principle of exponential decay applies to property rights. Drawing a line in time may be unjust, but any other action is practically worse.

We are all the descendants of thieves, and the world's resources are inequitably distributed, but we must begin the journey to tomorrow from the point where we are today. We cannot remake the past. We cannot, without violent disorder and suffering, give land and resources back to the "original" owners—who are dead anyway.

We cannot safely divide the wealth equitably among all present peoples, so long as people reproduce at different rates, because to do so would guarantee that our grandchildren—everyone's grandchildren—would have only a ruined world to inhabit.

Must Exclusion be Absolute?

To show the logical structure of the immigration problem I have ignored many factors that would enter into real decisions made in a real world. No matter how convincing the logic may be, it is probable that we would want, from time to time, to admit a few people from the outside to our lifeboat. Political refugees in particular are likely to cause us to make exceptions: We remember the Jewish refugees from Germany after 1933, and the Hungarian refugees after 1956. Moreover, the interests of national defense, broadly conceived, could justify admitting many men and women of unusual talents, whether refugees or not. (This raises the quality issue, which is not the subject of this essay.)

Such exceptions threaten to create runaway population growth inside the lifeboat, i.e., the receiving country. However, the threat can be neutralized by a population policy that includes immigration. An effective policy is one of flexible control.

Suppose, for example, that the nation has achieved a stable condition of ZPG, which (say) permits 1.5 million births yearly. We must suppose that an acceptable system of allocating birth-rights to potential parents is in effect. Now suppose that an inhumane regime in some other part of the world creates a horde of refugees, and that there is a widespread desire to admit some to our country. At the same time, we do not want to sabotage our population control system. Clearly, the rational path to pursue is the following. If we decide to admit 100,000 refugees this year we should compensate for this by reducing the allocation of birth-rights in the following year by a similar amount, that is, downward to a total of 1.4 million. In that way we could achieve both humanitarian and population control goals. (And the refugees would have to accept the population controls of the society that admits them. It is not inconceivable that they might be given proportionately fewer rights than the native population.)

In a democracy, the admission of immigrants should properly be voted on. But by whom? It is not obvious. The usual rule of a democracy is votes for all. But it can be questioned whether a universal franchise is the most just one in a case of this sort. Whatever benefits there are in the admission of immigrants presumably accrue to everyone. But the costs would be seen as falling most heavily on potential parents, some of whom would have to postpone or forego having their (next) child because of the influx of immigrants. The double question *Who benefits? Who pays?* suggests that a restriction of the usual democratic franchise would be appropriate and just in this case. Would our particular quasi-democratic form of government be flexible enough to institute such a novelty? If not, the majority might, out of humanitarian motives, impose an unacceptable burden (the foregoing of parenthood) on a minority, thus producing political instability.

Plainly many new problems will arise when we consciously face the immigration question and seek rational answers. No workable answers can be found if we ignore population problems. And—if the argument of this essay is correct—so long as there is no true world government to control reproduction everywhere it is impossible to survive in dignity if we are to be guided by spaceship ethics. Without a world government that is sovereign in reproductive matters mankind lives, in fact, on a number of sovereign lifeboats. For the foreseeable future survival demands that we govern our actions by the ethics of a lifeboat. Posterity will be ill served if we do not.

References

Anonymous. 1974. *Wall Street Journal* 19 Feb.

Borlaug, N. 1973. Civilization's future: a call for international granaries. *Bulletin of Atomic Science* 29: 7-15.

Boulding, K. 1966. The economics of the coming Spaceship Earth. *In* H. Jarrett, ed. *Environmental Quality in a Growing Economy.* Baltimore: John Hopkins Press.

Buchanan, W. 1973. Immigration statistics. *Equilibrium* 1(3): 16-19.

Davis, K. 1963. Population. *Scientific American* 209(3): 62-71.

Farvar, M.T., and J.P. Milton. 1972. *The Careless Technology.* Garden City, NY: Natural History Press.

Gregg, A. 1955. A medical aspect of the population problem. *Science* 121:681-682.

Hardin, G. 1966. Chap. 9 in *Biology: Its Principles and Implications*, 2nd ed. San Francisco: Freeman.

———. 1968. The tragedy of the commons. *Science* 162: 1243-1248.

———. 1969a. Page 18 in *Population, Evolution, and Birth Control*, 2nd ed. San Francisco: Freeman.

———. 1969b. The economics of wilderness. *Nat.Hist.* 78(6): 20-27.

———. 1972a. Pages 81-82 in *Exploring New Ethics for Survival: The Voyage of the Spaceship* Beagle. New York: Viking.

———. 1972b. Preserving quality on Spaceship Earth. *In* J.B. Trefethen, ed. *Transactions of the Thirty-Seventh North American Wildlife and Natural Resources Conference.* Wildlife Management Institute, Washington, D.C.

———. 1973. Chap. 23 in *Stalking the Wild Taboo.* Los Altos, CA: Kaufmann.

Harris, M. 1972. How green the revolution. *Nat.Hist.* 81(3): 28-30.

Langer, S.K. 1942. *Philosophy in a New Key*. Cambridge, MA: Harvard University Press.

Lansner, K. 1974. Should foreign aid begin at home? *Newsweek*, 11 Feb., p. 32.

Marx, K. 1875. Critique of the Gotha program. Page 388 in R.C. Tucker, ed. *The Marx-Engels Reader*. New York: Norton, 1972.

Ophuls, W. 1974. The scarcity society. *Harpers* 248(1487): 47-52.

Paddock, W.C. 1970. How green is the green revolution? *BioScience* 20: 897-902.

Paddock, W., and E. Paddock. 1973. *We Don't Know How*. Ames, IA: Iowa State University Press.

Paddock, W., and P. Paddock. 1967. *Famine—1975!* Boston: Little, Brown.

Wilkes, H.G. 1972. The green revolution. *Environment* 14(8): 32-39.

Questions for Discussion

1 Is it fair to say that nations should take responsibility for managing their own resources? Does it matter if some nations have exploited others in the past?

2 Hardin states that "Every life saved this year in a poor country diminishes the quality of life for subsequent generations." Is he right? If so, how powerful an argument is this against trying to save lives in poor countries?

Rich and Poor

Peter Singer

In the following article, Singer argues that citizens of affluent nations are morally obliged to give assistance to those who are starving up to the point at which such assistance would involve sacrificing something of equal moral worth. Since starvation is a much more serious evil than being deprived of some new clothing, or entertainment, etc., this would mean there is a positive obligation to give much more than what is commonly considered a virtuous amount.

★   ★   ★

Some Facts

...Consider these facts: by the most cautious estimates, 400 million people lack the calories, protein, vitamins and minerals needed for a normally healthy life. Millions are constantly hungry; others suffer from deficiency diseases and from infections they would be able to resist on a better diet. Children are worst affected. According to one estimate, 15 million children under five die every year from the combined effect of malnutrition and infection. In some areas, half the children born can be expected to die before their fifth birthday.

Nor is lack of food the only hardship of the poor. To give a broader picture, Robert McNamara, President of the World Bank, has suggested the term 'absolute poverty.' The poverty we are familiar with in industrialized nations is relative poverty—meaning that some citizens are poor, relative to the wealth enjoyed by their neighbours. People living in relative poverty in Australia might be quite comfortably off by comparison with old-age pensioners in Britain, and British old-age pensioners are not poor in comparison with the poverty that exists in Mali or Ethiopia. Absolute poverty, on the other hand, is poverty by any standard. In McNamara's words:

> Poverty at the absolute level...is life at the very margin of existence.
>
> The absolute poor are severely deprived human beings struggling to survive in a set of squalid and degraded circumstances almost beyond the power of our sophisticated imaginations and privileged circumstances to conceive.
>
> Compared to those fortunate enough to live in developed countries, individuals in the poorest countries have:
>
> An infant mortality rate eight times higher
>
> A life expectancy one-third lower
>
> An adult literacy rate 60% less
>
> A nutritional level, for one out of every two in the population, below acceptable standards; and for millions of infants, less protein than is sufficient to permit optimum development of the brain.

And McNamara has summed up absolute poverty as:

> a condition of life so characterized by malnutrition, illiteracy, disease, squalid surroundings, high infant mortality, and low life expectancy as to be beneath any reasonable definition of human decency.

Absolute poverty is, McNamara has said, responsible for the loss of countless lives, especially among infants and young children. When absolute poverty does not cause death it still causes misery of a kind not often seen in the affluent nations. Malnutrition in young children stunts both physical and mental development. It has been estimated that the health, growth, and learning capacity of nearly half the young children in developing countries are affected by malnutrition. Millions of people on poor diets suffer from deficiency diseases, like goitre, or blindness caused by a lack of vitamin A. The food value of what the poor eat is further reduced by parasites such as hookworm and ringworm, which are endemic in conditions of poor sanitation and health education.

Death and disease apart, absolute poverty remains a miserable condition of life, with inadequate food, shelter, clothing, sanitation, health services and education. According to World Bank estimates which define absolute poverty in terms of income levels insufficient to provide adequate nutrition, something like 800 million people—almost 40% of the people of developing countries—live in absolute poverty. Absolute poverty is probably the principal cause of human misery today.

This is the background situation, the situation that prevails on our planet all the time. It does not make headlines. People died from malnutrition and related diseases yesterday, and more will die tomorrow. The occasional droughts, cyclones, earthquakes and floods that take the lives of tens of thousands in one place and at one time are more newsworthy. They add greatly to the total amount of human suffering; but it is wrong to assume that when there are no major calamities reported, all is well.

The problem is not that the world cannot produce enough to feed and shelter its people. People in the poor countries consume, on average, 400 lbs of grain a year, while North Americans average more than 2000 lbs. The difference is caused by the fact that in the rich countries we feed most of our grain to animals, converting it into meat, milk and eggs. Because this is an inefficient process, wasting up to 95% of the food value of the animal feed, people in rich countries are responsible for the consumption of far more food than those in poor countries who eat few animal products. If we stopped feeding animals on grains, soybeans and fishmeal the amount of food saved would—if distributed to those who need it—be more than enough to end hunger throughout the world.

These facts about animal food do not mean that we can easily solve the world food problem by cutting down on animal products, but they show that the problem is essentially one of distribution rather than production. The world does produce enough food. Moreover the poorer nations themselves could produce far more if they made more use of improved agricultural techniques.

So why are people hungry? Poor people cannot afford to buy grain grown by American farmers. Poor farmers cannot afford to buy improved seeds, or fertilizers, or the machinery needed for drilling wells and pumping water. Only by transferring some of the wealth of the developed nations to the poor of the undeveloped nations can the situation be changed.

That this wealth exists is clear. Against the picture of absolute poverty that McNamara has painted, one might pose a picture of 'absolute affluence.' Those who are absolutely affluent are not necessarily affluent by comparison with their neighbours, but they are affluent by any reasonable definition of human needs. This means that they have more income than they need to provide themselves adequately with all the basic necessities of life. After buying food, shelter, clothing, necessary health services and education, the absolutely affluent are still able to spend money on luxuries. The absolutely affluent choose their food for the pleasures of the palate, not to stop hunger; they buy new clothes to look fashionable, not to keep warm; they move house to be in a better neighbourhood or have a play room for the children, not to keep out the rain; and after all this there is still money to spend on books and records, colour television, and overseas holidays.

At this stage I am making no ethical judgements about absolute affluence, merely pointing out that it exists. Its defining characteristic is a significant amount of income above the level necessary to provide for the basic human needs of oneself and one's dependents. By this standard Western Europe, North America, Japan, Australia, New Zealand and the oil-rich Middle Eastern states are all absolutely affluent, and so are many, if not all, of their citizens. The USSR and Eastern Europe might also be included on this list. To quote McNamara once more:

> The average citizen of a developed country enjoys wealth beyond the wildest dreams of the one billion people in countries with per capita incomes under $200....

These, therefore, are the countries—and individuals—who have wealth which they could, without threatening their own basic welfare, transfer to the absolutely poor.

At present, very little is being transferred. Members of the Organization of Petroleum Exporting Countries lead the way, giving an average of 2.1% of their Gross National Product. Apart from them, only Sweden, The Netherlands and Norway have reached the modest UN target of 0.7% of GNP. Britain gives 0.38% of its GNP in official development assistance and a small additional amount in unofficial aid from voluntary organizations. The total comes to less than £1 per month per person, and compares with 5.5% of GNP spent on alcohol, and 3% on tobacco. Other, even wealthier nations, give still less: Germany gives 0.27%, the United States 0.22% and Japan 0.21%.

The Moral Equivalent of Murder?

If these are the facts, we cannot avoid concluding that by not giving more than we do, people in rich countries are allowing those in poor countries to suffer from absolute poverty, with consequent malnutrition, ill health and death. This is not a conclusion which applies only to governments. It applies to each absolutely affluent individual, for each of us has the opportunity to do something about the situation; for instance, to give our time or money to voluntary organizations like Oxfam, War on Want, Freedom From Hunger, and so on. If then, allowing someone to die is not intrinsically different from killing someone, it would seem that we are all murderers.

Is this verdict too harsh? Many will reject it as self-evidently absurd. They would sooner take it as showing that allowing to die cannot be equivalent to killing than as showing that living in an affluent style without contributing to Oxfam is ethically equivalent to going over to India and shooting a few peasants. And no doubt, put as bluntly as that, the verdict *is* too harsh.

There are several significant differences between spending money on luxuries instead of using it to save lives, and deliberately shooting people.

First, the motivation will normally be different. Those who deliberately shoot others go out of their way to kill; they presumably want their victims dead, from malice, sadism, or some equally unpleasant motive. A person who buys a colour television set presumably wants to watch television in colour—not in itself a terrible thing. At worst, spending money on luxuries instead of giving it away indicates selfishness and indifference to the sufferings of others, characteristics which may be undesirable but are not compatible with actual malice or similar motives.

Second, it is not difficult for most of us to act in accordance with a rule against killing people: it is, on the other hand, very difficult to obey a rule which commands us to save all the lives we can. To live a comfortable, or even luxurious life it is not necessary to kill anyone; but it is necessary to allow some to die whom we might have saved, for the money that we need to live comfortably could have been given away. Thus the duty to avoid killing is much easier to discharge completely than the duty to save. Saving every life we could would mean cutting our standard of living down to the bare essentials needed to keep us alive. (Strictly, we would need to cut down to the minimum level compatible with

earning the income which, after providing for our needs, left us most to give away. Thus if my present position earns me, say, £10,000 a year, but requires me to spend £1,000 a year on dressing respectably and maintaining a car, I cannot save more people by giving away the car and clothes if that will mean taking a job which, although it does not involve me in these expenses, earns me only £5,000.) To discharge this duty completely would require a degree of moral heroism utterly different from what is required by mere avoidance of killing.

A third difference is the greater certainty of the outcome of shooting when compared with not giving aid. If I point a loaded gun at someone and pull the trigger, it is virtually certain that the person will be injured, if not killed; whereas the money that I could give might be spent on a project that turns out to be unsuccessful and helps no one.

Fourth, when people are shot there are identifiable individuals who have been harmed. We can point to them and to their grieving families. When I buy my colour television, I cannot know who my money would have saved if I had given it away. In a time of famine I may see dead bodies and grieving families on my new television, and I might not doubt that my money would have saved some of them; even then it is impossible to point to a body and say that had I not bought the set, that person would have survived.

Fifth, it might be said that the plight of the hungry is not my doing, and so I cannot be held responsible for it. The starving would have been starving if I had never existed. If I kill, however, I am responsible for my victims' deaths, for those people would not have died if I had not killed them.

These differences need not shake our previous conclusion that there is no intrinsic difference between killing and allowing to die. They are extrinsic differences, that is, differences normally but not necessarily associated with the distinction between killing and allowing to die. We can imagine cases in which someone allows another to die for malicious or sadistic reasons; we can imagine a world in which there are so few people needing assistance, and they are so easy to assist, that our duty not to allow people to die is as easily discharged as our duty not to kill; we can imagine situations in which the outcome of not helping is as sure as shooting; we can imagine cases in which we can identify the person we allow to die. We can even imagine a case of allowing to die in which, if I had not existed, the person would not have died—for instance, a case in which if I had not been in a position to help (though I don't help) someone else would have been in my position and would have helped.

[A] discussion of euthanasia illustrates the extrinsic nature of these differences, for they do not provide a basis for distinguishing active from passive euthanasia. If a doctor decides, in consultation with the parents, not to operate on—and thus to allow to die—a mongoloid infant with an intestinal blockage, his motivation will be similar to that of a doctor who gives a lethal injection rather than allow the infant to die. No extraordinary sacrifice or moral heroism will be required in either case. Not operating will just as certainly end in death as administering the injection. Allowing to die does have an identifiable victim. Finally, it may well be that the doctor is personally responsible for the death of the infant he decides not to operate upon, since he may know that if he had not taken this case, other doctors in the hospital would have operated.

Nevertheless, euthanasia is a special case, and very different from allowing people to starve to death. (The major difference being that when euthanasia is justifiable, death is a good thing.) The extrinsic differences which *normally* mark off killing and allowing to die do explain why we *normally* regard killing as much worse than allowing to die.

To explain our conventional ethical attitudes is not to justify them. Do the five dif-

ferences not only explain, but also justify, our attitudes? Let us consider them one by one:

(1) Take the lack of an identifiable victim first. Suppose that I am a travelling salesman, selling tinned food, and I learn that a batch of tins contains a contaminant, the known effect of which when consumed is to double the risk that the consumer will die from stomach cancer. Suppose I continue to sell the tins. My decision may have no identifiable victims. Some of those who eat the food will die from cancer. The proportion of consumers dying in this way will be twice that of the community at large, but which among the consumers died because they ate what I sold, and which would have contracted the disease anyway? It is impossible to tell; but surely this impossibility makes my decision no less reprehensible than it would have been had the contaminant had more readily detectable, though equally fatal, effects.

(2) The lack of certainty that by giving money I could save a life does reduce the wrongness of not giving, by comparison with deliberate killing; but it is insufficient to show that not giving is acceptable conduct. The motorist who speeds through pedestrian crossings, heedless of anyone who might be on them, is not a murderer. She may never actually hit a pedestrian; yet what she does is very wrong indeed.

(3) The notion of responsibility for acts rather than omissions is more puzzling. On the one hand we feel ourselves to be under a greater obligation to help those whose misfortunes we have caused. (It is for this reason that advocates of overseas aid often argue that Western nations have created the poverty of Third World nations, through forms of economic exploitation which go back to the colonial system.) On the other hand any consequentialist would insist that we are responsible for all the consequences of our actions, and if a consequence of my spending money on a luxury item is that someone dies, I am responsible for that death. It is true that

the person would have died even if I had never existed, but what is the relevance of that? The fact is that I do exist, and the consequentialist will say that our responsibilities derive from the world as it is, not as it might have been.

One way of making sense of the non-consequentialist view of responsibility is by basing it on a theory of rights of the kind proposed by John Locke or, more recently, Robert Nozick. If everyone has a right to life, and this right is a right *against* others who might threaten my life, but not a right *to* assistance from others when my life is in danger, then we can understand the feeling that we are responsible for acting to kill but not for omitting to save. The former violates the rights of others, the latter does not.

Should we accept such a theory of rights? If we build up our theory of rights by imagining, as Locke and Nozick do, individuals living independently from each other in a 'state of nature,' it may seem natural to adopt a conception of rights in which as long as each leaves the other alone, no rights are violated. I might, on this view, quite properly have maintained my independent existence if I had wished to do so. So if I do not make you any worse off than you would have been if I had had nothing at all to do with you, how can I have violated your rights? But why start from such an unhistorical, abstract and ultimately inexplicable idea as an independent individual? We now know that our ancestors were social beings long before they were human beings, and could not have developed the abilities and capacities of human beings if they had not been social beings first. In any case we are not, now, isolated individuals. If we consider people living together in a community, it is less easy to assume that rights must be restricted to rights against interference. We might, instead, adopt the view that taking rights to life seriously is incompatible with standing by and watching people die when one could easily save them.

(4) What of the difference in motivation? That a person does not positively wish for the death of another lessens the severity of the blame she deserves; but not by as much as our present attitudes to giving aid suggest. The behaviour of the speeding motorist is again comparable, for such motorists usually have no desire to kill anyone. They merely enjoy speeding and are indifferent to the consequences. Despite their lack of malice, those who kill with cars deserve not only blame but also severe punishment.

(5) Finally, the fact that to avoid killing people is normally not difficult, whereas to save all one could possibly save is heroic, must make an important difference to our attitude to failure to do what the respective principles demand. Not to kill is a minimum standard of acceptable conduct we can require of everyone; to save all one possibly could is not something that can realistically be required, especially not in societies accustomed to giving as little as ours do. Given the generally accepted standards, people who give, say, £100 a year to Oxfam are more aptly praised for above average generosity than blamed for giving less than they might. The appropriateness of praise and blame is, however, a separate issue from the rightness or wrongness of actions. The former evaluates the agent: the latter evaluates the action. Perhaps people who give £100 really ought to give at least £1,000, but to blame them for not giving more could be counterproductive. It might make them feel that what is required is too demanding, and if one is going to be blamed anyway, one might as well not give anything at all.

(That an ethic which put saving all one possibly can on the same footing as not killing would be an ethic for saints or heroes should not lead us to assume that the alternative must be an ethic which makes it obligatory not to kill, but puts us under no obligation to save anyone. There are positions in between these extremes, as we shall soon see.)

To summarize our discussion of the five differences which normally exist between killing and allowing to die, in the context of absolute poverty and overseas aid. The lack of an identifiable victim is of no moral significance, though it may play an important role in explaining our attitudes. The idea that we are directly responsible for those we kill, but not for those we do not help, depends on a questionable notion of responsibility, and may need to be based on a controversial theory of rights. Differences in certainty and motivation are ethically significant, and show that not aiding the poor is not to be condemned as murdering them; it could, however, be on a par with killing someone as a result of reckless driving, which is serious enough. Finally the difficulty of completely discharging the duty of saving all one possibly can makes it inappropriate to blame those who fall short of this target as we blame those who kill; but this does not show that the act itself is less serious. Nor does it indicate anything about those who, far from saving all they possibly can, make no effort to save anyone.

These conclusions suggest a new approach. Instead of attempting to deal with the contrast between affluence and poverty by comparing not saving with deliberate killing, let us consider afresh whether we have an obligation to assist those whose lives are in danger, and if so, how this obligation applies to the present world situation.

The Obligation to Assist

The Argument for an Obligation to Assist

The path from the library at my university to the Humanities lecture theatre passes a shallow ornamental pond. Suppose that on my way to give a lecture I notice that a small child has fallen in and is in danger of drowning. Would anyone deny that I ought to wade in and pull the child out? This will mean getting my clothes muddy, and either cancelling the lecture or delaying it until I can find something dry to change into; but compared with the avoidable death of a child this is insignificant.

A plausible principle that would support the judgement that I ought to pull the child out is this: if it is in our power to prevent something very bad happening, without thereby sacrificing anything of comparable moral significance, we ought to do it. This principle seems quite uncontroversial. It will obviously win the assent of consequentialists; but non-consequentialists should accept it too, because the injunction to prevent what is bad applies only when nothing comparably significant is at stake. Thus the principle cannot lead to the kinds of actions of which non-consequentialists strongly disapprove—serious violations of individual rights, injustice, broken promises, and so on. If a non-consequentialist regards any of these as comparable in moral significance to the bad thing that is to be prevented, he will automatically regard the principle as not applying in those cases in which the bad thing can only be prevented by violating rights, doing injustice, breaking promises, or whatever else is at stake. Most non-consequentialists hold that we ought to prevent what is bad and promote what is good. Their dispute with consequentialists lies in their insistence that this is not the sole ultimate ethical principle: that it is *an* ethical principle is not denied by any plausible ethical theory.

Nevertheless the uncontroversial appearance of the principle that we ought to prevent what is bad when we can do so without sacrificing anything of comparable moral significance is deceptive. If it were to be taken seriously and acted upon, our lives and our world would be fundamentally changed. For the principle applies, not just to rare situations in which one can save a child from a pond, but to the everyday situation in which we can assist those living in absolute poverty. In saying this I assume that absolute poverty, with its hunger and malnutrition, lack of shelter, illiteracy, disease, high infant mortality and low life expectancy, is a bad thing. And I assume that it is within the power of the affluent to reduce absolute poverty, without sacrificing anything of comparable moral significance. If these two assumptions and the principle we have been discussing are correct, we have an obligation to help those in absolute poverty which is no less strong than our obligation to rescue a drowning child from a pond. Not to help would be wrong, whether or not it is intrinsically equivalent to killing. Helping is not, as conventionally thought, a charitable act which it is praiseworthy to do, but not wrong to omit; it is something that everyone ought to do.

This is the argument for an obligation to assist. Set out more formally, it would look like this.

FIRST PREMISE: If we can prevent something bad without sacrificing anything of comparable significance, we ought to do it.

SECOND PREMISE: Absolute poverty is bad.

THIRD PREMISE: There is some absolute poverty we can prevent without sacrificing anything of comparable moral significance.

CONCLUSION: We ought to prevent some absolute poverty.

The first premise is the substantive moral premise on which the argument rests, and I have tried to show that it can be accepted by people who hold a variety of ethical positions.

The second premise is unlikely to be challenged. Absolute poverty is, as McNamara puts it, 'beneath any reasonable definition of human decency' and it would be hard to find a plausible ethical view which did not regard it as a bad thing.

The third premise is more controversial, even though it is cautiously framed. It claims only that some absolute poverty can be pre-

vented without the sacrifice of anything of comparable moral significance. It thus avoids the objection that any aid I can give is just 'drops in the ocean' for the point is not whether my personal contribution will make any noticeable impression on world poverty as a whole (of course it won't) but whether it will prevent some poverty. This is all the argument needs to sustain its conclusion, since the second premise says that any absolute poverty is bad, and not merely the total amount of absolute poverty. If without sacrificing anything of comparable moral significance we can provide just one family with the means to raise itself out of absolute poverty, the third premise is vindicated.

I have left the notion of moral significance unexamined in order to show that the argument does not depend on any specific values or ethical principles. I think the third premise is true for most people living in industrialized nations, on any defensible view of what is morally significant. Our affluence means that we have income we can dispose of without giving up the basic necessities of life, and we can use this income to reduce absolute poverty. Just how much we will think ourselves obliged to give up will depend on what we consider to be of comparable moral significance to the poverty we could prevent: colour television, stylish clothes, expensive dinners, a sophisticated stereo system, overseas holidays, a (second?) car, a larger house, private schools for our children.... For a utilitarian, none of these is likely to be of comparable significance to the reduction of absolute poverty; and those who are not utilitarians surely must, if they subscribe to the principle of universalizability, accept that at least *some* of these things are of far less moral significance than the absolute poverty that could be prevented by the money they cost. So the third premise seems to be true on any plausible ethical view—although the precise amount of absolute poverty that can be prevented before anything of moral significance is sacrificed will vary according to the ethical view one accepts.

Objections to the Argument

Taking care of our own Anyone who has worked to increase overseas aid will have come across the argument that we should look after those near us, our families and then the poor in our own country, before we think about poverty in distant places.

No doubt we do instinctively prefer to help those who are close to us. Few could stand by and watch a child drown; many can ignore a famine in Africa. But the question is not what we usually do, but what we ought to do, and it is difficult to see any sound moral justification for the view that distance, or community membership, makes a crucial difference to our obligation.

Consider, for instance, racial affinities. Should whites help poor whites before helping poor blacks? Most of us would reject such a suggestion out of hand: ...people's need for food has nothing to do with their race, and if blacks need food more than whites, it would be a violation of the principle of equal consideration to give preference to whites.

The same point applies to citizenship or nationhood. Every affluent nation has some relatively poor citizens, but absolute poverty is limited largely to the poor nations. Those living on the streets of Calcutta, or in a drought-stricken region of the Sahel, are experiencing poverty unknown in the West. Under these circumstances it would be wrong to decide that only those fortunate enough to be citizens of our own community will share our abundance.

We feel obligations of kinship more strongly than those of citizenship. Which parents could give away their last bowl of rice if their own children were starving? To do so would seem unnatural, contrary to our nature as biologically evolved beings—although whether it

would be wrong is another question altogether. In any case, we are not faced with that situation, but with one in which our own children are well-fed, well-clothed, well-educated, and would now like new bikes, a stereo set, or their own car. In these circumstances any special obligations we might have to our children have been fulfilled, and the needs of strangers make a stronger claim upon us.

The element of truth in the view that we should first take care of our own, lies in the advantage of a recognized system of responsibilities. When families and local communities look after their own poorer members, ties of affection and personal relationships achieve ends that would otherwise require a large, impersonal bureaucracy. Hence it would be absurd to propose that from now on we all regard ourselves as equally responsible for the welfare of everyone in the world; but the argument for an obligation to assist does not propose that. It applies only when some are in absolute poverty, and others can help without sacrificing anything of comparable moral significance. To allow one's own kin to sink into absolute poverty would be to sacrifice something of comparable significance; and before that point had been reached, the breakdown of the system of family and community responsibility would be a factor to weigh the balance in favour of a small degree of preference for family and community. This small degree of preference is, however, decisively outweighed by existing discrepancies in wealth and property.

Property rights Do people have a right to private property, a right which contradicts the view that they are under an obligation to give some of their wealth away to those in absolute poverty? According to some theories of rights (for instance, Robert Nozick's) provided one has acquired one's property without the use of unjust means like force and fraud, one may be entitled to enormous wealth while others starve. This individualistic conception of rights is in contrast to other views, like the early Christian doctrine to be found in the works of Thomas Aquinas, which holds that since property exists for the satisfaction of human needs, 'whatever a man has in superabundance is owed, of natural right, to the poor for their sustenance.' A socialist would also, of course, see wealth as belonging to the community rather than the individual, while utilitarians, whether socialist or not, would be prepared to override property rights to prevent great evils.

Does the argument for an obligation to assist others therefore presuppose one of these other theories of property rights, and not an individualistic theory like Nozick's? Not necessarily. A theory of property rights can insist on our *right* to retain wealth without pronouncing on whether the rich *ought* to give to the poor. Nozick, for example, rejects the use of compulsory means like taxation to redistribute income, but suggests that we can achieve the ends we deem morally desirable by voluntary means. So Nozick would reject the claim that rich people have an 'obligation' to give aid to the poor, in so far as this implies that the poor have a right to our aid, but might accept that giving is something we ought to do and failing to give, though within one's rights, is wrong—for rights is not all there is to ethics.

The argument for an obligation to assist can survive, with only minor modifications, even if we accept an individualistic theory of property rights. In any case, however, I do not think we should accept such a theory. It leaves too much to chance to be an acceptable ethical view. For instance, those whose forefathers happened to inhabit some sandy wastes around the Persian Gulf are now fabulously wealthy, because oil lay under those sands; while those whose forefathers settled on better land south of the Sahara live in absolute poverty, because of drought and bad harvests. Can this distribution be acceptable from an impartial point

of view? If we imagine ourselves about to begin life as a citizen of either Kuwait or Chad—but we do not know which—would we accept the principle that citizens of Kuwait are under no obligation to assist people living in Chad?

Population and the ethics of triage Perhaps the most serious objection to the argument that we have an obligation to assist is that since the major cause of absolute poverty is overpopulation, helping those now in poverty will only ensure that yet more people are born to live in poverty in the future.

In its most extreme form, this objection is taken to show that we should adopt a policy of 'triage.' The term comes from medical policies adopted in wartime. With too few doctors to cope with all the casualties, the wounded were divided into three categories: those who would probably survive without medical assistance, those who might survive if they received assistance, but otherwise probably would not, and those who even with medical assistance probably would not survive. Only those in the middle category were given medical assistance. The idea, of course, was to use limited medical resources as effectively as possible. For those in the first category, medical treatment was not strictly necessary; for those in the third category, it was likely to be useless. It has been suggested that we should apply the same policies to countries, according to their prospects of becoming self-sustaining. We would not aid countries which even without our help will soon be able to feed their populations. We would not aid countries which, even with our help, will not be able to limit their population to a level they can feed. We would aid those countries where our help might make the difference between success and failure in bringing food and population into balance.

Advocates of this theory are understandably reluctant to give a complete list of the countries they would place in the 'hopeless' category; but Bangladesh is often cited as an example. Adopting the policy of triage would, then, mean cutting off assistance to Bangladesh and allowing famine, disease and natural disasters to reduce the population of that country (now around 80 million) to the level at which it can provide adequately for all.

In support of this view Garrett Hardin has offered a metaphor: we in the rich nations are like the occupants of a crowded lifeboat adrift in a sea full of drowning people. If we try to save the drowning by bringing them aboard our boat will be overloaded and we shall all drown. Since it is better that some survive than none, we should leave the others to drown. In the world today, according to Hardin, 'lifeboat ethics' apply. The rich should leave the poor to starve, for otherwise the poor will drag the rich down with them.

Against this view, some writers have argued that overpopulation is a myth. The world produces ample food to feed its population, and could, according to some estimates, feed ten times as many. People are hungry not because there are too many but because of inequitable land distribution, the manipulation of Third World economies by the developed nations, wastage of food in the West, and so on.

Putting aside the controversial issue of the extent to which food production might one day be increased, it is true, as we have already seen, that the world now produces enough to feed its inhabitants—the amount lost by being fed to animals itself being enough to meet existing grain shortages. Nevertheless population growth cannot be ignored. Bangladesh could, with land reform and using better techniques, feed its present population of 80 million; but by the year 2000, according to World Bank estimates, its population will be 146 million. The enormous effort that will have to go into feeding an extra 66 million people, all added to the population within a quarter of a century, means that Bangladesh must develop at full speed to stay where she is. Other low income countries are in similar situations. By the end of the century, Ethiopia's population is expected to rise from 29 to 54 million; Somalia's from 3 to 7 million, India's from 620 to 958 million, Zaire's from 25 to 47 million. What will happen then? Population cannot grow indefinitely. It will be checked by a decline in birth rates or a rise in death rates. Those who advocate triage are proposing that we allow the population growth of some countries to be checked by a rise in death rates—that is, by increased malnutrition, and related diseases; by widespread famines; by increased infant mortality; and by epidemics of infectious diseases.

The consequences of triage on this scale are so horrible that we are inclined to reject it without further argument. How could we sit by our television sets, watching millions starve while we do nothing? Would not that...be the end of all notions of human equality and respect for human life? Don't people have a right to our assistance, irrespective of the consequences?

Anyone whose initial reaction to triage was not one of repugnance would be an unpleasant sort of person. Yet initial reactions based on strong feelings are not always reliable guides. Advocates of triage are rightly concerned with the long-term consequences of our actions. They say that helping the poor and starving now merely ensures more poor and starving in the future. When our capacity to help is finally unable to cope—as one day it must be—the suffering will be greater than it would be if we stopped helping them now. If this is correct, there is nothing we can do to prevent absolute starvation and poverty, in the long run, and so we have no obligation to assist. Nor does it seem reasonable to hold that under these circumstances people have a right to our assistance. If we do accept such a right, irrespective of the consequences, we are saying that, in Hardin's metaphor, we would continue to haul the drowning into our lifeboat until the boat sank and we all drowned.

If triage is to be rejected it must be tackled on its own ground, within the framework of consequentialist ethics. Here it is vulnerable. Any consequentialist ethics must take probability of outcome into account. A course of action that will certainly produce some benefit is to be preferred to an alternative course that may lead to a slightly larger benefit, but is equally likely to result in no benefit at all. Only if the greater magnitude of the uncertain benefit outweighs its uncertainty should we choose it. Better one certain unit of benefit than a 10% chance of 5 units; but better a 50% chance of 3 units than a single certain unit. The same principle applies when we are trying to avoid evils.

The policy of triage involves a certain, very great evil: population control by famine and disease. Tens of millions would die slowly. Hundreds of millions would continue to live in absolute poverty, at the very margin of existence. Against this prospect, advocates of the policy place a possible evil which is greater still: the same process of famine and disease, taking place in, say, fifty years time, when the world's population may be three times its present level, and the number who will die from famine, or struggle on in absolute poverty, will be that much greater. The question is: how probable is this forecast that continued assistance now will lead to greater disasters in the future?

Forecasts of population growth are notoriously fallible, and theories about the factors which affect it remain speculative. One theory, at least as plausible as any other, is that countries pass through a 'demographic transition' as their standard of living rises. When people are very poor and have no access to modern medicine their fertility is high, but population is kept in check by high death rates. The introduction of sanitation, modern medical techniques and other improvements reduces the death rate, but initially has little effect on the birth rate. Then population grows rapidly. Most poor countries are now in this phase. If standards of living continue to rise, however, couples begin to realize that to have the same number of children surviving to maturity as in the past, they do not need to give birth to as many children as their parents did. The need for children to provide economic support in old age diminishes. Improved education and the emancipation and employment of women also reduce the birthrate, and so population growth begins to level off. Most rich nations have reached this stage, and their populations are growing only very slowly.

If this theory is right, there is an alternative to the disasters accepted as inevitable by supporters of triage. We can assist poor countries to raise the living standards of the poorest members of their population. We can encourage the governments of these countries to enact land reform measures, improve education, and liberate women from a purely child-bearing role. We can also help other countries to make contraception and sterilization widely available. There is a fair chance that these measures will hasten the onset of the demographic transition and bring population growth down to a manageable level. Success cannot be guaranteed; but the evidence that improved economic security and education reduce population growth is strong enough to make triage ethically unacceptable. We cannot allow millions to die from starvation and disease when there is a reasonable probability that population can be brought under control without such horrors.

Population growth is therefore not a reason against giving overseas aid, although it should make us think about the kind of aid to give. Instead of food handouts, it may be better to give aid that hastens the demographic transition. This may mean agricultural assistance for the rural poor, or assistance with education, or the provision of contraceptive services. Whatever kind of aid proves most effective in specific circumstances, the obligation to assist is not reduced.

One awkward question remains. What should we do about a poor and already over-populated country which, for religious or nationalistic reasons, restricts the use of contraceptives and refuses to slow its population growth? Should we nevertheless offer development assistance? Or should we make our offer conditional on effective steps being taken to reduce the birthrate? To the latter course, some would object that putting conditions on aid is an attempt to impose our own ideas on independent sovereign nations. So it is—but is this imposition unjustifiable? If the argument for an obligation to assist is sound, we have an obligation to reduce absolute poverty; but we have no obligation to make sacrifices that, to the best of our knowledge, have no prospect of reducing poverty in the long run. Hence we have no obligation to assist countries whose governments have policies which will make our aid ineffective. This could be very harsh on poor citizens of these countries—for they may have no say in the government's policies—but we will help more people in the long run by using our resources where they are most effective. (The same principles may apply, incidentally, to countries that refuse to take other steps that could make assistance effective—like refusing to reform systems of land holding that impose intolerable burdens on poor tenant farmers.)

Leaving it to the government We often hear that overseas aid should be a government responsibility, not left to privately-run charities. Giving privately, it is said, allows the government to escape its responsibilities.

Since increasing government aid is the surest way of making a significant increase to the total amount of aid given, I would agree that the governments of affluent nations should give much more genuine, no strings attached, aid than they give now. One quarter of one percent of GNP is a scandalously small amount for a nation as wealthy as the United States to give. Even the official UN target of 0.7% seems much less than affluent nations can and should give—though it is a target few have reached. But is this a reason against each of us giving what we can privately, through voluntary agencies? To believe that it is seems to assume that the more people there are who give through voluntary agencies, the less likely it is that the government will do its part. Is this plausible? The opposite view—that if no one gives voluntarily the government will assume that its citizens are not in favour of overseas aid, and will cut its program accordingly—is more reasonable. In any case, unless there is a definite probability that by refusing to give we would be helping to bring about an increase in government assistance, refusing to give privately is wrong for the same reason that triage is wrong: it is a refusal to prevent a definite evil for the sake of a very uncertain gain. The onus of showing how a refusal to give privately will make the government give more is on those who refuse to give.

This is not to say that giving privately is enough. Certainly we should campaign for entirely new standards for both public and private overseas aid. We should also work for fairer trading arrangements between rich and poor countries, and less domination of the economies of poor countries by multinational corporations more concerned to produce profits for shareholders back home than food for the local poor. Perhaps it is more important to be politically active in the interests of the poor than to give to them oneself—but why not do both? Unfortunately many use the view that overseas aid is the government's responsibility as a reason against giving, but not as a reason for being politically active.

Too high a standard? The final objection to the argument for an obligation to assist is that it sets a standard so high that none but a saint could attain it. How many people can we really expect to give away everything not comparable in moral significance to the poverty their donation could relieve? For most of us, with commonsense views about what is of moral significance, this would mean a life of real austerity. Might it not be counterproductive to demand so much? Might not people say: 'As I can't do what is morally required anyway, I won't bother to give at all.' If, however, we were to set a more realistic standard, people might make a genuine effort to reach it. Thus setting a lower standard might actually result in more aid being given.

It is important to get the status of this objection clear. Its accuracy as a prediction of human behaviour is quite compatible with the argument that we are obliged to give to the point at which by giving more we sacrifice something of comparable moral significance. What would follow from the objection is that public advocacy of this standard of giving is undesirable. It would mean that in order to do the maximum to reduce absolute poverty, we should advocate a standard lower than the amount we think people really ought to give. Of course we ourselves—those of us who accept the original argument, with its higher standard—would know that we ought to do more than we publicly propose people ought to do, and we might actually give more than we urge others to give. There is no inconsistency here, since in both our private and our public behaviour we are trying to do what will most reduce absolute poverty.

For a consequentialist, this apparent conflict between public and private morality is always a possibility, and not in itself an indication that the underlying principle is wrong. The consequences of a principle are one thing, the consequences of publicly advocating it another.

Is it true that the standard set by our argument is so high as to be counterproductive?

There is not much evidence to go by, but discussions of the argument, with students and others, have led me to think it might be. On the other hand the conventionally accepted standard—a few coins in a collection tin when one is waved under your nose—is obviously far too low. What level should we advocate? Any figure will be arbitrary, but there may be something to be said for a round percentage of one's income like, say, 10%—more than a token donation, yet not so high as to be beyond all but saints. (This figure has the additional advantage of being reminiscent of the ancient tithe, or tenth, which was traditionally given to the church, whose responsibilities included care of the poor in one's local community. Perhaps the idea can be revived and applied to the global community.) Some families, of course, will find 10% a considerable strain on their finances. Others may be able to give more without difficulty. No figure should be advocated as a rigid minimum or maximum; but it seems safe to advocate that those earning average or above average incomes in affluent societies, unless they have an unusually large number of dependents or other special needs, ought to give a tenth of their income to reducing absolute poverty. By any reasonable ethical standards this is the minimum we ought to do, and we do wrong if we do less.

Questions for Discussion

1 Is Singer right that failing to provide assistance to those who are dying is virtually equivalent to killing people?

2 Is there any relevant moral difference between Singer's example of saving a child from drowning in a fountain on one's way to a lecture, and providing humanitarian aid to the many starving people in the world?

3 Does Singer provide an adequate response to the sort of argument raised by Hardin?

CHAPTER 4

Abortion

Abortion is an issue which is frequently and hotly debated, and upon which there seems to be very little consensus. Often the debate is put in terms of a conflict between the rights of an unborn fetus (I use that term loosely here, to cover all stages of development from fertilization of an egg to birth) and the rights of the woman in whose uterus the fetus exists. Traditionally, this debate has been largely between two views, commonly known as the "conservative" (or "pro-life") and the "liberal" (or "pro-choice") view. The conservative view asserts that a fetus is an innocent human being, and that all innocent human beings have an inviolable right to life. From this point of view, procuring an abortion is equivalent to murder—the taking of an innocent human life—and is never permissible (except perhaps to save another innocent life, such as the mother's). The liberal view, on the other hand, usually maintains that a fetus is not a full human being with rights, and that a woman's right to do as she chooses with her own body extends to choosing to have an abortion.

Between these views are a variety of views which might be described as "moderate." Whereas conservatives claim that abortion is always wrong, and liberals hold that abortion is always acceptable, what identifies a view as "moderate" is the belief that abortion is acceptable under some circumstances, but unacceptable under others. The difference might lie in areas such as the reasons a woman has for wanting an abortion (e.g., serious threats to her health or life prospects), the way in which the fetus was conceived (e.g., as a result of rape), or the stage of development of the fetus (e.g., implantation in the uterus, ability to feel pain, "quickening"—the first felt motions of the fetus, or "viability"—the point at which the fetus can survive outside the mother's uterus). Views which make the acceptability of abortion depend on whether the fetus has reached some specified stage of development are sometimes known as "drawing-the-line" types of moderate views.

Much of the discussion, then, has revolved around the question of when a fetus can be said to become a person, with the idea that only a person can properly be said to have "rights," such as the right to life. Does "personhood" occur at the moment of live birth, but not before? Is it at some set stage of fetal development, specifiable in terms of number of weeks? Is it at the moment of conception?

Some of this discussion, in turn, involves the question of what characteristics a being must have to be a "person." Is it a question of having a soul? Can we be sure that anyone has a soul, and if so, how do we know at what point we acquire it? Is it a question of the capacity to reason, or use language? If so, it should be noted that these capacities are not acquired until some time after birth, suggesting that infants (and perhaps some mentally handicapped adults) are not "persons." Should we treat "potential" persons as actual persons? But then how remote can the potential be? Is an unfertilized egg, or a sperm cell, a potential person in the requisite sense? Is personhood a question of viability—of when one is able to survive without external support? If so, would that mean that rational adults who require an iron lung or some such technological intervention to survive do not count as persons?

It is not easy to identify the characteristics which are required for a being to count as a person. This issue does not come up only in connection with abortion, however. A very similar debate is involved when one tries to decide how non-human animals should be treated. For that reason, more discussion of that aspect of the abortion issue will be covered in this book under the heading of the "Moral Status of Non-Human Animals."

Even people who agree that a fetus has rights may disagree about what that implies for the abortion debate. It is possible to maintain that the fetus has a right to life, but that that right is not absolute. There are decisions that societies make for the overall good which may predictably result in the deaths of some people—even decisions as trivial as raising the speed limit on highways. So there is at least some precedent for claiming that the right to life is not absolute. One might also argue that there is a limit to how much one person can be required to sacrifice so as to preserve the life of another, in which case it might turn out that a woman should not be required to carry a fetus to term, even if it has a right to life. (The question of what lengths a person is required to go to to save the life of another also comes up in connection with the obligations of the rich to help the poor, discussed in the chapter on "Distribution of Scarce Resources.") It may also become possible, as technology is developed, that a fetus may be removed from a woman's uterus without killing it, which might change the nature of the abortion issue. So there may still be room for debate even once the question of the moral status of the fetus is settled.

One other issue which should be mentioned along these lines is what is known as the "doctrine of double effect." According to this doctrine (originally employed by the Roman Catholic Church), it may be allowable to perform an action which will have results that would usually be unacceptable, under particular conditions. Specifically, the main requirement for the employment of this doctrine is that the "evil" must be a foreseen but unintended consequence of some other action which is itself good enough to outweigh the evil consequence. It is also considered important that the evil effect be another consequence of the same action, and not a means to the desired end. For example, bombing innocent civilians in a just war so as to demoralize the enemy and bring about victory would not be justified, since one is not allowed to kill civilians, but going on a bombing raid aimed at a military target, in the knowledge that some innocent civilians might also be killed, may be permissible.

The doctrine of double effect is often applied to abortion in cases where an operation is needed to save a pregnant woman's life, and it is foreseen that performing this operation is likely to kill the fetus. If one believes that killing a fetus is generally impermissible, one might apply the doctrine of double effect to allow the operation in such a case.

In addition to cases where the mother's health is endangered by the pregnancy, many people who are generally opposed to abortions believe they can be justified in cases where the pregnancy is the result of rape. If the reason for being opposed to abortion is related to a claim that the fetus has rights, this is a puzzling attitude. How could the details of how a fetus came into existence affect the rights it has once it is in existence? More likely, such a view reveals a belief that a woman can be expected to endure a pregnancy rather than abort because she is considered responsible for her condition, and people should bear the consequences of their own actions. Such a belief could explain why a pregnant woman would be freed of the responsibility in a case of rape, where she cannot be considered responsible. This raises questions about whether people who have actively tried to avoid pregnancy (e.g., by contraception) should be considered responsible if their preventive measures fail. There is also a question of whether it is fair for women to bear such consequences of their actions when the father is equally responsible.

The current Canadian legal situation concerning issues about unborn humans is extremely unsettled. The Supreme Court of Canada struck down the previously existing abortion legislation in 1988 on the grounds that it violated a woman's right to fair treatment (section 7 of the Charter of Rights). The decision left it unclear, however, whether the problem was in the particular law in question being too restrictive, or whether *any* law restricting abortions would be unconstitutional. There is not even agreement on whether Canada needs a law governing abortion at all. Since the arguments the judges consider often reveal much of the current thought on these issues, this chapter includes some of the legal reasoning employed by the Supreme Court of Canada in the case in which the old abortion law was struck down.

One other remark needs to be made in this connection, and that concerns the distinction between law and morality. It is possible that one could believe, for example, that abortion is immoral, and yet claim that it should *not* be illegal. Indeed, there are many things commonly thought to be immoral but not proper subjects of legislation (e.g., simple promise-breaking). Accordingly, it is useful when thinking about this issue to treat the question of whether abortion is immoral and the question of whether it should be illegal as separate questions.

Abortion, the Criminal Code, and the Morgentaler Decision

As things stand in Canada today, there is no federal law governing abortion. There was a part of the criminal code prohibiting abortions, except under specified conditions, until 1988. In that year, the Supreme Court of Canada, in the case of R. v. Morgentaler, Smoling and Scott, found that the law violated section 7 of the Charter of Rights, and was therefore unconstitutional. The following two articles contain the text of the original law, and some of the text of the Supreme Court decision which struck it down. Note that different justices on the Supreme Court who reached the same conclusion seem to have disagreed about which reasons for that conclusion were the most appealing.

★　★　★

Abortion in the Criminal Code (S.287)

PROCURING MISCARRIAGE / Woman procuring her own miscarriage / Definition of "means" / Exceptions / Information requirement / Definitions / "accredited hospital" / "approved hospital" / "board" / "Minister of Health" / "qualified medical practitioner" / "therapeutic abortion committee" / Requirement of consent not affected.

287. (1) Every one who, with intent to procure the miscarriage of a female person, whether or not she is pregnant, uses any means for the purpose of carrying out his intention is guilty of an indictable offence and liable to imprisonment for life.

(2) Every female person who, being pregnant, with intent to procure her own miscarriage, uses any means or permits any means to be used for the purpose of carrying out her intention is guilty of an indictable offence and liable to imprisonment for a term not exceeding two years.

(3) In this section, "means" includes

(a) the administration of a drug or other noxious thing;

(b) the use of an instrument; and

(c) manipulation of any kind.

(4) Subsections (1) and (2) do not apply to

(a) a qualified medical practitioner, other than a member of a therapeutic abortion committee for any hospital, who in good faith uses in an accredited or approved hospital any means for the purpose of carrying out his intention to procure the miscarriage of a female person, or

(b) a female person who, being pregnant, permits a qualified medical practitioner to use in an accredited or approved hospital any means for the purpose of carrying out her intention to procure her own miscarriage, if, before the use of those means, the therapeutic abortion committee for that accredited or approved hospital, by a majority of the members of the committee and at a meeting of the committee at which the case of the female person has been reviewed,

(c) has by certificate in writing stated that in its opinion the continuation of the pregnancy of the female person would or would be likely to endanger her life or health, and

(d) has caused a copy of such certificate to be given to the qualified medical practitioner.

(5) The Minister of Health of a province may by order

(*a*) require a therapeutic abortion committee for any hospital in that province, or any member thereof, to furnish him with a copy of any certificate described in paragraph (4)(*c*) issued by that committee, together with such other information relating to the circumstances surrounding the issue of that certificate as he may require, or

(*b*) require a medical practitioner who, in that province, has procured the miscarriage of any female person named in a certificate described in paragraph (4)(*c*), to furnish him with a copy of that certificate, together with such other information relating to the procuring of the miscarriage as he may require.

(6) For the purposes of subsections (4) and (5) and this subsection,

"accredited hospital" means a hospital accredited by the Canadian Council on Hospital Accreditation in which diagnostic services and medical, surgical and obstetrical treatment are provided;

"approved hospital" means a hospital in a province approved for the purposes of this section by the Minister of Health of that province;

"board" means the board of governors, management or directors, or the trustees, commission or other group of persons having the control and management of an accredited or approved hospital;

"Minister of Health" means

(*a*) in the Provinces of Ontario, Quebec, New Brunswick, Prince Edward Island, Manitoba and Newfoundland, the Minister of Health,

(*b*) in the Provinces of Nova Scotia and Saskatchewan, the Minister of Public Health, and

(*c*) in the Province of British Columbia, the Minister of Health Services and Hospital Insurance,

(*d*) in the Province of Alberta, the Minister of Hospitals and Medical Care,

(*e*) in the Yukon Territory and the Northwest Territories, the Minister of National Health and Welfare;

"qualified medical practitioner" means a person entitled to engage in the practice of medicine under the laws of the province in which the hospital referred to in subsection (4) is situated;

"therapeutic abortion committee" for any hospital means a committee, comprised of not less than three members each of whom is a qualified medical practitioner, appointed by the board of that hospital for the purpose of considering and determining questions relating to terminations of pregnancy within that hospital.

(7) Nothing in subsection (4) shall be construed as making unnecessary the obtaining of any authorization or consent that is or may be required, otherwise than under this Act, before any means are used for the purpose of carrying out an intention to procure the miscarriage of a female person. R.S., c. C-34, s. 251; 1974-75-76, c.93, s.22.1.

★　★　★

Morgentaler, Smoling and Scott v. The Queen

Supreme Court of Canada (1988) 44 D.L.R. (4th) 385

Chief Justice Dickson:

Although the "principles of fundamental justice" referred to in s. 7 have both a substantive and a procedural component,...it is not necessary in this appeal to evaluate the substantive content of s. 251 of the *Criminal Code*. My discussion will therefore be limited to various aspects of the administrative structure and procedure set down in s. 251 for access to therapeutic abortions.

In outline, s. 251 operates in the following manner. Subsection (1) creates an indictable offence for any person to use any means with the intent "to procure the miscarriage of a female person." Subsection (2) establishes a parallel indictable offence for any pregnant woman to use or to permit any means to be used with the intent "to procure her own miscarriage"....The crucial provision for the purposes of the present appeal is s.-s. (4) which states that the offences created in s.-ss. (1) and (2) "do not apply" in certain circumstances....

The procedure surrounding the defence is rather complex. A pregnant woman who desires to have an abortion must apply to the "therapeutic abortion committee" of an "accredited or approved hospital." Such a committee is empowered to issue a certificate in writing stating that in the opinion of a majority of the committee, the continuation of the pregnancy would be likely to endanger the woman's life or health. Once a copy of the certificate is given to a qualified medical practitioner who is not a member of the therapeutic abortion committee, he or she is permitted to perform an abortion on the pregnant woman and both the doctor and the woman are freed from any criminal liability....

As is so often the case in matters of interpretation, however, the straightforward reading of this statutory scheme is not fully revealing. In order to understand the true nature and scope of s. 251, it is necessary to investigate the practical operations of the provisions. The court has been provided with a myriad of factual submissions in this area. One of the most useful sources of information is the Badgley report [the final report of the Committee on the Operation of the Abortion Law issued in 1978]....

The Badgley report contains a wealth of detailed information which demonstrates ... that many of the most serious problems with the functioning of s. 251 are created by the procedural and administrative requirements established in the law.... [For example,] the seemingly neutral requirement of s. 251(4) that at least four physicians be available to authorize and to perform an abortion meant in practice that abortions would be absolutely unavailable in almost one quarter of all hospitals in Canada.

Other administrative and procedural requirements of s. 251(4) reduce the availability of therapeutic abortions even further. For the purposes of s. 251, therapeutic abortions can only be performed in "accredited" or "approved" hospitals.... [A]n "approved" hospital is one which a provincial minister of health has designated as such for the purposes of performing therapeutic abortions. The minister is under no obligation to grant any such approval. Furthermore, an "accredited" hospital must not only be accredited by the Canadian Council on Hospital Accreditation, it must also provide specific services. Many Canadian hospitals do not provide all of the required services, thereby being automatically disqualified from undertaking therapeutic abortions.... Moreover, even if a hospital is eligible to create a therapeutic abortion committee, there is no requirement in s. 251 that the hospital need do so....

...The requirement that therapeutic abortions be performed only in "accredited" or "approved" hospitals effectively means that the practical availability of the exculpatory provisions of s.-s. (4) may be heavily restricted, even denied, through provincial regulation....

A further flaw in the administrative system established in s. 251 is the failure to provide an adequate standard for therapeutic abortion committees which must determine when a therapeutic abortion should, as a matter of law, be granted. Subsection (4) states simply that a therapeutic abortion committee may grant a certificate when it determines that a continuation of a pregnancy would be likely to endanger the "life or health" of the pregnant woman. It was noted above that "health" is not defined for the purposes of the section....

...Various expert doctors testified at trial that therapeutic abortion committees apply widely differing definitions of health. For some committees, psychological health is a justification for therapeutic abortion; for others it is not. Some committees routinely refuse abortions to married women unless they are in physical danger, while for other committees it is possible for a married woman to show that she would suffer psychological harm if she continued with a pregnancy, thereby justifying an abortion. It is not typically possible for women to know in advance what standard of health will be applied by any given committee....

The combined effect of all of these problems with the procedure stipulated in s. 251 for access to therapeutic abortions is a failure to comply with the principles of fundamental justice.... One of the basic tenets of our system of criminal justice is that when Parliament creates a defence to a criminal charge, the defence should not be illusory or so difficult to attain as to be practically illusory. The criminal law is a very special form of governmental regulation, for it seeks to express our society's selective disapprobation of certain acts and omissions. When a defence is provided, especially a specifically-tailored defence to a particular charge, it is because the legislator has determined that the disapprobation of society is not warranted when the conditions of the defence are met.

Consider then the case of a pregnant married woman who wishes to apply for a therapeutic abortion certificate because she fears that her psychological health would be impaired seriously if she carried the fetus to term. The uncontroverted evidence appears that there are many areas in Canada where such a woman could simply not have access to a therapeutic abortion. She may be in an area where no hospital has four doctors; no therapeutic abortion committee can be created. Equally, she may live in a place where the treatment functions of the nearby hospitals do not satisfy the definition of "accredited hospital" in s. 251(6). Or she may be in a province where the provincial government has posed such stringent requirements on hospitals seeking to activate therapeutic abortion committees that no hospital can qualify. Alternatively, our hypothetical woman may confront a therapeutic abortion committee in her local hospital which defines "health" in purely physical terms or which refuses to countenance abortions for married women. In each of these cases, it is the administrative structures and procedures established by s. 251 itself that would in practice prevent the woman from gaining the benefit of the defence held out to her in s.251(4).

The facts indicate that many women do indeed confront these problems....

I conclude that the procedures created in s. 251 of the *Criminal Code* for obtaining a therapeutic abortion do not comport with the principles of fundamental justice. It is not necessary to determine whether s. 7 also contains a substantive content leading to the conclusion that, in some circumstances at least, the deprivation of a pregnant woman's right to security of the person can never comport with fundamental justice. Simply put, assuming Parliament can act, it must do so properly. For the reasons given earlier, the deprivation of security of the person caused by s. 251 as a whole is not in accordance with the second clause of s. 7.

Madam Justice Wilson:

At the heart of this appeal is the question whether a pregnant woman can, as a constitutional matter, be compelled by law to carry the fetus to term. The legislature has proceeded on the basis that she can be so compelled and, indeed, has made it a criminal offence punishable by imprisonment under s. 251 of the *Criminal Code*...for her or her physician to terminate the pregnancy unless the procedural requirements of the section are complied with.

My colleagues...have attacked those requirements in reasons which I have had the privilege of reading. They have found that the requirements do not comport with the principles of fundamental justice in the procedural sense and have concluded that, since they cannot be severed from the provisions creating the substantive offence, the whole of s. 251 must fall.

With all due respect, I think that the court must tackle the primary issue first. A consideration as to whether or not the procedural requirements for obtaining or performing an abortion comport with fundamental justice is purely academic if such requirements cannot as a constitutional matter be imposed at all. If a pregnant woman cannot, as a constitutional matter, be compelled by law to carry the fetus to term against her will, a review of the procedural requirements by which she may be compelled to do so seems pointless. Moreover, it would, in my opinion, be an exercise in futility for the legislature to expend its time and energy in attempting to remedy the defects in the procedural requirements unless it has some assurance that this process will, at the end of the day, result in the creation of a valid criminal offence. I turn, therefore, to what I believe is the central issue that must be addressed....

In order to ascertain the content of the right to liberty we must...commence with an analysis of the purpose of that right....We are invited, therefore, to consider the purpose of the Charter in general and of the right to liberty in particular.

The Charter is predicated on a particular conception of the place of the individual in society. An individual is not a totally independent entity disconnected from the society in which he or she lives. Neither, however, is the individual a mere cog in an impersonal machine in which his or her values, goals and aspirations are subordinated to those of the collectivity. The individual is a bit of both. The Charter reflects this reality by leaving a wide range of activities and decisions open to legitimate government control while at the same time placing limits on the proper scope of that control. Thus, the rights guaranteed in the Charter erect around each individual, metaphorically speaking, an invisible fence over which the state will not be allowed to trespass. The role of the courts is to map out, piece by piece, the parameters of the fence.

The Charter and the right to individual liberty guaranteed under it are inextricably tied to the concept of human dignity. Professor Neil MacCormick, *Legal Right and Social Democracy: Essays in Legal and Political Philosophy,* speaks of liberty as "a condition of human self-respect and of that contentment which resides in the ability to pursue one's own conception of a full and rewarding life." He says...:

> To be able to decide what to do and how to do it, to carry out one's own decisions and accept their consequences, seems to me essential to one's self-respect as a human being, and essential to the possibility of that contentment. Such self-respect and contentment are in my judgement fundamental goods for human beings, the worth of life itself being on condition of having or striving for them. If a person were deliberately denied the opportunity of self-respect and that contentment, he would suffer deprivation of his essential humanity....

The idea of human dignity finds expression in almost every right and freedom guaranteed in the Charter. Individuals are afforded the right to choose their own religion and their own philosophy of life, the right to choose with whom they will associate and how they will express themselves, the right to choose where they will live and what occupation they will pursue. These are all examples of the basic theory underlying the Charter, namely, that the state will respect choices made by individuals and, to the greatest extent possible, will avoid subordinating these choices to any one conception of the good life.

Thus, an aspect of the respect for human dignity on which the Charter is founded is the right to make fundamental personal decisions without interference from the state. This right is a crucial component of the right to liberty. Liberty...is a phrase capable of a broad range of meaning. In my view, this right, properly construed, grants the individual a degree of autonomy in making decisions of fundamental personal importance.

This view is consistent with the position I took in the case of *Jones v. The Queen* (1986).... One issue raised in that case was whether the right to liberty in s. 7 of the Charter included a parent's right to bring up his children in accordance with his conscientious beliefs. In concluding that it did I stated...:

> I believe that the framers of the Constitution in guaranteeing "liberty" as a fundamental value in a free and democratic society had in mind the freedom of the individual to develop and realize his potential to the full, to plan his own life to suit his own character, to make his own choices for good or ill, to be non-conformist, idiosyncratic and even eccentric—to be, in today's parlance, "his own person" and accountable as such. John Stuart Mill described it as "pursuing our own good in our own way." This, he believed, we should be free to do "so long as we do not attempt to deprive others of theirs or impede their efforts to obtain it." He added:
>
> > "Each is the guardian of his own health, whether bodily *or* mental or spiritual. Mankind are greater gainers by suffering each other to

> > live as seems good to themselves than by compelling each to live as seems good to the rest."

Liberty in a free and democratic society does not require the state to approve the personal decisions made by its citizens; it does, however, require the state to respect them....

...I would conclude, therefore, that the right to liberty contained in s. 7 guarantees to every individual a degree of personal autonomy over important decisions intimately affecting their private lives.

The question then becomes whether the decision of a woman to terminate her pregnancy falls within this class of protected decisions. I have no doubt that it does. This decision is one that will have profound psychological, economic and social consequences for the pregnant woman. The circumstances giving rise to it can be complex and varied and there may be, and usually are, powerful considerations militating in opposite directions. It is a decision that deeply reflects the way the woman thinks about herself and her relationship to others and to society at large. It is not just a medical decision; it is a profound social and ethical one as well. Her response to it will be the response of the whole person.

It is probably impossible for a man to respond, even imaginatively, to such a dilemma not just because it is outside the realm of his personal experience (although this is, of course, the case) but because he can relate to it only by objectifying it, thereby eliminating the subjective elements of the female psyche which are at the heart of the dilemma....

Given then that the right to liberty guaranteed by s. 7 of the Charter gives a woman the right to decide for herself whether or not to terminate her pregnancy, does s. 251 of the *Criminal Code* violate this right? Clearly it does. The purpose of the section is to take the decision away from the woman and give it to a committee. Furthermore, as the Chief Justice correctly points out, the committee bases its decision on "criteria entirely unrelated to [the pregnant woman's] priorities and aspirations." The fact that the decision whether a woman will be allowed to terminate her pregnancy is in the hands of a committee is just as great a violation of the woman's right to personal autonomy in decisions of an intimate and private nature as it would be if a committee were established to decide whether a woman should be allowed to continue her pregnancy. Both these arrangements violate the woman's right to liberty by deciding for her something that she has the right to decide for herself...

...[A]s the Chief Justice and Beetz J. point out, the present legislative scheme for the obtaining of an abortion clearly subjects pregnant women to considerable emotional stress as well as to unnecessary physical risk. I believe, however, that the flaw in the present legislative scheme goes much deeper than that. In essence, what it does is assert that the woman's capacity to reproduce is not to be subject to her own control. It is to be subject to the control of the state. She may not choose whether to exercise her existing capacity or not to exercise it. This is not, in my view, just a matter of interfering with her right to liberty in the sense (already discussed) of her right to personal autonomy in decision-making, it is a direct interference with her physical "person" as well. She is truly being treated as a means—a means to an end which she does not desire but over which she has no control. She is the passive recipient of a decision made by others as to whether her body is to be used to nurture a new life. Can there be anything that comports less with human dignity and self-respect? How can a woman in this position have any sense of security with respect to her person? I believe that s. 251 of the *Criminal Code* deprives the pregnant woman of her right to security of the person as well as her right to liberty.

Questions for Discussion

1 Justice Wilson argues that preventing a woman from controlling her own reproductive capacity (e.g., by requiring her to carry a pregnancy to term) treats her as merely a means to an end, and a "passive recipient of a decision made by others." Is she right, and if so, does that imply that it is morally forbidden to act in such a manner?

2 Justice Wilson states that "It is probably impossible for a man to respond, even imaginatively, to such a dilemma." Are men in a different situation from women who have never been pregnant, in this respect? Is abortion an issue which should be decided by women exclusively?

3 To what extent should the law take account of the fact that the same legal requirements may have a different impact on different people?

Bill C-43—Proposed Legislation

An Act Respecting Abortion

After the old abortion law was struck down, the government introduced a new bill concerning abortion. This new bill tried to take account of the Supreme Court's objections to the old law by, for example, dispensing with the requirement of approval by a hospital committee, which had in practice made abortions very difficult for many women to obtain. This bill was attacked by many pro-choice advocates for leaving ultimate control of women's reproduction in the hands of the medical profession, and by many pro-life advocates for making it too easy to meet the requirements for an abortion (especially by allowing mental and psychological health to be considered). This new proposal was never passed into law.

★　★　★

1. Sections 287 and 288 of the *Criminal Code* are repealed and the following substituted therefor:

"**287**. (1) Every *person who induces an abortion on a female person* is guilty of an indictable offence and liable to imprisonment for *a term not exceeding two* years, unless the abortion is induced by or under the direction of a medical practitioner who is of the opinion that, if the abortion were not induced, the health or life of the female person would be likely to be threatened.

(2) For the purposes of this section,

"health" includes, for greater certainty, physical, mental and psychological health;

"medical practitioner," in respect of an abortion induced in a province, means a person who is entitled to practise medicine under the laws of that province;

"opinion" means an opinion formed using generally accepted standards of the medical profession.

(3) For the purposes of this section and section 288, inducing an abortion does not include using a drug, device or other means on a female person that is likely to prevent implantation of a fertilized ovum.

Question for Discussion

1 Does there need to be a law concerning abortion?

On the Moral and Legal Status of Abortion

Mary Anne Warren

In this classic defense of the "liberal" position on abortion, Warren responds to the ideas of John T. Noonan, Jr., who claims that abortion is wrong because a fetus is a human. Warren argues that there is an important distinction between being "human" and being a "person." She claims that humanity is a matter of genetics, while "personhood" involves moral status, and that it is possible both that non-humans may be persons, and that humans may fail to be persons. In particular, Warren argues that a fetus is less person-like than "the average mature mammal, indeed the average fish," and correspondingly should be thought of as having even lower moral status. In a postscript which was added later, Warren responds to the charge that her argument must be rejected because it would justify killing not only fetuses, but new-born babies as well.

★　★　★

The question which we must answer in order to produce a satisfactory solution to the problem of the moral status of abortion is this: How are we to define the moral community, the set of beings with full and equal moral rights, such that we can decide whether a human fetus is a member of this community or not? What sort of entity, exactly, has the inalienable rights to life, liberty, and the pursuit of happiness? Jefferson attributed these rights to all *men*, and it may or may not be fair to suggest that he intended to attribute them *only* to men. Perhaps he ought to have attributed them to all human beings. If so, then we arrive, first, at Noonan's problem of defining what makes a being human, and, second, at the equally vital question which Noonan does not consider, namely, What reason is there for identifying the moral community with the set of all human beings, in whatever way we have chosen to define that term?

1. On the Definition of "Human"

One reason why this vital second question is so frequently overlooked in the debate over the moral status of abortion is that the term 'human' has two distinct, but not often distinguished, senses. This fact results in a slide of meaning, which serves to conceal the fallaciousness of the traditional argument that since (1) it is wrong to kill innocent human beings, and (2) fetuses are innocent human beings, then (3) it is wrong to kill fetuses. For if 'human' is used in the same sense in both (1) and (2) then, whichever of the two senses is meant, one of these premises is question-begging. And if it is used in two different senses then of course the conclusion doesn't follow.

Thus, (1) is a self-evident moral truth,[1] and avoids begging the question about abortion, only if 'human being' is used to mean something like 'a full-fledged member of the moral community.' (It may or may not also be meant to refer exclusively to members of the species *Homo sapiens*.) We may call this the *moral* sense of 'human.' It is not to be confused with what we will call the *genetic* sense, i.e., the sense in which *any* member of the species is a human being, and no member of any other species could be. If (1) is acceptable only if the moral sense is intended, (2) is non-question-begging only if what is intended is the genetic sense.

In "Deciding Who is Human," Noonan argues for the classification of fetuses with human beings by pointing to the presence of the full genetic code, and the potential capacity for rational thought.[2] It is clear that what he needs to show, for his version of the traditional argument to be valid, is that fetuses are human in the moral sense, the sense in which it is analytically true that all human beings have full moral rights. But, in the absence of any argument showing that whatever is genetically human is also morally human, and he gives none, nothing more than genetic humanity can be demonstrated by the presence of the human genetic code. And, as we will see, the *potential* capacity for rational thought can at most show that an entity has the potential for *becoming* human in the moral sense.

2. Defining the Moral Community

Can it be established that genetic humanity is sufficient for moral humanity? I think that there are very good reasons for not defiling the moral community in this way. I would like to suggest an alternative way of defining the moral community, which I will argue for only to the extent of explaining why it is, or should be, self-evident. The suggestion is simply that the moral community consists of all and only *people*, rather than all and only human beings,[3] and probably the best way of demonstrating its self-evidence is by considering the concept of personhood, to see what sorts of entity are and are not persons, and what the decision that a being is or is not a person implies about its moral rights.

What characteristics entitle an entity to be considered a person? This is obviously not the place to attempt a complete analysis of the concept of personhood, but we do not need such a fully adequate analysis just to determine whether and why a fetus is or isn't a person. All we need is a rough and approximate list of the most basic criteria of personhood, and some idea of which, or how many, of these an entity must satisfy in order to properly be considered a person.

In searching for such criteria, it is useful to look beyond the set of people with whom we are acquainted, and ask how we would decide whether a totally alien being was a person or not. (For we have no right to assume that genetic humanity is necessary for personhood.) Imagine a space traveler who lands on an unknown planet and encounters a race of beings utterly unlike any he has ever seen or heard of. If he wants to be sure of behaving morally toward these beings, he has to somehow decide whether they are people, and hence have full moral rights, or whether they are the sort of thing which he need not feel guilty about treating as, for example, a source of food.

How should he go about making this decision? If he has some anthropological background, he might look for such things as religion, art, and the manufacturing of tools, weapons, or shelters, since these factors have been used to distinguish our human from our prehuman ancestors, in what seems to be closer to the moral than the genetic sense of 'human.' And no doubt he would be right to consider the presence of such factors as good evidence that the alien beings were people, and morally human. It would, however, be overly anthropocentric of him to take the absence of these things as adequate evidence that they were not, since we can imagine people who have progressed beyond, or evolved without ever developing, these cultural characteristics.

I suggest that the traits which are most central to the concept of personhood, or humanity in the moral sense, are, very roughly, the following:

1. Consciousness (of objects and events external and/or internal to the being), and in particular the capacity to feel pain;
2. Reasoning (the *developed* capacity to solve new and relatively complex problems);
3. Self-motivated activity (activity which is relatively independent of either genetic or direct external control);
4. The capacity to communicate, by whatever means, messages of an indefinite variety of types, that is, not just with an indefinite number of possible contents, but on indefinitely many possible topics;
5. The presence of self-concepts, and self-awareness, either individual or racial, or both.

Admittedly, there are to apt to be a great many problems involved in formulating precise definitions of these criteria, let alone in developing universally valid behavioral criteria for deciding when they apply. But I will assume that both we and our explorer know approximately what (1)–(5) mean, and that he is also able to determine whether or not they apply. How, then, should he use his findings to decide whether or not the alien beings are people? We needn't suppose that an entity must have *all* of these attributes to be properly considered a person; (1) and (2) alone may well be sufficient for personhood, and quite probably (l)–(3) are sufficient. Neither do we need to insist that any one of these criteria is *necessary* for personhood, although once again (1) and (2) look like fairly good candidates for necessary conditions, as does (3), if 'activity' is construed so as to include the activity of reasoning.

All we need to claim, to demonstrate that a fetus is not a person, is that any being which satisfies *none* of (1)–(5) is certainly not a person. I consider this claim to be so obvious that I think anyone who denied it, and claimed that a being which satisfied none of (1)–(5) was a person all the same, would thereby demonstrate that he had no notion at all of what a person is—perhaps because he had confused the concept of a person with that of genetic humanity. If the opponents of abortion were to deny the appropriateness of these five criteria, I do not know what further arguments would convince them. We would probably have to admit that our conceptual schemes were indeed irreconcilably different, and that our dispute could not be settled objectively.

I do not expect this to happen, however, since I think that the concept of a person is one which is very nearly universal (to people), and that it is common to both proabortionists and antiabortionists, even though neither group has fully realized the relevance of this concept to the resolution of their dispute. Furthermore; I think that on reflection even the antiabortionists ought to agree not only that (1)–(5) are central to the concept of personhood, but also that it is a part of this concept that all and only people have full moral rights. The concept of a person is in part a moral concept; once we have admitted that x is a person we have recognized, even if we have not agreed to respect, x's right to be treated as a member of the moral community. It is true that the claim that x is a *human being* is more commonly voiced as part of an appeal to treat x decently than is the claim that x is a person, but this is either because 'human being' is here used in the sense which implies personhood, or because the genetic and moral sense of 'human' have been confused.

Now if (1)–(5) are indeed the primary criteria of personhood, then it is clear that genetic humanity is neither necessary nor sufficient for establishing that an entity is a person. Some human beings are not people, and there may well be people who are not human beings. A man or woman whose consciousness has been permanently obliterated but who remains alive is a human being which is no longer a person; defective human beings, with no appreciable mental capacity, are not and presumably never will be people; and a fetus is a human being which is not yet a person, and which therefore cannot coherently be said to have full moral rights. Citizens of the next century should be prepared to recognize highly advanced, self-aware robots or computers, should such be developed, and intelligent inhabitants of other worlds, should such be found, as people in the fullest sense, and to respect their moral rights. But to ascribe full moral rights to an entity which is not a person is as absurd as to ascribe moral obligations and responsibilities to such an entity.

3. Fetal Development and the Right to Life

Two problems arise in the application of these suggestions for the definition of the moral community to the determination of the precise moral status of a human fetus. Given that the paradigm example of a person is a normal adult human being, then (1) How like this paradigm, in particular how far advanced since conception, does a human being need to be before it begins to have a right to life by virtue, not of being fully a person as of yet, but of being *like* a person? and (2) To what extent, if any, does the fact that a fetus has the *potential* for becoming a person endow it with some of the same rights? Each of these questions requires some comment.

In answering the first question, we need not attempt a detailed consideration of the moral rights of organisms which are not developed enough, aware enough, intelligent enough, etc., to be considered people, but which resemble people in some respects. It does seem reasonable to suggest that the more like a person, in the relevant respects, a being is, the stronger is the case for regarding it as having a right to life, and indeed the stronger its right to life is. Thus we ought to take seriously the suggestion that, insofar as "the human individual develops biologically in a continuous fashion ... the rights of a human person might develop in the same way."[4] But we must keep in mind that the attributes which are relevant in determining whether or not an entity is enough like a person to be regarded as having some of the same moral rights are no different from those which are relevant to determining whether or not it is fully a person—i.e., are no different from (1)–(5)—and that being genetically human, or having recognizable human facial and other physical features, or detectable brain activity, or the capacity to survive outside the uterus, are simply not among these relevant attributes.

Thus it is clear that even though a seven- or eight-month fetus has features which make it apt to arouse in us almost the same powerful protective instinct as is commonly aroused by a small infant, nevertheless it is not significantly more personlike than is a very small embryo. It is *somewhat* more personlike; it can apparently feel and respond to pain, and it may even have a rudimentary form of consciousness, insofar as its brain is quite active. Nevertheless, it seems safe to say that it is not fully conscious, in the way that an infant of a few months is, and that it cannot reason, or communicate messages of indefinitely many sorts, does not engage in self-motivated activity, and has no self-awareness Thus, in the *relevant* respects, a fetus, even a fully developed one, is considerably less personlike than is the average mature mammal, indeed the average fish. And I think that a rational person must conclude that if the right to life of a fetus is to be based upon its resemblance to a person, then it cannot be said to have any more right to life than, let us say, a newborn guppy (which also seems to be capable of feeling pain), and that a right of that magnitude could never override a woman's right to obtain an abortion, at any stage of her pregnancy.

There may, of course, be other arguments in favor of placing legal limits upon the stage of pregnancy in which an abortion may be performed. Given the relative safety of the new techniques of artificially inducing labor during the third trimester, the danger to the woman's life or health is no longer such an argument. Neither is the fact that people tend to respond to the thought of abortion in the later stages of pregnancy with emotional repulsion, since mere emotional responses cannot take the place of moral reasoning in determining what ought to be permitted. Nor, finally, is the frequently heard argument that legalizing abortion, especially late in the pregnancy, may erode the level of respect for human life, leading, perhaps, to an increase in unjustified euthanasia and other crimes. For this threat, if it is a threat, can be better met by educating people to the kinds of moral distinctions which we are making here than by limiting access to abortion (which limitation may, in its disregard for the rights of women, be just as damaging to the level of respect for human rights).

Thus, since the fact that even a fully developed fetus is not personlike enough to have any significant right to life on the basis of its personlikeness shows that no legal restrictions upon the stage of pregnancy in which an abortion may be performed can be justified on the grounds that we should protect the rights of the older fetus; and since there is no other apparent justification for such restrictions, we may conclude that they are entirely unjustified. Whether or not it would be *indecent* (whatever that means) for a women in her seventh month to obtain an abortion just to avoid having to postpone a trip to Europe, it would not, in itself, be *immoral*, and therefore it ought to be permitted.

4. Potential Personhood and the Right to Life

We have seen that a fetus does not resemble a person in any way which can support the claim that it has even some of the same rights. But what about its *potential*, the fact that if nurtured and allowed to develop naturally it will very probably become a person? Doesn't that alone give it at least some right to life? It is hard to deny that the fact that an entity is a potential person is a strong prima facie reason for not destroying it; but we need not conclude from this that a potential person has a right to life, by virtue of that potential. It may be that our feeling that it is better, other things being equal, not to destroy a potential person is better explained by the fact that potential people are still (felt to be) an invaluable resource, not to be lightly squandered. Surely, if every speck of dust were a potential person, we would be much less apt to conclude that every potential person has a right to become actual.

Still, we do not need to insist that a potential person has no right to life whatever. There may well be something immoral, and not just imprudent, about wantonly destroying potential people, when doing so isn't necessary to protect anyone's rights. But even if a potential person does have some prima facie right to life, such a right could not possibly outweigh the right of a woman to obtain an abortion, since the rights of any actual person invariably outweigh those of any potential person, whenever the two conflict. Since this may not be immediately obvious in the case of a human fetus, let us look at another case.

Suppose that our space explorer falls into the hands of an alien culture, whose scientists decide to create a few hundred thousand or more human beings, by breaking his body into its component cells, and using these to create fully developed human beings, with, of course, his genetic code. We may imagine that each of these newly created men will have all of the original man's abilities, skills, knowledge, and so on, and also have an individual self-concept, in short that each of them will be a bona fide (though hardly unique) person. Imagine that the whole project will take only seconds, and that its chances of success are extremely high, and that our explorer knows all of this, and also knows that these people will be treated fairly. I maintain that in such a situation he would have every right to escape if he could, and thus to deprive all of these potential people of their potential lives; for his right to life outweighs all of theirs together, in spite of the fact that they are all genetically human, all innocent, and all have a very high probability of becoming people very soon, if only he refrains from acting.

Indeed, I think he would have a right to escape even if it were not his life which the alien scientists planned to take, but only a year of his freedom, or, indeed, only a day. Nor would he be obligated to stay if he had gotten captured (thus bringing all these people-potentials into existence) because of his own carelessness, or even if he had done so deliberately, knowing the consequences. Regardless of how he got captured, he is not morally obligated to remain in captivity for *any* period of time for the sake of permitting any number of potential people to come into actuality, so great is the margin by which one actual person's right to liberty outweighs whatever right to life even a hundred thousand potential people have. And it seems reasonable to conclude that the rights of a woman will outweigh by a similar margin whatever right to life a fetus may have by virtue of its potential personhood.

Thus, neither a fetus's resemblance to a person, nor its potential for becoming a person provides any basis whatever for the claim that it has any significant right to life. Consequently, a woman's right to protect her health, happiness, freedom, and even her life,[5] by terminating an unwanted pregnancy, will always override whatever right to life it may be appropriate to ascribe to a fetus, even a fully developed one. And thus, in the absence of any overwhelming social need for every possible child, the laws which restrict the right to obtain an abortion, or limit the period of pregnancy during which an abortion may be performed, are a wholly unjustified violation of a woman's most basic moral and constitutional rights.[6]

Postscript on Infanticide, February 26, 1982

One of the most troubling objections to the argument presented in this article is that it may appear to justify not only abortion but infanticide as well. A newborn infant is not a great deal more personlike than a nine-month fetus, and thus it might seem that if late-term abortion is sometimes justified, then infanticide must also be sometimes justified. Yet most people consider that infanticide is a form of murder, and thus never justified.

While it is important to appreciate the emotional force of this objection, its logical force is far less than it may seem at first glance. There are many reasons why infanticide is much more difficult to justify than abortion, even though if my argument is correct neither constitutes the killing of a person. In this country, and in this period of history, the deliberate killing of viable newborns is virtually never justified. This is in part because neonates are so very *close* to being persons that to kill them requires a very strong moral justification—as the killing of dolphins, whales, chimpanzees, and other highly personlike creatures. It is certainly wrong to kill such beings just for the sake of convenience, or financial profit, or "sport."

Another reason why infanticide is usually wrong, in our society, is that if the newborn's parents do not want it, or are unable to care for it, there are (in most cases) people who are able and eager to adopt it and to provide a good home for it. Many people wait years for the opportunity to adopt a child, and some are unable to do so even though there is every reason to believe that they would be good parents. The needless destruction of a viable infant inevitably deprives some person or persons of a source of great pleasure and satisfaction, perhaps severely impoverishing their lives. Furthermore, even if an infant is considered to be unadoptable (e.g., because of some extremely severe mental or physical handicap) it is still wrong in most cases to kill it. For most of us value the lives of infants, and would prefer to pay taxes to support orphanages and state institutions for the handicapped rather than to allow unwanted infants to be killed. So long as most people feel this way, and so long as our society can afford to provide care for infants which are unwanted or which have special needs that preclude home care, it is wrong to destroy any infant which has a chance of living a reasonably satisfactory life.

If these arguments show that infanticide is wrong, at least in this society, then why don't they also show that late-term abortion is wrong? After all, third trimester fetuses are also highly personlike, and many people value them and would much prefer that they be preserved; even at some cost to themselves. As a potential source of pleasure to some family, a viable fetus is just as valuable as a viable infant. But there is an obvious and crucial difference between the two cases: once the infant is born, its continued life cannot (except, perhaps, in very exceptional cases) pose any serious threat to the woman's life or health, since she is free to put it up for adoption, or, where this is impossible, to place it in a state-supported institution. While she might prefer that it die, rather than being raised by others, it is not clear that such a preference would constitute a right on her part. True, she may suffer greatly from the knowledge that her child will be thrown into the lottery of the adoption system, and that she will be unable to ensure its well-being, or even to know whether it is healthy, happy, doing well in school, etc.: for the law generally does not permit natural parents to remain in contact with their children, once they are adopted by another family. But there are surely better ways of dealing with these problems than by permitting infanticide in such cases. (It might help, for instance, if the natural parents of adopted children could at least receive some information about their progress, without necessarily being informed of the identity of the adopting family.)

In contrast, a pregnant woman's right to protect her own life and health clearly outweighs other people's desire that the fetus be preserved—just as, when a person's life or limb is threatened by some wild animal, and when the threat cannot be removed without killing the animal, the person's right to self-protection outweighs the desires of those who would prefer that the animal not be harmed. Thus, while the moment of birth may not mark any sharp discontinuity in the degree to which an infant possesses a right to life, it does mark the end of the mother's absolute right to determine its fate. Indeed, if and when a late-term abortion could be safely performed without killing the fetus, she would have no absolute right to insist on its death (e.g., if others wish to adopt it or pay for its care), for the same reason that she does not have a right to insist that a viable infant be killed.

It remains true that according to my argument neither abortion nor the killing of neonates is properly considered a form of murder. Perhaps it is understandable that the law should classify infanticide as murder or homicide, since there is no other existing legal category which adequately or conveniently expresses the force of our society's disapproval of this action. But the moral distinction remains, and it has several important consequences.

In the first place, it implies that when an infant is born into a society which—unlike ours—is so impoverished that it simply cannot care for it adequately without endangering the survival of existing persons, killing it or allowing it to die is not necessarily wrong—provided that there is no *other* society which is willing and able to provide such care. Most human societies, from those at the hunting and gathering stage of economic development to the highly civilized Greeks and Romans, have permitted the practice of infanticide under such unfortunate circumstances, and I would argue that it shows a serious lack of understanding to condemn them as morally backward for this reason alone.

In the second place, the argument implies that when an infant is born with such severe physical anomalies that its life would predictably be a very short and/or very miserable one, even with the most heroic of medical treatment, and where its parents do not choose to bear the often crushing emotional, financial and other burdens attendant upon the artificial prolongation of such a tragic life, it is not morally wrong to cease or withhold treatment, thus allowing the infant a painless death. It is wrong (and sometimes a form of murder) to practice involuntary euthanasia on persons, since they have the right to decide for themselves whether or not they wish to continue to live. But terminally ill neonates cannot make this decision for themselves, and

thus it is incumbent upon responsible persons to make the decision for them, as best they can. The mistaken belief that infanticide is always tantamount to murder is responsible for a great deal of unnecessary suffering, not just on the part of infants which are made to endure needlessly prolonged and painful deaths, but also on the part of parents, nurses, and other involved persons, who must watch infants suffering needlessly, helpless to end that suffering in the most humane way.

I am well aware that these conclusions, however modest and reasonable they may seem to some people, strike other people as morally monstrous, and that some people might even prefer to abandon their previous support for women's right to abortion rather than accept a theory which leads to such conclusions about infanticide. But all that these facts show is that abortion is not an isolated moral issue; to fully understand the moral status of abortion we may have to reconsider other moral issues as well, issues not just about infanticide and euthanasia, but also about the moral rights of women and of nonhuman animals. It is a philosopher's task to criticize mistaken beliefs which stand in the way of moral understanding, even when—perhaps especially when—those beliefs are popular and widespread. The belief that moral strictures against killing should apply equally to *all* genetically human entities, and *only* to genetically human entities, is such an error. The overcoming of this error will undoubtedly require long and often painful struggle; but it must be done.

Notes

1 Of course, the principle that it is (always) wrong to kill innocent human beings is in need of many other modifications, e.g., that it may be permissible to do so to save a greater number of other innocent human beings, but we may safely ignore these complications here.

2 John Noonan, "Deciding Who is Human," *Natural Law Forum*, 13 (1968), 135.

3 From here on, we will use 'human' to mean genetically human, since the moral sense seems closely connected to, and perhaps derived from, the assumption that genetic humanity is sufficient for membership in the moral community.

4 Thomas L. Hayes, "A Biological View," *Commonweal*, 85 (March 17, 1967), 677–78; quoted by Daniel Callahan, in *Abortion: Law, Choice and Morality* (London: Macmillan & Co., 1970).

5 That is, insofar as the death rate, for the woman, is higher for childbirth than for early abortion.

6 My thanks to the following people, who were kind enough to read and criticize an earlier version of this paper: Herbert Gold, Gene Glass, Anne Lauterbach, Judith Thomson, Mary Mothersill, and Timothy Binkley.

Questions for Discussion

1 In comparing a fetus and an average mature mammal, is it significant that a fetus is *potentially* a full person and the mammal is not? Are there cases where it would clearly be a mistake to treat a potential something as if it were actually already that something?

2 If Warren is right that fetuses are less personlike than mature mammals, does that mean we should count fetuses for less than we traditionally have, or that we should count mammals for more, or does it have no effect on moral status?

3 Is there any way to distinguish a fetus from a newborn baby in terms of personhood characteristics? Are there any *other* characteristics which might be used to assign different moral obligations to people concerning the two kinds of entities?

4 At what point does a human become sufficiently personlike to be a full right-holder? Are there any criteria of personhood which might be used in place of the ones Warren suggests?

Why Abortion is Immoral

Don Marquis

In this article, Marquis argues that what is wrong with killing a fetus is the same as what is wrong with killing an adult—in either case we are depriving the victim of a future. Accordingly, Marquis believes that abortion is, with rare exceptions, seriously immoral.

★ ★ ★

The view that abortion is, with rare exceptions, seriously immoral has received little support in the recent philosophical literature. No doubt most philosophers affiliated with secular institutions of higher education believe that the anti-abortion position is either a symptom of irrational religious dogma or a conclusion generated by seriously confused philosophical argument. The purpose of this essay is to undermine this general belief. This essay sets out an argument that purports to show, as well as any argument in ethics can show, that abortion is, except possibly in rare cases, seriously immoral, that it is in the same moral category as killing an innocent adult human being.

The argument is based on a major assumption. Many of the most insightful and careful writers on the ethics of abortion—such as Joel Feinberg, Michael Tooley, Mary Anne Warren, H. Tristram Engelhardt, Jr., L.W. Sumner, John T. Noonan, Jr., and Philip Devine[1]—believe that whether or not abortion is morally permissible stands or falls on whether or not a fetus is the sort of being whose life it is seriously wrong to end. The argument of this essay will assume, but not argue, that they are correct.

Also, this essay will neglect issues of great importance to a complete ethics of abortion. Some anti-abortionists will allow that certain abortions, such as abortion before implantation or abortion when the life of a woman is threatened by a pregnancy or abortion after rape, may be morally permissible. This essay will not explore the casuistry of these hard cases. The purpose of this essay is to develop a general argument for the claim that the overwhelming majority of deliberate abortions are seriously immoral.

★   ★   ★

A sketch of standard anti-abortion and pro-choice arguments exhibits how those arguments possess certain symmetries that explain why partisans of those positions are so convinced of the correctness of their own positions, why they are not successful in convincing their opponents, and why, to others, this issue seems to be unresolvable. An analysis of the nature of this standoff suggests a strategy for surmounting it.

Consider the way a typical anti-abortionist argues. She will argue or assert that life is present from the moment of conception or that fetuses look like babies or that fetuses possess a characteristic such as a genetic code that is both necessary and sufficient for being human. Anti-abortionists seem to believe that (1) the truth of all of these claims is quite obvious, and (2) establishing any of these claims is sufficient to show that abortion is morally akin to murder.

A standard pro-choice strategy exhibits similarities. The pro-choicer will argue or assert that fetuses are not persons or that fetuses are not rational agents or that fetuses are not social beings. Pro-choicers seem to believe that (1) the truth of any of these claims is quite obvious, and (2) establishing any of these claims is sufficient to show that an abortion is not a wrongful killing.

In fact, both the pro-choice and the anti-abortion claims do seem to be true, although

the "it looks like a baby" claim is more difficult to establish the earlier the pregnancy. We seem to have a standoff. How can it be resolved?

As everyone who has taken a bit of logic knows, if any of these arguments concerning abortion is a good argument, it requires not only some claim characterizing fetuses, but also some general moral principle that ties a characteristic of fetuses to having or not having the right to life or to some other moral characteristic that will generate the obligation or the lack of obligation not to end the life of a fetus. Accordingly, the arguments of the anti-abortionist and the pro-choicer need a bit of filling in to be regarded as adequate.

Note what each partisan will say. The anti-abortionist will claim that her position is supported by such generally accepted moral principles as "It is always prima facie seriously wrong to take a human life" or "It is always prima facie seriously wrong to end the life of a baby." Since these are generally accepted moral principles, her position is certainly not obviously wrong. The pro-choicer will claim that her position is supported by such plausible moral principles as "Being a person is what gives an individual intrinsic moral worth" or "It is only seriously prima facie wrong to take the life of a member of the human community." Since these are generally accepted moral principles, the pro-choice position is certainly not obviously wrong. Unfortunately, we have again arrived at a standoff.

Now, how might one deal with this standoff? The standard approach is to try to show how the moral principles of one's opponent lose their plausibility under analysis. It is easy to see how this is possible. On the one hand, the anti-abortionist will defend a moral principle concerning the wrongness of killing which tends to be broad in scope in order that even fetuses at an early stage of pregnancy will fall under it. The problem with broad principles is that they often embrace too much. In this particular instance, the principle "It is always prima facie wrong to take a human life" seems to entail that it is wrong to end the existence of a living human cancer-cell culture, on the grounds that the culture is both living and human. Therefore, it seems that the anti-abortionist's favored principle is too broad.

On the other hand, the pro-choicer wants to find a moral principle concerning the wrongness of killing which tends to be narrow in scope in order that fetuses will *not* fall under it. The problem with narrow principles is that they often do not embrace enough. Hence, the needed principles such as "It is prima facie seriously wrong to kill only persons" or "It is prima facie wrong to kill only rational agents" do not explain why it is wrong to kill infants or young children or the severely retarded or even perhaps the severely mentally ill. Therefore, we seem again to have a standoff. The anti-abortionist charges, not unreasonably, that pro-choice principles concerning killing are too narrow to be acceptable; the pro-choicer charges, not unreasonably, that anti-abortionist principles concerning killing are too broad to be acceptable.

Attempts by both sides to patch up the difficulties in their positions run into further difficulties. The anti-abortionist will try to remove the problem in her position by reformulating her principle concerning killing in terms of human beings. Now we end up with: "It is always prima facie seriously wrong to end the life of a human being." This principle has the advantage of avoiding the problem of the human cancer-cell culture counterexample. But this advantage is purchased at a high price. For although it is clear that a fetus is both human and alive, it is not at all clear that a fetus is a human *being*. There is at least something to be said for the view that something becomes a human being only after a process of development, and that therefore first trimester fetuses and perhaps all fetuses are not yet human beings. Hence, the anti-abortion-

ist, by this move, has merely exchanged one problem for another.[2]

The pro-choicer fares no better. She may attempt to find reasons why killing infants, young children, and the severely retarded is wrong which are independent of her major principle that is supposed to explain the wrongness of taking human life, but which will not also make abortion immoral. This is no easy task. Appeals to social utility will seem satisfactory only to those who resolve not to think of the enormous difficulties with a utilitarian account of the wrongness of killing and the significant social costs of preserving the lives of the unproductive.[3] A pro-choice strategy that extends the definition of 'person' to infants or even to young children seems just as arbitrary as an anti-abortion strategy that extends the definition of 'human being' to fetuses. Again, we find symmetries in the two positions and we arrive at a standoff.

There are even further problems that reflect symmetries in the two positions. In addition to counterexample problems, or the arbitrary application problems that can be exchanged for them, the standard anti-abortionist principle "It is prima facie seriously wrong to kill a human being," or one of its variants, can be objected to on the grounds of ambiguity. If 'human being' is taken to be a *biological* category, then the anti-abortionist is left with the problem of explaining why a merely biological category should make a moral difference. Why, it is asked, is it any more reasonable to base a moral conclusion on the number of chromosomes in one's cells than on the color of one's skin?[4] If 'human being', on the other hand, is taken to be a *moral* category, then the claim that a fetus is a human being cannot be taken to be a premise in the anti-abortion argument, for it is precisely what needs to be established. Hence, either the anti-abortionist's main category is a morally irrelevant, merely biological category, or it is of no use to the anti-abortionist in establishing (noncircularly, of course) that abortion is wrong.

Although this problem with the anti-abortionist position is often noticed, it is less often noticed that the pro-choice position suffers from an analogous problem. The principle "Only persons have the right to life" also suffers from an ambiguity. The term 'person' is typically defined in terms of psychological characteristics, although there will certainly be disagreement concerning which characteristics are most important Supposing that this matter can be settled, the pro-choicer is left with the problem of explaining why *psychological* characteristics should make a *moral* difference. If the pro-choicer should attempt to deal with this problem by claiming that an explanation is not necessary, that in fact we do treat such a cluster of psychological properties as having moral significance, the sharp-witted anti-abortionist should have a ready response. We do treat being both living and human as having moral significance. If it is legitimate for the pro-choicer to demand that the anti-abortionist provide an explanation of the connection between the biological character of being a human being and the wrongness of being killed (even though people accept this connection), then it is legitimate for the anti-abortionist to demand that the pro-choicer provide an explanation of the connection between psychological criteria for being a person and the wrongness of being killed (even though that connection is accepted).[5]...

[T]he pro-choicer cannot any more escape her problem by making person a purely moral category than the anti-abortionist could escape by the analogous move. For if person is a moral category, then the pro-choicer is left without the resources for establishing (non-circularly, of course) the claim that a fetus is not a person, which is an essential premise in her argument. Again, we have both a symmetry and a standoff between pro-choice and anti-abortion views.

Passions in the abortion debate run high. There are both plausibilities and difficulties with the standard positions. Accordingly, it is hardly surprising that partisans of either side embrace with fervor the moral generalizations that support the conclusions they pre-analytically favor, and reject with disdain the moral generalizations of their opponents as being subject to inescapable difficulties. It is easy to believe that the counterexamples to one's own moral principles are merely temporary difficulties that will dissolve in the wake of further philosophical search, and that the counterexamples to the principles of one's opponents are ... straightforward.... This might suggest to an impartial observer (if there are any) that the abortion issue is unresolvable. There is a way out of this apparent dialectical quandary. The moral generalizations of both sides are not quite correct. The generalizations hold for the most part, for the usual cases. This suggests that they are all *accidental* generalizations, that the moral claims made by those on both sides of the dispute do not touch on the *essence* of the matter.

This use of the distinction between essence and accident is not meant to invoke obscure metaphysical categories. Rather, it is intended to reflect the rather atheoretical nature of the abortion discussion. If the generalization a partisan in the abortion dispute adopts were derived from the reason why ending the life of a human being is wrong, then there could not be exceptions to that generalization unless some special case obtains in which there are even more powerful countervailing reasons. Such generalizations would not be merely accidental generalizations; they would point to, or be based upon, the essence of the wrongness of killing, what it is that makes killing wrong. All this suggests that a necessary condition of resolving the abortion controversy is a more theoretical account of the wrongness of killing. After all, if we merely believe, but do not understand, why killing adult human beings such as ourselves is wrong, how could we conceivably show that abortion is either immoral or permissible?

★   ★   ★

In order to develop such an account, we can start from the following unproblematic assumption concerning our own case: it is wrong to kill *us*. Why is it wrong?...

What primarily makes killing wrong is neither its effect on the murderer nor its effect on the victim's friends and relatives, but its effect on the victim. The loss of one's life is one of the greatest losses one can suffer. The loss of one's life deprives one of all the experiences, activities, projects, and enjoyments that would otherwise have constituted one's future. Therefore, killing someone is wrong, primarily because the killing inflicts (one of) the greatest possible losses on the victim. To describe this as the loss of life can be misleading, however. The change in my biological state does not by itself make killing me wrong. The effect of the loss of my biological life is the loss to me of all those activities, projects, experiences, and enjoyments which would otherwise have constituted my future personal life. These activities, projects, experiences, and enjoyments are either valuable for their own sakes or are means to something else that is valuable for its own sake. Some parts of my future are not valued by me now, but will come to be valued by me as I grow older and as my values and capacities change. When I am killed, I am deprived both of what I now value which would have been part of my future personal life, but also what I would come to value. Therefore, when I die, I am deprived of all of the value of my future. Inflicting this loss on me is ultimately what makes killing me wrong. This being the case, it would seem that what makes killing *any* adult human being prima facie seriously wrong is the loss of his or her future.[6]...

The claim that what makes killing wrong is the loss of the victim's future is directly supported by two considerations. In the first place, this theory explains why we regard killing as one of the worst of crimes. Killing is especially wrong, because it deprives the victim of more than perhaps any other crime. In the second place, people with AIDS or cancer who know they are dying believe, of course, that dying is a very bad thing for them. They believe that the loss of a future to them that they would otherwise have experienced is what makes their premature death a very bad thing for them. A better theory of the wrongness of killing would require a different natural property associated with killing which better fits with the attitudes of the dying. What could it be?

The view that what makes killing wrong is the loss to the victim of the value of the victim's future gains additional support when some of its implications are examined. In the first place, it is incompatible with the view that it is wrong to kill only beings who are biologically human. It is possible that there exists a different species from another planet whose members have a future like ours. Since having a future like that is what makes killing wrong, this theory entails that it would be wrong to kill members of such a species. Hence, this theory is opposed to the claim that only life that is biologically human has great moral worth, a claim which many anti-abortionists have seemed to adopt. This opposition, which this theory has in common with personhood theories, seems to be a merit of the theory.

In the second place, the claim that the loss of one's future is the wrong-making feature of one's being killed entails the possibility that the futures of some actual nonhuman mammals on our own planet are sufficiently like ours that it is seriously wrong to kill them also. Whether some animals do have the same right to life as human beings depends on adding to the account of the wrongness of killing some additional account of just what it is about my future or the futures of other adult human beings which makes it wrong to kill us. No such additional account will be offered in this essay. Undoubtedly, the provision of such an account would be a very difficult matter. Undoubtedly, any such account would be quite controversial. Hence, it surely should not reflect badly on this sketch of an elementary theory of the wrongness of killing that it is indeterminate with respect to some very difficult issues regarding animal rights.

In the third place, the claim that the loss of one's future is the wrong-making feature of one's being killed does not entail, as sanctity of human life theories do, that active euthanasia is wrong. Persons who are severely and incurably ill, who face a future of pain and despair, and who wish to die will not have suffered a loss if they are killed. It is, strictly speaking, the value of a human's future which makes killing wrong in this theory. This being so, killing does not necessarily wrong some persons who are sick and dying. Of course, there may be other reasons for a prohibition of active euthanasia, but that is another matter. Sanctity-of-human-life theories seem to hold that active euthanasia is seriously wrong even in an individual case where there seems to be good reason for it independently of public policy considerations. This consequence is most implausible, and it is a plus for the claim that the loss of a future of value is what makes killing wrong that it does not share this consequence.

In the fourth place, the account of the wrongness of killing defended in this essay does straightforwardly entail that it is prima facie seriously wrong to kill children and infants, for we do presume that they have futures of value. Since we do believe that it is wrong to kill defenseless little babies, it is important that a theory of the wrongness of killing easily account for this. Personhood

theories of the wrongness of killing, on the other hand, cannot straightforwardly account for the wrongness of killing infants and young children.[7] Hence, such theories must add special ad hoc accounts of the wrongness of killing the young. The plausibility of such ad hoc theories seems to be a function of how desperately one wants such theories to work. The claim that the primary wrong-making feature of a killing is the loss to the victim of the value of its future accounts for the wrongness of killing young children and infants directly; it makes the wrongness of such acts as obvious as we actually think it is. This is a further merit of this theory. Accordingly, it seems that this value of a future-like-ours theory of the wrongness of killing shares strengths of both sanctity-of-life and personhood accounts while avoiding weaknesses of both. In addition, it meshes with a central intuition concerning what makes killing wrong.

The claim that the primary wrong-making feature of a killing is the loss to the victim of the value of its future has obvious consequences for the ethics of abortion. The future of a standard fetus includes a set of experiences, projects, activities, and such which are identical with the futures of adult human beings and are identical with the futures of young children. Since the reason that is sufficient to explain why it is wrong to kill human beings after the time of birth is a reason that also applies to fetuses, it follows that abortion is prima facie seriously morally wrong....

★　★　★

How complete an account of the wrongness of killing does the value of a future-like-ours account have to be in order that the wrongness of abortion is a consequence? This account does not have to be an account of the necessary conditions for the wrongness of killing. Some persons in nursing homes may lack valuable human futures, yet it may be wrong to kill them for other reasons. Furthermore, this account does not obviously have to be the sole reason killing is wrong where the victim did have a valuable future. This analysis claims only that, for any killing where the victim did have a valuable future like ours, having that future by itself is sufficient to create the strong presumption that the killing is seriously wrong...

*   *   *

In this essay, it has been argued that the correct ethic of the wrongness of killing can be extended to fetal life and used to show that there is a strong presumption that any abortion is morally impermissible. If the ethic of killing adopted here entails, however, that contraception is also seriously immoral, then there would appear to be a difficulty with the analysis of this essay.

But this analysis does not entail that contraception is wrong. Of course, contraception prevents the actualization of a possible future of value. Hence, it follows from the claim that futures of value should be maximized that contraception is prima facie immoral. This obligation to maximize does not exist, however; furthermore, nothing in the ethics of killing in this paper entails that it does. The ethics of killing in this essay would entail that contraception is wrong only if something were denied a human future of value by contraception. Nothing at all is denied such a future by contraception, however....

At the time of contraception, there are hundreds of millions of sperm, one (released) ovum and millions of possible combinations of all of these. There is no actual combination at all. Is the subject of the loss to be a merely possible combination? Which one? This alternative does not yield an actual subject of harm either. Accordingly, the immorality of contraception is not entailed by the loss of a future-like-ours argument simply because there is no

nonarbitrarily identifiable subject of the loss in the case of contraception.

*   *   *

The purpose of this essay has been to set out an argument for the serious presumptive wrongness of abortion subject to the assumption that the moral permissibility of abortion stands or falls on the moral status of the fetus. Since a fetus possesses a property, the possession of which in adult human beings is sufficient to make killing an adult human being wrong, abortion is wrong. This way of dealing with the problem of abortion seems superior to other approaches to the ethics of abortion, because it rests on an ethics of killing which is close to self-evident, because the crucial morally relevant property clearly applies to fetuses, and because the argument avoids the usual equivocations on 'human life', 'human being', or 'person'. The argument rests neither on religious claims nor on Papal dogma. It is not subject to the objection of "speciesism." Its soundness is compatible with the moral permissibility of euthanasia and contraception. It deals with our intuitions concerning young children.

Finally, this analysis can be viewed as resolving a standard problem—indeed, the standard problem—concerning the ethics of abortion. Clearly, it is wrong to kill adult human beings. Clearly, it is not wrong to end the life of some arbitrarily chosen single human cell. Fetuses seem to be like arbitrarily chosen human cells in some respects and like adult humans in other respects. The problem of the ethics of abortion is the problem of determining the fetal property that settles this moral controversy. The thesis of this essay is that the problem of the ethics of abortion, so understood, is solvable.

Notes

1 Feinberg, "Abortion," in *Matters of Life and Death: New Introductory Essays in Moral Philosophy*, Tom

Regan, ed. (New York: Random House, 1986), pp. 256–293; Tooley, "Abortion and Infanticide," *Philosophy and Public Affairs*, II, 1 (1972): 37–65; Tooley, *Abortion and Infanticide* (New York: Oxford, 1984); Warren, "On the Moral and Legal Status of Abortion," *The Monist*, LVII, 1 (1973): 43–61; Engelhardt, "The Ontology of Abortion," *Ethics*, I, XXXIV, 3 (1974): 217–234; Sumner, *Abortion and Moral Theory* (Princeton: University Press, 1981); Noonan, "An Almost Absolute Value in History," in *The Morality of Abortion: Legal and Historical Perspectives*, Noonan, ed. (Cambridge: Harvard, 1970); and Devine, *The Ethics of Homicide* (Ithaca: Cornell, 1978).

2 For interesting discussions of this issue, see Warren Quinn, "Abortion: Identity and Loss," *Philosophy and Public Affairs*, XIII, 1 (1984): 24–54; and Lawrence C. Becker, "Human Being: The Boundaries of the Concept," *Philosophy and Public Affairs*, IV, 4 (1975): 334–359.

3 For example, see my "Ethics and the Elderly: Some Problems," in Stuart Spicker, Kathleen Woodward, and David Van Tassel, eds., *Aging and the Elderly: Humanistic Perspectives in Gerontology* (Atlantic Highlands, NJ: Humanities, 1978), pp. 341–355.

4 See Warren, *op. cit.*, and Tooley, "Abortion and Infanticide."

5 This seems to be the fatal flaw in Warren's treatment of this issue.

6 I have been most influenced on this matter by Jonathan Glover, *Causing Death and Saving Lives* (New York: Penguin, 1977), ch. 3; and Robert Young, "What Is So Wrong with Killing People?" *Philosophy*, LIV, 210 (1979): 515–528.

7 Feinberg, Tooley, Warren, and Engelhardt have all dealt with this problem.

Questions for Discussion

1 If what is wrong with killing is the loss of the victim's future, it might seem that killing a being with a longer future is worse than killing one with a shorter future. Is the death of a fetus worse than the death of, say, a five-year-old child? Would this view entail that the death of a fetus is worse than the death of its mother?

2 If a person deliberately kills a second person who, unknown to both of them, was going to be hit by a car and killed anyway a moment later, has the person who killed the second person done anything wrong? If so, and if what is wrong with killing is the loss of a future, how do we explain this?

3 Does it make a difference to Marquis' argument how likely it is that a fetus will survive to birth and beyond, without any interference?

A Defense of Abortion[1]

Judith Jarvis Thomson

*The traditional debate between conservatives, liberals, and "drawing-the-line"-type moderates has centred around whether a fetus is a person. In this landmark article, Thomson argues that abortion might be acceptable even if one grants that a fetus **is** a person. The central question here concerns the lengths to which one must go to protect the lives of others.*

★   ★   ★

Most opposition to abortion relies on the premise that the fetus is a human being, a person, from the moment of conception. The premise is argued for, but, as I think, not well. Take, for example, the most common argument. We are asked to notice that the development of a human being from conception through birth into childhood is continuous; then it is said that to draw a line, to choose a point in this development and say "before this point the thing is not a person, after this point it is a person" is to make an arbitrary choice, a choice for which in the nature of things no good reason can be given. It is concluded that the fetus is, or anyway that we had better say it is, a person from the moment of conception. But this conclusion does not follow. Similar things might be said about the development of an acorn into an oak tree, and it does not follow that acorns are oak trees, or that we had better say they are. Arguments of this form are sometimes called "slippery slope arguments"— the phrase is perhaps self-explanatory—and it is dismaying that opponents of abortion rely on them so heavily and uncritically.

I am inclined to agree, however, that the prospects for "drawing a line" in the development of the fetus look dim. I am inclined to think also that we shall probably have to agree that the fetus has already become a human person well before birth. Indeed, it comes as a surprise when one first learns how early in its life it begins to acquire human characteristics. By the tenth week, for example, it already has a face, arms and legs, fingers and toes; it has internal organs, and brain activity is detectable.[2] On the other hand, I think that the premise is false, that the fetus is not a person from the moment of conception. A newly fertilized ovum, a newly implanted clump of cells, is no more a person than an acorn is an oak tree. But I shall not discuss any of this. For it seems to me to be of great interest to ask what happens if, for the sake of argument, we allow the premise. How, precisely, are we supposed to get from there to the conclusion that abortion is morally impermissible? Opponents of abortion commonly spend most of their time establishing that the fetus is a person, and hardly any time explaining the step from there to the impermissibility of abortion.

Perhaps they think the step too simple and obvious to require much comment. Or perhaps instead they are simply being economical in argument. Many of those who defend abortion rely on the premise that the fetus is not a person, but only a bit of tissue that will become a person at birth; and why pay out more arguments than you have to? Whatever the explanation, I suggest that the step they take is neither easy nor obvious, that it calls for closer examination than it is commonly given, and that when we do give it this closer examination we shall feel inclined to reject it.

I propose, then, that we grant that the fetus is a person from the moment of conception. How does the argument go from here? Something like this, I take it. Every person has a right to life. So the fetus has a right to life. No doubt the mother has a right to decide what shall happen in and to her body; everyone would grant that. But surely a person's right to life is stronger and more stringent than the mother's right to decide what happens in and to her body, and so outweighs it. So the fetus may not be killed; an abortion may not be performed.

It sounds plausible. But now let me ask you to imagine this. You wake up in the morning and find yourself back to back in bed with an unconscious violinist. A famous unconscious violinist. He has been found to have a fatal kidney ailment, and the Society of Music Lovers has canvassed all the available medical records and found that you alone have the right blood type to help. They have therefore kidnapped you, and last night the violinist's circulatory system was plugged into yours, so that your kidneys can be used to extract poisons from his blood as well as your own. The director of the hospital now tells you, "Look, we're sorry the Society of Music Lovers did this to you—we would never have permitted it if we had known. But still, they did it, and the violinist now is plugged into you. To unplug you would be to kill him. But never mind, it's only for nine months. By then he will have recovered from his ailment, and can safely be unplugged from you." Is it morally incumbent on you to accede to this situation? No doubt it would be very nice of you if you did, a great kindness. But do you *have* to accede to it? What if it were not nine months, but nine years? Or longer still? What if the director of the hospital says, "Tough luck, I agree, but you've now got to stay in bed, with the violinist plugged into you, for the rest of your life. Because remember this. All persons have a right to life, and violinists are persons. Granted you have a right to decide what happens in and to your body, but a person's right to life outweighs your right to decide what happens in and to your body. So you cannot ever be unplugged from him." I imagine you would regard this as outrageous, which suggests that something really is wrong with that plausible-sounding argument I mentioned a moment ago.

In this case, of course, you were kidnapped; you didn't volunteer for the operation that plugged the violinist into your kidneys. Can those who oppose abortion on the ground I mentioned make an exception for a pregnancy due to rape? Certainly. They can say that persons have a right to life only if they didn't come into existence because of rape; or they can say that all persons have a right to life, but that some have less of a right to life than others, in particular, that those who came into existence because of rape have less. But these statements have a rather unpleasant sound. Surely the question of whether you have a right to life at all, or how much of it you have, shouldn't turn on the question of whether or not you are the product of a rape. And in fact the people who oppose abortion on the ground I mentioned do not make this distinction, and hence do not make an exception in case of rape.

Nor do they make an exception for a case in which the mother has to spend the nine months of her pregnancy in bed. They would agree that would be a great pity, and hard on the mother; but all the same, all persons have a right to life, the fetus is a person, and so on. I suspect, in fact, that they would not make an exception for a case in which, miraculously enough, the pregnancy went on for nine years, or even the rest of the mother's life.

Some won't even make an exception for a case in which continuation of the pregnancy is likely to shorten the mother's life; they regard abortion as impermissible even to save the mother's life. Such cases are nowadays very rare, and many opponents of abortion do not accept this extreme view. All the same, it is a good place to begin: a number of points of interest come out in respect to it.

1. Let us call the view that abortion is impermissible even to save the mother's life "the extreme view." I want to suggest first that it does not issue from the argument I mentioned earlier without the addition of some fairly powerful premises. Suppose a woman has become pregnant, and now learns that she has a cardiac condition such that she will die if she carries the baby to term. What may be done for her? The fetus, being a person, has a right to life, but as the mother is a person to, so has she a right to life. Presumably they have an equal right to life. How is it supposed to come out that an abortion may not be performed? If mother and child have an equal right to life, shouldn't we perhaps flip a coin? Or should we add to the mother's right to life her right to decide what happens in and to her body, which everybody seems to be ready to grant—the sum of her rights now outweighing the fetus' right to life?

The most familiar argument here is the following. We are told that performing the abortion would be directly killing[3] the child, whereas doing nothing would not be killing the mother, but only letting her die. Moreover, in killing the child, one would be killing an innocent person, for the child has committed no crime, and is not aiming at his mother's death. And then there are a variety of ways in which this might be continued. (1) But as directly killing an innocent person is always and absolutely impermissible, an abortion may not be performed. Or, (2) as directly killing an innocent person is murder, and murder is always and absolutely impermissible, an abortion may not be performed.[4] Or, (3) as one's duty to refrain from directly killing an innocent person is more stringent than one's duty to keep a person from dying, an abortion may not be performed. Or, (4) if one's only options are directly killing an innocent person or letting a person die, one must prefer letting the person die, and thus an abortion may not be performed.[5]

Some people seem to have thought that these are not further premises which must be added if the conclusion is to be reached, but that they follow from the very fact that an innocent person has a right to life.[6] But this seems to me to be a mistake, and perhaps the simplest way to show this is to bring out that while we must certainly grant that innocent persons have a right to life, the theses in (1) through (4) are all false. Take (2), for example. If directly killing an innocent person is murder, and thus is impermissible, then the mother's directly killing the innocent person inside her is murder, and thus is impermissible. But it cannot seriously be thought to be murder if the mother performs an abortion on herself to save her life. It cannot seriously be said that she *must* refrain, that she *must* sit passively by and wait for her death. Let us look again at the case of you and the violinist. There you are, in bed with the violinist, and the director of the hospital says to you, "It's all most distressing, and I deeply sympathize, but you see this is putting an additional strain on your kidneys, and you'll be dead within the month. But you have to stay where you are all the same. Because unplugging you would be directly killing an innocent violinist, and

that's murder, and that's impermissible." If anything in the world is true, it is that you do not commit murder, you do not do what is impermissible, if you reach around to your back and unplug yourself from that violinist to save your life.

The main focus of attention in writings on abortion has been on what a third party may or may not do in answer to a request from a woman for an abortion. This is in a way understandable. Things being as they are, there isn't much a woman can safely do to abort herself. So the question asked is what a third party may do, and what the mother may do, if it is mentioned at all, is deduced, almost as an afterthought, from what it is concluded that third parties may do. But it seems to me that to treat the matter in this way is to refuse to grant to the mother that very status of person which is so firmly insisted on for the fetus. For we cannot simply read off what a person may do from what a third party may do. Suppose you find yourself trapped in a tiny house with a growing child. I mean a very tiny house, and a rapidly growing child—you are already up against the wall of the house and in a few minutes you'll be crushed to death. The child on the other hand won't be crushed to death; if nothing is done to stop him from growing he'll be hurt, but in the end he'll simply burst open the house and walk out a free man. Now I could well understand it if a bystander were to say, "There's nothing we can do for you. We cannot choose between your life and his, we cannot be the ones to decide who is to live, we cannot intervene." But it cannot be concluded that you too can do nothing, that you cannot attack it to save your life. However innocent the child may be, you do not have to wait passively while it crushes you to death. Perhaps a pregnant woman is vaguely felt to have the status of house, to which we don't allow the right of self-defense. But if the woman houses the child, it should be remembered that she is a person who houses it.

I should perhaps stop to say explicitly that I am not claiming that people have a right to do anything whatever to save their lives. I think, rather, that there are drastic limits to the right of self-defense. If someone threatens you with death unless you torture someone else to death, I think you have not the right, even to save your life, to do so. But the case under consideration here is very different. In our case there are only two people involved, one whose life is threatened, and one who threatens it. Both are innocent: the one who is threatened is not threatened because of any fault, the one who threatens does not threaten because of any fault. For this reason we may feel that we bystanders cannot intervene. But the person threatened can.

In sum, a woman surely can defend her life against the threat to it posed by the un-born child, even if doing so involves its death. And this shows not merely that the theses in (1) through (4) are false; it shows also that the extreme view of abortion is false, and so we need not canvass any other possible ways of arriving at it from the argument I mentioned at the outset.

2. The extreme view could of course be weakened to say that while abortion is per-missible to save the mother's life, it may not be performed by a third party, but only by the mother herself. But this cannot be right ei-ther. For what we have to keep in mind is that the mother and the unborn child are not like two tenants in a small house which has, by an unfortunate mistake, been rented to both: the mother *owns* the house. The fact that she does adds to the offensiveness of deducing that the mother can do nothing from the supposition that third parties can do nothing. But it does more than this: it casts a bright light on the supposition that third parties can do nothing. Certainly it lets us see that a third party who says "I cannot choose between you" is fool-ing himself if he thinks this is impartiality. If Jones has found and fastened on a certain coat, which he needs to keep him from freezing, but which Smith also needs to keep him from freezing, then it is not impartiality that says "I cannot choose between you" when Smith owns the coat. Women have said again and again "This body is *my* body!" and they have reason to feel angry, reason to feel that it has been like shouting into the wind. Smith, af-ter all, is hardly likely to bless us if we say to him, "Of course it's your coat, anybody would grant that it is. But no one may choose be-tween you and Jones who is to have it."

We should really ask what it is that says "no one may choose" in the face of the fact that the body that houses the child is the mother's body. It may be simply a failure to appreciate this fact. But it may be something more interesting, namely the sense that one has a right to refuse to lay hands on people, even where it would be just and fair to do so, even where justice seems to require that some-body do so. Thus justice might call for some-body to get Smith's coat back from Jones, and yet you have a right to refuse to be the one to lay hands on Jones, a right to refuse to do physical violence to him. This, I think, must be granted. But then what should be said is not "no one may choose," but only "*I* cannot choose," and indeed not even this, but "*I* will not *act*," leaving it open that somebody else can or should, and in particular that anyone in a position of authority, with the job of se-curing people's rights, both can and should. So this is no difficulty. I have not been argu-ing that any given third party must accede to the mother's request that he perform an abor-tion to save her life, but only that he may.

I suppose that in some views of human life the mother's body is only on loan to her, the loan not being one which gives her any prior claim to it. One who held this view might well think it impartiality to say "I cannot choose." But I shall simply ignore this possi-bility. My own view is that if a human being has any just, prior claim to anything at all, he has a just, prior claim to his own body. And perhaps this needn't be argued for here anyway, since, as I mentioned, the arguments against abortion we are looking at do grant that the woman has a right to decide what happens in and to her body.

But although they do grant it, I have tried to show that they do not take seriously what is done in granting it. I suggest the same thing will reappear even more clearly when we turn away from cases in which the mother's life is at stake, and attend, as I propose we now do, to the vastly more common cases in which a woman wants an abortion for some less weighty reason than preserving her own life.

3. Where the mother's life is not at stake, the argument I mentioned at the outset seems to have a much stronger pull. "Everyone has a right to life, so the unborn person has a right to life." And isn't the child's right to life weightier than anything other than the mother's own right to life, which she might put forward as ground for an abortion?

This argument treats the right to life as if it were unproblematic. It is not, and this seems to me to be precisely the source of the mistake.

For we should now, at long last, ask what it comes to, to have a right to life. In some views having a right to life includes having a right to be given at least the bare minimum one needs for continued life. But suppose that what in fact *is* the bare minimum a man needs for continued life is something he has no right at all to be given? If I am sick unto death, and the only thing that will save my life is the touch of Henry Fonda's cool hand on my fevered brow, then all the same, I have no right to be given the touch of Henry Fonda's cool hand on my fevered brow. It would be frightfully nice of him to fly in from the West Coast to provide it. It would be less nice, though no doubt well meant, if my friends flew out to the West Coast and carried Henry Fonda back with them. But I have no right at all against anybody that he should do this for me.

Or again, to return to the story I told earlier, the fact that for continued life that violinist needs the continued use of your kidneys does not establish that he has a right to be given the continued use of your kidneys. He certainly has no right against you that *you* should give him continued use of your kidneys. For nobody has any right to use your kidneys unless you give him such a right; and nobody has the right against you that you shall give him this right—if you do allow him to go on using your kidneys, this is a kindness on your part, and not something he can claim from you as his due. Nor has he any right against anybody else that *they* should give him continued use of your kidneys. Certainly he had no right against the Society of Music Lovers that they should plug him into you in the first place. And if you now start to unplug yourself, having learned that you will otherwise have to spend nine years in bed with him, there is nobody in the world who must try to prevent you, in order to see to it that he is given something he has a right to be given.

Some people are rather stricter about the right to life. In their view, it does not include the right to be given anything, but amounts to, and only to, the right not to be killed by anybody. But here a related difficulty arises. If everybody is to refrain from killing that violinist, then everybody must refrain from doing a great many different sorts of things. Everybody must refrain from slitting his throat, everybody must refrain from shooting him, and everybody must refrain from unplugging you from him. But does he have a right against everybody that they shall refrain from unplugging you from him? To refrain from doing this is to allow him to continue to use your kidneys. It could be argued that he has a right against us that *we* should allow him to continue to use your kidneys. That is, while he had no right against us that we should give him the use of your kidneys, it might be argued that he anyway has a right against us that we shall not now intervene and deprive him of the use of your kidneys. I shall come back to third-party interventions later. But certainly the violinist has no right against you that *you* shall allow him to continue to use your kidneys. As I said, if you do allow him to use them, it is a kindness on your part, and not something you owe him.

The difficulty I point to here is not peculiar to the right to life. It reappears in connection with all the other natural rights; and it is something which an adequate account of rights must deal with. For present purposes it is enough just to draw attention to it. But I would stress that I am not arguing that people do not have a right to life—quite to the contrary, it seems to me that the primary control we must place on the acceptability of an account of rights is that it should turn out in that account to be a truth that all persons have a right to life. I am arguing only that having a right to life does not guarantee having either a right to be given the use of or a right to be allowed continued use of another person's body—even if one needs it for life itself. So the right to life will not serve the opponents of abortion in the very simple and clear way in which they seem to have thought it would.

4. There is another way to bring out the difficulty. In the most ordinary sort of case, to deprive someone of what he has a right to is to treat him unjustly. Suppose a boy and his small brother are jointly given a box of chocolates for Christmas. If the older boy takes the box and refuses to give his brother any of the chocolates, he is unjust to him, for the brother has been given a right to half of them. But suppose that, having learned that otherwise it means nine years in bed with that violinist, you unplug yourself from him. You surely are not being unjust to him, for you gave him no right to use your kidneys, and no one else can have given him any such right. But we have to notice that in unplugging yourself, you are killing him; and violinists, like everybody else,

have a right to life, and thus in the view we were considering just now, the right not to be killed. So here you do what he supposedly has a right you shall not do, but you do not act unjustly to him in doing it.

The emendation which may be made at this point is this: the right to life consists not in the right not to be killed, but rather in the right not to be killed unjustly. This runs a risk of circularity, but never mind: it would enable us to square the fact that the violinist has a right to life with the fact that you do not act unjustly toward him in unplugging yourself, thereby killing him. For if you do not kill him unjustly, you do not violate his right to life, and so it is no wonder you do him no injustice.

But if this emendation is accepted, the gap in the argument against abortion stares us plainly in the face: it is by no means enough to show that the fetus is a person, and to remind us that all persons have a right to life— we need to be shown also that killing the fetus violates its right to life, i.e., that abortion is unjust killing. And is it?

I suppose we may take it as a datum that in a case of pregnancy due to rape the mother has not given the unborn person a right to the use of her body for food and shelter. Indeed, in what pregnancy could it be supposed that the mother has given the unborn person such a right? It is not as if there were unborn persons drifting about the world, to whom a woman who wants a child says "I invite you in."

But it might be argued that there are other ways one can have acquired a right to the use of another person's body than by having been invited to use it by that person. Suppose a woman voluntarily indulges in intercourse, knowing of the chance it will issue in pregnancy, and then she does become pregnant; is she not in part responsible for the presence, in fact the very existence, of the unborn person inside her? No doubt she did not invite it in. But doesn't her partial responsibility for its being there itself give it a right to the use of her body?[7] If so, then her aborting it would be more like the boy's taking away the chocolates, and less like your unplugging yourself from the violinist—doing so would be depriving it of what it does have a right to, and thus would be doing it an injustice.

And then, too, it might be asked whether or not she can kill it even to save her own life: If she voluntarily called it into existence, how can she now kill it, even in self-defense?

The first thing to be said about this is that it is something new. Opponents of abortion have been so concerned to make out the independence of the fetus, in order to establish that it has a right to life, just as its mother does, that they have tended to overlook the possible support they might gain from making out that the fetus is *dependent* on the mother, in order to establish that she has a special kind of responsibility for it, a responsibility that gives it rights against her which are not possessed by any independent person—such as an ailing violinist who is a stranger to her.

On the other hand, this argument would give the unborn person a right to its mother's body only if her pregnancy resulted from a voluntary act, undertaken in full knowledge of the chance a pregnancy might result from it. It would leave out entirely the unborn person whose existence is due to rape. Pending the availability of some further argument, then, we would be left with the conclusion that unborn persons whose existence is due to rape have no right to the use of their mothers' bodies, and thus that aborting them is not depriving them of anything they have a right to and hence is not unjust killing.

And we should also notice that it is not at all plain that this argument really does go even as far as it purports to. For there are cases and cases, and the details make a difference. If the room is stuffy, and I therefore open a window to air it, and a burglar climbs in, it would be absurd to say, "Ah, now he can stay, she's given him a right to the use of her house—for she is partially responsible for his presence there, having voluntarily done what enabled him to get in, in full knowledge that there are such things as burglars, and that burglars burgle." It would be still more absurd to say this if I had had bars installed outside my windows, precisely to prevent burglars from getting in, and a burglar got in only because of a defect in the bars. It remains equally absurd if we imagine it is not a burglar who climbs in, but an innocent person who blunders or falls in. Again, suppose it were like this: people-seeds drift about in the air like pollen, and if you open your windows, one may drift in and take root in your carpets or upholstery. You don't want children, so you fix up your windows with fine mesh screens, the very best you can buy. As can happen, however, and on very, very rare occasions does happen, one of the screens is defective; and a seed drifts in and takes root. Does the person-plant who now develops have a right to the use of your house? Surely not—despite the fact that you voluntarily opened your windows, you knowingly kept carpets and upholstered furniture, and you knew that screens were sometimes defective. Someone may argue that you are responsible for its rooting, that it does have a right to your house, because after all you *could* have lived out your life with bare floors and furniture, or with sealed windows and doors. But this won't do—for by the same token anyone can avoid a pregnancy due to rape by having a hysterectomy, or anyway by never leaving home without a (reliable!) army.

It seems to me that the argument we are looking at can establish at most that there are *some* cases in which the unborn person has a right to the use of its mother's body, and therefore *some* cases in which abortion is unjust killing. There is room for much discussion and argument as to precisely which, if any. But I think we should sidestep this issue and leave it open, for at any rate the argument certainly does not establish that all abortion is unjust killing.

5. There is room for yet another argument here, however. We surely must all grant that there may be cases in which it would be morally indecent to detach a person from your body at the cost of his life. Suppose you learn that what the violinist needs is not nine years of your life, but only one hour: all you need do to save his life is to spend one hour in that bed with him. Suppose also that letting him use your kidneys for that one hour would not affect your health in the slightest. Admittedly you were kidnapped. Admittedly you did not give anyone permission to plug him into you. Nevertheless it seems to me plain you *ought* to allow him to use your kidneys for that hour—it would be indecent to refuse.

Again, suppose pregnancy lasted only an hour, and constituted no threat to life or health. And suppose that a woman becomes pregnant as a result of rape. Admittedly she did not voluntarily do anything to bring about the existence of a child. Admittedly she did nothing at all which would give the unborn person a right to the use of her body. All the same it might well be said, as in the newly emended violinist story, that she *ought* to allow it to remain for that hour—that it would be indecent of her to refuse.

Now some people are inclined to use the term "right" in such a way that it follows from the fact that you ought to allow a person to use your body for the hour he needs, that he has a right to use your body for the hour he needs, even though he has not been given that right by any person or act. They may say that it follows also that if you refuse, you act unjustly toward him. This use of the term is perhaps so common that it cannot be called wrong; nevertheless it seems to me to be an unfortunate loosening of what we would do better to keep a tight rein on. Suppose that box of chocolates I mentioned earlier has not been given to both boys jointly, but was given only to the older boy. There he sits, stolidly eating his way through the box, his small

brother watching enviously. Here we are likely to say "You ought not to be so mean. You ought to give your brother some of those chocolates." My own view is that it just does not follow from the truth of this that the brother has any right to any of the chocolates. If the boy refuses to give his brother any, he is greedy, stingy, callous—but not unjust. I suppose that the people I have in mind will say it does follow that the brother has a right to some of the chocolates, and thus that the boy does act unjustly if he refuses to give his brother any. But the effect of saying this is to obscure what we should keep distinct, namely the difference between the boy's refusal in this case and the boy's refusal in the earlier case, in which the box was given to both boys jointly, and in which the small brother thus had what was from any point of view clear title to half.

A further objection to so using the term "right" that from the fact that A ought to do a thing for B, it follows that B has a right against A that A do it for him, is that it is going to make the question of whether or not a man has a right to a thing turn on how easy it is to provide him with it; and this seems not merely unfortunate, but morally unacceptable. Take the case of Henry Fonda again. I said earlier that I had no right to the touch of his cool hand on my fevered brow, even though I needed it to save my life. I said it would be frightfully nice of him to fly in from the West Coast to provide me with it, but that I had no right against him that he should do so. But suppose he isn't on the West Coast. Suppose he has only to walk across the room, place a hand briefly on my brow—and lo, my life is saved. Then surely he ought to do it, it would be indecent to refuse. Is it to be said "Ah, well, it follows that in this case she has a right to the touch of his hand on her brow, and so it would be an injustice in him to refuse"? So that I have a right to it when it is easy for him to provide it, though no right when it's hard? It's rather a shocking idea that anyone's rights should fade away and disappear as it gets harder and harder to accord them to him.

So my own view is that even though you ought to let the violinist use your kidneys for the one hour he needs, we should not conclude that he has a right to do so—we should say that if you refuse, you are, like the boy who owns all the chocolates and will give none away, self-centered and callous, indecent in fact, but not unjust. And similarly, that even supposing a case in which a woman pregnant due to rape ought to allow the unborn person to use her body for the hour he needs, we should not conclude that he has a right to do so; we should conclude that she is self-centered, callous, indecent, but not unjust, if she refuses. The complaints are no less grave; they are just different. However, there is no need to insist on this point. If anyone does wish to deduce "he has a right" from "you ought," then all the same he must surely grant that there are cases in which it is not morally required of you that you allow that violinist to use your kidneys, and in which he does not have a right to use them, and in which you do not do him an injustice if you refuse. And so also for mother and unborn child. Except in such cases as the unborn person has a right to demand it—and we were leaving open the possibility that there may be such cases—nobody is morally *required* to make large sacrifices, of health, of all other interests and concerns, of all other duties and commitments, for nine years, or even for nine months, in order to keep another person alive.

6. We have in fact to distinguish between two kinds of Samaritan: the Good Samaritan and what we might call the Minimally Decent Samaritan. The story of the Good Samaritan, you will remember, goes like this:

> A certain man went down from Jerusalem to Jericho, and fell among thieves, which stripped him of his raiment, and wounded him, and departed, leaving him half dead.
> And by chance there came down a cer-

> tain priest that way; and when he saw him, he passed by on the other side.
> And likewise a Levite, when he was at the place, came and looked on him, and passed by on the other side.
> But a certain Samaritan, as he journeyed, came where he was; and when he saw him he had compassion on him.
> And went to him, and bound up his wounds, pouring in oil and wine, and set him on his own beast, and brought him to an inn, and took care of him.
> And on the morrow, when he departed, he took out two pence, and gave them to the host, and said unto him, "Take care of him; and whatsoever thou spendest more, when I come again, I will repay thee."
> (Luke 10:30–35)

The Good Samaritan went out of his way, at some cost to himself, to help one in need of it. We are not told what the options were, that is, whether or not the priest and the Levite could have helped by doing less than the Good Samaritan did, but assuming they could have, then the fact they did nothing at all shows they were not even Minimally Decent Samaritans, not because they were not Samaritans, but because they were not even minimally decent.

These things are a matter of degree, of course, but there is a difference, and it comes out perhaps most clearly in the story of Kitty Genovese, who, as you will remember, was murdered while thirty-eight people watched or listened, and did nothing at all to help her. A Good Samaritan would have rushed out to give direct assistance against the murderer. Or perhaps we had better allow that it would have been a Splendid Samaritan who did this, on the ground that it would have involved a risk of death for himself. But the thirty-eight not only did not do this, they did not even trouble to pick up a phone to call the police. Minimally Decent Samaritanism would call for doing at least that, and their not having done it was monstrous.

After telling the story of the Good Samaritan, Jesus said "Go, and do thou likewise." Perhaps he meant that we are morally required to act as the Good Samaritan did. Perhaps he was urging people to do more than is morally required of them. At all events it seems plain that it was not morally required of any of the thirty-eight that he rush out to give direct assistance at the risk of his own life, and that it is not morally required of anyone that he give long stretches of his life—nine years or nine months—to sustaining the life of a person who has no special right (we were leaving open the possibility of this) to demand it.

Indeed, with one rather striking class of exceptions, no one in any country in the world is *legally* required to do anywhere near as much as this for anyone else. The class of exceptions is obvious. My main concern here is not the state of the law in respect to abortion, but it is worth drawing attention to the fact that in no state in this country is any man compelled by law to be even a Minimally Decent Samaritan to any person; there is no law under which charges could be brought against the thirty-eight who stood by while Kitty Genovese died. By contrast, in most states in this country women are compelled by law to be not merely Minimally Decent Samaritans, but Good Samaritans to unborn persons inside them. This doesn't by itself settle anything one way or the other, because it may well be argued that there should be laws in this country—as there are in many European countries—compelling at least Minimally Decent Samaritanism.[8] But it does show that there is a gross injustice in the existing state of the law. And it shows also that the groups currently working against liberalization of abortion laws, in fact working toward having it declared unconstitutional for a state to permit abortion, had better start working for the adoption of Good Samaritan laws generally, or earn the charge that they are acting in bad faith.

I should think, myself, that Minimally Decent Samaritan laws would be one thing, Good Samaritan laws quite another, and in fact highly improper. But we are not here concerned with the law. What we should ask is not whether anybody should be compelled by law to be a Good Samaritan, but whether we must accede to a situation in which somebody is being compelled—by nature, perhaps—to be a Good Samaritan. We have, in other words, to look now at third-party interventions. I have been arguing that no person is morally required to make large sacrifices to sustain the life of another who has no right to demand them, and this even where the sacrifices do not include life itself; we are not morally required to be Good Samaritans or anyway Very Good Samaritans to one another. But what if a man cannot extricate himself from such a situation? What if he appeals to us to extricate him? It seems to me plain that there are cases in which we can, cases in which a Good Samaritan would extricate him. There you are, you were kidnapped, and nine years in bed with that violinist lie ahead of you. You have your own life to lead. You are sorry, but you simply cannot see giving up so much of your life to the sustaining of his. You cannot extricate yourself, and ask us to do so. I should have thought that—in light of his having no right to the use of your body—it was obvious that we do not have to accede to your being forced to give up so much. We can do what you ask. There is no injustice to the violinist in our doing so.

7. Following the lead of the opponents of abortion, I have throughout been speaking of the fetus merely as a person, and what I have been asking is whether or not the argument we began with, which proceeds only from the fetus' being a person, really does establish its conclusion. I have argued that it does not.

But of course there are arguments and arguments, and it may be said that I have simply fastened on the wrong one. It may be said that what is important is not merely the fact that the fetus is a person, but that it is a person for whom the woman has a special kind of responsibility issuing from the fact that she is its mother. And it might be argued that all my analogies are therefore irrelevant—for you do not have that special kind of responsibility for that violinist, Henry Fonda does not have that special kind of responsibility for me. And our attention might be drawn to the fact that men and women both *are* compelled by law to provide support for their children.

I have in effect dealt (briefly) with this argument in section 4 above; but a (still briefer) recapitulation now may be in order. Surely we do not have any such "special responsibility" for a person unless we have assumed it, explicitly or implicitly. If a set of parents do not try to prevent pregnancy, do not obtain an abortion, and then at the time of birth of the child do not put it out for adoption, but rather take it home with them, then they have assumed responsibility for it, they have given it rights, and they cannot *now* withdraw support from it at the cost of its life because they now find it difficult to go on providing for it. But if they have taken all reasonable precautions against having a child, they do not simply by virtue of their biological relationship to the child who comes into existence have a special responsibility for it. They may wish to assume responsibility for it, or they may not wish to. And I am suggesting that if assuming responsibility for it would require large sacrifices, then they may refuse. A Good Samaritan would not refuse—or anyway, a Splendid Samaritan, if the sacrifices that had to be made were enormous. But then so would a Good Samaritan assume responsibility for that violinist; so would Henry Fonda, if he is a Good Samaritan, fly in from the West Coast and assume responsibility for me.

8. My argument will be found unsatisfactory on two counts by many of those who want to regard abortion as morally permissible. First, while I do argue that abortion is not impermissible, I do not argue that it is always permissible. There may well be cases in which carrying the child to term requires only Minimally Decent Samaritanism of the mother, and this is a standard we must not fall below. I am inclined to think it a merit of my account precisely that it does *not* give a general yes or a general no. It allows for and supports our sense that, for example, a sick and desperately frightened fourteen-year-old schoolgirl, pregnant due to rape, may *of course* choose abortion, and that any law which rules this out is an insane law. And it also allows for and supports our sense that in other cases resort to abortion is even positively indecent. It would be indecent in the woman to request an abortion, and indecent in a doctor to perform it, if she is in her seventh month, and wants the abortion just to avoid the nuisance of postponing a trip abroad. The very fact that the arguments I have been drawing attention to treat all cases of abortion, or even all cases of abortion in which the mother's life is not at stake, as morally on a par ought to have made them suspect at the outset.

Secondly, while I am arguing for the permissibility of abortion in some cases, I am not arguing for the right to secure the death of the unborn child. It is easy to confuse these two things in that up to a certain point in the life of the fetus it is not able to survive outside the mother's body; hence removing it from her body guarantees its death. But they are importantly different. I have argued that you are not morally required to spend nine months in bed, sustaining the life of that violinist; but to say this is by no means to say that if, when you unplug yourself, there is a miracle and he survives, you then have a right to turn round and slit his throat. You may detach yourself even if this costs him his life; you have no right to be guaranteed his death, by some other means, if unplugging yourself does not kill him. There are some people who will feel dissatisfied by this feature of my argument. A woman may be utterly devastated by the thought of a child, a bit of herself, put out for adoption and never seen or heard of again. She may therefore want not merely that the child be detached from her, but more, that it die. Some opponents of abortion are inclined to regard this as beneath contempt—thereby showing insensitivity to what is surely a powerful source of despair. All the same, I agree that the desire for the child's death is not one which anybody may gratify, should it turn out to be possible to detach the child alive.

At this place, however, it should be remembered that we have only been pretending throughout that the fetus is a human being from the moment of conception. A very early abortion is surely not the killing of a person, and so is not dealt with by anything I have said here.

Notes

1 I am very much indebted to James Thomson for discussion, criticism, and many helpful suggestions.

2 Daniel Callahan, *Abortion: Law, Choice and Morality* (New York, 1970), p. 373. This book gives a fascinating survey of the available information on abortion. The Jewish tradition is surveyed in David M. Feldman, *Birth Control in Jewish Law* (New York, 1968), Part 5; the Catholic tradition in John T. Noonan, Jr., "An Almost Absolute Value in History," in *The Morality of Abortion*, ed. John T. Noonan, Jr. (Cambridge, Mass., 1970)....

3 The term "direct" in the arguments I refer to is a technical one. Roughly, what is meant by "direct killing" is either killing as an end in itself, or killing as a means of some end, for example, the end of saving someone else's life. See footnote 6 for an example of its use.

4 Cf. *Encyclical Letter of Pope Pius XI on Christian Marriage*, St. Paul Editions (Boston, n.d.), p. 32: "however much we may pity the mother whose health and even life is gravely imperiled in the performance of the duty allotted to her by nature, nevertheless what could ever be a sufficient reason for excusing in any way the direct murder of the innocent? This is precisely what we are dealing with here." Noonan (*The Morality of Abortion*, p. 43) reads this as follows: "What cause can ever avail to excuse in any way the direct killing of the innocent? For it is a question of that."

5 The thesis in (4) is in an interesting way weaker than those in (1), (2), and (3): they rule out abortion even in cases in which both mother and child will die if the abortion is not performed. By contrast, one who held the view expressed in (4) could consistently say that one needn't prefer letting two persons die to killing one.

6 Cf. the following passage from Pius XII, *Address to the Italian Catholic Society of Midwives*: "The baby in the maternal breast has the right to life immediately from God.—Hence there is no man, no human authority, no science, no medical, eugenic, social, economic or moral 'indication' which can establish or grant a valid juridical ground for a direct deliberate disposition of an innocent human life, that is a disposition which looks to its destruction either as an end or as a means to another end perhaps in itself not illicit.—The baby, still not born, is a man in the same degree and for the same reason as the mother" (quoted in Noonan, *The Morality of Abortion*, p. 45).

7 The need for a discussion of this argument was brought home to me by members of the Society for Ethical and Legal Philosophy, to whom this paper was originally presented.

8 For a discussion of the difficulties involved, and a survey of the European experience with such laws, see *The Good Samaritan and the Law*, ed. James M. Ratcliffe (New York, 1966).

Questions for Discussion

1 Is the "violinist" example a good analogy for a pregnant woman? In what ways are the cases alike, and in what ways are they unlike each other? What about the examples of people entering one's home through the window?

2 Is there a difference between the claim that it would be morally indecent for a person to deny a second person something, and the claim that the second person has a *right* to that thing? How should the notion of something's being "morally indecent" be interpreted?

Abortion Through a Feminist Ethics Lens

Susan Sherwin

*In this selection from her book, **No Longer Patient: Feminist Ethics and Health Care**, Sherwin argues that the issue of abortion is linked to the general struggle for women to overcome patriarchy and control their own sexuality and reproduction. Sherwin argues against the common view of pregnant women as mere passive containers of fetuses, or as adversaries of the fetuses. Instead, Sherwin claims we should focus on relationships for moral purposes, and ensure adequate support and health care so as to allow individual women to make their own choices concerning abortion and reproduction.*

★   ★   ★

Women and Abortion

The most obvious difference between feminist and nonfeminist approaches to abortion lies in the relative attention each gives in its analysis to the interests and experiences of women. Feminist analysis regards the effects of unwanted pregnancies on the lives of women individually and collectively as the central element in the moral examination of abortion; it is considered self-evident that the pregnant woman is the subject of principal concern in abortion decisions. In many nonfeminist accounts, however, not only is the pregnant woman not perceived as central, she is often rendered virtually invisible. Nonfeminist theorists, whether they support or oppose women's right to choose abortion, generally focus almost all their attention on the moral status of the fetus.[1]

In pursuing a distinctively feminist ethic, it is appropriate to begin with a look at the role of abortion in women's lives. The need for abortion can be very intense; no matter how appalling and dangerous the conditions, women from widely diverse cultures and historical periods have pursued abortions. No one denies that if abortion is not made legal, safe, and accessible in our society, women will seek out illegal and life-threatening abortions to terminate pregnancies they cannot accept. Antiabortion activists seem willing to accept this cost, although liberals definitely are not; feminists, who explicitly value women, judge the inevitable loss of women's lives that results from restrictive abortion policies to be a matter of fundamental concern.

Antiabortion campaigners imagine that women often make frivolous and irresponsible decisions about abortion, but feminists recognize that women have abortions for a wide variety of compelling reasons. Some women, for instance, find themselves seriously ill and incapacitated throughout pregnancy; they cannot continue in their jobs and may face insurmountable difficulties in fulfilling their responsibilities at home. Many employers and schools will not tolerate pregnancy in their employees or students, and not every woman is able to put her job, career, or studies on hold. Women of limited means may be unable to take adequate care of children they have already borne, and they may know that another mouth to feed will reduce their ability to provide for their existing children. Women who suffer from chronic disease, who believe themselves too young or too old to have children, or who are unable to maintain lasting relationships may recognize that they will not be able to care properly for a child when they face the decision. Some who are homeless, addicted to drugs, or diagnosed as carrying the AIDS virus may be unwilling to allow a child to enter the world with the handicaps that would result from the mother's condition. If the fetus is a result of rape or incest, then the psychological pain of carrying it may be unbearable, and the woman may recognize that her attitude to the child after birth will be tinged with bitterness. Some women learn that the fetuses that they carry have serious chromosomal anomalies and consider it best to prevent them from being born with a condition that is bound to cause them to suffer. Others, knowing the fathers to be brutal and violent, may be unwilling to subject a child to the beatings or incestuous attacks they anticipate; some may have no other realistic way to remove the child (or themselves) from the relationship.[2]

Finally, a woman may simply believe that bearing a child is incompatible with her life plans at the time. Continuing a pregnancy may have devastating repercussions throughout a woman's life. If the woman is young, then a pregnancy will likely reduce her chances of pursuing an education and hence limit her career and life opportunities: "The earlier a woman has a baby, it seems, the more likely she is to drop out of school; the less education she gets, the more likely she is to remain poorly paid, peripheral to the labor market, or unemployed, and the more children she will have" (Petchesky 1985, 150). In many circumstances, having a child will exacerbate the social and economic forces already stacked against a woman by virtue of her sex (and her race, class, age, sexual orientation, disabilities, and so forth). Access to abortion is necessary for many women if they are to escape the oppressive conditions of poverty.[3]

Whatever the specific reasons are for abortion, most feminists believe that the women concerned are in the best position to judge whether abortion is the appropriate response to a pregnancy. Because usually only the woman choosing abortion is properly situated to weigh all the relevant factors, most feminists resist attempts to offer general, abstract rules for determining when abortion is morally justified.[4] Women's personal deliberations about abortion involve contextually defined considerations that reflect their commitments to the needs and interests of everyone concerned, including themselves, the fetuses they carry, other members of their household, and so forth. Because no single formula is available for balancing these complex factors through all possible cases, it is vital that feminists insist on protecting each woman's right to come to her own conclusions and resist the attempts of other philosophers and moralists to set the agenda for these considerations. Feminists stress that women must be acknowledged as full moral agents, responsible for making moral decisions about their own pregnancies. Women may sometimes make mistakes in their moral judgments, but no one else can be assumed to have the authority to evaluate and overrule their judgments.[5]

Even without patriarchy, bearing a child would be a very important event in a woman's life, because it involves significant physical, emotional, social, and (usually) economic changes for her. The ability to exert control over the incidence, timing, and frequency of childbearing is often tied to a woman's ability to control most other things she values. Because we live in a patriarchal society, it is especially important to ensure that women have the authority to control their own reproduction.[6] Despite the diversity of opinion found among feminists on most other matters, most feminists agree that women must gain full control over their own reproductive lives if they are to free themselves from male dominance.[7]

Moreover, women's freedom to choose abortion is linked to their ability to control their own sexuality. Women's subordinate status often prevents them from refusing men sexual access to their bodies. If women cannot end the unwanted pregnancies that result from male sexual dominance, then their sexual vulnerability to particular men may increase, because caring for an(other) infant involves greater financial needs and reduced economic opportunities for women.[8] As a result, pregnancy often forces women to become dependent on particular men. Because a woman's dependence on a man is assumed to entail her continued sexual loyalty to him, restriction of abortion serves to commit women to remaining sexually accessible to particular men and thus helps to perpetuate the cycle of oppression.

In contrast to most nonfeminist accounts, feminist analyses of abortion direct attention to how women get pregnant. Those who reject abortion seem to believe that women can avoid unwanted pregnancies "simply" by avoiding sexual intercourse. These views show little appreciation for the power of sexual politics in a culture that oppresses women. Existing patterns of sexual dominance mean that women often have little control over their sexual lives. They may be subject to rape by their husbands, boyfriends, colleagues, employers, customers, fathers, brothers, uncles, and dates, as well as by strangers. Often the sexual coercion is not even recognized as such by the participants but is the price of continued "good will"—popularity, economic survival, peace, or simple acceptance. Many women have found themselves in circumstances where they do not feel free to refuse a man's demands for intercourse, either because he is holding a gun to her head or because he threatens to be emotionally hurt if she refuses (or both). Women are socialized to be compliant and accommodating, sensitive to the feelings of others, and frightened of physical power; men are socialized to take advantage of every opportunity to engage in sexual intercourse and to use sex to express dominance and power. Under such circumstances, it is difficult to argue that women could simply

"choose" to avoid heterosexual activity if they wish to avoid pregnancy. Catharine MacKinnon neatly sums it up: "The logic by which women are supposed to consent to sex [is]: preclude the alternatives, then call the remaining option 'her choice'" (MacKinnon 1989, 192).

Furthermore, women cannot rely on birth control to avoid pregnancy. No form of contraception that is fully safe and reliable is available, other than sterilization; because women may wish only to avoid pregnancy temporarily, not permanently, sterilization is not always an acceptable choice. The pill and the IUD are the most effective contraceptive means offered, but both involve significant health hazards to women and are quite dangerous for some.[9] No woman should spend the thirty to forty years of her reproductive life on either form of birth control. Further, both have been associated with subsequent problems of involuntary infertility, so they are far from optimal for women who seek to control the timing of their pregnancies.

The safest form of birth control involves the use of barrier methods (condoms and diaphragms) in combination with spermicidal foams or jelly. But these methods also pose difficulties for women. They are sometimes socially awkward to use. Young women are discouraged from preparing for sexual activity that might never happen and offered instead romantic models of spontaneous passion; few films or novels interrupt scenes of seduction for a partner to fetch contraceptives. Many women find their male partners unwilling to use barrier methods of contraception, and they often find themselves in no position to insist. Further, cost is a limiting factor for many women. Condoms and spermicides are expensive and are not covered under most health care plans.[10] Only one contraceptive option offers women safe and fully effective birth control: barrier methods with the back-up option of abortion.[11]

From a feminist perspective, the central moral feature of pregnancy is that it takes place in women's bodies and has profound effects on women's lives. Gender-neutral accounts of pregnancy are not available; pregnancy is explicitly a condition associated with the female body.[12] Because only women experience a need for abortion, policies about abortion affect women uniquely. Therefore, it is important to consider how proposed policies on abortion fit into general patterns of oppression for women. Unlike nonfeminist accounts, feminist ethics demands that the effects of abortion policies on the oppression of women be of principal consideration in our ethical evaluations.

The Fetus

In contrast to feminist ethics, most nonfeminist analysts believe that the moral acceptability of abortion turns entirely on the question of the moral status of the fetus. Even those who support women's right to choose abortion tend to accept the premise of the antiabortion proponents that abortion can be tolerated only if we can first prove that the fetus lacks full personhood.[13] Opponents of abortion demand that we define the status of the fetus either as a being that is valued in the same way as other humans and hence is entitled not to be killed or as a being that lacks in all value. Rather than challenging the logic of this formulation, many defenders of abortion have concentrated on showing that the fetus is indeed without significant value (Tooley 1972, Warren 1973); others, such as L.W. Sumner (1981), offer a more subtle account that reflects the gradual development of fetuses and distinguishes between early fetal stages, where the relevant criterion for personhood is absent, and later stages, where it is present. Thus the debate often rages between abortion opponents, who describe the fetus as an "innocent," vulnerable, morally

important, separate being whose life is threatened and who must be protected at all costs, and abortion supporters, who try to establish that fetuses are deficient in some critical respect and hence are outside the scope of the moral community. In both cases, however, the nature of the fetus as an independent being is said to determine the moral status of abortion.

The woman on whom the fetus depends for survival is considered as secondary (if she is considered at all) in these debates. The actual experiences and responsibilities of real women are not perceived as morally relevant to the debate, unless these women too, can be proved innocent by establishing that their pregnancies are a result of rape or incest.[14] In some contexts, women's role in gestation is literally reduced to that of "fetal containers"; the individual women disappear or are perceived simply as mechanical life-support systems.[15]

The current rhetoric against abortion stresses that the genetic makeup of the fetus is determined at conception and the genetic code is incontestably human. Lest there be any doubt about the humanity of the fetus, we are assailed with photographs of fetuses at various stages of development that demonstrate the early appearance of recognizably human characteristics, such as eyes, fingers, and toes. Modern ultrasound technology is used to obtain "baby's first picture" and stimulate bonding between pregnant women and their fetuses (Petchesky 1987). That the fetus in its early stages is microscopic, virtually indistinguishable to the untrained eye from fetuses of other species, and lacking in the capacities that make human life meaningful and valuable is not deemed relevant by the self-appointed defenders of the fetus. The antiabortion campaign is directed at evoking sympathetic attitudes toward a tiny, helpless being whose life is threatened by its own mother; the fetus is characterized as a being entangled in an adversarial relationship with the (presumably irresponsible) woman who carries it (Overall

1987). People are encouraged to identify with the "unborn child," not with the woman whose life is also at issue.

In the nonfeminist literature, both defenders and opponents of women's right to choose abortion agree that the difference between a late-term fetus and a newborn infant is "merely geographical" and cannot be considered morally significant. Daniel Callahan (1986), for instance, maintains a pro-choice stand but professes increasing uneasiness about this position in light of new medical and scientific developments that increase our knowledge of embryology and hasten the date of potential viability for fetuses; he insists that defenders of women's right to choose must come to terms with the question of the fetus and the effects of science on the fetus's prospects apart from the woman who carries it. Arguments that focus on the similarities between infants and fetuses, however, generally fail to acknowledge that a fetus inhabits a woman's body and is wholly dependent on her unique contribution to its maintenance, whereas a newborn is physically independent, although still in need of a lot of care.[16] One can only view the distinction between being in or out of a woman's womb as morally irrelevant if one discounts the perspective of the pregnant woman; feminists seem to be alone in recognizing the woman's perspective as morally important to the distinction.[17]

In antiabortion arguments, fetuses are identified as individuals; in our culture, which views the (abstract) individual as sacred, fetuses qua individuals are to be honored and preserved. Extraordinary claims are made to establish the individuality and moral agency of fetuses. At the same time, the women who carry these fetal individuals are viewed as passive hosts whose only significant role is to refrain from aborting or harming their fetuses. Because it is widely believed that a woman does not actually have to do anything to protect the life of her fetus, pregnancy is often

considered (abstractly) to be a tolerable burden to protect the life of an individual so like us.[18]

Medicine has played its part in supporting these attitudes. Fetal medicine is a rapidly expanding specialty, and it is commonplace in professional medical journals to find references to pregnant women as "the maternal environment." Fetal surgeons now have at their disposal a repertoire of sophisticated technology that can save the lives of dangerously ill fetuses; in light of the excitement of such heroic successes, it is perhaps understandable that women have disappeared from their view. These specialists see the fetuses as their patients, not the women who nurture the fetuses. As the "active" agents in saving fetal lives (unlike the pregnant women, whose role is seen as purely passive), doctors perceive themselves as developing independent relationships with the fetuses they treat. Barbara Katz Rothman observes: "The medical model of pregnancy, as an essentially parasitic and vaguely pathological relationship, encourages the physician to view the fetus and mother as two separate patients, and to see pregnancy as inherently a conflict of interests between the two" (Rothman 1986, 25).

Perhaps even more distressing than the tendency to ignore the woman's agency altogether and view her as a passive participant in the medically controlled events of pregnancy and childbirth is the growing practice of viewing women as genuine threats to the well-being of the fetus. Increasingly, women are described as irresponsible or hostile toward their fetuses, and the relationship between them is characterized as adversarial. Concern for the well-being of the fetus is taken as license for doctors to intervene to ensure that women comply with medical "advice." Courts are called upon to enforce the doctors' orders when moral pressure alone proves inadequate, and women are being coerced into undergoing unwanted cesarean deliveries and technologically monitored hospital births (Annas

1982; Rodgers 1989; Nelson and Milliken 1990). Some states have begun to imprison women for endangering their fetuses through drug abuse and other socially unacceptable behaviors (Annas 1986). Mary Ann Warren reports that a bill was recently introduced in an Australian state that makes women liable to criminal prosecution "if they are found to have smoked during pregnancy, eaten unhealthful foods, or taken any other action which can be shown to have adversely affected the development of the fetus" (Warren 1989, 60).

In other words, some physicians have joined antiabortion campaigners in fostering a cultural acceptance of the view that fetuses are distinct individuals who are physically, ontologically, and socially separate from the women whose bodies they inhabit and that they have their own distinct interests. In this picture, pregnant women are either ignored altogether or are viewed as deficient in some crucial respect, and hence they can be subject to coercion for the sake of their fetuses. In the former case, the interests of the women concerned are assumed to be identical with those of the fetus; in the latter, the women's interests are irrelevant, because they are perceived as immoral, unimportant, or unnatural. Focus on the fetus as an independent entity has led to presumptions that deny pregnant women their roles as active, independent, moral agents with a primary interest in what becomes of the fetuses they carry. The moral question of the fetus's status is quickly translated into a license to interfere with women's reproductive freedom.

A Feminist View of the Fetus

Because the public debate has been set up as a competition between the rights of women and those of fetuses, feminists have often felt pushed to reject claims of fetal value, in order to protect women's needs. As Kathryn Addelson (1987) has argued, however, view-ing abortion in this way "rips it out of the context of women's lives." Other accounts of fetal value are more plausible and less oppressive to women.

On a feminist account fetal development is examined in the context in which it occurs, within women's bodies, rather than in the isolation of imagined abstraction. Fetuses develop in specific pregnancies that occur in the lives of particular women. They are not individuals housed in generic female wombs or full persons at risk only because they are small and subject to the whims of women. Their very existence is relationally defined, reflecting their development within particular women's bodies; that relationship gives those women reason to be concerned about them. Many feminists argue against a perspective that regards the fetus as an independent being and suggest that a more accurate and valuable understanding of pregnancy would involve regarding the pregnant women "as a biological and social unit" (Rothman 1986, 25).

On this view, fetuses are morally significant, but their status is relational rather than absolute. Unlike other human beings, fetuses do not have any independent existence; their existence is uniquely tied to the support of a specific other. Most nonfeminist accounts have ignored the relational dimension of fetal development and have presumed that the moral status of fetuses could be resolved solely in terms of abstract, metaphysical criteria of personhood as applied to the fetus alone (Tooley 1972; Warren 1973). Throughout much of the nonfeminist literature, commentators argue that some set of properties (such as genetic heritage, moral agency, self-consciousness, language use, or self-determination) will entitle all who possess it to be granted the moral status of persons. They seek some feature by which we can neatly divide the world into moral persons (who are to be valued and protected) and others (who are not entitled to the same group privileges).

This vision, however, misinterprets what is involved in personhood and what is especially valued about persons. Personhood is a social category, not an isolated state. Persons are members of a community, and they should be valued in their concrete, discrete, and different states as specific individuals, not merely as conceptually undifferentiated entities. To be a morally significant category, personhood must involve personality as well as biological integrity.[19] It is not sufficient to consider persons simply as Kantian atoms of rationality, because persons are embodied, conscious beings with particular social histories. Annette Baier has developed a concept of persons as "second persons," which helps explain the sort of social dimension that seems fundamental to any moral notion of personhood:

> A person, perhaps, is best seen as one who was long enough dependent upon other persons to acquire the essential arts of personhood. Persons essentially are *second* persons, who grow up with other persons ... The fact that a person has a life *history,* and that a people collectively have a history depends upon the humbler fact that each person has a childhood in which a cultural heritage is transmitted, ready for adolescent rejection and adult discriminating, selection and contribution. Persons come after and before other persons (Baier 1985: 84–5).

Persons, in other words, are members of a social community that shapes and values them, and personhood is a relational concept that must be defined in terms of interactions and relationships with others.[20]

Because humans are fundamentally relational beings, it is important to remember that fetuses are characteristically limited in the "relationships" in which they can "participate"; within those relationships, they can make only the most restricted "contributions."[21] After birth human beings are capable of a much wider range of roles in relationships with a broad variety of partners; that very diversity of possibility and experience leads us to focus on the abstraction of the individual as a constant through all these different relationships. Until birth, however, no such variety is possible, so the fetus must be understood as part of a complex entity that includes the woman who currently sustains the fetus and who will, most likely, be principally responsible for it for many years to come.

A fetus is a unique sort of human entity, then, for it cannot form relationships freely with others, and others cannot readily form relationships with it. A fetus has a primary and particularly intimate sort of "relationship" with the woman in whose womb it developed; connections with any other persons are necessarily indirect and must be mediated through the pregnant woman. The relationship that exists between a woman and her fetus is clearly asymmetrical, because she is the only party to it who is capable of even considering whether the interaction should continue; further, the fetus is wholly dependent on the woman who sustains it, whereas she is quite capable of surviving without it.

Most feminist views of what is valuable about persons reflect the social nature of individual existence. No human, especially no fetus, can exist apart from relationships; efforts to speak of the fetus itself, as if it were not inseparable from the women in whom it develops, are distorting and dishonest. Fetuses have a unique physical status—within and dependent on particular women. That gives them also a unique social status. However much some might prefer it to be otherwise, no one other than the pregnant woman in question can do anything to support or harm a fetus without doing something to the woman who nurtures it. Because of this inexorable biological reality, the responsibility and privilege of determining a fetus's special social status and value must rest with the woman carrying it.

Many pregnancies occur to women who place a very high value on the lives of the particular fetuses they carry and choose to see their pregnancies through to term, despite the possible risks and costs involved; it would be wrong of anyone to force such a woman to terminate her pregnancy. Other women, or some of these same women at other times, value other things more highly (for example, their freedom, their health, or previous responsibilities that conflict with those generated by the pregnancies), and so they choose not to continue their pregnancies. The value that women ascribe to individual fetuses varies dramatically from case to case and may well change over the course of any particular pregnancy. The fact that fetal lives can neither be sustained nor destroyed without affecting the women who support them implies that whatever value others may attach to fetuses generally or to specific fetuses individually should not be allowed to outweigh the ranking that is assigned to them by the pregnant women themselves.

No absolute value attaches to fetuses apart from their relational status, which is determined in the context of their particular development. This is not the same, however, as saying that they have no value at all or that they have merely instrumental value, as some liberals suggest. The value that women place on their own fetuses is the sort of value that attaches to an emerging human relationship.

Nevertheless, fetuses are not persons, because they have not developed sufficiently in their capacity for social relationships to be persons in any morally significant sense (that is, they are not yet second persons). In this way they differ from newborns, who immediately begin to develop into persons by virtue of their place as subjects in human relationships; newborns are capable of some forms of communication and response. The moral status of fetuses is determined by the nature of their primary relationship and the value that is cre-

ated there. Therefore, feminist accounts of abortion emphasize the importance of protecting women's rights to continue or to terminate pregnancies as each sees fit.

The Politics of Abortion

Feminist accounts explore the connections between particular social policies and the general patterns of power relationships in our society. With respect to abortion in this framework, Mary Daly observes that "one hundred percent of the bishops who oppose the repeal of antiabortion laws are men and one hundred percent of the people who have abortions are women.... To be comprehended accurately, they [arguments against abortion] must be seen within the context of sexually hierarchical society" (Daly 1973, 106).

Antiabortion activists appeal to arguments about the unconditional value of human life. When we examine their rhetoric more closely, however, we find other ways of interpreting their agenda. In addition to their campaign to criminalize abortion, most abortion opponents condemn all forms of sexual relations outside of heterosexual marriage, and they tend to support patriarchal patterns of dominance within such marriages. Many are distressed that liberal abortion policies support permissive sexuality by allowing women to "get away with" sex outside of marriage. They perceive that ready access to abortion supports women's independence from men.[22]

Although nonfeminist participants in the abortion debates often discount the significance of its broader political dimensions, both feminists and antifeminists consider them crucial. The intensity of the antiabortion movement correlates closely with the increasing strength of feminism in achieving greater equality for women. The original American campaign against abortion can be traced to the middle of the nineteenth century, that is, to the time of the first significant feminist movement in the United States (Luker 1984). Today abortion is widely perceived as supportive of increased freedom and power for women. The campaign against abortion intensified in the 1970s, which was a period of renewed interest in feminism. As Rosalind Petchesky observes, the campaign rested on some powerful symbols: "To feminists and antifeminists alike, it came to represent the image of the 'emancipated woman' in her contemporary identity, focused on her education and work more than on marriage or childbearing; sexually active outside marriage and outside the disciplinary boundaries of the parental family; independently supporting herself and her children; and consciously espousing feminist ideas" (Petchesky 1986, 241). Clearly, much more than the lives of fetuses is at stake in the power struggle over abortion.

When we place abortion in the larger political context, we see that most of the groups active in the struggle to prohibit abortion also support other conservative measures to maintain the forms of dominance that characterize patriarchy (and often class and racial oppression as well). The movement against abortion is led by the Catholic church and other conservative religious institutions, which explicitly endorse not only fetal rights but also male dominance in the home and the church. Most opponents of abortion also oppose virtually all forms of birth control and all forms of sexuality other than monogamous, reproductive sex; usually, they also resist having women assume positions of authority in the dominant public institutions (Luker 1984). Typically, antiabortion activists support conservative economic measures that protect the interests of the privileged classes of society and ignore the needs of the oppressed and disadvantaged (Petchesky 1985). Although they stress their commitment to preserving life, many systematically work to dismantle key social programs that provide life necessities to the underclass. Moreover, some current campaigns against

abortion retain elements of the racism that dominated the North American abortion literature in the early years of the twentieth century, wherein abortion was opposed on the grounds that it amounted to racial suicide on the part of whites.[23]

In the eyes of its principal opponents, then, abortion is not an isolated practice; their opposition to abortion is central to a set of social values that runs counter to feminism's objectives. Hence antiabortion activists generally do not offer alternatives to abortion that support feminist interests in overturning the patterns of oppression that confront women. Most deny that there are any legitimate grounds for abortion, short of the need to save a woman's life—and some are not even persuaded by this criterion (Nicholson 1977). They believe that any pregnancy can and should be endured. If the mother is unable or unwilling to care for the child after birth, then they assume that adoption can be easily arranged.

It is doubtful, however, that adoptions are possible for every child whose mother cannot care for it. The world abounds with homeless orphans; even in the industrialized West, where there is a waiting list for adoption of healthy (white) babies, suitable homes cannot always be found for troubled adolescents, inner-city, AIDS babies, or many of the multiply handicapped children whose parents may have tried to care for them but whose marriages broke under the strain.

Furthermore, even if an infant were born healthy and could be readily adopted, we must recognize that surrendering one's child for adoption is an extremely difficult act for most women. The bond that commonly forms between women and their fetuses over the full term of pregnancy is intimate and often intense; many women find that it is not easily broken after birth. Psychologically, for many women adoption is a far more difficult response to unwanted pregnancies than abortion. Therefore, it is misleading to describe pregnancy as merely a nine-month commitment; for most women, seeing a pregnancy through to term involves a lifetime of responsibility and involvement with the resulting child and, in the overwhelming majority of cases, disproportionate burden on the woman through the child-rearing years. An ethics that cares about women would recognize that abortion is often the only acceptable recourse for them.

Expanding the Agenda

The injunction of feminist ethics to consider abortion in the context of other issues of power and oppression means that we need to look beyond the standard questions of its moral and legal acceptability. This implies, for instance, that we need to explore the moral imperatives of ensuring that abortion services are actually available to all women who seek them. Although medically approved abortions are technically recognized as legal (at least for the moment) in both Canada and the United States, many women who need abortions cannot obtain them; accessibility is still associated with wealth and privilege in many regions.[24] In Canada vast geographical areas offer no abortion services at all, so unless the women of those regions can afford to travel to urban clinics, they have no meaningful right to abortion. In the United States, where there is no universal health insurance, federal legislation (under the Hyde amendment) explicitly denies the use of public money for abortions. Full ethical discussion of abortion reveals the necessity of removing the economic, age, and racial barriers that currently restrict access to medically acceptable abortion services.[25]

The moral issues extend yet further. Feminism demands respect for women's choices; even if the legal and financial barriers could be surpassed, this condition may remain unmet. The focus of many political campaigns for abortion rights has been to make abortion a matter of medical, not personal, choice, suggesting that doctors (but not necessarily women) can be trusted to choose responsibly. Feminists must insist on respect for women's moral agency. Therefore, feminism requires that abortion services be provided in an atmosphere that is supportive of the choices that women make. This could be achieved by offering abortions in centers that deal with all matters of reproductive health in an open, patient-centered manner, where respectful counseling on all aspects of reproductive health is available.[26]

Furthermore, the moral issues surrounding abortion include questions of how women are treated when they seek abortions. All too frequently hospital-based abortions are provided by practitioners who are uneasy about their role and treat the women involved with hostility and resentment.[27] Health care workers involved in providing abortions must recognize that abortion is a legitimate option that should be carried out with respect and concern for the physical, psychological, and emotional well-being of the patient. In addition, we need to turn our moral attention to the effects of antiabortion protests on women. Increasingly, many antiabortion activists have personalized their attacks and focused their energies on harassing the women who enter and leave abortion clinics, thereby requiring them to pass a gauntlet of hostile protesters to obtain abortions. Such arrangements are not conducive to positive health care, so these protests, too, must be subject to moral criticism within the ethics of health care.

Feminist ethics promotes the value of reproductive freedom, which is defined as the condition under which women are able to make truly voluntary choices about their reproductive lives. Women must have control over their reproduction if patriarchal dominance over women is to be brought to an end. In addition to reliable and caring abortion services, then, women also need access to safe and effective birth control, which would provide them with other means of avoiding pregnancy.[28]

Moreover, we must raise questions about the politics of sexual domination in this context. Many men support women's right to abortion because they perceive that if women believe that they can engage in intercourse without having to accept an unwanted pregnancy, they will become more sexually available. Some of the women who oppose abortion resist it for this very reason; they do not want to support a practice that increases women's sexual vulnerability. Feminists need to develop an analysis of reproductive freedom that includes sexual freedom as it is defined by women, not men. Such an analysis would, for example, include women's right to refuse sex. Because this right can only be assured if women have power equal to men's and are not subject to domination because of their sex, women's freedom from oppression is itself an element of reproductive freedom. Finally, it is important to stress that feminist accounts do not deny that fetuses have value. They ask that fetuses be recognized as existing within women's pregnancies and not as separate, isolated entities. Feminists positively value fetuses that are wanted by the women who carry them; they vigorously oppose practices that force women to have abortions they do not want. No women should be subjected to coerced abortion or sterilization. Women must be assured of adequate financial and support services for the care of their children, so that they are not forced to abort fetuses that they would otherwise choose to carry. Further, voluntarily pregnant women should have access to suitable pre- and postnatal care and nutrition, lest wanted fetuses be unnecessarily harmed or lost.

Feminists perceive that far more could be done to protect and care for fetuses if the state directed its resources toward supporting women who choose to continue their pregnancies, rather than draining those resources to police the women who try to terminate undesired pregnancies. Unlike their conservative counterparts, feminists recognize that caring for the women who maintain the lives of fetuses is not only a more legitimate policy than is regulating them but also probably more effective at ensuring the health and well-being of more fetuses and, ultimately, of more infants.

In sum, then, feminist ethics demands that moral discussions of abortion reflect a broader agenda than is usually found in the arguments put forth by bioethicists. Only by reflecting on the meaning of ethical pronouncements on actual women's lives and the connections that exist between judgments on abortion and the conditions of domination and subordination can we come to an adequate understanding of the moral status of abortion in a particular society.

Notes

1 Technically, the term "fetus" does not cover the entire period of development. Medical practitioners prefer to distinguish between differing stages of development with such terms as "conceptus," "embryo" (and, recently, "pre-embryo"), and fetus. Because these distinctions are not relevant to the discussion here, I follow the course common to discussions in bioethics and feminism and use the term "fetus" to cover the entire period of development from conception to the end of pregnancy through either birth or abortion.

2 Bearing a child can keep a woman within a man's sphere of influence against her will. The Canadian news media were dominated in the summer of 1989 by the story of Chantel Daigle, a Quebec woman who faced injunctions granted to her former boyfriend by two lower courts against her choice of abortion before she was finally given permission for abortion by the Supreme Court of Canada. Daigle's explanation to the media of her determination to abort stressed her recognition that if she were forced to bear this child, she would never be free from the violent father's involvement in her life.

3 Feminists believe that it is wrong of society to make childbearing a significant cause of poverty in women, but the reality of our social and economic structures in North America is that it does. In addition to their campaigns for greater repro-

ductive freedom for women, feminists also struggle to ensure that women receive greater support
in child-rearing; in efforts to provide financial stability and support services to those who provide
care for children, feminists would welcome the
support of those in the antiabortion movement
who sincerely want to reduce the numbers of
abortions.

4 Among the exceptions here, see Overall (1987),
who seems willing to specify some conditions
under which abortion is immoral (78–79).

5 Critics continue to base the debate on the possibility that women might make frivolous abortion
decisions; hence they want feminists to agree to
setting boundaries on acceptable grounds for
choosing abortion. Feminists, however, should resist this injunction. There is no practical way of
drawing a line fairly in the abstract; cases that may
appear "frivolous" at a distance often turn out to
be substantive when the details are revealed. There
is no evidence to suggest that women actually
make the sorts of choices worried critics hypoth-
esize about: for example, the decision of a woman
eight months pregnant to abort because she wants
to take a trip or gets in "a tiff" with her partner.
These sorts of fantasies, on which demands to distinguish between legitimate and illegitimate personal reasons for choosing abortion rest, reflect an
offensive conception of women as irresponsible.
They ought not to be perpetuated. Women seeking moral guidance in their own deliberations
about choosing abortion do not find such hypothetical discussions of much use.

6 In her monumental historical analysis of the early
roots of Western patriarchy, Lerner (1986) determined that patriarchy began in the period from
3100 to 600 B.C, when men appropriated wom-
en's sexual and reproductive capacity; the earliest
states entrenched patriarchy by institutionalizing
the sexual and procreative subordination of
women to men.

7 Some women claim to be feminist yet oppose
abortion; some even claim to offer a feminist argument against abortion (see Callahan 1987). For
reasons that I develop in this chapter, I do not
believe a thorough feminist analysis can sustain a
restrictive abortion policy, although I do acknowledge that feminists need to be wary of some of
the arguments proposed in support of liberal policies on abortion.

8 The state could do a lot to ameliorate this condition. If it provided women with adequate financial support, removed the inequities in the labor
market, and provided affordable and reliable child
care, pregnancy need not so often lead to a woman's dependence on a particular man. That it does
not do so is evidence of the state's complicity in
maintaining women's subordinate position with
respect to men.

9 The IUD has proven so hazardous and prone to
lawsuits, it has been largely removed from the
market in the United States (Pappert 1986). It is
also disappearing from other Western countries
but is still being purchased by population-
control agencies for use in the developing world
(LaCheen 1986).

10 For a more detailed discussion of the limitations
of current contraceptive options, see Colodny
(1989); for the problems of cost, see esp. 34–35.

11 See Petchesky (1985), esp. chap. 5, where she
documents the risks and discomforts associated
with pill use and IUDs and the increasing rate at
which women are choosing the option of dia-
phragm or condom, with the option of early, legal abortions as backup.

12 Eisenstein (1988) has developed an interesting account of sexual politics, which identifies the pregnant body as the central element in the cultural
subordination of women. She argues that pregnancy (either actual or potential) is considered the
defining characteristic of all women, and because
it is not experienced by men, it is classified as deviance and considered grounds for different treatment.

13 Thomson (1971) is a notable exception to this
trend.

14 Because she was obviously involved in sexual activity, it is often concluded that the noncoerced
woman is not innocent but guilty. As such, she is
judged far less worthy than the innocent being she
carries within her. Some who oppose abortion
believe that an unwanted pregnancy is a suitable
punishment for "irresponsible" sex.

15 This seems reminiscent of Aristotle's view of
women as flowerpots where men implant the seed
with all the important genetic information and the
movement necessary for development and the
woman's job is that of passive gestation, like the
flowerpot. See Whitbeck (1973) and Lange
(1983).

16 Some are so preoccupied with the problem of fetuses being "stuck" in women's bodies that they
seek to avoid this geographical complication altogether, completely severing the ties between
woman and fetus. For example, Bernard Nathan-
son, an antiabortion activist with the zeal of a new
convert, eagerly anticipates the prospect of artificial wombs as alternative means for preserving the
lives of fetuses and "dismisses the traditional reverence for birth as merely 'mythology' and the act
of birth itself as an 'insignificant event'" (cited in
McDonnell 1984, 113).

17 Cf. Warren (1989) and Tooley (1972).

18 The definition of pregnancy as a purely passive
activity reaches its ghoulish conclusion in the increasing acceptability of sustaining brain-dead
women on life-support systems to continue their
functions as incubators until the fetus can be safely
delivered. For a discussion of this trend, see
Murphy (1989).

19 This apt phrasing is taken from Petchesky (1985),
342.

20 E.g., Held (1987) argues that personhood is a social status, created by the work of mothering persons.

21 Fetuses are almost wholly individuated by the
women who bear them. The fetal "contributions"
to the relationship are defined by the projections
and interpretations of the pregnant woman in the
latter stages of pregnancy, if she chooses to perceive fetal movements in purposeful ways (e.g., "it
likes classical music, spicy food, exercise").

22 See Luker (1984), esp. chaps. 6 and 7, and
Petchesky (1985), esp. chaps. 7 and 8, for documentation of these associations in the U.S.
antiabortion movement and Collins (1985), esp.
chap. 4, and McLaren and McLaren (1986) for
evidence of similar trends in the Canadian struggle.

23 See McLaren and McLaren (1986) and Petchesky
(1985).

24 When abortion was illegal, many women nonetheless managed to obtain abortions, but only the
relatively privileged women with money were able
to arrange safe, hygienic abortions; poor women
were often constrained to rely on dangerous, unacceptable services. In the United States court
rulings have ensured that rich and middle-class
women have, for the moment, relatively easy access to well-run clinics and hospitals, but because
public hospitals are mostly unwilling to offer abortion services and federal law prohibits the use of
Medicaid funding for abortion, many poor
women still find legal, safe abortions out of reach
(Petchesky 1985). In Canada, too, abortion services are most readily available to middle-class, urban, mature women. This suggests that financial
circumstances may be a more significant factor in
determining women's access to abortion than
abortion's legal status.

25 Some feminists suggest we seek recognition of the
legitimacy of non-medical abortion services. This
would reduce costs and increase access dramatically, with no apparent increase in risk as long as
services were provided by trained, responsible
practitioners who were concerned with the well-
being of their clients. It would also allow the possibility of increasing women's control over
abortion. See, e.g.. McDonnell (1984).

26 For a useful model of such a center, see Van
Wagner and Lee (1989).

27 A poignant collection of some women's unfortunate experiences with hospital abortions is offered
in *Telling Our Secrets,* produced by CARAL (1990).

28 Therefore, the Soviet model, in which abortions
have been relatively accessible, is also unacceptable, because there the unavailability of birth control forces women to rely on multiple abortions
to control their fertility.

Works Cited

Addelson, Kathryn Pyne. 1987. "Moral Passages." In
Women and Moral Theory, ed. Eva Feder Kittay and
Diana T. Meyers. Totowa, NJ: Rowman &
Littlefield.

Annas, George J. 1982. "Forced Cesareans: The
Unkindest Cut of All." *Hastings Center Report* 12
(3):16–17.

Annas, George J. 1986. "Pregnant Women as Fetal
Containers." *Hastings Center Report* 16 (6):13–14.

Baier, Annette C. 1985. *Postures of the Mind: Essays on
Mind and Morals.* Minneapolis: University of Min-
nesota Press.

Callahan, Daniel. 1986. "How Technology is Re-
framing the Abortion Debate." *Hastings Center Report,* 16 (l):33–42.

Callahan, Sidney. 1987. "A Pro-Life Feminist Makes Her Case." *Utne Reader,* March/April: 104–14.

CARAL/Halifax. 1990. *Telling Our Secrets: Abortion Stories from Nova Scotia.* Halifax, NS.: CARAL/ Halifax.

Collins, Anne. 1985. *The Big Evasion: Abortion, the Issue That Won't Go Away.* Toronto: Lester & OrpenDennys.

Colodny, Nikki. 1989. "The Politics of Birth Control in a Reproductive Rights Context." In *The Future of Human Reproduction,* ed. Christine Overall. Toronto: Women's Press.

Daly, Mary. 1973. *Beyond God the Father: Toward a Philosophy of Women's Liberation.* Boston: Beacon Press.

Eisenstein, Zillah R. 1988. *The Female Body and the Law.* Berkeley: University of California Press.

Held, Virginia. 1987. "Feminism and Moral Theory." In *Women and Moral Theory. See* Addelson 1987.

LaCheen, Cary. 1986. "Pharmaceuticals and Family Planning: Women are the Target." In *Adverse Effects: Women and the Pharmaceutical Industry,* ed. Kathleen McDonnell. Toronto: Women's Press.

Lange, Lynda. 1983. "Woman Is Not a Rational Animal: On Aristotle's Biology of Reproduction." In *Discovering Reality: Feminist Perspectives on Epistemology, Metaphysics, Methodology, and Philosophy of Science,* ed. by Sandra Harding and Merill Hintikka. Dordrecht, Neth.: D. Reidel.

Larner, Gerda. 1986. *The Creation of Patriarchy.* New York: Oxford.

Luker, Kristin. 1984. *Abortion and the Politics of Motherhood.* Berkeley: University of California Press.

MacKinnon, Catherine. 1989. *Toward a Feminist Theory of the State.* Cambridge, MA.: Harvard University Press.

McDonnell, Kathleen. 1984. *Not an Easy Choice: A Feminist Re-examines Abortion.* Toronto: Women's Press.

McLaren, Angus and Ariene Tigar McLaren. *1986. The Bedroom and the State: The Changing Practices and Politics of Contraception and Abortion in Canada, 1880-1980.* Toronto: McClelland & Stewart.

Murphy, Julien S. 1989. "Should Pregnancies be Sustained in Brain-Dead Women?: A Philosophical Discussion of Postmortem Pregnancy." In *Healing Technology: Feminist Perspectives,* ed. Kathryn Strother Ratcliff. Ann Arbor: University of Michigan Press.

Nelson, Lawrence J. and Nancy Milliken. 1990. "Compelled Medical Treatment of Pregnant Women: Life, Liberty, and Law in Conflict." In *Ethical Issues in the New Reproductive Technologies,* ed. Richard T. Hull. Belmont, Calif: Wadsworth.

Nicholson, Susan T. 1977. "The Roman Catholic Doctrine of Therapeutic Abortion." In *Feminism and Philosophy,* ed. Mary Vetterling-Braggin, Frederick A. Elliston, and Jane English. Totowa, NJ: Littlefield, Adams & Co.

Overall, Christine. 1987. *Ethics and Human Reproduction: A Feminist Analysis.* Boston: Allen & Unwin.

Pappert, Ann. 1986. "The Rise and Fall of the IUD." In *Adverse Effects. See* LaCheen 1986.

Petchesky, Rosalind Pollack. 1985. *Abortion and Woman's Choice: The State, Sexuality, and Reproductive Freedom.* Boston: Northeastern University Press.

Rodgers, Sandra. 1989. "Pregnancy as Justification for Loss of Juridical Autonomy." In *The Future of Human Reproduction. See* Colodny, 1989.

Rothman, Barbara Katz. 1986. "Commentary: When a Pregnant Woman Endangers Her Fetus." *Hastings Center Report* 16 (1):25.

Sumner, L.W. 1981. *Abortion and Moral Theory.* Princeton: Princeton University Press.

Thomson, Judith Jarvis. 1971. "A Defense of Abortion." *Philosophy and Public Affairs* 1(1): 47–66.

Tooley, Michael. 1972. "Abortion and Infanticide." *Philosophy and Public Affairs* 2 (1):37–65.

Van Wagner, Vicki and Bob Lee. "Principles into Practice: An Activist Vision of Feminist Reproductive Health Care." In *The Future of Human Reproduction. See* Colodny 1989.

Warren, Mary Ann. 1973. "On the Moral and Legal Status of Abortion." *The Monist* 57:43–61.

Warren, Mary Ann. 1989. "The Moral Significance of Birth." *Hypatia* 4:46–65.

Wertheimer, Roger. 1971. "Understanding the Abortion Argument." *Philosophy and Public Affairs* 1(1):67–95.

Witbeck, Carolyn. 1973. "Theories of Sex Difference." *Philosophical Forum* 5(1-2):54–80.

Questions for Discussion

1 Has Sherwin provided a good description of what is central to a "feminist" account? What other characteristics might be thought relevant to a definition of this concept?

2 Is Sherwin right that "Personhood is a social category, not an isolated state"? Are there any entities which deserve moral status, regardless of whether society acknowledges that status?

3 Is it true that there are no general rules about when an abortion is acceptable and when it is not? If individuals are to make decisions based on the particulars of their own situations, is it ever possible to offer moral criticism of another person?

An Excerpt from "Life's Dominion: An Argument About Abortion, Euthanasia, and Individual Freedom"

Ronald Dworkin

Ronald Dworkin has been one of the most influential writers of recent years in political philosophy and philosophy of law. In his 1993 book **Life's Dominion: An Argument About Abortion, Euthanasia, and Individual Freedom***, he turns his talents to an exploration of some contemporary moral issues. In the following excerpt, Dworkin argues that conservatives and liberals on abortion in fact share a commitment to a single principle—the desire to avoid what he calls "frustration of life." He claims that people with different views about abortion can be placed along a spectrum, depending on how they interpret this principle, and in particular on whether they place more emphasis on "natural investment" or "human investment" in lives.*

★　★　★

The Metric of Disrespect

I [shall] try to show how an understanding of the sacredness of human life allows us better to explain the two opposing attitudes toward abortion than does the traditional account, which supposes that these attitudes are based on different views about whether and when a fetus is a person with a right to life. I shall assume that conservatives and liberals all accept that in principle human life is inviolable in the sense I have defined [elsewhere], that any abortion involves a waste of human life and is therefore, in itself, a bad thing to happen, a shame. And I shall try to show how that assumption explains why the two sides both agree and disagree in the ways that they do.

I begin with their agreement. Conservatives and liberals both suppose ... that though abortion is always morally problematic and often morally wrong, it is worse on some occasions than on others. They suppose, in other words, that there are degrees of badness in the waste of human life. What measure are they assuming in those judgments? Let us put that question in a more general form. We all assume that some cases of premature death are greater tragedies than others, not only when we are puzzling about abortion, but in the context of many other events as well. Most of us would think it worse when a young woman dies in a plane crash than when an elderly man does, for example, or a boy than a middle-aged man. What measure of tragedy are we assuming when we think this? What measure should we assume?

... How should we measure and compare the waste of life, and therefore the insult to the sanctity of life, on different occasions?

We should consider, first, a simple and perhaps natural answer to that question. Life is wasted, on this simple view, when life is lost, so that the question of how much has been wasted by a premature death is answered by estimating how long the life cut short would probably otherwise have lasted. This simple answer seems to fit many of our intuitive convictions. It seems to explain the opinion I just mentioned, for example: that the death of a young woman in an airplane crash is worse than the death of an old man would be. The young woman would probably otherwise have had many more years left to live.

The simple answer is incomplete, because we can measure life—and therefore loss of life—in different ways. Should we take into account only the duration of life lost with no regard to its quality? Or should we take quality into account as well? Should we say that the loss of the young woman who died in the crash would be greater if she had been looking forward to a life full of promise and pleasure than if she was physically or psychologically handicapped in some permanent and grave way? Should we also take into account the loss her death would cause to the lives of others? Is the death of a parent of young children, or of a brilliant employer of large numbers of people, or of a musical genius, a worse waste of life than the death at the same age of someone whose life was equally satisfying to himself but less valuable to others?

We should not puzzle over these alternatives, however, because this simple answer, which measures waste of life only in terms of life lost, is unacceptable whether we define that loss only as duration of life or include quality of life or benefit to others. It is unac-

ceptable, in any of these forms, for two compelling reasons.

First, though the simple answer seems to fit some of our convictions, it contradicts other important and deeply held ones. If the waste of life were to be measured only in chronological terms, for example, then an early-stage abortion would be a worse insult to the sanctity of life, a worse instance of life being wasted, than a late-stage abortion. But almost everyone holds the contrary assumption: that the later the abortion—the more like a child the aborted fetus has already become—the worse it is. We take a similar view about the death of young children. It is terrible when an infant dies but worse, most people think, when a three-year-old child dies and worse still when an adolescent does. Almost no one thinks that the tragedy of premature death decreases in a linear way as age increases. Most people's sense of that tragedy, if it were rendered as a graph relating the degree of tragedy to the age at which death occurs, would slope upward from birth to some point in late childhood or early adolescence, then follow a flat line until at least very early middle age, and then slope down again toward extreme old age. Richard's murder of the princes in the Tower could have no parallel, for horror, in any act of infanticide.

Nor does the simple interpretation of how death wastes life fit our feelings better in the more elaborate forms I mentioned. Our common view that it is worse when a late-stage fetus is aborted or miscarries than an early-stage one, and worse when a ten-year-old child dies than an infant, makes no assumptions about the quality of the lives lost or their value for others.

The simple view of wasted life fails for a second, equally important reason. It wholly fails to explain the important truth I have several times emphasized: that though we treat human life as sacred, we do not treat it as incrementally good; we do not believe abstractly that the more human lives that are lived the better. The simple claim that a premature death is tragic only because life is lost—only because some period of life that might have been lived by someone will not be—gives us no more reason to grieve over an abortion or any premature death than we have to grieve over contraception or any other form of birth control. In both cases, less human life is lived than might otherwise be.

The "simple loss" view we have been considering is inadequate because it focuses only on future possibilities, on what will or will not happen in the future. It ignores the crucial truth that waste of life is often greater and more tragic because of what has already happened in the past. The death of an adolescent girl is worse than the death of an infant girl because the adolescent's death frustrates the investments she and others have already made in her life—the ambitions and expectations she constructed, the plans and projects she made, the love and interest and emotional involvement she formed for and with others, and they for and with her.

I shall use "frustration" (though the word has other associations) to describe this more complex measure of the waste of life because I can think of no better word to suggest the combination of past and future considerations that figure in our assessment of a tragic death. Most of us hold to something like the following set of instinctive assumptions about death and tragedy. We believe, as I said, that a successful human life has a certain natural course. It starts in mere biological development—conception, fetal development, and infancy—but it then extends into childhood, adolescence, and adult life in ways that are determined not just by biological formation but by social and individual training and choice, and that culminate in satisfying relationships and achievements of different kinds. It ends, after a normal life span, in a natural death. It is a waste of the natural and human creative in-

vestments that make up the story of a normal life when this normal progression is frustrated by premature death or in other ways. But how bad this is—how great the frustration—depends on the stage of life in which it occurs, because the frustration is greater if it takes place after rather than before the person has made a significant personal investment in his own life, and less if it occurs after any investment has been substantially fulfilled, or as substantially fulfilled as is anyway likely.

This more complex structure fits our convictions about tragedy better than the simple loss-of-life measure does. It explains why the death of an adolescent seems to us worse in most circumstances than the death of an infant. It also explains how we can consistently maintain that it is sometimes undesirable to create new human lives while still insisting that it is bad when any human life, once begun, ends prematurely. No frustration of life is involved when fewer rather than more human beings are born, because there is no creative investment in lives that never exist. But once a human life starts, a process has begun, and interrupting that process frustrates an adventure already under way.

So the idea that we deplore the frustration of life, not its mere absence, seems adequately to fit our general convictions about life, death, and tragedy. It also explains much of what we think about the particular tragedy of abortion. Both conservatives and liberals assume that in some circumstances abortion is more serious and more likely to be unjustifiable than in others. Notably, both agree that a late-term abortion is graver than an early-term one. We cannot explain this shared conviction simply on the ground that fetuses more closely resemble infants as pregnancy continues. People believe that abortion is not just emotionally more difficult but morally worse the later in pregnancy it occurs, and increasing resemblance alone has no moral significance. Nor can we explain the shared conviction by noticing that at some point in pregnancy a fetus becomes sentient. Most people think that abortion is morally worse early in the second trimester—well before sentience is possible—than early in the first one (several European nations, which permit abortion in the first but not the second trimester, have made that distinction part of their criminal law). And though that widely shared belief cannot be explained by the simple lost-life theory, the frustration thesis gives us a natural and compelling justification of it. Fetal development is a continuing creative process, a process that has barely begun at the instant of conception. Indeed, since genetic individuation is not yet complete at that point, we might say that the development of a unique human being has not started until approximately fourteen days later, at implantation. But after implantation, as fetal growth continues, the natural investment that would be wasted in an abortion grows steadily larger and more significant.

Human and Divine

So our sense that frustration rather than just loss compromises the inviolability of human life does seem helpful in explaining what unites most people about abortion. The more difficult question is whether it also helps in explaining what divides them. Let us begin our answer by posing another question. I just described a natural course of human life—beginning in conception, extending through birth and childhood, culminating in successful and engaged adulthood in which the natural biological investment and the personal human investment in that life are realized, and finally ending in natural death after a normal span of years. Life so understood can be frustrated in two main ways. It can be frustrated by premature death, which leaves any previous natural and personal investment unrealized. Or it can be frustrated by other forms of failure: by handicaps or poverty or misconceived projects or irredeemable mistakes or lack of training or even brute bad luck; any one of these may in different ways frustrate a person's opportunity to redeem his ambitions or otherwise to lead a full and flourishing life. Is premature death always, inevitably, a more serious frustration of life than any of these other forms of failure?

Decisions about abortion often raise this question. Suppose parents discover, early in the mother's pregnancy, that the fetus is genetically so deformed that the life it would lead after birth will inevitably be both short and sharply limited. They must decide whether it is a worse frustration of life if the gravely deformed fetus were to die at once—wasting the miracle of its creation and its development so far—or if it were to continue to grow in utero, to be born, and to live only a short and crippled life. We know that people divide about that question, and we now have a way to describe the division. On one view, immediate death of the fetus, even in a case like this one, is a more terrible frustration of the miracle of life than even a sharply diminished and brief infant life would be, for the latter would at least redeem some small part, however limited, of the natural investment. On the rival view, it would be a worse frustration of life to allow this fetal life to continue because that would add, to the sad waste of a deformed human's biological creation, the further, heartbreaking waste of personal emotional investments made in that life by others but principally by the child himself before his inevitable early death.

We should therefore consider this hypothesis: though almost everyone accepts the abstract principle that it is intrinsically bad when human life, once begun, is frustrated, people disagree about the best answer to the question of whether avoidable premature death is always or invariably the most serious possible frustration of life. Very conservative opinion, on this hypothesis, is grounded in the conviction that immediate death is inevitably a more serious frustration than any option that postpones death, even at the cost of greater frustration in other respects. Liberal opinion, on the same hypothesis, is grounded in the opposite conviction: that in some cases, at least, a choice for premature death minimizes the frustration of life and is therefore not a compromise of the principle that human life is sacred but, on the contrary, best respects that principle.

What reasons do people have for embracing one rather than the other of these positions? It seems plain that whatever they are, they are deep reasons, drawn consciously or unconsciously from a great network of other convictions about the point of life and the moral significance of death. If the hypothesis I just described holds—if conservatives and liberals disagree on whether premature death is always the worst frustration of life—then the disagreement must be in virtue of a more general contrast between religious and philosophical orientations.

So I offer another hypothesis. Almost everyone recognizes, as I have suggested, that a normal, successful human life is the product of two morally significant modes of creative investment in that life, the natural and the human. But people disagree about the relative importance of these modes, not just when abortion is in question but on many other mortal occasions as well. If you believe that the natural investment in a human life is transcendently important, that the gift of life itself is infinitely more significant than anything the person whose life it is may do for himself, important though that may be, you will also believe that a deliberate, premature death is the greatest frustration of life possible, no matter how limited or cramped or unsuccessful the continued life would be.[9] On the other hand, if you assign much greater relative importance to the human contribution to life's creative value, then you will consider the frustration of that contribution to be a more serious evil, and will accordingly see more point in deciding

that life should end before further significant human investment is doomed to frustration.

We can best understand some of our serious disagreements about abortion, in other words, as reflecting deep differences about the relative moral importance of the natural and human contributions to the inviolability of individual human lives. In fact, we can make a bolder version of that claim: we can best understand the full range of opinion about abortion, from the most conservative to the most liberal, by ranking each opinion about the relative gravity of the two forms of frustration along a range extending from one extreme position to the other—from treating any frustration of the biological investment as worse than any possible frustration of human investment, through more moderate and complex balances, to the opinion that frustrating mere biological investment in human life barely matters and that frustrating a human investment is always worse.

If we look at the controversy this way, it is hardly surprising that many people who hold views on the natural or biological end of that spectrum are fundamentalist or Roman Catholic or strongly religious in some other orthodox religious faith—people who believe that God is the author of everything natural and that each human fetus is a distinct instance of his most sublime achievement. Our hypothesis explains how orthodox religion can play a crucial role in forming people's opinions about abortion even if they do not believe that a fetus is a person with its own right to life.

That is a significant point. It is widely thought that religious opposition to abortion is premised on the conviction that every human fetus is a person with rights and interests of its own. It is therefore important to see that religious opposition to abortion need not be based on that assumption. I said [elsewhere] that many religious traditions, including Roman Catholicism for most of its history, based their opposition to abortion on the different assumption that human life has intrinsic value. The present hypothesis shows how that assumption can ground very fierce, even absolute, opposition to abortion. A strongly orthodox or fundamentalist person can insist that abortion is always morally wrong because the deliberate destruction of something created as sacred by God can never be redeemed by any human benefit.

This is not to suggest, however, that only conventionally religious people who believe in a creator God are conservatives about abortion. Many other people stand in awe of human reproduction as a natural miracle. Some of them ... embrace the mysterious but apparently powerful idea that the natural order is in itself purposive and commands respect as sacred. Some prominent conservationists, for example, though hardly religious in the conventional sense, seem to be deeply religious in that one and may be drawn a considerable distance toward the conservative end of the spectrum of opinion I described. They may well think that any frustration of the natural investment in human life is so grave a matter that it is rarely if ever justified—that the pulse in the mud★ is more profound than any other source of life's value. They might therefore be just as firmly opposed to aborting a seriously deformed fetus as any religiously orthodox conservative would be.

Nor does it follow, on the other hand, that everyone who is religious in an orthodox way or everyone who reveres nature is therefore conservative about abortion. As we have seen, many such people, who agree that unnecessary death is a great evil, are also sensitive to and emphatic about the intrinsic badness of the waste of human investment in life. They believe that the frustration of that contribu-

---

★ Dworkin elsewhere refers to poet David Plante, who "speaks of an elemental 'pulse in the mud' as the mysterious source of all life." (*Life's Dominion*, p. 79)

tion—for example, in the birth of a grievously deformed fetus whose investment in its own life is doomed to be frustrated—may in some circumstances be the worse of two evils, and they believe that their religious conviction or reverence for nature is not only consistent with but actually requires that position. Some of them take the same view about what many believe to be an even more problematic case: they say that their religious convictions entail that a woman should choose abortion rather than bear a child when that would jeopardize her investment in her own life.

I described extreme positions at two ends of the spectrum: that only natural investment counts in deciding whether abortion wastes human life, and that only human investment counts. In fact, very few people take either of these extreme positions. For most people, the balance is more complex and involves compromise and accommodation rather than giving absolute priority to avoiding frustration of either the natural or the human investment. People's opinions become progressively less conservative and more liberal as the balance they strike gives more weight to the importance of not frustrating the human investment in life; more liberal views emphasize, in various degrees, that a human life is created not just by divine or natural forces but also, in a different but still central way, by personal choice, training, commitment, and decision. The shift in emphasis leads liberals to see the crucial creative investment in life, the investment that must not be frustrated if at all possible, as extending far beyond conception and biological growth and well into a human being's adult life. On that liberal opinion, as I have already suggested, it may be more frustrating of life's miracle when an adult's ambitions, talents, training, and expectations are wasted because of an unforeseen and unwanted pregnancy than when a fetus dies before any significant investment of that kind has been made,

That is an exceptionally abstract description of my understanding of the controversy between conservative and liberal opinion. But it will become less abstract, for I shall try to show how the familiar differences between conservative and liberal views on abortion can be explained by the hypothesis that conservatives and liberals rank the two forms of frustration differently. We must not exaggerate that difference, however. It is a difference in emphasis, though an important one. Most people who take what I call a liberal view of abortion do not deny that the conception of a human life and its steady fetal development toward recognizable human form are matters of great moral importance that count as creative investments. That is why they agree with conservatives that as this natural investment continues, and the fetus develops toward the shape and capacity of an infant, abortion, which wastes that investment, is progressively an event more to be avoided or regretted. Many people who hold conservative opinions about abortion, for their part, recognize the importance of personal creative contributions to a human life; they, too, recognize that a premature death is worse when it occurs not in early infancy but after distinctly human investments of ambition and expectation and love have been made. Conservatives and liberals disagree not because one side wholly rejects a value the other thinks cardinal, but because they take different—sometimes dramatically different—positions about the relative importance of these values, which both recognize as fundamental and profound.

Conservative Exceptions: Reconsidering the Natural

I am defending the view that the debate over abortion should be understood as essentially about the following philosophical issue: is the frustration of a biological life, which wastes human life, nevertheless sometimes justified in order to avoid frustrating a human contribution to that life or to other people's lives, which would be a different kind of waste? If so, when and why? People who are very conservative about abortion answer the first of these questions No.

There is an even more extreme position, which holds that abortion is never justified, even when necessary to save the life of the mother. Though that is the official view of the Catholic church and of some other religious groups, only a small minority even of devout Catholics accept it, and even Justice Rehnquist, who dissented in *Roe* v. *Wade,* said that he had little doubt that it would be unconstitutional for states to prohibit abortion when a mother's life was at stake. So I have defined "very conservative" opinion to permit abortion in this circumstance. This exceedingly popular exception would be unacceptable to all conservatives ... if they really thought that a fetus is a person with protected rights and interests. It is morally and legally impermissible for any third party, such as a doctor, to murder one innocent person even to save the life of another one. But the exception is easily explicable if we understand conservative opinion as based on a view of the sanctity of life that gives strict priority to the divine or natural investment in life.

If either the mother or the fetus must die, then the tragedy of avoidable death and the loss of nature's investment in life is inevitable. But a choice in favor of the mother may well seem justified to very conservative people on the ground that a choice against her would in addition frustrate the personal and social investments in her life; even they want only to minimize the overall frustration of human life, and that requires saving the mother's life in this terrible situation.

The important debate is therefore between people who believe that abortion is permissible *only* when it is necessary to save the mother's life and people who believe that abortion may be morally permissible in other circumstances as well. I shall consider the further exceptions the latter group of people claim, beginning with those that are accepted even by people who regard themselves as moderately conservative about abortion and continuing to those associated with a distinctly liberal position.

Moderate conservatives believe that abortion is morally permissible to end a pregnancy that began in rape. Governor Buddy Roemer of Louisiana, for example, who has declared himself in favor of a ban on abortion, nevertheless vetoed an anti-abortion statute in 1991 because it excepted rape victims only in a manner that he said "dishonors women ... and unduly traumatizes victims of rape."[10] On the a-fetus-is-a-person view, an exception for rape is even harder to justify than an exception to protect the life of the mother. Why should a fetus be made to forfeit its right to live, and pay with its life, for the wrongdoing of someone else? But once again, the exception is much easier to understand when we shift from the claim of fetal personhood to a concern for protecting the divine or natural investment in human life. Very conservative people, who believe that the divine contribution to a human life is everything and the human contribution almost nothing beside it, believe that abortion is automatically and in every case the worst possible compromise of life's inviolability, and they do not recognize an exception for rape. But moderately conservative people, who believe that the natural contribution normally *outweighs* the human contribution, will find two features of rape that argue for an exception.

First, according to every prominent religion, rape is itself a brutal violation of God's law and will, and abortion may well seem less insulting to God's creative power when the life it ends itself began in such an insult. Though rape would not justify violating the rights of an innocent person, it could well diminish the horror conservatives feel at an abortion's deliberate frustration of God's investment in life.

In his opinion in *McRae* v. *Califano*, ... Judge John Dooling summarized testimony by Rabbi David Feldman: "In the stricter Jewish view abortion is a very serious matter permitted only where there is a threat to life, or to sanity, or a grave threat to mental health and physical well-being. Abortion for rape victims would be allowed, using a field and seed analogy: involuntary implantation of the seed imposes no duty to nourish the alien seed."[11]

Second, rape is a terrible desecration of its victim's investment in her own life, and even those who count a human investment in life as less important than God's or nature's may nevertheless recoil from so violent a frustration of that human investment. Rape is sickeningly, comprehensively contemptuous because it reduces a woman to a physical convenience, a creature whose importance is exhausted by her genital use, someone whose love and sense of self—aspects of personality particularly at stake in sex—have no significance whatsoever except as vehicles for sadistic degradation.

Requiring a woman to bear a child conceived in such an assault is especially destructive to her self-realization because it frustrates her creative choice not only in sex but in reproduction as well. In the ideal case, reproduction is a joint decision rooted in love and in a desire to continue one's life mixed with the life of another person. In Catholic tradition, and in the imagination of many people who are not Catholics, it is itself an offense against the sanctity of life to make love without that desire: that is the basis of many people's moral opposition to contraception. But we can dispute that sex is valuable only for reproduction, or creative only in that way—as most people do—while yet believing that sex is maximally creative when reproduction is contemplated and desired, and that reproduction frustrates creative power when it is neither. Of course, people in love often conceive by accident, and people not in love sometimes conceive deliberately, perhaps out of a misguided hope of finding love through children. Rape is not just the absence of contemplation and desire, however. For the victim, rape is the direct opposite of these, and if a child is conceived, it will be not only without the victim's desire to reproduce but in circumstances made especially horrible because of that possibility.

Moderate conservatives therefore find it difficult to insist that abortion is impermissible in cases of rape. It is sometimes said that conservatives who allow the rape exception but not, for example, an exception for unmarried teenagers whose lives would be ruined by childbirth must be motivated by a desire to punish unmarried women who have sex voluntarily. Though some conservatives may indeed believe that pregnancy is a fit punishment for sexual immorality, our hypothesis shows why conservatives who make only the rape exception do not necessarily hold that appalling view. The grounds on which I said conservatives might make an exception for rape do not extend so forcefully to pregnancies that follow voluntary intercourse. Though many religious people do think that unmarried sex also violates God's will, few consider it as grave as rape, and the argument that an unwanted pregnancy grotesquely frustrates a woman's creative role in framing her own life is weaker when the pregnancy follows voluntary sex. Of course, the difference would not be pertinent at all, as I said, if a fetus were a person with rights and interests of its own, because that person would be completely innocent whatever the nature or level of its mother's guilt.

Liberal Exceptions: Protecting Life in Earnest

Other, more permissive exceptions to the principle that abortion is wrong are associated with a generally liberal attitude toward abortion, and we should therefore expect, on the basis of the hypothesis we are testing, that they will reflect a greater respect for the human contribution to life and a correspondingly diminished concern with the natural. But we must not forget that people's attitudes about abortion range over a gradually changing spectrum from one extreme to the other, and that any sharp distinction between conservative and liberal camps is just an expository convenience.

Liberals think that abortion is permissible when the birth of a fetus would have a very bad effect on the quality of lives. The exceptions liberals recognize on that ground fall into two main groups: those that seek to avoid frustration of the life of the child, and those that seek to prevent frustration of the life of the mother and other family members.

Liberals believe that abortion is justified when it seems inevitable that the fetus, if born, will have a seriously frustrated life. That kind of justification is strongest, according to most liberals, when the frustration is caused by a very grave physical deformity that would make any life deprived, painful, frustrating for both child and parent, and, in any case, short. But many liberals also believe that abortion is justified when the family circumstances are so economically barren, or otherwise so unpromising, that any new life would be seriously stunted for that reason. It is important to understand that these exceptions are not based, as they might seem to be, on concern for the rights or interests of the fetus. It is a mistake to suppose that an early fetus has interests of its own; it especially makes no sense to argue that it might have an interest in being aborted. Perhaps we could understand that latter argument to mean that if the fetus does develop into a child, that child would be better off dead. But many liberals find abortion justified even when this is not so. I do not mean to deny that sometimes people would be better off dead—when they are in great and terminal pain, for example, or because their lives are otherwise irremediably frustrated.... But this is rarely true of children born into even very great poverty. Nor is it necessarily true even of children born with terrible, crippling handicaps who are doomed shortly to die; sometimes such children establish relationships and manage achievements that give content and meaning to their lives, and it becomes plain that it is in their interests, and in the interests of those who love and care for them, that they continue living as long as possible. The liberal judgment that abortion is justified when the prospects for life are especially bleak is based on a more impersonal judgment: that the child's existence would be intrinsically a bad thing, that it is regrettable that such a deprived and difficult life must be lived.

Sometimes this liberal judgment is wrongly taken to imply contempt for the lives of handicapped children or adults, or even as a suggestion, associated with loathsome Nazi eugenics, that society would be improved by the death of such people. That is a mistake twice over. First, ... the general question of the relative intrinsic tragedy of different events is very different from any question about the *rights* of people now living or about how they should be treated. The former is a question about the intrinsic goodness or evil of events, the latter about rights and fairness. Second, in any case, the liberal opinion about abortion of deformed fetuses in no way implies that it would be better if even grievously handicapped people were now to die. On the contrary, the very concern the liberal judgment embodies—respect for the human contribution to life and anxiety that it not be frustrated—normally sponsors exactly the opposite conclusion. The investment a seriously handicapped person makes in his own life, in his struggle to overcome his handicap as best he can, is intense, and the investment his family and others make is likely to be intense as well. The liberal position insists that these investments in life should be realized as fully as pos-

sible, for as long and as successfully as the handicapped person and his community together can manage; and liberals are even more likely than conservatives to support social legislation that promotes that end. One may think that in the worst of such cases it would have been better had the life in question never begun, that the investment we are so eager to redeem should never have been necessary. But that judgment does not detract from concern for handicapped people; on the contrary, it is rooted in the same fundamental respect for human investment in human life, the same horror at the investment being wasted.

The second distinctly liberal group of exceptions, which take into account the effects of pregnancy and childbirth on the lives of mothers and other family members, are even harder to justify on any presumption that includes the idea that a fetus is a person with rights and interests. But the popularity of these exceptions is immediately explicable once we recognize that they are based on respect for the intrinsic value of human life. Liberals are especially concerned about the waste of the human contribution to that value, and they believe that the waste of life, measured in frustration rather than mere loss, is very much greater when a teenage single mother's life is wrecked than when an early-stage fetus, in whose life human investment has thus far been negligible, ceases to live. That judgment does not, of course, depend on comparing the quality of the mother's life, if her fetus is aborted, with that of the child, had it been allowed to live. Recognizing the sanctity of life does not mean attempting to engineer fate so that the best possible lives are lived overall; it means, rather, not frustrating investments in life that have already been made. For that reason, liberal opinion cares more about the lives that people are now leading, lives in earnest, than about the possibility of other lives to come.

The prospects of a child and of its mother for a fulfilling life obviously each depend very much on the prospects of the other. A child whose birth frustrates the chances of its mother to redeem her own life or jeopardizes her ability to care for the rest of her family is likely, just for that reason, to have a more frustrating life itself. And though many people have become superb parents to disabled or disadvantaged children, and some extraordinary ones have found a special vocation in that responsibility, it will sometimes be a devastating blow to a parent's prospects to have a crippled child rather than a normal one, or a child whose bearing and care will seriously strain family resources.

This is only another instance of the difficulty any theoretical analysis of an intricate personal and social problem, like abortion, must face. Analysis can proceed only by abstraction, but abstraction, which ignores the complexity and interdependencies of real life, obscures much of the content on which each actual, concrete decision is made. So we have no formulas for actual decision but only, at best, a schema for understanding the arguments and decisions that we and other people make in real life. I have argued that we do badly, in understanding and evaluating these decisions and arguments, if we try to match them to procrustean assumptions about fetal personhood or rights. We do better to see them as reflecting more nuanced and individual judgments about how and why human life is sacred, and about which decision of life and death, in all the concrete circumstances, most respects what is really important about life.

There will be disagreement in these judgments, not only between large parties of opinion, like those I have been calling conservative and liberal, but within these parties as well. Indeed, very few people, even those who share the same religion and social and intellectual background, will agree in every case. Nor is it possible for anyone to compose a general theory of abortion, some careful weighing of different kinds or modes of life's frustration from which particular decisions could be generated to fit every concrete case. On the contrary, we discover what we think about these grave matters not in advance of having to decide on particular occasions, but in the course of and by making them.

... Seeing the abortion controversy in the fresh light I described will not, of course, end our disagreements about the morality of abortion, because these disagreements are deep and may be perpetual. But if that fresh light helps us to identify those disagreements as at bottom *spiritual,* that should help bring us together, because we have grown used to the idea, as I said, that real community is possible across deep religious divisions. We might hope for even more—not just for greater tolerance but for a more positive and healing realization: that what we share—our common commitment to the sanctity of life—is itself precious, a unifying ideal we can rescue from the decades of hate.

Notes

...

9 Many people who hold that view will make exceptions: for capital punishment, for example, and for killing the enemy in war. I cannot consider [here] the large and important question of how far these exceptions contradict the principle. But people who believe that the natural contribution to life is paramount for a particular reason—that God has created all life—will obviously not count these as contradictions if they also believe that executing murderers or killing enemy soldiers in a just war is also God's will.

10 See "Nation's Strictest Abortion Law Enacted in Louisiana Over Veto," *The New York Times,* June 19, 1991. The Louisiana legislature overrode Governor Roemer's veto, and the strict anti-abortion law it enacted has been held unconstitutional by two federal courts. See "Court Backs Overturning of Strict Abortion Law," *The New York Times,* September 23, 1992. In 1992, the Supreme Court refused to review a lower-court decision striking down a similar Guam statute. See Linda Greenhouse, "Guam Abortion Law; High Court Reaf-

firms Right to Regulate, but Not to Ban," *The New York Times*, December 6, 1992, D2.

11 491 F. Supp. 630 (1980), 696.

Questions for Discussion

1 Can there be a greater "frustration of life" than death?

2 If we could establish that people with different views on abortion all subscribe to the same prin-ciple, but interpret it differently, would that make it any more likely that we will be able to reach a universally acceptable solution to the abortion is-sue?

3 Does Dworkin's analysis make sense of differences in your intuitions about abortion in cases such as those where the mother's life is endangered, the pregnancy is the result of a rape, or the fetus is severely deformed? What role should intuitions about such cases play in deciding on the morality of abortion?

CHAPTER 5

Assisted Reproduction and Commodification

A number of techniques are now available to assist people with reproduction. These techniques are often referred to as "new reproductive technologies," but that name may not be particularly accurate. In some cases versions of the techniques have been around for centuries, so the "new" may be misleading, and although some of the techniques do involve sophisticated technology (such as synthetic hormone treatments, surgical techniques, and the use of expensive laboratory equipment), others involve only very simple, everyday sorts of technology. In any case, the increased availability and increased variety of techniques, together with the changes in scientific understanding which have accompanied them in recent years, have highlighted the need for ethical consideration of the issues which arise from these techniques.

Some people are moved by a general sort of uneasiness about tampering with things we do not understand fully, while others have confidence that any problems we encounter can be taken in stride and

resolved, with a greater gain than loss overall. Indeed, people's attitudes toward these techniques may reflect their general attitudes toward technology—some people believe we have gained greatly from technology with very little loss, whereas others believe technology has destroyed much which was valuable and threatens even greater destruction. Similarly, some people think we can change or stop our use of technology if we encounter problems, while others believe the technological age takes on a life of its own, and changes are very difficult or impossible to stop once they have begun. These differences in basic outlook on technology are reflected in the debate on techniques of assisted reproduction, but there are also more specific arguments in favour of and against the use of these techniques.

It might be useful to begin with a brief account of what the main techniques are which are at issue here. In order to make sense of how *assisted* reproduction works, it is first necessary to provide a brief account of how what might be called "natural" (unassisted) reproduction works.

Ordinary natural reproduction in humans occurs when healthy sperm cells, which come from males of the species, combine with healthy ova (or egg cells), which have been released from a female's ovaries ("ovulation"). This combining of sperm and ova is called "fertilization" or "conception." This fertilized egg (sometimes called a "zygote" or a "pre-embryo") then must travel through the female's fallopian tubes to her uterus, where it can implant and develop until birth. There is still much that is not known about exactly why reproduction does not always occur when the circumstances seem right (e.g., why a sperm cell and ovum may sometimes fail to combine, or why a zygote may fail to implant in the uterus). It *is* known, however, that natural reproduction cannot occur if there are no healthy sperm cells, or insufficient numbers of sperm cells, or if there are no healthy ova, or if ovulation does not occur, or if the fallopian tubes are blocked, or if a female does not have a functional uterus.

Different techniques of assisted reproduction enable people to deal with the different ways in which the natural reproduction process may go wrong. One technique for assisting reproduction is called artificial insemination. This technique involves a man's providing sperm-containing semen, through masturbation, which is then placed into a woman's upper vagina or uterus by means other than sexual intercourse. In its general outlines, this procedure does not require a very high level of technological sophistication—any vessel for transporting the semen and getting it to the woman's upper vagina will suffice. In practice, this technique is sometimes combined with some form of "treatment" of the semen, which may be done with the aim of increasing the sperm's tendency to

move ("motility"), so as to increase the chances of fertilization, or with the aim of affecting the sort of baby which is likely to result from pregnancy if it occurs (e.g., increasing the chances of the baby's being of a particular sex). The sperm may also be stored in a frozen state for a period of time prior to being used for artificial insemination. It should also be noted that the man who provides the sperm may be the husband or partner of the woman who is to become pregnant, in which case the procedure is known as AIH (Artificial Insemination by Husband), or some other man who donates sperm, in which case the procedure is known as DI (Donor Insemination) or AID (Artificial Insemination by Donor). Indeed, it is also possible to combine the sperm of more than one man for this procedure.

Another method of assisting reproduction involves inducing or enhancing ovulation. Sometimes, if a woman is not releasing eggs from the ovaries, changes in diet and activity level can bring about the internal changes required to begin ovulation. In other cases, ovulation can be induced by the introduction of synthetic hormones. Hormones may also be used to induce a woman's body to release more than the usual one ovum per month ("ovulation enhancement"). These procedures may make ova available for fertilization, but they can also be uncomfortable for the woman involved, and may involve the risk of serious side-effects. Furthermore, in cases in which more than one ovum is produced, each may become fertilized, leading to the possibility of multiple births, and also to conditions in which there is not enough room for any fetus to develop. Sometimes, in such cases, attempts may be made to abort some of the fetuses so as to allow others a chance to live, although these procedures may also involve risks. Ovulation induction or enhancement is often used in conjunction with other techniques, to increase the probability of fertilization.

A third technique for assisting reproduction is known as in vitro fertilization (IVF). "In vitro" literally means "in glass," as opposed to "in vivo," which is in a living body. The basic idea of this technique is that ova are removed from a woman's body and combined with sperm in a nutrient medium in a laboratory. This is generally done in a petri dish, but nevertheless resulting offspring are sometimes colloquially referred to as "test-tube babies." So as to improve the chances of a successful pregnancy, it is usual to try to fertilize several ova at once. If fertilization occurs, these fertilized eggs may then be allowed to develop to the eight-cell stage, at which point some of them may be placed inside a woman's uterus, while the rest are frozen and preserved. The idea is that those which are introduced into the uterus may implant and develop from there on as in a natural pregnancy. If the zygote does not implant, so that no pregnancy results, it may be possible to try again with one (or some) of the remaining pre-embryos.

It has been suggested that it might be possible to create an environment in which the entire development could occur within a laboratory, without requiring transfer to a woman's body ("ectogenesis"), or to enable the development to occur within a man's body rather than a woman's, but neither of those possibilities is technically feasible at the present time. As it is, IVF requires more sophisticated technology than the other main techniques of assisted reproduction, and there is limited evidence about its relative effectiveness. The first IVF child, Louise Brown, was born in Britain in 1978. The first IVF children (twin boys) born in Canada had been conceived in Britain, and were born in 1982, and the first IVF children (also twin boys) conceived and

born in Canada were born the following year. IVF is one of the better-known and most frequently discussed methods of assisted reproduction, although it is far from being the most frequently practiced.

The final type of technique of assisted reproduction to be discussed here is commonly known as "surrogate motherhood," although it is also sometimes called "contract motherhood" or "intrauterine adoption," and the arrangements to engage in it are sometimes referred to as "preconception agreements." The central notion here is simply that "a woman undertakes to conceive and bear a child with the understanding that it will be raised by someone else."[1] As such, there does not need to be any technological involvement here at all, and it has been suggested that surrogacy is at least as old as the Bible. People who want to acquire custody of a child through a preconception agreement but do not want to engage in sexual intercourse may make use of other techniques of assisted reproduction (such as AI or IVF) in connection with the preconception agreement. These agreements differ from ordinary adoption agreements in that the child to be adopted has not yet been conceived at the time of the agreement, and is conceived with the express intention of being turned over to the "commissioning" individual(s). It should also be noted that the woman who conceives and bears the child may be paid for doing so ("commercial surrogacy"), or may do it for non-monetary reasons. Furthermore, the woman who goes through the gestation process may also be the genetic mother, or the ovum may be donated by someone else.

★ ★ ★

There are many aspects to the debate about the ethical status of the techniques of assisted reproduction. People who support them tend to emphasize the improvement in individual well-being and expansion of autonomous choice involved in allowing people to have children as they choose. Indeed, it is sometimes claimed that people have a right to reproduce, and that it is unjust for some people to be denied this right simply because of a medical condition (infertility) or the circumstances of their lives.

Among the arguments raised in opposition to assisted reproduction are ones which focus on the impact on the family unit, and the "unnatural" element they introduce into the deeply personal process of reproduction. Some critics also point to questions about whether infertility should be viewed as a medical condition in need of treatment at all. The role of socialization in leading people to think that having children of their own is something to be particularly desired is often noted in this context.

Although many of the new reproductive technologies were originally developed for use in agriculture, their main benefit now is often taken to be the ability to enable infertile couples to have children. Definitions of infertility vary somewhat, but if we say that couples are affected by infertility if they are in their reproductive years, and have been unable to conceive after two years of cohabiting and not using contraception, then approximately 7 percent (or 1 in 14) of Canadian couples are affected by infertility. Those who favour the use of assisted reproduction often claim it is a valuable treatment for people suffering the often deeply felt frustration, sorrow, and stress of being infertile. It must be noted, however, that these techniques, once available, could possibly be used by people other than infertile couples. Single women and women past menopause (and therefore beyond the normal reproductive age for

women) might be able to use these techniques to have children without needing to have sex with a man, and lesbian couples might also be able to use these techniques in the same way. Indeed, the method of surrogate motherhood might even enable a single man to become a father without requiring sexual relations with or emotional commitments to a woman, and may allow a fertile woman who does not want to go through pregnancy nevertheless to become a mother of her own genetic offspring.

Many people take these possibilities to be indicative of one ethical problem these methods of assisting give rise to, that is that these methods seem to bring about changes in the traditional family. On some views, reproduction should take place only within families in which there is a man and a woman who together accept the responsibility of child-rearing. It might also be suggested that sex should be engaged in to bring loving people closer together in emotional or spiritual ways, and that children can be properly conceived only in such a context. Since the various techniques for assisting reproduction separate conception and pregnancy from the closeness of a sexual union, and ease the way for people who are not involved in male/female familial relationships to have children, it might be claimed that these techniques of assisted reproduction tend to undermine the family unit.

There are a variety of claims which might be made in response to such an argument. One sort of claim would be to accept the view that these techniques tend to undermine the traditional family unit, but reject the suggestion that this is a bad thing. Many people believe that the ideal of a "nuclear family" is itself responsible for a great deal of repression and injustice, and society would benefit from a shake-up of that institution. Even if the traditional family is not bad, it may be claimed that the effort to preserve it would not constitute enough of a good to warrant sacrificing the well-being which would stem from people's having more control over their ability to reproduce.

The argument which states that the techniques of assisted reproduction are bad for the family unit may also be challenged on empirical grounds. The argument suggested that the methods of assisted reproduction might tend to tear couples apart. It might be replied that, on the contrary, it is tensions surrounding infertility which are likely to tear couples apart. In helping couples to overcome such obstacles, and provide them with much-wanted children, these techniques may actually serve to enhance the sort of loving family relationship in question.

There may still be a nagging worry here that these methods of assisted reproduction are wrong, simply because they are unnatural. Philosophers tend to be wary of such claims, at least in the bold form stated here, because they require a great deal of understanding of what is "natural," and whether that which is natural is necessarily good. Indeed, it might be claimed that what is most natural for humans to do is to use our intelligence so as to acquire what we desire, as the various forms of assisted reproduction (and indeed all of medical science) attempt to do.

Nevertheless, it might be thought that assisted reproduction is significantly different from other uses of medical science. One reason which might be given for thinking that there is a difference has to do with the notion of "disease." It might be claimed that infertility is simply not a medical problem in the same way that, say, heart disease is. It is certainly not life-threatening, and indeed the various forms of assisted reproduction do not treat the root cause of the

problem—they simply treat the "symptom" of being unable to conceive. It should be noted that many conditions which frequently receive medical attention are not life-threatening, and that many treatments (e.g., eyeglasses, insulin) do not treat the root cause of the problem. If "disease" is defined as the inability to do that which human beings are normally able to do, then infertility would indeed seem to qualify as a disease. Of course that would not settle how great a priority infertility should be when compared with other medical conditions, but it might seem to deserve some weight. Perhaps, however, the proposed definition of "disease" is not the best one, and a better one can be utilized instead. In any case, clearly a certain amount of careful thought is required to identify the source of the feeling one might have that infertility is not a medical condition like other medical conditions.

One line of argument which has been put forward for the claim that infertility is different from other medical conditions has to do with the source of the view that infertility is a *problem*. It has been suggested that, in our society, women are valued much more if they have children than if they do not. Coupled with the fact that it is often very difficult to establish a meaningful relationship with children not one's own, this leads to a great deal of pressure for women to have children. Accordingly, women who are unable to conceive naturally might see themselves (and be seen by others) as somehow incomplete or inferior. On this view, the desire to have children is itself a product of socialization, not of any inherent drive to reproduce. Indeed, it might be thought that such socialization is detrimental to the real interests of women, and fails to value women sufficiently for their own sakes. It might then be thought that desires which are the product of such socialization need not be given much weight when it comes to deciding whether to "treat" infertility with new reproductive technologies. This would be particularly true if it could be established that these technologies have negative effects on the status of women, the cultural understanding of children, or the well-being of society as a whole.

Included among the concerns about possible negative effects are fears that women will come to be seen even more as mere "breeders." If it is thought that men exercise power over women through control of their sexuality and reproductive abilities, then increased technological control over reproduction by a primarily male-dominated medical community might be seen to enhance this domination.

These concerns tie in with another major cluster of objections to assisted reproduction, which has to do with the notion of "commodification." It has been suggested that these techniques increase the tendency for children to be seen as, in effect, things to be bought and sold, and for women's reproductive abilities to be reduced to mere market commodities as well. Of course, the strength of such arguments depends on the claim that some things are not appropriately treated as commodities. Such claims about commodification in an area where it is inappropriate are also at the core of debates about the ethics of prostitution, and provide the link within this chapter between assisted reproduction (surrogate motherhood in particular) and prostitution.

What sorts of things can properly be seen as commodities? Do people "own" their own genetic information, as conveyed in their gametes? Do fertility clinics "own" the products they deal with, or do they "belong to" the genetic parents, or those who are responsible for their creation? Are

there certain kinds of labour which should be exempt from market forces, and if so, why? Many people believe that it is inappropriate to have a market for sexual and reproductive "services." Accordingly, prostitution has been thought a moral wrong for centuries, and surrogate motherhood is sometimes seen to reflect similar moral flaws. Critics of this view have pressed issues, however, about exactly what it is about these kinds of labour which might distinguish them from other kinds. Indeed, it is sometimes claimed that women's sexual and reproductive labour has been denied its proper market value for centuries, and that prohibiting this kind of "commodification" would actually contribute to patriarchal domination. In any case, the issues surrounding the notion of "commodities" in human beings and human services connect the use of new reproductive technologies with a number of other human practices, including prostitution.

Beside worries about how commodification might affect attitudes in society, there are also worries that assisted reproduction might give rise to pressure toward intolerance of imperfection. The more control we have over reproduction, the more people might come to expect a physically and mentally "perfect" baby as a result. Furthermore, there may be questions about how the division of reproductive roles will affect the identity of the children, and their relationship to their parents. If one woman donates an ovum (the "genetic mother"), one man donates sperm (the "genetic father"), a second woman goes through the pregnancy and birth processes (the "gestational mother"), and the resulting child is raised by others (the "social parents," of whatever number and genders), who should we say are the child's "parents"?

One other issue which arises in connection with assisted reproduction has to do with the moral status of various sorts of entities. This issue, which is familiar from discussions of abortion and of the moral status of non-human animals, applies to assisted reproduction because of the way in which these techniques are exercised. For example, as was noted above, an IVF procedure generally involves the attempted fertilization of several ova, each of which is then allowed to develop to the eight-cell stage. If a pregnancy does not result from the first attempt, then some of the remaining zygotes might be used for a second attempt at pregnancy, and so on. But what if the first attempt *does* succeed? What then is to be done with the remaining zygotes? Is there an obligation to try to develop them into full-grown human beings? If so, who has that obligation? (Note that, in principle, *any* woman who meets basic health requirements could become a gestational mother for these zygotes.) Should they be viewed as the "property" of those who arranged for their existence, to be disposed of as they see fit? Can they be simply poured down the sink, or dumped in the garbage? Can they be allowed to develop a bit further, and then used for experimentation, or as sources of tissue for transplant into needy adults? The answers to such questions will depend heavily on beliefs about the moral status of such entities.

Finally, the existence of various techniques of assisted reproduction gives rise to issues about how large a portion of society's resources should be dedicated to such procedures, and about how we as a society should go about making decisions about these issues. The cost of many of these procedures might lead to a situation in which the ability to reproduce is shared unequally by rich and poor, unless society as a whole decides to fund them. Such societal decisions are made difficult by the fact that some people place tremendous value on the increased scope for autonomy and individual well-being new reproductive technologies seem to provide, while others believe such values are easily outweighed by the sorts of problems outlined above. Are some people's lives made better by the availability of techniques of assisted reproduction, and if so, is that improvement in people's lives worth the costs?

Note

1 *Proceed with Care: Final Report of the Royal Commission on New Reproductive Technologies*, p. 662.

Excerpts from "Proceed with Care"

Royal Commission on New Reproductive Technologies

In 1993, the Canadian Royal Commission on New Reproductive Technologies published its final report, entitled **Proceed with Care**. *The process of formulating this report had been extremely controversial—indeed, four of the original seven commissioners had gone to court to demand greater involvement with and access to the research process, several staff researchers chose to leave the commission, and several external researchers objected to the ways in which their work was treated by the commission. Nevertheless, the final report has been a focal point of discussion of the various forms of assisted reproduction since its publication. The 1250-page report is extremely wide-ranging, covering social attitudes, technical information, information about current Canadian practices in this area, ethical considerations, and policy recommendations. Its subjects of investigation include infertility and* *its causes, adoption, fertility drugs, assisted insemination, in vitro fertilization, embryo research, surrogate motherhood (called "preconception arrangements" by the commission), prenatal diagnosis, genetic engineering, and uses of fetal tissue. The following selections include remarks by the Commission which apply to the ethics of some of the most significant aspects of assisted reproduction.*

★ ★ ★

Infertility Treatments: Fertility Drugs

... The fertility drugs available today, when used alone, attempt to restore fertility by acting on various biological mechanisms in reproduction. They do not bypass any of the vital steps in the process that culminates in fertilization of an egg; instead, they attempt to correct disorders in women and men that can cause hormonal imbalance, or to reverse the effects of an illness that blocks fertility. Most fertility drugs on the market today fall into one of three broad categories: ovulation induction drugs, ovulation suppression drugs, and those used to treat male infertility.

... [The Commission's] comprehensive review showed that there has been a lack of systematic research on adverse side effects of ovulation induction drugs. Perhaps the most striking fact about the review is that it was the first comprehensive attempt ever in Canada to compile evidence on the adverse effects of ovulation induction drugs. The review showed that although these are immensely powerful drugs, there has been a relative vacuum in research attention directed to examining the results of their use; by contrast, drugs used for chemotherapy and cardiac arrhythmias are extensively reviewed. A commitment to the tenets of evidence-based medicine requires that this deficiency be remedied.

As with any medication, side effects occur in some women treated with ovulation induction drugs; in a small proportion of cases, serious health problems occur. The most serious side effect is a condition called ovarian hyperstimulation syndrome, which can be mild, moderate, or severe. Depending on the drug used, some women experience hot flushes, ovarian enlargement resulting in abdominal discomfort or pain, breast tenderness, dizziness, headache, nervousness, nausea or vomiting, fatigue, and visual disturbances. Women experiencing mild or moderate symptoms can be treated with rest, medication, and monitoring. However, the complications associated with severe cases (which occur in between 0.4 and 4 percent of cycles), though rare, can be life-threatening.[5] The highest risk of severe ovarian hyperstimulation syndrome is with the use of hMG. Women receiving ovulation induction drugs must therefore be monitored closely for signs of the syndrome, with careful attention paid to dosages, and steps must be taken to counteract the syndrome if it occurs.

Another of the adverse effects that has been shown clearly to result from ovulation induction drug use is an increased rate of multiple birth. The use of hMG carries the greatest risk, with multiple pregnancies reported in as many as 32 percent of women in some studies. The rate of multiple births in Canada has increased dramatically since the advent of fertility drug use. The statistics show a dramatic increase in the multiple-birth set rate in the 1980s and early 1990s as fertility drug and IVF use became more common. Recently published data for Canada between 1974 and 1990 show that the multiple-birth set rate rose from 912.8 in 1974 to 1,058.9 per 100,000 confinements in 1990. During this same period, the birth rate for triplets, quadruplets, and quintuplets rose from 8.3 to 21.7 per 100,000 confinements.[6] ...

It is logical to assume that fertility drug use is largely responsible for the increase in the multiple birth rate. Although a substantial per-

centage (38 percent) of all individuals born following *in vitro* fertilization in Canada are from
a multiple pregnancy, the absolute number of
IVF births for the Canadian population is still
small; thus, fertility drug use, particularly ovulation induction drugs, must have made a
greater contribution to the marked rise. As discussed [elsewhere], multiple pregnancies pose
significant risks for pregnant women, for the
fetuses, and for the eventual children, as well
as costs for the health care system and society
generally as these children grow up.

The possibility has also been raised that
fertility drug use could be associated with subsequent ovarian cancer. A large recent study
for the National Institute of Child Health and
Human Development found that the data
available at that time (January 1993) were inadequate to estimate whether there is an increased risk and, if so, its magnitude. However,
this possibility is a cause for concern, pointing to the need for further research.

In general terms, further research is
needed to provide full information on the
long-term health effects of fertility drug use
on women and their children. Although
clomiphene has been in use since the late
1960s, for example, only recently have any
data been available on its longer-term health
effects. There has been considerable conjecture
about the effects of clomiphene on the health
of children; in particular, an Australian study
raised the possibility of an increase in the occurrence of neural tube defects, but this has
not been confirmed in other studies or in a
large recent case-control study on this topic.[7]
Overall, studies of children at birth have
shown that the incidence of congenital
anomalies among the children of women who
took fertility drugs has been similar to that in
the general population.[8]

Ovulation Suppression Drugs

The second group of drugs used to treat infertility, ovulation suppression drugs, are used pri-

marily to treat women with endometriosis,
one of the risk factors associated with infertility. Ovulation suppression is a highly invasive
step, yet it is used, with no evidence that it is
effective, to treat a condition whose cause and
pathogenesis are not even understood, simply
in the hope that treatment will have an effect
on the woman's fertility. The drugs are used to
suppress her menstrual cycle for at least six
months, in the hope that the symptoms affecting fertility will subside and conception will be
more likely to occur once drug use is discontinued and menstrual cycles resume.

The Commission analyzed the data available in the worldwide literature on three types
of common ovulation suppression drugs—
danazol, norethindrone, and Gn-RH analogues—and their effect on endometriosis-
related infertility. Based on this analysis, it is
the Commission's assessment that the use of
danazol, norethindrone, Gn-RH analogues, or
any ovulation suppression drug is ineffective
in treating infertility thought to result from
endometriosis or unexplained infertility. Their
use should be discontinued, as they have moderate to severe side effects; moreover, they
eliminate the possibility of conceiving naturally for the duration of treatment. Such risks
should not be undertaken when there is evidence that the use of these drugs is ineffective.

Drugs to Treat Male Infertility

The Commission evaluated data on the drugs
used most often to treat male infertility; they
include clomiphene citrate, gonadotropin-
releasing hormone, oral kallikrein, bromo-
criptine, and androgens (male hormones).

SEMINAL DEFECTS

Since it is usual for a man's sperm count to
vary, an accurate diagnosis of a seminal defect
can be made only if several sperm samples are
collected over a period of time. Data collected

from Canadian academic infertility clinics show that in couples where the man had a seminal defect, 74 percent had oligospermia (reduced sperm count) and 26 percent had azoospermia (no sperm).

Azoospermia clearly results in infertility, but the relationship between low sperm count and male infertility is less clear. The partners of men with oligospermia have a live birth rate of 2 percent per month of unprotected intercourse, compared to about 20 to 25 percent for the population at large. Although 20 million sperm per millilitre is regarded as the dividing line between oligospermia and a normal sperm count, men with lower sperm counts (less than 5 million) have been known to conceive. Many physicians believe that as-yet-undetectable subfertility in the female partner adds to the problem in cases where a couple in which the man has oligospermia cannot conceive. This would help to explain why the partners of some men with low sperm counts are able to conceive while the partners of others cannot....

Need for research

Male infertility has been a neglected area in research, despite the fact that 24 percent of couples seen at Canadian infertility clinics are infertile because of a diagnosed problem in the male partner (see research volume, *Treatment of Infertility: Current Practices and Psychosocial Implications*). Medical science is unable to identity a specific cause for 30 to 40 percent of cases of male infertility, and researchers have estimated that only 11 percent of infertile men are potentially treatable at present. As we pointed out earlier, the area of male infertility warrants much greater research emphasis. Assigning a higher research priority to investigating male infertility would promote greater understanding of the causes, diagnoses, and treatments of seminal disorders and might enable a reduced use of treatments in female

partners who are fertile because of male infertility....

The data collected for the Commission on the practices of fertility clinics and attitudes of patients showed that counselling, information provision, and support for informed decision making do not measure up to patients' expectations with respect to informed choice or indeed to the standards set by physicians' professional organizations. The Commission also found that this information deficit seriously limits patients' ability to make decisions about their health. Without sufficient information about fertility drug treatment and its attendant risks, benefits, costs, and possible outcomes, patients must cope with added physical and psychological stresses....

Conclusion

Fertility drugs occupy a unique place in the infertility treatment spectrum. Many do not consider fertility drugs to be a "new reproductive technology," yet fertility drugs are developed and used to act on the same biological processes as new reproductive technologies, with the aim correcting some of the same disorders, and they have the same far-reaching implications—they could potentially affect not only the women who use them but also their children.

Fertility drugs are the most prevalent infertility treatment and are used in most other assisted conception techniques. The prevalence of fertility drug use makes it important to collect information on their short- and long-term outcomes. The side effects and long-term outcomes of fertility drug use have implications for society that are just as great as those of drugs used to treat heart disease or cancer. The evaluation of long-term outcomes is not easy, however, in part because the use of some drugs (especially clomiphene citrate) occurs most frequently outside the context of specialized treatment facilities, and in part because information on both the individuals receiving treatment and their children is relevant to this assessment.

It is not in society's interests that the use of these drugs continue without thorough and ongoing evaluation of their risks and effectiveness....

Infertility Treatments: Assisted Insemination

Effectiveness of AI

RISKS AND EFFECTIVENESS OF DONOR INSEMINATION

Statistics show that DI with frozen sperm, quarantined until the donor has been tested for infectious diseases, is the safest and most effective method of circumventing the lack of a male partner who is fertile. This is not surprising, as both the woman and the donor are presumably fertile, and no drug therapy, surgery, or other invasive procedures are required. In the past, frozen sperm was less viable than fresh sperm, but cryopreservation and insemination procedures have improved, and some recent studies show little difference in success rates between frozen and fresh sperm.

DI properly performed after appropriate testing of the donor poses no physical risks, but there may be psychological effects on the recipient, her partner, or both. DI pregnancies can be accompanied by feelings of ambivalence, fear, or nightmares for some women. Some women report being depressed after a DI birth, while their partners report feelings of guilt, impotence, and resentment (see research volume, *Treatment of Infertility: Assisted Reproductive Technologies*). Many of the psychological effects of DI can be minimized or avoided with proper counselling and informed consent before a woman or couple agrees to undergo the procedure; these and other related issues are discussed later in this chapter.

Issues in Sperm Donation, Collection, and Storage

The DI process begins with the donor. Studies show that men donate sperm for different reasons: altruism, for example, or a wish to "test" their fertility. Donors have been neglected in the study of DI, however, perhaps because they are wary of jeopardizing their anonymity and because current record-keeping practices make most of them impossible to contact. The donor's interests and responsibilities should not be ignored, however. Issues such as anonymity and informed consent, as well as the standards and practices of facilities that collect and use sperm, have implications for the donor's health and psychological well-being, as well as that of the recipient and her child.

DONOR ANONYMITY

One of the most controversial issues in DI is whether the donor should remain anonymous; the issue is also related to secrecy about the procedure (see section on Secrecy in DI Families). For decades, practitioners believed that anonymity made DI easier for everyone involved and have protected the identity of both the donor and the recipient. In interviews, many donors have said that they value the guarantee of anonymity because they want to ensure that they are not forced to assume the legal responsibilities of parenthood; they trust clinicians and sperm banks not to reveal their identity, and they have no interest in meeting recipients or their children. It has been argued that eliminating donor anonymity would make it more difficult to find men willing to donate sperm; in a national survey done for the Commission, men identified confidentiality as the number one condition for donating sperm. Most women and couples contemplating DI also prefer an anonymous donor, usually to avoid unwanted involvement by the donor in the life of family and the child. Although two

(2 of 33) AI programs surveyed by the Commission allow patients to designate a donor, few patients request this.

Donor anonymity may, however, work against the interests of DI children, for example if they want to know about their origins. Some DI children and parents told the Commission that without information about the donor, the children could feel cut off from their genetic origins, might be unaware of potential health problems, or might marry a blood relative unknowingly....

COMMERCIALIZATION

Commissioners are strongly opposed to commercializing human reproduction, as are Canadians generally. We heard clearly from Canadians that they are uncomfortable with any situation involving the development of reproductive technologies or services on the basis of their profit potential, particularly where only those with the means to pay can have access to them. In our view, no profit should be made from the selling of any reproductive material, including eggs, sperm, or zygotes/embryos, because of its ultimately dehumanizing effects. Two aspects are relevant here—payment for donors and sperm banking and distribution.

Payment for Donation. Because donors must spend considerable time giving a medical history, having a physical examination and coming back for repeated blood tests, and giving sperm samples, the Commission feels it is reasonable to compensate donors for their time and inconvenience. Such compensation should not be high enough, however, to provide a financial incentive to donate. What level of remuneration, if any, is appropriate for sperm "donation"? Most sperm donors in Canada receive money intended to reimburse their out-of-pocket expenses—currently around $75 per donation. This is unlikely to act as a financial inducement, given the inconvenience

involved, but we believe this level should not increase except perhaps to maintain its value relative to inflation.

Storage and Distribution. Another aspect of DI that lends itself to commercialization is the storing and distribution of sperm. The principle of non-commercialization means that commercial sperm banks are unacceptable in Canada, as are the purchase and use of sperm from commercial banks in other countries. In the United States, assisted insemination is a $164-million-per-year industry,[8] and data gathered by the Commission show that the potential exists for substantial profit in this country too—each sperm donation (for which the donor receives $75) produces 8 to 10 straws or containers of sperm, which are sold to practitioners for about $125 each. Since many women and couples undergoing DI have to pay in advance for a six-month supply of donor sperm—and are not reimbursed if a pregnancy occurs in an early cycle (see research volume, *Treatment of Infertility: Current Practices and Psychosocial Implications*)—sperm banks can potentially earn far more than it costs them to test, freeze, and transport sperm and maintain adequate records, despite the significant cost of stringent testing and detailed record keeping. Making a profit from sperm banking is unacceptable from the perspective of our guiding principles....

Issues in the Practice of Insemination

ACCESS TO TREATMENT

... The Commission believes that the criteria used to determine access to publicly funded medical services must be fair and applied equally to all. We believe this as one of our fundamental guiding principles, and we believe this because it reflects basic principles of human rights law. Nondiscrimination in the provision of public services is a clear requirement under the Canadian Charter and federal

Ethical Issues

and provincial human rights legislation, which prohibit discrimination on the basis of such historically disadvantaging factors as sex, marital status, sexual orientation, and social or economic status.

We do believe that it is within the purview of practitioners to make decisions about medical indications for services. That is their responsibility, and it is what they are trained to do. In the case of DI, however, there are no medical indications for this service, in that, other than in rare cases, it is performed on healthy women who are fertile. Whether heterosexual or homosexual, married or single, all women undergoing DI are in the same situation—they are unable to have a child, either because their partner is infertile or because they do not have a male partner. The Commission believes it is wrong to forbid some people access to medical services on the basis of social factors while others are permitted to use them: using criteria such as a woman's marital status or sexual orientation to determine access to DI, based on historical prejudices and stereotypes, amounts to discrimination as defined under human rights law and contravenes the Commission's guiding principle of equality. There is no intent to force any practitioner or clinic to provide new reproductive technologies if they do not wish to do so—our recommendations are to ensure that services provided and funded by provinces' health budgets are not offered in a discriminatory way contravening the Canadian Charter. Clearly, religious institutions exist and should not be forced to contravene their religious beliefs, but publicly supported health care should be delivered in a universal and non-discriminatory way.

The Commission recognizes that some Canadians are uneasy about family forms that might be facilitated by such access to AI. Our survey of national values and attitudes, for instance, found that the Canadians surveyed are most supportive of AI when it is used by a married, heterosexual couple, and least supportive when it is used by a lesbian couple. Almost half the people surveyed oppose or strongly oppose its use by single women.

Although most Canadians surveyed did not support lesbians having access to DI, to provide a service in a discriminatory way by denying access, without evidence that a resultant child would be harmed, is contrary to the Charter and also contravenes our ethic of care. The available evidence does not show different outcomes in children born to or raised by lesbians when compared to outcomes in children born to heterosexual women and couples.[13] Thus, the "best interests of the child" cannot be used as a reason to deny access simply because a woman is a lesbian. The ethic of care dictates that people should be treated equally unless there is evidence that others will be harmed....

Excluding single women or lesbians from DI programs not only contravenes their equality rights, it also puts their health at risk, by forcing them to resort to unsafe practices while heterosexual women in traditional marital relationships have access to safe and effective procedures. In both situations there is a strong desire for a child, but no male partner who is fertile; there is in fact no greater medical need in a woman whose partner has no sperm than in a woman who has no partner. If a service is to be available, women should be treated equally, unless there is good evidence that the best interests of the child will suffer. Current practice is inequitable and reflects discriminatory attitudes. The same standards of access to DI should apply to all women choosing this route to pregnancy and parenthood, to ensure that all can do so safely....

Familial and Societal Implications of DI

Complex issues face families formed using DI, and from them emerge new societal dilemmas. At the individual level, the secrecy surrounding DI can give rise to conflict within the DI family, but at the societal level it has also resulted in significant gaps in relevant research, legal direction, and record keeping. The legal status of DI families, what records should be required and who should have access to them, and how best to balance the needs of DI participants remain unaddressed in law or policy. Many DI participants liken their situation to that of adoptive families, so it is important to consider whether there are lessons to be learned from the evolution of Canada's adoption policies.

Surveys and research done for the Commission show that Canadians attach importance to having a genetic link between themselves and their children; we found that most Canadians would seek medical help to conceive before looking into adoption because of the importance of this link. Many aspects of Western and other cultures reflect as well as reinforce the importance of the genetic link between parent and child. As a result, many practitioners suggest that DI be kept secret, even from the child, to preserve the appearance that the family does not differ from most other families. Some clinics even require couples to sign a form stating that they will never tell anyone about their DI procedure. At the same time, our society values honesty and openness in personal relationships. This results in great ambivalence for many individuals involved, as secrecy often implies something to be ashamed of.

Parents deal with these pressures in different ways. There is a marked preference among recipients at the time of insemination to keep the procedure secret (although this may become more difficult as time passes and the child is growing up), and they are encouraged in this by our laws and medical standards. Secrecy is preferred because it seems to solve so many problems: the man's infertility is hidden, an image of normalcy is maintained, children do not grow up feeling different from their

peers, and any potential legal tangles are avoided. In addition, keeping it a secret sidesteps the issue of acknowledging a division between social and biological parenthood for these couples.

SECRECY IN DI FAMILIES

On the surface it would seem that secrecy about DI is fairly easy to maintain. Once conception has occurred, the pregnancy continues like any other. In the long run, however, the Commission found that secrecy places great strains on families. Parents must always remain on guard lest they give away the secret, and differences between father and child must be minimized or ignored. The father may feel incomplete or inadequate, but he has to suppress those feelings. Some fathers said they felt fraudulent about how they fit into the family narrative.

When Commission researchers interviewed married DI mothers, many expressed relief at finally being able to talk about the facts of their child's conception. They said they avoided talking about the issue at home, out of sensitivity for their husbands' feelings. Some women said they felt they were "living a lie," pretending that their husband was the genetic father of the children. Lesbian DI mothers told the Commission they did not feel the same pressure to keep their child's origins a secret because DI is more accepted in the lesbian community. Some said they paid a price for this openness—some were already estranged from parents and siblings who could not accept their sexual orientation, and undergoing DI added to the strain.

Commission research showed that maintaining secrecy about the means of conception can be contrary to the best interests of the child (see research volume, *The Prevalence of Infertility in Canada*). Adults born through DI reported that the decision to keep DI a secret was very damaging—they felt deceived and said they had always sensed that something was "wrong" in the family. Some told the Commission that they found out about the method of conception at a time of family crisis, such as divorce or death in the family—a time when secrets are difficult to keep. Discovering the truth in this way is doubly traumatic; the shock of discovery during an already stressful period is coupled with the realization that your parents had lied to you all your life.

Adoptive families used to be advised to keep this secret from the community and from the child; studies have since shown, however, that openness and honesty about adoption are healthier for all concerned.[17] Secrets kept within families put added pressure on marriages, and children often sense something is being hidden. Many professionals who have experience with adoption, such as social workers, psychologists, doctors, and sociologists who have seen the damage that secrets can cause, as well as some adoptees themselves, advocate openness about the fact of DI.[18]

Ultimately, the decision about whether and whom to tell should be made by the parents, as it is rooted in personal values and beliefs. However, given the long-term psychological and familial implications of secrecy, particularly for the resulting child, women and couples should make their decision based on full information and discussion about their options. Provision of information to the recipient about the issue should be a required part of the DI process....

Infertility Treatments: *In Vitro* Fertilization

The Views of Canadians

How IVF IS PAID FOR

The issue of public funding for IVF has been more controversial than that of funding for other infertility treatments, because it is very expensive, and because of questions about its effectiveness and safety. Even if these were known, however, many people opposed its public funding on the grounds that the health care system cannot afford the "luxury" of expensive, high-technology treatments for infertility, or because they felt it would divert attention and resources from other reproductive services or health priorities, including infertility prevention and basic prenatal care.

To those affected by it, however, infertility is not a trivial concern but a condition with potentially deep and lasting consequences for their well-being throughout their adult lives. We heard testimony that safe and effective procedures that could help those who are infertile should be included in the health care system, on the grounds that infertility is just as important in the lives of those affected as are many other conditions now treated in the health care system....

The Effectiveness of IVF

Answering the question "does the treatment work?" is seldom straightforward. For example, even couples who are fertile have a 4 percent chance of not conceiving in their first year of trying. It is therefore often difficult to tell whether an outcome (a pregnancy or birth) was the result of treatment or the result of the chance nature of fertility at work. If everyone in the treatment group were sterile, that is, unable to have a pregnancy without treatment, then any birth that occurred would obviously have been the result of receiving treatment. But the reality is that those having infertility treatment include a mix of people who are sterile and people with low fertility. To complicate matters even further, the proportion of these two groups will vary according to the diagnostic category.

This means that the number of births following treatment is not a direct measure of the effectiveness of treatment, because the likelihood of birth among the same or similar patients who have not had treatment must also be known—hence the need for a control group, which can be very difficult to assemble. Sometimes couples are willing to be their own control—accepting random assignment to a "waiting" group or postponing the beginning of treatment. But some couples are understandably unwilling to do this. Multicentre trials are therefore needed in order to generate large enough numbers to permit statistically significant and reliable conclusions to be drawn.

Despite these methodological difficulties, good information about the effectiveness of IVF is needed for decision making at both the societal and the individual level, and until the Commission investigated this area comprehensively, the existing information had simply not been collated and analyzed in one overall assessment, making rational decisions difficult or impossible.

At a societal level, policy makers and others making resource allocation decisions need good information about the effectiveness of medical procedures, the population to be served, and the cost and resource implications compared with the potential health benefits. Information about these elements helps to determine whether IVF should be offered and, if so, under what circumstances.

At the individual level, practitioners and couples have to take what is known about the broad effectiveness of IVF and apply it to the couple's specific circumstances to determine whether IVF is an appropriate treatment for them. To establish an accurate assessment of whether IVF is likely to work in their case, and whether the chance of a live birth is worth the risk of treatment, information about four elements is essential. These are

- *the natural force of pregnancy*—the couple's chance of conceiving naturally, given their age, diagnosis, and other relevant factors;

- *the effectiveness of treatment*—the couple's chance of conceiving with IVF, given their age, diagnosis, and other relevant factors;
- *the known risks of treatment*—including the short-term health implications and the possible long-term effects of treatment; and
- *the relative effectiveness, risk, and cost of alternative treatments or strategies.*

In the absence of information about each of these elements, practitioners and patients are unable to weigh the options, and patients cannot make informed choices.

Commissioners decided that if the evidence showed that IVF did not pass assessment after evaluating these four elements for a given diagnosis, we would recommend that it not be offered as a treatment for that diagnosis, regardless of the demand. If IVF showed promise with respect to a given category of diagnosis, but the evidence was not sufficient to demonstrate that it was more effective than receiving no treatment we would recommend that it be considered a priority for research. If the evidence derived from well-designed research studies showed that it was effective for a particular category of diagnosis, we would recommend that it be considered for funding as a medical service. However, the ethical, social, and legal implications would also have to be weighed in reaching an appropriate policy decision in this regard.

When assessing the effectiveness of IVF in achieving a live birth, it is important to keep in mind that natural conception rates in couples from the general population are also far from 100 percent. The average monthly chance of conception leading to a live birth is about 20 to 25 percent. There is a range in couples' ability to conceive, so that the peak conception rate is 33 percent in the first month of trying; then it falls quickly, settling to about 5 percent each month. Fertilization may occur more frequently than this, but about half of all fertilized eggs never result in a live birth....

[Our] review of the available evidence permitted two main conclusions about the effectiveness of IVF: First, IVF is effective only in cases of complete fallopian tube blockage resulting from tubal disease or defect, severe endometriosis, or previous surgical sterilization. IVF has not been proven effective for any of the other diagnoses it is currently being used for. Second, only IVF itself has been shown to be effective for blocked tubes—variations such as GIFT and ZIFT have not been shown to be of benefit.

Our data collation and analysis showed clearly that in 1990, more than a decade after IVF was first offered, IVF procedures for most infertility diagnoses fall into the category of not enough evidence—there simply is not enough reliable evidence to categorize them as effective or ineffective; we do not know if the treatment is more likely to result in a live birth than no treatment. This is not the same as saying that IVF does not work; rather, additional and better data are required before firm conclusions can be drawn about the appropriateness of IVF as a treatment for most types of infertility.

Our review of the evidence showed that IVF is effective when a woman has blocked fallopian tubes as a result of a disease, such as endometriosis, or surgical sterilization. By "effective" we do not mean that IVF will necessarily result in a live birth in every given case: however, when the results of treating many women with this diagnosis are taken together, IVF has been shown to be more effective (that is, more likely to result in a live birth) than receiving no treatment....

Risks of IVF

The second factor the Commission assessed in examining whether and under what conditions IVF should be provided were the risks involved. As noted earlier, no medical procedure can ever be entirely risk-free. There is, however, a need to reduce the risk to the minimum acceptable level while maintaining effectiveness. The risks outlined in this section are the known effects of IVF, which include multiple pregnancies and the risks of the drugs and procedures surrounding IVF.

Among the most serious risks of IVF are those associated with multiple pregnancy, a risk that is also associated with the use of the ovulation drugs, which are often used in conjunction with IVF (see Chapter 18). The usual practice in IVF is to transfer more than one zygote to the woman's uterus, as this increases the likelihood that at least one will implant; there have been reports of as many as seven zygotes being transferred at the same time, and often more than one implants and develops. Using American Fertility Society registry figures, which included both Canadian and U.S. data, the result of the practice is that about 30 percent of IVF deliveries, 24 percent of GIFT deliveries, and 23 percent of ZIFT deliveries are multiple, compared to a rate in the general population of about 1 percent. In fact, this way of counting understates the problem, as one confinement may give rise to several infants. For example, in Canada for 1991, although 23 percent of live birth confinements after IVF were multiple, one liveborn IVF child in three was part of a multiple birth (81 of 213 infants born after IVF or 38 percent). This is the more relevant statistic, because it is these individuals and their families who must deal with the consequences of multiple births.

Most of the multiple births reported in our survey of fertility programs were twins, with one set of triplets and one set of quadruplets. In a sample of this size (171 deliveries), however, no higher-order births would normally be expected—a set of triplets is expected to occur less than once in 10,000 deliveries, and a set of quadruplets less than once in a million deliveries.

Multiple pregnancies pose serious health risks for both women and their children. For women, multiple pregnancy increases the risk of anaemia, miscarriage, toxaemia, high blood pressure, kidney trouble, difficult delivery, and post-birth haemorrhage. In Canada, a woman carrying three or more fetuses usually spends the last 4 to 12 weeks of the pregnancy in hospital, and most undergo a Caesarian delivery with its attendant risks. Just as important, multiple pregnancies present risks for fetuses: miscarriage, accidents during delivery, and premature births are much more common in multiple pregnancies. Prematurity brings with it another risk—low birth weight. The incidence of low birth weight in the Canadian population is between 6 and 8 percent,[10] but studies have found that 12 percent of IVF singletons, 55 percent of IVF twins, and 94 percent of IVF triplet or higher-order births result in low birth weight (less than 2,500 grams). Moreover, one-third of triplets and higher-order births result in very low birth weight (less than 1,500 grams).[11]

The consequences of low birth weight can be serious and long-lasting: breathing problems are common in low birth weight infants, who are also more likely to have cerebral palsy, poor eyesight, short attention span, and poor learning skills as they grow up. Hyperactivity, reading difficulties, and poor coordination and motor skills in childhood are also more common. A three-year Canadian study of children with very low birth weights born between 1984 and 1986 found that 20 percent suffered some form of serious disability.[12] More recently, U.S. studies have shown that 25 percent[13] of very low birth weight children have serious disabilities, while an additional half have other problems, such as those requiring special education services.[14,15] In other words, a substantial proportion of very low birth weight children will need continuing attention

or care in varying degrees for a good part of their lives.

In addition to posing risks to the physical health of women and children, then, the consequences of multiple births can also strain the psychological and social health of the family after birth and place additional demands on the health, education, and social services systems. Parents of multiple-birth children cope with demands on their time, energy, and finances that are much greater than those of other parents. Although there are few Canadian studies of multiple-birth families, parents of "multiples" told the Commission that they had paid a price in raising their children. Despite the joy most parents derive from having children, these parents also felt overwhelmed by the demands on them. Families often need the support of paid and volunteer caregivers after the children leave hospital. In addition to pressures on the family, multiple births also involve added costs for health and social services systems. Provincial health insurance, for example, pays for the woman's longer hospital stay before and after birth, for Caesarian delivery, and for extended neonatal intensive care for the children.

Recognizing the risks involved in multiple pregnancies and the fact that if too many embryos implant they are all likely to die, some IVF clinics (5 of the 16 surveyed by the Commission) offer a procedure known as selective reduction in the situation of multiple pregnancy; some embryos are aborted to give the others a chance to survive. As well as ethical dilemmas, the procedure has risks, including loss of all the developing fetuses.

To avoid the physical and psychological risks of multiple pregnancy and selective reduction, Canadian associations of practitioners working in this field have recommended limits on the number of zygotes transferred, but they have not specified a standard. Most but not all IVF practitioners are now limiting the number of zygotes they transfer. Furthermore, the World Health Organization analysis of international data found that the live birth rate after IVF declines if more than three zygotes are transferred and the guidelines of the European Society of Human Reproduction limit the number of embryos transferred to three.

After considering the health risks to women, fetuses, and children, the emotional and financial costs, and the dubious benefits of transferring larger numbers of embryos, the Commission recommends that

> 108. No more than three zygotes be transferred during IVF procedures, and then only after counselling of the couple to ensure that they understand the possibility and implications of having triplets. Patients should give their consent in writing if more than one zygote is to be transferred and should be assured that no more than three will be transferred.

Drug risks

Most patients at Canadian IVF clinics undergo "stimulated" cycles; that is, ovulation induction drugs are used to stimulate the woman's ovaries to produce more than one egg. This increases the chances of at least one viable embryo being created *in vitro* and means that some can be frozen for use in a future cycle, thus avoiding the need for additional egg retrieval at that time while still giving another chance at pregnancy. We discussed what is known about the risks of fertility drug use [above]. As we noted [there], although ovulation induction drugs increase the number of eggs produced, their use can also make the uterus less hospitable to implantation; as a result, even if more zygotes can be created *in vitro*, fewer may survive transfer in a stimulated cycle.[16]

One Canadian clinic is currently conducting a trial to determine the effectiveness of "natural cycle" IVF without drugs; the one egg produced naturally during an unmedicated cycle is retrieved for fertilization. Although the drug risks are avoided and the uterus is more hospitable to implantation, only one egg is available for fertilization; thus, there is less of a chance of obtaining a viable zygote for transfer. U.S. statistics indicate that success rates for natural cycle IVF are increasing, but they are still less than half that of stimulated cycles.[17]

There is evidence, however, that the beneficial aspects of stimulated and unstimulated cycles can be combined to improve success rates and reduce risks. The ovaries are stimulated to produce multiple eggs, which are retrieved and fertilized and the zygotes cryopreserved until the woman's hormone levels have returned to normal. Then she has the opportunity to have one or two zygotes transferred, during several natural cycles if necessary, with only the one invasive egg retrieval procedure needed. Some believe that this is the only ethical way to perform IVF; drug risks are reduced, the chances of implantation are maximized, and only the most viable zygotes may be transferred. It is with this background that some physicians have expressed the view that cryopreservation of zygotes should be made mandatory in all IVF programs.

The question of whether frozen zygotes are as viable as fresh remains unanswered, but recent U.S. data show that the number of live births after fresh and frozen zygote transfer are similar.[18] Moreover, as cryopreservation techniques are refined, rates of successful transfer are increasing.[19] There appears to be no increase in spontaneous abortion or birth anomalies compared to pregnancies established with fresh zygotes, although more evidence is still required to confirm this.

The Commission believes that the benefits offered by cryopreserving zygotes for later implantation in an unstimulated cycle outweigh the risks. Cryopreservation reduces the use of ovulation induction drugs, gives more transfer opportunities during several cycles, and thus increases the likelihood of implantation. It also reduces the risks of multiple births resulting from the transfer of larger numbers of zygotes....

PROCEDURAL RISKS

All invasive procedures carry some risk of infection, bleeding, damage to internal tissues, and pain; IVF is no exception. In addition, the rate of extra-uterine pregnancies (ectopic or tubal pregnancies)—although quite low at a few percent—is still at least 25 times more common in IVF patients than in the general population. This may be because of the characteristics of IVF patients, however, rather than being a result of IVF procedures. Many IVF patients have tubal problems, are older, and have had trouble conceiving, so that the rate of ectopic pregnancy would be expected to be higher even if IVF had not been used. The Commission believes that data on the incidence of these various outcomes following IVF use—both ovulation induction and the procedure itself—should be collected by all facilities offering IVF. Having this information available will facilitate more informed decision making by patients, practitioners, regulators, and policy makers.

PSYCHOSOCIAL EFFECTS OF TREATMENT

Being treated for infertility is stressful and difficult for couples. Sociological studies carried out for the Commission showed high stress levels in couples involved in IVF treatment. How much of this stress is attributable to the treatment process and how much results from their infertility are hard to disentangle. An examination of 686 couples undergoing IVF found that patients ranked higher than the general population on a list of 29 symptoms of psychological distress. Although IVF treatment places couples under greater than normal pressure in a very personal part of their lives, the study also found that the vast majority of couples were well adjusted in terms

of marital happiness (see research volume, *Treatment of Infertility: Current Practices and Psychosocial Implications*). This supports the findings of other studies showing that infertility does not have a significant effect on the quality of marital life, but rather has indirect negative effects by lowering individuals' self-esteem and sense of control over their lives. The stress of repeated failures of treatment is particularly difficult for couples to deal with.

Social support, or the lack of it, plays an important role in reducing or adding to the stress felt by couples in treatment. Couples reported three common stress-causing situations: friends or family members asking each month whether the woman was pregnant yet; hints that the couple needed only to "relax" to get pregnant; and suggestions of folk cures to increase the couple's fertility. Women were more likely than their partners to discuss their infertility with others, but most women and men reported that they were not interested in taking part in support groups.

Since the female partners in couples undergoing IVF experience the most painful and invasive aspects of diagnostic and treatment procedures, not surprisingly women undergoing IVF report more stress than men do. Women also said they feared being dropped from the program if their bodies did not seem to be responding normally to treatment, and this created stress as well. The male partners tended to report more negative consequences on privacy and feelings of control.

Not all the psychosocial implications of IVF treatment are negative. The majority of IVF patients surveyed reported positive effects on their relationship with their partner and on their feelings about themselves. Even if treatment proved unsuccessful, they felt they had done everything they could to overcome their infertility.

One of the repeated messages we heard from Canadians was the need for information about longer-term risks and outcomes following IVF. As with most new medical treatments, the lack of follow-up data on IVF makes it difficult to determine whether there are any long-term adverse effects on women or children. Although some infertility practitioners have made great efforts, at present no organization or agency in Canada gathers information on the outcomes after IVF or tracks its effects over time. As described in our research volumes, record-keeping practices vary markedly among clinics and practitioners, with some clinics not even having data on whether a given IVF procedure resulted in a live birth.

One of the questions that must be asked about IVF is whether it poses any risk to the children born through its use. The many studies to date show no increased risk of congenital anomalies in IVF infants. One Australian study revealed a higher incidence of neural tube defects, but this result has not been confirmed by other studies, including a large recent case-control study by the National Institute of Child Health and Human Development.[20] We have already alluded to the high incidence of low birth weight infants following IVF, and perinatal death is three to four times higher for IVF births than for other births.[21] Because the technology is relatively new, however, long-term tracking of large numbers of IVF children has not yet been possible—the oldest child born as a result of the procedure is now 15.

It is essential that data on IVF—on treatment cycles, immediate outcomes, and long-term outcomes—be collected in a systematic and consistent manner. Data are needed to evaluate whether there are longer-term implications for women and what the actual outcomes are with respect to the health of IVF children as they grow up. To assess these out-

comes in the least intrusive manner would require linkage of coded IVF patient data bases with coded data on the same individuals from health-related and other data bases to draw conclusions about long-term outcomes for both women and their children (see section on Measuring Health Outcomes).

In summary, the Commission's review of the effectiveness and risks of *in vitro* fertilization showed that IVF is effective for one diagnostic category only—complete fallopian tube blockage—and that the risks of the technology, though real, are manageable from the perspective of service providers through the establishment of guidelines for practice and the careful monitoring of individual patients as treatment proceeds. From the perspective of individuals seeking treatment, however, each patient must make a fully informed decision about whether the identified level of risk is acceptable to her. It is therefore essential that anyone contemplating treatment be fully informed of what is known and what is not known about risks....

Preconception Arrangements

Views on Preconception Arrangements

... We found that opinions on this issue are diverse and difficult to catalogue, ranging from outright opposition to the practice, whatever form it might take, to acceptance and even encouragement of the practice by public policies to regulate it, to enforce contracts, and to provide medical services in support of it. Ranged between these positions are those who oppose commercial arrangements but would tolerate non-commercial arrangements, particularly in cases where the commissioning woman's health was the reason for seeking a preconception arrangement; those who would find commercial arrangements acceptable if certain safeguards or regulations were in place; and those who would not encourage or participate in a (non-commercial) preconception arrangement themselves but would not prohibit others from doing so. We examine this range of positions in the next three sections.

Those who hold that commercial preconception arrangements should be prohibited believe that they are inherently exploitive; that they treat children as commodities; that they are dehumanizing and degrading to women and their reproductive capacity; that they are harmful to the participants and to children born as a result of these arrangements; that they foster harmful social attitudes about the role and value of women, children, and families; and that they reinforce and perpetuate sexual inequality in our society. They also point out that such arrangements have significant implications for the gestational woman, who agrees on signing the contract to restrict her behaviour in certain ways (for example, with respect to smoking and drinking) and to abide by the commissioning couple's requirements for her pregnancy care (for example, to undergo tests such as amniocentesis). These arguments are examined in the next few pages.

Potential for Exploitation. Concerns about the exploitive nature of commercial preconception arrangements stem from several sources, in particular the social and economic disparities between gestational women and commissioning couples and the disproportionate assumption of risks and obligations by the parties to a preconception contract. These inequalities in power and resources, it is argued, make gestational women vulnerable to exploitation, no matter how willing they might be to participate, because they can never negotiate on an equal footing with the other parties.

A recurring concern we heard was that women willing to undertake gestational arrangements for others would be those who are economically vulnerable—that a woman who was well off financially would be most unlikely to agree to be a gestational mother. That this is often the case was borne out by our research, which revealed significant socioeconomic differences between commissioning women and gestational women. Although reliable data on participants are scarce, the information available shows that gestational women are younger, less well educated, and of lower income than commissioning couples. The study for the Law Reform Commission, for example, which examined data on 32 commissioning couples found that their overall age is much older than that of the gestational women: the youngest commissioning man, at age 35, and the youngest commissioning woman, at age 34, were both older than the oldest gestational woman, who was 33.

Commercial Preconception Contracts. The Commission examined preconception agreements drafted by U.S. commercial agencies. They contained some or all of the following provisions:

1. The gestational woman agrees to become pregnant using the commissioning man's sperm, to carry the fetus to term, and then to relinquish her parental rights and transfer custody of the child to the commissioning couple.

2. The gestational woman and her husband (if she has one) promise to take all steps necessary to have the commissioning man's name entered on the child's birth certificate as the father, and the gestational woman's husband agrees to renounce any legal presumption that he is the child's father.

3. The commissioning couple promises to pay the gestational woman a specified sum

(usually U.S.$10,000) when her maternal rights are terminated by a court order and provided he has custody of the child.

4. The parties agree that the specified fee can be reduced significantly if the woman miscarries or gives birth to a stillborn child. In the *Baby M* arrangement, for example, the gestational woman was to receive no payment if miscarriage occurred in the fourth month or earlier, and $1,000 if the fetus miscarried after the fourth month or was born dead.

5. The gestational woman promises that she will undergo amniocentesis.

6. The gestational woman agrees that she will not abort the fetus but that, if the commissioning couple decides on the basis of the amniocentesis results that they do not want the child to be born, she will have an abortion.

7. The gestational woman promises not to form a parent-child bond with the fetus.

8. The gestational woman agrees not to drink alcohol or to take any nonprescription, prescription, or illicit drugs without the permission of a physician specified in the agreement and otherwise to adhere to all medical instructions of the attending physician.

9. Should custody of the child be awarded to anyone not related to the commissioning couple (such as, for example, the gestational woman), the gestational woman and her husband promise to reimburse the commissioning couple for all sums they are ordered to pay in child support.

10. Should the commissioning man die before the child's birth, the gestational mother agrees to renounce her parental rights and to transfer custody of the child to his wife, if any. Should he not be married or should his wife also die before the child's birth, the gestational woman agrees to transfer custody to the person the commissioning couple has named in the arrangement.

11. The commissioning couple agrees to pay specified expenses incurred by the gestational woman, such as medical, hospitalization, laboratory and therapy expenses, travel, accommodation, and child care costs.

As a group, commissioning couples had a higher level of education than the gestational women; 88 percent of commissioning men and 79 percent of commissioning women had post-secondary degrees, compared to only 17 percent of gestational women. This was reflected in occupations with commissioning couples more likely to be professionals and to have higher incomes. Given the fees involved ($20,000 or more where fees to a broker and the gestational woman are involved), only the affluent can afford a preconception arrangement, so they are a highly select group and not typical of the general population.

Research in this area is of limited reliability in several respects; sample sizes were small, and the Law Reform Commission of Canada study was conducted in 1988. It showed nevertheless that most of the gestational women surveyed were married, usually to someone in a blue-collar occupation, most were of Protestant background, and almost all were Caucasian. Most of the women had not finished high school or had only high school education, and many did not work outside the home. The anecdotal accounts the Commission heard support this description of the situation of gestational mothers and their partners, suggesting that they tend to be of a lower socioeconomic status than commissioning couples and that payment is a major factor in their decision to participate.

Indeed, this contention is borne out by the experience of one broker in the United States. Only one woman a year came forward to be a gestational mother when arrangements were made on a volunteer basis. Once the broker began to offer payment, the number rose to 20 women per year within two years. Without the financial incentive, then, it can safely be assumed that there would be far fewer willing gestational women.

The inequalities between the gestational woman and the commissioning couple are reinforced by the involvement of brokers. Despite the neutrality of the term "broker," implying an intermediary between the parties, in fact commercial brokers usually represent the interests of the commissioning couple, who pay the broker's fee of U.S.$10,000 to $16,000. The inequality of the parties is then confirmed by the terms of the standard contract, in which the gestational woman agrees to accept all the risks of assisted conception and pregnancy—up to and including her own death—while abiding by behavioural and other rules established by the contract—including the requirement to submit to medical diagnosis and treatment at the commissioning couple's discretion.

The commissioning couple, by contrast, is obliged only to complete payment on delivery of the child and relinquishment of the gestational woman's maternal rights and transfer of custody. They can refuse to accept the child if it proves not to be the genetic offspring of the commissioning man, and there have even been reported cases of commissioning couples refusing to accept the child because it was of the "wrong" sex or had a congenital anomaly or disability.

Preconception contracts were of particular concern to many of the groups representing minority women who appeared before the Commission. They told us that they fear increased exploitation of lower-income women, a disproportionate number of whom are members of minority groups. The advent of purely gestational arrangements, moreover, raises the possibility of minority women being used by white couples to gestate their children, both here in Canada and in developing countries. This concern was raised, for example, by Immigrant and Visible Minority Women of British Columbia:

> With the rise of commercial surrogacy, and on the basis of current experience, we foresee devastating consequences for all poor women and for women of colour who are disproportionately represented among the poor ... We recommend that this Commission call for a ban on surrogacy. The costs in the increased potential for exploitation of women of colour by far outweigh any benefits that might accrue to affluent couples. (S. Thobani, Immigrant and Visible Minority Women of British Columbia, Public Hearings Transcripts, Vancouver, British Columbia, November 26, 1990.)

These concerns were given substance by reports that at least one U.S. broker is bringing women to the United States from overseas to act as gestational women; these women are not paid beyond their travel and living expenses, resulting in much lower costs for the commissioning couple. The same broker is also exploring the possibility of initiating the pregnancies overseas and bringing only the resulting children to the United States.

Non-financial forms of exploitation are also a danger, as many groups appearing before the Commission emphasized.

Dehumanizing and Degrading to Women. Apart from the question of whether commercial preconception arrangements are inherently exploitive, witnesses asked the Commission to consider the dehumanizing and degrading aspects of such agreement for the individual women who participate and for women generally:

> In the standard surrogacy arrangement the woman who ovulates, conceives, gestates, labours, and delivers a baby is not called "the mother." She is a mere "surrogate." The presumption is that the real mother is the wife/partner in the infertile couple. We

feel this is very degrading to the woman involved. (J. Lewicky, Alberta Federation of Women United for Families, Public Hearings Transcripts, Calgary, Alberta, September 14, 1990).

These aspects are certainly apparent in the contracts gestational mothers are asked to sign, which require them to waive their right to refuse medical treatment—a right guaranteed under the provisions of the *Canadian Charter of Rights and Freedoms* that protect every individual's "life, liberty and security of the person." Moreover, other values inherent in the Charter, such as women's right to autonomy and dignity (implied in section 7) and equality (section 15), would be offended by state legitimation or enforcement of preconception contracts:

> To ensure that the mother provides an appropriate environment for her "product," strict regulations are often placed on her diet, exercise, and intercourse with the male partner. The contracted mother may also be required to undergo medical treatment, including ultrasound, amniocentesis, and abortion, regardless of her wishes. Her right to refuse medical treatment is thus denied by the contract. If surrogacy contracts are made legally enforceable, a dangerous precedent will be set for the rights of all pregnant women. (Brief to the Commission from the Canadian Research Institute for the Advancement of Women, September 20, 1990.)

Harm to Participants and Children. Proponents of preconception arrangements downplay the concept of harm to the gestational mothers, arguing that they are free to decide whether to participate. Other witnesses, however, questioned this premise. pointing out that the circumstances surrounding such arrangements have the potential to lead to pressure or even coercion of women by husbands or partners in the interests of add-

ing to the household income. Even without direct coercion, they felt that, given the disparities in the income and social status of gestational women and commissioning couples, the choice in practice, is not "free." Family pressures in non-commercial situations may also undermine a woman's ability to decide freely whether to participate.

There may also be significant psychological implications for gestational mothers even if they have participated willingly. Pregnancy produces physical and hormonal changes in a woman's body that can affect her emotions and therefore have the capacity to alter her relationships with her partner and any other children she has. These changes may also affect her own thoughts and feelings about what she is doing and the fetus she is carrying. These effects cannot be predicted precisely before pregnancy begins; yet preconception contracts often require gestational mothers to certify in advance that they will not form a maternal bond with the fetus during the nine-month gestation period and will relinquish all ties to the child soon after birth.

Some who have investigated the practice contend that many gestational mothers seriously underestimate the emotional and psychological costs of giving up the child. In fact, there is a substantial body of medical, gynaecological, and psychological literature to support the view that the bonding that takes place during gestation should not be underestimated and that any forced separation between mother and child may result in lasting harm to the mother.

Some U.S. brokers have reported that gestational women tend to deny that the child they are carrying is their own and to see it as "belonging" to the commissioning couple. There is anecdotal evidence, however, that women who relinquish a child with little distress at the time can later suffer from the experience. The long-term effects of relinquishment simply are not known, although an analogy can be drawn to studies focussing on adoption. The evidence suggests that the effects of relinquishment including long-lasting grief, may be common to both practices.

If, on the other hand, the gestational mother decides not to relinquish the child, she may then have to cope with guilt or other feelings evoked by denying the commissioning couple the child they had anticipated. She could also face a court case over custody. Even if her attempt to keep the child is successful—whether because the commissioning couple does not challenge it or because she wins the custody case—she then faces the prospect of raising the child of another man with her husband or partner—or alone—with all the potential for strain on family relationships and finances that would entail.

For commissioning women, the benefits of such arrangements are not unambiguous. Society attaches great importance to the genetic link between fathers and children, and the woman may perceive this as pressure to agree to the man's desire to have a genetically related child. She may believe, for example, that this is something she "owes" her husband because of her feelings of inadequacy at not being able to carry his child herself. Several commissioning women have also reported difficulty dealing with what many would consider a fundamentally unacceptable situation—in essence, their husband having a child with another woman. In short, the voluntary participation of commissioning women, like that of gestational mothers, may be in doubt. Commissioning women too risk being coerced, even if the pressures are subtle, into agreeing to a preconception arrangement.

Other sources of strain can arise as the couple raises the child. Although with arrangements involving zygote transfer to a gestational woman both members of the couple would be related to the child, in most instances this is not the procedure used. As in donor insemination for male infertility, just

one member of the couple is genetically related to the child born as a result of a genetic-gestational arrangement. With donor insemination, it is the woman who is related to the child; with preconception arrangements using assisted insemination, however, it is the man. As discussed [elsewhere] on the use of donor gametes, this may result in the perception that the couple's relationships with the child are unequal. The child may also become a symbol and constant reminder of the woman's infertility.

Although they are not participants in the arrangement, the resulting children can also be affected profoundly by it. First, they have been created not as ends in themselves but to serve the needs of others and, at least in part, to fulfil the financial goals of the broker and possibly those of the gestational woman and her partner as well. Second, there is the issue of multiple parenthood when genetic, gestational, and social roles are separated as a result of a preconception arrangement—a situation that we know, based on experience with adoption, can have a significant impact on a child's personal and emotional development and sense of identity.

Commercial preconception arrangements are too recent a practice for there to be adults who began their lives under these circumstances. There are, however, several potentially harmful psychosocial implications for the children. Although the child may be very much wanted and loved, he or she has nonetheless been "bought at a price," which could make the child feel like a commodity that can be bought and sold, and create pressure for him or her to live up to his or her "purchase price."

Brokers have a service-oriented approach—their client is the commissioning couple, and the child is seen as a "product," as evidenced by the fact that the couple can opt out of the contract if the "product" is "defective." Also consistent with this approach is the fact that brokers generally do not screen prospective parents to ensure that the children will be going to suitable homes: ability to pay is the only prerequisite.

Finally, we have to consider the potential for conflict within families—for example, as a result of disapproval of the arrangement on the part of non-participating family members—and the effects this may have on children who feel, rightly or wrongly, that their existence is the source of the conflict.

The family of the gestational mother is also affected by her pregnancy. If she has other children, they see the child being given away and reportedly wonder whether they too could be relinquished by their parents. Her partner, if she has one, must make allowances for the physical and psychological changes of pregnancy, at the same time perhaps feeling resentful or jealous that his wife is carrying another man's child. Finally the gestational mother's parents may be affected by the loss of a child that they see as their grandchild.

Social Harms. Beyond the impact on those directly concerned, commercial preconception arrangements have an impact on society and on social perceptions of the role and value of women, families, and children. Many witnesses told the Commission, for example, that they fear that these arrangements will reinforce a social definition of women in terms of their ability to bear children and the perception of their bodies as vessels or tools designed to serve the interests of others.

We heard many concerns that preconception arrangements will alter society's understanding of parenthood, family, and parental responsibilities, reducing parenthood to a transaction—a deal depending solely on the will of the adults who make it—with the child as the product of the deal. This is clearly contrary to any notion of children as ends in themselves, as human beings with their own dignity and identity. Society's view of children

could be altered irrevocably as a result, with children being seen as a product, a commodity that can be bought and sold. By contrast, the trend in human rights over the past two decades has been toward increasing recognition of children as persons in their own right, not as parental property.

Sexual Inequality. Finally, we heard from Canadians that preconception arrangements perpetuate inequalities between men and women in our society, because they reinforce the idea that women's value is defined by serving men's needs and that men have a right to control women's bodies.

We live in a society that has been based, historically, on the idea that women's primary role is motherhood and that men have legal rights over women's bodies. Many of those who oppose commercial preconception arrangements do so on the grounds that they perpetuate the assumption that women's role and value in society are defined by their sexual and reproductive functions and reinforce the notion that men have a right to control these functions.

The principle of equality means that every member of the community is entitled to equal concern and respect. Commercial preconception arrangements diminish women's status as equal members of society by giving credence to a perception of women as being of value for a reproductive capacity that can be bought and sold.

AN ACCEPTABLE PRACTICE:
THE ARGUMENTS FOR COMMERCIAL
PRECONCEPTION ARRANGEMENTS

Those who believe that preconception agreements are an acceptable practice and warrant public policy support tend to argue from one of two general perspectives: the perspective of personal autonomy and rights or the perspective of medical necessity.

Personal Autonomy. The essence of the first argument is that a right to participate in a preconception arrangement is inherent in the right of couples to be free from state interference in their right to reproduce by sexual intercourse, which is protected by principles such as marital privacy and liberty. Proponents of this argument thus assert that there is a right to procreate, that those who cannot do so through sexual intercourse are entitled to use any other means at their disposal, and that people are entitled to the assistance of the state in exercising this right.

A second element of this perspective is the argument that a woman has a right to control her own body. Provided she is making a fully informed and free choice, it is argued, the state should not interfere in a woman's decision about whether to become a gestational woman:

> We strongly believe that a woman has the right to make the decision if she chooses to be a surrogate. (E. Mertick, Alberta Advisory Council on Women's Issues, Public Hearings Transcripts, Edmonton, Alberta, September 13, 1990.)

Medical Necessity. Several physicians' organizations and other groups appearing before the Commission saw assisted insemination and *in vitro* fertilization in support of preconception arrangements as acceptable and medically justifiable responses to certain types of infertility (such as an absent or malformed uterus) or medical conditions in the commissioning woman (severe hypertension, diabetes, or heart condition):

> We are in support of surrogacy in medically valid circumstances, that is a woman who has her uterus removed for some condition, who is not able to carry a child, who may have some condition that she would pass on to her child that would be life threatening to the child ... We neither support surrogacy for non-medical indica-

tions, nor do we support the commercialization of surrogacy agreements where valid medical indications may exist. (R. Reid, Society of Obstetricians and Gynaecologists of Canada and Canadian Fertility and Andrology Society, Public Hearings Transcripts, Montreal, Quebec, November 22, 1990.)

> [We are not suggesting] that surrogacy is either right or wrong ... [The question is] whether or not a true need exists for this technology. Many women find themselves incapable of reproducing due to loss of uterine function as a result of surgical intervention for malignant disease, especially carcinoma of the cervix, which affects women in the child-bearing ages. These women are frequently in the prime of child-bearing age and are suddenly deprived of uterine function but not of ovarian function. Such women are ideal candidates for surrogacy in order to achieve their own genetic offspring. (A. Yuzpe, Department of Obstetrics and Gynaecology, University of Western Ontario, Public Hearings Transcripts, London, Ontario, November 2, 1990.)

Commercial arrangements unacceptable, non-commercial may be acceptable

The Commission also heard testimony from Canadians who find the commercial aspects of preconception arrangements abhorrent but take a different approach to private, non-commercial arrangements. Several witnesses drew this kind of distinction between commercial and non-commercial arrangements:

> It has been an occasional practice cross-culturally and since time immemorial for women to bear children for other women known to them personally. These latter arrangements do not involve payment and often provide for continued interaction of all parties. [We do] not believe these arrangements pose problems for public values or the status of women. However, these

non-commercial arrangements should be distinguished from the socially novel practice of commercial preconception contracts involving third-party mediation between a woman and other parties desiring children. (Brief to the Commission from the Canadian Advisory Council on the Status of Women, March 28, 1991.)

Other witnesses who made this distinction pointed to two factors: the danger of driving a practice underground by making it illegal, and reluctance to deprive people of an option that might permit them to form a family.

The second factor reflects the view of significant numbers of Canadians, according to surveys conducted for the Commission. The surveys revealed that opinion about preconception arrangements varies considerably with the type of arrangement involved (commercial or non-commercial) and the circumstances that lead people to seek a preconception arrangement. There was, however, no consensus on whether and what types of preconception arrangements should be permitted.

One survey, for example, asked respondents whether a couple should consider a preconception arrangement if the woman had a medical condition that would be life-threatening if she became pregnant. Half the respondents (49 percent) disagreed with a preconception arrangement as the solution, 31 percent agreed, and 19 percent were neutral on the issue. In another survey, 58 percent of respondents disapproved and 23 percent approved of a preconception arrangement in the situation where the woman was infertile and the man's sperm was used to impregnate another woman.

The surveys showed that many Canadians do not wish to close the door on preconception arrangements, even if they would not participate themselves or would not advise others to do so. For example, 46 percent of respondents answering a general question (the situation of the couple was not described) said that

a person who is infertile should be able to consider the use of a preconception arrangement; 30 percent said this is something the person should not consider, and 24 percent remained neutral on the issue.

Finally, the surveys showed that a majority of respondents (61 percent) do not believe that preconception arrangements are likely to have significant impact on society, largely because they will not be used very often. This no doubt reflects the fact that a large majority of respondents said that they would not participate in a preconception arrangement; 90 percent of women surveyed said that it was unlikely they would become a gestational mother in such an arrangement, giving such reasons as "I couldn't give away a baby I gave birth to" and "I wouldn't undergo pregnancy and birth unless it was my child."

Recognition that it would be virtually impossible to enforce a law prohibiting private, non-commercial preconception arrangements is reflected in this and similar testimony:

> It should be emphasized that the Council does not endorse surrogacy as a means of obtaining a child. It does recognize, however, that surrogacy does exist and feels that any effort to ban it would merely send the practice underground ... [I]f it goes underground and is something over which there is no control whatsoever, the children and the women will be victims ... we don't see this as an ideal situation. (L. Newson, National Council of Women of Canada, Public Hearings Transcripts, Saskatoon, Saskatchewan, October 25, 1990.)

Given this situation, some witnesses argued, the best approach is to try to reduce the opportunities for abuse or exploitation and to provide for the interests of any children that are born:

> Our attitude is that surrogacy per se is not something that should be specifically encouraged, but also it should not be banned altogether. Therefore the general conclu-

sion we reached ... is that non-commercial, non-binding arrangements that of necessity must be based on generous, sincere motives should not be criminalized or otherwise banned ... We would acknowledge, therefore, the evidence of the existence of this practice and provide an appropriate legal response. (J. Dillon, Canadian Bar Association, Public Hearings Transcripts, Vancouver, British Columbia, November 27, 1990.)

Still others saw dangers in tolerating even non-commercial arrangements between close family members:

No, we do not accept surrogacy between sisters. We consider that the commodification of the human body is absolutely to be condemned. This is a basic ethical principle, but we believe that even in the case of sisters, it opens the door to other things. [Translation] (L. Fortin, Les Cercles de Fermières du Québec, Public Hearings Transcripts, Montreal, Quebec, November 22, 1990.)

The Commission's Assessment

As the preceding sections make clear, preconception arrangements cause ethical and legal issues that are neither straightforward nor easy to deal with. As Commissioners listened to the continuing debate about this practice, one conclusion became evident: proponents and opponents are not likely to change each other's minds about the ethical and social dimensions of preconception arrangements. Views on preconception arrangements are based on fundamentally different convictions about human nature and about how the world works or ought to work; therefore, assessments of the actual or potential implications of preconception arrangements for women, for children, for couples, and for our evolution as a society also differ.

COMMERCIAL ARRANGEMENTS

Using our ethical framework and standards, the Commission finds commercial preconception arrangements offensive on several grounds.

First, they offend human dignity by commodifying women's reproductive capacities and commodifying children; they contradict the principle that human reproduction should not be commercialized in any way. Second, we see actual and potential harms for families, for individual women and children, and for specific groups within society. Finally, we believe that public policy that condones or supports the establishment of adversarial relationships is fundamentally flawed; public policy should seek instead to support and encourage humane, non-conflictual family and social relationships. Any attempt to legitimize or support commercial preconception arrangements through public policy would represent the antithesis of this goal.

Commodification of Children and Reproduction. The fundamentally repugnant aspect of preconception arrangements is that they instrumentalize human beings through the deliberate act of creating a child for the express purpose of giving it up, usually in exchange for money. The premise of commercial preconception contracts is that a child is a product that can be bought and sold on the market. The moral point of view requires that people be treated as ends in themselves, not as a means to the ends of others. We must therefore uphold the value of children in and of themselves. Children are not a commodity, nor are they instruments to be used to serve the purposes of others. The commodification of children entailed by preconception arrangements ignores these essential values.

Moreover, commercial preconception arrangements commodify women's reproductive functions and place women in the situation of alienating aspects of themselves that should be inherently inalienable. A preconception contract obliges the gestational mother to sell an intimate aspect of her human functioning to provide someone else with a genetically related child; the capacity to become pregnant and bear a child is reduced to a marketable service. We do not allow people to give up their freedom and become slaves, even if they make a choice to do so, because of our collective conviction that this would negate the value we attach to human dignity and the inalienability of the person. Similarly, assigning a commercial value to the human function of reproduction would result eventually in a new and, in our view, undesirable social understanding of the value and dignity of women, their reproductive capacity, and their bodily integrity.

Commercial preconception contracts by their nature—the exchange of money for a child—contradict one of the fundamental tenets of the Commission's ethical framework. On these grounds alone, we could recommend prohibition of such arrangements, since we believe that all public policy in this field should be based on the principle of non-commercialization of reproduction.

The evidence is clear that in commercial preconception contracts the principal motivation of both the broker and the gestational woman is money. Far from being the idyllic situation portrayed by brokers—gestational woman as "altruistic angel" giving the gift of a child to a couple who is happy but infertile—commercial preconception contracts are business transactions. The child is a product being sold by one party and bought by the other.

Harms to Individuals. The Commission heard strong arguments that preconception arrangements are detrimental to the autonomy of gestational mothers. We concur. Far from enhancing the gestational woman's autonomy, as some have argued, the practice circum-

scribes and dictates the gestational woman's behaviour by specifying contractual obligations, including the obligation to be treated by medical personnel selected by the commissioning couple, to have an abortion if the commissioning couple so decides, and to renounce her maternal feelings and rights even before conception. Again, we believe there is clear evidence of the potential for coercion and exploitation of gestational women because of the disparities in power and resources between gestational women and commissioning couples.

A commissioning couple uses a woman as a vehicle to serve their own ends. As the New York State Task Force on Life and the Law observed, they seek the birth components of gestation from the gestational woman while denying the personal, emotional, and psychological dimensions of her experiences and self. If she succeeds in denying her emotional responses during this profound experience, she is dehumanized in the process. If she fails, her attachment to the child produces a conflict that cannot be resolved without anguish for all involved.

Moreover, informed choice is a necessary component of autonomy. As we have seen, however, brokers arranging preconception arrangements are not neutral intermediaries; they act in the interests of the commissioning couple. If the gestational mother has her own lawyer, it is often one recommended by the broker. Furthermore, since so little is known about the psychosocial effects of these arrangements on the participants and the resulting child, the woman's decision cannot be made in light of all the information that might influence it. All these factors undoubtedly undermine her capacity to exercise informed choice in deciding to enter a preconception arrangement.

We also conclude that concerns about negative psychosocial consequences for the gestational mother are well founded, particularly because it is impossible for her to predict, at the time she signs the contract, how she will feel about fulfilling its terms after the child has been born.

Even if fully informed choice were possible, society has established certain limits on what people are free to make choices about. Such situations are rare but central to our definition of the kind of society we want to live in. Thus, in a caring society, personal autonomy is not a value that trumps all others, and society may see fit to place limits on the exercise of free choice when the choice concerns an activity that society regards as fundamentally incompatible with values such as respect for human dignity and the inalienability of the person.

We heard the view that preconception arrangements enhance women's autonomy by giving substance to their right to control their own bodies—by allowing them to decide for themselves the meaning and social implications of their ability to bear children. We reject this argument. Although they are strongly held values, freedom and autonomy do not include the right to engage in activities that will result in harms to others, particularly, as in this case, to the child that is eventually born; the limits of autonomy become apparent when its exercise will harm others, as the commodification of children most certainly does.

Harm to children born as a result of these arrangements cannot be ignored. Commissioners reject the argument that these harms could be outweighed by the opportunity for life, as this argument assumes the very factor under deliberation—the child's conception and birth. We concur with the assessment of the New York State Task Force on Life and the Law: "The assessment for public policy occurs prior to conception when the ... arrangements are made. The issue then is not whether a particular child should be denied life, but whether children should be conceived in circumstances that would place them at

risk." Nor do we see any practical way of protecting the interests of the child that will eventually be born or even of ensuring that they are taken into account in negotiating and concluding a preconception arrangement.

Commercial preconception arrangements do produce benefits—but the benefits are to brokers and commissioning couples at the expense of the interests of vulnerable women and of children who had no part in the arrangement.

Harms to Society. We agree with those who argued that commercial preconception arrangements have potentially negative consequences not only for individuals but also for women collectively and for other groups in society. These arrangements reinforce social attitudes about motherhood as the role that defines women's status and value in society. Furthermore, preconception arrangements could create broad social harms by diminishing the dignity of reproduction and undermining society's commitment to the inherent value of children.

Even if the number of commercial preconception arrangements to date has been relatively small, over time such arrangements would be bound to have a detrimental effect on the way society perceives women, children, and reproduction generally.

In short we reject the notion that public policy can be based on a description of procreation in terms of a market production model—which is, essentially, that such arrangements should be permissible and legally enforceable because commissioning couples are willing to pay and gestational women are free to sell their labour. Second, we do not accept that the freedom to procreate automatically assumes a right to state support—whether in the form of enforceable contracts or publicly supported medical services—for the exercise of that right. Finally, we reject the arguments of proponents because they are premised on incomplete or inaccurate depictions of preconception arrangements, making them an inappropriate basis for public policy, which must take into account not only the interests of the participants, but also the other interests affected, including those of the resulting child, as well as the potential for individual and/or social harm.

We also reject the argument of medical necessity. We find it unacceptable that one party—the gestatlonal woman—should be called upon to bear all the medical risks of pregnancy and birth, and possibly those of *in vitro* fertilization and zygote transfer, while all benefits accrue to the commissioning couple. In no other circumstances does society accept that a healthy person be placed at medical risk for the benefit of someone else for money, even when that condition is life-threatening. In this case, the commissioning woman's infertility is not life-threatening.

The commonly understood motivation for commissioning couples to enter into a preconception arrangement is because the commissioning woman is unable to conceive and/or carry a fetus to term. This makes preconception arrangements appear as a last resort when infertility is untreatable or treatment has been unsuccessful. As we have seen, however, this is not always the case; not everyone who seeks a preconception arrangement is involuntarily infertile, a member of a couple, or even of childbearing age. But even in cases where it is true, preconception arrangements are not an acceptable remedy.

Goals of Public Policy. ... In some circumstances a preconception arrangement may seem a reasonable response to a particular situation. For example. where a woman has a serious health problem that prevents her from carrying a pregnancy, she might seek a gestational woman to carry a fetus conceived using the commissioning woman's eggs and her partner's sperm. Given the broader social harms we have described, however, we do not believe that using another woman's reproductive capacity is justifiable even in this situation, as difficult as it might be for the individuals involved to accept their inability to have a genetically related child.

We do not deny that a public response in the form of regulation could help to control some of the pressures and abuses identified with respect to preconception arrangements—for example, by requiring the provision of independent legal advice for gestational women or by making counselling mandatory for all parties to an arrangement. We are sceptical, however, that any regulatory scheme could ensure that all parties were able to make free and informed choices. Moreover, a regulatory approach by its nature would invite disputes and conflict.

Even if a regulatory system could be designed to overcome these obstacles, the deepest and most serious harms of preconception arrangements would remain. No regulatory system could remedy the basic affront to human dignity occasioned by the commodification of children and the commercialization of reproduction.

Non-Commercial Arrangements

The Commission's conclusions with respect to non-commercial preconception arrangements between family members or close friends are similar. We do not believe such arrangements should be undertaken, sanctioned, or encouraged. The motivation might be sincere and generous, but the arrangement still results in the commodification of a child and the reproductive process. Even if no money is involved, no one should have the right to make a "gift" of another human being; this is offensive to the human dignity of the child.

Non-commercial arrangements present the potential for coercion in the form of family pressure to participate. They also give rise to the possibility of damage to family relationships before or after the child is born, as well as even greater potential for confusion on the part of the child, because of continuing contact between the birth mother and the commissioning couple. Moreover, the arrangement still results in a healthy woman being placed at medical risk for the benefit of someone else.

At the same time, we recognize that the practice may continue to some degree and so demands a public policy response, particularly because of the uncertainties surrounding the legal status of a child born as a result of such an arrangement and the need to ensure that the child's best interests are served. We wish to make it clear, however, that our recommendations in this latter regard are not intended to sanction the practice, but simply to recognize that it is probably going to occur and that, in the absence of public policy, significant harm to children could result.

Recommendations

Commissioners are strongly of the view that preconception arrangements are unacceptable and do not warrant state support in any form that would signal acceptance or encouragement of them. We do not advise sanctions with respect to gestational mothers, however, as this would simply compound their vulnerability. While we recognize the vulnerability of couples who are infertile and their emotional needs, we believe that making payment for such arrangements should be prohibited. We also believe it is essential, in particular, to prohibit others from assisting in such arrangements—for example, brokers and physicians—by criminalizing the knowing provision of assistance....

Notes to "Infertility Treatments: Fertility Drugs"

5 Medical Research International. "Adverse Effects of Ovulatory Stimulants." Report submitted to the National Institute of Child Health and Human Development. Burlington: MRI, 1993.

6 Millar, W.J., S. Wadhera, and C. Nimrod. "Multiple Births: Trends and Patterns in Canada, 1974–1990." *Health Reports* 4 (3) (1992): 223–29.

7 Mills, J.L., et al. "Risk of Neural Tube Defects in Relation to Maternal Fertility and Fertility Drug Use." *Lancet* 336 (July 14, 1990): 103–104.

8 TERIS data base summary for clomiphene. Seattle: University of Washington, September 1992. The frequency of congenital anomalies was no greater than expected among infants of women who had been treated with clomiphene to induce ovulation in three cohort studies involving respectively 225, 340, and 935 children (Harlap, S. "Ovulation Induction and Congenital Malformations." *Lancet* (October 30, 1976): 961; Barrat, J., and D. Leger. "Avenir des grossesses obtenues après stimulation de l'ovulation." *Journal de Gynecologie, Obstetrique et Biologie de la Reproduction* 8 (1979): 333–42; Kurachi, K., et al. "Congenital Malformations of Newborn Infants After Clomiphene-Induced Ovulation." *Fertility and Sterility* 40 (2) (August 1983): 187–89) or in a case-control study of 4,904 infants with major congenital anomalies (Mili, F., M.J. Khoury, and X. Lu. "Clomiphene Citrate Use and the Risk of Birth Defects: A Population-Based Case-Control Study." *Geratology* 43 (5) (May 1991): 422–23).

Notes for "Infertility Treatments: Assisted Insemination"

8 United States. Congress. Office of Technology Assessment. *Artificial Insemination Practice in the United States: Summary of a 1987 Survey.* Washington: Office of Technology Assessment, 1988.

13 Golombok, S., and J. Rust. "The Warnock Report and Single Women: What About the Children?" *Journal of Medical Ethics* 12 (1986): 182–86.

17 Daly, K.J., and M.P. Sobol. "Adoption as an Alternative for Infertile Couples: Prospects and Trends." In Research Volumes of the Royal Commission on New Reproductive Technologies, 1993, p. 15.

18 Views expressed by the Toronto Branch of the Canadian Adoption Reunion Register, at the Commission's Public Hearings, Toronto, Ontario, November 20, 1990.

Notes for "Infertility Treatments: *In Vitro* Fertilization"

10 Millar, W.J. "Trends in Low Birthweight Canada 1971 to 1989." *Health Reports* 3 (4) (1991): 311–17.

11 Mickleburgh, R. "Rising Rate of Multiple Births Creates Burden for Taxpayers." *The Globe and Mail*, January 6, 1993, A6.

12 Lyons, J. "Tiny Tots: Prognosis Healthier as HSC Study Focuses on Underweight Babies." *Winnipeg Free Press*, August 17, 1992, C17.

13 Escobar, G.J., B. Littenberg, and D.B. Petitti. "Outcome Among Surviving Very Low Birthweight Infants: A Meta-Analysis." *Archives of Disease in Childhood* 66 (1991): 204–11.

14 Halsey, C.L., M.F. Collin, and C.L. Anderson. "Extremely Low Birth Weight Children and Their Peers: A Comparison of Preschool Performance." *Pediatrics* 91 (4) (April 1993): 807–11.

15 Eilers, B.L., et al. "Classroom Performance and Social Factors of Children with Birth Weights of 1250 Grams or Less: Follow-Up at 5 to 8 Years of Age." *Pediatrics* 77 (1986): 203–208.

16 Porter, J.B., P.J. Manberg, and, S.C. Hartz. "Statistics and Results of Assisted Reproductive Technologies." *Assisted Reproduction Reviews* 1 (1) (1991): 28–37.

17 Ibid.

18 McGuire, R. "Big Surprise; Frozen Embryos Make Better Babies." *The Medical Post*, December 1, 1992, p. 24.

19 There remains some question about the viability of cryopreserved embryos. Australia data indicate that the rate of clinical pregnancies is significantly improved when frozen and thawed embryos are implanted during natural cycles (cited in Mullen, M.A. "The Use of Human Embryos and Fetal Tissues: A Research Architecture." In Research Volumes of the Royal Commission on New Reproductive Technologies, 1993). Past studies have indicated that frozen embryos are only half as viable as fresh. A study published in the *New England Journal of Medicine* concluded that freezing embryos significantly reduces their capacity for implantation (Levran, D., et al. "Pregnancy Potential of Human Oocytes—The Effect of Cryopreservation." *New England Journal of Medicine* 323 (17) (October 25, 1990): 1153–56; and one researcher concluded that embryo freezing is much more difficult and time consuming and much less successful than might have been anticipated (Ashwood-Smith, M.J. "The Cryopreservation of Human Embryos." *Human Reproduction* 1 (5) (1986), p. 330).

20 Lancaster, P.A.L. "Congenital Malformations After In-Vitro Fertilisation." *Lancet* (December 12, 1987): 1392; Mills, J.I., et al., "Risk of Neural Tube Defects in Relation to Maternal Fertility and Fertility Drug Use." *Lancet* (July 14, 1990): 103–104.

21 Stephenson, P.A., and P.G. Svensson. "In Vitro Fertilisation and Infertility Care: A Primer for Health Planners." *International Journal of Health Sciences* 2 (3) (1991): 119–23.

Questions for Discussion

1 What restrictions, if any, should be placed on who gets access to new reproductive technologies?

2 Should the fact that a child is the product of assisted reproduction be kept "secret"?

3 Is it wrong for anyone to make a profit from involvement in assisted reproduction? Why or why not?

The Ethics of In Vitro Fertilization

Arthur L. Caplan

In this article, Arthur Caplan explores a number of new ethical problems which arise from our ability to manipulate nature, using new forms of assisted reproduction. He considers the question of whether infertility is the sort of condition which calls for medical attention in the first place, and raises a number of issues concerning social justice and the role of scientists, as well as the impact on the people directly affected by the use of new reproductive technologies.

★　★　★

Assisted Reproduction—A Cornucopia of Moral Muddles

There has been an explosion in recent years in the demand for and resources devoted to the treatment of infertility in the United States. Many parents have benefitted from the availability of new techniques such as artificial insemination, microsurgery, fertility drugs, and the various forms of what is generically known as "in vitro fertilization." At the same time, increases in the demand for and allocation of resources to the medical treatment of infertility raise profoundly disturbing and complex moral issues.

The scientific status of the current generation of infertility interventions remains unclear. Some commentators assert that it is obvious that artificial reproduction is still in its infancy. Others, usually more directly involved in providing the technology to patients, avow that the level of success is so high that many forms of artificial reproduction can be viewed only as therapies. The issue of whether medicine is capable of treating infertility is important not only for scientific reasons but also because basic moral issues concerning informed consent, liability for untoward results, and public policies concerning reimbursement pivot around the answer. Where should artificial reproduction be placed on the experiment/therapy continuum?

Little consensus exists either within the medical profession or among the general public as to the moral status of the entities that are the objects of a great deal of medical manipulation in any attempt to treat infertility: ova, sperm, and embryos. The ethics of manipulating, storing, or destroying reproductive materials raise basic questions about the moral status of possible and potential human beings.

It is not even clear whether infertility is or ought to be viewed as a disease requiring or meriting medical intervention. Many of the causes of infertility and many of the possible remedies are as much a function of social, cultural, and economic factors as they are physiologic or biologic abnormalities. Attitudes about conception, child rearing, and the nature of the family are greatly influenced by social and ethical beliefs concerning individual rights, the duties of marriage, and the desirability of passing on a particular set of genetic information into the next generation.

The treatment of infertility also raises basic questions concerning equity and justice. These fall roughly into two broad categories: questions of social justice and questions of individual justice.

Questions of Social Justice

At the social level, increasing amounts of scarce medical resources are being invested in the provision of services for those suffering from impaired fertility. It is estimated conservatively that the United States is now spending more than 200 million dollars annually on medical interventions intended to correct infertility. In the years from 1981 to 1983, more than 2 million visits were made to physicians in private practice by those seeking assistance regarding procreation.

Not only are many persons seeking help, but also an increasing proportion of medical resources are being devoted to this problem. The number of programs offering in vitro fertilization doubled in 1984 alone from 60 to 120. Private clinics whose sole interest is the provision of services to treat infertility have opened in many areas of the country.[1]

Increases in both the supply and demand for medical services to treat infertility can be expected to continue. The number of persons seeking medical assistance is still far below the number of persons in the general population estimated to have serious impairments for fertility.

The expenditure of scarce funds for health resources is not the only social issue raised by technologic progress with respect to reproduction. It is not uncommon for fertility services to be located in the same building, if not on the same floor, as services devoted to the termination of pregnancies. If this situation were not ironic enough in itself, it is surely odd to contemplate increases in the resources devoted to the alleviation of infertility at a time when millions of children in the United States and around the world lack parents as well as the basic necessities of life.

In the United States itself, there are still thousands of children who cannot be placed with either foster families or adoptive parents. This situation raises obvious issues of social justice and individual rights, particularly when many of the children requiring adoption have special physical, cognitive, and emotional needs.

Issues regarding the priority that should be given to the development of fertility-enhancing services are made all the more pressing at a time when both federal and state governments have been moving rapidly to institute cost-containment measures such as prospective payment and reimbursement by diagnosis related groups (DRGs). These efforts are likely to curtail sharply access to proven therapeutic services for the elderly, the disabled, and the poor, who depend on public expenditures for their care.

Questions of Individual Justice

At an individual or familial level, access to infertility services frequently is limited to those who can pay for them, either out of pocket or, in some cases, through private insurance. Access to services also is constrained by patient awareness of the existence of medical options, geography, and the ability to bear the often onerous financial, psychosocial, and time commitments associated with many of the available forms of assisted reproduction.

The proper role of the law and of the state in influencing or controlling individual decisions concerning reproduction is also a matter of much disagreement and dispute. Traditionally, American courts have been loathe to countenance any interference with matters pertaining to the family and individual decisions concerning procreation. As one philosopher has observed, parental decisions concerning children have been seen as "a right against all the rest of society to be indulged within wide limits,...immune from the scrutiny of and direction of others."[2]

However, in recent years, federal and state law has begun to acknowledge a powerful state interest in the welfare of children, particularly newborns. Child abuse statutes in many states have recently been revised and strengthened. The federal government has expressed its wish that children born with handicaps or congenital defects receive access to the same opportunities for medical assistance as would be available to other children. The traditional assumption in American law and morality that privacy provides an inviolate shield against intervention by other parties or the state has weakened somewhat in the face of increasing concern about protecting the interests of especially vulnerable human beings such as newborns and children and assuring that no one is subject to invidious discrimination on the basis of handicap, race, sex, or ethnic origin.[3]

The Growing Demand for Medical Assistance in Procreation

Infertility is a major problem in the United States. Almost one in six couples who have tried to conceive a child for 1 year fail to do so. Although the overall incidence of infertility appears to be relatively stable, the demand for infertility services is increasing rapidly.

The increase in demand for medical assistance in conceiving children is due to a variety of factors. Many couples have chosen to delay conception, thereby exposing themselves to the increased risks of infertility associated with aging. There appears to be some increase in the number of women encountering Iatrogenic fertility problems as a result of difficulties associated with various forms of birth control, such as intra-uterine devices (IUDs). Many women have entered the work force and, as a result, have been exposed to reproductive hazards and pollutants that may adversely affect fertility. Increases in the incidence of sexually transmitted diseases, especially pelvic inflammatory disease, have also produced a higher incidence of infertility among some subgroups within the general population.

The causes of increased demand for fertility services are not confined to physiologic factors. Couples who might have considered adoption in earlier decades are now turning in increasing numbers to the medical profession for assistance with respect to conception.

Moreover, there has been a dramatic increase in the availability of infertility services in the United States. Advances in diagnostic techniques such as laparoscopy and hormonal and genetic analysis also allow health care professionals to identify with increasing reliability those suffering from impairments in fertility.[4]

Attitudes toward human variability, the desirability of marriage and family, and the importance of biologic kinship between parent and child also play a powerful role in influencing the demand for medical assistance with respect to infertility. There is some evidence that parental expectations concerning pregnancy and reproduction have changed drastically during the past decade.

Lawsuits against and malpractice rates among those engaged in obstetrics have increased dramatically in recent years. Our society has come, whether wisely or not, to expect physicians to facilitate the conception of optimally healthy children at the conclusion of every pregnancy.

The power of medical intervention to influence procreation and reproduction challenges social norms concerning human differences and variability that are, at best, poorly understood by social scientists and moral philosophers. A growing emphasis on perfection in procreation and child rearing contributes to a situation in which those who are disabled, dysfunctional, or merely different from the norm may encounter increasing difficulties in securing social acceptance and material security. The availability of technologic methods for facilitating procreation in those for whom this would not have been an option in earlier times means that personal autonomy and individual choice are enhanced. However, it may also mean that such gains are purchased at the cost of lowering public tolerance for differences and diversity among individual human beings and about decisions concerning child-bearing, child rearing, childlessness, and disability.[5]

In Vitro Fertilization: A Case Study

Perhaps the most controversial and provocative of all the new forms of medically assisted reproduction available today is in vitro fertilization. Although it has been common practice for decades in the United States as well as in other nations to utilize sperm donated by either spouses or strangers for the purpose of facilitating procreation, it is only in the past 10 years that efforts have been made to utilize donated ova by various means in order to facilitate reproduction.

It is not merely the novelty of in vitro fertilization that makes it worthy of special comment and ethical reflection. The fact that in vitro fertilization is a technology that severs the traditional link between gestation and maternal identity raises serious and novel issues for both the law and morality. The prevailing ideology of equality, at least with respect to opportunity, in the United States makes it easy to overlook the fact that one of our society's most basic and fundamental beliefs about reproduction and the family is that the mothers of children are undeniably that, the mothers. Although it is true that artificial insemination by donor (AID) raises questions about paternal identity, the fact is that paternal identity, whether men like to admit it or not, has always been subject to a certain degree of uncertainty—with or without artificial insemination by donor.

Prior to the appearance of in vitro fertilization, there has never been any doubt, much less any empiric reason for doubting, that the woman who bore a child bore a direct familial relationship to that child. It is difficult to know exactly what the social reverberations of a technology capable of severing the tie between genetic relationship and gestation will be. However, the fact that this new technology can change a previously basic and undeniable reality of the human condition makes this particular technology worthy of serious and special moral consideration.

Standard In Vitro Fertilization

In vitro fertilization actually refers to a family of procedures that all involve the fertilization of an ovum outside of the human body. In the most commonly utilized technique, which might be termed "standard in vitro fertilization," one or more eggs are removed from the ovaries using a syringe known as a laparoscope. Egg cells are exceedingly small, so that the process of retrieval requires considerable skill and experience.

In many but not in all centers in which standard in vitro fertilization is practiced, the ovaries are stimulated artificially by hormones administered to the donor to produce more than one egg in the menstrual cycle. The eggs that are removed are subjected to microscopic inspection to determine which appears to be structurally most sound. One or more of the eggs is then fertilized in vitro using the husband's or a donor's sperm. The egg or eggs are then observed until they have grown to the eight-cell stage in an artificial medium. A decision is then made as to which of the developing embryos will be reimplanted into the prospective mother's womb.[6]

Reimplantation or, as it is often termed, "embryo transfer," also requires careful monitoring of the prospective mother in order to ascertain the optimal time for reimplanting the egg back into the uterus. Timing is critical to the success of reimplantation.

In some centers, some of the embryos that are produced are frozen for later use should the initial attempt at reimplantation fail. Techniques for freezing fertilized eggs at very low temperatures are well developed. The decision to freeze a fertilized egg allows for further efforts at reimplantation, but it also raises questions about the disposition of unused embryos.

The first successful use of standard in vitro fertilization took place in Britain in 1978. Since that time, nearly 1000 infants have been born utilizing this technique in the United

States, Australia, the Netherlands, and a number of other countries. The procedure generally costs between $3000 and $5000 per attempt. Several attempts are often required in order to achieve pregnancy. One recent report stated that out of 24,037 oocytes collected, 7722 resulted in fertilized embryos that were reimplanted in the mother's uterus. From this group, 590 children were born, among which were 56 twins, 7 triplets, and 1 set of quadruplets. These multiple births were a result of the simultaneous reimplantation of more than one embryo in order to increase the likelihood of a successful implantation and birth.[7]

These data indicate that the pregnancy rate achieved is about 25 per cent, although the number of pregnancies resulting in a liveborn child is less than 10 per cent. These figures are low, but it should be noted that they do not differ all that much from the rates of pregnancy and birth associated with sexual intercourse between fertile parents.[8]

Nonstandard In Vitro Fertilization

The techniques utilized in standard in vitro fertilization allow for a startling number of permutations and combinations with respect to the donors of sperm and eggs, the choice of a recipient to receive the embryos that result, and the choice of individuals to parent the children who are born as a result of these techniques. Donors of sperm or eggs may or may not be persons who are married. Women who cannot produce viable eggs or who for some reason are unwilling or unable to undergo the procedures necessary to perform laparoscopy may ask another woman to supply eggs for in vitro fertilization.

It is also possible to utilize women other than the biologic donor to serve as the "gestational mother" for a fertilized egg. These women may carry an embryo to term and then either keep the resulting child or turn it over to another party—either the biologic

donor or yet another person or persons. Because it is possible to freeze embryos, it is also possible to utilize in vitro fertilization techniques to produce a child after the death of the biologic donors or without the knowledge and consent of the biologic donors.

Nonstandard in vitro fertilization techniques allow for a division of the roles of mother and parent that was, quite simply, impossible before the appearance of these techniques. It is now possible to produce a child who has one set of biologic parents who may be either alive or dead and who provide eggs and sperm, another person or persons who are involved in pregnancy and gestation, and still a third person or persons who serve as the actual or social parent(s) of the child![9]

The fact that it is now possible to separate the biologic, gestational, and social aspects of mothering and parenting introduces a range of further novel possibilities concerning fertilization, reproduction, and birth. For example, frozen embryos not utilized for in vitro fertilization are available for research directly related to in vitro fertilization techniques or other medical purposes involving therapies not related to procreation (for example, the development of embryos in order to produce and harvest useful organic materials). Nonstandard in vitro fertilization techniques raise the possibility of remuneration of women for their services as either egg donors or gestational mothers, or, as the role is often termed, surrogates. The availability of standard and nonstandard in vitro fertilization techniques may facilitate the application of genetic engineering either for therapeutic purposes, aesthetic reasons, or even eugenic goals.

Major Policy Issues Raised by In Vitro Fertilization

The development of in vitro fertilization techniques of various types poses a direct and pressing challenge to public policy. At present, in vitro fertilization is still a relatively new medical modality, and as such, there are many aspects of the techniques utilized, including hormonal induction of ovulation, the freezing and storage of embryos, and the development of optimal media for embryo growth, in which further research is necessary. Little is known about the long-term psychosocial impacts of in vitro fertilization on children born by these methods or on the families who raise children produced by either standard or nonstandard in vitro fertilization techniques.[10]

Little formal supervision and regulation has been exercised to date by local, state, and federal authorities in the United States over the provision of in vitro fertilization as a therapy. At present, the only form of control over those who provide in vitro fertilization exists in the form of peer regulation through professional societies and individual collegial review. Few courts have ruled on matters pertaining to in vitro fertilization, and there are few legislative statutes that govern either research or therapy in this area....[11]

Major Ethical Issues Raised by In Vitro Fertilization

There is a tendency in the existing literature on in vitro fertilization to move directly to arguments about the moral implications of the nonstandard forms of the technique.[12] In many ways, this is understandable, because as noted earlier, the permutations and combinations of nonstandard in vitro fertilization techniques do allow for the separation of biologic, gestational, and parental functions, especially with respect to women, that pose enormous challenges to the legal system.

However, although issues pertaining to the moral acceptability of surrogacy, the desirability or undesirability of commercial relationships in nonstandard and standard forms of in vitro fertilization, and the policies that should be followed with regard to matters such as in-

heritance where in vitro fertilization embryos and children are concerned raise obvious moral and legal conundrums, it is not clear that these issues are actually the pivotal ones raised by advances in in vitro fertilization techniques. I suspect that moral matters regarding in vitro fertilization in terms of both research and therapy will actually hinge on the answers that are given to the following questions:

1. Is infertility a disease?
2. What counts as fair and equitable access to in vitro fertilization?
3. What is the moral status of a human embryo?

Is Infertility a Disease?

One common definition of disease often found in medical literature is that disease represents any deviation from the existing norms that prevail for human functioning.[13] Certainly, infertility, although not uncommon, is uncommon enough to qualify as abnormal or deviant relative to the average capacities and abilities of the human population.

Nonetheless, defining disease as abnormality has its own significant problems, not the least of which is that such a definition makes any physical or mental state at the tail ends of normal distributions diseases by definition. Thus, the state of being very tall, very smart, very dark-skinned, or very strong all qualify as diseases according to the abnormality criterion.

One way of avoiding including too much in the disease category is to restrict the definition of disease to those states that represent biologic dysfunction. According to this view, infertility would qualify as a disease because the relevant organ systems are not functioning as they presumably were designed to do.

However, again, a strictly biologic definition of disease flounders on empiric grounds. Not all dysfunctional bodily states constitute sources of symptoms or even problems for those who possess them. One can be afflicted with any number of dysfunctional states and attributes over the course of a normal life span without either knowing or caring very much about them one way or another. It seems odd to argue that a person who does not want children and who also has a low sperm count should be labeled as diseased.

Perhaps the most satisfying way to handle the problem of defining disease is to attempt a definition that captures both physiologic and patient perspectives. Disease would appear to refer to those dysfunctional states that a person recognizes or, if left untreated, will eventually come to recognize as dysfunctional either due to impairments in abilities or capacities as a result of noxious symptoms.[14]

Using a definition that recognizes both the biologic and psychosocial aspects of disease, it would appear defensible to argue that infertility is a disease that falls reasonably within medicine's purview. Although not all persons afflicted with fertility problems find this state distressing or limiting, many certainly do. Furthermore, although it is true that fertility and the ability to have children is a desire that is strongly mediated by social and cultural values, it is also true that this desire comes as close as can be to constituting a universal desire that can be found among every human society.

Indeed, it is the pervasiveness of the importance assigned to the ability to have offspring that provides one of the empiric warrants not only for labeling infertility as a disease but also for assigning its care and treatment a relatively high priority with respect to other disease states. If it is reasonable to include the capacity to bear children among those abilities and skills that constitute basic human goods, such as cognition, locomotion, and perception, infertility not only is a disease but also is one that should receive special attention and concern from physicians and those concerned with health policy.

What Counts As Fair and Equitable Access to In Vitro Fertilization?

If it is true that infertility is a disease that adversely affects a basic and important human capacity, it would seem important to assure access to efficacious and safe diagnostic, therapeutic, and palliative health care services that may contribute to the enhancement of this capacity. Indeed, infertility would appear to constitute so severe an impairment of a basic human capacity that, other things being equal, access to such services should not be contingent upon the individual patient's or family's ability to pay.

However, the major issue requiring resolution with respect to justice and equity in the allocation of resources for the diagnosis and treatment of infertility is not how much to spend or who should foot the bill, but rather whether the diagnostic and therapeutic techniques now in existence are safe and efficacious. Until the requisite empiric information for analyzing this issue has been obtained, it would be unethical to divert resources from other medical interventions already known to be safe and efficacious.

Moreover, although high priority should be accorded to the treatment of infertility, it should not be assumed that in vitro fertilization and other techniques are the only techniques that can be utilized to cope with the dysfunctional consequences of infertility or that the demonstration of a need for services thereby entails that any and all health care practitioners who wish to engage in treatment are thereby entitled to do so. Equity and fairness demand that those afflicted with the disease of infertility be aware of all options available to them, including adoption and foster parenting, and that public policy facilitate the utilization of those options. Equity and fairness also require that the resources devoted to in vitro fertilization and other techniques be used in the most efficient manner possible.

This may require that diagnostic and therapeutic services be regionalized and that funding be restricted to those centers that can demonstrate a high level of safety and efficacy with regard to in vitro fertilization techniques.[15]

What Is the Moral Status of a Human Embryo?

One of the most perplexing issues raised by the evolution of in vitro fertilization is the need to examine the moral standing that should be accorded to an embryo. Arguments about research on embryos and about the storage and disposition of embryos will ultimately pivot upon the moral status that should be accorded to these entities.

In general, the scientific and medical communities have tried to shy away from the suggestion that science has anything much to say about the questions of when life begins or what counts as a human being. Recent Congressional hearings on the question of the definition of life produced a barrage of disclaimers, dodges, and apologies from those scientists called upon to testify.

The unwillingness of many members of the scientific and medical communities to address squarely the issue of when life begins and what counts as a human being is perhaps not surprising. After all, the definition of human life raises theologic and psychologic issues that are difficult and disturbing to contemplate.

However, it is important to note that members of the scientific and medical communities have not been reticent about an analogous issue—when does human life end. The existence of brain death statutes in most states is evidence of the fact that the biomedical community has been willing to offer its expert opinion as to both the definition of death and the criteria that should be followed to assess whether a particular person meets this definition.[16]

The issues of when life begins and what entities count as human beings demand similar degrees of courage and attention from the biomedical community. Although biomedical scientists may not be able to formulate definitions of life and personhood among themselves that can command societal assent, they surely have a role to play in participating in the formulation of definitions and criteria that society will have to establish in order to cope with the existence of in vitro fertilization.

Two lessons should be learned from other attempts to define life and personhood in such arenas as the debates about abortion and animal experimentation. First, no single property is likely to serve as a distinct boundary for establishing the existence of personhood or even life. The criteria used in a definition are more likely to constitute a family or cluster of concepts.

Second, the definition of life and the criteria used to assess its presence do not end moral matters. Knowing when life begins and when personhood or humanity can be attributed to a particular entity provides only the starting point for arguments about what to do with embryos. It is still necessary to consider the rights, duties, and obligations of donors, prospective parents, and health care professionals in deciding what is to be done with and to embryos. However, it will not do for the biomedical community to continue to adopt an ostrich-like posture and proclaim that it has nothing whatsoever to contribute in the way of empiric information that might facilitate the formulation of an answer to the question of what moral status should be accorded to human embryos.

Conclusion

The evolution of medicine's capacity to assist those afflicted with impairments of fertility is an exciting and commendable prospect. However, enthusiasm for the techniques and for the benefit they can bring to those afflicted with a disease that impairs a fundamental and universally valued human capacity should not blind us to the fact that these techniques are still new, relatively poorly understood, and surrounded with uncertainty as to their efficacy and safety.

In vitro fertilization is not only a scientific and financial challenge to society but also a moral challenge. The possibility of separating the functions of biologic, gestational, and social parenting raises dilemmas of policy, law and regulation that have never before faced humankind. However, insufficient attention has been given to some of the basic moral issues that underlie much of the current fascination with, and fear of, in vitro fertilization. Given the implications of this technique for basic social institutions such as the family, kinship, and parenting, it is imperative that our regulatory, legal, and legislative responses to it be wise. We as a society must look much more carefully before we take a leap in any particular regulatory or legal direction.

Notes

1 Henahan, J. Fertilization: Embryo transfer procedures raise many questions. *J.A.M.A., 252*:877–882, 1984.

2 Schoeman, F. Rights of children, rights of parents and the moral basis of the family. *Ethics, 91*:6–19, 1980.

3 Murray, T., and Caplan, A. (eds.). *Which Babies Shall Live?* Clifton, New Jersey: Humana, 1985.

4 Grobstein, C., Flower, M. and Mendeloff, J. External human fertilization: An evaluation of policy. *Science, 222*:127–133, 1983.

5 Murray and Caplan (eds.). *Which Babies Shall Live?*

6 Blank, R. Making babies: The state of the art. *The Futurist, 19*:1–17, 1985; Warnock, M. *Report of the Committee of Inquiry into Human Fertilization and Embryology*, London: HMSO, 1984.

7 Hodgen, G. *The Need for Infertility Treatment. Testimony in Hearings on Human Embryo Transfer, Subcommittee on Investigations and Oversight, Committee*

on *Science and Technology*, US House of Representatives, August 8, 1984.

8 Sattaur, O. New conception threatened by old morality. *New Scientist, 103*:12–17, 1984.

9 Working Party, Council for Science and Society. *Human Procreation: Ethical Aspects of the New Techniques*, Oxford: Oxford University Press, 1984.

10 Warnock, M. *Report of the Committee of Inquiry into Human Fertilization and Embryology*, London: HMSO, 1984.

11 Annas, G. and Elias, S.. In vitro fertilization and embryo transfer: Medicolegal aspects of a new technique to create a family. *Family Law Quarterly, 17*:199–223, 1983.

12 Robertson, J.A. Procreative liberty and the control of conception, pregnancy and childbirth. *Virginia Law Review, 69*:20–80, 1983; Wadlington, W. Artificial conception: The challenge for family law. *Virginia Law Review, 69*:126–174, 1983.

13 Caplan, A., and Engelhardt, II, T. (eds.). *Concepts of Health and Disease*, Reading, Massachusetts: Addison-Wesley, 1981.

14 Caplan, A. Is aging a disease? *In* Spicker, S., and Ingman, S. (eds.), *Vitalizing Long-Term Care*, New York: Springer-Verlag, 1984, pp. 14–28.

15 Institute of Medicine. *Assessing Medical Technologies*, Washington, D.C.: National Academy Press, 1985.

16 Culver, C., and Gert, B. *Philosophy in Medicine*. New York, Oxford University Press, 1982.

Questions for Discussion

1 Is infertility a disease?

2 Is it ethical to invest considerable resources in producing new children when there are many children already living who need homes? Is it possible or desirable to change the common opinion that it is more desirable to raise one's own biological offspring?

3 What role should scientists play in deciding when life begins?

4 Is there reason to worry that increasing pressure to produce "optimal pregnancies" will lead to a lower tolerance of disability or difference in society?

Is Women's Labor a Commodity?

Elizabeth S. Anderson

One form of assisted reproduction which has attracted a great deal of philosophical attention is surrogate mother-hood, particularly when engaged in in exchange for money ("commercial surrogacy"). In the following influential article from 1990, Elizabeth Anderson argues that commercial surrogacy turns both children and women's repro-ductive capacities into commodities, and that this commodification is morally objectionable. In particular, she ar-gues that there are parental norms which govern the bringing of children into the world, which involve (among other things) certain emotional attachments, and that it is wrong to substitute the norms of the market for these parental norms.

★ ★ ★

In the past few years the practice of commer-cial surrogate motherhood has gained notori-ety as a method for acquiring children. A commercial surrogate mother is anyone who is paid money to bear a child for other peo-ple and terminate her parental rights, so that the others may raise the child as exclusively their own. The growth of commercial surro-gacy has raised with new urgency a class of concerns regarding the proper scope of the market. Some critics have objected to com-mercial surrogacy on the ground that it im-properly treats children and women's repro-ductive capacities as commodities.[1] The prospect of reducing children to consumer durables and women to baby factories surely inspires revulsion. But are there good reasons behind the revulsion? And is this an accurate description of what commercial surrogacy im-plies? This article offers a theory about what things are properly regarded as commodities which supports the claim that commercial sur-rogacy constitutes an unconscionable com-modification of children and of women's re-productive capacities.

What Is a Commodity?

The modern market can be characterized in terms of the legal and social norms by which it governs the production, exchange, and en-joyment of commodities. To say that some-thing is properly regarded as a commodity is to claim that the norms of the market are ap-propriate for regulating its production, ex-change, and enjoyment. To the extent that moral principles or ethical ideals preclude the application of market norms to a good, we may say that the good is not a (proper) com-modity.

Why should we object to the application of a market norm to the production or distri-bution of a good? One reason may be that to produce or distribute the good in accordance with the norm is to *fail to value it in an appro-priate way*. Consider, for example, a standard Kantian argument against slavery, or the commodification of persons. Slaves are treated in accordance with the market norm that owners may use commodities to satisfy their own interests without regard for the interests of the commodities themselves. To treat a per-son without regard for her interests is to fail to respect her. But slaves are persons who may not be merely used in this fashion, since as rational beings they possess a dignity which commands respect. In Kantian theory, the problem with slavery is that it treats beings worthy of *respect* as if they were worthy merely of *use*. "Respect" and "use" in this context denote what we may call different *modes of valuation*. We value things and persons in other ways than by respecting and using them. For example, love, admiration, honor, and appreciation constitute distinct modes of valuation. To value a thing or person in a distinctive way involves treating it in accordance with a particular set of norms. For example, courtesy expresses a mode of valuation we may call "civil respect," which differs from Kantian respect in that it calls for obedience to the rules of etiquette rather than to the categorical imperative.

Any ideal of human life includes a conception of how different things and persons should be valued. Let us reserve the term "use" to refer to the mode of valuation proper to commodities, which follows the market norm of treating things solely in accordance with the owner's nonmoral preferences. Then the Kantian argument against commodifying persons can be generalized to apply to many other cases. It can be argued that many objects which are worthy of a higher mode of valuation than use are not properly regarded as mere commodities.[2] Some current arguments against the colorization of classic black-and-white films take this form. Such films have been colorized by their owners in an attempt to enhance their market value by attracting audiences unused to black-and-white cinematography. But some opponents of the practice object that such treatment of the film classics fails to appreciate their aesthetic and historical value. True appreciation of these films would preclude this kind of crass commercial exploitation, which debases their aesthetic qualities in the name of profits. Here the argument rests on the claim that the goods in question are worthy of appreciation, not merely of use. The ideals which specify how one should value certain things are supported by a conception of human flourishing. Our lives are enriched and elevated by cultivating

and exercising the capacity to appreciate art. To fail to do so reflects poorly on ourselves. To fail to value things appropriately is to embody in one's life an inferior conception of human flourishing.[3]

These considerations support a general account of the sorts of things which are appropriately regarded as commodities. Commodities are those things which are properly treated in accordance with the norms of the modern market. We can question the application of market norms to the production, distribution, and enjoyment of a good by appealing to ethical ideals which support arguments that the good should be valued in some other way than use. Arguments of the latter sort claim that to allow certain market norms to govern our treatment of a thing expresses a mode of valuation not worthy of it. If the thing is to be valued appropriately, its production, exchange, and enjoyment must be removed from market norms and embedded in a different set of social relationships.

The Case of Commercial Surrogacy

Let us now consider the practice of commercial surrogate motherhood in the light of this theory of commodities. Surrogate motherhood as a commercial enterprise is based upon contracts involving three parties: the intended father, the broker, and the surrogate mother. The intended father agrees to pay a lawyer to find a suitable surrogate mother and make the requisite medical and legal arrangements for the conception and birth of the child, and for the transfer of legal custody to himself.[4] The surrogate mother agrees to become impregnated with the intended father's sperm, to carry the resulting child to term, and to relinquish her parental rights to it, transferring custody to the father in return for a fee and medical expenses. Both she and her husband (if she has one) agree not to form a parent-child bond with her child and to do everything necessary to effect the transfer of the child to the intended father. At current market prices, the lawyer arranging the contract can expect to gross $15,000 from the contract, while the surrogate mother can expect a $10,000 fee.[5]

The practice of commercial surrogacy has been defended on four main grounds. First, given the shortage of children available for adoption and the difficulty of qualifying as adoptive parents, it may represent the only hope for some people to be able to raise a family. Commercial surrogacy should be accepted as an effective means for realizing this highly significant good. Second, two fundamental human rights support commercial surrogacy: the right to procreate and freedom of contract. Fully informed autonomous adults should have the right to make whatever arrangements they wish for the use of their bodies and the reproduction of children, so long as the children themselves are not harmed. Third, the labor of the surrogate mother is said to be a labor of love. Her altruistic acts should be permitted and encouraged.[6] Finally, it is argued that commercial surrogacy is no different in its ethical implications from many already accepted practices which separate genetic, gestational, and social parenting, such as artificial insemination by donor, adoption, wet-nursing, and day care. Consistency demands that society accept this new practice as well.[7]

In opposition to these claims, I shall argue that commercial surrogacy does raise new ethical issues, since it represents an invasion of the market into a new sphere of conduct, that of specifically women's labor—that is, the labor of carrying children to term in pregnancy. When women's labor is treated as a commodity, the women who perform it are degraded. Furthermore, commercial surrogacy degrades children by reducing their status to that of commodities. Let us consider each of the goods of concern in surrogate motherhood—the child, and women's reproductive labor—to see how the commercialization of parenthood affects people's regard for them.

Children as Commodities

The most fundamental calling of parents to their children is to love them. Children are to be loved and cherished by their parents, not to be used or manipulated by them for merely personal advantage. Parental love can be understood as a passionate, unconditional commitment to nurture one's child, providing it with the care, affection, and guidance it needs to develop its capacities to maturity. This understanding of the way parents should value their children informs our interpretation of parental rights over their children. Parents' rights over their children are trusts, which they must always exercise for the sake of the child. This is not to deny that parents have their own aspirations in raising children. But the child's interests beyond subsistence are not definable independently of the flourishing of the family, which is the object of specifically parental aspirations. The proper exercise of parental rights includes those acts which promote their shared life as a family, which realize the shared interests of the parent and the child.

The norms of parental love carry implications for the ways other people should treat the relationship between parents and their children. If children are to be loved by their parents, then others should not attempt to compromise the integrity of parental love or work to suppress the emotions supporting the bond between parents and their children. If the rights to children should be understood as trusts, then if those rights are lost or relinquished, the duty of those in charge of transferring custody to others is to consult the best interests of the child.

Commercial surrogacy substitutes market norms for some of the norms of parental love. Most importantly, it requires us to understand parental rights no longer as trusts but as things more like property rights—that is, rights of use and disposal over the things owned. For in this practice the natural mother deliberately conceives a child with the intention of giving it up for material advantage. Her renunciation of parental responsibilities is not done for the child's sake, nor for the sake of fulfilling an interest she shares with the child, but typically for her own sake (and possibly, if "altruism" is a motive, for the intended parents' sakes). She and the couple who pay her to give up her parental rights over her child thus treat her rights as a kind of property right. They thereby treat the child itself as a kind of commodity, which may be properly bought and sold.

Commercial surrogacy insinuates the norms of commerce into the parental relationship in other ways. Whereas parental love is not supposed to be conditioned upon the child having particular characteristics, consumer demand is properly responsive to the characteristics of commodities. So the surrogate industry provides opportunities to adoptive couples to specify the height, I.Q., race, and other attributes of the surrogate mother, in the expectation that these traits will be passed on to the child.[8] Since no industry assigns agents to look after the "interests" of its commodities, no one represents the child's interests in the surrogate industry. The surrogate agency promotes the adoptive parents' interests and not the child's interests where matters of custody are concerned. Finally, as the agent of the adoptive parents, the broker has the task of policing the surrogate (natural) mother's relationship to her child, using persuasion, money, and the threat of a lawsuit to weaken and destroy whatever parental love she may develop for her child.[9]

All of these substitutions of market norms for parental norms represent ways of treating children as commodities which are degrading to them. Degradation occurs when something is treated in accordance with a lower mode of valuation than is proper to it. We value things

not just "more" or "less," but in qualitatively higher and lower ways. To love or respect someone is to value her in a higher way than one would if one merely used her. Children are properly loved by their parents and respected by others. Since children are valued as mere use-objects by the mother and the surrogate agency when they are sold to others, and by the adoptive parents when they seek to conform the child's genetic makeup to their own wishes, commercial surrogacy degrades children insofar as it treats them as commodities.[10]

One might argue that since the child is most likely to enter a loving home, no harm comes to it from permitting the natural mother to treat it as property. So the purchase and sale of infants is unobjectionable, at least from the point of view of children's interests.[11] But the sale of an infant has an expressive significance which this argument fails to recognize. By engaging in the transfer of children by sale, all of the parties to the surrogate contract express a set of attitudes toward children which undermine the norms of parental love. They all agree in treating the ties between a natural mother and her children as properly loosened by a monetary incentive. Would it be any wonder if a child born of a surrogacy agreement feared resale by parents who have such an attitude? And a child who knew how anxious her parents were that she have the "right" genetic makeup might fear that her parent's love was contingent upon her expression of these characteristics.[12]

The unsold children of surrogate mothers are also harmed by commercial surrogacy. The children of some surrogate mothers have reported their fears that they may be sold like their half-brother or half-sister, and express a sense of loss at being deprived of a sibling.[13] Furthermore, the widespread acceptance of commercial surrogacy would psychologically threaten all children. For it would change the way children are valued by people (parents and surrogate brokers)—from being loved by their parents and respected by others, to being sometimes used as objects of commercial profit-making.[14]

Proponents of commercial surrogacy have denied that the surrogate industry engages in the sale of children. For it is impossible to sell to someone what is already his own, and the child is already the father's own natural off-spring. The payment to the surrogate mother is not for her child, but for her services in carrying it to term.[15] The claim that the parties to the surrogate contract treat children as commodities, however, is based on the way they treat the *mother's* rights over her child. It is irrelevant that the natural father also has some rights over the child; what he pays for is exclusive rights to it. He would not pay her for the "service" of carrying the child to term if she refused to relinquish her parental rights to it. That the mother regards only her labor and not her child as requiring compensation is also irrelevant. No one would argue that the baker does not treat his bread as property just because he sees the income from its sale as compensation for his labor and expenses and not for the bread itself, which he doesn't care to keep. [16]

Defenders of commercial surrogacy have also claimed that it does not differ substantially from other already accepted parental practices. In the institutions of adoption and artificial insemination by donor (AID), it is claimed, we already grant parents the right to dispose of their children.[17] But these practices differ in significant respects from commercial surrogacy. The purpose of adoption is to provide a means for placing children in families when their parents cannot or will not discharge their parental responsibilities. It is not a sphere for the existence of a supposed parental right to dispose of one's children for profit. Even AID does not sanction the sale of fully formed human beings. The semen donor sells only a product of his body, not his child, and does not initiate the act of conception.

Two developments might seem to undermine the claim that commercial surrogacy constitutes a degrading commerce in children. The first is technological: the prospect of transplanting a human embryo into the womb of a genetically unrelated woman. If commercial surrogacy used women only as gestational mothers and not as genetic mothers, and if it was thought that only genetic and not gestational parents could properly claim that a child was "theirs," then the child born of a surrogate mother would not be hers to sell in the first place. The second is a legal development: the establishment of the proposed "consent-intent" definition of parenthood.[18] This would declare the legal parents of a child to be whoever consented to a procedure which leads to its birth, with the intent of assuming parental responsibilities for it. This rule would define away the problem of commerce in children by depriving the surrogate mother of any legal claim to her child at all, even if it was hers both genetically and gestationally.[19]

There are good reasons, however, not to undermine the place of genetic and gestational ties in these ways. Consider first the place of genetic ties. By upholding a system of involuntary (genetic) ties of obligation among people, even when the adults among them prefer to divide their rights and obligations in other ways, we help to secure children's interests in having an assured place in the world, which is more firm than the wills of their parents. Unlike the consent-intent rule, the principle of respecting genetic ties does not make the obligation to care for those whom one has created (intentionally or not) contingent upon an arbitrary desire to do so. It thus provides children with a set of preexisting social sanctions which give them a more secure place in the world. The genetic principle also places children in a far wider network of associations and obligations than the consent-intent rule sanctions. It supports the roles of grandparents and other relatives in the nurturing of children, and provides children with a possible focus of stability and an additional source of claims to care if their parents cannot sustain a well-functioning household.

In the next section I will defend the claims of gestational ties to children. To deny these claims, as commercial surrogacy does, is to deny the significance of reproductive labor to the mother who undergoes it and thereby to dehumanize and degrade the mother herself. Commercial surrogacy would be a corrupt practice even if it did not involve commerce in children.

Women's Labor as a Commodity

Commercial surrogacy attempts to transform what is specifically women's labor—the work of bringing forth children into the world—into a commodity. It does so by replacing the parental norms which usually govern the practice of gestating children with the economic norms which govern ordinary production processes. The application of commercial norms to women's labor reduces the surrogate mothers from persons worthy of respect and consideration to objects of mere use.

Respect and consideration are two distinct modes of valuation whose norms are violated by the practices of the surrogate industry. To respect a person is to treat her in accordance with principles she rationally accepts—principles consistent with the protection of her autonomy and her rational interests. To treat a person with consideration is to respond with sensitivity to her and to her emotional relations with others, refraining from manipulating or denigrating these for one's own purposes. Given the understanding of respect as a dispassionate, impersonal regard for people's interests, a different ethical concept—consideration —is needed to capture the engaged and sensitive regard we should have for people's emotional relationships. The failure of consideration on the part of the other parties to the

surrogacy contract explains the judgment that the contract is not simply disrespectful of the surrogate mother, but callous as well.[20]

The application of economic norms to the sphere of women's labor violates women's claims to respect and consideration in three ways. First, by requiring the surrogate mother to repress whatever parental love she feels for the child, these norms convert women's labor into a form of alienated labor. Second, by manipulating and denying legitimacy to the surrogate mother's evolving perspective on her own pregnancy, the norms of the market degrade her. Third, by taking advantage of the surrogate mother's noncommercial motivations without offering anything but what the norms of commerce demand in return, these norms leave her open to exploitation. The fact that these problems arise in the attempt to commercialize the labor of bearing children shows that women's labor is not properly regarded as a commodity.

The key to understanding these problems is the normal role of the emotions in noncommercialized pregnancies. Pregnancy is not simply a biological process but also a social practice. Many social expectations and considerations surround women's gestational labor, marking it off as an occasion for the parents to prepare themselves to welcome a new life into their family. For example, obstetricians use ultrasound not simply for diagnostic purposes but also to encourage maternal bonding with the fetus.[21] We can all recognize that it is good, although by no means inevitable, for loving bonds to be established between the mother and her child during this period.

In contrast with these practices, the surrogate industry follows the putting-out system of manufacturing. It provides some of the raw materials of production (the father's sperm) to the surrogate mother, who then engages in production of the child. Although her labor is subject to periodic supervision by her doctors and by the surrogate agency, the agency does not have physical control over the product of her labor as firms using the factory system do. Hence, as in all putting-out systems, the surrogate industry faces the problem of extracting the final product from the mother This problem is exacerbated by the fact that the social norms surrounding pregnancy are designed to encourage parental love for the child. The surrogate industry addresses this problem by requiring the mother to engage in a form of emotional labor.[22] In the surrogate contract, she agrees not to form or to attempt to form a parent-child relationship with her offspring.[23] Her labor is alienated, because she must divert it from the end which the social practices of pregnancy rightly promote— an emotional bond with her child. The surrogate contract thus replaces a norm of parenthood, that during pregnancy one create a loving attachment to one's child, with a norm of commercial production, that the producer shall not form any special emotional ties to her product.

The demand to deliberately alienate oneself from one's love for one's own child is a demand which can reasonably and decently be made of no one. Unless we were to remake pregnancy into a form of drudgery which is only performed for a wage, there is every reason to expect that many women who do sign a surrogate contract will, despite this fact, form a loving attachment to the child they bear. For this is what the social practices surrounding pregnancy encourage. Treating women's labor as just another kind of commercial production process violates the precious emotional ties which the mother may rightly and properly establish with her "product," the child, and thereby violates her claims to consideration.[24]

Commercial surrogacy is also a degrading practice. The surrogate mother, like all persons, has an independent evaluative perspective on her activities and relationships. The realization of her dignity demands that the other parties to the contract acknowledge rather than evade

the claims which her independent perspective makes upon them. But the surrogate industry has an interest in suppressing, manipulating, and trivializing her perspective, for there is an ever-present danger that she will see her involvement in her pregnancy from the perspective of a parent rather than from the perspective of a contract laborer.

How does this suppression and trivialization take place? The commercial promoters of surrogacy commonly describe the surrogate mothers as inanimate objects: mere "hatcheries," "plumbing," or "rented property"— things without emotions which could make claims on others.[25] They also refuse to acknowledge any responsibility for the consequences of the mother's emotional labor. Should she suffer psychologically from being forced to give up her child, the father is not liable to pay for therapy after her pregnancy, although he is liable for all other medical expenses following her pregnancy.[26]

The treatment and interpretation of surrogate mothers' grief raises the deepest problems of degradation. Most surrogate mothers experience grief upon giving up their children—in 10 percent of cases, seriously enough to require therapy.[27] Their grief is not compensated by the $10,000 fee they receive. Grief is not an intelligible response to a successful deal, but rather reflects the subject's judgment that she has suffered a grave and personal loss. Since not all cases of grief resolve themselves into cases of regret, it may be that some surrogate mothers do not regard their grief, in retrospect, as reflecting an authentic judgment on their part. But in the circumstances of emotional manipulation which pervade the surrogate industry, it is difficult to determine which interpretation of her grief more truly reflects the perspective of the surrogate mother. By insinuating a trivializing interpretation of her emotional responses to the prospect of losing her child, the surrogate agency may be able to manipulate her into accepting her fate without too much fuss, and may even succeed in substituting its interpretation of her emotions for her own. Since she has already signed a contract to perform emotional labor—to express or repress emotions which are dictated by the interests of the surrogate industry—this might not be a difficult task.[28] A considerate treatment of the mothers' grief, on the other hand, would take the evaluative basis of their grief seriously.

Some defenders of commercial surrogacy demand that the provision for terminating the surrogate mother's parental rights in her child be legally enforceable, so that peace of mind for the adoptive parents can be secured.[29] But the surrogate industry makes no corresponding provision for securing the peace of mind of the surrogate. She is expected to assume the risk of a transformation of her ethical and emotional perspective on herself and her child with the same impersonal detachment with which a futures trader assumes the risk of a fluctuation in the price of pork bellies. By applying the market norms of enforcing contracts to the surrogate mother's case, commercial surrogacy treats a moral transformation as if it were merely an economic change.[30]

The manipulation of the surrogate mother's emotions which is inherent in the surrogate parenting contract also leaves women open to grave forms of exploitation. A kind of exploitation occurs when one party to a transaction is oriented toward the exchange of "gift" values, while the other party operates in accordance with the norms of the market exchange of commodities. Gift values, which include love, gratitude, and appreciation of others, cannot be bought or obtained through piecemeal calculations of individual advantage. Their exchange requires a repudiation of a self-interested attitude, a willingness to give gifts to others without demanding some specific equivalent good in return each time one gives. The surrogate mother often operates according to the norms of gift relationships.

The surrogate agency, on the other hand, follows market norms. Its job is to get the best deal for its clients and itself, while leaving the surrogate mother to look after her own interests as best as she can. This situation puts the surrogate agencies in a position to manipulate the surrogate mothers' emotions to gain favorable terms for themselves. For example, agencies screen prospective surrogate mothers for submissiveness, and emphasize to them the importance of the motives of generosity and love. When applicants question some of the terms of the contract, the broker sometimes intimidates them by questioning their character and morality: if they were really generous and loving they would not be so solicitous about their own interests.[31]

Some evidence supports the claim that most surrogate mothers are motivated by emotional needs and vulnerabilities which lead them to view their labor as a form of gift and not a purely commercial exchange. Only 1 percent of applicants to surrogate agencies would become surrogate mothers for money alone; the others have emotional as well as financial reasons for applying. One psychiatrist believes that most, if not all, of the 35 percent of applicants who had had a previous abortion or given up a child for adoption wanted to become surrogate mothers in order to resolve their guilty feelings or deal with their unresolved loss by going through a process of losing a child again.[32] Women who feel that giving up another child is an effective way to punish themselves for past abortions, or a form of therapy for their emotional problems, are not likely to resist manipulation by surrogate brokers.

Many surrogate mothers see pregnancy as a way to feel "adequate," "appreciated," or "special." In other words, these women feel inadequate, unappreciated, or unadmired when they are not pregnant.[33] Lacking the power to achieve some worthwhile status in their own right, they must subordinate themselves to others' definitions of their proper place (as baby factories) in order to get from them the appreciation they need to attain a sense of self-worth. But the sense of self-worth one can attain under such circumstances is precarious and ultimately self-defeating. For example, those who seek gratitude on the part of the adoptive parents and some opportunity to share the joys of seeing their children grow discover all too often that the adoptive parents want nothing to do with them.[34] For while the surrogate mother sees in the arrangement some basis for establishing the personal ties she needs to sustain her emotionally, the adoptive couple sees it as an impersonal commercial contract, one of whose main advantages to them is that all ties between them and the surrogate are ended once the terms of the contract are fulfilled.[35] To them, her presence is a threat to marital unity and a competing object for the child's affections.

These considerations should lead us to question the model of altruism which is held up to women by the surrogacy industry. It is a strange form of altruism which demands such radical self-effacement, alienation from those whom one benefits, and the subordination of one's body, health, and emotional life to the independently defined interests of others.[36] Why should this model of "altruism" be held up to *women?* True altruism does not involve such subordination, but rather the autonomous and self-confident exercise of skill, talent, and judgment. (Consider the dedicated doctor.) The kind of altruism we see admired in surrogate mothers involves a lack of self-confidence, a feeling that one can be truly worthy only through self-effacement. This model of altruism, far from affirming the freedom and dignity of women, seems all too conveniently designed to keep their sense of self-worth hostage to the interests of a more privileged class.[37]

The primary distortions which arise from treating women's labor as a commodity—the surrogate mother's alienation from loved ones, her degradation, and her exploitation—stem from a common source. This is the failure to acknowledge and treat appropriately the surrogate mother's emotional engagement with her labor. Her labor is alienated, because she must suppress her emotional ties with her own child, and may be manipulated into reinterpreting these ties in a trivializing way. She is degraded, because her independent ethical perspective is denied, or demoted to the status of a cash sum. She is exploited, because her emotional needs and vulnerabilities are not treated as characteristics which call for consideration, but as factors which may be manipulated to encourage her to make a grave self-sacrifice to the broker's and adoptive couple's advantage. These considerations provide strong grounds for sustaining the claims of women's labor to its "product," the child. The attempt to redefine parenthood so as to strip women of parental claims to the children they bear does violence to their emotional engagement with the project of bringing children into the world.

Commercial Surrogacy, Freedom, and the Law

In the light of these ethical objections to commercial surrogacy, what position should the law take on the practice? At the very least, surrogate contracts should not be enforceable. Surrogate mothers should not be forced to relinquish their children if they have formed emotional bonds with them. Any other treatment of women's ties to the children they bear is degrading.

But I think these arguments support the stronger conclusion that commercial surrogate contracts should be illegal, and that surrogate agencies who arrange such contracts should be subject to criminal penalties.[38] Commercial surrogacy constitutes a degrading and harmful traffic in children, violates the dignity of women, and subjects both children and women to a serious risk of exploitation. But are these problems inherent in the practice of commercial surrogacy? Defenders of the practice have suggested three reforms intended to eliminate these problems: (1) give the surrogate mother the option of keeping her child after birth; (2) impose stringent regulations on private surrogate agencies; (3) replace private surrogate agencies with a state-run monopoly on surrogate arrangements. Let us consider each of these options in turn.

Some defenders of commercial surrogacy suggest that the problem of respecting the surrogate mother's potential attachment to her child can be solved by granting the surrogate mother the option to reserve her parental rights after birth.[39] But such an option would not significantly change the conditions of the surrogate mother's labor. Indeed, such a provision would pressure the agency to demean the mother's self-regard more than ever. Since it could not rely on the law to enforce the adoptive parents' wishes regardless of the surrogate's feelings, it would have to make sure that she assumed the perspective which it and its clients have of her: as "rented plumbing."

Could such dangers be avoided by careful regulation of the surrogate industry? Some have suggested that exploitation of women could be avoided by such measures as properly screening surrogates, setting low fixed fees (to avoid tempting women in financial duress), and requiring independent counsel for the surrogate mother.[40] But no one knows how to predict who will suffer grave psychological damage from surrogacy, and the main forms of duress encountered in the industry are emotional rather than financial. Furthermore, there is little hope that regulation would check the exploitation of surrogate mothers. The most significant encounters between the mothers and the surrogate agencies take place behind closed doors. It is impossible to regulate the multifarious ways in which brokers

can subtly manipulate the emotions of the vulnerable to their own advantage. Advocates of commercial surrogacy claim that their failure rate is extremely low, since only five out of the first five hundred cases were legally contested by surrogate mothers. But we do not know how many surrogate mothers were browbeaten into relinquishing their children, feel violated by their treatment, or would feel violated had their perspectives not been manipulated by the other parties to the contract. The dangers of exploiting women through commercial surrogacy are too great to ignore, and too deep to effectively regulate.

Could a state-run monopoly on surrogate arrangements eliminate the risk of degrading and exploiting surrogate mothers?[41] A nonprofit state agency would arguably have no incentive to exploit surrogates, and it would screen the adoptive parents for the sake of the best interests of the child. Nevertheless, as long as the surrogate mother is paid money to bear a child and terminate her parental rights, the commercial norms leading to her degradation still apply. For these norms are constitutive of our understanding of what the surrogate contract is for. Once such an arrangement becomes socially legitimized, these norms will govern the understandings of participants in the practice and of society at large, or at least compete powerfully with the rival parental norms. And what judgment do these norms make of a mother who, out of love for her child, decides that she cannot relinquish it? They blame her for commercial irresponsibility and flighty emotions. Her transformation of moral and emotional perspective, which she experiences as real but painful growth, looks like a capricious and selfish exercise of will from the standpoint of the market, which does not distinguish the deep commitments of love from arbitrary matters of taste.[42]

The fundamental problem with commercial surrogacy is that commercial norms are inherently manipulative when they are applied to the sphere of parental love. Manipulation occurs whenever norms are deployed to psychologically coerce others into a position where they cannot defend their own interests or articulate their own perspective without being charged with irresponsibility or immorality for doing so. A surrogate contract is inherently manipulative, since the very form of the contract invokes commercial norms which, whether upheld by the law or by social custom only, imply that the mother should feel guilty and irresponsible for loving her own child.

But hasn't the surrogate mother decided in advance that she is not interested in viewing her relationship to her child in this way? Regardless of her initial state of mind, once she enters the contract, she is not free to develop an autonomous perspective on her relationship with her child. She is contractually bound to manipulate her emotions to agree with the interests of the adoptive parents. Few things reach deeper into the self than a parent's evolving relationship with her own child. To lay claim to the course of this relationship in virtue of a cash payment constitutes a severe violation of the mother's personhood and a denial of the mother's autonomy.

Two final objections stand in the way of criminalizing commercial surrogacy. Prohibiting the practice might be thought to infringe two rights: the right of procreation, and the right to freedom of contract. Judge Harvey Sorkow, in upholding the legality and enforceability of commercial surrogate parenting contracts, based much of his argument on an interpretation of the freedom to procreate. He argued that the protection of the right to procreate requires the protection of noncoital means of procreation, including commercial surrogacy. The interests upheld by the creation of the family are the same, regardless of the means used to bring the family into existence.[43]

Sorkow asserts a blanket right to procreate, without carefully examining the specific human interests protected by such a right. The

interest protected by the right to procreate is that of being able to create and sustain a family life with some integrity. But the enforcement of surrogate contracts against the will of the mother destroys one family just as surely as it creates another. And the same interest which generates the right to procreate also generates an obligation to uphold the integrity of family life which constrains the exercise of this right.[44] To recognize the legality of commercial surrogate contracts would undermine the integrity of families by giving public sanction to a practice which expresses contempt for the moral and emotional ties which bind a mother to her children, legitimates the view that these ties are merely the product of arbitrary will, properly loosened by the offering of a monetary incentive, and fails to respect the claims of genetic and gestational ties to children which provide children with a more secure place in the world than commerce can supply.

The freedom of contract provides weaker grounds for supporting commercial surrogacy. This freedom is already constrained, notably in preventing the purchase and sale of human beings. Yet one might object that prohibiting surrogate contracts could undermine the status of women by implying that they do not have the competence to enter into and rationally discharge the obligations of commercial contracts. Insofar as the justification for prohibiting commercial surrogacy depends upon giving special regard to women's emotional ties to their children, it might be thought to suggest that women as a group are too emotional to subject themselves to the dispassionate discipline of the market. Then prohibiting surrogate contracts would be seen as an offensive, paternalistic interference with the autonomy of the surrogate mothers.

We have seen, however, that the content of the surrogate contract itself compromises the autonomy of surrogate mothers. It uses the norms of commerce in a manipulative way and commands the surrogate mothers to conform their emotions to the interests of the other parties to the contract. The surrogate industry fails to acknowledge the surrogate mothers as possessing an independent perspective worthy of consideration. And it takes advantage of motivations—such as self-effacing "'altruism'"—which women have formed under social conditions inconsistent with genuine autonomy. Hence the surrogate industry itself, far from expanding the realm of autonomy for women, actually undermines the external and internal conditions required for fully autonomous choice by women.

If commercial surrogate contracts were prohibited, this would be no cause for infertile couples to lose hope for raising a family. The option of adoption is still available, and every attempt should be made to open up opportunities for adoption to couples who do not meet standard requirements—for example, because of age. While there is a shortage of healthy white infants available for adoption, there is no shortage of children of other races, mixed-race children, and older and handicapped children who desperately need to be adopted. Leaders of the surrogate industry have proclaimed that commercial surrogacy may replace adoption as the method of choice for infertile couples who wish to raise families. But we should be wary of the racist and eugenic motivations which make some people rally to the surrogate industry at the expense of children who already exist and need homes.

The case of commercial surrogacy raises deep questions about the proper scope of the market in modern industrial societies. I have argued that there are principled grounds for rejecting the substitution of market norms for parental norms to govern the ways women bring children into the world. Such substitutions express ways of valuing mothers and children which reflect an inferior conception of human flourishing. When market norms are applied to the ways we allocate and understand parental rights and responsibilities, children are reduced from subjects of love to objects of use. When market norms are applied to the ways we treat and understand women's reproductive labor, women are reduced from subjects of respect and consideration to objects of use. If we are to retain the capacity to value children and women in ways consistent with a rich conception of human flourishing, we must resist the encroachment of the market upon the sphere of reproductive labor. Women's labor is *not* a commodity.

Notes

The author thanks David Anderson, Steven Darwall, Ezekiel Emanuel, Daniel Hausman, Don Herzog, Robert Nozick, Richard Pildes, John Rawls, Michael Sandel, Thomas Scanlon, and Howard Wial for helpful comments and criticisms.

1 See, for example, Gena Corea, *The Mother Machine* (New York: Harper and Row, 1985), pp. 216, 219; Angela Holder, "Surrogate Motherhood: Babies for Fun and Profit," *Case and Comment* 90 (1985): 3–11; and Margaret Jane Radin, "Market Inalienability," *Harvard Law Review* 100 (June 1987): 1849–1937.

2 The notion of valuing something more highly than another can be understood as follows. Some preferences are neither obligatory nor admirable. To value a thing as a mere use-object is to treat it solely in accordance with such nonethical preferences. To value a thing or person more highly than as a mere use-object is to recognize it as having some special intrinsic worth, in virtue of which we form preferences about how to treat the thing which we regard as obligatory or admirable. The person who truly appreciates art does not conceive of art merely as a thing which she can use as she pleases, but as something which commands appreciation. It would be contemptible to willfully destroy the aesthetic qualities of a work of art simply to satisfy some of one's nonethical preferences, and it is a mark of a cultivated and hence admirable person that she has preferences for appreciating art. This account of higher and lower modes of valuation is indebted to Charles Taylor's account of higher and lower values. See Charles Taylor, "The Diversity of Goods," in *Utilitarianism and Beyond*, ed. Amartya Sen and Bernard

Williams (Cambridge: Cambridge University Press, 1982), pp. 129–44.

3 This kind of argument shows why treating something as a commodity may be deplorable. Of course, more has to be said to justify prohibiting the commodification of a thing. I shall argue below that the considerations against the commodification of children and of women's labor are strong enough to justify prohibiting the practice of commercial surrogacy.

4 State laws against selling babies prevent the intended father's wife (if he has one) from being a party to the contract.

5 See Katie Marie Brophy, "A Surrogate Mother Contract to Bear a Child," *Journal of Family Law* 20 (1981–82): 263–91, and Noel Keane, "The Surrogate Parenting Contract," *Adelphia Law Journal* 2 (1983): 45–53, for examples and explanations of surrogate parenting contracts.

6 Mary Warnock, *A Question of Life* (Oxford: Blackwell, 1985), p. 45. This book reprints the Warnock Report on Human Fertilization and Embryology, which was commissioned by the British government for the purpose of recommending legislation concerning surrogacy and other issues. Although the Warnock Report mentions the promotion of altruism as one defense of surrogacy, it strongly condemns the practice overall.

7 John Robertson, "Surrogate Mothers: Not So Novel after All," *Hastings Center Report*, October 1983, pp. 28–34; John Harris, *The Value of Life* (Boston: Routledge and Kegan Paul, 1985).

8 See "No Other Hope for Having a Child," *Time,* 19 January 1987, pp. 50–51. Radin argues that women's traits are also commodified in this practice. See "Market Inalienability," pp. 1932–35.

9 Here I discuss the surrogate industry as it actually exists today. I will consider possible modifications of commercial surrogacy in the final section below.

10 Robert Nozick has objected that my claims about parental love appear to be culture-bound. Do not parents in the Third World, who rely on children to provide for the family subsistence, regard their children as economic goods? In promoting the livelihood of their families, however, such children need not be treated in accordance with market norms—that is, as commodities. In particular, such children usually remain a part of their families, and hence can still be loved by their parents.

But insofar as children are treated according to the norms of modern capitalist markets, this treatment is deplorable wherever it takes place.

11 See Elizabeth Landes and Richard Posner, "The Economics of the Baby Shortage," *Journal of Legal Studies* 7 (1978): 323–48, and Richard Posner, "The Regulation of the Market in Adoptions," *Boston University Law Review* 67 (1987): 59–72.

12 Of course, where children are concerned, it is irrelevant whether these fears are reasonable. One of the greatest fears of children is separation from their parents. Adopted children are already known to suffer from separation anxiety more acutely than children who remain with their natural mothers, for they feel that their original mothers did not love them. In adoption, the fact that the child would be even worse off if the mother did not give it up justifies her severing of ties and can help to rationalize this event to the child. But in the case of commercial surrogacy, the severing of ties is done not for the child's sake, but for the parents' sakes. In the adoption case there are explanations for the mother's action which may quell the child's doubts about being loved which are unavailable in the case of surrogacy.

13 Kay Longcope, "Surrogacy: Two Professionals on Each Side of Issue Give Their Arguments for Prohibition and Regulation," *Boston Globe,* 23 March 1987, pp. 18–19; and Iver Peterson, "Baby M Case: Surrogate Mothers Vent Feelings," *New York Times,* 2 March 1987, pp. B1, B4.

14 Herbert Krimmel, "The Case against Surrogate Parenting," *Hastings Center Report,* October 1983, pp. 35–37.

15 Judge Sorkow made this argument in ruling on the famous case of Baby M. See *In Re Baby M,* 217 N.J. Super 313. Reprinted in *Family Law Reporter* 13 (1987): 2001–30. Chief Justice Wilentz of the New Jersey Supreme Court overruled Sorkow's judgment. See *In the Matter of Baby M,* 109 N.J. 396, 537 A.2d 1227 (1988).

16 Sallyann Payton has observed that the law does not permit the sale of parental rights, only their relinquishment or forced termination by the state, and these acts are subject to court review for the sake of the child's best interests. But this legal technicality does not change the moral implications of the analogy with baby-selling. The mother is still paid to do what she can to relinquish her parental rights and to transfer custody of the child to the father. Whether or not the courts occasion-

ally prevent this from happening, the actions of the parties express a commercial orientation to children which is degrading and harmful to them. The New Jersey Supreme Court ruled that surrogacy contracts are void precisely because they assign custody without regard to the child's best interests. See *In the Matter of Baby M,* p. 1246.

17 Robertson, "Surrogate Mothers: Not So Novel after All," p. 32; Harris, *The Value of Life,* pp. 144–45.

18 See Philip Parker, "Surrogate Motherhood: The Interaction of Litigation, Legislation and Psychiatry," *International Journal of Law and Psychiatry* 5(1982): 341–54.

19 The consent-intent rule would not, however, change the fact that commercial surrogacy replaces parental norms with market norms. For the rule itself embodies the market norm which acknowledges only voluntary, contractual relations among people as having moral force. Whereas familial love invites children into a network of unwilled relationships broader than those they have with their parents, the willed contract creates an exclusive relationship between the parents and the child only.

20 I thank Steven Darwall and David Anderson for clarifying my thoughts on this point.

21 I am indebted to Dr. Ezekiel Emanuel for this point.

22 One engages in emotional labor when one is paid to express or repress certain emotions. On the concept of emotional labor and its consequences for workers, see Arlie Hochschild, *The Managed Heart* (Berkeley and Los Angeles: University of California Press, 1983).

23 Noel Keane and Dennis Breo, *The Surrogate Mother* (New York: Everest House, 1981), p. 291; Brophy, "A Surrogate Mother Contract," p. 267. The surrogate's husband is also required to agree to this clause of the contract.

24 One might ask why this argument does not extend to all cases in which one might form an emotional attachment to an object one has contracted to sell. If I sign a contract with you to sell my car to you, can I back out if I decide I am too emotionally attached to it? My argument is based upon the distinctive characteristics of parental love—a mode of valuation which should not be confused with less profound modes of valuation which generate sentimental attachments to

things. The degree to which other modes of valuation generate claims to consideration which tell against market norms remains an open question.

25 Corea, *The Mother Machine,* p. 222.

26 Keane and Breo, *The Surrogate Mother,* p. 292.

27 Kay Longcope, "Standing Up for Mary Beth," Boston Globe, 5 March 1987, p. 83; Daniel Goleman, "Motivations of Surrogate Mothers," *New York Times,* 20 January 1987, p. C1; Robertson, "Surrogate Mothers: Not So Novel after All," pp. 30, 34 n. 8. Neither the surrogate mothers themselves nor psychiatrists have been able to predict which women will experience such grief.

28 See Hochschild, *The Managed Heart,* for an important empirical study of the dynamics of commercialized emotional labor.

29 Keane and Breo, *The Surrogate Mother,* pp. 236–37.

30 For one account of how a surrogate mother who came to regret her decision viewed her own moral transformation, see Elizabeth Kane: *Birth Mother: The Story of America's First Legal Surrogate Mother* (San Diego: Harcourt Brace Jovanovich, 1988). I argue below that the implications of commodifying women's labor are not significantly changed even if the contract is unenforceable.

31 Susan Ince, "Inside the Surrogate Industry," in *Test-Tube Women,* ed. Rita Arditti, Ranate Duelli Klein, and Shelley Minden (Boston: Pandora Press, 1984), p. 110.

32 Philip Parker, "Motivation of Surrogate Mothers: Initial Findings," *American Journal of Psychiatry* 140 (1983): 117–18.

33 The surrogate broker Noel Keane is remarkably open about reporting the desperate emotional insecurities which shape the lives of so many surrogate mothers, while displaying little sensitivity to the implications of his taking advantage of these motivations to make his business a financial success. See especially Keane and Breo, *The Surrogate Mother,* pp. 247ff.

34 See, for example, the story of the surrogate mother Nancy Barrass in Anne Fleming, "Our Fascination with Baby M," *New York Times Magazine,* 29 March 1987, p. 38.

35 For evidence of these disparate perspectives, see Peterson, "Baby M Case: Surrogate Mothers Vent Feelings," p. B4.

36 The surrogate mother is required to obey all doctor's orders made in the interests of the child's health. (See Brophy, "A Surrogate Mother Contract"; Keane, "The Surrogate Parenting Contract"; and Ince, "Inside the Surrogate Industry.") These orders could include forcing her to give up her job, travel plans, and recreational activities. The doctor could confine her to bed, and order her to submit to surgery and take drugs. One can hardly exercise an autonomous choice over one's health if one could be held in breach of contract and liable for $35,000 damages for making a decision contrary to the wishes of one's doctor.

37 See Corea, *The Mother Machine,* pp. 227–33, and Christine Overall, *Ethics and Human Reproduction* (Boston: Allen and Unwin, 1987), pp. 122–28. Both emphasize the social conditions which undermine the claim that women choose to be surrogate mothers under conditions of autonomy.

38 Both of these conclusions follow the Warnock commission's recommendations. See Warnock, *A Question of Life,* pp. 43–44, 46–47. Since the surrogate mother is a victim of commercial surrogacy arrangements, she should not be prosecuted for entering into them. And my arguments are directed only against surrogacy as a commercial enterprise.

39 Barbara Cohen, "Surrogate Mothers: Whose Baby Is It?" *American Journal of Law and Medicine* 10 (1984): 282; Peter Singer and Deane Wells, *Making Babies* (New York: Scribner, 1985), pp. 106–7, 111.

40 Harris, *The Value of Life,* pp. 143–44, 156.

41 Singer and Wells support this recommendation in *Making Babies,* pp. 110–11. See also the dissenting opinion of the Warnock commission, *A Question of Life,* pp. 87–89.

42 See Fleming, "Our Fascination with Baby M," for a sensitive discussion of Americans' conflicting attitudes toward surrogate mothers who find they cannot give up their children.

43 *In Re Baby M,* p. 2022. See also Robertson, "Surrogate Mothers: Not So Novel after All," p. 32.

44 The Catholic Church makes this principle the fundamental basis for its own criticism of surrogate motherhood. See Congregation for the Doctrine of the Faith, "Instruction on Respect for Human Life In Its Origin and on the Dignity of Procreation: Replies to Certain Questions of the Day," reproduced in *New York Times,* 11 March 1987, pp. A14–A17.

Questions for Discussion

1 Can it be inconsiderate or disrespectful to treat people in ways they consent to? Does it matter if women enter into surrogacy arrangements because they are motivated by emotional needs and vulnerabilities?

2 If it is true that men who enter into surrogate contracts would not pay a woman "for the 'service' of carrying the child to term if she refused to relinquish her parental rights to it," does that establish that surrogacy arrangements really amount to the sale of children?

3 Is there a problem with commercial surrogacy because it fails to take adequate account of the emotional component of pregnancy and childbirth? Is it always wrong to engage people in "emotional labour"?

Exploitation or Empowerment?

Debating Surrogate Motherhood

Felicia Daunt

In the following article, Felicia Daunt argues that surrogate motherhood agreements, if regulated properly by law, have the capacity to further the empowerment of women rather than their oppression. She argues that women's special capabilities, such as gestation and birth, have traditionally been excluded from the marketplace, but that surrogate motherhood suggests a way in which such labour can come to be valued as it deserves to be. She also recommends that surrogacy arrangements be broken down into two distinct contracts. The first of these would pay a woman merely for undergoing artificial insemination and becoming pregnant. The second contract, according to which the woman would be paid for relinquishing the baby, should not be settled until after the birth of the child, leaving a woman with the legal option of turning down the second contract and keeping the child.

★ ★ ★

I. Introduction

Surrogate motherhood, whether we like it or not, is a growing industry in the United States and a budding industry here in Canada. As the infertility rate among middle-class women increases, due in part to women's increased presence in the work-force and their choice to delay having children, a corresponding increase in the demand for "adoptable" babies has made the waiting period for adoption unrealistic. An alternative to "stranger" adoption has emerged in the form of the surrogate motherhood contract, in the face of vehement opposition, both from some feminists, who foresee the increased oppression of women, and from (mostly male) traditionalists, who foresee the destruction of the nuclear family unit. For better or for worse, however, surrogacy is here to stay. Proper legislation is needed to allow the surrogacy contract to be a vehicle for the empowerment, not the oppression, of women.

Surrogacy contracts hold the potential to increase women's reproductive choices and to ensure that women's special capabilities receive recognition in the marketplace from which they have traditionally been excluded. Legislative control could eliminate the problems while retaining the benefits of this type of contract. We need to protect and extend women's right to make decisions. Feminists, in their effort to protect women from exploitation, must take care not to deny choices to women. We must beware our own paternalism. Women need legislative protection from the imbalance of bargaining power inherent in surrogate motherhood agreements, but should not be denied the measure of reproductive autonomy which would be stripped away by a complete banning or criminalization of surrogacy contracts.

II. Exploding Some Misconceptions

The existing debate on surrogate motherhood suffers at a basic level from flawed terminology, which both reflects and reinforces some misconceptions surrounding the current controversy. In the typical surrogate mother contract, the woman who bears the child is the child's *real* mother. Her egg is fertilized, and she carries the foetus to term and gives birth to her own baby. As Margaret Jane Radin observes, the label "surrogate mother" reflects the emphasis placed on the male genetic line: "Indeed, the very label we now give the birth mother reflects the father's ownership: she is a 'surrogate' for 'his' wife in her role of bearing 'his' child."[1] Similarly, in response to the characterization of surrogacy as baby-selling, the trial judge in the Baby M case unintentionally made the same point when he stated that a father "cannot buy what is already his."[2]

While the ovum donor situation, in which the gestational mother is not genetically related to the child, is a little more problematic, the perception of the gestational mother as nothing more than a host ignores the pregnancy and childbirth experience. Moreover, it ignores the bonds, both physical and psychological, that develop between the gestational mother and the baby she carries. The "host" characterization is indicative of a white, male, middle-aged, middle-class judicial understanding of the birthing process, *i.e.,* a complete lack of judicial desire to understand.

Another problematic development in the surrogate debate is that, while the above characterization focuses on the genetic relationship, in cases where the ovum donor is anonymous the genetic relationship is suddenly de-emphasized. Where there is *in vitro* fertilization using an anonymous donor's ovum, the donor has the same status as an anonymous sperm donor. The mere donation of an ovum does not create rights in the resulting child. It is only when the donating party wishes rights that rights are created. The desires of the gestational mother are subject to those of the donor. The gestational mother is seen as "donating" the end product, the child, in the same manner as the sperm donor donates the sperm or the ovum donor donates the ovum. Only an opinion based on the "neutral male model" could justify such a perception:

> In the political ideology based on the neutral male model—a model which takes the male body and male ethics as the norm—women are to be allowed to donate their children in exactly the same way that men donate their sperm. The all-male [Ontario Law Reform] commission stresses that the mother's importance to the child is merely genetic, and ignores the centrality of birthing, which has traditionally established a woman's relationship to a child.[3]

It is only by ignoring contextual issues that the gestational mother's importance to the child she bears, but to whom she is not genetically related, can be overlooked.

The typical surrogate motherhood contract, where the mother is genetically related to the child, is neither a new scientific phenomenon nor a new "reproductive technology." The surrogate mother bears a child the same way women have borne children since the beginning of time. There is no practical difference between the artificial insemination of a fertile woman with the sperm of a fertile man and the two having sexual intercourse with each other. To place the mother's impregnation under the heading of "reproductive technology" detours the discussion out of the realm of human interaction and attempts to justify the creation of a new legal category. As Roger Scruton states:

> Surrogate motherhood should be seen in its wider context—not as an answer to the problem of sterility, but as the outcome of a revision in moral perceptions, comparable to that foretold in *Brave New World*.... In surrogate motherhood the relation between mother and child ceases to issue from the very body of the mother and is severed from the experience of incarnation. The bond between mother and child is demystified, made clear, intelligible, scientific—and also provisional, revocable and of no more than contractual force.[4]

As long as the surrogacy arrangement is couched in scientific terminology, people like Scruton can draw this futuristic, science-fiction analogy. Does he feel the same way about the mother who gives her child up for adoption, a situation which is practically identical to surrogate motherhood, but for the payment of money? This demystified view does not result from the existence of surrogacy contracts, but from the scientific jargon associated with them. They are discussed in terms of "reproductive technology," allowing the great unwashed to forget the true nature of the subject, which has no more to do with science and technology than does a turkey baster.

The surrogate motherhood contract is not a "treatment for infertility"; neither the mother nor the father are infertile in the surrogacy arrangement. Typically, the biological father's wife is infertile, but hiring another woman to bear a child does not change her condition. To discuss the issue realistically, we must get the scientific bunk out of the debate. Scientific terminology only obscures the real problems and benefits inherent in the surrogacy arrangement. For this reason, I shall call the surrogate the "mother," the biological father the "father," and the biological father's wife the "adoptive mother."[5]

Even the contractual framework of the controversy is misleading. It completely disregards the contextual basis of the contract, that is, the use of a woman's reproductive capacity to produce a child. The special nature of both the woman and the child are ignored in any purely contractual discussion. Rather, the resolution of the dispute requires a combination of family and contract principles to give effect both to the reasoned nature of the agreement and to the uncertain, developmental, and vulnerable nature of the subject matter. As Richard Devlin notes, "contractual analysis is manifestly unsuited to the nature of the problem."[6] A surrogacy contract is not akin to an agreement for sale, but rather to an unusual type of custody and maintenance agreement entered before conception. The father agrees to support the mother while she is pregnant and to pay her a fee, in return for which she conceives, carries and gives birth to the child and then relinquishes all rights to custody and access.

However, it is important not to ignore the fundamental purpose of the surrogacy contract, which is not the rental of the womb, but the production of a child for the father's marriage in return for money. In this respect, it is akin to a contract for the sale of goods rather than the purchase of services. (Any other characterization of the contract is only trying to legitimize what seems to be basically "wrong.") For example, in the typical surrogacy contract, if artificial insemination is unsuccessful over about a six-month period, the would-be mother is paid nothing for her time. Also, she is paid no fee if she does get pregnant but subsequently miscarries.[7] The production of a baby to be parented by the father and the adoptive mother is therefore the purpose for which all parties enter the contract.

Because surrogacy contracts, at least in the United States, are arranged by private, free-enterprise agencies[8] who must cater to the paying party, they open the door to much potential abuse and exploitation of the gestational mother:

> Because these companies focus on the desires of the paying parties, they may neglect the treatment of the surrogate mother and the child.... Focusing on the satisfaction of the paying party leads to company policies that allow couples to insert individualized provisions into the standardized contract generally used. These provisions may range from limits on the surrogate's right to smoke or drink during pregnancy to the couple's presence at the delivery. No one knows how extreme these terms may be or how courts will enforce them.[9]

Further, "it is important to separate the natural and valid repugnancy towards agencies and other profiteers in the surrogate business from that of the act itself."[10] However, once stripped of the exploitative elements, both formal and substantive, surrogacy contracts do hold the potential to empower women, to increase women's reproductive choices and to ensure that women's special capabilities receive recognition in the marketplace from which they have traditionally been excluded.

III. Power Imbalance and Exploitation

For several reasons, people generally experience an almost instinctive distaste for the surrogate motherhood contract and for all the parties involved.[11] Foremost among these is the distaste for the commodification of babies and of women's reproductive capacity. As Prichard notes:

> [T]he mere description [of a "market for babies"] has a ring of parody to it as the incongruity of market notions and babies jars the reader ... the concern is that the special value we attribute to children de-

pends in part on the fact that they cannot be traded.[12]

At least part of the fear of surrogacy stems from a fear of the destruction of the traditional family unit, and the imagined social havoc which that would wreak. Women and children traditionally inhabit a place far removed from the marketplace. Their presence is reserved for the home, the private sphere. At least part of the revulsion of "commodification" comes from the tradition of separating "commodities," or the marketplace, from women and children. The disgust is analogous to the gut feeling one gets when faced with pod-like alien beings on Earth, or skeletons in your living room, or mushrooms growing on a couch. They just don't belong there. We don't really think about why this is: we are simply, instinctively revolted. But we must recognize that the revulsion comes from nurture, not nature.

Similarly, analogies between prostitution and surrogacy have been drawn to prove the undesirability of both.[13] After viewing the surrogacy industry from the inside, Susan Ince wrote:

> The language and process encountered in my experience within a surrogate company is consistent with the reproductive prostitution model described by [Andrea] Dworkin. The surrogate is paid for 'giving the man what his wife can't.' She 'loves being pregnant,' and is valued solely and temporarily for her reproductive capacity. After she 'enters the fold' she is removed from standard legal protections and is subject to a variety of abuses. She is generally considered to be mercenary, collecting large unearned fees for her services, but the terms of the system are in reality such that she may lose more permanent opportunities for employment, and may end up injured or dead with no compensation at all. Even the glowing descriptions of the surrogates sound remarkably like a happy hooker with a heart of gold.[14]

With the prostitution analogy comes the perception of something unnatural about the "perfect surrogate" who is maternal enough to love being pregnant, yet autonomous enough not to want to have anything to do with the baby after she is born. This analogy with prostitution causes the industry to advertise their "girls" in glowing language and to promote the "girl next door" image. As one industry representative said to Ince:

> [We want] to dispel the misconceptions people have about surrogates. I'm very sorry to say it, but they don't think our surrogates are nice girls like you. When people think surrogate, they think tight black satin slacks. I don't know why, but they do.[15]

Because prostitutes are perceived to be one of the most oppressed groups on earth, and because surrogacy is like prostitution, if surrogacy is allowed, surrogate mothers will therefore become oppressed. The easy solution is banning and criminalizing surrogacy contracts. Even defenders of surrogacy have felt the need to downplay the obvious analogy to prostitution. However, a good part of the oppression of prostitutes stems from the perceived illegality of prostitution itself. What emerges from Ince's article is that women who hire themselves out as surrogates are subjecting themselves to all kinds of abuses. While these are compelling arguments for governmental regulation of the industry to protect birth mothers, they are not convincing arguments for the abolition of the whole practice.

Similarly, would-be saviours of potential birth mothers espouse class imbalances as the reason for their distaste with surrogate motherhood contracts.[16] They see in these contracts the exploitation of poor and underprivileged women, and the exclusion of members of "undesirable" races from any potential economic gain. Conversely, they foresee the wide use of third-world women as breeding stock for white middle- and upper-class couples.[17] Both inclusion in and exclusion from the world of surrogacy are feared.

There is, of course the potential for gross exploitation of poor women who are willing to be used as breeders for rich couples. However, that potential remains so long as legislatures refuse to deal with the issue. The birth mother, who needs money, will always be in a poorer bargaining position than either the surrogacy agency or the adopting parents. Were these contracts subject to statutory conditions protecting the mother, the potential for abuse would be controlled. But as long as the area remains uncontrolled and within a free market framework, abuses can and will occur.

Moreover, underlying this concern that surrogacy will increase the oppression of women[18] is the premise that women's childbirth abilities should not have the status of a market commodity.

By increasing women's reproductive choices, by giving them a place in the market that has traditionally been denied, we can progress towards eliminating the power imbalance that currently exists between men and women.

The imbalance of bargaining power, and thus the potential to oppress women, is not nearly so great in the surrogacy context as that facing the already-pregnant woman considering giving her baby up for adoption. That woman is expected to make her decision facing economic disaster should she keep her baby. Not only can she expect no reward for giving her baby away to a wealthier couple, in most jurisdictions it is illegal for her to accept payment.

However, she does have the advantage of actually bearing her child before she makes the final decision to give her up. The surrogate mother is expected to decide even before she becomes pregnant. Also, most birth mothers under a surrogacy contract are disadvantaged by having no right of revocation after the baby

is born, unlike mothers giving their baby up for adoption. In Saskatchewan, the latter have 14 days to revoke their consent to adoption.[19]

What seems to make surrogacy "wrong" is the payment to the mother for bearing a child. As women have always done this for free, it is considered to be immoral to expect payment. Pregnant women are the only class of persons expected to perform unpaid labour. What at first blush seems to make surrogacy wrong can in fact signify a step toward balancing the power structure between the adoptive parents and the birth mother, and ultimately between all men and women....

V. Empowering Women with Surrogacy Contracts

Traditionally, women's role in society has had no value in the marketplace. Homemaking, sexual services, and bearing and raising children have all been unpaid labour. Women have had domestic responsibilities, but no corresponding rights. Prostitutes are perceived as a threat to this social order because they work outside the accepted societal framework and expect payment for performing a "wifely" duty.

To be paid for what they have always done for free would empower women and would increase the extent of their decision-making powers. Women have been denied a role in the marketplace in the past, so their role has come to be equated with that which is unmarketable, altruistic, their duty and responsibility, and therefore unpaid. To argue that a woman's reproductive capacity should remain noncommodified is to perpetuate that warped perception. As Radin notes (although she does not wholly adopt this persuasive view):

> [N]oncommodification of women's capabilities under current circumstances represents not a brave new world of human flourishing, but rather a perpetuation of the old order that submerges women in oppressive status relationships, in which per-

sonal identity as market-traders is the pre-rogative of males. We cannot make progress toward the noncommodification that might exist under ideal conditions of equality and freedom by trying to maintain non-commodification now under historically determined conditions of inequality and bondage.[30]

It is within our power to change that "historically determined condition." It is not too late to put a value on women's work.

This notion of duty perhaps explains why most people are shocked by the possibility that rich women might choose surrogacy even if they are not infertile.[31] That choice would make no practical difference to the gestational mother; her experience would be the same regardless of the motives of the adoptive mother. The revulsion for the adoptive mother's perceived choice not to bear her own child must therefore come from the perception that she is avoiding her "duty" as a woman to bear her husband's children. The mainstream view is that surrogacy should not increase her range of choice, that is, it should be available only to infertile women who have no other realistic choice. For it to be available to all women, without the saving factor of necessity, offends the sensibilities. The argument is equivalent to the old one used to deny women the choice of entering the workforce: women who have a husband capable of supporting them should not work.

The apparent immorality of remuneration for women's labour is in reality immoral itself, designed to keep women subservient. Payment is the difference between a slut and a whore. Slutting is bad because women are expected to reserve their sexual services for their husbands, but whoring is the greater of the two evils because women are expected to provide these services for free. Abolition of either surrogacy or prostitution denies women personal choices. Whether this is put in terms of "a woman's place" or discussed under the guise of protecting women from exploitation,

it denies women basic human rights. Although living in an oppressed state denies many women a "real" choice, a choice founded on the true freedom to make a decision based on the benefits available from each option, we cannot take away even an illusory choice. To do so still denies women the power of self-determination and of autonomy. It smacks of paternalism in the guise of protection. As Gail Pheterson, a prostitute, comments:

> Typically, [prostitution] abolitionists ... [say] that freedom and consciousness are exceptions within prostitution and that the majority of prostitutes are victimized women and children. But when asked whether a prostitute can ever be a self-determining agent, the abolitionists reply in the negative. Persons in the sex industry are thereby denied adult status.... They are defined as violated or trafficked persons whether or not they themselves experience or report abuse. If actually abused, prostitutes cannot demand recourse without implicating themselves as unworthy participants in illicit (*i.e.*, commercial) sex.[32]

Criminalizing prostitutes' work adds to their oppression. We must take care not to make the same mistake with surrogate mothers. We must allow all women to make adult decisions.

Legislative reform is the only way to avoid the abuse and exploitation of surrogate mothers. To ignore the problem is to consent through silence and inactivity to that abuse. Legislation must, however, recognize the special nature of the agreement and be designed to prevent abuse and exploitation. It must not in any way add to the existing abuse or oppression of mothers:

> A surrogacy contract involving the creation of life and the organization of families is simply not an unremarkable document providing for the transfer of commodities. The rules which govern most contracts should not be applied automatically to surrogacy contracts.[33]

For this reason, the Ontario Law Reform Commission recommendation that the adoptive parents be allowed the remedy of specific performance if the mother repudiates the contract[34] is completely reprehensible. She should at least be allowed the same revocation privilege as any woman considering giving up her child for adoption; moreover, this right should not be waivable through contract.[35]

Legislation must recognize the special nature of the relationship between mother and child and allow the mother to make the final decision. By taking the discussion out of a purely contractual framework—perhaps by imposing non-waivable statutory conditions—it becomes possible to empower the mother. To allow specific performance of this type of contract is to ignore its special nature. It is absolutely unthinkable that the law could force a fit mother to give up her child against her will. Were specific performance an available remedy, the whole contract would smack of slavery and treat women as nothing more than breeding stock.

Because the agreement concerns the production of a child, it is by its nature developmental, not constant, and therefore unsuited to regular contractual analysis. Over the four stages of the relationship[36] things change dramatically. At the time the agreement is reached (before conception), it is impossible to predict how the mother will react when faced with giving up a child. The main problem in drafting any legislation will be to decide "whether rights exercised at the agreement stage should control subsequent rights."[37] The agreement itself should reflect the changing nature of the subject matter. It is impossible to make an informed and reasoned consent to relinquish all rights to a child at a time when that child has not even been conceived.

Therefore, the agreement should take the form of two contracts. The first is an agreement that the mother will undergo artificial insemination, for which she should be paid and supported if she becomes pregnant. This creates a contract that truly is for the mother's services, and not for the sale of a baby.

The second agreement, to relinquish custody of the baby, should be entered into only after the baby is born. This will be a separate contract with separate remuneration, reflecting the differing nature of the decision from that involved in the first agreement. The mother should be given a statutory, non-waivable right of revocation for a specified time, as is any mother who gives up a child for adoption, whether private or public. Clearly this can be characterized as "baby-selling." but as I have argued, this is not as distasteful as it sounds.

Should the mother exercise her right of revocation, she would be liable to return any money paid under the second contract, as she would not have fulfilled her end of the bargain. She would not, however, be liable to return money paid under the first contract, as she would have fully performed her obligations thereunder. Because the adoptive parents have the greater bargaining power and the greater wealth, they should partly bear the risk of the mother deciding to keep the child. While the mother is not physically able to enter another surrogacy contract for some time, the adoptive parents are free to find another birth mother immediately. The father is, at least in part, paying to carry on his genetic line which is perpetuated whether or not he actually receives custody of the child.

In this manner, the legislature could empower women in surrogacy arrangements, while preventing abuse and exploitation, without denying either the mother or the adoptive mother any measure of reproductive autonomy.

VI. Conclusion: Empowering Surrogates and Prostitutes

Surrogacy is indeed akin to prostitution. Both surrogates and prostitutes are denied basic human rights by the society in which, and for whose benefit, they operate. At present, prostitutes are arguably the most oppressed group of people in the world. Because criminalization has driven prostitution underground, its practitioners find themselves abused by johns, pimps, and police.[38] It is submitted that criminalization of surrogacy will, in the long run, have the same effect, oppressing surrogates even more. What could be an honourable and empowering practice will become sleazy and abusive. Surrogate mothers need our protection, not our condemnation. Women need to be empowered, not enslaved.

Notes

1 M. Radin, "Market-Inalienability" (1987) 100 Harv. L. Rev. 1849 at 1929 n. 276.

2 *In Re Baby M*, 525 A. 2d 1128 at 1157 (N.J. Sup. Ct 1987), Sorkow J.

3 S. Brodribb, "Off the Pedestal and Onto the Block? Motherhood, Reproductive Technologies, and the Canadian State" (1986) 1 C.J.W.L. 407 at 420, referring to the Ontario Low Reform Commission, *Report on Human Artificial Reproduction and Related Matters*, (Toronto: Ministry of the Attorney General, 1985).

4 R. Scruton, "Ignore the Body, Lose Your Soul" *The [London] Times* (5 February 1985) 10.

5 See, for example, Devlin *infra*, note 6; Brodribb, *supra*, note 3; Radin, *supra*, note 1.

6 R. Devlin, "Baby M: The Contractual Legitimation of Misogyny" 10 R.F.L. (3d) 4 at 27.

7 S. Ince, "Inside the Surrogacy Industry" in R. Arditti, R. Klein, & S. Minden, eds. *Test-Tube Women: What Future of Motherhood?* (London: Pandora Press, 1984) 99 at 101.

8 See, for example, Ince *supra*, note 7; Devlin, *supra*, note 6; Mellown, *infra*, note 9; Knoppers & Sloss, *infra*, note 10; Prichard, *infra*, note 12; in England, M. Warnock, *A Question of Life: The Warnock Report on Human Fertilization and Embryology* (New York: B. Blackwell, 1985).

9 M.R. Mellown, "An Incomplete Picture: The Debate about Surrogate Motherhood" (1985) 8 Harv. Women's L.J. 231 at 237.

10 B. Knoppers and E. Sloss, "Recent Developments: Legislative Reforms in Reproductive Technology" (1986) 18 Ottawa L. Rev. 663 at 718.

11 See, for example, Radin, *supra*, note 1; Brodribb, *supra*, note 3.

12 J.R. Prichard, "A Market for Babies" (1984) 34 U.T.L.J. 341 at 347-52.

13 See, for example, A. Dworkin, *Right-Wing Women* New York: Perigee Books, 1983), Ince, *supra*, note 7; Brodribb, *supra*, note 3; Mellown, *supra*, note 9.

14 Ince, *supra*, note 7 at 115.

15 *Ibid.* at 105.

16 See, for example, Mellown, *supra*, note 9; Brodribb, *supra*, note 3; Radin *supra*, note 1.

17 See, for example, N.J. Wikler, "Society's Response to the New Reproductive Technologies: The Feminist Perspectives" (1986) 59 S. Cal. L. Rev. 1043.

18 See, for example, Radin, *supra*, note 1; Ince, *supra*, note 7; Brodribb, *supra*, note 3; Devlin, *supra*, note 6.

19 *The Adoption Act*, S.S. 1989-90, c. A-5.1, s. 8(2).

...

30 *Supra*, note 1 at 1916.

31 See, for example, M. Warnock, *A Question of Life: The Warnock Report on Human Fertilization and Embryology* (New York: B. Blackwell, 1985).

32 G. Pheterson, "Not Repeating History" in G. Pheterson, ed. *A Vindication of the Rights of Whores* (Seattle: The Seal Press, 1989) 2 at 14.

33 J. Dolgin, "Status and Contract in Surrogate Motherhood: An Illumination of the Surrogacy Debate" (1990) 38 Buffalo L. Rev. 515 at 547.

34 *Supra*, note 3 at 283.

35 Dolgin, *supra*, note 33 at 547; see also B. Stark, "Constitutional Analysis of the *Baby M* Decision" (1988) 11 Harv. Women's L.J. 19.

36 Stark, *ibid.* at 22. Stark suggests that the contract be divided into four stages:

(1) the agreement;
(2) insemination and conception;
(3) pregnancy and abortion; and
(4) determination of parental rights.

37 *Ibid.* at 36.

38 Pheterson, *supra*, note 32.

Questions for Discussion

1 Is surrogate motherhood a "new reproductive technology"? Is it a treatment for infertility?

2 Is a surrogacy contract more like an agreement to purchase services, or (as Daunt claims) like the sale of goods?

3 If a couple hires a surrogate, does it matter morally whether this is because the woman is infer-tile, or because she simply would rather pay than go through a pregnancy? Why or why not?

4 Does surrogate motherhood point the way for women to be paid for activities which for too long they have done for free?

5 Daunt suggests that women should be able to decide to keep children to whom they have given birth, regardless of any previous understanding about custody, and that women who exercise this option should still be paid for having gone through with the first part of the arrangement, being artificially inseminated. Is she right?

What's Wrong with Prostitution?

Igor Primoratz

Prostitution is widely believed to be morally wrong in some sense. After noting that fact, Igor Primoratz goes on to examine arguments which might be offered in support of that view. He considers arguments which hold that some things (e.g., sex) should simply not be for sale, that prostitution is degrading to, or contributes to the oppression of, women, and that prostitution is bad for the women engaged in it, and we have a paternalistic obligation to protect them from it. Primoratz argues that none of these arguments is convincing, and that in any case they apply equally to other kinds of practices which are not similarly condemned in our society. Accordingly, he concludes that we should consider prostitution to be morally acceptable, at least until someone offers a more convincing argument for the contrary opinion.

★ ★ ★

Over the last three decades the sexual morality of many Western societies has changed beyond recognition. Most of the prohibitions which made up the traditional, extremely restrictive outlook on sex that reigned supreme until the Fifties—the prohibitions of masturbation, pre-marital and extra-marital sex, promiscuity, homosexuality—are no longer seen as very serious or stringent or, indeed, as binding at all. But one or two traditional prohibitions are still with us. The moral ban on prostitution, in particular, does not seem to have been repealed or radically mitigated. To be sure, some of the old arguments against prostitution are hardly ever brought up these days; but then, several new ones are quite popular, at least in certain circles. Prostitution is no longer seen as the most extreme moral depravity a woman is capable of; but the view that it is at least seriously morally flawed, if not repugnant and intolerable, is still widely held. In this paper I want to look into some of the main arguments in support of this view and try to show that none of them is convincing.[1]

1. Positive Morality

The morality of this society and of most other societies today condemns prostitution in no uncertain terms; the facts of the condemnation and its various, sometimes quite serious and far-reaching consequences for those who practise it, are too well known to need to be recounted here. But what do these facts prove? Surely not that prostitution is wrong, only that positive morality of this and many other societies *deems it* wrong. With regard to prostitution, as with regard to any moral issue, we must surely attend to the distinction between positive morality, the morality prevalent in a society and expressed in its public opinion, its laws and the lives of its members, and critical morality, which is a set of moral principles, rules and values together with the reasoning behind them that an individual may adopt, not only to live by them, but also to apply them in judging critically the morality of any particular society, including his or her own.

To be sure, the importance, or even tenability, of this distinction has been denied; there have been authors (Emile Durkheim is a good example) who maintained that whatever a society holds to be right or wrong *is* right or wrong in that society. But the flaws of this position, which might be termed moral positivism or conventionalism, are obvious and fatal. One is that it implies that all philosophers, religion teachers, writers and social reformers who set out to criticize and reform the moral outlook of their societies were not merely wrong—all of them may, and some of them must have been wrong—but utterly misguided in what they were trying to do, for what they were trying to do logically cannot be done. There is no such thing as a radical moral critique of one's society (or any other society, for that matter). Another implausible implication of moral positivism is that the same action or practice can be both right (in one society) and wrong (in another). Thus prostitution was both morally unobjectionable (in ancient Greece) *and* a moral abomination (in nineteenth-century England). Finally, positive morality is often inconsistent. Prostitution is, again, a case in point. It has been pointed

out time and again that there is no morally significant difference between the common prostitute and the spouse in what used to be called a marriage of convenience. This kind of marriage, said Friedrich Engels, for example, 'turns often enough into the crassest prostitution—sometimes of both partners, but far more commonly of the woman, who only differs from the ordinary courtesan in that she does not let out her body on piecework as a wage worker, but sells it once and for all into slavery.'[2] The word 'slavery' is too strong, and it may not be the spouse's body that is being sold, but otherwise the point is well taken. How can positive morality condemn mercenary sex in one case, but not in the other?

I am not saying that this inconsistency cannot be explained. It can, if we attend to the social meaning of marriage and prostitution.[3] Both can be called 'sexual institutions', as both have to do with sex, both are institutional frameworks for satisfying sexual desire. But their social meaning is not the same. Throughout history, the most important social function of sex has been reproduction. Marriage has always been seen as the best institutional set-up for procreating and socializing the young. Accordingly, marriage is the central, most respected and most strongly supported among the sexual institutions, while other such institutions, such as concubinage or wife exchange, are the less supported and respected the more they are removed from marriage. Prostitution is at the other end of this range, for in prostitution

> both parties use sex for an end not socially functional, the one for pleasure, the other for money. To tie intercourse to sheer physical pleasure is to divorce it both from reproduction and from the sentimental primary type of relation which it symbolizes. To tie it to money ... does the same thing. (...) On both sides the relationship is merely a means to a private end....[4]

Both money and pleasure may be very important to the individuals concerned but, as merely individual objectives, have no social significance. Therefore, society accords prostitution neither support nor respect. The traditional Western sexual ethic considers sex as in itself morally problematic if not downright bad or sinful, and thus legitimate only as a means of procreation, and perhaps also of expression and reinforcement of emotions and attitudes usually associated with procreation. It is easy to see how Western society came to condemn and despise the practice of prostitution.

However, the inconsistency of condemning mercenary sex outside marriage but not within it still has not been explained. The missing part is the fact that society is concerned with practices and institutions, not with individuals; social morality judges primarily practices and institutions, and deals with individuals simply, and solely, by subsuming them under the roles defined by practices and institutions. If it were otherwise, if social morality were interested in, and capable of, relating to the individual and his or her actions in their particularity and complexity, as all serious and discerning moral thinking does, it could not fail to condemn mercenary sex within marriage no less than outside it. For it does not consider marriage valuable in itself, but as the proper framework for reproduction and the upbringing of offspring, and also, perhaps, as the framework that best sustains the emotions and attitudes helpful in the performance of these tasks. Therefore marital sex is not legitimate simply as marital, but as sex that serves the social purpose of marriage. When a person engages in sex within marriage, but fails to live up to this normative conception of the institution and has sex merely in order to secure the economic benefits of the married state, that is no less mercenary than the sex sold on the street to all comers, and accordingly no less wrong from the point of view of the sexual ethic to which society ad-

heres on the level of rules and roles, practices and institutions. Society does not see this because it cannot be bothered to look into the life, actions and motives of the individual. But that is surely reason enough not to bother with its pronouncements when attempting to settle an important moral question.

2. Paternalism

Paternalism is most commonly defined as 'the interference with a person's liberty of action justified by reasons referring exclusively to the welfare, good, happiness, needs, interests or values of the person being coerced.'[5] Philosophical discussions of paternalism have concentrated on paternalist legislation; for the most obvious, and often the most effective, kind of interference with an individual's liberty of action is by means of law. But paternalism can also be put forward as a moral position: it can be argued that the wrongness of doing something follows from the fact that doing it has serious adverse effects on the welfare, good, etc. of the agent and, having made that judgment, to exert the pressure of the moral sanction on the individuals concerned to get them to refrain from doing it. A popular way of arguing against prostitution is of this sort: it refers to such hazards of selling sex as (i) venereal diseases; (ii) unpleasant, humiliating, even violent behaviour of clients; (iii) exploitation by madams and pimps; (iv) the extremely low social status of prostitutes and the contempt and ostracism to which they are exposed. The facts showing that these are, indeed, the hazards of prostitution are well known; are they not enough to show that prostitution is bad and to be avoided?

A short way with this objection is to refuse to acknowledge the moral credentials of paternalism, and to say that what we have here is merely a prudential, not a moral argument against prostitution.

However, we may decide to accept that

paternalist considerations can be relevant to questions about what is morally right and wrong. In that case, the first thing to note about the paternalist argument is that it is an argument from *occupational* hazards and thus, if valid, valid only against prostitution as an *occupation*. For in addition to the professional prostitute, whose sole livelihood comes from mercenary sex, there is also the amateur, who is usually gainfully employed or married and engages in prostitution for additional income. The latter—also known as the secret prostitute—need not at all suffer from (iii) and (iv), and stands a much lower chance of being exposed to (i) and (ii). A reference to (iii) actually is not even an argument against professional prostitution, but merely against a particular, by no means necessary way of practising it; if a professional prostitute is likely to be exploited by a madam or pimp, then she should pursue the trade on her own.

But it is more important to note that the crucial, although indirect cause of all these hazards of professional prostitution is the negative attitude of society, the condemnation of prostitution by its morality and its laws. But for that, the prostitute could enjoy much better medical protection, much more effective police protection from abusive and aggressive behaviour of clients and legal protection from exploitation by pimps and madams, and her social status would be quite different. Thus the paternalist argument takes for granted the conventional moral condemnation of prostitution, and merely gives an additional reason for not engaging in something that has already been established as wrong. But we can and should refuse to take that for granted, because we can and should refuse to submit to positive morality as the arbiter of moral issues. If we do so, and if a good case for morally condemning commercial sex has still not been made out, as I am trying to show in this paper, then all these hazards should be seen as reasons for trying to disabuse society of the prejudices

against it and help to change the law and social conditions in general in which prostitutes work, in order radically to reduce, if not completely eliminate, such hazards.

However, there is one occupational hazard that has not been mentioned so far: one that cannot be blamed on unenlightened social morality, and would remain even if society were to treat prostitution as any other legitimate occupation. That is the danger to the sex life of the prostitute. As Lars Ericsson neatly puts it, 'Can one have a well-functioning sexual life if sex is what one lives by?'[6]

One way of tackling this particular paternalist objection is to say, with David A.J. Richards, that perhaps one can. Richards claims that there is no evidence that prostitution makes it impossible for those who practice it to have loving relationships, and adds that 'there is some evidence that prostitutes, as a class, are more sexually fulfilled than other American women.'[7] The last claim is based on a study in which 175 prostitutes were systematically interviewed, and which showed that 'they experienced orgasm and multiple orgasm more frequently in their personal, "non-commercial" intercourse than did the normal woman (as defined by Kinsey norms).'[8] Another, probably safer response is to point out, as Ericsson does, that the question is an empirical one and that, since there is no conclusive evidence either way, we are not in a position to draw any conclusion.[9]

My preferred response is different. I would rather grant the empirical claim that a life of prostitution is liable to wreck one's sex life, i.e., the minor premise of the argument, and then look a bit more closely into the major premise, the principle of paternalism. For there are two rather different versions of that principle. The weak version prevents the individual from acting on a choice that is not fully voluntary, either because the individual is permanently incompetent or because the choice in question is a result of ignorance of some important facts or made under extreme psychological or social pressure. Otherwise the individual is considered the sole qualified judge of his or her own welfare, good, happiness, needs, interests and values, and the choice is ultimately his or hers. Moreover, when a usually competent individual is prevented from acting on a choice that is either uninformed or made under extreme pressure, and is therefore not fully voluntary, that individual will, when the choice-impairing conditions no longer obtain agree that the paternalist interference was appropriate and legitimate, and perhaps even be grateful for it. Strong paternalism *is* meant to protect the individual from his or her voluntary choices, and therefore will not be legitimized by retrospective consent of the individual paternalized. The assumption is not that the individual is normally the proper judge of his or her own welfare, good, etc., but rather that someone else knows better where the individual's true welfare, good, etc. lie, and therefore has the right to force the individual to act in accordance with the latter, even though that means acting against his or her fully voluntary choice, which is said to be merely 'subjective' or 'arbitrary'. Obviously, the weak version of paternalism does not conflict with personal liberty, but should rather be seen as its corollary; for it does not protect the individual from choices that express his or her considered preferences and settled values, but only against his or her 'non-voluntary choices', choices the individual will subsequently disavow. Strong paternalism, on the other hand, is essentially opposed to individual liberty, and cannot be accepted by anyone who takes liberty seriously. Such paternalism smacks of intellectual and moral arrogance, and it is hard to see how it could ever be established by rational argument.[10]

Accordingly, if the argument from the dangers to the prostitute's sex life is not to be made rather implausible from the start, it ought to be put forward in terms of weak rather than strong paternalism. When put in these terms, however, it is not really an argument that prostitution is wrong because imprudent, but rather that it is wrong if and when it is taken up imprudently. It reminds us that persons permanently incompetent and those who still have not reached the age of consent should not (be allowed to) take up the life of prostitution and thereby most likely throw away the prospect of a good sex life. (They should not (be allowed to) become prostitutes for other reasons anyway.) As for a competent adult, the only legitimate paternalist interference with the choice of such a person to become a prostitute is to make sure that the choice is a free and informed one. But if an adult and sane person is fully apprised of the dangers of prostitution to the sex life of the prostitute and decides, without undue pressure of any sort, that the advantages of prostitution as an occupation are worth it, then it is neither imprudent nor wrong for that person to embark on the line of work chosen.[11] In such a case, as Mill put it, 'neither one person, nor any number of persons, is warranted in saying to another human creature of ripe years that he shall not do with his life for his own benefit what he chooses to do with it.'[12]

3. Some Things Just Are Not for Sale

In the eyes of many, by far the best argument against prostitution is brief and simple: some things just are not for sale, and sex is one of them.

It would be difficult not to go along with the first part of this argument. The belief that not everything can or should be bought and sold is extremely widespread, if not universal. The list of things not for sale is not exactly the same in all societies, but it seems that every society does have such a list, a list of 'blocked exchanges'.

The term is Michael Walzer's, and a discussion of such exchanges is an important part of his theory of justice. The central thesis of the theory is that there are several spheres of personal qualities and social goods, each autonomous, with its own criteria, procedures and agents of distribution. Injustice occurs when this autonomy is violated, when the borders are crossed and a sphere of goods becomes dominated by another in that the goods of the former are no longer distributed in accordance with its own criteria and procedures, but in accordance with those of the other sphere. The market is one such sphere—actually, the sphere with the strongest tendency to expand into, and dominate, other spheres of goods, at least in a modern capitalist society. But even this kind of society has an impressive list of things not for sale. The one Walzer offers as 'the full set of blocked exchanges in the United States today', but which would be valid for any contemporary liberal and democratic society, includes the sale of human beings (slavery), political power and office, criminal justice, freedom of speech, various prizes and honours, love and friendship, and more.'[13] This is, obviously, a mixed lot. In some cases, the very nature of a good rules out its being bought and sold (love, friendship); in others, that is precluded by the conventions which constitute it (prizes); in still others, the dominant conception of a certain sphere of social life prohibits the sale, as, for instance, our conception of the nature and purpose of the political process entails that political power and office must not be bought and sold. (To be sure, some of the things listed as a matter of fact are bought and sold. But that happens only on the black market, and the fact that the market is 'black', and that those who buy and sell there do so in secret, goes to show both the illegitimacy and the secondary, parasitic character of such transactions.) There is, thus, no single criterion by reference to which one could explain why all these items appear on the list, and why no other does.

What of sex? It is not on the list; for sex, unlike love, can, as a matter of fact, be bought and sold, and there is no single, generally accepted conception of sex that prohibits its sale and purchase. 'People who believe that sexual intercourse is morally tied to love and marriage are likely to favour a ban on prostitution ... (...) Sex can be sold only when it is understood in terms of pleasure and not exclusively in terms of married love ...'[14]

This is helpful, for it reminds us that the 'Not for sale' argument is elliptic; the understanding of sex that is presupposed must be explicated before the argument can be assessed. But the remark is also inaccurate, since it conflates two views of sex that are both historically and theoretically different: the traditional view, which originated in religion, that sex is legitimate only within marriage and as a means to procreation, and the more modern, secular, 'romantic' view that sex is to be valued only when it expresses and enhances a loving relationship. Let me look briefly into these two views in order to see whether a commitment to either does, indeed, commit one to favouring a ban on prostitution.

The first views sex as intrinsically inferior, sinful and shameful, and accepts it only when, and in so far as, it serves an important extrinsic purpose which cannot be attained by any other means: procreation. Moreover, the only proper framework for bringing up children is marriage; therefore sex is permissible only within marriage. These two statements make up the core of the traditional Christian understanding of sex, elaborated in the writings of St. Augustine and St. Thomas Aquinas, which has been by far the most important source of Western sexual ethics. To be sure, modern Christian thought and practice have broadened this view in various ways, in order to allow for the role of sex in expressing and enhancing conjugal love and care. Within the Catholic tradition this has been recognized as the 'unitive' function of sex in marriage; but that is a rather limited development, for it is still maintained that the two functions of sex, the unitive and the procreative, are inseparable.

Do those who are committed to this view of sex—and in contemporary Western societies, I suppose, only practising Catholics are—have to endorse the ban on prostitution? At a certain level, they obviously must think ill of it; for, as has often been pointed out, theirs is the most restrictive and repressive sexual ethics possible. It confines sex within the bounds of heterosexual, monogamous, exclusive, indissoluble marriage, and rules out sexual relations between any possible partners except husband and wife (as well as masturbation). Moreover, it restricts the legitimate sexual relations between the spouses to those that are 'by nature ordained' toward procreation. Prostitution or, more accurately, common prostitution, which is both non-marital and disconnected from procreation, would seem to be beyond the pale.

But then, even the legitimacy of marital and procreative sex is of a rather low order: as sex, it is intrinsically problematic; as marital and procreative, it is accepted as a necessary evil, an inevitable concession to fallen human nature. As St. Augustine says, 'any friend of wisdom and holy joys who lives a married life' would surely prefer to beget children without 'the lust that excites the indecent parts of the body', if it only were possible.[15] Therefore, if it turns out that accepting sex within marriage and for the purpose of procreation only is not concession enough, that human sexuality is so strong and unruly that it cannot be confined within these bounds and that attempts to confine it actually endanger the institution of marriage itself, the inevitable conclusion will be that further concession is in order. That is just the conclusion reached by many authors with regard to prostitution: it should be tolerated, for it provides a safety valve for a force which will otherwise subvert the institution of marriage

and destroy all the chastity and decency this institution makes possible. My favourite quotation is from Mandeville, who, of course, sees that as but another instance of the general truth that private vices are public benefits:

> If Courtezans and Strumpets were to be prosecuted with as much Rigour as some silly People would have it, what Locks or Bars would be sufficient to preserve the Honour of our Wives and Daughters? For 'tis not only that the Women in general would meet with far greater Temptations, and the Attempts to ensnare the Innocence of Virgins would seem more excusable to the sober part of Mankind than they do now: But some Men would grow outrageous, and Ravishing would become a common Crime. Where six or seven Thousand Sailors arrive at once, as it often happens at *Amsterdam*, that have seen none but their own Sex for many Months together, how is it to be suppos'd that honest Women should walk the Streets unmolested, if there were no Harlots to be had at reasonable Prices?(...) ...There is a Necessity of sacrificing one part of Womankind to preserve the other, and prevent a Filthiness of a more heinous Nature.[16]

That prostitution is indispensable for the stability and the very survival of marriage has not been pointed out only by cynics like Mandeville, misanthropes like Schopenhauer,[17] or godless rationalists like Lecky[18] and Russell;[19] it was acknowledged as a fact, and as one that entails that prostitution ought to be tolerated rather than suppressed, by St. Augustine and St. Thomas themselves.[20] Moreover, it has been confirmed by sociological study of human sexual behaviour, which shows that the majority of clients of prostitutes are married men who do not find complete sexual fulfillment within marriage, but are content to stay married provided they can have extramarital commercial sex as well.[21] Accordingly, even if one adopts the most conservative and restrictive view of sex there is, the view which ties sex to marriage and procreation, one need not, indeed should not condemn prostitution. One should rather take a tolerant attitude to it, knowing that it is twice removed from the ideal state of affairs, but that its demise would bring about something incomparably worse.

Another view which would seem to call for the condemnation of prostitution is the 'romantic' view of sex as essentially tied to love; for mercenary sex is normally as loveless as sex can ever get. The important thing to note is that whatever unfavourable judgement on prostitution is suggested by this view of sex, it will not be a judgment unfavourable to prostitution as such, but rather to prostitution as a type of loveless sex. It is the lovelessness, not the commercial nature of the practice that the 'romantic' objects to.

One response to this kind of objection would be to take on squarely the view of sex that generates it. One could, first, take a critical look at the arguments advanced in support of the view that sex should always be bound up with love; second, bring out the difficulties of the linkage, the tensions between love and sex which seem to make a stable and fruitful combination of the two rather unlikely; finally, argue for the superiority of loveless, noncommittal, 'plain sex' over sex that is bound up with love. All this has already been done by philosophers such as Alan Goldman and Russell Vannoy,[22] and probably by innumerable non-philosophers as well.

Another response would be to grant the validity of the 'romantic' view of sex, but only as a personal ideal, not a universally binding moral standard. This is the tack taken by Richards,[23] who points out that it would be signally misguided, indeed absurd, to try to enforce this particular ideal, based as it is 'on the cultivation of spontaneous romantic feeling.'[24] My preferred response to the 'romantic' objection is along these lines, but I would like to go a bit further, and emphasize that it is possible to appreciate the 'romantic' ideal

and at the same time not only grant that sex which falls short of it need not be wrong, but also allow that it can be positively good (without going as far as to claim that it is actually better than sex with love).

The 'romantic' typically points out the difference between sex with and without love. The former is a distinctively human, complex, rich and fruitful experience, and a matter of great importance; the latter is merely casual, a one-dimensional, barren experience that satisfies only for a short while and belongs to our animal nature. These differences are taken to show that sex with love is valuable, while loveless sex is not. This kind of reasoning has the following structure:

A is much better than B.
Therefore, B is no good at all.

In addition to being logically flawed, this line of reasoning, if it were to be applied in areas other than sex, would prove quite difficult to follow. For one thing, all but the very rich among us would die of hunger; for only the very rich can afford to take *all* their meals at the fanciest restaurants.[25]

Of course, B can be good, even if it is much less good than A. Loveless sex is a case in point. Moreover, other things being equal, it is better to be able to enjoy both loving and loveless sex than only the former. A person who enjoyed sex as part of loving relationships but was completely incapable of enjoying plain sex would seem to be missing out on something. To be sure, the 'romantic' rejection of plain sex often includes the claim that other things are not equal: that a person who indulges in plain sex thereby somehow damages, and ultimately destroys, his or her capacity for experiencing sex as an integral part of a loving relationship. This is a straightforward empirical claim about human psychology; and it is clearly false.

All this has to do with plain sex in general, rather than with its mercenary variety in particular. That is due to the general character of the 'romantic' objection to prostitution: prostitution is seen as flawed not on account of its commercial nature, but rather because it has nothing to do with love. Accordingly, as far as the 'romantic' view of sex is concerned, by exonerating plain sex, one also exonerates its commercial variety.

4. The Feminist Critique (a): Degradation of Women

In this section and the next I deal with what I have termed the 'feminist' objections to prostitution. This should not be taken to suggest that these objections are put forward only by feminists, nor that they are shared by all feminists. Contemporary discussion of the rights and wrongs of prostitution is for the most part a debate between those who hold that the sale of sex is just another service, in itself as legitimate as any other and not to be interfered with as long as no injustice, exploitation or fraud is involved, and those who deny this and claim that prostitution is essentially bound up with degradation or oppression of women. The particular concern for the role and status of women that motivates the latter position is clearly feminist; the former position can loosely be termed liberal. But there is a certain overlap: one of the currents of feminism is liberal feminism, and its adherents do not subscribe to the critique of prostitution advanced by feminists of other stripes, but rather think of it much as other liberals do, as morally unobjectionable in itself.[26] Incidentally, the position of liberal feminists seems to be more in tune with the way prostitutes themselves think of their occupation; but that may not count for much, as illiberal feminists are likely to dismiss the views of prostitutes as just another case of false consciousness.

One might want to take issue with the whole feminist approach to the question of prostitution as a question about women; for,

after all not all prostitutes are women. But this is not a promising tack; for, if not all, most of them are and always have been. So if prostitution involves either degradation or oppression, the great majority of those degraded or oppressed are women. But does it?

There is no denying that the belief that prostitution degrades those who practise it is very widespread. But this belief may be wrong. The question is: *Just why* should prostitution be considered degrading? There are four main answers: (i) because it is utterly impersonal; (ii) because the prostitute is reduced to a mere means; (iii) because of the intimate nature of the acts she performs for money; (iv) because she actually sells her body, herself. Let me look into each of these claims in turn.

(i) Prostitution is degrading because the relation between the prostitute and the client is completely impersonal. The client does not even perceive, let alone treat the prostitute as the person she is; he has no interest, no time for any of her personal characteristics, but relates to her merely as a source of sexual satisfaction, nothing more than a sex object.

One possible response to this is that prostitution need not be impersonal. There is, of course, the streetwalker who sells sex to all comers (or almost); but there is also the prostitute with a limited number of steady clients, with whom she develops quite personal relationships. So if the objection is to the impersonal character of the relation, the most that can be said is that a certain kind of prostitution is degrading, not that prostitution as such is. I do not want to make much of this, though. For although in this, as in many other services, there is the option of personalized service, the other, impersonal variety is typical.

My difficulty with the argument is more basic: I cannot see why the impersonal nature of a social transaction or relation makes that transaction or relation degrading. After all, the personal relations we have with others—with our family, friends and acquaintances——are just a small part (although the most important part) of our social life. The other part includes the overwhelming majority of our social transactions and relations which are, and have to be, quite impersonal. I do not have a personal relationship with the newspaper vendor, the bus driver, the shop assistant, and all those numerous other people I interact with in the course of a single day; and, as long as the basic decencies of social intercourse (which are purely formal and impersonal) are observed, there is nothing wrong with that. There is nothing wrong for me to think of and relate to the newspaper vendor as just that and, as far as I am concerned, nothing more. That our social relations must for the most part be impersonal may be merely a consequence of the scarcity of resources we invest in them. But it is inescapable in any but the smallest and simplest, so-called face-to-face society.

It may well be said that the selling and buying of newspapers and sex are quite different. While an impersonal attitude is unobjectionable in the former case, it is objectionable, because degrading, in the latter. But if this is the point, then the objection presupposes that sex ought to be personal; and that still has not been established. It need not be on any but the 'romantic' conception of sex; and I hope to have shown in the preceding section that the 'romantic' case against unromantic sex is not very strong.

The next two points are suggested in the following remarks by Russell:

> The intrusion of the economic motive into sex is always in a greater or lesser degree disastrous. Sexual relations should be a mutual delight, entered into solely from the spontaneous impulse of both parties. Where this is not the case, everything that is valuable is absent. To use another person in so intimate a manner is to be lacking in that respect for the human being as such, out of which all true morality must spring. (...) Morality in sexual relations, when it

is free from superstition, consists essentially of respect for the other person, and unwillingness to use that person solely as a means of personal gratification without regard to his or her desires.... Prostitution sins against this principle....[27]

(ii) Prostitution is said to degrade the prostitute because she is used as a means by the client. The client relates to the prostitute in a purely instrumental way: she is no more than a means to his sexual satisfaction. If so, is he not reducing her to a mere means, a thing, a sex object, and thereby degrading her?

If he were to rape her, that would indeed amount to treating her without regard to her desires, and thus to reducing, degrading her to a mere means. But as a customer rather than a rapist, he gets sexual satisfaction from her for a charge, on the basis of a mutual understanding, and she does her part of the bargain willingly. It is not true that he acts without regard to her desires. He does not satisfy her sexual desire; indeed, the prostitute does not desire that he should do so. But he does satisfy the one desire she has with regard to him: the desire for money. Their transaction is not 'a mutual delight, entered into solely from the spontaneous impulse of both parties', but rather a calculated exchange of goods of different order. But it does not offend against the principle of respect for human beings as such as long as it is free from coercion and fraud, and both sides get what they want.[28]

Most of our social transactions and relations are impersonal, and most are instrumental. There is nothing wrong with either an impersonal or instrumental way of relating to others as such. Just as the fact that A relates to B in a completely impersonal way is not tantamount to a violation of B's personhood, B's status as a person, so the fact that A relates to B in a purely instrumental way is not equivalent to A's reducing B to a mere means. In both cases B's informed and freely given consent absolves the relation of any such charge, and thereby also of the charge of degradation.

(iii) Sex is an intimate, perhaps the most intimate part of our lives. Should it not therefore be off limits to commercial considerations and transactions? And is it not degrading to perform something so intimate as a sex act with a complete stranger and for money?

It is not. As Ericsson points out,

> we are no more justified in devaluating the prostitute, who, for example, masturbates her customers, than we are in devaluating the assistant nurse, whose job it is to take care of the intimate hygiene of disabled patients. Both help to satisfy important human needs, and both get paid for doing so. That the harlot, in distinction to the nurse, intentionally gives her client pleasure is of course nothing that should be held against her![29]

It might be objected that the analogy is not valid, for there is an important asymmetry between pain and pleasure: the former has significantly greater moral weight than the latter. While it may be morally acceptable to cross the borders of intimacy in order to relieve pain or suffering, which is what the nurse does, that does not show that it is permissible to do so merely for the sake of giving pleasure, which is what the prostitute provides. But if so, what are we to say of a fairly good looking woman who undergoes plastic surgery and has her breasts enlarged (or made smaller) in order to become even more attractive and make her sex life richer and more pleasurable than it already is? Is she really doing something degrading and morally wrong?

(iv) Prostitution is degrading because what the prostitute sells is not simply and innocuously a service, as it may appear to a superficial look; actually, there is much truth in the old-fashioned way of speaking of her as a woman who 'sells herself'. And if *that* is not degrading, what is?

This point has been made in two different ways.

David Archard has recently argued that there is a sense in which the prostitute sells herself because of the roles and attitudes involved in the transaction:

> Sexual pleasure is not ... an innocent commodity. Always implicated in such pleasure is the performance of roles, both willing and unwilling. These roles range from the possibly benign ones of doer and done-to, through superior and subordinate to abaser and abased. Thus, when a man buys 'sex' he also buys a sexual role from his partner, and this involves the prostitute in being something more than simply the neutral exchanger of some commodity.

More specifically,

> if I buy (and you willingly sell) your allegiance, your obsequiousness, your flattery or your servility there is no easy distinction to be made between you as 'seller' and the 'good' you choose to sell. Your whole person is implicated in the exchange. So it is too with the sale of sex.[30]

However, commercial sex need not involve obsequiousness, flattery or servility, let alone allegiance, on the part of the prostitute. These attitudes, and the 'role' they might be thought to make up, are not its constitutive parts; whether, when, and to what degree they characterize the transaction is an empirical question that admits of no simple and general answer. Indeed, those who, knowingly or not, tend to approach the whole subject of sex from a 'romantic' point of view often say that sex with prostitutes is an impoverished, even sordid experience because of the impersonal, quick, mechanical, blunt way in which the prostitute goes about her job.

Moreover, some services that have nothing to do with sex tend to involve and are expected to involve some such attitudes on the part of the person providing the service. Examples would vary from culture to culture; the waiter and the hairdresser come to mind in ours. Now such attitudes are undoubtedly morally flawed; but that does not tell against any particular occupation in which they may be manifested, but rather against the attitudes themselves, the individuals who, perhaps unthinkingly, come to adopt them, and the social conventions that foster such attitudes.

Another way to try to show that the prostitute sells herself, rather than merely a service like any other, is to focus on the concept of self-identity. This is the tack taken by Carole Pateman. She first points out that the service provided by the prostitute is related in a much closer way to her body than is the case with any other service, for sex and sexuality are constitutive of the body, while the labour and skills hired out in other lines of work are not. 'Sexuality and the body are ... integrally connected to conceptions of femininity and masculinity, and all these are constitutive of our individuality, our sense of self-identity.'[31] Therefore, when sex becomes a commodity, so do bodies and selves.

But if so, what of our ethnic identity? When asked to say who they are, do not people normally bring up their ethnic identity as one of the most important things they need to mention? If it is granted that one's ethnic identity is also constitutive of one's individuality, one's sense of self-identity, what are we to say of a person who creates an item of authentic folk art and then sells it, or of a singer who gives a concert of folk music and charges for attendance? Are they also selling themselves, and thus doing something degrading and wrong?

The likely response will be to refuse to grant our ethnic identity the same significance for our self-identity that is claimed for gender. Although people typically refer to their ethnic identity when explaining who they are, there are also many exceptions. There are individuals who used to think of themselves in

such terms, but have come to repudiate, not merely their particular ethnic affiliation, but the very idea that ethnicity should be part of one's sense of who one is. There are also persons who have always felt that way (perhaps because that is how they were brought up to feel). They do not think of their own sense of self-identity as somehow incomplete, and neither should we. There are no analogous examples with regard to gender; we all think of ourselves as either men or women, and whatever particular conception one has of one's gender, the conception is closely connected with one's sexuality. Gender is much more basic than ethnicity, much more closely related to our sense of self-identity than ethnicity and anything else that may be thought relevant.

Perhaps it is.[32] But if that is reason enough to say that the prostitute sells her body and herself, and thus does something degrading and wrong, will not we have to say the same of the wet nurse and the surrogate mother? Their bodies and gender are no less involved in what they do than the body and gender of the prostitute; and they charge a fee, just as the prostitute does. I do not know that anybody has argued that there is something degrading, or otherwise morally wrong, in what the wet nurse does, nor that what she does is selling her body or herself, so I think she is a good counterexample to Pateman's argument.

The surrogate mother might be thought a less compelling one, for there has been considerable debate about the nature and moral standing of surrogacy. I do not need to go into all that, though.[33] The one objection to surrogacy relevant in the present context is 'that it is inconsistent with human dignity that a woman should use her uterus for financial profit and treat it as an incubator for someone else's child.'[34] However, it is not explained just why it should be thought inconsistent with human dignity to do that. Indeed, it is not clear how it could be, if it is not inconsistent with human dignity that a woman should use her breasts for financial profit and treat them as a source of nourishment for someone else's child. And if it is not, why should it be inconsistent with human dignity that a woman should use her sex organs and skills for financial profit and treat them as a source of pleasure for someone else?

5. The Feminist Critique (b): Oppression of Women

The other main feminist objection to prostitution is that it exemplifies and helps to maintain the oppression of women. This objection is much more often made than argued. It is frequently made by quoting the words of Simone de Beauvoir that the prostitute 'sums up all the forms of feminine slavery at once';[35] but de Beauvoir's chapter on prostitution, although quite good as a description of some of its main types, is short on argument and does nothing to show that prostitution as such must be implicated in the oppression of women.

An argument meant to establish that with regard to our society has recently been offered by Laurie Shrage. She expressly rejects the idea of discussing commercial sex in a 'cross-cultural' or 'trans-historical' way, and grants that it need not be oppressive to women in every conceivable or, indeed, every existing society. What she does claim is that in our society prostitution epitomizes and perpetuates certain basic cultural assumptions about men, women and sex which provide justification for the oppression of women in many domains of their lives, and in this way harm both prostitutes and women in general.[36]

There are four such cultural assumptions, which need not be held consciously but may be implicit in daily behaviour. A strong sex drive is a universal human trait. Sexual behaviour defines one's social identity, makes one a particular 'kind' of person: one is 'a homosexual', 'a prostitute', 'a loose woman'. Men

are 'naturally' dominant. In this connection, Shrage points out that the sex industry in our society caters almost exclusively to men, and 'even the relatively small number of male prostitutes at work serve a predominantly male consumer group.'[37] Finally, sexual contact pollutes and harms women.

The last claim is supported by a three-pronged argument. (i) In a woman, a history of sexual activity is not taken to suggest experience in a positive sense, expertise, high-quality sex. On the contrary, it is seen as a negative mark that marks off a certain kind of woman; women are valued for their 'innocence'. (ii) That sex with men is damaging to women is implicit in the vulgar language used to describe the sex act: 'a woman is "fucked", "screwed", "banged", "had", and so forth, and it is a man (a "prick") who does it to her.'[38] (iii) The same assumption is implicit in 'the metaphors we use' for the sex act. Here Shrage draws on Andrea Dworkin's book *Intercourse*, which invokes images of physical assault and imperialist domination and describes women having sexual intercourse with men as being not only entered or penetrated, but also 'split', 'invaded', 'occupied' and 'colonized' by men.

These cultural assumptions define the meaning of prostitution in our society. By tolerating prostitution, our society implies its acceptance of these assumptions, which legitimize and perpetuate the oppression of women and their marginality in all the main areas of social life. As for prostitutes and their clients, whatever their personal views of sex, men and women, they imply by their actions that they accept these assumptions and the practice they justify.

Now this argument is unobjectionable as far as it goes; but it does not go as far as Shrage means it to. In order to assess its real scope, we should first note that she repeatedly speaks of 'our' and 'our society's' toleration of prostitution, and refers to this toleration as the main ground for the conclusion that the cultural assumptions prostitution is said to epitomize in our society are indeed generally accepted in it. But toleration and acceptance are not quite the same; actually, toleration is normally defined as the putting up with something we *do not* accept. Moreover, prostitution is not tolerated at all. It is not tolerated legally: in the United States it is legal only in Nevada and illegal in all other states, while in the United Kingdom and elsewhere in the West, even though it is not against the law as such, various activities practically inseparable from it are. Some of these restrictions are quite crippling; for instance, as Marilyn G. Haft rightly says, 'to legalize prostitution while prohibiting solicitation* makes as much sense as encouraging free elections but prohibiting campaigning.'[39] It certainly is not tolerated morally; as I pointed out at the beginning, the condemnation of prostitution is one of the very few prohibitions of the traditional sexual morality that are still with us. It is still widely held that prostitution is seriously morally wrong, and the prostitute is subjected to considerable moral pressure, including the ultimate moral sanction, ostracism from decent society. That the practice is still with us is not for want of trying to suppress it, and therefore should not be taken as a sign that it is being tolerated.

Furthermore, not all the cultural assumptions prostitution in our society allegedly epitomizes and reinforces are really generally accepted. The first two—that human beings have a strong sex drive, and that one's sexual behaviour defines one's social identity—probably are. The other two assumptions—that men are 'naturally' dominant, and that sex with men harms women—are more important, for they make it possible to speak of oppression of women in this context. I am not so sure about the former; my impression is that at the very least it is no longer accepted quite as widely as it used to be a couple of

decades ago. And I think it is clear that the latter is not generally accepted in our society today. The evidence Shrage brings up to show that it is is far from compelling.

(i) It is probably true that the fact that a woman has a history of sexual activity is not generally appreciated as an indicator of experience and expertise, analogously to other activities. But whatever the explanation is—and one is certainly needed—I do not think that entails the other half of Shrage's diagnosis, namely that women are valued for their 'innocence'. That particular way of valuing women and the whole 'Madonna or harlot' outlook to which it belongs are well behind us as a society, although they characterize the sexual morality of some very traditional communities. A society which has made its peace with nonmarital sex in general and adolescent sex in particular to the extent that ours has could not possibly have persisted in valuing women for their 'innocence'.

(ii) Shrage draws on Robert Baker's analysis of the language used to refer to men, women and sex. Baker's point of departure is the claim that the way we talk about something reflects our conception of it; he looks into the ways we talk about sex and gender in order to discover what our conceptions of these are. With regard to sexual intercourse, it turns out that the vulgar verbs used to refer to it such as 'fuck', 'screw', 'lay', 'have' etc. display an interesting asymmetry: they require an active construction when the subject is a man, and a passive one when the subject is a woman. This reveals that we conceive of male and female roles in sex in different ways: the male is active, the female passive. Some of these verbs—'fuck', 'screw', 'have'—are also used metaphorically to indicate deceiving, taking advantage of, harming someone. This shows that we conceive of the male sexual role as that of harming the person in the female role, and of a person who plays the female sexual role as someone who is being harmed.[40]

---

* Editor's note: As Canada does.

This is both interesting and revealing, but what is revealed is not enough to support Shrage's case. Why is 'the standard view of sexual intercourse'[41] revealed not in the standard, but in the vulgar, i.e., substandard way of talking about it? After all, everybody, at least occasionally, talks about it in the standard way, while only some use the vulgar language too. Baker justifies his focusing on the latter by pointing out that the verbs which belong to the former, and are not used in the sense of inflicting harm as well, 'can take both females and males as subjects (in active constructions) and thus *do not pick out the female role*. This demonstrates that we conceive of sexual roles in such a way that only females are thought to be taken advantage of in intercourse.[42] It seems to me that the 'we' is quite problematic, and that all that these facts demonstrate is that some of us, namely those who speak of having sex with women as fucking or screwing them, also think of sex with them in these terms. Furthermore, the ways of talking about sex may be less fixed than Baker's analysis seems to suggest. According to Baker, sentences such as 'Jane fucked Dick', 'Jane screwed Dick' and 'Jane laid Dick', if taken in the literal sense, are not sentences in English. But the usage seems to have changed since his article was published; I have heard native speakers of English make such sentences without a single (linguistic) eyebrow being raised. The asymmetry seems to have lost ground. So the import of the facts analysed by Baker is much more limited than he and Shrage take it to be, and the facts themselves are less clear-cut and static too.

(iii) Shrage's third argument for the claim that our society thinks of sex with men as polluting and harmful to women is the weakest. Images of physical assault and imperialist domination certainly are not 'the metaphors we use for the act of sexual intercourse'; I do not know that anyone except Andrea Dworkin

does. The most likely reason people do not is that it would be silly to do so.

What all this shows, I think, is that there is no good reason to believe that our society adheres to a single conception of heterosexual sex, the conception defined by the four cultural assumptions Shrage describes, claims to be epitomized in, and reinforced by, prostitution, and wants to ascribe to every single case of commercial sex in our society as its 'political and social meaning', whatever the beliefs and values of the individuals concerned. Some members of our society think of heterosexual sex in terms of Shrage's four assumptions and some do not. Accordingly, there are in our society two rather different conceptions of prostitution, which in this context are best termed (a) prostitution as commercial screwing, and (b) prostitution as commercial sex *simpliciter*. What is their relative influence on the practice of prostitution in our society is a question for empirical research. Shrage rightly objects to the former for being implicated in the oppression of women in our society, and one need not be a feminist in order to agree. But that objection is not an objection to prostitution in our society as such.

6. Conclusion

I have taken a critical look at a number of arguments advanced to support the claim that prostitution stands morally condemned. If what I have been saying is right, none of these arguments is convincing.[43] Therefore, until some new and better ones are put forward, the conclusion must be that there is nothing morally wrong with it.[44] Writing about pornography—another practice which has been condemned and suppressed by traditional morality and religion, and has recently come under attack from feminist authors as well—G.L. Simons said that in a society which values liberty, 'social phenomena are, like individuals, innocent until proven guilty.'[45] So is prostitution.[46]

Ethical Issues

Notes

1 I am concerned only with prostitution in its primary, narrow sense of 'commercial' or 'mercenary sex', 'sex for money', and not with prostitution in the derived sense of 'use of one's ability or talent in a base or unworthy way'. The question I am asking is whether prostitution in the former, original sense is a case of prostitution in the latter, secondary sense.

2 F. Engels, *The Origin of the Family, Private Property and the State*, trans. A. West (Harmondsworth: Penguin, 1985), 102.

  The point was made as early as 1790; see M. Wollstonecraft, *Works*, J. Todd and M. Butler (eds) (London: William Pickering, 1989), V, 22, 129.

3 Here I am drawing on K. Davis, 'The Sociology of Prostitution', *Deviance*, S. Dinitz, R. R. Dynes and A. C. Clare (eds), 2nd ed. (New York: Oxford University Press, 1975).

4 Ibid., 328.

5 G. Dworkin, 'Paternalism', *The Monist* 56 (1972), 65.

6 L. Ericsson, 'Charges against Prostitution: An Attempt at a Philosophical Assessment', *Ethics* 90 (1979/80), 357.

7 D. A. J. Richards, *Sex, Drugs, Death, and the Law: An essay on Human Rights and Overcriminalization* (Totowa, NJ: Rowman and Littlefield, 1982), 113.

8 Ibid., 146 n. 251. The study referred to is described in W.B. Pomeroy, 'Some Aspects of Prostitution', *Journal of Sex Research* 1 (1965).

9 L. Ericsson, loc. cit.

10 For an analysis of the two kinds of paternalism, see J. Feinberg, 'Legal Paternalism', *Canadian Journal of Philosophy* 1 (1971).

11 Many authors who have written on prostitution as a 'social evil' have claimed that it is virtually never a freely chosen occupation, since various social conditions (lack of education, poverty, unemployment) force innumerable women into it. This argument makes it possible for Mrs. Warren (and many others) to condemn prostitution, while absolving the prostitute. But even if the empirical claim were true, it would not amount to an argument against prostitution, but only against the lack of alternatives to it.

12 J.S. Mill, *On Liberty*, C.V. Shields (ed.) (Indianapolis: Bobbs-Merrill, 1956), 93.

It was clear to Mill that his rejection of paternalism applied in the case of prostitution just as in any other case, but the way he says that is somewhat demure; see ibid., 120–122.

13 M. Walzer, *The Spheres of Justice* (New York: Basic Books, 1983), 100–103.

14 Ibid., 103. (The parts of the quotation I have deleted refer to religious prostitution, which is not the subject of this paper.)

15 Augustine, *Concerning the City of God*, trans. H. Bettenson (Harmondsworth: Penguin, 1972), Bk. 14, Ch. 16, 577.

16 B. Mandeville, *The Fable of the Bees*, F.B. Kaye (ed.) (Oxford University Press, 1957), Remark (H.), I, 95–96, 100.

  Mandeville discusses prostitution in detail in *A Modest Defence of Publick Stews: or, an Essay upon Whoring, As it is now practis'd in these Kingdoms* (London: A. Moore, 1724) (published anonymously). The argument I have quoted from the *Fable* is elaborated on pp. ii–iii, xi–xii, 39–52.

17 A. Schopenhauer, 'On Women', *Parerga and Paralipomena*, trans. E.F.J. Payne (Oxford: Oxford University Press, 1974), I, 623.

18 W.E.H. Lecky, *History of European Morals* (London: Longmans, Green & Co., 1869), II, 299–300.

19 B. Russell, *Marriage and Morals* (London: George Allen & Unwin, 1958), 116.

20 St. Augustine, *De ordine*, II, 4; St. Thomas Aquinas, *Summa theologiae*, 2a2ae, q. 10, art. 11.

21 H. Benjamin and R.E.L. Masters, *Prostitution and Morality* (London: Souvenir Press, 1965), 201.

22 See A. Goldman, 'Plain Sex', *Philosophy of Sex*, A. Soble (ed.) (Totowa, NJ: Littlefield, Adams & Co., 1980); R. Vannoy, *Sex without Love: A Philosophical Exploration* (Buffalo: Prometheus Books, 1980).

23 Op. cit., 99–104.

24 Ibid., 103–104.

25 For examples of this kind of reasoning and a detailed discussion of its structure, see J. Wilson, *Logic and Sexual Morality* (Harmondsworth: Penguin, 1965), 59–74.

26 See J.R. Richards, *The Sceptical Feminist: A Philosophical Enquiry* (London: Routledge & Kegan Paul, 1980), 198–202.

27 B. Russell, op. cit., 121–122.

28 Here I find Russell's version of the principle of respect for human beings as such more helpful than the classic, Kantian one (H.J. Paton, *The Moral Law: Kant's Groundwork of the Metaphysic of Morals* (London: Hutchinson, 1969), 90–93); for Russell puts it forward as an independent principle, while in Kant it cannot function on its own, but only when accepted together with other tenets of Kant's ethical theory, which one may well find problematic (cf. H.E. Jones, *Kant's Principle of Personality* (Madison: The University of Wisconsin Press, 1971)).

29 L. Ericsson, op. cit., 342.

30 D. Archard, 'Sex for Sale: The Morality of Prostitution', *Cogito* 3 (1989), 49–50.

31 C. Pateman, 'Defending Prostitution: Charges against Ericsson', *Ethics* 93 (1982/3), 562.

32 But see A. Appiah, '"But Would That still Be Me?": Notes on Gender, "Race", Ethnicity, as Sources of "Identity"', *The Journal of Philosophy* 87 (1990).

33 On the arguments pro and con see *Report of the Committee of Inquiry into Human Fertilization and Embryology* (London: HMSO, 1984), Ch. VIII; M. Warnock, 'The Artificial Family', and M. Lockwood, 'The Warnock Report: A Philosophical Appraisal', *Moral Dilemmas in Modern Medicine*, M. Lockwood (ed.) (Oxford University Press, 1985).

34 *Report*, 45.

35 S. de Beauvoir, *The Second Sex*, trans. and ed. H.M. Parshley (London: Pan Books, 1988), 569.

36 By 'our society' Shrage most of the time seems to mean contemporary American society, but toward the end of the paper claims to have discussed 'the meaning of commercial sex in modern Western culture' (L. Shrage, 'Should Feminists Oppose Prostitution?', *Ethics* 99 (1989/90), 361).

37 Ibid. 354.

38 Ibid. 355.

39 M.G. Haft, 'Hustling for Rights', *The Civil Liberties Review* 1 (1973/4), 20, quoted in A.M. Jaggar, 'Prostitution', *Philosophy of Sex*, A. Soble (ed.), 350.

40 See R. Baker, '"Pricks" and "Chicks": A Plea for "Persons"', *Philosophy and Sex*, R. Baker and F. Elliston (eds.) (Buffalo: Prometheus Books, 1975).

41 Ibid. 50.

42 Ibid. 61.

43 I have not discussed those arguments against prostitution which I think have been effectively refuted by others. See L. Ericsson, op. cit., on the arguments that prostitution exemplifies and reinforces commercialization of society, that it is an extreme case of the general inequality between men and women, that sex is much too basic and elementary in human life to be sold, and on the marxist critique of prostitution in general, and L.E. Lomasky, 'Gift Relations, Sexual Relations and Freedom', *The Philosophical Quarterly* 33 (1983), on the argument that commercial sex devalues sex given freely, as a gift.

44 That is, there is nothing morally wrong with it as long as the term 'morally wrong' is used in its robust sense, nicely captured, e.g., by Mill: 'We do not call anything wrong unless we mean to imply that a person ought to be punished in some way or other for doing it—if not by law, by the opinion of his fellow creatures; if not by opinion, by the reproaches of his own conscience' (*Utilitarianism*, G. Sher (ed.) (Indianapolis: Hackett, 1979), 47). This is the sense the term usually has in everyday moral discourse. When we say, e.g., that stealing is wrong, we normally do not mean to say merely that stealing falls short of the ideal way of relating to other people's property, or is not part of the good life, the best use one can put one's fingers to, or something one would recommend as a career to one's teenage daughter; we rather express our condemnation of stealing and imply that it is appropriate to apply the pressure of the moral sanction on those who steal. Of course, those given to using the term in some wider, watered-down sense may well come to the conclusion that prostitution is wrong after all.

45 G.L. Simons, *Pornography without Prejudice: A Reply to Objectors* (London: Abelard-Schuman, 1972), 96.

46 I have benefited from conversations on the subject of this paper with Carla Freccero and Bernard Gert, and from critical responses from audiences at Hull, Liverpool, Newcastle, St. Andrews and York, where I read this paper in December 1990/January 1991.

My greatest debt is to Antony Duff, Sandra Marshall, and Walter Sinnott-Armstrong, who read an earlier version of the paper and made a number of critical comments and suggestions for clarification and revision.

The paper was written during my stay at the Morrell Studies in Toleration project, Department of Politics, University of York, in the Winter and Spring terms of 1990/91. I would like to acknowledge with gratitude a research grant from the British Academy, which made that possible.

Questions for Discussion

1 What, if any, are the significant moral differences between the 'sexual institutions' of marriage and prostitution?

2 Is it any worse for a sexual relationship to be impersonal than a relationship with someone such as a newspaper vendor or a bus driver? If so, why?

3 Is something's being commonly perceived to be degrading sufficient to establish that it *is* degrading? What factors render an action degrading?

4 Is there a 'political and social meaning' to acts of commercialized sex? If so, what is it? Does it contribute to the oppression of women?

Markets in Women's Sexual Labor

Debra Satz

In this article, Debra Satz considers whether there is a difference between the sale of sexual capacities and the sale of other capacities (the "asymmetry thesis"). She rejects two kinds of arguments which suggest that prostitution is wrong, one based on its consequences in terms of welfare and efficiency, and one which claims prostitution is inherently alienating or harmful to human well-being. Satz offers a third kind of argument, however, which she claims does establish the wrongness of prostitution. This argument draws a connection between prostitution and the unequal status of women in society, by means of the image of prostitutes as sexual servants of men's needs.

★ ★ ★

There is a widely shared intuition that markets are inappropriate for some kinds of human endeavor: that some things simply should not be bought and sold. For example, virtually everyone believes that love and friendship should have no price. The sale of other human capacities is disputed, but many people believe that there is something about sexual and reproductive activities that makes their sale inappropriate. I have called the thesis supported by this intuition the asymmetry thesis.[1] Those who hold the asymmetry thesis believe that markets in reproduction and sex are asymmetric to other labor markets. They think that treating sexual and reproductive ca-

pacities as commodities, as goods to be developed and exchanged for a price, is worse than treating our other capacities as commodities. They think that there is something wrong with commercial surrogacy and prostitution that is not wrong with teaching and professional sports.

The intuition that there is a distinction between markets in different human capacities is a deep one, even among people who ultimately think that the distinction does not justify legally forbidding sales of reproductive capacity and sex. I accept this intuition, which I continue to probe in this article. In particular, I ask: What justifies taking an asymmetric attitude toward markets in our sexual capacities? What, if anything, is problematic about a woman selling her sexual as opposed to her secretarial labor? And, if the apparent asymmetry can be explained and justified, what implications follow for public policy?

In this article, I sketch and criticize two popular approaches to these questions. The first, which I call the economic approach, attributes the wrongness of prostitution to its consequences for efficiency or welfare. The important feature of this approach is its treatment of sex as a morally indifferent matter: sexual labor is not to be treated as a commodity if and only if such treatment fails to be efficient or welfare maximizing. The second, the "essentialist" approach, by contrast, stresses that sales of sexual labor are wrong because they are inherently alienating or damaging to human happiness. In contrast to these two ways of thinking about the immorality of prostitution, I will argue that the most plausible support for the asymmetry thesis stems from the role of commercialized sex and reproduction in sustaining a social world in which women form a subordinated group. Prostitution is wrong insofar as the sale of women's sexual labor reinforces broad patterns of sex discrimination. My argument thus stresses neither efficiency nor sexuality's intrinsic value but, rather, equality. In particular, I argue that contemporary prostitution contributes to, and also instantiates, the perception of women as socially inferior to men.

On the basis of my analysis of prostitution's wrongness, there is no simple conclusion as to what its legal status ought to be. Both criminalization and decriminalization may have the effect of exacerbating the inequalities in virtue of which I claim that prostitution is wrong. Nonetheless, my argument does have implications for the form of prostitution's regulation, if legal, and its prohibition and penalties, if illegal. Overall, my argument tends to support decriminalization.

The argument I will put forward here is qualified and tentative in its practical conclusions, but its theoretical point is not. I will argue that the most plausible account of prostitution's wrongness turns on its relationship to the pervasive social inequality between men and women. If, in fact, no causal relationship obtains between prostitution and gender inequality, then I do not think that prostitution is morally troubling.[2] This is a controversial claim. In my evaluation of prostitution, consideration of the actual social conditions which many, if not most, women face plays a crucial role. It will follow from my analysis that male prostitution raises distinct issues and is not connected to injustice in the same way as female prostitution.

On my view, prostitution is not wrong irrespective of its cultural and economic context. Moreover, prostitution is a complex phenomenon. I begin, accordingly, with the question, Who is a prostitute?

Who is a Prostitute?

While much has been written on the history of prostitution, and some empirical studies of prostitutes themselves have been undertaken, the few philosophers writing on this subject have tended to treat prostitution as if the term referred to something as obvious as "table."[3] But it does not. Not only is it hard to draw a sharp line between prostitution and practices which look like prostitution, but as historians of the subject have emphasized, prostitution today is also a very different phenomenon from earlier forms of commercial sex.[4] In particular, the idea of prostitution as a specialized occupation of an outcast and stigmatized group is of relatively recent origin.[5]

While all contemporary prostitutes are stigmatized as outsiders, prostitution itself has an internal hierarchy based on class, race, and gender. The majority of prostitutes—and all those who walk the streets—are poor. The majority of streetwalkers in the United States are poor black women. These women are a world apart from prostitution's upper tier. Consider three cases: a streetwalker in Boston, a call girl on Park Avenue, and a male prostitute in San Francisco's tenderloin district. In what way do these three lives resemble one another? Consider the three cases:

1. A fourteen-year-old girl prostitutes herself to support her boyfriend's heroin addiction. Later, she works the streets to support her own habit. She begins, like most teenage streetwalkers, to rely on a pimp for protection. She is uneducated and is frequently subjected to violence in her relationships and with her customers. She also receives no social security, no sick leave or maternity leave, and—most important—no control as to whether or not she has sex with a man. The latter is decided by her pimp.

2. Now imagine the life of a Park Avenue call girl. Many call girls drift into prostitution after "run of the mill promiscuity," led neither by material want nor lack of alternatives.[6] Some are young college graduates, who upon graduation earn money by prostitution while searching for other jobs. Call girls can earn between $30,000 and $100,000 annually. These women have control over the entire amount they earn as well as an unusual degree of independence, far greater than in most other forms of work. They can also decide who they wish to have sex with and when they wish to do so.[7] There is little resemblance between their lives and that of the Boston streetwalker.

3. Finally, consider the increasing number of male prostitutes. Most male prostitutes (but not all) sell sex to other men.[8] Often the men who buy such sex are themselves married. Unfortunately, there is little information on male prostitutes; it has not been well studied as either a historical or a contemporary phenomenon.[9] What we do know suggests that like their female counterparts, male prostitutes cover the economic spectrum. Two important differences between male and female prostitutes are that men are more likely to work only part time and that they are not generally subject to the violence of male pimps; they tend to work on their own.

Are these three cases distinct? Many critics of prostitution have assumed that all prostitutes were women who entered the practice under circumstances which included abuse and economic desperation. But that is a false assumption: the critics have mistaken a part of the practice for the whole.[10] For example, although women who walk the streets are the most visible, they constitute only about 20 percent of the prostitute population in the United States.[11]

The varying circumstances of prostitution are important because they force us to consider carefully what we think may be wrong with prostitution. For example, in the first case, the factors which seem crucial to our response of condemnation are the miserable background conditions, the prostitute's vulnerability to violence at the hands of her pimp or client, her age, and her lack of control over whether she has sex with a client. These conditions could be redressed through regulation without forbidding commercial sexual exchanges between consenting adults.[12] The second class of prostitution stands in sharp contrast. These women engage in what seems to be a voluntary activity, chosen among a range of decent alternatives. Many of these women sell their sexual capacities without coercion or regret. The third case rebuts arguments that prostitution has no other purpose than to subordinate women.

In the next section, I explore three alternative explanations of prostitution's wrongness, which I refer to respectively as economic, essentialist, and egalitarian.

What is Wrong with Prostitution?

The Economic Approach

Economists generally frame their questions about the best way to distribute a good without reference to its intrinsic qualities. They tend to focus on the quantitative features of a good and not its qualities.[13] Economists tend to endorse interference with a market in some good only when the results of that market are inefficient or have adverse effects on welfare.

An economic approach to prostitution does not specify a priori that certain sales are wrong: no act of commodification is ruled out in advance.[14] Rather, this approach focuses on the costs and benefits that accompany such sales. An economic approach to contracts will justify inalienability rules—rules which forbid individuals from entering into certain transactions—in cases where there are costly externalities to those transactions and in general where such transactions are inefficient. The economic approach thus supports the asymmetry thesis when the net social costs of prostitution are greater than the net social costs incurred by the sale of other human capacities.

What are the costs of prostitution? In the first place, the parties to a commercial sex transaction share possible costs of disease and guilt.[15] Prostitution also has costs to third parties: a man who frequents a prostitute dissipates financial resources which might otherwise be directed to his family; in a society which values intimate marriage, infidelity costs a man's wife or companion in terms of mistrust and suffering (and therefore prostitution may sometimes lead to marital instability); and prostitutes often have diseases which can be spread to others. Perhaps the largest third-party costs to prostitution are "moralisms":[16] many people find the practice morally offensive and are pained by its existence. (Note that 'moralisms' refers to people's preferences about moral issues and not to morality as such.)

The economic approach generates a contingent case for the asymmetry thesis, focusing on prostitution's "moral" costs in terms of public opinion or the welfare costs to prostitutes or the population as a whole (e.g., through the spread of diseases). Consideration of the limitations on sexual freedom which can be justified from a welfare standpoint can be illuminating and forces us to think about the actual effects of sexual regulations.[17] Nevertheless, I want to register three objections to this approach to justifying the asymmetry thesis.

First, and most obvious, both markets and contractual exchanges function within a regime of property rights and legal entitlements. The economic approach ignores the background system of distribution within which prostitution occurs. Some background systems, however, are unjust. How do we know whether prostitution itself is part of a morally acceptable system of property rights and entitlements?

Second, this type of approach seems disabled from making sense of distinctions between goods in cases where these distinctions do not seem to reflect mere differences in the net sum of costs and benefits. The sale of certain goods seems to many people simply unthinkable—human life, for example. While it may be possible to justify prohibitions on slavery by appeal to costs and benefits (and even count moralisms in the sum), the problem is that such justification makes contingent an outcome which reasonable people do not hold contingently. It also makes little sense, phenomenologically, to describe the moral repugnance people feel toward slavery as "just a cost."[18]

Let me elaborate this point. There seems to be a fundamental difference between the "goods" of my person and my external goods, a difference whose nature is not completely explained by appeal to information failures and externalities. "Human capital" is not just another form of capital. For example, my relationship with my body and my capacities is more intimate than my relationship with most external things. The economic approach fails to capture this distinction.

Richard Posner—one of the foremost practitioners of the economic approach to law—illustrates the limits of the economic approach when he views a rapist as a "sex thief."[19] He thus overlooks the fact that rape is a crime of violence and assault.[20] He also ignores the qualitative differences between my relationship with my body and my car. But that there are such differences is obvious. The circumstances in which I sell my capacities have a much more profound effect on who I am and who I become—through effects on my desires, capacities, and values—than the circumstances in which I sell my Honda Civic. Moreover, the idea of sovereignty over body and mind is closely related to the idea of personal integrity, which is a crucial element of any reasonable scheme of liberty. The liberty to exercise sovereignty over my car has a lesser place in any reasonable scheme of liberties than the liberty to be sovereign over my body and mind.[21]

Third, some goods seem to have a special status which requires that they be shielded from the market if their social meaning or role is to be preserved. The sale of citizenship rights or friendship does not simply produce costs and benefits: it transforms the nature of the goods sold. In this sense, the market is not a neutral mechanism of exchange: there are some goods whose sale transforms or destroys their initial meaning.

These objections resonate with objections to prostitution for which its wrongness is not adequately captured by summing up contingent welfare costs and benefits. These objections resonate with moralist and egalitarian concerns. Below I survey two other types of arguments which can be used to support the asymmetry thesis: (1) essentialist arguments that the sale of sexual labor is intrinsically wrong because it is alienating or contrary to human flourishing and happiness; and (2) my own egalitarian argument that the sale of sex is wrong because, given the background conditions within which it occurs, it tends to reinforce gender inequality. I thus claim that contemporary prostitution is wrong because it promotes injustice, and not because it makes people less happy.

The Essentialist Approach

Economists abstract from the qualities of the goods that they consider. By contrast essentialists hold that there is something intrinsic to the sphere of sex and intimacy that accounts for the distinction we mark between it and other types of labor. Prostitution is not wrong simply because it causes harm; prostitution constitutes a harm. Essentialists hold that there is some intrinsic property of sex which makes its commodification wrong. Specific arguments differ, however, in what they take this property to be. I will consider two popular versions of essentialism: the first stresses the close connection between sex and the self; the second stresses the close connection between sex and human flourishing. [22]

Some feminist critics of prostitution have argued that sexual and reproductive capacities are more crucially tied to the nature of our selves than our other capacities.[23] The sale of sex is taken to cut deeper into the self, to involve a more total alienation from the self. As Carole Pateman puts it, "When a prostitute contracts out use of her body she is thus selling *herself* in a very real sense. Women's selves are involved in prostitution in a different manner from the involvement of the self in other occupations."[24] The realization of women's selfhood requires, on this view, that some of the capacities embodied in their persons, including their sexuality, remain "market-inalienable."[25]

Consider an analogous strategy for accounting for the value of bodily integrity in terms of its relationship to our personhood.

It seems right to say that a world in which the boundaries of our bodies were not (more or less) secure would be a world in which our sense of self would be fundamentally shaken. Damage to, and violation of, our bodies affects us in a "deeper" way, a more significant way, than damage to our external properties. Robbing my body of a kidney is a violation different in kind than robbing my house of a stereo, however expensive. Distributing kidneys from healthy people to sick people through a lottery is a far different act than using a lottery to distribute door prizes.[26]

But this analogy can only be the first step in an argument in favor of treating either our organs or sexual capacities as market-inalienable. Most liberals think that individual sovereignty over mind and body is crucial for the exercise of fundamental liberties. Thus, in the absence of clear harms, most liberals would reject legal bans on voluntary sales of body parts or sexual capacities. Indeed, the usual justification of such bans is harm to self: such sales are presumed to be "desperate exchanges" that the individual herself would reasonably want to foreclose. American law blocks voluntary sales of individual organs and body parts but not sales of blood on the assumption that only the former sales are likely to be so harmful to the individual that given any reasonable alternative, she herself would refrain from such sales.

Whatever the plausibility of such a claim with respect to body parts, it is considerably weaker when applied to sex (or blood). There is no strong evidence that prostitution is, at least in the United States, a desperate exchange. In part this reflects the fact that the relationship people have with their sexual capacities is far more diverse than the relationship they have with their body parts. For some people, sexuality is a realm of ecstatic communion with another, for others it is little more than a sport or distraction. Some people will find consenting to be sexually used by another person enjoyable or adequately compensated by a wage. Even for the same person, sex can be the source of a range of experiences.

Of course, the point cannot simply be that, as an empirical matter, people have differing conceptions of sexuality. The critics of prostitution grant that. The point is whether, and within what range, this diversity is desirable.[27]

Let us assume, then, in the absence of compelling counterargument, that an individual can exercise sovereignty through the sale of her sexual capacities. Margaret Radin raises a distinct worry about the effects of widespread prostitution on human flourishing. Radin's argument stresses that widespread sex markets would promote inferior forms of personhood. She says that we can see this is the case if we "reflect on what we know now about human life and choose the best from among the conceptions available to us."[28] If prostitution were to become common, Radin argues, it would have adverse effects on a form of personhood which itself is intrinsically valuable. For example, if the signs of affection and intimacy were frequently detached from their usual meaning, such signs might well become more ambiguous and easy to manipulate. The marks of an intimate relationship (physical intimacy, terms of endearment, etc.) would no longer signal the existence of intimacy. In that case, by obscuring the nature of sexual relationships, prostitution might undermine our ability to apply the criteria for coercion and informational failure.[29] Individuals might more easily enter into damaging relationships and lead less fulfilling lives as a result.

Radin is committed to a form of perfectionism which rules out the social practice of prostitution as incompatible with the highest forms of human development and flourishing. But why should perfectionists condemn prostitution while tolerating practices such as monotonous assembly line work where human beings are often mere appendages to machines? Monotonous wage labor, moreover, is far more widespread than prostitution.[30] Can a consistent perfectionist give reasons for differentiating sexual markets from other labor markets?

It is difficult to draw a line between our various capacities such that only sexual and reproductive capacities are essential to the flourishing self. In a money economy like our own, we each sell the use of many human capacities. Writers sell the use of their ability to write, advertisers sell the use of their ability to write jingles, and musicians sell the use of their ability to write and perform symphonies. Aren't these capacities also closely tied to our personhood and its higher capacities?[31] Yet the mere alienation of the use of these capacities, even when widespread, does not seem to threaten personal flourishing.

An alternative version of the essentialist thesis views the commodification of sex as an assault on personal dignity.[32] Prostitution degrades the prostitute. Elizabeth Anderson, for example, discusses the effect of commodification on the nature of sex as a shared good, based on the recognition of mutual attraction. In commercial sex, each party now values the other only instrumentally, not intrinsically And, while both parties are thus prevented from enjoying a shared good, it is worse for the prostitute. The customer merely surrenders a certain amount of cash; the prostitute cedes her body: the prostitute is thus degraded to the status of a thing. Call this the degradation objection.

I share the intuition that the failure to treat others as persons is morally significant; it is wrong to treat people as mere things. But I am skeptical as to whether this intuition supports the conclusion that prostitution is wrong. Consider the contrast between slavery and prostitution. Slavery was, in Orlando Patterson's memorable phrase, a form of "social death": it denied to enslaved individuals the

ability to press claims, to be—in their own right—sources of value and interest. But the mere sale of the use of someone's capacities does not necessarily involve a failure of this kind, on the part of either the buyer or the seller.[33] Many forms of labor, perhaps most, cede some control of a person's body to others. Such control can range from requirements to be in a certain place at a certain time (e.g., reporting to the office), to requirements that a person (e.g., a professional athlete) eat certain foods and get certain amounts of sleep, or maintain good humor in the face of the offensive behavior of others (e.g., airline stewardesses). Some control of our capacities by others does not seem to be ipso facto destructive of our dignity.[34] Whether the purchase of a form of human labor power will have this negative consequence will depend on background social macrolevel and microlevel institutions. Minimum wages, worker participation and control, health and safety regulations, maternity and paternity leave, restrictions on specific performance, and the right to "exit" one's job are all features which attenuate the objectionable aspects of treating people's labor as a mere economic input. The advocates of prostitution's wrongness in virtue of its connection to self-hood, flourishing and degradation have not shown that a system of regulated prostitution would be unable to respond to their worries. In particular, they have not established that there is something wrong with prostitution irrespective of its cultural and historical context.

There is, however, another way of interpreting the degradation objection which draws a connection between the current practice of prostitution and the lesser social status of women.[35] This connection is not a matter of the logic of prostitution per se but of the fact that contemporary prostitution degrades women by treating them as the sexual servants of men. In current prostitution, prostitutes are overwhelmingly women and their clients are almost exclusively men. Prostitution, in conceiving of a class of women as needed to satisfy male sexual desire, represents women as sexual servants to men. The degradation objection, so understood, can be seen as a way of expressing an egalitarian concern since there is no reciprocal ideology which represents men as servicing women's sexual needs. It is to this egalitarian understanding of prostitution's wrongness that I turn in the next section.

The Egalitarian Approach

While the essentialists rightly call our attention to the different relation we have with our capacities and external things, they overstate the nature of the difference between our sexual capacities and our other capacities with respect to our personhood, flourishing, and dignity.[36] They are also insufficiently attentive to the background conditions in which commercial sex exchanges take place. A third account of prostitution's wrongness stresses its causal relationship to gender inequality. I have defended this line of argument with respect to markets in women's reproductive labor.[37] Can this argument be extended to cover prostitution as well?

The answer hinges in part on how we conceive of gender inequality. On my view, there are two important dimensions of gender inequality, often conflated. The first dimension concerns inequalities in the distribution of income, wealth, and opportunity. In most nations, including the United States, women form an economically and socially disadvantaged group. The statistics regarding these disadvantages, even in the United States, are grim.

1. *Income inequality.*—In 1992, given equal hours of work, women in the United States earned on average sixty-six cents for every dollar earned by a man.[38] Seventy-five percent of full-time working women (as opposed to

37 percent of full-time working men) earn less than twenty thousand dollars.[39]

2. *Job segregation.*—Women are less likely than men to fill socially rewarding, high-paying jobs. Despite the increasing entrance of women into previously gender-segregated occupations, 46 percent of all working women are employed in service and administrative support jobs such as secretaries, waitresses, and health aides. In the United States and Canada, the extent of job segregation in the lowest-paying occupations is increasing.[40]

3. *Poverty.*—In 1989, one out of five families were headed by women. One-third of such women-headed families live below the poverty line, which was $13,359 for a family of four in 1990.[41] In the United States, fathers currently owe mothers 24 billion dollars in unpaid child support.[42]

4. *Unequal division of labor in the family.*—Within the family, women spend disproportionate amounts of time on housework and rearing children. According to one recent study, wives employed full time outside the home do 70 percent of the housework; full-time housewives do 83 percent.[43] The unequal family division of labor is itself caused by and causes labor market inequality: given the lower wages of working women, it is more costly for men to participate in household labor.

Inequalities in income and opportunity form an important part of the backdrop against which prostitution must be viewed. While there are many possible routes into prostitution, the largest number of women who participate in it are poor, young, and uneducated. Labor market inequalities will be part of any plausible explanation of why many women "choose" to enter into prostitution.

The second dimension of gender inequality does not concern income and opportunity but status.[44] In many contemporary contexts, women are viewed and treated as inferior to men. This inferior treatment proceeds via several distinct mechanisms.

1. *Negative stereotyping.*—Stereotypes persist as to the types of jobs and responsibilities a woman can assume. Extensive studies have shown that people typically believe that men are more dominant, assertive, and instrumentally rational than women. Gender shapes beliefs about a person's capacities: women are thought to be less intelligent than their male equals.[45]

2. *Unequal power.*—Men are able to asymmetrically sanction women. The paradigm case of this is violence. Women are subjected to greater amounts of violence by men than is the reverse: every fifteen seconds a woman is battered in the United States. Battering causes more injury (excluding deaths) to women than car accidents, rape, and muggings combined.[46] Four million women a year are physically assaulted by their male partners.[47]

3. *Marginalization.*—People who are marginalized are excluded from, or absent from, core productive social roles in society—roles which convey self-respect and meaningful contribution.[48] At the extremes, marginalized women lack the means for their basic survival: they are dependent on state welfare or male partners to secure the basic necessities of life. Less severely marginalized women lack access to central and important social roles. Their activities are confined to peripheral spheres of social organization. For example, the total number of women who have served in Congress since its inception through 1992 is 134. The total number of men is 11,096. In one-third of governments worldwide, there are no women in the decision-making bodies of the country.[49]

4. *Stigma.*—A woman's gender is associated, in some contexts, with stigma, a badge of dishonor. Consider rape. In crimes of rape, the complainant's past behavior and character are central in determining whether a crime has actually occurred. This is not true of other crimes: "mail fraud" (pun intended) is not dismissed because of the bad judgment or naïveté of the victims. Society views rape differently, I suggest, because many people think that women really want to be forced into sex. Women's lower status thus influences the way that rape is seen.

Both forms of inequality—income inequality and status inequality—potentially bear on the question of prostitution's wrongness. Women's decisions to enter into prostitution must be viewed against the background of their unequal life chances and their unequal opportunities for income and rewarding work. The extent to which women face a highly constrained range of options will surely be relevant to whether, and to what degree, we view their choices as autonomous. Some women may actually loathe or judge as inferior the lives of prostitution they "choose." Economic inequality may thus shape prostitution.

We can also ask, Does prostitution itself shape employment inequalities between men and women? In general, whenever there are significant inequalities between groups, those on the disadvantageous side will be disproportionately allocated to subordinate positions. What they do, the positions they occupy, will serve to reinforce negative and disempowering images of themselves. In this sense, prostitution can have an effect on labor-market inequality, associating women with certain stereotypes. For example, images reinforced by prostitution may make it less likely for women to be hired in certain jobs. Admittedly the effect of prostitution on labor-market inequality, if it exists at all, will be small. Other roles which women disproportionately occupy—secretaries, housecleaners, babysitters, waitresses, and saleswomen—will be far more significant in reinforcing (as well as constituting) a gender-segregated division of labor.

I do not think it is plausible to attribute to prostitution a direct causal role in income inequality between men and women. But I believe that it is plausible to maintain that prostitution makes an important and direct contribution to women's inferior social status. Prostitution shapes and is itself shaped by custom and culture, by cultural meanings about the importance of sex, about the nature of women's sexuality and male desire.[50]

If prostitution is wrong it is because of its effects on how men perceive women and on how women perceive themselves. In our society, prostitution represents women as the sexual servants of men. It supports and embodies the widely held belief that men have strong sex drives which must be satisfied—largely through gaining access to some woman's body. This belief underlies the mistaken idea that prostitution is the "oldest" profession, since it is seen as a necessary consequence of human (i.e., male) nature. It also underlies the traditional conception of marriage, in which a man owned not only his wife's property but her body as well. It should not fail to startle us that until recently, most states did not recognize the possibility of "real rape" in marriage.[51] (Marital rape remains legal in two states: North Carolina and Oklahoma.)

Why is the idea that women must service men's sexual needs an image of inequality and not mere difference? My argument suggests that there are two primary, contextual reasons:

First, in our culture, there is no reciprocal social practice which represents men as serving women's sexual needs. Men are gigolos and paid escorts—but their sexuality is not seen as an independent capacity whose use women can buy. It is not part of the identity of a class of men that they will service women's sexual desires. Indeed, male prostitutes overwhelmingly service other men and not women. Men are not depicted as fully capable of commercially alienating their sexuality to women; but prostitution depicts women as sexual servants of men.

Second, the idea that prostitution embodies an idea of women as inferior is strongly suggested by the high incidence of rape and violence against prostitutes, as well as the fact that few men seek out or even contemplate prostitutes as potential marriage partners. While all women in our society are potential targets of rape and violence, the mortality rates for women engaged in streetwalking prostitution are roughly forty times higher than that of nonprostitute women.[52]

My suggestion is that prostitution depicts an image of gender inequality, by constituting one class of women as inferior. Prostitution is a "theater" of inequality—it displays for us a practice in which women are subordinated to men. This is especially the case where women are forcibly controlled by their (male) pimps. It follows from my conception of prostitution that it need not have such a negative effect when the prostitute is male. More research needs to be done on popular images and conceptions of gay male prostitutes, as well as on the extremely small number of male prostitutes who have women clients.

The negative image of women who participate in prostitution, the image of their inferior status, is objectionable in itself. It constitutes an important form of inequality—unequal status—based on attitudes of superiority and disrespect. Unfortunately, this form of inequality has largely been ignored by political philosophers and economists who have focused instead on inequalities in income and opportunity. Moreover, this form of inequality is not confined to prostitutes. I believe that the negative image of women prostitutes has third party effects: it shapes and influences the way women as a whole are seen. This hypothesis is, of course, an empirical one. It has not been tested largely because of the lack of studies of men who go to prostitutes. Most extant studies of prostitution examine the behavior and motivations of the women who enter into the practice, a fact which itself raises the suspicion that prostitution is viewed as "a problem about the women who are prostitutes ... [rather than] a problem about the men who demand to buy them."[53] In these studies, male gender identity is taken as a given.

To investigate prostitution's negative image effects on female prostitutes and on women generally we need research on the following questions: (1) What are the attitudes of men who visit women prostitutes toward prostitutes? How do their attitudes compare with the attitudes of men who do not visit prostitutes toward women prostitutes? (2) What are the attitudes of men who visit women prostitutes toward women generally? What are the attitudes of men who do not visit women prostitutes toward women generally? (3) What are the attitudes of women toward women prostitutes? (4) What are the attitudes of the men and women involved in prostitution toward themselves? (5) Given the large proportion of African-American women who participate in prostitution, in what ways does prostitution contribute to male attitudes toward these women? (6) Does prostitution contribute to or diminish the likelihood of crimes of sexual violence? (7) What can we learn about these questions through cross-national studies? How do attitudes in the United States about women prostitutes compare with those in countries with more egalitarian wage policies or less status inequality between men and women?

The answers to these questions will reflect social facts about our culture. Whatever plausibility there is to the hypothesis that prostitution causally contributes to gender status inequality, it gains this plausibility from its surrounding cultural context.

I can imagine hypothetical circumstances in which prostitution would not have a negative image effect, where it could mark a reclaiming of women's sexuality. Margo St. James and other members of Call Off Your Old Tired Ethics (COYOTE) have argued that prostitutes can function as sex therapists, fulfilling a legitimate social need as well as providing a source of experiment and alternative

conceptions of sexuality and gender.[54] I agree that in a different culture, with different assumptions about men's and women's gender identities, prostitution might not have unequalizing effects. But I think that St. James and others have minimized the cultural stereotypes that surround contemporary prostitution and their power over the shape of the practice. Prostitution, as we know it, is not separable from the larger surrounding culture which marginalizes, stereotypes, and stigmatizes women. Rather than providing an alternative conception of sexuality, I think that we need to look carefully at what men and women actually learn in prostitution. I do not believe that ethnographic studies of prostitution would support COYOTE's claim that prostitution contributes to images of women's dignity and equal standing.

If, through its negative image of women as sexual servants of men, prostitution reinforces women's inferior status in society, then it is wrong. Even though men can be and are prostitutes, I think that it is unlikely that we will find such negative image effects on men as a group. Individual men may be degraded in individual acts of prostitution: men as a group are not.

Granting all of the above, one objection to the equality approach to prostitution's wrongness remains. Is prostitution's negative image effect greater than that produced by other professions in which women largely service men, for example, secretarial labor? What is special about prostitution?

The negative image effect undoubtedly operates outside the domain of prostitution. But there are two significant differences between prostitution and other gender-segregated professions.

First, most people believe that prostitution, unlike secretarial work, is especially objectionable. Holding such moral views of prostitution constant, if prostitution continues to be primarily a female occupation, then the existence of prostitution will disproportionately fuel negative images of women.[55] Second, and relatedly, the particular image of women in prostitution is more of an image of inferiority than that of a secretary. The image embodies a greater amount of objectification, of representing the prostitute as an object without a will of her own. Prostitutes are far more likely to be victims of violence than are secretaries: as I mentioned, the mortality rate of women in prostitution is forty times that of other women. Prostitutes are also far more likely to be raped: a prostitute's "no" does not, to the male she services, mean no.

My claim is that, unless such arguments about prostitution's causal role in sustaining a form of gender inequality can be supported, I am not persuaded that something is morally wrong with markets in sex. In particular, I do not find arguments about the necessary relationship between commercial sex and diminished flourishing and degradation convincing. If prostitution is wrong, it is not because of its effects on happiness or personhood (effects which are shared with other forms of wage labor); rather, it is because the sale of women's sexual labor may have adverse consequences for achieving a significant form of equality between men and women. My argument for the asymmetry thesis, if correct, connects prostitution to injustice. I now turn to the question of whether, even if we assume that prostitution is wrong under current conditions, it should remain illegal.

Should Prostitution Be Legalized?

It is important to distinguish between prostitution's wrongness and the legal response that we are entitled to make to that wrongness. Even if prostitution is wrong, we may not be justified in prohibiting it if that prohibition makes the facts in virtue of which it is wrong worse, or if its costs are too great for other important values, such as autonomy and pri-

vacy. For example, even if someone accepts that the contemporary division of labor in the family is wrong, they may still reasonably object to government surveillance of the family's division of household chores. To determine whether such surveillance is justified, we need know more about the fundamental interests at stake, the costs of surveillance and the availability of alternative mechanisms for promoting equality in families. While I think that there is no acceptable view which would advocate governmental surveillance of family chores, there remain a range of plausible views about the appropriate scope of state intervention and, indeed, the appropriate scope of equality considerations.[56]

It is also important to keep in mind that in the case of prostitution, as with pornography and hate speech, narrowing the discussion of solutions to the single question of whether to ban or not to ban shows a poverty of imagination. There are many ways of challenging existing cultural values about the appropriate division of labor in the family and the nature of women's sexual and reproductive capacities—for example, education, consciousness-raising groups, changes in employee leave policies, comparable worth programs, etc. The law is not the only way to provide women with incentives to refrain from participating in prostitution. Nonetheless, we do need to decide what the best legal policy toward prostitution should be.

I begin with an assessment of the policy which we now have. The United States is one of the few developed Western countries which criminalizes prostitution.[57] Denmark, the Netherlands, West Germany, Sweden, Switzerland, and Austria all have legalized prostitution, although in some of these countries it is restricted by local ordinances.[58] Where prostitution is permitted, it is closely regulated.

Suppose that we accept that gender equality is a legitimate goal of social policy. The question is whether the current legal prohibition on prostitution in the United States promotes gender equality. The answer I think is that it clearly does not. The current legal policies in the United States arguably exacerbate the factors in virtue of which prostitution is wrong.

The current prohibition on prostitution renders the women who engage in the practice vulnerable. First, the participants in the practice seek assistance from pimps in lieu of the contractual and legal remedies which are denied them. Male pimps may protect women prostitutes from their customers and from the police, but the system of pimp-run prostitution has enormous negative effects on the women at the lowest rungs of prostitution. Second, prohibition of prostitution raises the dilemma of the "double bind": if we prevent prostitution without greater redistribution of income, wealth, and opportunities, we deprive poor women of one way—in some circumstances the only way—of improving their condition.[59] Analogously, we do not solve the problem of homelessness by criminalizing it.

Furthermore, women are disproportionately punished for engaging in commercial sex acts. Many state laws make it a worse crime to sell sex than to buy it. Consequently, pimps and clients ("johns") are rarely prosecuted. In some jurisdictions, patronizing a prostitute is not illegal. The record of arrests and convictions is also highly asymmetric. Ninety percent of all convicted prostitutes are women. Studies have shown that male prostitutes are arrested with less frequency than female prostitutes and receive shorter sentences. One study of the judicial processing of 2,859 male and female prostitutes found that judges were more likely to find defendants guilty if they were female.[60]

Nor does the current legal prohibition on prostitution unambiguously benefit women as a class because the cultural meaning of current governmental prohibition of prostitution is unclear. While an unrestricted regime of prostitution—a pricing system in women's sexual attributes—could have negative external consequences on women's self-perceptions and perceptions by men, state prohibition can also reflect a view of women which contributes to their inequality. For example, some people support state regulation because they believe that women's sexuality is for purposes of reproduction, a claim tied to traditional ideas about women's proper role.

There is an additional reason why banning prostitution seems an inadequate response to the problem of gender inequality and which suggests a lack of parallel with the case of commercial surrogacy. Banning prostitution would not by itself—does not—eliminate it. While there is reason to think that making commercial surrogacy arrangements illegal or unenforceable would diminish their occurrence, no such evidence exists about prostitution. No city has eliminated prostitution merely through criminalization. Instead, criminalized prostitution thrives as a black market activity in which pimps substitute for law as the mechanism for enforcing contracts. It thereby makes the lives of prostitutes worse than they might otherwise be and without clearly counteracting prostitution's largely negative image of women.

If we decide to ban prostitution, these problems must be addressed. If we decide not to ban prostitution (either by legalizing it or decriminalizing it), then we must be careful to regulate the practice to address its negative effects. Certain restrictions on advertising and recruitment will be needed in order to address the negative image effects that an unrestricted regime of prostitution would perpetuate. But the current regime of prostitution has negative effects on the prostitutes themselves. It places their sexual capacities largely under the control of men. In order to promote women's autonomy, the law needs to ensure that certain restrictions—in effect, a Bill of Rights for Women—are in place.[61]

1. No woman should be forced, either by law or by private persons, to have sex against her will. (Recall that it is only quite recently that the courts have recognized the existence of marital rape.) A woman who sells sex must be able to refuse to give it; she must not be coerced by law or private persons to perform.

2. No woman should be denied access, either by law or by private persons, to contraception or to treatment for sexually transmitted diseases, particularly AIDS, or to abortion (at least in the first trimester).

3. The law should ensure that a woman has adequate information before she agrees to sexual intercourse. The risks of venereal and other sexually transmitted diseases, the risks of pregnancy, and the laws protecting a woman's right to refuse sex should all be generally available.

4. Minimum age of consent laws for sexual intercourse should be enforced. These laws should ensure that women (and men) are protected from coercion and do not enter into sexual relationships until they are in a position to understand what they are consenting to.

5. The law should promote women's control over their own sexuality by prohibiting brokerage. If what is wrong with prostitution is its relation to gender inequality, then it is crucial that the law be brought to bear primarily on the men who profit from the use of women's sexual capacities.

Each of these principles is meant to establish and protect a woman's right to control her sexual and reproductive capacities and not to give control of these capacities to others. Each of these principles is meant to protect the conditions for women's consent to sex, whether commercial or not. Each of these principles also seeks to counter the degradation of women in prostitution by mitigating its nature as a form of female servitude. In addition, given that a woman's choices are shaped both by the range of available opportunities and by the distribution of entitlements in society, it is crucial to attend to the inferior economic position of women in American society and those social and economic factors which produce the unequal life chances of men and women.

Conclusion

If the arguments I have offered here are correct, then prostitution is wrong in virtue of its contributions to perpetuating a pervasive form of inequality. In different circumstances, with different assumptions about women and their role in society, I do not think that prostitution would be especially troubling—no more troubling than many other labor markets currently allowed. It follows, then, that in other circumstances, the asymmetry thesis would be denied or less strongly felt. While the idea that prostitution is intrinsically degrading is a powerful intuition (and like many such intuitions, it persists even after its proponents undergo what Richard Brandt has termed "cognitive therapy," in which errors of fact and inference are corrected), I believe that this intuition is itself bound up with well-entrenched views of male gender identity and women's sexual role in the context of that identity.[62] If we are troubled by prostitution, as I think we should be, then we should direct much of our energy to putting forward alternative models of egalitarian relations between men and women.

Notes

I am grateful to the support of a Rockefeller Fellowship at Princeton University's Center for Human Values. Earlier versions of this article were presented at Swarthmore College, Princeton University, and Oxford University. I am grateful to the audiences at these institutions and in particular to Elizabeth Anderson, Michael Blake, C.A.J. Coady, Amy Gutmann, George Kateb, Andrew Koppelman, Arthur Kuflik, Peter de Marneffe, Thomas Pogge, Adam Swift, Stuart White, and Elisabeth Wood. I also thank two anonymous reviewers at *Ethics,* as well as the editors of the journal.

Ethical Issues

1 Debra Satz, "Markets in Women's Reproductive Labor," *Philosophy and Public Affairs* 21 (1992): 107–31.

2 What would remain troubling would be the miserable and unjust background circumstances in which much prostitution occurs. That is, if there were gender equality between the sexes but a substantial group of very poor men and women were selling sex, this would indeed be troubling. We should be suspicious of any labor contract entered into under circumstances of desperation.

3 Laurie Shrage, "Should Feminists Oppose Prostitution?" *Ethics* 99 (1989): 347–61, is an important exception. See also her new book, *Moral Dilemmas of Feminism: Prostitution, Adultery and Abortion* (New York: Routledge, 1994).

4 The fact that monetary exchange plays a role in maintaining many intimate relationships is a point underscored by George Bernard Shaw in *Mrs. Warren's Profession* (New York: Garland, 1981).

5 Compare Judith Walkowitz, *Prostitution and Victorian Society* (Cambridge: Cambridge University Press, 1980); Ruth Rosen, *Prostitution in America: 1900–1918* (Baltimore: Johns Hopkins University Press, 1982); B. Hobson, *Uneasy Virtue: The Politics of Prostitution and the American Reform Tradition* (Chicago: University of Chicago Press, 1990).

6 John Decker, *Prostitution: Regulation and Control* (Littleton, Colo.: Rothman, 1979), p. 191.

7 Compare Harold Greenwald, *The Elegant Prostitute: A Social and Psychoanalytic Study* (New York: Walker, 1970), p. 10.

8 For discussion of male prostitutes who sell sex to women, see H. Smith and B. Van der Horst, "For Women Only—How It Feels to Be a Male Hooker," *Village Voice* (March 7, 1977). Dictionary and common usage tends to identify prostitutes with women. Men who sell sex to women are generally referred to as "gigolos," not "prostitutes." The former encompasses the sale of companionship as well as sex.

9 Male prostitutes merit only a dozen pages in John Decker's monumental study of prostitution. See also D. Drew and J. Drake, *Boys for Sale: A Sociological Study of Boy Prostitution* (Deer Park, N.Y.: Brown Book Co., 1969); D. Deisher, "Young Male Prostitutes," *Journal of American Medical Association* 212 (1970): 1661–66; Gita Sereny, *The Invisible Children: Child Prostitution in America, West Germany and Great Britain* (London: Deutsch,

1984). I am grateful to Vincent DiGirolamo for bringing these works to my attention.

10 Compare Kathleen Barry, *Female Sexual Slavery* (New York: Avon, 1979). If we consider prostitution as an international phenomenon, then a majority of prostitutes are desperately poor and abused women. Nevertheless, there is a significant minority who are not. Furthermore, if prostitution were legalized, it is possible that the minimum condition of prostitutes in at least some countries would be raised.

11 Priscilla Alexander, "Prostitution: A Difficult Issue for Feminists," in *Sex Work: Writings by Women in the Sex Industry*, ed. P. Alexander and F. Delacoste (Pittsburgh: Cleis, 1987).

12 Moreover, to the extent that the desperate background conditions are the problem it is not apparent that outlawing prostitution is the solution. Banning prostitution may only remove a poor woman's best option: it in no way eradicates the circumstances which led her to such a choice. See M. Radin, "Market-Inalienability," *Harvard Law Review* 100 (1987): 1849–1937, on the problem of the "double bind."

13 Sometimes the qualitative aspects of a good have quantitative effects and so for that reason need to be taken into account. It is difficult, e.g., to establish a market in used cars given the uncertainties of ascertaining their qualitative condition. Compare George Akerlof, "The Market for Lemons: Qualitative Uncertainty and the Market Mechanism," *Quarterly Journal of Economics* 84 (1970): 488–500.

14 For an attempt to understand human sexuality as a whole through the economic approach, see Richard Posner, *Sex and Reason* (Cambridge, Mass.: Harvard University Press, 1992).

15 Although two-thirds of prostitutes surveyed say that they have no regrets about choice of work. Compare Decker, pp. 165–66. This figure is hard to interpret, given the high costs of thinking that one has made a bad choice of occupation and the lack of decent employment alternatives for many prostitutes.

16 See Guido Calabresi and A. Douglas Melamed, "Property Rules, Liability Rules and Inalienability: One View of the Cathedral," *Harvard Law Review* 85 (1972): 1089–1128.

17 Economic analysis fails to justify the laws we now have regarding prostitution. See below.

18 See Radin, pp. 1884 ff.

19 Posner, *Sex and Reason*, p. 182. See also R. Posner, "An Economic Theory of the Criminal Law," *Columbia Law Review* 85 (1985): 1193–1231. "The prohibition against rape is to the sex and marriage 'market' as the prohibition against theft is to explicit markets in goods and services" (p. 1199).

20 His approach in fact suggests that rape be seen as a "benefit" to the rapist, a suggestion that I think we should be loathe to follow.

21 I do not mean to claim, however, that such sovereignty over the body is absolute.

22 This section draws from and enlarges upon Satz.

23 Prostitution is, however, an issue which continues to divide feminists as well as prostitutes and former prostitutes. On the one side, some feminists see prostitution as dehumanizing and alienating and linked to male domination. This is the view taken by the prostitute organization Women Hurt in Systems of Prostitution Engaged in Revolt (WHISPER). On the other side, some feminists see sex markets as affirming a woman's right to autonomy, sexual pleasure, and economic welfare. This is the view taken by the prostitute organization COYOTE.

24 Carole Pateman, *The Sexual Contract* (Stanford, Calif.: Stanford University Press, 1988), p. 207; emphasis added.

25 The phrase is Radin's.

26 J. Harris, "The Survival Lottery," *Philosophy* 50 (1975): 81–87.

27 As an example of the ways in which the diversity of sexual experience has been culturally productive, see Lynn Hunt, ed., *The Invention of Pornography* (New York: Zone, 1993). Many of the essays in this volume illustrate the ways in which pornography has historically contributed to broader social criticism.

28 Radin, p. 1884.

29 An objection along these lines is raised by Margaret Baldwin ("Split at the Root: Feminist Discourses of Law Reform," *Yale Journal of Law and Feminism* 5 [1992]: 47–120). Baldwin worries that prostitution undermines our ability to understand a woman's capacity to consent to sex. Baldwin asks, will a prostitute's consent to sex be seen as consent to a twenty dollar payment? Will courts determine sentences in rape trials involving prostitutes as the equivalent of parking fine violations (e.g., as another

twenty dollar payment)? Aren't prostitutes liable to have their fundamental interests in bodily integrity discounted? I think Baldwin's worry is a real one, especially in the context of the current stigmatization of prostitutes. It could be resolved, in part, by withholding information about a woman's profession from rape trials.

30 Radin is herself fairly consistent in her hostility to many forms of wage labor. She has a complicated view about decommodification in nonideal circumstances which I cannot discuss here.

31 Also notice that many forms of labor we make inalienable—e.g., bans on mercenaries—cannot be justified by that labor's relationship to our personhood.

32 Elizabeth Anderson, *Value in Ethics and Economics* (Cambridge, Mass.: Harvard University Press, 1993), p. 45.

33 Actually, the prostitute's humanity is a part of the sex transaction itself. Whereas Posner's economic approach places sex with another person on the same scale as sex with a sheep, for many people the latter is not a form of sex at all (*Sex and Reason*). Moreover, in its worst forms, the prostitute's humanity (and gender) may be crucial to the john's experience of himself as superior to her. See Catherine MacKinnon, *Toward a Feminist Theory of the State* (Cambridge, Mass.: Harvard University Press, 1989).

34 Although this statement might have to be qualified in the light of empirical research. Arlie Hochschild, e.g., has found that the sale of "emotional labor" by airline stewardesses and insurance salesmen distorts their responses to pain and frustration (*The Managed Heart: The Commercialization of Human Feeling* [New York: Basic, 1983]).

35 I owe this point to Elizabeth Anderson, who stressed the need to distinguish between different versions of the degradation objection and suggested some lines of interpretation (conversation with author, Oxford University, July 1994).

36 More generally, they raise questions about the desirability of a world in which people use and exploit each other as they use and exploit other natural objects, insofar as this is compatible with Pareto improvements.

37 See Satz.

38 U.S. Department of Labor, Women's Bureau (Washington, D.C.: Government Printing Office, 1992).

39 D. Taylor, "Women: An Analysis," in *Women: A World Report* (London: Methuen, 1985). Taylor reports that while on a world scale women "perform nearly two-thirds of all working hours [they] receive only one tenth of the world income and own less than one percent of world resources."

40 J. David-McNeil, "The Changing Economic Status of the Female Labor Force in Canada," in *Towards Equity: Proceedings of a Colloquium on the Economic Status of Women in the Labor Market*, ed. Economic Council of Canada (Ottawa: Canadian Government Publication Centre, 1985).

41 S. Rix, ed., *The American Woman, 1990–91* (New York: Norton, 1990), cited in Woman's Action Coalition, ed., *WAC Stats: The Facts about Women* (New York: New Press, 1993), p. 41.

42 Report of the Federal Office of Child Support Enforcement, 1990.

43 Rix, ed. Note also that the time women spend doing housework has not declined since the 1920s despite the invention of labor saving technologies (e.g., laundry machines and dishwashers).

44 My views about this aspect of gender inequality have been greatly clarified in discussions and correspondence with Elizabeth Anderson and Elisabeth Wood during 1994.

45 See Paul Rosenkrantz, Susan Vogel, Helen Bees, Inge Broverman, and David Broverman, "Sex-Role Stereotypes and Self-Concepts in College Students, *Journal of Consulting and Clinical Psychology* 32 (1968): 286–95.

46 L. Heise, "Gender Violence as a Health Issue" (Violence, Health and Development Project. Center for Women's Global Leadership, Rutgers University, New Brunswick, N.J., 1992).

47 L. Heise, "Violence against Women: The Missing Agenda," in *Women's Health: A Global Perspective* (New York: Westview, 1992), cited in Woman's Action Coalition, ed., p. 55. More than one-third of female homicide victims are killed by their husbands or boyfriends.

48 I am indebted here to the discussion of Iris Young in *Justice and the Politics of Difference* (Princeton, N.J.: Princeton University Press, 1990).

49 Ruth Leger Sivard, *Women ... a World Survey* (Washington, D.C.: World Priorities, 1955).

50 Shrage ("Should Feminists Oppose Prostitution?") argues that prostitution perpetuates the following beliefs which oppress women: (1) the universal possession of a potent sex drive; (2) the "natural" dominance of men; (3) the pollution of women by sexual contact; and (4) the reification of sexual practice.

51 Susan Estrich, *Real Rape* (Cambridge, Mass.: Harvard University Press, 1987).

52 Baldwin, p. 75. Compare the Canadian Report on Prostitution and Pornography; also M. Silbert, "Sexual Assault on Prostitutes," research report to the *National Center for the Prevention and Control of Rape*, November 1980, for a study of street prostitutes in which 70 percent of those surveyed reported that they had been raped while walking the streets.

53 Carole Pateman, "Defending Prostitution: Charges against Ericsson," *Ethics* 93 (1983): 561–65, p. 563.

54 See also, S. Schwartzenbach. "Contractarians and Feminists Debate Prostitution," *New York University Review of Law and Social Change* 18 (1990–91): 103–30.

55 I owe this point to Arthur Kuflik.

56 For example, does the fact that racist joke telling reinforces negative stereotypes and perpetuates racial prejudice and inequality justify legal bans on such joke telling? What are the limits on what we can justifiably use the state to do in the name of equality? This is a difficult question. I only note here that arguments which justify state banning of prostitution can be consistent with the endorsement of stringent protections for speech. This is because speech and expression are arguably connected with basic fundamental human interests—with forming and articulating conceptions of value, with gathering information, with testifying on matters of conscience—in a way that prostitution (and some speech, e.g., commercial speech) is not. Even if we assume, as I think we should, that people have fundamental interests in having control over certain aspects of their bodies and lives, it does not follow that they have a fundamental interest in being free to sell themselves, their body parts, or any of their particular capacities.

57 Prostitution is legalized only in several jurisdictions in Nevada.

58 These countries have more pay equity between men and women than does the United States. This might be taken to undermine an argument about prostitution's role in contributing to income inequality. Moreover, women's status is lower in some societies which repress prostitution (such as

those of the Islamic nations) than in those which do not (such as those of the Scandinavian nations). But given the variety of cultural, economic, and political factors and mechanisms which need to be taken into account, we need to be very careful in drawing hasty conclusions. Legalizing prostitution might have negative effects on gender equality in the United States, even if legal prostitution does not correlate with gender inequality in other countries. There are many differences between the United States and European societies which make it implausible to think that one factor can alone be explanatory with respect to gender inequality.

59 Radin, pp. 1915 ff.

60 J. Lindquist et al., "Judicial Processing of Males and Females Charged with Prostitution," *Journal of Criminal Justice* 17 (1989): 277–91. Several state laws banning prostitution have been challenged on equal protection grounds. These statistics support the idea that prostitution's negative image effect has disproportionate bearing on male and female prostitutes.

61 In this section, I have benefited from reading Cass Sunstein, "Gender Difference, Reproduction and the Law" (University of Chicago Law School, 1992, unpublished manuscript). Sunstein believes that someone committed to gender equality will, most likely, advocate a legal ban on prostitution.

62 Richard B. Brandt, *A Theory of the Good and the Right* (Oxford: Clarendon, 1979).

Questions for Discussion

1 In what ways is the sale of one's sexual capacities akin to the sale of one's body parts (e.g., a kidney)? In what ways are they unlike each other?

2 Could it be that prostitution is morally wrong in our society when engaged in by women, but not when engaged in by men?

3 Does prostitution contribute to the unequal status of women by reinforcing the image of women as sexual servants of men's strong sexual needs?

CHAPTER 6

Euthanasia

Life itself is one of the central values of common-sense morality, and in most cases very little doubt arises about this. However, there are some cases in which it is not quite so obvious how valuable a given life is, or even sometimes whether a being counts as a living person at all. Some of these sorts of questions arise in connection with the issues of abortion and assisted reproduction, but this chapter will focus on aspects of these questions which arise at the other end of life, and in particular the issue of euthanasia.

The concept of euthanasia (also sometimes known loosely as "mercy killing") has been around for centuries, and it has even been practiced for centuries, but recent developments have changed the nature of euthanasia and, correspondingly, revived interest in the ethical problems it poses. Modern technology has made it possible to keep the body "alive" under a variety of circumstances which once would have been directly linked with death. Correspondingly, some people have come to fear a drawn-

out life, being kept alive by technology, more than they fear death itself. At the same time, there has been a growth in interest about the changing nature of the practice of medicine, and doctors who were once simply assumed to "know best" have found themselves increasingly under scrutiny. Ethical thought has had to struggle to keep up with these developments. Many of the issues here tend to involve deep questions about what makes life valuable. If we could know what it is that makes life valuable, then it would be easier to decide what lengths one is required to go to in order to sustain it, or indeed whether it is permissible to take deliberate steps to end a person's life in some circumstances. Perhaps more than any other single practical issue, euthanasia forces us to take on the stereotypical philosophical question, "What is the meaning of life?"

The word "euthanasia" comes from ancient Greek meaning "good death," and still carries some shades of meaning from that origin, but its meaning has changed somewhat in the context of the modern debate. Indeed, one of the controversial aspects of the modern debate involves finding an adequate characterization of what euthanasia means. It is generally understood to refer to the inducement of a gentle, easy death so as to avoid an unreasonable amount of suffering, or a loss of dignity.

The main reasons offered to justify hastening death or refusing to prolong life have to do with the best interests of a person, or the desire to treat people with dignity and respect. A person who is in great pain may be considered "better off dead," although of course we do not really know what it is like to be dead. Can a life ever be "not worth living"? Alternatively, the decision may be based on a belief that certain conditions threaten the dignity of people, either because they reduce them to states in which they are not capable of doing what they previously could, or simply because they are too physically intrusive. Finally, one important sort of case involving dignity concerns the belief that human beings should have "autonomy" (the ability to govern themselves). That could mean that they should be allowed to decide for themselves what is to happen in their lives. In this case, it may be morally required that we accept people's decisions if they decide they want to end their own lives. (One problematic possibility this raises is that a person may decide to die so as to avoid becoming a burden on friends and family.)

There are several distinctions which have traditionally been raised in connection with euthanasia. Perhaps the most basic of these is a distinction between killing a person, and letting a person die (sometimes described as "active" versus "passive" euthanasia). Many people believe that it is sometimes permissible to refrain from taking steps which would prolong a life, but that it is never permissible to take active steps to hasten the end of a life. (Indeed, some people use the word euthanasia only for those cases in which active steps are taken, and not for "letting die.") It might be claimed that actively killing a person amounts to "playing God," and allowing such killings might lead people (including health care professionals, who are presumed to be dedicated to preserving life and health) to lower the value they place on human life in other contexts (the "slippery slope" argument). Simply letting someone die, when there doesn't seem to be much for that person to live for, is not considered to have the same dire consequences.

On the other side of this issue, one might argue that refraining from life-sustaining treatment and waiting for natural death may sometimes be less humane than bringing about a quick and painless death. If the reason for refusing to prolong life is that the person whose life it is is suffering greatly, for example, it might seem kinder to put such a person "out of his or her misery." People on this side of the issue deny that there is any relevant difference between passive and active euthanasia. (Note: both sides can agree that there could be cases in which both passive and active euthanasia would be wrong.)

Another important distinction in this area is that between "voluntary" and "nonvoluntary" euthanasia. A voluntary decision about death is one in which the decision-maker is considered competent to make decisions regarding his or her own life. In such cases, many people would say that we have to respect the autonomy of that person, and accept the decision (although of course this obligation might not reach so far as to require us to take positive steps to bring it about, if the person is not able to bring it about without our help). Some writers have suggested that in cases of competent individuals, the right to life should be understood to extend to the "right to death."

The more complicated cases here involve people who are not able to make decisions for themselves. Such people cannot act voluntarily, and so a decision to perform euthanasia would have to be non-voluntary. (Note: it might also be possible to perform euthanasia on a person against that person's own stated desires, which might be called "involuntary euthanasia." Most people would find this generally unacceptable, however, and it is not discussed much in the literature.)

There are a variety of reasons why people may be unable to express a view regarding their own fate. One extreme circumstance would be one in which the person is unconscious. People may also be considered incompetent to make such a decision if, for example, they are too young, or suffer from some mental impairment which leaves them unable to understand their situation.

How are we to go about deciding whether euthanasia can be performed on a person not competent to speak for him or herself? There are two main types of standards which have been applied to such cases. The first, called the "best interests" standard, requires the decision-makers to decide what they believe to be in the best interests of the incompetent person and act accordingly. Of course different decision-makers might have different ideas about what makes for a good life, and so this standard may yield different results depending on who is using it. There is, however, some precedent for the state's assuming a duty to look after the best interests of those who cannot look after themselves, for example by protecting children from abusive parents.

The "substituted judgement" standard maintains that the decision properly belongs to the individual involved, because of that person's rights to autonomy and privacy. However, since that person is unable to decide, the task of the decision-maker should be to figure out what the individual *would* decide if he or she were competent to do so. This may or may not correspond to the decision-maker's own opinion about what would be best for that person.

There may be cases in which the calculation of what a person would decide is made easier by an opinion raised by that person before becoming incompetent. Although it is true that people sometimes change their minds, there is at least some reason to think that a request such as "If I am ever in condition *x*, please let me die" should be heeded if the person does indeed end up in condition *x*. The acceptability of this sort of statement has been tested in many places by the making of a so-called "living will."

In many cases, however, the individual concerned was never competent, or did not express a clear preference. It might be very difficult to apply the substituted judgement standard in such cases. Indeed, asking people to decide what they would do if they were not who they are, or were in very different circumstances, is always going to be difficult, although it might be the best approach available.

One final issue which needs to be raised about non-voluntary euthanasia is that of who is to make the decision. Should it be the family of the individual affected? The attending physicians? A hospital ethics committee? The courts? Each may have some advantages over the others. Of course, if all agree, there may be no problem, but conflicts are inevitable, and this also raises difficult problems.

The selections which follow address some of the key aspects of the euthanasia debate, first in a fairly abstract philosophical way, and then by reference to a couple of prominent recent Canadian cases.

Voluntary Active Euthanasia

Dan W. Brock

Beginning with an observation of an apparent consensus on the view that patients should be allowed to refuse treatment, or have treatment discontinued, Brock argues that we should also be willing to accept voluntary active euthanasia and assisted suicide. He claims that self-determination and individual well-being both support not only passive but active euthanasia, and that there are no compelling reasons for distinguishing the two. Brock also argues against the view that it is always morally wrong to kill an innocent person deliberately, and he considers and rejects a number of arguments which raise concerns about the consequences of euthanasia on both the medical profession, and society in general.

★   ★   ★

Since the case of Karen Quinlan first seized public attention fifteen years ago, no issue in biomedical ethics has been more prominent than the debate about forgoing life-sustaining treatment. Controversy continues regarding some aspects of that debate, such as forgoing life-sustaining nutrition and hydration, and relevant law varies some from state to state. Nevertheless, I believe it is possible to identify an emerging consensus that competent patients, or the surrogates of incompetent patients, should be permitted to weigh the benefits and burdens of alternative treatments, including the alternative of no treatment, according to the patient's values, and either to refuse any treatment or to select from among available alternative treatments. This consensus is reflected in bioethics scholarship, in reports of prestigious bodies such as the President's Commission for the Study of Ethical Problems in Medicine, The Hastings Center, and the American Medical Association, in a large body of judicial decisions in courts around the country, and finally in the beliefs and practices of health care professionals who care for dying patients.[1]

More recently, significant public and professional attention has shifted from life-sustaining treatment to euthanasia—more specifically, voluntary active euthanasia—and to physician-assisted suicide. Several factors have contributed to the increased interest in euthanasia. In the Netherlands, it has been openly practiced by physicians for several years with the acceptance of the country's highest court.[2] In 1988 there was an unsuccessful attempt to get the question of whether it should be made legally permissible on the ballot in California. In November 1991 voters in the state of Washington defeated a widely publicized referendum proposal to legalize both voluntary active euthanasia and physician-assisted suicide. Finally, some cases of this kind, such as "It's Over, Debbie," described in the *Journal of the American Medical Association*, the "suicide machine" of Dr. Jack Kevorkian, and the cancer patient "Diane" of Dr. Timothy Quill, have captured wide public and professional attention.[3] Unfortunately, the first two of these cases were sufficiently problematic that even most supporters of euthanasia or assisted suicide did not defend the physicians' actions in them. As a result, the subsequent debate they spawned has often shed more heat than light. My aim is to increase the light, and perhaps as well to reduce the heat, on this important subject by formulating and evaluating the central ethical arguments for and against voluntary active euthanasia and physician-assisted suicide. My evaluation of the arguments leads me, with reservations to be noted, to support permitting both practices. My primary aim, however, is not to argue for euthanasia, but to identify confusions in some common arguments, and problematic assumptions and claims that need more defense or data in others. The issues are considerably more complex than either supporters or opponents often make out; my hope is to advance the debate by focusing attention on what I believe the real issues under discussion should be.

In the recent bioethics literature some have endorsed physician-assisted suicide but not euthanasia.[4] Are they sufficiently different that the moral arguments for one often do not apply to the other? A paradigm case of physician-assisted suicide is a patient's ending his or her life with a lethal dose of a medication requested of and provided by a physician for that purpose. A paradigm case of voluntary active euthanasia is a physician's administering the lethal dose, often because the patient is unable to do so. The only difference that need exist between the two is the person who actually administers the lethal dose—the physician or the patient. In each, the physician plays an active and necessary causal role.

In physician-assisted suicide the patient acts last (for example, Janet Adkins herself pushed the button after Dr. Kevorkian hooked her up to his suicide machine), whereas in euthanasia the physician acts last by performing the physical equivalent of pushing the button. In both cases, however, the choice rests fully with the patient. In both the patient acts last in the sense of retaining the right to change his or her mind until the point at which the lethal process becomes irreversible. How could there be a substantial moral difference between the two based only on this small difference in the part played by the physician in the causal process resulting in death? Of course, it might be held that the moral dif-

ference is clear and important—in euthanasia the physician kills the patient whereas in physician-assisted suicide the patient kills him- or herself. But this is misleading at best. In assisted suicide the physician and patient together kill the patient. To see this, suppose a physician supplied a lethal dose to a patient with the knowledge and intent that the patient will wrongfully administer it to another. We would have no difficulty in morality or the law recognizing this as a case of joint action to kill for which both are responsible.

If there is no significant, intrinsic moral difference between the two, it is also difficult to see why public or legal policy should permit one but not the other; worries about abuse or about giving anyone dominion over the lives of others apply equally to either. As a result, I will take the arguments evaluated below to apply to both and will focus on euthanasia.

My concern here will be with *voluntary* euthanasia only—that is, with the case in which a clearly competent patient makes a fully voluntary and persistent request for aid in dying. Involuntary euthanasia, in which a competent patient explicitly refuses or opposes receiving euthanasia, and nonvoluntary euthanasia, in which a patient is incompetent and unable to express his or her wishes about euthanasia, will be considered here only as potential unwanted side-effects of permitting voluntary euthanasia. I emphasize as well that I am concerned with *active* euthanasia, not withholding or withdrawing life-sustaining treatment, which some commentators characterize as "passive euthanasia." Finally, I will be concerned with euthanasia where the motive of those who perform it is to respect the wishes of the patient and to provide the patient with a "good death," though one important issue is whether a change in legal policy could restrict the performance of euthanasia to only those cases.

A last introductory point is that I will be examining only secular arguments about euthanasia, though of course many people's attitudes to it are inextricable from their religious views. The policy issue is only whether euthanasia should be permissible, and no one who has religious objections to it should be required to take any part in it, though of course this would not fully satisfy some opponents.

The Central Ethical Argument for Voluntary Active Euthanasia

The central ethical argument for euthanasia is familiar. It is that the very same two fundamental ethical values supporting the consensus on patients' rights to decide about life-sustaining treatment also support the ethical permissibility of euthanasia. These values are individual self-determination or autonomy and individual well-being. By self-determination as it bears on euthanasia, I mean people's interest in making important decisions about their lives for themselves according to their own values or conceptions of a good life, and in being left free to act on those decisions. Self-determination is valuable because it permits people to form and live in accordance with their own conception of a good life, at least within the bounds of justice and consistent with others doing so as well. In exercising self-determination people take responsibility for their lives and for the kinds of persons they become. A central aspect of human dignity lies in people's capacity to direct their lives in this way. The value of exercising self-determination presupposes some minimum of decisionmaking capacities or competence, which thus limits the scope of euthanasia supported by self-determination; it cannot justifiably be administered, for example, in cases of serious dementia or treatable clinical depression.

Does the value of individual self-determination extend to the time and manner of one's death? Most people are very concerned about the nature of the last stage of their lives. This reflects not just a fear of experiencing substan-

tial suffering when dying, but also a desire to retain dignity and control during this last period of life. Death is today increasingly preceded by a long period of significant physical and mental decline, due in part to the technological interventions of modern medicine. Many people adjust to these disabilities and find meaning and value in new activities and ways. Others find the impairments and burdens in the last stage of their lives at some point sufficiently great to make life no longer worth living. For many patients near death, maintaining the quality of one's life, avoiding great suffering, maintaining one's dignity, and insuring that others remember us as we wish them to become of paramount importance and outweigh merely extending one's life. But there is no single, objectively correct answer for everyone as to when, if at all, one's life becomes all things considered a burden and unwanted. If self-determination is a fundamental value, then the great variability among people on this question makes it especially important that individuals control the manner, circumstances, and timing of their dying and death.

The other main value that supports euthanasia is individual well-being. It might seem that individual well-being conflicts with a person's self-determination when the person requests euthanasia. Life itself is commonly taken to be a central good for persons, often valued for its own sake, as well as necessary for pursuit of all other goods within a life. But when a competent patient decides to forgo all further life-sustaining treatment then the patient, either explicitly or implicitly, commonly decides that the best life possible for him or her with treatment is of sufficiently poor quality that it is worse than no further life at all. Life is no longer considered a benefit by the patient, but has now become a burden. The same judgment underlies a request for euthanasia: continued life is seen by the patient as no longer a benefit, but now a burden. Especially in the often severely compromised and debilitated states of many critically ill or dying patients, there is no objective standard, but only the competent patient's judgment of whether continued life is no longer a benefit.

Of course, sometimes there are conditions, such as clinical depression, that call into question whether the patient has made a competent choice, either to forgo life-sustaining treatment or to seek euthanasia, and then the patient's choice need not be evidence that continued life is no longer a benefit for him or her. Just as with decisions about treatment, a determination of incompetence can warrant not honoring the patient's choice; in the case of treatment, we then transfer decisional authority to a surrogate, though in the case of voluntary active euthanasia a determination that the patient is incompetent means that choice is not possible.

The value or right of self-determination does not entitle patients to compel physicians to act contrary to their own moral or professional values. Physicians are moral and professional agents whose own self-determination or integrity should be respected as well. If performing euthanasia became legally permissible, but conflicted with a particular physician's reasonable understanding of his or her moral or professional responsibilities, the care of a patient who requested euthanasia should be transferred to another.

Most opponents do not deny that there are some cases in which the values of patient self-determination and well-being support euthanasia. Instead, they commonly offer two kinds of arguments against it that on their view outweigh or override this support. The first kind of argument is that in any individual case where considerations of the patient's self-determination and well-being do support euthanasia, it is nevertheless always ethically wrong or impermissible. The second kind of argument grants that in some individual cases euthanasia may *not* be ethically wrong, but maintains nonetheless that public and legal policy should

never permit it. The first kind of argument focuses on features of any individual case of euthanasia, while the second kind focuses on social or legal policy. In the next section I consider the first kind of argument.

Euthanasia is the Deliberate Killing of an Innocent Person

The claim that any individual instance of euthanasia is a case of deliberate killing of an innocent person is, with only minor qualifications, correct. Unlike forgoing life-sustaining treatment, commonly understood as allowing to die, euthanasia is clearly killing, defined as depriving of life or causing the death of a living being. While providing morphine for pain relief at doses where the risk of respiratory depression and an earlier death may be a foreseen but unintended side effect of treating the patient's pain, in a case of euthanasia the patient's death is deliberate or intended even if in both the physician's ultimate end may be respecting the patient's wishes. If the deliberate killing of an innocent person is wrong, euthanasia would be nearly always impermissible.

In the context of medicine, the ethical prohibition against deliberately killing the innocent derives some of its plausibility from the belief that nothing in the currently accepted practice of medicine is deliberate killing. Thus, in commenting on the "It's Over, Debbie" case, four prominent physicians and bioethicists could entitle their paper "Doctors Must Not Kill."[5] The belief that doctors do not in fact kill requires the corollary belief that forgoing life-sustaining treatment, whether by not starting or by stopping treatment, is allowing to die, not killing. Common though this view is, I shall argue that it is confused and mistaken.

Why is the common view mistaken? Consider the case of a patient terminally ill with ALS disease. She is completely respirator dependent with no hope of ever being weaned.

She is unquestionably competent but finds her condition intolerable and persistently requests to be removed from the respirator and allowed to die. Most people and physicians would agree that the patient's physician should respect the patient's wishes and remove her from the respirator, though this will certainly cause the patient's death. The common understanding is that the physician thereby allows the patient to die. But is that correct?

Suppose the patient has a greedy and hostile son who mistakenly believes that his mother will never decide to stop her life-sustaining treatment and that even if she did her physician would not remove her from the respirator. Afraid that his inheritance will be dissipated by a long and expensive hospitalization, he enters his mother's room while she is sedated, extubates her, and she dies. Shortly thereafter the medical staff discovers what he has done and confronts the son. He replies, "I didn't kill her, I merely allowed her to die. It was her ALS disease that caused her death." I think this would rightly be dismissed as transparent sophistry—the son went into his mother's room and deliberately killed her. But, of course, the son performed just the same physical actions, did just the same thing, that the physician would have done. If that is so, then doesn't the physician also kill the patient when he extubates her?

I underline immediately that there are important ethical differences between what the physician and the greedy son do. First, the physician acts with the patient's consent whereas the son does not. Second, the physician acts with a good motive—to respect the patient's wishes and self-determination—whereas the son acts with a bad motive—to protect his own inheritance. Third, the physician acts in a social role through which he is legally authorized to carry out the patient's wishes regarding treatment whereas the son has no such authorization. These and perhaps other ethically important differences show that

what the physician did was morally justified whereas what the son did was morally wrong. What they do *not* show, however, is that the son killed while the physician allowed to die. One can either kill or allow to die with or without consent, with a good or bad motive, within or outside of a social role that authorizes one to do so.

The difference between killing and allowing to die that I have been implicitly appealing to here is roughly that between acts and omissions resulting in death.[6] Both the physician and the greedy son act in a manner intended to cause death, do cause death, and so both kill. One reason this conclusion is resisted is that on a different understanding of the distinction between killing and allowing to die, what the physician does is allow to die. In this account, the mother's ALS is a lethal disease whose normal progression is being held back or blocked by the life-sustaining respirator treatment. Removing this artificial intervention is then viewed as standing aside and allowing the patient to die of her underlying disease. I have argued elsewhere that this alternative account is deeply problematic, in part because it commits us to accepting that what the greedy son does is to allow to die, not kill.[7] Here, I want to note two other reasons why the conclusion that stopping life support is killing is resisted.

The first reason is that killing is often understood, especially within medicine, as unjustified causing of death; in medicine it is thought to be done only accidentally or negligently. It is also increasingly widely accepted that a physician is ethically justified in stopping life support in a case like that of the ALS patient. But if these two beliefs are correct, then what the physician does cannot be killing, and so must be allowing to die. Killing patients is not, to put it flippantly, understood to be part of physicians' job description. What is mistaken in this line of reasoning is the assumption that all killings are *unjustified* causings of death. Instead, some killings are ethically justified, including many instances of stopping life support.

Another reason for resisting the conclusion that stopping life support is often killing is that it is psychologically uncomfortable. Suppose the physician had stopped the ALS patient's respirator and had made the son's claim, "I didn't kill her, I merely allowed her to die. It was her ALS disease that caused her death." The clue to the psychological role here is how naturally the "merely" modifies "allowed her to die." The characterization as allowing to die is meant to shift felt responsibility away from the agent—the physician—and to the lethal disease process. Other language common in death and dying contexts plays a similar role; "letting nature take its course" or "stopping prolonging the dying process" both seem to shift responsibility from the physician who stops life support to the fatal disease process. However psychologically helpful these conceptualizations may be in making the difficult responsibility of a physician's role in the patient's death bearable, they nevertheless are confusions. Both physicians and family members can instead be helped to understand that it is the patient's decision and consent to stopping treatment that limits their responsibility for the patient's death and that shifts that responsibility to the patient.

Many who accept the difference between killing and allowing to die as the distinction between acts and omissions resulting in death have gone on to argue that killing is not in itself morally different from allowing to die.[8] In this account, very roughly, one kills when one performs an action that causes the death of a person (we are in a boat, you cannot swim, I push you overboard, and you drown), and one allows to die when one has the ability and opportunity to prevent the death of another, knows this, and omits doing so, with the result that the person dies (we are in a boat, you cannot swim, you fall overboard, I don't throw you an available life ring, and you

drown). Those who see no moral difference between killing and allowing to die typically employ the strategy of comparing cases that differ in these and no other potentially morally important respects. This will allow people to consider whether the mere difference that one is a case of killing and the other of allowing to die matters morally, or whether instead it is other features that make most cases of killing worse than most instances of allowing to die. Here is such a pair of cases:

> *Case 1.* A very gravely ill patient is brought to a hospital emergency room and sent up to the ICU. The patient begins to develop respiratory failure that is likely to require intubation very soon. At that point the patient's family members and long-standing physician arrive at the ICU and inform the ICU staff that there had been extensive discussion about future care with the patient when he was unquestionably competent. Given his grave and terminal illness, as well as his state of debilitation, the patient had firmly rejected being placed on a respirator under any circumstances, and the family and physician produce the patient's advance directive to that effect. The ICU staff do not intubate the patient, who dies of respiratory failure.

> *Case 2.* The same as Case 1 except that the family and physician are slightly delayed in traffic and arrive shortly after the patient has been intubated and placed on the respirator. The ICU staff extubate the patient, who dies of respiratory failure.

In Case 1 the patient is allowed to die, in Case 2 he is killed, but it is hard to see why what is done in Case 2 is significantly different morally than what is done in Case 1. It must be other factors that make most killings worse than most allowings to die, and if so, euthanasia cannot be wrong simply because it is killing instead of allowing to die.

Suppose both my arguments are mistaken. Suppose that killing is worse than allowing to die and that withdrawing life support is not killing, although euthanasia is. Euthanasia still need not for that reason be morally wrong. To see this, we need to determine the basic principle for the moral evaluation of killing persons. What is it that makes paradigm cases of wrongful killing wrongful? One very plausible answer is that killing denies the victim something that he or she values greatly—continued life or a future. Moreover, since continued life is necessary for pursuing any of a person's plans and purposes, killing brings the frustration of all of these plans and desires as well. In a nutshell, wrongful killing deprives a person of a valued future, and of all the person wanted and planned to do in that future.

A natural expression of this account of the wrongness of killing is that people have a moral right not to be killed.[9] But in this account of the wrongness of killing, the right not to be killed, like other rights, should be waivable when the person makes a competent decision that continued life is no longer wanted or a good, but is instead worse than no further life at all. In this view, euthanasia is properly understood as a case of a person having waived his or her right not to be killed.

This rights view of the wrongness of killing is not, of course, universally shared. Many people's moral views about killing have their origins in religious views that human life comes from God and cannot be justifiably destroyed or taken away, either by the person whose life it is or by another. But in a pluralistic society like our own with a strong commitment to freedom of religion, public policy should not be grounded in religious beliefs which many in that society reject. I turn now to the general evaluation of public policy on euthanasia.

Would the Bad Consequences of Euthanasia Outweigh the Good?

The argument against euthanasia at the policy level is stronger than at the level of individual

cases, though even here I believe the case is ultimately unpersuasive or at best indecisive. The policy level is the place where the main issues lie, however, and where moral considerations that might override arguments in favor of euthanasia will be found, if they are found anywhere. It is important to note two kinds of disagreement about the consequences for public policy of permitting euthanasia. First, there is empirical or factual disagreement about what the consequences would be. This disagreement is greatly exacerbated by the lack of firm data on the issue. Second, since on any reasonable assessment there would be both good and bad consequences, there are moral disagreements about the relative importance of different effects. In addition to these two sources of disagreement, there is also no single, well-specified policy proposal for legalizing euthanasia on which policy assessments can focus. But without such specification, and especially without explicit procedures for protecting against well-intentioned misuse and ill-intentioned abuse, the consequences for policy are largely speculative. Despite these difficulties, a preliminary account of the main likely good and bad consequences is possible. This should help clarify where better data or more moral analysis and argument are needed, as well as where policy safeguards must be developed.

Potential Good Consequences of Permitting Euthanasia

What are the likely good consequences? First, if euthanasia were permitted it would be possible to respect the self-determination of competent patients who want it, but now cannot get it because of its illegality. We simply do not know how many such patients and people there are. In the Netherlands, with a population of about 14.5 million (in 1987), estimates in a recent study were that about 1,900 cases of voluntary active euthanasia or physician-assisted suicide occur annually. No straightforward extrapolation to the United States is possible for many reasons, among them that we do not know how many people here who want euthanasia now get it, despite its illegality. Even with better data on the number of persons who want euthanasia but cannot get it, significant moral disagreement would remain about how much weight should be given to any instance of failure to respect a person's self-determination in this way.

One important factor substantially affecting the number of persons who would seek euthanasia is the extent to which an alternative is available. The widespread acceptance in the law, social policy, and medical practice of the right of a competent patient to forgo life-sustaining treatment suggests that the number of competent persons in the United States who would want euthanasia if it were permitted is probably relatively small.

A second good consequence of making euthanasia legally permissible benefits a much larger group. Polls have shown that a majority of the American public believes that people should have a right to obtain euthanasia if they want it.[10] No doubt the vast majority of those who support this right to euthanasia will never in fact come to want euthanasia for themselves. Nevertheless, making it legally permissible would reassure many people that if they ever do want euthanasia they would be able to obtain it. This reassurance would supplement the broader control over the process of dying given by the right to decide about life-sustaining treatment. Having fire insurance on one's house benefits all who have it, not just those whose houses actually burn down, by reassuring them that in the unlikely event of their house burning down, they will receive the money needed to rebuild it. Likewise, the legalization of euthanasia can be thought of as a kind of insurance policy against being forced to endure a protracted dying process that one has come to find burdensome and unwanted, especially when there is no life-sustaining treatment to forgo. The strong concern about losing control of their care expressed by many people who face serious illness likely to end in death suggests that they give substantial importance to the legalization of euthanasia as a means of maintaining this control.

A third good consequence of the legalization of euthanasia concerns patients whose dying is filled with severe and unrelievable pain or suffering. When there is a life-sustaining treatment that, if forgone, will lead relatively quickly to death, then doing so can bring an end to these patients' suffering without recourse to euthanasia. For patients receiving no such treatment, however, euthanasia may be the only release from their otherwise prolonged suffering and agony. This argument from mercy has always been the strongest argument for euthanasia in those cases to which it applies.[11]

The importance of relieving pain and suffering is less controversial than is the frequency with which patients are forced to undergo untreatable agony that only euthanasia could relieve. If we focus first on suffering caused by physical pain, it is crucial to distinguish pain that *could* be adequately relieved with modern methods of pain control, though it in fact is not, from pain that is relievable only by death.[12] For a variety of reasons, including some physicians' fear of hastening the patient's death, as well as the lack of a publicly accessible means for assessing the amount of the patient's pain, many patients suffer pain that could be, but is not, relieved.

Specialists in pain control, as for example the pain of terminally ill cancer patients, argue that there are very few patients whose pain could not be adequately controlled, though sometimes at the cost of so sedating them that they are effectively unable to interact with other people or their environment. Thus, the argument from mercy in cases of physical pain can probably be met in a large majority of cases by providing adequate measures of pain relief. This should be a high priority, whatever our legal policy on euthanasia—the relief of pain and suffering has long been, quite properly, one of the central goals of medicine. Those cases in which pain could be effectively relieved, but in fact is not, should only count significantly in favor of legalizing euthanasia if all reasonable efforts to change pain management techniques have been tried and have failed.

Dying patients often undergo substantial psychological suffering that is not fully or even principally the result of physical pain.[13] The knowledge about how to relieve this suffering is much more limited than in the case of relieving pain, and efforts to do so are probably more often unsuccessful. If the argument from mercy is extended to patients experiencing great and unrelievable psychological suffering, the numbers of patients to which it applies are much greater.

One last good consequence of legalizing euthanasia is that once death has been accepted, it is often more humane to end life quickly and peacefully, when that is what the patient wants. Such a death will often be seen as better than a more prolonged one. People who suffer a sudden and unexpected death, for example by dying quickly or in their sleep from a heart attack or stroke, are often considered lucky to have died in this way. We care about how we die in part because we care about how others remember us, and we hope they will remember us as we were in "good times" with them and not as we might be when disease has robbed us of our dignity as human beings. As with much in the treatment and care of the dying, people's concerns differ in this respect, but for at least some people, euthanasia will be a more humane death than what they have often experienced with other loved ones and might otherwise expect for themselves.

Some opponents of euthanasia challenge how much importance should be given to any

of these good consequences of permitting it, or even whether some would be good consequences at all. But more frequently, opponents cite a number of bad consequences that permitting euthanasia would or could produce, and it is to their assessment that I now turn.

Potential Bad Consequences of Permitting Euthanasia

Some of the arguments against permitting euthanasia are aimed specifically against physicians, while others are aimed against anyone being permitted to perform it. I shall first consider one argument of the former sort. Permitting physicians to perform euthanasia, it is said, would be incompatible with their fundamental moral and professional commitment as healers to care for patients and to protect life. Moreover if euthanasia by physicians became common, patients would come to fear that a medication was intended not to treat or care [sic], but instead to kill, and would thus lose trust in their physicians. This position was forcefully stated in a paper by Willard Gaylin and his colleagues:

> The very soul of medicine is on trial ... This issue touches medicine at its moral center; if this moral center collapses, if physicians become killers or are even licensed to kill, the profession—and, therewith, each physician—will never again be worthy of trust and respect as healer and comforter and protector of life in all its frailty.

These authors go on to make clear that, while they oppose permitting anyone to perform euthanasia, their special concern is with physicians doing so:

> We call on fellow physicians to say that they will not deliberately kill. We must also say to each of our fellow physicians that we will not tolerate killing of patients and that we shall take disciplinary action against doctors who kill. And we must say to the

broader community that if it insists on tolerating or legalizing active euthanasia, it will have to find nonphysicians to do its killing.[14]

If permitting physicians to kill would undermine the very "moral center" of medicine, then almost certainly physicians should not be permitted to perform euthanasia. But how persuasive is this claim? Patients should not fear, as a consequence of permitting *voluntary* active euthanasia, that their physicians will substitute a lethal injection for what patients want and believe is part of their care. If active euthanasia is restricted to cases in which it is truly voluntary, then no patient should fear getting it unless she or he has voluntarily requested it. (The fear that we might in time also come to accept nonvoluntary, or even involuntary, active euthanasia is a slippery slope worry I address below.) Patients' trust of their physicians could be increased, not eroded, by knowledge that physicians will provide aid in dying when patients seek it.

Might Gaylin and his colleagues nevertheless be correct in their claim that the moral center of medicine would collapse if physicians were to become killers? This question raises what at the deepest level should be the guiding aims of medicine, a question that obviously cannot be fully explored here. But I do want to say enough to indicate the direction that I believe an appropriate response to this challenge should take. In spelling out above what I called the positive argument for voluntary active euthanasia, I suggested that two principal values—respecting patients' self-determination and promoting their well-being—underlie the consensus that competent patients, or the surrogates of incompetent patients, are entitled to refuse any life-sustaining treatment and to choose from among available alternative treatments. It is the commitment to these two values in guiding physicians' actions as healers, comforters, and protectors of their patients' lives that should be at the "moral center" of medicine, and these two values support physicians' administering euthanasia when their patients make competent requests for it.

What should not be at that moral center is a commitment to preserving patients' lives as such, without regard to whether those patients want their lives preserved or judge their preservation a benefit to them. Vitalism has been rejected by most physicians, and despite some statements that suggest it, is almost certainly not what Gaylin and colleagues intended. One of them, Leon Kass, has elaborated elsewhere the view that medicine is a moral profession whose proper aim is "the naturally given end of health," understood as the wholeness and well-working of the human being; "for the physician, at least, human life in living bodies commands respect and reverence—*by its very nature.*" Kass continues, "the deepest ethical principle restraining the physician's power is not the autonomy or freedom of the patient; neither is it his own compassion or good intention. Rather, it is the dignity and mysterious power of human life itself."[15] I believe Kass is in the end mistaken about the proper account of the aims of medicine and the limits on physicians' power, but this difficult issue will certainly be one of the central themes in the continuing debate about euthanasia.

A second bad consequence that some foresee is that permitting euthanasia would weaken society's commitment to provide optimal care for dying patients. We live at a time in which the control of health care costs has become, and is likely to continue to be, the dominant focus of health care policy. If euthanasia is seen as a cheaper alternative to adequate care and treatment, then we might become less scrupulous about providing sometimes costly support and other services to dying patients. Particularly if our society comes to embrace deeper and more explicit rationing of health care, frail, elderly, and dying patients will need to be strong and effective advocates for their own health care and other needs, although they are hardly in a position to do this. We should do nothing to weaken their ability to obtain adequate care and services.

This second worry is difficult to assess because there is little firm evidence about the likelihood of the feared erosion in the care of dying patients. There are at least two reasons, however, for skepticism about this argument. The first is that the same worry could have been directed at recognizing patients' or surrogates' rights to forgo life sustaining treatment, yet there is no persuasive evidence that recognizing the right to refuse treatment has caused a serious erosion in the quality of care of dying patients. The second reason for skepticism about this worry is that only a very small proportion of deaths would occur from euthanasia if it were permitted. In the Netherlands, where euthanasia under specified circumstances is permitted by the courts, though not authorized by statute, the best estimate of the proportion of overall deaths that result from it is about 2 percent.[16] Thus, the vast majority of critically ill and dying patients will not request it, and so will still have to be cared for by physicians, families, and others. Permitting euthanasia should not diminish people's commitment and concern to maintain and improve the care of these patients.

A third possible bad consequence of permitting euthanasia (or even a public discourse in which strong support for euthanasia is evident) is to threaten the progress made in securing the rights of patients or their surrogates to decide about and to refuse life-sustaining treatment.[17] This progress has been made against the backdrop of a clear and firm legal prohibition of euthanasia, which has provided a relatively bright line limiting the dominion of others over patients' lives. It has therefore been an important reassurance to concerns about how the authority to take steps ending life might be misused, abused, or wrongly extended.

Many supporters of the right of patients or their surrogates to refuse treatment strongly oppose euthanasia, and if forced to choose might well withdraw their support of the right to refuse treatment rather than accept euthanasia. Public policy in the last fifteen years has generally let life-sustaining treatment decisions be made in health care settings between physicians and patients or their surrogates, and without the involvement of the courts. However, if euthanasia is made legally permissible greater involvement of the courts is likely, which could in turn extend to a greater court involvement in life-sustaining treatment decisions. Most agree, however, that increased involvement of the courts in these decisions would be undesirable, as it would make sound decisionmaking more cumbersome and difficult without sufficient compensating benefits.

As with the second potential bad consequence of permitting euthanasia, this third consideration too is speculative and difficult to assess. The feared erosion of patients' or surrogates' rights to decide about life-sustaining treatment, together with greater court involvement in those decisions, are both possible. However, I believe there is reason to discount this general worry. The legal rights of competent patients and, to a lesser degree, surrogates of incompetent patients to decide about treatment are very firmly embedded in a long line of informed consent and life-sustaining treatment cases, and are not likely to be eroded by a debate over, or even acceptance of, euthanasia. It will not be accepted without safeguards that reassure the public about abuse, and if that debate shows the need for similar safeguards for some life-sustaining treatment decisions they should be adopted there as well. In neither case are the only possible safeguards greater court involvement, as the recent growth of institutional ethics committees shows.

The fourth potential bad consequence of permitting euthanasia has been developed by David Velleman and turns on the subtle point that making a new option or choice available to people can sometimes make them worse off, even if once they have the choice they go on to choose what is best for them.[18] Ordinarily, people's continued existence is viewed by them as given, a fixed condition with which they must cope. Making euthanasia available to people as an option denies them the alternative of staying alive by default. If people are offered the option of euthanasia, their continued existence is now a choice for which they can be held responsible and which they can be asked by others to justify. We care, and are right to care, about being able to justify ourselves to others. To the extent that our society is unsympathetic to justifying a severely dependent or impaired existence, a heavy psychological burden of proof may be placed on patients who think their terminal illness or chronic infirmity is not a sufficient reason for dying. Even if they otherwise view their life as worth living, the opinion of others around them that it is not can threaten their reason for living and make euthanasia a rational choice. Thus the existence of the option be comes a subtle pressure to request it.

This argument correctly identifies the reason why offering some patients the option of euthanasia would not benefit them. Velleman takes it not as a reason for opposing all euthanasia, but for restricting it to circumstances where there are "unmistakable and overpowering reasons for persons to want the option of euthanasia," and for denying the option in all other cases. But there are at least three reasons why such restriction may not be warranted. First, polls and other evidence support that most Americans believe euthanasia should be permitted (though the recent defeat of the referendum to permit it in the state of Washington raises some doubt about this support). Thus, many more people seem to want the choice than would be made worse off by getting it. Second, if giving people the option of ending their life really makes them worse off, then we should not only prohibit euthanasia, but also take back from people the right they now have to decide about life-sustaining treatment. The feared harmful effect should already have occurred from securing people's right to refuse life-sustaining treatment, yet there is no evidence of any such widespread harm or any broad public desire to rescind that right. Third, since there is a wide range of conditions in which reasonable people can and do disagree about whether they would want continued life, it is not possible to restrict the permissibility of euthanasia as narrowly as Velleman suggests without thereby denying it to most persons who would want it; to permit it only in cases in which virtually everyone would want it would be to deny it to most who would want it.

A fifth potential bad consequence of making euthanasia legally permissible is that it might weaken the general legal prohibition of homicide. This prohibition is so fundamental to civilized society, it is argued, that we should do nothing that erodes it. If most cases of stopping life-support are killing, as I have already argued, then the court cases permitting such killing have already in effect weakened this prohibition. However, neither the courts nor most people have seen these cases as killing and so as challenging the prohibition of homicide. The courts have usually grounded patients' or their surrogates' rights to refuse life-sustaining treatment in rights to privacy, liberty, self-determination, or bodily integrity, not in exceptions to homicide laws.

Legal permission for physicians or others to perform euthanasia could not be grounded in patients' rights to decide about medical treatment. Permitting euthanasia would require qualifying, at least in effect, the legal prohibition against homicide, a prohibition that in general does not allow the consent of the victim to justify or excuse the act. Nevertheless, the very same fundamental basis of the right to decide about life-sustaining treatment—respecting a person's self-determination—does support euthanasia as well. Individual self-determination has long been a well-entrenched and fundamental value in the law, and so extending it to euthanasia would not require appeal to novel legal values or principles. That suicide or attempted suicide is no longer a criminal offense in virtually all states indicates an acceptance of individual self-determination in the taking of one's own life analogous to that required for voluntary active euthanasia. The legal prohibition (in most states) of assisting in suicide and the refusal in the law to accept the consent of the victim as a possible justification of homicide are both arguably a result of difficulties in the legal process of establishing the consent of the victim after the fact. If procedures can be designed that clearly establish the voluntariness of the person's request for euthanasia, it would under those procedures represent a carefully circumscribed qualification on the legal prohibition of homicide. Nevertheless, some remaining worries about this weakening can be captured in the final potential bad consequence, to which I will now turn.

This final potential bad consequence is the central concern of many opponents of euthanasia and, I believe, is the most serious objection to a legal policy permitting it. According to this "slippery slope" worry, although active euthanasia may be morally permissible in cases in which it is unequivocally voluntary and the patient finds his or her condition unbearable, a legal policy permitting euthanasia would inevitably lead to active euthanasia being performed in many other cases in which it would be morally wrong. To prevent those other wrongful cases of euthanasia we should not permit even morally justified performance of it.

Slippery slope arguments of this form are problematic and difficult to evaluate.[19] From one perspective, they are the last refuge of conservative defenders of the status quo. When all the opponent's objections to the wrongness of euthanasia itself have been met, the opponent then shifts ground and acknowledges both that it is not in itself wrong and that a legal policy which resulted only in its being performed would not be bad. Nevertheless, the opponent maintains, it should still not be permitted because doing so would result in its being performed in other cases in which it is not voluntary and would be wrong. In this argument's most extreme form, permitting euthanasia is the first and fateful step down the slippery slope to Nazism. Once on the slope we will be unable to get off.

Now it cannot be denied that it is *possible* that permitting euthanasia could have these fateful consequences, but that cannot be enough to warrant prohibiting it if it is otherwise justified. A similar *possible* slippery slope worry could have been raised to securing competent patients' rights to decide about life support, but recent history shows such a worry would have been unfounded. It must be relevant how likely it is that we will end with horrendous consequences and an unjustified practice of euthanasia. How *likely* and *widespread* would the abuses and unwarranted extensions of permitting it be? By abuses, I mean the performance of euthanasia that fails to satisfy the conditions required for voluntary active euthanasia, for example, if the patient has been subtly pressured to accept it. By unwarranted extensions of policy, I mean later changes in legal policy to permit not just voluntary euthanasia, but also euthanasia in cases in which, for example, it need not be fully voluntary. Opponents of voluntary euthanasia on slippery slope grounds have not provided the data or evidence necessary to turn their speculative concerns into well-grounded likelihoods.

It is at least clear, however, that both the character and likelihood of abuses of a legal policy permitting euthanasia depend in significant part on the procedures put in place to protect against them. I will not try to detail fully what such procedures might be, but will just give some examples of what they might include:

1. The patient should be provided with all relevant information about his or her medical condition, current prognosis, available alternative treatments, and the prognosis of each.
2. Procedures should ensure that the patient's request for euthanasia is stable or enduring (a brief waiting period could be required) and fully voluntary (an advocate for the patient might be appointed to ensure this).
3. All reasonable alternatives must have been explored for improving the patient's quality of life and relieving any pain or suffering.
4. A psychiatric evaluation should ensure that the patient's request is not the result of a treatable psychological impairment such as depression.[20]

These examples of procedural safeguards are all designed to ensure that the patient's choice is fully informed, voluntary, and competent, and so a true exercise of self-determination. Other proposals for euthanasia would restrict its permissibility further—for example, to the terminally ill—a restriction that cannot be supported by self-determination. Such additional restrictions might, however, be justified by concern for limiting potential harms from abuse. At the same time, it is important not to impose procedural or substantive safeguards so restrictive as to make euthanasia impermissible or practically infeasible in a wide range of justified cases.

These examples of procedural safeguards make clear that it is possible to substantially reduce, though not to eliminate, the potential for abuse of a policy permitting voluntary active euthanasia. Any legalization of the practice should be accompanied by a well-considered set of procedural safeguards together with

an ongoing evaluation of its use. Introducing euthanasia into only a few states could be a form of carefully limited and controlled social experiment that would give us evidence about the benefits and harms of the practice. Even then firm and uncontroversial data may remain elusive, as the continuing controversy over what has taken place in the Netherlands in recent years indicates.[21]

The Slip into Nonvoluntary Euthanasia

While I believe slippery slope worries can largely be limited by making necessary distinctions both in principle and in practice, one slippery slope concern is legitimate. There is reason to expect that legalization of voluntary active euthanasia might soon be followed by strong pressure to legalize some nonvoluntary euthanasia of incompetent patients unable to express their own wishes. Respecting a person's self-determination and recognizing that continued life is not always of value to a person can support not only voluntary active euthanasia, but some non-voluntary euthanasia as well. These are the same values that ground competent patients' right to refuse life-sustaining treatment. Recent history here is instructive. In the medical ethics literature, in the courts since Quinlan, and in norms of medical practice, that right has been extended to incompetent patients and exercised by a surrogate who is to decide as the patient would have decided in the circumstances if competent.[22] It has been held unreasonable to continue life-sustaining treatment that the patient would not have wanted just because the patient now lacks the capacity to tell us that. Life-sustaining treatment for incompetent patients is today frequently forgone on the basis of a surrogate's decision, or less frequently on the basis of an advance directive executed by the patient while still competent. The very same logic that has extended the right to refuse life-sustaining treatment from a competent patient to the surrogate of an incompetent patient (acting with or without a formal advance directive from the patient) may well extend the scope of active euthanasia. The argument will be, Why continue to force unwanted life on patients just because they have now lost the capacity to request euthanasia from us?

A related phenomenon may reinforce this slippery slope concern. In the Netherlands, what the courts have sanctioned has been clearly restricted to voluntary euthanasia. In itself, this serves as some evidence that permitting it need *not* lead to permitting the nonvoluntary variety. There is some indication, however, that for many Dutch physicians euthanasia is no longer viewed as a special action, set apart from their usual practice and restricted only to competent persons.[23] Instead, it is seen as one end of a spectrum of caring for dying patients. When viewed in this way it will be difficult to deny euthanasia to a patient for whom it is seen as the best or most appropriate form of care simply because that patient is now incompetent and cannot request it.

Even if voluntary active euthanasia should slip into nonvoluntary active euthanasia, with surrogates acting for incompetent patients, the ethical evaluation is more complex than many opponents of euthanasia allow. Just as in the case of surrogates' decisions to forgo life-sustaining treatment for incompetent patients, so also surrogates' decisions to request euthanasia for incompetent persons would often accurately reflect what the incompetent person would have wanted and would deny the person nothing that he or she would have considered worth having. Making nonvoluntary active euthanasia legally permissible, however, would greatly enlarge the number of patients on whom it might be performed and substantially enlarge the potential for misuse and abuse. As noted above, frail and debilitated elderly people, often demented or otherwise incompetent and thereby unable to defend and assert their own interests, may be especially vulnerable to unwanted euthanasia.

For some people, this risk is more than sufficient reason to oppose the legalization of voluntary euthanasia. But while we should in general be cautious about inferring much from the experience in the Netherlands to what our own experience in the United States might be, there may be one important lesson that we can learn from them. One commentator has noted that in the Netherlands families of incompetent patients have less authority than do families in the United States to act as surrogates for incompetent patients in making decisions to forgo life-sustaining treatment.[24] From the Dutch perspective, it may be we in the United States who are *already* on the slippery slope in having given surrogates broad authority to forgo life-sustaining treatment for incompetent persons. In this view, the more important moral divide, and the more important with regard to potential for abuse, is not between forgoing life-sustaining treatment and euthanasia, but instead between voluntary and nonvoluntary performance of either. If this is correct, then the more important issue is ensuring the appropriate principles and procedural safeguards for the exercise of decision-making authority by surrogates for incompetent persons in *all* decisions at the end of life. This may be the correct response to slippery slope worries about euthanasia.

I have cited both good and bad consequences that have been thought likely from a policy change permitting voluntary active euthanasia, and have tried to evaluate their likelihood and relative importance. Nevertheless, as I noted earlier, reasonable disagreement remains both about the consequences of permitting euthanasia and about which of these consequences are more important. The depth and strength of public and professional debate about whether, all things considered, permitting euthanasia would be desirable or undesirable reflects these disagreements. While my own view is that the balance of considerations supports permitting the practice, my principal purpose here has been to clarify the main issues.

The Role of Physicians

If euthanasia is made legally permissible, should physicians take part in it? Should only physicians be permitted to perform it, as is the case in the Netherlands? In discussing whether euthanasia is incompatible with medicine's commitment to curing, caring for, and comforting patients, I argued that it is not at odds with a proper understanding of the aims of medicine, and so need not undermine patients' trust in their physicians. If that argument is correct, then physicians probably should not be prohibited, either by law or by professional norms, from taking part in a legally permissible practice of euthanasia (nor, of course, should they be compelled to do so if their personal or professional scruples forbid it). Most physicians in the Netherlands appear not to understand euthanasia to be incompatible with their professional commitments.

Sometimes patients who would be able to end their lives on their own nevertheless seek the assistance of physicians. Physician involvement in such cases may have important benefits to patients and others beyond simply assuring the use of effective means. Historically in the United States suicide has carried a strong negative stigma that many today believe unwarranted. Seeking a physician's assistance, or what can almost seem a physician's blessing, may be a way of trying to remove that stigma and show others that the decision for suicide was made with due seriousness and was justified under the circumstances. The physician's involvement provides a kind of social approval, or more accurately helps counter what would otherwise be unwarranted social disapproval.

There are also at least two reasons for restricting the practice of euthanasia to physicians only. First, physicians would inevitably be involved in some of the important procedural safeguards necessary to a defensible practice, such as seeing to it that the patient is well-informed about his or her condition, prognosis, and possible treatments, and ensuring that all reasonable means have been taken to improve the quality of the patient's life. Second, and probably more important, one necessary protection against abuse of the practice is to limit the persons given authority to perform it, so that they can be held accountable for their exercise of that authority. Physicians, whose training and professional norms give some assurance that they would perform euthanasia responsibly, are an appropriate group of persons to whom the practice may be restricted.

Acknowledgments

Earlier versions of this paper were presented at the American Philosophical Association Central Division meetings (at which David Velleman provided extremely helpful comments), Massachusetts General Hospital, Yale University School of Medicine, Princeton University, Brown University, and as the Brin Lecture at The Johns Hopkins School of Medicine. I am grateful to the audiences on each of these occasions, to several anonymous reviewers, and to Norman Daniels for helpful comments. The paper was completed while I was a Fellow in the Program in Ethics and the Professions at Harvard University.

References

1 President's Commission for the Study of Ethical Problems in Medicine and Biomedical and Behavioral Research, *Deciding to Forego Life-Sustaining Treatment* (Washington, D.C.: U.S. Government Printing Office, 1983); The Hastings Center, *Guidelines on the Termination of Life-Sustaining Treatment and Care of the Dying* (Bloomington: Indiana University Press, 1987); *Current Opinions of the Council on Ethical and Judicial Affairs of the Ameri-*

can Medical Association—1989: Withholding or Withdrawing Life-Prolonging Treatment (Chicago: American Medical Association, 1989); George Annas and Leonard Glantz, "The Right of Elderly Patients to Refuse Life-Sustaining Treatment," *Millbank Memorial Quarterly* 64, suppl. 2 (1986): 95–162; Robert F. Weir, *Abating Treatment with Critically Ill Patients* (New York: Oxford University Press, 1989); Sidney J. Wanzer et al. "The Physician's Responsibility toward Hopelessly Ill Patients," *NEJM* 310 (1984): 955–59.

2 M.A.M. de Wachter, "Active Euthanasia in the Netherlands," *JAMA* 262, no. 23 (1989): 3315–19.

3 Anonymous, "It's Over, Debbie," *JAMA* 259 (1988): 272; Timothy E. Quill, " Death and Dignity," *NEJM* 322 (1990): 1881–83.

4 Wanzer et al., "The Physician's Responsibility toward Hopelessly Ill Patients: A Second Look," *NEJM* 320 (1989): 844–49.

5 Willard Gaylin, Leon R. Kass, Edmund D. Pellegrino, and Mark Siegler, "Doctors Must Not Kill," *JAMA* 259 (1988): 2139–40.

6 Bonnie Steinbock, ed., *Killing and Allowing to Die* (Englewood Cliffs, N.J.: Prentice Hall, 1980).

7 Dan W. Brock, "Forgoing Food and Water: Is It Killing?" In *By No Extraordinary Means: The Choice to Forgo Life-Sustaining Food and Water*, ed. Joanne Lynn (Bloomington: Indiana University Press, 1986), pp. 117–31.

8 James Rachels, "Active and Passive Euthanasia," *NEJM* 292 (1975): 78–80; Michael Tooley, *Abortion and Infanticide* (Oxford: Oxford University Press, 1983). In my paper, "Taking Human Life," *Ethics* 95 (1985): 851–65, I argue in more detail that killing in itself is not morally different from allowing to die and defend the strategy of argument employed in this and the succeeding two paragraphs in the text.

9 Dan W. Brock, "Moral Rights and Permissible Killing," in *Ethical Issues Relating to Life and Death*, ed. John Ladd (New York: Oxford University Press, 1979), pp. 94–117.

10 P. Painton and E. Taylor, "Love or Let Die," *Time*, 19 March 1990, pp. 62–71; *Boston Globe*/Harvard University Poll, *Boston Globe*, 3 November 1991.

11 James Rachels, *The End of Life* (Oxford: Oxford University Press, 1986).

12 Marcia Angell, "The Quality of Mercy," *NEJM* 306 (1982): 98–99; M. Donovan, P. Dillon, and L. Mcguire, "Incidence and Characteristics of Pain in a Sample of Medical-Surgical Inpatients," *Pain* 30 (1987): 69–78.

13 Eric Cassell, *The Nature of Suffering and the Goals of Medicine* (New York: Oxford University Press, 1991).

14 Gaylin, et al., "Doctors Must Not Kill."

15 Leon R. Kass, "Neither for Love Nor Money: Why Doctors Must Not Kill," *The Public Interest* 94 (1989): 25–46; cf. also his *Toward a More Natural Science: Biology and Human Affairs* (New York: The Free Press, 1985), chs. 6–9.

16 Paul. J. Van der Maas et al., "Euthanasia and Other Medical Decisions Concerning the End of Life," *Lancet* 338 (1991): 669–74.

17 Susan M. Wolf, "Holding the Line on Euthanasia," Special Supplement, *Hastings Center Report* 19, no. 1 (1989): 13–15.

18 My formulation of this argument derives from David Velleman's statement of it in his commentary on an earlier version of this paper delivered at the American Philosophical Association Central Division meetings; a similar point was made to me by Elisha Milgram in discussion on another occasion. For more general development of the point see Thomas Schelling, *The Strategy of Conflict* (Cambridge, Mass.: Harvard University Press, 1960); and Gerald Dworkin, "Is More Choice Better Than Less?" in *The Theory and Practice of Autonomy* (Cambridge: Cambridge University Press, 1988).

19 Frederick Schauer, "Slippery Slopes," *Harvard Law Review* 99 (1985): 361–83; Wibren van der Burg, "The Slippery Slope Argument," *Ethics* 102 (October 1991): 42–65.

20 There is evidence that physicians commonly fail to diagnose depression. See Robert I. Misbin, "Physicians Aid in Dying," *NEJM* 325 (1991): 1304–7.

21 Richard Fenigsen, "A Case against Dutch Euthanasia," Special Supplement, *Hastings Center Report* 19, no. 1 (1989): 22–30.

22 Allen E. Buchanan and Dan W. Brock, *Deciding for Others: The Ethics of Surrogate Decisionmaking* (Cambridge: Cambridge University Press, 1989).

23 Van der Maas et al., "Euthanasia and Other Medical Decisions."

24 Margaret P. Battin, "Seven Caveats Concerning the Discussion of Euthanasia in Holland," *American Philosophical Association Newsletter on Philosophy and Medicine* 89, no. 2 (1990).

Questions for Discussion

1 Does it make sense to say that a greedy son who disconnects his mother's life support so as to inherit is killing her, while a doctor who disconnects a woman's life support because she says she no longer wants to live is "merely letting die"?

2 Is a policy allowing euthanasia analogous to fire insurance, in the sense of comforting those who think they might need it in the future, as well as those who actually do need it?

3 Would allowing doctors to perform voluntary active euthanasia cause irrevocable harm to our understanding of the role of health-care professionals, and to our ability to trust doctors?

When Self-Determination Runs Amok

Daniel Callahan

In the following selection, Callahan argues that allowing (active) euthanasia would be a serious moral mistake. He considers four general types of arguments which have been offered in favour of (active) euthanasia (one based on self-determination and well-being, one based on the lack of distinction between killing and allowing to die, one based on skepticism about harmful consequences for society, and one based on the belief that euthanasia is consistent with good medical practice) and argues that each of them is badly flawed.

★   ★   ★

The euthanasia debate is not just another moral debate, one in a long list of arguments in our pluralistic society. It is profoundly emblematic of three important turning points in Western thought. The first is that of the legitimate conditions under which one person can kill another. The acceptance of voluntary active euthanasia would morally sanction what can only be called "consenting adult killing." By that term I mean the killing of one person by another in the name of their mutual right to be killer and killed if they freely agree to play those roles. This turn flies in the face of a longstanding effort to limit the circumstances under which one person can take the life of another, from efforts to control the free flow of guns and arms, to abolish capital punishment, and to more tightly control warfare. Euthanasia would add a whole new category

of killing to a society that already has too many excuses to indulge itself in that way.

The second turning point lies in the meaning and limits of self-determination. The acceptance of euthanasia would sanction a view of autonomy holding that individuals may, in the name of their own private, idiosyncratic view of the good life, call upon others, including such institutions as medicine, to help them pursue that life, even at the risk of harm to the common good. This works against the idea that the meaning and scope of our own right to lead our own lives must be conditioned by and be compatible with, the good of the community which is more than an aggregate of self-directing individuals.

The third turning point is to be found in the claim being made upon medicine: it should be prepared to make its skills available to individuals to help them achieve their private vision of the good life. This puts medicine in the business of promoting the individualistic pursuit of general human happiness and well-being. It would overturn the traditional belief that medicine should limit its domain to promoting and preserving human health, redirecting it instead to the relief of that suffering which stems from life itself; not merely from a sick body.

I believe that, at each of these three turning points, proponents of euthanasia push us in the wrong direction. Arguments in favor of euthanasia fall into four general categories, which I will take up in turn: (1) the moral claim of individual self-determination and well-being; (2) the moral irrelevance of the difference between killing and allowing to die; (3) the supposed paucity of evidence to show likely harmful consequences of legalized euthanasia; and (4) the compatibility of euthanasia and medical practice.

Self-Determination

Central to most arguments for euthanasia is the principle of self-determination. People are presumed to have an interest in deciding for themselves, according to their own beliefs about what makes life good, how they will conduct their lives. That is an important value, but the question in the euthanasia context is, What does it mean and how far should it extend? If it were a question of suicide, where a person takes her own life without assistance from another, that principle might be pertinent, at least for debate. But euthanasia is not that limited a matter. The self-determination in that case can only be effected by the moral and physical assistance of another. Euthanasia is thus no longer a matter only of self-determination, but of a mutual, social decision between two people, the one to be killed and the other to do the killing.

How are we to make the moral move from

my right of self-determination to some doctor's right to kill me—from *my* right to *his* right? Where does the doctor's moral warrant to kill come from? Ought doctors to be able to kill anyone they want as long as permission is given by competent persons? Is our right to life just like a piece of property to be given away or alienated if the price (happiness, relief of suffering) is right? And then to be destroyed with our permission once alienated?

In answer to all those questions, I will say this: I have yet to hear a plausible argument why it should be permissible for us to put this kind of power in the hands of another, whether a doctor or anyone else. The idea that we can waive our right to life, and then give to another the power to take that life, requires a justification yet to be provided by anyone.

Slavery was long ago outlawed on the ground that one person should not have the right to own another, even with the other's permission. Why? Because it is a fundamental moral wrong for one person to give over his life and fate to another, whatever the good consequences, and no less a wrong for another person to have that kind of total, final power. Like slavery, dueling was long ago banned on similar grounds: even free, competent individuals should not have the power to kill each other, whatever their motives, whatever the circumstances. Consenting adult killing, like consenting adult slavery or degradation, is a strange route to human dignity.

There is another problem as well. If doctors, once sanctioned to carry out euthanasia, are to be themselves responsible moral agents—not simply hired hands with lethal injections at the ready—then they must have their own *independent* moral grounds to kill those who request such services. What do I mean? As those who favor euthanasia are quick to point out, some people want it because their life has become so burdensome it no longer seems worth living.

The doctor will have a difficulty at this point. The degree and intensity to which people suffer from their diseases and their dying, and whether they find life more of a burden than a benefit, has very little directly to do with the nature or extent of their actual physical condition. Three people can have the same condition, but only one will find the suffering unbearable. People suffer, but suffering is as much a function of the values of individuals as it is of the physical causes of that suffering. Inevitably in that circumstance, the doctor will in effect be treating the patient's values. To be responsible, the doctor would have to share those values. The doctor would have to decide, on her own, whether the patient's life was "no longer worth living."

But how could a doctor possibly know that or make such a judgment? Just because the patient said so? I raise this question because, while in Holland at [a] euthanasia conference ... the doctors present agreed that there is no objective way of measuring or judging the claims of patients that their suffering is unbearable. And if it is difficult to measure suffering, how much more difficult to determine the value of a patient's statement that her life is not worth living?

However one might want to answer such questions, the very need to ask them, to inquire into the physician's responsibility and grounds for medical and moral judgment, points out the social nature of the decision. Euthanasia is not a private matter of self-determination. It is an act that requires two people to make it possible, and a complicit society to make it acceptable.

Killing and Allowing to Die

Against common opinion, the argument is sometimes made that there is no moral difference between stopping life-sustaining treatment and more active forms of killing, such as lethal injection. Instead I would contend that the notion that there is no morally significant difference between omission and commission is just wrong. Consider in its broad implications what the eradication of the distinction implies: that death from disease has been banished, leaving only the actions of physicians in terminating treatment as the cause of death. Biology, which used to bring about death, has apparently been displaced by human agency. Doctors have finally, I suppose, thus genuinely become gods, now doing what nature and the deities once did.

What is the mistake here? It lies in confusing causality and culpability and in failing to note the way in which human societies have overlaid natural causes with moral rules and interpretations. Causality (by which I mean the direct physical causes of death) and culpability (by which I mean our attribution of moral responsibility to human actions) are confused under three circumstances.

They are confused, first, when the action of a physician in stopping treatment of a patient with an underlying lethal disease is construed as *causing* death. On the contrary, the physician's omission can only bring about death on the condition that the patient's disease will kill him in the absence of treatment. We may hold the physician morally responsible for the death, if we have morally judged such actions wrongful omissions. But it confuses reality and moral judgment to see an omitted action as having the same causal status as one that directly kills. A lethal injection will kill both a healthy person and a sick person. A physician's omitted treatment will have no effect on a healthy person. Turn off the machine on me, a healthy person, and nothing will happen. It will only, in contrast, bring the life of a sick person to an end because of an underlying fatal disease.

Causality and culpability are confused, second, when we fail to note that judgments of moral responsibility and culpability are human constructs. By that I mean that we human beings, after moral reflection, have decided to call some actions right or wrong, and to devise moral rules to deal with them. When physicians could do nothing to stop death, they were not held responsible for it. When, with medical progress, they began to have some power over death—but only its timing and circumstances, not its ultimate inevitability—moral rules were devised to set forth their obligations. Natural causes of death were not thereby banished. They were, instead, overlaid with a medical ethics designed to determine moral culpability in deploying medical power.

To confuse the judgments of this ethics with the physical causes of death—which is the connotation of the word *kill*—is to confuse nature and human action. People will, one way or another, die of some disease; death will have dominion over all of us. To say that a doctor "kills" a patient by allowing this to happen should only be understood as a moral judgment about the licitness of his omission, nothing more. We can, as a fashion of speech only, talk about a doctor *killing* a patient by omitting treatment he should have provided. It is a fashion of speech precisely because it is the underlying disease that brings death when treatment is omitted; that is its cause, not the physician's omission. It is a misuse of the word killing to use it when a doctor stops a treatment he believes will no longer benefit the patient—when, that is, he steps aside to allow an eventually inevitable death to occur now rather than later. The only deaths that human beings invented are those that come from direct killing—when, with a lethal injection, we both cause death and are morally responsible for it. In the case of omissions, we do not cause death even if we may be judged morally responsible for it.

This difference between causality and culpability also helps us see why a doctor who has omitted a treatment he should have provided has "killed" that patient while another doctor—performing precisely the same act of omission on another patient in different circumstances—does not kill her, but only allows her to die. The difference is that we have come, by moral convention and conviction, to classify unauthorized or illegitimate omissions as acts of "killing." We call them "killing" in the expanded sense of the term: a culpable action that permits the real cause of death, the underlying disease, to proceed to its lethal conclusion. By contrast, the doctor who, at the patient's request, omits or terminates unwanted treatment does not kill at all. Her underlying disease, not his action, is the physical cause of death; and we have agreed to consider actions of that kind to be morally licit. He thus can truly be said to have "allowed" her to die.

If we fail to maintain the distinction between killing and allowing to die, moreover, there are some disturbing possibilities. The first would be to confirm many physicians in their already too-powerful belief that, when patients die or when physicians stop treatment because of the futility of continuing it, they are somehow both morally and physically responsible for the deaths that follow. That notion needs to be abolished, not strengthened. It needlessly and wrongly burdens the physician, to whom should not be attributed the powers of the gods. The second possibility would be that, in every case where a doctor judges medical treatment no longer effective in prolonging life, a quick and direct killing of the patient would be seen as the next, most reasonable step, on grounds of both humaneness and economics. I do not see how that logic could easily be rejected.

Calculating the Consequences

When concerns about the adverse social consequences of permitting euthanasia are raised, its advocates tend to dismiss them as unfounded and overly speculative. On the contrary, recent data about the Dutch experience suggests that such concerns are right on target. From my own discussions in Holland, and from ... articles on that subject ... I believe we can now fully see most of the *likely* consequences of legal euthansia.

Three consequences seem almost certain, in this or any other country: the inevitability of some abuse of the law; the difficulty of precisely writing, and then enforcing, the law; and the inherent slipperiness of the moral reasons for legalizing euthanasia in the first place.

Why is abuse inevitable? One reason is that almost all laws on delicate, controversial matters are to some extent abused. This happens because not everyone will agree with the law as written and will bend it, or ignore it, if they can get away with it. From explicit admissions to me by Dutch proponents of euthanasia, and from the corroborating information provided by the Remmelink Report and the outside studies of Carlos Gomez and John Keown, I am convinced that in the Netherlands there are a substantial number of cases of nonvoluntary euthanasia, that is, euthanasia undertaken without the explicit permission of the person being killed. The other reason abuse is inevitable is that the law is likely to have a low enforcement priority in the criminal justice system. Like other laws of similar status, unless there is an unrelenting and harsh willingness to pursue abuse, violations will ordinarily be tolerated. The worst thing to me about my experience in Holland was the casual, seemingly indifferent attitude toward abuse. I think that would happen everywhere.

Why would it be hard to precisely write, and then enforce, the law? The Dutch speak about the requirement of "unbearable" suffering, but admit that such a term is just about indefinable, a highly subjective matter admitting of no objective standards. A requirement for outside opinion is nice, but it is easy to find complaisant colleagues. A requirement that a medical condition be "terminal" will

run aground on the notorious difficulties of knowing when an illness is actually terminal.

Apart from those technical problems there is a more profound worry. I see no way, even in principle, to write or enforce a meaningful law that can guarantee effective procedural safeguards. The reason is obvious yet almost always overlooked. The euthanasia transaction will ordinarily take place within the boundaries of the private and confidential doctor-patient relationship. No one can possibly know what takes place in that context unless the doctor chooses to reveal it. In Holland, less than 10 percent of the physicians report their acts of euthanasia and do so with almost complete legal impunity. There is no reason why the situation should be any better elsewhere. Doctors will have their own reasons for keeping euthanasia secret, and some patients will have no less a motive for wanting it concealed.

I would mention, finally, that the moral logic of the motives for euthanasia contain within them the ingredients of abuse. The two standard motives for euthanasia and assisted suicide are said to be our right of self-determination, and our claim upon the mercy of others, especially doctors, to relieve our suffering. These two motives are typically spliced together and presented as a single justification. Yet if they are considered independently—and there is no inherent reason why they must be linked—they reveal serious problems. It is said that a competent, adult person should have a right to euthanasia for the relief of suffering. But why must the person be suffering? Does not that stipulation already compromise the principle of self-determination? How can self-determination have any limits? Whatever the person's motives may be, why are they not sufficient?

Consider next the person who is suffering but not competent, who is perhaps demented or mentally retarded. The standard argument would deny euthanasia to that person. But why? If a person is suffering but not competent, then it would seem grossly unfair to deny relief solely on the grounds of incompetence. Are the incompetent less entitled to relief from suffering than the competent? Will it only be affluent, middle-class people, mentally fit and savvy about working the medical system, who can qualify? Do the incompetent suffer less because of their incompetence?

Considered from these angles, there are no good moral reasons to limit euthanasia once the principle of taking life for that purpose has been legitimated. If we really believe in self-determination, then any competent person should have a right to be killed by a doctor for any reason that suits him. If we believe in the relief of suffering, then it seems cruel and capricious to deny it to the incompetent. There is, in short, no reasonable or logical stopping point once the turn has been made down the road to euthanasia, which could soon turn into a convenient and commodious expressway.

Euthanasia and Medical Practice

A fourth kind of argument one often hears both in the Netherlands and in this country is that euthanasia and assisted suicide are perfectly compatible with the aims of medicine. I would note at the very outset that a physician who participates in another person's suicide already abuses medicine. Apart from depression (the main statistical cause of suicide), people commit suicide because they find life empty, oppressive, or meaningless. Their judgment is a judgment about the value of continued life, not only about health (even if they are sick). Are doctors now to be given the right to make judgments about the kinds of life worth living and to give their blessing to suicide for those they judge wanting? What conceivable competence, technical or moral, could doctors claim to play such a role? Are we to medicalize suicide, turning judgments about its worth and value into one more clinical issue? Yes, those are rhetorical questions.

Yet they bring us to the core of the problem of euthanasia and medicine. The great temptation of modern medicine, not always resisted, is to move beyond the promotion and preservation of health into the boundless realm of general human happiness and well-being. The root problem of illness and morality is both medical and philosophical or religious. "Why must I die?" can be asked as a technical, biological question or as a question about the meaning of life. When medicine tries to respond to the latter, which it is always under pressure to do, it moves beyond its proper role.

It is not medicine's place to lift from us the burden of that suffering which turns on the meaning we assign to the decay of the body and its eventual death. It is not medicine's place to determine when lives are not worth living or when the burden of life is too great to be borne. Doctors have no conceivable way of evaluating such claims on the part of patients, and they should have no right to act in response to them. Medicine should try to relieve human suffering, but only that suffering which is brought on by illness and dying as biological phenomena, not that suffering which comes from anguish or despair at the human condition.

Doctors ought to relieve those forms of suffering that medically accompany serious illness and the threat of death. They should relieve pain, do what they can to allay anxiety and uncertainty, and be a comforting presence. As sensitive human beings, doctors should be prepared to respond to patients who ask why they must die, or die in pain. But here the doctor and the patient are at the same level. The doctor may have no better answer to those old questions than anyone else, and certainly no special insight from his training as a physician. It would be terrible for physicians to forget this, and to think that in a swift, lethal injection, medicine has found its own answer to the riddle of life. It would be a false answer, given by the wrong people. It would be no less a false answer for patients. They should neither ask medicine to put its own vocation at risk to serve their private interests, nor think that the answer to suffering is to be killed by another. The problem is precisely that, too often in human history, killing has seemed the quick, efficient way to put aside that which burdens us. It rarely helps, and too often simply adds to one evil still another. That is what I believe euthanasia would accomplish. It is self-determination run amok.

Questions for Discussion

1 Does the fact that more than one person is involved in each case of euthanasia mean that it is not really a case of self-determination?

2 Should the right to self-determination extend to legalizing duelling and selling oneself into slavery? If not, are there any relevant differences between these cases and that of euthanasia?

3 Callahan distinguishes suffering which stems from "life itself" from that which stems "merely from a sick body." Can this distinction be maintained? Is he right that medicine should be concerned only with biologically based suffering?

4 Callahan says, "If we really believe in self-determination, then any competent person should have a right to be killed by a doctor for any reason that suits him. If we believe in the relief of suffering, then it seems cruel and capricious to deny it to the incompetent." Is he right? If so, does that establish that we should reject the arguments for active euthanasia which are based on self-determination and suffering?

Rodriguez v. Canada (A.G.)

Excerpts from the Judgement

Supreme Court of Canada

In 1993, a 42-year-old woman named Sue Rodriguez went to the Supreme Court of Canada with her claim that she should be allowed to have a qualified physician set up "technological means by which she might, when she is no longer able to enjoy life, by her own hand, at the time of her own choosing, end her life." Ms. Rodriguez was suffering from amyotrophic lateral sclerosis ("ALS," also known as "Lou Gehrig's Disease"), which is a disease in which the sufferer's abilities to swallow, speak, walk, and move without assistance deteriorate, and for which there is no cure. Because of this condition, Ms. Rodriguez would be unable to end her life by her own hand without assistance. She claimed that the law (s. 241(b) of the Criminal Code) prohibiting the giving of assistance to commit suicide violated her rights and thus should be struck down as being unconstitutional. The particular aspects of the Constitution cited to support her case were s. 7, which states "everyone has the right to life, liberty, and security of the person and the right not to be deprived thereof except in accordance with the principles of fundamental justice," s. 12, which provides for protection against cruel and unusual treatment or punishment, and s. 15, which guarantees equal treatment. In short, Ms. Rodriguez claimed that her rights to liberty and security of the person included the right to choose the time and manner of her death, and that able-bodied Canadians are able to exercise that right without external assistance (attempted suicide was decriminalized in 1972). Since she could exercise the same right as other Canadians only with assistance, she claimed the law prohibiting such assistance violated her right to equality.

If Rodriguez succeeded in persuading the court that her rights were violated by the law, she would still have to establish that her rights should win out over any legitimate public goals the law prohibiting assisted suicide might achieve, because s. 1 of the Charter states that "The Canadian Charter of Rights and Freedoms guarantees the rights and freedoms set out in it subject only to such reasonable limits prescribed by law as can be demonstrably justified in a free and democratic society." Accordingly, the court had to decide whether the right to liberty and security of the person extended to the right to end one's life, whether the prevention of assisted suicide amounted to discrimination against people with disabilities such as those of Ms. Rodriguez, and whether, if it did, such violations of her rights could be justified by the reasonable demands of a democratic society. In the end, the court decided by a 5–4 margin that the law against assisted suicide was consistent with the constitution, and so Ms. Rodriguez lost her case. Different justices gave different reasons for their decisions, the main points of which are included here. The first opinion offered is from Chief Justice Lamer, who supports Ms. Rodriguez's claim. Justice Sopinka then offers the opinion of the majority, against Ms. Rodriguez. Justices McLachlin and Cory then each present their own reasons for disagreeing with the majority, and favouring Ms. Rodriguez's claims.

As a further note: having failed in her attempt to have assisted suicide legalized, Ms. Rodriguez nevertheless went ahead and ended her life some months later, and no criminal charges have been laid in connection with that assisted suicide.

★   ★   ★

Lamer, C.J.—

(c) Section 241(b) of the *Criminal Code*

Section 241(b) creates an inequality since it prevents persons physically unable to end their lives unassisted from choosing suicide when that option is in principle available to other members of the public. This inequality is moreover imposed on persons unable to end their lives unassisted solely because of a physical disability, a personal characteristic which is among the grounds of discrimination listed in s. 15(1) of the *Charter*. Furthermore, in my opinion the inequality may be characterized as a burden or disadvantage, since it limits the ability of those who are subject to this inequality to take and act upon fundamental decisions regarding their lives and persons. For them, the principle of self-determination has been limited.

(i) An Inequality

It seems clear that s. 241(b) of the *Criminal Code* creates an inequality in that it prevents persons who are or will become incapable of committing suicide without assistance from choosing that option in accordance with law, whereas those capable of ending their lives unassisted may decide to commit suicide in Canada without contravening the law. Since

1972, attempted suicide has ceased to be a crime in Canada....

I accept that s. 241(b) was never intended to create such an inequality, and that that provision, which contains no distinction based on personal characteristics, does at first sight treat all individuals in the same way. ...[H]owever, saying this does not dispose of the argument that the provision creates inequality. Even if this was not the legislature's intent, and although s. 241(b) does not contain any provision specifically applicable to persons with disabilities, the fact remains that such persons, those who are or will become incapable of committing suicide unassisted, are on account of their disability affected by s. 241(b) of the *Criminal Code* differently from others.

I note in passing that in *Canadian Odeon Theatres Ltd. v. Saskatchewan Human Rights Commission*[*] ... the Saskatchewan Court of Appeal, in connection with discrimination based on a physical disability, has demonstrated the absurdity of the argument that there is no discrimination where persons with disabilities receive the same treatment as the general public. Commenting on this argument, Vancise J.A. stated (at p. 741):

> If that interpretation of the meaning of discrimination in s. 12(1)(b) is correct then

---

[*] Editor's note: Case citations omitted throughout.

the right not to be discriminated against for physical disability protected by the Code is meaningless. If that interpretation is correct, I can conceive of no situation in which a disabled person could be discriminated against in the use of accommodation, services or facilities which are offered to the public. If that interpretation is correct, the owner of a public facility, who offers washroom facilities of the same kind offered to the public generally to a disabled person or offers any other service notwithstanding that it cannot be used by a wheelchair reliant person, will then be found to have discharged his obligation under the Code. A physically reliant person does not, in my opinion, acquire an equal opportunity to utilize facilities or services which are of no use to him or her. Identical treatment does not necessarily mean equal treatment or lack of discrimination.

In short, although at first sight persons who cannot commit suicide and those who can are given identical treatment under s. 241(b) of the *Criminal Code*, they are nevertheless treated unequally since by the effect of that provision persons unable to commit suicide without assistance are deprived of any ability to commit suicide in a way which is not unlawful, whereas s. 241(b) does not have that effect on those able to end their lives without assistance.

The question then is whether this inequality is discriminatory....

To determine whether the inequality created by s. 241(b) of the *Criminal Code* is discriminatory, it must first be determined whether the effect of that provision is to impose on certain persons or groups of persons a disadvantage or burden or to deprive them of an advantage, benefit and so on. It must then be determined whether that deprivation is imposed by or by the effect of a personal characteristic listed in s. 15(1) of the *Charter*, or a similar characteristic.

(ii) Disadvantage or Burden

Does the fact that one is unable to commit suicide in accordance with law constitute a disadvantage or burden giving rise to application of s. 15(1) of the *Charter*?

First, it should be pointed out that the advantage which the appellant claims to be deprived of is not the option of committing suicide as such. She does not argue that suicide is a benefit which she is deprived of by the effect of s. 241(b) of the *Criminal Code*. What the appellant is arguing is that she will be deprived of the right to choose suicide, of her ability to decide on the conduct of her life herself.

In *Turpin* ... this Court recognized that being deprived of the right to choose could be a disadvantage or burden for the purposes of an analysis under s. 15(1) of the *Charter*. The difference in treatment in question in that case resulted from the right certain accused had, but the appellants did not, to opt for trial before a judge alone or trial before a judge and jury. Concluding that loss of this right could disadvantage the appellants, Wilson J. adopted at pp. 1329–30 the observations of the Ontario Court of Appeal, which had stated:

> What we are faced with in this case is not so much whether one form of trial is more advantageous than another, i.e., whether a person charged with murder is better protected by a judge and jury trial or by a trial by judge alone. Rather, the question is whether having that *choice* is an advantage in the sense of a benefit of the law. Mr. Gold, on behalf of the respondents in this case, suggested that it is the having of the option, "the ability to elect one's mode of trial" that was a benefit which accused persons charged with murder in Alberta had over accused persons charged with murder elsewhere in Canada. We have to agree with that submission. [Emphasis in original.]

Can the right to choose at issue here, that is the right to choose suicide, be described as an advantage of which the appellant is being deprived? In my opinion, the Court should answer this question without reference to the philosophical and theological considerations fuelling the debate on the morality of suicide or euthanasia. It should consider the question before it from a legal perspective ... while keeping in mind that the *Charter* has established the essentially secular nature of Canadian society and the central place of freedom of conscience in the operation of our institutions As Dickson J. said in *Big M Drug Mart*, at p. 336:

> A truly free society is one which can accommodate a wide variety of beliefs, diversity of tastes and pursuits, customs and codes of conduct. A free society is one which aims at equality with respect to the enjoyment of fundamental freedoms and I say this without any reliance upon s. 15 of the *Charter*.

He went on to add (at p. 346):

> It should also be noted ... that an emphasis on individual conscience and individual judgment also lies at the heart of our democratic political tradition. The ability of each citizen to make free and informed decisions is the absolute prerequisite for the legitimacy, acceptability, and efficacy of our system of self-government.

In medical matters, the common law recognizes to a very large degree the right of each individual to make decisions regarding his or her own person, despite the sometimes serious consequences of such choices. In *Ciarlariello v. Schacter*, ... Cory J., for this Court recently restated the right of a patient to decide on the treatment he is prepared to undergo (at p. 135):

> It should not be forgotten that every patient has a right to bodily integrity. This encompasses the right to determine what medical procedures will be accepted and the extent to which they will be accepted.

Everyone has the right to decide what is to be done to one's own body. This includes the right to be free from medical treatment to which the individual does not consent. This concept of individual autonomy is fundamental to the common law

Like the *Charter* itself in several of its provisions, therefore, the common law recognized the fundamental importance of individual autonomy and self-determination in our legal system. That does not mean that these values are absolute. However, in my opinion s. 15(1) requires that limitations on these fundamental values should be distributed with a measure of equality.

In this connection, and without expressing any opinion on the moral value of suicide, I am forced to conclude that the fact that persons unable to end their own lives cannot choose suicide because they do not legally have access to assistance is—in legal terms—a disadvantage giving rise to the application of s. 15(1) of the *Charter*. Is this disadvantage based on a personal characteristic covered by s. 15(1)?

(d) Personal Characteristic

In *Andrews*, ... McIntyre J. stated that the first characteristic of discrimination is that it is "a distinction ... based on grounds relating to personal characteristics of the individual or group" (p. 174). Can it be said that the distinction here is "based" on grounds relating to a personal characteristic covered by s. 15(1)? In my view, if s. 15(1) is to be applied to adverse effect discrimination, as McIntyre J. implies, the definition given in *Andrews* should not be taken too literally. I adopt in this regard the observations of Linden J.A., who said in dissent in *Egan and Nesbit v. Canada* ... at p. 196:

> While a distinction must be based on grounds relating to personal characteristics of the individual or group in order to be discriminatory, the words "based on" do

not mean that the distinction must be designed with reference to those grounds. Rather, the relevant consideration is whether the distinction affects the individual or group in a manner related to their personal characteristics....

In other words, the difference in treatment must be closely related to the personal characteristic of the person or group of persons. In the case at bar, there can be no doubt as to the existence of such a connection. It is only on account of their physical disability that persons unable to commit suicide unassisted are unequally affected by s. 241(b) of the *Criminal Code*. The distinction is therefore unquestionably "based" on this personal characteristic. Is it a characteristic covered by s. 15(1)?

A physical disability is among the personal characteristics listed in s. 15(1) of the *Charter*. There is therefore no need to consider at length the connection between the ground of distinction at issue here and the general purpose of s. 15, namely elimination of discrimination against groups who are victims of stereotypes, disadvantages or prejudices. No one would seriously question the fact that persons with disabilities are the subject of unfavourable treatment in Canadian society, a fact confirmed by the presence of this personal characteristic on the list of unlawful grounds of this discrimination given in s. 15(1) of the *Charter*. In *Andrews*, ... McIntyre J. said (at p. 175):

> The enumerated grounds do ... reflect the most common and probably the most socially destructive and historically practised bases of discrimination and must, in the words of s. 15(1), receive particular attention.

There is also no need to undertake any lengthy demonstration in order to show that persons so physically disabled that they are or will become unable to end their own lives without assistance, even assuming that all the usual means of committing suicide are avail-able to them, fall within the classes of persons with disabilities covered by s. 15(1) of the *Charter*, which contains no definition of the phrase "physical disability". Persons whose movement is so limited are even to some degree the classic case of what is meant by a person with a disability in ordinary speech. I prefer to postpone to a later occasion the task of defining the meaning of the phrase "physical disability" for the purposes of s. 15(1).

It is moreover clear that the class of persons with physical disabilities is broader than that of persons unable to end their lives unassisted. In other words, some persons with physical disabilities are treated unequally by the effect of s. 241(b) of the *Criminal Code*, but not all persons, nor undoubtedly the majority of persons with disabilities, are so treated. The fact that this is not a bar to a remedy under s. 15(1) seems to me to have been clearly decided by *Brooks v. Canada Safeway Ltd.* ... and *Janzen v. Platy Enterprises Ltd.*....

In *Brooks*, the question was whether unfavourable treatment on account of pregnancy could be regarded as sex discrimination. Responding to the argument that this was not so because all women were not affected by this discriminatory provision, Dickson C.J. said (at p. 1247):

> I am not persuaded by the argument that discrimination on the basis of pregnancy cannot amount to sex discrimination because not all women are pregnant at any one time. While pregnancy-based discrimination only affects part of an identifiable group, it does not affect anyone who is not a member of the group. Many, if not most, claims of partial discrimination fit this pattern. As numerous decisions and authors have made clear, this fact does not make the impugned distinction any less discriminating.

In *Janzen* this Court had to determine whether sexual harassment was a form of sex discrimination. The Court of Appeal had accepted the argument that since all women were not affected by this type of behaviour, no discrimination had resulted. Dickson C.J. rejected this argument as follows (at pp. 1288–89):

> If a finding of discrimination required that every individual in the affected group be treated identically, legislative protection against discrimination would be of little or no value. It is rare that a discriminatory action is so bluntly expressed as to treat all members of the relevant group identically.

(e) Conclusion

For all these reasons, I conclude that s. 241(b) of the *Criminal Code* infringes the right to equality guaranteed in s. 15(1) of the *Charter*. This provision has a discriminatory effect on persons who are or will become incapable of committing suicide themselves, even assuming that all the usual means are available to them, because due to an irrelevant personal characteristic such persons are subject to limitations on their ability to take fundamental decisions regarding their lives and persons that are not imposed on other members of Canadian society. I now turn to considering s. 241(b) in light of s. 1.

(2) Section 1

(a) Introduction

Having found s. 241(b) of the Code to infringe s. 15 of the *Charter*, it is now necessary to determine if this infringement may be justified under s. 1. The onus under s. 1 is on the state to demonstrate that an infringement on a *Charter* right is demonstrably justified in a free and democratic country. The standard that the state must satisfy under s. 1 is now well established and consists of the two branches first outlined in *R. v. Oakes* ... The first branch of the test considers the validity of the legislative objective, while the second branch considers the validity of the means chosen to achieve that objective.

(b) Legislative Objective

The appellant does not appear to dispute that the legislation in question is aimed at the protection of persons who may be vulnerable to the influence of others in deciding whether, when and how to terminate their lives. The trial judge referred to this constituency in the following terms:

> ... those who may at a moment of weakness, or when they are unable to respond or unable to make competent value judgments, may find themselves at risk at the hand of others who may, with the best or with the worst of motives, aid and abet in the termination of life. Section 241 protects the young, the innocent, the mentally incompetent, the depressed, and all those other individuals in our society who at a particular moment in time decide the termination of their life is a course that they should follow for whatever reason.

I accept this characterization. However, while s. 241(b) has always been intended for the protection of such vulnerable people, the context in which this provision operated was altered when, in 1972, Parliament removed the offence of attempted suicide from the *Criminal Code*. The evidence suggests that the offence of attempted suicide was repealed in order to reflect the prevailing societal view that suicide was an issue related more to health and social policy than to the ambit of the criminal justice system. Parliament by so doing was acknowledging that the threat of jail offered minimal deterrence to a person intent on terminating his or her life.

I also take the repeal of the offence of attempted suicide to indicate Parliament's unwillingness to enforce the protection of a group containing many vulnerable people (i.e., those contemplating suicide) over and against the freely determined will of an individual set on terminating his or her life. Self-determination was now considered the paramount factor in the state regulation of suicide. If no external interference or intervention could be demonstrated, the act of attempting suicide could no longer give rise to criminal liability. Where such interference and intervention was present, and therefore the evidence of self-determination less reliable, the offence of assisted suicide could then be triggered.

As I noted above, however, s. 241(b), while remaining facially neutral in its application, now gave rise to a deleterious effect on the options open to persons with physical disabilities, whose very ability to exercise self-determination is premised on the assistance of others. In other words, can it be said that the intent of Parliament in retaining s. 241(b) after repealing the offence of attempted suicide was to acknowledge the primacy of self-determination for physically able people alone? Are the physically incapacitated, whether by reason of illness, age or disability, by definition more likely to be vulnerable than the physically able? These are the vexing questions posed by the continued existence of the offence of assisted suicide in the wake of the repeal of the attempted suicide provision.

The objective of s. 241(b) also must be considered in the larger context of the legal framework which regulates the control individuals may exercise over the timing and circumstances of their death. For example, it is now established that patients may compel their physicians not to provide them with life-sustaining treatment ... and patients undergoing life-support treatment may compel their physicians to discontinue such treatment ... even where such decisions may lead directly to death. The rationale underlying these decisions is the promotion of individual autonomy ... An individual's right to control his or her own body does not cease to obtain merely because that individual has become dependent on others for the physical maintenance of that body; indeed, in such circumstances, this type of autonomy is often most critical to an individual's feeling of self-worth and dignity. As R. Dworkin concisely stated in his recent study, *Life's Dominion: An Argument About Abortion, Euthanasia, and Individual Freedom* (1993), at p. 217: "Making someone die in a way that others approve, but he believes a horrifying contradiction of his life, is a devastating, odious form of tyranny."

I also wish to stress, however, that the scope of self-determination with respect to bodily integrity in our society is never absolute. While there may be no limitations on the treatments which a patient may refuse or discontinue, there are always limits on the treatment which a patient may demand, and to which the patient will be legally permitted to consent. Palliative care, for example, which is made available to ease pain and suffering in the terminal stages of an illness even though the effect of the treatment may be to significantly shorten life, may not necessarily be made available to a person with a chronic illness but whose death is not imminent: see M.A. Somerville, "Pain and Suffering at Interfaces of Medicine and Law" (1986), 36 U.T.L.J. 286, at pp. 299–301. Most important of these limits is s. 14 of the *Criminal Code*, which stipulates that an individual may not validly consent to have death inflicted on him or her. Additionally, it is well established that, under the common law, there are circumstances under which an individual's consent to an assault against him or her will not be recognized ...

With these limitations in mind, I conclude that the objective of s. 241(b) of the Code may properly be characterized as the protection of vulnerable people, whether they are consenting or not, from the intervention of others in decisions respecting the planning and commission of the act of suicide. Underlying this legislative purpose is the principle of preservation of life. Section 241(b) has, therefore, a clearly pressing and substantial legislative objective. For that reason, I find the provision satisfies the first branch of the *Oakes* test. However, I hasten to add that the repeal of the offence of attempted suicide demonstrates that Parliament will no longer preserve human life at the cost of depriving physically able individuals of their right to self-determination. The question to which I must now turn is whether, given the importance of the legislative objective, Parliament is justified in depriving persons with disabilities of their right to an equal measure of self-determination.

(c) Proportionality

The second branch of the test under s. 1 considers whether a reasonable balance has been struck between the legislative objective and the means chosen to achieve that objective. There are three different components to this inquiry. The first component requires that the means chosen to achieve the objective are rational, fair and not arbitrary. The second component requires that the means impair as minimally as is reasonably possible the right in question. Finally, the third component requires the assessment of whether the infringement on the right is sufficiently proportional to the importance of the objective that is sought to be achieved. Only if the legislation survives each of these components may the limitation of the *Charter* right or freedom be found justifiable under s. 1.

(i) Rational Connection

The first component of the proportionality test requires that the means chosen to fulfil the legislative objective be carefully designed to meet the objective. Can it be said that a provision which prohibits a person from aiding or abetting another's suicide has been carefully designed to protect vulnerable people? The government has argued that an absolute prohibition on assisted suicide is necessary as there is no practicable way for the government to divine what the motives of those assisting in a suicide might be. The compassionately motivated, in other words, cannot be distinguished from the corrupt. In light of the irrevocable nature of the act of suicide, the government contends that, in the final analysis, it is necessary and justifiable to thwart the self-determination of some persons with physical disabilities in order to assure the protection of all those who may be vulnerable to being pressured or coerced into committing suicide.

I find that the prohibition of assisted suicide is rationally connected to the objective of protecting vulnerable persons who may be contemplating terminating their own life. As a result of the operation of s. 241(b), it is clear that no one may coercively "assist" another to commit suicide without facing criminal sanction. The limitation of this prohibition to those who require assistance to terminate their own life is, to a certain extent, irrational, since it is based on the untenable assumption that those who require assistance will necessarily be more vulnerable to coercion or other undue influence. As a result, there is no way, under the present legislation, to distinguish between those people whose freely chosen will it is to terminate their life, and those people who are potentially being pressured or coerced by others. Vulnerability, in a sense, is simply imposed on all people who happen to be physically unable to commit suicide independently and the right to choose suicide is therefore removed from this entire class of persons.

This question, however, suggests a problem not so much with the rationality of the means chosen by the state to achieve its objective, but rather with the overbroad nature of the means chosen. The vulnerable are effectively protected under s. 241(b), but so, it would appear, are those who are not vulnerable, who do not wish the state's protection, but who are brought within the operation of s. 241(b) solely as a result of a physical disability. The question of overbreadth in such circumstances is properly dealt with under the second component of the proportionality test.

(ii) Minimal Impairment

Under the second component of the proportionality test, the question that must be answered is whether the provision in question was carefully designed to impair the equality rights of the appellant as little as reasonably possible....

In Reference re ss. 193 and 195.1(i)(c) of the *Criminal Code* (Man.) ... at p. 1199, which also dealt with a provision of the *Criminal Code* reflecting a policy compromise premised on moral values, I stated that Parliament must be afforded a measure of flexibility in its policy choices:

> The role of this Court is not to second-guess the wisdom of policy choices made by our legislators. Prostitution, and specifically, the solicitation for the purpose thereof, is an especially contentious and at times morally laden issue, requiring the weighing of competing political pressures. The issue for this Court to determine is not whether Parliament has weighed those pressures and interests wisely, but rather whether the limit they have imposed on a *Charter* right or freedom is reasonable and justified.

The offence of assisted suicide also may be characterized as "contentious" and "morally laden"; consequently, I think it would be wrong for this Court to unduly circumscribe the ambit of options open to Parliament in addressing the "competing political pressures" that will factor in to such decision-making.

In *R. v. Chaulk*, ... I stated that "Parliament may not have chosen the absolutely *least* intrusive means of meeting its objective, but it has chosen from a range of means which impair s. 11(d) as little as is reasonably possible. Within this range of means it is virtually impossible to know, let alone be sure, which means violate *Charter* rights the *least*." (Emphasis in original.) Similarly, the question to be answered in this case is whether the equal-

ity rights of the appellant have been impaired as little as reasonably possible. In so doing, the concern for the intricate and delicate function of Parliament to choose between differing reasonable policy options, some of which may impair a particular individual or group's rights more than others, should not be misconstrued as providing Parliament with a license for indifference to whatever *Charter* rights it deems necessary....

It was argued that if assisted suicide were permitted even in limited circumstances, then there would be reason to fear that homicide of the terminally ill and persons with physical disabilities could be readily disguised as assisted suicide and that, as a result, the most vulnerable people would be left most exposed to this grave threat. There may indeed be cause for such concern. Sadly, increasingly less value appears to be placed in our society on the lives of those who, for reason of illness, age or disability, can no longer control the use of their bodies. Such sentiments are often, unfortunately, shared by persons with physical disabilities themselves, who often feel they are merely a burden and expense to their families or on society as a whole. Moreover, as the intervener COPOH (Coalition of Provincial Organizations of the Handicapped) observed in its written submissions, "[t]he negative stereotypes and attitudes which exist about the lack of value and quality inherent in the life of a person with a disability are particularly dangerous in this context because they tend to support the conclusion that a suicide was carried out in response to those factors rather than because of pressure, coercion or duress".

The principal fear is that the decriminalization of assisted suicide will increase the risk of persons with physical disabilities being manipulated by others. This "slippery slope" argument appeared to be the central justification behind the Law Reform Commission of Canada's recommendation not to repeal this provision. The Commission stated the following in its Working Paper 28, *Euthanasia, Aiding Suicide and Cessation of Treatment* (1982), at p. 46:

> The principal consideration in terms of legislative policy, and the deciding one for the Commission, remains that of possible abuses. There is, first of all, a real danger that the procedure developed to allow the death of those who are a burden to themselves may be gradually diverted from its original purpose and eventually used as well to eliminate those who are a burden to others or to society. There is also the constant danger that the subject's consent to euthanasia may not really be a perfectly free and voluntary act.

While I share a deep concern over the subtle and overt pressures that may be brought to bear on such persons if assisted suicide is decriminalized, even in limited circumstances, I do not think legislation that deprives a disadvantaged group of the right to equality can be justified solely on such speculative grounds, no matter how well intentioned. Similar dangers to the ones outlined above have surrounded the decriminalization of attempted suicide as well. It is impossible to know the degree of pressure or intimidation a physically able person may have been under when deciding to commit suicide. The truth is that we simply do not and cannot know the range of implications that allowing some form of assisted suicide will have for persons with physical disabilities. What we do know and cannot ignore is the anguish of those in the position of Ms. Rodriguez. Respecting the consent of those in her position may necessarily imply running the risk that the consent will have been obtained improperly. The proper role of the legal system in these circumstances is to provide safeguards to ensure that the consent in question is as independent and informed as is reasonably possible.

The fear of a "slippery slope" cannot, in my view, justify the over-inclusive reach of the *Criminal Code* to encompass not only people who may be vulnerable to the pressure of others but also persons with no evidence of vulnerability, and, in the case of the appellant, persons where there is positive evidence of freely determined consent. Sue Rodriguez is and will remain mentally competent. She has testified at trial to the fact that she alone, in consultation with her physicians, wishes to control the decision-making regarding the timing and circumstances of her death. I see no reason to disbelieve her, nor has the Crown suggested that she is being wrongfully influenced by anyone. Ms. Rodriguez has also emphasized that she remains and wishes to remain free not to avail herself of the opportunity to end her own life should that be her eventual choice. The issue here is whether Parliament is justified in denying her the ability to make this choice lawfully, as could any physically able person.

While s. 241(b) restricts the equality rights of all those people who are physically unable to commit suicide without assistance, the choice for a mentally competent but physically disabled person who additionally suffers from a terminal illness is, I think, different from the choice of an individual whose disability is not life-threatening; in other words, for Ms. Rodriguez, tragically, the choice is not whether to live as she is or to die, but rather when and how to experience a death that is inexorably impending. I do not, however, by observing this distinction, mean to suggest that the terminally ill are immune from vulnerability, or that they are less likely to be influenced by the intervention of others whatever their motives. Indeed, there is substantial evidence that people in this position may be susceptible to certain types of vulnerability that others are not. Further, it should not be assumed that a person with a physical disability who chooses suicide is doing so only as a result of the incapacity. It must be acknowledged that mentally competent people who commit suicide do so for a wide variety of motives, irrespective of their physical condition or life expectancy.

The law, in its present form, takes no account of the particular risks and interests that may be at issue in these differing contexts. The Law Reform Commission used the distinction between these differing contexts to justify its recommendation not to decriminalize assisted suicide in the Working Paper 28, supra, at pp. 53–54:

> the prohibition in section 224 is not restricted solely to the case of the terminally ill patient, for whom we can only have sympathy, or solely to his physician or a member of his family who helps him to put an end to his suffering. The section is more general and applies to a variety of situations for which it is much more difficult to feel sympathy. Consider, for example, a recent incident, that of inciting to mass suicide. What of the person who takes advantage of another's depressed state to encourage him to commit suicide, for his own financial benefit? What of the person who, knowing an adolescent's suicidal tendencies, provides him with large enough quantities of drugs to kill him? The "accomplice" in these cases cannot be considered morally blameless. Nor can one conclude that the criminal law should not punish such conduct. To decriminalize completely the act of aiding, abetting or counselling suicide would therefore not be a valid legislative policy....

I agree with the importance of distinguishing between the situation where a person is aided in his or her decision to commit suicide and the situation where the decision itself is a product of someone else's influence. However, I fail to see how preventing against abuse in one context must result in denying self-determination in another. I remain unpersuaded by the government's apparent contention that it is not possible to design legislation that is somewhere in between complete decriminalization and absolute prohibition.

In my view, there is a range of options from which Parliament may choose in seeking to safeguard the interests of the vulnerable and still ensure the equal right to self-determination of persons with physical disabilities. The criteria for assuring the free and independent consent of Ms. Rodriguez set out in McEachern C.J.'s dissenting reasons in the Court of Appeal seem designed to address such concerns though they relate only to terminally ill persons. Regardless of the safeguards Parliament may wish to adopt, however, I find that an absolute prohibition that is indifferent to the individual or the circumstances in question cannot satisfy the constitutional duty on the government to impair the rights of persons with physical disabilities as little as reasonably possible. Section 241(b) cannot survive the minimal impairment component of the proportionality test, and therefore I need not proceed to the third component of the proportionality test. As a result, I find the infringement of s. 15 by this provision cannot be saved under s. 1....

VI. Disposition

I would answer the constitutional questions as follows:

1. Does s. 241(b) of the *Criminal Code of Canada* infringe or deny, in whole or in part, the rights and freedoms guaranteed by ss. 7, 12 and 15(1) of the *Canadian Charter of Rights and Freedoms*?

Answer: Yes.

2. If so, is it justified by s. 1 of the *Canadian Charter of Rights and Freedoms* and therefore not inconsistent with the *Constitution Act, 1982*?

Answer: No.

I would therefore allow the appeal, with costs to the appellant against the Attorneys General of British Columbia and Canada, and declare s. 241(b) to be of no force or effect, on the condition that the effect of this declaration be suspended for one year from the date of this judgment. During that one-year suspension period, a constitutional exemption from s. 241(b) may be granted by a superior court on application ... In the case of Ms. Rodriguez, in light of the factual record before this Court, it is not necessary for her to make application to a superior court. As long as she satisfies the conditions outlined above, she is granted the constitutional exemption and may proceed as she wishes....

The judgment of La Forest, Sopinka, Gonthier, Iacobucci and Major JJ. was delivered by

Sopinka J.—I have read the reasons of the Chief Justice and those of McLachlin J. herein. The result of the reasons of my colleagues is that all persons who by reason of disability are unable to commit suicide have a right under the *Canadian Charter of Rights and Freedoms* to be free from government interference in procuring the assistance of others to take their life.... I must respectfully disagree with the conclusion reached by my colleagues and with their reasons.

I. Section 7

The most substantial issue in this appeal is whether s. 241(b) infringes s. 7 in that it inhibits the appellant in controlling the timing and manner of her death. I conclude that while the section impinges on the security interest of the appellant, any resulting deprivation is not contrary to the principles of fundamental justice. I would come to the same conclusion with respect to any liberty interest which may be involved.

Section 7 of the *Charter* provides as follows:

> 7. Everyone has the right to life, liberty and security of the person and the right not to be deprived thereof except in accordance with the principles of fundamental justice.

The appellant argues that, by prohibiting anyone from assisting her to end her life when her illness has rendered her incapable of terminating her life without such assistance, by threat of criminal sanction, s. 241(b) deprives her of both her liberty and her security of the person. The appellant asserts that her application is based upon (a) the right to live her remaining life with the inherent dignity of a human person, (b) the right to control what happens to her body while she is living, and (c) the right to be free from governmental interference in making fundamental personal decisions concerning the terminal stages of her life. The first two of these asserted rights can be seen to invoke both liberty and security of the person; the latter is more closely associated with only the liberty interest.

(a) Life, Liberty and Security of the Person

The appellant seeks a remedy which would assure her some control over the time and manner of her death. While she supports her claim on the ground that her liberty and security of the person interests are engaged, a consideration of these interests cannot be divorced from the sanctity of life, which is one of the three *Charter* values protected by s. 7.

None of these values prevail a priori over the others. All must be taken into account in determining the content of the principles of fundamental justice and there is no basis for imposing a greater burden on the propounder of one value as against that imposed on another.

Section 7 involves two stages of analysis. The first is as to the values at stake with respect to the individual. The second is concerned with possible limitations of those values when considered in conformity with fundamental justice. In assessing the first aspect, we may do so by considering whether there has been a violation of Ms. Rodriguez's security of the person and we must consider this in light of the other values I have mentioned....

[After rejecting some arguments which purport to show that the protections of s. 7 do not apply to the case of Ms. Rodriguez, Sopinka J. continues:]

I find more merit in the argument that security of the person, by its nature, cannot encompass a right to take action that will end one's life as security of the person is intrinsically concerned with the well-being of the living person. This argument focuses on the generally held and deeply rooted belief in our society that human life is sacred or inviolable (which terms I use in the non-religious sense described by Dworkin (*Life's Dominion: An Argument About Abortion, Euthanasia, and Individual Freedom* (1993) to mean that human life is seen to have a deep intrinsic value of its own). As members of a society based upon respect for the intrinsic value of human life and on the inherent dignity of every human being, can we incorporate within the Constitution which embodies our most fundamental values a right to terminate one's own life in any circumstances? This question in turn evokes other queries of fundamental importance such as the degree to which our conception of the sanctity of life includes notions of quality of life as well.

Sanctity of life, as we will see, has been understood historically as excluding freedom of choice in the self-infliction of death and certainly in the involvement of others in carrying out that choice. At the very least, no new consensus has emerged in society opposing the right of the state to regulate the involvement of others in exercising power over individuals ending their lives.

The appellant suggests that for the terminally ill, the choice is one of time and manner of death rather than death itself since the latter is inevitable. I disagree. Rather it is one of choosing death instead of allowing natural forces to run their course. The time and precise manner of death remain unknown until death actually occurs. There can be no certainty in forecasting the precise circumstances of a death. Death is, for all mortals, inevitable. Even when death appears imminent, seeking to control the manner and timing of one's death constitutes a conscious choice of death over life. It follows that life as a value is engaged even in the case of the terminally ill who seek to choose death over life.

Indeed, it has been abundantly pointed out that such persons are particularly vulnerable as to their life and will to live and great concern has been expressed as to their adequate protection, as will be further set forth.

I do not draw from this that in such circumstances life as a value must prevail over security of person or liberty as these have been understood under the *Charter*, but that it is one of the values engaged in the present case.

What, then, can security of the person be said to encompass in the context of this case? ...

In my view, ... the judgments of this Court in *Morgentaler* can be seen to encompass a notion of personal autonomy involving, at the very least, control over one's bodily integrity free from state interference and freedom from state-imposed psychological and emotional stress.... Lamer J. also expressed this view, stating ... that "[s]ection 7 is also implicated when the state restricts individuals' security of the person by interfering with, or removing from them, control over their physical or mental integrity". There is no question, then, that personal autonomy, at least with respect to the right to make choices concerning one's own body, control over one's physical and psychological integrity, and basic human dignity are encompassed within security of the person, at least to the extent of freedom from criminal prohibitions which interfere with these.

The effect of the prohibition in s. 241(b) is to prevent the appellant from having assistance to commit suicide when she is no longer able to do so on her own. She fears that she will be required to live until the deterioration from her disease is such that she will die as a result of choking, suffocation or pneumonia caused by aspiration of food or secretions. She will be totally dependent upon machines to perform her bodily functions and completely dependent upon others. Throughout this time, she will remain mentally competent and able to appreciate all that is happening to her. Although palliative care may be available to ease the pain and other physical discomfort which she will experience, the appellant fears the sedating effects of such drugs and argues, in any event, that they will not prevent the psychological and emotional distress which will result from being in a situation of utter dependence and loss of dignity. That there is a right to choose how one's body will be dealt with, even in the context of beneficial medical treatment, has long been recognized by the common law. To impose medical treatment on one who refuses it constitutes battery, and our common law has recognized the right to demand that medical treatment which would extend life be withheld or withdrawn. In my view, these considerations lead to the conclusion that the prohibition in s. 241(b) deprives the appellant of autonomy over her person and causes her physical pain and psychological stress in a manner which impinges on the security of her person. The appellant's security interest (considered in the context of the life and liberty interest) is therefore engaged, and it is necessary to determine whether there has been any deprivation thereof that is not in accordance with the principles of fundamental justice.

(b) The Principles of Fundamental Justice

In approaching this step of the analysis in this most difficult and troubling problem, I am impressed with the caveat expressed by the American scholar, L. Tribe, in his text *American Constitutional Law* (2nd ed. 1988). He states, at pp. 1370–71:

> The right of a patient to accelerate death as such—rather than merely to have medical procedures held in abeyance so that disease processes can work their natural course—depends on a broader conception of individual rights than any contained in common law principles. A right to determine when and how to die would have to rest on constitutional principles of privacy and personhood or on broad, perhaps paradoxical, conceptions of self-determination.

Although these notions have not taken hold in the courts, the judiciary's silence regarding such constitutional principles probably reflects a concern that, once recognized, rights to die might be uncontainable and might prove susceptible to grave abuse, more than it suggests that courts cannot be persuaded that self-determination and personhood may include a right to dictate the circumstances under which life is to be ended. In any event, whatever the reason for the absence in the courts of expansive notions about self-determination, the resulting deference to legislatures may prove wise in light of the complex character of the rights at stake and the significant potential that, without careful statutory guidelines and gradually evolved procedural controls, legalizing euthanasia, rather than respecting people, may endanger personhood.

On the one hand, the Court must be conscious of its proper role in the constitutional make-up of our form of democratic government and not seek to make fundamental changes to long-standing policy on the basis of general constitutional principles and its own view of the wisdom of legislation. On the other hand, the Court has not only the power but the duty to deal with this question if it appears that the *Charter* has been violated. The power to review legislation to determine whether it conforms to the *Charter* extends to not only procedural matters but also substantive issues. The principles of fundamental justice leave a great deal of scope for personal judgment and the Court must be careful that they do not become principles which are of fundamental justice in the eye of the beholder only.

In this case, it is not disputed that in general s. 241(b) is valid and desirable legislation which fulfils the government's objectives of preserving life and protecting the vulnerable. The complaint is that the legislation is over-inclusive because it does not exclude from the reach of the prohibition those in the situation of the appellant who are terminally ill, mentally competent, but cannot commit suicide on their own. It is also argued that the extension of the prohibition to the appellant is arbitrary and unfair as suicide itself is not unlawful, and the common law allows a physician to withhold or withdraw life-saving or life-maintaining treatment on the patient's instructions and to administer palliative care which has the effect of hastening death. The issue is whether, given this legal context, the existence of a criminal prohibition on assisting suicide for one in the appellant's situation is contrary to principles of fundamental justice.

Discerning the principles of fundamental justice with which deprivation of life, liberty or security of the person must accord, in order to withstand constitutional scrutiny, is not an easy task. A mere common law rule does not suffice to constitute a principle of fundamental justice, rather, as the term implies, principles upon which there is some consensus that they are vital or fundamental to our societal notion of justice are required. Principles of fundamental justice must not, however, be so broad as to be no more than vague generalizations about what our society considers to be ethical or moral. They must be capable of being identified with some precision and applied to situations in a manner which yields an understandable result. They must also, in my view, be legal principles. The now familiar words of Lamer J. (as he then was) in *Re B.C. Motor Vehicle Act*, ... are as follows:

> Consequently, the principles of fundamental justice are to be found in the basic tenets and principles, not only of our judicial

process, but also of the other components of our legal system.

> ... the proper approach to the determination of the principles of fundamental justice is quite simply one in which, as Professor L. Tremblay has written, "future growth will be based on historical roots"....

Whether any given principle may be said to be a principle of fundamental justice within the meaning of s. 7 will rest upon an analysis of the nature, sources, rationale and essential role of that principle within the judicial process and in our legal system, as it evolves.

This Court has often stated that in discerning the principles of fundamental justice governing a particular case, it is helpful to look at the common law and legislative history of the offence in question (*Re B.C. Motor Vehicle Act* and *Morgentaler* ... and *R. v. Swain* ...). It is not sufficient, however, merely to conduct a historical review and conclude that because neither Parliament nor the various medical associations had ever expressed a view that assisted suicide should be decriminalized, that to prohibit it could not be said to be contrary to the principles of fundamental justice. Such an approach would be problematic for two reasons. First, a strictly historical analysis will always lead to the conclusion in a case such as this that the deprivation is in accordance with fundamental justice as the legislation will not have kept pace with advances in medical technology. Second, such reasoning is somewhat circular, in that it relies on the continuing existence of the prohibition to find the prohibition to be fundamentally just.

The way to resolve these problems is not to avoid the historical analysis, but to make sure that one is looking not just at the existence of the practice itself (i.e., the continued criminalization of assisted suicide) but at the rationale behind that practice and the principles which underlie it.

The appellant asserts that it is a principle of fundamental justice that the human dignity and autonomy of individuals be respected, and that to subject her to needless suffering in this manner is to rob her of her dignity.... Respect for human dignity underlies many of the rights and freedoms in the *Charter*.

That respect for human dignity is one of the underlying principles upon which our society is based is unquestioned. I have difficulty, however, in characterizing this in itself as a principle of fundamental justice within the meaning of s. 7. While respect for human dignity is the genesis for many principles of fundamental justice, not every law that fails to accord such respect runs afoul of these principles. To state that "respect for human dignity and autonomy" is a principle of fundamental justice, then, is essentially to state that the deprivation of the appellant's security of the person is contrary to principles of fundamental justice because it deprives her of security of the person. This interpretation would equate security of the person with a principle of fundamental justice and render the latter redundant.

I cannot subscribe to the opinion expressed by my colleague, McLachlin J., that the state interest is an inappropriate consideration in recognizing the principles of fundamental justice in this case. This Court has affirmed that in arriving at these principles, a balancing of the interest of the state and the individual is required....

The interests in the area with which we are here concerned involve particularly delicate balancing, and, as Wilson J. has demonstrated, the various common law countries have approached it in rather different ways. I do not wish to undertake the invidious task of examining which is the better way. All seem to me to be reasonable approaches, but what is important is that the *Charter* provisions seem to me to be deeply anchored in previous Canadian experience. By this, I do not mean that we must remain prisoners of our past. I do mean, however, that in continuing to grope for

the best balance in specific contexts, we must begin with our own experience....

Where the deprivation of the right in question does little or nothing to enhance the state's interest (whatever it may be), it seems to me that a breach of fundamental justice will be made out, as the individual's rights will have been deprived for no valid purpose. This is, to my mind, essentially the type of analysis which E. Colvin advocates in his article "Section Seven of the *Canadian Charter of Rights and Freedoms*" (1989), 68 Can. Bar Rev. 560, and which was carried out in *Morgentaler*. That is, both Dickson C.J. and Beetz J. were of the view that at least some of the restrictions placed upon access to abortion had no relevance to the state objective of protecting the foetus while protecting the life and health of the mother. In that regard the restrictions were arbitrary or unfair. It follows that before one can determine that a statutory provision is contrary to fundamental justice, the relationship between the provision and the state interest must be considered. One cannot conclude that a particular limit is arbitrary because (in the words of my colleague, McLachlin J. ...) "it bears no relation to, or is inconsistent with, the objective that lies behind the legislation" without considering the state interest and the societal concerns which it reflects.

The issue here, then, can be characterized as being whether the blanket prohibition on assisted suicide is arbitrary or unfair in that it is unrelated to the state's interest in protecting the vulnerable, and that it lacks a foundation in the legal tradition and societal beliefs which are said to be represented by the prohibition.

Section 241(b) has as its purpose the protection of the vulnerable who might be induced in moments of weakness to commit suicide. This purpose is grounded in the state interest in protecting life and reflects the policy of the state that human life should not be depreciated by allowing life to be taken. This policy finds expression not only in the provisions of our *Criminal Code* which prohibit murder and other violent acts against others notwithstanding the consent of the victim, but also in the policy against capital punishment and, until its repeal, attempted suicide. This is not only a policy of the state, however, but is part of our fundamental conception of the sanctity of human life. The Law Reform Commission expressed this philosophy appropriately in its Working Paper 28, *Euthanasia, Aiding Suicide and Cessation of Treatment* (1982), at p. 36:

> Preservation of human life is acknowledged to be a fundamental value of our society. Historically, our criminal law has changed very little on this point. Generally speaking, it sanctions the principle of the sanctity of human life. Over the years, however, law has come to temper the apparent absolutism of the principle, to delineate its intrinsic limitations and to define its true dimensions.

As is noted in the above passage, the principle of sanctity of life is no longer seen to require that all human life be preserved at all costs. Rather, it has come to be understood, at least by some, as encompassing quality of life considerations, and to be subject to certain limitations and qualifications reflective of personal autonomy and dignity....

Unlike the situation with the partial decriminalization of abortion, the decriminalization of attempted suicide cannot be said to represent a consensus by Parliament or by Canadians in general that the autonomy interest of those wishing to kill themselves is paramount to the state interest in protecting the life of its citizens. Rather, the matter of suicide was seen to have its roots and its solutions in sciences outside the law, and for that reason not to mandate a legal remedy....

(ii) Medical Care at the End of Life

Canadian courts have recognized a common law right of patients to refuse consent to medical treatment, or to demand that treatment, once commenced, be withdrawn or discontinued ... This right has been specifically recognized to exist even if the withdrawal from or refusal of treatment may result in death ... The United States Supreme Court has also recently recognized that the right to refuse life-sustaining medical treatment is an aspect of the liberty interest protected by the Fourteenth Amendment ... However, that Court also enunciated the view that when a patient was unconscious and thus unable to express her own views, the state was justified in requiring compelling evidence that withdrawal of treatment was in fact what the patient would have requested had she been competent.

The House of Lords has also had occasion very recently to address the matter of withdrawal of treatment. In *Airedale N.H.S. Trust v. Bland*, ... their Lordships authorized the withdrawal of artificial feeding from a 17-year-old boy who was in a persistent vegetative state as a result of injuries suffered in soccer riots, upon the consent of his parents. Persistence in a vegetative state was found not to be beneficial to the patient and the principle of sanctity of life, which was not absolute, was therefore found not to be violated by the withdrawal of treatment.

Although the issue was not before them, their Lordships nevertheless commented on the distinction between withdrawal of treatment and active euthanasia. Lord Keith stated ... that though the principle of sanctity of life is not an absolute one, "it forbids the taking of active measures to cut short the life of a terminally ill patient". Lord Goff also emphasized this distinction, stressing that the law draws a crucial distinction between active and passive euthanasia. He stated as follows, at pp. 368–69:

> ... the former [passive euthanasia] may be lawful, either because the doctor is giving effect to his patient's wishes by withholding the treatment or care, or even in cer-

tain circumstances in which (on principles which I shall describe) the patient is incapacitated from stating whether or not he gives his consent. But it is not lawful for a doctor to administer a drug to his patient to bring about his death, even though that course is prompted by a humanitarian desire to end his suffering, however great that suffering may be.... So to act is to cross the Rubicon which runs between on the one hand the care of the living patient and on the other hand euthanasia—actively causing his death to avoid or to end his suffering.... It is of course well known that there are many responsible members of our society who believe that euthanasia should be made lawful; but that result could, I believe, only be achieved by legislation which expresses the democratic will that so fundamental a change should be made in our law, and can, if enacted, ensure that such legalised killing can only be carried out subject to appropriate supervision and control. It is true that the drawing of this distinction may lead to a charge of hypocrisy; because it can be asked why, if the doctor, by discontinuing treatment, is entitled in consequence to let his patient die, it should not be lawful to put him out his misery straight away, in a more humane manner, by a lethal injection, rather than let him linger on in pain until he dies. But the law does not feel able to authorise euthanasia, even in circumstances such as these; for once euthanasia is recognised as lawful in these circumstances, it is difficult to see any logical basis for excluding it in others.

Following Working Paper 28, the Law Reform Commission recommended in its 1983 *Report to the Minister of Justice* that the *Criminal Code* be amended to provide that the homicide provisions not be interpreted as requiring a physician to undertake medical treatment against the wishes of a patient, or to continue medical treatment when such treatment "has become therapeutically useless", or from requiring a physician to "cease adminis-

tering appropriate palliative care intended to eliminate or to relieve the suffering of a person, for the sole reason that such care or measures are likely to shorten the life expectancy of this person" (Report 20, *Euthanasia, Aiding Suicide and Cessation of Treatment* (1983), at pp. 34–35).

The Law Reform Commission had discussed in the Working Paper the possibility of the decriminalization of assisted suicide in the following terms, at pp. 53–54:

> First of all, the prohibition in [s. 241] is not restricted solely to the case of the terminally ill patient, for whom we can only have sympathy, or solely to his physician or a member of his family who helps him to put an end to his suffering. The section is more general and applies to a variety of situations for which it is much more difficult to feel sympathy. Consider, for example, a recent incident, that of inciting to mass suicide. What of the person who takes advantage of another's depressed state to encourage him to commit suicide, for his own financial benefit? What of the person who, knowing an adolescent's suicidal tendencies, provides him with large enough quantities of drugs to kill him? The "accomplice" in these cases cannot be considered morally blameless. Nor can one conclude that the criminal law should not punish such conduct. To decriminalize completely the act of aiding, abetting or counselling suicide would therefore not be a valid legislative policy. But could it be in the case of the terminally ill?

The probable reason why legislation has not made an exception for the terminally ill lies in the fear of the excesses or abuses to which liberalization of the existing law could lead. As in the case of "compassionate murder", decriminalization of aiding suicide would be based on the humanitarian nature of the motive leading the person to provide such aid, counsel or encouragement. As in the case of compassionate murder, moreover, the law may legitimately fear the difficulties involved in determining the true motivation of the person committing the act.

Aiding or counselling a person to commit suicide, on the one hand, and homicide, on the other, are sometimes extremely closely related. Consider, for example, the doctor who holds the glass of poison and pours the contents into the patient's mouth. Is he aiding him to commit suicide? Or is he committing homicide, since the victim's willingness to die is legally immaterial? There is reason to fear that homicide of the terminally ill for ignoble motives may readily be disguised as aiding suicide....

It can be seen, therefore, that while both the House of Lords, and the Law Reform Commission of Canada have great sympathy for the plight of those who wish to end their lives so as to avoid significant suffering, neither has been prepared to recognize that the active assistance of a third party in carrying out this desire should be condoned, even for the terminally ill. The basis for this refusal is twofold it seems—first, the active participation by one individual in the death of another is intrinsically morally and legally wrong, and second, there is no certainty that abuses can be prevented by anything less than a complete prohibition. Creating an exception for the terminally ill might therefore frustrate the purpose of the legislation of protecting the vulnerable because adequate guidelines to control abuse are difficult or impossible to develop.

... In the Netherlands, although assisted suicide and voluntary active euthanasia are officially illegal, prosecutions will not be laid so long as there is compliance with medically established guidelines. Critics of the Dutch approach point to evidence suggesting that involuntary active euthanasia (which is not permitted by the guidelines) is being practised to an increasing degree. This worrisome trend supports the view that a relaxation of the absolute prohibition takes us down "the slippery slope"....

(iv) Conclusion on Principles of Fundamental Justice

... Canada and other Western democracies recognize and apply the principle of the sanctity of life as a general principle which is subject to limited and narrow exceptions in situations in which notions of personal autonomy and dignity must prevail. However, these same societies continue to draw distinctions between passive and active forms of intervention in the dying process, and with very few exceptions, prohibit assisted suicide in situations akin to that of the appellant. The task then becomes to identify the rationales upon which these distinctions are based and to determine whether they are constitutionally supportable.

The distinction between withdrawing treatment upon a patient's request, such as occurred in the *Nancy B.* case, on the one hand, and assisted suicide on the other has been criticized as resting on a legal fiction—that is, the distinction between active and passive forms of treatment. The criticism is based on the fact that the withdrawal of life supportive measures is done with the knowledge that death will ensue, just as is assisting suicide, and that death does in fact ensue as a result of the action taken. See, for example, the Harvard Law Review note "Physician-Assisted Suicide and the Right to Die with Assistance" (1992), 105 Harv. L. Rev. 2021, at pp. 2030–31.

Other commentators, however, uphold the distinction on the basis that in the case of withdrawal of treatment, the death is "natural"— the artificial forces of medical technology which have kept the patient alive are removed and nature takes its course. In the case of assisted suicide or euthanasia, however, the course of nature is interrupted, and death results directly from the human action taken (E. W. Keyserlingk, Sanctity of Life or Quality of Life in the Context of Ethics, Medicine and Law (1979), a study paper for the Law Reform Commission of Canada's Protection of Life Series). The Law Reform Commission calls this distinction "fundamental" (at p. 19 of the Working Paper 28).

Whether or not one agrees that the active vs. passive distinction is maintainable, however, the fact remains that under our common law, the physician has no choice but to accept the patient's instructions to discontinue treatment. To continue to treat the patient when the patient has withdrawn consent to that treatment constitutes battery (*Ciarlariello* and *Nancy B.*, ...). The doctor is therefore not required to make a choice which will result in the patient's death as he would be if he chose to assist a suicide or to perform active euthanasia.

The fact that doctors may deliver palliative care to terminally ill patients without fear of sanction, it is argued, attenuates to an even greater degree any legitimate distinction which can be drawn between assisted suicide and what are currently acceptable forms of medical treatment. The administration of drugs designed for pain control in dosages which the physician knows will hasten death constitutes active contribution to death by any standard. However, the distinction drawn here is one based upon intention—in the case of palliative care the intention is to ease pain, which has the effect of hastening death, while in the case of assisted suicide, the intention is undeniably to cause death. The Law Reform Commission, although it recommended the continued criminal prohibition of both euthanasia and assisted suicide, stated, at p. 70 of the Working Paper, that a doctor should never refuse palliative care to a terminally ill person only because it may hasten death. In my view, distinctions based upon intent are important, and in fact form the basis of our criminal law. While factually the distinction may, at times, be difficult to draw, legally it is clear. The fact that in some cases, the third party will, under the guise of palliative care, commit euthanasia or assist in suicide and go unsanctioned due to the difficulty of proof cannot be said to render the existence of the prohibition fundamentally unjust.

The principles of fundamental justice cannot be created for the occasion to reflect the court's dislike or distaste of a particular statute. While the principles of fundamental justice are concerned with more than process, reference must be made to principles which are "fundamental" in the sense that they would have general acceptance among reasonable people. From the review that I have conducted above, I am unable to discern anything approaching unanimity with respect to the issue before us. Regardless of one's personal views as to whether the distinctions drawn between withdrawal of treatment and palliative care, on the one hand, and assisted suicide on the other are practically compelling, the fact remains that these distinctions are maintained and can be persuasively defended. To the extent that there is a consensus, it is that human life must be respected and we must be careful not to undermine the institutions that protect it.

This consensus finds legal expression in our legal system which prohibits capital punishment. This prohibition is supported, in part, on the basis that allowing the state to kill will cheapen the value of human life and thus the state will serve in a sense as a role model for individuals in society. The prohibition against assisted suicide serves a similar purpose. In upholding the respect for life, it may discourage those who consider that life is unbearable at a particular moment, or who perceive themselves to be a burden upon others, from committing suicide. To permit a physician to lawfully participate in taking life would send a signal that there are circumstances in which the state approves of suicide.

I also place some significance in the fact that the official position of various medical associations is against decriminalizing assisted suicide (Canadian Medical Association, British Medical Association, Council of Ethical and Judicial Affairs of the American Medical

Association, World Medical Association and the American Nurses Association). Given the concerns about abuse that have been expressed and the great difficulty in creating appropriate safeguards to prevent these, it can not be said that the blanket prohibition on assisted suicide is arbitrary or unfair, or that it is not reflective of fundamental values at play in our society. I am thus unable to find that any principle of fundamental justice is violated by S. 241(b).

II. Section 12

Section 12 of the *Charter* provides as follows:

> 12. Everyone has the right not to be subjected to any cruel and unusual treatment or punishment.

In order to come within the protection of s. 12, the appellant must demonstrate two things: first, that she is subjected to treatment or punishment at the hands of the state, and second, that such treatment or punishment is cruel and unusual. In this case, the appellant alleges that the prohibition on assisted suicide has the effect of imposing upon her cruel and unusual treatment in that the prohibition subjects her to prolonged suffering until her natural death or requires that she end her life at an earlier point while she can still do so without help. In my opinion, it cannot be said that the appellant is subjected by the state to any form of punishment within the meaning of s. 12. The question of whether the appellant is subjected to "treatment", however, is less clear....

For the purposes of the present analysis, I am prepared to assume that "treatment" within the meaning of s. 12 may include that imposed by the state in contexts other than that of a penal or quasi-penal nature. However, it is my view that a mere prohibition by the state on certain action, without more, cannot constitute "treatment" under s. 12. By this I should not be taken as deciding that only positive

state actions can be considered to be treatment under s. 12; there may well be situations in which a prohibition on certain types of actions may be "treatment" as was suggested by Dickson J. of the New Brunswick Court of Queen's Bench in *Carlston v. New Brunswick (Solicitor General)* ... who was prepared to consider whether a complete ban on smoking in prisons would be "treatment" under s. 12. The distinction between that case and [others the court considered], and the situation in the present appeal, however, is that in the cited cases the individual is in some way within the special administrative control of the state. In the present case, the appellant is simply subject to the edicts of the *Criminal Code*, as are all other individuals in society. The fact that, because of the personal situation in which she finds herself, a particular prohibition impacts upon her in a manner which causes her suffering does not subject her to "treatment" at the hands of the state. The starving person who is prohibited by threat of criminal sanction from "stealing a mouthful of bread" is likewise not subjected to "treatment" within the meaning of s. 12 by reason of the theft provisions of the Code, nor is the heroin addict who is prohibited from possessing heroin by the provisions of the Narcotic Control Act, R.S.C., 1985, c. N-1. There must be some more active state process in operation, involving an exercise of state control over the individual, in order for the state action in question, whether it be positive action, inaction or prohibition, to constitute 'treatment" under s. 12. In my view, to hold that the criminal prohibition in s. 241(b), without the appellant being in any way subject to the state administrative or justice system, falls within the bounds of s. 12 stretches the ordinary meaning of being "subjected to ... treatment" by the state.

For these reasons, in my view s. 241(b) does not violate s. 12.

III. Section 15

The Chief Justice concludes that disabled persons who are unable to commit suicide without assistance are discriminated against contrary to s. 15 in that they are deprived of a benefit or subjected to a burden by virtue of s. 241(b) of the *Criminal Code*. Two difficult and important issues arise with respect to this application of s. 15:

(1) whether a claim by the terminally ill who cannot commit suicide without assistance can be supported on the ground that s. 241(b) discriminates against all disabled persons who are unable to commit suicide without assistance;

(2) whether deprivation of the ability to choose suicide is a benefit or burden within the meaning of s. 15 of the *Charter*.

These issues would require the Court to make fundamental findings concerning the scope of s. 15. Since I am of the opinion that any infringement is clearly saved under s. 1 of the *Charter*, I prefer not to decide these issues in this case. They are better left to a case in which they are essential to its resolution. Rather, I will assume that s. 15 of the *Charter* is infringed and consider the application of s. 1.

IV. Section 1

I agree with the Chief Justice that s. 241(b) has "a clearly pressing and substantial legislative objective" grounded in the respect for and the desire to protect human life, a fundamental *Charter* value. I elaborated on the purpose of s. 241(b) earlier in these reasons in my discussion of s. 7.

On the issue of proportionality, which is the second factor to be considered under s. 1, it could hardly be suggested that a prohibition on giving assistance to commit suicide is not rationally connected to the purpose of s. 241(b). The Chief Justice does not suggest otherwise. Section 241(b) protects all individuals against the control of others over their lives. To introduce an exception to this blanket pro-

tection for certain groups would create an inequality. As I have sought to demonstrate in my discussion of s. 7, this protection is grounded on a substantial consensus among western countries, medical organizations and our own Law Reform Commission that in order to effectively protect life and those who are vulnerable in society, a prohibition without exception on the giving of assistance to commit suicide is the best approach. Attempts to fine tune this approach by creating exceptions have been unsatisfactory and have tended to support the theory of the "slippery slope". The formulation of safeguards to prevent excesses has been unsatisfactory and has failed to allay fears that a relaxation of the clear standard set by the law will undermine the protection of life and will lead to abuses of the exception. The recent Working Paper of the Law Reform Commission, quoted above, bears repeating here:

> The probable reason why legislation has not made an exception for the terminally ill lies in the fear of the excesses or abuses to which liberalization of the existing law could lead. As in the case of "compassionate murder", decriminalization of aiding suicide would be based on the humanitarian nature of the motive leading the person to provide such aid, counsel or encouragement. As in the case of compassionate murder, moreover, the law may legitimately fear the difficulties involved in determining the true motivation of the person committing the act.

The foregoing is also the answer to the submission that the impugned legislation is overbroad. There is no halfway measure that could be relied upon with assurance to fully achieve the legislation's purpose; first, because the purpose extends to the protection of the life of the terminally ill. Part of this purpose, as I have explained above, is to discourage the terminally ill from choosing death over life. Secondly, even if the latter consideration can be stripped from the legislative purpose, we have no assurance that the exception can be made to limit the taking of life to those who are terminally ill and genuinely desire death.

I wholeheartedly agree with the Chief Justice that in dealing with this "contentious" and "morally laden" issue, Parliament must be accorded some flexibility. In these circumstances, the question to be answered is, to repeat the words of La Forest J., quoted by the Chief Justice, from *Tetreault-Gadoury v. Canada* ... whether the government can "show that it had a reasonable basis for concluding that it has complied with the requirement of minimal impairment". In light of the significant support for the type of legislation under attack in this case and the contentious and complex nature of the issues, I find that the government had a reasonable basis for concluding that it had complied with the requirement of minimum impairment. This satisfies this branch of the proportionality test and it is not the proper function of this Court to speculate as to whether other alternatives available to Parliament might have been preferable.

It follows from the above that I am satisfied that the final aspect of the proportionality test, balance between the restriction and the government objective, is also met. I conclude, therefore, that any infringement of s. 15 is clearly justified under s. 1 of the *Charter*.

V. Disposition

I agree with the sentiments expressed by the justices of the British Columbia Court of Appeal—this case is an upsetting one from a personal perspective. I have the deepest sympathy for the appellant and her family, as I am sure do all of my colleagues, and I am aware that the denial of her application by this Court may prevent her from managing the manner of her death. I have, however, concluded that the prohibition occasioned by s. 241(b) is not contrary to the provisions of the *Charter*.

In the result, the appeal is dismissed, but without costs.

The constitutional questions are answered as follows:

1. Does s. 241(b) of the *Criminal Code of Canada* infringe or deny, in whole or in part, the rights and freedoms guaranteed by ss. 7, 12 and 15(1) of the *Canadian Charter of Rights and Freedoms*?

Answer: No, except as to s. 15 in respect of which an infringement is assumed.

2. If so, is it justified by s. 1 of the *Canadian Charter of Rights and Freedoms* and therefore not inconsistent with the Constitution Act, 1982?

Answer: As to ss. 7 and 12, no answer is required. As to s. 15, the answer is yes....

McLachlin J. (dissenting)—I have read the reasons of the Chief Justice. Persuasive as they are, I am of the view that this is not at base a case about discrimination under s. 15 of the *Canadian Charter of Rights and Freedoms*, and that to treat it as such may deflect the equality jurisprudence from the true focus of s. 15—"to remedy or prevent discrimination against groups subject to stereotyping, historical disadvantage and political and social prejudice in Canadian society": *R. v. Swain* ... I see this rather as a case about the manner in which the state may limit the right of a person to make decisions about her body under s. 7 of the *Charter*. I prefer to base my analysis on that ground.

I have also had the benefit of reading the reasons of my colleague Sopinka J. I am in agreement with much that he says. We share the view that s. 241(b) infringes the right in s. 7 of the *Charter* to security of the person, a concept which encompasses the notions of dignity and the right to privacy. Sopinka J. concludes that this infringement is in accordance with the principles of fundamental justice, because the infringement is necessary to prevent deaths which may not truly be consented to. It is on this point that I part company with him. In my view, the denial to Sue Rodriguez of a choice available to others cannot be justified. The potential for abuse is amply guarded against by existing provisions in the *Criminal Code*, as supplemented by the condition of judicial authorization, and ultimately, it is hoped, revised legislation. I cannot agree that the failure of Parliament to address the problem of the terminally ill is determinative of this appeal. Nor do I agree that the fact that medically assisted suicide has not been widely accepted elsewhere bars Sue Rodriguez's claim. Since the advent of the *Charter*, this Court has been called upon to decide many issues which formerly lay fallow. If a law offends the *Charter*, this Court has no choice but to so declare.

... In the present case, Parliament has put into force a legislative scheme which does not bar suicide but criminalizes the act of assisting suicide. The effect of this is to deny to some people the choice of ending their lives solely because they are physically unable to do so. This deprives Sue Rodriguez of her security of the person (the right to make decisions concerning her own body, which affect only her own body) in a way that offends the principles of fundamental justice, thereby violating s. 7 of the *Charter*. The violation cannot be saved under s. 1. This is precisely the logic which led the majority of this Court to strike down the abortion provisions of the *Criminal Code* in *Morgentaler*. In that case, Parliament had set up a scheme authorizing therapeutic abortion. The effect of the provisions was in fact to deny or delay therapeutic abortions to some women. This was held to violate s. 7 because it deprived some women of the right to deal with their own bodies as they chose thereby infringing their security of the person, in a manner which did not comport with the principles of fundamental justice. Parliament could not advance an interest capable of justifying this arbitrary legislative scheme, and,

accordingly, the law was not saved under s. 1 of the *Charter*.

Section 7 of the Charter

Section 7 of the *Charter* provides:

> 7. Everyone has the right to life, liberty and security of the person and the right not to be deprived thereof except in accordance with the principles of fundamental justice.

It is established that s. 7 of the *Charter* protects the right of each person to make decisions concerning his or her body ... This flows from the fact that decisions about one's body involve "security of the person" which s. 7 safeguards against state interference which is not in accordance with the principles of fundamental justice. Security of the person has an element of personal autonomy, protecting the dignity and privacy of individuals with respect to decisions concerning their own body. It is part of the persona and dignity of the human being that he or she have the autonomy to decide what is best for his or her body. This is in accordance with the fact, alluded to by McEachern C.J.B.C. below, that "s. 7 was enacted for the purpose of ensuring human dignity and individual control, so long as it harms no one else" ...

As Wilson J. wrote in *Morgentaler* ... at p. 164:

> The *Charter* is predicated on a particular conception of the place of the individual in society. An individual is not a totally independent entity disconnected from the society in which he or she lives. Neither, however, is the individual a mere cog in an impersonal machine in which his or her values, goals and aspirations are subordinated to those of the collectivity. The individual is a bit of both. The *Charter* reflects this reality by leaving a wide range of activities and decisions open to legitimate government control while at the same time placing limits on the proper scope of that control.

Section 7 of the *Charter* mandates that if the state limits what people do with their bodies, the state must do so in a way which does not violate the principles of fundamental justice ... It requires the court to inquire into whether the manner in which the state has chosen to limit what one does with one's body violates the principles of fundamental justice. The question on this appeal is whether, having chosen to limit the right to do with one's body what one chooses by s. 241(b) of the *Criminal Code*, Parliament has acted in a manner which comports with the principles of fundamental justice.

This brings us to the next question: what are the principles of fundamental justice? They are, we are told, the basic tenets of our legal system whose function is to ensure that state intrusions on life, liberty and security of the person are effected in a manner which comports with our historic, and evolving, notions of fairness and justice ... Without defining the entire content of the phrase "principles of fundamental justice", it is sufficient for the purposes of this case to note that a legislative scheme which limits the right of a person to deal with her body as she chooses may violate the principles of fundamental justice under s. 7 of the *Charter* if the limit is arbitrary. A particular limit will be arbitrary if it bears no relation to, or is inconsistent with, the objective that lies behind the legislation. This was the foundation of the decision of the majority of this Court in *Morgentaler* ...

This brings us to the critical issue in the case. Does the fact that the legal regime which regulates suicide denies to Sue Rodriguez the right to commit suicide because of her physical incapacity, render the scheme arbitrary and hence in violation of s. 7? Under the scheme Parliament has set up, the physically able person is legally allowed to end his or her life; he or she cannot be criminally penalized for attempting or committing suicide. But the person who is physically unable to accomplish the act is not similarly allowed to end her life. This is the effect of s. 241(b) of the *Criminal Code*, which criminalizes the act of assisting a person to commit suicide and which may render the person who desires to commit suicide a conspirator to that crime. Assuming without deciding that Parliament could criminalize all suicides, whether assisted or not, does the fact that suicide is not criminal make the criminalization of all assistance in suicide arbitrary?

My colleague Sopinka J. has noted that the decriminalization of suicide reflects Parliament's decision that the matter is best left to sciences outside the law. He suggests that it does not reveal any consensus that the autonomy interest of those who wish to end their lives is paramount to a state interest in protecting life. I agree. But this conclusion begs the question. What is the difference between suicide and assisted suicide that justifies making the one lawful and the other a crime, that justifies allowing some this choice, while denying it to others?

The answer to this question depends on whether the denial to Sue Rodriguez of what is available to others can be justified. It is argued that the denial to Sue Rodriguez of the capacity to treat her body in a way available to the physically able is justified because to permit assisted suicide will open the doors, if not the floodgates, to the killing of disabled persons who may not truly consent to death. The argument is essentially this. There may be no reason on the facts of Sue Rodriguez's case for denying to her the choice to end her life, a choice that those physically able have available to them. Nevertheless, she must be denied that choice because of the danger that other people may wrongfully abuse the power they have over the weak and ill, and may end the lives of these persons against their consent. Thus, Sue Rodriguez is asked to bear the burden of the chance that other people in other situations may act criminally to kill others or improperly sway them to suicide. She is asked to serve as a scapegoat.

The merits of this argument may fall for consideration at the next stage of the analysis, where the question is whether a limit imposed contrary to the principles of fundamental justice may nevertheless be saved under s. 1 of the *Charter* as a limit demonstrably justified in a free and democratic society. But they have no place in the s. 7 analysis that must be undertaken on this appeal. When one is considering whether a law breaches the principles of fundamental justice under s. 7 by reason of arbitrariness, the focus is on whether a legislative scheme infringes a particular person's protected interests in a way that cannot be justified having regard to the objective of this scheme. The principles of fundamental justice require that each person, considered individually, be treated fairly by the law. The fear that abuse may arise if an individual is permitted that which she is wrongly denied plays no part at this initial stage. In short, it does not accord with the principles of fundamental justice that Sue Rodriguez be disallowed what is available to others merely because it is possible that other people, at some other time, may suffer, not what she seeks, but an act of killing without true consent. As Lamer C.J. stated in *Swain* ...

> It is not appropriate for the state to thwart the exercise of the accused's right by attempting to bring societal interests into the principles of fundamental justice and to thereby limit an accused's s. 7 rights. Societal interests are to be dealt with under s. 1 of the *Charter*, where the Crown has the burden of proving that the impugned law is demonstrably justified in a free and democratic society. In other words, it is my view that any balancing of societal interests against the individual right guaranteed by s. 7 should take place within the confines of s. 1 of the *Charter*.

I add that it is not generally appropriate that the complainant be obliged to negate

societal interests at the s. 7 stage, where the burden lies upon her, but that the matter be left for s. 1, where the burden lies on the state.

As my colleague Sopinka J. notes, this Court has held that the principles of fundamental justice may in some cases reflect a balance between the interests of the individual and those of the state. This depends upon the character of the principle of fundamental justice at issue. Where, for instance, the Court is considering whether it accords with fundamental justice to permit the fingerprinting of a person who has been arrested but not yet convicted (*R. v. Beare* ...) or the propriety of a particular change in correctional law which has the effect of depriving a prisoner of a liberty interest (*Cunningham v. Canada* ...), it may be that the alleged principle will be comprehensible only if the state's interest is taken into account at the s. 7 stage. The *Charter* complainant may be called upon to bear the onus of showing that long-established or prima facie necessary practices do not accord with the principles of fundamental justice. The inquiry whether a legislative scheme is arbitrary raises different concerns. The state will always bear the burden of establishing the propriety of an arbitrary legislative scheme, once a complainant has shown it is arbitrary. It will do so at the s. 1 stage, where the state bears the onus, and where the public concerns which might save an arbitrary scheme are relevant. This is precisely the way the majority judgments in *Morgentaler* treated the issues that arose there; it is the way I think the Court should proceed in this case.

It is also argued that Sue Rodriguez must be denied the right to treat her body as others are permitted to do, because the state has an interest in absolutely forbidding anyone to help end the life of another. As my colleague Sopinka J. would have it: "... active participation by one individual in the death of another is intrinsically morally and legally wrong" ... The answer to this is that Parliament has not exhibited a consistent intention to criminalize acts which cause the death of another. Individuals are not subject to criminal penalty when their omissions cause the death of another. Those who are under a legal duty to provide the "necessaries of life" are not subject to criminal penalty where a breach of this duty causes death, if a lawful excuse is made out, for instance the consent of the party who dies, or incapacity to provide: see *Criminal Code*, s. 215. Again, killing in self-defence is not culpable. Thus there is no absolute rule that causing or assisting in the death of another is criminally wrong. Criminal culpability depends on the circumstances in which the death is brought about or assisted. The law has long recognized that if there is a valid justification for bringing about someone's death, the person who does so will not be held criminally responsible. In the case of Sue Rodriguez, there is arguably such a justification— the justification of giving her the capacity to end her life which able-bodied people have as a matter of course, and the justification of her clear consent and desire to end her life at a time when, in her view, it makes no sense to continue living it. So the argument that the prohibition on assisted suicide is justified because the state has an interest in absolutely criminalizing any wilful act which contributes to the death of another is of no assistance.

This conclusion meets the contention that only passive assistance—the withdrawal of support necessary to life—should be permitted. If the justification for helping someone to end life is established, I cannot accept that it matters whether the act is "passive"—the withdrawal of support necessary to sustain life—or "active"—the provision of a means to permit a person of sound mind to choose to end his or her life with dignity.

Certain of the interveners raise the concern that the striking down of s. 241(b) might demean the value of life. But what value is there in life without the choice to do what one wants with one's life, one might counter. One's life includes one's death. Different people hold

different views on life and on what devalues it. For some, the choice to end one's life with dignity is infinitely preferable to the inevitable pain and diminishment of a long, slow decline. Section 7 protects that choice against arbitrary state action which would remove it.

In summary, the law draws a distinction between suicide and assisted suicide. The latter is criminal, the former is not. The effect of the distinction is to prevent people like Sue Rodriguez from exercising the autonomy over their bodies available to other people. The distinction, to borrow the language of the Law Reform Commission of Canada, "is difficult to justify on grounds of logic alone": Working Paper 28, *Euthanasia, Aiding Suicide and Cessation of Treatment* (1982), at p. 53. In short, it is arbitrary. The objective that motivates the legislative scheme that Parliament has enacted to treat suicide is not reflected in its treatment of assisted suicide. It follows that the s. 241(b) prohibition violates the fundamental principles of justice and that s. 7 is breached.

Section 1 of the Charter

A law which violates the principles of fundamental justice under s. 7 of the *Charter* may be saved under s. 1 of the *Charter* if the state proves that it is "reasonable ... [and] demonstrably justified in a free and democratic society".

The first thing which the state must show is that the law serves an objective important enough to outweigh the seriousness of the infringement of individual liberties. What then is the objective of the provision of the *Criminal Code* which criminalizes the act of assisting another to commit suicide? It cannot be the prevention of suicide, since Parliament has decriminalized suicide. It cannot be the prevention of the physical act of assisting in bringing about death, since, as discussed above, in many circumstances that act is not a crime. The true objective, it seems, is a practical one. It is the fear that if people are allowed to assist other people in committing suicide, the power will be abused in a way that may lead to the killing of those who have not truly and of their free will consented to death. It is this concern which my colleague Sopinka J. underscores in saying that the purpose of s. 241(b) is "the protection of the vulnerable who might be induced in moments of weakness to commit suicide" (p. 595).

This justification for s. 241(b) embraces two distinct concerns. The first is the fear that unless assisted suicide is prohibited, it will be used as cloak, not for suicide, but for murder. Viewed thus, the objective of the prohibition is not to prohibit what it purports to prohibit, namely assistance in suicide, but to prohibit another crime, murder or other forms of culpable homicide.

I entertain considerable doubt whether a law which infringes the principles of fundamental justice can be found to be reasonable and demonstrably justified on the sole ground that crimes other than those which it prohibits may become more frequent if it is not present. In Canada it is not clear that such a provision is necessary; there is a sufficient remedy in the offences of culpable homicide. Nevertheless, the fear cannot be dismissed cavalierly; there is some evidence from foreign jurisdictions indicating that legal codes which permit assisted suicide may be linked to cases of involuntary deaths of the aging and disabled.

The second concern is that even where consent to death is given, the consent may not in fact be voluntary. There is concern that individuals will, for example, consent while in the grips of transitory depression. There is also concern that the decision to end one's life may have been influenced by others. It is argued that to permit assisted suicide will permit people, some well intentioned, some malicious, to bring undue influence to bear on the vulnerable person, thereby provoking a suicide which would otherwise not have occurred.

The obvious response to this concern is that the same dangers are present in any suicide. People are led to commit suicide while in the throes of depression and it is not regarded as criminal conduct. Moreover, this appeal is concerned with s. 241(b) of the *Criminal Code*. Section 241(a), which prohibits counselling in suicide, remains in force even if it is found that s. 241(b) is unconstitutional. But bearing in mind the peculiar vulnerability of the physically disabled, it might be facile to leave the question there. The danger of transitory or improperly induced consent must be squarely faced.

The concern for deaths produced by outside influence or depression centre on the concept of consent. If a person of sound mind, fully aware of all relevant circumstances, comes to the decision to end her life at a certain point, as Sue Rodriguez has, it is difficult to argue that the criminal law should operate to prevent her, given that it does not so operate in the case of others throughout society. The fear is that a person who does not consent may be murdered, or that the consent of a vulnerable person may be improperly procured.

Are these fears, real as they are, sufficient to override Sue Rodriguez's entitlement under s. 7 of the *Charter* to end her life in the manner and at the time of her choosing? If the absolute prohibition on assisted suicide were truly necessary to ensure that killings without consent or with improperly obtained consent did not occur, the answer might well be affirmative. If, on the other hand, the safeguards in the existing law, supplemented by directives such as those proposed by McEachern C.J. below are sufficient to meet the concerns about false consent, withholding from Sue Rodriguez the choice to end her life, which is enjoyed by able-bodied persons, is neither necessary nor justified.

In my view, the existing provisions in the *Criminal Code* go a considerable distance to meeting the concerns of lack of consent and improperly obtained consent. A person who causes the death of an ill or handicapped person without that person's consent can be prosecuted under the provisions for culpable homicide. The cause of death having been established, it will be for the person who administered the cause to establish that the death was really a suicide, to which the deceased consented. The existence of a criminal penalty for those unable to establish this should be sufficient to deter killings without consent or where consent is unclear. As noted above, counselling suicide would also remain a criminal offence under s. 241(a). Thus the bringing of undue influence upon a vulnerable person would remain prohibited.

These provisions may be supplemented, by way of a remedy on this appeal, by a further stipulation requiring court orders to permit the assistance of suicide in a particular case. The judge must be satisfied that the consent is freely given with a full appreciation of all the circumstances. This will ensure that only those who truly desire to bring their lives to an end obtain assistance. While this may be to ask more of Ms. Rodriguez than is asked of the physically able person who seeks to commit suicide, the additional precautions are arguably justified by the peculiar vulnerability of the person who is physically unable to take her own life.

I conclude that the infringement of s. 7 of the *Charter* by s. 241(b) has not been shown to be demonstrably justified under s. 1 of the *Charter*.

The Respective Roles of Parliament and the Courts

It was strenuously argued that it was the role of Parliament to deal with assisted suicide and that the Court should not enter on the question. These arguments echo the views of the justices of the majority of the Court of Appeal below. Hollinrake J.A. stated: "it is my

view in areas with public opinion at either extreme, and which involve basically philosophical and not legal considerations, it is proper that the matter be left in the hands of Parliament as historically has been the case" (p. 177). Proudfoot J.A. added: "On the material available to us, we are in no position to assess the consensus in Canada with respect to assisted suicide.... I would leave to Parliament the responsibility of taking the pulse of the nation" (p. 186).

Were the task before me that of taking the pulse of the nation, I too should quail, although as a matter of constitutional obligation, a court faced with a *Charter* breach may not enjoy the luxury of choosing what it will and will not decide. I do not, however, see this as the task which faces the Court in this case. We were not asked to second guess Parliament's objective of criminalizing the assistance of suicide. Our task was the much more modest one of determining whether, given the legislative scheme regulating suicide which Parliament has put in place, the denial to Sue Rodriguez of the ability to end her life is arbitrary and hence amounts to a limit on her security of the person which does not comport with the principles of fundamental justice. Parliament in fact has chosen to legislate on suicide. It has set up a scheme which makes suicide lawful, but which makes assisted suicide criminal. The only question is whether Parliament, having chosen to act in this sensitive area touching the autonomy of people over their bodies, has done so in a way which is fundamentally fair to all. The focus is not on why Parliament has acted, but on the way in which it has acted....

I would answer the constitutional questions as proposed by the Chief Justice.

The following are the reasons delivered by

Cory J. (dissenting)—I have read the excellent reasons of the Chief Justice and Justices Sopinka and McLachlin. I am in agreement with the disposition of this appeal proposed by the Chief Justice, substantially for the reasons put forward both by the Chief Justice and McLachlin J. The bases for my conclusion can be briefly stated.

At the outset I would observe that all parties to this debate take the same basic position, namely that human life is fundamentally important to our democratic society. Those opposed to the relief sought by Sue Rodriguez seek to uphold the impugned provisions of the *Criminal Code* on the grounds that it assists society to preserve human life. Those supporting her position recognize the importance of preserving the essential dignity of human life, which includes the right of Sue Rodriguez to die with dignity.

Section 7 of the *Canadian Charter of Rights and Freedoms* has granted the constitutional right to Canadians to life, liberty and the security of the person. It is a provision which emphasizes the innate dignity of human existence. This Court in considering s. 7 of the *Charter* has frequently recognized the importance of human dignity in our society. See, for example, *Re B.C. Motor Vehicle Act*, [1985] ... and *R. v. Morgentaler* ...

The life of an individual must include dying. Dying is the final act in the drama of life. If, as I believe, dying is an integral part of living, then as a part of life it is entitled to the constitutional protection provided by s. 7. It follows that the right to die with dignity should be as well protected as is any other aspect of the right to life. State prohibitions that would force a dreadful, painful death on a rational but incapacitated terminally ill patient are an affront to human dignity.

In this regard it was conceded by those opposing this application that it was open to a patient of sound mind to refuse treatment even though that refusal would inevitably result in death. It follows that it is the right of those who are sound in mind to choose death with dignity rather than accepting life preserving treatment. The right of a patient to refuse treatment arising from the common law concept of bodily integrity was recently recognized by this Court in *Ciarlariello v. Schacter* ...

I can see no difference between permitting a patient of sound mind to choose death with dignity by refusing treatment and permitting a patient of sound mind who is terminally ill to choose death with dignity by terminating life preserving treatment, even if, because of incapacity, that step has to be physically taken by another on her instructions. Nor can I see any reason for failing to extend that same permission so that a terminally ill patient facing death may put an end to her life through the intermediary of another, as suggested by Sue Rodriguez. The right to choose death is open to patients who are not physically handicapped. There is no reason for denying that choice to those that are....

I would therefore dispose of the appeal in the manner suggested by the Chief Justice.

Appeal dismissed, Lamer C.J. and L'Heureux-Dube, Gory and McLachlin JJ. dissenting.

Questions for Discussion

1 Is there a "right to commit suicide"? Can such a right be derived from a right to life or a right to security of the person?

2 If all people receive the same treatment by the law, but some people are unable to make use of that treatment because of a physical disability, are those with the disability being discriminated against in a morally objectionable way?

3 Suppose Sue Rodriguez had a right to assisted suicide. Would it be acceptable for the government to prevent her from exercising that right out of a fear of abuse, and harm to others?

Assisted Suicide, Causality and the Supreme Court of Canada

Edward W. Keyserlingk

In the following article, Edward W. Keyserlingk offers a critical assessment of the Supreme Court decision in the Rodriguez case. He distinguishes several different senses of causality in the context of life and death, and claims that the majority decision hinged on what he calls the "standard causality" model. Keyserlingk argues that this model is flawed, and that we should accept instead what he calls the "normative causality" analysis.

★ ★ ★

Introduction

Physicians, nurses and family members are often hesitant about terminating a patient's life support measures, either when requested (now or in advance) by the patient, or when supporting a permanently unconscious patient's life is judged by others to have become "futile". Their reluctance can have a variety of explanations, the most obvious being the enormity of the decision in view of the patient's resulting death. Concern may also arise with regard to the issue of futility: Has life support really become futile in this case? What are or should be the criteria for determining futility? Who should make such a determination?

A third concern which frequently arises is that stopping life support is often seen as equivalent to causing the patient's death. It looks and feels, at least to some of those involved, especially the team members who actually stop the respirator or remove the feeding tubes, as if one is killing the patient. After all, it is sometimes said, if we had not stopped the life support, the patient would have continued to live, or at least would not have died then. Whatever qualms exist will typically be moral ones, though at times accompanied by vague or explicit fears about criminal or civil liability.

Responses from ethics and law to questions about causality in the context of life and death decisions may arguably be grouped into three major views or strands. They are not in every respect mutually exclusive, and in some respects that which distinguishes the views and their proponents is more a question of emphasis and level of analysis than of diametrically opposed positions. With that proviso, the views can legitimately be separated for purposes of analysis and comparison. The first position will be labelled in this paper as the "standard causality" view or explanation. The second will be designated the "empirical causality" view. The third will be referred to here as the "normative causality" position.

Of interest in this paper are the causality stances adopted in the majority judgment of the Supreme Court of Canada in *Rodriguez* v. *Canada (A.G.)*.[1] By focusing almost exclusively on the matter of causality, this comment will not directly address the core of the *Rodriguez* judgment, which dealt primarily with constitutional issues. Nevertheless, in that decision the assumptions and stances on the matter of criminal liability for causing death implicitly or explicitly contributed to the conclusions about whether assisted suicide should be allowed for Sue Rodriguez. Although the three positions to be examined are as much positions on ultimate criminal liability as they are positions on causality, it is the latter, and its role in criminal liability, which is of primary interest in this paper.

I. The "Standard Causality" Position

What will be described under the label of "standard causality" is not, strictly speaking, a "position" on causation, and certainly not a coherent one. It could more accurately be characterized as a series of somewhat incoherent elements and stances comprising the present state of the law on criminal liability in this area. Among the elements in addition to but-for causality are those of intent and distinctions between act/omission, natural/artificial and lawful/unlawful. The "standard causality" view can best be described by applying it to the five different circumstances which follow. A *competent patient* is entitled to refuse or terminate life-supporting treatment, and to continue to provide it in the face of such a (present or advance) refusal would constitute assault. To terminate treatment is therefore not interpreted as causing the patient's death, but simply as allowing the patient to die by respecting his or her autonomy or right to self-determination. To stop a respirator in this situation, for example, is regarded as letting the patient die, not as killing him or her; as an omission, not as an act; as simply passive euthanasia, not as active euthanasia.[2]

If it is established that a patient is *permanently unconscious,* then a family member is entitled to request that futile life support measures be stopped. The cause of death in such cases is said to be the patient's disease or condition, which medicine is powerless to alter, not the act of stopping the respirator. What is involved here is commonly said to be more in the nature of an omission than an act.[3]

A terminally ill patient may (possibly "must") be provided with an appropriate form and amount of *pain medication* to control that patient's pain, even if death is thereby "indirectly" hastened. Because the physician has a duty to alleviate pain, and because it is the alleviation of pain that he or she intends and not to cause the patient's death, then here too the cause of death is said to be the patient's disease or condition, not the pain medication.[4]

The "standard causality" explanation goes on to distinguish all three of the above situations from those of *assisted suicide* and *voluntary euthanasia.* Assisted suicide is prohibited by paragraph 241(*b*) of the *Criminal Code* and is considered by many to be immoral because to so assist is at least to participate in causing another's death. As for voluntary active euthanasia, the final act causing death is that of the doctor, nurse or family member. Death from assisted suicide includes an "act" of assistance, not merely an omission. Death from active euthanasia is by the "act" of another who is no longer simply "omitting", for example, respirator support. In both cases, death is not natural, that is, it is not caused by the patient's disease or condition.

II. The "Empirical Causality" Position

The second view, labelled in this paper as the "empirical causality" position, takes a different tack. Though ethically, legally and logically persuasive for many, the first or "standard causality" explanation is not uniformly reassuring for health care practitioners at the deeper experiential level. Some continue to feel that it is counter-intuitive and does not account for the widely shared belief that their decisions and activities in *all* five circumstances are in some manner, to at least some extent, causative of the deaths which follow.

Similarly, but more emphatically, a number of philosophers, jurists and others maintain that the withdrawal of life support is as much a cause of death as assisted suicide and active euthanasia. After all, they claim, stopping a life-supporting respirator is the empirical cause, the cause-in-fact, of the death. Had the life support system not been terminated, the patient would not have died, or at least would not have died then. It is therefore suggested by those who espouse this second view that assisted suicide, and possibly voluntary euthanasia as well, should be as ethically and legally allowable as are competent refusals of life support, family decisions to stop life support on grounds of futility, and the provision of appropriate pain control even if death is hastened. Those espousing this view tend not to be impressed by counter-arguments against the decriminalization of assisted suicide which highlight the potential dangers of abuse or the added pressures on the vulnerable and those who believe that they are a burden to their family or friends.[5] Others come to the opposite conclusion for the same reason. In effect, they agree that in all these circumstances death is being caused by the act of another and not solely by the patient's disease or condition. However, for that very reason, they maintain that patient and family autonomy concerning life-sustaining technology and pain control measures should be restricted because otherwise they will lead inevitably to the decriminalization of assisted suicide and voluntary euthanasia.

III. A "Normative Causality" Approach

The third position, the one advocated in this paper, is labelled here as a "normative causality" view. A more comprehensive label would be "a normative approach to criminal liability". It is suggested that both the first and second positions are inadequate and much in need of further qualification. First of all, the "standard causality" view is deficient in that it does not acknowledge that stopping a life-supporting respirator is indeed the empirical, scientific or "but-for" cause of death. In such cases, it is not sufficient to claim that the disease or the patient's condition is the cause of death. While

this is particularly evident when the patient is not terminally ill, even if terminally ill, the patient would not otherwise have died at that time. In the final analysis, criminal liability for causing death cannot simply be based upon distinctions between acts and omissions. After all, in medical practice it is by no means clear whether the relevant practice, for instance, of switching off a respirator or stopping medical feeding and hydration, is an act or an omission. In this regard, the third position takes more seriously the experience and hesitations of some health care professionals referred to above, though it does not stop there.

Compared to the second or "empirical causality" view, however, the third position emphasizes not simply scientific causality, the cause-in-fact of a death, but normative or legal causality as well. This more nuanced and comprehensive analysis holds that empirical, scientific or "but-for" causality cannot alone account for what distinguishes assisted suicide from voluntary euthanasia, or what distinguishes both from withdrawal of life support or appropriate pain control resulting in death. Nor can empirical causality alone serve as the basis for deciding upon the criminality of assisted suicide or voluntary euthanasia. Other elements of greater moral and legal significance are, especially, those of duty, legality and estimates of the social consequences of decriminalization.

Act/omission distinctions are not solely determinative of criminal or tort liability. When there is a duty to act, failure to do so could make the omission actionable. However, "whether there is such a duty to act is a legal conclusion. not a matter of policy-free factfinding."[6] Causality in law is, in the final analysis, a normative or policy choice. To stop a life-supporting respirator at a competent patient's request, or because life support has become futile, is legal. However, if life support is neither refused nor futile, then a court could find that the physician's act (or omission) was the legal cause of the patient's death. In both cases, the physician's act is the empirical cause-in-fact of the death. Concluding in the first case that the patient's condition was the cause of death is, from the perspective of this normative causality analysis, only a shorthand affirmation, a policy-based conclusion, that a court would not find the physician liable or responsible for the consequences which occurred, that the act was not the legal or proximate cause of death.[7]

As for the provision of appropriate pain control, from the perspective of this third normative position a similar analysis applies. In effect, our society, criminal law and courts have made an implicit policy decision that it is acceptable in view of medicine's mandate to relieve suffering, to provide pain control measures sufficient for its alleviation, even if they also hasten death. The normative and legal criterion is not whether death is caused, but whether the dosage is appropriate for that person's pain.

IV. Normative Concerns about Assisted Suicide

What then can distinguish withdrawing life support treatment from assisted suicide? What could justify imposing criminal liability for the latter but not for the former? From the perspective of this "normative causality" analysis, such justification is not found by stating that the withdrawal of life support is an "omission" and assisted suicide is a "provision" (of death assistance). There are arguably three main policy justifications for maintaining criminal liability for assisted suicide.

One possible policy justification is the traditional ground of protecting a vulnerable minority, the psychologically unsound.[8] Some who accept this as a valid concern claim that it does not justify the prohibition of assisting the suicides of rational persons.[9] Others respond that rational suicide may be rare and

may often be the result of failure to recognize treatable depression or to provide effective pain management. Furthermore, it is suggested that the social sanctioning of rational suicide and assisted suicide may result in an increase in irrational suicide and irrational assisted suicide, and put increased pressure on the elderly and those who feel that they are burdensome to kill themselves or request suicide assistance.[10]

A second policy reason advanced for maintaining the criminal liability of assisted suicide is that assisted suicide could be used as a way of disguising murder. That was the reasoning behind the formulation in the American Law Institute's *Model Penal Code,* which made causation of suicide criminal homicide if it involved force, duration or deception.[11] This same concern influenced the Law Reform Commission of Canada to propose the maintenance of criminal liability for aiding suicide.[12] The number of reported cases in which persons who caused suicide were charged with murder, or could have been, makes this concern a legitimate one.[13]

A third policy argument made against decriminalizing assisted suicide is that distinguishing assisted suicide from voluntary euthanasia can be so difficult that legalizing the former could lead to condoning the latter. Whether or not one subscribes to the view of Joseph Fletcher that voluntary euthanasia is simply a form of suicide,[14] there clearly are circumstances in which the activities involved make it hard to distinguish the two. Consider, for example, the physician who places the glass with a lethal dosage beside the patient, or hands it to the patient unable to lift it, or pours it down the throat of a patient unable to hold the glass. Who performs the final act, the one that results in death?

Clearly, the strength of this argument depends upon the ability to establish the undesirability of a policy permitting voluntary euthanasia independent of cause-in-fact similarities with assisted suicide, and even if the latter could be justified in some respects. One plausible policy concern is that, in the case of euthanasia, the final act leading to death is caused by the doctor (or whomever), not the patient, whereas in assisted suicide causality is shared. There are, as well, legitimate concerns about whether voluntary euthanasia conditions, guidelines, safeguards and procedures could ever be devised and enforced in a manner that adequately protects vulnerable patients. Such concerns are similar to those raised in regard to assisted suicide, but are arguably more serious in the context of euthanasia.

V. The "Standard Causality" Position in *Rodriguez*

How does the majority judgment in *Rodriguez* deal with the matter of causing death in all five circumstances indicated above, particularly that of assisted suicide, which is its primary focus? On which of the three views outlined above does that judgment rely?

The majority judgment written by Mr. Justice Sopinka generally reflects what this paper has labelled the "standard causality" position. He stated that the assisted suicide that Sue Rodriguez was seeking was contrary to the historical understanding of the sanctity of life, one of the values protected by section 7 of the *Canadian Charter of Rights and Freedoms*.[15] It is "choosing death instead of allowing natural forces to run their course."[16] The implication is that, by contrast, when life-supporting treatment is refused or stopped, death *is* the result of natural forces and is not caused by the physician who stops the respirator.

Mr. Justice Sopinka rejected the argument that paragraph 241(*b*) of the *Criminal Code* is over-inclusive and contrary to the principles of fundamental justice since the prohibition of assisted suicide extends to those unable to commit suicide on their own.[17] He stated that the prohibition is one aspect of an appropriate balance between, on the one hand, the

valid interest of the State in preserving life and protecting the vulnerable, and on the other hand, the autonomy and dignity of the individual. That conclusion was based upon several arguments. First of all, the blanket prohibition of assisted suicide has not been revised to date by Parliament, and the decriminalization of attempted suicide did not signify a societal condonation of suicide. Secondly, the blanket prohibition of assisted suicide is the norm in Western democracies, none of which has yet found it to be unconstitutional, and there is no consensus in favour of decriminalizing assisted suicide. Thirdly, the serious concerns about appropriate safeguards, should exceptions be permitted, justify the blanket prohibition. Fourthly, on the basis of personal autonomy and dignity, there are some narrow exceptions permitted to the sanctity of life principle.

For our purposes we need only consider here the fourth point. Mr. Justice Sopinka acknowledged[18] that courts and commentators have established the right of patients to refuse treatment even if its withdrawal results in death, the right of family members to have such treatment stopped if it has become "futile" or "therapeutically useless", and the legitimacy of appropriate palliative care even if death is thereby hastened. Here again, the majority opinion appears to favour the "standard causality" position in the arguments made and sources selected to support the view that while the former are legitimate exceptions, assisted suicide and euthanasia are not. At the same time, however, there is some acknowledgement of the distinction between empirical and normative causality.

Mr. Justice Sopinka cited with approval the recent House of Lords decision in *Airedale N.H.S.* v. *Bland,* which allowed the withdrawal of medical feeding from a patient in a persistent vegetative state with the consent of the patient's parents, but which rejected "the taking of active measures to cut short the life of a terminally ill patient."[19] On the one hand, the rejection of active euthanasia in that decision appears to be based on a presumed cause-in-fact distinction between active and passive euthanasia, rather than on policy considerations supporting the illegality of active euthanasia, regardless of whether the physician's act is an empirical cause of death in both active and passive euthanasia.

On the other hand, there is a suggestion that despite the professed Rubicon between active and passive euthanasia on cause-in-fact grounds, it could nevertheless be crossed in some instances were it not for the inability to prevent abuses. Mr. Justice Sopinka noted approvingly that the basis for the rejection of active euthanasia in *Airedale* (and of assisted suicide by the Law Reform Commission of Canada) "is twofold it seems—first, the active participation by one individual in the death of another is intrinsically morally and legally wrong, and second, there is no certainty that abuses can be prevented by anything less than a complete prohibition."[20]

What this somewhat inconsistent view appears to mean is that, on the one hand, a third party's empirical causing of death from active euthanasia makes it intrinsically wrong, but if a way could be found to prevent abuses, then despite the empirical causing of death and the inherent immorality, that cause-in-fact would no longer be considered the legal or proximate cause of death. A more straightforward analysis, from the perspective of "normative causality", would not assign immorality or illegality on the basis of third party empirical causing of death, but on the basis of other normative policy reasons such as the danger of abuses.

There is yet another example of ambiguity in the majority opinion regarding causality of death and the distinction between active and passive forms of treatment. Justice Sopinka stated that there are two competing viewpoints.[21] One view finds that in both with-

drawal of life support and assisted suicide, death is foreseen and does follow as a result of the action taken. This is essentially what this paper has labelled the "empirical causality" position. The other view claims that in withdrawal of life support, "the death is 'natural'— the artificial forces of medical technology are removed and nature takes its course,"[22] whereas in the case of assisted suicide, "the course of nature is interrupted, and death results *directly* from the human action taken."[23] This is in effect what this paper has designated the "standard causality" position.[24]

Regardless of which view one adopts, Sopinka J. concluded that the physician must nonetheless respect the patient's instructions and "is therefore not required to make a choice which will result in the patient's death as he would be if he chose to assist a suicide or to perform active euthanasia."[25] In effect, however, this conclusion is consistent only with the "standard causality" position. After all, even though requested by the patient, the physician's withdrawal of life support is the empirical cause-in-fact of death and remains a choice that will "result in the patient's death."[26] If, on the other hand, Mr. Justice Sopinka meant that the physician's withdrawal of life support in that case is not the "legal" cause of the patient's death, since the normative policy in this case gives precedence to patient autonomy, then his position would be consistent with what has been designated in this paper as the "normative causality" position.

It may not be far-fetched to claim that the very fact that the majority judgment placed as much emphasis as it did on the matter of societal consensus is an implicit acceptance of the "normative causality" position. Although Mr. Justice Sopinka concluded that there is at present no societal consensus in favour of decriminalizing assisted suicide, he implied that should there be evidence of such a consensus, the blanket prohibition against it could be modified.[27] The judgment appears to accept that in assisted suicide the physician's act is a cause-in-fact of the patient's death (a choice resulting in the patient's death). Therefore, to envisage the possibility of its decriminalization, in at least some circumstances, means that in the event of decriminalization the physician's assistance would not constitute a culpable, normative or legal cause of death. By Sopinka J.'s own reasoning, it could become an instance of a justifiable cause of death.

VI. Intention and Normative Causality

We come, finally, to the subject of intent. Mr. Justice Sopinka acknowledged that, "[t]he administration of drugs for pain control in dosages which the physician knows will hasten death constitutes active contribution to death by any standard."[28] He went on to distinguish such palliative care from assisted suicide on the basis of intent: "However, the distinction drawn here is one based upon intention—in the case of palliative care the intention is to ease pain, which has the effect of hastening death, while in the case of assisted suicide, the intention is undeniably to cause death."[29]

This analysis is in one respect similar to the "normative causality" view. It acknowledges in effect that a physician's pain control treatment, if it hastens death, is for that reason a cause-in-fact of the patient's death, just as it would be in assisted suicide. It is, of course, the case that, in the psychological sense, a physician would typically intend something different in each case: pain control in the first, and death in the second.

However, from the perspective of causality and criminal liability, what makes intent culpable in the legal sense is the intent to commit an unlawful act, not merely the intent to cause death *per se.* The normative question is whether or not causing death in a particular instance is legally justified or not, and whether or not the physician is acting in a legally protected manner. The prior norma-

tive policy choice made by our society, criminal law and courts is that causing (hastening) death in the pain control circumstance is acceptable in view of the medical mandate to alleviate suffering, and is therefore not an unlawful act. Similarly, causing death by terminating life support at a competent patient's request is not unlawful in view of that patient's right to refuse it.

What relieves the physician of culpable intent is not simply that there is no intent to cause death, but more to the point, there is no intent to commit an illegal act. Death is in fact being caused, and the physician knows it and may even desire it, but assuming the dosage is appropriate for that patient's pain control, there is no intent to commit an unlawful act. Equally, what at present makes the intent culpable in assisted suicide is not the intent to assist the taking of life *per se,* but the intent to commit a presently unlawful act, to act in a legally prohibited manner. What brands that act as lawful or unlawful at a point in time are the same normative or policy-based considerations which lead to deciding which of several causes of death will be considered "the" cause of death for legal purposes. A society's values and norms are not static and will always be subject to challenges and evolution. On the one hand, defining what ought to be criminal acts merely by reference to what is presently unlawful is inadequate and circular. On the other hand, new normative and social considerations may well justify the existing prohibition.

Conclusion

What then does the "normative causality" analysis add in comparison to the essentially "standard causality" approach reflected in the majority judgment of Mr. Justice Sopinka? In some respects, not a great deal. No claim can reasonably be made that the Supreme Court would have concluded otherwise had a more overt "normative causality" approach been adopted. Nor would the reasons advanced in support of that conclusion necessarily have been significantly different. After all, normative policy factors, such as concerns about abuse, played at least as significant a role in the decision to maintain the blanket prohibition of assisted suicide as did assigning (shared) causality for death to the assisting physician. As for the "normative causality" analysis, merely because it finds empirical causation of death in withdrawal of life support, assisted suicide and active euthanasia, does not necessarily mean that this approach is inherently more inclined to promote the decriminalization of assisted suicide and active euthanasia. Normative reasons such as fears of abuse, or an increased risk to vulnerable patients, can be just as, or even more, persuasive from this "normative causality" outlook.

Nevertheless, there are arguably at least two important correctives which a "normative causality" analysis could have added to this decision. First of all, by acknowledging empirical causality in all five circumstances considered, the judgment would have been more reflective of the perceptions of many physicians and family members who have to make the decisions about stopping life support and administering appropriate but lethal pain control. Secondly, by acknowledging that the common denominator in all five circumstances is the physician's act (or omission) causing death in an empirical, but-for sense, the focus could have been more directly on how they are arguably distinct for other normative reasons. They are not likely to be seriously weighed by law reformers, legislators and courts until a more sophisticated and comprehensive approach to the relationship between causality and criminal liability is adopted.

Notes

The research for this paper was supported in part by grant #806-92-0008, awarded by the Social Sciences and Humanities Research Council of Canada.

1 [1993] 3 S.C.R. 519, (*sub nom. Rodriguez v. British Columbia (A.G.)*) 107 D.L.R. (4th) 342 [hereinafter *Rodriguez* cited to S.C.R.]. Due to space limitations, this comment will not consider the causality stances of the three minority judgments.

2 *Nancy B.* v. *Hôtel-Dieu de Québec*, [1992] R.J.Q. 361, 86 D.L.R. (4th) 385 (Sup. Ct.); *Mallette* v. *Shulman* (1990), 72 O.R. (2d) 417, 67 D.L.R. (4th) 321 (C.A.); *Cruzan* v. *Director, Missouri Department of Health*, 497 U.S. 261 (1990).

3 *Airedale N.H.S. Trust* v. *Bland*, [1993] 1 All E.R. 821, [1993] 2 W.L.R. 316 [hereinafter *Airedale*].

4 Law Reform Commission of Canada, *Euthanasia, Aiding Suicide and Cessation of Treatment* (Report No. 20) (Hull, Que.: Supply & Services Canada, 1983).

5 J. Rachels, *The End of Life: Euthanasia and Morality* (New York: Oxford University Press, 1986); D. Brock, "Voluntary Active Euthanasia" (1992) 22: 2 Hastings Center Rep. 10; Note, "Physician-Assisted Suicide and the Right to Die with Assistance" (1992) 105 Harv. L. Rev. 2021.

6 Note, *ibid.* at 2029. This in substance is the position of Lamer C.J. in *Rodriguez, supra* note 1 at 561.

7 Note, *ibid.* at 2030. See also, D.W. Brock, "Forgoing Life-Sustaining Food and Water: Is It Killing?" in J. Lynn, ed., *By No Extraordinary Means: The Choice to Forgo Life Sustaining Food and Water* (Bloomington, Ind.: University Press, 1986) 117.

8 As has been noted, historically in Anglo-American common law there were two other grounds for the assertion of state interest in preventing suicide and prohibiting suicide assistance. One was religious belief, which served as the basis of the denial of funeral rites to suicides. Another was sovereign cupidity, as evidenced by the forfeiture of a suicide's goods, in the feudal period, to his liege lord, and by the fourteenth century, to the coffers of the Crown. In present-day secular societies, only the third historical ground, namely the protection of the vulnerable, merits consideration. See M.T. CeloCruz, "Aid-in-Dying:

Ethical Issues

Should We Decriminalize Physician-Assisted Suicide and Physician-Committed Euthanasia?" (1992) 18 Am. J. Law & Med. 369 at 373–76.

9   *Ibid.* at 397.

10 See Y. Kamisar, "Are Laws against Assisted Suicide Unconstitutional?" (1993) 23: 3 Hastings Center Rep. 32 at 37.

11 *Model Penal Code* § 210.5(1) (Proposed Official Draft 1962).

12 *Supra* note 4.

13 For numerous examples, see C.D. Shaffer, "Criminal Liability for Assisting Suicide" (1986) 86 Colum. L. Rev. 348 at 364–66.

14 *Morals and Medicine* (Boston: Beacon Press, 1954).

15 Part I of the *Constitution Act, 1982*, being Schedule B to the *Canada Act 1982* (U.K.), 1982, c. 11 [hereinafter the *Charter*]. See *Rodriguez, supra* note 1 at 585.

16 *Rodriguez, ibid.* at 586.

17 *Ibid.* at 584.

18 *Ibid.* at 598–601, 606–607.

19 *Ibid.* at 598, citing *Airedale, supra* note 3.

20 *Ibid.* at 601.

21 *Ibid.* at 606.

22 *Ibid.*

23 *Ibid.* [emphasis in original].

24 Mr. Justice Sopinka cited (*ibid.* at 606) a study paper written by this writer for the Law Reform Commission of Canada in support of the "standard causality" approach, namely, *Sanctity of Life or Quality of Life in the Context of Ethics, Medicine and Law* (Ottawa: Supply & Services Canada, 1979). That was indeed the analysis this writer proposed

at that time. However, as readers of this comment will be aware, that is no longer the case.

25 *Rodriguez, ibid.*

26 *Ibid.*

27 The reliance upon and determinations about societal consensus on the subject of issues as contentious and evolving as assisted suicide is laudable in principle, but in practice has its dangers and limits. A first problem concerns the weight that should be assigned to such consensus in formulating and revising law and public policy, assuming consensus can be found. A second problem is where one should look to find it. It is by no means evident that legislation, court decisions or law reform commissions in this country or other western democracies reflect present-day societal views. Current polls may seem to be more reliable sources. They appear to reflect considerable and growing support for the decriminalization of assisted suicide, and suggest that legislation on this subject in Western democracies is increasingly unreflective of public consensus. On the other hand, polls may not themselves be reliable in view of ambiguities in both questions and responses. A referendum may appear to be an accurate indication of public stances, but it too can be prone to the same ambiguities and reflects only the views of those who voted.

28 *Rodriguez, supra* note 1 at 607.

29 *Ibid.*

Questions for Discussion

1 Is Keyserlingk right that the "standard causality" position is made up of "a series of incoherent elements and stances"?

2 Does whether an action is considered the cause of an event depend on policy considerations (i.e., normative judgements)?

The Case of Robert and Tracy Latimer

Rudy Krutzen

In October of 1993, Robert Latimer arranged things so that his 12-year-old daughter Tracy, who had suffered from a severe case of cerebral palsy throughout her life, would die of carbon monoxide poisoning. Since Tracy was unable to communicate, and since Robert Latimer was ostensibly acting so as to provide her with a merciful death, this might be seen as a case of non-voluntary active euthanasia. The ensuing murder trial became the focus of a great deal of attention, emotion, and debate. In the following paper, Rudy Krutzen argues that Robert Latimer did the right thing, and for the right reason. He claims that those who are severely disabled, as Tracy Latimer was, need our help to die as well as to live, and that we must not shy away from making difficult quality-of-life decisions. His discussion encompasses concerns that allowing such actions might lead to abuse of the disabled, or to a slippery slope concerning euthanasia in general, but he claims that all such arguments fall short of the mark.

★ ★ ★

Tracy Latimer was born in North Battleford, Saskatchewan, in 1982. She died painlessly at the hands of her father from carbon monoxide poisoning on October 24, 1993. These are the obituary facts. Behind them lies a story of two persons, one of whom, Tracy, was victimized by her biology, the other, Robert, her father, who was punished by a judicial system for loving his daughter more than he feared it.

A damaged brain at birth foretold a life of utter dependency. Tracy's mind never developed. She could not sit up, talk, or feed herself. Cerebral palsy had strangled her movements and twisted her body. Surgeons fought back, snipping muscles and wiring her spine straight.

At four months, Tracy began having seizures every minute she was awake.... Doctors, after experimenting with a variety of anticonvulsants—phenobarbital, Depakene, Dilantin, Tegretol—finally put her on Rivotril, a drug similar to Valium, with sedative effects. Tracy's seizures eventually dropped to five or six each day. While she could roll over, her reflexes were not responsive and she showed no signs of learning to crawl.

Tracy wore diapers and often needed suppositories to unplug her bowels. Feeding her took about half an hour. She had trouble swallowing....Vomiting was a problem throughout her life.

Tracy had her first operation when she was four. It was now clear that she had a severe case of cerebral palsy, that she was what is known as a totally body-involved, spastic quad. Her damaged brain was sending abnormal signals to all parts of her body, triggering spastic muscle responses that, combined with her seizures, wrenched her frame into twisted, frozen positions. To help relieve tension at her hips and keep them from dislocating ... orthopaedic surgeons in Saskatoon cut the abductor muscles at the top of Tracy's legs.... [As a result] she lost the ability to kick her legs.

The seizures continued.... Doctors decided to cut the muscles in her toes, on the outside of her knees, and again at the top of her legs, and put her in a plaster body cast for six weeks in an attempt to keep her body straight. About seventy-five per cent of "totally involved" children develop an abnormal curvature in the spine, called scoliosis. Another seventy-five per cent develop either a partially or a fully dislocated hip. Tracy had developed both.... By 1989, her back was curved to the right at a fifty-degree angle, into a C shape. This put pressure on her lungs, forcing liquid inside and causing frequent bronchial infections.

Tracy's spine had reached a seventy-three-degree angle in the months leading up to her fourth and final operation in August, 1992. [Anne] Dzus [a paediatric orthopaedic surgeon in Saskatoon] opened up her back, placed two long stainless steel rods one on either side of her backbone, and drilled them into place at the pelvis. Steel cable was wrapped around each vertebra and then pulled around the rods and tied.

The operation was a qualified success.... But the steel rods and cables left her "like a board," says Laura [her mother]. "She was never the same again." Sleeping became a problem. Her left side developed angry bedsores so the Latimers had to shift Tracy to her other side at regular intervals, which was painful as her right hip was fully dislocated.

On October 12, Laura took Tracy to Saskatoon for the last time.... Dzus felt strongly that the hip required surgery... Even if they went ahead and fixed Tracy's hip, Dzus had cautioned that the procedure could leave her in "incredible" pain.... There was nothing to prevent the other hip from dislocating later on, and in the meantime something else could go wrong. "They said they were just treating the symptoms, they weren't treating her problems," recalled Laura.... "There was no end to the surgeries that Tracy was going to have to have." They both felt trapped.... Five days later Tracy was dead.[1]

Robert Latimer did the right thing and for the right reason. In the circumstances, he did what every rational and compassionate person would do and ought to do. The alternative, namely, to continue to subject Tracy to a never-ending schedule of treatment that could do nothing to commute the merciless sentence her biology imposed on her—as both the current law and moral fundamentalists would have

her father do—would be to subject her to cruel and unusual punishment.[2] And that is morally reprehensible and barbaric.

The law disagrees. But that is not surprising. Legal justice and moral justice do not always coincide. Sometimes the law is morally blind—as this case tragically demonstrates—and when it is, it needs to be changed. *It is not because justice matters that we care—rather, it is because we care that justice matters.* Just when and how the law should be changed is a moral, not a legal, matter. It is not the law that determines what is morally right; it is what is morally right that determines what the law should be and how it should be interpreted and applied. This is why blind obedience to the law is morally objectionable.

The foregoing is not the only reason why it is a mistake to think that following the law will ensure that justice is done. Another is that the legal system arbitrarily insists on being its own judge and jury with respect to the question of whether its own laws are just. Juries, for example, have the moral right, and the *de facto* power, to ignore the law if they think it is unjust. But according to the legal system as it is presently constituted, it is illegal for the judge to disclose this crucial fact to the jury. This is not a minor point, for it shows there is a built-in injustice in the justice system that precludes the jury from making a *morally* responsible decision. The end result of this sort of deceit is that the very elements essential in making morally just decisions—love and compassion—the very kind of evidence that differentiates what Robert Latimer did from what Susan Smith did in South Carolina, are all inexcusably excluded from the court's deliberations. In Latimer's case this meant he could not be legally acquitted even if every member of the jury agreed that what he did was morally justified! Hard cases, they say, make bad laws; what is conveniently ignored is that bad laws make hard cases more difficult and tragic than they need be.

It is no wonder the vast majority of Canadians are morally outraged by the verdict. And rightly so. Not everyone, however, agrees.

The Question of Punishment

The reaction of some has been ambivalent. For reasons discussed below, many have been reluctant to commit themselves one way or the other on the question of whether Robert Latimer did the right thing. Uneasy about approving of what he did and at the same time reluctant to categorically condemn his action, they have fastened instead on the question of the appropriateness of the severity of the court's sentence. Their concern in this regard is understandable, for in comparison with the charges brought against others in similar cases, and in light of their subsequent suspended sentences, Latimer's sentence of life imprisonment (without eligibility for parole for 10 years) for second degree murder is clearly more vengeful than just.

On May 15, 1993, Michael W. Power (35) and Cheryl M. Meyers (36) killed Cheryl's 67-year-old father who was dying of terminal brain and lung cancer. Not wanting to undergo the undignified and painful suffering that his wife Rita had undergone before she died of cancer in August 1991, he repeatedly requested that they not let him suffer the way his wife had. Finally, with apparently only a few hours to live, they smothered him with a pillow. Charged originally with second degree murder, they eventually pleaded guilty to manslaughter. On December 23, 1994, a Nova Scotia Supreme Court judge, Justice Felix Cacchione, found that the common-law couple had "acted out of compassion, mercy and love" and gave them a suspended sentence. They were placed on three years probation and ordered to put in 150 hours of community service.[3]

On March 2, 1995, 81-year-old Jean Brush, the survivor of a failed double-suicide pact, pleaded guilty to the lesser charge of manslaughter after admitting she had stabbed to death her ailing husband of 58 years. Judge Bernd Zabel of the Ontario Court's Provincial Division gave her a suspended sentence and placed her on probation for 18 months.[4]

Although both judges are empowered by the law to impose the maximum sentence of life imprisonment for manslaughter, neither did. Neither was blinded by 'the letter of the law' to the 'spirit of the law'. Both recognized the exceptional circumstances in which the defendants found themselves, both recognized the defendants acted out of mercy, love and compassion, both acknowledged that incarceration would not serve the ends of justice, and both acknowledged that the defendants' inerasable knowledge of what they had done left them with a greater loss than any legal punishment the courts might impose could extract. The same judicial enlightenment was notably absent in the judicial proceedings in Latimer's case. Unlike his Eastern colleagues, Randy Kirkham, the prosecutor in the Latimer case, deliberately followed 'the letter of the law' to the letter, ignored the exceptional circumstances of the case, and charged Latimer with first-degree murder. After the trial, with the inflated righteousness of a legal zealot, and despite all the evidence to the contrary presented during the trial, he steadfastly continued to describe Latimer as a "callous, cold, calculated and heartless" murderer who had taken it upon himself to play God in order "to make his own life easier".[5] As this unfounded and prejudicial characterization of Latimer demonstrates, Kirkham, unlike the God he invoked, was obviously not willing to see justice tempered with mercy. When tempering justice with mercy is viewed as tantamount to tampering with justice, it is not surprising that Latimer was treated unjustly.[6]

Although Latimer's inequitable treatment before the law is a matter of legitimate and serious concern, it ought not to deflect attention from the central issue which is whether Robert Latimer was morally justified, in the circumstances, in killing his severely disabled 12-year-old daughter, Tracy. The question of whether he deserves to be punished arises only if what he did was in fact immoral. If he was morally justified in ending his daughter's ineradicable, pointless pain and suffering, he deserves neither to be punished nor rebuked. The claim that he ought to be punished, but not as severely as the law demands, makes no sense if what he did was morally justified. It is equivalent to arguing that someone can be justifiably legally punished for doing what is morally right! But this is absurd. And yet this is precisely what has happened in this case and why the majority of Canadians are condemning the jury's verdict as a travesty of justice.

Society cannot have it both ways. If what he did was wrong, he deserves to be punished. If he did what was right, he deserves to be lauded for his moral courage and not punished for it. There is no in-between.

The Matter of Consent

Those who condemn Latimer are quick to point out that although there are obvious surface similarities between his case and those cited above and the more widely publicized case of Sue Rodriguez with which it is often compared, there is a significant difference between them. The difference is that the severity of Tracy's cerebral palsy was such that she had neither the intellectual ability to comprehend the alternatives of life or death nor the ability to give vocal or written consent to have her life ended. Even sympathetic supporters of Latimer admit to being bothered by the fact she was unable to give consent to having her father kill her. But they ought not to be. For while the matter of consent is of crucial import in the aforementioned cases, in Tracy's case it is simply irrelevant. The worry about the absence of consent on her part only makes sense if she had been capable of giving consent and had refused to do so. But of course she could do neither.

This does not mean her father and/or mother were not justified in deciding for her what was in her best interest. They had made this decision for her every day of her life.

To insist, as some do, that, in the absence of consent on her part, her parents had no right to make decisions on her behalf, is both irrational and morally perverse. For it is to say that because Tracy was never able to consent to *treatment*—never able to say "yes"—that her parents, knowing her cerebral palsy could never be 'cured', were *wrong* in consenting on her behalf to all the medications, drugs, treatments and operations that kept her alive for 12 years. Yet, these are the very same people who, while condemning Robert for acting without Tracy's consent, are absolutely convinced that the *right* thing to have done would have been to continue to pump her full of drugs and to subject her to a series of decreasingly effective salvage operations as long as these assaults on her body kept her alive, despite the fact Tracy was unable to *refuse* to give consent—unable to say "no"!

The same twisted logic surfaces amongst those who claim that when Latimer took it upon himself to decide what was in the best interests of Tracy he was 'playing God'. While they do not think Latimer is qualified to play the role of God, they have no doubt about their own qualifications and ability to play the part of the Almighty. One might well ask: How is it all those who so confidently insist it is impossible for Robert Latimer to know what is in the best interests of Tracy, are so certain *they do know* what is in her best interests? Their unbounded self-righteous conceit does a disservice to us all. It is a thinly disguised attempt to absolve us from the moral responsibility that is ours alone. We have to play God; there is no alternative, for we are the only gods there are.

Armed with the insight of hindsight, some have succumbed to the temptation to blame the medical profession for the predicament

Latimer eventually found himself in. Had the attending physician not resuscitated Tracy in her infancy, had he 'let her die', the ensuing tragic series of events that led to her death would never have occurred. There is no doubt that for some, like Tracy, the only thing better than an early death is not to have been born at all. But she was born and unfortunately there was no way of telling at birth she would be one of the unfortunate 10% at the extreme end of the spectrum of those afflicted with cerebral palsy, that she would suffer the deprivations of severe mental retardation, the painful involuntary contraction of all the muscles in her body, and be subject to recurring seizures. Blaming the medical profession for what happened 12 years later may help in venting one's anger at Nature's indifference to Tracy's plight but it is a pointless and irrational exercise. The only villains in this case are those who, despite the present day knowledge of the everyday horrors of Tracy's life, heartlessly insist that Tracy should have been *forced* to live out her tortured life to the bitter end.

It is not always easy to live and it is not always easy to die either. Sometimes people need help to live and sometimes they need help to die. Tracy needed both. She could not live without help and she could not die without help either. Tracy was fortunate she had loving, caring, and compassionate parents who unselfishly gave her the help she needed to both live and die.

The Abuse of the Disabled

The prosecutor's claim that a verdict of "not guilty" would signal "open season on the disabled" is not only absurd but demeans and insults us all. It is a cheap shot. It implies the able-bodied, unlike the disabled, are all closet Nazis held in check only by the law!

Tracy's cerebral palsy was not, and is not, the issue. Tracy and her parents had lived with that fact twenty-four hours a day for twelve

years. During that time they could have abandoned her, neglected her, or mistreated her. But they did none of these things. Nor did they make life easier for themselves by putting their daughter into an institution and letting others look after her. Instead, they accepted her for who and what she was, kept her and tended to her every need knowing full well that their countless daily sacrifices and tender loving care could not overturn the merciless sentence Tracy's biology had imposed upon her.

But in the end it was the pain—the unmanageable, unbearable, and unredeeming pain—that neither they nor Tracy could live with. It was because the relentless pain she was suffering was *pointless*, that no good would come from it, that her father mercifully ended her life. There is nothing strange about this. Nor is it difficult to understand. People will consent to painful procedures and treatment if that is indeed the only way they can achieve a desirable good such as health or the birth of a baby. But no one in their right mind would consent to being subjected to painful and crippling procedures out of which no good could come. The fact that Tracy was neither intellectually nor vocally equipped to express this axiom of commonsense is no reason to think Tracy was any different from anyone else in this regard. Nor was this severe disability of hers an excuse to treat her as a human guinea pig.

That the disabled who see Tracy's death as a threat to their own survival are prepared to countenance and, indeed, to vociferously insist, that Tracy's parents and society should sanction and enforce the continuation of this kind of inhuman medical experimentation on Tracy, speaks volumes about the cruel selfishness that passes for compassion by those who would have us refrain from ending Tracy's senseless suffering. *They* are the ones who are the real villains in this drama. The very care and compassion they insist they have a right to expect from others, they themselves are not prepared to extend to others! Sadly, the only compassion they are interested in is that which is directed at themselves.[7]

Afraid that they themselves will be unwillingly put to death, the disabled demand that no one who wants to end their life should be allowed to do so and that such persons should be *compelled* instead to live out their lives to the bitter end. But this fear on the part of the disabled is a red-herring in the euthanasia debate. No one is arguing that it is morally justified to end a life worth living. Nor is anyone arguing that the disabled be killed regardless of whether they want to continue to live. That would be absurd. However, to compel someone who wishes to die, to continue to live, is just as absurd, barbaric, and unjustified.

The self-centred rhetoric of spokespersons for the disabled is itself a form of abuse; it politicalizes what is a universal problem. Abuse is not a problem that only affects the disabled. To talk as if it were, makes about as much sense as the claim that racial discrimination is a Jewish issue—namely, none! Despite all the rhetoric one hears to the contrary, racism is not a skin disease; it is not some sort of inbred racial defect of a particular race; nor is it a peculiar affliction inherent in a particular economic class; and neither is it some sort of genetic disorder. It is none of these things. It is rather a universal *human* failing born of moral weakness and ignorance of oneself, others, and the world in which we live. The same is true, *mutatis mutandis*, of all forms of unjust discrimination. Unlike justice, injustice is blind; it is ageless, colour-blind, gender-neutral, and racially and biologically indifferent; it is indifferent to the differences between men and women, young and old, heterosexuals and homosexuals, theists and atheists, blacks and whites, the disabled and the able-bodied, the intelligent and the not-so-intelligent, the poor and the rich, and so on. Moreover, the perpetrators of unjust discrimination are no more identifiable by their biological characteristics and/or their membership in some socially constructed category than are its victims. This is why unjust discrimination is the multifaceted universal problem it is and why it is a problem that concerns us *all*.

Abusive discrimination, in whatever form it surfaces, is a wrong that needs to be righted. Spokespersons for organizations for the disabled have uniformly expressed their relief that Latimer was prosecuted and found guilty—if not of first degree murder at least of murder in the second degree. Underlying their relief is their conviction that the only satisfactory or acceptable safeguard against abuse is the rigid enforcement of some system of sanctions that would admit of no exceptions and that would thereby eliminate even the possibility of abuse. This is the same sort of muddled reasoning that guides those who would have us solve abuses of Medicare or unemployment insurance programs, for example, by abolishing such programs. Such drastic measures would certainly be effective—one cannot abuse what does not exist. However, it would also effectively punish everyone for the misdeeds of a few—a form of abuse worse than that which it is intended to rectify! The same holds true for euthanasia. Categorically condemning euthanasia, regardless of a person's condition, wishes, or circumstances, punishes us all for the possible abuses of a few. This stretches our common sense of justice beyond recognition.

The Rhetoric of Slippery-Slope Arguments

What the disabled and others fear is that if Latimer is not punished, if the killing of his daughter is exempted from the general condemnation of the killing of innocent persons, then the lives of all of us are at risk. We will have begun to descend a slippery slope which will inevitably land us in moral chaos. This is the fear and the rhetorical means by which many have tried to justify their heartless and unforgiving condemnation of Latimer.

Slippery-slope arguments are notoriously slippery arguments. They can have a positive or a negative function. Their positive function is to persuade people that the step they are contemplating taking is both rational and morally permissible. The thrust of *positive* slippery-slope arguments is to bring about needed moral reforms and change the status quo. Alternatively, *negative* slippery-slope arguments are designed to maintain the status quo by dissuading people from taking a step in a certain direction on the grounds that the proposed change would only make things worse than they already are.

The standard use of slippery-slope arguments is the negative one of 'painting the Devil on the wall.' As such they are easy to formulate but difficult to substantiate. The following is typical:

> Once a single brick is removed from the dam protecting the sanctity of all life, the entire dam is liable to collapse and every life is at risk.... From the killing of a malformed infant, it is only one slippery step to the elimination of cripples or senile people in advanced stages of degeneration. From there it is only one further step to the destruction of other 'undesirables' burdening society.[8]

The prosecutor's claim that a "not guilty" verdict in the Latimer case would signal "open season on the disabled" is a variation on the same theme. In both cases the claim is that one thing leads to another and before we know it we will find ourselves in a state of moral anarchy.

What makes such slippery-slope arguments particularly slippery is that it is easy to slip into thinking that because the moral anarchy depicted in the argument is a *logical* possibility it is therefore a *real* possibility. But these, however, are two distinct claims. It is one thing to argue that once we begin to descend the slope the *possibility* exists that we will continue to slide until the bottom is reached but quite another to argue that, *as a matter of fact,* no

foothold *can* be carved out on the slope and that sliding to the bottom is inevitable. Showing that something *might* happen does not prove that it *must* or *will* happen.

It is not up to others to show that what might happen could not happen. The onus is on the prosecutor, the spokespersons for the disabled, and others of the same persuasion, to demonstrate that what *might* happen *will* happen. In light of the absence of such evidence their appeal to the slippery-slope is nothing more than empty rhetoric—not that that matters to them. Their bluster knows no end. With an arrogance born of ignorance, they shamelessly continue to insist that the rest of us—unlike themselves!—lack the requisite intelligence, knowledge, and moral character to know when, where, and how, to carve out a foothold on the slope. Suffice it to say, their lack of confidence in the ability of the rest of us to make morally discriminating judgments is based less on fact than it is on their own apparent incompetency in this regard. Most people with moral commonsense have no difficulty in carving out a foothold on the slope, of drawing a line between the Latimers and Susan Smiths of this world.

Drawing The Line

Perplexed and bothered by the complexities involved in drawing the line at one point rather than another, the question invariably raised is: "Where are we to draw the line?" One common response to this question is that *no* line ought to be drawn at all. But this is not the solution to the problem many think it is. It is not a solution because it is impossible *not* to draw a line at some point or other. Refusing to draw a line just means the line is being drawn at one or the other extreme ends of the spectrum rather than at some disputed point in between.

Refusing to draw a line does not solve our problems. It simply ignores them. However, ignoring a problem is no solution. If anything, it makes matters worse. Not the least of the problems this kind of pseudo-solution creates is that it compromises our moral integrity. Worse, the pretence that such decisions are not made is both unrealistic and hypocritical. The harsh realities of life force us to make decisions of one kind or another—to make 'quality of life' decisions—whether we want to or not. Such decisions are made all the time in medicine. As well, political decisions regarding health care are 'quality of life' decisions even though they are not explicitly described as such. Nevertheless that is what they are. The pretence that such decisions are not made is a strained denial of reality.

The choice, then, that confronts us, is not whether we ought to make 'quality of life' decisions, but whether we ought to make unfounded and/or unsympathetic decisions, or whether we ought to make the most rational and compassionate 'quality of life' decisions we can in the circumstances.

Whenever we make 'quality of life' decisions—wherever we decide to draw the line— we have no guarantee we are drawing the line in the right place. Without the 20-20 vision of hindsight, it is impossible to be absolutely certain beforehand that our decision *is* the correct decision. *Without the foresight of hindsight, perfection is impossible.* Only after the decision is made and acted upon will we know for certain whether we made the right decision. But this is no excuse for shirking our moral responsibility and not doing the best we can. The alternative is to refrain from making a decision but this, to repeat, is to make a decision by default. In particular, it is to opt for a continuation of the status-quo state of affairs that generated our moral uneasiness and concern in the first place.

'Quality of Life' Decisions

There is no abstract, impersonal, mechanical, decision procedure by means of which we can

determine someone's 'quality of life'. But that is not to say that we cannot make 'quality of life' decisions. We make them all the time— in medicine and in politics. And we make them on a *comparative* basis—on the basis of the wisdom of our common life-experiences and observations.

The 'quality of one's life' is a matter of *degree*. That is, the 'quality of one's life' depends upon the degree to which one can realize the physical and mental capabilities that are characteristic of our species. Understood in this sense, judgments about the quality of one's life are an *objective* matter.

The 'politically correct' would have us believe otherwise. Ms. Priti Shah, a lawyer with the Canadian Disability Rights Council, for example, would have us believe that the marked difference between the public's anger and unmitigated condemnation of Susan Smith's cold-blooded murder of her two young sons and the public's sympathy for Robert Latimer is indicative of a widespread prejudice in society against the disabled. "Who are we", she asks rhetorically, "to say that because the Smith boys were able-bodied that their lives were better than Tracy's? This is a classic imposition of a stereotype."[9] Shah's confused comment—and it is not uncommon—is counter-productive to what is in the best interests of the disabled. It is precisely because the disabled are disabled, are vulnerable, that the need for ensuring their welfare arises. And yet when their differences and vulnerability are tellingly described, these descriptive truths are resentfully dismissed as oppressive!

Ms. Shah and the disabled she represents are understandably sensitive to 'quality of life' decisions. But the fact that the disabled are disabled is not a prejudice but a physical fact. The simple fact is that on a comparative 'quality of life' scale, the greater one's disability, the less the objective quality of one's life. This is an unalterable fact of life. The disabled may not like it but it is a fact they have to live with.

Nothing they can say or do can change the fact of their disability and the diminished quality of life it entails.

However, the question of the quality of life that one objectively has is distinct from the question of whether the quality of life one has is worth living. Whereas the former is an *objective* judgment, the latter is an individual *subjective* judgment. Whether a life of a certain quality is worth living will vary depending upon whose life it is and what price the individual is prepared to pay to live it. As well, those whose lives are inextricably interwoven with the lives of those who, like Tracy, are incapable of making this decision for themselves also have to pay a price and it too has to be factored into the decision-making process. Religious fanatics and rule-bound moralists may not like it, but moral commonsense clearly recognizes that life at any price is not worth the cost. Those who object conveniently forget that *no price is too high to pay for those who do not have to pay it nor is anything impossible for those who do not have to do it.*

The Role of Emotions

Morality is not a game that one can choose to play or not play. We can play it well or play it poorly, but play it we must. It is, if you will, a game within the game of life—which is why we are life-long participants in it whether we like it or not. It is what differentiates us from non-human animals.

It is not a simple or easy game to play. To play it well requires both intelligence and emotional maturity. The importance of the latter cannot be overemphasized. If we did not care, if we were emotional eunuchs—unmoved by the pain and suffering of others—and if moral reasoning was simply an intellectual exercise in logical thinking, the consequences of our actions would still count, but none would 'matter' in the ways in which they do. As it is, we are not the sort of one-dimensional, rational

androids that moral absolutists with their rigid principles would have us be. We both think and feel, and the commonsense moral judgments that people with commonsense ordinarily make realistically reflect this duality of our nature. The more morally mature and astute recognize that if it were not for our ability to reason, the actual and potential consequences of our actions would be unintelligible to us but they also recognize that if we were not the sentient, compassionate and caring beings we are, the moral significance of these consequences would be equally incomprehensible. Both characteristics are an integral part of what it is to be moral. In the absence of either morality is impossible.

It is in recognition of this fact that our ordinary moral judgments are infused with intelligence and compassion in a way that reflects the dynamic and flexible interplay that exists between reason and emotion in our daily lives. At their best, our commonsense moral judgments are a rational expression of our emotional concerns. At their worst, they signal the difficulty involved in achieving the requisite equilibrium between feeling and thought, between the spirit and the letter of what it means to be a responsible moral human being.

Serving on a jury does not mean one has been granted 'time out' from playing the moral game. There are no 'time outs' in playing the moral game even when one is serving on a jury. If anything, members of a jury have a special moral duty to see to it that *justice* and not just 'the law' is served. In the Latimer case, members of the jury did just the opposite. In following the judge's orders not to let their emotions play a part in their deliberations and in agreeing to be guided solely by reason and the law, the members of the jury morally castrated and dehumanized themselves in the process.

The demand that we disown our emotions, that we pretend we have ice-water in our veins, that we act as if we were nothing more than thinking computers, is a moral death-wish. It is reason that enables us to correctly identify the moisture on Tracy's cheeks as drops of salt water, but the recognition that these droplets of salt water are tears, or more, that they are tears of pain or sadness rather than tears of laughter or joy, is an insight of the heart and not the head.

Thoughts without feelings are like lamps without oil—useless. This is why we do not turn to computers, no matter how advanced they may be, for moral guidance. A computer may recount a joke, but it fails to see the joke's humour. And that is the problem—computers are devoid of emotion; they cannot laugh or cry and hence are incapable of sympathy and compassion. *Without reason the facts are senseless and without compassion they are barren.* In the absence of either, morality is impossible.

In bringing in a guilty verdict the jury members demonstrated a lack of moral courage —the very sort of moral courage that Robert Latimer displayed when he did what he was morally obligated to do despite its illegality. It is no defence to protest: "We were only following orders—legal orders that were given by a legally authorized authority, namely, the presiding judge." This is just another example of the *Eichmann Defence,* the defence Adolf Eichmann gave when tried as a war criminal for his part in the Holocaust. But Eichmann's defence, "I was just following orders," did not morally excuse him from what he did and neither does it morally excuse the jury from the injustice they have inflicted upon Robert Latimer and his family.

Misplaced Duty and Compassion

Obsessed with what will (or might) happen if we *do* certain things, little thought is being given to what will (or might) happen if we *don't* do certain things. It is time we did. To know what will happen we need only look at what is already happening. For unless the laws governing euthanasia are changed, the future will resemble the present, only more so.

If something is not done to help the dying die, more and more people will be faced with the situation of a loved one being kept alive long after any hope of recovery is possible. In a recent letter to the editor of *The Globe and Mail,* Cyril Kalin describes how twice in her life family members were mistreated because of some medical personnel's misguided sense of duty to their patient. "My father," she writes,

> was 86 years old and in the last stages of lung cancer when a religious nurse in the Los Angeles hospital where he was a patient took it upon herself to defy his doctor's prescription for four-hourly administrating of a painkiller. This was on the grounds that if continued it could lead to his death. It took actual threats to the hospital on my part to have the doctor's instructions reinstated.
>
> The second case was my 39-year-old daughter, this time in the Columbia-Presbyterian Hospital in New York City.
>
> She had had a flat brain trace for a week and when I arrived there I found that the attending doctor had prescribed, and she had been given, antibiotics to fight her infection. Again I had to resort to violent protest before anyone had the guts and intelligence to let the girl die.
>
> This particular doctor actually admitted that "these people here are paranoid about pulling the plug."[10]

Physicians have a duty to do for their patients what needs to be done. But this is no excuse for a physician to insist on aggressive treatment far beyond the point when the patient can hope to benefit. There are times when nothing should be done. And there are times, as in Tracy's case, when patients should be given the treatment that ends all treatment.

If we *do not* legally help those who wish to die, the Sue Rodriguezs of this world, to say nothing of those with AIDS, will seek and receive the help they need outside the law. If the law is not changed, caregivers will continue to find themselves in guilt-ridden no-win situations. Jane Doe (a pseudonym) spoke for many when she wrote of her own conflicting feelings in keeping her daughter alive.

> I consider myself a conscientious parent. I wake up every morning at 6 a.m. to help my daughter to get ready for the day. She has a degenerative neurological disease. So, I have to change her diapers, dress her, get her up, feed her breakfast and offer her liquids. She is virtually helpless, and I hate to think about how she feels lying there in bed, waiting for me to come.
>
> I don't really know how she feels because I'm not able to have conversations with her. She can no longer speak....
>
> Most kids with her disability are dead by her age. I believe she is still alive because of the care I've given her. When she has pneumonia [and she has had it countless times], I sleep by her bed on the floor, so I can get up to turn her over every half-hour. If I have to, I'll clap her back to break up the congestion, and sometimes I'll use an eyedropper to give her water....
>
> It seems like I pull her through one illness only to face another. I'm the one who resolutely keeps her alive....
>
> Of course, I know that if I even once withheld antibiotics from her, or wasn't so ever-vigilant, she would die. But I can't stand to see her suffer. Yet I can honestly admit that if there was a pill or a shot— *and no legal strings attached to its use—she would have received it long ago.*
>
> I keep on thinking about our old dog that we put to sleep last year when her cancer, arthritis and heart condition all caught up with her. I patted her head and looked deep into her eyes as the shot the vet gave her took effect. This dog and I were pals, and I still miss her, but I don't regret the choice that was made.
>
> For my daughter, the situation is more problematic, legally and morally. So I go on....
>
> Now my daughter is on the waiting list for a group home.... I know that I can't go on any longer after so many years or

> rally the specialized help she needs forever.... I feel I'm imposing a death sentence on her by sending her there, but society supports this kind of decision....
>
> I can easily understand what Robert Latimer was thinking the day his daughter died.[11]

In the end, Jane's misplaced compassion for her daughter will betray them both. Her daughter will die in an institution. Uprooted from her home, from her familiar surroundings, deprived of the ever-ready sound, sight, and touch of her mother, she will die— alone—amidst a sea of strangers. And Jane will bear the nagging guilt of knowing she did not do what she knows she should and would have done had it not been for the law. Her lack of moral courage in this regard is understandable. It is also regrettable.

A Parliamentary 'Free Vote'—A Matter of Individual Conscience

Under our parliamentary system the political solution to seemingly insoluble moral issues is to allow members of parliament a 'free vote' whenever, if ever, legislation on such matters is brought before the House of Commons for a vote. A 'free vote' means members are no longer constrained by Party affiliation and can vote according to the dictates of their own individual consciences. There are several problems with this approach, not the least of which are the following.

First, if Robert Latimer's conscience is dismissed as an illegitimate moral authority, what reason is there to believe that the conscience of a Member of Parliament is any more morally reliable? If anything, Latimer's conscience, given his unique, intimate, knowledge and care of Tracy, is better informed than the conscience of any member of parliament could possibly be.

Second, the claim that the collective consciences of members of parliament ought to be accepted as morally authoritative is just a reformulation of the undergraduate myth that what is morally right is whatever is accepted or approved of by the majority. Despite its widespread popularity, this view of right and wrong is false, for it entails the self-defeating presupposition that the truth in moral matters is just a matter of opinion; it conflates the distinction between belief and knowledge; it renders the fact of moral disagreements and the idea of moral progress unintelligible; it tolerates acts of intolerable intolerance; it makes cross-cultural moral judgments impossible; and it attributes to the majority a moral infallibility that is belied by the historical facts. The aforementioned inconsistencies and absurdities also bedevil the 'subjectivist' interpretation of moral judgments according to which the approval of the majority is replaced by a moral standard of every individual's own making.

Third, once parliamentarians are free of party discipline and free of the responsibility of having to represent the predominant view of their constituents, once they are free to vote as they personally see fit, Parliament's vote is a crapshoot.[12] It ought not to be; moral truth is not a popularity contest. Moral judgments, like scientific judgments, are only as sound as the evidence and arguments on which they rest.

Conclusion

Those who have condemned Robert Latimer have done so on the basis of reasons and arguments that cannot be sustained. Their reasons and arguments lack both intellectual merit and genuine compassion. I do not deny the problems that abuse presents, nor the slipperiness of the slopes on which we constantly find ourselves, nor the difficulty in drawing lines fairly, nor the agony of the finality of quality-of-life decisions, nor the fallibility of both our thoughts and feelings. What I do deny is the legitimacy of these concerns in the case of Robert and Tracy Latimer.

Being moral is not easy; it is fraught with risk and ambivalent decisions, with ignorance

and unfounded convictions, with imperfect knowledge, misguided compassion and frayed courage. More needs to be said and done,[13] but in the meantime we would do well to remember the following:

While moral common sense is unnecessary in heaven and pointless in hell, it is indispensable in life.

Notes

1 Bruce Hutchinson, "Latimer's Choice," *Saturday Night,* March, 1995, pp. 37–43. This is the most detailed, accurate, account in print (that I am aware of) of the history of Tracy's medical condition and of what she and her family went through during the 12 years of her life. In light of the facts recounted by Hutchinson, it defies comprehension that another journalist, Linda Goyette, an editorial writer with the *Edmonton Journal,* could write without any sense of wrongdoing:

> It's odd that we vilify a South Carolina woman for the murder of two sons while we offer infinite sympathy to a Saskatchewan father who committed the same crime.... What was the difference between Michael and Alexander Smith and Tracy Latimer? Not humanity. Only human intelligence. [Quoted in "Reactions," *The Globe and Mail,* November 25, 1994.]

Goyette's comment, based as it is on an appalling ignorance of the most basic facts distinguishing the two cases, deserves to be dismissed for the asinine comment it is. Unfortunately, she is not alone in her ignorance.

2 A moral fundamentalist is one who believes (a) that to be moral is to be rational, (b) that to be rational is to be a person of principle, (c) that moral principles are absolute and universally valid, and (d) that moral principles, as edicts of reason, always 'trump' the dictates of the heart. "Do good and avoid evil" is an indisputable moral axiom and should not be confused with, for example, the moral principle: "The intentional killing of an innocent person is always wrong." Unlike the former, the latter is disputable. It is, for the reasons given in the text, indisputably false.

3 *The Daily News,* December 24, 1994; *The Chronicle-Herald,* December, 1994.

4 *The Globe and Mail,* March 3, 1995.

5 *The Star Phoenix,* November 16, 1994.

6 Evidence has now surfaced that Kirkham, with the aid of the RCMP, had no moral qualms about tampering with justice when it served his own legal ends! "Cpl. Nick Hartle 'collaborated' with Kirkham in preparing [a] questionnaire used to gather information on prospective jurors' religion, their position on abortion and mercy killing, and whether they had any family members or 'close associates' with disabilities." This information was not disclosed "to the sheriff, the trial justice or the defence" [*The Star Phoenix,* October 31, 1995]. The Justice Department is conducting an internal investigation. In the meantime, Kirkham has been suspended with pay!

7 Not every disabled person is as embittered by their disability, or is as cynical about the motivation of their care givers and/or the general public's commitment to their welfare, as the statements of spokespersons for organizations on their behalf suggest. The words of Valerie Baker express a very different attitude:

> People ask me if I feel threatened by what he did to his daughter. Like Tracy, I too have cerebral palsy, but any comparison made between the two of us would be like comparing apples and oranges. I live independently, holding a master's degree, and am capable of making my own way in the world.
>
> I feel sorry for disabled people who condemn Latimer. It's difficult to understand why they feel threatened by this act of compassion. No one is advocating the killing of anyone simply because they have a disability. However, we do need to have deep compassion which will allow us to do what is right for our fellow humans.
>
> I only pray that if I become profoundly disabled, there would be a Latimer with me. [*The Province,* February 26, 1995. From the *Kitchener Waterloo Record.*]

8 Immanuel Jacobovits, "Jewish Views on Infanticide," in Marvin Kohl, ed. *Infanticide and the Value of Life* (Buffalo, New York: Prometheus Books, 1978), p. 28.

9 *The Star Phoenix,* November 22, 1994.

10 *The Globe and Mail,* Saturday, December 3, 1994.

11 *The Globe and Mail,* Tuesday, November 22, 1994, my italics.

12 A striking illustration of the dangers of relying on the political process to provide moral insight and leadership on the issues of euthanasia and assisted suicide is found in *Of Life and Death: Report of the Special Senate Committee on Euthanasia and Assisted Suicide* (June, 1995.) The majority of the seven-member Senate committee basically recommended maintaining the status quo even though national opinion polls have repeatedly shown that 70% (and in British Columbia and Quebec, 80%) of Canadians favour changing the current federal law's prohibition of euthanasia and assisted suicide. But as John Hofsess, executive director of The Right to Die Society of Canada, pointedly notes:

> The committee's witnesses... inverted these ratios. Of the 250 who appeared before the senators, roughly seven in 10 opposed any change of the law. Thus we have, at best, 30 per cent of the witnesses representing 70 to 80 per cent of Canadians, and 70 per cent of the witnesses representing 17 to 20 per cent of the population. [*The Globe and Mail,* May 4, 1995.]

The significance of these numbers becomes quickly apparent when one reads the report and discovers that it consists of a series of often repetitive alternative summary statements of 'on the one hand' but 'on the other hand' types of 'argument', with no reasons being given for accepting the arguments of those who opposed change other than the fact that their submissions *outnumbered* those in favour of changing the status quo.

13 More is said and done in a book I am currently writing, *Moral Sanity (Why Ethics Ought Not To Be Taught As It Is),* in which I articulate and defend what I call, "A Caring Theory of Justice: An Ethic of Informed Commonsense."

Questions for Discussion

1 Is it true that making the decision to help an incompetent person die is in principle no different from making any other decision aimed at the person's best interests?

2 Would it make a moral difference if Latimer had caused his daughter's death by, say, withholding some medication, rather than actively exposing her to a poisonous substance?

3 Are those who claim that acceptance of Latimer's actions amounts to "open season on the disabled" themselves guilty of a type of abuse? What moral weight, if any, should be attached to the fears of the disabled that such an acceptance will prove harmful to them?

CHAPTER 7

Free Expression, Censorship, and Pornography

It has become a commonplace of what might be called "modern liberal democracies" that freedom of expression is an important right of each individual. This right has not always been officially recognized in the history of these nations, and there is a long history of debate over it. Indeed, in many parts of the world today this right is not recognized, although it is enshrined in the rights documents of most international organizations including the United Nations. It is sometimes thought that nations can be divided into those which are politically advanced enough to recognize this right, and those which are not. However, all societies place *some* restrictions on the content and form of what people may say, and the circumstances in which they are allowed to say it, so the situation is not quite as straightforward as it might seem.

In Canada, legal limitations on speech include: government guidelines on broadcasting and advertising; laws against libel, slander, and perjury; a law against distribution of hate propaganda; restrictions concerning the publication of official secrets, especially in time of war or other such emergency; and the prohibition of speech acts such as the famous example of yelling "Fire!" in a crowded theatre.

There may appear to be overwhelming justifications for at least some of these restrictions on speech. Other values, such as national security, need to be protected in society, and it is quite possible that some of these may appear to be of more pressing importance than individual speech. From a philosophical perspective, however, interesting questions arise about what these values might be which can conflict with the right to free speech. Asking these questions also requires one to ask *why* free speech is considered valuable in the first place—what value is *that* right supposed to protect? And once one has admitted that the right is not absolute, it then becomes an interesting question where the limits are. Not surprisingly, there are some cases in which it is not clear which side of the principle a given form of expression lies on, and people disagree about whether certain sorts of acts constitute protected speech acts or not.

Any restriction on freedom of expression, especially in a written or visual form, may be considered censorship. Such restriction need not take the form of an outright prohibition of the work, although some people would want to reserve use of the word for this case. Other actions which might be considered censorship include making it more difficult for people to gain access to certain materials (by such measures as restrictions on manner and places of sale, or heavy taxation, or even restrictions on the language of communication), or allowing only some individuals to have access to certain materials (such as those over a certain age). A fairly recent proposal in the United States (the so-called "Minneapolis Ordinance") suggested the alternative of allowing people who believe they have been harmed by pornography to sue the producers and/or distributors of those materials for damages. All of these provisions can be more or less restrictive, and these gradations of degree can have a significant impact on the accessibility of the materials concerned. It is worth bearing in mind that even in this sense censorship is not a clear-cut issue.

The main debates about censorship, however, revolve around certain sorts of expression, and the question of whether they should be considered protected speech. One prominent area of this dispute has to do with the notion of "hate literature" or "hate propaganda." The Canadian Criminal Code contains provisions (Sections 318 and 319) against advocating genocide and against public incitement of hatred against any identifiable group. What reasons can be given for prohibiting people from stating their beliefs publicly in these areas? Are these reasons strong enough to justify the very intrusive measures of the criminal law? Should we be willing to trust the machinery

of the law to administer this law wisely, or is there too much danger that the rights of some individuals will be violated? Perhaps most importantly, what sorts of statements would violate the provision? How "public" does an incitement need to be, and what is to count as an "identifiable group"? These are some of the questions at stake here, and they tend to involve a balance between the right to free expression and perhaps the right to privacy as well, on the one hand, and various social goods such as public order, and perhaps rights of unspecifiable members of various potential target groups, on the other.

Another prominent area of dispute concerning free expression has to do with the notion of obscenity and the maintenance of public moral standards. Many people have argued that any society must protect its moral standards in order to survive. Similarly, it might be argued that a society has an obligation to do all it can to help its members flourish as human beings, and this may include watching out for their moral interests (in a sort of gentle paternalism). If these beliefs are correct, they may provide a justification for limitations on the freedom of expression when such expressions may tend to compromise the moral standards of the society. On the other hand, one might believe that society as a whole benefits when people are allowed to challenge its existing beliefs. Also, there is the question of whether we want to trust the machinery of the law to decide which particular expressions are permissible.

This issue of the protection of public morals leads naturally to a discussion of pornography. This is perhaps the most hotly debated subject within the issue of freedom of expression. Yet there is little agreement about what pornography *is*, or even whether it is best understood as a form of expression at all.

Is producing pornography an instance of free speech? In the classic cases, free speech has been understood as an attempt to put forward an unpopular political view or challenge to prevailing beliefs. It seems clear that producers of pornography are usually driven by a desire to provide entertainment, and/or to make a profit, more than by any political motives, although there are inevitably cases where the distinction is not clear. Does it matter for the purposes of free speech what the intention of the speaker is? And who gets to decide what the "real" intention is? If intention is important, then it may well be that at least some pornography does not amount to protected speech, and the "censorship" debate may be short-circuited.

It is worth noting some of the difficulties in even finding a definition of the term "pornography." The word itself comes from ancient Greek and means, literally, speaking and writing about the lives of prostitutes (and, by extension, their patrons). Its modern meaning has clearly changed somewhat, but there is disagreement about its proper usage. At some times "pornography" has been taken to refer to sexually explicit depictions that are still within prevailing social standards, as contrasted with "obscenity." Recently, however, it has been more common (especially in the light of feminist criticism) to use "pornography" to refer to unacceptable forms of sexual depiction, as opposed to "erotica," which may be equally explicit but not be considered offensive. There is still considerable disagreement, however, about what is "offensive."

Some people view any very explicit sexual materials as unacceptable, while others believe there must be further elements present. Examples of such other elements might include: the conjunction of violence with sex, the presence of the *intent* to arouse, the presence of something that tells

lies about human sexuality, or the inclusion of elements that seem to recommend degrading or abusive behaviour. Some people might wonder whether these elements are necessary features of pornography, or just indicators that pornography may be present. Indeed, some would deny that materials need to be sexually explicit in order to be "pornographic"—for example, the use of women's bodies to sell commercial products might be viewed as pornographic even if the depiction is not overtly sexual. It is also possible to ask for clarification of some of the crucial terms, such as defining what constitutes a "lie" about human sexuality, or what sorts of behaviour are degrading. One interesting question one might ask is: Can a person be degraded (and thereby harmed) even if that person does not perceive the activity to be degrading? This question introduces the notion of "false consciousness." This notion also leads to other questions about when a person can be understood to have consented to his or her participation in the production of pornography. Does it matter how many other meaningful options were available? Does it matter if the person "consenting" is a child? Is there a reliable way to ensure that the producers use models, etc., *only* for things to which they have consented?

Clearly, finding a definition of pornography is itself a difficult problem. It is worth noting, in reading various authors' views about pornography, that they may have different definitions of the term in mind.

Often discussions of pornography have focused not on whether it is bad in itself, but rather on whether large-scale availability of pornography will have bad consequences. As suggested above, some people worry that the presence of pornography tends to undermine the general moral fabric of a society, including (for example, in contemporary Canada) providing a chal-

lenge to the traditional vision of the nuclear family.

Some people who *want* to challenge
traditional values nevertheless worry about
the consequences of pornography. For example, there is the concern that consumption of pornography tends to encourage
men (or at least some men) to commit
sexual assault. Alternatively, it has been
suggested that pornography might provide
an alternative sort of sexual release for
would-be rapists, and thereby actually reduce the incidence of sexual assault. There
has been quite a bit of interesting research
aimed at trying to determine whether pornography does tend to have these effects,
and the resulting evidence is unclear. People on each side of the issue can cite studies that seem to provide some support for
their views. But it is also not clear how
much of the issue hinges on such research.

It might be argued that even if only one
man were led to commit rape as a result of
consuming pornography, that would be
enough reason to justify censorship. This
sort of assertion raises complex questions
about how to balance foreseen risks to
some individuals with expected benefits to
large numbers of others. In the case at
hand, it might be argued that the severe
harm of being sexually assaulted could not
be outweighed by *any* number of people
who benefit from the "entertainment"
value of pornography. It should be noted,
however, that people *might* be inspired to
commit violent crimes by a wide variety of
stimuli (many of which would not be seen
as stimulating in this way by most members
of society), and it could be asked whether
it is possible or desirable to try to control
every possible such source.

Many people would argue that even if
pornography does not directly induce men
to commit sexual assault, it does help foster attitudes toward sexuality, and toward

women in general, which society would be
better off without. Indeed, it is generally
assumed that what people see or read has
an effect on how they think and act. That
is why some people recommend reading
great literature and why many parents try
to monitor the television programs their
children watch. It might seem surprising if
pornography did not have some effect on
the thoughts and actions of those who consume it. It is very difficult to tell how significant such an effect might be, however,
and in particular whether the effect is significant enough (and undesirable enough)
to warrant bringing in the coercive force of
the criminal law. Trying to censor materials
for such reasons might also lead to limitations on romance novels, violent films, ad-
vertisements, and many other facets of
popular culture. One might believe that
such limitations would be a good idea, but
it is not a decision to be taken lightly.

There are a few other aspects of expression which have received increased attention in recent years. One of these has to do
with the notion that some kinds of communication are "politically incorrect." Such
communications are thought to demonstrate either a deliberate or negligent lack
of sensitivity to the interests of traditionally
oppressed groups. Sometimes the claim is
that one has used terms or images offensive to particular people, perhaps without
realizing the emotional connotations of
those terms or images for some people.
Sometimes the claim is that particular kinds
of expression suggest unquestioned dominant beliefs about certain groups which in
fact contain negative stereotypes. Related
to this last point, it is sometimes suggested
that dominant groups within a society have
a tendency to impose their own views of
various cultural groups, even on members
of those groups themselves, thereby "appropriating" the distinctive voices of those

groups. Each of these kinds of "politically incorrect" speech is thought to harm the members of the groups involved, and therefore it is thought that some restrictions might be appropriate on such speech. These need not be legal restrictions, but it is sometimes thought appropriate to encourage publishers not to publish works which contain such appropriation or insensitivity, art galleries not to exhibit such works, and educational institutions not to include any materials containing such features in their curricula or discussions.

There is one other aspect of the free speech debate which deserves mention, and it is one which arises due to advances in technology. This aspect is the issue of censorship or control of material on computer networks (such as "the Internet"). These networks are set up in such a way that anybody who "subscribes" can "surf the net" and read materials on a vast array of topics, retrieve pictures, and contribute his or her own "postings." People with an interest in a particular topic can establish a "site" on that topic, and anybody who has access to the network can then "visit" the site, read what is being said, and contribute his or her own ideas.

Since anybody with access to the network can post anything he or she wants (and indeed, postings may be completely unrelated to the supposed topic of the site), issues arise as to whether there should be any control over this medium, and if so, whether such control is possible. Should access to the Internet be limited? If so, on what basis? As things stand, it seems to be limited solely on the basis of who has the financial ability to purchase the computer technology required, and to pay whatever fees may be involved in subscribing and paying for air time. Perhaps it is unfair that the less wealthy are denied access to this medium of the future, in which case one might

wonder whether anything can be done to universalize access. For example, schools or public libraries might provide free access to the public. On the other hand, we might think access should be restricted more than it is. For example, it might be thought that children under a certain age should not be allowed access, at least to some sites. Similarly, it might be thought that it should be forbidden to post certain sorts of materials (e.g., racist materials, or materials of a sexually explicit nature).

To some extent, these problems arise because of some uncertainty as to the status of these communications. In some ways, Internet discussions seem to resemble private conversations between individuals who choose to participate. Such private conversations are often thought to be beyond the scope of any legalistic interferences, and thus there may be some precedent for the protection of Internet speech on this model. On the other hand, Internet discussions also seem to resemble broadcasts (as in television or radio), since messages conveyed may reach a mass audience, comprised of people who may be completely unknown to the person sending the message. Broadcasts have often been thought to be suitable subjects for some sort of restriction on free speech, and thus if Internet communications are looked at in this way, they too may be thought proper subjects of some sort of restriction. In which way is it best to understand this new medium?

More specific issues have arisen about the *sorts* of expression which might be thought candidates for censorship on the Internet. The best known examples involve the transmission of sexually explicit materials (words and pictures) and racist messages, which are readily accessible for a variety of people, including children. These are not the only issues the Internet gives rise to, however. A couple of examples might serve to illustrate other issues.

In 1993 and 1994, a ban was in effect on the publication of material concerning a case then current in the courts, the case of Karla Homolka. Newspapers, television and radio stations, etc., were prohibited from informing their audiences about the latest facts in the case. Some people with access to the Internet, however, acquired information about what was going on during the trial and posted it on the Internet. Did such behaviour violate the publication ban? In the event, some law enforcement officials considered that it did, and took steps to shut down the access of those posting the information, but again issues arise here as to how we should understand the nature of the communication.

Another issue which raises questions about the nature of communication on the Internet has arisen in 1996. Some musicians had taken to using the Net as a way of exchanging information about songs they had learned to play. Thus, if one wanted to know how to play a song from one's favourite recording, one could post a request, and somebody else who knew how to play it might write back a detailed answer to the request. A major record company took exception to this practice, however, claiming that many of the songs involved were copy-

righted, and that such exchange of information violated the rights of the composers of the music and of the company which controlled the rights. This might have been thought especially true in cases where the information about how to play a given song was also available for a fee from the company concerned (e.g., by purchasing the sheet music). Here, questions arise as to whether the postings involved should be considered private exchanges of information, where musicians merely help each other out, or whether they should be thought of as exchanges of a commodity that someone owns and which should not be exchanged without the consent of the owner.

Many of the issues raised in connection with free expression today are essentially the same as issues which have been raised for years. Sometimes, however, these issues take on a new aspect in light of developments in technology and of earlier discussions and (possibly resultant) changes in the state of societal understandings. Once in a while, completely new issues arise in connection with freedom of expression. Such situations might call out for public decision and action, but careful philosophical consideration beforehand can only improve the quality of the eventual decision and action.

R. v. Keegstra

Supreme Court of Canada, Chief Justice Dickson

One kind of speech which many people think it appropriate for the government to control is hate literature (also known as "hate propaganda"). Canada has a law (section 319 of the Criminal Code) which forbids hate propaganda. One of the first serious legal tests of this legislation in court was in the case of R. v. Keegstra, which went to the Supreme Court of Canada in 1990. Keegstra had been a teacher who had taught his classes that the Holocaust did not occur, and that there was a world-wide Jewish conspiracy. The issue before the court was whether a law limiting the ability to put forward hate propaganda infringes the right to freedom of expression (section 2(b) of the Charter of Rights and Freedoms), and, if so, whether such a limitation can nevertheless be "demonstrably justified in a free and democratic society" (as required by section 1 of the Charter). In the following excerpt from his opinion for the majority in that case, Chief Justice Dickson considers whether it can be established that 1) hate propaganda causes harm, 2) the limitation on hate propaganda does not cut too deeply into the values the right to freedom of expression is meant to protect (which requires some discussion of what those values are), and 3) whether the existing law is a proportional response to the foreseen harm.

★   ★   ★

[T]he presence of hate propaganda in Canada is sufficiently substantial to warrant concern. Disquiet caused by the existence of such material is not simply the product of its effectiveness, however, but stems from the very real harm which it causes. Essentially, there are two sorts of injury caused by hate propaganda. First, there is the harm done to members of the target group. It is indisputable that the emotional damage caused by words may be of grave psychological and social consequence. In the context of sexual harassment, for example, this Court has found that words can in themselves constitute harassment.... In a similar manner, words and writings that wilfully promote hatred can constitute a serious attack on persons belonging to a racial or religious group....

A second harmful effect of hate propaganda which is of pressing and substantial concern is its influence upon society at large.... It is...not inconceivable that the active dissemination of hate propaganda can attract individuals to its cause, and in the process create serious discord between various cultural groups in society. Moreover, the alteration of views held by the recipients of hate propaganda may occur subtly, and is not always attendant upon conscious acceptance of the communicated ideas. Even if the message of hate propaganda is outwardly rejected, there is evidence that its premise of racial or religious inferiority may persist in a recipient's mind as an idea that holds some truth, an incipient effect not to be entirely discounted....

In my opinion, it would be impossible to deny that Parliament's objective in enacting s. 319(2) is of the utmost importance. Parliament has recognized the substantial harm that can flow from hate propaganda, and in trying to prevent the pain suffered by target group members and to reduce racial, ethnic and religious tension in Canada has decided to suppress the wilful promotion of hatred against identifiable groups....

At the core of freedom of expression lies the need to ensure that truth and the common good are attained, whether in scientific and artistic endeavors or in the process of determining the best course to take in our political affairs. Since truth and the ideal form of political and social organization can rarely, if at all, be identified with absolute certainty, it is difficult to prohibit expression without impeding the free exchange of potentially valuable information. Nevertheless, the argument from truth does not provide convincing support for the protection of hate propaganda. Taken to its extreme, this argument would require us to permit the communication of all expression, it being impossible to know with absolute certainty which factual statements are true, or which ideas obtain the greatest good. The problem with this extreme position, however, is that the greater the degree of certainty that a statement is erroneous or mendacious, the less its value in the quest for truth. Indeed, expression can be used to the detriment of our search for truth; the state should not be the sole arbiter of truth, but neither should we overplay the view that rationality will overcome all falsehoods in the unregulated marketplace of ideas. There is very little chance that statements intended to promote hatred against an identifiable group are true, or that their vision of society will lead to a better world. To portray such statements as crucial to truth and the betterment of the political and social milieu is therefore misguided.

Another component central to the rationale underlying s. 2(*b*) concerns the vital role of free expression as a means of ensuring individuals the ability to gain self-fulfillment by developing and articulating thoughts and ideas as they see fit. It is true that s. 319(2) inhibits this process among those individuals whose expression it limits, and hence arguably works against freedom of expression values. On the other hand, such self-autonomy stems in part from one's ability to articulate and nurture an identity derived from membership in a cultural or religious group. The message put forth by individuals who fall within the ambit of s. 319(2) represents a most extreme opposition to the idea that members of identifiable groups should enjoy this aspect of the s. 2(*b*) benefit. The extent to which the unhindered promotion of this message furthers free expression values must therefore be tempered insofar as it advocates with inordinate vitriol an intolerance and prejudice which views as execrable the process of individual self-development and human flourishing among all members of society.

Moving on to a third strain of thought said to justify the protection of free expression, one's attention is brought specially to the political realm. The connection between freedom of expression and the political process is perhaps the linchpin of the s. 2(*b*) guarantee, and the nature of this connection is largely derived from the Canadian commitment to democracy. Freedom of expression is a crucial aspect of the democratic commitment, not merely because it permits the best policies to be chosen from among a wide array of proffered options, but additionally because it helps to ensure that participation in the political process is open to all persons. Such open participation must involve to a substantial degree the notion that all persons are equally deserving of respect and dignity. The state therefore cannot act to hinder or condemn a political view without to some extent harming the openness of Canadian democracy and its associated tenet of equality for all.

The suppression of hate propaganda undeniably muzzles the participation of a few individuals in the democratic process, and hence detracts somewhat from free expression values, but the degree of this limitation is not substantial. I am aware that the use of strong language in political and social debate—indeed, perhaps even language intended to promote hatred—is an unavoidable part of the democratic process. Moreover, I recognize that hate propaganda is expression of a type which would generally be categorized as "political," thus putatively placing it at the heart of the principle extolling freedom of expression as vital to the democratic process. Nonetheless, expression can work to undermine our commitment to democracy where employed to propagate ideas anathemic to democratic values. Hate propaganda works in just such a way, arguing as it does for a society in which the democratic process is subverted and individuals are denied respect and dignity simply because of racial or religious characteristics. This brand of expressive activity is thus wholly inimical to the democratic aspirations of the free expression guarantee.

Indeed, one may quite plausibly contend that it is through rejecting hate propaganda that the state can best encourage the protection of values central to freedom of expression, while simultaneously demonstrating dislike for the vision forwarded by hate-mongers. In this regard, the reaction to various types of expression by a democratic government may be perceived as meaningful expression on behalf of the vast majority of citizens. I do not wish to be construed as saying that an infringement of s. 2(*b*) can be justified under s. 1 merely because it is the product of a democratic process; the Charter will not permit even the democratically elected legislature to restrict the rights and freedoms crucial to a free and democratic society. What I do wish to emphasize, however, is that one must be careful not to accept blindly that the suppression of expression must always and unremittingly detract from values central to freedom of expression....

I am very reluctant to attach anything but the highest importance to expression relevant to political matters. But given the unparalleled vigour with which hate propaganda repudiates and undermines democratic values, and in particular its condemnation of the view that all citizens need be treated with equal respect and dignity so as to make participation in the political process meaningful, I am unable to see the protection of such expression as integral to the democratic ideal so central to the s. 2(*b*) rationale. Together with my comments as to the tenuous link between communications covered by s. 319(2) and other values at the core of the free expression guarantee, this conclusion leads me to disagree with the opinion of McLachlin J. [in dissent] that the expression at stake in this appeal mandates the most solicitous degree of constitutional protection. In my view, hate propaganda should not be accorded the greatest of weight in the s. 1 analysis.

As a caveat, it must be emphasized that the protection of extreme statements, even where they attack those principles underlying the freedom of expression, is not completely divorced from the aims of s. 2(*b*) of the Charter. As noted already, suppressing the expression covered by s. 319(2) does to some extent weaken these principles. It can also be argued that it is partly through a clash with extreme and erroneous views that truth and the democratic vision remain vigorous and alive.... In this regard, judicial pronouncements strongly advocating the importance of free expression values might be seen as helping to expose prejudiced statements as valueless even while striking down legislative restrictions that proscribe such expression. Additionally, condon-

ing a democracy's collective decision to protect itself from certain types of expression may lead to a slippery slope on which encroachments on expression central to s. 2(*b*) values are permitted. To guard against such a result, the protection of communications virulently unsupportive of free expression values may be necessary in order to ensure that expression more compatible with these values is never unjustifiably limited.

None of these arguments is devoid of merit, and each must be taken into account in determining whether an infringement of s. 2(*b*) can be justified under s. 1. It need not be, however, that they apply equally or with the greatest of strength in every instance. As I have said already, I am of the opinion that hate propaganda contributes little to the aspirations of Canadians or Canada in either the quest for truth, the promotion of individual self-development or the protection and fostering of a vibrant democracy where the participation of all individuals is accepted and encouraged. While I cannot conclude that hate propaganda deserves only marginal protection under the s. 1 analysis, I can take cognizance of the fact that limitations upon hate propaganda are directed at a special category of expression which strays some distance from the spirit of s. 2(*b*), and hence conclude that "restrictions on expression of this kind might be easier to justify than other infringements of s. 2(*b*)."...

Having made some preliminary comments as to the nature of the expression at stake in this appeal, it is now possible to ask whether s. 319(2) is an acceptably proportional response to Parliament's valid objective. As stated above [this part of the case is set out in Part I], the proportionality aspect of the *Oakes* test requires the Court to decide whether the impugned state action: i) is rationally connected to the objective; ii) minimally impairs the Charter right or freedom at issue; and iii) does not produce effects of such severity so as to make the impairment unjustifiable....

Section 319(2) makes the wilful promotion of hatred against identifiable groups an indictable offence, indicating Parliament's serious concern about the effects of such activity. Those who would uphold the provision argue that the criminal prohibition of hate propaganda obviously bears a rational connection to the legitimate Parliamentary objective of protecting target group members and fostering harmonious social relations in a community dedicated to equality and multiculturalism. I agree, for in my opinion it would be difficult to deny that the suppression of hate propaganda reduces the harm such expression does to individuals who belong to identifiable groups and to relations between various cultural and religious groups in Canadian society.

Doubts have been raised, however, as to whether the actual effect of s. 319(2) is to undermine any rational connection between it and Parliament's objective.... [T]here are three primary ways in which the effect of the impugned legislation might be seen as an irrational means of carrying out the Parliamentary purpose. First, it is argued that the provision may actually promote the cause of hate-mongers by earning them extensive media attention. In this vein, it is also suggested that persons accused of intentionally promoting hatred often see themselves as martyrs, and may actually generate sympathy from the community in the role of underdogs engaged in battle against the immense powers of the state. Second, the public may view the suppression of expression by the government with suspicion, making it possible that such expression— even if it is hate propaganda—is perceived as containing an element of truth. Finally, it is often noted...that Germany in the 1920s and 1930s possessed and used hate propaganda laws similar to those existing in Canada, and yet these laws did nothing to stop the triumph of a racist philosophy under the Nazis.

If s. 319(2) can be said to have no impact in the quest to achieve Parliament's admirable objectives, or in fact works in opposition to these objectives, then I agree that the provision could be described as "arbitrary, unfair or based on irrational considerations,."... In my view, however, the position that there is no strong and evident connection between the criminalization of hate propaganda and its suppression is unconvincing....

It is undeniable that media attention has been extensive on those occasions when s. 319(2) has been used. Yet from my perspective, s. 319(2) serves to illustrate to the public the severe reprobation with which society holds messages of hate directed towards racial and religious groups. The existence of a particular criminal law, and the process of holding a trial when that law is used, is thus itself a form of expression, and the message sent out is that hate propaganda is harmful to target group members and threatening to a harmonious society....

In this context, it can also be said that government suppression of hate propaganda will not make the expression attractive and hence increase acceptance of its contents. Similarly, it is very doubtful that Canadians will have sympathy for either propagators of hatred or their ideas. Governmental disapproval of hate propaganda does not invariably result in dignifying the suppressed ideology. Pornography is not dignified by its suppression, nor are defamatory statements against individuals seen as meritorious because the common law lends its support to their prohibition....

As for the use of hate propaganda laws in pre-World War Two Germany, I am skeptical as to the relevance of the observation that legislation similar to s. 319(2) proved ineffective in curbing the racism of the Nazis. No one is contending that hate propaganda laws can in themselves prevent the tragedy of a Holocaust.... Rather, hate propaganda laws are one part of a free and democratic society's bid to prevent the spread of racism, and their rational connection to this objective must be seen in such a context....

...[I]n light of the great importance of Parliament's objective and the discounted value of the expression at issue I find that the terms of s. 319(2) create a narrowly confined offence which suffers from neither overbreadth nor vagueness. This interpretation stems largely from my view that the provision possesses a stringent *mens rea* requirement, necessitating either an intent to promote hatred or knowledge of the substantial certainty of such, and is also strongly supported by the conclusion that the meaning of the word "hatred" is restricted to the most severe and deeply-felt form of opprobrium. Additionally, however, the conclusion that s. 319(2) represents a minimal impairment of the freedom of expression gains credence through the exclusion of private conversation from its scope, the need for the promotion of hatred to focus upon an identifiable group and the presence of the s. 319(3) defences. [These are: (a) truth; (b) good faith opinion on a religious matter; (c) public interest; (d) good faith attempt to point out, so as to remove, matters producing feelings of hatred toward an identifiable group.] As for the argument that other modes of combatting hate propaganda eclipse the need for a criminal provision, it is eminently reasonable to utilize more than one type of legislative tool in working to prevent the spread of racist expression and its resultant harm....

The third branch of the proportionality test entails a weighing of the importance of the state objective against the effect of limits imposed upon a Charter right or guarantee. Even if the purpose of the limiting measure is substantial and the first two components of the proportionality test are satisfied, the deleterious effects of a limit may be too great to permit the infringement of the right or guarantee in issue.

I have examined closely the significance of the freedom of expression values threatened by s. 319(2) and the importance of the objective which lies behind the criminal prohibition. It will by now be quite clear that I do not view the infringement of s. 2(*b*) by s. 319(2) as a restriction of the most serious kind. The expressive activity at which this provision aims is of a special category, a category only tenuously connected with the values underlying the guarantee of freedom of speech. Moreover, the narrowly drawn terms of s. 319(2) and its defences prevent the prohibition of expression lying outside of this narrow category. Consequently, the suppression of hate propaganda affected by s. 319(2) represents an impairment of the individual's freedom of expression which is not of a most serious nature.

It is also apposite to stress yet again the enormous importance of the objective fueling s. 319(2), an objective of such magnitude as to support even the severe response of criminal prohibition. Few concerns can be as central to the concept of a free and democratic society as the dissipation of racism, and the especially strong value which Canadian society attaches to this goal must never be forgotten in assessing the effects of an impugned legislative measure. When the purpose of s. 319(2) is thus recognized, I have little trouble in finding that its effects, involving as they do the restriction of expression largely removed from the heart of free expression values, are not of such a deleterious nature as to outweigh any advantage gleaned from the limitation of s. 2(*b*).

Questions for Discussion

1 What values is the right to freedom of expression meant to protect?

2 In considering the view that complete freedom of expression must be allowed so as to increase the chances of truth emerging, Dickson claims that "the greater the degree of certainty that a statement is erroneous or mendacious, the less its value in the quest for truth," and he suggests that

some kinds of expression may actually work to the detriment of truth. Is he right about this? Is it a good idea to empower a government to make decisions about when a given kind of speech is unlikely to contribute to the quest for truth?

3 Is Dickson correct that allowing certain kinds of speech could lead to a greater infringement of the

values free expression protects than limiting them by law would?

4 Could the sorts of arguments Dickson puts forward for limiting hate propaganda be applied to the issue of pornography? Could pornography be seen as a kind of hate propaganda, with women as the objects of hatred?

Hate Propaganda and Charter Rights

L.W. Sumner

In this article, L.W. Sumner summarizes the different positions Canadian courts have taken on the subject of hate propaganda. He then uses his analysis to draw out some points about the nature of rights within the Canadian Charter of Rights and Freedoms, and the role of consequentialist considerations in interpreting rights.

★ ★ ★

Hate literature is deeply problematic for liberal societies because it exposes an awkward conflict between two of their most cherished values. On the one hand, the dissemination of racist propaganda, however odious it might be, seems to fit easily within the definition of political speech. Racists typically have a political agenda, and the public circulation of their views is an indispensable means of carrying out that agenda. The freedom to advocate deeply held political convictions is one of the cornerstones of a liberal democracy. Classically, the vigorous protection of this freedom has been claimed to yield a number of important pay-offs, both individual and social. For the holders of such convictions this freedom provides an essential means of self-expression or self-fulfilment and ensures their opportunity to participate effectively in the democratic process, while for the public at large it plays the crucial role of exposing comfortable orthodoxies to productive challenge and criticism. While the individual benefits derived from freedom of expression may not vary with the content of the ideas being expressed, the so-

cial benefits may actually be greatest when the convictions in question are unpopular, unsettling, irritating, or even offensive. In any polity what gets labelled as propaganda is by definition controversial or heterodox. Liberals will therefore assign a high value to political propaganda, and will take special pains to protect the right of citizens to circulate it freely.

On the other hand, the public expression of hatred or contempt for minorities can cause those groups demonstrable harm. No society is free of racism, and the unhindered circulation of propaganda which portrays visible minorities as inferior or despicable is likely to encourage the spread of this poison. The immediate result for the target groups will be diminished self-esteem and a questioning of the extent to which they are valued members of the social order. This may in turn encourage a response of quietism or passivity—a reluctance to compete too vigorously for conspicuous social positions, or to press claims of social justice, lest success breed a backlash of resentment and hostility. Those who are not so easily intimidated may none the less find their progress impeded by discrimination which is reinforced by derogatory racial stereotypes. Nor do the indignities stop there: enmity or contempt are likely also to be expressed in racial taunts or slurs, social ostracism, the desecration of sacred places, and personal violence.

Hate propaganda therefore forces liberals to choose between protecting individual liberty and promoting social equality. The stakes are high, since any choice they make will necessarily circumscribe or curtail some important basic rights. For Canadians this conflict takes an especially acute form. In common with a number of European jurisdictions, but in sharp contrast to the United States, Canada has a criminal statute governing the dissemination of hate propaganda. Recent judicial challenges to this statute have highlighted its seeming inconsistency with the constitutional guarantee of freedom of expression. In examining these challenges, and their ultimate resolution by the courts, my principal aim is to draw some conclusions concerning the nature and grounding of basic legal rights. But I have a further purpose as well. For years I accepted the civil libertarian case against the criminalization of hate propaganda, not on grounds of abstract right but out of the purely pragmatic conviction that the social costs of attempting to control the circulation of this kind of material were likely to be higher than the costs of leaving it unhindered. Now I am no longer quite so sure, and I want to try to explain (and also understand) why I have come to change my mind.

1. The Criminal Code and the Charter

Under s. 319(2) of the Canadian Criminal Code 'every one who, by communicating statements, other than in private conversation, wilfully promotes hatred against any identifiable group' is guilty of an offence carrying a maximum penalty of imprisonment for two years.[1] For the purpose of this section an 'identifiable group' is defined as 'any section of the public distinguished by colour, race, religion or ethnic origin'. Section 319(3) then adds the following schedule of defences:

> No person shall be convicted of an offence under subsection (2)
> (a) if he establishes that the statements communicated were true;
> (b) if, in good faith, he expressed or attempted to establish by argument an opinion upon a religious subject;
> (c) if the statements were relevant to any subject of public interest, the discussion of which was for the public benefit, and if on reasonable grounds he believed them to be true; or
> (d) if in good faith, he intended to point out, for the purpose of removal, matters producing or tending to produce feelings of hatred towards an identifiable group in Canada.

Meanwhile, s. 2 of the Canadian Charter of Rights and Freedoms states that 'everyone has the following fundamental freedoms: ... (b) freedom of thought, belief, opinion and expression, including freedom of the press and other media of communication'.[2] Under s. 1 of the Charter these freedoms are 'subject only to such reasonable limits prescribed by law as can be demonstrably justified in a free and democratic society'.

The materials for a Charter challenge to the hate propaganda statute are therefore ready to hand. So far this challenge has been raised in two cases: *Keegstra* and *Andrews*.[3] James Keegstra was convicted under s. 319(2) of making anti-Semitic comments to his high school students, while Donald Andrews was convicted under the same section of publishing and distributing a white supremacist periodical known as the Nationalist Reporter. Both convictions were appealed, and both appeals turned in part on the claim that s. 319(2) is an unjustifiable infringement of s. 2(b) of the

Charter. At this second stage, the paths followed by the two cases diverged. In *Keegstra* the Alberta Court of Appeal accepted this argument (among others) and quashed Keegstra's conviction, while in *Andrews* the Ontario Court of Appeal rejected the argument and upheld Andrews's conviction. Both cases were appealed to the Supreme Court, where s. 319(2) was upheld by a majority of 4–3.[4] Andrews's conviction was confirmed, while Keegstra was eventually committed to trial a second time on the original charges. He was convicted once again.

It would be tiresome to rehearse all of the Charter issues which have surfaced, both at trial and on appeal, in the two cases. Fortunately, there is general agreement among all the courts involved that two questions are paramount:

> *The section 2 issue:* Does s. 319(2) infringe the right of freedom of expression protected by s. 2(b) of the Charter?
>
> *The section 1 issue:* If so, does this infringement fall within the 'reasonable limits' of s. 1 of the Charter?

These two questions yield three possible decision paths, all of which have been pursued during the various stages of adjudication of the two cases. As the flow chart on p. 481 shows, there are two paths which result in upholding s. 319(2) but only one which leads to striking it down. There are also two different ways of sorting the various opinions in *Keegstra* and *Andrews*. One looks only to their ultimate conclusion: do they hold the hate propaganda statute to be an unjustifiable infringement of the Charter right of freedom of expression? This line of division separates the various supporters of the statute (those on the two outside paths) from its opponents (those on the middle path). The other way looks strictly to their handling of the s. 2 issue: do they hold the hate propaganda statute to be any infringement of the Charter right at all? On this question

some of the statute's supporters (those on the left-hand path) agree with its opponents (still the middle path). Both lines of division raise interesting issues concerning the nature and grounding of fundamental rights. These issues will be explored in the next two sections.

2. The Balancing Act

All parties to the judicial debate agree on some fundamental points. The purpose of s. 319(2) of the Criminal Code is to protect racial, ethnic, and religious minorities against the harms which are likely to result from the spread of contempt or enmity directed toward them. Equal respect for minorities is an important value in a liberal society. The purpose of s. 2(b) of the Charter is to protect freedom of expression, especially where the ideas or opinions being expressed are unpopular or offensive. Freedom of expression is also an important value in a liberal society. Where hate propaganda is concerned, these values appear to conflict. Any resolution of this conflict will necessarily favour one value at the expense of the other.

The defenders of the hate propaganda statute declare themselves willing, in this instance, to limit freedom of expression in order to safeguard equal respect. Contrariwise, its attackers declare themselves willing, in this instance, to put the latter at risk in order to protect the former. Although the two sides to the debate reach opposed conclusions, they both get there by engaging in the same exercise of balancing the two values in question against one another. The lower-court judgments in *Keegstra* and *Andrews* are full of this language of balancing,[5] as are both the majority and minority opinions for the Supreme Court. Writing for the majority, Dickson CJ speaks of 'finding the correct balance between prohibiting hate propaganda and ensuring freedom of expression'.[6] But the most elaborate and developed account of the balancing act is provided by McLachlin J., writing for the minority:

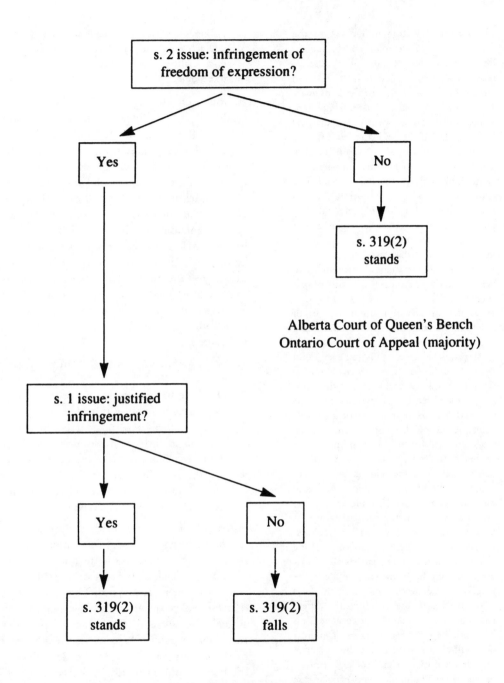

s. 2 issue: infringement of freedom of expression?

Yes

No

s. 319(2) stands

Alberta Court of Queen's Bench
Ontario Court of Appeal (majority)

s. 1 issue: justified infringement?

Yes

No

s. 319(2) stands

s. 319(2) falls

Ontario Court of Appeal
(minority)
Supreme Court (majority)

Alberta Court of Appeal
Supreme Court (minority)

The Court's function under s. 1 of the *Charter* is that of weighing and balancing. Before reaching s. 1, the Court must already have determined that the law in question infringes a right or freedom guaranteed by the *Charter*. The infringement alone, however, does not mandate that the law must fall. If the limit the law imposes on the right infringed is 'reasonable' and 'can be demonstrably justified in a free and democratic society', the law is valid. The demonstration of this justification, the burden of which lies on the state, involves proving that there are other rights or interests which outweigh the right infringed in the context of that case.

The task which judges are required to perform under s. 1 is essentially one of balancing. On the one hand lies a violation or limitation of a fundamental right or freedom. On the other lies a conflicting objective which the state asserts is of greater importance than the full exercise of the right or freedom, of sufficient importance that it is reasonable and 'demonstrably justified' that the limitation should be imposed. The exercise is one of great difficulty, requiring the judge to make value judgments. In this task logic and precedent are but of limited assistance. What must be determinative in the end is the court's judgment, based on an understanding of the values our society is built on and the interests at stake in the particular case. As Wilson J. has pointed out in [the] *Edmonton Journal*, this judgment cannot be made in the abstract. Rather than speak of values as though they were Platonic ideals, the judge must situate the analysis in the facts of the particular case, weighing the different values represented in that context. Thus it cannot be said that freedom of expression will always prevail over the objective of individual dignity and social harmony, or vice versa. The result in a particular case will depend on weighing the significance of the infringement on freedom of expression represented by the law in question, against the importance of the counter-

vailing objectives, the likelihood the law will achieve those objectives, and the proportionality of the scope of the law to those objectives.[7]

Although Dickson CJ and McLachlin J. eventually come to contrary conclusions about s. 319(2) (he is on the left-hand path, she on the middle), they agree on the nature, and the necessity, of the balancing exercise. Implicitly or explicitly, this agreement runs through all of the various judgments, at every level, in *Keegstra* and *Andrews*. In each instance, the ultimate conclusion reached concerning the status of s. 319(2) reflects an opinion about the balance which it strikes between protecting minorities, on the one hand, and safeguarding freedom of expression, on the other. There is also general agreement concerning the questions to be raised in the course of the balancing exercise:[8]

1. Is the objective of s. 319(s) an important one?
2. Does the statute employ measures reasonably likely to achieve this objective?
3. Do these measures impair freedom of expression as little as possible in order for them to achieve the statute's objective?
4. Are the resulting costs to freedom of expression proportional to the expected gains from achieving this objective?

Since all parties agree on the importance of safeguarding equal respect for minorities, the main points of contention are questions (2)–(4). The judicial opponents of s. 319(2) advance two main arguments. The first is that the criminal prosecution of hatemongers may actually be self-defeating, since it provides them with a public platform for the advocacy of their opinions.[9] In reply, the defenders of the statute point primarily to the symbolic effect of prosecution as a means of expressing social condemnation of hate propaganda.[10]

The opponents' second argument is that, in its present form, s. 319(2) is too broadly

drawn and thus trenches too much on freedom of expression.[11] Its defenders deny this,
citing the various restrictions and defences incorporated into the law:[12]

1. The communication must be public;
   s. 319(2) does not apply to private conversation.
2. The 'identifiable groups' protected are limited to sections of the public distinguished
   by colour, race, religion, or ethnic origin.
3. The promotion of hatred must be 'wilful',
   i.e., intentional. The offence is therefore
   one of specific intent, requiring at the very
   least some awareness on the part of the
   agent of the likely effects of the expression. Mere recklessness with respect to
   those effects will not suffice.
4. Establishing the truth of the statements
   communicated constitutes an absolute defence.
5. Opinions expressed in good faith on religious subjects are excluded from prosecution.
6. A 'public benefit' defence is available.
7. Publicizing hate propaganda for the purpose of combatting it is not an offence.
8. The consent of the Attorney-General is
   required for a prosecution under s. 319(2).

Thus are the terms of the debate set. It should
be obvious by now that, at bottom, this is an
argument about public policy. Where two important social values conflict we are forced to
seek an acceptable trade-off between them.
This is precisely what the courts are doing in
all their talk of 'balancing'. The optimal trade-
off, or balance, is that at which any further
gains in one of the values would be outweighed by greater losses in the other. Freedom of expression would be better protected
were there no legal constraints whatever on
the circulation of hate propaganda, while the
security of minority groups would be more
effectively safeguarded by legislation a good
deal more restrictive than s. 319(2). Some-

where between these extremes we seek a balance point at which the greater protection for
minorities afforded by stronger legislation
would be outweighed by the chilling effect on
political speech, while the greater protection
for expression afforded by weaker legislation
would be outweighed by the increase in racial hatred. Whether s. 319(2) properly locates
that balance point is, of course, open to legitimate doubt. That is what the judicial debate concerning the constitutionality of the
statute is all about.

That legislation regulating hate propaganda
should aim to strike such a balance has been
understood from the beginning. The Special
Committee on Hate Propaganda in Canada
(hereafter referred to as the Cohen Committee), whose 1966 report led to the enactment
of the Canadian legislation, formulated the issue in the following terms:

> The prevailing view in Canada is that free-
> dom of expression is a qualified right, rep-
> resenting the balance that must be struck
> between the social interest in the full and
> frank discussion necessary to a free society
> on the one hand, and the social interests
> in public order and individual and group
> reputation on the other.[13]

In striking this balance, the Committee's view
was that the higher priority should be assigned
to freedom of expression:

> as among conflicting values, preference
> must always be given to freedom of expres-
> sion rather than to legal prohibitions di-
> rected at abuses of it. This is not to say that
> freedom of expression is regarded as an ab-
> solute, but only to insist that it will be es-
> teemed more highly and weighted more
> significantly in the legislative scales, so that
> legal markings of the borderline areas [be-
> tween 'legitimate' and 'illegitimate' public
> discussion] will always be such as to per-
> mit liberty even at the cost of occasional
> license ... legislation should be so drafted
> as to permit the maximum freedom of ex-

pression consistent with its purpose and the needs of a free society.[14]

What the Cohen Committee recommended, in effect, is that we begin with an initial presumption in favour of unfettered freedom of expression, and then impose the least extensive restrictions necessary in order to safeguard social values of equal importance. The question to be asked for every proposed restriction, therefore, is whether the marginal gain in the rival value is worth purchasing at the marginal cost to freedom of expression. Section 319 followed the Committee's recommendations in all essential respects, especially in the relatively high threshold which it established for successful prosecution.

If this is the correct way to understand the exercise of balancing (and what else could it be?), then it falls into an argumentative pattern familiar to moral or political philosophers. We have located the optimal balance between conflicting values when the costs of a departure in either direction exceed its benefits. But in that case the optimal balance is that point any departure from which will result in a net loss of value, i.e., the point at which the sum total of the values in question is maximized. Philosophers have a name—consequentialism—for the kind of moral/political theory which tells us always to prefer the outcome which maximizes value on the whole. It is an interesting feature of the judicial debate about s. 319(2) that all of its parties appear to agree on this consequentialist methodology.

This may seem a surprising result. After all, on the surface of it the Charter does not have the look of a consequentialist document. How then does it happen that in Charter adjudication judges come to behave as consequentialists? A full answer to this question would take us much too far afield, but it is easy to see in very rough outline how such an answer would go. The political function of the Charter is to confer a special degree of legal protection on

a set of selected social values by entrenching them as constitutionally guaranteed rights. Which values are to be protected in this way is itself a policy question, the best mix presumably being that which best safeguards the flourishing of a liberal democratic society. Whatever the favoured values may be, however, they will be capable of conflicting both with one another and with other values which do not enjoy the same degree of constitutional protection. These conflicts will require interpretation of the abstract and perfunctory formulae enshrined in the Charter, interpretation which will perforce be carried out not by politicians but by judges. When judges are confronted by legislation which protects some significant social value but appears to trench on a Charter right, and when they have no unambiguous precedent to guide them, then it is difficult to see how they might proceed other than by seeking a reasonable balance between the values in conflict. But in that case their objective will be the resolution of the conflict which promises to yield the best outcome on the whole.

There is in this an important lesson about the nature and role of rights.[15] Legal rights are best regarded as instruments whose function is to safeguard important individual and social values. They are morally justified when they perform this function well—that is, when they strike an optimal, or at least an acceptable, balance among the values in question. It follows from this that rights cannot be the ultimate premises of moral/political argument; rather, they follow as conclusions from premises specifying the values which they are to protect, plus some understanding of how these values are to be weighed against one another. What may on the surface appear to be appeals to abstract right, therefore, are to be understood on a deeper level as consequentialist arguments concerning matters of public policy. In this respect constitutional adjudication conforms to the general pattern of moral/political argument, in which the good is prior to, and foundational for, the right.

What may be disquieting in all this is not that conflicting values need to be commensurated, nor that the optimal balance is the maximizing option, but that it is judges who are carrying out this entire exercise. Unlike politicians they are not answerable to the electorate, and unlike special committees or commissions they have little opportunity to collect empirical data. How can they be expected to reach informed judgments on large questions of social policy, such as the trade-off between freedom of expression and racial toleration, and how can they be held responsible for the judgments they do reach? The worry about information may be somewhat alleviated by reflecting that, while judges have little opportunity to engage in primary research themselves, they can and do avail themselves of the findings of others. Doubtless their conclusions remain to a large degree intuitive; these are, as we say, judgment calls. However this may be, the role of judges as practising consequentialists seems to come with the territory. The abstract rights of the Charter cry out for interpretation, and much of this interpretation will necessarily take the form of defining them in socially optimal ways. If we do not give this job to judges, then to whom might we entrust it?

3. Internal v. External Limits

Earlier, I distinguished two different ways in which the judicial opinions on s. 319(2) could be classified. The first of these we can now identify as the outcome of the consequentialist cost/benefit balancing, which settles the constitutionality issue. This line of division, as I said then, separates the friends of the hate propaganda statute from its foes, the former taking the view that the marginal loss in freedom of expression is outweighed by the marginal gain in protection for minorities, the latter being of

contrary mind. The second line of division concerns the different routes by which the friends of the statute reach their common destination. Here the crucial question is *not* whether s. 319(2) is an unjustifiable infringement of the s. 2(b) right of freedom of expression—for all its friends agree that it is not—but whether it is any infringement of that right at all. This is the issue which divided the Ontario Court of Appeal in *Andrews*. The majority, consisting of Grange and Krever JJA, agree with Quigley J. of the Alberta Court of Queen's Bench in *Keegstra* that s. 319(2) does not infringe s. 2(b). Cory JA, delivering the minority opinion in *Andrews,* agrees with the Alberta Court of Appeal in *Keegstra* that it does (unlike the Alberta Court, he then finds that the infringement is justified under the terms of s. 1).

As Grange JA observes, 'Everything depends on the interpretation of "freedom of expression" in the Charter.'[16] On the face of it, the various rights guaranteed by s. 2 are unqualified: 'Everyone has the following fundamental freedoms: ... (b) freedom of thought, belief, opinion and expression'. Not 'freedom of expression, except in the following circumstances' but just 'freedom of expression', full stop. Notwithstanding this absolutist language, however, Grange JA and the others of like mind take the view that the right delineated by s. 2(b) is not absolute. Leaving the hate propaganda issue to one side, they claim that the right does not protect expression which is obscene, seditious, or libellous. Grange JA includes group defamation among the forms of unprotected expression: 'in my view [s. 2(b)] never was intended to and does not give constitutional protection to hate-mongering such as that of the appellants ... I simply do not believe [s. 319(2)] offends the traditional protection of the freedom of speech or s. 2(b) of the Charter.'[17] Quigley J. takes the same view: 'In my opinion, the words "freedom of expression" as used in s. 2(b) of the Charter does [*sic*] not mean an absolute freedom permitting an unbridged [*sic*] right of speech or expression. In particular, I hold that [s. 319(2)] of the *Criminal Code* does not infringe upon the freedom of expression granted by s. 2(b) of the Charter.'[18]

After his discussion of the same issue, Cory JA comes to exactly the opposite conclusion: 'Offensive as it may seem, the expressions used in the case at bar do come within the purview of s. 2(b) of the Charter.'[19] In their treatment of the hate propaganda cases, therefore, the lower courts offered two quite different interpretations of s. 2(b). On the wide interpretation it simply means what it appears to say: the right to freedom of expression is unqualified. Since s. 319(2) clearly qualifies that right, it clearly infringes s. 2(b); the issue of its validity must then be referred to s. 1.[20] On the narrow interpretation, by contrast, s. 2(b) already includes a number of implicit qualifications, so that obscenity, sedition, and defamation (including group defamation) are excluded from its scope. On this reading s. 319(2) does not trench on the s. 2(b) right and so need not be justified by reference to s. 1.

The legal issues raised by these competing interpretations are interesting and important. One of them is whether the various specific sections of the Charter are to be read as incorporating rights extant in pre-existing jurisprudence, or whether the Charter starts with a clean slate. If the former view is taken, then, since freedom of expression was clearly not absolute in the pre-Charter era, s. 2(b) will be read as implicitly qualified. If the latter view is preferred then these internal limits are not dictated, and the right may be read as having a much broader scope. A related issue concerns the structural difference between the Charter and the American Bill of Rights. Because the latter contains no analogue to s. 1, the limits which are judicially imposed on the scope of its abstract rights must often be treated as internal and implicit. If similar limits are then read into the various rights enumerated by the

Charter, the function of s. 1 may thereby be pre-empted. The wide interpretation of s. 2 may therefore be thought to be more congruent with the unique character of the Charter, since it reserves to s. 1 the inevitable task of balancing conflicting values.

Such, in any case, was the view ultimately taken by the Supreme Court, where both the majority and minority agreed on the wide interpretation, and on the balancing role of s. 1. Following the line of analysis it had laid out in commercial expression cases,[21] the Court favoured 'a large and liberal interpretation' of s. 2(b), under which any activity will qualify as expression as long as it 'conveys or attempts to convey a meaning', regardless of the content of that meaning.[22] All expression in turn falls under the protection of s. 2(b), unless it takes a physically violent form. Since hate propaganda is not normally communicated in a violent manner, s. 2(b) guarantees a right to disseminate it.[23] The question whether that right is overridden by a competing consideration of equal or greater importance is then referred to s. 1. On that question the Court, of course, divided, the majority agreeing with Cory JA of the Ontario Court of Appeal, the minority siding with the Alberta Court.

To a philosopher's eyes, it can be a little difficult to make out just what is at stake in this judicial debate concerning the scope of the right guaranteed by s. 2(b) of the Charter. After all, when they get down to cases all the friends of the hate propaganda statute defend it on the same substantive ground, namely that it strikes a reasonable balance between freedom of expression and the protection of minorities. They are therefore united on the important moral/political conclusion, and seemingly divided only on the legal gloss to be placed on it. One party takes its cost/benefit balancing to show that s. 319(2) does not infringe s. 2(b) in the first place, while the other uses precisely the same calculation to establish that the infringement of s. 2(b) falls within the 'reasonable limits' of s. 1. Since both parties agree that s. 319(2) is consistent with the Charter, why does it matter which construction of the constitutional issues they choose?

I can imagine a legal reason for thinking that it matters: assigning a robust balancing role to s. 1 might be thought to provide a more coherent interpretation of the Charter as a whole. However, I can also see a philosophical reason for favouring the narrower reading of s. 2(b). The question is whether we should regard the right to freedom of expression as internally limited or as overridden by a competing right. On the former view the right to circulate hate propaganda has no Charter protection; on the latter view it does have such protection but it is trumped by a right of greater weight, namely the right of minorities to be protected against racial hatred. Now in many contexts this distinction can make a normative difference. I have the right to walk along a public footpath but no right to insist that you get out of my way if you happen to be using the same path. Because you infringe no right on my part, you owe me no compensation for forcing me to detour around you. By contrast, I have ownership rights over my land but the municipal government may have the right to expropriate that land for a public project. Because the expropriation infringes my property right, I am owed compensation for my loss. The philosophical point is that where a genuine right is justifiably infringed it does not simply vanish, as though it had never existed in the first place. Rather, something of normative significance has occurred, which may entitle the rightholder to remedial action. No remedy of any kind would be owed, however, where there was no right in the first place.

The Supreme Court now seems irreversibly committed to a 'broad, inclusive approach to the protected sphere of free expression',[24] leaving the strength of the protection in a particular instance to be determined by reference

to s. 1.[25] It has therefore determined that racists have a constitutionally protected right to circulate hate propaganda, but that this right may be justifiably infringed in order to protect their intended victims. Is the Court then prepared to acknowledge that Keegstra and Andrews are owed compensation for their normative loss? Apparently not, since the Court is willing to see them convicted of a criminal offence. But then how does this resolution of their cases differ substantively from finding that hate propaganda is a form of expression no one has a right to engage in, so that its restriction is no infringement of right in the first place?

We have already seen that strictly juridical considerations might incline us toward the wide interpretation of s. 2(b), and the corresponding activist role for s. 1, as ingredients in the best interpretation of the Charter as a distinctive constitutional document. However, there is another way of thinking about the interpretive issue. Suppose we ask the same question all the courts are asking in deciding whether to uphold s. 319(2) or to strike it down, namely which alternative will make for the better public policy. Suppose further, for a moment, that there is a good consequentialist case for legislation like s. 319(2). In that case, which interpretive approach is more likely to enhance the objective of the legislation, which is to discourage the circulation of hate propaganda? Will it be more effective to concede hatemongers a legal right to disseminate their views, which the State is justified in infringing, or to deny them that right in the first place? Put in these terms, the narrow interpretation of s. 2(b), with its internal limits on freedom of expression, may be found morally and politically preferable to the wide interpretation, which relies on the external controls of s. 1.

To say no more about the interpretive question would leave a misleading impression of the degree of constitutional protection which the Supreme Court is actually prepared to accord to hate propaganda. On the one hand, the entire Court shares the official view that all (non-violent) expression falls under the protection of s. 2(b), regardless of its content. On the other hand, the majority also holds that hate propaganda merits only relatively weak protection, because of its content.[26] Writing for the majority, Dickson CJ argues that the expression prohibited by s. 319(2) is only 'tenuously connected to the values underlying s. 2(b)'—namely, the collective search for truth, individual self-development, and the effective participation of all citizens in the political process. Now this conclusion is certainly open to dispute (it is disputed by the minority).[27] But its quite explicit effect is to weaken the s. 2(b) protection of hate propaganda; as Dickson CJ puts it, this material 'should not be accorded the greatest of weight in the s. 1 analysis'.[28] While hate propaganda falls within the scope of constitutionally protected expression, it is located on the periphery of this domain rather than at its core. The threshold is therefore lowered for a successful s. 1 argument in favour of limiting the s. 2(b) right: competing values deemed to be sufficiently weighty to override the right in this case might be too slight to limit a form of expression which has been accorded a higher initial degree of protection.

The Court majority is therefore somewhat at odds with itself over the issue of content restrictions on political expression. Why the particular content of hate propaganda should suffice to diminish its constitutional protection, but not to remove it altogether, remains unexplained. However, it seems obvious that the line taken by the majority foreordains the outcome of its s. 1 analysis of the hate propaganda statute; if the threshold has already been lowered then it is scarcely surprising that the majority is able to find an argument which surmounts it. As McLachlin J. points out on behalf of the minority, the entire argument

appears to be circular: 'If one starts from the premise that the speech covered by s. 319(2) is dangerous and without value, then it is simple to conclude that none of the commonly-offered justifications for protecting freedom of expression are served by it.'[29] Certainly the majority's approach does rather compromise its commitment to the wide interpretation of s. 2(b). It now appears that the broader the domain of the Charter right the thinner the protection it affords, at least around the edges.[30]

4. Hate Propaganda and Civil Liberties

Whether the limits on freedom of expression are already implicit in s. 2(b) or are imposed by s. 1, it is clear that there are such limits. It also seems clear from the adjudication of *Keegstra* and *Andrews* that the proper location of these limits is ultimately a question of public policy. The hate propaganda statute is consistent with the Charter if and only if it strikes a reasonable balance between the two important social values in conflict. We are therefore left with the substantive issue: does the statute protect minorities from vilification at too high a cost to freedom of expression?

Like the Supreme Court minority and the Alberta Court of Appeal, civil libertarians answer this question in the affirmative. They are able to marshal some very powerful considerations in favour of their position.[31] They claim that during the twenty years of its life s. 319(2) has had no discernible effect on the level of racial intolerance in Canada, or even on the circulation of hate propaganda. Indeed, by providing priceless publicity for their odious views, court proceedings against hatemongers may well have worsened the position of the very groups which the legislation purports to protect. However this may be, the law has certainly had a chilling effect on political speech, all the more so because it has tended to be applied not against the racist bigots which the Cohen Committee had in mind but against innocent or even progressive parties. If there were some way of deleting hate propaganda without thereby endangering other forms of political expression then, the civil libertarians say, they might have no objection to criminal legislation. But it is Utopian to think that a law, however carefully drafted, will not be abused and misapplied in practice. In that case, even if it does succeed in protecting minorities against discrimination, this success will come at an unacceptably high cost.

These are very forceful arguments, the selfsame arguments which I used to accept. Now I find myself no longer able to do so, at least with my former level of confidence. What has led me to part company on this issue with my usual civil libertarian allies? For one thing, with the prosecution of Keegstra and Andrews the hate propaganda statute is now being used against its rightful targets, namely the tireless merchants of racial enmity. Since the statute has now survived constitutional challenge, it might well begin to have just the sort of chilling effect on hate propaganda itself which the Cohen Committee had in mind.

More importantly, I have latterly come to be more impressed by the depth and tenacity of the intolerance towards racial and ethnic minorities which is both felt and openly expressed by a great many otherwise perfectly ordinary Canadians. While I do not believe that most of these people are as obsessive in their bigotry as Keegstra or Andrews, I fear that they provide a very fertile ground indeed for the seeds of enmity sown by the dedicated hatemongers. There is no shortage of opportunists aiming to cultivate this potential audience. In Vancouver a telephone hotline provides interested callers with a variety of recorded messages claiming that the Holocaust is a Jewish hoax, that a Jewish conspiracy controls the media, and that nonwhite 'aliens' are importing crime and social problems as they immigrate to Canada. In Toronto a similar

service dishes out racist slurs against native people. Furthermore, there is some evidence that racial intolerance is on the increase in Canada. For the past eight years the League for Human Rights of B'nai Brith Canada has polled attitudes toward minority groups. Much to their dismay, the researchers have discovered 'an increased willingness on the part of the population to express prejudicial opinions about all minorities'.[32]

I have also been struck by what I perceive to be a shift of target for Canadian racial hatred. While the old guard, like Keegstra and Andrews, still rant on about the Jews, most bigots now seem at least equally concerned with francophones, or native peoples, or blacks, or Asians. It is arguable, indeed is often argued, that Canadian Jews are now secure enough not to need special protection against anti-Semitic propaganda.[33] Be this as it may, the same cannot be claimed for blacks or Métis or Sikhs. These socially marginalized and relatively powerless groups, it seems to me, are at genuine risk of harm from the racist attitudes of employers, landlords, police, bureaucrats, and thugs. Early in 1992 police arrested a group of neo-Nazi skinheads minutes before they were going to fire-bomb an apartment occupied by a black family in Montreal, where there have been a number of clashes between gangs of blacks and white neo-Nazis. Since 1988 white police officers in Toronto have shot eight black civilians, some fatally. In Manitoba an inquiry into the justice system found it riddled with prejudice against native peoples, while a Quebec coroner's report found a 'totally unacceptable' level of racism in the Montreal police force. It does not seem far-fetched to think that the racial attitudes which have been manifested in these and other ways are capable of being reinforced and legitimized by the negative portrayal of visible minorities in hate propaganda.

Canadian racism is not an isolated phenomenon. Stimulated by a deepening economic recession, expressions of racial intolerance, and perhaps also the level of intolerance itself, are on the increase in most industrialized societies. In the United States the incidence of hate crimes rose to a record level in 1991, while the number of active hate groups showed a similar surge.[34] According to a European Parliament report, as many as 70,000 racial attacks occur annually in the United Kingdom, which is plagued by an especially 'high level of racial harassment and violence'.[35] In western Europe similar violence against racial and ethnic minorities is on the upswing in Germany, and in such models of decency and social justice as Belgium and Sweden, while in the East the collapse of communism has allowed the resurgence of old nationalist rivalries often marked by intolerance and xenophobia. Furthermore, racist platforms are finding their way more and more into the political mainstream, led by the electoral successes of right-wing parties in France and Germany which have openly targeted immigrant populations. Everywhere, it seems, blaming visible minorities for our social and economic ills is becoming politically respectable.

When we keep before us a vivid sense of the corrosive effects of racism on those who are its actual or potential victims, then it seems to me that there is no convincing case against some form of criminal legislation governing hate propaganda. In order to minimize the impact of such legislation on freedom of expression, it will need to establish a very high threshold for successful prosecution. However, when we bear in mind the safeguards built into s. 319(2), it also seems to me that there is no convincing case against the statute in its present form. It is already a well-established fact that the right to express one's opinions is not absolute. In Canada defamatory libel against individuals is a criminal offence.[36] Section 319(2) seeks to extend the same protection to certain specified groups. That racial, religious, and ethnic groups are in need of

such protection was accepted by the Cohen Committee in 1966. Following a survey of some materials being circulated in the years 1963–5, the Committee came to the following conclusion:

> It is evident from the foregoing that there exists in Canada a small number of persons and a somewhat larger number of organizations, extremist in method and dedicated to the preaching and spreading of hatred and contempt against certain identifiable minority groups in Canada.[37]

And again:

> The amount of hate propaganda presently being disseminated and its measurable effects probably are not sufficient to justify a description of the problem as one of crisis or near crisis proportions. Nevertheless the problem is a serious one. We believe that, given a certain set of socio-economic circumstances, such as a deepening of the emotional tensions or the setting in of a severe business recession, public susceptibility might well increase significantly. Moreover, the potential psychological and social damage of hate propaganda, both to a desensitized majority and to sensitive minority groups, is incalculable.[38]

Sadly, the Committee's fears have been borne out during these recessionary times a quarter of a century later. During the intervening years neither the incidence nor the intensity of Canadian racism seems to have diminished. There still appear to be a distressingly large number of Canadians whose dislike for one or more minority groups is sufficiently deep and persistent to be capable of being fanned into open enmity by demagogues and hatemongers, should they be permitted a platform from which to spread their message. It is true that the prosecution of racists may have the unintended effect of providing them with just such a platform. However, their conviction will also send a clear signal that the fomenting of hatred through the circulation of racist literature will not be tolerated in a liberal society. To tolerate it in the interest of freedom of expression would inevitably be to confer upon it a certain degree of legitimacy. This is something no society can afford to do, if it wishes to safeguard the status of minorities as equal citizens.[39]

Doubtless, s. 319(2) is not perfect as it stands.[40] The very small number of prosecutions under the section tends to show that its safeguards for freedom of expression have been quite effective. If anything, the hate propaganda law might be drawn somewhat more broadly than at present. One change worth consideration is expansion of the range of protected groups, at least far enough to include all those embraced by s. 15 of the Charter, which would add the further distinguishing features of sex, age, and disability, but perhaps farther still, so as to encompass groups identified by sexual orientation. If the scope of the statute were widened in this way then the circulation of hate propaganda against women would become a criminal matter. In that case, the expanded version of s. 319(2) might better accomplish the only legitimate work to be done by an obscenity statute. Since not all material promoting hatred against women has sexual content, and since not all sexually explicit material portrays women in a degrading way, hate propaganda legislation could provide a more focused instrument against the objectionable forms of pornography.[41]

I advance these proposals with diffidence; indeed, I defend the present version of s. 319(2) with equal diffidence. I am not at all certain of the case in favour of hate propaganda legislation, not nearly as certain as I once was of the case against it. But my earlier diagnosis of the nature of the debate goes some way toward both explaining and justifying my present state of mind. If at bottom this is a public policy issue, and if the best policy is the one which strikes the best balance between competing social values, then a view on either side of the issue reflects a highly speculative consequentialist calculation. Since none of the parties to the debate has a secure command over the relevant empirical data, it would seem to behove all of us to hold our views with considerable modesty and circumspection. I am acutely conscious of having provided very little evidence to support the various factual claims I made above: that minority groups in Canada today are vulnerable to racist propaganda, that the criminal law can provide some of the protection they need, that effective legislation need not trench too deeply on freedom of expression, and so on. But then the civil libertarians on the other side of the question have provided equally scanty support for their claims: that the existing law has been ineffective or counter-productive, that the abuses to which any such law is subject will more than cancel out any benefits it might yield, and so on. The difference between us is that their confidence in their view of the matter seems unassailable. It is this tone of absolute conviction which I find hardest to understand. Like everyone else who addresses this issue, their arguments are empirical and pragmatic. How then can they be so sure they are right?

Notes

1 RSC 1985, c. C-46. After the cases discussed below had reached the appeal stage, the previous s. 281.2 (RSC 1970, C. C-34) was renumbered as s. 319. For uniformity of reference, I have converted all citations to the new numbering.

2 Part I of the Constitution Act 1982, being Schedule B of the Canada Act 1982 (UK) 1982, c. 11.

3 *R. v. Keegstra* (1988) 43 CCC (3d) 150, reversing (1984) 19 CCC (3d) 254 (referred to hereafter as *Keegstra* (1988) and (1984) respectively); *R. v. Andrews* (1988) 43 CCC (3d) 193 (hereafter *Andrews(1988)*). *R. v. Zundel* (1987) 31 CCC (3d) 97 raised a similar challenge to the then s. 177 (now s. 181) of the Criminal Code; it will here be disregarded.

4 *R. v. Keegstra* (1990) 3 SCR 697; *R. v. Andrews* (1990) SCR 870 (hereafter *Keegstra* (1990) and *Andrews* (1990) respectively).

5 See e.g. *Keegstra* (1984), 274–5, and *Keegstra* (1988), 171, 176.

6 *Keegstra* (1990), 754; cf. 734, 735.

7 Ibid. 844–5; cf. 846, 848, 863–5.

8 Following *R. v. Oakes* (1986) 1 SCR 103.

9 *Keegstra* (1988), 174; (1990), 852–3.

10 *Keegstra* (1990), 769.

11 *Keegstra* (1988), 175–8; (1990), 844–65.

12 The following list is adapted from *Keegstra* (1984), 274. See also *Keegstra* (1990), 772–83; *Andrews* (1988), 216–19; and Law Reform Commission of Canada, *Hate Propaganda* (Working Paper 50, 1986), 30–8.

13 House of Commons, *Report of the Special Committee on Hate Propaganda in Canada* (1966), 61 (referred to hereafter as the Cohen Committee Report). See also Law Reform Commission, *Hate Propaganda*, ch. 2, s. I, 'Freedom of Expression versus Freedom from Hate: The Search for a Balance'.

14 Cohen Committee Report, 61.

15 A lesson which I have urged in *The Moral Foundation of Rights* (Clarendon Press, Oxford, 1987).

16 *Andrews* (1988), 221.

17 Ibid.

18 *Keegstra* (1984), 268.

19 *Andrews* (1988), 210.

20 The Alberta Court of Appeal, of course, also uses the wide interpretation, but then parts company with the friends of the hate propaganda statute by holding its infringement of s. 2(b) to be unjustified under the terms of s. 1. See *Keegstra* (1988), 162ff.

21 *Ford v. Quebec (Attorney General* (1988) 2 SCR 712; *Irwin Toy Ltd. v. Quebec (Attorney General)* (1989) 1 SCR 927.

22 *Keegstra* (1990), 728–9.

23 Ibid. 730–3, 829–31.

24 *Irwin Toy* (1989), 970.

25 Since deciding *Keegstra* and *Andrews*, the Court has reconfirmed this commitment in *R. v. Butler*, where the form of expression at stake is pornography.

26 *Keegstra* (1990), 759–67.

27 Ibid. 840–2.

28 Ibid. 765.

29 Ibid. 841.

30 The Court has located at least two other forms of expression at the periphery of the Charter right: communication for the purpose of prostitution (in *Reference re ss. 193 and 195.1(1)(c) of the Criminal Code (Man.)* (1990)1 SCR 1123), and pornography (in *Butler*).

31 See e.g. A. Alan Borovoy, *When Freedoms Collide: The Case for Our Civil Liberties* (Lester & Orpen Dennys, Toronto, 1988), 40–53.

32 *Toronto Star*, 22 Feb. 1992.

33 It is worth noting, however, that in 1991 reported incidents of anti-Semitism in Canada were 42% higher than two years earlier (see ibid.).

34 *The Globe and Mail*, 25 Feb. 1992.

35 Ibid. 12 Oct. 1990.

36 Criminal Code, ss. 297–317.

37 Cohen Committee Report, 25.

38 Ibid. 59.

39 The expressive purpose of hate propaganda legislation was well understood by the Cohen Committee. In their opinion, such legislation 'sets out as a solemn public judgment that the holding up of identifiable groups to hatred or contempt is inherently likely to dispose the rest of the public to violence against the members of these groups and inherently likely to expose them to loss of respect among their fellow men' (Report, 64–5).

40 It is, however, noteworthy that the Law Reform Commission recommended only minor changes in it; see *Hate Propaganda*, 39–41.

41 This is, however, less likely to happen now that the Supreme Court has upheld the obscenity statute in *Butler*.

Questions for Discussion

1 Is Sumner right that both supporters and opponents of hate propaganda legislation approach the issue in a consequentialist manner?

2 Are obscene, seditious, or defamatory speech kinds of expression which should be covered by

a right to free expression at all? If so, but they are limited by competing values, are the would-be speakers owed any compensation for the infringement of their right?

3 The Canadian hate propaganda legislation prohibits the wilful promotion of hatred against "any identifiable group." Is this description too broad? Which groups, specifically, should be protected by this legislation?

4 Does the strength of the argument against hate propaganda legislation depend on the "depth and tenacity of the intolerance towards racial and ethnic minorities which is both felt and openly expressed by a great many otherwise perfectly ordinary Canadians"?

Diversity and Creativity

Excerpt from "Selling Illusions: The Cult of Multiculturalism in Canada"

Neil Bissoondath

*Some forms of expression have been labelled as "politically incorrect" because they contain messages (explicitly or implicitly) which portray groups of people in a negative light. In this selection from his book **Selling Illusions**, Neil Bissoondath examines a few examples of specific forms of speech which some people have thought should be banned for such reasons. Bissoondath argues in favour of a balanced treatment of these texts, with careful attention to historical setting to possible unacceptable hidden assumptions. However, he argues against the concept of banning any such materials, and points out some ridiculous lengths to which such a policy could be taken. Bissoondath also offers some remarks about the notion that groups of people may have a distinctive voice which should not be "appropriated" by members of different groups, particularly of more dominant groups in society.*

★ ★ ★

Art is a passion of the mind. And the imagination works best when it is most free. Western writers have always felt free to be eclectic in their selection of theme, setting, form; Western visual artists have, in this century, been happily raiding the visual storehouses of Africa, Asia, the Philippines. I am sure that we must grant ourselves an equal freedom.

Salman Rushdie,
Imaginary Homelands[1]

How easy it is, in life and in art, to give and to take offence.

The language is littered with the corpses of unworthy terminology: the mentally or physically handicapped are now the mentally or physically challenged; AIDS victims have become People with AIDS (suggesting that we must now talk of People with Accidents); failures are now defined as incomplete successes, and companies no longer fire or lay off people, they downsize and destaff. U.S. real-estate advertisers are now advised to avoid red-light words such as "executive" (which could be racist, since most corporate executives are white), "master bedroom" (which could be suggestive of slavery), "walk-in closet" (which might offend those who cannot walk) and "spectacular view" (which might offend those who cannot see).

And a Canadian publisher, Douglas Gibson of McClelland & Stewart Ltd., relishes the following story: In a speech to an industry convention, Mr. Gibson, a clever and witty man, attacked the federal government's tax on books by saying, "Those who tax reading must be people who find reading taxing." The line was greeted with laughter and applause. But afterward, one person approached him to register displeasure. "That was a clever line," the man said. "Many people laughed. I did not. I'm dyslexic. It's not nice to imply that people who have a hard time reading are stupid."

It is a particularly perilous time for those who work with words. Speech and copy writers, journalists, academics and novelists must exercise greater than usual caution in the selection of their words. Even if, for the writer, a word such as "candle" means simply a stick of wax used to provide illumination, it will be taken by many to mean much more than it says, so that, for instance, if a power outage in a novel should prompt a male character to offer a candle to a female character, his action may be interpreted as a form of sexual aggression. It is one consequence of literature courses around the world that teach students to seek significance in every word, comma and period. There is little scope for essays and dissertations, after all, if a candle is just a candle. A candle must be more than itself if it is to bear the weight of ideology.

In her short story "Labour Day Dinner," Alice Munro writes: "Ruth is wearing a white shirt belonging to her brother, his striped pyjama bottoms, and a monumental black turban. She looks like a proud but good-natured Sikh."[2]

Proud *but* good-natured?

The harmless conjunction could, if one so wished, unleash a torrent of ill-feeling, for it could be construed as implying that proud Sikhs are not on the whole good-natured; it could be taken as indicative of distrust of Sikh pride—indeed, distrust of any minority group with a sense of self.

But to read all of this into the innocent conjunction, to suspect Ms. Munro of harbouring hostilities, one must be prey to particularly febrile sensitivities. One must be governed by a sense of historical and ethnic injustice married to a refusal to understand or forgive. One must be able to see behind that "but" a mental convergence between Ms. Munro and those who mistreated the passengers of the *Komagata Maru* in 1914. One must be in love, then, with one's own victimhood. Sikhs, happily, have far greater problems to worry about, and they are a people on the whole too proud to be silly. Unfortunately, such silliness—the obsessive desire to seek offence and the obsessive desire to avoid giving it—are rampant elsewhere, sprouting vigorously in the upturned soil of the multicultural land.

Sometimes, the twists and turns of sensitivities being unpredictable, even the greatest of care is insufficient. Inoffensiveness can never be taken for granted.

Consider, for instance, "The Hockey Sweater," Roch Carrier's classic story of life in a small Quebec town in the late Forties. It is a simple and effective tale that depicts, through the neatly captured voice of a child, a life governed by the imperatives of school, church and hockey:

> The winters of my childhood were long, long, seasons. We lived in three places—the school, the church and the skating rink—but our real life was on the skating-rink.... [S]chool was ... a quiet place where we could prepare for the next hockey game, lay out our next strategies. As for church, we found there the tranquility of God: there we forgot school and dreamed about the next hockey game. Through our daydreams it might happen that we would recite a prayer: we would ask God to help us play as well as Maurice Richard.[3]

When the boy—who, like his friends, worships the Montreal Canadiens—outgrows his Canadiens hockey sweater, his mother orders a new one from the Eaton's mail-order department. The store mistakenly supplies a Toronto

Maple Leafs sweater. Forced to wear it because his mother fears offending Monsieur Eaton, an *anglais*, the boy's anger flares on the ice after he is given what he considers an unfair penalty. He smashes his stick in frustration, only to be confronted by the young vicar:

> "My child," he said, "just because you're wearing a new Toronto Maple Leafs sweater unlike the others, it doesn't mean you're going to make the laws around here. A proper young man doesn't lose his temper. Now take off your skates and go to the church and ask God to forgive you."
>
> Wearing my Maple Leafs sweater I went to the church, where I prayed to God; I asked him to send, as quickly as possible, moths that would eat up my Toronto Maple Leafs sweater.

"The Hockey Sweater" is a charming story that reveals much about the sporting and religious life of Quebec as well as, more generally, about the mythology of hockey in Canada. It speaks to many, even to those not enamoured of hockey. One would not expect it to upset anyone.

But it may be that expectations exist in order to be demolished.

Some years after its initial appearance, the publishers received a letter requesting permission to include the story in a new anthology for schools. The letter requested "some minor changes" in view of the fact that the anthology would be used "by elementary students from varying backgrounds and religions"; specifically, it requested the deletion of all references to God and was accompanied by photocopies of the relevant pages with the offending words scratched out.

More recently, the novelist Alberto Manguel wrote of his own experience with an offending word.[4] Invited to contribute to the introduction of a book on the immigrant experience, he wrote that "Canada has been perceived as a land of noble savages..." To his consternation, the word "savages" was taken

out and replaced by the word "natives." This was done at the insistence of the publisher's native liaison officer, "who considered the use of the word 'savage' unacceptable 'in any context.'" He or she was apparently unfamiliar with the eighteenth-century literary concept of the noble savage, to which Mr. Manguel was referring. "To change the wording," Mr. Manguel points out, "to prettify the concept by replacing 'savage' with 'native' is an arrogant attempt to modify history.... Language is inextricable from the society that uses it; we are defined by our vocabulary, by the words we used and by the words we use."

Censorship is nothing new in this world. It appears everywhere in one guise or another, for reasons that are not always ill-meaning but are nearly always misguided.

William Shakespeare's *The Merchant of Venice* is a particular favourite of the censors. While Shylock's portrayed viciousness is seen as the product of anti-Semitism, his moving plea for recognition of his humanity remains largely ignored. I was only ten or eleven when I first read the play (for a primary school production that never materialized), and from the beginning the portrait of Shylock struck me as moving and complex, a compelling reminder that even though human beings may be turned into brutes by circumstance and experience, they remain human beings. This is an unsettling truth, for it challenges the satisfying prejudices we all harbour. We do not have to like or even forgive the brutes among us, but we ignore their humanity at our own peril.

And yet the play has caused problems in classrooms. As Bernie M. Farber, national director for community relations for the Canadian Jewish Congress, has written, Shylock's redeeming qualities are of no importance "to the 14-year-old Jewish student who, after viewing a production of *The Merchant of Venice* a few months ago, had pennies and gum wrappers pelted at him by other students. And it makes little difference to the dozens of Jewish students who have been referred to as 'Jewish dog,' 'Jew devil' and 'Shylock,' or have had swastikas carved in their desks or coins thrown at them as a result of youthful insensitivities following the play's reading in class."[5]

Such actions would suggest, though, that the problem is not with the play but with the way in which it is presented. Shylock, properly explored, would not bring taunts to Jewish students but a new sympathy, a recognition of the viciousness to which Jews[6] have historically been subjected. No better vehicle exists for an exploration of anti-Semitism. The Canadian Jewish Congress, as Mr. Farber makes clear, does not call for the banning of the play, as others have done, but does insist that its full context be explored, its perspectives on prejudice and bigotry stressed.

This is the only sensible approach to controversial works, but it requires a basic trust in the instincts and intelligence of teachers and students. It requires a trust that free people can think for themselves, can examine different points of view and, with appropriate guidance, come to appropriate conclusions.

This is not a trust that Mr. Victor Doerksen, a Conservative member of the Alberta legislature, is prepared to extend. In March 1994, during national Freedom to Read Week (the irony would, in all likelihood, have been lost on the Honorable Member), he delivered an eight-hundred-name petition to the legislature demanding that John Steinbeck's *Of Mice and Men* be banned from all Alberta school libraries. The petition called on the government "not to allow literature in the education system that is intolerant of any religion, including Christianity, or demeans or profanes the name of God and Jesus Christ."[7] Although admitting he has not read the 118-page novel, Mr. Doerksen nevertheless insisted that it uses "profane words" 198 times. (The thought does occur to me that Mr. Doerksen may in fact be doing the students a favour. Banning the book may be the one infallible

way to ensure that they read it—surreptitiously, without guidance, seeking out only the titillating or "offensive" parts...)

John Steinbeck is not the only Nobel prize winner to merit such treatment from people like Mr. Doerksen, though. The use of the word "fuck," so shocking to students' sensibilities, has prompted calls for the banning of Aleksandr Solzhenitsyn's *One Day in the Life of Ivan Denisovich*; as has the use of the word "nigger "in William Golding's *Lord of the Flies,* Harper Lee's *To Kill a Mockingbird* and Mark Twain's *Huckleberry Finn.* Closer to home, the sexuality in Margaret Laurence's *The Diviners* frequently proves too offensive to bear, as do W.P. Kinsella's depictions of natives.

Of course, we have never been a country entirely devoted to the idea of freedom of speech. Once Mr. Doerksen's political career is over, he can always seek employment among the ranks of the literary critics hired by Canada Customs to protect us from the literary depravities flooding in from abroad, all those books that promote "a homosexual lifestyle" (whatever that is), debase the family and demean Christian values, books that just might contravene our hate laws, such as Salman Rushdie's *The Satanic Verses,* which was "delayed" by Customs so that its critics could judge the work's literary merits.

In this atmosphere, even the warnings of the past must be handled with care, as Reform Party MP for Okanagan Centre Werner Schmidt found out when his constituency newsletter quoted Adolf Hitler: "What luck for rulers that men do not think."[8] The resulting furore—the Canadian Jewish Congress condemned the use of a mass-murderer's words in an MP's newsletter as "highly offensive" and "inexcusable"—led to quick apologies from party leader Preston Manning and an extraordinary statement from a chastened Mr. Schmidt: "I would never have put it in there personally because I don't think a person who has such an odious history or background should ever be quoted."[9] Any use of

Hitler's name or words is bound to be controversial, but do we not do ourselves a disservice by refusing ever to quote him? The lessons to be drawn from a life like Hitler's are many and varied. Ugliness, like beauty, has much to impart.

In the face of these cases, and of hundreds like them, the request to delete God from "The Hockey Sweater" seems minor. But the attitude implicit in the request—that literature must be shaped and sanitized in order to avoid all possibility of giving offence—is now making itself felt in ways that are exquisitely mind-boggling for writers. Many gods other than He of the Old and New Testaments have been erected: ethnic gods, gender gods. They all have their defenders. They all claim their victims....

Appropriation of Voice

The urge to segregate first made itself felt in the Canadian literary community in 1987 when a nasty spat developed among the editors of the Women's Press in Toronto. A proposed short-story anthology ran into trouble when objections were raised, in part by Marlene Philip,[22] concerning certain of the stories already contracted for publication. The problem was simple: white female writers had written from the viewpoint of black female characters; they had "appropriated" the experiences of women already exploited in a society dominated by white males. The white writers had, in telling the stories of black women, practised a kind of cultural imperialism. The house, a vital and necessary publisher, split viciously over the issue. A kind of in-house coup ensued. Locks were changed, jobs were lost.

But this was just the beginning. Soon other demands were made: not only must whites not write about blacks, but men must not write about women, non-natives about natives, and so on, all based on the claim that if you haven't lived the life, you don't have the right to write about it. And the writer who dares to explore the territory deemed not his or her own becomes a thief, open to charges of racism, sexism, imperialism from people who object to being portrayed in ways other than they would portray themselves—and self-portraits, let us face it, tend to be free of blemishes....

In an article in *Brick* magazine, writer Dionne Brand accuses my portrayals of women and blacks of simply revalidating the myths of "Eurocentric discourse," of drawing "only the stereotype so helpful in white domination," of filtering their voices "through the Eurocentric screen of racist, sexist discourse." Further, "[i]n producing a Neil Bissoondath to denounce the cultural appropriation critique, the white cultural establishment produces a dark face to dismiss and discredit all the other dark faces and simultaneously to confirm and reinscribe that colonial representation which is essential to racial domination."[23]

... The accusations levelled against me and a variety of other artists across the country have in the end little to do with racism or sexism or any other "ism." These are simply convenient hooks that have much more to do with the revealed hollowness of armchair revolutionary ideology. Challenged where it hurts most, those who see themselves in my characters hit back like children, with a stunning if typical simple-mindedness. All artistic expression—whether a book, a painting or a museum exhibition—demands a certain subtlety of mind, a certain emotional nakedness, if it is to be understood. Ideologues, pushed by often legitimate grievances into a mind-numbing self-righteousness, have neither. Living by received ideas, they bend and simplify the complexities of life to suit their own ideological preoccupations. They seek to cow everyone else into accepting their visions and their timetables.

Those who seek to subordinate art, its functions and its freedoms to sexual, racial or religious politics seek nothing less than to impose their own ideological visions on the imaginative expressions of others. They claim rights for themselves that they would deny to those who do not share their view of the world.

In this society, the charge of racism is a particularly virulent one. There are few who do not recognize racism as an evil, making it a charge easily levelled by those who interpret the world through the colour of their skin, by those who are "racialized." Declaring themselves anti-racists, they ironically share a racial vision of life with the architects and defenders of apartheid. I would suggest that to define yourself by your colour is to be racist, just as to define yourself by your gender is sexist; it is to reduce the complexity of human beings to formulae. I would further suggest that imposed political ideology distorts reality, and that sharpened racial ideology distorts the soul.

Notes

1 Salman Rushdie, *Imaginary Homelands*, p. 20.

2 Alice Munro, "Labour Day Dinner" in *The Moons of Jupiter* (Toronto: Penguin Books, 1986), p. 150.

3 Roch Carrier, "The Hockey Sweater," trans. by Sheila Fischman, in *Breaking Through*, ed. John Borovilos (Toronto: Prentice-Hall, 1990).

4 Alberto Manguel, "To deny the past is worse than foolish," *The Globe and Mail*, April 28, 1994.

5 Bernie M. Farber, "Merchant of Venice has made young Jewish students suffer," *Montreal Gazette*, November 5, 1993.

6 Even the term "Jew" is problematic. Centuries of anti-Semitism have made it a term of abuse, so that popular sensitivities now prefer to refer to "Jewish persons." I found myself reassured, though, while listening to a speech by former Israeli defence minister Ariel Sharon, who had no hesitation in referring to himself as a Jew, [and] to his people as Jews. While some will choose to see this, particularly from Sharon, as a mark of belligerence, I prefer to see it as a sign of pride: to allow the word to be expropriated by hatemongers is to betray a little part of yourself.

7 "School ban urged for Steinbeck novel," *The Globe and Mail*, March 2, 1994.

8 Portia Priegert, "MP was wrong to quote Hitler in newsletter: Manning," Canadian Press, *Montreal Gazette*, February 10, 1994.

9 Ibid.

...

22 See M. Nourbese Philip, "Gut Issues in Babylon" in *Frontiers* (Stratford: The Mercury Press, 1992), p. 211.

23 Dionne Brand, "Who Can Speak for Whom?" *Brick*, no. 46, summer 1993, p. 19.

Questions for Discussion

1 Are some works of literature too offensive or dangerous to specific groups to be used at all for educational purposes, or is any work in principle suitable, provided "that its full context be explored, its perspectives on prejudice and bigotry stressed"? Does it matter what level of education a work is being considered for?

2 Under what circumstances would it be appropriate to quote people with an "odious history or background," such as Adolf Hitler? Under what circumstances would it be inappropriate?

3 In what way might "appropriating" the voice of a particular culture harm that culture or the members of it? Does the danger of "appropriation" mean that people should never write about (or from the perspective of) members of different cultural groups?

Freedom of Expression and Choice of Language

Leslie Green

One aspect of the freedom of expression issue which has been prominent particularly in Canada concerns the importance of the ability to communicate in the language of one's choice. In this selection, Leslie Green considers the relationship between regulations concerning the language used for expression, and restrictions on freedom of expression itself. He considers several arguments against the view that language is merely a neutral medium of

Ethical Issues

communication, adding nothing to the message conveyed. First, Green notes that there may be cases where exact translation is impossible, due to differences in connotation and semantics, and he then raises the more significant point that choice of language affects the audience one will be able to reach with one's communication. Nevertheless, he argues that the most significant reason why language should not be seen as merely a meaning-neutral code is that choice of language also plays an expressive role of its own, given the way in which language is often linked to cultural and political identity.

★ ★ ★

1. The Problem

In linguistically divided countries, governments often regulate the use of language; they make some languages official, they restrict others, they impose linguistic requirements on educational or professional qualifications, and so on. My question is this: Do sound principles of free expression direct or constrain such regulation?

The issue is a familiar one to Canadians whose federal government requires the use of French and English for certain purposes, and whose provincial governments have often restricted one or the other. Historically, French and languages other than English bore the brunt of deliberate repression, but nationalist governments in Quebec have recently turned the tables and banned, in certain contexts, the use of English and other languages. Quebec's Charter of the French Language, for example, made French the sole official language of that province, and prohibited non-French commercial publicity, firm names and, with certain exceptions, public signs.[1]

In a series of important and highly controversial judgments, the Supreme Court of Canada struck down some of these provisions as inconsistent with the guarantees of free expression found both in the entrenched Canadian Charter of Rights and Freedoms and also in Quebec's provincial human rights statute. These decisions were generally admired by English Canadians and, not surprisingly, deplored by the Quebec French. In consequence, the government of Quebec used its power under the Charter to derogate from the free expression guarantees, a decision that they may, in retrospect, have regretted. That action quickly polarized public sentiment and was among the factors making it impossible for Quebec to secure the agreement of all the majority-anglophone provinces on constitutional amendments which would have given it more control over its cultural affairs. Perhaps the linguistic division of opinion on the cases was to be expected. More surprising, however, was the political division, for the decisions did not attract much support from liberal and left-wing academics either. They were disappointed to see the Court protecting commercial expression and to see it assisting a historically powerful group (English Quebeckers) against a historically weaker one (French Quebeckers). Groups who are normally friends of free expression were thus surprisingly hostile to the Supreme Court's defence of it in these cases.

Part of the puzzle is explained by the fact that these cases involved commercial signs and that there are many liberals whose commitment to free expression does not reach that far. But it is, I think, quite wrong to let one's views about commercial expression occlude the broader issue here. First, some of the grounds on which Quebec defended its legislation (for instance, that its government enjoyed 'democratic legitimacy', i.e., was elected) would permit the restriction of noncommercial expression as well. Second, some Quebec nationalists thought—and still think—that the impugned legislation did not go far enough in restricting English. Finally, the will to regulate more broadly was in any case manifest in the proposal of the Montreal Catholic School Commission to ban languages other than French from the playgrounds and corridors of their schools. None of this is resolved by one's views about commercial expression, so by focusing solely on that aspect liberals lost the opportunity to test their views more fully.

Still, it is not *obvious* that a sound view of free expression should protect choice of language. (And here I mean morally, and not just legally, sound.) Indeed, some Canadians regard that suggestion as a kind of legalistic joke, rather as if one argued that the Oleomargarine Act, in requiring margarine to be dyed orange, wrongfully discriminates on grounds of colour. But I want to suggest that this is mistaken and that free expression does properly extend so far as to protect choice of language.

Principles of free expression protect expressive acts by imposing disabilities or duties on people, and they do so *in order to* protect such acts. The question whether freedom or expression protects choice of language thus needs to be distinguished from a broader question: Are there *any* principles of political morality that direct or constrain the regulation of language?

The questions are importantly different. Governments should not, for instance, act irrationally. Since there is no evidence that Quebec's restrictions on external commercial signs would do more good than harm that is enough to impugn them, at least morally and perhaps constitutionally as well. But that is not an argument derived from free expression. Likewise, it is wrong to pay English-speaking workers more than French-speaking workers when language is irrelevant to the job. But the wrong is one of discrimination, not the violation of freedom of expression. Again, it would be wrong to punish people for speaking French at home. But the evil here is just that in prohibiting a harmless activity it restricts their personal liberty.

Principles of rationality, non-discrimination, and personal liberty will in such ways often protect language use indirectly, as fall-out from their central aims. Free expression plays an independent role only if it enhances these protections, if it protects language beyond what can be expected from other principles of political morality (Greenawalt 1989: 9–10). That is the sort of principle I want to explore here.

I follow Scanlon in regarding an expressive act as 'any act that is intended by its agent to communicate to one or more persons some proposition or attitude' (Scanlon 1972: 206). Expressive acts are thus all those that bear the communicative intentions of some agent, whom for sake of simplicity we shall call the speaker. This must not, however, be taken to imply that all expressive acts are speech acts: writing, signalling, playing music, painting, etc. can all be expressive, as can some criminal acts, including acts of terrorism and civil disobedience. Much fruitless debate in political theory is inspired by the narrow language of the First Amendment to the American Constitution which protects 'freedom of speech, or of the press'. This has given rise to many unedifying attempts to distinguish speech and action. In contrast, section 2 of the Canadian Charter, like many other human rights documents, casts the net more broadly to catch: 'freedom of thought, belief, opinion and expression, including freedom of press and other media of communication' (Canadian Charter, 1982). That is, I think, a better way to demarcate the territory. Such unity as exists in the area flows, not from the fact that these are all in some obscure sense forms of 'speech', but rather that they are all expressive.

Generally, an act counts as expressive only if it attempts to get others to understand or share some proposition or attitude, and only if it does this communicatively, that is, by trying to get them to recognize that it is done with that intention.[2] I say, 'proposition or attitude', because it would be a poor and excessively rationalistic view of human communication to think that it only serves the communication of truths. The contents of communicative acts are quite diverse: we attempt to communicate to others, not only propositions or ideas to be believed, but attitudes and values to be shared. In the case of artistic expression, for example, communicative intent is hardly ever propositional. Attitudes, values, and dispositions all enter into our common life in important ways and are transmitted in part through their expression. In any case, so far as the Charter is concerned, the cognitive and the affective are both accommodated by the language itself which distinguishes the terms 'thought,' 'belief,' and 'opinion' from the more general notion of 'expression'.

The reasons for protecting such acts are, I believe, several and are grounded in the interests of speakers, of their audiences, and of the general public. Attempts to reduce these intersecting and sometimes competing considerations to a monistic theory have not met with great success,[3] for a cluster of different kinds of interests is at stake here. Surely consequentialist considerations, such as J.S. Mill's claim that free expression promotes knowledge of the truth, have weight (Mill 1962: ch. 2). At the same time, it fosters and expresses both collective and individual autonomy: it serves democratic decision making, artistic and cultural endeavor, the expression of individual identity, and so on. Interestingly, the Supreme Court of Canada has explicitly endorsed such a pluralistic account of the grounds of free expression (*Irwin Toy* at 976–7; *Ford* at 712) and that is the view I shall adopt here.

I do want to reiterate, however, that the interests at stake in free expression are not, on this view, just individual ones. They have an important social dimension, recognition of which is, contrary to the allegations of some theorists, deeply rooted in the liberal tradition. Mill, for example, held that: 'Were an opinion a personal possession of no value except to the owner; if to be obstructed in the enjoyment of it were simply a private injury, it would make some difference whether the injury was inflicted only on a few persons or on many' (Mill 1962: 142). But, he continued, the restriction of opinion harms not just the individual but the public interest, and it is not just for the sake of a single speaker that we protect expression. To prevent even one person from speaking is wrong, not mainly because of the value of this liberty to her or to him, but because of the contribution it makes to the common good.

Meiklejohn took the public interest justification even further, denying the speaker's interest any independent moral importance at all: 'What is essential is not that everyone should speak, but that everything worth saying shall be said' (Meiklejohn, 1960: 26). Of course, principles of free expression do not require that everyone should speak; at most they require that everyone has the opportunity to speak or remain silent. And the connection between what is worth saying and what is worth protecting is more complex than Meiklejohn allows. We do not want to claim that a speaker's interest in uttering a banal, commonplace ideal should count for little merely on the ground that, having been said before, its contribution to the public interest is slight. Indeed, a single-minded concern that, as Meiklejohn puts it, 'everything worth saying shall be said', could easily lead to the violation of what we normally think of as paradigm rights of free expression. We do not believe that only those things worth saying should be permitted to be said nor even that scarce resources should be apportioned among speakers according to how socially valuable their views are. Moreover, in some cases we do regard it as important that everyone has an opportunity to speak, even if that means that the amount of time devoted to the worthless and the worthwhile is about the same. Meiklejohn thought his argument a democratic one, but the notion that everyone should speak in fact has deep roots in democratic theory, beginning with the classical Greek notion of *isogoria*. While the public interest is essential to understanding the full importance of freedom of expression, there is also an individual interest that cannot be discounted.

2. Medium and Message

There is an objection, however, to thinking that choice of language should be protected by such principles. They protect expressive acts in virtue of their expressive character; but not all features of such acts *are* expressive. For example, it is commonly thought that free expression does not protect the time, manner, or place of expression. Thus the regulation of radio frequencies, or the quality and supply of paper during war time, or the chemical additives present in artists' paints and materials, may all have effects on the character and quality of expressive acts, and may at the margin even inhibit some forms of expression and promote others. But, according to the proposed distinction they would count as regulation of the media of communication only and not of the message itself. These normally bear, the argument goes, on the form rather than content of expression. Likewise, it may be said, whether the medium of expression is French, English, or Cree, the message remains invariant, so restrictions of medium need not offend principles of free expression.

That was how one Canadian court saw the issue. In *Irwin Toy,* a case testing the constitutionality of legislation restricting advertising directed at children, Hugessen, ACJ. introduced a distinction which was to prove pivotal. He said, 'The late Dr McLuhan notwithstanding, message and medium are, in law, two very different things' (*Irwin Toy* at 58). He held that a legislature which regulates or restricts the

medium in which some message is communicated is not regulating or restricting the message itself and thus cannot be said to be regulating or restricting any expressive act.

This reasoning also dominates the trial judgment in *Devine* which, though overturned on appeal, nicely puts the objection we now consider. Dugas, J. applied the distinction between medium and message to the case of language: 'Language, after all, is nothing more than a code of written or oral signs, used by those who know it to communicate with each other' (*Devine* at 375). Prohibiting the use of a particular code, he stated, does not therefore interfere with the communicative intention, for any other code might be used to express the same propositions or attitudes. Hence 'Freedom of expression does not include the freedom to choose the language of expression' (*Devine* at 379).

There are many interesting and important aspects of these judgments that we need not consider here. What I do want to focus on is the central distinction between medium and message and the use to which it was put. The reasoning seems to have gone something like this:

1. Only expressive acts are candidates for the protection of freedom of expression;
2. A language is nothing more than a content-neutral code;
3. Thus, restricting the choice of language cannot restrict any expressive act.

Now I have already endorsed (1) and suggested some of the reasons one might have for protecting such acts, so let us turn to (2). The word 'code' which I draw from the judgment is unhappy, suggesting as it does an artificial medium used in place of a natural language. The fact that the same meaning may be borne by a sentence spoken in English and the same English sentence sent over the wire in Morse code would hardly suffice to establish the semantic equivalence of that sentence and its best French translation. There are codes and then there are 'codes'. We must take care not to become enchanted with the jargon of some fashionable linguistic theory. The sense in (2) just amounts to this: it is roughly true that anything that can be said in English can also be said in French. But, as we shall see below, the fact that this is only *roughly* true allowed the Supreme Court of Canada in *Ford* to reject (2) and the inference drawn from it. That result was not too surprising, for there were plenty of other clouds on the horizon for this distinction, at least as a matter of law.

First, medium of communication is expressly mentioned in the Charter as being included in the guarantees of section 2. It is true that, in that context, the central cases of such media are the press and airwaves, but neither the language of the constitution nor the decided cases inhibits its development by analogy. Even if medium is distinct from message, in at least some cases the Canadian constitution finds reasons for protecting both.

Second, the following words of an earlier Supreme Court judgment suggest a view of language as something more than a content-neutral code:

> The importance of language rights is grounded in the essential role that language plays in human existence, development and dignity. It is through language that we are able to form concepts; to structure and order the world around us. Language bridges the gap between isolation and community, allowing human beings to delineate the rights and duties they hold in respect of one another, and thus to live in society. (*Reference re: Manitoba Language Rights* at 19)

Finally, and perhaps most important for present purposes, this view of language seemed inconsistent with the very statute the trial judge was attempting to interpret. For its preamble opens with the ringing declaration that 'the French language ... is the instrument by which that people [i.e., Quebeckers] has articulated its identity' (Charter of the French

Language, 1977). As Boudreault J. shrewdly observed in the trial judgement in *Ford,* this makes it very difficult to suppose that the *legislators* conceived of language merely as a neutral code and thus that they intended that the Act should regulate its use only in that respect (*Ford* at 724).

So in deciding as it did, the Supreme Court certainly had a reasonable footing: nothing in Canadian law prohibited their finding that freedom of expression includes the freedom to choose one's language and there was enough directing them along that path. But was it, in the end, a wise decision? Can it be defended in principle? I turn now to examine three arguments to that conclusion.

3. A Semantic Argument

One of the arguments the Supreme Court accepted, and one that has an obvious appeal, is to deny the premise of the objection. If it is wrong to think of a natural language as a content-neutral code, then it is wrong to think that regulating the code is not regulating content. Thus, in *Ford* the Court unanimously rejected (2) in the following words:

> Language is so intimately related to the form and content of expression that there cannot be true freedom of expression by means of language if one is prohibited from using the language of one's choice. Language is not merely a means or medium of expression; it colors the content and meaning of expression[4] (*Ford* at 748).

The Court thus exploits the inevitable haziness of the boundary between medium and message. That what can be said in French can also be said in English is only *roughly* true because choice of language colours the content and meaning of expression. Language is not, therefore, a content-neutral code.

Was the Court right about that? It is true that the expressive power of language varies, and that exact synonymy may be unavailable in some cases. Considering cultural resonance and sonorities, it would be hard to say that there are no semantic differences between the roughly equivalent idioms, *'filer à l'anglais'* and 'to take French leave'. Language does in such cases colour the meaning of the expression.

But is this sufficiently important and pervasive to bring choice of language under the comprehensive protection of free expression? I do not think so. Valerie Ford's offence, after all, was to have displayed the word 'wool' alongside 'laine' in the window of her wool shop. It is surely not to secure against any possible semantic slippage that we would defend her right to freedom of expression. This is not to deny that such slippage can occur, even in the context of commercial signs. A *'depanneur'* is not exactly a 'convenience store'. The differences in meaning are real; but they are occasional and do not matter much. If we are about to impose duties and disabilities on people as a matter of general policy, we must make sure that the stakes are high enough to warrant it. To show that language does in some cases flavour the meaning of expression will not warrant adopting a general policy of protecting choice of language just in order to catch such cases of heteronymy. The availability of circumlocutions, or the adoption of some foreign word and terms, would be a satisfactory alternative.

For this reason the tempting analogy with obscenity is misguided. One might initially be inclined to regard choice of natural language as being on a par with choice of tone or force and, reasoning along the lines of the US Supreme Court in *Cohen* v. *California,* argue that to restrict language is to restrict a whole mode of communication. But to exclude obscene or vulgar speech from the protections of free expression *is* to remove a distinctive tool, one which might prove useful or even necessary in circumstances that cannot easily be isolated in advance.[5] The potential heteronymy of French and English near-equivalents is neither

as pervasive nor as undirectional as the power of vulgar speech, so the analogy is unhelpful. There just is not a general linguistic tone or pragmatic effect that accrues to speaking English in the way that one might be thought to accrue to speaking vulgarly. So while it is certainly true as a descriptive matter that semantic slippage occurs, it is hard to endorse the normative thesis that this is what ought to bring choice of language under the protective umbrella of free expression.

4. An Instrumental Argument

A better route to the protection of choice of language is surely the instrumental one. Restricting the use of certain languages simply cuts off potential audiences or makes it more difficult to reach them, and that harms one of the core interests underlying freedom of expression on any plausible account.

To take a clear example: suppose a government restricted the language in which political commentary might appear in the newspapers, requiring that all published criticism of its policies to be in Ojibway, while favourable comment could be in any language. What matters here is not the possible semantic slippage, but the closing down of channels of communication by restricting both speakers and their potential audiences.

Now this argument bears, one must concede, less heavily on requirements than on prohibitions. Canada's Official Languages Act of 1969, for example, requires various officials and Government agencies to use both French and English, and Quebec's Charter of the French Language makes wide use of such requirements in order to promote the use of French in the working world. And they do so partly for instrumental reasons that are ultimately based on audience interests. The Charter of the French Language, for example, seeks to establish French as the normal working language of commerce and Government in Quebec thereby directly protecting the substantial interest that the francophone majority has in being able to understand communications of all sorts. It is important to note, moreover, that the audience interest is not exhausted by the immediate benefits of intelligible communication. It is well-known that patterns of language use will also have substantial secondary effects on people's life chances, including their opportunities for education, occupational advancement, and social and geographic mobility.

In the case of intended audiences, speakers will generally aim to communicate in a language that the audience understands. We should not, however, assume on that basis that everyone's interests can be best served without any regulation of language at all. The free market can fail in language as it can elsewhere. When the audience is linguistically fragmented there may be complex problems of co-ordination involved in finding a common language. When the minorities are bi- or multilingual there is the potential for collective action problems in sustaining the use of minority languages, and there is the risk of majorities oppressing linguistic minorities. None the less, it is easy to see why speakers have an interest in the freedom to use the language that they feel is best suited to their audiences. Unintended audiences also have an interest in the intelligibility of communication, however. It matters not only what others say to you, but what is being said generally. Since speakers have weaker, and in some cases no, incentives to serve the needs of unintended audiences, this may provide another reason for required use.

Might one argue that forcing someone to use a language other than the one he or she would otherwise use in that context limits the speaker's choice of medium and therefore must, at the very least, call for a persuasive justification? To assess this claim, one must investigate more closely the structure of speaker's

interest. In part, it derives from the intended audience's interest in intelligible communication: the intention to reach them is frustrated if one cannot do so. But we are not now considering a case in which the speaker's audience is limited by prohibition, but only a case in which the potential audience is expanded. A requirement that commercial signs and publicity be in French as well as another language, for example, does not inhibit the speaker's capacity to communicate with the audience at which the signs are directed. Could a speaker wish that a certain audience *not* receive a particular communication? No doubt, although plausible cases will turn, not on freedom of expression, but on the right to privacy.

The instrumental argument for protection for choice of language is thus an important one, though it may fail in some circumstances. Widespread individual bilingualism, or even the availability of convenient translation, lessens its force. A more discriminating policy of protecting choice of language where it is necessary for effective communication might answer to the same concerns and have fewer costs. And over time languages can be learned, so the need to do so stimulates investment in language learning. Quebec's language regime weighs less heavily on the anglophone community now than it would have done twenty years ago. Such are the limitations on the instrumental argument, so it seems unlikely that general protection for choice of language could be completely defended on instrumental grounds alone.

5. An Expressive Argument

There is, however, a third and independent reply to the objection that language is merely a non-expressive medium of communication, one noticed though not much elaborated by Supreme Court. Choice of language should be protected because it is an expression of identity and individuality:

It is, as the preamble of the Charter of the French Language itself indicates, a means by which a people may express its cultural identity. It is also the means by which the individual may express his or her personal identity and sense of individuality *(Devine* at 375).

This is an aspect of the romantic, as opposed to rationalist, tradition in free expression. Its context is not the forum or market-place of ideas, but rather the organic relations between an individual and his or her community. I say this is an independent objection, for it may succeed even where the instrumental argument fails, and even when the thesis of content-neutrality holds.

Returning now to the argument set out in section 2, above, we can see a further mistake. The thesis of content-neutrality does not show that a natural language is 'nothing more than a code'. Compare the following inference:

4. A flag is a piece of cloth,
5. Therefore, a flag is nothing more than a piece of cloth.

The conclusion does not follow because a flag can be both a piece of cloth *and* something more than a piece of cloth. Likewise, a language can be a content-neutral code *and* something more than a content-neutral code. If the something more makes it expressive, then the fact that it may also appropriately be described as a neutral code cannot change that.

To be still more precise, we do not even need to show that language is something more than a neutral code in order to justify the protection we want to accord it. Even if it were true that a natural language is nothing but a neutral code, and even if restrictions on language would not restrict the potential audience, the argument given above would still be invalid. For consider:

6. Choice of language is a candidate for protection of free expression only if it is an expressive act;
7. Language is nothing more than a neutral code;
8. So, freedom of expression does not include freedom to choose language of expression.

Even if (7) were true, (8) would still not follow, for (8) is about *choice* of language, and not about language itself. The error thus lies not just in the arguable falsehood of (7), but in an equivocation between 'language' as an abstract entity and 'choice of language' as an act. Invoking again our earlier analogy, we might compare:

9. Waving a flag is a candidate for protection of free expression only if it is an expressive act;
10. A flag is nothing more than a piece of cloth;
11. So, freedom of expression does not include freedom to wave a flag.

Here, the fallacy is patent, for the supposed truth of (10) plainly has nothing whatever to do with (11). A flag, like a language, is not an act of any kind, let alone an expressive one. But *speaking* a particular language, like *waving* a flag, is indeed an act and very possibly expressive. Thus, the purported distinction between medium and message is irrelevant. The fact, if it be one, that medium and message are two different things does not even begin to show that choice of medium cannot be intended to convey a message.

It is important to distinguish between the expressive argument defended here and the semantic argument that I rejected above. Suppose it were permitted to say 'Long live a free Quebec!' but prohibited to say *'Vive le Québec libre!'* What is most significant: the fact that there are nuances of meaning, historical and cultural resonances, poetics of sound present in *'Vive'* but absent from 'long live'? I doubt it. The significance of choice of language here lies not in what it says but in what it shows. Saying it in French is a doubly political act, for the propositional content is backed up by the fact that the utterance displays the legitimacy of the language and its relation to nationhood.

The argument we are pursuing is a normative one, but it does depend on certain social facts. It fails unless it actually is the case that language use has a social or individual meaning. This cannot be established *a priori*. But at least in Canada there is plenty of evidence that in many contexts it does. As I said earlier, the expressive function of language was not missed even by the legislators. The Charter of the French Language begins, 'Whereas the French language, the distinctive language of a people that is in the majority French-speaking, is the instrument by which that people has articulated its identity'....[6] What is distinctively nationalistic here is merely the suggestion that a group of people who are only 'in the majority' francophone constitute '*a* people'. The reality in a pluralistic society is that language choice permits each people to express its identity. The way this is done is largely a social creation, governed by convention, context and history.[7] In Canada, choice of language bears a number of meanings, of which ethnic identification and political affirmation are the most important.

Those who choose to use a particular language often thereby signal their sense of identification with an ethnic or cultural group. This is most commonly true of minority language speakers in circumstances where use of their language imposes some social or economic cost. The language establishes a link with an intended audience, a link which simultaneously invokes a boundary between those inside and those outside the group. This mark of distinction is often a source of value to minority language speakers, and legitimately so. Notice that ethnic identification

may be expressed even by those who are monolingual minority-language speakers. The notion of 'choice' in play may well be an attenuated one. For language use to have the expressive character I have attributed to it, it is not necessary that a person deliberately use one language and avoid another in circumstances where options are available. The expressive act need not be, for example, speaking Italian instead of English, but simply speaking Italian instead of remaining silent or allowing others to speak on one's behalf.

Language may also be an expression of political identity. Quebec's policies of *francisation* express not only a boundary-defining sense of common feeling, but also a political position which celebrates the distinctiveness of Quebec society and its aspirations for autonomy. It is no accident that minority language use is often a political marker, and not surprising that suppression of such languages is often undertaken with political aims in mind. The various forms of compulsion to which Estonian, Croatian, or Welsh speakers have been subject by their governments was motivated by a desire to suppress social formations which embody and promote nationalist politics.[8] That repression was unjust, but it was not ill-informed: use of those languages was indeed a political act.

Here again, the consequences of requiring the use of a certain language are likely to differ from those of prohibiting the use of others. The decision *not* to use a particular language may in some circumstances be expressive: it may be an act of resistance. In other cases, it may be understood that to use a particular language is not necessarily to identify with the ethnic group whose language it characteristically is, nor to endorse any political view. A language may simply be, and be understood to be, a *lingua franca*. Moreover, the burden of required use may be partly alleviated by the division of labour. Organizations like companies and bureaucracies may have the power to arrange their affairs so that, for example, only those willing to use English must do so. And where the regulations apply directly to individuals, they often do so only for limited contexts and purposes. This is not to deny that required use is ever onerous. When language has become politically charged with the burden of nationality, use of language is almost inevitably an expressive act. Both prohibitions and requirements on use limit that expression, though generally in different degrees.

Unlike the semantic thesis, the expressive thesis is pervasive; the use of a language may have an expressive function without regard to subject matter. The sign in Valerie Ford's shop had a social and political significance quite apart from its semantic content. Indeed, Quebec nationalists have often correctly noticed that the use of English by merchants is not purely a matter of commercial expediency but is in part a collective *non placet*, sometimes even a political provocation. To denounce it in one breath and then in the next defend prohibitions on English on the ground that they merely regulate a neutral code is either blindness or hypocrisy.

Since this expressive character may break out at any point, even on a commercial sign, there seems to be no way one might adopt narrower protections to serve the same ends. Unlike the instrumental argument, the expressive argument is capable of supporting broader principles. The strongest objection to this argument is rather different. It is that the interests at stake are not sufficiently weighty or general to warrant holding others duty-bound to protect them or disabling them from infringing them. Is that a credible position? The power of ethnicity and nationality in organizing personal identity, the widely felt need for rootedness, and the structuring power of culture all suggest that identification with an ethnic group may be a substantial human good. Expressing such identification is good to the extent that it constitutes, reinforces and adapts it.

Perhaps one might object that these interests, though powerful, are purely private. A follower of Chafee, for example, might be tempted in that direction. He saw the underlying values of free expression to be these:

> There is an individual interest, the need of men to express their opinions on matters vital to them if life is to be worth living, and a social interest in the attainment of truth, so that the country may not only adopt the wisest course of action but carry it out in the wisest way[9] (Chafee 1964: 33).

Ignoring the social interest, Chafee thought, leads people systematically to underestimate the importance of free speech. But his view of what the social interest actually comprises is an implausibly narrower one. The expressive need is not merely individual, nor is the social interest merely that of attaining the truth. Sound public policy is to be guided, not merely by the true, but by the good. There is a common interest in a regime which enables and supports the expression and exploration of ethnic identities, at least when these help structure valuable forms of life. Not only is this good in itself, but it indirectly contributes to a climate of ethnic tolerance and to the public good of linguistic security, so that each may speak his or her mother tongue without unfair pressure to conform. The expressive interest is thus of general value and not what Mill called a 'personal possession'; its violation is not merely a 'private injury' (Mill 1962).

It is here, I think, that one finds the deepest and most important roots of free expression and why, of the three arguments I have canvassed, the expressive one is so important in completing the case for protecting choice of language.

Notes

This paper was first published in *Law and Policy* 13(1991), pp. 215–229. Versions of this paper were read to a conference on freedom of expression at

McMaster University, Hamilton, Ontario, and at the Boalt Hall School of Law, University of California, Berkeley. I am grateful to the participants, and to the editors and referees of *Law and Policy* for helpful criticism.

1 The Original Act, R.S.Q. 1977, c. C-11, provides that 'Except as may be provided under this act or the regulations of the *Office de la langue française,* signs and posters and commercial advertising shall be solely in the official [i.e. French] language'. Similarly s. 69 prohibits non-French firm names. Section 51 exempts publicity carried in publications circulating in languages other than French, and religious, political, ideological, or humanitarian communications provided that they are not of commercial character (s. 59). Nor does it apply to small businesses of less than four employees, to publicity for the cultural activities of non-French ethnic groups, or to business specializing in foreign or ethnic goods!

2 The qualification is necessary because an act can try to get others to share a belief in some other way. If A wants B to think it is cold in the room, A can achieve this communicatively, e.g., by telling B that it is cold, or non-communicatively, e.g., by opening a window and making B cold. The second does not require for its success that B recognize A's intention in opening the window, and thus is not a communicative act in the sense under discussion here.

3 Alexander Meiklejohn, for instance, thought that speech should be protected only when it can be reliably thought to promote self-government. Thus it excludes commercial radio broadcasts: 'The radio, as we now have it, is not cultivating those qualities of taste, of reasoned judgment, of integrity, of loyalty, of mutual understanding upon which the enterprise of self-government depends. On the contrary, it is a mighty force for breaking them down' (Meiklejohn 1960: 87). What would he have thought of comic books, pop music, or television?

4 There is in fact a complication in the judgment, for while the above passage suggests that choice of language is protected because regulation of language is regulation of content, the Court also says that the reference in s. 2 to freedom of 'thought', 'belief', and 'opinion' shows that the *Charter's* protections *go beyond* what it calls 'mere content', or at least 'content of expression in its narrow sense'.

5 Cf. *Kopyto* per Corry, JA, at 226: 'Hyperbole and colourful, perhaps even disrespectful language, may be the necessary touchstone to fire the interest and imagination of the public to the need for reform, and to suggest the manner in which that reform may be achieved'. Per Goodman, JA, at 259 'The expression of an opinion which may be lawfully expressed in mild, polite, temperate, or scholarly language does not become unlawful because it is expressed in crude, vulgar, impolite, or acerbic words'.

6 The equally authoritative French version reads: 'Langue distinctive d'un peuple majoritairement francophone, la langue française permet au peuple québécois d'exprimer son identité'.

7 The context-dependence of meaning provides an illustration of the limits of abstract argument in political philosophy. One cannot resolve these issues solely by appeal to our concepts of 'expression', 'language', etc. It is no thesis of mine that choice of language is always, universally, or necessarily, protected by principles of free expression. I am merely trying to identify cases in which it is. Does this need to attend to context suggest that language is ill-suited for protection by constitutionally entrenched rights? I make no claims about that here: the question turns on the nature of rights, and on moral and institutional arguments for putting certain matters beyond the reach of ordinary politics. The issues are well known. But I might note one general point. One might object that, in view of the social character of our interests in language, it *must* be an inappropriate matter for rights, for they only protect individuated interests. The objection is too hasty, for it elides a number of interestingly different ways in which interests may fail to be fully individuated. For example, individuals may have rights to certain collective goods. See, Green (1991) and cf. Réaume (1988).

8 Political affirmation is often but not always coincident with ethnic identification. Some bilingual Canadians use their second official language in post offices or at border crossings in order to make a political statement without thereby intending to express any sense of ethnic identification with the other group.

9 The passage refers to the interests protected by the First Amendment to the American Constitution, but there is no evidence that Chafee thought that there were any important expressive interests not protected by that document.

References

Chafee, Zechariah (1964), *Free Speech in the United States* (Harvard University Press, Cambridge, Mass.).

Green, Leslie (1991), 'Two Views of Collective Rights', *Canadian Journal of Law and Jurisprudence,* 4: 315–27.

Greenawalt, Kent (1989), *Speech, Crime, and the Uses of Language* (Oxford University Press, New York).

Meiklejohn, Alexander (1960), *Political Freedom: The Constitutional Powers of the People* (Oxford University Press, New York).

Mill, John Stuart (1962), *Utilitarianism, On Liberty, Essay on Bentham* ed. Mary Warnock (New American Library, New York).

Réaume, Denise (1988), 'Individuals, Groups, and Rights to Public Goods', *University of Toronto Law Journal,* 38:1–28.

Scanlon, Thomas (1972), 'A Theory of Freedom of Expression', *Philosophy and Public Affairs,* 1: 204–26.

Cases Cited

Cohen *v.* California (1971) 403 US 15.

Devine *c.* PG Québec et PG du Canada mis en cause (1982) CS 355 (Can.)

Ford *v.* AG Quebec (1984) 18 DLR (4th) 711 (Can.)

Ford *v.* AG Quebec (1988) 2 SCR 712 (Can.)

Irwin Toy Ltd. *c.* PG du Québec et Gilles Moreau (1982) CS 96 (Can.)

Reference re: Manitoba Language Rights (1985) 19 DLR (4th) 1 (Can.)

R. *v.* Kopyto (1988) 47 DLR (4th) 213 (Ont CA) (Can.)

Statutes Cited

Canadian Charter of Rights and Freedoms s. 2(b), Part I of the Constitution Act of 1982 being Schedule B of the Canada Act of 1982 (UK), 1982, chap. 11.

Charter of the French Language RSQ 1977 c.C-11 (Can.).

Official Languages Act of 1969.

Questions for Discussion

1 Is language more than a "content-neutral code" in which various messages can be expressed? If so, what else is it?

2 To what extent does freedom of expression include the freedom to choose one's audience, and to be assured access to it?

Whose Body? Whose Self?

Beyond Pornography

Myrna Kostash

In this article, Kostash maintains that pornography should not be considered simply a matter of expression, on a par with the expression of political dissidence. She argues that women are right to fear pornography and that, although there are reasons to be concerned about any form of censorship, pornography should be added to the list of cases in which the freedom of expression is not absolute.

★   ★   ★

Annals of the Boys' Club. When Larry Flynt, publisher of *Hustler* magazine, was convicted a few years ago of obscenity charges in the United States, several luminaries of the arts world, including novelist Gore Vidal and filmmaker Woody Allen, came to his defence.

They called him an "American dissident," a designation which made their association of his tribulation with that of Soviet dissidents, Andrei Sakharov and Alexander Solzhenitsyn, irresistible. "Look," they were saying, liberal banners unfurled, "the authoritarian Soviet state represses free thought, the puritanical American state represses sexual expression." The implication was clear: those who would defend the fastnesses of the human imagination must take a stand here, at the line where the bureaucratic thought-police decree their interests (in this case, sexual discipline) have been trespassed.

It shall be left up to the reader to judge the appropriateness of the comparison between the situation of Soviet intellectuals and an American skin-magazine publisher, but this much can be said: the possibility that a pornographer is a *victim* of society is the fruit of a mid-Sixties mentality. Which is to say of a pre-feminist mentality. For it is thanks to the feminist movement of the last decade that we are now in a position to understand that obscenity and pornography, far from being a release from the sexual repression that bedevils our culture, do in fact trade in the same coin: contempt for women and traffic in our sexuality.

Larry Flynt is no dissident. He is a pimp.

★　★　★

Unfortunately, this perception alone resolves nothing. For women, the current debate about what does and does not represent sexual and intellectual freedom spins around a truly anguishing dilemma. On the one hand, the historical challenge (up to and including the sexual liberation skirmishes of the Sixties) to age-old taboos that govern sexual behaviour have been moments in women's ongoing struggle with the patriarchy—its family, its marketplace, its state. One has only to think of the exuberance with which the women's movement smashed the conspiratorial silence

that had muffled the issues of female masturbation, female orgasm and lesbianism to understand how campaigns for the right to sexual self-expression have served us well.

When we have repudiated notions of "virginity" and "chastity," have denounced the sexual double standard ("Higamous, hogamous, women are monogamous; hogamous, higamous, men are polygamous"), have exposed the fallacies of "biological destiny," have censured the publicization of female masochism, we have in effect joined the struggle for the right to determine the nature and practice of our own sexuality.

In so doing, we have stood up in the same forum with those who, for instance, defended the publication of *Lady Chatterly's Lover* or *Body Politic*, or the distribution of *Pretty Baby*, or liberal amendments to the Criminal Code. This, then, is the anguish and the confusion: now *Hustler* and worse have entered the forum, on the grounds that pornography too smashes taboos and constraints. Do we feminists contradict ourselves when we say we hate and fear it?

The dilemma is deepened by the compelling arguments of civil libertarians that the "freedom to read," and indeed the "freedom of the imagination," are in the public interest, even when these freedoms are employed to produce or consume pornography. This is all the more cogent when the freedom to read comes under attack, as in the case of Ontario school boards' banning of Margaret Laurence's *The Diviners* from school bookshelves; and the freedom to publish, as in parliamentary denunciations of the Canada Council's funding of publishers of "pornographic" poetry, "offensive to anyone with even a shred of decency," an idiotic allusion to Talonbooks and the work of poet bill bissett.[1] And when a small-town Ontario newspaper complains that such writers' "offerings are nothing more than a succession of gutter language, usually not even in sentence structure,"[2] we see how perilously close the attack on the allegedly pornographic comes to an attack on the artistic avant-garde as a whole.

Well, we say, *we* know what we mean by "pornography" and it isn't bill bissett; fair enough, but we are not in control of the public definition. *They* are, the MPs, the police, the judges—and feminists, as well as civil libertarians, have every right to fear that *their* definition casts a wide net indeed: shall we see public burnings of *Our Bodies, Our Selves?*

No, say the civil libertarians, not if we insist that the freedom to read and to publish is absolute and indivisible. Feminists cannot have it both ways—the restrictions on the distribution of "snuff" films, for instance, but the lifting of restrictions on, say, the Official Secrets Act.

On the other hand, of course, are the demands of the women's liberation movement. Reproductive freedoms: access to safe abortion and birth control and the right to give birth without trauma and insult. Freedom from rape and sexual abuse. Lesbian rights. Day care. Maternity rights, and so on. All those instances of the decolonization of our bodies.

How can we take these up and *not* hate and fear pornography?

Pornography: "the representation of sexual images, often including ridicule and violence, which degrades human beings for the purpose of entertaining or selling products."[3] The definition must be attempted, just as the definition of other modes of oppression and exploitation—racism, sexism, imperialism—have been risked and from that have entered our political lexicon. Else we risk wallowing in the subjectivities of perception, ambivalence and other temptations of liberalism ("Obscenity is in the eye of the beholder"), as though pornography does not take place out there in society, in social transactions between men and women. Pornography: from the Greek "to write about prostitution." At its root, then, the mercantile notion of the (usually) female body

as a commodity. The territory of a commercial transaction. Pornography: a graphic metaphor for sex as the power that one (male) person wields over the destiny of another and the hostility that such an imbalance of power provokes.

What are its elements? Sadomasochism: the woman's body is subjected to various bondages, abuses, humiliations, from which she is often seen to extract her own pleasure. Misogyny: contempt for the female and her chastisement. Fascism: the male "lover" is frequently costumed as a militaristic superman, triumphing over the female subhuman, particularly where she is non-Aryan. Phallocentrism: the pornographic scenario is organized, overwhelmingly, around the penis and its ejaculation. Voyeurism: the deployment of the woman's body so as to excite the viewer.

What is its message? That sexual violence is pleasurable to men and that women desire or at least expect this violence. That women are "bad," their femaleness ridiculous, even foul, their submission appropriate. That male sexual (and political) satisfaction requires the diminution of female energy.

The images. The female torso disappears into a meat grinder. The woman, bound and gagged, splayed across the bed. The concubine, trussed up like a chicken, and raped. The girl-child, receiving foamy "come" on her eyelids and cheeks.

Enough.

Now begins the hard part. Must not our definition—images of ridicule and violence—also include the ostensibly artistic, the "art" photography of a Les Krims (a breast, cut off, is stuck to a table and dribbles blood) or the "arresting" acrylics of a James Spenser (a woman in black lace panties, her languid nudity an advertisement for her availability and for the flesh's uselessness, her body long since deprived of animation)? Must not our definition—for the purpose of entertainment or selling products—include almost the whole of popular culture and mass advertising in which the fragments of the female body are made to represent the desirability of a given product for consumption or for sale? Must not our definition—that which degrades the human being—now also include all those representations of coercion in which one person loses power to another's (aggressive) will, images which are pervasive in a male supremacist culture, which is to say are present in the merely sexist and in the pleasurably erotic?[4]

The definition, it turns out—but has anybody another that is more useful?—includes just about the whole of the iconography of everyday heterosexual life. The question becomes: what is *not* pornographic?

The answer to that lies in the realms of the utopian, or at best in the purely intimate or in the pockets of feminist subculture. For the non-pornographic, or the erotic, is about our, women's, vision of the sexually *possible*. In the best of possible worlds how would we represent sex? (What would art look like? Publicity? Movies?) With tenderness, affection, respect, with humour, playfulness. We would take delight in the sensuous detail, we would caress, we would be open psychically to the "lunar," to that part of our nervous system which is intuitional, which apprehends patterns, which is artistic. The "erotica" which corresponds to this ideal would represent freely chosen sexual behaviour in which the partners would serve each other's (and Eros's!) pleasure equally and in which the "I love you" is made flesh. How does it go? "With this body I thee honour...."

Feminist descriptions of the non-pornographic are necessarily as vague, evasive, dreamy as this for we have only recently allowed ourselves the luxury of contemplating sexual happiness, as opposed to the sexual terror of our environment. It is not easily done. Everywhere we turn we see our need for "romance" distorted as the ostensibly "erotic," which is in fact a thinly-veiled invitation to

further violence. I'm thinking of the movies in which "provocative" women are murdered; blue jeans ads in which young girls are offered up to adult men; fashion layouts in which the limbs of the models are bruised in the jaws of snarling dogs. This is the so-called "pretty porn," the means by which the pornographic fantasy, heretofore closeted in hard-core literature and imagery, acquires access to the broad public. "Pretty porn" softens us up, as it were; it creates a tolerance for the explicitly sadistic and, like a callous, dulls our nerve endings so that we are no longer repelled. The image has become normal. Full frontal female nudity—this used to be considered porn—is now a standard of the Hollywood film and *Playboy*; the horse we flogged in the early Seventies now seems positively pastoral compared to the stuff in cellophane wrappers. For women, such de-sensitization is grotesque: we have somehow to make our way through the city *as though* pornography had nothing to do with us. For to acknowledge that it does is to let in the nightmare: "to be unknown, and hated," as Susan Griffin writes.[5]

But let it in we must, for to know the nature of the beast is the end of illusion and the beginnings of politics. Consider: *Hustler* magazine has seven million readers a month; six of ten bestselling monthlies are "men's entertainment" magazines; there are 260 different periodicals available in the United States devoted to child porn; pornography, in short, is a $4 billion industry.[6] Is this a problem for women? It is true that, even in Canada, rape is increasingly accompanied by sexual sadism and mutilation. Now where do rapists get their ideas? While current research on the relationship between pornography and aggression is far from conclusive, one way or the other, we do know that more than 50 studies involving 10,000 children have demonstrated over the years a consistent relationship between the amount of television violence consumed by the child and her/his level of aggression.[7] We have it from Drs. Neil Malamuth and James Check at the University of Manitoba that when "effects of pornographic violence were assessed in responses to a lengthy questionnaire the findings indicated that heightened aggressiveness persists for at least a week."[8]

Of course, as it has been said, women do not need "proof" of laboratory research to know that the pervasiveness of the pornographic image is a threat to our well-being. In the image is an education: by it, men and women alike are instructed in the power men have over women, a power which extends along the whole desperate continuum of male privilege, from conjugal rights to pimping, from sexual harassment to rape-murder. By it women themselves are blamed for what has happened to them: we are venal, we are stupid, we are uppity, we deserve what we get.

The *political* content of these representations of sexuality—that male authority is normal and can only be challenged at enormous risk—is obscured by the fact that, in our culture, relations of dominance and submission between men and women are seen as *sexy*. Power is an eroticized event, masked as titillation. Which is to say it is experienced as something intimate, domestic, personal. We literally don't see it. Two men are grappling on the floor, fingers at the throat, teeth biting into flesh: they are fighting. A man and a woman are grappling on the floor, teeth bared and her clothing ripped: they are making love.

★ ★ ★

Having come this far in our disillusionment, our work is cut out for us. Some feminist groups, organized explicitly to challenge the *consensus* that the pervasiveness of porn represents, have taken the beast by the horns. In San Francisco, Women Against Violence in Pornography and the Media (WAVPM) have picketed shops selling *Hustler*, have conducted tours for women through the Tenderloin, the porn district (no more averting our eyes from the scenarios of our humiliation), have put together a consciousness-raising slideshow and guided women through the "speaking bitterness" sessions which follow. In Toronto, Women Against Violence Against Women (WAVAW) demonstrated at Metro and City executive committee meetings to demand that the film *Snuff*[9] be banned. Twenty men and women invaded the cinema, smashed the projector and staged a sit-in until five of their number were arrested. And all over North America similar groups have demonstrated to "take back the night" from the merchants of sexual ghoulishness, repeatedly making the connection between porn and all other violence done women—rape, battery, forced sterilization, back-alley abortions—that cements the foundations of our social structures.

Such campaigns immediately raise the hackles of those to whom the issue of pornography is one not of sexual politics (who has the power to do what to whom) but of society's right to uncensored opinion. Briefly, they argue that "the realm of the imagination should not be subject to government control"[10] and that one must always be careful to draw the line between "personal" rights (we do have the right to freedom from physical attack, say) and "intellectual" rights (we all have the right to say aloud what we think without fear of reprisal). Even those who are as nauseated as any WAVAW member by pornography point out that men do not rape just because they see pictures, for the pictures are simply "metaphors" for what is already taking place in society. Besides, as long as women have little political power *qua* women, the demand for censorship of pornographic materials reproduces our powerlessness: somebody else, not us, will be the censors. In any event, as Alberta's attorney general put it to the Alberta Status of Women, "...it is impossible to pass a law or laws governing every imaginable human activity. Laws unfortunately do not prevent all undesirable activity, but merely make them illegal."

In reply, feminists have argued that the claim that pornography exists solely in the realms of the imagination or of self-expression is specious: it is an extensively public phenomenon, an *event* in the social situation of the sexes. Certainly the Nazis understood this when, having occupied Poland, they flooded the bookstalls with porn to demoralize the population. And certain disenchanted Scandinavians understand it when, for all the availability of "liberating" porn, they still refer to themselves as "sexual invalids" and admit that from 1960 to 1978 rape was up 60 percent.[11]

Feminists have further argued that the right to "free speech" in practice extends only to those who have the money to buy it: the publishers, the producers, the politicians, the consumers. Those without money, women's groups for instance, must resort to other practices—leafleting, picketing, rallying, marching—which are, of course, denounced by liberals as "interferences" in the freedom of speech. Feminists ask: *whose* freedom?

All kinds of limitations already exist on "freedom of speech": laws relating to libel, slander, perjury, copyright, advertising, incitement. We accept them; *we* acknowledge that this freedom is not absolute. Therefore, the "right" to produce and consume pornography must be curtailed if our *women's* right to freedom from slander and injury is to be respected.[12]

In any event, it comes down to this: the woman's liberation movement, like all collectivist appeals to social transformation, is impatient with the claims of civil libertarians. It seeks not mere individual rights but social justice.

Justice must be seen to be done. It is within the *realpolitik* of the streetwise women's movement that each woman activist make her own decision about what she is prepared to do to smash the gloomy tyranny of porn.

Already the agenda is drawn up. Consumer campaigns, public education, vigilante squads, agit-prop (protests that provoke public debate). Feminist-informed research (to establish once and for all the connection between pornography and behaviour). Agitation for changes in the law relating to obscenity, as in "a law based on new standards which would entrench the physical and sexual autonomy of women and children within the law"[13] (although it is debatable how that which is not true in society—the sexual autonomy of women and children—can be guaranteed by law).

Feminists must also refine their arguments with their critics. There remains the longstanding liberal defence of pornography as an "isolated act," harmlessly "indulged in" by individuals free to choose their own "lifestyle." Feminists say: we want to live in an order where what we do and think has consequences. Leftists, ostensibly pro-feminist, have defended pornography on the various grounds that it is a "revolutionary aesthetic" (in which case it is the social protest of an idiot), that it is the "erotica" of the working class (in fact, pornography is a capitalist success story and is consumed overwhelmingly by middle-class men), that *Penthouse*, say, is anti-establishment (in fact, the fantasies purveyed by skin magazines *replicate* the deadening relations of the family place, the workplace, the marketplace). Rightists, lining up to burn skin magazines and smash rock records, are, however, on a moral crusade against sexual explicitness and are no friends of women. Against the feminist demand for women's right to sexual self-determination, the Right poses the stability of the patriarchal family, the iniquity of homosexuality and the sanctity of the chaste. We have been through that scenario before.

Through such refinements, women in the anti-porn movement may even come to a vision of what is possible beyond pornography. Pornography celebrates the atomization and irresponsibility of the person in the pretence that what one does as a sexual being has nothing to do with anything else, neither with the sexual partner nor with society. Beyond this morbidity, the gentle, laughing, administering embrace of sensual camaraderie presents itself: the longed-for alternative to the social tyrannies of passivity and mechanization. Beyond pornography lies the *polis*, the political space of the aggrieved in which we may finally overwhelm those forces that would circumscribe our vigour and our compassion.

★   ★   ★

At the University of California in Berkeley I am sitting in a journalism class. The instructor, writer Valerie Miner, has invited a representative from WAVPM to present the "consciousness-raising" slideshow on pornography. We watch it in disbelieving silence. Then the class is split up—the male students are invited to discuss the presentation in a separate room.

The women talk. So *that's* pornography. I've never really looked. Do men *really* want it? You know, it isn't just weirdos buying this stuff, it's our brothers and boyfriends (six, ten, fifteen million a month!), they're harbouring these fantasies, it's like a, well, barrier between us, isn't it? Do we have to accept it? How do we teach our men that this stuff hurts us without alienating them? Wait a minute, there's a "porn" for women, too: all those romances of the super-feminine heroine overpowered by the dark, passionate lover. Remember *Wuthering Heights*? (Giggles)

I am thinking: my God, women have to be *taught* to like and live with men; our first, instinctual feeling toward them is fear.

Fear. The discussion takes an interesting turn. Away from the pornographic images we have just seen to anecdotes about fear. One story after another. Of being followed. Of obscene phone calls. Of being afraid to live alone, to go out at night, to answer the door-bell. "Women are such scairdy cats," the women say. "Why are we so dumb, so afraid all the time?" And then more stories.

Fear. Suddenly all the intellectual and political anguish provoked by the threat of pornography has dissolved into one simple perception. Pornography is about women being afraid. While there is pornography, we are not safe. It is not a question of learning to "live with it": we are dying with it.

Notes

1 Quoted in *ACP Notebook*, No. 13 (July 1978), p. 2.

2 *Ibid.*, p. 8.

3 Valerie Miner, "Fantasies and Nightmares: The Red-Blooded Mass Media," unpublished paper, p. 3.

4 I am aware that almost all discussion of the issue of pornography concerns itself only with the photographic image, as though we accept the written word and the painting as "self-expression" but the unmediated image—the ultra-realistic depiction of gross materiality, not form—as dangerous and offensive. The photograph seems to reproduce reality and erases the distinction between fantasy and what is actually possible. Since this is true of any photograph, the next question is: is *any* photographic representation of women in a male supremacist culture *ipso facto* sexist and exploitative? Two British writers pursue this. "Pornography is a site for the struggle over the representations of women.... Is it more acceptable to view the image of a woman at work than a nude playmate? Why?" (Mary Bos and Jill Pack, "Porn, Law and Politics," *Camerawork* No. 18). Perhaps because work, for all its exploitation of the worker's labour power, does not *as an image* deny the dignity of the worker. The image of the female, however, has carried the burden of meaning of everything from original sin to commodity fetishism. The image of the female connotes venality.

5 Susan Griffin, *Rape: The Power of Consciousness* (New York: Harper and Row, 1979), p. 51.

6 The figures are American. No Canadian ones are available.

7 Miner, op. cit., p. 11.

8 *New York Times*, September 30, 1980.

9 The film purports to show the actual mutilation and death of an actress.

10 The Writers' Union of Canada, "Obscenity Brief" (in respect to Bill C-51), January 1970.

11 Cited in "Fallout from the Sexual Revolution," *Maclean's*, 1981.

12 It is worth noting, however, that in the eleven years since the enactment of the Hate Propaganda Act (governing the "irrational and malicious abuse of certain identifiable minority groups" or an attack on such groups in "abusive, insulting, scurrilous and false terms") there have been only two charges laid under it. The first was against people distributing "Yankee Go Home" leaflets at a Shriners' Parade in Toronto. The second was against two men distributing anti-French Canadian handbills. In the latter case an appeal resulted in an acquittal. Cited in "Group Defamation in Canada," Jeanne Hutson, *Carleton Journalism Review*, Winter 1980.

13 Debra Lewis, *Kinesis*, April–May, 1979.

Questions for Discussion

1 Is there any way to distinguish between the "expression" of political dissidents, or of artists, on the one hand, and the "expression" of producers of pornography, on the other?

2 Is Kostash right that the message of pornography is that femaleness is ridiculous or bad, and that women desire or expect sexual violence?

3 Is Kostash right that pornography is a matter of sexual politics and power relationships in society, and not simply "fantasies" or "entertainment" lying solely in the realm of imagination?

Excerpts from "Pornography: The Other Side"

Ferrel Christensen

*Ferrel Christensen is one of the leaders of Educators and Counsellors Against Censorship. In these selections from his **Pornography: The Other Side**, he criticizes some of the arguments which have been raised against pornography.*

★ ★ ★

In the continuing clamor over pornography, the claims most often heard are these: (1) it is evil so it should be banned, and (2) it is evil but censorship is a greater evil. The other side—that pornography is not in itself morally bad—is rarely defended. The purpose of this essay is to present some of the evidence for that other side. In fact, it will be argued that the current anti-pornography campaign is in many ways itself morally evil. This will be a startling claim to many, but that is largely because they have been given so little opportunity to see the whole picture. Actually, pornography itself is not the fundamental issue; opposition to it is only a symptom of more general beliefs about sex that are tragically mistaken. Though such a complex subject cannot be completely circumscribed in one short essay, most of the essentials of the debate are treated here.

Standard Moral Objections: Debasement and Exploitation

In the next few sections we will look briefly at some of the reasons commonly given in making the claim that pornography is *intrinsically* evil; i.e., that it is bad in itself, independently of any good or ill it might later lead to. The question of whether it causes harmful attitudes or behavior in those who use it will be delayed until the second half of this essay. Let us begin by making the following observation: that where beliefs are produced by nonrational influences, such as wishful thinking or indoctrination, the mind typically attempts to create a rational basis for them, after the fact. As an example, certain human cultures have a tradition of disfiguring the teeth (blackening them, filing them down, even knocking them out); and when people of one such group were asked why that should be a desirable thing to do, they replied that having natural-looking teeth would make them "like *animals.*" A large arsenal of such rationalizations has been employed in the attempt to justify this society's traditional attitudes about sexuality, including pornography. In general, now, one thing that exposes an argument as a mere rationalization is the fact that it is so clearly fallacious, once it is actually examined. Often, for instance, those who employ it wouldn't think of making the same claim in relevantly similar situations. (Animals eat food and care for their young; does that mean humans should not? The capacity to destroy all life is uniquely human—does that mean it would be a good thing to do?) In other cases, the reasoning is seen to require a distortion of the facts in order to be convincing. Indeed, some such claims are virtually empty of factual content: they are mere shibboleths, which one has learned to say on cue but which describe nothing in reality. This is exactly the situation, we shall see, in regard to the standard moral objections against pornography. They all reveal an any-stick-will-do abandonment of critical judgement.

To begin with a variation on the "animal" *motif,* a common charge against pornography is that it is "dehumanizing." On the contrary, nothing is any more human than sexual fantasies and feelings, along with their representation and vicarious enjoyment in various media of expression. If anyone is trying to de-

humanize us in this regard, it is those who would denigrate our sexuality and its celebration: they are denying a significant part of our humanity. As was hinted above, this sort of argument is evidently based on the assumption that anything uniquely or specially human is good, or that whatever is typical of animals is inferior. And once again, it is absurd. Alas, selfishness, arrogance and hatred are as human as generosity and compassion. It may be that we have a greater capacity than other animals for emotions such as the latter, but the same is true of the former. Those who employ the argument know little about human *or* animal nature. They typically assume that things like love, sex with love, monogamy or long-term bonding are peculiarly human, but they are wrong on every count.

The reasoning is often based on an erroneous view that animals and humans are utterly different in their natures: moved by blind instinct vs. emotion and intelligence. In truth, all the dissimilarities are differences in degree, not in kind—mostly degree of intelligence. Even conscience (guilt, etc.) is found in some other animals, as any dog-owner should know. But even if some traits are uniquely human, that does not mean they are good; they must be evaluated on their own merits. A second belief sometimes underlying this assumption is a misunderstanding of evolution: the idea that it is a benevolent force whose goal is to produce ever more noble creatures. But this is contrary to all of our scientific understanding. For example, once more, romantic love is not an emotion that nature values for its own sake; its ultimate "purpose" is the same as that of lust, to help propagate the species or the genes. None of this implies that there *are* no noble feelings, of course. What does constitute genuine goodness and moral rightness has already been briefly mentioned here, and will continue to be discussed.

Another standard accusation is that the persons involved in sexually explicit portrayals are thereby treated "like objects." Now, it isn't at all clear what this is supposed to mean. Or even whether it means anything at all, once again. It has come to be repeated so ritualistically, without explanation, that it appears to have no more descriptive content than "son of a bitch": it expresses the speaker's anger or contempt but nothing more. After all, "sex object" sounds like a contradiction in terms: objects don't have sexuality, but people do. Of course, to charge angrily that pornography treats people as sexual *beings* would have no negative impact, so that isn't said. Notice in this connection how seductively easy name-calling is. Anything can be made to sound awful by an appropriate choice of epithets. For example, one might charge that in a love relationship, or a movie about one, human beings are treated as "emotionally security blankets." Or it might be said that to expect sexual exclusivity from a mate is to treat him or her like private property, i.e., like an object one possesses. Such claims would be no more mindless than this familiar rhetoric.

Nevertheless, let us examine various things that might be meant by the objectification charge, to see if any of them are at all cogent. Sometimes what is intended is fetched pretty far. For example, there is the claim that since pornographic photos or movies are themselves objects, those who are portrayed in them are *ipso facto* treated or regarded as objects by the viewer. It doesn't seem to occur to those who talk this way that the same charge would apply equally well to pictures, movies and books of any *other* kind, including love stories. With similar foolishness, it might be alleged that a little girl's doll treats people as passive objects to be used and manipulated.

At other times, what the objection alludes to is the fact that those depicted in sexual materials are not personally known to the reader or viewer, or that the sex portrayed is itself between strangers. (Sex with a stranger is an extremely common fantasy of both men and women, and whirlwind romance with a stranger is *the* major love-story theme.) Here the claim is that sex, even fantasy sex, with someone one doesn't already know intimately is "impersonal" or "depersonalized," hence treats the other as an object rather than a person. That non-sequitur evidently rests on an equivocation between the words "person" and "personal": the latter refers either to what is unique or to what is not publicly shared about an individual, the former to the general fact of personhood. In this confused thinking, then, if one is not treated as a uniquely special person one is not treated as a person at all. The absurdity of the argument is also evident from the fact that it would render objectionable most *non*-sexual interactions with other people, along with (again) all other media presentations. Consider how bizarre it would be, for instance, to say that giving compassionate help to someone is depersonalized, treats that person as an object, if she or he is a stranger. If pornography *or* "casual" sex is to be condemned, it will have to be on more rational grounds than these.

At least part of the motive for all the talk about objects, clearly, is the fact that the human body is involved; it is (among other things) a physical object. And the portrayal of the body, hinting at or engaged in the physical activity of sex, is a central characteristic of pornography, while the arousal or satisfaction of desires toward the body is its *raison d'être*. Hence it seems pretty obvious that our long standing tradition of devaluing the physical body, and physical sex in particular, underlies this charge. But it is a serious and destructive error. Having a body is just as much a part of being a person as is having intelligence or emotions. Attraction to the former no more treats someone as a non-person than does attraction to one of the latter. Some of those who use the "object" rhetoric sound as if they have been alienated from their own bodies, from an essential part of their being.

Once again, most of that tradition about the body is dead and buried in the 1980s, with its emphasis on beauty and bodily health; only the suspicions about sex linger on. The result is an inconsistency of attitude that is revealed by the claim before us. For pictures of clothed people are no less pictures of bodies—the clothes themselves are mere inanimate objects. And video movies of, say, exercise classes (a bunch of "anonymous panting playthings"?) are just as much a focus on the physical body and its activities as is one involving sexual activity. But charges of treating people as objects are never raised against them. To realize how contradictory common thinking is on this matter, one has only to consider the general importance of close physical contact in human life: deprecatory remarks about the body are never made when the subject is the value of just being held. In a similar vein, a lover of things like painting and ballet would never grant that their purely physical nature makes them an unfitting source of emotional gratification.

As for the gratification itself—the pleasure or satisfaction derived from various sources like these—standard beliefs on this topic reveal parallel confusions. For instance, the traditional claim that sexual feelings are "merely physical" while others are "spiritual" is another serious error. One has only to reflect carefully on some of these other emotions to realize that they are also physical sensations; they are merely felt in a different part of the body, notably the face and chest. And as has already been hinted, *all* of our feelings are mediated by chemicals in the brain. Love and lust belong equally to the body and the soul. Along with the sharp dichotomy between humans and animals, the picture of a noble soul trying to control a rebellious body is obsolete, if not morally obstructive.

Sometimes the claim of objectification takes forms that are particularly fatuous. It is said, for example, that pornography reduces its subjects to a "collection of body parts."[1] Go

look through any of a great number of *non*erotic magazines, and you will find ads and articles featuring pictures of hair, ears, feet, hands, etc., all by themselves. (They may be selling anklets or fungicide, or discussing the cause of lower back pain.) But they are never condemned for reducing people to their organs. The real reason for attacking the showing of sex organs, once again, is that they alone among body parts are considered shameful. Moreover, it is certainly not the case that displaying them all by themselves is the point of pornography. Most males and a small minority of females are biologically primed to focus especially on them, but only as part of the wider bodily *gestalt*. (The face is another body part, it should be noticed, and special attraction to it is universal.) In fact, it is the traditional aversion to nudity that comes closest to fitting the derogatory description under discussion. By decreeing that only certain parts may be shown or appreciated, it divides them off from the rest; it prevents us from enjoying our whole selves. In any case, the biologically healthy attraction to certain areas of the body is no more degrading to a person than interest in his or her personality, intelligence or moral character—no one would charge that a special interest in one of the latter carves a person up into pieces.

This leads us to another way of interpreting the "object" charge, one that clearly is intended by some who make it. It isn't the fact that pornography displays bodies and bodily activities, but that they are *all* it presents, that is supposed to "objectify" those involved. It treats people as if they were "*nothing but* sexual objects," the claim is often worded. Similar charges abound. Pornography presents a "one-dimensional view of life," it is said; it "reduces its subjects to their bodies and their physical appetites, rather than treating them as whole human beings," or "carries the tacit message that sex is all they're good for." Now it is quite true that most pornography has a very limited scope; it contains little else besides sex. (To some, in fact, that is a defining characteristic of it.) This is due in part to the fact that overt sexuality has traditionally been excluded from socially respectable portrayals of human experience; it has been driven out into a realm by itself. But it does not follow from its limited content that pornography treats its subjects as if they were nothing but sexual entities.

The absurdity of this new charge, together with its rationalizing nature, is once again revealed by the fact that no similar claim is made in analogous cases. All of our media presentations, to a greater or lesser degree, are specialized in their content. From sporting events to symphonies, they portray a "one-dimensional view of life" indeed—and many people spend an awful lot of their time enjoying such things. But is there anything wrong with that? Among the periodicals you will find magazines specializing in sports, food, romance, entertainment, hobbies, fashion, etc. Shall we say that such publications don't portray people as whole human beings? Do fashion magazines, for example, turn their models into human mannequins, just a bunch of clothing racks? (To mimic some of the purpler prose we hear denouncing pornography.) For that matter, do traditional movies and novels, which scrupulously avoid frank eroticism, deny our completeness by ignoring *that* important aspect of us? Human wholeness in no way precludes focusing on one aspect of ourselves at a time. And if there is some *special* reason why sex should only be portrayed in combination with other things, this argument again fails to give it. Fallacious arguments about personhood aside, these parallel cases also reveal that many who complain pornography portrays nothing but sex would find its explicitness offensive regardless of the rest of the content; for some this objection is only a pretext.

Underlying this charge against pornography, very often, is the wider claim that sexual desire toward another person, or even mutu-

ally between persons, is "objectifying" unless certain other sorts of feeling are present as well. But its status as a rationalization is also clear. We never hear the converse claim, that (say) desiring another's companionship but not his or her sexuality treats that individual as less than a whole person—even though the interest is no less partial. More generally, the fact that certain aspects of an individual should be of special or sole interest to someone does not imply that that person has no other human worth. Shall we say that students treat a professor as a mere intellect-object, because their only reason for coming to her or him is to learn about (say) history or logic? Does their limited interest mean they think that's all he or she is good for? Only ideologically induced blindness leads people to say such things in a sexual context.

It is instructive to consider one specific example of the "whole person" charge. (From Beatrice Faust's book *Women, Sex and Pornography*. Overall, Ms. Faust's treatment of the subject is unusually level-headed and well informed.) Contrasting the similar scenes of men watching a stripper and young women getting excited over a rock music star, the writer says, "Men react impersonally to the stripper's body and sexual aura; girls react to the pop star as a person, not as a sexy body." Aside from its standard confusion of being personal with being a person, even the distinction this statement makes regarding the former is spurious. Male celebrities standardly report that before they achieved that status they got no special attention from women—yet they haven't changed *as persons*. Nor is there anything particularly personal about the star's highly contrived aura or stage persona; the girls are excited by the artificial image and high status of an individual they've never even met. In fact, one's body is clearly more unique and intrinsic to one's self than status or fame; it is *more* personal. But the important point here is that there is nothing disrespectful about the reaction to the star *or* to the stripper. Neither in any intelligent sense treats him or her as other than a complete human being.

There is one more thing that could be meant, and manifestly often is meant, by the charge that pornography treats people as objects. It is that those who enjoy such presentations do not care about the welfare of the subjects portrayed, about their needs or feelings as human beings. There is only one thing to be said in response to this charge: it is a vicious libel. Sexual desire, including its expressions involving pornography, represents a need, not an attitude. And there is nothing intrinsically uncaring about a need—though of course, any need can be accompanied by callous attitudes or pursued in a callous way. On the part of some, the error here would seem to lie in confusing romantic love with human love: they think that feeling sexual desire without the former sort of emotional involvement just *is* being cold and uncaring. Now, human love is the essence of morality, whereas romantic attachment is only one need or desire among many. For a person who feels the latter yearning, it is important that it be met, but it is no more inherently noble than any other interpersonal need. The truth in this matter, in fact, is just the reverse of what has been charged. It is those who despise the sexual and emotional makeup of others—their greater need for sex, or greater emotional independence, or both—who reveal a lack of caring and human concern.

Closely similar to the accusation of callousness is another that often accompanies it. Explicitly sexual presentations, it is said, "exploit" their subjects; the latter are simply "used" for the gratification of one's own selfish desires. Once again, the underlying attitudes here transcend the specific issue of pornography. Of all the things that people desire for themselves, and all the ways in which they wish to satisfy needs or get pleasure from others, it is uniquely the sexual ones that are

regarded in this culture as inherently selfish. This has become such a kneejerk response, in fact, that people don't stop to ask whether the charge is really appropriate in a given case. So let us remind ourselves of the meaning of the word: to exploit a person is to get something from him or her in a way that is hurtful or unfair. Whatever else may be good or bad about the situation, if it is consensual and equally beneficial, it is not exploitive. To illustrate this inconsistency of attitudes toward different sources of pleasure, consider something one observes not infrequently: a woman's eyes lighting up at the sight of a cute baby in a magazine or on TV. "Oh, what a darling little thing!" she may say, focusing intently. She is getting pleasure for herself from the visual experience, and perhaps fantasizing getting pleasure from a real child. Is this being exploitive? Does it mean she regards babies as mere objects for her gratification? Of course not. Indeed, her desires include *sharing* pleasure with the infant of her fantasy.

Yet it is no different from this, for normal persons, in the sexual enjoyment of others—whether in fantasy or in real life. Sexual desire is fundamentally a desire for mutual pleasure. Nothing is any more gratifying, or more sexually exciting, than to have one's erotic interest returned. Hence it is hardly surprising that the commonest theme of male-oriented erotic movies is that of women who are uninhibited in seeking sex. She wants him the same way he wants her! Its appeal rests precisely on the fact that it makes the need and pleasure equal and mutual. To be sure, attempts to satisfy sexual needs can and often do employ exploitive means. (Though this seems to be less common in sex-positive cultures, where satisfying such needs is much less difficult. To a degree, at least, the attitude that sex is exploitive is self-fulfilling.) People with unmet needs will often settle for less than the mutual ideal. But this is true of all other strong desires as well, including romantic love—as is made plain by the scheming manipulations so often engaged in by jealous or insecure spouses and lovers. In fact, it is germane to point out here that false moral charges are themselves used in the selfish manipulation of other persons. If some can convince others that the latter's desires are ignoble, they can more easily get what they want instead. This motive seems to underlie a lot of negative attitudes involving sexuality; the reader should keep it in mind as we continue.

Sometimes sexually frank performances and materials are called exploitive on the grounds that, even if all those directly involved enjoy their experience, it still offends the deep feelings of others to know they exist. "Sex is sacred and personal," it is said; "its privacy should not be violated." These third-party arguments are often tinged with hypocrisy. It is the censors who want to invade the personal lives of others, to tell them what they may participate in making or what they may use even in private. More to the point, once again, it is hard to see why we shouldn't apply the same reasoning to many other things. Does a television show like *The Waltons* exploit families or family living? Does it invade family privacy? (What could be more sacred or personal than that?) Such comparisons make it clear that sex and nudity are covered up because they are considered shameful, not because they are seen as sacred. Feelings of shame are the reason sex is regarded as private and personal, not the other way around. And those conditioned feelings have no more ultimate claim on our moral values than any other taboos we have inherited. Even with these emotions as they now are, however, the argument is fallacious. Both drama and psychology texts lay bare the most personal of human affairs; but so far from being evil, that can be highly rewarding. What is apt to be bad, by contrast, is invading the privacy of individuals in real life, in contrast to staged portrayals. Consider the television cameras staring brazenly at a grief-stricken couple

as they watch their daughter die in the explosion of the Challenger: *that* is obscene.

The notion of exploitation also appears in a different sort of claim, one involving the commercial aspect of most pornography. The idea that making money by portraying sex is illegitimate has become so common that the term "sexploitation" is recognized by everyone. We hear nothing about commercial exploitation of the family, however, even though programs like *The Cosby Show* presumably make a lot of money for their sponsors. "Porn makes profit from women's bodies!" shouts one slogan. And the construction industry makes money from the bodies of men—what does *that* tell us? Actors and models of every other type perform their services for pay, and make money for their employers, to almost no one's dismay. No reason why sex should be so different in this regard is ever given. In a similar vein, the buying of sexual materials is often equated with the buying of sex itself. Yet we never hear it said that spending money to read or watch love stories makes a "commodity" of love. Sex is also said to be besmirched when erotic portrayals appear in magazines that are full of advertising for consumer goods—ignoring the fact that magazines on any other subject are also loaded with such ads. The attempt to sell things by associating them directly with sex, love, friendship, or anything else people find desirable is standard in advertising these days. That is arguably objectionable, but is not immediately relevant to our topic.

In addition to claims that it is immoral, pornography is frequently accused of being inherently bad in other ways. Explicit sex is "ugly," it is said, or "not really erotic." Beyond the failure to realize how fully mere conditioning is responsible for their aesthetic reactions, what these speakers reveal is their ego-centredness. "My tastes, the tastes of my group, are true and beautiful; what turns me on is genuinely erotic. But as for you...."[2] On the other hand, much of the explicitly erotic literature and movies traditionally produced would seem inferior to the tastes of nearly everyone: they are very cheaply made. But clearly, this is an artifact of the low level of social acceptability of really explicit pornography. If it were even as "respectable" as media violence has always been (consider the high levels of both artistic excellence and brutality in, say, *Hill Street Blues*), much more of it would be produced by those who make quality films and magazines—as is indeed already the case for mildly and implicitly sexual productions.

In a similar vein, many detractors of pornography decry the sad tawdriness of the peep-show parlors. In this they are partly right, though perhaps not in the way they think. There you will often find men who are painfully shy or sexually inhibited, men whom women regard as unattractive or as losers, military men cut off from other sources of female companionship, men who are physically or psychologically impaired, old and middle-aged men whose biological cravings defy social dogma by yearning for young women, young men whose female acquaintances don't want sex, and so on. What they all have in common is a powerful need and an inability, temporary or long-term, to get "the real thing." So they accept a poor substitute, a commercial fantasy. (And it's said that *they* are exploiters, of the women who make money from their plight!) Sad and tawdry indeed. But what is amazing is not the pornography-foes' indifference to that suffering: "Let them eat cake" is often the attitude of those not in need toward those who are. Nor is it their failure to grant that a poor substitute is better than nothing at all. It is the tacit or explicit message that somehow pornography is the cause of the sad situation. Like many another social epiphenomenon, it gets the blame for problems whose real source lies in nature or in the structure of society.

The supply of arguments for the intrinsic badness of sexual explicitness goes on and on, but the foregoing are common and representative. And they are all worthless. The fact is that all the standard "moral" arguments against pornography and sex for its own sake are logical fallacies of one kind or another. That such patent rationalizations have been convincing to so many is a testament to the power of socialization, once again. It is very, very difficult even to recognize the real sources of, much less to consciously overcome, the beliefs one has been indoctrinated with and the feelings one has been conditioned to have; they seem so natural, so obviously right. But the price humanity has always had to pay for such blindness is a terrible one. Summoning the will to be honest in this regard is not only the moral thing but the only intelligent thing to do, for the sake of the welfare of all—as we shall continue to see.

Degrading Content

Another special issue which is often aired regarding sexual portrayals is that of degradation. Or at least that of women: just as there is a tradition of special concern over violence against them, there is a wider view that affronts to the dignity of women are more reprehensible than those affecting men. Now, the primary topic discussed in this essay so far has been whether or not sexual openness or explicitness is degrading in itself; that general question needs no further treatment. But it is often charged that much pornography is genuinely debasing, over and above its sexual frankness. In fact, many anti-pornography groups claim that they are not opposed to portrayals of nudity or sexual behavior as such; it is merely the degrading ones that they abhor—though they insist that the latter are very common. For example, the conservative Commission on Pornography appointed by US Attorney-General Edwin Meese declared in its *Final Report* that non-violent but degrading material "constitutes somewhere between the predominant and the overwhelming portion of what is currently standard fare heterosexual pornography."[3] That charge, involving as it does specific types of sexual depiction, does require further analysis.

Actually, this new claim is very often highly misleading, if not deliberately deceitful. "We're only opposed to *degrading* sex" certainly sounds reasonable, and is manifestly designed to reassure the public that its makers aren't just motivated by traditional prudishness. When we read the fine print, however, it frequently turns out that most of what they include under this rubric *is* objected to for its sexual content; scenes that are at all explicit (e.g., with genital close-ups) rather than soft-focus or merely suggestive, or that don't contain sufficient aesthetic content or affectionateness, or whose sole purpose is to display nudity (pin-ups), etc. Some of these people are simply not being honest about their views. Others' attitudes do differ from traditional ones, but only in degree, only in the amount of explicitness or disinhibition or unredeemed sex they find tolerable.

There is one charge in this category that is worthy of special mention. It derives from the fact, discussed earlier, that the women of pornography typically display strong sexual desire or responsiveness; they show high levels of excitement and enthusiasm, engaging in sex readily and enjoying a variety of sexual acts or partners or both. The accusation is made, not only that this misrepresents women in general, but that it is degrading to them to be portrayed in such a manner. Often those who make the charge engage in hyperbole or distortion, saying pornography views women as "dirty whores," or at least as "nymphomaniacs" who are "hysterical" over sex. And once again, some even insist the debasement is deliberate, motivated by a desire to degrade all women. It has already been pointed out here

that sexual fantasies don't make a statement of fact about any real women, much less about all. But what if they did? Are such depictions really degrading to anyone?

What is most astonishing about these accusations, in this day and age, is their totally unselfconscious endorsement of a double standard of sexual behavior. The men of pornography are equally randy and uninhibited—a fact that the accusers occasionally admit, as an afterthought. But it is only complained that women are shown as "sexually undiscriminating" and "hypersexual." And only women are said to be degraded by being so portrayed. It is even alleged that such depictions will lead to a loss of respect for women (but not men) in general, hence to sexist discrimination and mistreatment of numerous kinds. This is absurd; such treatment certainly might be caused by the double standard these people embrace, but it can hardly be blamed on portrayals that treat men and women alike. The main point here, however, is this: it is not at all genuinely degrading, to a man *or* to a woman, to be or to be seen as highly sexual. A strong love of sex is no more evil than a strong love of sports, or of music. To have erotic desires that are lower than average may (or may not) be unfortunate, but no one considers it morally evil; an unusually high enthusiasm for sex should be regarded no differently. Only those who find such enthusiasm bad would object to anyone's being "stereotyped" as having it; otherwise it would be no worse than being represented as honest, or as liking lasagna....

Many charges of degradation in pornography are straightforward extensions of the traditional attitude that sex itself is degrading. But there are claims, involving certain special types of portrayal, that the debasement is independent of the sexual content. The Meese Commission listed three general kinds of depiction that they felt encompass the "degrading" category: portraying persons as "existing solely for the sexual satisfaction of others," or as being "in decidedly subordinate roles," or engaging "in sexual practices which would to most people be considered humiliating."[4] As described, such scenes might indeed be objectionable; it will be of value for us to consider these cases one at a time.

That first phrase, unfortunately, is more rhetorical than descriptive; it isn't at all clear what it comes to, and no examples were given. But charges of this type are often levelled against pornography, including ordinary pinups. And they are generally absurd. Though posing for a photograph of any kind typically involves making oneself as appealing as possible, only in the case of pictures of nude females is this considered a sign of existing merely to satisfy others. Another standard complaint is about portrayals of fellatio. These people are usually stone silent about those of cunnilingus, even though they are also a staple of hard-core sex films: that shows a man giving pleasure to a woman. But neither act is at all totally one-sided, since, once again, such a large factor in sexual excitement is the excitement of the other person.

In other contexts, what is seemingly meant by rhetoric like this is the flip side of that "nymphomaniac" charge. This time, on the grounds that no woman would engage so readily in sex, or in so much sex or in certain types of sex, for her own enjoyment, it is concluded that she is doing it only to satisfy men. That is to say, many insist on re-interpreting scenes of highly sexed women as cases of the women merely accommodating the men. They are reading traditional stereotypes of females as passive, compliant and non-sexual into scenes where they are obviously anything but; the "nymphomaniac" charges are exaggerated but at least more honest. Quite naturally, now, men fantasize about women who enjoy sharing things they themselves would like. But equally, women's romantic fantasies typically have men engaging in and enjoying things that the women want. So the main

problem here is this: in some people's eyes, a fantasy doesn't count as portraying equality between the sexes unless it involves men's desires becoming like women's, rather than the other way around. But there is nothing genuinely wrong with either. For all that, even the fact that male tastes are typically celebrated in pornography is hardly inevitable. The laws of the marketplace decree that a larger female interest in sexual portrayals would change their content—a process that has already begun in the case of video movies.

This is not to deny that a one-sided selfishness is ever found in pornography—or in real sex. There certainly are men and women whose pleasure in receiving things from the opposite gender (security, affection, *or* sex) is not contingent upon the latter's pleasure. But only a small proportion of pornography genuinely reflects these attitudes. This is so in spite of the fact that the making of such materials, unlike that portraying women's fantasies, has been left largely in the hands of people whose social sensitivities are not very keen. But even if certain depictions do contain a one-sided concern for male pleasure, it is a gross exaggeration to describe them in terms like "existing only to serve men," or even to consider them degrading rather than merely selfish and inconsiderate. And they can hardly compare to the message of this society's chivalric sexism, that women's needs and wishes are more noble than those of men. Indeed, it is precisely the failure of pornography to accede to this social attitude that so distresses traditionalists and some feminists.

Actually, the charge under discussion here is only one manifestation of a wider distortion in the views of sexist feminists. They claim that women in this society are constantly serving men, whereas men never do anything to help or please women. This is a complex topic, but there is far less truth to that claim than is commonly supposed. Indeed, their perception of such things often contains a further double standard. If men are shown being solicitous to women—e.g., opening doors for them—the "message" is that women are helpless children; if they are shown doing things for men, it is that women exist only to serve. In summary, this first category of "degrading" pornography is almost wholly the product of the sorts of paranoia and excuse-fishing that we have encountered before. We will have to look elsewhere for examples of genuine debasement.

★   ★   ★

Let us turn to the second alleged type of degrading portrayal, in which someone is shown in a definitely subordinate role. Objections to this kind of thing arise from concern over traditional male dominance and female passivity. This is a problem that must not be taken lightly; eliminating the power imbalance between the sexes is central to the cause of equality for women. Unfortunately, some have become hypersensitive to the issue, reading such imbalances into innocent situations. And they have done this with a vengeance in the case of pornography. For example, it is often claimed that emotional passivity, not just the physical stillness required in posing for a camera, is reflected in ordinary pin-ups. And a reclining nude is said to be doubly passive and helpless—never mind that the only comfortable way to have sex is lying down, to them the posture represents submission, not sex. (On the question of whether the "missionary position" subordinates women, of course, the extremist feminists and the traditionalists part company.) This mindset also leads to some revealing doublethink. For instance, if a male is shown having consensual sex with more than one female, they're automatically his "harem"; if it is a woman with two or more men, it's a "gang rape."

One of the more incredible charges of this type is that sexual portrayals of interracial couples are racist, no matter how equally they are actually depicted. (This is also ironic, since in earlier years a common objection to men's magazines was that they were racist for only showing white women.) The rationale here is that the social power imbalance between the different races means that any such depiction inherently involves dominance. If that conclusion followed, it would bode even worse for a *real* sexual relationship between members of different races, including marriage. What makes this claim especially disturbing is the fact that abhorrence of interracial sex is such an integral part of real racism. "Would you want your sister to marry one?" used to be the presumed clincher in defenses of segregation. And under Hollywood's old Hays Code, not only sex but any depiction of interracial couples was strictly prohibited. If racial dominance is really endorsed, in pornography or anywhere else, that certainly is bad. But the idea that depicting interracial sexuality is inherently evil is itself tinged with racism.

False charges aside, it certainly is true that some pornography depicts men who are dominant and women who are passive, to one degree or another. In this, however, it is merely reflecting the reality in this culture: from dating to kissing and embracing to sex itself, males are still forced by female passivity to take the more active role. (Notice then how this particular objection clashes with an earlier one: it comes dangerously close to complaining that pornography is *too* true to life!) Moreover, sexual depictions of this type are only doing what others often do, from adventure stories to romance novels. To single out sexual portrayals for special blame for something that is so universal reveals that the real objections lie elsewhere. (The footnote on p. 330 of the Commission's *Final Report* suggests that they were desperate to find power imbalances. The alleged pornographic theme, "He is ready to take. She is ready to be taken," describes equally well the large majority of love scenes in romantic novels and movies.) In fact, however, pornography on the whole treats women and men more alike and more equal than the entertainment media in general do. So far from being passive, once again, most of the women portrayed in it are sexually assertive.

This was borne out by the study of hard-core videotapes made in Vancouver. It found that in only fourteen percent of the sexual scenes was the activity less than completely mutual; in these, the team of male and female coders felt that at least one of the participants was playing "a more dominant or directive role," "a more assertive role in directing the course of the interaction." In nearly half of these cases the woman was more dominant than the man—which sounds more egalitarian than mainstream movies. Notice also that this description doesn't sound particularly serious; extreme subordination was evidently quite uncommon. That being so, it isn't clear that even this much dominance is very objectionable. Many independent women report that they sometimes like to be dominated in the bedroom—"but not anywhere else!" Evidently, they do not see this as having consequences for their non-sexual lives. If they are right, a mild power imbalance in depictions of sexual activity is not a threat to women's equality. Notice also that this attitude appears to be part of a more general one: women often speak of the emotional value of being held by a man, but not of *doing* the holding. It is not clear that there is anything bad about this, however. Only those who feel threatened by all gender differences will automatically reject it.

What about that small minority of cases of extreme dominance in sexual portrayals, then? They fall into several categories, which will need to be considered separately.... First of all, there is the standard macho novel. Liberally sprinkled with scenes of rape and men pushing women around, they certainly are objectionable for their portrayal of women, *and* men. Most of these would not rightly be classed as pornography, since sex is not their central focus. As for those that would, the point here is that they are only the erotic segment of a larger category of fantasies, those expressing the power-desires of lower class males. Denied access to the money and status of the entrenched social structure, these men compensate with a tough-guy self image. So the characters in these stories ride roughshod over other males as well; general dominance is the theme, not just the subjection of women. To pretend, as many do, that this mistreatment of women is a natural outgrowth of the portrayal of sex is a serious distortion of the facts. Its cause and cure lie elsewhere.

Another variety of genuine subjugation involves a special paraphilia. What is known as "dominance and submission" is practiced by a tiny sexual subculture. (*The Story of O* provides a well-known illustration. This and another paraphilic specialization, "bondage and discipline," are often both classed as subcategories of sadomasochism.) The causes of such desires are obscure. The Freudian hypothesis that they trace back to the love-and-helplessness relationship of a child to its parents is plausible, but hard evidence is not easy to get. What does seem clear is that they are not in general produced by a wider desire to subjugate women, as some have charged. Indeed, the majority of the males in this category desire the submissive role. (They want a "dominatrix.") This is reportedly reflected in the sexual materials published for these people: in a survey of such magazines, one researcher found submissive males in roughly thirty percent more of the cases.[5] The extremist claim that "porn is about power, not about sex" is absurd, once again; but it is even false in regard to paraphilic dominance and submission. For the individuals who have these feelings, power or its lack is what *causes* sexual arousal. The former is only a means to the latter—just the reverse of this charge.

But isn't that sort of activity, or its portrayal, evil nonetheless? To answer, we must realize again that paraphilic behavior like this is nearly always just play-acting; it is practiced by mutual consent and for mutual enjoyment. Moreover, its practitioners' non-sexual lives tend to be quite normal. Disturbing to others though they naturally are, these desires are not in general a reflection of forces or feelings that are a threat, to women or anyone else. And they certainly are not common. One study of "adult" book shops in New York City found that about seventeen percent of their magazine covers depicted bondage or domination, but this figure is misleadingly high. First, materials that cater to more unusual sexual tastes are concentrated in these stores; the big-selling sex magazines are sold in more socially acceptable outlets. Second, this particular survey counted titles, rather than separate issues or the number of copies of the latter; but publications portraying more deviant activities tend to be produced only once (in spite of the "Vol. 1, No. 1" they may carry).[6] Unlike the last one, this variety of depicted dominance should be of little concern to the women's movement.

The oppression of women by men down through history is a fact to be deplored. But feminists too frequently ignore the power that women exercise over men. Humans are highly social beings, whose behavior is more often influenced by the opinions of others than by superior physical strength. And in the matter of controlling others through approval and disapproval, women exercise very great power. This influence is especially great in the formative years of early childhood, since the bulk of socialization at that age is done by women: mothers, day-care workers, school teachers, etc. More directly, women have traditionally controlled men by getting other men to do it for them, from gallant knights vying for their favors to modern politicians vying for their votes. In fact, an often-effective way of exercising power over others is precisely by exaggerating one's lack of power, by playing

victim. Social reality is much more complex than feminist theories generally allow.

The power of women is nowhere more in evidence than in regard to love and sex: the fact that this culture's moral standards match the needs of its females better than those of its males has been mentioned here repeatedly. In the last century, the women's "purity crusade" created laws against pornography, prostitution and male homosexual acts, also birth control and abortion. Without a single vote, the women involved were able to shame male legislators into doing what the crusaders perceived as being in women's best interests.[7] It is certainly true that the extreme double standard maintained previous to that time by the males in power was oppressive to women; but the comstockery that replaced it was oppressive to everyone. In a more direct way, men's greater need for sex puts control into the hands of women. "All that power," marvels Ms. Friday in describing the control this gives adolescent females over their male peers. Some women are oblivious to this situation, while others exploit it—just as some males exploit females' greater need for love.

The manner in which these facts are reflected in sexual fantasies is extremely important to our discussion. For once more, their purpose is often to make the world seem better than it is in real life. Hence it is not surprising that some male fantasies would "turn the tables" in this relationship. Those occasional scenes in which a woman is so strongly aroused that she begs for sex make a transparently clear statement of male powerlessness in this regard. Similarly, pornographic portrayals in which men dominate women—*and* those that are the other way around—appear to represent attempts by males to cope with the feelings of helplessness and frustration. Such things must be understood for what they really are, not simplemindedly denounced as yet another manifestation of patriarchy.

Notes

1 For those who have seen it, the one thing in all the world that is best described by this familiar rhetoric is artist Judy Chicago's tableful of plastic vaginas, *The Dinner Party*. But male sexual desire isn't involved, so it is politically acceptable to many if not all feminist foes of pornography. Had it appeared in *Hustler* instead of in feminist circles, it would no doubt be standardly cited by them as a paradigm of the male objectification of women. Traditionalists, of course, are scandalized by it.

2 To satisfy the reader's curiosity, the explicit scenes of hard-core pornography do not appeal to me; I find them very unaesthetic. (I also detest the taste of baked squash and fresh onions.) But I have decent, caring friends who get great pleasure from them, including some who use them to augment loving marital relationships.

3 From pp. 334–5 in the *Final Report* of the Attorney General's Commission on Pornography (hereafter, *AGCP*).

4 P. 331. The religiously conservative Meese Commission was of course silent about the subordination of women many insist is endorsed by the Bible.

5 From Alan Soble's *Pornography: Marxism, Feminism and the Future of Sexuality*, p. 19.

6 The survey was by Dietz and Evans, in the *American Journal of Psychiatry*, 139:11. (Having been co-authored by one of the commissioners, this article may also throw more light on the question of which acts they considered non-dominating but still degrading; see the chart on p. 1494.) The information that such magazines are not produced only once is from Robin Badgley *et al.*, *Sexual Offences Against Children*.

7 For example, see Sheila Rothman's book *Woman's Proper Place*.

Questions for Discussion

1 Much of Christensen's argument takes the form of a comparison of pornography with other aspects of popular culture, suggesting pornography is no more offensive. Christensen uses this to claim pornography is acceptable. Could one use the same point to establish that much of popular culture should be changed?

2 One of Christensen's points is that those who attack pornography have been influenced by an unreasonable traditional view that a woman's nudity is more degrading than a man's nudity, or that the same actions or attitudes can be shameful in a woman but not in a man. Is he right? Does it matter to his argument whether most consumers of the pornography see it in those terms?

Pornography is a Civil Rights Issue

Andrea Dworkin

Andrea Dworkin is one of the best known feminist supporters of legal measures against pornography. She and Catharine MacKinnon were the framers of the "Minneapolis Ordinance." This ordinance was designed to make trafficking in pornography a violation of civil rights (for which a victim might sue) rather than an obscenity offense. She was called as a witness before the United States Attorney General's Commission on Pornography to present her views. The following is taken from her testimony before that commission.

★   ★   ★

MS DWORKIN: Thank you very much. My name is Andrea Dworkin. I am a citizen of the United States, and in this country where I live, every year millions and millions of pictures are being made of women with our legs spread. We are called beaver, we are called pussy, our genitals are tied up, they are pasted, makeup is put on them to make them pop out of a page at a male viewer. Millions and millions of pictures are made of us in postures of

Ethical Issues

submission and sexual access so that our vaginas are exposed for penetration, our anuses are exposed for penetration, our throats are used as if they are genitals for penetration. In this country where I live as a citizen real rapes are on film and are being sold in the marketplace. And the major motif of pornography as a form of entertainment is that women are raped and violated and humiliated until we discover that we like it and at that point we ask for more.

In this country where I live as a citizen, women are penetrated by animals and objects for public entertainment, women are urinated on and defecated on, women and girls are used interchangeably so that grown women are made up to look like five- or six-year-old children surrounded by toys, presented in mainstream pornographic publications for anal penetration. There are magazines in which adult women are presented with their pubic areas shaved so that they resemble children.

In this country where I live, there is a trafficking in pornography that exploits mentally and physically disabled women, women who are maimed; there is amputee pornography, a trade in women who have been maimed in that way, as if that is a sexual fetish for men. In this country where I live, there is a trade in racism as a form of sexual pleasure, so that the plantation is presented as a form of sexual gratification for the black woman slave who asks please to be abused, please to be raped, please to be hurt. Black skin is presented as if it is a female genital, and all the violence and the abuse and the humiliation that is in general directed against female genitals is directed against the black skin of women in pornography.

Asian women in the country where I live are tied from trees and hung from ceilings and hung from doorways as a form of public entertainment. There is a concentration camp pornography in this country where I live, where the concentration camp and the atrocities that occurred there are presented as existing for the sexual pleasure of the victim, of the woman, who orgasms to the real abuses that occurred, not very long ago in history.

In the country where I live as a citizen, there is pornography of the humiliation of women where every single way of humiliating a human being is taken to be a form of sexual pleasure for the viewer and for the victim; where women are covered with filth, including feces, including mud, including paint, including blood, including semen; where women are tortured for the sexual pleasure of those who watch and do the torture, where women are murdered for the sexual pleasure of murdering women, and this material exists because it is fun, because it is entertainment, because it is a form of pleasure, and there are those who say it is a form of freedom.

Certainly it is freedom for those who do it. Certainly it is freedom for those who use it as entertainment, but we are also asked to believe that it is freedom for those to whom it is done.

Then this entertainment is taken, and it is used on other women, women who aren't in the pornography, to force those women into prostitution, to make them imitate the acts in the pornography. The women in the pornography, sixty-five to seventy percent of them we believe are victims of incest or child sexual abuse. They are poor women; they are not women who have opportunities in this society. They are frequently runaways who are picked up by pimps and exploited. They are frequently raped, the rapes are filmed, they are kept in prostitution by blackmail. The pornography is used on prostitutes by johns who expect them to replicate the sexual acts in the pornography, no matter how damaging it is.

Pornography is used in rape—to plan it, to execute it, to choreograph it, to engender the excitement to commit the act. Pornography is used in gang rape against women. We see an increase since the release of *Deep Throat* in throat rape—where women show up in emergency rooms because men believe they can penetrate, deep-thrust, to the bottom of a woman's throat. We see increasing use of all elements of pornography in battery, which is the most commonly committed violent crime in this country, including the rape of women by animals, including maiming, including heavy bondage, including outright torture.

We have seen in the last eight years an increase in the use of cameras in rapes. And those rapes are filmed and then they are put on the marketplace and they are protected speech—they are real rapes.

We see a use of pornography in the harassment of women on jobs, especially in nontraditional jobs, in the harassment of women in education, to create terror and compliance in the home, which as you know is the most dangerous place for women in this society, where more violence is committed against women than anywhere else. We see pornography used to create harassment of women and children in neighborhoods that are saturated with pornography, where people come from other parts of the city and then prey on the populations of people who live in those neighborhoods, and that increases physical attack and verbal assault.

We see pornography having introduced a profit motive into rape. We see that filmed rapes are protected speech. We see the centrality of pornography in serial murders. There *are* snuff films. We see boys imitating pornography. We see the average age of rapists going down. We are beginning to see gang rapes in elementary schools committed by elementary school age boys imitating pornography.

We see sexual assault after death where frequently the pornography is the motive for the murder because the man believes that he will get a particular kind of sexual pleasure having sex with a woman after she is dead.

We see a major trade in women, we see the torture of women as a form of entertainment, and we see women also suffering the injury of objectification—that is to say we are

dehumanized. We are treated as if we are subhuman, and that is a precondition for violence against us.

I live in a country where if you film any act of humiliation or torture, and the victim is a woman, the film is both entertainment and it is protected speech. Now that tells me something about what it means to be a woman citizen in this country, and the meaning of being second class.

When your rape is entertainment, your worthlessness is absolute. You have reached the nadir of social worthlessness. The civil impact of pornography on women is staggering. It keeps us socially silent, it keeps us socially compliant, it keeps us afraid in neighborhoods; and it creates a vast hopelessness for women, a vast despair. One lives inside a nightmare of sexual abuse that is both actual and potential, and you have the great joy of knowing that your nightmare is someone else's freedom and someone else's fun.

Now, a great deal has happened in this country to legitimize pornography in the last ten to fifteen years. There are people who are responsible for the fact that pornography is now a legitimate form of public entertainment.

Number one, the lobby of lawyers who work for the pornographers; the fact that the pornographers pay lawyers big bucks to fight for them, not just in the courts, but in public, in the public dialogue; the fact that lawyers interpret constitutional principles in light of the profit interest of the pornographers.

Number two, the collusion of the American Civil Liberties Union with the pornographers, which includes taking money from them. It includes using buildings that pornographers own and not paying rent, it includes using pornography in benefits to raise money. It includes not only defending them in court but also doing publicity for them, including organizing events for them, as the Hugh Hefner First Amendment Awards is organized by ACLU people for *Playboy*. It includes publishing in their magazines. It includes deriving great pride and economic benefit from working privately for the pornographers, while publicly pretending to be a disinterested advocate of civil liberties and free speech.

I want you to contrast the behavior of the ACLU in relation to the pornographers with their activities in relation to the Klan and the Nazis. The ACLU pretends to understand that they are all equally pernicious. But do ACLU people publish in the Klan newsletter? No. Do they go to Nazi social events? No. Do they go to cocktail parties at Nazi headquarters? No, they don't, at least not yet.

Finally, they have colluded in this sense, that they have convinced many of us that the standard for speech is what I would call a repulsion standard. That is to say we find the most repulsive person in the society and we defend him. I say we find the most powerless people in this society, and we defend *them*. That's the way we increase rights of speech in this society.

A third group that colludes to legitimize pornography are publishers and the so-called legitimate media. They pretend to believe that under this system of law there is a First Amendment that is indivisible and absolute, which it has never been.

As you know, the First Amendment protects speech that has already been expressed from state interference. That means it protects those who own media. There is no affirmative responsibility to open communications to those who are powerless in the society at large.

As a result, the owners of media, the newspapers, the TV networks, are comfortable with having women's bodies defined as the speech of pimps, because they are protecting their rights to profit as owners, and they think that that is what the First Amendment is for.

I am ashamed to say that people in my profession, writers, have also colluded with the pornographers. We provide their so-called so-

cially redeeming value, and they wrap the tortured bodies of women in the work that we do.

Fourth, politicians have colluded with the pornographers in municipalities all over this country. They do it in these ways:

Zoning laws do not keep pornography out of cities. They are an official legal permission to traffic in pornography. And as a result politicians are able to denounce pornography moralistically while protecting it through zoning laws.

Zoning laws impose pornography on poor neighborhoods, on working-class neighborhoods, on neighborhoods where people of color live, and all of those people have to deal with the increase in crime, the terrible harassment, the degradation of the quality of life in their neighborhoods, and the politicians get to protect the property values of the rich. There is an equal protection issue here: why the state makes some people pay so other people can profit.

But that issue has never been raised. We have never been able to sue a city under the equal protection theory, because lawyers are on the other side. Lawyers belong primarily to pornographers, and the people who live in these neighborhoods that are saturated with pornography are powerless people. They don't even have power in their own municipalities.

In addition, what pornographers do in municipalities is that they buy land that is targeted for development by cities. They hold that land hostage. They develop political power through negotiating around that land. They make huge profits, and they get influence in local city governments.

Five, not finally but next to the last, a great colluder with the pornographers was the last presidential Commission on Obscenity and Pornography. They were very effective in legitimizing pornography in this country. They appeared to be looking for a proverbial ax murderer who would watch pornography and within twenty-four or forty-eight hours go out and kill someone in a horrible and clear way. The country is saturated with pornography, and saturated with violence against women, and saturated with the interfacing of the two. And the Commission didn't find it.

None of the scientific research that they relied on to come to their conclusions is worth anything today. It's all invalid. I ask you to take seriously the fact that society does not exist in a laboratory, that we are talking about real things that happen to real people, and that's what we are asking you to take some responsibility for.

Finally, the ultimate colluders in the legitimizing of pornography, of course, are the consumers. In 1979 we had a $4-billion-a-year industry in this country. By 1985 it was an $8-billion-a-year industry. Those consumers include men in all walks of life: lawyers, politicians, writers, professors, owners of media, police, doctors, maybe even commissioners on presidential commissions. No one really knows, do they?

And no matter where we look, we can't find the consumers. But what we learn is the meaning of first-class citizenship, and the meaning of first-class citizenship is that you can use your authority as men and as professionals to protect pornography both by developing arguments to protect it and by using real social and economic power to protect it.

And as a result of all this, the harm to women remains invisible; even though we have the bodies, the harm to women remains invisible. Underlying the invisibility of this harm is an assumption that what is done to women is natural, that even if a woman is forced to do something, somehow it falls within the sphere of her natural responsibilities as a woman. When the same things are done to boys, those things are perceived as an outrage. They are called unnatural.

But if you force a woman to do something that she was born to do, then the violence to her is not perceived as a real violation of her.

In addition, the harm to women of pornography is invisible because most sexual abuse still occurs in private, even though we have this photographic documentation of it, called the pornography industry.

Women are extremely isolated, women don't have credibility, women are not believed by people who make social policy.

In addition, the harm of pornography remains invisible because women have been historically excluded from the protections of the Constitution; and as a result, the violations of our human rights, when they don't occur the same way violations to men occur, have not been recognized or taken seriously, and we do not have remedies for them under law.

In addition, pornography is invisible in its harm to women because women are poorer than men and many of the women exploited in pornography are very poor, many of them illiterate, and also because there is a great deal of female compliance with brutality, and the compliance is based on fear, it's based on powerlessness and it is based on a reaction to the very real violence of the pornographers.

Finally, the harm is invisible because of the smile, because women are made to smile, women aren't just made to do the sex acts. We are made to smile while we do them.

So you will find in pornography women penetrating themselves with swords or daggers, and you will see the smile. You will see things that cannot be done to a human being and that are done to men only in political circumstances of torture, and you will see a woman forced to smile.

And this smile will be believed, and the injury done to her as a human being, to her body and to her heart and to her soul, will not be believed.

Now, we have been told that we have an argument here about speech, not about women being hurt. And yet the emblem of that argument is a woman bound and gagged and we are supposed to believe that that is speech. Who is that speech for? We have women being tortured and we are told that that is somebody's speech? Whose speech is it? It's the speech of the pimp, it is not the speech of a woman. The only words we hear in pornography from women are that women want to be hurt, ask to be hurt, like to be raped, get sexual pleasure from sexual violence; and even when a woman is covered in filth, we are supposed to believe that her speech is that she likes it and she wants more of it.

The reality for women in this society is that pornography creates silence for women. The pornographers silence women. Our bodies are their language. Their speech is made out of our exploitation, our subservience, our injury and our pain, and they can't say anything without hurting us, and when you protect them, you protect only their right to exploit and hurt us.

Pornography is a civil rights issue for women because pornography sexualizes inequality, because it turns women into subhuman creatures.

Pornography is a civil rights issue for women because it is the systematic exploitation of a group of people because of a condition of birth. Pornography creates bigotry and hostility and aggression towards all women, targets all women, without exception.

Pornography is the suppression of us through sexual exploitation and abuse, so that we have no real means to achieve civil equality; and the issue here is simple, it is not complex. People are being hurt, and you can help them or you can help those who are hurting them. We need civil rights legislation, legislation that recognizes pornography as a violation of the civil rights of women.

We need it because civil rights legislation recognizes the fact that the harm here is to human beings. We need that recognition. We need civil rights legislation because it puts the power to act in the hands of the people who have been forced into pornographized pow-

erlessness, and that's a special kind of powerlessness, that's a powerlessness that is supposed to be a form of sexual pleasure.

We need civil rights legislation because only those to whom it has happened know what has happened. They are the people who are the experts. They have the knowledge. They know what has happened, how it's happened; only they can really articulate, from beginning to end, the reality of pornography as a human rights injury. We need civil rights legislation because it gives us something back after what the pornographers have taken from us.

The motivation to fight back keeps people alive. People need it for their dignity, for their ability to continue to exist as citizens in a country that needs their creativity and needs their presence and needs the existence that has been taken from them by the pornographers. We need civil rights legislation because, as social policy, it says to a population of people that they have human worth, they have human worth, that this society recognizes that they have human worth.

We need it because it's the only legislative remedy thus far that is drawn narrowly enough to confront the human rights issues for people who are are being exploited and discriminated against, without becoming an instrument of police power to suppress real expression.

We need the civil rights legislation because the process of civil discovery is a very important one, and it will give us a great deal of information for potential criminal prosecutions, against organized crime, against pornographers, and I ask you to look at the example of the Southern Poverty Law Center and their Klanwatch Project, which has used civil suits to get criminal indictments against the Klan.

Finally, we need civil rights legislation because the only really dirty word in this society is the word "women," and a civil rights approach says that this society repudiates the brutalization of women.

We are against obscenity laws. We don't want them. I want you to understand why, whether you end up agreeing or not.

Number one, the pornographers use obscenity laws as part of their formula for making pornography. All they need to do is provide some literary, artistic, political or scientific value and they can hang women from the rafters. As long as they manage to meet that formula, it doesn't matter what they do to women.

And in the old days, when obscenity laws were still being enforced, in many places—for instance the most sadomasochistic pornography—the genitals were always covered because if the genitals were always covered, that wouldn't kick off a police prosecution.

Number two, the use of the prurient interest standard—however that standard is construed in this new era, when the Supreme Court has taken two synonyms, "lasciviousness" and "lust," and said that they mean different things, which is mind-boggling in and of itself. Whatever prurient interest is construed to mean, the reaction of jurors to material—whether they are supposed to be aroused or whether they are not allowed to be aroused, whatever the instructions of the court—has nothing to do with the objective reality of what is happening to women in pornography.

The third reason that obscenity law cannot work for us is: what do community standards mean in a society when violence against women is pandemic, when according to the FBI a woman is battered every eighteen seconds and it's the most commonly committed violent crime in the country? What would community standards have meant in the segregated South? What would community standards have meant as we approached the atrocity of Nazi Germany? What are community standards in a society where women are persecuted for being women and pornography is a form of political persecution?

Obscenity laws are also woman-hating in their construction. Their basic presumption is that it's women's bodies that are dirty. The standards of obscenity law don't acknowledge the reality of the technology. They were drawn up in a society where obscenity was construed to be essentially writing and drawing; and now what we have is mass production in a way that real people are being hurt, and the consumption of real people by a real technology, and obscenity laws are not adequate to that reality.

Finally, obscenity laws, at the discretion of police and prosecutors, will keep obscenity out of the public view, but it remains available to men in private. It remains available to individual men, it remains available to all-male groups; and whenever it is used, it still creates bigotry, hostility and aggression towards all women. It's still used in sexual abuse as part of sexual abuse. It's still made through coercion, through blackmail and through exploitation.

I am going to ask you to do several things. The first thing I am going to ask you to do is listen to women who want to talk to you about what has happened to them. Please listen to them. They know, they know how this works. You are asking people to speculate; they know, it has happened to them....

Questions for Discussion

1 Dworkin suggests that it is impossible to separate pornography from a whole pattern of power imbalances and violence against women in our society. Is she right?

2 Should legislation concerning pornography be framed in terms of violation of civil rights, rather than obscenity?

Feminism, Moralism, and Pornography

Ellen Willis

Willis writes from a feminist perspective, but is very suspicious of any attempts to censor pornography. She warns against a tendency to repeat elements of the traditional views of the proper role of women in the current feminist campaign against pornography. She also raises some questions about how those who are opposing pornography try to define what they are opposed to.

★   ★   ★

For women, life is an ongoing good cop–bad cop routine. The good cops are marriage, motherhood, and that courtly old gentleman, chivalry. Just cooperate, they say (crossing their fingers), and we'll go easy on you. You'll never have to earn a living or open a door. We'll even get you some romantic love. But you'd better not get stubborn, or you'll have to deal with our friend rape, and he's a real terror; we just can't control him.

Pornography often functions as a bad cop. If rape warns that without the protection of one man we are fair game for all, the hard-core pornographic image suggests that the alternative to being a wife is being a whore. As women become more "criminal," the cops call for nastier reinforcements; the proliferation of lurid, violent porn (symbolic rape) is a form of backlash. But one can be a solid citizen and still be shocked (naively or hypocritically) by police brutality. However widely condoned, rape is illegal. However loudly people proclaim that pornography is as wholesome as granola, the essence of its appeal is that emotionally it remains taboo. It is from their very contempt for the rules that bad cops derive their power to terrorize (and the covert approbation of solid citizens who would love to break the rules themselves). The line between a bad cop and outlaw is tenuous. Both rape and pornography reflect a male outlaw mentality that rejects the conventions of romance and insists, bluntly, that women are cunts. The crucial

difference between the conservative's moral indignation at rape, or at *Hustler*, and the feminist's political outrage is the latter's understanding that the problem is not bad cops or outlaws but cops and the law.

Unfortunately, the current women's campaign against pornography seems determined to blur this difference. Feminist criticism of sexist and misogynist pornography is nothing new; porn is an obvious target insofar as it contributes to larger patterns of oppression—the reduction of the female body to a commodity (the paradigm being prostitution), the sexual intimidation that makes women regard the public streets as enemy territory (the paradigm being rape), sexist images, and propaganda in general. But what is happening now is different. By playing games with the English language, anti-porn activists are managing to rationalize as feminism a single-issue movement divorced from any larger political context and rooted in conservative moral assumptions that are all the more dangerous for being unacknowledged.

When I first heard there was a group called Women Against Pornography, I twitched. Could I define myself as Against Pornography? Not really. In itself, pornography—which, my dictionary and I agree, means any image or description intended or used to arouse sexual desire—does not strike me as the proper object of a political crusade. As the most cursory observation suggests, there are many varieties of porn, some pernicious, some more or less benign. About the only generalization one can make is that pornography is the return of the repressed, of feelings and fantasies driven underground by a culture that atomizes sexuality, defining love as a noble affair of the heart and mind, lust as a base animal urge centered in unmentionable organs. Prurience—the state of mind I associate with pornography—implies a sense of sex as forbidden, secretive pleasure, isolated from any emotional or social context. I imagine that in utopia, porn would wither away along with the state, heroin, and Coca-Cola. At present, however, the sexual impulses that pornography appeals to are part of virtually everyone's psychology. For obvious political and cultural reasons nearly all porn is sexist in that it is the product of a male imagination and aimed at a male market; women are less likely to be consciously interested in pornography, or to indulge that interest, or to find porn that turns them on. But anyone who thinks women are simply indifferent to pornography has never watched a bunch of adolescent girls pass around a trashy novel. Over the years I've enjoyed various pieces of pornography—some of them of the sleazy Forty-second Street paperback sort—and so have most women I know. Fantasy, after all, is more flexible than reality, and women have learned, as a matter of survival, to be adept at shaping male fantasies to their own purposes. If feminists define pornography, per se, as the enemy, the result will be to make a lot of women ashamed of their sexual feelings and afraid to be honest about them. And the last thing women need is more sexual shame, guilt, and hypocrisy—this time served up as feminism.

So why ignore qualitative distinctions and in effect condemn all pornography as equally bad? WAP organizers answer—or finesse—this question by redefining pornography. They maintain that pornography is not really about sex but about violence against women. Or, in a more colorful formulation, "Pornography is the theory, rape is the practice." Part of the argument is that pornography causes violence; much is made of the fact that Charles Manson and David Berkowitz had porn collections. This is the sort of inverted logic that presumes marijuana to be dangerous because most heroin addicts started with it. It is men's hostility toward women—combined with their power to express that hostility and for the most part get away with it—that causes sexual violence. Pornography that gives sadistic fantasies concrete shape—and, in today's atmosphere, social legitimacy—may well encourage suggestible men to act them out. But if *Hustler* were to vanish from the shelves tomorrow, I doubt that rape or wife-beating statistics would decline.

Even more problematic is the idea that pornography depicts violence rather than sex. Since porn is by definition overtly sexual, while most of it is not overtly violent, this equation requires some fancy explaining. The conference WAP held in September was in part devoted to this task. Robin Morgan and Gloria Steinem addressed it by attempting to distinguish pornography from erotica. According to this argument, erotica (whose etymological root is "eros," or sexual love) expresses an integrated sexuality based on mutual affection and desire between equals; pornography (which comes from another Greek root—"porne," meaning prostitute) reflects a dehumanized sexuality based on male domination and exploitation of women. The distinction sounds promising, but it doesn't hold up. The accepted meaning of erotica is literature or pictures with sexual themes; it may or may not serve the essentially utilitarian function of pornography. Because it is less specific, less suggestive of actual sexual activity, "erotica" is regularly used as a euphemism for "classy porn." Pornography expressed in literary language or expensive photography and consumed by the upper middle class is "erotica";

the cheap stuff, which can't pretend to any purpose but getting people off, is smut. The erotica-versus-porn approach evades the (embarrassing?) question of how porn is *used*. It endorses the portrayal of sex as we might like it to be and condemns the portrayal of sex as it too often is, whether in action or only in fantasy. But if pornography is to arouse, it must appeal to the feelings we have, not those that by some utopian standard we ought to have. Sex in this culture has been so deeply politicized that it is impossible to make clear-cut distinctions between "authentic" sexual impulses and those conditioned by patriarchy. Between, say, *Ulysses* at one end and *Snuff* at the other, erotica/pornography conveys all sorts of mixed messages that elicit complicated and private responses. In practice, attempts to sort out good erotica from bad porn inevitably come down to "What turns me on is erotic; what turns you on is pornographic."

It would be clearer and more logical simply to acknowledge that some sexual images are offensive and some are not. But logic and clarity are irrelevant—or rather, inimical—to the underlying aim of the anti-porners, which is to vent the emotions traditionally associated with the word "pornography." As I've suggested, there is a social and psychic link between pornography and rape. In terms of patriarchal morality both are expressions of male lust, which is presumed to be innately vicious, and offenses to the putative sexual innocence of "good" women. But feminists supposedly begin with different assumptions—that men's confusion of sexual desire with predatory aggression reflects a sexist system, not male biology; that there are no good (chaste) or bad (lustful) women, just women who are, like men, sexual beings. From this standpoint, to lump pornography with rape is dangerously simplistic. Rape is a violent physical assault. Pornography can be a psychic assault, both in its content and in its public intrusions on our attention, but for women as for men it can also

be a source of erotic pleasure. A woman who is raped is a victim; a woman who enjoys pornography (even if that means enjoying a rape fantasy) is in a sense a rebel, insisting on an aspect of her sexuality that has been defined as a male preserve. Insofar as pornography glorifies male supremacy and sexual alienation, it is deeply reactionary. But in rejecting sexual repression and hypocrisy—which have inflicted even more damage on women than on men— it expresses a radical impulse.

That this impulse still needs defending, even among feminists, is evident from the sexual attitudes that have surfaced in the anti-porn movement. In the movement's rhetoric pornography is a code word for vicious male lust. To the objection that some women get off on porn, the standard reply is that this only shows how thoroughly women have been brainwashed by male values—though a WAP leaflet goes so far as to suggest that women who claim to like pornography are lying to avoid male opprobrium. (Note the good-girl-versus-bad-girl theme, reappearing as healthy-versus-sick, or honest-versus-devious; for "brainwashed" read "seduced.") And the view of sex that most often emerges from talk about "erotica" is as sentimental and euphemistic as the word itself: lovemaking should be beautiful, romantic, soft, nice, and devoid of messiness, vulgarity, impulses to power, or indeed aggression of any sort. Above all, the emphasis should be on *relationships*, not (yuck) *organs*. This goody-goody concept of eroticism is not feminist but feminine. It is precisely sex as an aggressive, unladylike activity, an expression of violent and unpretty emotion, an exercise of erotic power, and a specifically genital experience that has been taboo for women. Nor are we supposed to admit that we, too, have sadistic impulses, that our sexual fantasies may reflect forbidden urges to turn the tables and get revenge on men. (When a woman is aroused by a rape fantasy, is she perhaps identifying with the rapist as well as the victim?)

At the WAP conference lesbian separatists argued that pornography reflects patriarchal sexual relations; patriarchal sexual relations are based on male power backed by force; ergo, pornography is violent. This dubious syllogism, which could as easily be applied to romantic novels, reduces the whole issue to hopeless mush. If all manifestations of patriarchal sexuality are violent, then opposition to violence cannot explain why pornography (rather than romantic novels) should be singled out as a target. Besides, such reductionism allows women no basis for distinguishing between consensual heterosexuality and rape. But this is precisely its point; as a number of women at the conference put it, "In a patriarchy, all sex with men is pornographic." Of course, to attack pornography, and at the same time equate it with heterosexual sex, is implicitly to condemn not only women who like pornography, but women who sleep with men. This is familiar ground. The argument that straight women collaborate with the enemy has often been, among other things, a relatively polite way of saying that they consort with the beast. At the conference I couldn't help feeling that proponents of the separatist line were talking like the modern equivalents of women who, in an era when straightforward prudery was socially acceptable, joined convents to escape men's rude sexual demands. It seemed to me that their revulsion against heterosexuality was serving as the thinnest of covers for disgust with sex itself. In any case, sanitized feminine sexuality, whether straight or gay, is as limited as the predatory masculine kind and as central to women's oppression; a major function of misogynist pornography is to scare us into embracing it. As a further incentive, the good cops stand ready to assure us that we are indeed morally superior to men, that in our sweetness and nonviolence (read passivity and powerlessness) is our strength.

Women are understandably tempted to believe this comforting myth. Self-righteousness has always been a feminine weapon, a permissible way to make men feel bad. Ironically, it is socially acceptable for women to display fierce aggression in their crusades against male vice, which serve as an outlet for female anger without threatening male power. The temperance movement, which made alcohol the symbol of male violence, did not improve the position of women; substituting porn for demon rum won't work either. One reason it won't is that it bolsters the good girl—bad girl split. Overtly or by implication it isolates women who like porn or "pornographic" sex or who work in the sex industry. WAP has refused to take a position on prostitution, yet its activities—particularly its support for cleaning up Times Square—will affect prostitutes' lives. Prostitution raises its own set of complicated questions. But it is clearly not in women's interest to pit "good" feminists against "bad" whores (or topless dancers, or models for skin magazines).

So far, the issue that has dominated public debate on the anti-porn campaign is its potential threat to free speech. Here too the movement's arguments have been full of contradictions. Susan Brownmiller and other WAP organizers claim not to advocate censorship and dismiss the civil liberties issue as a red herring dragged in by men who don't want to face the fact that pornography oppresses women. Yet at the same time, WAP endorses the Supreme Court's contention that obscenity is not protected speech, a doctrine I—and most civil libertarians—regard as a clear infringement of First Amendment rights. Brownmiller insists that the First Amendment was designed to protect political dissent, not expressions of woman-hating violence. But to make such a distinction is to defeat the amendment's purpose, since it implicitly cedes to the government the right to define "political." (Has there ever been a government willing to admit that its opponents are anything more than anti-social troublemakers?) Anyway, it makes no sense to oppose pornography on the grounds that it's sexist propaganda, then turn around and argue that it's not political. Nor will libertarians be reassured by WAP's statement that "We want to change the definition of obscenity so that it focuses on violence, not sex." Whatever their focus, obscenity laws deny the right of free expression to those who transgress official standards of propriety—and personally, I don't find WAP's standards significantly less oppressive than Warren Burger's. Not that it matters, since WAP's fantasies about influencing the definition of obscenity are appallingly naive. The basic purpose of obscenity laws is and always has been to reinforce cultural taboos on sexuality and suppress feminism, homosexuality, and other forms of sexual dissidence. No pornographer has ever been punished for being a woman-hater, but not too long ago information about female sexuality, contraception, and abortion was assumed to be obscene. In a male supremacist society the only obscenity law that will not be used against women is no law at all.

As an alternative to an outright ban on pornography, Brownmiller and others have advocated restricting its display. There is a plausible case to be made for the idea that anti-woman images displayed so prominently that they are impossible to avoid are coercive, a form of active harassment that oversteps the bounds of free speech. But aside from the evasion involved in simply equating pornography with misogyny or sexual sadism, there are no legal or logical grounds for treating sexist material any differently from (for example) racist or anti-Semitic propaganda; an equitable law would have to prohibit any kind of public defamation. And the very thought of such a sweeping law has to make anyone with an imagination nervous. Could Catholics claim they were being harassed by nasty depictions of the pope? Could Russian refugees argue

that the display of Communist literature was a form of psychological torture? Would pro-abortion material be taken off the shelves on the grounds that it defamed the unborn? I'd rather not find out.

At the moment the First Amendment issue remains hypothetical; the movement has concentrated on raising the issue of pornography through demonstrations and other public actions. This is certainly a legitimate strategy. Still, I find myself more and more disturbed by the tenor of antipornography actions and the sort of consciousness they promote; increasingly their focus has shifted from rational feminist criticism of specific targets to generalized, demagogic moral outrage. Picketing an anti-woman movie, defacing an exploitative billboard, or boycotting a record company to protest its misogynist album covers conveys one kind of message, mass marches Against Pornography quite another. Similarly, there is a difference between telling the neighborhood news dealer why it pisses us off to have *Penthouse* shoved in our faces and choosing as a prime target every right-thinking politician's symbol of big-city sin, Times Square.

In contrast to the abortion rights movement, which is struggling against a tidal wave of energy from the other direction, the anti-porn campaign is respectable. It gets approving press and cooperation from the New York City government, which has its own stake (promoting tourism, making the Clinton area safe for gentrification) in cleaning up Times Square. It has begun to attract women whose perspective on other matters is in no way feminist ("I'm anti-abortion," a participant in WAP's march on Times Square told a reporter, "but this is something I can get into"). Despite the insistence of WAP organizers that they support sexual freedom, their line appeals to the anti-sexual emotions that feed the backlash. Whether they know it or not, they are doing the good cops' dirty work.

Question for Discussion

1 Is Willis right to suggest that feminists should view the distinction between "erotica" and "pornography" as being dangerously close to the traditional dichotomy of "good girls" and "bad girls"?

2 Willis states that "there are no legal or logical grounds for treating sexist material any differently from (for example) racist or anti-Semitic propaganda," and then goes on to express concern about the extremes to which any law aimed at prohibiting all defamation might be taken. What light, if any, do her concerns here shed on the hate propaganda debate?

Censorship and the Internet

Selections from "The Economist"

A new medium of expression can give rise to new aspects of the issues surrounding freedom of expression. One such new medium is made up of computer on-line networks such as the Internet. The "cyberspace" created by such networks combines elements of what have traditionally been private communication devices such as telephones with the capacity to reach mass audiences typical of media such as radio and television. A number of concerns have arisen about how people, and in particular children, can be given access to the advantageous aspects of cyberspace without being exposed to what are deemed undesirable aspects. The following commentaries explore a number of aspects of this issue.

* * *

Only Disconnect

Can Pornography in Cyberspace Be Regulated?

Censorship is an ugly word. But even liberal societies accept the need for governments to uphold some standards of public decency and, in particular, to shield children from exposure to the worst obscenities. Almost everywhere, governments restrict what can be pumped out on radio, film and television, or down the telephone line, or in books and periodicals. Should cyberspace be any different?

There is no obvious reason to exempt the Internet and other computer networks from restrictions that society chooses to clamp on other forms of communication. But neither is there reason to treat cyberspace less liberally than other media—by means, for instance, [of one proposed bill which would] threaten people who send "indecent" words or pictures via

computers with a fine of $100,000 and up to two years in prison. This is clumsy and heavy-handed. Such a law could kill the chances of the Internet developing into a superb vehicle for free speech and open communications....

The alternative proposed by many supporters of the Internet is self-control. They put their faith in software programs that block access to pornographic "sites" on the Internet, or in senders voluntarily labelling Internet material that is not appropriate for children. Some commercial services, such as America Online, already allow parents to make some "adult" areas off-limits to children. These private (as opposed to official) remedies are welcome, though it remains to be seen how well they will work. The trouble is that all of them place the technical burden of screening cyberspace's offerings on users (lists of "indecent" sites would require constant updating), and they take no account of regional differences in the definition of obscenity (stuff that is deemed obscene in America might be considered tame in Denmark, risqué in Britain and outrageous in Saudi Arabia).

The Difference Between Cannot and Should Not

Why then not regulate the Net like other media? Nerds, who revere the anarchic character of the Net, think any interference whatever is wrong. More telling, they claim (convenient, this) that the Internet cannot be policed even if it should be.

Certainly, the Net is more difficult to regulate than traditional media. It is unfettered by national boundaries. More important, once connected to it, all you need to become a large-scale supplier of pornography is a personal computer. Governments can control the output of TV stations by withholding licences; they can raid presses or close cinemas. Policing the millions of computer-owners who might want to post something nasty in cyberspace does indeed seem impossible.

Nonetheless, the view that nothing can be done is probably wrong—and, for the Internet's own sake, it had better be. If current proposals are any guide, rules of an extremely illiberal sort are a likelier outcome in many countries than the present free-for-all, if that remains the only choice. So here is a better idea. It concentrates on the role of Internet "access providers", the firms that make their living by hooking local subscribers on to the Net. Some current proposals aim to make these providers liable for infringements they cannot prevent: even if it were desirable (which it isn't), providers could not monitor millions of files each day, screening out everything that might be deemed objectionable. But there is another approach.

Make it a regulator's job, guided by users' complaints, to surf the Net looking out for material that would be prohibited if supplied in traditional ways. When such material is discovered, access providers could be alerted, and required to deny users entry to the sites concerned. Safeguards would be needed: the regulator's actions would have to be overseen by a court, with opportunities for legal challenge. Other protections could be built in.

The limits of any such scheme are clear. First, regulators could control only those providers that fall within their national jurisdiction. At the greater expense of an international (as opposed to local) telephone call, a porn-seeker could find an unregulated provider based abroad. A determined censor would then need to block access to those foreign providers—a large and worrying extension of his powers. As the cost of telecommunications continues to fall, this loophole will grow, and the dilemma for those wishing to balance desirable regulation against broader freedoms will be more painful.

The scheme is flawed in other respects too. Some parts of public cyberspace (notably live chat areas and broadcast e-mail) may be impossible to regulate even in this limited way. And no matter how great its appetite for obscenity, no regulator could hope to find all, or even most, offending sites. However, to judge the idea by these standards would be silly. Existing regimes of media regulation are themselves extremely imperfect. When they make sense, it is certainly not because they prevent all contact with prohibited material. It is because they make obscenity more difficult to find, especially by accident; and because this greater difficulty (especially where children are concerned) serves a social purpose. With a little ingenuity, a similar result can be achieved in cyberspace.

★ ★ ★

Censorship in Cyberspace

A Bad Idea, Even if Pornographers Love the Internet

If you were to listen only to its enthusiasts, you might think that the Internet and the associated world of on-line computer networks are at the very least the best thing since, say, the Renaissance; they deliver a cornucopia of information and intellectual excitement to the desktop or living room of anyone with a computer and modem. If you listened only to its detractors, on the other hand, you might feel that the on-line world has become merely a transmitter of smut and fantasy, making use of electronic ubiquity to bypass laws against pornography and to flout public decency.

Both views are flawed. Sadly for the Renaissance bunch, *Penthouse* magazine claims the record for the Internet's most visited "site". But the detractors err more. A bill [proposed in] America's Senate would make it a crime to send "indecent" material on-line. A similar bill [proposed] in the New Zealand parliament would do the same with material sent for profit. And Singapore, whose illiberal government controls the island's only Internet gateway, has warned that it will police cyberspace and prosecute those posting subversive material.

The issues in these cases are complex, and not to be confused with a simple choice between free speech and censorship. Almost all societies choose to impose some limits—on libel, say, or inciting racial hatred—to what can be said in public. The issue is whether a network such as the Internet requires special, sterner laws to enforce such limits. Even now, "cyberspace" is not above the law, and nor should it be: if you threaten President Clinton by electronic mail, it is just as criminal as doing so by post. A fraudulent sale is no less of an offence if it is conducted on-line. Nor are theft, sexual harassment or even trespassing.

However, there are at least two reasons to wonder whether cyberspace can be governed adequately by existing laws. First, as the debate about pornography reveals, the Internet throws up jurisdictional problems. It is seamlessly global; whether a place on it is physically located in Atlanta or Amsterdam matters little to a cybernaut, who can "visit" either with a click of the mouse. What is legal in Amsterdam may not be legal in Atlanta. The prurient citizen who sees the Net as a way to evade the moral rules of a prudish government (or, awkwardly, the dissident seeking to evade censorship by a dictator) could hardly hope for a more convenient way of doing so.

The second difficulty is that existing regulatory models do not fit the anarchic world of cyberspace at all well. Electronic mail—private messages between individuals—may resemble the postal system, but it could just as easily be compared to the telephone. "Newsgroups"— some 14,000 channels of open discussion, ranging from computer arcana to radical politics (with a lot of sex thrown in for good measure)—look more like a broadcast medium. The World Wide Web, the multimedia portion of the Net, where companies and others display information, is perhaps most like a newsagent, with tens of thousands of magazines on display. Finally, there are software and document archives, which might be compared to libraries.

This is why simply banning the "transmission" of indecent material ... is such a bad idea. By treating as identical widely different classes of information and exchange, it encroaches too far on freedom. Private communication between adults is almost always a matter for them alone. In broadcasting, in contrast, there is a risk to the innocent bystander (your 12-year-old daughter, let us say, cruises the Net to find out why dinosaurs died out and stumbles instead across some horrifying sexual perversion). The Internet contains all these forms of communication, plus many in between. Laws that failed to discriminate between them would at best be unworkable, at worst a severe encroachment on liberty.

Different, But Also the Same

Framing laws that are sufficiently discriminating could be a nightmare, and until they are confident of their ability to do so, governments should suppress their instinct to censor. Existing laws, for all their jurisdictional inadequacies, are not powerless. And there is meanwhile a certain amount that legitimate users of the Internet could do to protect the innocent.

The electronic *Penthouse*, for example, lists the countries where its content would be forbidden, and asks visitors from those countries

not to look. *Playboy* "warns" electronic visitors that naked women are ahead. If the online industry is wise, it will head off bad legislation by enlarging on such ideas, for example by making it easier for parents to control what children do on-line. The film and videogame industries already subject themselves to a rating system. Commercial services, such as Prodigy and America Online, define services that children are not supposed to enter without parental approval.

This is hardly a panacea; since most parents need computer-literate offspring to guide them to the Internet, many children will circumvent such prohibitions. But these children can probably get their hands on a dirty magazine, too. In many other ways, cyberspace is a microcosm of the ordinary world, with all the same mingled potential for good or bad. It cannot, and should not, be wished away by over-hasty legislation.

★ ★ ★

Sex on the Internet

When Bavaria Wrinkles Its Nose, Must the Whole World Catch a Cold?

Remember how the Internet was going to corrupt young people by evading laws, parents and policemen to import pornography weightlessly and unstoppably through cyberspace? Well, a funny thing has just happened. On Christmas eve the Internet became a way of importing censorship instead. A prosecutor in Munich told CompuServe, a company that provides its global subscribers with access to the Internet, that about 200 of the Net's sex-related "newsgroups" violated German law, particularly laws designed to protect minors. CompuServe thereupon shut off access to the newsgroups. But not only in Germany. Because the firm had no technical way to tailor Internet content just for German subscribers

(it holds most of its content in computers in Ohio), it was forced to apply the rule everywhere in the world, imposing upon all of its 4m subscribers the standards deemed appropriate for seven-year-old Bavarians.

The reaction from denizens of the Internet was predictably hysterical. Cyberlibertarians warned that this was the first horseman of the coming censorship apocalypse. Surely, they fretted, if a German censor can dictate what CompuServe subscribers around the world can see, the day when Saudi Arabia can do the same is just around the corner. They exaggerate. But the CompuServe fiasco does underline two lessons about the emerging world of cyberspace. The first is that (contrary to much nerdish opinion) this domain can, will and should be regulated, just like other media from magazines to television. The second is that ... regulation ought to be at the point of delivery, not origin—to control, if need be, what people take off the Internet, not what they put on it.

There is no case for putting cyberspace above the law just because it is a new medium. If a country, state, or locality decides for reasons of its own to ban, say, explicit images of sex or restrict them to adults only, the Internet should not be an unpoliceable loophole simply by virtue of its technical complexity. But the decisions of one community should not limit the freedoms of another. If a Swede chooses, as allowed by Swedish law, to put a bit of cyberporn on a Swedish computer connected to the Internet, a Tennessee postal inspector should have no right to prosecute, no matter how offended he may be when he downloads the stuff in Nashville. After all, in the cyberspace metaphor, the inspector "went" to the Swedish computer to get the pictures, instructing the computer to send them along the Internet's open lines to his home. If anyone broke the law, he did, for "importing" banned material.

If the same Tennessee inspector had requested the images through the post, he might have a more valid complaint: at least then the Swede would have had to consciously send the porn to a place where it was banned. But on the Internet, geography gets blurred. In most cases, there is no way in which the Swedish computer can tell where a request comes from.

Gradually, a Solution

There is, however, one part of the Internet that does know where a user is. This is the on-ramp, or "access provider", the company that provides the local modems and other connections through which users drive on to the Internet. Big providers such as CompuServe have banks of modems in thousands of cities and regions around the world, as do hundreds of smaller local firms providing the same service. These firms know what the local law is, and could filter some Internet content as demanded by it. At present few bother.

The actions of the Munich prosecutor suggest that these firms will now have to start bothering, lest one jurisdiction after another takes exception until some international lowest common denominator of censorship is reached, with no words or pictures offensive to any religion, smut sentry, or government allowed on the Internet. That would, at the very least, be bad for business, which is why CompuServe is already working feverishly to come up with the technical means to tailor its offerings to local laws. Corporate self-interest meets local regulation; with a little luck and a lot of effort, cyberspace can, it seems, be controlled sensibly after all.

Questions for Discussion

1 Is any regulation required for cyberspace? If so, should voluntary self-censorship and market forces be given a chance to control it, or should it be done by governments? If by government regulation, who should be held liable for infringements?

2 Does the international nature of cyberspace require changes in the way we understand the relationships between different jurisdictions? In what senses, if any, is the world "getting smaller"? Is this a good thing, or a bad thing?

CHAPTER 8

Multiculturalism, Nationalism, and Aboriginal Rights

It is still fairly common to refer to the relationships between Canada as a whole and the various cultures to which individual Canadians belong in terms of the image of the "Canadian Mosaic." This is contrasted with the image of a "melting pot" in which people merge their identities to become all one new culture. In the "mosaic" model, each group maintains its own identity while at the same time it joins with other groups. The result is "multiculturalism"—a plurality of cultures (or sub-cultures) within the whole.

This may sound like a very appealing ideal, but it is not without problems. For one thing, there may be cases in which conflict arises because different cultural groups want or need things which are not compatible. It is difficult to provide a systematic, non-discriminatory method for adjudicating such issues.

Another problem is that cultures may need positive steps on the part of government in order to preserve their integrity, or sometimes to continue to survive at all.

Even with the goal of a multicultural mosaic, there may well be a dominant culture which tends to submerge others. To what extent is society at large obliged to provide assistance for particular cultures? Is this simply a matter for market forces, in which it is left up to individual members of the culture in question to decide whether to take the steps necessary to preserve it, or to assimilate into the "dominant culture"? Or should the government provide, for example, financial support for cultural institutions? And should the government make allowances in its own dictates for cultural difference, such as allowing Sikhs to wear turbans when doing so deviates from the standard RCMP uniform?

It might make a difference, in answering these questions, which cultural group's fate is at stake. One might think that, from a legal point of view, there is no distinction between people on the basis of culture in Canada today, but that is not entirely accurate. For example, the Separate School Board system across the country ensures the continuation of Catholic and (in Québec) Protestant education, but does not necessarily make similar provisions for other faiths. Furthermore, there are enshrined protections for some linguistic groups and not others. Part of the legacy of the Trudeau government of the late 1960s and 1970s is official bilingualism, according to which individuals are to be guaranteed access to services (at least from the government) in either French or English anywhere in the country. Similarly, various government sources of money are available for both official languages in places where they constitute a minority language.

Why are these groups protected rather than others? Is it simply a matter of numbers? Would that mean, for example, that in parts of the country where languages other than the two "official" languages (say, Ukrainian or Chinese) are very common, the government should make sure it accommodates these groups? Is it rather a matter of history—the idea that Canada was "founded" by these groups, which therefore have a special entitlement to protection? In that case, one might well ask what the status should be of various First Nations languages, such as Ojibway and Cree.

These issues have been prominent in Canadian political life for a long time, and at times seem to threaten to tear the country apart. Moreover, they are not unique to Canada—there are many countries in the world which have struggled to find the right balance between cultural diversity and national homogeneity. Sometimes—as in Yugoslavia and Ireland—these struggles have taken the form of bloody warfare, and even attempts to draw boundaries and establish separate nations have often proven messy and complicated.

This chapter will explore some aspects of this issue, concentrating on the Canadian experience. In this country, the most obvious

cultural distinction historically has been that between the French and the English. Even within that distinction, there has been the issue of who should be allowed to speak for the French—the combination of Francophone Canadians, including those living in predominantly English-speaking parts of the country, or the province of Québec, in which French is the majority language. The French-English distinction is not the only one within this country, however, and others have been getting more attention in recent years. Issues about turban-wearing RCMP officers or reparations for rights violations of Japanese Canadians during the war also have received considerable attention.

Another complex and important set of issues has to do with the cultural integrity of the various groups of aboriginal peoples in Canada. Historically, these groups stand in a very different relation to the dominant culture than do any of the cultures which have immigrated to this land. Indeed, part of the complexity of the issues connected with aboriginal rights today has to do with questions of what happens when different cultures, complete with different understandings of things such as the relationship between people and the land they live on, come into contact with each other. Is the dominant culture entitled to impose its understandings and its interpretations of laws and principles on the other culture?

Aboriginal people have also always been treated differently by Canadian law. Treaties (where they exist) were often interpreted to suit the purposes of the government and non-aboriginal settlers and developers rather than the aboriginal peoples, or were blatantly violated. Also, the government has taken direct control of many aspects of the lives of aboriginal people through the Indian Act. Many would argue that these facts have contributed greatly to the social problems facing aboriginal people today. What steps, if any, is the government obliged to take to reverse the effects of these policies? To what extent should members of a present generation feel obliged to compensate for past injustices? Are aboriginal groups entitled to "self-determination" (or "self-government"), and if so, what does that mean within a broader Canadian context?

These are some of the most important issues connected with the relationships between individuals, the cultures they belong to, and society as a whole. Some of these issues pose serious questions for political theory in general. Can a society such as Canada's, with its traditional emphasis on tolerance and the value of individual choice, find an appropriate place for the value of cultural membership and one's

identification as a member of a group? Is there room for the existence of officially recognized "distinct societies" within one nation? Can justice be satisfied purely in terms of individual rights, or should society take notice of such things as "collective rights"? Can protection of cultural groups be consistent with the ideal of a "colour-blind" Constitution which advocates equality for all? To what extent can cultural groups violate equality rights in order to preserve their identity (for example, by drawing distinctions between women and men within the cultural group)? Is the very concept of an individual right the product of a specific culture, which should not be applied wholesale to other cultures?

All of these questions are touched upon in the readings which follow.

Multiculturalism and Objectivity

Susan Haack

In this article, Haack outlines a number of different meanings of the term "multiculturalism," and argues that we should be in favour of multiculturalism on some interpretations of the term, but opposed to it on other interpretations. In particular, she offers a critical assessment of the claim that the very notions of knowledge, truth, fact, and evidence are culturally specific.

★ ★ ★

Truth is rarely pure and never simple. Modern life would be intolerable if it were either.

> Algernon, in Oscar Wilde's
> *The Importance of Being Earnest*

Multiculturalism seems such an engaging idea and yet, somehow, threatening. Why do I, like many people, feel so ambivalent about it? The explanation is not, after all, so hard to find: the term "multiculturalism" is multiply ambiguous. Sometimes it is used to refer to the

kinds of societies where people from different cultural backgrounds live together, to characteristic problems that arise in such circumstances, and, sometimes, to the idea that the dominant culture should not impose unnecessarily on the sensibilities of minority culture(s)—*social multiculturalism*. Sometimes "multiculturalism" is used to refer to the idea that it is desirable for students to know about other cultures than their own (sometimes, that it is especially desirable in multicultural societies in the sense just explained, for students to know something about the cultures of those with whom they live)—*pluralistic educational multiculturalism*. Sometimes, again, "multiculturalism" is used to refer to the idea that students (especially, that students from minority groups in multicultural societies) should be educated in *their own* culture—*particularistic educational multiculturalism*. And sometimes "multiculturalism" is used to refer to the idea that the dominant culture is not, or should not be, "privileged" (in the contemporary American context, this is often expressed as the claim that "Western culture" should not be privileged)—*philosophical multiculturalism*.

Already, since pluralistic and particularistic educational multiculturalism are in tension— if the latter is interpreted as suggesting that students should be educated *exclusively* in their own culture, they are downright incompatible—we have not only different, but potentially conflicting, uses. But it is impossible to avoid making matters even more complicated by identifying another dimension of ambiguity, this time in the term "culture." Some of the ambiguities are familiar: think of Snow's distinction of the "two cultures," the scientific and the literary; think of the difference between "British culture" construed as referring to Shakespeare, Handel, Eliot, and so on, or as referring to soccer, fish and chips, warm beer, perennial miners' strikes, and so forth. Recall that, despite our membership in the Common Market, we British still have some difficulty thinking of ourselves, as opposed to those foreigners across the Channel, as "Europeans," but would agree with the French in finding the idea that American culture is "European" somewhat comical; and that "Europe" blurs together a great variety of racial types, languages, ways of life—as "Africa" does, or "Asia."

Beyond these familiar kinds of fuzziness, however, is a recent, crucial shift of meaning,

a shift just barely hinted at in my characterization of philosophical multiculturalism. Initially, with philosophical multiculturalism, the contrast seems to be between the majority culture in a multicultural society and minority culture(s)—as it might be, between the majority Hindu culture of India, say, and Muslim and Christian minorities; or, in this country, between the *soi-disant* "European" culture of the majority (actually itself pretty varied), and many and varied not-even-distantly-European minority cultures. But of late "Western culture" has come to refer to anything associated with what is taken to be the dominant class of contemporary American society, and the theme is that *this* "culture" should not be privileged over the "cultures" of what are taken to be oppressed, marginalized, disadvantaged classes—classes identified in terms of color, sex, and sexual orientation. The scare quotes here are intended to signal that the term "culture" has been extended far beyond anything its ordinary elasticity permits; for, so far from respecting the usual contrast of culture with nature, we are now to take "black" or "female" as designating cultures.

Diane Ravitch, distinguishing pluralistic and particularistic conceptions of multiculturalism, urges the value of the former and the dangers of the latter. Daniel Bonevac, distinguishing liberal and illiberal multiculturalism, complains of a "bait and switch" operation replacing the liberal by the illiberal. Richard Bernstein writes of a *dérapage*, or slide, from a benign to an alarming kind of multiculturalism. Mary Lefkowitz distinguishes multiculturalism, of which she approves, from uniculturalism and anticulturalism, of which she does not. Lefkowitz's tripartite distinction reflects the fact that we need to accommodate both a shift from pluralism to particularism, and a shift from an ordinary, vague, ambiguous, but maybe just-barely-serviceable notion of differing and overlapping cultures, to the more-than-debatable notion of cultures of the dominant and the oppressed, "cultures" identified by race, sex, etc.—from multiculturalism to counter-culturalism, as I shall say. The first shift was already accommodated in my original fourfold distinction; accommodating the second shift gives us eight distinguishable positions; for example, besides philosophical multiculturalism, *philosophical counter-culturalism*. In principle, that is: in practice it is often far from clear which of these is being proposed. It is part of the particularists' strategy to blur the distinction between their position and the pluralists', and it is part of the counter-culturalists' strategy to blur the differences between their use of "Western culture" and more ordinary uses. Bernstein's word is certainly a good one for this conceptually slippery situation.

I mention social multiculturalism only to put it aside. It raises hard questions, even in the practically and morally more straightforward cases where social multiculturalism is not the result of conquest or a territorial decision imposed from outside, but of immigration: that Muslim girls in British schools should not be obliged to wear gym uniforms which are, by their standards, immodest, is easy enough, but it is very far from obvious that the same tolerance should extend to, say, recognition of polygamous marriages, or to banning *The Satanic Verses*. But such social and political questions fall outside the scope of this essay.

The claim of pluralistic educational multiculturalism is true. It *is* desirable for people to know about other cultures than their own. (As I write this sentence, though, newly struck by that deceptively straightforward-sounding phrase, "their own," I am reminded of Dewey's observation that "the typical American is himself ... international and interracial in his makeup.") Pluralistic educational multiculturalism is desirable, but it is not easily achieved—a more-than-superficial knowledge of another culture is likely to require some fluency in another language; and it is not

easily combined with ensuring that students acquire the other knowledge and skills they will need. Still, awareness that others do things differently and take different beliefs for granted helps one to discriminate the conventional from the non-conventional in one's own practice and thinking, to avoid the "rightly are they called 'pigs'" syndrome. And yes, knowledge of the customs of minority communities within a multicultural society can, surely, contribute to the accomplishment of a mutually tolerable, or, with good luck and good will, a mutually enriching, *modus vivendi*.

The claim of particularistic educational multiculturalism is false, and for some of the same reasons that pluralistic educational multiculturalism is true (and, for some of the same reasons that pluralistic educational multiculturalism is likely to contribute to mutual tolerance, particularistic educational multiculturalism runs the risk of contributing to mutual *intolerance* and resentment.) Sometimes particularistic educational multiculturalism is defended by appeal to the argument that it will raise students' self-esteem. But this is wrong-headed not only in its presupposition that raising students' self-esteem is a proximal goal of education but, more fundamentally, in its failure to acknowledge that a sense of self-worth is likely to be better founded on mastery of some difficult discipline than on ethnic boosterism, and that students can be inspired to achievement by the example of people of very different backgrounds from their own— as, for example, W.E.B. Dubois testifies that he was by his education in the classics of European literature.

Sometimes, again, particularistic educational multiculturalism is defended by appeal to the idea that students are unfairly disadvantaged unless they are educated in "their" cultural traditions. At the purely pragmatic level, this calls for a candid acknowledgment that children of immigrant parents are, on the contrary, likely to find themselves disadvantaged if their education does not make them familiar with the customs and practices of their new country. It also calls for a plain statement that it is surely untrue that only persons of Chinese descent can really master Confucius, or only persons of Greek descent, Homer, or only persons of French descent, Balzac, and so forth. I don't understand or appreciate Peirce any the less, for instance, because, unlike myself, he was American; nor Bacon any the more because, like myself, he was English.

Turning, now, to philosophical multiculturalism, I note that part of what is at stake may be the thought that when, as pluralistic educational multiculturalism reasonably urges, students are taught something of cultures other than their own, it should be *with respect*. It can be granted without further ado that all persons should be treated with respect; and that it is undesirable to encourage an attitude of suspicion or disrespect for what is unfamiliar merely because it is unfamiliar. But it doesn't follow, and neither is it true, that all opinions, practices, institutions, traditions, are equally deserving of respect. One of the benefits of knowing that others take for granted quite different opinions and practices than oneself is that it enables one to understand more of what is conventional and what is not in one's own practice and belief a benefit that would be sacrificed by an uncritical relativism that found *all* comparisons to be odious.

Let me try to find an example that will not touch on any local sensibilities. I find much to admire in the life of the Kalahari bushmen: their closeness to the natural world, the vigor of their cave paintings, their delight in music and dancing, their taking for granted, in the extraordinary harshness of their conditions of life, that "if one eats, all eat." And thinking about the remarkable ingenuity of the triple-jointed poisoned arrows with which they hunt their game, I am set to wondering in a new way about what the social or intellectual conditions were that led to the rise of modern science in seventeenth-century Europe. But it doesn't follow, and neither is it true, that Bushman myths about the origin of the world or the causes of the seasons, and so forth, are on a par with the best scientific theorizing.

Rather than consider all four forms of counter-culturalism, allow me to turn my attention, now, directly to philosophical counter-culturalism. Further disambiguation is still needed, since the "privilege" that is being denied may be ethical, aesthetic, epistemological, or all three. Of these, I shall consider only the third, henceforth dubbed *epistemological counter-culturalism*. "Western culture," the thought is, has been largely the work of white, heterosexual men, and consequently gives an undeserved authority to *their* ways of knowing or seeing things, and serves *their* interests. The first phrase hints that there are black or female or homosexual "ways of knowing," an idea which seems to me not only false, but of the essence of racism or sexism; the second marks the connection with radical philosophies which deny the possibility of separating knowledge and power, inquiry and advocacy.

The point of epistemological counter-culturalism is to "contest" the [allegedly] undeserved [alleged] epistemic "privilege" of white males. Thus, Wahneema Lubiano tells us that "strong multiculturalism" is "not about the liberal tolerance of difference, but about the contestation of differences"; Mike Cole urges that multiculturalism "must push against the forces of oppression, be they centered on race, class, gender or all three"; and Naomi Scheman suggests that "a useful umbrella under which to shelter diverse projects [of "feminist epistemology"] would be that of 'anti-masculinism' by analogy with anti-racism," a link which, she continues, "points to the necessity for any feminist epistemology to be simultaneously committed to challenging the other sorts of bias that may be found within the dominant practices of acquiring, justifying, and accounting for knowledge."

Epistemological counter-culturalism rests on misconceptions about knowledge, society, power, and objectivity. These are, most importantly: first, that epistemic standards, standards of good evidence, justified belief, *bona fide* knowledge, are culture- or community-bound; and, second, that inquiry is inevitably disguisedly political. The first of these is dispiritingly skeptical in tendency, and the second is outright scary: if all inquiry really were political, there would be no difference between knowledge and propaganda, between inquiry and rhetorical bullying. Unfortunately, however, the fact that a thesis is dispiriting or scary is not in itself a reason for supposing it false; so it is necessary to articulate why these misconceptions *are* misconceptions.

Let me begin by distinguishing two projects in which epistemology may engage: articulating criteria of what constitutes justification of or good evidence for a belief, and giving guidelines for the conduct of inquiry. (Though these are frequently run together in contemporary epistemology, they are, though of course related, as different as criteria for judging roses are from instructions for growing them.)

One source of the first epistemological counter-culturalist thesis, that epistemic standards are culture- or community-bound, may have been the perception that neither of the traditionally rival theories of epistemic justification—foundationalism and coherentism—is acceptable, and the conviction that the only alternative is to resort to some kind of contextualism, according to which epistemic justification is context- or community-bound. Another source has been Kuhn's observation that proponents of rival scientific paradigms disagree even about what constitutes evidence, which has suggested the parallel conclusion, within the philosophy of science, that epistemic standards are paradigm-bound.

I agree that neither foundationalism nor coherentism will do. Foundationalism founders on its failure to identify a class of basic beliefs which could plausibly be claimed both to be justified exclusively by experience, and to be sufficient to support all other justified beliefs; coherentism founders on its failure, consistently with its claim that justification is a relation exclusively among beliefs, to acknowledge any role to experience in empirical justification. But contextualism is not the only, or the most plausible, alternative. A theory intermediate between foundationalism and coherentism, which allows the relevance of experience to empirical justification without requiring any beliefs to be justified by experience alone, and which allows pervasive mutual support among beliefs without requiring that empirical justification be a matter exclusively of relations among beliefs, can avoid the difficulties of both foundationalism and coherentism. In this intermediate theory (I call it, more accurately than euphoniously, "foundherentist"), the model of evidential support is—not, as much recent epistemology has supposed, a mathematical proof—but a crossword puzzle. The clues are the analogue of experiential evidence, and already-completed intersecting entries the analogue of reasons, of the subject's background beliefs.

Rather than suggesting the context- or paradigm-dependence of standards of evidence, this model suggests how deep-seated disagreement in background beliefs will give rise to disagreements about what evidence counts as relevant. Suppose you and I are working on the same crossword puzzle. You think, given your solution to 7 across, that the fact that a solution to 2 down ends in an "E" is evidence in its favor; I, given my solution to 7 across, that the fact that it ends in an "S" is evidence in its favor. There is no real relativity of standards; we are both trying to fit the entry to its clue and to other relevant entries. Compare the case where you and I are both on an appointments committee; you think this candidate should be ruled out on the grounds that his handwriting indicates he is not to be trusted; I think graphology is bunk and scoff at your "evidence." Once again, there is no real relativity of standards, only disagreement in background beliefs.

A distinction is called for here which parallels a hitherto-unremarked ambiguity in the counter-culturalists' talk of "privilege." Epistemological counter-culturalism may be straightforwardly relativist, maintaining that epistemic standards are not only community-bound, but also conventional, so that there is no sense to the question, whether these or those are better; or tribalist, maintaining that epistemic standards are community-bound, but that "ours" are best. Epistemological counter-culturalists of the former, relativist, stripe are committed to the claim that *no* standards, those of "Western culture" included, are privileged; those of the latter, tribalist, stripe are committed to the claim that *their*, non-"Western," standards are privileged.

Implicit in what has been said thus far, but needing to be made explicit, is the thought that an adequate epistemology will require a logical dimension (in its account of relations of evidential support); a personal dimension (in its recognition that you and I may believe the same thing, and yet I be justified and you unjustified, and that empirical justification depends ultimately on the subject's experience); and a dimension focused on human nature (in its recognition that our notion of the evidence of the senses presupposes that, for all normal human beings, the senses are a source of information about the world).

One source of the second epistemological counter-culturalist thesis, that knowledge is inherently political, has been the perception that inquiry is in some epistemologically important sense social. And in a sense, indeed, it is. Each of us, as a knowing subject, is pervasively dependent on others; and scientific in-

quiry has been as successful as it has in part because of its social character, of the cooperative and competitive engagement of many persons, both within and across generations. So, yes, let me add that an adequate epistemology will also require a social dimension (but, also, that none of "black" or "female" or "homosexual" can plausibly be supposed to identify an epistemic community).

But these observations about the epistemic interdependence of knowing subjects and the social character of scientific inquiry, rather than suggesting the conclusion that knowledge is inherently political, suggest, on the contrary, that one of the (of course, fallible and imperfect) mechanisms by means of which bias gets detected and corrected—in scientific theorizing, and, though less systematically, in inquiry generally—is by means of competition between supporters of rival theories or approaches.

Another source of the idea that knowledge is inherently political has been the perception that racist, sexist, etc., ideas have sometimes come to be accepted, not because they were well-supported by evidence, but because of unjustifiable prejudices and preconceptions. (Hence the astonishing outbreak of sneer quotes—"knowledge," "fact," "evidence," "rationality," and so forth—in recent radical epistemology.) Racist or sexist ideas have, indeed, sometimes passed for known fact or established theory; and sometimes, no doubt, at least part of the explanation of how this came about is that those ideas' being accepted served the interests of the more powerful race or sex. But the inference from the true premise that what has passed for known fact or objective evidence is no such thing, to the conclusion that the notions of knowledge, fact, evidence, etc., are ideological humbug, is manifestly invalid. Indeed, this invalid inference—I call it *the "passes for" fallacy*—is not only fallacious, but also pragmatically self-defeating. For if, as the conclusion has it, the notions of knowledge, fact, relevant evidence, and so forth were really no more than ideological humbug, then the premise, that racist or sexist theories have sometimes been accepted on inadequate evidence, would itself be undermined.

In short, one can perfectly well acknowledge the shortcomings of foundationalism and coherentism, human inquirers' pervasive epistemic dependence on one another, the social character of scientific inquiry, the complexity and fallibility of all human cognitive activity, the corruption of some claims to truth, without being obliged to grant either that epistemic standards are community- or culture-relative, or that inquiry is invariably political.

One way to put it, using the vocabulary of "objectivity" and its several contrasts, would be this: a truth-claim is either true or else false, true or false objectively, that is, independently of whether you or I or anybody believes it. But there is of course no guarantee that all truth-claims are *true*. Standards of evidence are objective, that is, a person is more or less justified in believing something, and a scientific theory is more or less warranted, depending on how good his, or the, evidence is—and "how good," here, does *not* mean "how good by the standards of community C." But of course inquirers are not always perfectly objective, that is, they do not always seek out all the evidence they can, nor assess the worth of their evidence fairly.

"In order to reason well ..., it is absolutely necessary to possess ... such virtues as intellectual honesty and ... a real love of truth." C.S. Peirce distinguished genuine inquiry from "sham reasoning," that is, pseudo-inquiry aimed not at finding the truth but at making a case for some conclusion fixed in advance. And if sham reasoning becomes commonplace, he predicted, people come "to look on reasoning as mainly decorative," and "man loses his conceptions of truth and of reasoning." And that, it seems to me, is the philo-sophical *débâcle* taking place before our eyes; genuine inquiry is so complex and difficult, and advocacy "research" has become so commonplace, that our grip on the concepts of truth and reason is being loosened—as the ubiquitous "passes for" fallacy, and all those dismissive sneer quotes, suggest.

This is to be much regretted; and not least because honest, thorough inquiry—reasoned pursuit of the truth—is the best defense against racist and sexist stereotypes. To the anticipated objection that reasoned pursuit of the truth is a "Western" ideal, I shall say only that, "Western" or not, it is an ideal of nearly incalculable value to humanity.

The appropriate philosophical response (after, of course, patiently pointing out that one could not discover by honest inquiry that there is no such thing as honest inquiry, that it could not be really-and-truly true that "truth" is no more than ideological humbug, etc.), is to try to articulate an epistemology which can recognize the subtleties of the structure of evidence and the complexity, revisability, and fallibility of inquiry. That, at any rate, is what I have tried to do.

Questions for Discussion

1 Are there objective standards of such things as knowledge and evidence, or is the common view that there are such standards merely an instance of a privileged group imposing its standards on others?

2 Does Haack's crossword puzzle analogy succeed at providing a model of how there can be great differences in beliefs based on individuals' backgrounds, yet still be objective right answers?

3 Is the concept of a "culture" too fuzzy to make multiculturalism a coherent notion?

4 Is Haack right that the claim of pluralistic educational multiculturalism is true, but that of particularistic educational multiculturalism is false? Why or why not?

The Limits of Diversity

Excerpt from "Selling Illusions: The Cult of Multiculturalism in Canada"

Neil Bissoondath

*Neil Bissoondath, the child of East Indian parents, is a writer who was raised in Trinidad, and then moved to Canada. His book, **Selling Illusions: The Cult of Multiculturalism in Canada**, offers a number of critiques of the policy of multiculturalism. In this selection, he argues that Canada must demand respect for its own cultural ideals, and place limits on the lengths to which it goes in accommodating diversity.*

★ ★ ★

In the West Indies, long and boisterous parties, on the whole, inconvenience no one. They are held at houses, both inside and outside. Neighbours tend to be invited; children sleep where they fall. Food and drink are in plentiful supply, music is loud and lively, meant not as background filler but as foreground incentive to dance. There is nothing sedate about the archetypal West Indian party. So central is "a good time" to the West Indian sense of self that someone—not a West Indian—once wryly commented that she had the impression that parties, and not calypso or reggae, were the great West Indian contribution to world culture. Booming music, the yelp and rumble of excited voices, the tramp of dancing feet are accepted as an integral part of the region's cultural life.

Transfer this to, say, Toronto or Vancouver—not to a house surrounded by an extensive yard but to an apartment hemmed in by other apartments. Transfer the music, the dancing, the shouting—everything but the fact that the neighbours, unknown and uncommunicative, are likely to be invited. It takes little imagination to appreciate the tensions that may, and do, arise.

A simple lack of consideration for the rights of others? Yes—but it may be, as some claim, that everything is political. The view has frequently been expressed to me that, in view

of the importance of parties in West Indian culture, and considering the official policy of multicultural preservation in Canada, complaints about noise or demands that stereo volumes be lowered can be justifiably viewed as a form of cultural aggression. Changing the tone of the party, the argument goes, results in a lessening of its Caribbean character, and is therefore a sign of cultural intolerance. Implicit in this view is the idea that everything deemed cultural is sacred—as well as the idea that the surrounding society must fully accommodate itself to displays, no matter how disruptive, of cultural life. In this atmosphere, a party is no longer just a party; it becomes a form of cultural expression and therefore under political and legal protection.

This is an admittedly aggressive interpretation of multicultural philosophy, but it is neither far-fetched nor fully indefensible. Open-ended political policy is, almost without exception, subject to an endless stretching of the envelope: there will always be someone—or some group—attempting to go further than anyone else has gone before.

In 1992, the Ontario College of Physicians and Surgeons expressed concern over a rise, unexplained and unexpected, in the number of requests for infibulation, otherwise known as female circumcision. The procedure, long viewed in western culture as a kind of mutilation, involves "cutting off a young girl's external genital parts, including the clitoris. In some countries, it includes stitching closed the vulva until marriage, leaving a small opening for urination and menstrual flow.... Various health risks have been linked to it, including immediate serious bleeding, recurring infections, pain during intercourse, hemorrhaging during childbirth and infertility.... Charles Kayzze, head of Ottawa's African Resource Centre, believes it is being performed here by members of the community. In some cases, he says, families are sending their children to Africa to have it done."[1]

The result is the reduction of the woman to the status of machine, capable of production but mechanically, with no pleasure in the process. This, however, is an unabashedly "Eurocentric" view of infibulation.

A more culturally sensitive view is presented in an article for the *Globe and Mail*[2] by Christine Hodge, a Canadian working for the United Nations World Food Program in Chad. She tells of a woman named Khadidja Ahmat Rahmasaleh, head of nutritional services in the ministry of social affairs and promotion of the family. Ms. Rahmasaleh, a Muslim, is an intelligent, educated and "forward-thinking" woman dedicated to the traditions of her tribe, her family and her God. But this is not all she is. She has spent five years at university in Italy. She is familiar with the ways of the West, and seeks "to incorporate the ways of two worlds that often seem at logger-heads." Her experiences and studies in Italy convinced her that circumcision "was neither necessary nor right."

And yet, to Ms. Hodge's disappointment, Ms. Rahmasaleh's two daughters, ages seven and nine, decided to undergo the procedure—at the daughters' own request: "Because they were not circumcised, they were not considered to be women. Their friends refused to let them join in games and conversations." Cut off from the life of the community, the girls grew sullen and depressed—and to be cut off

from the community in Chad is to risk more than a social life, it is to risk life itself. It was the community that had raised the funds to send Ms. Rahmasaleh to Italy; the community that would provide sustenance in time of inevitable famine; the community that would tend to the children in the event of their mother's death. To leave the girls uncircumcised and, so, alienated from the community, was to sever a vital lifeline.

For any mother, but particularly for a Chadean mother cognizant of her family's uncertain circumstances, it was an intolerable situation. Ms. Rahmasaleh decided the girls would undergo neither of the two traditional procedures—infibulation, in which the entire external genitalia are cut off and the wound sewn up; or the less radical excision of the clitoris and labia major, which would remove sexual pleasure but diminish health risks. She devised instead a method—a pin-prick to the clitoris—that would satisfy the ceremonial need to draw blood while leaving her children intact—unpleasant, no doubt, but not mutilating.

Despite opposition—her own mother and aunts insisted the girls' clitorises be removed—her method, a blending of the old idea with the new, was employed, as it was again later on for her ten-year-old niece.

Ms. Hodge, although not present, was yet able to witness the procedure and the ensuing celebrations through the miracle of technology: everything had been videotaped. She ends her article still opposed to female circumcision—she does not flinch from the word "barbaric"—but with a greater appreciation of the context that prompts its continuance.

And that, in the end, is the point: context is everything. How far, in the Canadian context, do we go in accommodation? Female circumcision is clearly a vital, traditional rite of passage to womanhood for these Chadean women. Do we, in rejecting it, impose an uncontextualized, "Eurocentric" value on certain ethnic groups? Should we, under certain circumstances (a sterile operating room, trained medical personnel), respect the right of certain women to undergo what we see as mutilation? And what of those cultures in which male offspring are vital? Do we permit the use of the available technology to permit sex-selection? But multiculturalism ends where our notions of human rights and dignity begin—and therein lies the thorny question of limits.

The Multiculturalism Act suggests no limits to the accommodation offered to different cultural practices, so that a few years ago a Muslim group in Toronto demanded, in the name of respect for its culture, the right to opt out of the Canadian judicial system in favour of Islamic law, a body of thought fundamental to the life and cultural outlook of its practising members. In the opinion of their spokesmen, this right should be a given in a truly multicultural society. It is not an argument without philosophical merit (on practical grounds, it's a different matter) and one that evokes questions of the larger context: how far can multiculturalism be taken? Can Canada accommodate citizens whose loyalties do not encompass its long-established legal system? It is a sensitive topic.

On January 18, 1994, talk-show host Jane Hawtin of CFRB Radio in Toronto posed the following question: "Should Canada relax its rules and laws to accommodate the Muslim culture?"[3] The question arose from the Montreal case in which a girl had been sodomized by her stepfather and also from a case in Edmonton in which a judge permitted the marriage of a fourteen-year-old pregnant girl. In both cases the judges "cited Muslim values for their leniency." The question—based, as one man said, on "certain preconceived notions about Islam"—prompted protest from some Toronto Muslims. And yet, it is precisely because those "preconceived notions" exist that the question should be asked, the notions debated and cleared up, limits established.

The same could be said about a proposal from a group of women's organizations that sought to overturn a policy that directed police to always lay charges in wife-assault cases.[4] One of the great victories in the battle against violence against women, the policy had come to be seen as inadequate, or even counterproductive, in helping to protect immigrant women and women from visible minorities. The principal reason given for the proposed change was that, because police and the courts seem to deal more harshly with minority groups, assaulted women who call the authorities face ostracization from their own communities. Moreover, "[w]omen, especially from the black community, just simply don't call the police because they are afraid of the consequences for their partner." The answer, the women's groups suggested, was in establishing "tailor-made charging policies by ethnic or racial group, municipality by municipality."

The proposal is one of divisiveness fraught with complexity and rich with racist possibilities. It does not address the inadequacies of the present approach but simply attempts to sidestep them in unwieldy fashion with a show of essentially meaningless cultural and racial sensitivity.

While the acceptance of female circumcision and sex-selection, and the establishment of a separate legal system for Muslims, are virtual impossibilities—they take the right to "opt out" to unacceptable extremes—the racial segregation of schools apparently is not. This is an idea that writer Cecil Foster has described as "sweeping through the Canadian black community. It calls for black-focused public schools, where the curriculum, teachers and emphasis would be primarily black, or 'Afrocentric,' to use the current buzzword."[5]

The drive to segregation is a deep-seated one, prompted by the alienation of black students from the school system. "The textbooks exclude them," Mr. Foster writes, "and the teachers and principals are usually white and uncaring. The entire attitude of the public education system makes them feel set apart by negative stereotypes that black students, for example, are more fulfilled on the basketball court than in the physics lab."

While this view ignores the role of the family—black American novelist Leon Forrest once pointed out that there is "a problem in Afro-American society these days: if a woman has a niece and a nephew, she'll give the niece a copy of a Toni Morrison book and take the nephew to the Bulls game"[6]—the consequence is a drop-out rate for black students two or three times higher than for the general student population. It is, by any stretch of the imagination, a worrisome trend, and the temptation to establish schools where a black staff would provide positive role models, "living proof in the classrooms, playgrounds and principals' offices that blacks are capable of achieving great things," must be seductive. Mr. Foster quotes the words of Mr. Vernon Farrell, chairman of the African-Heritage Educators Network: "Black-focused schools will cause students to reflect on shared history, social relationships, belief systems, social practices and collective responses to political and economic realities. Above all, students will develop a sense of identity, critical consciousness and belonging." All the things, in other words, that multiculturalism was supposed to provide and has not.

This construction of a safer world, the withdrawal into it, is a sign of despair. It indicates dissatisfactions with the world as it is and a lack of faith that the system can ever acquire legitimacy. The despair is not difficult to understand. It comes from the evisceration that follows years of anger and fatigue—both of which emerge from living constantly with society's stereotypical brushings. A black youth commits a crime and all black youths must suffer the suspicion of the streets: the wary eyes, the tensed bodies, the wide berths. How many people react in similar fashion to white or Asian youths in the aftermath of a crime committed by one of their number? As educator and activist Lennox Farrell wrote in a letter to *The Globe and Mail* following the murder of Georgina Leimonis in a Toronto restaurant, "I must ... mourn for the collective loss of innocence experienced by some young men who, wherever they go, get the stare, the attitude, the comments from total strangers, simply because they look like other young men involved in criminal activities; other young men who are black."[7] The dream of flight, of retreat, is a plea for security, an urge that is understandable but also, by its very nature, self-defeating, even when it is presented as principle, clothed in buzzwords.

Buzzwords are dangerous creatures. They disguise with quasi-intellectual terminology the true nature of the topic they pretend to describe; they lend a respectability, an apparent complexity, to essentially simplistic ideas. An "Afrocentric" or "black-focused" school system, racially segregated, racially staffed, would simply be a return to the past: to the racial separations of the American south; to the separate but (un)equal approaches of apartheid. It might produce higher grades—and even that is debatable[8]—but would it prepare students for the wider world? It might facilitate the acquisition of knowledge, but would it facilitate the socialization necessary to life beyond the comforting confines of its walls?

A separate education system is an illusory answer to the problems faced by black youth in our society. It would solve nothing, and when students graduate they would inevitably feel the falling away of its racial comforts. It would merely provide a context for withdrawal from society, while the problems—racial and otherwise—can be solved only by engagement with it. It is, in the end, as Mr. Foster points out, simply a recipe for self-ghettoization.

Unlike infibulation and sex-selection, a racially segregated school system is a topic of serious and prolonged discussion. It is an idea that, to many, has great merit. It is not to me. Racial segregation has never been a pretty thing; it has betrayed more than it has aided. Moreover, if we give black parents the right to send their children to all-black schools, do we also give the right to white parents to send their children to all-white schools? And does not such an approach spell the death of any ideal of a multi-racial, multi-ethnic society?

One does not surrender to problems; one grapples with them. Problems exist in the public school system; the needs of many of its students are not being met. It is in that arena, then, and not in the artificial creation of a separate one, that the solutions must be found.

Because we have failed to establish the limits of diversity, because we have so blithely accepted the mentality of division, we find ourselves lost in a confusion of values. Multiculturalism has made us fearful of defining acceptable boundaries; it has caused us to confuse the establishment of circumscription with a lack of respect. And so we find ourselves in danger of accepting, in its name, a slide into ethical chaos. We say no to voluntary infibulation, but consider saying yes to voluntary racial segregation.

How selectively, in our confusion, we judge our evils.

Personal disruptiveness, female circumcision, a separate legal system, racial segregation: it may seem that I am here compiling a catalogue of the worst aspects of multiculturalism. And so, I suppose, I am. None of these excesses in itself constitutes an indictment, but taken together they illustrate the psychology of divisiveness without limits. Excesses cannot be denied; they too are part of the fabric and must be reckoned with. Together they pose the question of how far we, or any society, can go in accommodating diversity. It is the excesses, of demand or of action, that push the boundaries; they challenge basic notions in ways uncomfortable but necessary. The difficulty is in gauging the validity of excess—but to gauge one must first have a sense of one's own beliefs, one's own limits.

There is a logic to these excesses. It is a logic indicative of a certain disdain for the legal and ethical values that shape, and are shaped by, Canadian society—and therefore for Canadian society itself. And why should this not be so, given that the picture the country transmits of itself is one that appears to diminish a unified whole in favour of an ever-fraying mosaic? There may be more communities in the "community of communities" than former prime minister Joe Clark suspects, or is prepared to contend with.

If Canada, as an historical, social, legal and cultural concept, does not demand respect for itself and its ideals, why should any respect be expected?

Notes

1 Sherri Davis Barron, "Doctors draw up policy on female circumcision," *Toronto Star*, January 6, 1992.

2 Christine Hodge, "Throwing away the circumcision knife," *The Globe and Mail*, January 15, 1994.

3 *NOW* magazine, Toronto, January 27–February, 1994.

4 Sean Fine, "End sought to mandatory charges in wife-abuse cases," *The Globe and Mail*, January 27, 1994.

5 Cecil Foster, "All black schools: more ghettoes?" *The Globe and Mail*, September 30, 1993.

6 Quoted in "Visible Man," an article on Ralph Ellison, by David Remnick, *The New Yorker*, March 14, 1994, p. 38.

7 *The Globe and Mail*, April 13, 1994.

8 See James Traub, "Can Separate Be Equal?" *Harper's*, June 1994.

Questions for Discussion

1 Should toleration of diversity extend to accepting cultural practices such as female circumcision, which in the mainstream Canadian context is seen as mutilation motivated by a mistaken view of the worth of women? Where, if at all, should we draw the line beyond which practices will not be tolerated, regardless of their worth to particular cultures?

2 Is it ever acceptable to have different legal practices for different cultural groups within a single society?

Excerpt from "Multiculturalism and 'The Politics of Recognition'"

Charles Taylor

Charles Taylor is one of the leading advocates of a political philosophy called "communitarianism." This view challenges liberalism, partly on the grounds that liberals do not pay sufficient attention to the ways in which individuals depend on communities in which they are situated. In this excerpt from the inaugural volume of the University Center for Human Values at Princeton University, Taylor focuses on the importance of recognition and the demands it places on societies committed to equal dignity, but also to "authenticity" in identity. In particular, he considers how we should recognize the worth of different cultures.

★   ★   ★

A number of strands in contemporary politics turn on the need, sometimes the demand, for *recognition*. The need, it can be argued, is one of the driving forces behind nationalist movements in politics. And the demand comes to the fore in a number of ways in today's politics, on behalf of minority or "subaltern" groups, in some forms of feminism and in what is today called the politics of "multiculturalism."

The demand for recognition in these latter cases is given urgency by the supposed links between recognition and identity, where this latter term designates something like a person's understanding of who they are, of their fundamental defining characteristics as a human being. The thesis is that our identity is partly shaped by recognition or its absence, often by the misrecognition of others, and so a person or group of people can suffer real damage, real distortion, if the people or society around them mirror back to them a confining or demeaning or contemptible picture of themselves. Nonrecognition or misrecognition can inflict harm, can be a form of oppression, imprisoning someone in a false, distorted, and reduced mode of being.

Thus some feminists have argued that women in patriarchal societies have been induced to adopt a depreciatory image of themselves. They have internalized a picture of their own inferiority, so that even when some of the objective obstacles to their advancement fall away, they may be incapable of taking advantage of the new opportunities. And beyond this, they are condemned to suffer the pain of low self-esteem. An analogous point has been made in relation to blacks: that white society has for generations projected a demeaning image of them, which some of them have been unable to resist adopting. Their own self-depreciation, on this view, becomes one of the most potent instruments of their own oppression. Their first task ought to be to purge themselves of this imposed and destructive identity. Recently, a similar point has been made in relation to indigenous and colonized people in general. It is held that since 1492 Europeans have projected an image of such people as somehow inferior, "uncivilized," and through the force of conquest have often been able to impose this image on the conquered. The figure of Caliban has been held to epitomize this crushing portrait of contempt of New World aboriginals.

Within these perspectives, misrecognition shows not just a lack of due respect. It can inflict a grievous wound, saddling its victims with a crippling self-hatred. Due recognition is not just a courtesy we owe people. It is a vital human need.

In order to examine some of the issues that have arisen here, I'd like to take a step back, achieve a little distance, and look first at how this discourse of recognition and identity came to seem familiar, or at least readily understandable, to us. For it was not always so, and our ancestors of more than a couple of centuries ago would have stared at us uncomprehendingly if we had used these terms in their current sense. How did we get started on this?

Hegel comes to mind right off, with his famous dialectic of the master and the slave. This is an important stage, but we need to go a little farther back to see how this passage came to have the sense it did. What changed to make this kind of talk have sense for us?

We can distinguish two changes that together have made the modern preoccupation with identity and recognition inevitable. The first is the collapse of social hierarchies, which used to be the basis for honor. I am using *honor* in the ancien régime sense in which it is intrinsically linked to inequalities. For some to have honor in this sense, it is essential that not everyone have it. This is the sense in which Montesquieu uses it in his description

of monarchy. Honor is intrinsically a matter of "préférences."[1] It is also the sense in which we use the term when we speak of honoring someone by giving her some public award, for example, the Order of Canada. Clearly, this award would be without worth if tomorrow we decided to give it to every adult Canadian.

As against this notion of honor, we have the modern notion of dignity, now used in a universalist and egalitarian sense, where we talk of the inherent "dignity of human beings," or of citizen dignity. The underlying premise here is that everyone shares in it.[2] It is obvious that this concept of dignity is the only one compatible with a democratic society, and that it was inevitable that the old concept of honor was superseded. But this has also meant that the forms of equal recognition have been essential to democratic culture. For instance, that everyone be called "Mr.," "Mrs.," or "Miss," rather than some people being called "Lord" or "Lady" and others simply by their surnames—or, even more demeaning, by their first names—has been thought essential in some democratic societies, such as the United States. More recently, for similar reasons, "Mrs." and "Miss" have been collapsed into "Ms." Democracy has ushered in a politics of equal recognition, which has taken various forms over the years, and has now returned in the form of demands for the equal status of cultures and of genders.

But the importance of recognition has been modified and intensified by the new understanding of individual identity that emerges at the end of the eighteenth century. We might speak of an *individualized* identity, one that is particular to me, and that I discover in myself. This notion arises along with an ideal, that of being true to myself and my own particular way of being. Following Lionel Trilling's usage in his brilliant study, I will speak of this as the ideal of "authenticity."[3]

. . .

Ethical Issues

II

[T]he discourse of recognition has become familiar to us, on two levels: First, in the intimate sphere, where we understand the formation of identity and the self as taking place in a continuing dialogue and struggle with significant others. And then in the public sphere, where a politics of equal recognition has come to play a bigger and bigger role. Certain feminist theories have tried to show the links between the two spheres.[14]

I want to concentrate here on the public sphere, and try to work out what a politics of equal recognition has meant and could mean.

In fact, it has come to mean two rather different things, connected, respectively, with the two major changes I have been describing. With the move from honor to dignity has come a politics of universalism, emphasizing the equal dignity of all citizens, and the content of this politics has been the equalization of rights and entitlements. What is to be avoided at all costs is the existence of "first-class" and "second-class" citizens. Naturally, the actual detailed measures justified by this principle have varied greatly, and have often been controversial. For some, equalization has affected only civil rights and voting rights; for others, it has extended into the socioeconomic sphere. People who are systematically handicapped by poverty from making the most of their citizenship rights are deemed on this view to have been relegated to second-class status, necessitating remedial action through equalization. But through all the differences of interpretation, the principle of equal citizenship has come to be universally accepted. Every position, no matter how reactionary, is now defended under the colors of this principle. Its greatest, most recent victory was won by the civil rights movement of the 1960s in the United States. It is worth noting that even the adversaries of extending voting rights to blacks in the southern states found some pretext consistent with universalism, such as "tests" to be administered to would-be voters at the time of registration.

By contrast, the second change, the development of the modern notion of identity, has given rise to a politics of difference. There is, of course, a universalist basis to this as well, making for the overlap and confusion between the two. *Everyone* should be recognized for his or her unique identity. But recognition here means something else. With the politics of equal dignity, what is established is meant to be universally the same, an identical basket of rights and immunities; with the politics of difference, what we are asked to recognize is the unique identity of this individual or group, their distinctness from everyone else. The idea is that it is precisely this distinctness that has been ignored, glossed over, assimilated to a dominant or majority identity. And this assimilation is the cardinal sin against the ideal of authenticity.[15]

Now underlying the demand is a principle of universal equality. The politics of difference is full of denunciations of discrimination and refusals of second-class citizenship. This gives the principle of universal equality a point of entry within the politics of dignity. But once inside, as it were, its demands are hard to assimilate to that politics. For it asks that we give acknowledgment and status to something that is not universally shared. Or, otherwise put, we give due acknowledgment only to what is universally present—everyone has an identity—through recognizing what is peculiar to each. The universal demand powers an acknowledgment of specificity.

The politics of difference grows organically out of the politics of universal dignity through one of those shifts with which we are long familiar, where a new understanding of the human social condition imparts a radically new meaning to an old principle. Just as a view of human beings as conditioned by their socioeconomic plight changed the understanding of second-class citizenship, so that this category came to include, for example, people in inherited poverty traps, so here the understanding of identity as formed in interchange, and as possibly so malformed, introduces a new form of second-class status into our purview. As in the present case, the socioeconomic redefinition justified social programs that were highly controversial. For those who had not gone along with this changed definition of equal status, the various redistributive programs and special opportunities offered to certain populations seemed a form of undue favoritism.

Similar conflicts arise today around the politics of difference. Where the politics of universal dignity fought for forms of nondiscrimination that were quite "blind" to the ways in which citizens differ, the politics of difference often redefines nondiscrimination as requiring that we make these distinctions the basis of differential treatment. So members of aboriginal bands will get certain rights and powers not enjoyed by other Canadians, if the demands for native self-government are finally agreed on, and certain minorities will get the right to exclude others in order to preserve their cultural integrity, and so on.

To proponents of the original politics of dignity, this can seem like a reversal, a betrayal, a simple negation of their cherished principle. Attempts are therefore made to mediate, to show how some of these measures meant to accommodate minorities can after all be justified on the original basis of dignity. These arguments can be successful up to a point. For instance, some of the (apparently) most flagrant departures from "difference-blindness" are reverse discrimination measures, affording people from previously unfavored groups a competitive advantage for jobs or places in universities. This practice has been justified on the grounds that historical discrimination has created a pattern within which the unfavored struggle at a disadvantage. Reverse discrimi-

nation is defended as a temporary measure that will eventually level the playing field and allow the old "blind" rules to come back into force in a way that doesn't disadvantage anyone. This argument seems cogent enough—wherever its factual basis is sound. But it won't justify some of the measures now urged on the grounds of difference, the goal of which is not to bring us back to an eventual "difference-blind" social space but, on the contrary, to maintain and cherish distinctness, not just now but forever. After all, if we're concerned with identity, then what is more legitimate than one's aspiration that it never be lost?[16]

So even though one politics springs from the other, by one of those shifts in the definition of key terms with which we're familiar, the two diverge quite seriously from each other. One basis for the divergence comes out even more clearly when we go beyond what each requires that we acknowledge—certain universal rights in one case, a particular identity on the other—and look at the underlying intuitions of value.

The politics of equal dignity is based on the idea that all humans are equally worthy of respect. It is underpinned by a notion of what in human beings commands respect, however we may try to shy away from this "metaphysical" background. For Kant, whose use of the term *dignity* was one of the earliest influential evocations of this idea, what commanded respect in us was our status as rational agents, capable of directing our lives through principles.[17] Something like this has been the basis for our intuitions of equal dignity ever since, though the detailed definition of it may have changed.

Thus, what is picked out as of worth here is a *universal human potential,* a capacity that all humans share. This potential, rather than anything a person may have made of it, is what ensures that each person deserves respect. Indeed, our sense of the importance of potentiality reaches so far that we extend this protection even to people who through some circumstance that has befallen them are incapable of realizing their potential in the normal way—handicapped people, or those in a coma, for instance.

In the case of the politics of difference, we might also say that a universal potential is at its basis, namely, the potential for forming and defining one's own identity, as an individual, and also as a culture. This potentiality must be respected equally in everyone. But at least in the intercultural context, a stronger demand has recently arisen: that one accord equal respect to actually evolved cultures. Critiques of European or white domination, to the effect that they have not only suppressed but failed to appreciate other cultures, consider these depreciatory judgments not only factually mistaken but somehow morally wrong. When Saul Bellow is famously quoted as saying something like, "When the Zulus produce a Tolstoy we will read him,"[18] this is taken as a quintessential statement of European arrogance, not just because Bellow is allegedly being *de facto* insensitive to the value of Zulu culture, but frequently also because it is seen to reflect a denial in principle of human equality. The possibility that the Zulus, while having the same potential for culture formation as anyone else, might nevertheless have come up with a culture that is less valuable than others is ruled out from the start. Even to entertain this possibility is to deny human equality. Bellow's error here, then, would not be a (possibly insensitive) particular mistake in evaluation, but a denial of a fundamental principle.

To the extent that this stronger reproach is in play, the demand for equal recognition extends beyond an acknowledgment of the equal value of all humans potentially, and comes to include the equal value of what they have made of this potential in fact. This creates a serious problem, as we shall see below.

These two modes of politics, then, both based on the notion of equal respect, come into conflict. For one, the principle of equal respect requires that we treat people in a difference-blind fashion. The fundamental intuition that humans command this respect focuses on what is the same in all. For the other, we have to recognize and even foster particularity. The reproach the first makes to the second is just that it violates the principle of nondiscrimination. The reproach the second makes to the first is that it negates identity by forcing people into a homogeneous mold that is untrue to them. This would be bad enough if the mold were itself neutral—nobody's mold in particular. But the complaint generally goes further. The claim is that the supposedly neutral set of difference-blind principles of the politics of equal dignity is in fact a reflection of one hegemonic culture. As it turns out, then, only the minority or suppressed cultures are being forced to take alien form. Consequently, the supposedly fair and difference-blind society is not only inhuman (because suppressing identities) but also, in a subtle and unconscious way, itself highly discriminatory.[19]

This last attack is the cruelest and most upsetting of all. The liberalism of equal dignity seems to have to assume that there are some universal, difference-blind principles. Even though we may not have defined them yet, the project of defining them remains alive and essential. Different theories may be put forward and contested—and a number have been proposed in our day[20]—but the shared assumption of the different theories is that one such theory is right.

The charge leveled by the most radical forms of the politics of difference is that "blind" liberalisms are themselves the reflection of particular cultures. And the worrying thought is that this bias might not just be a contingent weakness of all hitherto proposed theories, that the very idea of such a liberalism may be a kind of pragmatic contradiction, a particularism masquerading as the universal....

IV

[The form of liberalism which simply looks to an equality of rights accorded to its citizens] has come under attack by radical proponents of the politics of difference as in some way unable to give due acknowledgment to distinctness. Are the critics correct?

The fact is that there are forms of this liberalism of equal rights that in the minds of their own proponents can give only a very restricted acknowledgment of distinct cultural identities. The notion that any of the standard schedules of rights might apply differently in one cultural context than they do in another, that their application might have to take account of different collective goals, is considered quite unacceptable. The issue, then, is whether this restrictive view of equal rights is the only possible interpretation. If it is, then it would seem that the accusation of homogenization is well founded. But perhaps it is not. I think it is not, and perhaps the best way to lay out the issue is to see it in the context of the Canadian case, where this question has played a role in the impending breakup of the country. In fact, two conceptions of rights-liberalism have confronted each other, albeit in confused fashion, throughout the long and inconclusive constitutional debates of recent years.

The issue came to the fore because of the adoption in 1982 of the Canadian Charter of Rights, which aligned our political system in this regard with the American one in having a schedule of rights offering a basis for judicial review of legislation at all levels of government. The question had to arise how to relate this schedule to the claims for distinctness put forward by French Canadians, and particularly Quebeckers, on the one hand, and aboriginal peoples on the other. Here what was at stake was the desire of these peoples for survival, and their consequent demand for certain forms of autonomy in their self-government, as well as the ability to adopt certain kinds of legislation deemed necessary for survival.

For instance, Quebec has passed a number of laws in the field of language. One regulates who can send their children to English-language schools (not francophones or immigrants); another requires that businesses with more than fifty employees be run in French; a third outlaws commercial signage in any language other than French. In other words, restrictions have been placed on Quebeckers by their government, in the name of their collective goal of survival, which in other Canadian communities might easily be disallowed by virtue of the Charter.[29] The fundamental question was: Is this variation acceptable or not?

The issue was finally raised by a proposed constitutional amendment, named after the site of the conference where it was first drafted, Meech Lake. The Meech amendment proposed to recognize Quebec as a "distinct society," and wanted to make this recognition one of the bases for judicial interpretation of the rest of the constitution, including the Charter. This seemed to open up the possibility for variation in its interpretation in different parts of the country. For many, such variation was fundamentally unacceptable. Examining why brings us to the heart of the question of how rights-liberalism is related to diversity.

The Canadian Charter follows the trend of the last half of the twentieth century, and gives a basis for judicial review on two basic scores. First, it defines a set of individual rights that are very similar to those protected in other charters and bills of rights in Western democracies, for example, in the United States and Europe. Second, it guarantees equal treatment of citizens in a variety of respects, or, alternatively put, it protects against discriminatory treatment on a number of irrelevant grounds, such as race or sex. There is a lot more in our Charter, including provisions for linguistic rights and aboriginal rights, that could be understood as according powers to collectivities, but the two themes I singled out dominate in the public consciousness.

This is no accident. These two kinds of provisions are now quite common in entrenched schedules of rights that provide the basis for judicial review. In this sense, the Western world, perhaps the world as a whole, is following American precedent. The Americans were the first to write out and entrench a bill of rights, which they did during the ratification of their Constitution and as a condition of its successful outcome. One might argue that they weren't entirely clear on judicial review as a method of securing those rights, but this rapidly became the practice. The first amendments protected individuals, and sometimes state governments,[30] against encroachment by the new federal government. It was after the Civil War, in the period of triumphant Reconstruction, and particularly with the Fourteenth Amendment, which called for "equal protection" for all citizens under the laws, that the theme of nondiscrimination became central to judicial review. But this theme is now on a par with the older norm of the defense of individual rights, and in public consciousness perhaps even ahead.

For a number of people in "English Canada," a political society's espousing certain collective goals threatens to run against both of these basic provisions of our Charter, or indeed any acceptable bill of rights. First, the collective goals may require restrictions on the behavior of individuals that may violate their rights. For many nonfrancophone Canadians, both inside and outside Quebec, this feared outcome had already materialized with Quebec's language legislation. For instance, Quebec legislation prescribes, as already mentioned, the type of school to which parents can send their children; and in the most famous instance, it forbids certain kinds of commercial signage. This latter provision was actually struck down by the Supreme Court as contrary to the Quebec Bill of Rights, as

well as the Charter, and only reenacted through the invocation of a clause in the Charter that permits legislatures in certain cases to override decisions of the courts relative to the Charter for a limited period of time (the so-called notwithstanding clause).

But second, even if overriding individual rights were not possible, espousing collective goals on behalf of a national group can be thought to be inherently discriminatory. In the modern world it will always be the case that not all those living as citizens under a certain jurisdiction will belong to the national group thus favored. This in itself could be thought to provoke discrimination. But beyond this, the pursuit of the collective end will probably involve treating insiders and outsiders differently. Thus the schooling provisions of Law 101 forbid (roughly speaking) francophones and immigrants to send their children to English-language schools, but allow Canadian anglophones to do so.

This sense that the Charter clashes with basic Quebec policy was one of the grounds of opposition in the rest of Canada to the Meech Lake accord. The cause for concern was the distinct society clause, and the common demand for amendment was that the Charter be "protected" against this clause, or take precedence over it. There was undoubtedly in this opposition a certain amount of old-style anti-Quebec prejudice, but there was also a serious philosophical point, which we need to articulate here.

Those who take the view that individual rights must always come first, and, along with nondiscrimination provisions, must take precedence over collective goals, are often speaking from a liberal perspective that has become more and more widespread in the Anglo-American world. Its source is, of course, the United States, and it has recently been elaborated and defended by some of the best philosophical and legal minds in that society, including John Rawls, Ronald Dworkin,

Bruce Ackerman, and others.[31] There are various formulations of the main idea, but perhaps the one that encapsulates most clearly the point that is relevant to us is the one expressed by Dworkin in his short paper entitled "Liberalism."[32]

Dworkin makes a distinction between two kinds of moral commitment. We all have views about the ends of life, about what constitutes a good life, which we and others ought to strive for. But we also acknowledge a commitment to deal fairly and equally with each other, regardless of how we conceive our ends. We might call this latter commitment "procedural," while commitments concerning the ends of life are "substantive." Dworkin claims that a liberal society is one that as a society adopts no particular substantive view about the ends of life. The society is, rather, united around a strong procedural commitment to treat people with equal respect. The reason that the polity as such can espouse no substantive view, cannot, for instance, allow that one of the goals of legislation should be to make people virtuous in one or another meaning of that term, is that this would involve a violation of its procedural norm. For, given the diversity of modern societies, it would unfailingly be the case that some people and not others would be committed to the favored conception of virtue. They might be in a majority; indeed, it is very likely that they would be, for otherwise a democratic society probably would not espouse their view. Nevertheless, this view would not be everyone's view, and in espousing this substantive outlook the society would not be treating the dissident minority with equal respect. It would be saying to them, in effect, "your view is not as valuable, in the eyes of this polity, as that of your more numerous compatriots."

There are very profound philosophical assumptions underlying this view of liberalism, which is rooted in the thought of Immanuel Kant. Among other features, this view understands human dignity to consist largely in autonomy, that is, in the ability of each person to determine for himself or herself a view of the good life. Dignity is associated less with any particular understanding of the good life, such that someone's departure from this would detract from his or her own dignity, than with the power to consider and espouse for oneself some view or other. We are not respecting this power equally in all subjects, it is claimed, if we raise the outcome of some people's deliberations officially over that of others. A liberal society must remain neutral on the good life, and restrict itself to ensuring that however they see things, citizens deal fairly with each other and the state deals equally with all.

The popularity of this view of the human agent as primarily a subject of self-determining or self-expressive choice helps to explain why this model of liberalism is so strong. But we must also consider that it has been urged with great force and intelligence by liberal thinkers in the United States, and precisely in the context of constitutional doctrines of judicial review.[33] Thus it is not surprising that the idea has become widespread, well beyond those who might subscribe to a specific Kantian philosophy, that a liberal society cannot accommodate publicly espoused notions of the good. This is the conception, as Michael Sandel has noted, of the "procedural republic," which has a very strong hold on the political agenda in the United States, and which has helped to place increasing emphasis on judicial review on the basis of constitutional texts at the expense of the ordinary political process of building majorities with a view to legislative action.[34]

But a society with collective goals like Quebec's violates this model. It is axiomatic for Quebec governments that the survival and flourishing of French culture in Quebec is a good. Political society is not neutral between those who value remaining true to the culture of our ancestors and those who might want to cut loose in the name of some individual goal of self-development. It might be argued that one could after all capture a goal like *survivance* for a proceduralist liberal society. One could consider the French language, for instance, as a collective resource that individuals might want to make use of, and act for its preservation, just as one does for clean air or green spaces. But this can't capture the full thrust of policies designed for cultural survival. It is not just a matter of having the French language available for those who might choose it. This might be seen to be the goal of some of the measures of federal bilingualism over the last twenty years. But it also involves making sure that there is a community of people here in the future that will want to avail itself of the opportunity to use the French language. Policies aimed at survival actively seek to *create* members of the community, for instance, in their assuring that future generations continue to identify as French-speakers. There is no way that these policies could be seen as just providing a facility to already existing people.

Quebeckers, therefore, and those who give similar importance to this kind of collective goal, tend to opt for a rather different model of a liberal society. On their view, a society can be organized around a definition of the good life, without this being seen as a depreciation of those who do not personally share this definition. Where the nature of the good requires that it be sought in common, this is the reason for its being a matter of public policy. According to this conception, a liberal society singles itself out as such by the way in which it treats minorities, including those who do not share public definitions of the good, and above all by the rights it accords to all of its members. But now the rights in question are conceived to be the fundamental and crucial ones that have been recognized as such from the very beginning of the liberal tradition: rights to life, liberty, due process, free

speech, free practice of religion, and so on. On this model, there is a dangerous overlooking of an essential boundary in speaking of fundamental rights to things like commercial signage in the language of one's choice. One has to distinguish the fundamental liberties, those that should never be infringed and therefore ought to be unassailably entrenched, on one hand, from privileges and immunities that are important, but that can be revoked or restricted for reasons of public policy—although one would need a strong reason to do this—on the other.

A society with strong collective goals can be liberal, on this view, provided it is also capable of respecting diversity, especially when dealing with those who do not share its common goals; and provided it can offer adequate safeguards for fundamental rights. There will undoubtedly be tensions and difficulties in pursuing these objectives together, but such a pursuit is not impossible, and the problems are not in principle greater than those encountered by any liberal society that has to combine, for example, liberty and equality, or prosperity and justice.

Here are two incompatible views of liberal society. One of the great sources of our present disharmony is that the two views have squared off against each other in the last decade. The resistance to the "distinct society" that called for precedence to be given to the Charter came in part from a spreading procedural outlook in English Canada. From this point of view, attributing the goal of promoting Quebec's distinct society to a government is to acknowledge a collective goal, and this move had to be neutralized by being subordinated to the existing Charter. From the standpoint of Quebec, this attempt to impose a procedural model of liberalism not only would deprive the distinct society clause of some of its force as a rule of interpretation, but bespoke a rejection of the model of liberalism on which this society was founded. Each society misperceived the other throughout the Meech Lake debate. But here both perceived each other accurately—and didn't like what they saw. The rest of Canada saw that the distinct society clause legitimated collective goals. And Quebec saw that the move to give the Charter precedence imposed a form of liberal society that was alien to it, and to which Quebec could never accommodate itself without surrendering its identity.[35]

I have delved deeply into this case because it seems to me to illustrate the fundamental questions. There is a form of the politics of equal respect, as enshrined in a liberalism of rights, that is inhospitable to difference, because (a) it insists on uniform application of the rules defining these rights, without exception, and (b) it is suspicious of collective goals. Of course, this doesn't mean that this model seeks to abolish cultural differences. This would be an absurd accusation. But I call it inhospitable to difference because it can't accommodate what the members of distinct societies really aspire to, which is survival. This is (b) a collective goal, which (a) almost inevitably will call for some variations in the kinds of law we deem permissible from one cultural context to another, as the Quebec case clearly shows.

I think this form of liberalism is guilty as charged by the proponents of a politics of difference. Fortunately, however, there are other models of liberal society that take a different line on (a) and (b). These forms do call for the invariant defense of *certain* rights, of course. There would be no question of cultural differences determining the application of *habeas corpus,* for example. But they distinguish these fundamental rights from the broad range of immunities and presumptions of uniform treatment that have sprung up in modern cultures of judicial review. They are willing to weigh the importance of certain forms of uniform treatment against the importance of cultural survival, and opt sometimes in favor of

the latter. They are thus in the end not procedural models of liberalism, but are grounded very much on judgments about what makes a good life—judgments in which the integrity of cultures has an important place.

Although I cannot argue it here, obviously I would endorse this kind of model. Indisputably, though, more and more societies today are turning out to be multicultural, in the sense of including more than one cultural community that wants to survive. The rigidities of procedural liberalism may rapidly become impractical in tomorrow's world.

V

The politics of equal respect, then, at least in this more hospitable variant, can be cleared of the charge of homogenizing difference. But there is another way of formulating the charge that is harder to rebut. In this form, however, it perhaps ought not to be rebutted, or so I want to argue.

The charge I'm thinking of here is provoked by the claim sometimes made on behalf of "difference-blind" liberalism that it can offer a neutral ground on which people of all cultures can meet and coexist. On this view, it is necessary to make a certain number of distinctions—between what is public and what is private, for instance, or between politics and religion—and only then can one relegate the contentious differences to a sphere that does not impinge on the political.

But a controversy like that over Salman Rushdie's *Satanic Verses* shows how wrong this view is. For mainstream Islam, there is no question of separating politics and religion the way we have come to expect in Western liberal society. Liberalism is not a possible meeting ground for all cultures, but is the political expression of one range of cultures, and quite incompatible with other ranges. Moreover, as many Muslims are well aware, Western liberalism is not so much an expression of the secular, postreligious outlook that happens to be popular among liberal *intellectuals* as a more organic outgrowth of Christianity—at least as seen from the alternative vantage point of Islam. The division of church and state goes back to the earliest days of Christian civilization. The early forms of the separation were very different from ours, but the basis was laid for modern developments. The very term *secular* was originally part of the Christian vocabulary.[36]

All this is to say that liberalism can't and shouldn't claim complete cultural neutrality. Liberalism is also a fighting creed. The hospitable variant I espouse, as well as the most rigid forms, has to draw the line. There will be variations when it comes to applying the schedule of rights, but not where incitement to assassination is concerned. But this should not be seen as a contradiction. Substantive distinctions of this kind are inescapable in politics, and at least the nonprocedural liberalism I was describing is fully ready to accept this.

But the controversy is nevertheless disturbing. It is so for the reason I mentioned above: that all societies are becoming increasingly multicultural, while at the same time becoming more porous. Indeed, these two developments go together. Their porousness means that they are more open to multinational migration; more of their members live the life of diaspora, whose center is elsewhere. In these circumstances, there is something awkward about replying simply, "This is how we do things here." This reply must be made in cases like the Rushdie controversy, where "how we do things" covers issues such as the right to life and to freedom of speech. The awkwardness arises from the fact that there are substantial numbers of people who are citizens and also belong to the culture that calls into question our philosophical boundaries. The challenge is to deal with their sense of marginalization without compromising our basic political principles.

This brings us to the issue of multiculturalism as it is often debated today, which has a lot to do with the imposition of some cultures on others, and with the assumed superiority that powers this imposition. Western liberal societies are thought to be supremely guilty in this regard, partly because of their colonial past, and partly because of their marginalization of segments of their populations that stem from other cultures. It is in this context that the reply "this is how we do things here" can seem crude and insensitive. Even if, in the nature of things, compromise is close to impossible here—one either forbids murder or allows it—the attitude presumed by the reply is seen as one of contempt. Often, in fact, this presumption is correct. Thus we arrive again at the issue of recognition.

Recognition of equal value was not what was at stake—at least in a strong sense—in the preceding section. There it was a question of whether cultural survival will be acknowledged as a legitimate goal, whether collective ends will be allowed as legitimate considerations in judicial review, or for other purposes of major social policy. The demand there was that we let cultures defend themselves, within reasonable bounds. But the further demand we are looking at here is that we all *recognize* the equal value of different cultures; that we not only let them survive, but acknowledge their *worth*.

What sense can be made of this demand? In a way, it has been operative in an unformulated state for some time. The politics of nationalism has been powered for well over a century in part by the sense that people have had of being despised or respected by others around them. Multinational societies can break up, in large part because of a lack of (perceived) recognition of the equal worth of one group by another. This is at present, I believe, the case in Canada—though my diagnosis will certainly be challenged by some. On the international scene, the tremendous sensitivity of certain supposedly closed societies to world opinion—as shown in their reactions to findings of, say, Amnesty International, or in their attempts through UNESCO to build a new world information order—attests to the importance of external recognition.

But all this is still *an sich,* not *für sich,* to use Hegelian jargon. The actors themselves are often the first to deny that they are moved by such considerations, and plead other factors, like inequality, exploitation, and injustice, as their motives. Very few Quebec independentists, for instance, can accept that what is mainly winning them their fight is a lack of recognition on the part of English Canada.

What is new, therefore, is that the demand for recognition is now explicit. And it has been made explicit, in the way I indicated above, by the spread of the idea that we are formed by recognition. We could say that, thanks to this idea, misrecognition has now graduated to the rank of a harm that can be hardheadedly enumerated along with the ones mentioned in the previous paragraph.

One of the key authors in this transition is undoubtedly the late Frantz Fanon, whose influential *Les Damnés de la Terre (The Wretched of the Earth)*[37] argued that the major weapon of the colonizers was the imposition of their image of the colonized on the subjugated people. These latter, in order to be free, must first of all purge themselves of these depreciating self-images. Fanon recommended violence as the way to this freedom, matching the original violence of the alien imposition. Not all those who have drawn from Fanon have followed him in this, but the notion that there is a struggle for a changed self-image, which takes place both within the subjugated and against the dominator, has been very widely applied. The idea has become crucial to certain strands of feminism, and is also a very important element in the contemporary debate about multiculturalism.

The main locus of this debate is the world of education in a broad sense. One important focus is university humanities departments, where demands are made to alter, enlarge, or scrap the "canon" of accredited authors on the grounds that the one presently favored consists almost entirely of "dead white males." A greater place ought to be made for women, and for people of non-European races and cultures. A second focus is the secondary schools, where an attempt is being made, for instance, to develop Afrocentric curricula for pupils in mainly black schools.

The reason for these proposed changes is not, or not mainly, that all students may be missing something important through the exclusion of a certain gender or certain races or cultures, but rather that women and students from the excluded groups are given, either directly or by omission, a demeaning picture of themselves, as though all creativity and worth inhered in males of European provenance. Enlarging and changing the curriculum is therefore essential not so much in the name of a broader culture for everyone as in order to give due recognition to the hitherto excluded. The background premise of these demands is that recognition forges identity, particularly in its Fanonist application: dominant groups tend to entrench their hegemony by inculcating an image of inferiority in the subjugated. The struggle for freedom and equality must therefore pass through a revision of these images. Multicultural curricula are meant to help in this process of revision.

Although it is not often stated clearly, the logic behind some of these demands seems to depend upon a premise that we owe equal respect to all cultures. This emerges from the nature of the reproach made to the designers of traditional curricula. The claim is that the judgments of worth on which these latter were supposedly based were in fact corrupt, were marred by narrowness or insensitivity or, even worse, a desire to downgrade the excluded. The implication seems to be that absent these distorting factors, true judgments of value of different works would place all cultures more or less on the same footing. Of course, the attack could come from a more radical, neo-Nietzschean standpoint, which questions the very status of judgments of worth as such, but short of this extreme step (whose coherence I doubt), the presumption seems to be of equal worth.

I would like to maintain that there is something valid in this presumption, but that the presumption is by no means unproblematic, and involves something like an act of faith. As a presumption, the claim is that all human cultures that have animated whole societies over some considerable stretch of time have something important to say to all human beings. I have worded it in this way to exclude partial cultural milieux within a society, as well as short phases of a major culture. There is no reason to believe that, for instance, the different art forms of a given culture should all be of equal, or even of considerable, value; and every culture can go through phases of decadence.

But when I call this claim a "presumption," I mean that it is a starting hypothesis with which we ought to approach the study of any other culture. The validity of the claim has to be demonstrated concretely in the actual study of the culture. Indeed, for a culture sufficiently different from our own, we may have only the foggiest idea *ex ante* of in what its valuable contribution might consist. Because, for a sufficiently different culture, the very understanding of what it is to be of worth will be strange and unfamiliar to us. To approach, say, a raga with the presumptions of value implicit in the well-tempered clavier would be forever to miss the point. What has to happen is what Gadamer has called a "fusion of horizons."[38] We learn to move in a broader horizon, within which what we have formerly taken for granted as the background to valuation can be situated as one possibility alongside the different background of the for-

merly unfamiliar culture. The "fusion of horizons" operates through our developing new vocabularies of comparison, by means of which we can articulate these contrasts.[39] So that if and when we ultimately find substantive support for our initial presumption, it is on the basis of an understanding of what constitutes worth that we couldn't possibly have had at the beginning. We have reached the judgment partly through transforming our standards.

We might want to argue that we owe all cultures a presumption of this kind. I will explain later on what I think this claim might be based. From this point of view, withholding the presumption might be seen as the fruit merely of prejudice or of ill-will. It might even be tantamount to a denial of equal status. Something like this might lie behind the accusation leveled by supporters of multiculturalism against defenders of the traditional canon. Supposing that their reluctance to enlarge the canon comes from a mixture of prejudice and ill-will, the multiculturalists charge them with the arrogance of assuming their own superiority over formerly subject peoples.

This presumption would help explain why the demands of multiculturalism build on the already established principles of the politics of equal respect. If withholding the presumption is tantamount to a denial of equality, and if important consequences flow for people's identity from the absence of recognition, then a case can be made for insisting on the universalization of the presumption as a logical extension of the politics of dignity. Just as all must have equal civil rights, and equal voting rights, regardless of race or culture, so all should enjoy the presumption that their traditional culture has value. This extension, however logically it may seem to flow from the accepted norms of equal dignity, fits uneasily within them, as described in Section II, because it challenges the "difference-blindness" that was central to them. Yet it does indeed seem to flow from them, albeit uneasily.

I am not sure about the validity of demanding this presumption as a right. But we can leave this issue aside, because the demand made seems to be much stronger. The claim seems to be that a proper respect for equality requires more than a presumption that further study will make us see things this way, but actual judgments of equal worth applied to the customs and creations of these different cultures. Such judgments seem to be implicit in the demand that certain works be included in the canon, and in the implication that these works have not been included earlier only because of prejudice or ill-will or the desire to dominate. (Of course, the demand for inclusion is *logically* separable from a claim of equal worth. The demand could be: Include these because they're ours, even though they may well be inferior. But this is not how the people making the demand talk.)

But there is something very wrong with the demand in this form. It makes sense to demand as a matter of right that we approach the study of certain cultures with a presumption of their value, as described above. But it can't make sense to demand as a matter of right that we come up with a final concluding judgment that their value is great, or equal to others'. That is, if the judgment of value is to register something independent of our own wills and desires, it cannot be dictated by a principle of ethics. On examination, either we will find something of great value in culture C, or we will not. But it makes no more sense to demand that we do so than it does to demand that we find the earth round or flat, the temperature of the air hot or cold.

I have stated this rather flatly, when as everyone knows there is a vigorous controversy over the "objectivity" of judgments in this field, and whether there is a "truth of the matter" here, as there seems to be in natural science, or, indeed, whether even in natural

science "objectivity" is a mirage. I do not have space to address this here. I have discussed it somewhat elsewhere.[40] I don't have much sympathy for these forms of subjectivism, which I think are shot through with confusion. But there seems to be some special confusion in invoking them in this context. The moral and political thrust of the complaint concerns unjustified judgments of inferior status allegedly made of nonhegemonic cultures. But if those judgments are ultimately a question of the human will, then the issue of justification falls away. One doesn't, properly speaking, make judgments that can be right or wrong; one expresses liking or dislike, one endorses or rejects another culture. But then the complaint must shift to address the refusal to endorse, and the validity or invalidity of judgments here has nothing to do with it.

Then, however, the act of declaring another culture's creations to be of worth and the act of declaring oneself on their side, even if their creations aren't all that impressive, become indistinguishable. The difference is only in the packaging. Yet the first is normally understood as a genuine expression of respect, the second often as unsufferable patronizing. The supposed beneficiaries of the politics of recognition, the people who might actually benefit from acknowledgment, make a crucial distinction between the two acts. They know that they want respect, not condescension. Any theory that wipes out the distinction seems at least *prima facie* to be distorting crucial facets of the reality it purports to deal with.

In fact, subjectivist, half-baked neo-Nietzschean theories are quite often invoked in this debate. Deriving frequently from Foucault or Derrida, they claim that all judgments of worth are based on standards that are ultimately imposed by and further entrench structures of power. It should be clear why these theories proliferate here. A favorable judgment on demand is nonsense, unless some such theories are valid. Moreover, the giving of such a judgment on demand is an act of breathtaking condescension. No one can really mean it as a genuine act of respect. It is more in the nature of a pretend act of respect given on the insistence of its supposed beneficiary. Objectively, such an act involves contempt for the latter's intelligence. To be an object of such an act of respect demeans. The proponents of neo-Nietzschean theories hope to escape this whole nexus of hypocrisy by turning the entire issue into one of power and counterpower. Then the question is no more one of respect, but of taking sides, of solidarity. But this is hardly a satisfactory solution, because in taking sides they miss the driving force of this kind of politics, which is precisely the search for recognition and respect.

Moreover, even if one could demand it of them, the last thing one wants at this stage from Eurocentered intellectuals is positive judgments of the worth of cultures that they have not intensively studied. For real judgments of worth suppose a fused horizon of standards, as we have seen; they suppose that we have been transformed by the study of the other, so that we are not simply judging by our original familiar standards. A favorable judgment made prematurely would be not only condescending but ethnocentric. It would praise the other for being like us.

Here is another severe problem with much of the politics of multiculturalism. The peremptory demand for favorable judgments of worth is paradoxically—perhaps one should say tragically—homogenizing. For it implies that we already have the standards to make such judgments. The standards we have, however, are those of North Atlantic civilization. And so the judgments implicitly and unconsciously will cram the others into our categories. For instance, we will think of their "artists" as creating "works," which we then can include in our canon. By implicitly invoking our standards to judge all civilizations

and cultures, the politics of difference can end up making everyone the same.[41]

In this form, the demand for equal recognition is unacceptable. But the story doesn't simply end there. The enemies of multiculturalism in the American academy have perceived this weakness, and have used this as an excuse to turn their backs on the problem. But this won't do. A response like that attributed to Bellow which I quoted above, to the effect that we will be glad to read the Zulu Tolstoy when he comes along, shows the depths of ethnocentricity. First, there is the implicit assumption that excellence has to take forms familiar to us: the Zulus should produce a Tolstoy. Second, we are assuming that their contribution is yet to be made (when the Zulus produce a Tolstoy. . .). These two assumptions obviously go hand in hand. If they have to produce our kind of excellence, then obviously their only hope lies in the future. Roger Kimball puts it more crudely: "The multiculturalists notwithstanding, the choice facing us today is not between a 'repressive' Western culture and a multicultural paradise, but between culture and barbarism. Civilization is not a gift, it is an achievement—a fragile achievement that needs constantly to be shored up and defended from besiegers inside and out."[42]

There must be something midway between the inauthentic and homogenizing demand for recognition of equal worth, on the one hand, and the self-immurement within ethnocentric standards, on the other. There are other cultures, and we have to live together more and more, both on a world scale and commingled in each individual society.

What there is is the presumption of equal worth I described above: a stance we take in embarking on the study of the other. Perhaps we don't need to ask whether it's something that others can demand from us as a right. We might simply ask whether this is the way we ought to approach others.

Well, is it? How can this presumption be grounded? One ground that has been proposed is a religious one. Herder, for instance, had a view of divine providence, according to which all this variety of culture was not a mere accident but was meant to bring about a greater harmony. I can't rule out such a view. But merely on the human level, one could argue that it is reasonable to suppose that cultures that have provided the horizon of meaning for large numbers of human beings, of diverse characters and temperaments, over a long period of time—that have, in other words, articulated their sense of the good, the holy, the admirable—are almost certain to have something that deserves our admiration and respect, even if it is accompanied by much that we have to abhor and reject. Perhaps one could put it another way: it would take a supreme arrogance to discount this possibility *a priori*.

There is perhaps after all a moral issue here. We only need a sense of our own limited part in the whole human story to accept the presumption. It is only arrogance, or some analogous moral failing, that can deprive us of this. But what the presumption requires of us is not peremptory and inauthentic judgments of equal value, but a willingness to be open to comparative cultural study of the kind that must displace our horizons in the resulting fusions. What it requires above all is an admission that we are very far away from that ultimate horizon from which the relative worth of different cultures might be evident. This would mean breaking with an illusion that still holds many "multiculturalists"—as well as their most bitter opponents—in its grip.[43]

Notes

1 "La nature de l'honneur est de demander des préférences et des distinctions...." Montesquieu, *De l'esprit des lois*, Bk. 3, chap. 7.

2 The significance of this move from "honor" to "dignity" is interestingly discussed by Peter Berger in his "On the Obsolescence of the Concept of Honour," in *Revisions: Changing Perspectives in Moral Philosophy*, ed. Stanley Hauerwas and Alasdair MacIntyre (Notre Dame, Ind.: University of Notre Dame Press, 1983), pp. 172–81.

3 Lionel Trilling, *Sincerity and Authenticity* (New York: Norton, 1969).

. . .

14 There are a number of strands that have linked these two levels, but perhaps special prominence in recent years has been given to a psychoanalytically oriented feminism, which roots social inequalities in the early upbringing of men and women. See, for instance, Nancy Chodorow, *Feminism and Psychoanalytic Theory* (New Haven: Yale University Press, 1989); and Jessica Benjamin, *Bonds of Love: Psychoanalysis, Feminism and the Problem of Domination* (New York: Pantheon, 1988).

15 A prime example of this charge from a feminist perspective is Carol Gilligan's critique of Lawrence Kohlberg's theory of moral development, for presenting a view of human development that privileges only one facet of moral reasoning, precisely the one that tends to predominate in boys rather than girls. See Gilligan, *In a Different Voice* (Cambridge, Mass.: Harvard University Press, 1982).

16 Will Kymlicka, in his very interesting and tightly argued book *Liberalism, Community and Culture* (Oxford: Clarendon Press, 1989), tries to argue for a kind of politics of difference, notably in relation to aboriginal rights in Canada, but from a basis that is firmly within a theory of liberal neutrality. He wants to argue on the basis of certain cultural needs—minimally, the need for an integral and undamaged cultural language with which one can define and pursue his or her own conception of the good life. In certain circumstances, with disadvantaged populations, the integrity of the culture may require that we accord them more resources or rights than others. The argument is quite parallel to that made in relation to socio-economic inequalities that I mentioned above.

But where Kymlicka's interesting argument fails to recapture the actual demands made by the groups concerned—say Indian bands in Canada, or French-speaking Canadians—is with respect to their goal of survival. Kymlicka's reasoning is valid (perhaps) for *existing* people who find themselves trapped within a culture under pressure, and can flourish within it or not at all. But it doesn't justify measures designed to ensure survival through indefinite future generations. For the populations concerned, however, that is what is at stake. We need only think of the historical resonance of "la survivance" among French Canadians.

17 See Kant, *Grundlegung der Metaphysik der Sitten* (Berlin: Gruyter, 1968; reprint of the Berlin Academy edition), p. 434.

18 I have no idea whether this statement was actually made in this form by Saul Bellow, or by anyone else. I report it only because it captures a widespread attitude, which is, of course, why the story had currency in the first place.

19 One hears both kinds of reproach today. In the context of some modes of feminism and multiculturalism, the claim is the strong one, that the hegemonic culture discriminates. In the Soviet Union, however, alongside a similar reproach leveled at the hegemonic Great Russian culture, one also hears the complaint that Marxist-Leninist communism has been an alien imposition on all equally, even on Russia itself. The communist mold, on this view, has been truly nobody's. Solzhenitsyn has made this claim, but it is voiced by Russians of a great many different persuasions today, and has something to do with the extraordinary phenomenon of an empire that has broken apart through the quasi-secession of its metropolitan society.

20 See John Rawls, *A Theory of Justice* (Cambridge, Mass.: Harvard University Press, 1971); Ronald Dworkin, *Taking Rights Seriously* (London: Duckworth, 1977) and *A Matter of Principle* (Cambridge, Mass.: Harvard University Press, 1985); and Jürgen Habermas, *Theri des kommunikativen Handelns* (Frankfurt: Suhrkamp, 1981).

...

29 The Supreme Court of Canada did strike down one of these provisions, the one forbidding commercial signage in languages other than French. But in their judgment the justices agreed that it would have been quite reasonable to demand that all signs be in French, even though accompanied by another language. In other words, it was permissible in their view for Quebec to outlaw unilingual English signs. The need to protect and promote the French language in the Quebec context would have justified it. Presumably this would mean that legislative restrictions on the language of signs in another province might well be struck down for some quite other reason.

Incidentally, the signage provisions are still in force in Quebec, because of a provision of the Charter that in certain cases allows legislatures to override judgments of the courts for a restricted period.

30 For instance, the First Amendment, which forbade Congress to establish any religion, was not originally meant to separate church and state as such. It was enacted at a time when many states had established churches, and it was plainly meant to prevent the new federal government from interfering with or overruling these local arrangements. It was only later, after the Fourteenth Amendment, following the so-called Incorporation doctrine, that these restrictions on the federal government were held to have been extended to all governments, at any level.

31 Rawls, *A Theory of Justice* and "Justice as Fairness: Political Not Metaphysical," *Philosophy & Public Affairs* 14 (1985): 223–51; Dworkin, *Taking Rights Seriously* and "Liberalism," in *Public and Private Morality*, ed. Stuart Hampshire (Cambridge: Cambridge University Press, 1978); Bruce Ackerman, *Social Justice in the Liberal State* (New Haven: Yale University Press, 1980).

32 Dworkin, "Liberalism."

33 See, for instance, the arguments deployed by Laurence Tribe in his *Abortion: The Clash of Absolutes* (New York: Norton, 1990).

34 Michael Sandel, "The Procedural Republic and the Unencumbered Self," *Political Theory* 12 (1984): 81-96.

35 See Guy Laforest, "L'esprit de 1982," in *Le Québec et la restructuration du Canada, 1980–1992*, ed. Louis Balthasar, Guy Laforest, and Vincent Lemieux (Quebec: Septentrion, 1991).

36 The point is well argued in Larry Siedentop, "Liberalism: The Christian Connection," *Times Literary Supplement*, 24–30 March 1989, p. 308. I have also discussed these issues in "The Rushdie Controversy," in *Public Culture* 2, no. 1 (Fall 1989): 118–22.

37 (Paris: Maspero, 1961).

38 *Wahrheit und Methode* (Tübingen: Mohr, 1975), pp. 289–90.

39 I have discussed what is involved here at greater length in "Comparison, History, Truth," in *Myth and Philosophy*, ed. Frank Reynolds and David

Tracy (Albany: State University of New York Press, 1990); and in "Understanding and Ethnocentricity," in *Philosophy and the Human Sciences* (Cambridge: Cambridge University Press, 1985).

40 See part 1 of *Sources of the Self.*

41 The same homogenizing assumptions underlie the negative reaction that many people have to claims to superiority in some definite respect on behalf of Western civilization, say in regard to natural science. But it is absurd to cavil at such claims in principle. If all cultures have made a contribution of worth, it cannot be that these are identical, or even embody the same kind of worth. To expect this would be to vastly underestimate the differences. In the end, the presumption of worth imagines a universe in which different cultures complement each other with quite different kinds of contribution. This picture not only is compatible with, but demands judgments of, superiority-in-a-certain-respect.

42 "Tenured Radicals," *New Criterion*, January 1991, p. 13.

43 There is a very interesting critique of both extreme camps, from which I have borrowed in this discussion, in Benjamin Lee, "Towards a Critical Internationalism" (forthcoming).

Questions for Discussion

1 Do different cultures each have equal worth?

2 Should "liberalism" be thought of as a neutral way of dealing with the competing claims of different cultures? Does it represent a culture of its own which might conflict with other cultures?

3 Does misrecognition damage the self-esteem of those misrecognized? If so, what precautions should people take to avoid misrecognizing others, and what steps is it morally acceptable to take for those who believe they have been misrecognized to reclaim their image?

4 Is it legitimate for groups to pursue collective goals, even when the means for doing so involve establishing different procedures for members of different groups? If so, how should we distinguish protections which can be sacrificed from rights which cannot be infringed?

Liberalism in Culturally Plural Societies

Excerpt from "Liberalism, Community, and Culture"

Will Kymlicka

The following is excerpted from a book in which Will Kymlicka tries to find the appropriate value of community within a liberal framework.

★   ★   ★

So far...I have not made any explicit distinction between two different kinds, or different aspects, of community. On the one hand, there is the political community, within which individuals exercise the rights and responsibilities entailed by the framework of liberal justice. People who reside within the same political community are fellow citizens. On the other hand, there is the cultural community, within which individuals form and revise their aims and ambitions. People within the same cultural community share a culture, a language and history which defines their cultural membership.

Now clearly these two may simply be aspects of the same community: those people who have the same citizenship may also have the same cultural membership. A political community may be coextensive with one cultural community, as is envisaged in the 'nation-state,' and this seems to be the situation implicitly assumed in most contemporary political theory. But the two forms of community may not coincide: the political community may contain two or more groups of people who have different cultures, speaking different languages, developing different cultural traditions. This is the situation in multinational, or culturally plural, states, and these form the vast majority of the world's states (Connor, 1972 pp. 319-21, van den Berghe, 1981 p. 62).

How should liberals respond to a situation of cultural plurality? Clearly the answer depends on the role cultural membership plays in liberal theory. But this is not a simple matter, and immediately raises a number of questions. What does it mean for people to 'belong' to a cultural community—to what extent are individuals' interests tied to, or their very sense of identity dependent on, a particular culture? And what follows from the fact that people belong to different cultures—do people have a legitimate interest in ensuring the continuation of their own culture, even if other cultures are available in the political community? If they do have such an interest, is it an interest which needs to be given independent recognition in a theory of justice?

These are all questions which arise most pressingly in a culturally plural state, but they go to the heart of the liberal conception of the relationship between self and community. And they give rise to an important political issue: the rights of minority cultures. In [what follows] I use the question of minority rights, and in particular the rights of the aboriginal population in Canada and the United States, as a focal point for exploring these questions about the role of cultural membership in liberal theory.

Aboriginal rights are a part of political life in North America, and perhaps they are the most familiar example of minority rights to the Anglo-American world. Yet they are very much at odds with some of our common self-perceptions. While the United States is often viewed as a 'melting-pot,' without permanently distinct minority cultures, this is clearly not true of the aboriginal population. There is a system of reservations for the American Indian population, within which the members of particular Indian communities have been able (to a greater or lesser degree) to protect their culture. But their ability to do so has rested on having, as a community, unusual rights and powers. The reservations form special political jurisdictions over which Indian communities have certain guaranteed powers, and within which non-Indian Americans have restricted mobility, property, and voting rights.

This scheme for the protection of a minority culture is often treated as an exception, an issue which arises prior to, or outside the bounds· of, liberal theory. But it is far from unique in contemporary liberal democracies. It is similar to legislation which establishes special political and social rights for aboriginal peoples in Canada, New Zealand, and Australia as well. And these are similar to many of the special measures of political and cultural autonomy for minorities in the multicultural countries of Western Europe, such as Belgium and Switzerland. And if we look beyond Western liberal democracies to many African, or Eastern-bloc, countries, the story is very similar. On all continents, in countries of all ideological stripes, we find cultural minorities that have a distinct legal and political status. In these countries, individuals are incorporated into the state, not 'universally' (i.e. so that each individual citizen stands in the same direct relationship to the state), but 'consociationally' (i.e. through membership in one or other of the cultural communities). Under consociational modes of incorporation, the nature of people's rights, and the opportunities for exercising them, tend to vary with the particular cultural community into which they are incorporated. And the justification for these measures focuses on their role in allowing minority cultures to develop their distinct cultural life, an ability insufficiently protected by 'universal' modes of incorporation.

How should liberals respond to these kinds of measures for minority cultures? They may seem, at first glance, to be inconsistent with liberal theories of justice, and that indeed is the common presumption. But, if so, that is a serious matter, for these measures have been important to the political legitimacy, and very stability, of many multicultural countries. Wars have been fought in order to gain or protect these measures. Removing them would have a profound effect on the political culture of these countries, and on the lives of the members of the minority cultures.

It's surprising, then, that liberal theorists haven't explicitly defended, or even discussed, this implication of their theories....

Why is it commonly supposed that liberals must oppose special status for minority cultures? Liberal opposition is often explained in terms of an alleged conflict between individual and collective rights. This is exhibited in recent debates concerning the constitutional definition of the special status of the aboriginal peoples of Canada (i.e. Indian, Inuit, and Métis). This special status was recognized, but left undefined, in Section 35 of the 1982 Constitution Act. Greater specification of this status was to be reached through a series of annual constitutional conferences between government and aboriginal leaders. There was a general consensus that aboriginal peoples should be self-governing, in contrast to the paternalistic legislation under which reservation life had been regulated in detail for decades. But aboriginal leaders said that the principle of aboriginal self-government must include the recognition of certain collective rights, rights which need to be weighed alongside and balanced against more traditional individual rights. For example, self-government would include the ability of aboriginal communities to restrict the mobility, property, and voting rights of non-aboriginal people.

Many government officials, on the other hand, demanded that aboriginal self-government operate in a way that leaves intact the structure of individual rights guaranteed elsewhere in the constitution. So the initial agreement soon gave way to disagreement over the relationship between individual and collective rights. (These differences have, so far, proven too great to overcome, and the constitutional rights of aboriginal peoples in Canada remain undefined.)

The accepted wisdom is that liberals must oppose any proposals for self-government which would limit individual rights in the name of collective rights. I think that is a mistake, one that has caused serious harm to the aboriginal population of North America, and to the members of minority cultures in other liberal democracies. This chapter will explore some of the reasons why liberals have opposed collective rights for minority cultures.[1] ...

What explains the common liberal opposition to such minority rights? It's not difficult to see why liberals have opposed them. Liberalism, as I've presented it, is characterized both by a certain kind of *individualism*— that is, individuals are viewed as the ultimate units of moral worth, as having moral standing as ends in themselves, as 'self-originating sources of valid claims' (Rawls 1980 p. 543); and by a certain kind of *egalitarianism*—that is, every individual has an equal moral status, and hence is to be treated as an equal by the government, with equal concern and respect (Dworkin 1983 p. 24; Rawls 1971 p. 511). Since individuals have ultimate moral status, and since each individual is to be respected as an equal by the government, liberals have demanded that each individual have equal rights and entitlements. Liberals have disagreed amongst themselves as to what these rights should be, because they have different views about what it is to treat people with equal concern and respect. But most would accept that these rights should include rights to mobility, to personal property, and to political participation in one's community. The new Canadian Charter of Rights and Freedoms embodies these liberal principles, guaranteeing such rights to every citizen, regardless of race or sex, ethnicity or language, etc. (Asch, pp. 86-7; Schwartz ch. 1).

There seems to be no room within the moral ontology of liberalism for the idea of collective rights. The community, unlike the individual, is not a 'self-originating source of valid claims.' Once individuals have been treated as equals, with the respect and concern owed them as moral beings, there is no further obligation to treat the communities to which they belong as equals. The community has no moral existence or claims of its own. It is not that community is unimportant to the liberal, but simply that it is important for what it contributes to the lives of individuals, and so cannot ultimately conflict with the claims of individuals. Individual and collective rights cannot compete for the same moral space, in liberal theory, since the value of the collective derives from its contribution to the value of individual lives.

The constitutional embodiment of these liberal principles, in Canada and elsewhere, has played an important role in many of liberalism's greatest achievements in fighting against unjust legislation. For example, in the *Brown v. Board of Education* case, ([1954] 347 US 483), the Fourteenth Amendment of the American Constitution, guaranteeing equal protection of the law to all its citizens, was used to strike down legislation that segregated blacks in the American South. The 'separate but equal' doctrine which had governed racial segregation in the United States for sixty years denied blacks the equal protection of the law. That case dealt solely with segregated school facilities, but it was a major impetus behind the removal of other segregationist legislation in the 1950s, the passage of the Civil Rights and Voting Rights Acts in the 1960s, and the development

of mandatory busing, 'head start,' and affirmative action programs in the 1970s; which in turn were the catalyst for similar programs to benefit other groups—Hispanics, women, the handicapped, etc. Indeed, "its educative and moral impact in areas other than public education and, in fact, its whole thrust toward equality and opportunity for all men has been of immeasurable importance" (Kaplan p. 228). The 'thrust' of this movement was sufficiently powerful to shape non-discrimination and equal protection legislation in countries around the world, and it provided the model for various international covenants on human rights (especially the Convention on the Elimination of All Forms of Racial Discrimination, adopted by the UN General Assembly in 1965). It also underlies the prominent philosophical accounts of liberal equality.

The history of these developments is one of the high points of Western liberalism in the twentieth century, for there is a powerful ideal of equality at work here in the political morality of the community—the idea that every citizen has a right to full and equal participation in the political, economic, and cultural life of the country, without regard to race, sex, religion, physical handicap—without regard to any of the classifications which have traditionally kept people separate and behind.

The logical conclusion of these liberal principles seems to be a 'colour-blind' constitution—the removal of all legislation differentiating people in terms of race or ethnicity (except for temporary measures, like affirmative action, which are believed necessary to reach a colour-blind society). Liberal equality requires the 'universal' mode of incorporating citizens into the state. And this indeed has often been the conclusion drawn by courts in Canada and the United States.

This movement exercised an enormous influence on Canadian Indian policy as well (Berger 1984 p. 94). The desirability of a colour-blind constitution was the explicit motivation behind the 1969 proposals for reforming the Indian Act in Canada. In 1968 Pierre Trudeau was elected Prime Minister of Canada on a platform of social justice that was clearly influenced by the American political movements. Canada didn't have a policy of segregating blacks, but it did have something which looked very similar. As in the United States, the native Indian population was predominantly living on segregated reserves, and was subject to a complex array of legislation which treated Indians and non-Indians differentially. While every Indian had the right to live on the land of her band, there were restrictions on her ability to use the land, or dispose of her estate as she saw fit, and there was a total prohibition on any alienation of the land. The reservation system also placed restrictions on the mobility, residence, and voting rights of non-Indians in the Indian territory; and in the case of voting rights, the restriction remained even when the non-Indian married into the Indian community. There were, in other words, two kinds of Canadian citizenship, Indian and non-Indian, with different rights and duties, differential access to public services, and different opportunities for participating in the various institutions of Canadian government.

Dismantling this system was one of the top priorities of Trudeau's 'Just Society' policy, and early in 1969 the government released a White Paper on Indian Policy which recommended an end to the special constitutional status of Indians (DIAND 1969). The government proposed that the reservation system, which had protected Indian communities from assimilation, be dismantled. Indians would not, of course, be compelled to disperse and assimilate. They would be free to choose to associate with one another, and co-ordinate the way they used their resources in the market, so as to preserve their way of life. Freedom of association is one of the individual rights to be universally guaranteed in a colour-blind con-

stitution. But they would receive no legal or constitutional help in their efforts. Legislation discriminating against non-Indians in terms of property-rights, mobility rights, or political rights would not be allowed.

From its very conception to the choice of language in the final draft, the policy reflected the powerful influence of the ideal of racial equality which was developing in the United States and the United Nations. Paraphrasing UN human rights instruments, the authors said that the policy rested "upon the fundamental right of Indian people to full and equal participation in the cultural, social, economic and political life in Canada," and this required that the legislative and constitutional bases of discrimination be removed (DIAND 1969 pp. 201-2). Echoing the *Brown* decision, the policy proposed that Indians no longer receive separate services from separate agencies, because "separate but equal services do not provide truly equal treatment" (DIAND 1969 p. 204). Echoing Justice Harlan's famous dictum that the American Constitution should be colour-blind, the Canadian proposal said that "The ultimate aim of removing the specific references to Indians from the constitution may take some time, but it is a goal to be kept constantly in view" (DIAND 1969 p. 202). Perhaps it was the weight of all this normative authority that gave the authors such a sense of righteousness. It is, they said, 'self-evident' that the constitution should be colour-blind, an "undeniable part of equality" that Indians should have equal access to common services; "There can be no argument.... It is right" (DIAND 1969 pp. 202-3).

It is worth emphasizing that the issue was not about temporary measures to help Indians overcome their disadvantaged position in the broader society. While not all liberals are prepared to allow even temporary measures which differentiate on the basis of race or ethnicity, the government proposal followed the more common view that measures such as affirmative action are acceptable. But they are acceptable precisely because they are viewed as appropriate or necessary means to the pursuit of the ideal of a colour-blind constitution. Affirmative action of this sort appeals to the values embodied in that ideal, not to competing values. The issue posed by the special status of Canada's Indians, therefore, was not that of affirmative action, but "whether the granting of permanent political rights to a special class of citizens (rather than special rights on a temporary basis) is possible within an ideology that maintains the principle of equality of consideration" (Asch p. 76). And for the liberal architects of the 1969 proposal, the answer was that liberal equality was incompatible with the permanent assigning of collective rights to a minority culture.

The proposal was immediately applauded by the media, even by opposition parties, as a triumph for liberal justice. Indians, on the other hand, were furious, and after six months of bitter and occasionally violent Indian protest, the policy was withdrawn. In the words of one commentator, the policy was a response "to white liberal demands from the public, not to Indian demands" (Weaver 1981 p. 196). But liberals have only reluctantly retreated from that policy, despite the almost unanimous opposition it received from the Indians themselves. Liberals fear that any deviation from the strict principle of equal individual rights would be the first step down the road to apartheid, to a system where some individuals are viewed as first-class citizens and others only second-class, in virtue of their race or ethnic affiliation. These fears are strengthened when liberals see white South African leaders invoke minority rights in defence of their system of apartheid, and compare their system of tribal homelands to our system of Indian reservations and homelands (*International Herald* p. 2; *Toronto Star* p. B3). If we allow Indians to discriminate against non-Indians in the name of their collective rights, how can we criticize white South Africans for discriminating against blacks in the name of their collective rights?...

The crucial difference between blacks and the aboriginal peoples of North America is, of course, that the latter value their separation from the mainstream life and culture of North America. Separation is not always perceived as a 'badge of inferiority.' Indeed, it is sometimes forgotten that the American Supreme Court recognized this in the *Brown* desegregation case. The Court did not reject the 'separate but equal' doctrine on any universal grounds. The Court ruled that, in the particular circumstances of contemporary American white-black relations, segregation was perceived as a 'badge of inferiority.' The lower motivation of black children in their segregated schools was a crucial factor in their decision. But in Canada, segregation has always been viewed as a defence of a highly valued cultural heritage. It is forced *integration* that is perceived as a badge of inferiority by Indians, damaging their motivation. While there are no special problems about motivation on segregated reserve schools, the drop-out rate for Indians in integrated high schools was over 90 per cent, and in most areas was 100 per cent for post-secondary education (Cardinal 1977 p. 194; Gross p. 238).

Michael Gross distinguishes the case of blacks and Indians this way:

> Where blacks have been forcibly *excluded* (segregated) from white society by law, Indians—aboriginal peoples with their own cultures, languages, religions and territories—have been forcibly *included* (integrated) into that society by law. That is what the [Senate Subcommittee on Indian Education] meant by coercive assimilation—the practice of compelling, through submersion, an ethnic, cultural, and linguistic minority to shed its uniqueness and mingle with the rest of society. (Gross p. 244)

Gross argues that the "integration of Indian children in white-dominated schools had the same negative educational and emotional effects which segregation was held to have on blacks in *Brown*" (Gross p. 245). Therefore, the 'underlying principle' which struck down legislated segregation of blacks (i.e. that racial classifications harmful to a racial minority are unconstitutional) would also strike down legislated integration of Indians (Gross p. 248).[2] Assimilation for the Indians, like segregation for the blacks, is a badge of inferiority which, in the words of the Senate Subcommittee, fails "to recognize the importance and validity of the Indian community" and which results in a "dismal record" of "negative self-image [and] low achievement" as the "classroom and the school [become] a kind of battleground where the Indian child attempts to protect his integrity and identity as an individual by defeating the purposes of the school" (Gross p. 242). Similar situations arise when Indians have to assimilate later in life, e.g. at work.

But to say that segregation is preferred by the Indians is not to say it is, or even could be, the natural result of the interplay of preferences in the market. On the contrary, the viability of Indian communities depends on coercively restricting the mobility, residence, and political rights of both Indians and non-Indians. It is this which raises the need for the minority rights that are decried by many liberals, rights that go beyond non-discrimination and affirmative action.

These special needs are met, in Canada, by two different forms of aboriginal community arrangements (Asch, ch. 7). In the reservations of southern Canada, where the population is high and land scarce, the stability of Indian communities is made possible by denying non-Indians the right to purchase or reside on Indian lands (unless given special permission). In the north, however, they are creating political arrangements for the Indian and Inuit population which would have none of these restrictions. Under these arrangements, non-aboriginal people will be free to

take jobs, buy land, and reside as long as they want; the inhospitality of the environment ensures that aboriginal people are not likely to be outnumbered by non-aboriginal permanent residents. However, northern Canada is rich in resources, and development projects will often bring in huge influxes of temporary resident workers. While very few, if any, of these workers are likely to remain in the north for more than seven years, so that the aboriginal people will continue to constitute the majority of permanent residents, at any one time non-aboriginal people may well form the majority. If non-aboriginal transient workers were allowed to vote, they would probably decide to use public money to provide amenities for themselves—movie theatres, dish antennas for television reception, even a Las Vegas-styled resort. Since many aboriginal people in the north are dependent on short-term work projects due to the seasonal nature of most economic activity in the area, such a policy could force them to move into localities dominated by whites, and to work and live in another culture, in a different language. Transient residents might also use their voting power to demand that public services and education be provided in their own language, at the expense of the provision of services and education in aboriginal languages.[3]

To guard against this, aboriginal leaders have proposed a three-to-ten-year residency requirement before one becomes eligible to vote for, or hold, public office, and a guaranteed 30 per cent aboriginal representation in the regional government, with veto power over legislation affecting crucial aboriginal interests. If this scheme proved unable to protect aboriginal communities, they would have the power to impose even greater restrictions, most likely on immigration, and thereby move closer to the southern model, which avoids the necessity of restricting voting rights by simply denying non-aboriginal people a chance to gain residence. In other words, there is a continuum of possibilities, involving greater or lesser guarantees of power for aboriginal people, and greater or lesser restrictions on the mobility and political rights of non–aboriginal people (see Bartlett, and Lyon pp. 48–65, for some of the variants). Aboriginal groups have demanded the restrictions they believe to be necessary to protect their communities.

Historically, the evidence is that when the land on which aboriginal communities are based became desirable for white settlement and development, the only thing which prevented the undesired disintegration of the community was legally entrenched non-alienability of land. Indeed the most common way of breaking open stubbornly held Indian land for white settlement was to force the Indians to take individual title to alienable land, making the pressure on some individuals to sell almost unbearable, partly because Indians were financially deprived (and hence in need of money to meet the basic needs of the family), and also because they were culturally ill-equipped to understand the consequences of having (or selling) title to land (Sanders 1983a pp. 4-12; Kronowitz *et al.* pp. 530-1; MacMeekin p. 1239). Such measures to endow individual title are usually justified as giving Indians greater choice. The White Paper, for example, proclaimed that "full and true equality calls for Indian control and ownership of reserve land... [this] carries with it the free choice of use, retention, or of disposition" (DIAND 1969 p. 209). The Minister responsible for the policy said he was only trying to give Indians the same freedom to manage their own affairs as other Canadians (Bowles *et al.* p. 215). But Indians have as much free choice over the use of their land as the average renter has over her public-housing apartment. Indeed rather more, since the Indian bands are like cooperatively-managed apartment buildings. Moreover, unlike renters, Indians get a per capita share of the band's funds if they choose to leave the reservation. The reservation system can thus combine considerable freedom of individual choice over the use of one's resources with protection of the community from the disintegrating effects of the collective action problem that would result were the costs of maintaining the community borne individually. Whatever the motivation for the endowing of individual title, the effect has been to sacrifice the Indian community in order to protect the mobility rights of individual non-Indians.

But the reservation system causes a problem in the case of mixed marriages. Every member of an Indian band has the right to reside on the band reserve—not the right to buy land on the reserve, since that land can't be bought or sold, but the right to be allocated a plot of land to live on. If the band population grew at a natural rate from purely intra-band marriages, there wouldn't be a problem. But when there are a substantial number of marriages to people from outside the band, if the majority of such mixed couples prefer to live on the reserve (as they do), then there will soon be a problem of overcrowding. Unless there is the possibility of expanding the land-base, some mechanism is needed to control the membership.

In the United States, they use a blood criterion. Only those with a certain proportion of Indian blood can be full members of the band, so non-Indian spouses never acquire membership, nor do the children if they have less than the required proportion. Nonmembers never acquire the right to participate in band government, and should the Indian spouse die, they have no right to residence and so can be evicted; while non-member children must leave the reserve at the age of eighteen. In Canada, the obvious drawbacks of the blood criterion are replaced by a kinship system; everyone in a nuclear family has the same status. If one person in the family has membership, they all do, and so all have full non-contingent rights of residence and participation in band government. Clearly, however, not every mixed family can have membership—that would create over-population. If some non-Indians gain membership for themselves and their children by marrying an Indian, there must also be some Indians who give up membership for themselves and their children by marrying a non-Indian. In Canada, until recently it has been Indian women who lose status upon entering into a mixed marriage.

There is an obvious trade-off here—sexual equality for family integrity. There are other models for regulating membership (Sanders 1972 pp. 83-7; Manyfingers) some of which are more equitable. But all options have this in common; if the land-base is fixed and over-population threatens, some Indians will not legally be able to marry a non-Indian and have him or her move in and become a full and equal member of the community. Again, there is a continuum of possibilities involved: some proposals allow non-Indian spouses to vote but not to hold office, others allow non-member spouses and children to remain after the death of the Indian spouse but not to vote, etc. (DIAND, 1982). In all cases there are restrictions on the marriage and voting rights of both Indians and non-Indians: these are viewed as the concomitants of the reservation system needed to protect Indian cultural communities.

There are also controversial measures concerning language rights. The Charter of Rights and Freedoms guarantees to all Canadian citizens the right to a public education in either of the two official languages (English or French), and to deal with all levels of government in either of these languages, where numbers permit. Aboriginal leaders have sought exemption from this. Allowing new residents in the community to receive education and public services in English would weaken the long-term viability of the community. Not only will new residents not have to fully integrate into the minority culture, the establishment of an anglophone infrastructure will attract new anglophone arrivals who may have no interest in even partial integration into the aboriginal community. This is a concern for French-Canadians in Quebec, who want to limit access to English-language schools for people moving into the province. On the other hand, parents will demand their right to a publicly funded education in English so that their children will not be at a disadvantage if they choose to enter the historically dominant and privileged social, political, and economic life in English Canada.

This is just a partial survey of some of the aspects of the aboriginal rights question in Canada. The arrangements are not uniform across the country, and they are all in a state of flux as a result of the unfinished constitutional negotiations. But we can at least get a sense of the basic issues raised for a liberal theory of justice. The common element in all these measures is that some of the recognized rights and liberties of liberal citizenship are limited, and unequally distributed, in order to preserve a minority culture. And we could tell similar stories about the goals and effects of minority rights schemes in other countries, notwithstanding their many variations.

As we've seen, many liberals treat these measures as obviously unjust, and as simple disguises for the perpetuation of ethnic or racial inequality. But once we recognize the differences between these measures and the segregation of blacks, judgements of fairness become more complex, and our intuitions concerning individual and collective measures may be divided.

What underlies this conflict of intuitions? At first glance, someone might suppose that the conflict is between 'respect for the individual' and 'respect for the group.' On this view, to endorse minority rights at the expense of individual rights would be to value the group over the individual. But there is another, and I believe more accurate, view of our intuitions. On this view, both sides of the dilemma concern respect for the individual. The problem is that there are two kinds of respect for individuals at stake here, both of which have intuitive force.

If we respect Indians as Indians, that is to say, as members of a distinct cultural community, then we must recognize the importance to them of their cultural heritage, and we must recognize the legitimacy of claims made by them for the protection of that culture. These claims deserve attention, even if they conflict with some of the requirements of the Charter of Rights. It may not seem right, for example, that aboriginal homelands in the north must be scrapped just because they require a few migrant workers to be temporarily disenfranchised at the local level. It doesn't seem fair for the Indian and Inuit population to be deprived of their cultural community just because a few whites wish to exercise their mobility rights fully throughout the country. If aboriginal peoples can preserve their cultural life by extending residency requirements for non-aboriginal people, or restricting the alienability of the land-base, doesn't that seem a fair and reasonable request? To give every Canadian equal citizenship rights without regard to race or ethnicity, given the vulnerability of aboriginal communities to the decisions of the non-aboriginal majority, does not seem to treat Indians and Inuit with equal respect. For it ignores a potentially devastating problem faced by aboriginal people, but not by English-Canadians—the loss of cultural membership. To insist that this problem be recognized and fairly dealt with hardly sounds like an insistence on racial or ethnic privilege.

Yet if we respect people as Canadians, that is to say as citizens of the common political community, then we must recognize the importance of being able to claim the rights of equal citizenship. Limitations on, and unequal distribution of, individual rights clearly impose burdens. One can readily understand the feeling of discrimination that occurs when an Indian woman is told she can't get a publicly funded education in English for her child (or when a white man is told that he can't vote in the community he resides in or contributes to).

There is, I think, a genuine conflict of institutions here, and it is a conflict between two different considerations involved in showing respect for persons. People are owed respect as citizens and as members of cultural communities. In many situations, the two are perfectly compatible, and in fact may coincide. But in culturally plural societies, differential citizenship rights may be needed to protect a cultural community from unwanted disintegration. If so, then the demands of citizenship and cultural membership pull in different directions. Both matter, and neither seems reducible to the other. (Indeed, when Charles Taylor wanted to illustrate the ultimate plurality of moral value, he chose precisely this conflict between equality for Indians *qua* members of a cultural community and equality for Indians *qua* citizens of the political community: C. Taylor 1988 p. 25.)

The special status of aboriginal people can be viewed as an acceptable, if imperfect, resolution of this conflict. Such conflicts are, in fact, endemic to the day-to-day politics of culturally plural societies, and various schemes of minority rights can be understood and evaluated in this light.

Liberalism, as commonly interpreted, doesn't recognize the legitimacy of one half of this dilemma. It gives no independent weight to our cultural membership, and hence demands equal rights of citizenship, regardless of the consequences for the existence of minority cultures. As Taylor has said: "The modern notion of equality will suffer no differences in the field of opportunity which individuals have before them. Before they choose, individuals must be interchangeable; or alternatively put, any differences must be chosen" (C. Taylor 1979 p. 132). This conception of equality gives no recognition to individuals' cultural membership, and if it operates in a culturally plural country, then it tends to produce a single culture for the whole of the political community, and the undesired assimilation of distinct minority cultural communities. The continued existence of such communities may require restrictions on choice and differentials in opportunity. If liberal equality requires equal citizenship rights, and equal access to a common 'field of opportunity,' then some minority cultures are endangered. And this, I believe, does not respond to our intuitions about the importance of our cultural membership.

If we are troubled by this failure of liberal theories to do justice to our institutions about the importance of cultural membership, two responses are possible. One response is to say that liberals have misinterpreted the role that cultural membership can or must play in their own theory. On this view, the correct interpretation of liberalism does not require universal incorporation or a colour-blind constitution, and liberals should accept the possible legitimacy of minority rights. The other response is to accept that liberalism accords no role to cultural membership, and precludes minority rights, but then say that liberalism is incomplete, or perhaps entirely inapplicable to the case of minority rights at stake. On this view, we should seek some other moral theory or set of values which will recognize the importance of cultural membership and the legitimacy of minority rights.

Supporters of aboriginal self-government in Canada have tended to adopt this second approach, defending aboriginal rights *against* liberalism. Liberalism is said to be incomplete or inapplicable for a number of reasons: some claim that the aboriginal population has special rights because their ancestors were here first (Cardinal 1969; Dene Nation; Robinson and Quinney); others claim that Indians and Inuit are properly viewed as 'peoples' under inter-

national law, and so have the right of self-determination (Sanders 1983*a* pp. 21-5; Robinson and Quinney pp. 141-2; L.C. Green p. 346); some claim that aboriginal peoples have a different value system, emphasizing the community rather than the individual, and hence group rights rather than individual rights (Ponting and Gibbins 1986 p. 216; Little Bear, Boldt, and Long p. xvi; Svensson pp. 451-2); yet others suggest that aboriginal communities *themselves* have certain rights, because groups as well as individuals have legitimate moral claims (Boldt and Long 1985 pp. 343-5). These are all common ways of defending aboriginal rights against liberalism, by locating our intuitions in favour of them in some non-liberal theory of rights or values.[4]

However, I think that the first response—the attempt to reconcile minority rights and liberal equality—is worth considering, whether one's first commitment is to liberalism, or to minority rights....

The current liberal hostility to minority rights is, I [shall] argue, misguided. However, it is not the result of any simple or obvious mistake, and identifying the problem requires looking deep into the liberal view of the self and community. And even if we recognize the problem, there is no simple or obvious way to correct it within a liberal theory of justice. The issue for liberal theory is not as simple as Trudeau once suggested, in response to a question about his reasons for advancing and then withdrawing the 1969 proposal:

> We had perhaps the prejudices of small 'l' liberals and white men at that who thought that equality meant the same law for everybody, and that's why as a result of this we said 'well let's abolish the Indian Act and make Indians citizens of Canada like everyone else. And let's let Indians dispose of their lands just like every other Canadian. And let's make sure that Indians can get their rights, education, health and so on, from the governments like every other Ca-

nadian.' But we learned in the process we were a bit too abstract, we were not perhaps pragmatic enough or understanding enough. (Quoted in Weaver 1981 p. 185.)

I shall argue that the problem isn't just one of pragmatism or prejudice. The idea of collective rights for minority cultures doesn't just conflict with the pre-reflective habits or prejudices of liberals. It seems in direct conflict with some of the most fundamental liberal principles, even in their most theoretically sophisticated formulations. And so the search for a liberal defence of minority rights will take us back into the heart of liberal theory....

Notes

1 One terminological point concerning the specific example of minority rights or special status that I am using: the issue of minority rights is raised in many countries by the presence of aboriginal peoples who have been conquered, colonized, or simply overrun by settlers from other countries and continents. The rights of Canada's aboriginal peoples are, therefore, representative of a major class of minority rights questions. However, the term 'aboriginal rights' is sometimes used in a more restricted sense, to refer solely to those rights which flow from original occupancy of the land. Hence some writers distinguish between the 'aboriginal rights' of aboriginal peoples (e.g. land claims) and their 'national rights,' 'minority rights,' or 'human rights' (e.g. to cultural freedom, self-determination, language rights, etc.)—e.g. Barsh and Henderson 1982 p. 76. But this restricted usage is uncommon, and I shall be using 'aboriginal rights' to refer to the rights of aboriginal peoples, not simply to those rights which aboriginal people have because they are the original occupants of the land.

One of the most important aspects of minority rights claims concerns the ability of minority cultures to restrict the mobility or voting rights of non-members. In the context of Canada's aboriginal people, this is invariably phrased as a matter of whether aboriginal communities can restrict the rights of 'whites.' The historical basis for this usage is obvious, and it has become an unquestioned part of the political vocabulary of the debate over aboriginal rights. But it is important to note that 'whites' is not being used as a racial

term—many people who are racially white have become members of aboriginal communities (by marriage or adoption), and Canadians who are not members of aboriginal communities have diverse racial ancestry (including aboriginal ancestry). The terms 'aboriginal' and 'white' refer to cultural membership, not race. 'White' has simply become a general label for those Canadians who are not members of aboriginal communities. Hence many of the aboriginal people who demand restrictions on the mobility of 'whites' have some white ancestry, and many of the people whose mobility is being restricted have some aboriginal (or black, or Asian, etc.) ancestry.

2 Similarly, the principles underlying the Supreme Court decisions which struck down legislation redrawing political boundaries so as to *exclude* blacks from political subdivisions (e.g. *Gomillion v. Lightfoot* [1960] 364 US 339) would seem to argue against legislation to *include* Indians in political subdivisions which are unrepresentative and therefore harmful to their interests (Gross p. 250).

3 This is precisely what happened to the Métis in Manitoba, and to the Hispanic population in the American Southwest, during the second half of the nineteenth century. These groups formed a majority in their respective regions, and had rights to public services and education in their own languages. But once their regions became incorporated into the larger Canadian and American federations, these groups became outnumbered by anglophone settlers, who quickly proceeded to take away those rights (see J. Weinstein pp. 46-7 on the Métis; Glazer 1975 p. 25 and 1983 p. 277 on the Spanish-speaking population of the Southwest). Aboriginal self-government proposals have been designed with these dangers and historical precedents in mind. (J. Weinstein p. 47; Purich p. 229).

4 I shall discuss the weakness of the last two arguments (about the different value systems of aboriginal peoples, and the moral standing of communities) [elsewhere]. I am unsure what to say about the first two, partly because they in fact have many variants, some of which contradict others. But I should say something about them, since they are important not only in Canada, but in the emerging international norms concerning aboriginal rights.

The fact of original occupancy is invoked to defend at least two different aboriginal claims. The first is 'aboriginal title' (i.e. ownership or usufructuary rights over land and natural resources), the second is sovereignty. I'll discuss sovereignty together with the self-determination argument, since they raise similar questions of international law.

The 'aboriginal title' claim, by itself, does not justify permanent special political status, unless it is further claimed that "the ownership of the land is the fundamental concept on which other rights, including the right to self-government, are based" (Sanders, 1983*b* pp. 328–9). This is in fact the argument amongst some aboriginal groups whose land-base is secure and legally recognized. However, the emphasis on aboriginal title raises a number of questions. Firstly, it is far from clear why it matters who first acquired a piece of land, unless one is inclined to a Nozick-like theory of justice (Lyons; McDonald 1976). Aboriginal communities were, of course, unjustly deprived of much of their land when whites settled, and those injustices have lingering effects which warrant some form of compensation. But that is not yet a reason why the ultimate goal shouldn't be some form of equality of resources for all the citizens of the country, rather than any permanent special status. Secondly, if self-government is supposed to flow from aboriginal title, then there may not be any grounds to demand that the federal government fund aboriginal self-government (Lyon pp. 13-14). Finally, it won't justify either land or self-government for some aboriginal groups, who for various (and often historically arbitrary) reasons lack recognizable title (Robinson and Quinney pp. 51, 86; Opekokew).

The sovereignty claim says that because aboriginal nations were here first, and have not officially relinquished their sovereignty, therefore, as a matter of international law, domestic Canadian law does not apply to aboriginal communities. Any relationship between the federal government and the aboriginal communities must be concluded by what are essentially state-to-state treaties. On the self-determination view, aboriginal peoples are entitled to the same right to self-determination that previously colonized peoples claim under Article 1 of the International Covenant on Civil and Political Rights. The two views often go hand in hand (e.g. Robinson and Quinney), but they are distinct, since aboriginal communities could have sovereignty even if they are not 'peoples' under international law, or they could be 'peoples' even if they do not have sovereignty under international law.

However, neither claim has heretofore been explicitly recognized in international law. Aboriginal

rights have instead been viewed as coming under Article 27 of the Covenant, dealing with minority rights (see e.g. United Nations 1983 pp. 94-104), which is roughly how I have been treating them. Most aboriginal leaders have been concerned to change that pattern (see e.g. Sanders 1983*b* pp. 21–5; Barsh 1983 pp. 91-5, 1986 pp. 376-7; Kronowitz *et al.* pp. 598-600; L.C. Green p. 346; Robinson and Quinney pp. 141-2), although some people have thought Article 27 sufficient (e.g. Svensson p. 438). Aboriginal advocates rightly point out that international rulings have been quite arbitrary in limiting the recognition of sovereignty or peoplehood to overseas colonies (the 'Blue Water Thesis'), while denying it to internal groups who share many of the same historical and social features (e.g. Barsh 1983 pp. 84-91).

But since advocates of self-determination and sovereignty views are not in fact seeking a sovereign state, it is not immediately clear what rests on the distinction between Article 1 and Article 27 rights. Article 27 has occasionally been interpreted as merely requiring non-discrimination against minorities. But the recent Capotorti report on the international protection of minority rights decisively rejects that view, and insists that special measures for minority cultures are required for 'factual equality,' and that such measures are as important as non-discrimination in 'defending fundamental human rights' (Capotorti pp. 40-1, 98-9). If the goal is not a sovereign state, then Article 27 may be as good as Article 1 in arguing for the right of minority cultures to freely develop and express their own culture. As Wirsing notes, recent changes in the interpretation of Article 27 go 'some distance towards closing the gap' between the expectations of minority cultures and the concessions of the international community (Wirsing 1980 p. 228). And while elimination of the 'Blue Water Thesis' in regard to the definition of 'peoples' would eliminate some arbitrariness, it would also essentially eliminate the category of 'minorities' (most groups which have sought special measures under Article 27 would constitute peoples, not minorities, according to the definitions offered by some aboriginal groups—e.g. the Mikmaq proposal quoted in Barsh 1983 p. 94.)

One worry aboriginals have about Article 27, even on an expansive reading, concerns not the content of the rights it may accord to minorities, but the question of who *delegates* the rights. They are aware of the vulnerability created by the American system of aboriginal rights, in which self-government "is a gift, not a right...a question of policy and politics" (Kronowitz *et al.* pp. 533, 535; cf. Barsh 1983 p. 103). Some aboriginal leaders believe that claims to sovereignty are needed to avoid this vulnerability (see e.g. Robinson and Quinney p. 123). But others say that such claims heighten misunderstanding and prevent the negotiation of adequate guarantees. "The maximum height on the government side is generated by the word 'sovereignty'; and on the aboriginal side, by the word 'delegated.' Somewhere between the two lies an area of potential agreement" (M. Dunn p. 37).

Since Article 1 has not been applied to the aboriginal peoples of North America, and since Article 27 may still be too weak, some aboriginal groups have been pressing for the recognition of a specifically aboriginal category between those of 'peoples' and 'minorities,' in which self-determination is neither sovereign nor delegated (see Moore pp. 27-8; Kronowitz *et al.* pp. 612-20; Barsh 1986 pp. 376-8; Sanders 1983*b* pp. 28-9). The question of whether self-government is delegated or not is clearly important, but it is somewhat distinct from the questions I am addressing. If aboriginal rights to self-determination are not delegated, or indeed if aboriginal communities retain their legal sovereignty, then aboriginals should be able to reject the substantive provisions of a Canadian government proposal for self-government, should they view them as unjust. My question is the prior one of evaluating the justice of the provisions. And it may be that the same substantive provisions would be just whether aboriginal groups are viewed as peoples, or as minorities, or as their own third category. The different categories would affect not only the justice of their claims, but their domestic and international ability to negotiate for those just claims.

Even if aboriginal peoples have substantive claims which cannot be derived from Article 27, in virtue of aboriginal title or legal sovereignty, it is still important for liberals to determine what is owed minorities under that article. Even if aboriginal peoples have special rights beyond those owed them as a minority culture, liberals should ask what they (or other minorities) are owed just in virtue of plural cultural membership. In any event, it is doubtful whether all North American aboriginal groups could qualify as sovereign or self-determining peoples under international law. So a liberal defence of minority rights, if one can be found, would be a helpful argument for many aboriginal groups, and may be the only argument available for some of the groups.

References

Asch, M. (1984). *Home and Native Land: Aboriginal Rights and the Canadian Constitution.* Toronto: Methuen.

Barsh, R. (1983). 'Indigenous North America and Contemporary International Law.' *Oregon Law Review.* Vol. 62.

————. (1986). 'Indigenous Peoples: An Emerging Object of International Law.' *American Journal of International Law.* Vol 80.

Barsh, R., and Henderson, J.Y. (1982). 'Aboriginal Rights, Treaty Rights, and Human Rights: Indian Tribes and Constitutional Renewal.' *Journal of Canadian Studies.* Vol 17.

Bartlett, R. (1986). *Subjugation, Self-Management and Self-Government of Aboriginal Lands and Resources in Canada.* Kingston, Ont.: Institute of Intergovernmental Relations.

Berger, T. (1984). 'Towards the Regime of Tolerance.' In *Political Thought in Canada: Contemporary Perspectives.* Ed. S. Brooks. Toronto: Irwin Publishing.

Boldt, M., and Long, J.A. (1985). 'Tribal Philosophies and the Canadian Charter of Rights and Freedoms.' In *The Quest for Justice: Aboriginal People and Aboriginal Rights.* Eds. Boldt, M., and Long, J.A. Toronto: University of Toronto Press.

Bowles, R., Hanley, J., Hodgins, B., and Rawlyk, G. (1972). *The Indian: Assimilation, Integration or Separation?* Scarborough, Ont.: Prentice-Hall.

Capotorti, F. (1979). *Study on the Rights of Persons Belonging to Ethnic, Religious and Linguistic Minorities.* UN Doc. E/CN 4/Sub. 2/384 Rev. 1.

Cardinal, H. (1969). *The Unjust Society.* Edmonton: Hurtig Publishers.

————. (1977). *The Rebirth of Canada's Indians.* Edmonton: Hurtig Publishers.

Connor, W. (1972). 'Nation-Building or Nation-Destroying?' *World Politics,* Vol. 24.

Dene Nation (1977). 'A Proposal to the Government and People of Canada.' In *Dene Nation: The Colony Within.* Ed. M. Watkins. Toronto: University of Toronto Press.

DIAND (Department of Indian Affairs and Northern Development). (1969). 'A Statement of the Government of Canada on Indian Policy.' In Bowles *et al.* (1972).

————. (1982). 'The Elimination of Sex Discrimination from the Indian Act.' R32-59/1982. Ottawa.

Dunn, M. (1986). *Access to Survival: A Perspective on Aboriginal Self-Government for the Constituency of the Native Council of Canada*. Kingston, Ont.: Institute of Intergovernmental Relations.

Dworkin, R. (1983). 'In Defense of Equality.' *Social Philosophy and Policy*, Vol. 1.

Glazer, N. (1975). *Affirmative Discrimination: Ethnic Inequality and Public Policy*. New York: Basic Books.

————. (1983). *Ethnic Dilemmas: 1964–1982*. Cambridge, Mass.: Harvard University Press.

Green, L.C. (1983). 'Aboriginal Peoples, International Law and the Canadian Charter of Rights and Freedoms.' *Canadian Bar Review*, Vol. 61.

Gross, M. (1973). 'Indian Control for Quality Indian Education.' *North Dakota Law Review*, Vol. 49.

International Herald Tribune (1985). 'Botha Rejects Plea From Within Party to End Home School Segregation.' 3 Oct.

Kaplan, J. (1964). 'Comment on "The Decade of School Desegregation".' *Columbia Law Review*, Vol. 64.

Kronowitz, R., Lichtman, J., McSloy, S., and Olsen, M. (1987). 'Toward Consent and Cooperation: Reconsidering the Political Status of Indian Nations.' *Harvard Civil Rights–Civil Liberties Review*, Vol. 22.

Little Bear, L., Boldt, M., and Long, J. (1984). *Pathways to Self-Determination: Canadian Indians and the Canadian State*. Toronto: University of Toronto Press.

Lyon, N. (1984). *Aboriginal Self-Government: Rights of Citizenship and Access to Government Services*. Kingston, Ont.: Institute of Intergovernmental Relations.

Lyons, D. (1981). 'The New Indian Claims and Original Rights to Land.' In *Reading Nozick: Essays on Anarchy, State and Utopia*. Ed. J. Paul. Totowa, NJ.: Rowman and Littlefield.

McDonald, M. (1976). 'Aboriginal Rights.' In *Contemporary Issues in Political Philosophy*. Eds. W. Shea and J. King-Farlow. New York: Science History Publications.

MacMeekin, D. (1969). 'Red, White and *Gray*: Equal Protection and the American Indian.' *Stanford Law Review*, Vol. 21.

Manyfingers, M. (1986). 'Determination of Indian Band Membership: An Examination of Political Will.' *Canadian Journal of Native Studies*, Vol. 6.

Moore, K. (1984). *The Will to Survive: Native People and the Constitution*. Val d'Or, Que.: Hyperborea Publishings.

Opekokew, D. (1987). *The Political and Legal Inequalities Among Aboriginal Peoples in Canada*. Kingston, Ont.: Institute of Intergovernmental Affairs.

Ponting, J., and Gibbins, R. (1986). 'An Assessment of the Probable Impact of Aboriginal Self-Government in Canada.' In *The Politics of Gender, Ethnicity, and Language in Canada*. Eds. A. Cairns and C. Williams. Toronto: University of Toronto Press.

Rawls, J. (1971). *A Theory of Justice*. London: Oxford University Press.

————. (1980). 'Kantian Constructivism in Moral Theory.' *Journal of Philosophy*. Vol. 77.

Robinson, E., and Quinney, H. (1985). *The Infested Blanket: Canada's Constitution—Genocide of Indian Nations*. Winnipeg: Queenston House.

Sanders, D. (1972). 'The Bill of Rights and Indian Status.' *University of British Columbia Law Review*. Vol. 7.

————. (1983*a*). 'The Re-Emergence of Indigenous Questions in International Law.' *Canadian Human Rights Yearbook 1983*. Toronto: Carswell.

————. (1983*b*). 'The Rights of the Aboriginal Peoples of Canada.' *Canadian Bar Review*. Vol. 61.

Schwartz, B. (1986). *First Principles, Second Thoughts: Aboriginal Peoples, Constitutional Reform and Canadian Statecraft*. Montreal: The Institute for Research on Public Policy.

Svensson, F. (1979). 'Liberal Democracy and Group Rights: The Legacy of Individualism and Its Impact on American Indian Tribes.' *Political Studies*. Vol. 27.

Taylor, C. (1979). *Hegel and Modern Society*. Cambridge: Cambridge University Press.

————. (1988). *Justice After Virtue*. Legal Theory Workshop Series, Faculty of Law, University of Toronto. WS 1987-88 no. 3.

Toronto Star (1986). 'Botha's Warning.' 28 Sept.

United Nations Human Rights Committee. (1983). *Considerations of Reports Submitted by States Parties under Article 40 of the Covenant: Canada*. CCPR/C/1/Add. 62.

van de Berghe, P. (1981). *The Ethnic Phenomenon*. New York: Elsevier.

Weaver, S. (1981). *Making Canadian Indian Policy*. Toronto: University of Toronto Press.

Weinstein, J. (1986). *Aboriginal Self-Determination off a Land Base*. Kingston, Ont.: Institute of Intergovernmental Relations.

Wirsig, R. (1980). 'Cultural Minorities: Is the World Ready to Protect Them?' *Canadian Review of Studies in Nationalism.* Vol 7.

Questions for Discussion

1 Should liberals oppose any proposals which would limit individual rights in the name of collective rights?

2 Is community valuable only for what it contributes to the lives of individuals?

Justice in Our Time

Pierre E. Trudeau

In June of 1969, the Canadian government issued a "Statement of the Government of Canada on Indian Policy" (commonly known as the "White Paper"), in which it proposed to repeal all laws suggesting differential treatment of aboriginal peoples, and phase out the Department of Indian Affairs. This statement marked an important turning point in the history of aboriginal peoples in the country. In a famous speech a little over a month after the statement's release, Prime Minister Trudeau tried to explain the government's position.

★ ★ ★

Remarks on Aboriginal and Treaty Rights.

Excerpts from a Speech Given August 8th, 1969, Vancouver, British Columbia

I think Canadians are not too proud about their past in the way in which they treated the Indian population of Canada and I don't think we have very great cause to be proud.

We have set the Indians apart as a race. We've set them apart in our laws. We've set them apart in the ways the governments will deal with them. They're not citizens of the province as the rest of us are. They are wards of the federal government. They get their services from the federal government rather than from the provincial or municipal governments. They have been set apart in law. They have been set apart in the relations with government and they've been set apart socially too.

So this year we came up with a proposal. It's a policy paper on the Indian problem. It proposes a set of solutions. It doesn't impose them on anybody. It proposes them—not only to the Indians but to all Canadians—not only to their federal representatives but to the provincial representatives too and it says we're at the crossroads. We can go on treating the Indians as having a special status. We can go on adding bricks of discrimination around the ghetto in which they live and at the same time perhaps helping them preserve certain cultural traits and certain ancestral rights. Or we can say you're at a crossroads—the time is now to decide whether the Indians will be a race apart in Canada or whether they will be Canadians of full status. And this is a difficult choice. It must be a very agonizing choice to the Indian peoples themselves because, on the one hand, they realize that if they come into the society as total citizens they will be equal under the law but they risk losing certain of their traditions, certain aspects of a culture and perhaps even certain of their basic rights and this is a very difficult choice for them to make and I don't think we want to try and force the pace on them any more than we can force it on the rest of Canadians but here again is a choice which is in our minds whether Canadians as a whole want to continue treating the Indian population as something outside, a group of Canadians with which we have treaties, a group of Canadians who have as the Indians, many of them claim, aboriginal rights or whether we will say well forget the past and begin today and this is a tremendously difficult choice because, if—well one of the things the Indian bands often refer to are their aboriginal rights and in our policy, the way we propose it, we say we won't recognize aboriginal rights. We will recognize treaty rights. We will recognize forms of contract which have been made with the Indian people by the Crown and we will try to bring justice in that area and this will mean that perhaps the treaties shouldn't go on forever. It's inconceivable, I think, that in a given society one section of the society have a treaty with the other section of the society. We must be all equal under the laws and we must not sign treaties amongst ourselves and many of these treaties, indeed, would have less and less significance in the future anyhow but things that in the past were covered by treaties like things like so much twine or so much gun powder and which haven't been paid this must be paid. But I don't think that we should encourage the Indians to feel that their treaties should last forever within Canada so that they be able to receive their twine or their gun powder. They should become Canadians as all other Canadians and if they are prosperous and wealthy they will be treated like the prosperous and wealthy and they will be paying taxes for the other Canadians who are not so prosperous and not so wealthy whether they be Indians or English Canadians or French or Maritimers and this is the only basis on which I see our society can develop as equals. But aboriginal rights, this really means saying, "We were here before you. You came and you took the land from us and perhaps you cheated us by giving us some worthless things in return for vast expanses of land and we want to re-open this question. We want you to preserve our aboriginal rights and to restore them to us." And our answer—it may not be the right one and may not be one which is accepted but it will be up to all of you people to make your minds up and to choose for or against it and to discuss with the Indians—our answer is "no."

If we think of restoring aboriginal rights to the Indians well what about the French who were defeated at the Plains of Abraham? Shouldn't we restore rights to them? And what about though the Acadians who were deported—shouldn't we compensate for this? And what about the other Canadians, the immigrants? What about the Japanese Canadians who were so badly treated at the end or during the last war? What can we do to redeem the past? I can only say as President Kennedy said when he was asked about what he would do to compensate for the injustices that the Negroes had received in American society. We will be just in our time. This is all we can do. We must be just today.

Questions for Discussion

1 Is Trudeau right to suggest that it is impossible to make up for past injustices, and that we must simply start now and be "just in our time"?

2 Are there any relevant differences between the government's relationship to aboriginal peoples, and to other minorities in Canada?

Indian Women and the Law in Canada: Citizens Minus

Kathleen Jamieson

The government's position in the White Paper met with an unforeseen amount of opposition, especially from aboriginal leaders, in light of which the White Paper was eventually withdrawn. In the first of the two following excerpts, Kathleen Jamieson describes this reaction. In the other excerpt, she outlines the political climate surrounding the legal case of Jeannette Lavell a couple of years later. The Indian Act had specified that Indian women who married non-Indians lost their status as Indians, whereas men who married non-Indians bestowed their Indian status on their spouses. Lavell protested this apparent violation of her equality rights, and the resulting Supreme Court case is a classic example of conflict of legal principles, with significant political overtones.

★   ★   ★

The Minister of Indian Affairs, Jean Chrétien, in what came to be called the "White Paper," proposed a new deal for Indians. This policy paper deplored the disadvantaged position of Indians and suggested to remedy this a total revision of the Indian Act and the gradual phasing out of the Department of Indian Affairs over five years; the paper also proposed that there should be increased provincial involvement (which had been suggested in the Hawthorne-Tremblay Report) in the Administration of Indian Affairs. It is significant, if not ominous, in the light of subsequent provincial government reaction to the issue of Indian women's rights, that this paper begins: "To be an Indian is to be a man with a man's needs and abilities."[1]

Some eighteen meetings on changes to the Act had been held with Indians prior to this proposal. When the Indians were presented with the "White Paper" on June 25, 1969, however, there was an immediate and outright rejection of its content. In the first reaction of June 26th, ten Indian Chiefs from across Canada issued a statement declaring that though they did not question the Minister's "good will" they could only "view this as a

policy designed to divest us of our aboriginal, residual and statutory rights. If we accept this policy and in the process lose our rights and our lands, we become willing partners in cultural genocide."[2]

"It is apparent to us," they said, "that while there was a show of consultation, neither the Minister nor his Department really heard and understood the Indian people."[3]

At this time two factors strengthened the Indians' position. First, Indians' aspirations to special rights based on aboriginal rights had been given a strong impetus by the imminent settlement of the Alaska native land claims by the US government. Secondly, the formation of the National Indian Brotherhood with a membership limited to status Indians in 1968 also seemed to make for a more united Indian political front than had hitherto been possible. It was ironical, though perhaps inevitable, that successful political cohesion depended on Indian Act categories.

The "White Paper," however, had provided real cause for alarm in that it did indeed seem to attempt to play down treaty rights and deny aboriginal land rights: "These aboriginal claims to land are so general and undefined that it is not realistic to think of them as specific claims capable of remedy except through a policy and program that will end injustice to Indians as members of the Canadian community."[4]

Prime Minister Trudeau fanned the flames by stating two months later in a speech in Vancouver: "But aboriginal rights, this really means saying, 'We were here before you!'... Our answer...is 'no.'" He then defended the "White Paper" as an attempt to rescue Indians from "the ghetto in which they live."[5] "Canadians," he said, "were not proud of their treatment of Indians in the past and had no reason to be so," but he promised, "We will be just in our time. This is all we can do. We must be just today."[6]

But to the Indians this was not justice and this government was not really saying anything new. The "Just Society" and the policy of "integration" which Prime Minister Trudeau and his government were now espousing were only another formulation of assimilation, which had always been the stated intention of every Canadian government. The difference was that Indians were now determined that they would no longer be dictated to by anyone....

The [Lavell] case, which became a political vehicle for both the government and the Indians, came before the Supreme Court of Canada in 1973, when Jeannette Lavell contested her loss of Indian Status under the section 12(1)(b) of the Indian Act. The basis of the case...was that the discriminatory provisions of this section of the Indian Act were contrary to the Canadian Bill of Rights.

The government had just published a "White Paper" proposing that the Indian Act should be phased out.[7] But a strong Indian political front was emerging, apparently determined to wring from the government redress for past injustices. Insistence on the retention of the Indian Act was regarded as a crucial part of this strategy by the Indian leaders. As

Harold Cardinal put it, "We do not want the Indian Act retained because it is a good piece of legislation; it isn't. It is discriminatory from start to finish. But it is a lever in our hands and an embarrassment to the government, as it should be.... We would rather continue to live in bondage under the *Indian Act* than surrender our sacred rights."[8] The Indian Act was thus transformed from the legal instrument of oppression which it had been since its inception into a repository of sacred rights for Indians. The opposition of Indian leaders to the claim of Lavell became a matter of policy to be pursued at all cost by government and Indians together because it endangered the Indian Act.

Jeannette Lavell lost her case, but the consequences were far-reaching. The issue of Indian women's status under section 12(1)(b) acquired, for many people, the dimensions of a moral dilemma—the rights of all Indians against the rights of a minority of Indians, i.e. Indian women. The case created a united Indian front on the "untouchable" nature of the Indian Act. And finally, the federal government's eagerness to support the major Indian political associations (most of which seem to have almost exclusively male executives and memberships) against Lavell established a basis for continued government-Indian interaction, which had been in deadlock since the conflict over the government "White Paper" of 1969. The rapport generated during the Lavell case was, after a short period of gestation, to give birth in 1975 to a joint NIB-Cabinet consultative committee to revise the Indian Act.

The government gave an undertaking to the NIB that no part of the Indian Act would be changed until revision of the whole Act is complete, after full process of consultation. The result of this gentleman's agreement has been that until very recently, a powerful blanket of silence was imposed on discussion of the status of Indian women and the topic began to assume an extra dimension. It became taboo and unwise in certain circles even to mention the subject. Despite the fact that the Indian Act continues to discriminate against them on the basis of race, sex and marital status, and is contrary to the most fundamental principles of human rights, Indian women who have dared to speak out against it have been seen by many as somehow threatening the "human rights" of Indians as a whole.

The fact that Indian women in Canada who have lost their status are expected to accept this oppression compounds and perpetuates the injustice and has clear parallels in other societies where discriminatory practices and legislation permit the victimization of one group by another....

A curious twist to the issue has now developed. Despite the fact that Section 12(1)(b) is part of an Indian Act which was developed by previous federal governments without consultation with the Indian peoples, and despite the fact that this kind of discrimination against Indian women was never part of Indian cultural tradition, ... the government is now placing the onus for the continuing existence of this discrimination squarely on the shoulders of the Indians and their representatives, the NIB.

Thus we find in a nationally-read newspaper the recent headline: "Indians' leaders warned to halt discrimination against women." The article then begins, "Justice Minister Ronald Basford has warned Indian leaders that Parliament is not going to tolerate 'for too long' the discrimination against women contained in the Indian Act."[9]

The Honourable Marc Lalonde, the Minister responsible for the Status of Women, in February 1978, informed a meeting of women delegates from across Canada that the issue of discrimination against Indian women is complicated and that "Discrimination against women is a scandal but imposing the cultural standards of white society on native society would be another scandal."[10]

This "two scandals" argument is another version of the "moral dilemma," but this time discrimination against women is argued as being Indian custom and for the government to impose other values prohibiting discrimination would be scandalous.

Of the many and varied arguments that have been used to justify the continued existence of this legislation, this product of the 1970s is the most insidious.

Notes

1 Government of Canada, *Statement of the Government of Canada on Indian Policy, 1969* (Ottawa, 1969), p. 3

2 National Indian Brotherhood, *Statement on the Proposed New "Indian Policy,"* press release, July [sic] 26, 1969.

3 Ibid., p. 5

4 Government of Canada, op. cit., p. 11

5 Cumming, Peter A. and Mickenberg, Neil H., *Native Rights in Canada* 2nd edition (Toronto: Indian-Eskimo Association of Canada in association with General Pulishing Co., 1972), p. 263

6 Ibid.

7 Chrétien, Hon. Jean, *Indian Policy, Statement of the Government of Canada* (Ottawa, 1969). Afterwards called the "White Paper."

8 Cardinal, Harold, *The Unjust Society* (Edmonton: M.G. Hurtig, 1961), p. 140.

9 *The Globe and Mail*, May 26, 1977.

10 *The Globe and Mail*, February 17, 1978.

Questions for Discussion

1 Should cultural groups within Canada have the power to enforce measures which seem to conflict with equality rights, in the interests of cultural integrity?

Aboriginal Rights

Michael McDonald

In this article, Michael McDonald considers how the "entitlement theory" approach to the acquisition of property, as outlined by Robert Nozick, might apply to aboriginal rights. According to this view, it seems that aboriginal peoples justly acquired the land, and then had it unjustly taken from them, suggesting those original rights have never been relinquished. McDonald considers a number of arguments which might be offered against this defense of aboriginal rights, and claims that they all fail, but he concludes that the entitlement theory itself, which underlies the argument, is deeply flawed. Nevertheless, he concludes that we should accept aboriginal rights claims as if the entitlement theory held, until such time as a truly just system of distribution is put in place throughout the country.

* * *

How would you respond to the question "What sorts of treatment do the native peoples of Canada deserve?"

Since native peoples are amongst the most underprivileged Canadians, you might respond on the basis of your attitude to the poor. Thus, if you believe that Canadians should have welfare rights, then you would claim that Indians like other Canadians should not be allowed to fall below some national standard of minimum welfare. You may believe that this is best done through providing a guaranteed annual income or through the provision of various goods (such as food and housing) and various services (such as medical care and job training). You would then find yourself in agreement with Prime Minister Trudeau who in 1969 said that native people

> ... should become Canadians as all other Canadians and if they are prosperous and wealthy they will be treated like the prosperous and wealthy and they will be paying taxes for the other Canadians who are not so prosperous and not so wealthy whether they be Indians or English Canadians or French or Maritimers and this is the only basis on which I see our society can develop as equals.

On the other hand, another person might make a libertarian response and deny that anyone has a right to welfare. He might argue that no one deserves "free passage"—that everyone should work his own way. The debate would then be joined over a whole set of familiar issues. What are the relative merits of free enterprise and planned economies? What does "equal opportunity" involve? How much may the government interfere in citizens' lives? And so the argument will wend its way over time-worn paths until one or both of you get tired and change the subject.

A very effective way of changing the subject is changing it so that you both wind up on opposite sides of the original question with you arguing against any special treatment for "the poor Indians" and your libertarian opponent demanding that they receive significant advantages from white society. I think this reversal is likely to happen if you shift the topic from welfare rights to aboriginal rights. Topic shifts of this sort, those which get the attacker and defender of a particular *status quo* to change places, very often provide interesting material for the political philosopher. Such is the case with aboriginal rights.

I. Entitlement Theory

What is the reason for this reversal in position?

I would suggest that there is something different about the ways in which we ground welfare and aboriginal rights. That is, when we argue for someone's having a welfare right we usually base our arguments on quite different sorts of premises than when we argue for aboriginal rights. The initial problem is then to characterize these sorts of differences.

Fortunately, this task has been made easier by the recent publication of *Anarchy, State, and Utopia* (New York, 1974) by Robert Nozick, who defends Locke's libertarian political philosophy. He argues that neither more nor less than the minimum or night watchman state of *laissez-faire* economics can be justified. In the course of this argument, he has to explain how people may legitimately have the exclusive use of various things, i.e., how they may come to own things. It is this discussion of "justice in holdings" that sheds light on the salient differences between welfare and aboriginal rights.

According to Nozick there are two primary ways in which I can have a just holding. If the object is unowned, I may under certain conditions come to own it; this is called "justice in the original acquisition of holdings." If the object is owned, then its owner may under certain conditions transfer it to me; this is called "justice in the transfer of holdings." Thus, for example, if you want to find out if the Atlantic salmon in my freezer is mine, you would want to know how I came to have the fish in my freezer: if I caught it, stole it, bought it, received it as a gift, etc. In short, you would ask for a history of ownership. The fish is mine if its original acquisition was just, and all subsequent transfers, if any, are also just. Insofar as you can trace this history, you can determine if I have *clear* title. To the extent that you cannot trace this history, it is not clearly mine, e.g., if all you know

is that a friend gave it to me but you have no way of knowing how he got it, you can't say for certain that it really is mine.

If you get a clear history and then find that the original acquisition or one of the subsequent transfers was unjust, then you or someone else has the problem of deciding how to rectify this injustice in holdings. The rectification of injustice in holdings is the third part of Nozick's theory of just ownership. Thus, if you find out that my generous friend stole the salmon from a seafood store, you'll have to decide whether or not you should tell me to return it.

Now let us imagine that you decide to settle the question of my ownership of the salmon by using welfare principles solely. Let us assume that whatever welfare criterion you intend to use will only apply to the two of us in this case. First, you appeal to "need." You say that you are hungry and desperately short of protein, while I am not; since needs should be satisfied, you should have the fish. Say that I ignore that plea, so you try a hedonic appeal: you claim that you will enjoy eating the salmon much more than I will; hence, by the greatest happiness principle, you should have the salmon. It is not difficult in either appeal to imagine how I would have to respond to prove that I have a better title to the fish according to the criterion used. I would argue that I am needier than you or that I would really enjoy it more than you. Further it is not difficult to imagine the two criteria coming into conflict: you need the protein, but I would enjoy the dinner more. Then we would have to sort out which criterion takes precedence, e.g., that needs take precedence over wants. It is also not difficult to foresee some of the problems we might have in applying these considerations: how can I compare my need or enjoyment with yours, how can we properly take into account the effects of giving the fish to you or to me on each of our future needs or enjoyments, how do we know what counts as a "need" as opposed to what counts as a "want"? These are all problems which make up the bulk of philosophical debate about utilitarianism.

In our argument about who has the better welfare claim to the fish we proceed in a quite different way than we did earlier in trying to decide if the fish was a just holding of mine. Then we asked if the salmon had been justly acquired by me or justly transferred to me; in short, we looked backwards in time to see how the fish came into my possession. In the second case, we applied welfare criteria by looking to our present and future conditions to decide the issue according to our relative positions on the scale of need or enjoyment. Two major differences in the determination of ownership stand out in these cases: these are different attitudes to (a) the past and the future, and (b) the characteristics of the affected parties. Both (a) and (b) require some further explanation.

Regarding (a), we have seen that what mattered in determining justice in holdings were the acquisitions and transfers of the object; that is to say, the principle for the determination of ownership was *historical*. In the use of welfare criteria, we looked only at present and future considerations, viz. the relative degrees to which my or your having the fish would meet present and future needs or yield present and future enjoyment. Here we decided who owned the salmon on the basis of *end-results. Our* approach in the second case was *a*historical.

Regarding (b), you will recall that in the application of the welfare criteria we were concerned with the degree to which each of us had or lacked certain characteristics: if you were needier or would enjoy it more, then the fish should be yours. We were concerned in this case with the resulting patterns of the alternative distributions. In the first case, however, we proceeded without reference to patterns. There were no characteristics (such

as need) which I might or might not have that would be determinative of the question of my ownership. It mattered not why I caught the fish (e.g., that I was trying to satisfy my hunger or pass the time of day) or even what I would do with it (e.g., eat it, throw it back in the stream, or use it for fertilizer). Nor did it matter why someone transferred it to me (e.g., because I paid for it, because I am his son, or because he simply felt like it). In fact it doesn't even matter if I have a freezer full of Atlantic salmon and you have none or even no food at all. Justice in holdings is *unpatterned* in that there is no natural dimension (what I call a "characteristic") or set of dimensions according to which the distribution of goods should take place.

II. Aboriginal Rights

We can now see how Nozick's approach to justice in holdings, which he calls "entitlement theory," ties in with the topic of aboriginal rights. Aboriginal rights are none other than original acquisition rights which haven't been transferred to anyone else. To defend the aboriginal rights of Canada's native peoples necessarily involves us in presenting a theory of original acquisition. Moreover, we must be willing to defend our theory of original acquisition against not only rival theories of original acquisition, but also against non-entitlement theories of ownership.

At the beginning of this paper, the argument about providing help to native people was carried on between a person who held a non-entitlement theory of the distribution of goods and one who held an entitlement theory. As you recall, one argued that native people should be helped on the basis of need. This, we have just seen, is an argument based on end-results and patterns. The other disputant argued that native people were not entitled to help. This argument is essentially historical and unpatterned.

Introducing aboriginal rights into the argument forced a change in the disputants' positions because it introduced a historical and unpatterned basis for the native people's entitlement. Now it was possible for the libertarian defender of property rights to argue that the natives had been dealt a historic injustice which stands in need of rectification. The defender of welfare rights must reject this approach, not because native people shouldn't receive significant benefits, but because in his view the only true basis for the reception of benefits is need. That is, he was arguing that benefits should be distributed in a patterned way with a view to the end-results achievable.

Now it is important to realize that we cannot simply let the disputants "agree to disagree." In practical terms, we are talking about claims to at least half of Canada. According to Peter Cumming and Neil Mickenberg in the second edition of *Native Rights in Canada* (Toronto, 1972), aboriginal claims have been superseded by treaties for less than one half of Canada. This would leave standing aboriginal claims to British Columbia, Quebec, the Maritimes, the Yukon, and parts of the Northwest Territories. Think of what this means to established settlements and to plans for Northern development. Remember, too, that "the natives are restless": they have been pressing their claims in the courts (in 1973 the Supreme Court of Canada split four to three against admitting an aboriginal claim), over the bargaining table (in Quebec native people have received a large cash and land settlement for allowing the James Bay Project to proceed in a scaled down form), at the barricades (in British Columbia), and before a royal commission (Mr. Justice Berger is carrying out an investigation of the effect of the proposed Mackenzie Valley Pipeline on native peoples). The questions of aboriginal rights is a real, not an ivory-tower, question.

In my examination of this question, I do not intend to say much more about non-entitlement theories except by way of contrast to entitlement theories. I shall instead focus on various problems that I see in the application of Nozickian and Lockean entitlement theories to the question of aboriginal rights in Canada. I will argue that some of the problems anticipated in such an application of entitlement theory can be adequately handled, but that other problems—particularly those at the core—are much more difficult and may well be insurmountable.

I shall proceed by presenting a number of objections to an entitlement defence of aboriginal rights. I shall first state the objection in the broad and general way it occurs in non-philosophical discussion. Here I have tried to draw upon statements made by politicians, lawyers, and native people, as well as from discussions I've had with students and colleagues. This response will consist, first, in sorting out various objections that have been confused and run together in the non-philosophical context. After that, I shall see what kind of reply can be made within an entitlement theory. I have tried to give each objection a name which suggests the sort of objection made and renders the arguments easier to remember. This mnemonic aid is important because the arguments are often interrelated and used together for or against aboriginal rights.

A. The Vandals Argument

This is the kind of argument that Trudeau has used:

> If we think of restoring aboriginal rights to the Indians, well, what about the French who were defeated at the Plains of Abraham? Shouldn't we restore rights to them? What about the Acadians who were deported—shouldn't we compensate for this? And what about the other Canadians, the immigrants? What about the Japanese Canadians who were so badly treated at the end [of] or during the last war?

A similar position was taken by many Americans in response to James Forman's demand that American churches and synagogues pay $500 million as reparations for years of slavery. In his book, *The Case for Black Reparations* (New York, 1973), Yale law professor Boris Bittker cites the *New York Times* response to Forman: "There is neither wealth nor wisdom enough in the world to compensate for all the wrongs in history."

An objector might ask if the descendants of the Roman victims of the Vandals' sack of Rome in 453 A.D. should be able to sue the Vandals' descendants? Here, however, we see the need to distinguish two separate objections. The first is what I shall call "Historical Disentanglement," and the second "Arbitrariness."

A.1. Historical Disentanglement. The first objection rests on practical difficulties in sorting out historical issues. The problem is to find out who is a descendant of the victims of an injustice and who is a descendant of the perpetrators of that injustice. In the Vandals' case the problems seem well-nigh insuperable. Even if some sorting out is possible, there will probably be enough intermarriage to confuse most cases thoroughly. Intermarriage has been alleged [to be] a serious barrier to reparations to blacks in the United States.

In the case we are considering, however,—that of native Canadians—we can get some powerful assistance from the facts. A quarter of a million Indians are registered under the Indian Act of 1951 as members of recognized bands. While we may have problems with the fairness of some of the provisions of that Act (e.g., Indian women who marry non-Indian males are deregistered and non-Indian females who marry Indian males are automatically registered), the fact remains that we have an accurate, though somewhat incomplete, record of many descendants of the purported victims of injustice. The cases of the unregistered Indians and of the Métis are more difficult, but

we have two important facts which will help disentangle matters. First, these people have regarded themselves as native people. And secondly, they have been regarded by white Canadians as natives insofar as they have been objects of the same informal extra-legal distinctions (including racial prejudices) as those under the Indian Act. It should not prove to be too difficult to arrive at a consensus on who is or is not a native person amongst the Métis and other unregistered claimants of this status.

This, of course, leaves the question of tracing the descendants of those purported to have violated aboriginal title. Here again the facts help us—in this case it is the legal fact that only the Crown could seize land. In the case of New France, we can regard the Crown as the inheritor of whatever title France had to aboriginal lands.

It is also possible that we might in hard cases make use of a test Nozick suggests for determining the descendants of victims and perpetrators on the grounds that *persistent* inequalities are most likely a result of historical injustice. (While Nozick does not suggest "persistency" as a criterion here, I think it might make his suggestion more plausible.)

A.2. Arbitrariness. The second distinct element in the Vandals Argument is that suggestion that the defender of aboriginal rights wants to make an arbitrary and invidious distinction between rectifying the injustices done to aboriginal peoples and the injustices done to non-aboriginal Canadians. This is, I think, what Trudeau was asking, namely, how could we defend rectifying the injustices done to the Indians and ignore the injustices done by our nation to the French, the Acadians, and Japanese?

Trudeau goes on to say that we cannot "redeem the past"; we can only be "just in our time." This seems to let us argue that if we can't wholly rectify all the injustices we have ever done, then we needn't rectify any. The most favourable interpretation that I can put on Trudeau's conclusion is that we may have to face a multiplicity of competing claims of all sorts including a number of competing claims for the rectification of past injustices. We may then not be able to do everything that we ought ideally to do; in an imperfect world we may have to pay our most morally pressing debts in full and make only token payments on the remainder. There need be no arbitrariness in the recognition of aboriginal rights, for we can still recognise other past and present injustices. We may not be able to fully satisfy all the claims for rectification, but that isn't arbitrary either—there is no obligation to do more than one can.

B. The Forefathers Argument

There is another way of taking Trudeau's conclusion that we cannot redeem the past, and that is to say that we are only responsible for our sins and not for the sins of our fathers. How can I be blamed for what my French-Canadian ancestors did to the Indians of New France? How can anyone do more than be just in his own time?

Let's sort out this argument.

B.1. Backwards Causation. The first thing to clarify is whether saying that I ought to rectify injustice X involves saying that I am one of X's causes. If my children ruin my neighbor's prize roses, may I not have an obligation to make reparations? If I do, it needn't be the case that in so doing I am admitting that it was I who tramped through the roses. I may not even have to admit that it was somehow my fault that my children were in the garden. I may have told my children to stay out of the garden. Moreover, I may have done the best I can to instill in them a sense of respect for others' property. Then there is nothing more I should have done. (After all, there are outward bounds like child abuse for determining how far a parent can go in instructing his children.) Indeed my children

may not have acted deliberately, purposely, or even intentionally; it was an accident pure and simple, for which even they are not to blame. But there it is: the roses are ruined, and I am the one who should set it right.

The point is that "responsibility" can be used in a variety of ways. Sometimes it is used to indicate causality, in which case contemporaneousness or precedence in time is essential. But in the rose garden case, it was used to indicate who was *liable* for damages. The concept of liability is most highly developed within the law, but we do use it outside the law in our ordinary attributions or moral responsibility. The question then is whether anyone today has liability for the past violations (if any) of aboriginal rights.

There is a further confusion in this argument. This is to claim that backwards causation must be involved because I can only have obligations of my own making. Thus, I could have an obligation to contemporary native peoples respecting aboriginal rights only if I had undertaken to respect these rights, i.e., if I made a promise to or contract with their ancestors. It will take only a moment's reflection, however, to see that many obligations we have are not entered into voluntarily (or involuntarily either), e.g., not to kill, to express gratitude for favours received, to be kind, and to be honest.

B.2. Benefits Received. In (B.1.) I didn't really so much respond to the Forefathers Argument as clear the way for a response to it. That liability-responsibility is different from causal-responsibility is important; nevertheless, it does not tell us if Canadians today have liability-responsibility for violations of aboriginal title. Neither does knowing that all obligations are not of our own making tell us if the rectification of this putative injustice is our responsibility.

A much more telling response is an analogy with the receipt of stolen goods. If person *A* steals person *B*'s watch and then makes a present of it to *C*, do we think that *C* has an obligation to return it to *B* even though he had no idea that he was in receipt of stolen goods when he accepted the watch? Surely, the answer is "Yes!" We might go on to say that *A* owes *C* something (an apology at minimum) for inconveniencing and embarrassing him. We would, I think, give the same answer even if the thief *A* can't recompense *C* (say that *A* is now dead). It is worth noting here that no one is blaming *C* for *A*'s stealing *B*'s watch or even for unwittingly accepting stolen property. *C* needn't feel any guilt about either of these matters. He should, however, feel guilt if he doesn't return the watch to *B*. l see no reason to change our views about returning the watch if instead of talking about *B* and *C* we talk about their heirs. I would not extend this to *A*'s heirs, however, who presumably have not benefitted either from *A*'s theft itself, or the gift of the watch to *C*.

The parallels with the case of aboriginal rights should be fairly obvious. Non-Indians have in Canada benefitted (albeit in very unequal degrees) from the noncompensated supercession of aboriginal title. This is not to say that non-Indians *today* refused to compensate native people for the loss of aboriginal rights *during* the last and preceding centuries. These non-Indians certainly can't be held responsible for being born into this society or for immigrating to it. In this respect, breast-beating over what has been done to the "poor native" is neither due nor appropriate. Guilt is appropriate only if nothing is done to remedy injustices in the treatment of native people including, in particular, the rectification of past injustices.

Of course, the case for reparations becomes more difficult if we change the analogy somewhat. For example, what, if anything, does *C* owe *B* if after *C* receives the watch he loses it? It would be different if *C* were keeping *B*'s watch in trust for *B*, for then he could well be

responsible for not losing it. This problem posed by lost or ruined articles seems quite likely to occur with the passage of significant periods of time. If we are talking about *C*'s and *B*'s great-grandchildren, the odds are that by this time the watch has been lost or no longer works.

That is, I think, the kind of thing that Bittker has in mind when he says that there would be no case for reparations to blacks if in the period since the Civil War there had been an unbroken ascent up to a present state of genuine equality. That is, the argument here is that reparations are not due if the relative advantage seized by the act of injustice gets lost or equalised in the course of history, so that it no longer makes any difference. It is *not* crucial to this argument that *both* the benefits accruing to the oppressors and their heirs and the evils suffered by the victims and their heirs no longer remain. It is enough to have the first without the second.

B.3. Inheritance. There is a way of taking the Forefathers Argument that avoids the reply just advanced (B.2.). There I argued that if you can inherit benefits, you can inherit burdens chargeable against those benefits. This is like having to pay estate taxes and creditors before receiving an inheritance. As we have just seen, if you inherit nothing, you do not have any obligation (save, perhaps, "a debt of honour") to pay any debts chargeable against the estate. This suggests that there would be no aboriginal rights if there were no rights to make bequests; that is, aboriginal rights disappear if no one may rightfully inherit anything.

Native people could use this as an effective *ad hominem* argument in pressing their case. They could say to the rich and powerful in our society that Indians and Inuit will give up their claims to aboriginal rights if the rich and powerful will surrender all the property that they have inherited. This would not mean the end of private property but only the aspect of it—which I call "bequeathability." Other aspects of private property would remain (viz. rights of alienability, exclusive use, security, management, income, and so forth) but these "standard incidents" of property would be limited to the life of the holder. (To make this suggestion effective, we would have to set a limit to the life of corporations, for under our laws these "artificial persons" can be immortal.)

C. The Double Wrong Argument

The objection here is that to rectify one injustice another will have to be done, so that in rectifying the injustice done to the native people an injustice will have to be done to non-native Canadians by taking away from them land or the profit therefrom which they have in good faith purchased and improved. Moreover, the settlement of aboriginal claims will impose an enormous burden on those who in some cases are already disadvantaged.

The main response to this has already been made in the Forefathers Argument (B.2). No one has a right to receive and retain what is not another's to give. "Good faith" here excuses one from complicity in the original theft: one is not to blame for the theft, so one needn't feel guilty about it. It does not excuse one from returning the stolen goods or the equivalent. Remember that we are working within the context of entitlement theory; justice in holding demands, justice in acquisition, and transfers. To give weight to the claims of those who have unjust holdings is just the sort of thing end-result theorists would do.

Nevertheless, the entitlement theorist can reduce the practical force of this objection by pointing out that third party beneficiaries (here, non-Indian and non-Inuit property owners) must return what remains of that which was wrongfully transferred to them. Given the ravages of time, one may not have to surrender any of one's own goods in making this repara-

tion because nothing of value remains. I say "may not" because among the benefits received from the stolen property is that there is less drain on one's own resources. Thus, in the watch analogy, *C* or his heirs may benefit from not having to purchase watches of their own because they have the use of the watch stolen from *B*. So if the watch breaks after a few years while in *C*'s possession, *B* might ask for rent for the use of his watch over the years before it broke. If *C* is now bankrupt, there may be little *B* can get (unless it is the case that entitlement theory would demand that *C* work the rent off). If it is the case that in addition to bankruptcy *C* also dies, then *B* cannot demand that *C*'s would-be heirs pay for it out of their own justly acquired resources (including working the debt off). Death without the transmission of a benefice would seem on the entitlement theory to end the case for repayment simply because the unjust holding no longer exists. Presumably, in this wealthy nation, most of the benefit has been transmitted to us.

A final remark on the plight of the small property holder. According to the principles of rectification of injustice in holdings, it surely must be the case that those who have benefitted most from unjust holdings owe more than those who have benefitted least. Keeping in mind the complications about inheritance discussed earlier, it should be the case that in a society like ours, in which most wealth—especially capital—remains concentrated in a few families, the wealthiest would have the most to lose by the recognition of aboriginal rights. Here I would think especially of those who have benefitted most from the exploitation of natural resources (like gas, oil, and minerals) in the areas in question, particularly Alberta, the North, and B.C. Of course, it has already been argued (B.3.) that these same people have the most to lose by denying aboriginal claims for they would thereby undermine their own claims to inherited wealth.

D. The Sovereignty Argument

In an article in *The Globe and Mail* (21 February 1973), Cumming has suggested that one possible reason for the Government's reluctance to recognise aboriginal rights is the fear that in so doing there would be a recognition of aboriginal sovereignty over the lands in question, to wit, Trudeau's reference to the Plains of Abraham. This is evident, too, in the same speech when Trudeau says, "It's inconceivable, I think, that in a given society one section of society have a treaty with another section of society." Trudeau is not the only politician in Canada's history to express concern about holding the country together; this is a country which has been plagued by threats of separatism—from Quebec, the West, and the Maritimes.

If it is the case that the recognition of aboriginal rights would necessarily involve a recognition of a separate aboriginal nation or nations then it is not clear what an entitlement theorist like Nozick would say. Nozick's invisible hand explanation of the emergence of a dominant protection agency as the (minimal) state never comes to grips with the fact that there is more than one nation in this complicated world. The fact of nationalism should also have some effect on Nozick's proposal for utopia—allowing diverse experiments in types of communities *within* a single nation. Are nationalists entirely wrong when they think that they must have control over the state and not just over the community? Another interesting way of putting this question is to ask what sorts of self-determination (determination particularly of a group's identity) are not possible in a libertarian society. Leaving aside these complex and difficult questions, it is possible to argue that if sovereignty is an issue here, then surely we must talk about more than justice in holdings.

The simplest way of dealing with this objection is to deny, as Cummings does, that sovereignty and property rights are connected except in an indirect way. In ordinary disputes over land ownership, neither claimant is trying to set up an independent nation. The adjudication usually follows the laws of the nation in which the property is situated. Although in a few difficult cases there can be arguments about which of two nation's laws are applicable, the dispute is primarily about ownership and only secondarily about sovereignty. It should be pointed out that no less an entitlement theorist [than] Locke claimed that rights to property are quite independent of rights to rule, for he maintained that property rights should survive changes in government including violent changes brought about by war.

E. The Litigation Argument

The general argument here is that claims to aboriginal title are unlike ordinary property claims. They are not amenable to the usual sorts of tests used by the courts to decide property rights. In particular many aboriginal claims are such as to deny courts the use of a most effective procedure for deciding between rival claims in cases where due to the passage of time both records are missing and memories are uncertain, namely, "prescription" which is "the operation of time as a vestitive fact." If this is correct, then how can anyone maintain that aboriginal claims can be settled in the same way as ordinary disputes about ownership? Indeed, how can anyone maintain that they are property rights at all?

This argument can be taken in part as a necessary corrective to the oversimplified reply that I just advanced against the Sovereignty Argument. There I argued that sovereignty and property were different kinds of rights. This may have left the impression that all property rights are alike and that aboriginal rights are like other property-rights. Neither of these contentions is true.

I agree with A.M. Honore that "property" is probably best thought of in terms of a list of "the standard incidents of ownership." This would be a list of the rights which a property owner has in the standard, full-blown case. It would include rights of physical possession, use, derivation of profit and capital, security, management, and so forth. One would probably also have to say something about the duties of ownership as well, in particular the prohibition of harmful use. If some of these incidents are missing in a particular case, we could still talk about "property-rights." In fact all the Indian treaties deny Indians the liberty of converting their reserves into capital, i.e., they may not alienate their lands, only the Crown may. In this sense, reserves could be seen as belonging to a particular people in perpetuity, not just to its present-day occupants; thus, future generations would have patrimonial rights. Aboriginal land claims involve the same kind of arrangement. (I should add here that if a whole people, conceived as a group extending across time into the future, can have property rights, then such right might well play havoc with many of the positions that Nozick defends on the basis of actions in a free market).

So part of my reply to this argument is that while aboriginal titles may lack some of the standard incidents of property it may well be possible to still think of them as property rights. To properly establish this reply would require a great deal more space than I presently have. I think more needs to be said, however, about this argument along somewhat different lines.

First, there is the issue of "prescription." In the law it is the case that the passage of time can extinguish or establish ownership. This is determined by time limits established by custom or statute. For example, in some jurisdictions if you have made use of part of someone else's land as a right-of-way for twenty years, then the courts will uphold your right to continue to do so and thus bar the landowner from preventing your passage. Thus time has

given you a right you formerly did not have and extinguished a property-right that the landowner had. The point of prescription is quite straightforward: the passage of time is used as a conclusive evidence because it simplifies the work of the courts in determining ownership. Thus, the jurist Savigny said, "All property is founded in adverse possession ripened by prescription."

The problem for aboriginal claims is that in many cases the land claimed is not now and has not been occupied by the claimants at all or on an exclusive basis for many years more than the limits set by law for the extinguishment of title. Yet it seems unfair therefore to deny title even though it is fair to do so in ordinary cases. In ordinary cases the law protects the property-owner's exercise of his property-rights before the period of prescription has elapsed. That is, if he wants to prevent his title from lapsing, he need only take action. Thus, in the right-of-way case, the property-owner can put up a "no trespassing" sign before the twenty years are out; this completely extinguishes your claim to a legally guaranteed right-of-way. If it is illegal to post the sign, then using the passage of time to effect a transfer of title would be unfair. The parallel here is that native peoples have not been given an opportunity to present their aboriginal claims, either through the courts or directly to government.

Secondly, the Litigation Argument does raise important doubts about the appropriate *forum* for the determination of the value and extent of various aboriginal claims. Cummings say that "the court is by far the least appropriate forum for dealing with aboriginal rights" because "litigation is expensive, time-consuming, and abounds with technical difficulties." He proposes instead that there be direct negotiations between the government and native people. Thus, this is essentially a practical, not an in-principle concern.

Thirdly, the Litigation Argument hints at a problem which will concern us in the next and final section. The problem, as seen from the perspective of this Argument, concerns the relationship between particular property-rights and the existing legal system. One way of finding the general area of difficulty is to ask if there can be property without laws. If there cannot be property without laws (as has been argued by generations of contractarians, Kant among them), then is property merely a creature of law? If property-rights can only be created and destroyed by law, what must be said about the entitlement theorists' claim that we have a natural right to "estate" in addition to "life and liberty"? In the next section I will consider some of these questions.

F. The Acquisition Arguments

Thus far, in all the objections and replies, I have tried to apply entitlement theory to the question of aboriginal rights. If I am right, then a number of interesting and plausible objections to entitlement theory and its application can be answered. In neither the objections nor the replies have I asked if native people actually have a claim to these lands on the basis of just original acquisition; for the sake of argument I have assumed that they do, and then gone to ask whether such claims should be recognised. Obviously, if native people in general or in particular did *not* make a just original acquisition of the land, the whole case for aboriginal rights fails. This would now show that all the native people's claims to land ownership are null and void, but it would remove the most important and the largest claims.

There is more than this practical issue at stake here. The whole entitlement theory rests on original acquisition. If the justice of an original acquisition is called into question then so also, Nozick says, are all subsequent transfers. If *all* original acquisitions can be called into question, then, perhaps, all claims to property rights are challengeable. One way of calling all aboriginal acquisitions into question

is to deny that sense can be made of the concept of "original acquisition." Another way would be to deny that original acquisition as imagined by entitlement theorists can be a basis for rightful ownership.

So now I will turn to the "keystone" issue. I should say that some of the sharpest criticisms of the original acquisition doctrine come from Nozick himself. He writes in an almost ironic, or shall I say, "contrapuntal" way that involves the reader and enlivens debate. I will present four objections and responses. The responses, I should indicate, are partial and do not, I think, save entitlement theory (though, curiously enough, they save aboriginal rights).

F.1. The Jus Tertii Argument. One way of challenging aboriginal rights *within* the framework of entitlement theory is to deny that the Indians and Inuit had made original and just acquisition. This could be denied on the grounds that Indians and Inuit weren't the first human beings in Canada and that Indians and Inuit acquired the northern half of this continent by force. In any event, given the lack of records of property acquisition, it could be claimed that no one can know for certain if the native people's ancestors acquired the lands justly as either first possessors or as a result of just transfer. This would at the very least make aboriginal claims suspect.

The argument presented here rests on a claim like the following: if Bill's acquisition of Blackacres from Alice is unjust, then Chuck's acquisition of the land from Bill need not follow the rules of just transfer in order to get as good, or better, title than Bill has to Blackacres. The underlying contention is that if title is, so to speak, "spoiled" at any point the property is simply up for grabs. Here I am assuming that the just owner Alice is not laying claim to Blackacres and that Chuck is in no way acting on behalf of Alice. The question is not, then, one of Chuck's rectifying an injustice done to Alice by Bill. The objection rests on the contention that gives Alice's not laying or transferring her claim to another, Bill's act of injustice returns Blackacres to an ownerless situation from which Chuck may claim it.

Before questioning this contention, I would note that even accepting this reasoning there still is a difference between showing that Bill's title is spoiled and raising a suspicion that it may not be clear. In some cases, it simply is impossible for a possessor to prove that he has clear title; however, this does not mean that others can prove that he does not. Surely the burden of proof rests on those who charge wrongful possession.

Now as to the argument itself, it is worth noting that the practice under common law is not to establish ownership *absolutely* but *only relatively*, i.e., to decide who has a *better* right to possess. It would, I believe, be the case that a court would hold that Bill has a better title to Blackacres than Chuck and Alice has a better title to Blackacres than Bill. Regardless of the court's decision, it is certainly more convenient for a court to decide matters in this relative way (adjudicating only between the rival claims presented to it) rather than trying to do this once and for all (which would involve ruling on every conceivable claim). In this case, the court would settle the dispute between Bill and Chuck leaving it to others such as Alice to bring suit separately.

Which approach should an entitlement theorist adopt—that unjust acquisition or transfer returns the object to an ownerless condition or that it simply "weakens" the possessor's title? I wonder if in answering this question we will have to fall back on utilitarian considerations, e.g., about which procedure would be the most orderly and least disruptive for a given society. I am not sure how this question would be decided on purely entitlement grounds. That is, I don't know what *natural* rights to the ownership of Blackacres are held by Bill as opposed to Chuck. I would suspect that this cannot be

determined without a *policy* decision about the rules governing property. Entitlement theory does not say which is the appropriate way of deciding ownership in this case. If this is right then it indicates an important gap in entitlement theory, for it means that the theory of justice in holdings has to be patched up by resorting to utilitarianism.

Apropos the question of aboriginal rights, it would seem that if we proceed on the basis of who has better title rather than on the basis of who has absolute title, then native people's claims would seem to be stronger than those of successive possessors.

F.2. The Spoilage Argument. In *The Second Treatise of Government*, Locke presents an objection to his view of justice in original acquisition:

> That if gathering the Acorns, or other Fruits of the Earth, &c. makes a right to them, then any one may *ingross* as much as he will.

Locke says that this is not so; one may take "as much as one can make use of to any advantage of life before it spoils ... Whatever is beyond this, is more than his share and belongs to others." Locke grounds this limitation of original acquisition on God's will: "Nothing was made by God for Man to spoil or destroy." Yet it is clear that God's will is not capricious, for as Locke says earlier:

> God, who hath given the World to Men in common, hath also given them reason to make use of it to the best advantage of life and convenience.

Men then have a right to self-preservation which entitles them to take the means thereto, viz. by acquiring the necessaries of life. Self-preservation grounds appropriation and sets limits to it.

Now it could be argued that the spoilage provision sets the limits too widely in that it allows me to refuse to share my bounty with my starving neighbours so long as I can use that bounty for "the best advantage of [my] life and convenience." Matters are weighted heavily in favour of the propertied and against those without property. But let us for the sake of argument accept spoilage as an outward limit of just original acquisition. We can then ask whether native peoples violated the spoilage principle in acquiring these lands. If they did and if the Europeans who came here could make use of the wasted portions, then aboriginal claims may be defensible on the grounds of wastage.

If this question is answerable, it would have to be on the basis of historical evidence; however, it is fair for the philosopher to ask about the determination of the criteria for wastage and spoilage: by what marks do we identify something as waste? Here it is tempting to ask if the thing in question is used for anyone's benefit. But will any minute amount of incremental benefit suffice to justify ownership or must there be some standard margin of benefit for this use to count here for title? Must there also be standards of efficient use? Would there be a combined standard, e.g., "Makes the best use of X for the greatest benefit"? Any benefit or efficiency standard would seem to be hopelessly utilitarian and redistributivist. On the other hand, having no standards at all would effectively deny a right of self-preservation to those without property and the correlative duty to share for the propertied.

If we try to fix on some mid-point (i.e., having a spoilage provision which is compatible with entitlement theory), then the question is how to justify our selection of standards on an entitlement basis. This is a particularly troublesome question in the case of aboriginal rights. In many cases an advanced agricultural and industrialised economy came into contact with a hunting, fishing, and gathering economy. The patterns of resource use were bound to be different. What would appear as under-utilisation in one economy might appear as over-utilisation in the other.

Clearly Canada's native peoples made ingenious use of the often harsh environment, but their uses could not support the numbers of people that present-day uses can. (In this paper I am being deliberately silent about how much longer we can continue our use-patterns.) However, if we move in the direction of giving title to the Europeans rather than the native peoples, then we would have to surrender our ownership claims to any society which could support more people here more efficiently. This seems quite obviously in direct opposition to the whole thrust of an *entitlement* theory: if I am entitled to something, if it's *mine*, then I should within the limit of non-harmfulness be able to use it as efficiently or as inefficiently as I wish for whosoever's advantage I choose. This would accord with Nozick's slogan: "From each as they choose, to each as they are chosen."

Tentatively, then, if we are willing to deny the right of self-preservation and more especially the correlative duty of sharing when necessary to provide it, then we can still hold the entitlement theory and so avoid the conceptual difficulties posed by the spoilage principle.

F.3. The "Proviso" Argument. Spoilage is not the only limit Locke sets to original acquisition; he also suggests what Nozick calls "the Lockean Proviso," namely that there be "enough and as good left in common for others." This Nozick says, "is meant to ensure that the position of others is not worsened." Thus, we can imagine a parallel argument to the Spoilage Argument being advanced against aboriginal rights on the grounds that aboriginal possession violated the enough-and-as-good proviso.

Factually, this is going to be a tricky argument to work out for not only must it be shown that the native people did not leave enough and as good to the immigrants, but also that the immigrants have taken just enough to rectify this violation of the proviso.

This will be very hard to prove, given the relative wealth of natives and immigrants. At present, indeed, native people could justifiably argue that the immigrants haven't left enough and as good to them.

Here, as in the Spoilage Argument, there are serious conceptual problems in determining the appropriate criteria. Nozick advances two interpretations of the Proviso:

> Someone may be made worse off by another's appropriation in two ways: first by losing the opportunity to improve his situation by a particular appropriation or anyone, and second, by no longer being able to use freely (without appropriation) what he previously could.

Nozick accepts the second or "weaker requirement" and not the first or "the stringent requirement." The difference between the two seems to be between characterizing the proviso as applying to appropriation (ownership) or to use. But then it must be remembered that earlier Nozick says that "the central core of the notion of a property right in X is "the right to determine what shall be done with X." If I have a right to use X, then would I not have a property right in X?

Be that as it may, Nozick argues that those who are unable to appropriate (because everything is now owned) are likely to be compensated for this restriction on their liberty by having their prospects increased by a system which allows (virtually unlimited) private acquisition. Nozick says the free market will make up for their loss of acquisition and/or use rights. The point is to compensate these people enough for not being able to appropriate or use what they could have had they been born earlier. Nozick suggests that the level of compensation can be determined by getting "an estimate of the general economic importance of appropriation."

But this, I suggest, won't do for several reasons. First, if this isn't forcing on someone a kind of compensation that he doesn't want, then in the case of those who really want to make acquisitions the state will have to take something away from various property-owners. Secondly, as my colleague Jan Narveson has argued, the level of compensation will probably have to be set high enough to amount to a tidy guaranteed annual income. Thirdly, it isn't clear how much compensation is to be given to any particular propertyless person. Does he get as much as he would have been likely to get if he were in the position of the last person who acquired property or as much as if he were the first person to acquire property? In either case, the primary basis for distribution (his acquisitiveness) seems suspiciously patterned. Fourth, if the benefits of a free market economy really do provide enough compensation, then why does it seem so unlikely that anyone who has more than a little property, e.g., E.P. Taylor, would want to change places with one of these people who can't acquire any property because everything is owned?

All of which suggests that on a *pure* entitlement theory—one which is based on historical entitlement—there would be no room for the Proviso. On a pure entitlement theory if you are born after all the accessible and useful unowned objects have been taken up by your predecessors, you are simply out of luck. The denial of the Proviso would also seem to be in agreement with Nozick's criticisms of Rawls' contention that a system of natural liberties allows distribution on morally arbitrary grounds—that the distribution of natural talents is not on the basis of desert leads Rawls to design the social system to compensate for this "arbitrariness" by favouring (other things being equal) the least talented in the distribution of goods. Nozick criticises this as a "manna-from-heaven" model that totally ignores who has made these goods, i.e., Rawls ignores the crucial fact of historical entitlement. Similarly, the Proviso seems to ignore the crucial fact of appropriation.

Finally, as in the Spoilage Argument, we can ask what it is to leave "enough and as good"? If the standard is *usability*, then do we adopt the native peoples' idea of what is usable or the non-native immigrants? If we defend the latter, then in effect we are denying native peoples their ways of life. According to the Proviso, this would seem to demand that we compensate the native peoples for that loss. Yet is that something for which adequate compensation is possible other than allowing them to maintain their standards of use and so their way of life? Would not "the base line for comparison" be very high indeed then?

F.4. The Invalid Acquisition Arguments. In both the Spoilage and Proviso Arguments, aboriginal title was challenged on the grounds that Indians and Inuit had acquired too much, i.e., more than they were entitled to acquire. It is possible to raise a different objection by claiming that they failed to acquire anything or scarcely anything at all. The heart of this contention is that native peoples did not perform the appropriate acquisitive acts. We get a variety of objections of this kind based on different views of what is an appropriate act of acquisition, that is depending on what sorts of human actions bring things out of a state of ownerlessness into a state of property. Before trying to get this argument off the ground, it is worth noting that both Nozick and Locke start with the assumption that before individual acquisition things are in an ownerless condition (the *res nullis* doctrine); there is another school of thought that assumes that before private acquisition takes place, things are held in common by all men (the *res communae* doctrine).

The major problem in raising this objection is fixing on some kind(s) of action that can be plausibly regarded as acts of original acquisition, i.e., upon the *rites* that generate property *rights*. Nozick raises very serious problems about Locke's criterion for owner-ship, namely that one owns that with which one has mixed one's labour. He asks about the boundaries of such an acquisition:

> If a private astronaut clears a place on Mars, has he mixed his labour with (so that he comes to own) the whole planet, the whole uninhabited universe, or just a particular plot?

Nozick also asks why mixing one's labour with something isn't simply throwing one's labour away, and if it isn't, then why should one have title to more than the value (if any) added by one's labour? If "mixing labour" is the acquisitive act, then surely these and related questions must be convincingly answered if entitlement theory is to proceed.

We have already seen that if usage is made the standard there are serious problems in determining whose standard of use should prevail. In fact, it would seem that an entitlement theorist should shy away from recognising usage as the acquisitive action, for anyone could take your title to X away from you by finding a better use of X (if you are already using it) or putting it to use for the first time (if you haven't used it yet). I would think that an entitlement theorist should say that it is solely up to X's owner whether and to what use X shall be put. Yet it is Locke who denies that the Indians of America have any ownership rights beyond what they use for food and clothing; English settlers have rights to the land itself because they till it. In short, Locke denies aboriginal rights because the Indians don't use the land in the same way as the English immigrants.

Perhaps, then, it will be suggested that acquisitive actions are *conventional*—literally consisting in the conventions (customs or laws) of a particular people. Thus in one society you own only what you actually have in hand or on your person at the moment, while in another you own whatever bears your mark, and in still another society you own only those things entered in the central ownership registry. Of course, there will be problems when societies with different ownership conventions each want to make exclusive use of the same objects. Each society (assuming no overlap in conventions) can say that the other society's people haven't really acquired the goods in question because of a failure to follow the appropriate conventions. I do not see how an entitlement theorist can say which set of conventions (in part, presumably, adopted for non-arbitrary reasons having to do with different patterns of usage) should prevail on the basis of entitlement theory; it seems to me that he must resort to patterned and, in the end, possibly redistributivist considerations. I think it is on the basis of these considerations that our society will have to deal with the contention (if it can be proven) that the Indian treaties are invalid because the whites and the Indians had totally different conceptions of ownership.

Conclusions

First, I hope to have shown in my consideration of entitlement theory that a number of plausible objections to it (A) through (E), can be answered. These are essentially peripheral objections. Once we get to the core of the theory, however, serious and, I would maintain, insurmountable problems arise. The entitlement theory of original acquisition cannot be maintained without resort to non-entitlement considerations—patterns, end-results, and pure conventions. To cleanse

entitlement theory of these additions will make it so unattractive that it cannot be accepted as a theory of justice in holdings.

Secondly, and somewhat surprisingly, I think that I have made out the case for aboriginal rights. I claim that this country ought to recognise aboriginal rights *on the basis of original acquisition*. Of course, this conclusion depends on the validity of my claim that the only rationale that is advanced and is plausible for the present system of holdings in Canada is entitlement theory. I contend that it is on the basis of entitlement theory alone, that we could ever hope to justify the way in which most holdings are distributed in Canada. Just because entitlement theory won't work does not mean that our society won't proceed as if it does. The argument for aboriginal rights is provisional. But it ought to obtain until we are willing to redistribute holdings in this country on a truly just basis.

Questions for Discussion

1 Do McDonald's arguments establish that past injustices cannot simply be ignored? Would his arguments be sufficient to refute the "just in our time" policy Trudeau advocates?

2 Can theories of justice (such as the entitlement theory, or whatever "truly just" system of distribution we come up with to replace it) simply be applied to aboriginal peoples, or must we take note of the fact that aboriginal cultures might not accept the dominant culture's notions of justice or ownership? Is it appropriate to consider *how* to divide ownership of things such as land, when some people do not believe land can be owned at all?

Aboriginal Peoples and the Canadian Charter

Mary Ellen Turpel

The following is excerpted from an article in which Turpel raises doubts about the applicability of a legal system based on a particular culture (European) to other cultures, in particular those of aboriginal peoples.

★   ★   ★

The Rights Paradigm

The whole fabric of rights discourse constitutes the more subtle level at which the undifferentiated legal framework displays its cultural imagery. The struggle over the division of social, political, and economic power in Canadian society has been formulated by the Charter as a set of rights claims or as a dispute over rights in order to give it constitutional currency. Even multiculturalism operates as an interpretive rider on rights analysis in the Charter. Sections 25 and 27 of the Charter, the interpretation provisions on aboriginal and treaty rights and multiculturalism, are said to take account of cultural differences in constitutional human rights conflicts.[1] It is significant to note that these are provisions within a rights-focused framework of legal analysis. Consequently, any consideration of cultural differences suggested by sections 25 and 27 will be formulated within the predetermined mode of reasoning, central to Anglo-European legal discourse, of rights claims or claims against the state. These provisions do attempt to address differences or "otherness," from within the dominant or prevalent method of resolving legal conflicts. It is noteworthy, however, that they are construed as exceptional or special provisions within the rights-based dominant style of analysis. Hence, we are in the realm of the special, exceptional, or "other" in section 25, and arguably in section 27, rather than in the realm of the fun-

damentally different, incongruous, or incommensurable. Arguments for multiculturalism are particularly offensive because they presume differences to be "minority" matters that are manageable, interpretively, from within the majority-conceived scheme of the Charter. This is an aberration to aboriginal people because it does not recognize the fundamental challenge presented by cultural difference to the rights approach to social conflicts.[2]

Because the rights regime is dominant, sanctioned and elevated as the supreme law, it must filter all conflicts through its categories and conceptual apparatus. The rights regime dominates the culturally different interpretive communities by using its own conceptual framework to apply the provisions of the Charter to "others" even though these provisions may be interpreted in a "special" way. It decides for those it doesn't understand, using a framework that undermines their objectives. It performs a levitation trick by transforming differences into rights within the supreme law of Canada.

To what extent can a rights paradigm of analysis be viable universally? Is it shared by culturally different peoples? I suggest that the "rights" analysis and imagery is a projection of an exclusionary cultural or political self-image. In situating this assertion in the context of aboriginal peoples, I am faced with the fact that rights discourse has been widely appropriated by aboriginal peoples in struggles

Ethical Issues

against the effects of colonialism, and that we have been encouraged to do so. Here it is important to distinguish arguments that are made for aboriginal peoples by legal scholars who do not share a common ancestry or culture with those for whom they write, from the much smaller body of literature by aboriginal persons.[3] This distinction is critical because just as cultural difference is acknowledged, aboriginal peoples are faced with a response, at least from the legal community that is ostensibly "supportive," that unwittingly perpetuates their domination through a false reconciliation of differences. For example, in the introduction to a pair of recent articles by W. Pentney, one finds a general disclaimer to the effect that his work on the Charter was written from the perspective of a supporter and that it is entirely conceivable that many aboriginal peoples would not share/understand his perspective.[4] However, in the text, this modesty seems to be effaced by the legal analysis advanced. He constructs an argument that by-passes cultural differences and advances a thesis that assumes that if only better legal tests were developed to balance collective and individual rights, and more care were taken to define aboriginal rights, the problems with the culturally hegemonic self-image of the Charter could be conceivably resolved.[5] The task is frequently formulated as one of better thinking, more rigorous analysis, and consciousness-building in order to decide how to "apply" the constitution to aboriginal peoples. This style, even, as here, in its best-intentioned form, has provoked frustration and criticism from aboriginal writers, many of whom would suggest that the legal arguments simply mask social and political conflicts between aboriginal peoples and the Canadian state, concealing the painful experiences of aboriginal peoples under bureaucratic rule. An expression of the sense of domination felt by aboriginal people when someone from "outside" the cultural framework sets out to solve and reconcile con-

flicts is expressed in an article by Patricia Monture.[6] She writes:

> Following this tradition of oral history and storytelling, I want to share one of my experiences with you. Like most other academics, I spent at least a little bit of my time going to conferences, listening to other people, and learning and sharing what we are thinking. This is a story about a conference I attended, a legal conference, that I want to tell you. It is also a story about anger. My anger is not unique to this conference; it is paralleled at many other conferences I have been to and the classes I have been to, most other days in my life, so it is an important story.... [She relates her reaction to a discussion of a racial incident].... *This is my life.* I do not have any control over the pain and brutality of living the life of a dispossessed person. I cannot control when that pain is going to enter my life. I had gone away for this conference quite settled with having to deal with racism, pure and simple. But, I was not ready to have my pain appropriated. I am pretty possessive about my pain. It is my pain. I worked hard for it. Some days it is all I have. Some days it is the only thing I can feel. Do not try to take that away from me too. That was what was happening to me in that discussion. My pain was being taken away from me and put on the table and poked and prodded with these sticks, these hypotheticals. "Let's see what happened next." I felt very much under a microscope, even if it was not my own personal experience that was being examined.[7]

Monture's description of pain at having racism discussed dispassionately, or as a technical or unconflicted analysis is interesting because it points to the inability of legal categories and descriptions to account for the lived experiences of aboriginal peoples in Canada. Moreover, it suggests the possibility that assistance aimed at human rights progress may actually be part of the oppression aboriginal peoples experience.[8]

It is interesting to me that, in other disciplines, apart from law, cultural differences have been approached in a way that is contrary to current legal analyses. They have not been "interpreted" as gaps in one's knowledge of a discipline or discourse, waiting to be filled with conceptual bridges and extensions, but rather as irreconcilable or irreducible elements of human relations. Barbara Johnson, for example, in a recent work on literary theory, observes the following of her experience of difference:

> If I perceive my ignorance as a gap in knowledge instead of an imperative that changes the very nature of what I think I know, then I do not truly experience my ignorance. The surprise of otherness is that moment when a new form of ignorance is suddenly activated as an imperative.[9]

The perception of cultural difference as an imperative that may loosen or shift the paradigm of knowledge, rather than a cognitive gap to be filled, is one that has not yet been taken seriously in legal analysis or interpretation vis-à-vis the cultural differences of aboriginal peoples. What would the implications of a Johnson-type sensibility be for the legal discourse? I contend that it would problematize the conceptual basis of the rights paradigm in Canadian legal analysis because concepts, such as the rule of law, human rights, and judicial impartiality, would be seen more as culturally-specific beliefs rather than universally applicable concepts. As Raymond Williams suggests of this shift for political theory and literature:

> When the most basic concepts—the concepts, as it is said, from which we begin—are suddenly seen to be not concepts but problems, not analytic problems either but historical movements that are still unresolved, there is no sense listening to their sonorous summons or their resounding clashes. We have only, if we can, to recover the substance from which their forms were cas[t].[10]

Williams captures, in my view, the effect of the imperative of cultural difference. When we think of cultural differences between aboriginal peoples and the Canadian state and its legal system, we must think of these as problems of conceptual reference for which there is no common grounding or authoritative foothold. Necessarily, we can't "decide" the substance of cultural differences from a position of a particular institutional and conceptual cultural framework; each culture is capable of sensitivity to the basic condition of difference, and should develop cross-cultural relations accordingly. To what extent is the rights paradigm of constitutional analysis a conceptual framework for the toleration of, or sensitivity toward, cultural difference? To answer this question at least two lines of inquiry need to be pursued: what is the conceptual-historical basis of the rights paradigm, and how do aboriginal peoples use rights terminology?

The human rights paradigm in Canadian constitutional discourse is clearly a product of the political theories of natural rights developed in Europe during the seventeenth century. Despite recurring references to a collectivist orientation of society, most often cited in attempts to differentiate Canada from the United States, individualism arguably derived from Locke and Hobbes underpins the Charter.[11] While I do not want to suggest that an exploration of the origins of the paradigm is dispositive in any way, it does seem significant that the rights conception developed in Europe, and especially for Canadian constitutional purposes, in England in the later seventeenth century. Moreover, the conceptual basis of rights analysis in notions of property and exclusive ownership are critical factors in the tension between rights discourse and cultural difference.

Thomas Hobbes and John Locke developed theories of "natural rights" based on the argument that one key purpose for entering civil society was the protection of private

Ethical Issues

property. Locke suggested that every *man* (and emphasis should be on *man* because Locke should be infamous for his theory that society was naturally patriarchal) possesses a right of property ownership. This right, he reasoned, flowed logically from the fact that human beings are God's property. He argued that people enter into "civil society" for the central, and negatively conceived, purpose of protecting their interest or claim to private property against random attack from other persons.

The idea of the absolute right to property, as an exclusive zone of ownership, capable of being transmitted through the family (through males according to the doctrine of "primo-genitor"), is arguably the cornerstone of the idea of rights in Anglo-American law. Rights are seen as a special zone of exclusion where the individual is protected against harm from others. Obviously, this is a highly individualistic and negative concept of social life based on the fear of attack on one's "private" sphere. It provides something of a basis, however, for all ideas about rights—the idea that there is a zone of absolute individual rights where the individual can do what she chooses. As Roberto Unger has suggested:

> The right is a loaded gun that the right-holder may shoot at will in his corner of town.... The property right was the very model of right generally. The consolidated property right had to be a zone of absolute discretion. In this zone, the right-holder could avoid any tangle to claims to mutual responsibility. It was natural that this conception of right should be extended to all rights.[12]

The imagery of the property-based right to exclude surfaces rather revealingly in Charter rights jurisprudence. With property rights metaphors at hand, the Supreme Court of Canada in the recent *Morgentaler* case on the Criminal Code provisions on abortion, suggested that

> [t]he Charter is predicated on a particular conception of the place of the individual in

society. An individual is not a totally independent entity disconnected from the society in which he or she lives. Neither, however, is the individual a mere cog in an impersonal machine in which his or her values, goals, and aspirations are subordinated to those of the collectivity. The individual is a bit of both. The Charter reflects this reality by leaving a wide range of activities and decisions open to legitimate government control while at the same time placing limits on the proper scope of that control. Thus, the rights guaranteed in the Charter erect around each individual, metaphorically speaking, an invisible fence over which the state will not be allowed to trespass.... The role of the courts is to map out, piece by piece, the parameters of the fence.[13]

The metaphors of the fence, mapping, and trespassings are so property-specific and exclusionary in character that they can only be construed as symptoms of acute Locke-jaw.

Notions of protection from social/legal intrusion, a classical concept of liberty, seem to have a common conceptual origin in or nexus with property rights. The idea that rights are necessary to protect one's "rightful" corner of town, to restrain the ill-intentioned from depriving someone of their corner, is also an important justificatory argument for rights claims in contemporary legal and political theory. The extension of this notion of a natural right to property to other forms of social relations (and conceptions of the private) arguably precedes the rights paradigm formalized in the Charter. It emphasizes a liberal conception of social life where the maximization of wealth and happiness through self-interest is the guiding creed. Ironically, liberal notions of property and self-interest regulate the general character of Canadian political discourse. They are likewise evident in legal texts and in their interpretation where debates over individualism and collectivism find expression.[14]

There is no policy that is purely individualistic or purely collectivist. A binary coupling of these characteristics implies a kind of dialectical hierarchy. I would suggest that the individual description is integrally privileged in the rights paradigm and that collectivist considerations are merely supplementary. However, I would take issue with some scholars on their projection of "society" as an either-or, and caution against an attempt to typify, for example, an aboriginal society in such a fashion.[15]

The Canadian human rights system, and in particular the Charter, having been distanced in time from what I would construe as the conceptual basis of rights theories—that is, the natural right to individual ownership of property—seems a little less hostile to and perhaps even supportive of cultural difference, especially since so much is said of aboriginal matters in the context of interpretations of provisions of the Charter. Some scholars argue extensively that the Charter has recognized certain collective rights, such as aboriginal rights and language rights, and that this has taken legal conceptions of rights in Canada far beyond the "individualistic" basis of rights that find their origin in property notions.

There are two aspects of the collective rights stream of legal scholarship on the Charter that I would call into question in the context of cultural difference. The first is the tendency to conceptualize collective rights, and arguments for collectivist considerations, as "oughts": perhaps persuasive, but at this point only apologies for suggested directions. Scholars in this camp serve as wishful legislative "spin doctors." The second is the extent to which these arguments are responsive to cultural differences vis-à-vis aboriginal peoples when made on their behalf, presuming that aboriginal peoples can unproblematically engage in the abstract, adversarial legal process for the "granting" of such rights. In other words, the problem, identified earlier, is that of using an(other) language and conceptual apparatus (the Canadian legal system) to further an understanding of a different system of belief.

On the first issue, I would suggest that if current political and economic arrangements are any indication, the scope for respect of cultural differences is more theoretical than actual in the case of aboriginal peoples.[16] The main difference which is tolerated, albeit with considerable strain, in Canadian federalism is the French linguistic/cultural difference inside of Quebec and, to a lesser extent, outside of that province. Indeed, the tale of two founding nations present at Confederation, accepted uncritically in Canadian legal discourse, while often trotted out in support of "collective rights"-style arguments, is a position particularly disrespectful of the cultural and political differences of aboriginal peoples.[17] For the most part, Canada is defined politically as two primary and distinct cultures and languages that form the centrepiece of nationhood, with multiple decorator cultures as embellishing addenda. This is not to belittle the differences that have been nominally formalized in legislation, but to question why cultural difference means different compared with either or both of the two privileged solitudes.[18]

One can understand why aboriginal peoples reacted so strongly to the distinct society clause, section 2(1)(b), of the 1987 constitutional (Meech Lake) accord.[19] As the Assembly of First Nations suggested in their reaction to the clause:

> It perpetuates the idea of a duality in Canada and strengthens the myth that the French and English peoples are the foundation of Canada. It neglects the original inhabitants and distorts history. It is as if the peoples of the first nations never existed. It suggests that historically and presently as well the French peoples in Quebec form the *only* distinct society in Canada. The amendment fails to give explicit constitutional recognition to the existence of first nations as distinct societies that also

form a fundamental characteristic of Canada....We were told for five years that governments are reluctant to entrench undefined self-government of aboriginal peoples in the constitution. Yet, here is an equally vague idea of a "distinct society" unanimously agreed to and allowed to be left to the courts for interpretation.[20]

Apart from the apparent subterfuge of the Meech Lake Accord, the collective rights position is put forth with built-in restrictions in legal scholarship. For example, Joseph Magnet, in an article on collective rights, suggests that

[t]he spirit of Canada's constitution is rooted in the principle of bi-nationality. Canada's federal system proceeds directly from the requirements of a bi-national state.[21]

Perhaps the tolerance of a collective difference within Confederation is the result of the scope of that difference. Could it be that differences will be tolerated, respected, and even formally enshrined provided they are differences arising from a common (European) ancestry?

Some arguments for collective rights view them as logical extensions of real—that is, individual rights. In this line of reasoning, individual rights serve as the conceptual source of collective rights. Hence, by common sense, constitutional provisions that protect individual rights will protect collectivities. Even those of such persuasion would not seriously suggest that the Charter is strictly (textually) an individualist document.[22] But the extent to which one can argue that there is any framework, conceptual and institutional, within which to seek recognition of such diverse collective-based interests is, in my view, very limited at present. Furthermore, the extent to which it would be desirable to do so, especially for aboriginal peoples, is questionable given the issue raised earlier of the ability of the rights paradigm to deal with cultural differences. As Canada pins multiculturalism on its chest, the dominant European culture continues presumptively to set the terms of tolerance for collective differences.

Notes

1 These sections provide:

> Section 25: The guarantees in this Charter of certain rights and freedoms shall not be construed so as to abrogate or derogate from any aboriginal, treaty or other rights or freedoms that pertain to the aboriginal peoples of Canada including (1) any right of freedoms that have been recognized by the Royal Proclamation of October 7, 1763, and (b) any rights or freedoms that now exist by way of land claims agreements or may be so acquired.
>
> Section 27: This Charter shall be interpreted in a manner consistent with the preservation and enhancement of the multicultural heritage of Canadians.

Also, section 35, in Part II of the Constitution Act, 1982, provides:

> (1) The existing aboriginal and treaty rights of the aboriginal peoples of Canada are herby recognized and affirmed.
> (2) In this Act, aboriginal peoples of Canada includes the Indian, Inuit and Métis peoples of Canada.
> (3) For greater certainty, in subsection (1) "treaty rights" includes rights that now exist by way of land claims agreements or may be so acquired.
> (4) Notwithstanding any other provision of this Act, the aboriginal and treaty rights referred to in subsection (1) are guaranteed equally to male and female persons.

2 As D. Sanders, "Article 27 and Aboriginal Peoples of Canada," (in *Multiculturalism and the Charter: A Legal Perspective.* Toronto: Carswell, 1987.) suggests (p. 156),

> Frequently Indian leaders have rejected the terms "ethnic" or "cultural minority" as inadequate to describe the special situation of indigenous peoples. They assert a uniqueness which they feel is denied by terms that equate them to Irish Catholics or Chinese. The rejection of such categories was rather sharply put by Brooklyn

Rivera, the Miskito Indian leader from Nicaragua, when he said "Ethnic groups run restaurants; we are nations of people."

3 Examples in the former category are numerous and part of a growth industry. See, as a sampling, Cumming, "Rights of Indigenous Peoples: A Comparative Analysis" (1974), 68 *ASIL Proc.* 265; B. Morse, *Aboriginal Self-Government in Australia and Canada* (Kingston: Institute of Intergovernmental Relations, 1984); Sanders, "Aboriginal Peoples and the Constitution" (1981), 19 *Alberta L.R.* 410; Slattery, "The Constitutional Guarantee of Aboriginal and Treaty Rights" (1983), 8 *Queens L.J.* 232; and Wildsmith, "Pre-Confederation Treaties," in Morse, ed., *Aboriginal Peoples and the Law* (Ottawa: Carleton University Press, 1985), 122. Scholarship in the aboriginal community includes, as a sampling, B. Richardson, ed. *Drumbeat: Anger and Renewal in Indian Country* (Summerhill Press, 1989); G. Manuel and M. Posluns, *The Fourth World: An Indian Reality* (Don Mills: Collier-Macmillan, 1974); V. Deloria, Jr. and C. Lytle, *The Nations Within: The Past and Future of American Indian Sovereignty* (New York: Pantheon Books, 1984); Henderson, "Unravelling the Riddle of Aboriginal Title" (1977), 5 *Am. Indian L. Rev.* 75; Chartier, "Aboriginal Rights and Land Issues: The Métis Perspective," in Boldt and Long, eds., *The Quest for Justice: Aboriginal Peoples and Aboriginal Rights* (Toronto: University of Toronto Press, 1985), 54; Monture, see infra note [6]; and Gunn-Allen, *The Sacred Hoop* (Boston: Beacon Press, 1986).

4 William Pentney, "The Rights of the Aboriginal Peoples of Canada in the Constitution Act, 1982: Part I—The Interpretive Prism of Section 25" (1988), 22 *U.B.C.L.Rev.* 21, and "Part II Section 35: The Substantive Guarantee" (1988) 22 *U.B.C.L.Rev.* 207.

5 Pentney, ibid., in Part II, at 278, concludes by suggesting that:

The key challenge that remains is to translate the theoretical generalities presented here into arguments in concrete cases, for it is only by this process that sections 25 and 35 of the Constitution Act, 1982 can serve to enhance the rights of the aboriginal peoples of Canada.

And in Part I, at 59, he concludes that:

The illustrations...should operate in a Charter case. It is an interpretive prism,

and the refraction which it provides will protect the rights and freedoms of the aboriginal peoples of Canada.

6 Patricia Monture, "Ka-Nin-Geh-Heh-Gah-E-Sa-Nonh-Yah-Gah" (1986), 2 *C.J.W.L.* 159.

7 Ibid., at 160 and 163-64.

8 For an explanation of this idea in another cultural context, see A.D. Freeman, "Legitimizing Racial Discrimination Through Anti-discrimination Law: A Critical Review of Supreme Court Doctrine" (1978), 62 *Minn.L.Rev.* 1049. Freeman's dialogue (at 1049-50, footnotes omitted) in his analysis attempts to capture he ironical effect of anti-discrimination law:

THE LAW: "Black American rejoice! Racial Discrimination has now become illegal."
BLACK AMERICANS: "Great, we who have no jobs want them. We who have lousy jobs want better ones. We whose kids go to black schools want to choose integrated schools if we think that would be better for our kids, or want enough money to make our own schools work. We want political power roughly proportionate to our population. And many of us want houses in the suburbs."
THE LAW: "You can't have any of those things. You can't assert your claim against society in general, but only against a named discriminator, and you've got to show that you are an individual victim of that discrimination and that you were intentionally discriminated against. And be sure to demonstrate how that discrimination has caused your problem, for any remedy must be co-extensive with the violation. Be careful your claim does not impinge on some other cherished American value, like local autonomy of the suburbs, or previously distributed vested rights, or selection on the basis of merit. Most important, do not demand any remedy involving racial balance or proportionality; to recognize such claims would be racist."

9 Barbara Johnson, *A World of Difference.*

10 Raymond Williams, *Marxism and Literature*, (Oxford: Oxford University Press, 1981), at 213.

11 Whose two most important works, respectively are: John Locke, *Two Treatises of Civil Government* (1690) and Thomas Hobbes, *Leviathan* (1651)

12 Roberto Unger, *The Critical Legal Studies Movement* (Cambridge: Harvard University Press, 1986), at 36 and 38.

13 Madame Justice Wilson writing in *Morgentaler, Smoling & Scott v. The Queen & Attorney General of Canada*, [1988] 1 S.C.R. 30, at 164; (1988) 82 N.R. 1, at 116; and (1988) 44 D.L.R. (4th) 385, at 485.

14 I do not want to get embroiled in the individualist versus collectivist description of Canadian society. See for example Patrick Monahan, *Politics and the Constitution: The Charter, Federalism and the Supreme Court of Canada* (Toronto: Carswell, 1987).

15 Ibid. Although Monahan does not explicitly do so, his employment of the metaphor of society, which implies a kind of totality of Canada, would seem to overlook cultural differences and their relation to the binary of individual versus collective.

16 Here I would note that the scholarly legal arguments suggesting Canada is a society respectful of difference, and indeed built on it, are largely reflective of a body of historical work along the same theme. It is interesting to me that this body of literature tends to focus on French-English differences ("two solitudes") as the primary cultural difference in Canada, generally effacing the arguably more radical (non-European) difference between either of those cultures and the First Nations. See, for example, A.R.M. Lower, "Two Ways of Life: The Primary Antithesis of Canadian History," in R. Cook, C. Brown and C. Berger, eds., *Contemporary Approaches to Canadian History* (Toronto: University of Toronto Press, 1987), at 1.

17 See Manuel and Posluns, *The Fourth World*, supra note [3], who ask:

> Why should there be a different kind of equality for us Indian people than for the other groups of Canadians who share both a common history and a common territory in the way a province occupies a single territory? Yet I can only imagine that our relationship with this land and with one another is far deeper and more complex than the relationship between the people of any province and their institutions, or one another. Nor can the Indian peoples be brushed off with the multicultural broom to join the diverse ethnic

groups that compose the Third Element of Canada, that is, those who are neither French nor English.

18 I am reminded of the bitter closing remarks of Métis leader Jim Sinclair at the final failed sessions of First Ministers' constitutional discussions on Aboriginal Rights in March 1986 when he prophesied that the Prime Minister and Premiers who had rejected aboriginal peoples would soon "take care of their own" and bring Quebec explicitly into constitutional agreement. Of course, within a year, that same congenial confederation family left Meech Lake with an accord recognizing Quebec as a distinct society in Canada.

19 This section of the Accord provides that the Constitution of Canada shall be interpreted in a manner consistent with "the recognition that Quebec constitutes within Canada a distinct society."

20 Assembly of First Nations, position paper on the Meech Lake Accord, 1987 (unpublished).

21 Joseph Magnet, "Collective Rights, Cultural Autonomy and the Canadian State" (1986), 32 *McGill L.J.* 170, at 172.

22 The individualist-collectivist debate in many ways betrays the descriptive poverty of so much constitutional scholarship. Two absolutist, parable-like claims are cast as either/or. Evidently, scholars feel quite strongly that one or the other should prevail. However, I would question the validity of this restricting choice and its cultural relativity. See Monahan, supra note [14], at 95, and Schwartz, *First Principles, Second Thoughts: Aboriginal Peoples, Constitutional Reform and Canadian Statecraft* (Montreal: Institute for Research on Public Policy, 1986), at 366.

Questions for Discussion

1 Is Turpel correct that human rights are not universal, but rather products of a particular culture which cannot properly be imposed on other cultures?

2 Is it true that merely engaging in the legal dialogue in which the majority culture deals, forces members of minority cultures to abandon their cultural understandings of the world? If so, what consequences does this have for the possibility of communication across cultures?

Canadian Nationalism and the Distinctiveness Fetish

Thomas Hurka

Many of the issues surrounding multiculturalism revolve around the presence of many cultures within one nation. Questions can also be raised, however, about the allegiance many people feel to one nation rather than another (which might be called "nationalism"). In this article, Thomas Hurka examines Canadian nationalism. He claims that such nationalism is often framed in terms of what is distinct about Canada, but he argues that this is a mistaken (and even somewhat "nasty") way to think about nationalism.

★ ★ ★

Canadians care about medicare; it's a source of national pride and central to our attachment to Canada. Some Canadians care especially about medicare because they think it's distinctive of Canada, at least as compared with the United States. But it's an odd idea: that we should care most about what's distinctively Canadian, as so many discussions of Canadian nationalism assume. Would medicare matter less if the U.S. had it too?

It isn't hard to imagine. John F. Kennedy might not have been assassinated in 1963; Hubert Humphrey might have been elected president in 1968. Either might have instituted full medicare in the U.S. If he had, our own medicare would be less distinctive. To think Canadian nationalism must focus on what's distinctively Canadian is to think Canadian medicare would then be less important. But that's to misunderstand the basis of healthy national feelings.

Nationalism is a form of partiality, of caring more about some people than about others. A Canadian nationalist cares more about relieving poverty among his fellow Canadians than among foreigners; he wants immigration policy decided mainly by its effects on people now in Canada. In this respect nationalism is like other forms of partiality, such as caring more about your spouse or children than about strangers, and can be understood by analogy with them.

If you care specially about your spouse, it's partly for some of their qualities: their intelligence, trustworthiness, and so on. But you know these qualities aren't unique. Other people have them, some even to a higher degree. What attaches you specially to your spouse is something that isn't a quality in the normal sense. It's their having participated with you in a shared history. No one else, no matter how intelligent or trustworthy, could be the very person you fell in love with that summer, who helped you through that depression, and who did all those other things with you.

Nationalism has a similar basis. A Canadian nationalist thinks Canada has good qualities, like a commitment to tolerance and equality. But he needn't think Canada is the best country in the world. What ties him specially to his fellow-Canadians is something historical: that they grew up with him here, experiencing the same weather and TV shows, electing and then despising the same politicians.

That's why it wouldn't matter if the U.S. too had medicare. Canadian medicare would still be a good thing about Canada, and it would still be part of our history. It would be something we developed, from Tommy Douglas and Emmett Hall through the Canada Health Act. It would be something we've all participated in, both as users of medicare and as contributors to it. American medicare might be similar, but it wouldn't be the system we've lived with here.

So it's a mistake to tie Canadian nationalism to distinctively Canadian qualities. And it isn't a harmless mistake. It's had several destructive effects on Canadian national life.

First, it's led many Canadians to embrace false beliefs about their country. It's often said that Canada is, distinctively, a country of diverse regions, not just Quebec compared to English Canada but every province compared to the others. But do we really believe that, say, Nova Scotia is more different from Alberta than Scotland is from England, or than northern India is from southern India? Reverting to medicare, do we think we're the only country in the world with social programs?

Some nationalists recognize that in the world as a whole Canada is a fairly average industrial democracy. But they say the point isn't to be distinctive in the world. It's to be distinctive in North America, to be an egalitarian or sharing society in the same region as the U.S. That's because the U.S. isn't just another country. It's our immensely powerful neighbour and the source of our constant existential question: why aren't we part of them? Only as distinct from the behemoth to the south does Canada have a reason to exist.

But there's no such existential question. Canadians have no interest in joining the U.S., as they show repeatedly in opinion polls. And it's not because of any bogus ideas about distinctiveness. (They root for Canadian sprinters at the Olympics without wondering whether they sprint in a distinctively Canadian way.) Think again about your spouse and children. Do you face a constant question about whether to join the family next door, just because they have a bigger house or more money? Of course not. You're attached to your

family by a history your neighbours don't share, and that's attachment enough.

Second, the distinctiveness fetish has corrupted Canadian politics, offering an all-purpose counter to any proposal: "That will lead to the Americanization of Canada." This counter is used by the left to oppose privatization and deficit-cutting and by the right to oppose employment equity and the Charter of Rights. But if something American is bad, it has to be bad for some reason other than that it's American. So let's hear that other reason. And may some American things not be good?

Or consider Prime Minister Jean Chrétien's remark that Canada without Quebec is unthinkable. It assumes that Canada is thinkable only if it's distinct from the U.S., and will be less distinct without Quebec. But the assumption, again, is false. Canada without Quebec would be a smaller Canada; it would lack, tragically, many people who participated in our history. But it would have no more reason to break up than a family would after one member runs away.

Also corrupted is commentary on the arts, which often assumes the main point of Canadian art is to express what's distinctively Canadian. This view is hard to apply to arts like music. How does a classical violinist play Beethoven in a distinctively Canadian way? And it's even constricting when applied to literature. There are uniquely Canadian experiences, and literature that captures them can be as great as any literature anywhere. But there are also universal experiences, such as falling in love, aging, and death. Writing exploring those experiences can likewise be great; if it's by a Canadian, that makes it ours.

Canadian nationalism hasn't always been based on ideas about distinctiveness. Think of the nationalism of the years following the Second World War, based on Canada's participation in that war. Canadians of the late 1940s didn't think they had fought in a war no one else had fought, or even fought in a distinctive way. It was enough that they—people with a common history—had fought alongside other nations and fought well.

This older nationalism was healthier than any current version based on distinctiveness. To care that your nation's good qualities be distinctive is to care both that your nation have them and that other nations do not. (The second, by the logic of distinctiveness, is just as important as the first.) But isn't it nasty to want other nations not to share your own's good qualities. Isn't it a kind of malice?

Distinctiveness nationalists should ask themselves whether they aren't prone to this malice. Do they take a kind of comfort from the violence and inequality of the U.S., just because they make Canada different? Are they partly pleased when Newt Gingrich and Pat Buchanan have political successes in the U.S., because they wouldn't have them here? If so, their ill-wishing only works through the nasty logic of distinctiveness.

But Canadian nationalism needn't be nasty. We can, while recognizing Canada's weaknesses, treasure its good qualities and hope other nations share them. We can want all na-

tions to respect human rights and practise tolerance; we can hope the U.S. one day becomes less violent and even institutes medicare. If it does, Canada will be less distinctive. But that won't matter to Canadians freed of fraudulent ideas about distinctiveness and attached to each other, as to their families, by the solid bond of a common history.

Questions for Discussion

1 To what extent are relationships of love and friendship based on a shared history? What other factors come into play? Is a sense of nationalism like or unlike love and friendship in this regard?

2 Could the fact that geographical regions differ in things such as climate and resources justify a sense that residents of one area can be distinct from residents of other areas? Can such differences account for the importance of "distinctiveness" to nationalism?

3 Is it a mistake for Canadian nationalists to focus on ways in which Canada is different from the United States?

4 Is Hurka right that being a Canadian nationalist amounts to caring more about Canadians than about other people? If so, is Canadian nationalism morally justifiable?

CHAPTER 9

Ethics and the Use of Violence

Of the many capacities common to human beings, the capacity to act violently toward other human beings is often thought to be among the worst. Nevertheless, many people believe that there are situations in which the use of physical force against other humans can be justified. These situations might include cases of individual self-defense, cases of individual or state punishment of wrongdoing, and cases of "just warfare," perhaps even including justified acts of terrorism. This chapter will examine several of these aspects of the allegedly justified use of violence.

Some background information about the traditional debates on these issues might help in understanding the ensuing discussions. I begin with the so-called "just war theory," which attempts to specify the conditions under which a war can justifiably be fought.

The "just war" tradition, as it is now understood, had its roots among some of the classic Christian theologians, such as Augustine, Aquinas, Vitoria and Suarez. The

general problem stemmed from the fact that it was considered a sin to harm or kill other human beings, and yet war inevitably involved such harm or killing. One clear policy option, then, was "pacifism," or the view that one should not engage in the use of force under any circumstances, and in particular one should never engage in war.

On the other hand, questions arise about how one should respond if somebody else is violating the prohibition against harming and killing. If I see an innocent person being threatened by the injustice of another, and I could do something to protect that innocent person, do I not have some sort of obligation to do what I can to protect the person? If the answer in general is "Yes, I do have such an obligation," then what becomes of that obligation if the only means I have for stopping the injustice is the use of force? If the force were directed at me, perhaps I could claim a right to self-defense. Could there be some analogy with self-defense which would justify the use of force against an unjust aggressor?

The classic theologians believed that there could be conditions under which the use of force would be justified. They were concerned, however, to maintain the force of the basic prohibition on killing and harming. Accordingly, "just war theory" developed as a way of trying to specify, as carefully as possible, the conditions which would allow the use of force, or, as it in fact developed, to specify conditions under which the use of force would *not* be justified.

Although there are some disagreements within the tradition, classic just war theory can be generally understood as containing two distinct requirements. One of these concerns the conditions which must be present if a decision to wage war is to be justified. This phase is sometimes known as the "just cause" aspect of just war theory, or "jus ad bellum." It has three main elements. The first of these elements is that there must be substantial aggression on the part of another, so that the amount of good, or justice, to be promoted by the waging of war can outweigh the harm which will result if war is not waged. One consequence of this principle is that it is often thought that wars must be defensive rather than aggressive if they are to be ethically acceptable. The second element is that all peaceful methods of ending the aggression must have been tried, and must all have failed, leaving war as the only recourse. Finally, there must be a reasonable chance that the attempt at stopping the aggression will succeed, so that one is not merely throwing energies and lives away in a hopeless cause.

The second requirement for a war to be just, according to just war theory, concerns the manner in which war is conducted ("just means," or "jus in bello"). Even if all the requirements of a just cause of war are satisfied, a war might still be ethically unacceptable if it is not conducted in an ac-

ceptable manner. In particular, there are two key elements which have been thought relevant to this phase of the theory. The first condition specified by the theory for the just conduct of a war is that the harm resulting from the conduct of the war must be proportionate to the objective to be obtained. The other, and more commonly discussed, of these elements concerns a distinction between combatants and non-combatants (or "non-innocents" and "innocents"). In order for the conduct of a war to be considered justified, just war theory specifies that harm to innocents should not be directly intended as an end or a means. One aspect of this involves an application of the "doctrine of double effect" (discussed also in the chapter on abortion). This doctrine specifies conditions under which it may be morally acceptable to bring about consequences one would usually be morally required to avoid. Specifically, an action which brings about such "bad" consequences may be morally acceptable if the action also has "good" consequences which outweigh the bad, and the bad consequences are not a means to the good. In relation to just war theory, this might mean that it is sometimes acceptable to perform actions which one foresees will bring about the deaths of innocent people, although the intentional killing of innocents is always unacceptable. For example, it might be held that bombing a number of civilians so as to demoralize the enemy and hasten the end of the war is unacceptable, because doing so would be intending the death of innocent civilians as a means, but that it could be acceptable to authorize a bombing run aimed at a legitimate military target (e.g., a munitions factory), even if one foresees that some of the bombs may go astray and end up killing innocent civilians.

Many problems have been raised concerning just war theory. For example, some people have questioned whether it is possible to draw a clear enough distinction between aggressors and defenders, and others have raised doubts about how we are to distinguish innocents from non-innocents. Similarly, people have wondered whether it really makes a difference whether innocents are killed intentionally, or if their deaths are merely a foreseen but unintended consequence of an otherwise good action. Furthermore, there are questions about how to decide how much aggression justifies military intervention, and about what sorts of rights can legitimately be defended by the use of lethal force. Furthermore, there are people who maintain that war is not justified under any conditions, others who claim that we simply cannot know enough to be confident that a given situation is one in which war is justified, and, at the other extreme, people who claim that a war can be justified even if all these conditions are not satisfied.

One specific sort of use of violence which has attracted philosophical attention is terrorism. Does the term "terrorism" apply to political assassination? Does it include acts of sabotage, directed at property rather than persons? Can there be non-violent terrorism? Can terrorism be conducted by recognized governments? Is terrorism more like criminal activity, or like acts of war? Is there any way to distinguish morally bad "terrorists" from morally good "freedom fighters"? Both the conceptual and ethical analysis of terrorism have proven rich subjects for philosophers.

Another use of force which has received a great deal of philosophical attention is the use of coercive force by the government against its citizens in terms of the criminal law. Is the state justified in punishing those who break its laws? If so, under what circumstances is punishment justified, what goals should it seek to achieve, and what

principles should apply to determine who should be punished and to what extent?

Some people, who might be thought to fit into the camp of "anarchists," hold that it is never legitimate for the state to exercise coercive force over its citizens. Among the majority of philosophers who have rejected this view, there have been two traditional approaches to the justification of punishment. One of these holds that punishment is justified, when it is, by the good consequences it has for society. This approach to punishment has most commonly been associated with the ethical theory of utilitarianism, although one could be a utilitarian with regard to punishment without accepting that ethical theory for other purposes. The other main approach to punishment is known as "retributivism," and the idea of this approach is that punishment is in some way fitting as a response to wrongdoing, perhaps to restore the balance the wrongdoing disturbed, or perhaps simply to repay evil with evil.

Although the utilitarian theory of punishment holds that the loss of liberty or other harm to the person punished is itself an evil, the theory also maintains that this evil might be outweighed by good effects such punishment would also have. There are several different kinds of consequences which a utilitarian might look to to justify punishment. First of all, and perhaps most obviously, there is the notion of deterring people from committing crimes. The belief here might be that people are likely to pursue their own interests, even at the expense of others, and of social order in general. To avoid such infringement of social order and of people's interests, it might be thought that people must be given a reason to think that performing such damaging actions would *not* be in their own interests. The threat of punishment might serve that purpose.

In addition to deterrence, it might be thought that punishment can have good effects for society by keeping dangerous individuals away from vulnerable prospective victims. Furthermore, it might be hoped that punishment may be able to "reform" prisoners, so that they emerge from prison having "learned their lesson," and no longer posing a threat to society. One further, and related, perspective on punishment holds that punishment benefits the community by reinforcing the moral principles of society, and perhaps educating both the criminal and the rest of society as to the right moral principles.

Opponents of the utilitarian approach to punishment sometimes argue that it fails to achieve its objectives. For example, it might be claimed that people who are tempted to commit crimes are often in the midst of passion, and so the possibility of being punished does not enter their considerations as a deterrent, or that, if the possibility of punishment does enter their considerations, they are likely to conclude that they will manage to "get away with it," and thus again the threat of punishment will fail to deter. Similarly, people might be skeptical about the likelihood of criminals being rehabilitated by their punishment, or of the moral education being effective. Indeed, people might wonder whether society should take on the responsibility of determining what moral principles should be taught at all.

Furthermore, opponents of the utilitarian approach to punishment sometimes argue that the methods it advocates might not be justified even if they were likely to succeed. For example, there might be cases where people have not yet committed any crimes, but are considered to be high risks of doing so. Would it be appropriate to lock up such people so as to protect the interests of the innocent members of society? Or

perhaps even more starkly, there could be cases in which subjecting people who are commonly believed to be guilty of some crime but are in fact known to be completely innocent to some sort of painful condition might fulfill the goals of deterrence and public education. If the infliction of harm is justified by good social consequences, then it might seem that punishing the innocent could occasionally be justified on the basis of its good effects on others. Yet many people believe that the punishment of the innocent (if it makes conceptual sense at all) is inherently unjust. Similarly, it might be that the kinds of punishments which would be most effective as deterrents would be disproportional to the amount of wrongdoing involved. For example, if there were an area in which people were creating a problem by parking illegally, and these people were not deterred by the existing fines, it might be suggested that more serious penalties would get people to stop parking illegally. Suppose, for instance, that the penalty for illegal parking were changed to twenty years in prison without parole. Such a "draconian" punishment might prove very effective at deterring people from parking illegally, yet many people might believe that an injustice would be committed if anyone were actually convicted and sentenced to this new punishment.

The retributive theory of punishment seems to have an advantage here in that it can ensure that innocent people are not liable to punishment. This theory asserts that the "punishment must fit the crime" in terms of severity, and so people who have done nothing wrong cannot justly be punished at all. In the classic version of retributivism, the punishment was supposed to be equivalent to the harm imposed by the wrong-doing. This version of retributivism is known as the "lex talionis," and is perhaps most clearly understood in terms of the biblical injunction to punish wrongdo-ers with "an eye for an eye, a tooth for a tooth."

The lex talionis encounters difficulties in connection with some crimes. Perhaps most obviously, a mass murderer cannot have more than one life taken away in return. More generally, there may be things peo-ple have done which cannot, in principle, be "done to" them. For example, people who are convicted of treason or espionage cannot be subjected to treason or espio-nage themselves. Other concerns about the lex talionis involve the observation that the same treatment (e.g., loss of an eye) may not have the same impact on different peo-ple (in the extreme, it will have a different effect on people who only have one eye than on those with two, but more gener-ally, it may be that some people value their stereoscopic vision more, or have a lower pain threshold, etc.), or the general ques-tion about whether such treatment may not be too barbaric for modern sensibilities.

The retributivist need not be committed to the lex talionis, however. The claim that punishment should be proportional to the amount of wrongdoing involved need not mean that the amount of punishment must be equal to the amount of harm caused— all that is required is that more serious crimes receive more serious punishments than less serious ones.

Even at that, there are questions which have been raised about the retributivist ac-count of punishment. Suppose that, in a particular situation, no good consequences could be expected from a given act of pun-ishment, either for the person punished or for society in general. Would it still be a good thing to punish the criminal? If so, why? Punishment cannot, as a general rule,

restore things to the way they were before the crime was committed. Furthermore, making the punishment fit the amount of wrongdoing might require more insight into the moral lives of individuals than any-one is capable of. Two people who have committed the same type of action may not be equally morally culpable. Indeed, it might seem that retributivism requires peo-ple to be punished in accordance with all the wrongdoing in their lives, yet making judgements about the moral goodness of the entire lives of others seems a daunting task.

Many people believe that it is morally acceptable for the state to use its coercive power to punish those who break its laws, but the justification of such a practice of punishment proves elusive. Some people have tried to combine the best elements of the various accounts of punishment dis-cussed here into one more appealing whole, but it has proven difficult to get widespread agreement to any such hybrid theory of punishment as well. This chapter contains some of the Canadian Law Reform Commis-sion's reflections on the purpose of the crim-inal law and the justification of punishment, as well as some reflections on the particular problems posed for the criminal justice sys-tem by the presence of different cultural groups within society, such as Aboriginal groups, which have not always received equal treatment by the legal system.

Perhaps there are no justifiable uses of force by one human being against another. If there are such justifiable uses, perhaps they all have similar justifications, or per-haps they depend on a variety of ethical principles for support. It is hoped that this chapter will cast light on some dimensions of the many ethical problems related to the use of force and violence.

Reconciling Pacifists and Just War Theorists

James P. Sterba

Traditional debate on the issue of the use of violence for war has focused on two camps. One camp has set out what is called "Just War Theory," which claims that war can be justified if certain conditions are met. The other camp has favoured a view called "pacifism," which is usually understood to be the position that violent war cannot be justified. In this paper, Sterba argues that these two traditional rivals can in fact be reconciled. In order to bring about this reconciliation, he discusses and discards several different versions of pacifism, until he ends with a version of what he calls "anti-war pacifism." He also considers various just war theories, and claims we must insist on a stringent theory, which would justify very few of the wars which have actually taken place. Finally, Sterba claims that these most appealing versions of each theory in fact agree that war would be justified in a few rare cases, but only in those cases.

★ ★ ★

Traditionally pacifism and just war theory have represented radically opposed responses to aggression. Pacifism has been interpreted to rule out any use of violence in response to aggression. Just war theory has been interpreted to permit a measured use of violence in response to aggression.[1] It has been thought that the two views might sometimes agree in particular cases, for example, that pacifists and just war theorists might unconditionally oppose nuclear war, but beyond that it has been generally held that the two views lead to radically opposed recommendations. In this paper, I hope to show that this is not the case. I will argue that pacifism and just war theory, in their most morally defensible interpretations, can be substantially reconciled both in theory and practice.

In traditional just war theory there are two basic elements: an account of just cause and an account of just means. Just cause is usually specified as follows:

1) There must be substantial aggression.
2) Nonbelligerent correctives must be either hopeless or too costly.
3) Belligerent correctives must be neither hopeless nor too costly.

Needless to say, the notion of substantial aggression is a bit fuzzy, but it is generally understood to be the type of aggression that violates people's most fundamental rights. To suggest some specific examples of what is and is not substantial aggression, usually the taking of hostages is regarded as substantial aggression, while the nationalization of particular firms owned by foreigners is not so regarded. But even when substantial aggression occurs, frequently nonbelligerent correctives are neither hopeless nor too costly. And even when nonbelligerent correctives are either hopeless or too costly, in order for there to be a just cause, belligerent correctives must be neither hopeless nor too costly.

Traditional just war theory assumes, however, that there are just causes and goes on to specify just means as imposing two requirements:

1) Harm to innocents should not be directly intended as an end or a means.
2) The harm resulting from the belligerent means should not be disproportionate to the particular defensive objective to be attained.

While the just means conditions apply to each defensive action, the just cause conditions must be met by the conflict as a whole.

It is important to note that these requirements of just cause and just means are not essentially about war at all. Essentially, they constitute a theory of just defense that can apply to war but can also apply to a wide range of defensive actions short of war. Of course, what needs to be determined is whether these requirements can be justified. Since just war theory is usually opposed to pacifism, to secure a non-question-begging justification for the theory and its requirements we need to proceed as much as possible from premises that are common to pacifists and just war theorists alike. The difficulty here is that there is not just one form of pacifism, but many. So we need to determine which form of pacifism is most morally defensible.

Now, when most people think of pacifism they tend to identify it with a theory of nonviolence. We can call this view "nonviolent pacifism." It maintains that:

> Any use of violence against other human beings is morally prohibited.

It has been plausibly argued, however, that this form of pacifism is incoherent. In a well-known article, Jan Narveson rejects nonviolent pacifism as incoherent because it recognizes a right to life yet rules out any use of force in defense of that right.[2] The view is incoherent, Narveson claims, because having a right entails the legitimacy of using force in defense of that right, at least on some occasions.

Given the cogency of objections of this sort, some have opted for a form of pacifism that does not rule out all violence, but only lethal violence. We can call this view "non-lethal pacifism." It maintains that:

> Any lethal use of force against other human beings is morally prohibited.

In defense of nonlethal pacifism, Cheyney Ryan has argued that there is a substantial issue between the pacifist and the nonpacifist concerning whether we can or should create the necessary distance between ourselves and other human beings in order to make the act of killing possible.[3] To illustrate, Ryan cites George Orwell's reluctance to shoot at an enemy soldier who jumped out of a trench and ran along the top of a parapet half-dressed and holding up his trousers with both hands. Ryan contends that what kept Orwell from shooting was that he couldn't think of the soldier as a thing rather than as a fellow human being.

However, it is not clear that Orwell's encounter supports nonlethal pacifism. For it may be that what kept Orwell from shooting the enemy soldier was not his inability to think of the soldier as a thing rather than as a fellow human being, but rather his inability to think of the soldier who was holding up his trousers with both hands as a threat or a combatant. Under this interpretation, Orwell's decision not to shoot would accord well with the requirements of just war theory.

Let us suppose, however, that someone is attempting to take your life. Why does that permit you, the defender of nonlethal pacifism might ask, to kill the person making the attempt? The most cogent response, it seems to me, is that killing in such a case is not evil, or at least not morally evil, because anyone who is wrongfully engaged in an attempt upon your life has already forfeited his or her right to life by engaging in such aggression.[4] So, provided that you are reasonably certain that the aggressor is wrongfully engaged in an attempt upon your life, you would be morally justified in killing, assuming that it is the only way of saving your own life.

There is, however, a form of pacifism that remains untouched by the criticisms I have raised against both nonviolent pacifism and nonlethal pacifism. This form of pacifism neither prohibits all violence nor even all uses of lethal force. We can call the view "anti-war pacifism" because it holds that:

> Any participation in the massive use of lethal force in warfare is morally prohibited.[5]

In defense of anti-war pacifism, it is undeniable that wars have brought enormous amounts of death and destruction in their wake and that many of those who have perished in them have been noncombatants or innocents. In fact, the tendency of modern wars has been to produce higher and higher proportions of noncombatant casualties, making it more and more difficult to justify participation in such wars. At the same time, strategies for nonbelligerent conflict resolution are rarely intensively developed and explored before nations choose to go to war, making it all but impossible to justify participation in such wars.[6]

To determine whether the requirements of just war theory can be reconciled with those of anti-war pacifism, however, we need to consider whether we should distinguish between harm intentionally inflicted upon innocents and harm whose infliction on innocents is merely foreseen. On the one hand, we could favor a uniform restriction against the infliction of harm upon innocents that ignores the intended/foreseen distinction. On the other hand, we could favor a differential restriction which is more severe against the intentional infliction of harm upon innocents, but is less severe against the infliction of harm that is merely foreseen. What needs to be determined, therefore, is whether there is any rationale for favoring this differential restriction on harm over a uniform restriction. But this presupposes that we can, in practice, distinguish between what is foreseen and what is intended, and some have challenged whether this can be done. So first we need to address this challenge.

Now the practical test that is frequently appealed to in order to distinguish between foreseen and intended elements of an action is the Counterfactual Test. According to this test, two questions are relevant:

1) Would you have performed the action if only the good consequences would have resulted and not the evil consequences?
2) Would you have performed the action if only the evil consequences resulted and not the good consequences?

If an agent answers 'Yes' to the first question and 'No' to the second, some would conclude that (1) the action is an intended means to the good consequences, (2) the good consequences are an intended end, and (3) the evil consequences are merely foreseen.

But how well does this Counterfactual Test work? Douglas Lackey has argued that the test gives the wrong result in any case where the 'act that produces an evil effect produces a larger good effect'.[7] Lackey cites the bombing of Hiroshima as an example. That bombing is generally thought to have had two effects: the killing of Japanese civilians and the shortening of the war. Now suppose we were to ask:

(1) Would Truman have dropped the bomb if only the shortening of the war would have resulted but not the killing of the Japanese civilians?
(2) Would Truman have dropped the bomb if only the Japanese civilians would have been killed and the war not shortened?

And suppose that the answer to the first question is that Truman would have dropped the bomb if only the shortening of the war would have resulted but not the killing of the Japanese civilians, and that the answer to the second question is that Truman would not have dropped the bomb if only the Japanese civilians would have been killed and the war not shortened. Lackey concludes from this that the killing of civilians at Hiroshima, self-evidently a means for shortening the war, is by the

Counterfactual Test classified not as a means but as a mere foreseen consequence. On these grounds, Lackey rejects the Counterfactual Test as an effective device for distinguishing between the foreseen and the intended consequences of an action.

Unfortunately, this is to reject the Counterfactual Test only because one expects too much from it. It is to expect the test to determine all of the following:

(1) Whether the action is an intended means to the good consequences;
(2) Whether the good consequences are an intended end of the action;
(3) Whether the evil consequences are simply foreseen consequences.

In fact, this test is only capable of meeting the first two of these expectations. And the test clearly succeeds in doing this for Lackey's own example, where the test shows the bombing of Hiroshima to be an intended means to shortening the war, and shortening the war an intended consequence of the action.

To determine whether the evil consequences are simply foreseen consequences, however, an additional test is needed, which I shall call the Nonexplanation Test. According to this test, the relevant question is:

> Does the bringing about of the evil consequences help explain why the agent undertook the action as a means to the good consequences?

If the answer is 'No,' that is, if the bringing about of the evil consequences does not help explain why the agent undertook the action as a means to the good consequences, the evil consequences are merely foreseen. But if the answer is 'Yes,' the evil consequences are an intended means to the good consequences.

Of course, there is no guaranteed procedure for arriving at an answer to the Nonexplanation Test. Nevertheless, when we are in doubt concerning whether the evil conse-

quences of an act are simply foreseen, seeking an answer to the Nonexplanation Test will tend to be the best way of reasonably resolving that doubt. For example, applied to Lackey's example, the Nonexplanation Test comes up with a 'Yes,' since the evil consequences in this example do help explain why the bombing was undertaken to shorten the war. For according to the usual account, Truman ordered the bombing to bring about civilian deaths which by their impact upon Japanese morale were expected to shorten the war. So, by the Nonexplanation Test, the civilian deaths were an intended means to the good consequences of shortening the war.[8]

Assuming, then, that we can distinguish in practice between harm intentionally inflicted upon innocents and harm whose infliction on innocents is merely foreseen, we need to determine whether there is any rationale for favoring a differential restriction that is more severe against the intentional infliction of harm upon innocents but is less severe against the infliction of harm that is merely foreseen over a uniform restriction against the infliction of harm upon innocents that ignores the intended/foreseen distinction.

Let us first examine the question from the perspective of those suffering the harm. Initially, it might appear to matter little whether the harm would be intended or just foreseen by those who cause it. From the perspective of those suffering harm, it might appear that what matters is simply that the overall amount of harm be restricted irrespective of whether it is foreseen or intended. But consider: Don't those who suffer harm have more reason to protest when the harm is done to them by agents who are directly engaged in causing harm to them than when the harm is done incidentally by agents whose ends and means are good? Don't we have more reason to protest when we are being used by others than when we are affected by them only incidentally?

Moreover, if we examine the question from the perspective of those causing harm, additional support for this line of reasoning can be found. For it would seem that we have more reason to protest a restriction against foreseen harm than we have reason to protest a comparable restriction against intended harm. This is because a restriction against foreseen harm limits our actions when our ends and means are good, whereas a restriction against intended harm only limits our actions when our ends or means are evil or harmful, and it would seem that we have greater grounds for acting when both our ends and means are good than when they are not. Consequently, because we have more reason to protest when we are being used by others than when we are being affected by them only incidentally, and because we have more reason to act when both our ends and means are good than when they are not, we should favor the foreseen/intended distinction that is incorporated into just means.

It might be objected, however, that at least sometimes we could produce greater good overall by violating the foreseen/intended distinction of just means and acting with the evil means of intentionally harming innocents. On this account, it might be argued that it should be permissible at least sometimes to intentionally harm innocents in order to achieve greater good overall.

Now, it seems to me that this objection is well-taken insofar as it is directed against an absolute restriction upon intentional harm to innocents. It seems clear that there are exceptions to such a restriction when intentional harm to innocents is:

1) trivial (e.g., as in the case of stepping on someone's foot to get out of a crowded subway),
2) easily reparable (e.g., as in the case of lying to a temporarily depressed friend to keep her from committing suicide), or

3) greatly outweighed by the consequences of the action, especially to innocent people (e.g., as in the case of shooting one of two hundred civilian hostages to prevent in the only way possible the execution of all two hundred).

Yet while we need to recognize these exceptions to an absolute restriction upon intentional harm to innocents, there is good reason not to permit simply maximizing good consequences overall, because that would place unacceptable burdens upon particular individuals. More specifically, it would be an unacceptable burden on innocents to allow them to be intentionally harmed in cases other than the exceptions we have just enumerated. And, allowing for these exceptions, we would still have reason to favor a differential restriction against harming innocents that is more severe against the intentional infliction of harm upon innocents but is less severe against the infliction of harm upon innocents that is merely foreseen. Again, the main grounds for this preference are that we would have more reason to protest when we are being used by others than when we are being affected by them only incidentally, and more reason to act when both our ends and means are good than when they are not.

So far, I have argued that there are grounds for favoring a differential restriction on harm to innocents that is more severe against intended harm and less severe against foreseen harm. I have further argued that this restriction is not absolute so that when the evil intended is trivial, easily reparable or greatly outweighed by the consequences, intentional harm to innocents can be justified. Moreover, there is no reason to think that anti-war pacifists would reject either of these conclusions. Anti-war pacifists are opposed to any participation in the massive use of lethal force in warfare, yet this need not conflict with the commitment of just war theorists to a differential but nonabsolute restriction on harm to innocents as a require-ment of just means.[9] Where just war theory goes wrong, according to anti-war pacifists, is not in its restriction on harming innocents but rather in its failure to adequately determine when belligerent correctives are too costly to constitute a just cause or lacking in the propor-tionality required by just means. According to anti-war pacifists, just war theory provides in-sufficient restraint in both of these areas. Now to evaluate this criticism, we need to consider the following cases:

Case (1) where only the intentional or fore-seen killing of an unjust aggressor would pre-vent one's own death.[10]

Case (2) where only the intentional or fore-seen killing of an unjust aggressor and the foreseen killing of one innocent bystander would prevent one's own death and that of five other innocent people.

Case (3) where only the intentional or foreseen killing of an unjust aggressor and the foreseen killing of one innocent bystander would pre-vent the death of five innocent people.

Case (4) where only the intentional or fore-seen killing of an unjust aggressor and the foreseen killing of five innocent people would prevent the death of two innocent people.

Case (5) where only the intentional or fore-seen killing of an unjust aggressor and the foreseen killing of five innocent people would prevent the death of two innocent people and ensure certain liberties or other values for a larger group of people.

Let us discuss each of these cases in turn.

Case (1) seems to present no problems. In the first place, anti-war pacifists have adopted their view because they are convinced that there are instances of justified killing. And, in this case, the only person killed is an unjust aggressor. So surely anti-war pacifists would have to agree with just war theorists that one can justifiably kill an unjust aggressor if it is the only way to save one's life.

Case (2). Here we do have the foreseen killing of an innocent person as well as the killing of the unjust aggressor, but since it is the only way to save one's own life and the lives of five other innocent people, anti-war pacifists and just war theorists alike would have reason to judge it morally permissible. In this case, the intended life-saving benefits to six innocent people surely would outweigh the foreseen death of one innocent person.

Case (3). In this case, despite the fact that we lack the justification of self-defense, sav-ing the lives of five innocent people in the only way possible should still provide anti-war pacifists and just war theorists with sufficient grounds for granting the moral permissibility of killing an unjust aggressor, even when the killing of an innocent person is a foreseen consequence. In this case, the intended life-saving benefits to five innocent people would still outweigh the foreseen death of one in-nocent person.

Case (4). In this case, neither anti-war pacifists nor just war theorists would find the cost and proportionality requirements of just war theory to be met. Too many innocent people would have to be killed to save too few. Here the fact that the deaths of the in-nocents would be merely foreseen does not outweigh the fact that we would have to ac-cept the deaths of five innocents in order to be able to save two.

Case (5). The interpretation of this case is crucial. Up to this point in previous cases, we have simply been counting the number of in-nocent deaths involved in each case and opt-ing for the solution that minimizes the loss of innocent lives that would result. In this case, we are asked to sanction a greater loss of in-nocent lives in order to preserve certain lib-erties or other values for a larger group of people.

Now, some just war theorists have ac-cepted the legitimacy of trade-offs of just this sort, thereby giving credence to the charge that their theory provides insufficient restraints on just cause and just means.[11] These just war theorists have argued that when interpreting the cost and proportionality requirements of just war theory, we cannot simply do some type of utilitarian calculation weighing lives against lives, presumably not even weighing innocent lives against innocent lives, but that moral values such as liberty and the preferability of certain ways of life must also be taken into account.

But it is unclear how this argument is supposed to go. Surely we might argue that in order to preserve certain freedoms or values in our own society, we are justified in taking defensive actions that have as their foreseen consequence a lessening of freedom in the aggressor's society. For example, our resistance might cause a crackdown on dissidents in the aggressor's society. But it is a further step to justify taking defensive actions that have as their foreseen consequence the greater loss of innocent lives in the aggressor's society than any loss of innocent lives that would thereby be prevented in one's own society. Such trade-offs would not be acceptable even if failure to take such defensive actions would also result in the loss of important liberties in our own society. Thus, for example, even if Lithuania could effectively free itself from the Soviet Union by infiltrating into Moscow several bands of saboteurs who would then attack several military and government installations in Moscow, causing an enormous loss of innocent lives, such trade-offs would not be justified. If the cost and proportionality requirements of just cause and just means are to be met, we must save more innocent lives than we cause to be lost, we must preserve more liberty and other goods than we cause to be destroyed, and we must not kill innocents, even indirectly, simply to preserve important liberties.[12]

Of course, sometimes our lives and liberties are threatened together. Or better, if we are unwilling to give up our liberties then our lives might be threatened as well. Nevertheless, if we are justified in our use of lethal force to defend ourselves in cases that will indirectly kill innocents, it is because our lives are also threatened, not simply our liberties. And the same holds for when we are defending others.

What this shows is that the constraints imposed by just war theory on the use of belligerent correctives are actually much more severe than anti-war pacifists have tended to recognize.[13] In determining when belligerent correctives are too costly to constitute a just cause or are lacking in the proportionality required by just means, just war theory under its most morally defensible interpretation 1) allows the use of belligerent means only when they minimize the loss of innocent lives overall, and 2) allows innocent lives to be threatened only to prevent the loss of innocent lives, not simply to prevent the loss of liberties or other goods.

Now, it might be objected that all that I have shown through the analysis of the above five cases is that killing in defense of oneself or others is morally permissible, not that it is morally required or morally obligatory. That is true. I have not established any obligation to respond to aggression with lethal force in these cases, but only that it is morally permissible to do so. For one thing, it is difficult to ground an obligation to use lethal force on self-defense alone, as would be required in Case 1. Obligations to oneself appear to have an optional quality that is absent from obligations to others. In Cases 2 and 3, however, the use of lethal force would save the lives of others, and here I contend it would be morally obligatory if either the proposed use of lethal force required only a relatively small personal sacrifice from us or if we were fairly bound by convention or a mutual defense agreement to come to the aid of those whose lives we could save. In such cases, I think we can justifiably speak of a moral obligation to kill in defense of others.

Another aspect of cases 1-3 to which someone might object is that it is the wrongful actions of others that put us into situations where I am claiming that we are morally justified in killing.[14] But for the actions of unjust aggressors, we would not be in situations where I am claiming that we are morally permitted or required to kill.

Yet doesn't something like this happen in a wide range of cases when wrongful actions are performed? Suppose I am on the way to the bank to deposit money from a fundraiser, and someone accosts me and threatens to shoot if I don't hand over the money. If I do hand over the money, I would be forced to do something I don't want to do, something that involves a loss to myself and others. But surely it is morally permissible for me to hand over the money in this case. And it may even be morally required for me to do so if resistance would lead to the shooting of others in addition to myself. So it does seem that bad people, by altering the consequences of our actions, can alter our obligations as well. What our obligations are under nonideal conditions are different from what they would be under ideal conditions. If a group of thugs comes into this room and makes it very clear that they intend to shoot me if each of you doesn't give them one dollar, I think, and I would hope that you would also think, that each of you now has an obligation to give the thugs one dollar, when before you had no such obligation. Likewise, I think that the actions of unjust aggressors can put us into situations where it is morally permissible or even morally required for us to kill when before it was not.

Now it might be contended that anti-war pacifists would concede the moral permissibility of cases 1-3, but still maintain that any participation in the massive use of lethal force in warfare is morally prohibited. The scale of the conflict, anti-war pacifists might contend, makes all the difference. Of course, if this simply means that many large-scale conflicts will

have effects that bear no resemblance to cases 1-3, this can hardly be denied. Still, it is possible for some large-scale conflicts to bear a proportionate resemblance to the above cases. For example, it can plausibly be argued that India's military action against Pakistan in Bangladesh and the Tanzanian incursion into Uganda during the rule of Idi Amin resemble case 3 in their effects upon innocents. What this shows is that anti-war pacifists are not justified in regarding every participation in the massive use of lethal force in warfare as morally prohibited. Instead, anti-war pacifists must allow that at least in some real-life cases, wars and other large-scale military operations both have been and will be morally permissible.

This concession from anti-war pacifists, however, needs to be matched by a comparable concession from just war theorists themselves, because too frequently they have interpreted their theory in morally indefensible ways. I have argued that when just war theory is given a morally defensible interpretation, the theory favors a strong just means prohibition against intentionally harming innocents. I have also argued that the theory favors the use of belligerent means only when such means 1) minimize the loss of innocent lives overall, and 2) threaten innocent lives only to prevent the loss of innocent lives, not simply to prevent the loss of liberties or other goods. Obviously, just war theory, so understood, is going to place severe restrictions on the use of belligerent means in warfare. In fact, most of the actual uses of belligerent means in warfare that have occurred turn out to be unjustified. For example, the U.S. involvement in Nicaragua, El Salvador and Panama, Soviet involvement in Afganistan, Israeli involvement in the West Bank and the Gaza Strip all violate the just cause and just means provisions of just war theory as I have defended them. Even the recent U.S.-led war against Iraq violated both the just cause and just means provisions of just war theory.[15] In fact, one strains to find examples of justified applications of just war theory in recent history. Two examples I have already referred to are India's military action against Pakistan in Bangladesh and the Tanzanian incursion into Uganda during the rule of Idi Amin. But after mentioning these two examples it is difficult to go on. What this shows is that when just war theory and anti-war pacifism are given their most morally defensible interpretations, both views can be reconciled. In this reconciliation, the few wars and large-scale conflicts that meet the stringent requirements of just war theory are the only wars and large-scale conflicts to which anti-war pacifists cannot justifiably object. We can call the view that emerges from this reconciliation "just war pacifism."[16] It is the view which claims that due to the stringent requirements of just war theory, only very rarely will participation in a massive use of lethal force in warfare be morally justified. It is the view on which I rest my case for the reconciliation of pacifism and just war theory.[17]

Notes

An earlier version of this paper was presented as the presidential address for 1990 National Meeting of Concerned Philosophers for Peace at which time I received many helpful suggestions. In particular, I would like to thank Timo Airaksinen, Joseph Boyle, Laurence Bove, Duane Cady, Sheldon Cohen, Barry Gan, Robert Holmes, Robert Johansen, Janet Kourany, Douglas Lackey, Robert Phillips, Ronald Santoni, Jonathan Schonsheck, Paula Smithka and Richard Werner.

1 Some would say with too generous a measure.

2 Jan Narveson, "Pacifism: A Philosophical Analysis," *Ethics*, (1965), pp. 259-71.

3 Cheyney Ryan, "Self-Defense, Pacifism and the Possibility of Killing" *Ethics*, (1983), pp. 514-524. Also reprinted in James P. Sterba, *The Ethics of War and Nuclear Deterrence* (Belmont, CA: Wadsworth Publishing Co. 1985).

4 Alternatively, one might concede that even in this case killing is morally evil, but still contend that it is morally justified because it is the lesser of two evils.

5 For two challenging defenses of this view, see Duane L. Cady, *From Warism to Pacifism* (Philadelphia: Temple University Press, 1989) and Robert L. Holmes, *On War and Morality* (Princeton: Princeton University Press, 1989).

6 See Cady, *op. cit.*, pp. 51, 89ff; and Holmes, *op cit.*, p. 278.

7 Douglas P. Lackey, 'The Moral Irrelevance of the Counterforce/Counter-value Distinction,' *The Monist* (1987). pp. 255-276. For a similar view, see Susan Levine, 'Does the "Counterfactual Test" Work for Distinguishing a Means from a Foreseen Concomitant?', *Journal of Value Inquiry* (1984), pp. 155-7.

8 This Nonexplanation Test also solves a related problem of distinguishing foreseen from intended consequences, as noted by Charles Fried. (Charles Fried, *Right and Wrong* [Cambridge, MA: Harvard University Press, 1978], pp. 23-4) Fried was concerned with the following example, first discussed by Philippa Foot (Philippa Foot, 'The Problem of Abortion and the Doctrine of Double Effect,' *Oxford Review* 5 [1967], pp. 5-15): 'Imagine that a fat person who is leading a party of spelunkers gets herself stuck in the mouth of a cave in which flood waters are rising. The trapped party of spelunkers just happens to have a stick of dynamite with which they can blast the fat person out of the mouth of the cave; either they use the dynamite or they all drown, the fat person with them.' Now suppose someone made the claim that using the dynamite was simply a means of freeing the party of spelunkers and that the death of the fat person was just a foreseen side-effect. Fried's problem is that while he rejects this account of the action, he can find no way of successfully challenging it. What he clearly needs is the Nonexplanation Test. For suppose we employ the test and ask whether the death of the fat person helps explain why the dynamite was used to free the spelunkers from the cave; the answer we get is clearly 'Yes.' For how else could the use of the dynamite free the party of spelunkers from the cave except by removing the fat person from the mouth of the cave in such a way as to cause her death? It follows, according to the Nonexplanation Test, that the death of the fat person is a means intended for freeing the party of spelunkers and not merely a foreseen consequence of the use of the dynamite.

9 This is because the just means restrictions protect innocents quite well against the infliction of intentional harm.

10 By an "unjust aggressor" I mean someone who the defender is reasonably certain is wrongfully engaged in an attempt upon her life or the lives of other innocent people.

11 See, for example, William V. O'Brien, *The Conduct of Just and Limited* (Praeger Publishers, 1981) and John Courtney Murray, *Morality and Modern War*, Council on Religion and International Affairs, 1959.

12 Of course, we would not be causing innocent lives to be lost or goods to be destroyed in the relevant sense with respect to those who knowingly have chosen to sacrifice their lives and goods in defense of a just cause. Thus, it is always possible for people to say "Give me liberty or give me death." What we cannot do, however, is make this choice for other people.

13 And more severe than some just war theorists have tended to recognize.

14 See Holmes, *op. cit.*, pp. 208-211.

15 The just cause provision was violated because the extremely effective economic sanctions were not given enough time to work. It was estimated that when compared to past economic blockades, the blockade against Iraq had a near 100% chance of success if given about a year to work. (See *New York Times*, January 14, 1991.) The just means provision was violated because the number of combatant and noncombatant deaths were disproportionate. As many as 150,000 Iraqi soldiers were killed according to U.S. intelligence sources.

16 For another use of this term, see Kenneth H. Wenker, "Just War Pacifism," *Proceedings of the American Catholic Philosophical Association* (1983) pp.

135-141. For a defense of a similar view to my own, which is considered by the author to be a defense of pacifism, see Richard Norman. "The Case for Pacifism," *Journal of Applied Philosophy* (1988). pp. 197-210.

17 Of course, more needs to be done to specify the requirement of just war pacifism. One fruitful way to further specify these requirements is to appeal to a hypothetical social contract decision procedure as has been done with respect to other practical problems. Here I have simply tried to establish the defensibility of just war pacifism without appealing to any such procedure. Yet once the defensibility of just war pacifism has been established, such a decision procedure will prove quite useful in working out its particular requirements.

Questions for Discussion

1 Can Just War Theory be used to justify fighting which goes beyond defending lives, to defending important liberties?

2 Does it make a significant moral difference whether one intends a good result from one's action but foresees the loss of innocent lives as another consequence, or one intends the loss of innocent lives as a means of obtaining a good consequence? If so, is the difference significant enough to mean that one is acceptable and the other is not? Can they be adequately distinguished?

3 What is the most morally defensible version of pacifism? Would this most defensible version have to concede that war can be morally acceptable in some circumstances?

From Maternal Thinking to Peace Politics

Sara Ruddick

Women have often contributed a distinctive voice to discussions of the ethics of violence and warfare. One strand of this contribution focuses on the traditional role of women as caretakers and nurturers, which appears to be in conflict with warfare. In the following selection, Sara Ruddick draws on the traditional function of "mothering" (which she claims is commonly, but not necessarily, done by women) to find resources which might be used to promote a politics of peace.

★   ★   ★

Mothering/nurturing is a vital force and process establishing relationships through the universe. Exploring and analyzing the nature of all components involved in a nurturing activity puts one in touch with life extending itself. . . . We can choose to be mothers, nurturing and transforming a new space for a new people in a new time.

Bernice Johnson Reagon

Peace the great meaning has not been
  defined.
When we say peace as a word, war
As a flare of fire leaps across our eyes.
We went to this school. Think war;
Cancel war, we were taught.
What is left is peace.
No, peace is not left, it is no cancelling;
The fierce and human peace is our deep
  power
Born to us of wish and responsibility.

Muriel Rukeyser

In this essay I talk about a journey, a "progress," from a "womanly" practice and way of knowing to a liberatory standpoint. Specifically, I plot a move from maternal thinking to peace politics.

First, a word about "war" and "peace." No one can provide easy answers to haunting questions about when and how to fight. I believe that violence is addictive, that the effectiveness of violence is consistently exaggerated, and that the short- and long-term costs of organized violence—economic, social, psychological, and physical—are routinely underestimated. Meanwhile, the multiple rewards and effectiveness of "nonviolence" are underrated, misreported, and misunderstood. But it is arrogant to urge nonviolent confrontation, let alone nonviolent reconciliation and cooperation from a distance, whether in El Salvador, South Africa, Ireland, or Palestine and Israel.

"War" is both the quintessential expression of violence and its most attractive representative. I believe that the ways of thinking that

invalidate militarism will also undermine more covert and pervasive violence. "War" is familiar; the myriad forms of nonviolent confrontation, cooperation, and reconciliation that would be "peace" are still to be invented. I believe that to imagine forms of nonviolent resistance and cooperation is to imagine new personal and civic relationships to abuse and neglect. Hence in concentrating on the relationship of mothers to war, I believe that I am also talking about less dramatic, maternal relationships to closer "enemies."

Although nonviolent action rarely succeeds without global outrage and resources, the conditions of peace and resistance are local. I speak as a citizen of the United States, a nation that, as I see it, frequently, even habitually, enters the social and natural world as an armed, invasive, exploitative conqueror. Within this nation, governments and communities "throw away," quarantine, track, and abuse their more vulnerable, assaulted, or troubled members. Whether moved by outright greed and racist bigotry or paralyzed by passivity, self-preoccupation, and despair, these governments and communities routinely fail to respond to the promise of birth, fail to provide the shelter, healing, and sustenance on which mothering depends. In the midst of this many-faceted violence, maternal thinkers and feminist ethicists can contribute in distinctive ways to imagining and creating "peace."

I begin with a question. How might it be possible to intensify the contradiction between mothering and violence and to articulate the connections between mothering and nonviolence so that mothers would be more apt to move from maternal thinking to peace politics?

The opposition between mothers and war is legendary. Mothering begins with birth and promises life; militaries require organized, deliberate killing. A mother preserves the bodies, nurtures the psychic growth, and disciplines the consciences of children; military enterprises deliberately endanger the bodies, psyches, and consciences that mothers protect. On the face of it, war and other organized violence threaten every aspect of mothering work—sheltering, protecting, attending, feeding, maintaining connections on which children depend. Understandably, the figure of the mater dolorosa—the mother of sorrows—is central to subversive war narrative. Just warriors know that war is hateful and cruel, but it is the mater dolorosa who refuses to subordinate the pain to a warrior's tale of just cause and victory. For her war remains a catastrophe that overshadows whatever purposes lie behind it. The mater dolorosa's vision of war as unredeemed suffering among the ruins takes on new poignancy as nuclear and advanced "conventional" weapons force us to imagine wars that threaten all human and global life.

If military endeavors seem a betrayal of maternal commitments, nonviolent action can seem their natural extension. Maternal "peacefulness" is not a sweet, appeasing gentleness but a way of living in which people demand a great deal of each other. When mothers fight with their children or on their behalf, when they teach their children ways of fighting safely without being trampled on or trampling on others, they engage in nonviolent action. Many individual mothers abuse their children; in most cultures children suffer from accepted but abusive practices; some cultures may legitimate systematic maternal abuse. Nonetheless, some maternal practices are sufficiently governed by principles of nonviolence to offer one model for nonviolent relationships. This does not mean that in these practices mothers achieve the nonviolence to which they aspire. Since children are vulnerable and the vulnerable are subject to abuse and neglect, mothers may be more than usually tempted by sadism, self-indulgent aggression, and self-protective indifference to the real needs of demanding children. It is maternal *commitment* to care for rather than assault or abandon children—whatever failure, guilt, and despair follows in that commitment's wake—that illuminates more public struggles to live nonviolently.

Yet mothers are not "peaceful." Wherever there are wars, mothers support and supply soldiers and, if encouraged, often become fierce and effective fighters themselves. Mothers are as apt as other people to welcome the excitements of violence—rewards of community solidarity, and promise of meaningful sacrifice. War also offers many mothers who suffer from discriminatory economic and social policies distinctive opportunities for adventure and material gain; "peace"-time military service often appears to provide their adolescent children with jobs, social discipline, education, and training that are unavailable or prohibitively expensive in civilian society.

Yet the myth of maternal peacefulness remains alluring. Mothers may be willing warriors, but war is their enemy, nonviolence often their practice. Precisely because mothers have played their supportive parts in military scripts, their refusal to perform might prompt a rewriting of the plot. Hence the urgency of my question: Can the contradictions between mothering and violence, the connections between mothering and nonviolence be made sufficiently visible, audible, disturbing, and promising to turn maternal thinking into an instrument of peace politics?

Different Voices, Standpoints, and "Feminist Ethics"

My particular project, plotting a progress from maternal thinking to peace politics, is an instance of a more general transformative endeavor—namely, the transformation of "womanly" stances into feminist or liberatory standpoints. Several feminist philosophers have suggested that people who engage in "caring labor" acquire a distinctive epistemological stance, a "rationality of care."[1] Mothering is both an instance of caring labor and intertwined with many other kinds of caring such as homemaking, kin work,[2] nursing, tending the frail elderly, and teaching small children. Hence maternal thinking—a congeries of metaphysical attitude, cognitive capacities, and values that arises from mothering—is one element of the "rationality of care."

Although societies differ in their ways of distributing the pleasures and burdens of mothering or caring labor, and although individual women and men are variously interested in and capable of these kinds of work, there is nothing distinctively feminine about mothering, nursing, or any other form of caretaking. There is, for example, no reason why men cannot engage in mothering, and many men already do. Nonetheless, maternal work, and more generally caring labor, have historically been the provenance [sic] of women. Maternal thinking and the rationality of care are therefore construed—and celebrated or minimized—as "womanly" achievements.

Accordingly, feminist psychologists and critics who identify values or ways of knowing associated with *women* typically attribute the differences they discover at least partly to the effect on women of the caring work they have undertaken. Conversely, certain feminists have cited the value of mothering and caretaking or of maternal thinking and the "rationality of care" in order to argue that women's perspectives offer a "standpoint" from which to criticize dominant values and invent new ones. At the least women's perspectives and voices should be included in any adequate moral or psychological theory. Many feminists make a stronger claim: the destructiveness and "perversion" of dominant values is intertwined with "abstract masculinity," while the values and relationships that would characterize more just and caring societies are intertwined with "caring femininity."[3]

But just as women (and men) who are mothers have not proved "peaceful," women generally have not reliably extended the do-

main of care beyond class, race, or neighborhood. Nor have they (we) consistently engaged in struggles for political liberty and economic and racial justice. (There are small, fluctuating "gender gaps" between women's and men's support of various progressive issues—perhaps especially peace and ecology. I am not, however, interested in women's possible, marginal superiority to men.) Nor are women's values and relationships reliably feminist. Women's work and stories are not only shaped by, but also often contribute to the exploitation of caretakers and the subordination of women. Women (as well as men) identify care with self-sacrifice, or responsiveness to need with pleasing others.[4] Despite the efforts of feminist and lesbian mothers, women (as well as men) embed the idea of maternity in a heterosexist, sexually conservative ideology. Women have to fight against women (as well as men) to acquire the power to refuse maternal work. If they become mothers, they have to resist women's (as well as men's) reductive definitions of their pleasures and needs as only maternal.[5] Any "feminine" standpoint that feminists might celebrate is yet to be achieved.

Nonetheless, "different voice" critics who set out to identify women's values and perspectives almost always[6] take themselves to be engaged in a feminist project. ("Different voice" theorists is a shorthand label for any critic, reader, or theorist who attempts to identify perspectives or ways of knowing associated with women. The label draws on Carol Gilligan's work *In a Different Voice* and was suggested by Nancy Goldberger, coauthor of *Women's Ways of Knowing*.) Most important, they normally aim to create a liberatory standpoint that at least is compatible with feminism and at best is an extension and expression of militant feminist vision. Their effort to *transform* a "womanly" stance into a liberatory and feminist standpoint is an essay in "feminist ethics."[7]

Although different voice critics may find it impossible to separate their feminist commitments from their respect for women's voices, many of the actual voices currently dominant within North American feminism have serious misgivings about their transformative enterprise. These skeptical feminists claim that the idea of "womanly" difference will be used against women and is in any case empirically unfounded, exclusionary, ethnocentric, and sentimental. On their view "women" have been historically produced in asymmetrical opposition to a "masculinity" intertwined with racial privilege and defined in conjunction with Reason and Power. Nothing to these women can be named outside of oppressive patriarchal and ethnocentric definitions of "women"—no "womanly" work, "women's" oppression, or female bodily experience. Women might speak and be spoken of once all hierarchical gender distinctions were laid to rest—but then "women's" different voices, if not "women" themselves, would be fading relics that should be buried not resurrected.

I do not directly address these feminist challenges here, but they have prompted me to review my particular project—plotting a progress from maternal thinking to peace politics—and to reread others' essays in transformative "feminist ethics" in order to get a clearer sense of what I (we?) have been about. In retrospect, I now discern three overlapping moments in the transformation of maternal thinking: heuristic representation of the "womanly" stance, which includes antiracist elements; a diagnosis of flaws, including tendencies to racism, within, not apart from, the stance represented; and a transformative encounter with feminism and women's politics of resistance. I also see these moments in others' efforts to transform the "womanly" into the liberatory.

Heuristic Representation: Maternal Peacefulness

A "heuristic" representation serves both to discover and to reveal particular desirable aspects of the practices of thinking represented. Thus I represent maternal thinking *as if* it were already peaceful in order to discover and reveal the peacefulness I hope and believe to be there. It is not surprising that my rendition of maternal thinking contrasts in detail and as a whole with military thinking. For example, on my view, the attentive love of mothering requires concrete cognition, tolerance for ambivalence and ambiguity, receptiveness to change, and recognition of the limits of control. Mothers are apt to acquire a variegated concept of "nature" as at best beneficent, hospitable to goodness, and at worst a respected negotiating partner. These and many other capacities and attitudes provoked by mothering contrast with the abstractions and certainties of militarist thinking and with the exploitative attitudes toward human and nonhuman nature characteristic of militarism and the instrumental technocracy on which it depends.

More generally, I read—as I believe any antimilitarist could read—the "alternative epistemologies" that Margaret Urban Walker identifies in feminist ethics as opposed to militarism. "Attention to the particular," where attention is interlaced with disciplined caring, is inimical to the creation of "throwaway" people and "killable" enemies. Nonviolent activists have to construct morally relevant understandings that are "contextual and narrative"; just-war theorists rely on abstract causes, state boundaries, and rules of war. Military orders depend on both hierarchy and selfless bonding; nonviolent struggle envisions a future when moral deliberation will become "a site of expression and communication" where partners in conflict neither dominate nor submit.[8]

My articulations of maternal thinking and my readings of feminist ethics are not simply inventions. I try as best as I can to "cling" to the only data I have: honest memory, candid conversation, and the widest range of accurate reading and mother watching that I can manage. But no story of mothering is independent of the motives of the teller. I am obsessed with deliberate, organized, legitimate violence. I am determined to tell one story of maternal thinking that is ready to be turned into a story of peace.

I choose to look at mothering through the lens of nonviolence. I then "discover"—amid incontrovertible evidence of maternal abandonment and assault—a typical maternal struggle to create nonviolent forms of cooperation and conflict. I see women and men who are powerless, powerfully and passionately engaged with vulnerable and provocative children, making "peace." Resisting their own and others' violence, these mothers of both sexes sustain responsive relationships with their children despite disappointments, anger, and often radical differences in style and value.

In a similar vein I look for "sturdily antimilitarist" conceptions of bodies and bodily life that might be called forth both by working with children and by an appreciation of the giving of birth on which all mothering depends. Central to the antimilitarist conception of bodiliness I propose is a celebration of natality—the human activities of giving and receiving birth. I take the complex physical and social relations of birth giver and infant—the exquisite conjunction of radical interdependency and emergent individual separateness—as emblematic of the nonviolent connections through difference that mothers of both sexes struggle to sustain. Describing mothering as a sustained response to the promise of birth, I "see" mothers welcoming bodily life as a locus of pleasure and origin of will.

If my readings of mothering are sufficiently detailed and accurate, they should provoke in some other mothers a self-respecting, surprised recognition of antimilitarist tendencies and principles of nonviolence latent in their work and thought. Since mothers differ from each other in all the individual and social ways that people differ, it will take many

versions of maternal thinking, some radically different from mine, to inspire among varieties of mothers the surprised recognition I aim for. Yet, granted the promise of that variety, it seems reasonable to hope that antimilitarist representations of maternal work and thinking will strengthen the "peacefulness" of individuals and contribute to the wider recognition of an active, unsentimental, civic, antimilitarist maternal identity.

Diagnosis: Maternal Militarism

Heuristic representations of the sort I propose can seem perilously close to mystifying ideology. In order to ward off obfuscation and to insist on the need for change, I try to identify specific sources of maternal militarism within the practices of good enough, potentially peaceful mothers. For example, alongside a "sturdily antimilitarist" conception of bodily life I put a more familiar maternal conception of bodies which is incipiently militarist. A careful, caring welcome of bodily life and respect for bodily integrity is central to maternal nonviolence. Yet even the most benign mother may sometimes take her own and her children's "nature," their willful embodied being, as an enemy to be conquered. In times of rapid change or social crisis, a superstitious terror of the "stranger" can fuel an otherwise temperate mother's rage to control "disorderly," dirty, lustful, bodily life at home. Only in the most malignant forms of maternal thinking are children's bodies conceived as the site of pain and domination, the place where sadistic or terror-driven mothers enact their will. But many ordinary, good enough mothers struggle against their own compulsion for order and their drive to dominate unruly, "disobedient" children.

A maternal struggle to achieve a welcoming response to bodily life is emblematic of struggles to extend publicly maternal nonviolence. Just as mothers have to learn not to hurt or dominate what is strange and threatening in their own children, they also have to *strive* to respect and negotiate with alien and often frightening people outside their "own" circle. This is not surprising. Mothering typically begins with a passionate commitment to particular children and the particular people they live among. Although in a daily way mothers may try to create a peace worth keeping—one that is as free as possible from greed, domination, and injustice—domestic justice does not translate easily beyond the families and cultures in which it originates. Just because they hold themselves responsible for preserving the traditions and integrity, sometimes even the survival, of their social group, many mothers will fiercely support violence against the "enemy" (and therefore against the enemy's children) who seems to threaten their "ways," community, or state. At their not uncommon worst, parochial mothers engage in outright racist battle behind the shield of neighborhood and family.

Some mothers learn to hold their passionate loyalty to particular children in creative tension with a sympathy for other children, including those who are strange or strangers. Even these mothers may nonetheless counsel their children to embrace the violence that their state or political leaders tell them is necessary. Mothers train children in the ways of obedience that enable them at least to survive and at best to flourish—but also to "serve" when "called" by employers or governments. Despite their responsibility for training, many mothers are expected to delegate "difficult" policy decisions to fathers and public officials. To the extent that they have complied with the deauthorization of their authority, they will be ill-prepared for independent-minded resistance to their government's or political group's militarist policies in a time of "emergency." By contrast, committed patriotic sacrifice to the whole nation, to all "our boys," can seem a generous extension of the parochial loyalties of most mothers' lives.

In *Lest Innocent Blood Be Shed*, an account of nonviolent resistance and rescue in a French village during the second world war, Phillip Hallie identified three habits of mind and will that enabled citizens of Le Chambon to appreciate and resist the evils of Nazi racism while many more of their well-intentioned compatriots refused to see or were unable to act. According to Hallie, "lucid knowledge, awareness of the pain of others, and stubborn decision dissipated for the Chambonnais the Night and Fog that inhabited the minds of so many people in Europe, and in the world at large, in 1942."[9] Conversely—adapting Hallie's praise to the purposes of diagnosis—maternal parochialism prevents many mothers from seeing, let alone caring about, the pain of distant or different others. Willingness to abdicate "difficult" decisions to public officials produces ignorance rather than "lucid knowledge" of the real character and motives of war-making and of the painful consequences for "others" of the policies of one's own government. A cultural expectation that mothers will weep for war but can do nothing to stop it makes "stubborn decisiveness" unlikely.

Maternal peacefulness is an empowering myth. At its center is the promise of birth: every body counts, every body is a testament of hope. To violate bodies—to starve, terrorize, mutilate, damage, or abandon them—is to violate birth's promise. At its best, mothering represents a disciplined commitment to the promise of birth and a sustained refusal to countenance its violation. But good enough mothers—like other, good enough women and men—protect themselves from lucidity and therefore from responsibility. The peacefulness of mothering as we know it is entwined with the abstract loyalties on which war depends, the racialism in which war flourishes, and the apolitical privacy that lets dominators and racists have their way. There is no sharp division between the Good Mother of Peace and her fearful, greedy, or dominating sister. The heuristic representation of mothers as peaceful is inseparable from the diagnosis of mothers as militarist. It is the same work, the same thinking, ready for and requiring transformation. It is precisely at the point of felt contradiction, at the intersection of the promise of birth and its violation, that a transformative encounter might occur.

Toward Lucidity, Compassion, and Decision

When I first began thinking about mothers, I was more concerned with what feminists could bring to maternal thinking than with what mothers could bring to the world. I construed mothering and feminism oppositionally. I wrote as a mother who believed that feminism trivialized or simplified the challenges of maternal work. But I also wrote as a feminist daughter who believed that feminism might manage to rescue a damaged and flawed maternity. As a feminist I wrote suspiciously of the very practices and thinking that as a mother I was determined to honor. Yet, so great (at that time) was some feminists' fear of—and other feminists' need of—a mother's voice, that my daughterly suspicion was barely heard.

I am no stranger to feminist fear of mothering. Of all the essentialist identities to which "women" have been subject, the conflation of "the female" with heterosexual (or lesbian?) mothering may well be the most fearsome. Given a sorry history in which so many women's bodies and dreams have been destroyed by enforced and repressive "motherhood," it is not surprising that feminists have not found it easy to hear, let alone to speak in, a maternal voice. Adrienne Rich may have been the first to name feminist matrophobia and the consequent feminist desire to perform "radical surgery" in order to cut oneself away from the mother who "stands for the victim, the unfree women."[10] Peace activist Ynestra King elaborates this feminist rejection: "Each of us

is familiar as daughters with maternal practice, but most of us in becoming feminists have rejected the self-sacrificing, altruistic, infinitely forgiving, martyred unconditionally loving mother—for this is how I saw my mother—have rejected that mother in *ourselves* as the part of ourselves which is complicit in our own oppression."[11]

Feminists have good reason to reject a maternal identity that is still enmeshed in patriarchal and heterosexist institutions and that has often been legally, physically, and psychologically forced on women who would otherwise reject it. This reasoned and conscious resistance to patriarchal institutions of motherhood is intertwined with less conscious fears. As we have learned from Dorothy Dinnerstein and other psychoanalytic feminists, in societies where almost all mothers are women, few people overcome the fears and unfulfilled fantasies of Bad/Good, Devouring/All Providing Maternal Creatures. If, as Marianne Hirsch[12] and others have argued, feminists are especially ambivalent about power, authority, conflict, and anger, they may also be especially liable to what Nancy Chodorow and Susan Contratto have called "The Fantasy of the Perfect Mother," with its attendant fear of maternal power and anger at maternal powerlessness.[13] Like Men of Reason, feminists who honor choice and control may be threatened by the unpredictability and vulnerability of children and by the stark physicality and radical dependencies of birth giving.

Yet, however grounded their (our) rejection or deep their (our) fears, feminists cannot afford to leave mothering alone. Just because "mother" has been a fearsome crystallized female identity, mothering must be reconstituted as an enabling human work. Moreover, for many women mothering and giving birth are sex-expressive sex-affirming constitutive identities. To the extent that feminists adopt an exclusively and excluding daughterly stance, these women will either reject feminism or accept their alienation as mothers within feminism just as they accepted their alienation as women within other movements and institutions that ignored or trivialized "womanly" experience.[14] By contrast, a mother-respecting feminism in which mothers (who are also daughters or sons) are speaking subjects, in which daughters (who are sometimes mothers) are attuned to maternal voices, can confront in the name of mothers the damages as well as the pleasures of mothering.

When I now imagine mothers' transformative encounter with feminism, feminism is mother-inclusive, and therefore the meeting is not intrinsically oppositional. A mother-inclusive feminism can avoid the arrogance of setting out to "rescue" militarist mothers from "their" insularity and denial. Various forms of peacefulness are at least as latent in mothering as in feminist practices. Both feminist and mothering practices are drawn to militarist power and domination; each practice has its resources for resisting its own and others' militarism. It is the conjunction of feminist and maternal consciousness, of maternal sympathies and feminist solidarity, that might shift the balance within maternal practices from denial to lucid knowledge, from parochialism to awareness of others' suffering, and from compliance to stubborn, decisive capacities to act.[15]

For example, women and men acquiring feminist consciousness tend to focus on the impact in their lives of norms of femininity and masculinity. They come to recognize that the stories they have been told and tell themselves about what it means to "be a woman" are mystifying and destructive. Central among these stories about women are various tales of female mothering: women are "naturally" suited for maternal work and men cannot be mothers; unless widowed, mothers should be married or at least heterosexual; mother love is free of anger and ambivalence; good mothers are unself-

ish; children's demands are consuming and therefore mothers shouldn't, and in a just world needn't, "work"; mothers can't pilot airplanes, don't like to sell or repair heavy machines, can't dedicate themselves to an art or command soldiers in combat ... and on and on. In unraveling these and other stories, mothers acquiring feminist consciousness may well be prompted to explore undefensively their ambitions and sexual desires and in particular to describe realistically the angers and ambivalences of maternal love. As they ferret out the dominant myths of mothering, they may be able to confront the political conditions—what Adrienne Rich called the "institutions of motherhood" —that exact from them unnecessary sacrifices of pleasure and power.

Whatever the tensions and ambivalence of individual mothers acquiring feminist consciousness, a mother-respecting feminism brings a public and nearly inescapable lucidity to bear on its particular culture's mode of mothering. This feminist-inspired lucidity undercuts many kinds of violence in mothers' lives. Most obviously feminists name the abuses mothers suffer from lovers, employers, husbands, and strangers. Equally important, they recognize mothers' tendencies to "submit" or, even worse, to get their children to submit to or take the blame for the violence they suffer, perhaps especially when that violence is perpetrated by a father or a mother's lover. Feminists also look at *maternal* violence, and name the domineering or sadistic tendencies often barely concealed by the demands of discipline. But mother-respecting feminists look at mothers with a compassionate eye. They acknowledge the complex ambivalences of maternal passion, the poverty and desperation that often lie behind men's or women's maternal abuse or neglect, and the repressive and punitive control of female sexuality and birth giving that squander women's capacity to cherish their own or their children's bodily being. Most important, feminists move on from identifying and analyzing in order to create policies and spaces that offer mothers the minimal economic means and physical safety to take care of themselves and those they care for—to start again.

Mothers who "see" personal violences they previously denied, may find themselves seeing through the fantasies and moralities that justify organized public violence. Feminists have revealed the ways in which the "masculinity" for which men are rewarded is intertwined with the domination and violence that masculinity permits.[16] Militarist discourse is preeminent among the discourses of "masculinity"; as much as men have made war, war has made "men" as we know them. But if war is "manly," it is also "womanly." Many women are thrilled by the armed yet vulnerable Just Warrior who confronts Death on an illusory Battlefield. It is a feminine heroine "behind the lines" who keeps the "home fire burning" and with it the rare and increasingly outdated division between homes and battlefields, civilian and Soldier. A newly perceptive woman may suspect that myths of Heroic Deaths camouflage the realities of war's random, accidental, fratricidal killings as well as the cruelly vicious murder that making war permits. She may recognize that the fiction of a soldier's Battlefield is belied by the myriad soldier-civilian "relationships" created by distant bombings, fire torchings, search and destroy missions, forced relocations, prostitution, rape, torture, and pillage.

Mothers who begin to tease apart the fantasies of hero and battlefield that have buttressed their faith in war, are more likely to suspect the Men in Power and Defense Intellectuals in whom they have trusted. Evil Enemies, National interests, emergencies, conspiracies, and other worst-case scenarios are all vulnerable to their lucid, knowing gaze. When joined with a traditional commitment to protect, lucid knowledge may inspire mothers to protest policies that threaten their own

children—thus adding distinctive maternal voices and energies to antinuclear and ecological politics. Increasing *habits* of lucidity might also enable mothers—against the odds of media distortion—to acknowledge the violence of their own government's military and economic policies.

But lucidity alone cannot inspire a maternal compassion that can undercut the ethnic rivalry or racist phobia that fuels violence. Mothers have to learn to apprehend, to appreciate, to identify with the suffering of "other" mothers and children if they are to act against the violence that "others" suffer or to fight the injustices to which violence is so often a response. Imaginative compassion is hard won. Differences among people—of race, class, wealth, gender, sexual preference, nationality, religion, and education—are typically more obvious and almost always more deeply felt than similarities. Of the many differences among people there may be none more painful than the difference between a mother who expects to be able to provide for her children's needs, share in their pleasures, and mitigate their unhappiness and a mother who expects that despite her efforts her children will be hungry, frightened, brutalized by bigotry, or humiliated and disabled by the hidden as well as the evident injuries of class. Moreover, mothers are committed to their children; every fragile, emerging, cross-cultural maternal identification is threatened by any division that sets one people and its children against another. We should read with astonishment the literary and historical record of maternal identification with "other" mothers and their children—including those of the "enemy." Despite the pull of parochial loyalty, fear, and distorting fantasy, at least some mothers can see in "other" and "enemy" mothers a real, particular, and variant form of the passionate attachments and connections that determine the shapes of their own lives.

Interpreted heuristically, cross-cultural maternal compassion[17] is evidence that the difficult discipline of attentive love central to maternal thinking can be tentatively if imperfectly extended. An attentive mother is pained by her children's pain but does not confuse the two separable sufferings or inflict on her child her own distinct, adult and motherly sorrow. She comforts her child and therefore *indirectly* herself. Similarly, cross-cultural mothers do not pretend that they share, or even fully understand, another's suffering. It is sufficient that they imaginatively apprehend another's pain as painful, that they are pained by the other's pain, and that they act to relieve the *other's* suffering and only indirectly their own. Although they may be prompted by shame or guilt, as well as by outrage and sorrow, they do not let their self-preoccupations hinder their power to act.

I believe that a feminist ideal of solidarity with women who struggle against violence can inform and strengthen existing yet fragile maternal compassion. A principal obstacle to compassion for the different "other" is that difference is so often created in a nexus of domination and oppression, outrage and shame. Sympathy is sabotaged by injustice; conversely, to adapt a phrase of Alice Walker's, only justice can stop the curse of mutual hate and fear.[18] Early feminist ideals of sisterhood that assumed a "common" oppression or experience of caretaking mystified real divisions among women and the damages of oppression.[19] A more recent feminist ideal of solidarity aims for a cross-cultural alliance among and identification with just those women who are resisting violence and abuse. Because ideals of solidarity are sex/gender-expressive, mothers would be inspired as women to identify with other women who, as mothers, strive to create for themselves and their children the conditions for dignified work, self-governance, effective love, and pleasure. (Men who are mothers take on themselves something of the feminine condition.

See *Maternal Thinking*, chapter 2. They would therefore also identify to some extent with other women mothers.) Because these ideals legitimize women's struggle against specific injustices and abuse (as well as against more "natural" disaster), mothers moved by solidarity could be prompted to move beyond their shame, fear, or even their self-interest. A sex/gender-expressive extension of compassion and action will be more likely if there are actual existing struggles of women in resistance that can call forth and utilize acts of solidarity.

Fortunately in recent years, movements of women in resistance have developed in countries as different as South Africa, Chile, East Germany, England, Israel, Palestine, and the United States.[20] A women's politics of resistance begins by affirming "womanly" obligations and then demands that governments or communities respect the conditions necessary for "womanly" work and love. For example, women are responsible for children's health; in the name of their maternal duty they call on their government to halt nuclear testing which, epitomizing its general unhealthiness, leaves strontium 90 in women's milk. Since women feed families, they "riot" for bread. Since (mostly) women actively nurse the sick, women organize not only for better pay but also for conditions that will allow them to do their work effectively. Since women are responsible for protective mothering, in Argentina, Chile and across Latin America, Madres publicly and dramatically protest the "disappearing"—the kidnapping, torturing, mutilating, and murdering—of their children.

Women in resistance create new values of activity and stubborn decisiveness. When women carry pictures of their loved ones in the public plazas of a police state, chain themselves to their capitol building's fence, put pillowcases and photographs up against the barbed-wire fences of missile bases, or create open alliances among "enemy" mothers, they translate the symbols of attachment into political speech.

Insisting that their governors name and take responsibility for the injuries they risk and inflict, they speak a "woman's language" of loyalty, love and outrage; but they speak with a public anger in a public place in ways they were never meant to do. They are the heirs of the mater dolorosa, taking active, decisive, public responsibility for restoring a world in which their children can survive. As they fulfill expectations of femininity they also violate them, transforming, even as they act on the meanings of maternity and womanliness.

In a utopian mood I have envisioned a "feminist, maternal peace politics" made up of mothers, mother-inclusive feminists, and women in resistance. Feminist, maternal peacemakers draw on the history and traditions of women to create a *politics* of peace. They are inspired by the act and symbol of birth and by the passionate labor of women who throughout most of history have borne the primary responsibility for protection and care. Yet because they are feminists, these peacemakers subvert mythical divisions between women and men, private care and public justice, that hobble both mothering and peacemaking. Men become mothers and mothers invent new models and styles of public, nonviolent resistance and cooperation that are suitable to their particular temperament, personal history, social location, and economic resources.

The forms and ideologies of a feminist, maternal peace politics are various and just being invented. Yet even in its inchoate forms this politics is transforming the maternal imagination, creating in mothers new capacities to know, care, and act. This is not to say that feminist mothers or feminist and mother-identified men and women are the only or the loudest voices of peace. Many voices, wills, and projects are needed; there need be no competition for best peacemaker. It is enough that mothers who have hitherto played their parts in the scripts of the violent now move from maternal thinking to peace politics, thus contributing in

their own distinctively maternal ways to the many-faceted, polymorphous, collective effort to make a peace worth keeping.

Notes

1 For an excellent account of "standpoint" theories that rely on the idea of "caring labor," see Sandra Harding, *The Science Question in Feminism* (Ithaca, N.Y.: Cornell University Press, 1986). I rely especially on Nancy Hartsock, "The Feminist Standpoint: Developing the Ground for a Specifically Feminist Historical Materialism," which is now the last chapter of her *Money, Sex and Power* (New York: Longman, 1983). I have also used Hilary Rose, "Hand, Brain and Heart," *Signs* 9.1 (1983), 73-91, and "Women's Work, Women's Knowledge" in Ann Oakley and Juliet Mitchell, eds., *What is Feminism?* (New York: Pantheon, 1983), 161-184. There are many other accounts of the rationality of care with differing emphases. Two more recent interesting articles are Patricia Hill Collins, "The Social Construction of Black Feminist Thought," *Signs* 14, no. 4 (Spring 1989), and Joan Tronto, "Beyond Gender Difference to a Theory of Care," *Signs* 12.4 (1987), 644-663. Drawing on very different traditions and methodologies, Carol Gilligan and Nel Noddings also develop "care" perspectives. For Gilligan and Gilligan et al., see *In a Different Voice, Mapping the Moral Domain*, and *Making Connections* (Cambridge, Mass.: Harvard University Press, 1982, 1989, 1990). For Nel Noddings see *Caring* and *Women and Evil* (Berkeley: University of California Press, 1984, 1989).

2 Michaela de Leonardo, "The Female World of Cards and Holidays: Women, Families and the Work of Kinship," *Signs* 12, no. 3 (1987), 440-453.

3 I am relying especially on Nancy Hartsock's language.

4 These examples are Carol Gilligan's, *In a Different Voice*.

5 See Barbara Christian: mothering offers "an insight into the preciousness of life," "because women are *reduced* to the function of mother, which often results in their loss of a sense of self, the gift of seeing the world from [a maternal] angle is lost to them and their communities"—"An Angle of Seeing Motherhood," in *Black Feminist Criticism* (New York: Pergamon, 1985), 246.

6 A clear exception is Carol McMillan, *Women, Reason, and Nature* (Princeton, N.J.: Princeton University Press, 1982). While a "partisan of women," McMillan is explicitly antifeminist.

7 There are many other definitions and tasks of "feminist ethics," for example, elucidating feminist values or assessing moral concepts implied by or useful to feminist politics.

8 These phrases are from Margaret Urban Walker, "Moral Understanding: Alternative 'Epistemology' for a Feminist Ethics," in E. Browning Cole and Susan Coultrap-McQuin, eds., *Explorations in Feminist Ethics: Theory and Practice* (Bloomington: Indiana University Press, 1992), 165-175.

9 Phillip Hallie, *Lest Innocent Blood Be Shed* (New York: Harper & Row, 1979), 104.

10 Adrienne Rich, *Of Woman Born* (New York: Norton, 1978), 236.

11 Ynestra King, talk at the Columbia Seminar on Women and Society, Spring 1983.

12 Throughout these paragraphs I am relying extensively on the readings, analysis, and political insights of Marianne Hirsch's *Mother-Daughter Plot: Narrative, Psychoanalysis, Feminism* (Bloomington: Indiana University Press, 1989), especially chapter five. This book promises to create a new relationship, publicly and for me personally between mothering and feminism (Bloomington: Indiana University Press, 1989).

13 Nancy Chodorow and Susan Contratto, "The Fantasy of the Perfect Mother" in Barrie Thorne and Marilyn Yalon, eds., *Rethinking the Family* (New York: Longman, 1982).

14 According to Marianne Hirsch, a "daughterly-feminism" that casts mothers as object or other can be subject to maternal critique of the sort that white feminists in the United States have been subjected to by women of color; Western feminists, by Third World women; and middle-class feminists, by working-class women.

15 Internationally and in the United States, feminism is a multifaceted social movement in the process of change and self-definition. I intend my remarks about feminism to be neutral and inclusive though I am sure they will seem ethnocentric or biased to some feminists. I hope that it is not necessary for my purposes to distinguish kinds of feminism: gynocentric, egalitarian, lesbian, individualist, relational, liberal, Third World, socialist, Marxist, radical, etc.

16 As Carol Cohn has pointed out: Feminists aim to "destabilize, delegitimize, and dismantle patriarchal discourses—to render their systems, methods, and presumptions unable to retain their dominance and power and thus to open spaces for other voices to be heard." "Emasculating America's Linguistic Deterrent" in Adrienne Harris and Ynestra King, eds., *Rocking the Ship of State* (Boulder: Westview Press, 1989), 155.

17 "Compassion" differs from "pity." The compassionate person does not feel superior to the sufferer for whom she has compassion. Nor does she separate herself from the sufferer's fate. On the other hand, compassion is not quite "empathy" or what Carol Gilligan and Grant Wiggins call "co-feeling." The compassionate person does not, and should not try to, actually share the others' suffering. Such appropriation almost always leads to misunderstanding and romantic, masochistic, or mystifying identifications. The compassionate person is pained by another's distinct and separate pain and acts to relieve both pains. On the importance of presumed equality to suffering see Simone Weil: "Whoever does not know just how far necessity and a fickle fortune hold the human soul under their domination cannot treat as his equals, nor love as himself, those whom chance has separated from him by an abyss. The diversity of the limitations to which men are subject creates the illusion that there are different species among them who cannot communicate with one another. Only he who knows the empire of might and knows how not to respect it is capable of love and justice." Simone Weil, "The *Iliad*, Poem of Might," in George A. Panichas, ed., *Simone Weil Reader* (Mt. Kisko, N.Y.: Moyer Bell Limited, 1977). See also Lawrence Blum on the importance of equality to compassion, on the dangers of the compassionate relationship, and on the necessity of sharing another's pleasures as well as pain. "Compassion," in Amelie Rorty, ed., *Explaining Emotions* (Berkeley: University of California Press, 1980). On the meaning and development of compassion, Carol Gilligan and Grant Wiggins, "The Origins of Morality and Early Childhood Relationships," in Carol Gilligan, Janie Victoria Ward, and Jill McLean Taylor, eds., *Remapping the Moral Domain* (Cambridge, Mass.: Harvard University Press, 1988) 11-140.

18 Alice Walker, "Only Justice Can Stop a Curse," in *Reweaving the Web of Life*, Pam McAllister, ed., (Philadelphia: New Society Publishers, 1982), 262-266.

19 In "Relating to Privilege," Aida Hurtado has spoken of a common oppression that women suffer but that takes different forms for white women and women of color. While white women are seduced by white men, women of color are rejected by them. But both are dominated and oppressed. Although this common identification may work cross racially for women's subordination to men, and although many mothers suffer as women in relation to men, mothers seem to me more ineradicably divided by differences in the violence they suffer or perpetrate and differences in the resources they have to resist violence and provide for their children. *Signs* 14.4, (1989), 833–855. Maureen Reddy has written of the ways in which, in some African American writing, maternal bonding creates a degree of alliance between Black and white women. "Reading White in Black: Biracial Relationships in several Black Women's Novels," manuscript, courtesy of the author.

20 For an interesting and different discussion of these movements see Ann Snitow, "A Gender Diary"

in Adrienne Harris and Ynestra King, eds., *Rocking the Ship of State: Toward a Feminist Peace Politics* (Boulder, Colo.: Westview Press, 1989).

Questions for Discussion

1 Ruddick identifies many different, and sometimes conflicting, practices and dispositions characteristic of motherhood. She then wants to focus on some and discard others, for the purposes of developing peace politics. In what way, if any, are the remaining traits still best thought of as "maternal"?

2 Is the tendency of mothers to protect their children more likely to lead to their accepting the need to defend their territory, by military force if necessary, or to extend their desire to protect so as to include the children of others, in a way which argues against military force? Is one of these possibilities more reasonable or more desirable than the other?

War, Innocence, and Theories of Sovereignty

Michael Green

Traditional just war theory has relied heavily on a distinction between combatants and "innocents." In this article, Michael Green outlines the view of sovereignty which was current when this theory was first formulated, but then traces some historical changes (in particular around the French Revolution) to the understanding of sovereignty, and explores their implications for just war theory. In particular, he argues that the definition of "innocents" has changed, and with it the nature of warfare.

★　★　★

1. Introduction

The question of who may and who may not be a legitimate target in war has been a recurring subject of discussion among philosophers. The problem has been formulated as one of distinguishing between those who are innocent and those who are not in terms of their responsibility or lack of responsibility for the initiation or conduct of war. However, the connection between one's determination of

who bears responsibility for a political act and one's conception of political sovereignty has been generally ignored. In this paper I wish to argue that a major paradigm shift in the conception of sovereignty occurred during the French Revolution and that, as a result of this, a major shift in the way in which political responsibility was assigned occurred. This in turn led to a reassessment of the distinction between innocence and noninnocence and thus

Ethical Issues

to a change in the way it was thought permissible to wage war. Failure to recognize this has led many philosophers in their discussions of the conditions for a just war to rely upon models that apply only upon certain conditions and within certain circumstances and not, as they maintain, in all circumstances in which there is a war. I will begin by distinguishing two conceptions of sovereignty and showing how responsibility in and for war is assigned in each. I will then detail some of the difficulties arising from current discussions of noncombatant immunity that arise from an insufficient appreciation of these two ways of assigning responsibility. Finally, in the last section I will briefly suggest an alternative formulation of the problem and an approach that doesn't get bogged down in questions of responsibility.

2. War and Political Communities

Human beings tend to organize themselves into groups. There have been times when there were very few armed conflicts among such groups.[1] Neolithic villages were by and large unwalled. However, at other times the resort to armed conflict has been the accepted way of relating to another group. Not every kind of group conflict, though, constitutes war. Among some groups, a young man with sufficient daring could recruit others to go forth in pursuit of plunder and honor. This was a private act of those individuals and not an act of the whole community.[2] Violence in this case would not yet be a political act of one group against another. It would become so when different communities consolidated into a single political community headed by institutions conceived of as exercising power in the name of the whole community. The use of armed force against another group would then become a political act of one community against another. When this occurs, the nature of the conflict changes significantly.

Success becomes dependent upon the adequacy of teamwork, organization, and command within the political community and not just upon the weapons used.[3] The way in which this political authority is exercised conditions the way in which war is waged. Of the many ways of political organization open to human beings, two are of concern to us for our present discussion, for they gave rise in the West to two distinct ways of conceptualizing war and of assigning responsibility for it.

One type of political community holds that society ought to be based upon centralized and hierarchically organized political institutions and authorities. According to the variant of this tradition that has been strongest in the West, political institutions are divinely instituted and have the aim of upholding natural law, which is that part of God's eternal law that applies to human beings. Rulers were supposed to do this by formulating positive laws that adapt the dictates of natural law to the particular circumstances of the subjects over which they rule. It was recognized that custom could create law. However, custom was supposed to be subordinated to the natural law created by God. In this hierarchical conception of legitimacy, authority ran from God to natural law through the king to his administrators and then to the people. Government was not thought of as an instrument of the people but of God.[4] In creating them, God designed certain moral purposes for these states to serve. They were obliged to seek the common welfare of their citizens and to defend their citizens against unjust aggressors. All individuals were thought to have been corrupted by original sin. The state was established to maintain by force and coercion sufficient order to minimize the harms that sinful individuals might inflict on one another. It was God's agent for punishing the wicked. A ruler held his position in trust and upon condition that he uphold the moral order of the universe. Since the ruler derived his legitimacy from God, he was thought of as God's designated agent. God had entrusted him with the guardianship of a certain people. Government was not subordinate to the people, but the people to government. The people were to keep within their proper places and to obey their rulers. Indeed, there was little feeling between the people and their government.[5] Since the chain of authority on this view was from God to government to people, the people had no part to play in legitimizing, commanding, or controlling the activities of the government. Thus, their contribution to these were minimal and so was their responsibility for them. One cannot be held responsible for what one cannot and is not obligated to control.

This conception of political authority engendered its own conception of war. Since political acts were the province of the king and since war was a political act, it was the king's concern. The army was the king's army, and war was conceptualized as a clash of rulers. There was not much that the people could do about war except keep out of the way. In such a centralized state, the army consisted of professionals, often with specialized weapons. One of the fullest developments of this was the mailed knight. With the use of firearms, though, he was replaced by an army consisting of aristocratic officers and mercenaries. Both of these represented heavy investments and thus were not wasted unnecessarily.[6] Given this social organization, it was difficult to recruit citizen soldiers, and it was often dangerous to political authorities for them to arm their subjects. Working within this paradigm, war was, from the end of the Thirty Year's War to the French Revolution, conducted upon a limited scale and for limited objectives, usually territorial.[7] It was fought by professional soldiers according to a code of chivalry and certain agreed upon conventions and formalities. There were generally agreed upon rules for (1) treating noncombatants and

prisoners; (2) regulating the means of destruction; (3) arranging parleys, truces and safe-conducts; (4) levying extractions upon conquered territories; (5) conducting and terminating sieges; and (6) giving military honors to defeated troops. War was essentially the art of strategy. This was a form of war appropriate to a hierarchically organized society.

It was within this context that the traditional theory of just war developed. The view that a legitimate end justified the use of any and every means was rejected, and attempts were made to determine how a war ought to be conducted. A perennial problem in this regard was whether (and, if so, how) a distinction could be drawn between those who could be legitimately killed in war and those who could not. It was thought that killing innocent individuals was murder and hence wrong. The presumption was that an individual had a right to life and liberty and thus ought not to forfeit these without very good reason. Thus, the moral problem was twofold. First one had to distinguish between those who were morally legitimate military targets and those who were not. Then one had to show why the initial presumption to life and liberty remained in force in the second case but not in the first. In accordance with the theory of hierarchical sovereignty, it was held that certain groups of individuals were immune because they were not responsible for the prosecution of the war.[8] The question became, who was and who was not responsible for the war by taking an active part in the injustice? Within this perspective, St. Augustine argued that the soldiers of an army of a state acting aggressively were innocent. For such an individual, obedience to political authority was a duty.[9] A soldier was merely an agent or instrument of the public authority. He was merely following orders. Thus, since a person cannot be responsible for the evil consequences arising from the performance of his duty, the soldier was not responsible for the killing of others. The responsibilities lay solely with the sovereign who acted unjustly by instigating the war.[10] An aggressive war was due primarily to the evil intentions of a certain ruler, and thus in the strict sense only he was guilty of breaking the law and so forfeiting his right to life. War was basically a conflict between the will of the aggressive ruler (and possibly others involved in the decision) and the will of God which was being upheld by and through those opposing this aggressor. Innocence was granted to all those who did not participate actively in the act of aggression. Such individuals could be slain only as an unfortunate and indirect result of an attack on an unjust aggressor. Given the conception of political authority as coming down from above, this made perfectly good sense. Political authorities were responsible for war so that therefore it was the king and his [army which were responsible for war.]

After the French Revolution, war was fundamentally different because political authority and thus responsibility were conceptualized in a fundamentally different manner. In the new paradigm, war became a conflict among nations and peoples involving the total mobilization of those nations.[11] The French Revolution started the totalization of warfare by instituting the draft and involving the whole population in the war. It was natural to save what was thought of as a republic grounded in the will of the people by creating a people's army—a citizens' militia in which everyone was a soldier of some sort contributing to the war effort. A democratic nation required citizen soldiers to defend it. This was made explicit in a law passed on August 23, 1793, by the revolutionary French National Convention, which stated:

> The young men shall fight; married men shall forge weapons and transport supplies; women will make tents and clothes and will serve in the hospitals; the children will make up old linen into lint; the old men will have themselves carried into the public square to rouse the courage of the fighting men, to preach hatred of kings and the unity of the Republic.[12]

The basis for democracy was the citizen soldier. In Machiavelli, Guibert, Montesquieu, Rousseau, Mobly, Marx, and Engels one finds variations of this view.[13] Such an army was the surest safeguard against tyranny. In the American Revolution the citizen soldiers also played an important part. The Minutemen did not fight in strict formation or wear distinctive uniforms. The musket had helped to undermine the medieval order by ending the era of the knight. However, it was not until rifles could be mass produced that the citizen soldier could come into his own. As long as the rifle remained a specialized weapon available only to an elite, the citizens were at a disadvantage in any conflict. The citizen soldier came to his own in the American Civil War, and it was then that a new type of warfare began to develop.

Sherman's slash-and-burn path has been understood in several ways by different thinkers. Dombrowski argues that Sherman held that moral principles don't apply in war.[14] Walzer argues that he held the view that if the end was justified then any means deemed necessary in pursuit of this end was justified.[15] Neither captures what is primary to Sherman's notion that "war is hell." Hell is a place in which moral notions do apply. The guilty are punished with all the fury of pain and torment that they have unleashed on others and hence deserve. Sherman justified his actions as follows:

> we are not only fighting hostile armies, but a hostile people and must make old and young, rich and poor, feel the hard hand of war, as well as the organized armies.[16]

General Grant understood the Civil War in similar terms. As one biographer of Grant states:

Above all he understood that he was engaged in a people's war, and that the people as well as the armies of the South must be conquered before the war could end.[17]

The people of a nation became responsible for the initiation and conduct of war once political authority came to be seen as grounded in the will of the people. According to anthropologists, humankind's earliest ancestors survived because of their ability to cooperate and work cohesively in groups.[18] Individuals that have been deprived of human contact for long periods of time begin to lose many of their human traits. Feral children almost always fail to develop these traits.[19] Individuals have organized themselves into many different kinds of groups and have developed many different forms of life within these groups. The primary mechanism for maintaining group cohesion and functional unity is some sort of political process, an ongoing process of mutual adjustment and realignment of individuals within the political community. A political community gets its legitimacy from the consent (implicit and explicit) of its members. As Walzer correctly points out:

> politics depends on a shared history, communal sentiment, accepted conventions—upon some extended version of Aristotle's friendship.[20]

Groups of individuals that have radically different norms, values, and understandings can seldom function as one people. They often lack mutual understanding and trust and thus are unable to work together as a unity. This horizontal contract constitutes the nation.[21] It is a political community and not isolated individuals or radically different forms of life that agree to be governed as one body. The state, on the other hand, is a vertical contract. It is between the members of a nation and its government. This creates a certain form of government that ideally gives effect to the will of the people or nation. A legitimate government serves as an instrument established by collective decision in order to give effect to the collective wishes of a nation.

The movement toward mass participation, that is, democracy based upon nation-states in which the will of the people is supposed to direct government, provided one of the basic grounds from which mass war developed. In democracy, sovereignty (and hence power and control) belonged in theory to the people as a whole. Government derived its just powers from the consent of the governed and decisions affecting the welfare of the nation were decided by representatives who were as close as possible to the will of the people as a whole. This mass participation applied not only to political processes during peace but also in war. The nation was supposed to defend itself because it consisted of citizen soldiers—individuals who could in a moments notice shift from civilian to soldier. Napoleon could mobilize the resources of his state for war more fully than anyone before and thus could bring an enormous concentration of force to bear on the enemy only because a new kind of politics based on nation-states had developed. This new politics could enlist the whole citizen body for war.[22] With this new politics:

> the policy of a nation though maintained and enforced by her soldiers and sailors is not fashioned by them but by the civilian population.[23]

After the French Revolution, the chain of authority was conceptualized differently. It went from the people to the government so that now the people were thought of as the source of the legitimate activities of their government. The contributions of the people were (in theory) maximal and thus so was their responsibility.[24] A group that explicitly, knowingly, and willingly formulated a policy and then delegated and directed another to carry it out bore responsibility for it. Aggressive war was conceptualized on the model of a group of individuals who had sworn an oath toward each other to take every possible step to kill or enslave the members of another group. The conceptualization of the moral problem was also changed drastically. In the paradigm based on a hierarchical mode of political organization, there was the initial assumption of innocence and it was guilt that had to be proven. Now, there is the presumption of guilt on the part of all the members of the opposing group. Sherman's position was that since war is a group conspiracy, every member of the group is guilty. Thus, since the members of this group have unleashed a horrible and bloody whirlwind of violence, they deserve to feel the "heavy hand" of war and have this horrible and bloody whirlwind of violence unleashed upon them, as is only just. Many current discussions of the distinction between innocents and noninnocents rely implicitly upon the first paradigm in which it is assumed that a citizen is a passive bystander of the policies of his government. This raises serious questions about the range of applicability of such discussions and their relevance to modern times. To show this, I will now turn to an examination of some of these arguments.

3. Innocents and Noninnocents

Walzer's discussion of just and unjust wars is typical in many respects and will serve to highlight the difficulties that emerge from ignoring the social-political construction of responsibility and innocence. First it should be noted that he, like many modern philosophers, lumps together primitive wars (fought by individuals with bows and unfeathered arrows), the combat of aristocratic warriors, the limited wars of the eighteenth century, and modern ones as if war were always the same. He claims that the "modern characteristics of war are a product of war itself," thereby implying that war is (in its essence?) always the same.[25] Is there an essentialist metaphysics at work

here? Is the mathematical model of philosophical definition lurking in the background? Part of the problem in the treatment of war by philosophers is an insufficient appreciation of history and of the developmental character of human social institutions. Leaving this aside, let us turn to his analysis of the essence of war. The overall pattern of his argument is to argue first that the nation, that is, the people, are merely passive participants in war. Then he argues that governments are the source of aggression when it takes place. Upon this basis, he argues that the nation is innocent while the government isn't so that war can be waged justifiably only against the latter. Let us look at each of these steps in more detail.

The first step is to argue for the passivity of the people of a country in war. He argues that soldiers are forced into combat, and so are not responsible for the war itself.[26] We don't blame a soldier for fighting for his government. He is not thought of as a member of a robber band, a willful wrongdoer, but as a loyal and obedient subject and citizen.[27] Soldiers are mere pawns of war.[28] The war conventions are for armies of victims and not of free humans.[29] Most soldiers do not identify themselves as warriors nor is fighting their chosen occupation.[30] Most of the time they haven't chosen the combat and discipline they endure. They have a minimum of freedom and responsibility.[31] These same assumptions can be found in a whole host of other philosophers. Thus, Holmes argues that those who do the killing have "little or no say in the overall enterprise."[32] Fullinwider uses two analogies to conceptualize the relation between a nation and its army. In one case the relation between a nation and its army is like that between an individual who is cheering on an aggressor and the aggressor himself. In another case it is like that between an individual who is on the sideline observing an aggressor he has sent out and the person who is actually committing the act of aggression.[33] Mack also characterizes the relation between the nation and its army in one of two ways. He thinks that this relation is like that between a person "who happens to be walking just behind"[34] an aggressor and that aggressor or like that between an individual "who is not participating in any way in"[35] the aggression and the aggressor who is actually committing the act of aggression.[36] Nagel takes the passivity so far that he seems, at least by implication, to hold that only the guns themselves are active aggressors![37]

The second step is to pin the aggression on the government so that the political authorities bear the responsibility for it. Thus, Walzer argues that the legalist paradigm, which might lead one to believe that one nation (and not just their governments) was in conflict with another, uses a domestic analogy in which war is thought of as being like armed robbery or murder.[38] He rejects this analogy as inappropriate to the relation between nations. To refute it, he gives the example of the Greeks' war against Melos, in which an oligarchy refused to let the generals address a popular assembly. He draws the general conclusion that aggression is initially the work of political leaders.[39] In a similar vein Holmes states that government leaders are the "initiators of wrong."[40] Fullinwider, Mack, and Nagel in their analogies seem to also identify the aggressor with the government and not with the people, who are often thought of as merely innocent bystanders.

The third step in the argument is that war should be waged against a government and not the people of a nation. Thus Walzer argues that the men and women who lead their people into war are the ones who should be held accountable for that war.[41] Leaders are individuals who act for the sake of other people and in their name.[42] Thus, punishment should be directed toward such political leaders and others who actually control the government and make key decisions.[43] They are the source rather than the recipient of superior orders.[44]

There is a basic right to life so that no one can be forced to fight or to risk his life. No one can be threatened with war or warred against unless, through some act of his own, he has surrendered or lost his rights.[45] Thus, one may not attack or injure innocent bystanders or third parties, but only attackers.[46] Deterrence is like attempting to prevent a murder by threatening to kill the family and friends of every murderer.[47] Those who have lost their rights do so only because of their warlike activities. All those not fighting and not engaged in supplying those who are with the means of fighting ought not be attacked because they retain their innocence.[48] Those providing food to the troops are doing nothing warlike so have done nothing that entails the loss of their rights.[49] In an interesting contrast with the declaration of the French Assembly, he argues that women, children, and old men are not participants in the war and hence not legitimate objects of attack.[50] He asks how the people of Hiroshima could be said to have forfeited their rights to life. Neither paying their taxes, sending their sons into battle, nor even celebrating the victory of Pearl Harbor is sufficient to make these people liable to a direct attack.[51] However, here he hedges his bets a little because communities in "extreme emergencies" are allowed to kill innocents.[52] Mack also allows innocents to be justly killed under certain circumstances. However, Holmes, in opposition to positions like these, argues that since innocents will always be killed in war, war itself is immoral. Despite the differences in their final conclusions, one finds the common assumption of the passivity of the people of a nation. Such people are "led" into war, and have no or little control over the government (which acts instead of the people) and its key decisions. They are often like innocent bystanders (such as family member and friends) or third parties, who are forced to become soldiers by having their lives nationalized, and who have to kill individuals who are similarly the victims of their state. These assumptions seem true enough for a nation under despotic rule or which is organized in accordance with the theory of hierarchical sovereignty. Indeed, one must wonder how much these discussions of war were shaped by the Vietnam war in which most of the above assumptions were probably appropriate.

Yet there is a tension in Walzer's view that will bring to light some of the problems with this way of viewing war within the modern context. Walzer argues that the moral standing of a state depends on:

> ... the reality of the common life it protects and the extent to which the sacrifices required by that protection are willingly accepted and thought worthwhile.[53]

This seems more to describe a democratic state in which soldiers are not mere pawns but are voluntary contributors to a cause they deem worthwhile. He argues that the dominant value in international society is the survival and independence of separate political communities—"communities of men and women that freely shape their own destiny."[54] Such individuals share a way of life developed by their ancestors that is passed on to their children. A world in which entire people are enslaved and massacred is literally unbearable.[55] Individuals have a right to build a common life and to risk their lives only when they freely choose to do so.[56] This picture is in conflict with his previous one. He discusses the example of a war between Russia and Finland. This latter country was a democracy and the government's decision to fight had overwhelming support. In respect to this case, he argues that the decision to go to war should be made by the men and women who will have to endure the war that follows.[57] Here again he has an underlying image of passivity—the people must endure (not wage) the war. Yet at the same time his argument relies

upon a nonpassive stance upon the part of the population. A citizens' militia was to be responsible for its own defense. Indeed, delegating this responsibility to the government was a risky business, since the government could very easily turn such a concentration of force on its own citizens. This same assumption of passivity is found at other points. He states that "political integration and civic discipline make cities in which inhabitants expect to be defended and are prepared to endure a siege."[58] Again they don't expect to defend themselves but to be defended. The former is probably a more accurate description of many conflicts than the latter.

At one point he does say that "in a perfect democracy all who cooperated in planning, initiating and waging war would be responsible."[59] He might have discussed Thucydides's account of the Greek war against Sicily. The Greek assembly deliberated upon, discussed, and finally reached a decision on the question of whether or not to go to war. After reaching a consensus, they with great enthusiasm sent their generals (some of whom thought the whole thing folly) to invade Sicily. This is exactly how war has become conceptualized according to the new paradigm represented by Sherman and others. In a perfect democracy, though, this would implicate everyone, and Walzer's distinction between those who are innocent and those who are not would no longer hold. His claim that the people of a democratic government are not guilty of aggressive war and thus are not to blame for it because it is not their war seems very paradoxical—if not downright contradictory.[60] One might well ask to what extent such a nation was actually democratic. This is as paradoxical as his statement that democracy is a "factor only insofar as it increases the legitimacy of the state and then the effectiveness of its coercive power."[61] Democracy is supposed to function to minimize the coerciveness of government by making it subordinate to the wishes of the nation and not to increase its coerciveness. In a perfect democracy each and every person would be equally and fully responsible for the actions of his government. Each would be equally responsible because each would in theory be an equal participant in the political process insofar as each would count as one and no more than one. Each would be fully responsible, because if the method of consent has been in operation, each has agreed to the decision reached by that method, or, if not that, to be bound by whatever decision was reached by that method. Since each individual would be politically responsible either by actively participating or by withdrawing and allowing the decision to be made, and since each would do this voluntarily and purposively with all available knowledge of what they were doing, each and every individual would become morally and politically responsible for the decision so made.

Walzer's assertion that dissenters would be absolved of responsibility is also not at all clear.[62] In classical democratic theory, dissenters were still bound by the decisions of the majority, a commitment that was made in the original contract by which the government was formed. To adapt an argument from Locke's Second Treatise, if after having obtained the age at which one can "shift for oneself" (to use Locke's phrase) an individual chooses to remain within a country, then that person has given implicit consent to be bound by and to uphold the general will as expressed by the majority. As long, then, as the government is legitimate and it expresses the general will, then one is bound to support its decisions. One is still, though, at liberty to try and change the opinions of the majority.

Walzer's further claim that if a country is not a perfect democracy, then responsibility for war falls mainly on the government officials is also not obvious.[63] Even if the government is tyrannical, it is not clear that according to democratic theory the people are to be ab-

solved of responsibility for the acts of their government. Locke reserved to the people a right of revolution by which the people not only may but indeed ought to overthrow and resist a tyrannical government in which an individual or group attempts to substitute its will for the general will or one in which power has been usurped by an individual or group without consulting the people. Insofar, then, as the nation doesn't oppose such a government, it thereby lends legitimacy to it and its actions so that it comes to express the general will of that people. Within democratic theory, it is not clear that even children, the insane, and the mentally handicapped are innocent. These have guardians who represent their interests. These guardians are still bound by and to the general will of the society in which they find themselves in representing their interests. Thus, even if as a matter of fact political authorities are responsible for most wars and citizens are usually forced into being soldiers against their will, it is not clear that this absolves them from responsibility if they were responsible for letting themselves be put in circumstances in which they are so passive. Walzer asserts that holding civilians responsible for their government assimilates:

> ordinary men and women to their government as if the two really made a totality and it judges them in a totalitarian way.[64]

The assimilation of people to their government can occur in one of two ways. Either the government is primary and the people are made to conform to it, or the people are primary and the government is made to conform to [them]. Only the first is the way of totalitarianism in which the government becomes a total institution attempting to control all aspects of a people's lives.

There is an instance, though, in which he seems to recognize the possibility of a war between the will of one people and the will of another. This is in his discussion of guerilla war. In such a war, "the people are defending themselves."[65] It involves a "special form of *levée en masse* authorized from below."[66] In this kind of war the civilian support for war is "more direct" than merely voting for a candidate. Such a war depends upon winning "a very substantial popular support" for the guerrillas.[68] A high degree of support makes them legitimate rulers of the country.[69] The contrast between merely voting and being directly involved is one between passivity and activity and raises the question of the extent to which a country in which individuals play such a passive role would be anything more than a democracy in name only. However, he argues:

> if the *levée en masse* is a reality then war cannot be fought because no distinction between combatants and noncombatants would be possible in the actual fighting.[70]

He also argues that political hostility does not make people enemies, for if it did, then there would be no civilian immunity except when wars are fought in neutral countries.[71] Walzer's arguments beg the question. He assumes the validity of a distinction when it is the possibility of making that very distinction that is at issue. If the distinction between combatants and noncombatants breaks down because everyone is a combatant, then his conclusion that war may not be waged doesn't follow. The universalization of the combatant role is the typical condition of modern war according to Sherman and his tradition. The concepts of a nation in arms and a citizens' army were part of the thought of proponents of liberal democracy as well as of proponents of communism, such as Engels and Sorel. It is not at all clear that this type of war is so atypical when one considers the importance of wars between basic forms of life. Genocidal wars, such as those waged against the Native Americans in the nineteenth century, ideological and religious wars, such as those waged against the radical Protestants in the sixteenth century, and

civil wars, such as that waged by the North against the South, are not uncommon forms of warfare. What is at issue typically in such conflicts are whole ways of life between which there cannot be any compromise, according to the participants in the respective forms of life. Walzer's whole concept of returning to normal life would be meaningless when one becomes unable to do those things that make life worthwhile because an attempt has been made to eradicate one's way of life. He recognizes this but fails to see that in some circumstances this conflicts with his concept of returning to normal life. He might have examined the government policy toward Native Americans in the nineteenth century to see the limitations of this position. Walzer's doctrine that hostilities cease when a country is subjugated makes sense only when the conqueror makes minimal demands on the conquered, such as the demand to pay tribute or taxes, while leaving the other aspects of the way of life of the subjugated people alone. Otherwise, it becomes an attempt to eradicate a way of life and a nation—a crime that is according to Walzer of the worst kind.

The basic problem is whether the theory of democratic sovereignty sketched above allows one to treat the people of a democratic nation as passive victims of their government. From the point of view of the theory of democratic sovereignty, it is not, as Nagel argues,[72] just the soldiers engaged in fighting who are to be considered a threat. As Murphy points out, it certainly seems odd to consider the soldiers, but not the ones that order them into action, guilty.[73] Indeed, an army is more than a mass of individuals with guns. It has a chain of command and controls that directs its activities and keeps it together as a functioning whole. These are in many ways the most important part of an army, just as the nervous system is the most important part of an organism. Thus, not just the front line soldiers but anyone who is, as Murphy states, anywhere in "the chain of command or responsibility—from top to bottom" is part of the threat.[74] Thus, those directing the war effort may not claim innocence. What is important is to trace the chain of agency that holds "together under the notion of who it is that is engaged in an attempt to destroy you."[75] Most civilians, he assumes, would be merely contributing causes but not part of the chain of command. However, it is not so clear that this chain of command and responsibility need be as narrowly drawn as he thinks. Indeed, contributing as a causal link in the chain of events that enables an individual to function as a soldier isn't really the most important contribution to war when it is seen as a political act. Interestingly enough, he states later that the "enemy can plausibly be expanded to include all those who are criminal accomplices," or, as he also states, to those "with a stake in the venture."[76] In the democratic theory of sovereignty sketched above, the army is the instrument of the government and the government in turn is the instrument of the nation or people. Within such a system the deployment of the army depends upon the commands of the government but these depend in turn upon the commands of the people. Within this system, war is like a conspiracy among a group of people to direct violence upon another group. As the army is the agent of the government and under its control and command, so the government is under the control and command of the people. In the case of a conspiracy sending out hired killers, the killers are merely instruments of the persons who are sending them out. They are merely extensions of the common will expressed in the consensus reached by the group. Without this, the killers would not become a threat nor would they remain one. The individuals sending out the killer are not passive as Fullinwider's and Mack's examples suggest. Instead they are actively recruiting other assassins and issuing them directives to kill and, as citizen soldiers,

taking up arms themselves when necessary. The threat is the whole complexly organized system that generates the assassins and sends them forth. If the government and the military are the expressions of the general will or common consensus of the nation, then the threat is between one nation and another nation. The aggressive nation is organized as a whole for military purposes. It is this organized whole that is a threat to the citizens of the other state and not just each and every individual. Indeed, the war is only going to be brought to an end when this system of organization is disrupted so that the aggressive nation no longer has the will to fight. It is through its soldiers and armaments that one nation can become a threat to another one. From the point of view of the theory of democratic sovereignty, one can remove the threat only by going to the heart of the matter, the will of the people waging the war, and rendering the system unwilling to perform as a whole. Civil wars often take on characteristics of people's wars. Vietnam took on many of the characteristics of a people's war in which, as Christensen states, "the distinctions between civilians and combatants, women with children and combatants and unarmed individuals and combatants frequently" broke down.[77] Thus, Nagel's assertion that civilians are "harmless"[78] and that they have "nothing to do with the threat"[79] is not true in all circumstances. Neither is his statement that it is only the government and the military that constitute the threat.[80] Under the appropriate conditions, the entire nation can, contrary to Wasserstrom,[81] be culpable, that is, responsible for a war's initiation and conduct. This also calls into doubt Holmes's argument that war will always involve killing the innocent.

4. An Alternative Approach

My aim in this paper has been to show that war is a complex social institution and that conceptualizations of innocence and non-innocence occur within the context of a host of assumptions concerning the organization of political power and of the relation between a nation and its government. My aim has not been to glorify war nor to argue that one of the two paradigms distinguished in this paper is preferable to another. That the above discussions of war were framed in terms of a passive citizenry is indicative of the modern sense of alienation from political processes and calls into question the extent to which these processes are actually democratic in any manner except in name only. The history of warfare in the twentieth century is one in which centralized authority gains control over the military and replaces the citizen soldier with specialized troops equipped with specialized weapons.[82] This itself is indicative of the decline of democracy or of a failure to realize it completely. Individuals are treated as if they were still citizen soldiers, for example, by being targeted by atomic weapons, when in fact they no longer have the ability to function as such. The terms in which individuals are conceptualized (as actively involved citizen soldiers determining policy) no longer corresponds to their actual condition (passive individuals merely reacting to government policy). Thus, at the center of the views presented by these philosophers there is a fundamental truth. Yet there are other times and circumstances in which such assumptions may not be valid.

It should not be assumed, though, that the acceptance of the democratic theory of sovereignty and the recognition of the nonexistence of a distinction between the innocent and noninnocent, entails that one may legitimately wage war in any manner conceivable and against every conceivable individual. A full development of how these consequences can be avoided is beyond the limits of this paper, but I can briefly sketch its outlines.

Independent of questions of innocence or noninnocence, nations will wish to limit war

so that the possibility of their nation being totally destroyed is minimized, or at least significantly reduced. Most will wish that enough of their country remain so that their country can be rebuilt and their way of life continued after hostilities. A nation will wish to preserve its cultural, educational, and religious sites, its reproductive capacity (traditionally represented by women and children), and its nonmilitary economic assets. Thus, it will wish to restrict war as far as possible to military and military-related activities, and it will wish actions against these to be circumscribed by rules of appropriate conduct. However, no nation can expect other nations to grant these protections unless it is willing to grant similar protections to them through formal agreements. It is through such agreements as the Geneva Conventions and United Nation Declarations that such protections are publicly granted to those that enter into these agreements. Such a process captures more accurately how historically civilian immunity has developed.[83] Nations wish the perpetuation and furtherance of their own way of life. Since they claim self-perpetuation, independence, and sovereignty for themselves and since fairness requires that similar cases be treated similarly, it follows that they must grant similar self-perpetuation, independence, and sovereignty to other nations. Thus, nations have an obligation to attempt to create through formal agreements a community of nations, that is, an international system within which each and every nation has a place and may flourish. They should endeavor to create a framework that fosters mutual understanding, trust, and respect, allows for the social, economic, and cultural development of each nation, and is conducive to reconciliation among warring nations.[84] This is done by formalizing the relations among nations by subjecting them to rules and regulations so that a common core of expectations and procedures can be developed upon which mutual trust, understanding, communication, and assistance can hopefully be built. The creation of such a community of nations is fostered in part by preventing, through formal agreements, war from becoming a duel to the death and from becoming conducted in such a way that reconciliation becomes difficult, if not impossible. From this point of view, the whole question of innocence and non-innocence seems to be rendered irrelevant.

Beyond this there are other reasons for replacing violent means of conflict resolution with nonviolent ones. Given the tendency of government to become concerned more with its own survival than with the survival of the nation and to develop specialized weapons and forces to enforce its will, the question becomes, What is the best way for a nation to take back its ability to defend itself both from outside invaders and from its own government? The problem should not be to get people to think they can wash their hands of the situation because of their supposed innocence (which is an illusion under current conceptualizations), but to get them to assume their responsibilities and when necessary be able and willing to take direct action against such aggressive powers. One who takes democracy seriously holds that no government can maintain itself without the implicit or explicit, coerced or free, support and cooperation of the nation over which that government claims authority. The self-defense of a nation then depends upon developing mechanisms for mobilizing the ultimate source of government—the people as a whole—in order to withhold this support from illegitimate governments and governmental activities and from invading forces. The option of having some armed and some not (upon which the innocence-noninnocence distinction depends) seems incompatible with an active democratic way of life. The options are between training all the citizens in mechanisms of violent resistance and turning them all into traditional soldiers or training them in mechanisms of nonviolent resistance and turning them all first and foremost into active citizens. Between universalizing the ability to inflict violence or superseding violence. The ancient Greeks as well as several Native American tribes made sure that warriors who were fresh from the slaughter of battle underwent rites of purification before they were reincorporated and readmitted into the community. They recognized the fundamental incompatibility of the two modes of life. In our times it seems we are less clear about which mode of life is most compatible with human communal existence and democratic citizenship and responsibility.[85]

Notes

1 Robert Anchor, "War and the Social Order," in *Humanities in Society* 5 (1982): 9-28.

2 H.H. Turney-High, *Primitive War: Its Practice and Concepts*, (Columbia, S.C.: University of South Carolina Press, 1971).

3 *Primitive War: Its Practice and Concepts*, p. 23.

4 Joseph C. McKenna, "Ethics and War: A Catholic View," in *American Political Scientist Review* 54 (1960): 649.

5 R.R. Palmer, "Frederick the Great, Guibert, Bulow: From Dynastic to National War," in Peter Paret, ed., *Makers of Modern Strategy*, (Princeton: Princeton University Press, 1986), pp. 91-123.

6 G.E. Rothenberg, "Maurice of Nassau, Gustavus Adolphus, Raimondo Montecuccoli, and the 'Military Revolution' of the Seventeenth Century," in Peter Paret, ed., *Makers of Modern Strategy*, pp. 32-64.

7 Theodore Ropp, *War In The Modern World*, (New York: MacMillan, 1962).

8 R.S. Hartigan, *The Forgotten Victim: A History of the Civilian* (Chicago: Precedent Publishing, Inc., 1982).

9 R.S. Hartigan, "St. Augustine On War and Killing: The Problem of the Innocent," in *Journal of the History of Ideas* 27 (1977): 195-204.

10 St. Augustine, *De Civitate Dei*, translated by Marcus Dods (New York: Modern Library, 1950), I, 21, p. 27.

11 Peter Paret, "Napoleon and the Revolution in War," in Paret, ed., *Makers of Modern Strategy*, pp. 123-43.

12 Quoted in Hoffman Nickerson, *The Armed Horde 1793-1939* (New York: G.P. Putnam's Sons, 1940), p. 64. One can find a similar statement made by the Vietcong. See Michael Walzer, *Just and Unjust Wars* New York: Basic Books, 1977), p. 180.

13 R.R. Palmer, "Frederick the Great, Guibert, Bulow: From Dynastic to National War," in Paret, ed., *Makers of Modern Strategy*, p. 107ff; and S. Neumann and M. von Hagen, "Engels and Marx on Revolution, War, and the Army in Society," in Paret, ed. *Makers of Modern Strategy*, pp. 262-81.

14 D.A. Dombrowski, "What does 'War Is Hell' Mean?," in *The International Journal of Applied Philosophy* 1 (1983): 19-24.

15 Michael Walzer, *Just and Unjust Wars*, pp. 30, 32, 204, and 230.

16 Quoted in R.F. Weigley, *The American Way of War* (New York: MacMillan, 1973), p. 150.

17 *The American Way of War*, p. 149.

18 C.H. Cooley, *Social Organization* (New York: Charles Scribner's Sons, 1925); Ralph Linton, *The Study of Man* (New York: Appleton-Century-Crofts, 1936); and Patricia Mische, "Passage From Nationalism: A Personal Journey," in *Philosophy* 16 (1980): 215-38.

19 J.A.L. Singh and Robert M. Zingg, *Wolf-Children and Feral Man* (New York: Harper & Row, 1966).

20 M. Walzer, "The Moral Standing of States: A Response to Four Critics," in *Philosophy & Public Affairs* 9 (1980): 229.

21 Gerald Doppelt, "Walzer's Theory of Morality in International Relations," in *Philosophy & Public Affairs* 8 (1978): 3-26.

22 J.L. Thompson, "The Logic of War," in *International Journal of Moral and Social Studies* 1 (1986): 32.

23 Quoted in John Ford, "The Morality of Obliteration Bombing," in R.A. Wasserstrom, ed., *War and Morality* (Belmont, Cal.: Wadsworth, 1970): p. 351.

24 I am quite aware that democracies usually do not function in practice as they are supposed to in theory. In this section and the next I wish to deal only with the theoretical development of democracy. In the last section, I will turn to the importance of the fact that democracies often do not function as they should.

25 Walzer, *Just and Unjust Wars*, p. 35.

26 *Just and Unjust Wars*, p. 38.

27 *Just and Unjust Wars*, p. 39.

28 *Just and Unjust Wars*, p. 40.

29 *Just and Unjust Wars*, p. 45.

30 *Just and Unjust Wars*, p. 138.

31 *Just and Unjust Wars*, p. 305.

32 Robert Holmes, *On War and Morality* (Princeton: Princeton University Press, 1989), p. 186.

33 R.K. Fullinwider, "War and Innocence," in *Philosophy & Public Affairs* 5 (1975): 90-97.

34 Eric Mack, "Three Ways to Kill Innocent Bystanders," in *Social Philosophy & Policy* 3 (1985): 1-26.

35 Mack, "Three Ways to Kill Innocent Bystanders": 3.

36 "Three Ways to Kill Innocent Bystanders": 1-26.

37 Thomas Nagel, "War and Massacre," in *Philosophy & Public Affairs* 1 (1972): 141n.

38 *Just and Unjust Wars*, p. 58.

39 *Just and Unjust Wars*, p. 289.

40 *On War and Morality*, p. 187.

41 *Just and Unjust Wars*, p. 289.

42 *Just and Unjust Wars*, p. 290.

43 *Just and Unjust Wars*, p. 291. See also p. 273n.

44 *Just and Unjust Wars*, p. 291.

45 *Just and Unjust Wars*, p. 135.

46 *Just and Unjust Wars*, p. 137.

47 *Just and Unjust Wars*, p. 272.

48 *Just and Unjust Wars*, p. 145.

49 *Just and Unjust Wars*, p. 146.

50 *Just and Unjust Wars*, p. 43.

51 *Just and Unjust Wars*, p. 264. This ignores the extent to which the Japanese political system works on the basis of consensus and that the Japanese

entrance into World War II was based on unanimity. See Takeshi Ishida, *Japanese Political Culture* (New Brunswick, N.J.: Transaction Books, 1983), pp. 87-115.

52 *Just and Unjust Wars*, p. 254.

53 *Just and Unjust Wars*, p. 54.

54 *Just and Unjust Wars*, p. 72.

55 *Just and Unjust Wars*, p. 254.

56 *Just and Unjust Wars*, p. 61.

57 *Just and Unjust Wars*, p. 71.

58 *Just and Unjust Wars*, p. 163.

59 *Just and Unjust Wars*, p. 299.

60 *Just and Unjust Wars*, p. 302.

61 *Just and Unjust Wars*, p. 35.

62 *Just and Unjust Wars*, p. 300.

63 *Just and Unjust Wars*, p. 301.

64 *Just and Unjust Wars*, p. 261.

65 *Just and Unjust Wars*, p. 180.

66 *Just and Unjust Wars*, p. 185.

67 *Just and Unjust Wars*, p. 185.

68 *Just and Unjust Wars*, p. 195.

69 *Just and Unjust Wars*, p. 196.

70 *Just and Unjust Wars*, p. 187.

71 *Just and Unjust Wars*, p. 202.

72 "War and Massacre," pp. 123-44.

73 J.G. Murphy, "The Killing of the Innocent," *Monist* 57 (1973): 532.

74 "The Killing of the Innocent": 532.

75 "The Killing of the Innocent": 533.

76 "The Killing of the Innocent": 538.

77 W.N. Christensen and John King-Farlow, "Aquinas and the Justification of War," in *The Thomist* 35 (1971): 94-112.

78 "War and Massacre," p. 128.

79 "War and Massacre," p. 138.

80 "War and Massacre," p. 139.

81 Wasserstrom, "On The Morality of War: A Preliminary Inquiry," in Wasserstrom, ed., *War and Morality*, pp. 78-102.

82 The conflict between democratic and authoritarian tendencies in the military in World War I and the eventual victory of the latter over the former is treated by Robert Axelrod in *The Evolution of Cooperation* (New York: Basic Books, 1984).

83 R.S. Hartigan, "Noncombatant Immunity: Reflections on Its Origins and Present Status," in *The Review of Politics* 29 (1966): 219.

84 Robert Barry, "Just War Theory and the Logic of Reconciliation," in *New Scholasticism* 54 (1980): 129-52.

85 For a development of the concept of nonviolence as a mode of life, an idea hinted at by Holmes, and its relation to democracy as a way of life, see again Ishida, *Japanese Political Culture*.

Questions for Discussion

1 Are citizens of a democracy which is engaged in hostile acts "innocent"? Are soldiers who are "following orders"?

2 Are ordinary citizens of a democracy who are in favour of war in which it is engaged any more "responsible" for it than those who oppose the war?

3 Does a nation have not only a right, but an obligation, to ensure that the sovereign does not impose its own will in place of that of the people? If so, what implications does this have for the notions of innocence and warfare?

Excerpt from "Meeting New Challenges: Canada's Response to a New Generation of Peacekeeping"

The Senate of Canada

The twentieth century saw the rise of the notion that the international community should take responsibility for reducing violence between nations, rather than leaving individual nations with a free hand to decide how to promote their own perceived interests. One prominent development of this attempt at international control, developed after World War II, has been the "peacekeeping" force, which can provide a buffer between competing forces, supervise ceasefires and contentious elections, observe withdrawals, and assist with the provision of humanitarian aid. Canada has been particularly prominent in the role of peacekeeper, and indeed by 1993 was the only country in the world to have contributed to every United Nations peacekeeping venture, as well as having contributed to a number of international peacekeeping missions outside United Nations auspices. Altogether, Canada had contributed to over 30 missions, involving approximately 100,000 Canadians. The estimated total cost to Canada of these missions is in the neighbourhood of 21 billion dollars. Many questions have been raised about the extent to which peacekeeping missions have been beneficial, the degree to which it is in Canada's interests to continue to support them, and the general future of peacekeeping given a number of changes which have occurred in the international community. In 1993, the Canadian Standing Committee on Foreign Affairs filed a report summarizing the changes on the world political scene and examining the history and future of Canada's commitment to peacekeeping. The following is an excerpt from that report.

★　★　★

I. A New Era: What Does It Mean For Canada?

The world has entered a new historical era. The Cold War, which for 40 years provided a grim structure to the conduct of international relations, has been swept away with the death of communism in the Soviet Union and the collapse of the Soviet empire. The prayers of the western alliance have been answered; the consequences, however, have surprised many of the West's policy makers and left them searching—not always very effectively—for new ways to deal with the aftermath of tyranny and empire.

One challenge relates to the nature of this new era. President George Bush of the United States was bold enough to predict a new world order. His bravado has been met with considerable scepticism, especially from more pessi-

mistic analysts of international affairs, who have grumbled, sometimes cogently, about the greater likelihood of world disorder.[1] Ian Smart, a former executive director of the Royal Institute of International Affairs in Britain, has suggested that the decades between 1950 and 1980, when East–West confrontation and the balance of nuclear terror imposed stasis on international relations, amounted to a holiday for diplomats. But, he adds, "the holiday is over. We are reverting to a world of more mobile action and alignment."[2]

The members of the Senate Subcommittee on Security and National Defence prefer to remain cautious about labelling the new era. At the very least, however, the Subcommittee agrees that it is a period of profound transition. Already, the world has experienced a sweeping restructuring of alliances. Currently, it is witnessing various efforts to forge new or better international instruments to grapple more effectively with a complex of demanding challenges.

In seeking to understand the transition—and what Canada's responses should be—it is relevant to review the more obvious trends in contemporary world affairs, which are shaping the contours of the new era. These trends can be summarized as follows:

first,   the diffusion of power;

second, the crisis of the state;

third,   the rise of ethnicity and religion;

fourth,   the expanding meaning of security; and

fifth,   the increasing resort to multilateral principles and organizations.

Among the most significant consequences of these trends are the demands they create for the exercise of collective security. As a tool of collective security and international diplomacy, peacekeeping is changing to meet some of these demands. Peacekeeping has entered its second generation and, as the following chapters demonstrate, the new generation promises to be very different from the first.

Accordingly, Canada ought to use this transition to rethink its cherished commitment to peacekeeping. The proposal that this be done in no way reflects on the value of peacekeeping as it was practised during the Cold War, nor does it reflect on the abilities of the Canadian Forces; they were demonstrably good at a good thing. But the world has changed, so Canada must change. Canadians must reflect even on what is good—Canada's contribution to international peacekeeping—to discover both whether it is still relevant and, if so, how it might be improved. In order to do this, it is important to consider the five major trends of the new era outlined above.

(1) The Diffusion of Power

The foremost currency of international relations has always been power. Power, at its most basic level, is the ability of one party or actor to get other parties to behave in a certain way. To do this, states exercise a vast array of political, economic and military levers. The bipolar world of the Cold War saw power put to use in an intense contest of wills between the two superpowers, the Soviet Union and the United States, when every international event was either influenced by their rivalry or filtered through its lens.

That bipolar world has been replaced by a much more complex world in which power has been diffused. Different spheres of world politics have different distributions of power—some of them multipolar, some as much influenced by private actors as by states, and some spheres, such as nuclear weapons, remaining largely bipolar in distribution.[3] In economics, which is gaining increasing significance as a factor in assessing power, multipolarity appears to be the trend, with new regional blocs emerging. Several of these blocs enjoy, or are in the process of developing, competitive industrial bases. Each of them has its own dominant powers, all of which are pursuing influence and, in some cases, hegemony.

The end of the Cold War has not been marked by a concentration of power in the United States. Yet arguably the United States remains a superpower by virtue of its overwhelming military might, its continuing economic strength and diversity, its immense cultural appeal in the broadest sense of that word, as well as because of more intangible factors such as the prestige of having led the Western alliance during the Cold War, and the simple yet subtle expectation on the part of both Americans and foreigners that it will continue to offer leadership. Nevertheless, the United States is retrenching and reconsidering its global interests, with an urgency heightened by domestic pressures.

(2) The Crisis of the Nation State

The second trend, which may be the principal challenge of the new era, is the crisis of the nation state. The term itself, as one witness before the Subcommittee observed, has always been a misnomer since over 90 percent of the states in the world are multi-ethnic. (9:15)[4] A state is a legal entity with one status (or internal peace or order) maintained ultimately by a unitary or federal government. Nations are vaguer: groups of substantial numbers of people who share a culture, a language, a religion, a history, or all four. Most large countries are not unitary nations but multinational states. Some nations—like the Kurds, Palestinians, Armenians, Basques, or the Crees—have no state. Only in a very few countries, like Japan, do the limits of the nation coincide with the frontiers of the state.[5]

The frontiers of most of Africa's 50-odd states were drawn by the great powers at the Berlin Conference in 1884 with little concern for the ethnic, linguistic or cultural affinities of the Africans. The borders of most of the modern Middle East are equally artificial, derived from the division of spoils between the French and British after the Ottoman Empire crumbled during World War I.

Yet, as the British political theorist Lord Acton wrote in 1907:

> The greatest adversary of the rights of nationality is the modern theory of nationality. By making the State and the nation commensurate with each other in theory, it reduces practically to a subject condition all other nationalities that may be within the boundary. It cannot admit them to an equality with the ruling nation which constitutes the State, because the State would then cease to be national, which would be a contradiction of the principle of its existence. According, therefore, to the degree of

> humanity and civilisation in that dominant body which claims all the rights of the community, the inferior races are exterminated, or reduced to servitude, or outlawed, or put in a condition of dependence.[6]

The current crisis has its roots in the enormous proliferation of states which followed the Second World War. Fully two-thirds of the contemporary roster have been established since 1945. At the end of World War II, there were barely 60 states, 50 of them signatories to the UN Charter. Through the process of decolonization, that number increased to almost 160 by the end of the Cold War in 1988. More recently, with the breakup of Yugoslavia and the Soviet Union, the number is over 180 and climbing.

Whether all the most recent creations will be capable of sustained self-governance is moot. During the Cold War, a number of states survived largely because of infusions of aid from their former colonial masters or from one or the other superpower as the price of alliance. In the new era, with less generous subsidization and with the advent of a number of internal pressures ranging from ethnic conflict to drug trafficking, their political sustainability is doubtful. The results could be debilitating both for the citizens of those states and for the international community, faced with the tasks of providing peacekeeping and humanitarian assistance and of coping with refugees. Already, some observers have been moved to write:

> From Haiti in the Western Hemisphere to the remnants of Yugoslavia, from Somalia, Sudan and Liberia in Africa to Cambodia in Southeast Asia, a disturbing new phenomenon is emerging: the failed nation state, utterly incapable of sustaining itself as a member of the international community.[7]

Somalia is an especially apt illustration of the phenomenon. William Millward, an Arab studies expert who testified before the Subcommittee, described Somalia as a nation in search of a state, noting that the country is "relatively homogenous ethnically, linguistically, religiously, and culturally...." (9:14) Nevertheless, Somalia has not had a functioning central government since early 1991.

> The breakdown of central authority has brought virtually the entire population of Somalia into conflict in one way or another. A vicious cycle of insecurity and hunger is at work in Somalia. Lack of security prevents the delivery of food, while food shortages contribute to the level of violence and insecurity. Meanwhile, refugees from the senseless killing and the famine have exported the problem to the neighbouring states. (9:14)

The situation is similar in Ethiopia, where the destiny of the region of Eritrea has been the focus of an extended and violent clash, and in Sudan, where famine and the government's relentless attacks on minority rights are together propelling that country toward anarchy. Throughout the Horn of Africa, political instability, the collapse of central authority, inter-ethnic or internecine conflict and rampant militarism, combined with prolonged drought, are creating conditions of mass starvation and chaos.

(3) The Rise of Ethnicity and Religion

The issue of the nation state takes on revived significance because of the (re)emergence of ethnicity, nationalism and religion as political forces. Ethnic groups exist everywhere; indeed, everyone belongs to at least one such group. They are essentially synonymous with the "nation"—people sharing a culture: traditions, language, sometimes religion. Although dynamic, ethnic and national groupings have never ceased to exist. Yet, during the Cold War, they were largely ignored or actively suppressed because of the overriding, intense superpower rivalry.

In the current era, many groups have begun to reassert their identities, often with objectives that are highly political. Unfortunately, as Allan Kagedan, a Soviet nationalities expert, told the Subcommittee, "the politicization of ethnicity often leads to violence."(9:16) Political ethnicity or nationalism can be seen as a basic need:

> the need is to belong together in a coherent and stable community. Such a need is normally satisfied by the family, the neighbourhood, the religious community. In the last century and a half such institutions all over the world have had to bear the brunt of violent social and intellectual change, and it is no accident that nationalism was at its most intense where and when such institutions had little resilience and were ill-prepared to withstand the powerful attacks to which they became exposed.[8]

Some ethnic groups seek self-determination or autonomy within a multinational state or simply rights of expression and political participation equal to those of other citizens or groups. They use legal or constitutional mechanisms to that end. One such example would be the Czech and Slovak Federated Republic. Following a fair and democratic referendum, the two republics have decided that their futures lie apart.

Yet other groups have demonstrated ugly and unsettling objectives, allowing long-simmering hatreds to boil over and permitting vengeance to govern the means and ends of political life. Dr. Kagedan told the Subcommittee:

> eastern Europe and central Eurasia, freed of communist control, have fallen prey to a history of ethnic enmity which has left the region strewn with conflicting territorial claims, tales of massacres, hostile ethnic stereotypes and contemporary scores to be settled.(9:17)

The war between Armenia and Azerbaijan over Ngorno-Karabakh is being waged with the echoes of the 1915 Turkish massacre of Armenians still ringing in the ears of combatants on both sides, while some of the historical echoes in the desperate struggle raging in the former Yugoslavia date back to the 14th century. In the latter case, some groups, employing a practice known as "ethnic cleansing," have been forcibly expelling others by terror and murder. When hatred of this intensity is combined with political will and powerful weapons, the results are disastrous.

Yet such intensity argues more strongly for forbearance and early efforts at conciliation—"preventive diplomacy"—by the international community; qualities which were not much in evidence in the early stages of the crisis in the former Yugoslavia. Professor Edith Klein, an authority on Yugoslavia at York University, has noted that "the intense pressure put on the international community" to extend early recognition to Slovenia and Croatia "preempted setting in place any kind of conflict resolution procedure."(6:27)

Hence, the blame for the difficulties of effective peacekeeping at this juncture in ex-Yugoslavia should really be affixed to the inadequacies of earlier diplomatic efforts—when the domestic political considerations of various foreign states overrode the process of reconciliation. The peacekeeping efforts now being made in the former Yugoslavia are a direct result of that failure and an object lesson for other cases where ethnic conflict threatens the viability of multinational states.

(4) The Expanding Scope of Security

The fourth trend of the new era is the expanding scope of security. Preserving and promoting security means fostering those conditions that create and maintain stability, while still allowing legitimate change. Threats to security, therefore, are those which disturb or impede the necessary conditions.

The Cold War approach to security was to determine as well as possible both a state's military capabilities and its intentions. The overwhelming emphasis was on issues related to the military balance between the superpowers. The root causes of conflict were perceived to be superpower rivalry and the arms race.

In the post-Cold War era, the definition of security is expanding. Issues that were of concern during the Cold War, such as nuclear proliferation and arms races, still carry great weight—witness the anxiety about the command and control of nuclear weapons in the former Soviet Union. However, security no longer is considered an exclusively state-based concept any more than national armies are perceived as the only instigators of serious conflict. Military issues still matter, but no longer are they the paramount factor which they used to be.

Yet the end of the Cold War alone does not explain the enlarged scope of security. The fact that disparate and often non-military conditions may serve as catalysts of tension or trigger actual conflict is not a new phenomenon. What has changed is the way the world perceives such conflicts or threats of conflict. The communications revolution—the phenomenon of the "global village"—has magnified the impact of such strife everywhere. Consequently, in the discussion of emerging security issues that follows the most salient factor may well be the increasing visibility of all these issues as much as the issues themselves.

One of the new issues to emerge as a security concern has been humanitarian aid, especially to areas affected by conflicts or natural disasters. The international community no longer finds it easy to ignore the fate of large numbers of suffering humanity—even when the causes are due to internal conflict. Moral rectitude and public pressure have influenced decision makers to make at least some effort to alleviate suffering. UN Under Secretary-General for Humanitarian Affairs, Jan Eliasson, told the Subcommittee of a new concept of "the solidarity of people in need" as a means of balancing the diverging claims of national sovereignty and international interference.

The decision by the UN Security Council, on December 3, 1992, to send a U.S.-led force to Somalia to create a "secure environment for humanitarian relief operations" marks, according to some observers, a landmark in the development of humanitarian law.[9] For the first time, a Security Council resolution stated that "the magnitude of the human tragedy caused by the conflict in Somalia" by itself constituted "a threat to international peace and security," justifying outside intervention.[10]

Increasingly, the international community appears to recognize the welfare of suffering people and the urgency of their plight. Moreover, with the Cold War abated, there are fewer ideological or geostrategic barriers to interceding. The major inhibition now relates to states' willingness to use their resources for this purpose. Nevertheless, it is difficult to limit intervention to humanitarian affairs without addressing in some way the underlying political conflict. Indeed, it probably is vital that the causes be dealt with, once a decision on international intervention has been taken, for the alternative may simply be a recurrence of the problems in an even graver form.

Another set of issues of increasing concern within the international community, which are being described more often as a security matter, are human rights and democratic development. In a speech to the 47th session of the United Nations General Assembly, the Honourable Barbara McDougall, Secretary of State for External Affairs, described "three fundamental weaknesses" within nation states "that can cause disputes that go beyond their borders: (i) the absence or abuse of fundamental human rights; (ii) the absence of a developed

system of democratic values and institutions; and (iii) an inability to make responsible choices in the management of public policy."[11]

Unfortunately, the Minister was unable to meet with the Subcommittee to discuss in greater depth the weaknesses she had outlined. The Subcommittee does not find itself in entire agreement with Ms. McDougall. While the Subcommittee accepts that democratic development may be a laudable long-term goal, it notes that in Western societies institutions of civil society preceded the advent of democracy or even democratic values by generations. It may be, rather, that democratic institutions can operate effectively only after a foundation of law and order has been established and accepted by the society as a whole. Indeed, too heavy and impatient an emphasis on democracy may prove to be counterproductive both to the maintenance of international peace and security and to the achievement of viable democracies. A senior UN official recently observed indirectly to another parliamentary committee,

> Many people have accepted a game—democracy—which, when it comes right down to it, they don't want to play. In many parts of the world, people think they cannot afford to lose and so when the results of democracy are unacceptable they demand their own country or state where they are sure to win. In the former USSR, everyone wants to be sovereign.[12]

At the same time, the Subcommittee believes that Western governments should be concerned to encourage the legal and institutional basis for healthy and sustainable civil societies elsewhere in the world. Such a basis is crucial if a more tolerant approach to diversity is to be followed in states, the great majority of which are likely to remain multi-ethnic rather than unitary in composition. The emphasis, therefore, should be on good governance, which admits of both diversity and power-sharing, and on securing the rights of minorities rather than on early elections as a panacea, a general cure for all the political ills of mankind.

A third emerging security issue is the vast problem associated with refugees and other displaced peoples. This issue has been brought to the fore by several of the trends described above. The lot of refugees is seen as an unacceptable deprivation of the security of the person with the potential to create destabilizing situations which, by definition, will involve other countries. Moreover, the countries most affected by refugee issues have gained new voices and new leverage within the international community.

Finally, security is also now being seen to include a complex range of economic and environmental factors. That widespread economic distress can lead to political instability and even to international conflict is not a particularly new concept. More recent is the recognition that environmental decline can also occasionally lead directly to conflict—for example, when scarce water resources must be shared. Generally, however, the environment's impact on nations' security "is felt in the downward pull on economic performance and, therefore, on political stability."[13]

(5) Multilateral Diplomacy

Inevitably, the new, broader security agenda will encourage an increased emphasis on multilateralism. Three main reasons may be cited:

First, as noted above, the number of states is increasing and thus the number with a stake in any issue area. The effect of this fragmentation actually has been to increase the interdependence of states. But although more states are demanding to be included in the process of negotiation and decision-making, "interdependence does not mean harmony; rather, it often means unevenly balanced mutual dependence." Nevertheless, states will search "for

the forum that defines the scope of an issue in the manner best suiting their interests."[14]

Second, the past few years have seen a proliferation on the international agenda of issues, that cut across national boundaries and require collective action and international cooperation. These include environmental concerns such as global warming and acid rain, debt crises, health epidemics, the drug trade, the protection of human rights, refugee movements, and terrorism.

Third, in the new era, no one state alone either can or will be able to afford the costs of providing all the necessary support and assistance, whatever the issue might be. In order to create a pool of resources big enough to accomplish all the tasks that are agreed upon, a significant number of other states and organizations will have to be involved.

Given that diplomacy increasingly will be practised in a multilateral context, the United Nations will become a leading forum of discussion and negotiation and, less certainly but most likely, an important vehicle for providing aid and resources. Regional organizations also may play more important roles.

Aleksandr Belonogov, Russian Ambassador to Canada and former Soviet Ambassador to the United Nations, told the Subcommittee that the Cold War held the effectiveness of the United Nations in check. With its passing ends "a state of semi-paralysis in its most important but politically most delicate sphere of international security." (5:6) Already, the new-found consensus among the five permanent members of the Security Council has spawned a series of initiatives in several regional conflicts that previously had been impervious to progress. These have included the decolonization of Namibia, mediation efforts throughout Central America, and the movements toward peace in Afghanistan, Angola, Cambodia, and Mozambique.

Canada's Interests

Changes in international relations over the past few years have been dramatic. The obvious question which these changes raise for Canada is whether Canadian policies should change as well. What are Canada's interests in this new period of transition?

Historically, Canada has justified its activity in peacekeeping as an expression of an overarching policy of helping to maintain international peace and security. In the discussion above, it was noted that security now encompasses stability and economic well-being, as well as more traditional military considerations. Although striving to promote international security certainly contains elements of altruism, it is anchored in two quite pragmatic considerations of fundamental importance to Canada's own security. First, widespread respect for the rule of law makes the world safer and more predictable. Second, Canadians will be more secure if Canada is a stable and prosperous society within a community of stable and prosperous societies.

Collective security, in principle, means creating and maintaining international peace and security by regulating and enforcing appropriate international relations through the rule of law and by encouraging the prosperity of individual states within that framework. Accordingly, collective security is a chief pillar of Canada's foreign policy; peacekeeping acts as a buttress to that pillar. William Barton, former Canadian Ambassador to the United Nations, summarized this position for the Subcommittee: "Canadian participation in peacekeeping has made a substantial and valuable contribution to the attainment of international peace and security and thus to our foreign policy goals and the national interest."(5:11)

Professor Harold Klepak of the Collège militaire royal de St-Jean observed that, as the Canadian military presence in Europe diminishes, Canada will be seeking new kinds of op-portunities to play a role and influence events on the world stage. Canada's expertise in peacekeeping is an obvious asset in such a strategy.

> From a military point of view, particularly now that we have withdrawn from Europe to all intents and purposes, peacekeeping is the only major area of Canadian military activity that is not continental.... peacekeeping is what we do that is not with the United States and therefore may provide a role in terms of keeping our forces abreast not so much with modern technology as with what is happening in the world in cooperative efforts on a multilateral basis. As multilateralism is the basis of Canadian interests historically, that is an important point. (3:11)

Professor Klepak's final observation is an accurate characterization of the period since 1945. Multilateral institutions provide channels for the pursuit of many of Canada's foreign policy objectives. As a middle power, Canada frequently has interests similar to those of other middle powers. Acting alone, it may have only a limited capacity to achieve its goals. However, when Canada acts in concert with a group of middle powers, Canada can both influence the goals of that group and contribute to the resources and weight of the group.

Moreover, Canada has had a special reason to emphasize a multilateral approach in its international diplomacy. As a middle power with innumerable ties to the United States, Canada always has been concerned to create countervailing ties to offset American influence. The conviction has been that in multilateral forums, Canada would find, among other states, allies for its positions, and as a group they, in turn, could influence U.S. policies. This notion of a countervail is a tradition in Canadian foreign policy, and should be maintained, not for its sentimental value, but because it remains a rational direction for policy given the unique constraints that Canada faces.

However, especially at a time of increasing American participation in multilateral institutions of peace and security, it is in Canada's interest to increase its own involvement in these institutions in order to take advantage of American resources, while at the same time trying to ensure that American participation does not overwhelm the legitimate interests of middle and smaller powers.

There are other reasons for Canadian involvement. Professor David Cox of Queen's University suggested that Canada has achieved certain side benefits from the practice of peacekeeping.

> Peacekeeping has helped Canada to establish itself as a leading proponent of cooperative approaches to international security.... peacekeeping, and with it the image of a responsible internationalist state, raises Canada's profile and strengthens our position across a broad range of international diplomatic negotiations. (6:6)

The Subcommittee accepts this argument, but it questions whether either Canada's politicians or its diplomats are making full use of the leverage Canadian activities could provide. A generation in Cyprus and intense involvement in Yugoslavia must surely indicate our ongoing contribution to European security. Perhaps more credit, and therefore more benefits, could be gained from these activities in various multilateral and bilateral dealings.

Professor Cox remarked also that peacekeeping had become an important element in shaping the Canadian identity:

> [P]eacekeeping, which is really the most visible manifestation of Canada's international diplomacy, identifies Canada to Canadians. It makes us aware of our international orientation, of an orientation that is distinctively and perhaps uniquely Canadian.(6:6)

The final traditional Canadian interest in pursuing an active profile in peacekeeping was the benefits it provided the military. A predecessor of this Subcommittee, the Senate Special Committee on National Defence, heard from General Paul Manson, the Chief of Defence Staff in 1987, that "there is no question that we welcome the opportunity to send our people to the United Nations peacekeeping operations." He went on to explain that the training that peacekeeping offers is difficult to provide in an artificial setting, and he especially emphasized its importance for junior leaders in the Canadian Forces.[15]

This point was reconfirmed on more than one occasion during the Subcommittee's proceedings, but Major-General Clive Milner, the former Commander of the UN Force in Cyprus, may have put it most succinctly when he said:

> There is nothing like the completion of a six-month or one-year assignment to a United Nations mission by a Canadian officer or soldier to raise his morale, because he feels that he has done something for himself, for his unit, for his uniform, for his country and for the world at large. There is a tremendous feeling of satisfaction when that young man or young woman comes home and is able to say, 'I helped keep the peace. I may have helped save lives. I helped people in distress, people who were much worse off than I am....' As an individual it raises morale. Collectively as a unit it certainly does, and therefore it contributes to the well-being of the Canadian Forces at large.(10:14)

The foregoing provides a summary of the main reasons for Canada's active participation in international peacekeeping over the years—Canada's interests in peacekeeping. This report will seek to explore, along with what has changed in the world since the end of the Cold War, what changes Canada should adopt with respect to its peacekeeping activity.

We have mentioned the Subcommittee's conviction that, in trying to assess this question, the inherent virtue of the activity or even our abilities at it are not sufficient reason to warrant its continuation. Alex Morrison, of the Canadian Institute of Strategic Studies, who has a great deal of peacekeeping experience, suggested that Canada contributed to peacekeeping: "because it was good."(7:20) While this may have been an adequate response during the initial phase of peacekeeping—the phase which bears a distinctively Canadian stamp because of the efforts of statesmen like Lester Pearson and Howard Green and Paul Martin to make it work—it no longer is adequate as we move into an era when demands for Canadian involvement multiply, when missions may require larger forces, when the risks are greater, and when the complexity and nuances of the various missions have all significantly increased.

In the past there appears to have been a proclivity on the part of successive Canadian governments to participate in every peacekeeping mission. They did not decide to participate lightly, without weighing the relevant factors, but the decisions increasingly came to be taken in a context in which Canada's record and reputation were never far removed from the minds of the decision-makers. A Canadian military historian, J.L. Granatstein, has made this point; he quotes the late distinguished scholar of Canadian foreign policy, John Holmes:

> 'Ours is not a divine mission to mediate. Our hand is strengthened by acknowledged success, but it is weakened if planting the maple leaf becomes the priority'. Too often Canada's participation in peacekeeping operations (PKOs) has had some of this 'planting the flag' idea about it, a sense that we must maintain our record as the country that has served on more PKOs than any other—whether or not those operations made sense, had much chance of success, or exposed our servicemen and servicewomen to unnecessary risks in an unstable area of the world.[16]

The Subcommittee also notes Professor Granatstein's admonition that "for too many Canadians peacekeeping has become a substitute for policy and thought."[17] In this report, we seek to set forth factors which ought to be taken into account as the Government strives to achieve a policy to guide Canada's participation in peacekeeping in the complex new era in which we live.

V. Meeting the Challenge

A distinguished critic once wrote, "The most a critic can do is to sort out those aging ideas that get encrusted round past creative achievement and clog the proper working of the imagination in changing times." It is in this sense that the Subcommittee has approached its work. Whether our efforts will be regarded as helpful, we leave to historians. But we do hope that this report will serve as a cogent critique of current international efforts in peacekeeping and, in turn, prompt action, or reaction, by policymakers as they assess Canada's future role in international peace and security.

In concluding this report, the first major point the Subcommittee wishes to emphasize is that, in the new era, there are likely to be many occasions for Canadian involvement in different kinds of peacekeeping operations, some of which will be much more complicated and dangerous than any in the past. In responding to these opportunities, Canada will not be able to do all that it did in the past; for example, it will not be able to participate in every mission that is requested of it. Indeed, it ought not to be involved if its interests or resources dictate otherwise.

Moreover, in what Canada does undertake, it will have to alter its approaches. First, regardless of participation in actual operations, Canada should help to define how peacekeeping is to be practised in this new era. Second, it is time for Canada to define its own interests clearly. Third, the record of the Canadian

Forces has been good, but the situations faced are changing so that new responses are needed.

In the first instance, the Subcommittee was impressed by evidence which suggests that the world has changed dramatically and that one of the changes has been that peacekeeping has moved from being a relatively peripheral affair to being front and centre in the conduct of international relations. Yet, despite its greater importance and despite the explosion of new operations, the institutions and infrastructure of peacekeeping remain much the same.

There are, however, still more fundamental issues which need to be addressed. The principal threat to peace now is nationalist aggression or national disintegration. But the politically confused situation confronting the West is producing, as one analyst of international relations put it, "a confusion in values."

> At the moment there is some consensus with regard to the rights of states in relation to each other, that is, nonaggression, and with the rights of individuals in relation to states, that is, basic political liberties. But there is growing confusion with regard to the rights of groups in relation to states and in relation to each other.[1]

It may be, as another analyst has suggested, that a compass will be found in the Holocaust's enduring lesson, namely "that sovereignty in a seamless new world no longer allows a regime to destroy its own citizens with impunity or indifference and that a truly peaceful planet must outlaw aggression within borders as well as across them."[2]

Certainly, there needs to be a concerted effort by the international community to forge a new system of collective action to redress such outrages. At the same time, there must also be a recognition of "the complexity of such intervention, of external culpability in tragedies such as Somalia, and of the dangers of neo-imperial aggrandizement."[3] Canada has a role to play in these debates, and it is an important role.

Consider the first of the complicating factors—the complexity of intervention. Even where the intervention is strictly humanitarian—without any direct strategic advantage, such as in Somalia—the complexities may yet prove to be too great for the international community to resolve. John Watson, the executive director of Care Canada, observed at a recent meeting:

> Somalia is not an anomaly; whole areas of the world could revert to tribalism and chaos. In these situations, humanitarian aid is the most that can be managed. The trouble is that far from being a peacemaker, aid can act as a catalyst of conflict.

But once intervention takes place, the world is immediately faced by two serious problems: (a) how is it possible to intervene without becoming embroiled in local conflicts and, (b) how is it possible *not* to address in some way the underlying political conflicts that gave rise to such misery?

A distinction needs to be drawn between humanitarian efforts which are little more than palliative and designed chiefly to make people in the West feel better and more effective operations. It may be Canadians need to fortify themselves against the argument that something should or even can be done in all the conflict situations around the world. That would be tantamount to making policy by television. The Arab studies expert, William Millward, reminded the Subcommittee:

> [W]e have to be careful here not to give ourselves an exaggerated sense of mission; that our mission really is to transfer from our own domestic experience to other parts of the world that are so radically different culturally, the same measures, standards, institutions, and values.(9:22)

Moreover, in some situations, involvement would not only be pointless, it could be counterproductive because it could put Canadian soldiers and civilians at risk, while making a bad situation abroad worse. Sadly, we may have to face the fact that there is tragedy in the world every day and that there is not always a great deal that we can do about it.

What Canada must do is to help improve the UN's capacity to identify prospective horrors like Somalia before they become running sores on the conscience of the international community. It is clear that help is needed when Canadians are treated to stories on CBC television about negligence and "historic failure" on the part of the UN with respect to Somalia itself. It is dispiriting to hear people such as Canada's former Ambassador to the UN, Stephen Lewis, charge that, although the Secretary-General obtained a "first-class" person in Jan Eliasson to head the new Department of Humanitarian Assistance, he has not permitted him any of the additional people needed, so that the department is a "disaster."[4] Nor did the UN heed the many warnings about impending disaster, including those of the Secretary-General's Special Representative for Somalia, Mohamed Sahnoun. But when Mr. Sahnoun dared to criticize the world body's shortcomings publicly, he was summarily dismissed by the Secretary-General.

This is the kind of example that undermines the UN's credibility at a critical stage in its history. There is no other organization like it. It cannot be reinvented. But what Canada, a long-time and ardent supporter, must do is to insist on a full inquiry concerning the UN's role in the Somali crisis in an effort to find out what can be done to improve the early warning mechanisms of the UN so that the kinds of gross oversights the CBC exposed are not repeated.

A great deal more must also be done to improve the institutions and infrastructure of peacekeeping and of peace and security as a whole. Precisely because, for the foreseeable future, much of the world will remain beyond order and control, the need for effective multilateral institutions is vital. At critical moments, they could make the difference between a complete breakdown in security in entire regions of the world.

Here is where the world's interest and Canada's coincide: it is in Canada's interest to encourage a strong multilateral system and, particularly, a revitalized United Nations. Much of the new optimism surrounding UN institutions has resulted from the end of the Cold War and the waning of ideology as a major factor in international politics. In a less ideological age, Canada's traditional pragmatic approach offers a political version of comparative advantage.

First, Canada should continue to press for strengthened UN capacities in preventive diplomacy, peacemaking, and peacekeeping. Central to this are more resources which translate into better financial arrangements at the UN and a keener appreciation among great powers like the United States of their financial responsibilities for maintaining the peace as fervently as they pursued the Cold War. Canada should press for a command and control system and a military presence at the UN that inspires respect. It should strive for a revamped support system to replace supply and logistics arrangements which often have resulted in poor supply flow and inadequate stocks. Canada should encourage attempts to ensure the effective coordination of large operations with diverse components. It should insist on the standardization of UN military operations around the world.

Canada should also do everything in its power to strengthen the various regional organizations, to make them more effective in coping with breaking emergencies. The CSCE is one example, but to date a very imperfect one. In a recent address to the CSCE, the Secretary of State for External Affairs, the Hon. Barbara McDougall, indicated Canada's compassionate concern for the plight of the people of the former Yugoslavia, while firmly rebuking the states of the CSCE for idleness:

Ethical Issues

The 1992 Helsinki Document weighs about half a kilo but does not even mention the torment in Bosnia-Hercegovina. During the weeks that our officials negotiated and bickered over the political statement, thousands were killed in Bosnia-Hercegovina.[5]

Second, Canada also should do better at defining its own interests. It will be impossible for Canada to participate in every peacekeeping operation. The Government will have to choose and will have to justify its choices to a knowledgeable and concerned Canadian public. There will always be a clamour from one group or another for Canadian involvement—such are the dynamics of a democratic and multicultural society. But only if the Government delineates a clear set of criteria—a set of criteria that takes into account the complexities of the new era—will it be able to defend its choices.

One criterion should be whether the conflict has direct implications for Canada's security. A serious threat in the Middle East, for example, probably would meet that criterion. Another would be whether the conflict affects a significant trading partner or, if not, whether it has implications for any other of Canada's trading partners and whether they might respond favourably in other ways—if the appropriate linkages were drawn—to Canada's participation. Still another factor should be humanitarian concerns. The complication here is that situations involving mass sickness and starvation may arise because of socio-economic collapse or political strife. When deciding whether or not to intervene in such situations the government should determine whether it aims to provide only short-term treatment for the symptoms or whether it aspires to correct the underlying socio-economic and political circumstances.

Regardless of the particular arguments for engaging in "peacekeeping" in any situation, one question always ought to be asked: what is the likelihood of achieving the specified goal within a reasonable period of time? While recognizing that any major action entails some uncertainty, the Subcommittee believes that Canada ought to resist participating in undertakings with unspecified goals or where failure seems almost inevitable.

Third, the Canadian Forces should alter its approach. Canada has had an exemplary record in peacekeeping. In fact, it is the sole military activity which Canadians fully support. It identifies Canada to the rest of the world. But what has worked well in the past will not necessarily serve us well in the future. The Canadian Forces do not want to be caught in the position either of fighting the last war or planning for the last peacekeeping expedition. Since the founding of NATO, following the Second World War, the *raison d'etre* of Canada's land forces has been its European commitment. This commitment, in turn, has provided the justification for maintaining a general purpose force. Today, in a new era, Canada should be prepared to employ its troops on a regular basis in peacekeeping pursuits, provided the criteria for participation are clear and are applied rigorously. It should explore the idea of a rapid reaction force which could be deployed with alacrity in order to lay the groundwork for a successful operation, whereafter it would be withdrawn. It should also reconsider the way its armed forces are trained.

Canada should behave as a committed realist. Canadians cherish their record of being present at the creation of the United Nations and active participants in finding ways and means to help the organization function more effectively. Today, when the possibility of rethinking some of the basic concepts and techniques of the United Nations is at hand, our presence and participation is welcomed. The answers we give could have profound implications for the shape of Canada's armed forces, the practice of future peacekeeping, and the evolution of the United Nations.

Chapter 9: Ethics and the Use of Violence

Notes to "I. A New Era: What Does It Mean For Canada?"

1 Earl C. Ravenal, "The Case for Adjustment", *Foreign Policy*, Winter 1990-91; Theo Sommer, "A World Beyond Order and Control", *Guardian Weekly*, April 28, 1991; William Pfaff, "Redefining World Power", *Foreign Affairs*, America and the World, 1990-91; Joseph S. Nye, Jr., "What New World Order?", *Foreign Affairs*, Spring 1992.

2 Ian Smart, "The World in Flux", *Behind the Headlines*, Canadian Institute of International Affairs, 1990, pp. 3-4.

3 Joseph S. Nye, Jr., "Soft Power", *Foreign Policy*, Fall 1990, pp. 156-59.

4 *Proceedings of the Senate Sub-Committee on Security and National Defence*, November 25, 1992, Issue 9, page 15. Hence forward all references to the Proceedings will be bracketed in the text itself as shown above (9:15).

5 Glenn Frankel, "Decline Of The Nation-State", *The Guardian Weekly*, December 2, 1990.

6 Lord Acton, "Nationality" from *The History of Freedom and Other Essays*, pp. 192-93.

7 Gerald B. Helman and Steven R. Ratner, "Saving Failed States", *Foreign Policy*, Winter 1992-93, p. 3.

8 Elie Kedourie, *Nationalism*, London, 1960, p. 101.

9 Paul Lewis, "First U.N. Goal Is Security: Political Outlook is Murky", *The New York Times*, December 4, 1992.

10 Paul Lewis, "Painting Nations Blue", *The New York Times*, December, 1992.

11 *Address by the Honourable Barbara McDougall to the 47th Session of the United Nations General Assembly*, New York, September 24, 1992, 92/46, pp. 3-4.

12 Robert Miller, "Recent Visit to the United Nations," *Memorandum to Members of the House of Commons Standing Committee on External Affairs and International Trade*, November 17, 1992, p. 5.

13 Jessica Tuchman Matthews, "Redefining Security", *Foreign Affairs*, Spring 1989, p. 166.

14 Joseph S. Nye, Jr., "Soft Power", *Foreign Policy*, p. 158.

15 Report of the Special Committee of the Senate On National Defence, *Canada's Land Forces*, October 1989, p. 83.

16 J.L. Granatstein, "Peacekeeping: Did Canada Make a Difference? And What Difference Did Peacekeeping Make to Canada?" in *Making a Difference? Canada's Foreign Policy in a Changing World Order*, ed. by John English and Norman Hillmer, 1992, p. 223.

17 *Ibid.*, p. 234.

Notes to "V. Meeting the Challenge"

1 Lawrence Freedman, "Order and Disorder in the New World", *Foreign Affairs, America and the World*, 1991-92, p. 30.

2 Roger Morris, "A New Foreign Policy for a New Era", *The New York Times*, December 9, 1992.

3 *Ibid.*

4 "UN bungling and delays blamed for suffering in Somalia" Prime Time News, CBC Television, December 15, 1992.

5 *An Address by The Honourable Barbara McDougall, Secretary of State for External Affairs, to the Conference on Security and Cooperation in Europe Summit in Helsinki, Finland*, July 9, 1992. p. 1.

Questions for Discussion

1 To what extent should the provision of humanitarian aid to other countries be linked to involvement with underlying political conflicts, or with human rights enforcement? Why?

2 Should Canada become involved in peacekeeping operations only when it perceives some direct threat to its security or other important interests? To what extent is altruism a compelling reason for Canadian involvement in peacekeeping?

3 What should the role of the United Nations be, given the changes in world political arrangements outlined by the Committee? How should Canada go about trying to influence the role of the United Nations?

Challenging the Domestic Analogy

A Critique of Killing in Self-Defense

Joseph Kunkel

The use of force which is perhaps most commonly accepted is that required for self-defense. Indeed, the apparent legitimacy of that use of force has been used as an analogy to justify certain kinds of warfare. In this article, Joseph Kunkel offers a critical examination of the justification of self-defense, and argues that neither it nor its extension to war can be upheld.

★ ★ ★

Introduction

Killing an aggressor in private self-defense is often claimed intuitively to be morally justified. Michael Walzer, for instance, uses the self-evidence of this domestic norm as grounds for approving wars fought against aggressors. "Individual rights (to life and liberty)," he says, "underlie the most important judgments that we make about war."[1] By contrast, morally restraining oneself from killing, in a case of self-defense, has been subjected to extensive ethical criticism.

With this context in mind, I set out to review the rational arguments favoring killing an aggressor in private self-defense. To my surprise I found the arguments generally inconclusive. If the argumentation is indeed weak, then those who wish to justify war based upon this domestic analogy need to find another moral presupposition to bolster their position.

In this paper I review and critique these arguments. I have limited the question to killing in private self-defense. Public self-defense—for example, capital punishment, war, and police activity—introduces additional issues that would best be taken up only after reviewing the clearer private case. Critiquing the arguments in support of killing in private self-defense is not the same as arguing that such killing is wrong; still, as I will show, it

does shift the strength of moral force in that direction.

I shall begin by anticipating a few potential ambiguities. Violence has frequently been equated with force. 'Force', however, applies to geophysical as well as to human phenomena. For example, electricity, the wind, flowing waters, and earth tremors are called forces. By contrast, as Newton Garver has shown, 'violence' stems from the same root as 'violation.'[2] Violence or a violation is more than a simple demonstration of force, like gravity; violence carries a connotation of destructiveness. Accordingly, high winds are sometimes called 'violent,' but in a geophysical sense. When I use 'violence' here I mean it in a moral sense, a violation of one person by purposive, destructive harm to another. For instance a surgeon's forced entry into another person's body may do physical harm, but if the surgeon's purpose is healing, and the patient tacitly consents, there is no moral violence.

Self-defense is first and foremost a defense. Defending oneself is natural and moral. An ethical dilemma arises only when one uses violence to defend against violence. The difficulty comes in returning violence for violence when doing violence is considered wrong. The classic ethical case of returning violence for violence is killing in self-defense when the defensive killing is not purely accidental.

This paper addresses the justification for killing in response to a violent threat to life; I do not address justifications for forms of self-defense short of killing the attacker. The paradigm case is an encounter in which a human aggressor threatens the life of a victim. The emphasis is on the aggressor's *threat to kill* the victim. Without violent response to this threat, the result may be the victim's death. The victim, however, is not certain that her death will occur, but is certain that her life is genuinely threatened. In response to this life-threatening provocation the victim, or a third-party bystander, kills the aggressor in self-defense. The question for us is whether this killing in private self-defense is morally justified.

There are four types of arguments given to justify killing an aggressor in private self-defense: consequentialism, forfeiture of rights, deontology, and double effect. Each form of argument is examined and counterargued below. With one restricted exception, the arguments are found insufficient to justify killing in private self-defense. In the process of counterarguing I maintain that a satisfactory argument must be sufficiently precise so as only to include the victim's killing of the aggressor and not also to justify the aggressor's killing of the victim. I begin with the consequentialist arguments.

Consequentialism

The utilitarian justification for killing in self-defense over killing in general is vague. This stems in part from the conceptual difficulty utilitarians encounter in formulating what has traditionally been called the human right to life, or the right not to be killed. Utilitarians tend to view human life as equivalent to biological life, something humans share naturally with plants and animals. When life is restricted to conscious life, plants but not animals are excluded. Life is thus significant, in classical utilitarianism, for the pleasures and pains that accrue. In this sense ceasing to live, as in being instantaneously killed, does not constitute an additional pain but rather a cessation of pleasures and pains.

A person killed enters into the utility calculus only when one either looks at the total view or counts up the side-effects. Under the total view, killing in a torturously painful manner would be wrong. However, killing an unhappy person quickly adds to the maximization of pleasure in the universe, and killing a happy person subtracts from that maximization. Killing the aggressor in self-defense, accordingly, would be justified only if the original victim were happy and the aggressor unhappy. Among side-effects may be listed effects on family and friends, loss to the community of contributions from the deceased, hatred aroused, and the undermining of the sense of security of others.[3] But these side-effects cut both ways, affecting the victim who kills in self-defense as well as the aggressor who is killed. Both may have had family and friends, and the one killed may have made a larger contribution to society if still alive. So killing in self-defense under classical utilitarian criteria does not automatically favor the victim.

With serial killers and with deranged individuals who open fire on crowds of people or on children at play, the situation changes. Results favor the killing of such attackers by the threatened victims or by others. In these instances it is the multiple murders that weight the consequences toward defense of the victims. Such examples, however, cannot serve as models for evaluating single aggressor-victim situations.

Another consequentialist approach is found in what Peter Singer and others call preference utilitarianism.[4] The preference refers to the person's desire to go on living. The position maintains that killing a self-conscious being is worse than killing a conscious being, and among self-conscious beings killing a person with a preference for continued life is worse than killing a person having no such preference. So, all side-effects being equal, persons can be killed justifiably if they do not desire to go on living. In cases of self-defense, however, the situation is less clear. The act of aggression with a deadly weapon does not in itself display the aggressor's own preference for living or not living. Thus preference utilitarianism, like classical utilitarianism, does not always favor killing the aggressor over the victim in cases of private self-defense. Some cases appear to favor killing the aggressor, and others the victim.

Philip Montague shifts away from preferences to behaviors, and defends a utilitarian rule called forced choice.[5] With behaviorism as his starting point, he first broadens the self-defensive descriptors to include innocent aggressors and self-preservation situations. He then claims, "[W]hen faced with a forced choice between lives, it is sometimes permissible to kill some number of persons in order to save the lives of others."[6] In particular, Montague is attempting to distinguish people who are innocent victims from those displaying "threatening and aggressive behavior." The difficulty is the ensuing ambiguity as soon as the victim moves to defend herself. Does not the victim then behave in a threatening and aggressive manner toward the original aggressor? If so, is not the aggressor also forced to choose between lives as soon as the victim behaviorally creates a life-threatening situation for the aggressor? Would not the aggressor-become-victim be justified, according to the same forced choice rule, in killing the victim-become-aggressor? Forced choice thus resembles "the fastest gun" in the Old West.

Montague tries to circumvent this difficulty by distinguishing provoked from unprovoked behavior. Provoked [sic] behavior he calls "*culpable* behavior." The aggressor is thus viewed as culpable, the victim as innocent.

Such designations, however, are highly subjective. They ignore previous events, personal histories, undisclosed intentions. In one-to-one encounters they encourage each participant to be what John Yoder calls a "judge, prosecutor, and executioner in one's own case."[7] Self-righteousness may be allowed to supersede judicious balance.

An analogous difficulty has plagued the justification of wars fought in defense of the innocent. This is partly offset by use of functional descriptors to separate those who are culpable and "combatants" from those who are innocent and "noncombatants."[8] Still, such a differentiation does not settle who are the aggressors and who are the non-aggressors.

No terms similar to 'combatants' and 'noncombatants' have yet been found applicable for private encounters. Whose behavior, for example, is culpable when two people fight in a barroom, when family members feud in an apartment, when householders keep revolvers on their nightstands, or when pharmacists place loaded guns under the counter? Is the innocent person the one who draws second but shoots first? Unless such descriptors are made available, the distinction between culpable and innocent behavior is practically meaningless for situations of private self-defense.

Cheyney Ryan takes another tack in differentiating between the aggressor and the victim.[9] Ryan suggests that the asymmetry of roles between the aggressor and the victim can best be brought out by the notion of responsibility. "When Aggressor threatens Victim," Ryan says, "his actions have created a situation in which *someone's* life will be lost (he hopes Victim's)." The aggressor is thus responsible for the situation, while the victim only determines "*whose* life will be lost." By appealing to self-defense, then, a person is saying that the aggressor is the one responsible for the loss of life. However, Ryan's analysis only works if there is a necessary connection between the aggressor's opening thrust and the boomeranging lethal ending. Yoder shows there are other options, including natural disruptions of the sequence, interventions, talking downs, disarmings, and even unsuccessful killings.[10] Options short of killing the aggressor are thus sufficiently available to indicate that the self-defending victim normally has more responsibility for the result than merely choosing "whose life will be lost."

Forfeiture of Rights

The second kind or argumentation involves forfeiture of rights. This argument goes back at least to John Locke. Locke maintains a view that natural rights, including the right not to be killed, are inherently part of being human. Natural rights are inalienable, unconditional, and universally applicable. But when these rights are violated, Locke says, the violator is placed outside the state of nature, forfeiting his natural rights and falling into a state of war. An aggressor who threatens the life of a victim is thus portrayed as an "outlaw," a person outside the natural constraints of morality and the constitutional bounds of law.

There is an obvious difficulty with this view. Since natural rights are said to be based on nature, how can they be forfeited? Surely they can be grossly violated, but that does not establish a natural basis for loss of possession. Based on a natural foundation for rights, Locke's forfeiture claim runs counter to the inherent inalienability: if rights are natural and inalienable, how can an individual forfeit them?

A way around this problem is to ground rights not on nature but on a social contract, which can be broken. Many contractarians, like Locke, build the social contract on a basis of natural rights, and then the problem remains. But if, as in Hobbes, the contract is the foundation for morality, then moral rights are lost whenever the contract or moral promise is broken. Accordingly, if one attacks another person one ceases to be protected by moral restraints. This loss of moral restraints, of course, would appear to cut both ways, in that one who has forfeited moral rights may *ipso facto* no longer be obligated to respect the rights of others with whom she is no longer under moral contract. For example, if a woman aggressor loses her right to life, does she not also lose her duty to preserve life? May she then not kill amorally with impunity? This, ironically, would also impact on the case of the serial killer.

Additional troubling questions arise for the theory of forfeiture.[11] Does a violation of any right constitute sufficient grounds for the forfeiture of all rights? Locke, for instance, lists robbery as sufficient grounds. Or are some rights more fundamental than others? If fundamental rights are forfeited by aggressors, are all rights and consequent duties forfeited? If an aggressor physically harms a victim, does the aggressor forfeit his right not to be tortured or maimed? If in abusing the victim he unfairly violates a criminal statute, does he as an outlaw forfeit his right to be treated fairly under the law? Are aggressors presumed guilty until proven innocent? Are rights, laws, and morality only for the virtuous, with immorality and unlawfulness the standard for the nonvirtuous? If the aggressor is immobilized in the process of an unsuccessful act of aggression, can the victim nevertheless at will kill the defenseless aggressor that has forfeited the right not to be killed? If not, why not? How long does the forfeiture last? Does the attacker reacquire forfeited rights upon immobilization, after police arrival, or only after repudiation of the bad intention? In cases of capital punishment, does the newly convicted criminal again forfeit his right to life after having reacquired that right while preparing for trial? Then, too, most of the above questions repeat themselves as the condemned prisoner awaits execution. Some of these questions are disposed of in a practical way by legislatures, judges, and juries; however, from a theoretical standpoint the forfeiture claim adds more problems than it solves, and thus would not seem adequate as an argument favoring killing in private self-defense.

Deontology

The third type of argumentation flows out of the Kantian tradition. The common interpretation is that killing in self-defense, private or public, is moral. The argument is that killing an aggressor who is threatening the life of an innocent victim is in accord with the Kantian principle of respecting other human beings as equals.[12] What does this imply? At the very least it implies that the duty not to kill or the right not to be killed is not absolute. The reason, some say, is that there is a prior duty to preserve life. In this instance, however, by killing an assailant one is not preserving all lives.

Perhaps the prior duty is to self-defense. Or better, maybe W.D. Ross is correct in arguing that all rights and duties are prima facie rather than absolute.[13] Ross argues that in morally conflictive situations multiple duties are incumbent on us because of the complex relationships we have with one another. In conflictive situations, therefore, one right may be overridden by another right that is said to be more stringent than the first. In situations of self-defense, the argument claims, the aggressor has a right not to be killed, but this is overridden by the more stringent right (or duty) of the victim to be defended. To use more compelling terminology, the victim's or a third-party bystander's duty or obligation not to kill is overridden by the more stringent duty to defend the life of the victim. The issue is not any defense of the life of the victim, but defense with a deadly force. The claim is being made that the duty to kill in self-defense is more stringent than the duty not to kill.

If this is true, at least two troubling conclusions result. First, if it is a duty to kill in self-defense, then not killing, as in the case of

radical pacifism, is immoral. Therefore those who universalize the maxim "Do not kill" in a supererogatory manner are violating a more stringent duty to kill in self-defense, unless, of course, there is another (as yet unnamed) principle that overrides self-defense. Secondly, if preserving one's life overrides the obligation not to kill, the aggressor becomes duty-bound to kill the victim-become-aggressor and the victim becomes duty-bound to kill the aggressor. In other words, as soon as the victim or a third-party bystander moves to kill the aggressor, the aggressor becomes obligated to defend her own life. Thus victim, bystander, and aggressor-become-victim are all acting to defend human lives. A society founded on such a principle would have all defenders and no aggressors, and Hobbes's nightmarish natural condition of humanity would become a sanctioned reality. In response, most ethicists modify the situational context in which the right to life is overridden, by requiring the obligation not to kill to be less stringent only when the self-defending victim is innocent and the aggressor culpable. Such a modification, however, requires further explication either through reasons of innocence or forfeiture, two arguments previously discussed and found wanting, or through specification, an argument we shall presently address.

Specification purports to justify killing in private self-defense by delimiting or specifying the right not to be killed.[14] What supporters of specification say is that no one has a right not to be killed; instead one has a right not to be murdered, that is, a right not to be killed unjustly. What this amounts to saying is that killing is only wrong when one kills unjustly. Accordingly, victim may kill aggressor whenever it is not unjust to do so. Why? Because it is not unjust. When? Whenever what Judith Thomson calls the "factual specification" permits. But when does the factual specification permit killing?[15] When, for instance, the aggressor is trying to kill the victim who, in turn, can preserve his life only by killing the aggressor. Or when the aggressor is innocent, demented, and displaying behavior that seems deadly to others. Or when a deadly threat is posed by someone's culpable recklessness or negligence. Or sometimes in the case of rape or mugging. The list goes on and on, complicating rather than simplifying. Moreover, specifying factors does not entail the justification of the specifications that make killing permissible. In fact, the factors are justified by a principle that is itself established by recourse to the same factors. But such circular reasoning is not the only problem. The whole purpose of introducing duties as a foundation for morality is defeated when duties are made contingent upon right or just factual specifications, as opposed to wrong or unjust ones. What are duties, for example, if we have duties only not to be tortured unjustly, not to be held in slavery unjustly, not to be discriminated against unjustly, or not to steal unjustly? Under such specifications duties derived from more basic principles cease to be the determinants of morality. So specification, like forfeiture, turns out to be an unsatisfactory way of discriminating the innocent from the guilty.

Double Effect

The final form of argumentation used to justify killing in private self-defense is the principle of double effect as embodied in natural law ethics. Natural law proponents admit killing is evil. However, under the principle of double effect a single act with double—good and evil—effects is permitted, provided four conditions are simultaneously met. The conditions are: (1) The act, exclusive of the evil effect, must be good; (2) The person acting must have a right intention; (3) The evil effect may not be the means to the good effect; and (4) There must be a proportionate grave reason for acting.

As applied to situations of private self-defense the first condition requires that preserving one's life in a threatening situation not be evil for other reasons, which in the victim's case under consideration it is not. The second condition strives to introduce harmony into a threatening situation, and is met in preserving one's life, provided some effort at mediating differences is undertaken. The fourth condition, proportionate grave reason, is met by the threat to one's life. The third condition, however, is not as readily met. If the victim preserves her life by killing her assailant, then killing her assailant becomes the means for saving her life, and condition three is violated. Admittedly there are a few instances in which the killing is purely accidental, as when an assailant who is pushed to the ground hits his head and dies of a concussion. But the usual case involves a lethal wounding by the victim that is not accidental; such a killing, in turn, seems to be the direct means to the intended end.

Some authors circumvent this assessment by arguing that in cases of self-defense the death of the aggressor is foreseen but not intended. Only when the killing is *intended* as the means to the end, they say, is Condition Three violated. Their argument rests on the meaning of intention as applied to situations of self-defense.[16] They follow St. Thomas Aquinas in arguing that "moral acts take their species according to what is intended and not according to what is beside the intention...."[17] Therefore, if only self-defense is intended then self-defense alone figures in the morality of the act. Killing may be foreseen, but unless it is actually intended it is not morally culpable. In this way the third condition is rewritten as:

> (3a) The evil effect may not be intended as the means to the good effect.

If we grant this to be a plausible interpretation of double effect, preserving one's life becomes the acceptable intended act, and killing the aggressor is said to be foreseen, but not intended. Killing in private self-defense could therefore be justified by this interpretation of double effect.

The argument, however, has two drawbacks. The first drawback is that once self-defense is stressed as a personal intention—independent of the universal duty we discussed previously—any person, victim or aggressor, can claim the intention for self-defense over killing in situations of private lethal conflict. Either the victim-become-defender or the aggressor-become-defender could foresee the killing of the other person, while supposedly not intending it. In response to this criticism proponents of double effect can refer to the necessity of meeting all four conditions as a precondition for the justification of an action. Thus an aggressor-become-defender also needs to have a right intention, to be performing an action that is not in itself evil, and to have a proportionately grave reason for acting in order for his action to be moral. In the paradigm case we are examining, if the aggressor intends to threaten the life of a victim, then the other three conditions cannot be met. However, if the threat is merely behavioral, as in displaying a gun during a robbery but with no intention of using it, or perhaps with only an intention to shoot over people's heads, then it is possible that a subsequent self-defensive reaction by the aggressor-become-defender could meet all four conditions for a moral action. For example, a robber with a gun may be committing an evil act in entering a pharmacy, but the evil act is robbery, or robbery with a lethal weapon, not murder. If the pharmacist reacts by pulling a gun and firing, the robber is then placed in an entirely different situation, one of self-defense. At that point the robber-become-victim could intend preservation of life and fulfill all four conditions of double effect. So in some instances double effect does not work, because it exonerates the aggressor-become-victim as well as the victim-become-defender.

The second drawback revolves around how intentions that are morally acceptable can be objectively distinguished from those that are not. For example, if the victim-become-defender shoots the aggressor in the head, chest, or back, and claims an intention only for self-defense, how can this intention be objectively supported against what might appear to others as an intended killing? In a few cases, such as when a person is first securely restrained and then killed, the murderous intention appears obvious, unless, of course, the murderer is judged mentally insane. But if the victim regularly carries a concealed weapon, or keeps a loaded revolver near the cash register, and shoots the aggressor with no warning, it is not clear whether the intention is preservation of life, or preservation of one's property and/or protection of one's turf. The latter intentions run counter to having a proportionate grave reason for killing. In other cases, such as when the shooting is preceded by a fight, or when the victim is challenging the aggressor to "make my day," a question can be raised about the right intention of the victim. On the other hand, if the aggressor puts herself in the same conflictive situation several times, as in the case of a serial killer, the objectivity of the intention becomes obvious. Applying double effect, therefore, turns out to be more complicated than was immediately evident. With four conditions needing to be met, killing in private self-defense is sometimes justified and sometimes not justified by one interpretation of the principle of double effect.

Conclusion

I have argued that, with this one carefully construed exception, killing in private self-defense is not justified by the arguments given in its support. Have I therefore proven that such killing is for the most part unjustifiable? Ryan says no. He claims that negating the arguments that purport to justify private self-defense only establishes "that we do not *know* if killing is justified or not."[18] He says that until arguments are given in support of the right not to be killed, skepticism reigns and individuals are free to choose either principle.

Is Ryan correct? Do the counterarguments lead only to moral skepticism regarding killing or not killing? Hardly. Rather, a moral obligation remains, but what it is follows upon one's ethical orientation. Under consequentialism, for instance, if the rules for forced choice and culpable behavior do not hold, the system reverts to calculating the costs and benefits accruing to the victim and aggressor in each instance. Such a method does not provide a solid basis for arguing that killing in self-defense is usually justified. Neither does it justify an individual in choosing either killing or not killing. Moral obligation, under consequentialism, always depends upon the results, not the individual's choice. Under forfeiture of rights, when the forfeiture argument is negated the case for not killing is bolstered. If there are no sufficient grounds for arguing that the right not to be killed can be forfeited, then the right not to be killed remains pervasively in force. Under deontology, if specification muddies the reasoning, we are left to search for another principle to decide the issue of killing or not killing. But if the overrider or stringency claims are countered, killing in private self-defense is not justified, and the duty not to kill remains in force. Under the principle of double effect, killing is admitted to be evil. The evil, however, is allowed when four conditions are met; when all four conditions are not met, the evil act is disallowed. So right or wrong depends upon the particular intentions formed and the specific circumstances involved.

To sum up, almost all the arguments given in support of killing in private self-defense are unsatisfactory. This conclusion does not necessitate that every killing in self-defense is therefore immoral. To make the latter claim requires

proof that private killings are not justified, and that type of argument too appears not to be forthcoming. At present there is no definitive moral argument for or against killing in private self-defense.

The suggestion that individuals can therefore choose to kill or not to kill in self-defense is indefensible. What happens morally depends upon one's ethical orientation. Some orientations do not allow killing in self-defense. Others do, but under restrictive circumstances. What is clear is that being allowed to kill in order to avoid being killed is not morally self-evident.

The morality of going to war is also affected by the lack of a definitive argument for killing in private self-defense. To the extent the domestic analogy is a prerequisite for proving that war against aggressors is justified, then going to war in self-defense may not be justified. Those wishing to justify war, therefore, must either settle for a highly restrictive set of satisfying conditions—more restrictive than the elastic set of just-war conditions now in vogue—or develop an alternate moral foundation for approving war. A third option would be to present a definitive argument for killing in private self-defense. To ignore these issues is to revert to an amoral, Hobbesian powerplay.

Notes

1 Michael Walzer, *Just and Unjust Wars: A Moral Argument With Historical Illustrations* (New York: Basic Books, 1977). p.54. See also Jeffrie Murphy, "The Killing of the Innocent," *The Monist* Vol. 57 (1973), p. 535.

2 Newton Garver, "What Violence Is," *Philosophy for a New Generation* Eds. A. Bierman and J. Gould (New York: Macmillan, 4th ed., 1981). pp. 217-228. The article is here revised from its original appearance in *The Nation* (June 24, 1968), pp. 817-822.

3 Jonathan Glover, *Causing Death and Saving Lives* (New York: Penguin Books, 1977), p. 114.

4 Peter Singer, "Killing Humans and Killing Animals," *Inquiry*, Vol. 22 (1979), pp. 145-56, and *Practical Ethics* (Cambridge: Cambridge University Press, 1979), pp. 72-84.

5 Philip Montague, "Self-Defense and Choosing Between Lives," *Philosophical Studies*, Vol. 40 (1981), pp. 207-219.

6 Montague, *op. cit.*, p. 211. The remaining quotes from Montague are from this same page.

7 John Yoder, "'What Would You Do If...?' An Exercise in Situation Ethics," *The Journal of Religious Ethics*, Vol. 2.2 (Fall, 1974), p. 85.

8 See, for example: Jeffrie Murphy, *op. cit.*, pp. 527-536.

9 Cheyney Ryan, "Self-Defense, Pacifism, and the Possibility of Killing," *Ethics*, Vol. 93, (1982-1983), pp. 515-520.

10 Yoder, *op. cit.*, pp. 90-94.

11 For these questions I am especially indebted to Hugo Bedau, "Capital Punishment." *Matters of Life and Death*, Ed. Tom Regan (New York: Random House. 2nd ed., 1986), pp. 177-181, and to Judith Thomson, "Self-Defense and Rights." *The Lindley Lecture* (U. of Kansas, April 5, 1976), pp. 3-6. See also Ryan, *op. cit.*, pp. 510-512, and George Fletcher, "The Right to Life," *The Monist*, Vol. 63, (1980), pp. 142-145.

12 See, for example, Alan Donagan, *The Theory of Morality* (Chicago: U. of Chicago Press, 1977), pp. 72-74.

13 W.D. Ross, *The Right and The Good* (Oxford: Clarendon Press, 1930), pp. 19-20ff.

14 For this argument and counter-argument I am especially indebted to Judith Thomson. See Thomson, *op. cit.*, p. 6-12.

15 Thomson, *op. cit.*, p. 7.

16 See, for example, Germain Grise, "Toward a Consistent Natural-Law Ethics of Killing," *The American Journal of Jurisprudence*, Vol. 15 (1970), pp. 73-96, and Joseph M. Boyle, Jr. "Toward Understanding the Principle of Double Effect," *Ethics*, Vol. 90 (1979-1980) pp. 527-538.

17 St. Thomas Aquinas, *The Summa Theologica*, Trans. Fathers of English Dominican Province (New York: Benziger Brothers, 1948), Vol. II-II, Quest. 64, Art 7.

18 Ryan, *op. cit.* p. 520.

Questions for Discussion

1 Suppose one person appears to threaten the life of another (e.g., by showing a gun), and the second person responds with force. Can the first person legitimately see this use of force as an aggressive act, and respond defensively ("aggressor-become-victim," in Kunkel's terms)? Does it matter if the first person had no intention of harming the second (e.g., if the gun was not loaded, or if the person planned to shoot over the head of the second)?

2 Does it make sense to say that one can respond with force to an aggressor because in committing the act of aggression that person has forfeited his or her rights? If so, what rights, specifically, are forfeited, and under what conditions?

3 Is it possible to justify the use of lethal force in self-defense?

Excerpts from "Our Criminal Law"

Law Reform Commission of Canada

In 1976, the Law Reform Commission of Canada offered a brief pamphlet which touched on the deep issues surrounding the justification of the criminal law and punishment. The following selections indicate the general view of the Commission at that time, that the law cannot be justified on the grounds of deterrence, rehabilitation, or retribution, but rather serves the purpose of reinforcing the moral and social values of society.

★ ★ ★

I. Coping with Crime

We live today in anxious times. Inflation, unemployment, strikes, pollution, crime—these trouble every free society. But crime falls in a special category. Crime threatens individual security, frightens us personally and makes us fearful for our own survival. Such fear can lead to excess reaction, oppression and injustice. Societies that want freedom, justice and security face few greater challenges than that of how to cope with crime.

Coping with crime is a two-sided problem for a just society. Crime uncoped with is unjust: to the victim, to potential victims and to all of us. Crime wrongly coped with is also unjust: criminal law—the state against the individual—is always on the cutting edge of the abuse of power. Between these two extremes justice must keep a balance.

Balance means rationality. To get to grips with crime rationally, we have to keep our heads, not hit out blindly, and not mistake activity for action. We must avoid being misled by fears, frustrations or false expectations, however natural they may be.

Fear of crime is natural. Of all the things that frighten us—accidents, diseases, natural disasters—crime has a particular place. It wears a human face. Other things happen, crime is done deliberately. Hijacking, bombing, kidnapping and so on do not just occur, they are planned. And planned increasingly perhaps: at any rate there is a growing sense in Canada and many other countries of crisis about crime. Small wonder crime brings fear.

Crime brings frustration too. Common sense suggests that stopping crime is simple, and yet it seems to keep on rising no matter what we do. Criminology has still not discovered the cause or cure. All it has found is that our present cures work badly. So we end up frustrated with our criminal law for not delivering the goods and not satisfying our expectations.

Expectations are maybe to blame. We expect the law to protect us and reduce the volume of crime, yet, as we know, the vast majority of crimes are not cleared up. For every crime prosecuted there may be ten reported and forty unreported. Reducing this 'dark number' of crime would need more police, better equipment, greater willingness to report incidents and to help the authorities, and also a very different criminal law. The kind of law we have can never guarantee protection—in general it only moves in *after* the event and bolts the door after the horse has escaped. Our criminal law looks to the past. Protection comes from looking to the future.

II. Trying to Control the Future

Looking to the future—admittedly our law does try to do this. It tries by means of sentence and punishment. It seeks to deter potential criminals and rehabilitate the actual offender.

Unfortunately success is doubtful. Deterrence and reform are not wholly effective. Take deterrence. Some criminals are irrationally undeterrable, some just like to gamble, and some consider crime a worthwhile risk because the chance of being caught is slight. Above all, our society has too much respect for freedom and humanity to countenance measures stern enough to make deterrence really bite. Or take reform. It is hard to rehabilitate offenders without being sure what it is to *habilitate* them. And once again our respect for freedom and humanity rules out mind-altering techniques that operate mechanically and by clockwork-orange methods. In short, the very nature of our society prevents our criminal law from fully organizing the future.

Organizing the future though, is not the major function of the criminal law. It has a different, more important role. After all, even if the nature of our free society limits criminal law's impact on crime, we still need criminal law. Even if we cannot control the future, this does not mean we must ignore the present and the past. We still need to do something about wrongful acts: to register our social disapproval, to publicly denounce them and to re-affirm the values violated by them. Criminal law is not geared only to the future; it also serves to throw light on the present—by underlining crucial social values.

III. Criminal Law and Values

Criminal law, then, primarily has to do with values. Naturally, for crime itself is nothing more nor less than conduct seriously contrary to our values. Crimes are acts not only punishable by law but also *meriting* punishment. As Fitzjames Stephen said, the ordinary citizen views crime as an act "forbidden by law and revolting to the moral sentiments of society". Crimes are not just forbidden, they are also wrong.

As such—as wrongful acts—they demand response. Suppose a murder is committed in our midst: we must respond as human beings and as social creatures. First, "no man is an island" and every person's death diminishes all other persons: to do nothing and ignore this fact is to be less than human. Second, murder tramples on our society's basic values about human life: to do nothing is tantamount to condoning it and saying murder is all right. To be fully human and to hold certain values means responding when they are violated. Such violation requires public condemnation, and this is preeminently the job of criminal law.

This job—condemning crime—is not an end in itself. It is part of the larger aim of producing a society fit to live in. Such a society is less one where people are too frightened to commit crimes than one where people have too much respect for one another to commit them. Fostering this kind of personal respect is a major aim of parents, teachers, churches,

and all other socializing agents. One such agent, though far less important than the others, is the criminal law. In its own way the criminal law reenforces lessons about our social values, instills respect for them and expresses disapproval for their violation. This—what some call "general deterrence"—is the moral, educative role of criminal law....

VI. Reshaping Criminal Law

... We have to see that parents, families, schools, churches, local communities and all other socializing agencies do their job of teaching and instilling fundamental values. Too often when these abandon their responsibilities, the cry is heard for law to do the task. The truth is, however, that theirs is the primary responsibility. Criminal law is but a last resort.

2. The Role of Criminal Law

Criminal law, then, comes in by way of last resort. As such, it provides, as argued earlier, a necessary response to wrongful behaviour. Not that the business of the criminal law is simply retribution. That notion is too complex morally and philosophically to provide a justification for the criminal law. Besides, making sin reap its own reward is no fit enterprise for mere mortal men and women. Like Blackstone we prefer to leave this to "the Supreme Being".

Nor is the business of the criminal law the enforcement of morality. Though wrong behaviour is the target, its wrongfulness or immorality is only a necessary condition, not a sufficient one. First, no one can *make* another person moral. The criminal law certainly cannot. Indeed the state and its legal institutions cannot really handle morality. Second, not all individual behaviour concerns the law. The state has no place in some activities of the nation. Its place concerns activities harmful to other individuals and to society itself.

Not that the function of the criminal law is to protect from harm in any direct and simple way. Much as we might like to think that it protects society through deterrence and rehabilitation, the efficacy of both these methods is problematic. Besides, desirable as it may be, mere protection from harm is not what we want of criminal law. After all, mere non-commission of crimes will not wholly satisfy. To satisfy, the non-commission must result from the view that crimes should not be committed. In short, we want a society where people think they *ought* not to be criminals.

In truth, the criminal law is fundamentally a *moral* system. It may be crude, it may have faults, it may be rough and ready, but basically it is a system of applied morality and justice.

It serves to underline those values necessary, or else important, to society. When acts occur that seriously transgress essential values, like the sanctity of life, society must speak out and reaffirm those values. This is the true role of criminal law.

Questions for Discussion

1 The Commission states that, when a murder has been committed, "to do nothing is tantamount to condoning it and saying that murder is all right." Is this true? Why or why not?

2 The Commission asserts that the criminal law is not effective as a deterrent, nor as a rehabilitative agent, and that nobody short of a divine being should attempt retribution. The Commission's conclusion is that the purpose of the criminal law is to underline, or reinforce, social values. Is this the proper role of the criminal law?

Excerpt from
"Aboriginal Peoples and Criminal Justice"

Law Reform Commission of Canada

In addition to general questions about the justification of the coercive power of the state, there are specific issues which arise in Canada concerning the application of the justice system to cultural or religious minorities, and Aboriginal peoples in particular. The central question here is whether these groups have received equal access to justice. In addition to concerns that the implementation of the system has been biased in various ways against aboriginal people, leading to a spiral of disruption of individual lives, there is a concern that one culture has simply imposed its notions of justice on another. In its report of December, 1991, the Law Reform Commission of Canada considered these issues, and the advisability of creating separate Aboriginal-designed and -run criminal justice systems. The following are excerpts from that report.

★   ★   ★

Chapter Two: The Aboriginal Perspective on Criminal Justice

Aboriginal communities number in the several hundreds and each has had a distinctive experience of the Canadian criminal justice system. Given this diversity, there is necessar-

ily some oversimplification in the following general description of Aboriginal perceptions and aspirations. Nevertheless, we have been struck by the remarkably uniform picture of the system that has been drawn by Aboriginal speakers and writers.

I. Aboriginal Perceptions

From the Aboriginal perspective, the criminal justice system is an alien one, imposed by the dominant white society. Wherever they turn or are shuttled throughout the system, Aboriginal offenders, victims or witnesses encounter a sea of white faces. Not surprisingly, they regard the system as deeply insensitive to their traditions and values: many view it as unremittingly racist.

Abuse of power and the distorted exercise of discretion are identified time and again as principal defects of the system. The police are often seen by Aboriginal people as a foreign, military presence descending on communities to wreak havoc and take people away. Far from being a source of stability and security, the force is feared by them even when its services are necessary to restore a modicum of social peace to the community.

For those living in remote and reserve communities, the entire court apparatus, quite literally, appears to descend from the sky—an impression that serves to magnify their feelings of isolation and erects barriers to their attaining an understanding of the system.

The process is in reality incomprehensible to those who speak only Aboriginal languages, especially where little or no effort is made to provide adequate interpretation services. Even the English- or French-speaking inhabitants find the language of the courts and lawyers difficult to understand. Understanding is more than a problem of mere language. Aboriginal persons contend that virtually all of the primary actors in the process (police, lawyers, judges, correctional personnel) patronize them and consistently fail to explain adequately what the process requires of them or what is going to happen to them. Even those who are prepared to acknowledge certain well-intentioned aspects of the present system nevertheless conclude that the system has utterly failed.

Such efforts as have been made to involve the community in the administration of justice are seen as puny and insignificant, and there is little optimism about the future. Elders see the community's young people as the primary victims of the system—cut adrift by it and removed from the community's support as well as from its spiritual and cultural traditions. They recount experiences of children taken from their communities at an early age who later emerge, hardened from the court and correctional processes and ultimately beyond the reach of even imaginative initiatives designed to promote rehabilitation.

Evident and understandable weariness and frustration attend any discussion of approaches to fixing the system or setting it right. For Aboriginal persons, the system presents an unending course of barriers and obstacles, with no avenues of effective complaint or redress. Their sense of injustice is bottomless. They have little or no confidence in the legal profession or in the judiciary to bring about justice or to effect a just resolution of any particular dispute in which they are involved. If the truth be told, most have given up on the criminal justice system.

II. Aboriginal Aspirations

Aboriginal people have a vision of a justice system that is sensitive to their customs, traditions and beliefs. This vision is a natural outgrowth of their aspirations to self-government and sovereignty. They desire a criminal justice system that is Aboriginal-designed, -run and -populated, from top to bottom.

Undoubtedly there are many contrasting visions as to what constitutes an Aboriginal justice system, but fundamental is the belief that the system must be faithful to Aboriginal traditions and cultural values, while adapting them to modern society. Hence, a formal Aboriginal justice system would evince appropriate respect for community Elders and leaders, give heed to the requirements of Aboriginal spirituality and pay homage to the relation of humankind to the land and to nature.

The Aboriginal vision of justice gives preeminence to the interests of the collectivity, its overall orientation being holistic and integrative. Thus, it is community-based, stressing mediation and conciliation while seeking an acknowledgement of responsibility from those who transgress the norms of their society. While working toward a reconciliation between the offender and the victim, an Aboriginal justice system would pursue the larger objective of reintegrating the offender into the community as a whole.

The Aboriginal vision challenges both common and civil law concepts. Statute law becomes less important. Within an Aboriginal justice system, laws would not be uniform or homogeneous; they would vary from community to community, depending on customary practices. Customary law would be the binding force promoting harmony within the community.

While possessing common general characteristics, an Aboriginal justice system would of necessity be pluralistic. What such a system would actually look like is unclear. This haziness is a source of frustration. Much essential detail is missing, and Aboriginal people are hesitant to provide that detail, not because they are incapable of providing it—some communities have well-developed and well-articulated models—but because, in their view, they should not have to do so. They aspire to local control. Their contention is essentially: "Give us the keys. Let us control the system. We can hardly do worse than you have."

Chapter Four: The Desirability of Aboriginal Justice Systems

Highlights

Aboriginal communities that are identified by the legitimate representatives of Aboriginal peoples as being willing and capable should have the authority to establish Aboriginal justice systems. The federal and provincial governments should enter into negotiations to transfer such authority to those Aboriginal communities.

In the course of our consultations on this Reference, one participant, Ovide Mercredi, eloquently expressed a view that was widely shared by others with whom we met:

> One of the problems that I see is the perception that the criminal justice system is near-perfect but can maybe be made a little more perfect by making some changes to it over a period of time to allow for the concerns and the rights of Aboriginal people. The real issue is what some people have called cultural imperialism, where one group of people who are distinct make a decision for all other people.... If you look at it in the context of law, police, court and corrections, and you ask yourself: "Can we improve upon the system?" Well, my response is, quite frankly, you can't. Our experiences are such that, if you make it more representative, it's still your law that would apply, it would still be your police forces that would enforce the laws, it would still be your courts that would interpret them, and it would still be your corrections system that houses the people that go through the court system. It would not be our language that is used in the system. It would not be our laws. It would not be our traditions, our customs or our values that decide what happens in the system. That is what I mean by cultural imperialism. So a more representative system, where we have more Indian judges, more Indian lawyers, more Indian clerks of the court, more Indian correctional officers or more Indian managers of the correctional system is not the solution. So what we have to do, in my view, is take off that imperial hat, if that's possible, and find alternatives to the existing system....[16]

New, imaginative solutions offer a brighter promise of enlisting the support and respect of Aboriginal people as well as ensuring equal access and equitable treatment. The time has come to co-operate in the creation of Aboriginal-controlled systems of justice, for which many possible models exist.[17]

We recognize that the call for completely separate justice systems is part of a political agenda primarily concerned with self-government. We need not enter that debate. Aboriginal-controlled justice systems have merits quite apart from political considerations.

It is often contended that Aboriginal crime arises from the marginalization of Aboriginal societies as a result of colonization.[18] According to that theory, as control of their own destinies has been removed from Aboriginal people, suicide rates have climbed, crime has increased and their societies have broken down. The steps necessary to solve these problems go well beyond criminal justice reform. As LaPrairie has noted: "Deflecting responsibility to the criminal justice system rather than addressing fundamental problems of social and economic disparity as reflected in reserve life, almost assures the continuation of the problems."[19]

Nonetheless, the criminal justice system itself has contributed to the process of marginalization. In traditional Aboriginal societies, "[l]eaders remained leaders only as long as they held the respect of their community."[20] Respect for Elders was "the social glue holding people together in relatively peaceful obedience to commonly accepted rules."[21] However, we are told that "the very presence of our courts has taken away a critical forum in which wisdom can be demonstrated and respect earned."[22] Increasingly, participants in the criminal justice system are questioning whether this cultural hegemony is necessary.

Broadly speaking, we believe that criminal law and procedure should impose the same requirements on all members of society, what-

ever their private beliefs. However, we also feel that the distinct historical position of Aboriginal persons justifies departing from that general principle. As a general rule, all those coming to or residing in Canada should accept Canadian rules, and the outer limit of allowable behaviour should be set by the criminal law. However, the Aboriginal peoples did not come to Canada. Canada came to them. They have constitutional recognition and treaty rights that set them apart from all other Canadians.

> The Algonquins have lived in the valley of the Ottawa River at least as long as the French have lived in France or the English have lived in England. Before there was a Canada, before Cartier sailed his small ship up the great river, Algonquins lived in, occupied, used, and defended their home in the Ottawa Valley.[23]

To the reality of different constitutional status may be added the feature of cultural difference. Many Aboriginal cultures are essentially non-adversarial. As a result of this different cultural orientation, we are told that they are less likely to be able to use the protections of our justice system, such as the presumption of innocence:

> Amongst the Mohawk, one of the most serious of crimes is lying, which would include not acknowledging those acts of which you were properly accused ... [I]t is likely that the offence with which they are charged is less serious to them than lying about their involvement in it, precisely what a "not guilty" plea would represent for them.[24]

The effects of cultural difference may be noted at various stages. In the preparation of pre-sentence reports, or in consideration of parole applications, Aboriginal offenders often fare poorly:

> What we may be missing is the fact that the offender behaves as he does because

our *techniques* of rehabilitation, of "healing", may not only be very different, but also traditionally improper. His refusal may stem not from indifference or from amorality but from *allegiance* to ethical precepts which we have not seen.[25]

Some Aboriginal communities, we are told, wish to be given the opportunity to rehabilitate offenders and reincorporate them into their societies. They contend that, as constituted, our justice system interferes with that process and our criminal courts cannot serve as a substitute for the community: "Since a person can only be shamed by someone who is respected and looked up to, this cannot be effected by a travelling court.[26] For these communities, sending an offender to jail delays the time when reintegration with the community can start. It may also cause an offender to become isolated from the community and more defiant;[27] indeed, imprisonment can allow the offender to avoid more distasteful options.[28]

These Aboriginal desires may be difficult for some observers to square with the squalid reality that exists in the most depressed, demoralized and crime-ridden reserve communities. Such an analysis, however, is ultimately self-defeating. We believe that, where suitable conditions exist, new approaches should be adopted.

Upon examination, we have concluded that the present system fails the Aboriginal peoples and contributes to their difficulties. The problems with the criminal justice system, for the most part, are obvious and long-standing. It is a system that, for Aboriginal people, is plagued with difficulties arising from its remoteness—a term that encompasses not only physical separation but also conceptual and cultural distance. Cultural distance is also manifest in different attitudes to legal control and to the legal environment. Aboriginal peoples continue to believe in the superiority of their traditional methods for resolving disputes

and maintaining social order. It is those ancient ways that, ironically, provide the new approaches and concepts of law that the Minister has urged us to explore.

Recommendation

2. Aboriginal communities identified by the legitimate representatives of Aboriginal peoples as being willing and capable should have the authority to establish Aboriginal justice systems. The federal and provincial governments should enter into negotiations to transfer that authority to those Aboriginal communities.

Notes

16 Ovide Mercredi, Remarks (Law Reform Commission of Canada Consultation, Edmonton, Alberta, March 1991).

17 One description of the spectrum of possible court models for Aboriginal persons in Canada is offered in *Justice on Trial, supra,* note 14 at 11-2 to 11-5.

18 See, *e.g.,* Mary Hyde and Carol LaPrairie, *Amerindian Police Crime Prevention.* Working Paper No. 1987-21 (Ottawa: Solicitor General Canada. 1987), which characterizes Aboriginal crime as a product of social disorganization derived from colonization and dependency. To the same effect. see Michael Jackson, "Locking up Natives in Canada" (1989) 23 U.B.C.L.Rev. 215 at 218-19; Lawrence J. Barkwell, David N. Chartrand, David N. Gray et al., "Devalued People: The Status of the Métis in the Justice System" (1989) 9:1 Can. J. of Native Studies 121; Havemann et al., *supra,* note 11; Nova Scotia, Royal Commission on the Donald Marshall, Jr., Prosecution. *The Mi'kmaq and Criminal Justice in Nova Scotia: A Research Study* by Scott Clark, vol. 3 (Halifax: The Commission, 1989), especially General Finding 2 at 69 (Chair: T.A. Hickman) [hereinafter Marshall Inquiry. vol. 3]; *Northern Frontier, Northern Homeland: The Report of the MacKenzie Valley Pipeline Inquiry,* vol. 1 (Ottawa: Supply and Services Canada, 1977) at 152 (Commissioner: Thomas R. Berger).

19 Carol LaPrairie, *If Tribal Courts Are the Solution, What Is the Problem?* (Consultation Document prepared for the Department of the Attorney General, Province of Nova Scotia. January 1990) at viii [unpublished].

20 Michael Coyle. "Traditional Indian Justice in Ontario: A Role for the Present?" (1986) 24 Osgoode Hall L.J. 605 at 614.

21 Rupert Ross, "Cultural Blindness and the Justice System in Remote Native Communities" (Address to the "Sharing Common Ground" Conference on Aboriginal Policing Services, Edmonton, May 1990) at 13. Our consultants have made similar observations from their own experience.

22 Ross, *ibid*. In Nova Scotia, Royal Commission on the Donald Marshall, Jr., Prosecution. *Consultative Conference on Discrimination against Natives and Blacks in the Criminal Justice System and the Role of the Attorney General*, vol. 7 (Halifax: The Commission, 1989) at 27 (Chair: T.A. Hickman) [hereinafter Marshall Inquiry, vol. 7], Judge Coutu. Co-ordinating Judge for the Itinerant Court of the District of Abitibi, stated: "What is important is not the system we adopt, but that the Native communities regain the social control they have lost because of the changes they have suffered since the coming of Europeans in America."

23 Chief Greg Sarazin, "220 Years of Broken Promises" in Boyce Richardson, ed., *Drumbeat: Anger and Renewal in Indian Country* (Toronto: Summerhill, 1989) at 169 [hereinafter *Drumbeat*].

24 Rupert Ross, "Leaving Our White Eyes Behind: The Sentencing of Native Accused" [1989] 3 C.N.L.R. 1 at 9. Further, "[t]he traditionally minded Aboriginal personal is predisposed to avoid conflict and argument and will shy away from confrontation. Even if a not guilty plea has been entered, the Aboriginal person may not provide the court *or even his counsel* with evidence unfavourable to the opposing witnesses": Indig-enous Bar Association, *The Criminal Code and Aboriginal People* (Paper prepared for the Law Reform Commission of Canada, 1991) at 21 [unpublished] [hereinafter IBA]. Similarly, Aboriginal persons may make bad witnesses, either in their own defence or for the prosecution, because "it is perceived as ethically wrong to say hostile, critical, implicitly angry things about someone *in their presence*": Ross, *ibid*. at 6.

25 Ross, *supra*, note 21 at 10.

26 Submission of the Sandy Lake Band to the Ontario Ministry of the Attorney General, quoted in Ross, *supra*, note 21 at 12.

27 Submission of the Alexander Tribal Government to *Justice on Trial*, *supra*, note 14 at 6-43.

28 See Michael Jackson, *In Search of the Pathways to Justice: Alternative Dispute Resolution in Aboriginal Communities* (Paper prepared for the Law Reform Commission of Canada, 1991) at 82-83 [unpublished].

Questions for Discussion

1 Is the adversarial justice system as practiced in Canada culturally biased? If so, must questions about the justification and methodology of the criminal justice system be raised separately for each minority group? Do Aboriginal peoples have a special status in this regard?

2 How should the rights and interests of an accused individual be balanced against the rights and interests of a community which operates its own criminal justice system? Should the accused have the right to choose which criminal justice system they wish to be tried under?

What Is Terrorism?

Igor Primoratz

"Terrorism" is a familiar term, but it is difficult to specify exactly what it is. Is it a kind of crime, or a kind of warfare? Can it be aimed at property, or must it be aimed at human life? Can it be perpetrated by recognized governments ("state terrorism")? In this essay, Igor Primoratz tries to answer these and a number of other questions in the attempt to isolate the concept of terrorism.

★ ★ ★

The phenomenon of terrorism raises numerous questions. Some are theoretical: What are its causes, and what are its various effects? Others are practical: What is to be done about it? Should terrorism be tackled directly, or is the only really promising way of dealing with it to attend to the grievances that give rise to it? Still others are moral: Just what is it that makes terrorism so thoroughly morally repugnant to most of us? Could it be justifiable under certain circumstances, or is it absolutely wrong? Philosophers are likely to be most interested in the last sort of question. This paper is an attempt at a definition of terrorism that will capture the trait, or traits, of terrorism which cause most of us to view it with repugnance.

Obviously, the definition I am after will be rather narrow in comparison to a great many definitions one finds in history and social sciences. There the tendency seems to be to apply the word to political assassination, and sometimes even to political violence of any sort. However, a conception of terrorism that lumps together the assassination of Reinhard Heydrich, the *Reichsprotektor* of Bohemia and the burning to death of a woman and her baby riding on an inter-city bus,[1] can be of no use in moral thinking.

Terrorism and Violence

Etymologically, 'terrorism' derives from 'terror'. Originally the word meant a system, or regime, of terror: at first that imposed by the Jacobins, who applied the word to themselves without any negative connotations; subsequently it came to be applied to any policy or regime of the sort and to suggest a strongly negative attitude, as it generally does today. Since I am seeking a definition that will cover both a single act and a policy of terrorism, I suggest we put aside the notions of 'system' and 'regime', but preserve the connection with terror. Terrorism is meant to cause terror (extreme fear) and, when successful, does so. But if someone did something likely to cause terror in others with no further aim, just for the fun of it, I think we would not see that as a case of terrorism. Terrorism is intimidation with a purpose: the terror is meant to cause others to do things they would otherwise not do. Terrorism is coercive intimidation.

This is just the definition offered by Carl Wellman in his paper 'On Terrorism Itself': "the use or attempted use of terror as a means of coercion".[2] Wellman remarks that violence often enters the picture, as it is one of the most effective ways of causing terror, but hastens to add that "the ethics of terrorism is not a mere footnote to the ethics of violence because violence is not essential to terrorism and, in fact, most acts of terrorism are nonviolent".[3] I agree that the ethics of terrorism is more than a footnote to the ethics of violence, but not for the reason adduced by Wellman. It seems to me that it would not make much sense to speak of 'non-violent terrorism' (in the sense which also excludes threats of violence). Wellman has three counter-examples, none of which strikes me as convincing. One is a judge who sentences a convicted criminal to death in order to deter potential criminals. I should think that execution is one of the more violent things we can do to a person (except, of course, if one accepts the definition of violence as 'the illegitimate use of force', which I find most unhelpful). Then there is blackmail, in which the fear of exposure is used as a means of intimidation. I think we would need to know just how serious the harm caused by the exposure would be in particular cases. If the harm threatened were great, and if violent actions characteristically inflict great harm in a striking manner, as Wellman rightly says, then to blackmail would indeed be to threaten violence. Finally, Wellman says:

> I must confess I often engage in nonviolent terrorism myself, for I often threaten

to flunk any student who hands in his paper after the due date. Anyone who doubts that my acts are genuine instances of terrorism is invited to observe the unwillingness of my students to hand in assigned papers on time in the absence of any such threat and the panic in my classroom when I issue my ultimatum.[4]

This sounds quite fanciful. But if Wellman's students are indeed as given to panic and terror as he suggests, and if to be flunked in his course is indeed such a great and dramatically inflicted harm that their reaction is understandable, then Wellman's threat is a threat of violence after all. It is not terrorism, though; nor is the meting out of the death penalty to a convicted criminal—for the reason to which I now come.

Indiscriminate Violence

It is often said that the most distinctive characteristic of terrorism is that it employs violence indiscriminately. This is certainly not true if construed literally; for the terrorist does not strike blindly and pointlessly, left and right, but rather plans his actions carefully, weighing his options and trying for the course of action that will best promote his objective at the lowest cost to himself. But the claim is true, and of crucial importance, if taken to refer to the terrorist's failure to discriminate between the guilty and the innocent, and to respect the immunity of the latter.

Terrorism has a certain basic structure. It has not one, but two targets: the immediate, direct target, which is of secondary importance, and the indirect target, which is really important. This indirect strategy is a feature of our everyday life, and there is nothing wrong with it as such. But when the indirect, but really important, aim is to force someone to do something they would otherwise not do, when this is to be achieved by intimidation, and when intimidation is effected by using

violence against innocent people—by killing, maiming, or otherwise severely harming them—or by threatening to do so, then the indirect strategy is that of terrorism. Usually, the primary and secondary targets are different persons or groups of people, but they may also be the same person or persons, as in blackmail. The person or persons who constitute the primary, but indirect, target of the terrorist, may or may not be innocent themselves; what is essential is that those who are made his secondary, but direct target, are. Thus terrorists may attack a group of civilians with the aim of intimidating the civilian population at large and getting it to leave a certain area. Or they may attack such a group with the purpose of cowing the government into accepting their demands, as is usually the case in airplane hijacking.

What is the sense in which the direct victims of the terrorist are 'innocent'? They have not *done* anything the terrorist could adduce as a justification of what he does to them. They are not attacking him, and thus he cannot justify his action as one of self-defence. They are not engaged in war against him, and therefore he cannot say that he is merely fighting in a war himself. They are not responsible, in any plausible sense of the word, for the (real or alleged) injustice, suffering, deprivation, which is inflicted on him or on those whose cause he has embraced, and which is so enormous that it could justify a violent response. Or, if they are, he is not in a position to know that.

I have said that one can lose one's immunity by being responsible for 'real or alleged' injustice or suffering because I am not speaking of innocence and immunity from a point of view different from, and independent of, that of the terrorist. Adopting such an approach would mean introducing an unacceptable degree of relativity into discussions of terrorism. The killing of Aldo Moro, for instance, would then be seen as terroristic by most of us: for, whatever we might think of Moro's policies, most of us surely do not consider them so extremely unjust and morally intolerable as to make him deserve to die on account of them; that is, most of us think of Moro as innocent in the relevant sense and therefore immune against killing. But the Red Brigades would deny that, and claim that what they did was political assassination, not terrorism; for they judged his policies quite differently. If we adopted this approach, we would have to grant that, to paraphrase *the* cliché about terrorism, one person's terrorist is another person's political assassin. I will not grant that; accordingly, what I am saying is that being responsible for a merely alleged injustice—an injustice that is alleged by the terrorist, but not recognized as such by anyone else—will be enough for losing one's immunity. Just as immunity is lost not only by fighting in an unjust war, but by fighting in any war—this is the grain of truth contained in Napoleon's notorious remark that "soldiers are made to be killed"—so it can be lost not only by holding political office in a gravely unjust government, but by holding such office in any government. As King Umberto I of Italy said after an unsuccessful attempt on his life, this kind of risk is part of the job. Of course, I am talking of 'innocence' and 'immunity' in a very specific, restricted sense: the sense relevant to the question of defining terrorism and distinguishing it from such things as war and political assassination. I am doing this to emphasize that the terrorist's victim is innocent from *the terrorist's own point of view*, i.e. innocent even if we grant the terrorist his assessment of the policies he supposes. I am not implying that as soon as an opponent of a certain regime has satisfied himself that the regime is utterly and intolerably unjust, he has a moral *carte blanche* to kill and maim its officials, but only that if he does so, his actions will not be terrorism, but political assassination. But nothing stands in the way of our condemning him, if we reject his

judgment of the moral standing of the regime. To show that an action is not terrorism but political assassination is neither to justify nor to excuse it.

I have also said that the terrorist's immediate victims are not responsible "in any plausible sense of the word" for the injustice and suffering to which the terrorist objects. Some terrorists are not at all bothered by that. Others are; they sometimes attempt to deny that their victims are innocent. But their arguments are based on a conception of responsibility so wide and undifferentiated that it enables them to say—as Emile Henry, a French anarchist who planted a bomb in a Paris café in 1894, did—"There are no innocents!" Such arguments may carry conviction with the terrorists who advance them, but are rightly found preposterous by almost everyone else.

Since terrorism is indiscriminate in the sense specified—since it does not discriminate between the guilty and the innocent—it is also indiscriminate in another sense: it is unpredictable. One can never count on keeping clear of the terrorist by not doing the things the terrorist objects to: for example, by not joining the army or the police, or by avoiding political office. One can never know whether, at any time and in any place, one will become a target of a terrorist attack.

Walter Laqueur objects to this way of defining terrorism:

> ... Many terrorist groups have been quite indiscriminate in the choice of their victims, for they assume that the slaughter of innocents would sow panic, give them publicity and help to destabilize the state and society. However, elsewhere terrorist operations have been quite selective. It can hardly be argued that President Sadat, the Pope, Aldo Moro or Indira Gandhi were arbitrary targets. Therefore, the argument that terrorist violence is by its nature random, and that innocence is the quintessential condition for the choice of victims,

cannot be accepted as a general proposition; this would imply that there is a conscious selection process on the part of the terrorist, that they give immunity to the 'guilty' and choose only the innocents.[5]

Neither of the two arguments is convincing. To take the latter first, the way Laqueur presents it contains a contradiction: if it is claimed that terrorist violence is *random*, then it cannot be also claimed that it is directed *solely* against the innocent, while the guilty are given immunity. What *is* claimed is that the defining feature of terrorism, and the reason why many of us find it extremely morally repugnant, is its failure to discriminate between the innocent and the guilty, and its consequent failure to respect the immunity of the former and to concentrate exclusively on the latter. The terrorist does not take on the army or the police, nor does he attempt to kill a political official, but chooses, say, to plant a bomb in a city bus, either because that is so much easier or, perhaps, because that will better serve his cause. He knows that his victims are civilians, but that is no good reason for him not to do it. If a couple of soldiers get on the bus along with the civilians and get killed as well, he will not see that as a fly in the ointment, but will either consider it irrelevant, or welcome it as an unexpected bonus. As for Laqueur's first argument, it is predicated either on a definition of terrorism that includes political assassination, and is thus question-begging, or on the assumption that every act of a terrorist is a terrorist act, which is absurd. The Red Brigades, for instance, were a terrorist organization, for they committed many terrorist acts; but when they abducted and killed Aldo Moro, that was political assassination, not terrorism. A similar confusion was conspicuous in the Israeli media a couple of years ago, when suicide attacks on the Israeli Army carried out by Shiite terrorists were uniformly described as 'terrorist attacks'.

This targeting of the innocent is the essential trait of terrorism, both conceptually and morally. The distinction between guilt and innocence is one of the basic distinctions in the moral experience of most of us. Most of us require that the infliction of serious harm on someone be justified in terms of some free, deliberate action on their part. If this cannot be done, people are innocent in the relevant sense, and thus immune against the infliction of such harm. A paper on the definition of terrorism is not the right context for establishing this claim. But I would not be greatly tempted to try to prove it in any context. The belief that innocence implies a far-reaching (though perhaps not absolute) immunity against the infliction of severe harm is a brute fact of the moral experience of most of us; for those who find it compelling, it is as simple and compelling as anything, and certainly more so than anything that might be brought up as a supporting argument. Accordingly, as Michael Walzer has put it, "the theoretical problem is not to describe how immunity is gained, but how it is lost. We are all immune to start with; our right not to be attacked is a feature of normal human relationships".[6] One may lose this immunity by attacking someone else, or by enlisting in the army in time of war, or by joining security services, or holding office in a regime or an organization that is resisted by violence because of its unjust, or allegedly unjust, policies. But one who has done none of the above is innocent of anything that might plausibly be brought up as a justification for a violent attack on him, or a threat of such an attack, and is thus immune against it. When he is attacked nevertheless, with the aim of cowing him, or someone else, into a course of action that otherwise would not be undertaken, that is terrorism. Terrorism is different, both conceptually and morally, from violence employed in self-defence, from war in general and guerrilla war in particular, and from political assassination.[7]

The next three points are suggested by C.A.J. Coady's definition of a terrorist act as:

> a political act, ordinarily committed by an organized group, which involves the intentional killing or other severe harming of non-combatants or the threat of the same or intentional severe damage to the property of non-combatants or the threat of the same.[8]

Violence Against Persons and Against Property

The violence perpetrated by terrorists is typically killing, maiming or otherwise severely harming their victims. Must terrorist violence be directed against persons? According to Coady's definition, it need not. Suppose a terrorist organization decided to stop killing and maiming people, and took to destroying valuable works of art instead. Or suppose it started destroying the crops which were the only source of livelihood of a village. Would that mean giving up terrorism for a non-terrorist struggle, or would it rather be substituting one terrorist method for another? In the latter case, I think, we would still speak of terrorism—because the destruction of property would threaten people's lives. In the former case, however, the word 'terrorism' might no longer seem appropriate. As Jenny Teichman puts it, "it may indeed be grossly unfair and unjust to destroy the property of non-combatants, but unless that property is needed for life itself it isn't terroristic. For one thing it is not likely to produce terror—only fury".[9]

Terrorism and Terror

While Wellman wants to preserve the connection between terrorism and terror, but to disconnect terrorism from violence, Coady's definition suggests the opposite: terrorism is a type of violence which, indeed, often causes terror, but this is "an insight into the sociology of terrorism" and should not be included

in the definition. The connection is merely contingent. After all, all uses of political violence effect some degree of fear.[10]

That is true, but I think there is an important difference between the sort of violence most of us would want to call terrorist and other kinds of violence, where the fear caused is either a less important objective, or not an objective at all, but merely a welcome byproduct. In terrorism proper, the causing of fear and coercion through fear is *the* objective. Even if the crucial role of coercion through fear is not important enough from a theoretical point of view to single out this particular type of violence, things look different from a moral point of view. Most of us feel that terrorism is so very wrong primarily, but not solely, because it is violence inflicted on the innocent; the element of intimidation and coercion through intimidation is an *additional* ground for moral condemnation, an insult added to injury.[11]

Terrorism: Political and Non-political, State and Anti-state

Terrorism is often defined in various unjustifiably restrictive ways. The identification of terrorism with political terrorism, as in the definition offered by Coady, is quite typical. But the method of coercive intimidation by infliction of violence on innocent persons has often been used in non-political contexts: one can speak of religious terrorism (e.g. that of the Hizb Allah) and criminal terrorism (e.g. that of the Mafia). Even more restrictive are definitions couched in terms of *who* uses terrorism. Terrorism is often presented as a method employed solely by rebels and revolutionaries; state terrorism is thus defined out of existence:

> Throwing a bomb is bad,
> Dropping a bomb is good;
> Terror, no need to add,
> Depends on who's wearing the hood.[12]

This may be good propaganda, but it is poor analysis. The word 'terrorism' was originally used to refer to the 'Reign of Terror' set up by the Jacobins, i.e. to a particular case of *state* terrorism. And even the most enlightened, liberal, democratic states have occasionally engaged in terrorism: witness the bombing of Dresden and Hamburg, Hiroshima and Nagasaki. In all these cases the targets were neither military nor industrial, but rather major centres of civilian population of enemy countries; the objective was to destroy the morale and break the will of the population and in that way either ensure victory (over Germany) or shorten the war (against Japan). This kind of bombing has come to be known as 'terror bombing'. Furthermore, there is a type of state, the totalitarian state, whose most fundamental principle is permanent, institutionalized terrorism. For nothing less than such terrorism, exercised by the omnipotent state and, in particular, its secret police in an utterly unpredictable manner, and embodied in "the true central institution of totalitarian organizational power", the concentration camp (Hannah Arendt), would do as a means of an attempt at total domination of society.[13]

Amoralism

A number of authors claim that terrorism is essentially amoral. Thus Paul Wilkinson writes:

> What fundamentally distinguishes terrorism from other forms of organised violence is not simply its severity but its features of amorality and antinomianism. Terrorists either profess indifference to existing moral codes or else claim exemption from all such obligations. Political terror, if it is waged consciously and deliberately, is implicitly prepared to sacrifice all moral and humanitarian considerations for the sake of some political end.[14]

To be sure, many terrorists seem to be oblivious to the moral aspects of their actions. Some terrorists or fellow-travellers even flaunt their amoralism, as did the nineteenth-century anarchist writer Laurent Tailhade: "What do the victims matter if the gesture is beautiful!" But such attitudes are by no means universal; terrorism of the left, at least, can claim a rich apologetic tradition. Views on terrorism advanced in the writings of Bakunin, Nechaev, Trotsky and Marcuse, were developed in response to moral criticism; they are couched in moral terms, and exhibit the formal traits widely considered to be definitive of moral views: they are action-guiding, universalizable, and of overriding importance to those who hold them. These authors do not reject morality as such, but rather conventional morality; and in the same breath they proclaim 'the interest of the Revolution' to be the supreme *moral* law. Their views may not amount to a convincing moral position (I, for one, am not convinced), but they do amount to *a* moral position. To hold otherwise is to confuse one's own moral outlook with the moral point of view as such.[15]

Summing Up

The preceding remarks lead up to the following definition of terrorism: the deliberate use of violence, or threat of its use, against innocent people, with the aim of intimidating them, or other people, into a course of action they otherwise would not take.

Let me summarize the most important points about this definition.

1. Terrorism has a certain structure. It has two targets, the primary and secondary. The latter target is directly hit, but the objective is to get at the former, to intimidate the person or persons who are the primary target into doing things they otherwise would not do. Sometimes the same person or group of persons is both the primary and secondary target; but ordinarily the two targets are different (groups of) people.

2. The secondary target, which is hit directly, is innocent people. Thus terrorism is distinguished both from war in general, and guerrilla war in particular, in which the innocent (non-combatants, civilians) are not deliberately attacked, and from political assassination, whose victims—political officials and police officers—are responsible for certain policies and their enforcement. This, of course, does not mean that an army cannot engage in terrorism; many armies have done so. Nor does it mean that political assassination does not often intimidate the government or the public, or is not often meant to do so.

3. The connection of 'terrorism' with 'terror' and 'terrorizing' is preserved.

4. The definition covers both political and non-political (e.g. religious, criminal) terrorism.

5. With regard to political terrorism, it makes it possible to speak both of state and non-state terrorism, of revolutionary and counter-revolutionary terrorism, terrorism of the left and of the right. The definition is politically neutral.

6. It is also morally neutral. I believe it captures what many of us find so repugnant in terrorism. But it is not a definitional *fiat* that begs the moral question at issue (the way the definition of violence as the illegitimate use of force does, for example). It does not make moral condemnation of terrorism analytically true, its moral defence analytically false, or the question about its moral standing a self-answering one.

7. Some are likely to find the definition too restrictive, and to want to apply the word to other sorts of violence. It may well be that, as a matter of fact, the word is used in a wider sense most of the time. But I trust it will be generally (although not universally) agreed that the actions covered by the definition are indeed terroristic. I suspect that most of those likely to deny this will want to define terrorism in terms of who employs it and to what

ultimate purpose. If so, I am not worried. Those who claim that who is a terrorist, and who a freedom fighter, depends on who is wearing the hood, or what its colour is, are not promising partners for a serious discussion anyway.

One final remark: the definition of terrorism I have suggested is accurate and helpful with regard to the actions, policies and organizations in the twentieth century which most of us would want to describe as terrorist. Large-scale terrorism in the sense defined is very much a phenomenon of our time. To be sure, the targeting of the innocent as a means of coercive intimidation was occasionally advocated and practised in the nineteenth century as well: advocated, for instance, by the radical democrat Karl Heinzen,[16] practised in particular in the last decades of the century by some Irish nationalists and some of the anarchists who believed in the "propaganda by deed". But most of those who were called, and often called themselves, terrorists, throughout the last century—most anarchists, various revolutionary groups in Russia—did not practise terrorism in this sense, but rather engaged in political assassination. Russian revolutionaries in particular were given to constant probing of the moral questions raised by their struggle. They accepted the use of violence only unwillingly, and generally insisted that it be employed sparingly; in the words of P.L. Lavrov, "not one drop of unnecessary blood shall be spilled". They considered assassination of some of the most prominent officials of the oppressive regime as a grave sin that must be committed, but must also be expiated by dying on the gallows. They would never contemplate deliberate killing and maiming of the innocent; if a planned assassination turned out to involve deaths of innocent people as an inevitable side effect, they called off the action, even if that meant taking an extreme risk to themselves.[17] The moral distance between them and present-day terrorists is immense. Accordingly, I think it would be helpful to restrict the word 'terrorist' to the latter, rather than apply it to both and then distinguish between them in some such terms as 'direct' and 'indirect' or 'individual' and 'mass' terrorism.[18]

This shift away from assassination of chiefs of state and other high political officials to indiscriminate attacks on the innocent, which took place at the beginning of our century, can be explained in more than one way. Walter Laqueur points out that "in the twentieth century, human life became cheaper; the belief gained ground that the end justified all means, and that humanity was a bourgeois prejudice".[19] Edward Hyams offers a different explanation: "chiefs of state are more carefully guarded than they used to be, and revolutionaries have learnt that the elimination of individual leaders is apt to resemble driving out Satan with Beelzebub".[20] There may be still other causes; but I will not go into this question, for it can be answered only by empirical research. I am mentioning this change only in order to emphasize the limited applicability of the definition of terrorism I have suggested.

Acknowledgement

I would like to thank Dr. David George for helpful comments on an earlier version of this paper.

Notes

1 Cf. W. Laqueur (1987) *The Age of Terrorism* (Boston, Little, Brown & Co.), pp. 21, 127.

2 C. Wellman (1979) On terrorism itself, *The Journal of Value Inquiry*, 13, p. 250.

3 Ibid., p. 251.

4 Ibid., p. 252.

5 W. Laqueur, op. cit., pp. 143-144.

6 M. Walzer (1980) *Just and Unjust Wars* (Harmondsworth, Penguin Books), p. 145 n.

7 This is, obviously, rather general. When applying the distinction between the guilty and the innocent in these three areas, one will have to make it more specific. What are the criteria for ascribing and apportioning responsibility for the policies of an organization or a regime? Does the distinction, when applied to war, boil down to one between combatants and non-combatants? In the latter context, in particular, numerous borderline cases are likely to arise: Is a soldier on leave from his unit guilty or innocent, a legitimate or an illegitimate target? What of a soldier who has been drafted against his will, who holds the war waged by his country to be wrong, and always shoots above the heads of enemy soldiers? What of a worker in an ammunition factory? What of a civilian whose work is not involved in his country's war effort, but who actively supports that effort by participating in war-mongering rallies, contributing generously to government war loans, etc.? However, I will not go into such matters here, for doing so would no longer be elaborating a definition, but rather engaging in substantive moral thinking. Another reason is that such problems, insofar as they concern war, have been discussed in a very helpful way by T. Nagel ((1971/2) War and massacre, *Philosophy and Public Affairs*, 1), J.G. Murphy ((1973) The killing of the innocent, *The Monist*, 57), M. Walzer (op. cit.) and J. Teichman ((1986) *Pacifism and the Just War* (Oxford, Blackwell)).

8 C.A.J. Coady, (1985) The morality of terrorism, *Philosophy*, 60, p. 52.

9 J. Teichman, op. cit., p. 92.

10 C.A.J. Coady, op. cit., p. 53.

11 This should not be taken to suggest a simplistic, overly rationalistic picture of terrorism: a picture of the terrorist making a clearly specified threat to his primary target, who then rationally considers the matter and comes to the conclusion that it pays to comply. This picture may fit some cases of terrorism, but it certainly does not fit others. For terrorism very often aims at setting off long and complex social processes, involving much irrational behavior, that are meant to disorient the public and destabilize various social arrangements and institutions, if not social life in general (on this, see, e.g. T.P. Thornton (1964). Terror as a weapon of political agitation, in: H. Eckstein (Ed.) *Internal War* (New York, The Free Press)). However, intimidation plays a central role in such cases

as well, while the ultimate aim of the terrorist is, again, to make those who constitute his primary target do things they would otherwise not do. Thus such cases do not call for a revision of the definition of terrorism as a type of coercion through intimidation.

12 R. Woddis, Ethics for Everyman, quoted in C.A.J. Coady, op. cit., p. 47.

13 See H. Arendt (1958) *The Origins of Totalitarianism*, 2nd edn. (Cleveland, The World Publication Co.), Ch. 12-13.

14 P. Wilkinson (1974) *Political Terrorism* (London, Macmillan), pp. 16-17.

15 I deal with this point in some detail in 'On the Ethics of Terrorism', forthcoming in the *Proceedings of the 14th World Congress in Philosophy of Law and Social Philosophy*, Edinburgh, August 17-23, 1989.

16 See his essay, Murder in: W. Laqueur (Ed.) (1978) *The Terrorism Reader* (New York, New American Library).

17 See, e.g. Z. Ivianski (1989), The moral issue: some aspects of individual terror, in: D.C. Rapoport &

Y. Alexander (Eds.), *The Morality of Terrorism*, 2nd edn. (New York, Columbia University Press).

18 The first distinction is advanced, e.g. by E. Hyams (1974) *Terrorists and Terrorism* (New York, St. Martin's Press), pp. 9-11; the second is usually made in Marxist literature.

19 W. Laqueur, op. cit., p. 84.

20 E. Hyams, op. cit., p. 166.

Questions for Discussion

1 Is there a significant difference between political assassination and terrorism? What do they have in common, and what are their differences (if any)?

2 Can there be non-violent terrorism (e.g., blackmail)?

3 Primoratz specifies that the direct victims of terrorism must be innocent from "the terrorist's own point of view," but then rejects the assertion made by some terrorists that "there are no innocents" by saying, "such arguments may carry conviction with the terrorists who advance them, but are rightly found preposterous by anyone else." Are these consistent?

Terrorism, Self-Defense, and Whistleblowing

Laura Westra

One fundamental question about terrorism is whether it is ever morally acceptable. In this paper, Laura Westra examines this question from a Kantian ethical perspective. Westra tries to put forward the strongest case that can be made in favour of (some) terrorism from this perspective, which sees it as related to the notion of self-defense, but she concludes that terrorism is always morally unacceptable.

★   ★   ★

In a recent paper given at a Symposium on terrorism, Thomas Hill, Jr., discussed "Making Exceptions Without Abandoning the Principle: Or How a Kantian Might Think about Terrorism." His argument, however, after acknowledging that "terrorists of course often claim to have morally worthy ends and also means that are morally justified in the con-

text," and further stating that "some such claims deserve a serious hearing,"[1] goes on to deal with the related question of

> ... what one may justifiably do in response to morally indefensible terrorism.[2]

Most terrorist acts are—he says—undefensible. Now, since my sympathies lie with the

Ethical Issues

Kantians in most discussions of problems in interhuman ethics, I thought I would take up the challenge and see what—if anything—can be said in defense of the terrorist, from the Kantian standpoint. I believe, for reasons that will become apparent in the next two sections, that neither a consequentialist defense of terrorism nor a contractarian one stands up under scrutiny, and Narveson makes this clear in his paper on "Terrorism and Morality."[3] On the other hand, the Kantian perspective is the only one which might permit a somewhat favorable analysis, although even that will not succeed in justifying terrorist activity.

I will take that stance and attempt an analysis that will at least permit a somewhat broader understanding of terrorism, and a clear position on what is permissible in response to terrorist violence. In the first section, I will explore the meaning and form of terrorism, in the second, I will ask the question whether terrorism can be morally defensible by sketching a view of it as a particular form of self-defense and, in the third part, I will argue for the grounds of this specific self-defense and consider whether it might also be viewed as a form of whistle-blowing. I will conclude with a brief suggestion on state-terrorism.

1. What is Terrorism?

> ... terrorism can be neither murder which is purely private and has no political significance, nor war, which is entirely public and overt, but which the terrorist's partly would be incapable of winning.[4]

Notwithstanding the strenuous efforts of many to simply dismiss terrorism as nothing but a different form of organized crime, philosophers persist in thinking about certain recalcitrant features of terrorism that point to another possible interpretation. This does not imply that terrorism is viewed as permissible or even less as morally appropriate. It simply means that there are certain aspects of terror-

ism that invite philosophical analysis, as they appear to be radically different from regular criminal activities. These differences come through at several levels. Some of these are: a) the actual form that terrorist operations take; b) the aims of their activities; and c) the alleged motive of these activities.

The latter, c), is perhaps the most important of the three. Unlike common criminals, whose aim is to promote personal or—at best—group economic gain through illegal and immoral acts, the terrorist claims universalizable principles as his motive. Even if gain is involved and demanded, it is not meant for luxury (whether individual or group), but for the sustenance of the "cause," whatever it might be. Their motive might be primarily "to affect political arrangements of the community in question,"[5] and it ought to be a "political motive, the ingredient which turns the use of violence into terrorism."[6] In fact, a strong political motive is a necessary, although possibly not a sufficient component to turn violence into terrorism. Paul Gilbert suggests that even political intent is not sufficient; his example, even a robber who contributes to party funds, is not a terrorist. The specifying "differentia," he believes, is that "the terrorist intends to wage a war, and would wage open civil war were the balance of power appropriate," primarily as a challenge to a "state's claim to rule a particular territory."[7]

It is important to clarify the meaning of terrorism, not only in order to judge its moral status (if any), but also in order to assess which form of response might be appropriate or justifiable on the part of a state. It is worth noting, in passing, that in general, it seems as though many states, such as the U.S. for instance, take the paradoxical stance of *both* branding terrorists as "criminals," and, at the same time, reacting to them in war-like fashion. By contrast, we can see the painstaking legal approach to the conviction and punishment of war criminals who are carefully isolated and tried by due process of law. Of course, the fact that some governments react to terrorism as if it were war is not an argument for the acceptance of terrorism as war. It is—however—an indication that many so view it and many more are willing to accept this implicit judgement.

I think it is safe to say that what determines that violent acts should be labeled "terrorism," rather than "crime" or "random violence," is a political stance of a special kind, namely, one aimed at forcing a government hostile to the terrorists' territorial claims or freedom claims, to change its position by the strongest means possible, short of waging an actual war (which is beyond their capacity). In essence, the terrorist does not engage in either civil war or revolution, although the results he advocates may be similar to those of either. As Glover puts it, "The violence or the threats have to be of the kind that can strike terror into people."[8] He further remarks that "political violence" is the central feature of terrorism, thus we cannot limit ourselves to a consideration of its standard cases, but need to consider state terrorism as well.

This discussion does not point to a precise, easily defined picture, but to a rather elastic, multidimensional cluster of activities, loosely joined by their commonality of aims and intent. Aims and intents are closely tied, and this raises the question of the state of affairs he wishes to bring about. It is this "vision," this belief that impels him to act in violent ways as the only avenue left to bring about an eminently desirable state of affairs. Now if we allow consequentialist considerations to influence our understanding of terrorist action, we appear to be committed to a utilitarian framework of some sort. The terrorist's aim is to bring about a certain (changed) state of affairs, thus we need to consider the proposed and projected results of his activities. Narveson argues that a possible justification might be to view them as a last re-

sort option, thus as "a means of social change." That would extend to terrorism the sort of justification which a just war claims. Yet a just war ought to be primarily a war of self defense against unprovoked and unjustified attack, whereas terrorist acts are primarily meant to be attacks, not defense, thus the core meaning of "just war" cannot simply be extended to cover "just" or "justifiable" terrorist activity without much more analysis and argument (if at all).[9]

What remains present is the desirability of the state of affairs the terrorist aims to bring about, although this is a separate, though intimately connected issue. A recent example, and a clear statement can be seen in the speech of Mr. Arafat (PLO) to the General Assembly of the United Nations:

> Finally, I say to our people: "The dawn approaches. Victory is at hand. I see the homeland in your holy stones. I see the flag of our independent Palestine fluttering over the hills of our beloved homeland." (*Globe and Mail*, Dec. 14, 1988)

As Narveson rightly sees it, in order for the vision to even begin to justify violent action, one would need pretty strong evidence that the just ends that will be achieved will a) be "tolerably clear and coherent," and b) consist in "improvements in respect to justice."[10] Consequentialist reasoning is less than successful in identifying the clear, coherent, improved, just aims of terrorist action, and I think that Narveson is correct in implying that (somewhat like Marxist revolutionaries) terrorists are often better at decrying present states of affairs than they are at specifying the all-pervasive, just improvement in which their efforts would culminate.

These difficulties point to the fact that human fallibility and incapacity to accurately assess long-term consequences (a common failing of utilitarianism in other contexts as well), indicate that a possible justification of terrorism, even if one existed, could not be based on utilitarian grounds.

Finally, what of the actual form their operations take? Annette Baier vigorously argues that modern life and even human life throughout history is and has been an exercise in various and multifaceted forms of violence, some of it possessing the seal of approval of the authority in power. The latter, she says, is not easy to distinguish from so-called "illegitimate" violence:

> The important moral questions have always been "Whom or what may I assault and kill?" not "May I assault and kill."[11]

If we accept, as I think we must, her indictment of displays of leashed violence as not only acceptable but representative of a country, violence and coercion of all sorts within families, as well as within and without the framework of states and nations, even violence in "sacrifices" for religious purposes, then it is correct to say, as she does, that we have little ground for "righteous indignation." Yet to simply say, look at what we do routinely, legitimately, and what has been done throughout the ages, and don't be too quick to cast stones at terrorists, would be to use a fallacious form of argument, almost a textbook example of a two-wrongs fallacy, and Baier does not do this. She does however make a strong case for the great difficulty of separating "morally acceptable" from unacceptable violence. I have suggested a somewhat parallel argument for the difficulties of isolating those who can truly be termed "innocents" in a just war (if such a war were possible), fought with discriminating weaponry.[12]

Yet we must admit that terrorists not only employ violence, but use this violence indiscriminately, and worse. Not only are innocents killed as in war, with a sort of "double-effect" justification, but they are often deliberately sought out because of their greater value as "standard bearers,"[13] to use Baier's felicitous

expression, to announce their aims, their plans, and confirm their involvement. If the terrorist's aim is to perpetrate violence and other acts which "...have to be the kind that can strike *terror* into people," as we have seen, then the more random and horribly inappropriate their violence, the "better" or more successful their efforts will be.

This approach of the terrorist will destroy even the tenuous hold on morality a so-called "just" war might have, at least if it attempts to discriminate between innocents and non-innocents. Thus even if we attempt to assimilate terrorist acts to war, rather than criminal activity, they lack, at least prima facie the sort of justification which is adduced for 1) a just war (because of the difficulty of viewing their actions as self-defense), and 2) justice in war (because they fail to comply with the primary rule of war morality: the conscientious effort to discriminate between lawful and unlawful targets of legitimate violence).

2. Can Terrorism Be Morally Defensible? (Self-Defense and Self-Defense₁)

Onora O'Neill argues that "moral problems" emerge or are perceived within the context of a specific moral doctrine, although they are "to some extent independent of theories, even if our apprehension of them is theory-dependent."[14] She warns:

> But it is not enough for writing in applied ethics to seek reasoned resolutions of problems, while assuming that the specifications of the problems are given.[15]

Therefore, in order to shed light on terrorism as such, we need to start by analyzing it without too strong an assumption that our ideological framework, which condemns some forms of violence while sanctioning others, is necessarily the correct one. It may well be the case that our instinctive or intuitive revulsion against terrorism will prove to be justified; nevertheless our first step must be to question it.

We have seen the difficulties arising from an attempted utilitarian defense of terrorist acts. Can they be justified on any other ground? I have argued that violence can be justified in cases of self-defense and in small, contained wars of liberation, fought only with discriminating weapons.[16] The generally accepted meaning of self-defense is simply one's response to an immediate, violent and grave threat to one's life or one's (physical) integrity (although Walzer, for instance, sees even personal space as defensible, for individuals or nations, see ft. 9).

What about other values, such as "liberation," for instance? The question is whether life is the ultimate value, the only one that permits violent self-defense on our part, or whether certain specific requirements of life's quality possess equal, or even superior value. The whole notion of comparing other "values" to life is not one which permits easy answers. Frey, for instance, asks whether "human dignity" is a "commensurable or incommensurable value."[17] Ultimately, he argues that as we plainly raise questions about both life and human dignity by comparing them to other possible values we might prefer to uphold or foster, then a scale has to be found against which these might be measured. He finds this scale in quantity measured in economic terms. Others, such as Scherer, disagree and opt for a hierarchical scale for the values themselves, as an acceptable, and preferable alternative.[18]

What about a conflict between life and human dignity? No economic comparison is possible and there are serious difficulties, common, for instance, in geriatric problems arising in health care. In these cases, the conflict is often resolved in favor of autonomy/dignity, rather than mere life as physical existence. An example might be the taking of extraordinary measures to keep elderly or dying patients in pain, or terminal, just barely alive, either

against their earlier (expressed) wishes, or against the informed, respectful wishes of family members. Often, in such cases, it is judged that the higher value is that of the dignity and personal (rather than merely physical) integrity of the patient, and therefore heroic measures are discontinued. Other examples might be the Jehovah's Witness' conscious choice to preserve his own autonomous moral choices (thus, once again his personal integrity) even at the cost of his life, understood as mere biological survival. The freedom of belief and worship, fundamental in modern Western Societies, at least as an ideal, demands that such autonomous choices be protected in rational individuals even if—by their own choices—they forfeit their existence.

As it is impossible to assign monetary value to the preference of the Jehovah's Witness, it seems clear that, with reference to the debate mentioned, Scherer, not Frey, has the right of it, and that hierarchical ranking of values is not only possible, but accepted and practiced.

At this point it might be best to pause in order to unpack the meaning of a key term I have used repeatedly, that is, "integrity" and "personal integrity." I understand the notion to imply cohesiveness of beliefs and autonomous decision making capacity in this context, rather than moral integrity or honesty. It is close to what Kant would say about "ends in themselves" possessing dignity. Hill cites Kant, defining the latter as an "unconditional and incomparable worth ... that ... admits of no equivalent." As such it is an unconditional value, it is "above all price." Further, Hill refers to the second formulation of the Categorical Imperative ("That we must always treat humanity as an end in itself"), as the "dignity principle."[19] It would seem perhaps simpler for me to simply speak of "dignity," but I will persist in my use of "integrity," although it is not particularly more useful in this context than the other term, but because it is preferable in contexts transcending interhuman ethics and the Kantian imperatives, as I have shown elsewhere. In a word, "integrity" lends itself better to the context of individuals and wholes lacking human rationality.[20]

To return now to the question of value-ranking, and if a hierarchical scale is at all acceptable, then it might be possible to argue for a different reading of the terrorist position. As we saw, the self-defense justification which is available to the participant of a just war (of self-defense), is not available to the terrorist, as he initiates violence, rather than reacting to it in a just and proportionate manner. But this objection is only pertinent if we limit the value that we deem defensible by violent means to physical existence only. The question that arises is if personal integrity and autonomy, understood as a basic universally held human value comprising the right to hold beliefs and to practice these beliefs (provided they do not harm others),—have we a corresponding right to "self-defense" (let us call it self-defense$_1$) which extends beyond our physical person in some way? Cases such as that of the Jehovah's Witness seem to imply that we do. The more difficult question is how we can defend such a value (and right) morally, and I will return to that point later. For now, further remarks are in order on the question of personal integrity and self-defense. Narveson, for instance, argues for the following "cases, from most to least plausible, as situations justifying violence," thus for values whose defense is permissible:

1. Immediate prevention of injury to self—out-and-out Self-Defense.

2. Immediate prevention of injury to others—out-and-out Other Defense.

3. Longer Range or indirect defense of self or others.

4. Securing of necessary conditions of a minimally acceptable life when no other means is possible.

5. Promoting a better life for oneself, some favored group, or humankind at large, over and beyond what is called for by (1–4).[21]

Now what I am suggesting is that "better life," when it entails the freedom to act in accordance with one's beliefs, might fit better under Narveson's headings 1 and 2, according to whether they are ours or those of our family and community. The first step in that direction might be the attempt to fit personal integrity (thus self-defense$_1$) under 3 or 4 (i.e., "long range or indirect defense," or "securing of necessary conditions of a minimally acceptable life"). Clearly, the possibility of making this move depends on what we view as "minimally acceptable life," as it is a somewhat ambiguous expression like any reference to "harming" and its prevention, in this context. Their interpretation depends on a previous decision to accept "physical life" as the ultimate value, or to permit personal integrity (or the "dignity principle" in Kantian terms) to hold the prior position. On the question of violence and the defense of values, Annette Baier asks:

> Do we, on reflection, prefer that people meekly tolerate oppression, dispossession, non-recognition, indignity? Do we, for example admire the weakness with which women for so long put up not just with domination, but with male violence in and out of the home?[22]

She does not suggest that violence is appropriate in all cases of "oppression" or "non-recognition," but she sees a gradual increase in justification, based on a) the terrorist's history of non-violent attempts to secure freedom or justice, and b) the plausibility of his claim that he represents the case of the group, not just his own injustice. Yet, all in all, she still concludes:

> The fact that the terrorist and his people have suffered inhumane treatment does not justify, but might excuse, his inhumanity.[23]

I am not sure I am ready to go even that far; I simply want to start by defending the possibility that other values, not only biological life, may be defensible. Further, that some of these values may be deemed to be at least as important if not more important than life itself, and that might be non-material and non-quantifiable to some extent (although "oppression" and "indignity" may represent both an attitude which affects one as a person, and be translated in demeaning, even violent actions), perhaps also intellectual or spiritual; at any rate indicative of human personal integrity as previously detailed.

To return once again to the terrorist's motive and aim, we have seen it is not defensible on consequentialist grounds: it is not sufficient to claim that a "better" future or life is envisioned, without enough specificity to be able to compare utilities and disutilities in the "before" and "after" scenarios. Therefore, from a utilitarian standpoint, the terrorist loses whatever (weak) "moral leg" he might have had to stand on at the outset. And if the envisioned consequences of his activity cannot help his defense, then only his motive remains to offer a possible justification. Therefore, I have attempted a somewhat Kantian defense of personal integrity (autonomy/dignity) as a value or cluster of values which can form the basis of a right of self-defense, superior even to normal (i.e. "life") self-defense.

Now, even if it is granted that there might be a value which is superior to that of simple biological life, there is no ground *yet*, for the claim that evidence is thereby justifiable in its defense. To extend the earlier parallel, it would be—minimally—like claiming that the Jehovah's Witness not only has a right to self-defense, and thus can morally refuse medical help intended to sustain his biological existence at the cost of his personal integrity, and freedom of choice, but *also* that he has the moral right to turn around, if he can, and strike dead the doctor or nurse who is forc-

ing a blood transfusion upon him. This is a claim that cannot be made without further argument (if at all), and I will turn to an examination of that position in the next section.

3. Terrorism as Self-Defense₁ and Whistleblowing

Let us return to the previous example: is it basically flawed? After all, the doctor or nurse attempting to fulfill her mandate to save lives (even at the expense of the principles, beliefs and choices of the recalcitrant patient) has an indubitable benevolent motive: she has a commitment to the patient's "best interests" and is acting out of goodwill, and viewing the patient as an "end" not means to some other goal. This is in direct conflict with what the terrorist intends: since the days of the inquisition, no one has succeeded in claiming that we do "good" to people by torturing them, by harming or killing them, even if we do so in order to instill justice, or a "better" way of life.

But even with these differences, a disturbing element remains: how far can the patient go to defend his spiritual or personal integrity, if others will not allow him to act autonomously? And is that (i.e., self-defense₁) close enough to self-defense to offer the same justification, or even a better sort of justification for violence? Perhaps the best way to approach this difficult question is to start by a mention of well-known cases when principles and human dignity and autonomy have been chosen over existence. The cases of Joan of Arc and all Christian martyrs fit that description, as do those of many heroes. However saints and martyrs are inappropriate examples: the innocent lives they sacrifice are their own, thus—as they cannot continue to exist to practice their autonomous choices—they really can't be said to die in self-defense₁. Rather, they can be seen as dying for their principles, or perhaps in order that others may have the right to choose those principles and thereby live autonomous lives, although their own integrity appears usually to be their primary motive. "I will not worship idols" is a strong declaration which clearly puts personal integrity above all things. And yet, it is far from obvious that any martyr would have willingly killed the tyrant who insisted on the idols, even if she could have done so.

Perhaps then serious harm to others represents the boundary beyond which one may not go even in defense of the—admittedly—highest value. But this appears to be self-contradictory, because the reason why regular self-defense permits (unintended, but necessary) killing, is that it was deemed to be a defense of the ultimate value (i.e. biological life).

If we replace this ultimate with another, why can we not, regretfully, kill for its sake, if all else fails? The reason may be that biological life may not be the highest value, but it represents the ground of all other possible values, including the ultimate one. Further, the forfeit of our physical life is not a reversible harm: it is absolutely final, and perhaps this is not true of "harm" to our personal integrity. One can thwart our ability to practice what we believe in, but our spirituality cannot be taken away; whether we are allowed to practice them or not, our beliefs and principles are our own.[24] And that is why it is not morally right for the Jehovah's Witness to defend his own integrity by attacking the doctor. If she waits until he is unconscious or even if she forces him to have the transfusion while he is conscious but incapable of preventing it, she does not take his beliefs away, although she violates his freedom of choice. Surely no one, not even the deity could possibly claim the patient sinned or made the wrong choice by abandoning his principles, under those circumstances. In fact—I am told—a doctor who transfused a fetus whose life was in danger against the expressed wishes of the mother, a Jehovah's Witness, was eventually thanked by the mother after a safe delivery, for allowing her to persist in her stance, while forcing the life-saving procedure on the baby.

Thus it seems that even though the spiritual value of personal integrity may be the higher one, and we have the right to it and also to defend it, a violent defense does not appear justifiable. Spiritual and intellectual values are not such that they can be taken from us *in toto* (at least without physical assault involving surgical or chemical means, perhaps). If we are temporarily prevented from holding on to our integrity, we may still regain it, once the coercive power is removed or ceases, unlike life, which cannot be temporarily withheld. Therefore, even if one grants the argument that makes self-defense$_1$ superior to self-defense because of the higher value it defends, it is still not right *ipso facto* to defend that value through violence, a rather "inconclusive" conclusion to the argument, up to this point.

Still, terrorism, when it is the "real thing" as far as defensible motives are concerned, brings to our attention some important facts, often forgotten: favorable consequences or rational self-interest are not the only principles that move us to action or which are morally defensible. On the contrary, even that ultimate "prudential" value, life, is and can be viewed as secondary, under the sway of deeply held beliefs, strong enough to define and delimit personal integrity, while providing the basis for autonomous choices. For instance, virginity may be viewed as a quaint past condition, or as a present temporary inconvenience by a female college student determined to affirm her sexual liberation today, but to a nun faced with possible rape, it may be seen as a necessary defining condition of her integrity and her personhood: a virgin is what she *is*, even more fundamentally than being a biological existent.

Thus, rather than viewing the terrorist as an irrational contractor, or a misguided utilitarian whose calculus does not really add-up, it might be more accurate to view him as an uncompromising Kantian, at least insofar as his motives and principles are concerned. However, just like the consequentialist who decides to drop an atomic bomb in order to discourage the enemy and terminate the war, he is wrong when he assumes that his justifiable motive permits unjustifiable means in its defense. We can grant that terrorism is not simply a crime, and even understand it, most of the time, as self-defense, possibly moved by a justifiable desire to see universalizable principles upheld and to continue to live in a way which is consonant with his personal integrity and which permits the exercise of his autonomy.

In that case, the terrorist is not immoral in his aim or his motive. Still, even if self-defense$_1$ is as strong a position as self-defense itself, both need to be proportionate, that is, neither must exceed the requirements of *defense*, rather than result in inappropriate *offense*. Nagel suggests that "absolutism" (deontology) demands that limits be posed even to just war activities in both a) the target of such activities, and b) the form of the activity.[25] The terrorist act is wrong in both a) and b). Proportionality is not present in his defense, and if it were possible for him to retaliate by depriving his oppressor of the freedom and autonomy he is deprived of now, he could legitimately respond to repression, restraint, deprivation, by restraining, depriving and coercing and repressing in turn. Annette Baier acknowledges that,

> People who have been dispossessed, degraded, humiliated, but whose spirit has not been broken, understandably want to proclaim their grievances, whether or not they expect their proclamations to advance their cause.[26]

This, incidentally is, once again, what consequentialist and rational contractor theories do not appear to take into consideration. It seems to me that it is their right, possibly even their duty, in the sense that those who blow the whistle on immoral practices of powerful institutions indeed have not only the right but also the duty to do so, particularly when the public interest is severely affected. However, just like the terrorists, the harm the whistleblowers may justly inflict on the powerful (but guilty) bodies they attack, may not be violent in turn. Baier is indeed correct in pointing out that—for instance—the corporation which sanctions the spewing of toxic wastes into our water and air is doing violence.[27]

My point is that to blow the whistle on such activities and call public attention to them in every way possible is the duty of those who become aware of their evil-doing—that is—in every way possible other than committing violent actions, such as poisoning them in turn. We might be in sympathy with their feelings, applaud their motive, but I think we must stop short of terming their actions morally defensible, should they do so.

The crux of the problem then is to be found neither in the consequences, nor in the possible "rationality" (understood in the limited sense of relation of means to ends) of the terrorist, but rather in his right to principles and beliefs, to his own integrity *and* to a proportionate defense of these. The meaning of self-defense$_1$, however, must be clearly understood as such that it does not exceed the requirements of protection of such integrity. It is here that the greatest problem emerges: when all noisy, noticeable, but non-violent means have been tried (and failed), what can the terrorist justly do? The argument that only violence and horror captures our attention, and thus that of the media, is a reasonably strong one, but not totally accurate: Gandhi's approach surely did both and it is also not easily forgotten, with the arrival of the next catastrophe or bloodbath the media reports. Unfortunately, I don't know the answer to this final problem and to point to education and consciousness raising, as in the case for women's rights, appears hopelessly slow and inadequate: easy enough to suggest, from the perspective of a reasonably free and safe existence.

4. Conclusion

I have argued that the terrorist is 1) engaging in self-defense of a special sort (self-defense$_1$), which provides limited justification for counter-attack, and that 2) his position is akin to that of the whistleblower, in that he is engaging in "Violent Demonstrations"[28] to bring immoral action to the attention of the public and to denounce the power and authority that sanctions and practices it.

However, much as his motives and his position are both morally justifiable, if attacks to his integrity, repression of his autonomy and so on, are truly present; his means, if indiscriminate and disproportionate, are not. This is sad, as it brings home once again the powerlessness of individuals and minority groups in so-called democratic and just societies. To continue with the somewhat Kantian analysis I have suggested, the only recourse which would be left to the conscientious terrorist, would be self-directed violence (such as the hunger strikes in Ireland and elsewhere). Kant forbids suicide generally, and offers the single example of a morally correct one, in that of Seneca, dying to defend freedom and autonomy, in the hope that his death may encourage others to overcome oppression.[29] Thomas Hill cites Kant's *Groundwork* for his position on suicide. He adds:

> He later says that to avoid suicide is a "perfect" or exceptionless duty, but he admits that it is an open question for casuistry whether we should count as *suicide* the deliberate sacrifice of oneself to avoid an unjust death sentence or the madness and death inevitable from the bite of a rabid dog.[30]

In essence then, the moral message to the would-be terrorist, would be, if you have tried everything else and you deeply believe in your cause as moral and just, and you further believe that only violence may bring your cause the attention it justly deserves, then practice that violence on yourself, not on others; not only will you remain a moral person, but you will in fact, become a hero. Hard advice, and probably not too popular with terrorists, and a weak conclusion to this discussion. On the other hand, a stronger conclusion can be drawn from this line of argument, in regard to State terrorism instead. Lacking both self-defense$_1$, powerlessness, and the moral requirements of whistleblowing as motives, a State's retaliatory violence is not permissible. If a State wishes to treat well-organized, large groups of terrorists as waging war, then they are bound by the rules of just wars (the use of discriminate weaponry, the prohibitions against harming non-combatants, and the like). If—on the other hand—they wish to denounce terrorism as crime, then each and every terrorist retains his human rights to respect, representation and due process of the law, and his punishment must fit the rules that govern the crime he has committed, after he is proven guilty. No summary condemnation and punishment can be morally justified.

Notes

1 Thomas Hill, Jr., "Making Exceptions without Abandoning the Principle: Or How a Kantian Might Think About Terrorism," unpublished paper, read at Symposium on Terrorism, at Bowling Green State University, Nov. 20, 1988; p. 1.

2 Ibid., p. 2.

3 Jan Narveson, "Terrorism and Morality," paper read at Symposium (as above).

4 Ibid., p. 3.

5 Ibid., p. 1.

6 Paul Gilbert, "Terrorism: War or Crime?" unpublished paper read at the XVIII World Congress of Philosophy, Brighton, England, Aug. 26, 1988; p. 5.

7 Ibid., p. 6.

8 Jonathan Glover, "State Terrorism," paper read at Symposium on Terrorism, as above, p. 1.

9 I cannot get into a detailed analysis of Just War theory in this context. It is clear, however, that the question of *jus ad bellum* needs to be settled before that of *jus in bello*. Most of those who write on the Just War question seem to take the answer to the first question to be primarily "self-defense" mainly, but not exclusively, in the territorial sense. Walzer for instance, says: "A man has certain rights in his home ... because neither his life nor his liberty is secure unless there exists some physical space he is safe from intrusion. Similarly again, the right of a nation or a people not to be invaded derives from the common life its members have made." (M. Walzer, *Just and Unjust Wars*, New York: Basic Books, 1977, p. 55); Theodore Roszak instead cites Augustine; after describing what is blamed *in* a war (desire to harm, cruelty, revengefulness, lust of domination), he says: "...and often to punish these things wars are waged justly by the good against those who resist with violence." (*Contra Faustum*, Bk XII, lxxiv; T. Roszak, "A Just War Analysis of Two Types of Deterrence," in *Nuclear Deterrence*, University of Chicago Press, Chicago, 1985).

10 Narveson, op. cit., p. 9.

11 Annette C. Baier, "Violent Demonstrations," paper read at Symposium as above, p. 7.

12 Laura Westra, "On War and Innocence," in *Dialogue*, Winter 1986 Issue.

13 Baier, op. cit.; she says, "...like the soldier, she (the terrorist) has standard bearers at least in the rear. Indeed, she is a sort of standard-bearer, using her victims as a sort of living flare," p. 4.

14 Onora O'Neill, "How Can We Individuate Moral Problems?" in *Social Policy and Conflict Resolution*, Bowling Green Studies in Applied Philosophy, 1984 (Vol. VI), p. 106.

15 Ibid., p. 114.

16 Westra, op. cit.

17 R.G. Frey, "Conflict and Resolution: On Values and Trade-Offs," in *Social Policy and Conflict Resolution*, op. cit., pp. 1–2.

18 D. Scherer, "Some Simple Rational Conflict Resolution Procedures for Incommensurable Values," in op. cit.

19 Hill, op. cit., p. 11.

20 Laura Westra, "Ecology and Animals: Is There a Joint Ethic of Respect?" starts to lay the foundation for the argument which is then completed in "'Respect,' 'Dignity' and 'Integrity': An Environmental Proposal for Ethics." The former is in *Environmental Ethics*, Fall 1989, the latter in *Epistemologia, The Journal for the Philosophy of Science*, XII (1989), pp. 91–124.

21 Narveson, op. cit., p. 6.

22 Baier, op. cit., p. 12.

23 Ibid., p. 15.

24 I am indebted to Shawn St. Clair for calling my attention to this point.

25 Thomas Nagel, "War and Massacre," in *War and Moral Responsibility*, Philosophy and Public Affairs Reader, Princeton University Press, Princeton, 1974, p. 13.

26 Baier, op. cit., p. 2.

27 Ibid., p. 14.

28 Ibid.

29 Hill, op. cit., p. 12.

30 Ibid.

Questions for Discussion

1 Could terrorism ever be seen as a kind of legitimate self-defense?

2 If one person is ignoring the legitimate autonomous wishes of another, what can the second justifiably do to the first so as to protect his or her autonomy? (Cf. the example of a Jehovah's Witness being forced to undergo a blood transfusion.)

Acknowledgements

I acknowledge the support of the University of Regina and the assistance of Richard Bruce.

Chapter 1: The Moral Status of Non-Human Animals

Canadian law against cruelty to animals.

J. Feinberg, "The Rights of Animals and Unborn Generations," in his *Rights, Justice, and the Bounds of Liberty: Essays in Social Philosophy* (Princeton, NJ: Princeton University Press, 1980), pp. 159–184; first published in W.T. Blackstone (ed.) *Philosophy and Environmental Crisis* (Athens, GA: University of Georgia Press, 1974), pp. 43–68. Reprinted with permission.

P. Singer, "Animal Liberation," originally in *New York Review of Books*, April 1973, pp. 17–21 as a review of S. Godlovith, R. Godlovith, and J. Jarris (eds.) *Animals, Men and Morals* [reprinted in many places including D. VanDeVeer & C. Pierce (eds.) *People, Penguins, and Plastic Trees: Basic Issues in Environmental Ethics*, pp. 24–32]. Reprinted with the permission of the author.

R. Crisp, "Utilitarianism and Vegetarianism," in *The International Journal of Applied Philosophy*, Vol. 4, No. 1, Spring 1988, pp. 41–49. Reprinted with permission.

P. Harrison, "Do Animals Feel Pain?" in *Philosophy*, Vol. 66 (1991), pp. 25–40. Reprinted with the permission of Cambridge University Press.

G. Varner, "The Prospects for Consensus and Convergence in the Animal Rights Debate," in *Hastings Center Report* 24, no. 1 (January–February 1994), pp. 24–28. Reprinted with the permission of the Center and the author.

J. Barber, "Trapped," in *Domino* (Globe and Mail Magazine), Sept. 1990, pp. 81–83, 98, 100, and 102.

Chapter 2: Ethics and the Environment

Law Reform Commission of Canada, "Crimes Against the Environment."

A. Naess, "Identification as a Source of Deep Ecological Attitudes," in Michael Tobias (ed.), *Deep Ecology* (San Marcos, CA: Avant Books, 1988), pp. 256–71.

A. Salleh, "Deeper Than Deep Ecology: The Eco-Feminist Connection," in *Environmental Ethics*, Vol. 6, No. 4, Winter 1984, pp. 339–345. Reprinted with permission.

P. Elder, "Legal Rights for Nature: The Wrong Answer to the Right(s) Question," in R. Bradley and S. Duguid (eds.), *Environmental Ethics: Volume II* (Burnaby, BC: Institute for the Humanities, Simon Fraser University, 1989), pp. 107–119 [previous version in *Osgoode Hall Law Journal*, Vol. 22, No. 2, pp. 285–295.] Reprinted with permission.

J. Narveson, "Resources and Environmental Policy," presented to the WMU Center for the Study of Ethics in Society on November 21, 1994 and published by the Center for the Study of Ethics in Society, Western Michigan University. Reprinted with the permission of the author.

N. Myers, selection from *The Sinking Ark* (Oxford: Pergamon Press, 1980), pp. 3–13, 27–31.

T. Govier, "New and Future People: What Should We Do About Future People?", in *American Philosophical Quarterly*, 1979, pp. 399–413. Reprinted with permission.

Chapter 3: Distribution of Scarce Resources

R. Nozick, selections from *Anarchy, State and Utopia* (New York, NY: Basic Books, 1974). © 1994 by Basic Books, Inc. Reprinted by permission of Basic Books, a division of HarperCollins Publishers Inc.

K. Nielsen, edited selections from *Equality and Liberty: A Defense of Radical Egalitarianism* (Totowa, NJ: Rowman & Allanheld Publishers, 1985). Reprinted with the permission of the author.

World Health Organization, definition of "health."

R. Munson, "Allocating Scarce Medical Resources; Selection Committee for Dialysis." © 1995 by Ronald Munson. From Ronald Munson, *Intervention and Reflection: Basic Issues in Medical Ethics, 5th Edition.* Wadsworth Publishing Company: Belmont, California, 1995. Reprinted with permission.

N. Daniels, "Four Unsolved Rationing Problems: A Challenge," in *Hastings Center Report* 24, no. 4 (1994), pp. 27–29. Reprinted with the permission of the Center and the author.

J. La Puma and E.F. Lawlor, "Quality-Adjusted Life-Years: Ethical Implications for Physicians and Policymakers," in *Journal of the American Medical Association*, Vol. 263, No. 21 (June 6, 1990), pp. 2917–2921. Copyright 1990, American Medical Association. Reprinted with permission.

G. Hardin, "Living on a Lifeboat," *BioScience* 25. © 1975 American Institute of Biological Sciences [reprinted in many collections, including J.E. White (ed.) *Contemporary Moral Problems*, 3rd Edition, pp. 185–197]. Reprinted with permission.

P. Singer, "Rich and Poor," in Singer, *Practical Ethics* (Cambridge: Cambridge University Press, 1979), pp. 158–181. Reprinted with the permission of Cambridge University Press.

Chapter 4: Abortion

Abortion in the Criminal Code (S.287) and Supreme Court of Canada, "Morgentaler, Smoling and Scott v. The Queen."

Bill C-43—Proposed Legislation.

M. Warren, "On the Moral and Legal Status of Abortion," in *The Monist*, Vol 57, No. 1 (LaSalle, Illinois).

D. Marquis, "Why Abortion is Immoral," in *The Journal of Philosophy*, LXXXVI, 4 (April 1989), pp. 183–202. Reprinted with the permission of both the *Journal* and the author.

J. Thomson, "A Defense of Abortion," in *Philosophy and Public Affairs*, Vol. 1, No. 1 (copyright 1976 by Princeton University Press), pp. 47–66. Reprinted by permission of Princeton University Press.

S. Sherwin, "Abortion Through a Feminist Ethics Lens," in Sherwin, *No Longer Patient: Feminist Ethics and Health Care* (Philadelphia, PA: Temple University Press, 1992), pp. 83–98. Reprinted with the permission of both Temple University Press and the author.

R. Dworkin, selection from *Life's Dominion: An Argument About Abortion, Euthanasia, and Individual Freedom*, pp. 84–101. Copyright 1993 by Ronald Dworkin. Reprinted with the permission of Alfred A. Knopf Inc.

Chapter 5: Assisted Reproduction and Commodification

Royal Commission on New Reproductive Technology, selection from "Proceed with Care," Privy Council Office. Reproduced with the permission of Minister of Supply and Services Canada, 1996.

A. Caplan, "The Ethics of In Vitro Fertilization," [in R. T. Hull (ed.) *Ethical Issues in the New Reproductive Technologies* (Belmont, CA: Wadsworth, 1990), pp. 96–109]; originally in *Primary Care*, 1986, 13:2, pp. 241–253. Reprinted with the permission of W.B. Saunders Co., Philadelphia and the author.

E. Anderson, "Is Women's Labor a Commodity?" in *Philosophy and Public Affairs*, Vol. 19, No. 1, Winter 1990, pp. 71–92. © 1990 by Princeton University Press. Reprinted by permission of Princeton University Press.

F. Daunt, "Exploitation or Empowerment? Debating Surrogate Motherhood," in *Saskatchewan Law Review*, Vol. 55, 1991, pp. 415–428. Reprinted with permission.

I. Primoratz, "What's Wrong with Prostitution?" in *Philosophy*, Vol. 68 (1993), pp. 159–182. Reprinted with the permission of Cambridge University Press.

D. Satz, "Markets in Women's Sexual Labor," in *Ethics* 106 (October 1995), pp. 63–85. Reprinted with the permission of The University of Chicago Press and the author.

Chapter 6: Euthanasia

D. Brock, "Voluntary Active Euthanasia," in *Hastings Center Report*, March-April 1992, pp. 10–

22. Reprinted with permission of the Center and the author.

D. Callahan, "When Self-Determination Runs Amok," in *Hastings Center Report*, March-April 1992, pp. 52–55. Reprinted with the permission of the Center and the author.

Supreme Court of Canada, selection from "Rodriguez v. Canada (A.G.)."

E. Keyserlingk, "Assisted Suicide, Causality and the Supreme Court of Canada" (1994) 39 McGill L.J. 708. Reprinted with permission.

R. Krutzen, "The Case of Robert and Tracy Latimer." Reprinted with permission.

Chapter 7: Free Speech, Censorship, and Pornography

Supreme Court of Canada, selection from "R. v. Keegstra."

L. W. Sumner, "Hate Propaganda and Charter Rights," from *Free Expression; Essays in Law and Philosophy* (Oxford: Clarendon Press, 1994), pp. 153–174.

N. Bissoondath, selection from *Selling Illusions: The Cult of Multiculturalism in Canada* (Toronto: Penguin Books Canada, 1994), pp. 145–170. Copyright Neil Bissoondath 1994. Reprinted by permission of Penguin Books Canada Ltd.

L. Green, "Freedom of Expression and Choice of Language," 13 *Law and Policy* (1991), pp. 215–29. © Blackwell Publishers, UK. Reprinted with permission.

M. Kostash, "Whose Body? Whose Self?: Beyond Pornography," in M. Fitzgerald, C. Guberman, and L. Wolfe (eds.), *Still Ain't Satisfied!: Canadian Feminism Today* (Toronto: The Women's Press, 1982), pp. 43–54. Reprinted with permission.

F. Christensen, selection from *Pornography: The Other Side.* © 1990 by Praeger Publishers, Westport, CT. Reproduced with permission of Greenwood Publishing Group, Inc., Westport, CT.

A. Dworkin, "Pornography is a Civil Rights Issue," from *Letters From A War Zone, Writings 1976–1987* (New York: E.P. Dutton, a division of Penguin, 1989), pp. 276–307. © 1989 Andrea Dworkin. Reprinted with permission.

E. Willis, "Feminism, Moralism, and Pornography" [in A. Snitow, C. Stansell, & S. Thompson (eds.), *Powers of Desire: The Politics of Sexuality* (New York: New Feminist Library, Monthly Review Press, 1983), pp. 460–467]; originally in the *Village Voice*, Oct. and Nov. 1979 [copyright Ellen Willis]. Reprinted with permission.

The Economist, Leaders: "Only Disconnect" (*The Economist*, July 1, 1995, pp. 16–17), "Censorship in Cyberspace" (*The Economist*, April 8, 1995, pp. 16–17) and "Sex on the Internet" (*The Economist*, January 6, 1996, p. 18). © 199_ The Economist Newspaper Group, Inc. Reprinted with permission.

Chapter 8: Multiculturalism, Nationalism and Aboriginal Rights

S. Haack, "Multiculturalism and Objectivity." Copyright 1995 Susan Haack. This article originally appeared in the *Partisan Review*, Vol. 62, No. 3, 1995, and is reprinted with permission.

N. Bissoondath, selection from *Selling Illusions: The Cult of Multiculturalism in Canada* (Toronto: Penguin Books Canada, 1994). Copyright N. Bissoondath 1994. Reprinted by permission of Penguin Books Canada Ltd.

C. Taylor, selection from *Multiculturalism and 'The Politics of Recognition'; An Essay by Charles Taylor* (Princeton, NJ: Princeton University Press), pp. 25–28, 37–44 and 51–73. Reprinted with the permission of the author.

W. Kymlicka, "Liberalism in Culturally Plural Societies," (somewhat edited) Ch. 7 of Kymlicka, *Liberalism, Community, and Culture* (Oxford: Clarendon Press, 1989), pp. 135–161. Reprinted with the author's permission.

P. Trudeau, "Justice In Our Time" speech, printed in P. A. Cumming & N. H. Mickenberg (eds.), *Native Rights in Canada*, 2nd Edition (Toronto: Indian-Eskimo Association of Canada, in assoc. with General Publishing Co. Ltd., 1972), pp. 331–332. Reprinted with permission.

K. Jamieson, *Indian Women and the Law in Canada: Citizens Minus* (Ottawa: Minister of Supply and

Services, 1978), pp. 77–78 and pp. 2–4. Reprinted with permission.

M. McDonald, "Aboriginal Rights," from W. Shea and John King-Farlow (eds.), *Contemporary Issues in Political Philosophy* (New York: Academic Publications Inc.), pp. 269–286. Reprinted with the permission of the author.

M. E. Turpel, selection from "Aboriginal Peoples and the Canadian Charter: Interpretive Monopolies, Cultural Differences," from R.F. Devlin (ed.), *Constitutional Interpretation* (Toronto: Emond Montgomery Publications Ltd) pp. 126–131. Reprinted with permission.

T. Hurka, "Canadian Nationalism and the Distinctiveness Fetish." Reprinted with the permission of the author. A shortened version of this article appeared in *The Globe and Mail* on May 11, 1996.

Chapter 9: Ethics and the Use of Violence

J. Sterba, "Reconciling Pacifists and Just War Theorists," from Duane L. Cady and Richard Werner (eds.), *Just War, Nonviolence and Nuclear Deterrence: Philosophers on War and Peace*, pp. 35–50. © Concerned Philosophers for Peace, 1991. Information on this and other books from Concerned Philosophers for Peace and on its newsletter can be obtained from: Concerned Philosophers for Peace, Department of Philosophy, University of N. Carolina at Charlotte, 9201 University City Blvd., Charlotte, NC 28223-0001. Reprinted with permission.

S. Ruddick, "From Maternal Thinking to Peace Politics," from Eve Browning Cole and Susan Coultrap-McQuin (eds.), *Explorations in Feminist Ethics; Theory and Practice* (Bloomington: Indiana University Press, 1992), pp. 141–155. Reprinted with permission.

M. Green, "War, Innocence and Theories of Sovereignty," in *Social Theory and Practice*, Vol. 18, no. 1, Spring 1992), pp. 39–62. © *Social Theory and Practice*. Reprinted with permission.

The Senate of Canada, "Meeting New Challenges: Canada's Response to a New Generation of Peacekeeping," transcribed from a report of a standing committee of the Senate of Canada.

J. Kunkel, "Challenging the Domestic Analogy: A Critique of Killing in Self-Defense," from Duane L. Cady and Richard Werner (eds.), *Just War, Nonviolence and Nuclear Deterrence*, pp. 51–64. © Concerned Philosophers For Peace, 1991. Reprinted with permission.

Law Reform Commission of Canada, selection from "Our Criminal Law."

Law Reform Commission of Canada, selection from "Aboriginal Peoples and Criminal Justice," Justice Canada. Reproduced with the permission of Minister of Supply and Services Canada 1996.

I. Primoratz, "What Is Terrorism?" in *Journal of Applied Philosophy*, Vol. 7, No. 2, 1990, pp. 129–138. Reprinted with permission.

L. Westra, "Terrorism, Self-Defense, and Whistle-Blowing," in *Journal of Social Philosophy*, Vol. 20, No. 3, 1989, pp. 46–58. Reprinted by permission of the *Journal of Social Philosophy*.

* * *

The Editor of this book and the Publisher have made every attempt to locate the authors of the copyrighted material or their heirs or assigns, and would be grateful for information that would allow them to correct any errors or omissions in a subsequent edition of the work.